CRITICAL SURVEY
OF
LONG FICTION

CRITICAL SURVEY

OF

LONG FICTION

Second Revised Edition

Volume 6

V. S. Pritchett - August Strindberg

Editor, Second Revised Edition
Carl Rollyson
Baruch College, City University of New York

Editor, First Edition. English and Foreign Language Series
Frank N. Magill

SALEM PRESS, INC.
Pasadena, California   Hackensack, New Jersey

Managing Editor: Christina J. Moose
Research Supervisor: Jeffry Jensen
Acquisitions Editor: Mark Rehn
Photograph Editor: Karrie Hyatt
Manuscript Editors: Lauren M. D'Andrea, Doug Long
Research Assistant: Jun Ohnuki
Production Editor: Cynthia Beres
Layout: William Zimmerman
Graphics: Yasmine Cordoba

Some of the essays in this work, which have been updated, originally appeared in the following Salem Press publications: *Critical Survey of Long Fiction, English Language Series, Revised Edition* (1991), *Critical Survey of Long Fiction, Foreign Language Series* (1984).

Library of Congress Cataloging-in-Publication Data

Critical survey of long fiction / editor, Carl Rollyson ; editor, English and foreign language series, Frank N. Magill.—2nd rev. ed.

p. cm.

"The current reference work both updates and substantially adds to the previous editions of the Critical survey from which it is partially drawn: the Critical survey of long fiction. English language series, revised edition (1991) and the Critical survey of long fiction. Foreign language series (1984)"—Publisher's note.

Includes bibliographical references and index.

ISBN 0-89356-888-0 (v. 6 : alk. paper) — ISBN 0-89356-882-1 (set : alk. paper)

1. Fiction—History and criticism. 2. Fiction—Bio-bibliography—Dictionaries. I. Rollyson, Carl E. (Carl Edmund) II. Magill, Frank Northen, 1907-1997.

PN3451.C75 2000
809.3—dc21   00-020195

First Printing

CONTENTS

CRITICAL SURVEY
OF
LONG FICTION

V. S. PRITCHETT

Born: Ipswich, England; December 16, 1900
Died: London, England; March 20, 1997

PRINCIPAL LONG FICTION

Claire Drummer, 1929
Shirley Sanz, 1932 (also known as *Elopement into Exile*)
Nothing Like Leather, 1935
Dead Man Leading, 1937
Mr. Beluncle, 1951

OTHER LITERARY FORMS

V. S. Pritchett is recognized above all as a master of the short story. His stories rely less on plot than on character—character revealed principally through dialogue. Many of Pritchett's stories were first published in magazines; they have been collected, however, in more than a dozen volumes.

Pritchett is also widely known as a travel writer and a literary critic and biographer. As the former, he produced several works, among which *The Spanish Temper* (1954) was perhaps most highly praised. *The Offensive Traveller* (1964; also known as *Foreign Faces*) collected numerous previously published travel essays. Pritchett's literary biographies include *Balzac: A Biography* (1973), *The Gentle Barbarian: The Life and Work of Turgenev* (1977), and *Chekhov: A Spirit Set Free* (1988). His criticism ranges across more than four decades, from *In My Good Books* (1942) to *A Man of Letters* (1985).

Two autobiographical works by Pritchett, *A Cab at the Door* (1968) and *Midnight Oil* (1972) are regarded as classics of the genre.

ACHIEVEMENTS

During the second half of the twentieth century, Pritchett's readership and influence in the United States grew considerably. After the 1950's, his stories appeared frequently in *The New Yorker*, and selections of his reviews appeared yearly in *The New York Review of Books*. He was the Christian Gauss Lecturer at Princeton University (1953), writer-in-

residence at Smith College (1966), Beckman Professor at the University of California at Berkeley (1962), and visiting professor at Brandeis University (1968). His fiction and criticism alike were enjoyed and praised by American critics—his fiction for its social comedy, acute characterization, and subtle manner, his criticism for its focus, lucidity, and balance. As a "literary journalist," he has been compared to Edmund Wilson, and his sentences, whether in fiction or nonfiction, are thought to be among the best written in English in the twentieth century. In England, he was an elder statesman of letters, many times honored. He was the Clark Lecturer at Cambridge University (1969) and was awarded a D.Litt. by Leeds University (1972). He served as president of the British Association of Poets, Playwrights, Editors, Essayists, and Novelists (PEN) in 1970 and of the International PEN Club in 1974. He was the recipient of two awards for nonfiction, the Heinemann in 1969 and the International PEN Club in 1974. He was a Fellow of the Royal Society of Literature and an hon-

(Nancy Crampton)

orary member of the American Academy of Arts and Letters. In 1969, he was made a Commander of the British Empire, and in 1975, he was knighted.

BIOGRAPHY

In December of 1900, in lodgings over a toy shop in Ipswich, England, Victor Sawdon Pritchett was born, the first child of Beatrice Martin and Walter Pritchett, who had met in the milliner's shop where they both worked. The marriage apparently began passionately, three children following quickly after Victor, but because of Walter's many business misadventures and his conversion to Christian Science, the marriage was soon unsettled and its passion converted to quarrelsomeness. Although the Pritchetts were not shiftless, their household was often shifted about: By the time Pritchett was twelve, the family had moved around London at least fourteen times, usually so that Walter Pritchett could escape creditors, twice to hide his bankruptcy. Beatrice Pritchett lived in constant fear of creditors—once denying her identity on opening the door to an officer attempting to serve a writ—and in outspoken jealousy of the "other women" in her husband's life—his mother, his business partner ("Miss H"), and Mary Baker Eddy.

Because the family never stayed in one place for long, Pritchett felt that he belonged nowhere, that he was an outsider everywhere but in his own, rather strange, family. Besides moving with his parents, he was sent at intervals to his grandparents in Yorkshire, an arrangement contrived, apparently, to ease the burden on Walter Pritchett's purse. New problems complicated their home life from 1910, when in Camberwell, Walter was converted to Christian Science. His conversion brought on quarrels with Beatrice about "that woman" which lasted well into the night, and later his business failed. After a year's separation, during which time Pritchett formed a vague idea that he would become a painter, Beatrice and the children rejoined Walter in Dulwich, where he had established an art needlework trade with his former bookkeeper, Miss H.

Until he moved to Dulwich, Pritchett had received only sporadic schooling, and then only in rough Methodist and penny-a-day schools, because his father

did not trouble himself about the children's education. Finally, Beatrice grew impatient with Walter's ruminations over the prospectuses from Eton and Harrow, for which Pritchett would never have qualified because, among other things, he knew no Latin, and she enrolled him in Rosendale Road School. There he was awarded John Ruskin's *Modern Painters* for one of his paintings, and there too, under a man named Bartlett, he read his first literature. He promptly began to read whatever he could find, having decided to become a writer. He became known in the family as "Dirty Poet" and "Professor." Two years later, to impress Miss H, his father allowed him to sit for an examination for a scholarship to the Strand School (Streatham), which he failed. Pritchett identifies this failure in *A Cab at the Door* as a turning point in his life, for he believed that had he won the scholarship, he surely would have continued at a university and died as a writer. Instead, at Miss H's expense, he entered Alleyn's School, a London grammar school founded to educate the lower middle classes. There he learned that he was good at languages, and he also enjoyed a few classroom successes with his writing. Around this time, he sprained his ankle, and this accident was the occasion of his first hearing the Christian Science argument from his father. Not long afterward, Pritchett professed his belief in it, probably out of a need to please his father, but his faith seems never to have been very strong. Church provided a social outlet for him, the children otherwise not being allowed to go out.

In 1916, at the instigation of his grandfather, Pritchett was taken from school and put to work as a clerk in a London leather-manufacturing firm. After fighting with another clerk on the office floor, he was promoted out of the office to learn the other phases of the trade. For four years he commuted into London, so happy with the idea of thoroughly learning a trade that for a while he abandoned his literary ambitions. At the end of 1920, however, he fell ill, and when he recovered, he did not go back to the leather business but instead went to Paris, which he had dreamed of doing for several years.

With two hundred pounds saved from his earnings and a typewriter from his father, Pritchett arrived in

Paris in the spring of 1921. He found a job as a photographer's assistant and settled joyfully into Parisian life. Christian Science had taught him that sex should be avoided as the chief avenue of Animal Magnetism, the force that created the illusion of Evil, but by this time, it is fair to say, he was tormented by his virginity. Finally, he managed a brief affair with a Danish girl, who soon after returned to Denmark and married another man. Pritchett had a few other friends, mostly from the church, but he knew no writers, least of all the American expatriates. He spent most of his time alone, continuing the autodidacticism which for the most part had been his education; it was in his room, remembering author J. M. Barrie's advice to write about small things, that he began his career as a writer. His first three sketches were taken almost immediately by *The Saturday Westminster, Time and Tide*, and *The Christian Science Monitor*. Soon he was emboldened to quit the photographer's shop for a job as a shellac salesman. He was happy to be part of the workaday city, to walk the streets with his samples, but he sold nothing and was fired. Once again, he began to write and to place articles, but then his luck changed, he ran out of money, and *The Christian Science Monitor* did not pay him for a series of articles he had written. When he was on the verge of starvation, he was fed by his landlady and given money by friends. Storing his belongings in Paris, he returned to England, two years after leaving, to see the London editor of *The Christian Science Monitor*.

In Paris, Pritchett had proven to himself and to his father that he could lead an independent and manly life as a writer, so once back in London, he looked for regular work writing. At *The Christian Science Monitor*, the new editor was not immediately forthcoming, but eventually he paid Pritchett and gave him a trial assignment in Ireland, where Pritchett met Æ, James Stephens, Sean O'Casey, and William Butler Yeats himself, with whom he argued about George Bernard Shaw. In Ireland, too, he fell in love with another journalist and rashly married her after agreeing to go to Spain for *The Christian Science Monitor*. He did not much like his role as foreign correspondent because he disliked politics, preferring instead to write about places, people, customs, and manners. Tiring of journalism, he began to write short stories, none of which was published for several years. Over a period of three years of writing from Ireland, Spain, and the United States, his writing (by his own account) had grown self-conscious and contorted. At long last, *The Christian Science Monitor* tired of it and fired him.

In London again, Pritchett sustained himself by translating business letters for a foreign language school, serving as the librarian to the Bath Club for one pound a week, and selling a few stories and sketches. Unable to find a publisher for a collection of sketches, poor, and inspired by D. H. Lawrence's *Sea and Sardinia* (1921), he decided to walk across Spain and write a book about it upon his return to England. *Marching Spain* (1928) sold only six hundred copies before it was remaindered, but it won Pritchett two contracts, one for a book of stories and another for a novel. In the meantime, he was hired again by *The Christian Science Monitor*, this time as a reviewer, a job he kept until he published "The Saint" in the 1930's and was fired for the last time. Also in 1928, he began what proved to be a long association with *New Statesman* (he eventually became the director), published a few stories in *The Fortnightly Review*, and became the novel reviewer for *The Spectator*. In 1929, his first novel, *Claire Drummer*, was published, and his first book of stories, *The Spanish Virgin and Other Stories*, followed in 1930. The book of stories surprised everyone by selling three thousand copies; the novel sold fewer than a thousand.

Throughout the 1920's, Pritchett and his wife had been separated much of the time, partly because she was pursuing an acting career. By the 1930's, Pritchett had earned some measure of peace and security from his writing, but it was not until 1934 that the transiency and emotional tension which had characterized his entire life were relieved. In this year, he met Dorothy Rudge Roberts, who, after his divorce in 1936, became his second wife. It was not merely to fulfill a tedious convention that he dedicated all of his subsequent books to her, for—believing that love released the tension responsible for his bad writing—it was to her and their marriage that he attributed the great burst of creativity that overtook him. Through the 1930's he published three more novels, but, as portended by the response to *The Spanish Virgin*, it was in the short story that he excelled. During the war years, he gardened and reviewed books; in the 1950's, he published his only truly successful novel, *Mr. Beluncle*, and *The Spanish Temper*, which is generally thought to be one of the best books ever written on Spain; throughout the 1960's, 1970's, and 1980's he continued to write stories and reviews. He also completed two volumes of memoirs in 1968 and 1971.

Pritchett continued to live in London with his wife until his death there at the age of ninety-six. The critical praise he received for his 1988 biography, *Chekhov*, was testimony to the fact that even as he approached ninety he remained a masterful scholar and wordsmith.

ANALYSIS

Two central forces shaped V. S. Pritchett's artistry: his family and his urge to break away from it. The picture that Pritchett gives of his home life in *A Cab at the Door* is of a fantastic edifice of dreams, resounding with the words of Walter Pritchett—self-complacent, moralizing, and sometimes angry words. The family life Walter tried to create was a fantasy that Beatrice chipped away at. She wailed jealous complaints and remonstrated; she told stories about dead relatives, dead pets, and dead royalty; above all, she told jokes which ended with her bursting into hysterical laughter, rocking on her chair, and peering out at her audience from behind spread fingers, her skirts hoisted above her knees and her bloomers showing. If his father's words imprisoned the young Pritchett, his mother's opened a chink into the world where people voiced their feelings and cried, and where, most important, they laughed.

When Pritchett began to read widely, he discovered fictions other than his father's and was led to a consideration of the worlds which prompted them. (That he thought there was some literal place where life was better is demonstrated by his early desire to travel.) It is characteristic of his imagination that as a young man going to work in London he was re-

minded of Charles Dickens, rather than of London when reading Dickens, and that as a septuagenarian he described himself as two people—the writer, "the prosing man at the desk," and the other self, "the valet who dogs him and does the living" (*Midnight Oil*). For Pritchett, in short, life followed art, and this order of things is important for understanding the writer.

Probably because his interest in literature arose suddenly from his recognition that print is like paint, that it can create pictures which open onto other perspectives, his writing is predominantly descriptive, his narrative perhaps more lyric than dramatic. Added to his visual acuity is a good ear for dialect, developed from adjusting his own language to whatever new neighborhood he found himself in as a boy and from speaking French and Spanish as a young man. The mundane world, consequently, is richly evoked in his works. He is not primarily concerned with recording the details of the external world, however, for he is too much of an essentialist in purpose and too richly comic in manner to be preoccupied with strict representationalism. Like the Victorians, he studies characters in a social setting; like Dickens and Thomas Hardy, his first-loved novelists, he concerns himself with the social environment as a condition of character. Place and class are important as limiters—of experience, language, and the stuff of fantasy. He evokes them with selected, exaggerated, and often symbolic images, usually visual, and by the words the characters speak. There is perhaps no twentieth century writer as adept as Pritchett at representing society through these brilliant half-strokes. Yet, in the sense of upholding the value—whether mythical, political, or moral—of one class above another, he is ultimately one of the least class-conscious of English writers. His authorial position is class-free, his attitude independent.

His real divergence from social realism is most obvious in his characters, who ring true, but not because they are singly imitative of individuals with whom one might rub shoulders in the real world. The eccentrics who populate his books are instead caricatures through which are enacted certain emotional, intellectual, and aesthetic problems. The conflicting versions of the world created by the various characters produce a collision at the climax which is often understated and ironic, and perhaps it is the frequency of this "silent" climax that has led to the charge by critics that Pritchett's plotting is weak. Then, too, character and situation above all capture his attention. In a relatively static fashion, one resembling portraiture more than dramatic literature, he touches and retouches his central point.

The unifying theme of Pritchett's fiction concerns dreaming as an ambiguous mechanism of the imagination, for it can lead either to freedom or to imprisonment. According to their way of dreaming, his characters fall loosely into two categories. The first is the egotist. He has many faces, but essentially he is the one who, as is said of Mr. Beluncle, never dreams at all—except when he is awake. Usually he is treated humorously, under a Dickensian light, and when there is an objective narrator, in the Meredithian manner: incisively, ironically, and epigrammatically. The egotist, by placing himself at the center of things and acting out his dreams, tries to negate the three-dimensional world. His dreams are for the most part unrealizable and his version of the world untenable, and he appears comically two-dimensional as a result. The second character type, the artist, recognizes and belongs to the world where perspectives shift. Like the egotist, he dreams, but, unlike the egotist's desires, his longings and aspirations are curbed by an awareness of actual conditions. He is, moreover, capable of holding contradictory dreams, or accounts of the world, in his mind at the same time.

DEAD MAN LEADING

Pritchett's first three novels draw upon his experiences in Ireland, Spain, and London. They were not successful, and in *Midnight Oil* he writes that they were "machines for conveying [his] characters into a trap." In *Dead Man Leading*, he tried something new. Instead of looking for essences in the stuff of his own experience, he concocted a material world to convey the essence of masochism. His idea, that explorers are motivated by masochism, he inferred from reading biographies; his setting, Brazil, was known to him only through literature. To pick up mundane de-

tails he read missionaries' diaries and talked about Manaos with a drunk businessman on leave, and to fix the setting clearly in mind, he made a small model of the river in his garden. This method of writing the book is partly responsible for both its strengths and its weaknesses. It is overloaded with the pop-Freudianism that infects the literature of the 1930's and is too imitative in its symbolism, whether consciously or not, of Joseph Conrad. Still, it shows an uncommon force of imagination in other respects and a strong narrative power, and—being a symbolic tale approaching psychological allegory—it sheds light on his other works.

The story concerns an expedition by three men, each of whom is an egotist of sorts. The first is Charles Wright, a famous explorer, now middle-aged, who is making the expedition to complete a former, aborted one. The second is Harry Johnson, the chosen companion of Wright, a young Englishman who works in the Brazilian timber industry and uses his leaves to explore the far reaches of the world. He and Wright are "camp companions," initiates into the thoroughly masculine world where women are "bad luck." The third is Gilbert Phillips, who stands outside their circle, a stranger to their code. He envied Harry when they were boys together, and now, as a journalist, he is trying to acquire courage by following bold men. These characters—especially Wright and Johnson—are less persuasive as people than as Freudian symbols.

Despite Wright's nominal leadership, Johnson is at the head of the group. The expedition, which occurs in three stages (not counting the long expository flashback), is a primal regression into the interior of Johnson's being, a gradual peeling-back of his adult self. The flashback, in which we learn that Johnson has had an affair with Wright's stepdaughter, Lucy, and is now burdened with guilt and a desire for self-punishment, lays the foundation for the analysis of his puritanical, masochistic psychology, according to which Wright and Lucy (to whom Wright had been attracted before marrying her mother) serve as father and mother surrogates. Through the first stage of the expedition, the journey upriver with Phillips to meet Wright, Johnson grows feverish and, in an irrational effort to avoid Wright, tries to persuade Phillips to disembark and strike out over land. When they do rendezvous with Wright, Johnson is put to bed in the house of a whiskey-besotted Cockney named Calcott, who entertains him while Wright and Phillips are off hunting turtle eggs. He encourages Johnson in his misogyny ("all women are dagoes") and insists that Johnson is there to look for his father, a missionary who slept in the same room before disappearing into the jungle years earlier. Calcott's Portuguese confidant, Jose Silva, lends support to Calcott by pretending to be the voice of the dead man in a seance arranged for Johnson's benefit. When Phillips and Wright are detained for several days by a storm and Johnson grows impatient to try his luck, Silva, thinking there might be gold in it for him, encourages Johnson to set out and to take him along. When Phillips and Wright return, then, Johnson is gone—now leading the expedition.

The second stage consists of Johnson's trip with Silva. Johnson, making a conscious decision neither to flee his friends nor to follow his father, simply goes on without turning back. Loosened from the "net" the minds of others cast over him, he drifts into a world where the birds whistle "like boys" and Silva chatters and frolics in the sand. Silva is like a boy-genie (an "artist," the narrator calls him) released by Harry's subconscious to grant his deepest wishes. After several days, however, Johnson is overtaken and, in a strained reunion with Wright, breaks down, regressing to an angry child wishing for the death of his father. Wright, attempting to restore harmony, invites him to go out hunting. While they are spearing fish in a mudhole, a jaguar surprises them and, in the panic of the moment, Wright shoots himself. By the time Johnson is able to bring him in, Wright is dead. Characteristically, Johnson thinks this accident has been caused by his own weakness and that his weakness has been brought upon him by Lucy. He now feels "that he had no longer a self, that he was scattered, disintegrated—nothing."

So begins the third and final stage of the expedition. Johnson's idea, if he has one, is to walk until he encounters the South American Indians who are presumed to have killed his father. Although Phillips has lost his interest in the expedition with the death of Wright, he has promised Lucy, with whom he also has had an affair, that he will take care of Johnson. Consequently, when Silva and the crew turn back, Phillips follows him overland, hoping to save him from the ultimate solitude of the grave. At first, Johnson tolerates his company, but after a few days, Phillips conceives the idea that he intends to leave him behind. When Phillips is nearly dead of thirst, Johnson decides to search for water, leaving a note and his gun behind. Roused from delirium before Johnson is out of sight, Phillips believes he is being abandoned and fires at him. Johnson is last seen looking back at Phillips before turning and automatically marking a trail he will not follow back. Without Phillips, representative perhaps of the social aspect of the ego, Johnson is finally alone, free to rejoin his father, death.

The setting, seemingly so important to the action, is largely created by images drawn from the characters' private states of mind. When England to Gilbert is a fresh memory, for example, the wake of the boat is "like an old mat" and the "slow clapping" of vultures' wings is "like dusty and ragged rugs being shaken." Later, when he is obsessed with keeping the fire low, the vultures wheeling overhead are "like two bits of charred paper tossed up by the draught of a fire." As it is imagined by the characters, the setting helps to describe and explain their motivations. As a stage for playing out a psychological drama, it is nowhere better adapted to the purpose than in the chapter presenting Wright's death. In the topography, the mudhole, and the appearance of the jaguar, the imagery binds character to setting, and the action expresses subconscious desires.

The role of language in shaping the world surfaces as an explicit theme in each stage of the expedition. In the first, Silva speaks in the "voice" of Johnson's father and in the second in the voice of the child within. By a Freudian model, Silva can be understood as the voice of Johnson's ego, at one time speaking out of the super-ego and at another out of the id. In the third stage of the expedition, when Johnson feels disintegrated, Silva is absent. In this last stage, Johnson and Phillips develop a special camaraderie, complete with its own vocabulary, which the narrator explains at some length. First they coin new words for the essentials of their life—"water" becoming "mud," for example—then they abbreviate them, and then they lapse into nearly total silence. This loss of society, of language, of the vocabulary necessary for cultivating the physical world, parallels Johnson's regression.

As analyzed in *Dead Man Leading*, the desire to explore is masochistic, and masochism arises from the sexual guilt produced by puritanism. Puritanism, Walter Allen has noted, is Pritchett's main study, and in no other book is his recurring theme more evident. Yet Pritchett's attitude toward Johnson's puritanism and toward Johnson himself is not clear. Although Johnson behaves ridiculously, he is not treated as a comic character. Indeed, Pritchett creates a good deal of sympathy for him, portraying him as a troubled, possibly even tragic, hero. Certainly, by doing what others cannot do, he is great: He cuts through the world of social convention and conscious activity directly into the world of unadulterated egotism, into the dream world where accidents really do make wishes come true. In this sense, Johnson is like Beluncle, an artist of egotism. The general ambivalence of the authorial attitude toward Johnson, however, is probably caused by the thorny subject matter: the relationships among father, mother, and son, which Pritchett eventually mastered in late middle-age.

MR. BELUNCLE

It was not until 1951, after a decade of book-reviewing and short-story writing, that Pritchett published his next novel. *Mr. Beluncle* is concerned with what he calls in *Midnight Oil* his "obsessive subject": his father. *Dead Man Leading* was concerned with this obsessive subject, too, but the father in question was not drawn directly from Pritchett's own, and it was the son's, not the father's, story. In *Mr. Beluncle*, however, there is an unmistakable portrait of Walter Pritchett. Pritchett's manner in this book is not, as it had been in *Dead Man Leading*, to approach his subject and character earnestly but to create an attitude, which can be termed "objective sympathy," out of a barbed, epigrammatic wit reminiscent of George Meredith. Both books concern the quality of the indi-

vidual's imagination and the power of dreaming, but *Mr. Beluncle* is far superior, its subject and manner being natural to Pritchett's genius and fully under control. Indeed, all of Pritchett's strengths are united in *Mr. Beluncle* to produce what is surely his finest novel.

Compared to *Dead Man Leading*, so like a boy's adventure story, *Mr. Beluncle* is a quiet book. Both books are, in a sense, character studies, but in *Dead Man Leading*, to the extent that it is psychological allegory, the primary means of characterization is action, while in *Mr. Beluncle*, it is portraiture. *Mr. Beluncle* works largely through long gazes at Beluncle penetrated by a quick narrative omniscience, through set presentations of monologues and incremental repetition of ritualized behavior, and through a panorama of supporting characters. Many of the minor characters are eccentrics in their own right, but in the narrative, they serve Mr. Beluncle in his fantastic egotism.

Mr. Beluncle occupies two domains, in each of which he possesses a helpmate and a family. At home, it is his wife, Ethel, and his sons, Henry, George, and Leslie. At work, it is his business partner, Mrs. Linda Truslove, his junior partner, Mr. Everard Chilly, and his typist. At home, he is a tyrant, self-complacently moralizing to his family, filling his drawers with expensive clothing while neglecting to give Ethel housekeeping money, and refusing to allow the family members to go out alone or to have friends. A fleshy man himself, he does not want them to leave him because he feels diminished; they are "like vultures pulling his flesh off him." At work, he is a fake, busying himself with writing aphorisms on slips of paper, daydreaming about a new house, issuing commands, and driving the company car over to the showroom. It is in fact Mrs. Truslove who runs the company, who has bought the car, and who has tried to save the business from Beluncle's extravagances.

Mrs. Truslove has been in love with Beluncle for years and subject to his persuasions, but it is not she who basically enables him to live in his house of delusion. That role is reserved for his other "mistress," the Church of the Last Purification. With its easy transcendentalism and its central doctrine that evil is illusory, the religion has enabled him to dismiss as illusory anything unpleasant and to achieve such a degree of self-importance that God, like his family and associates, serves him. "God is a radio station," he asserts in an expansive moment; "God is Supply," in a moment of financial need. His most immediate need, he thinks, is another new house; having heard that in the Father's house are many mansions, he is certain that "one has been prepared" for him. Especially congenial to his sensibility is the church's equating evil and sex. A very clean man married to a somewhat slovenly woman, Beluncle finds it "hard to realize that woman is a Divine Idea." Because his "sexual instinct interfered with the acquisitive," he is gratified by church doctrine, since, as Lady Roads, head of the local church, says, "it takes sex out of love." His way is thus clear to express it more naturally, by using his attractiveness to women (his sister, his mother, Lady Roads, Mrs. Truslove, and Mrs. Robinson, a tearoom manageress) to seduce them out of their money. He manages everything with charm and righteousness, always depending on God, who is (as Mrs. Truslove thinks of it) the "joker in his pack." The story is about the collapse of his house of cards.

Beluncle's huge capacity for dreaming has produced his success to date, but it is the very thing which destroys him in the end. Encouraged to daydream by the transcendental aspect of Purification theology, he ignores factual circumstances. Accountants, for example, amaze him because they actually believe the figures on paper. "You can add it up this way, you can add it up that way and every time you get a different answer," he opines and adds, "As Shakespeare says, it's all in your mind." Mrs. Truslove, though, is one who believes the figures on paper, and because she is finished loving him, signals her intention of withdrawing from the business. At home, he has disappointments too. Chief among them is his son Henry, who without Beluncle's knowledge has fallen in love with the stationmaster's daughter, Mary Phibbs. When Beluncle confronts Henry with the "idea" of Mary, the boy is unable to stand up to him, but, in defeat and humiliation, he flings the more cutting decision at him: He has no intention of

entering the business. Thus, Beluncle's dream for his son, who would have belonged to him forever and brought him a girl with money for the business, collapses. Yet, the more the world submits evidence that his dreams are ashes, the harder he clings to them. All that is needed, he thinks, is a miracle to vindicate and save him, so when Judy Dykes, the crippled sister of Mrs. Truslove, is brought to her feet by the verbal assault of a fanatical newspaper vendor, he launches into a new round of expenditures. Instead of saving him, this miracle completes his ruin. It calls into question the soundness of the Purification, for Judy's recovery is the prelude to her death, and once she is gone, Mrs. Truslove is free to pursue a new life. When Mr. Beluncle receives word of Judy's death, he is prompted to make his first and last speech in his new board room, to an imaginary board of directors. He begins by denying the death. "It's a mistake, a dream and—by the way, I'll give you a thought there, where is the dream when you wake up?"

Everyone in *Mr. Beluncle* dreams: Judy Dykes that she will walk, Mrs. Truslove that someday something will come of her love for Beluncle, Henry that he will free himself from his father. Each character attempts to force reality to conform to the dream: Judy Dykes by accumulating fashionable shoes; Mrs. Truslove by using the business as a marriage; Henry by loading the slender figure of Mary Phibbs with his many nameless desires. Judy dies, however, and Mrs. Truslove parts with her desire for Beluncle, which has been "exhausted by the imagination." Henry, who has imitated his father in many respects, observes Mary's reaction to his declaration that he has lost his faith and realizes for the first time that she is "not an extension of himself, but another human being." Everyone wakes up to find the dream gone, except for Mr. Beluncle, who uses language to keep it alive.

If the quality of the individual's dream is the moral topic of the book, then the manner by which language serves the imagination is its aesthetic corollary. Mr. Beluncle's extraordinary force of personality expresses itself by his physical substance and demeanor but also, and more important, by his words. He is a man who likes to roll words in his mouth like fine chocolates and bestow his thoughts on those around him like a king. Never mind that what he says is absurd, his manner convinces. To Mr. Chilly, one of Beluncle's admirable traits is his ability to "make a statement and then appear to lean physically upon it." One thought uttered, he is hoisted to another, word by word exchanging fact for fancy, as if to speak were to make the world anew. To Beluncle, the narrator explains, talking is "a way of turning realities into unrealities," and placing written messages, such as "Eternity = Now," next to letters from creditors is typical of his way of doing business. In various other ways, too, the fundamental connection between dreaming and speaking, image and word, is emphasized. One major way is by the character of Henry, who imitates his father in his love of the creative power of language, especially when he is with Mary Phibbs. To her, he tells stories about his family, improved by an artistic juggling of detail, without noticing that she hates them because of "their importance to him and his pride in them"—because, basically, of their self-centeredness. Other characters, too, spin their wishful accounts of the world.

A second, more symbolic way in which the role of language in projecting the dream world surfaces is in two characters who exist primarily as "voices"—a technique Pritchett had practiced in *Dead Man Leading*. One is the youngest Beluncle boy, Leslie, who emerges in the middle of the book to utter the blunt, innermost thoughts of the family which are ordinarily blurred by Beluncle's rich discourse; the other is Mary's sister. Leslie attaches himself to Henry in one key scene in the garden, and Mary's sister sleeps with her and teases her with the things that Mary is afraid to think directly. Henry and Mary do not, however, give in entirely to this dream voice, as does Harry Johnson. Rather, they hear it along with another one, that of the waking world, and out of the two they harmonize a public voice. Mr. Beluncle, unlike them, is afraid of hearing two voices. He is afraid of the inner voice, because it whispers to him of his own mortality, but he is also afraid of the outer voice, because it denies the complete gratification of his infantile desires. A puritan who has adopted a transcendental explanation of human nature in order to live

with himself, he has succeeded, it would seem, in killing one of the voices—exactly which one is moot. It is enough to say that his inner voice has been made public, that his dream is his life. Thus, he is one-dimensional, hollow, his ego merely an expanding shell.

That Henry hears two voices makes possible a doubling of perspective which will eventually lead him out of egotistic confinement into artistic freedom. Henry is the foil to Beluncle's charlatanry, the nascent artist of the book, and clearly the autobiographical character; what is especially remarkable about the book is that he never nudges Beluncle out of the limelight. For being an autobiographical novel of sorts, and one incorporating elements of comedy, *Mr. Beluncle* is surprisingly unconcerned in any overt way with the triumph of son over father, youth over age. In this, his major study of egotism, Pritchett never forgets that the archetypal egotist in his private imagination is his father. If his earliest desire was to surmount him, then he succeeds in this novel, not by assuming center stage himself, not by painting himself large, but by reducing himself, by exercising the artist's negative capability to create one of the most memorable eccentrics in English literature.

Linda F. Tunick

OTHER MAJOR WORKS

SHORT FICTION: *The Spanish Virgin and Other Stories*, 1930; *You Make Your Own Life and Other Stories*, 1938; *It May Never Happen and Other Stories*, 1945; *Collected Stories*, 1956; *The Sailor, the Sense of Humour, and Other Stories*, 1956 (also known as *The Saint and Other Stories*, 1966); *When My Girl Comes Home*, 1961; *The Key to My Heart*, 1963; *Blind Love and Other Stories*, 1969; *The Camberwell Beauty and Other Stories*, 1974; *Selected Stories*, 1978; *The Fly in the Ointment*, 1978; *On the Edge of the Cliff*, 1979; *Collected Stories*, 1982; *More Collected Stories*, 1983; *A Careless Widow and Other Stories*, 1989; *Complete Collected Stories*, 1990.

NONFICTION: *Marching Spain*, 1928; *In My Good Books*, 1942; *The Living Novel and Later Appreciations*, 1946; *Why Do I Write? An Exchange of Views Between Elizabeth Bowen, Graham Greene, and V. S.*

Pritchett, 1948; *Books in General*, 1953; *The Spanish Temper*, 1954; *London Perceived*, 1962; *The Offensive Traveller*, 1964 (also known as *Foreign Faces*); *New York Proclaimed*, 1965; *The Working Novelist*, 1965; *Shakespeare: The Comprehensive Soul*, 1965; *Dublin: A Portrait*, 1967; *A Cab at the Door*, 1968; *George Meredith and English Comedy*, 1970; *Midnight Oil*, 1972; *Balzac: A Biography*, 1973; *The Gentle Barbarian: The Life and Work of Turgenev*, 1977; *The Myth Makers: Literary Essays*, 1979; *The Tale Bearers: Literary Essays*, 1980; *The Other Side of the Frontier: A V. S. Pritchett Reader*, 1984; *A Man of Letters*, 1985; *Chekhov: A Spirit Set Free*, 1988; *Lasting Impressions*, 1990; *The Complete Essays*, 1991; *Balzac*, 1992.

BIBLIOGRAPHY

Baldwin, Dean R. *V. S. Pritchett*. Boston: Twayne, 1987. A useful introduction for the beginning reader of Pritchett. Acknowledges him as a master of the short story, but also examines his novels and nonfiction works. A sympathetic study, noting that Pritchett deserves more attention than he has received.

Lane, Denis, and Rita Stein, eds. *Modern British Literature*. Vol. 5. New York: Frederick Ungar, 1985. The chapter on Pritchett gives a concise, appreciative overview of his work, naming his strengths as a creative and intelligent writer. Discusses a review by Douglas A. Hughes of Pritchett's collection of short stories, *On the Edge of the Cliff*. According to Lane and Stein, these short stories earn for Pritchett credit as the "finest short story writer of our time."

Lucas, John. "V. S. Pritchett." In *Great Writers of the English Language: Novelists and Prose Writers*, edited by James Vinson. New York: St. Martin's Press, 1979. Lucas acknowledges Pritchett as a "distinguished man of letters" and cites as an example *The Tale Bearers*, considered by many to be the standard in its field. Rates *Dead Man Leading* as Pritchett's finest novel, but considers his short stories more impressive. Also discusses Pritchett's two autobiographical novels, *A Cab at the Door* and *Midnight Oil*.

Stinson, John J. *V. S. Pritchett: A Study of the Short Fiction*. New York: Twayne, 1992. The paucity of criticism focusing on Pritchett's mastery of the short-story form is somewhat rectified by this slim volume. Stinson lacks space to comment on all—or even most—of the stories, but he does a good job of hitting the high points (in chronological order). The volume also reprints an interview with Pritchett, as well as Pritchett's own essay, "A Writer's Tale," about his literary influences. The book concludes by reprising previously published criticism by short-story practitioners Eudora Welty and William Trevor, and an original assessment by Professor Douglas A. Hughes.

Vannatta, Dennis P., ed. *The English Short Story, 1945-1980: A Critical History*. Boston: Twayne, 1985. Discusses Pritchett's short stories in the context of his contemporaries. Contains some thoughtful analyses of individual stories with appreciation for Pritchett's singular characters and the comedy in his writing.

FREDERIC PROKOSCH

Born: Madison, Wisconsin; May 17, 1908
Died: Plan de Grasse, France; June 2, 1989

PRINCIPAL LONG FICTION

The Asiatics, 1935
The Seven Who Fled, 1937
Night of the Poor, 1939
The Skies of Europe, 1941
The Conspirators, 1943
Age of Thunder, 1945
The Idols of the Cave, 1946
Storm and Echo, 1948
Nine Days to Mukalla, 1953
A Tale for Midnight, 1955
A Ballad of Love, 1960
The Seven Sisters, 1962
The Dark Dancer, 1964
The Wreck of the "Cassandra," 1966

The Missolonghi Manuscript, 1968
America, My Wilderness, 1972

OTHER LITERARY FORMS

Frederic Prokosch published five books of poetry. Some of his poems enjoyed a transitory popularity and appeared in anthologies, notably those of Oscar Williams. In addition, he translated the love sonnets of Louise Labé in 1947, some of the poetry of Friedrich Hölderlin in 1943, and Euripides' *Medea* (431 B.C.E.) in 1947.

Many of the poems in his first collection, *The Assassins* (1936), celebrate places and journeys and aspire to create an exotic mood. The collection also contains one of his most anthologized poems, "The Dolls," where Prokosch writes at his musical best of the sweet, crescent-eyed shapes, which, reaching into the poet's "secret night," become the "furies" of his sleep. Dylan Thomas later parodied this poem, giving to his own poem the title "The Molls."

Prokosch's second volume of poems, *The Carnival* (1938), depends less on the dazzling imagery of geography and more on the ordinary things of life and was an attempt, according to the author, to convey the darkness of the prewar decade, as in "Fable," where the "rippled snow is tracked with blood,/ And my love lies cold in the burning wood." The volume contains a long, autobiographical "Ode" that describes the phases of Prokosch's first thirty years of life and his various discoveries (of fairy tales, his body, the past, Asia). His "Nocturne," beginning "Close my darling both your eyes,/ Let your arm lie still at last," shares similarities with W. H. Auden's well-known poem "Lay your sleeping head, my love,/ Human on my faithless arm."

The poems contained in *Death at Sea* (1940) concern the plight of the individual in a chaotic world. In "The Festival," for example, a pair of lovers who are apparently homosexual note the "coming tempest" and follow "Silent the paths of longing and regret/ Which all our learning taught us to despise"; the

(Library of Congress)

poem is set against a backdrop of earrings trembling in the dark and fairies huddling by a bridge.

Reviewers were not kind to Prokosch the poet, and time itself has been still less kind. Although he assembled an anthology, *Chosen Poems*, in 1944, it was not until 1983 that he published his next volume of verse, *The Sea*, a collection of sonnets that once again reflects Prokosch's fascination with geography.

Finally, in 1983, Prokosch published his memoirs, *Voices*, a series of vignettes in which many of the literary giants of the twentieth century appear in a decidedly unheroic light.

ACHIEVEMENTS

Prokosch is said to have created the novel of geography, a distillate of the reflective travelogue.

More than half of his sixteen novels fall into this category, and even those that do not are dominated in some way by the theme of geography and involve cosmopolitan, travel-loving characters. With the publication of his first novel, *The Asiatics*, in 1935, a book highlighted by Asian scenes and attitudes when other American novelists were writing realistic novels set in their own country, Prokosch achieved instant fame and maintained a high reputation for approximately the next ten years. William Butler Yeats was deeply struck by Prokosch's poetic gifts, and André Gide, Thomas Mann, and Albert Camus all praised his works during his stellar decade. Even his later works were praised by W. Somerset Maugham, Thornton Wilder, and Marianne Moore. *The Asiatics*, which was translated into seventeen foreign languages and was even more popular in Europe than in the United States, would remain in print for more than fifty years. *The Seven Who Fled* won the Harper Novel Prize, awarded by a panel of judges consisting of Thornton Wilder, Sinclair Lewis, and Louis Bromfield. In 1944, Warner Bros. made *The Conspirators* into a motion picture starring Hedy Lamarr and Paul Henreid.

Radcliffe Squires has observed that Prokosch's recurring theme—the death-defying search for truth in travel—began to seem irrelevant to a postwar generation looking for stability in suburbia. Subsequently, his novels were not so much condemned by the critics as they were ignored. Nevertheless, no complete discussion of twentieth century literature can afford to gloss over the fictional subgenre pioneered by the wunderkind Prokosch, the novel of geography.

BIOGRAPHY

Frederic Prokosch was born in Madison, Wisconsin, on May 17, 1908, the middle child of three children born to Eduard and Mathilde Depprich Prokosch. His father, who had left Austria to escape a duel, was professor of Germanic philology at the University of Wisconsin, and his mother was an accomplished pianist. In 1913, Eduard Prokosch assumed a position at the University of Texas at Austin, which he lost six years later as a result of the anti-German hysteria that followed World War I.

Prokosch was sent in 1914 to spend a year in Europe, visiting his grandfather in Austria and attending private schools there and in Munich. His Austrian-Slavic-Germanic ancestry and his early acquaintance with European culture encouraged Prokosch's cosmopolitan spirit and love for geography. As a child, he developed an interest in fairy tales, and this he credits for his fascination as a novelist with picaresque and allegorical characters who strive inexorably for fulfillment.

In 1920, the family moved to Bryn Mawr, where Prokosch attended high school; in 1922, he entered Haverford College. In college, he became an athlete, particularly in tennis and squash, which, indeed, he did not abandon for years to come; he won the national squash championship of France in 1939 and that of Sweden in 1944. An avid lepidopterist, in later years he became as dexterous wielding his butterfly net as he had been with a racket.

After receiving his first master's degree from Haverford in 1928, Prokosch proceeded to earn a second one from King's College, Cambridge, in 1930. Two years later, he earned his doctorate at Yale. While a doctoral student, Prokosch taught English (from 1931 to 1933), continuing as a research fellow in 1934. The following year, *The Asiatics* appeared, and he returned to England, later visiting Africa and Asia. In 1936 and 1937, he was teaching at New York University, but when in 1937 he received both a Guggenheim Fellowship and the Harper Novel Prize of $7,500, he abandoned teaching altogether. He was then at the apogee of his renown as a writer, and he could write from Prague in 1937 that one of his main interests was "trying to avoid the vulgarizations of money and publicity." Ironically, the vagaries of the reading public would facilitate this goal considerably in coming years.

After the fall of France, Prokosch spent two years in Lisbon, which served as the setting for *The Conspirators*. When the United States entered the war, Prokosch returned home to enter government service in the Office of War Information and then spent two years (1943 to 1944) as an attache in the American Legation in Stockholm. After the war, he went to Rome (1947 to 1953), where, on a Fulbright Scholarship (1951 to 1952), he researched in the Vatican Library the material for his first attempt at a historical novel, *A Tale for Midnight*, about the Renaissance Cenci family.

The 1960's found Prokosch living in Paris; he finally settled in Grasse in the south of France. He continued his writing—now largely ignored by critics—and indulged his interest in rare books. Between 1968 and 1970, he printed and bound a series of elegant gift books, each containing a single poem by a well-known modern writer; these books' imprints dated the printing between 1933 and 1940, making them collectors' items. Eventually Nicolas Barker exposed these "self-forgeries" and Prokosch admitted to the books' late date. Prokosch died in June, 1989, in Plan de Grasse, France.

ANALYSIS

The creator of the novel of geography, Frederic Prokosch was a lover of travel and even of maps themselves. In *America, My Wilderness*, he defines the place-name as a "talisman that guides us through the terror of anonymity," and his novelist's fascination with place-names is, at its best, lyrical and evocative, at its worst, pedantic and tedious. It follows that such a lover of the places of this world would be a proponent of internationalism, and in most of his novels written after 1940, Prokosch urged his American readers to abandon their isolationism and to nurture links and bonds with the other peoples of the world.

All of Prokosch's fiction is an attempt in some way to probe the spiritual malaise characteristic of the twentieth century. In his novels of the 1930's, there is an abiding, non-Western fatalism. A sense of impending doom for the world saturates *The Asiatics* as the natives philosophize to the young American traveler about the resignation implicit in the Asian personality. This doom is counterbalanced by the lyrical nature of the writing and by the luxuriance of detail, however, and the beguiling, unutterable beauty of life strains to prevail even in these prewar novels. When the fear and foreboding of the 1930's was eventually replaced by worldwide optimism after the war, the tenor of Prokosch's novels changed in tune

with the times. In *Storm and Echo*, the emphasis is on Africa as a new continent rather than on Asia as a dying one, and the hint of a positive note in the destiny of humankind is unmistakable.

THE ASIATICS

In the picaresque narrative of *The Asiatics*, the nameless young American hero crosses the entire Asian continent from Lebanon to China. The character of the hero is elusive and vague, and many of the secondary characters with whom he forms friendships—friendships that are sometimes intense but always temporary—seem to take on more life than he. The hero is jailed in Turkey and suffers a plane crash in Iran, but always keeps his mind open and unbiased in order to soak up all the aphorisms proffered him both by the Asians and by the Western travelers whom he encounters. There is a chillingly prophetic mood to the novel; Asia is old and tired and waiting for death. When the hero enters a snowy-domed *dagoba* in Kandy and begins to converse with an old monk, it is of the coming of the twenty-fifth Buddha and of the accompanying dissolution of the world into Nirvana that they speak. The novel never ceases to analyze and emphasize the decadence and resignation of the enigma that is Asia.

THE SEVEN WHO FLED

In *The Seven Who Fled*, Prokosch weaves an allegory around a group of seven travelers, each representing a country in Europe (England, France, Spain, Germany, Austria, Belgium, and Russia), set adrift in the hostile vastness of Chinese Turkestan. After their caravan reaches Aqsu from Kashgar, the two German-speaking geologists are put into prison by local authorities; two others are kept as hostages; the Frenchman de la Scaze falls prey to a fever. Only the Englishman Layeville and de la Scaze's beautiful Spanish wife are free to proceed; the former joins a caravan to Tibet, and the latter continues eastward on a caravan in the company of Dr. Liu, a wealthy Chinese merchant. Much of the first half of the book details the disintegration and eventual death of Layeville in the icy summits of Tibet. In his relationship with the barbaric and tantalizing Tansang, his Turgot guide whose powerful face combines the strengths of "a young man, a woman and a child," Layeville feels the possibility of a renewal of his spirit, but he loses his last chance when Tansang dies.

Like Layeville and Tansang, the hostages back in Aqsu, the Russian Serafimov (an inarticulate bear of a man) and the Belgian thief Goupilliere, form an uneasy pair. When Serafimov is rejected by the Russian prostitute Madame Tastin while his companion Goupilliere is accepted, Serafimov consummates his hatred for the Belgian by murdering him. The two geologists, the German Wildenbruch (who worships heroism and ambition) and the blond, angelic Austrian Von Wald, escape from prison together and travel to Shanghai, where the tubercular Wildenbruch departs for home and Von Wald decides to remain. The last pair, the most mismatched of all, are Paul and Olivia de la Scaze. Olivia, who abandons her husband in Aqsu, comes under the complete control of Dr. Liu and ends up joining a house of prostitution in Shanghai. Paul recovers from his fever, eventually catches cholera from a dancing girl, and dies.

Although the seven characters do not correspond exactly to the seven cardinal sins of medieval theology, each sin is very much in evidence. Certainly sloth is implied in the flight of the seven from the responsibilities of their European lives to the distractions of adventure abroad. Lust is evident in Layeville's reminiscences of homosexuality, in Olivia's eventual choice of occupation, and in Serafimov's obsession with Madame Tastin. Wildenbruch feels envy for the innocence of Von Wald, and only Von Wald seems relatively immune to the ravages of the deadly sins.

NINE DAYS TO MUKALLA

Nine Days to Mukalla is the story of four plane-crash survivors who make their way from an island in the Indian Ocean to Mukalla in Arabia (now Saudi Arabia, Yemen, and the Persian Gulf states), where they will be able to get a boat for Aden and return to civilization. The novel employs the rich, evocative style that characterizes Prokosch's best work and allegorizes the contrasting sensibilities of the four victims lost in a mysterious Arabia, which, in its capacity to distill good and evil, "reveals the human skeleton." The group is composed of two Englishwomen, Miss Todd and Sylvia Howard; and two

Americans, an archaeologist, Dr. Moss, and David Gilbert, who is the only survivor by the end of the novel. David, described by Miss Todd as not quite a typical American, seems symbolic of a new, postwar, cosmopolitan America. Miss Todd, although she dies early in the narrative, possesses such great vitality that her spirit persists throughout the novel. It is the gift of her jewelry to David that enables him to reach Mukalla successfully. Dr. Moss is Miss Todd's foil, and just as the party's Bedouin guide thinks of Miss Todd as their good spirit, Moss is viewed by him as their bad spirit. He steals some of Miss Todd's jewels, abandons the party in his own interest, and is finally murdered in the desert. The primness of Sylvia Howard, the sketchiest of the four characters, is broken down in the Arabian desert, and before she dies of exhaustion when she actually reaches Mukalla, she asks David to make love to her.

THE SEVEN SISTERS

The Seven Sisters is Prokosch's first novel in which an American setting (Bishop's Neck, Maryland) is handled as powerfully as the foreign settings are in his earlier works. Each of the seven Nightingale sisters has a story, and the story of each sheds light on the character of Peter, an orphan who lives with the family. Peter is another of Prokosch's searching artists, but this time, untypically for Prokosch, his search ends in a kind of maturity. Five of the seven sisters, after frantic struggles, gradually achieve a kind of maturity as well.

The death of one of the sisters, young Elizabeth, who succumbs to a snake bite while still innocent, signals the real start of the action of the novel, suggesting a world divested of its innocence. The oldest sister, the repressed Augusta, marries a neighboring aristocrat, recognizes that the marriage is a mistake, and returns to her parents' home. Daphne leaves home dressed as a boy, falls in with a lesbian, meets a runaway New Yorker named Pancho, loses him to another man and to death, rejects the lesbian, and returns home. The elfin and visionary Grace never leaves home, but follows the advice of a ouija board, becomes pregnant, and goes to a cave, where she dies in the act of childbirth.

Consuelo, Barbara, and Freya, in the company of

Peter and their mother, go to Europe. Consuelo links up with a Hungarian refugee. Blonde, beautiful Barbara marries a wealthy, aging Italian prince, falls in love with his handsome nephew, and ends up, after losing both, praying for forgiveness for her vanity and pride. Freya gives up her career as a painter and goes to Brazil as a social worker, where she perishes in the jungle. It is the character of Peter that acts as the cohesive force in the novel; it is with him that the novel begins and ends.

THE SKIES OF EUROPE

The Skies of Europe is Prokosch's first realistic novel and covers the events that led up to World War II. Philip, a young American journalist, loves Saskia, a failed artist who does not love him. The novel abounds in characters who are unsuccessful artists and neglected poets; one such unnamed character seems intended to represent Hitler. *The Skies of Europe* has affinities with a later novel, *A Ballad of Love*, Prokosch's most nearly autobiographical novel, his "portrait of the artist as a young man." It is, moreover, a portrait of a *defeated* artist. The hero, Henry, is a poet who grows up in Austria, Texas, and Wisconsin and becomes involved in a disastrous love affair similar to those in *The Skies of Europe* and *The Idols of the Cave*.

WORLD WAR II NOVELS

Three of Prokosch's novels are set against the backdrop of World War II. *The Conspirators*, which takes place in a wartime Lisbon filled with refugees and reeking of espionage, relates the detection and murder of a Nazi agent. Its atmosphere of historical change is haunting, and the degree of conventional suspense is rare in Prokosch's work. *Age of Thunder*, dedicated to the memory of Antoine de Saint-Exupéry, is not as realistic or as successful as *The Conspirators* and suffers from a preponderance of sketchily drawn characters, whereas the latter concentrates on a select few. As in all of Prokosch's novels, many of the scenes are brilliant, and they faithfully evoke the hypnotic atmosphere of war, but the dreamlike mission of the hero, Jean-Nicholas, through the Haute-Savoie seems to lack significance in the overall picture of the war. *The Idols of the Cave* makes use of the wartime atmosphere of New

York as *The Conspirators* did with Lisbon. The city's brooding and sinister air is such that it almost overpowers the reader, and the unsuccessful love-story plot is little more than a duplication of that of *The Skies of Europe*.

NIGHT OF THE POOR

Night of the Poor, the title of which was taken from a painting by Diego Rivera, is perhaps the author's weakest novel and amounts to little more than a conventional travelogue. It is the first of Prokosch's novels that has an American setting, and American place-names are savored and enumerated to such an extent that they tax the reader's patience. The plot chronicles the travels of Tom on his way to Texas after the death of an uncle in Wisconsin, and the gamut of depravity and inhumanity that he encounters on the way. Thirty-three years later, Prokosch would rework the same idea in *America, My Wilderness*, dressing it up with generous amounts of Surrealism and modernistic bizarrerie. After the murder of his uncle in the Middle West, a half-black outcast named Pancho Krauss wanders from the Atlantic to the Pacific, savoring the "slow transition of one landscape into another."

STORM AND ECHO

Storm and Echo follows the pattern of Prokosch's first two novels, and the landscape of Africa is even more brilliantly painted than that of Asia in his earlier novels. There is a Conradian power in this tale of an American's search for a mysterious friend who has gone off to Mount Nagala. Central Africa is typically fraught with dangers of all kinds, but the friend is found (albeit as a corpse impaled upon a rock), and the protagonist emerges victorious over his own death wish.

HISTORICAL NOVELS

Prokosch's historical novels include *A Tale for Midnight, The Dark Dancer*, and *The Missolonghi Manuscript*. The first, characterized by its author as "dedicated to storytelling per se and above all," seems to be just that, chronicling the murder of Count Francesco Cenci in 1599 by his wife and children and stressing the effect of the crime on the main conspirator, his daughter Beatrice. Its portrayal of sixteenth century Rome as plague-ridden, flood-ridden, and sin-ridden is graphic and effective. *The Dark Dancer* is laid in seventeenth century India at the zenith of the Mogul Golden Age, when Emperor Shah Jahan built the Taj Mahal for his wife Arjumand. The Emperor, however, is dispossessed of his empire by his sons, even as he himself had murdered to secure it, and gets to see the monumental building only when, as a prisoner, he is too weary even to admire it. *The Missolonghi Manuscript*, which purports to be the long-lost memoirs of Lord Byron unearthed by an American professor, is the strongest of Prokosch's postwar novels. Praiseworthy for its sensitive probing of Byron's personality and for its historical accuracy, the book is perhaps flawed by its overemphasis on the homosexual side of Byron's undeniably bisexual lifestyle.

THE WRECK OF THE "CASSANDRA"

The Wreck of the "Cassandra" is similar to *Nine Days to Mukalla*, but lacks the latter's allegorical sweep. Here, nine survivors of a shipwreck somewhere between Hong Kong and Australia reach a large island and settle down idyllically for a short time before the spirit of the island distills their personalities into various shades of good and evil. The presence of hostile natives adds to the tensions in the group, they confront one another violently, and some of their number are lost before their inevitable rescue.

Prokosch is destined to be remembered, if not as a great novelist, as a pioneer of the novel of geography and as an internationalist, one who focused on the exotica of faraway lands but always called his fellow Americans to abandon their parochialism and recognize the underlying unity of humankind.

Jack Shreve

OTHER MAJOR WORKS

POETRY: *The Assassins*, 1936; *The Carnival: Poems*, 1938; *Death at Sea: Poems*, 1940; *Chosen Poems*, 1944; *The Sea*, 1983; *Voices*, 1983 (verse memoir).

TRANSLATIONS: *Some Poems of Friedrich Hölderlin*, 1943; *Love Sonnets of Louise Labé*, 1947; *Medea* in *Greek Plays in Modern Translation*, 1947 (Dudley Fitts, editor).

BIBLIOGRAPHY

Austen, Roger. *Playing the Game: The Homosexual Novel in America*. Indianapolis: Bobbs-Merrill, 1977. Contains a useful discussion of Prokosch, situating him in the context of twentieth century literature.

Bishop, John Peale. *The Collected Essays of John Peale Bishop*. Edited by Edmund Wilson. New York: Charles Scribner's Sons, 1948. "Final Dreading" is Bishop's favorable poetry review of Prokosch's *The Assassins*, his first book of poems. Refers to Prokosch's extensive travels and their influence on these poems and concludes with a brief commentary on Prokosch's technique and his relationship to Oswald Spengler and Saint-John Perse.

Carpenter, Richard C. "The Novels of Frederic Prokosch." *College English* 18 (1957): 261-267. Provides much insight into the development of Prokosch's novelistic style. An appreciative essay by a sympathetic critic of Prokosch.

Marowski, Daniel G., and Roger Matuz, eds. *Contemporary Literary Criticism*. Vol. 48. Detroit: Gale Research, 1988. The entry on Prokosch presents an overview of his works, citing him as a "highly regarded novelist" who gained prominence in the 1930's. Included is a sampling of reviews, mostly favorable, of his earlier works (*The Asiatics, The Assassins, The Seven Who Fled*), as well as later works, such as *The Missolonghi Manuscript* and his memoir, *Voices,* in which he addresses his literary displacement.

Quartermain, Peter, ed. *Dictionary of Literary Biography*. Vol. 48. Detroit: Gale Research, 1986. Provides a selected checklist of Prokosch's works, giving more emphasis to his poetry, although he is better known as a novelist. Discusses his poems between 1920 and the mid-1940's. Also includes background information on Prokosch, including his numerous travels, and some brief commentary on his novels.

Squires, Radcliffe. *Frederic Prokosch*. New York: Twayne, 1964. Presents Prokosch's works in a chronological format and is useful as a critical introduction. Squires focuses on the timeless quali-

ties of "interplay of emotion and intellect" in Prokosch's work but acknowledges that his writing
was a "casualty" of World War II, which changed
the values of the reading public. A selected bibliography is provided.

MARCEL PROUST

Born: Auteuil, France; July 10, 1871
Died: Paris, France; November 18, 1922

PRINCIPAL LONG FICTION

Du côté de chez Swann, 1913 (*Swann's Way*, 1922)
À l'ombre des jeunes filles en fleurs, 1919 (*Within
    a Budding Grove*, 1924)
Le Côté de Guermantes, 1920-1921 (*The
    Guermantes Way*, 1925)
Sodome et Gomorrhe, 1922 (*Cities of the Plain*,
    1927)
La Prisonnière, 1925 (*The Captive*, 1929)
Albertine disparue, 1925 (*The Sweet Cheat Gone*,
    1930)
Le Temps retrouvé, 1927 (*Time Regained*, 1931)
À la recherche du temps perdu, 1913-1927 (collec-
    tive title for all of the above, *Remembrance of
    Things Past*, 1922-1931, 1981)
Jean Santeuil, 1952 (English translation, 1955)

OTHER LITERARY FORMS

In addition to his magnum opus, *Remembrance of
Things Past*, Marcel Proust wrote a number of less
well-known works. His first book, *Les Plaisirs et les
jours* (1896; *Pleasures and Regrets*, 1948), a collection of stories and some verse, was published in
1896. Its primary value lies in its preliminary statement of themes that are developed more fully in *Remembrance of Things Past*, as Edmund Wilson has
pointed out in *Axel's Castle* (1931).

Proust's fascination with John Ruskin led to pref-
aces for and translations of Ruskin's *The Bible of
Amiens* (1880-1885) in 1904 and of his *Sesame and
Lilies* (1865) in 1906. Before turning his full at-

tention to the novel, Proust also wrote a series of
parodies of his favorite French writers, which were
published in *Le Figaro*. Of considerable interest to
Proust scholars is *Contre Sainte-Beuve* (*By Way of
Sainte-Beuve*, 1958), written in 1908 but not published until 1954. In it, Proust uses a variety of essays, autobiographical pieces, and fiction to attack
criticism that claims to be scientific and objective.
Proust argues instead that only memory and the unconscious can break through the barriers of habit that
impede art. Of somewhat less interest is *Pastiches et
mélanges*, a volume of miscellaneous pieces published in 1919. Proust's brother, Robert, collected
magazine and newspaper articles written by Proust
as late as 1921 and published them in *Chroniques*
(1927).

ACHIEVEMENTS

Proust's monumental achievement in writing *Remembrance of Things Past* consists not simply in the
work's multivolume length or the complexity of the
extended and intermingled lives of its characters,
although these elements alone are impressive. It is
above all the intense psychological realism with
which the novel's characters—particularly the author's alter ego, Marcel—are rendered that has influenced other writers and has drawn critical acclaim.
That "realism" is internal: Proust was fascinated by
the interplay between external events and the mind,
especially by the way human perception synthesizes
and interprets events in time—by "the symbolic om-
nitemporality of an event fixed in a remembering
consciousness," as Erich Auerbach put it. These concerns are reflected in much of twentieth century literature—notably in the works of James Joyce, Thomas
Mann, and Virginia Woolf—and Proust may be said
to have introduced their full exposition in his magnum opus.

Although, at the beginning of his writing career,
Proust received little recognition outside his literary
milieu, he was awarded the Prix Goncourt in 1919 for
Within a Budding Grove. This recognition helped establish him as a serious and significant author, and
since his death, his reputation and influence have
continued to grow.

BIOGRAPHY

Marcel Proust was born in Auteuil, a suburb of Paris, on July 10, 1871. He was the son of the happily married Dr. Adrien Proust and Jeanne Weil. Adrien Proust had left the devoutly Catholic home of his candlemaker father in Illiers to go to Paris, where he ultimately found acclaim as a professor and hygienist. Adrien's family returned to Illiers, the "Combray" of *Remembrance of Things Past*, for frequent holidays. The home there of Adrien's sister, Elisabeth, became the model for the famous house and garden of Marcel's Aunt Léonie. Marcel's mother was the daughter of a wealthy Jewish family from Lorraine. Although Marcel was baptized a Catholic, he remained close to his mother's family throughout his life. His novels reveal little interest in religion other than aesthetic pleasure in church architecture, and Proust practiced no religion during his adult life.

From his birth, Proust was plagued by ill health; indeed, his parents feared he would die shortly after his birth. In spite of careful attention given to his well-being, he suffered a severe attack of asthma at the age of nine. Such frailty doubtless contributed to his acute sensitivity. While both his father and younger brother, Robert (later also a doctor), were committed to science, duty, and routine, Marcel and his mother were of a more emotional, artistic, and intellectual sensibility.

Poor health did not restrict Proust's movement entirely. He attended the Lycée Condorcet, and during his years there (1882-1889), he played in the gardens of the Champs-Elysées, where he fell in love with Marie de Banardaky. Although he had numerous friendships at school, even at that early age he found pleasure in the solitary task of writing. That did not, however, prevent him from attending the salons of his classmates' mothers. At the age of seventeen, Proust had already entered the world of Parisian society that he would depict so brilliantly in *Remembrance of Things Past*.

After receiving his *baccalauréat* in 1889, Proust volunteered for his one year of military duty. It was one of the happiest, most "normal" years of his life. He became friends with Gaston Arman de Caillavet, one of the models for Robert de Saint-Loup. On his return to Paris, he studied at the Sorbonne and at the École des Sciences Politiques, where he was deeply influenced by the lectures of the French philosopher Henri Bergson. In spite of his father's wish that he enter diplomatic service, Proust found himself more attracted to the worlds of society and literature. He became a favorite in the salons of both the haute bourgeoisie and the nobility. At the salon of Madame Arman de Caillavet, he met Anatole France, a meeting that provided the model in part for Bergotte. Although women such as the Comtesse Greffulhe and Princess Mathilde provided invaluable opportunities for Proust to observe the mannerisms and style of the pinnacle of Parisian society, it was perhaps the salon of Madame Straus, widow of Georges Bizet and mother of Marcel's Condorcet friend, Jacques, that was most influential in Proust's development. Madame Straus was noted for her beauty and wit, and along with the Comtesse de Chevigné, she contributed significantly to the characterization of the chief denizen of Proust's fictional Parisian suburb Faubourg Saint-Germain, Madame de Guermantes.

In his mid-twenties, Proust gradually withdrew from the brilliant world he had both participated in and observed so carefully. From an early age he had felt that artistic endeavor and social life were largely incompatible; he may also have grown disillusioned with the vanities of high society.

During these early years of maturity, Proust developed intense platonic relationships with both men and women. His sexual interest was primarily in men. Among his earliest affairs was one with Reynaldo Hahn, a composer. It was Comte Robert de Montesquiou, however, who served as chief model for Proust's greatest homosexual character, the Baron de Charlus. Perhaps Proust's most compelling involvement was with Alfred Agostinelli, who served as his chauffeur and secretary. Agostinelli, who enrolled in aviation school under the name "Marcel Swann," drowned as the result of an airplane crash off the French coast in 1914. It has been suggested frequently that Proust's tortured experience with Agostinelli was the inspiration for the characterization of Albertine.

Proust's father died in 1903, and his mother's death in 1905 left Proust utterly grief-stricken. Yet within a year after his mother's death, he began an early version of *Remembrance of Things Past*. In the remaining years of that decade, he wrote widely, penning parodies, some fiction, and essays in criticism. In January, 1909, Proust returned on a snowy evening to the warmth of his kitchen for a cup of tea and dry toast; while idly savoring the humble repast, he involuntarily recalled precious childhood memories. The significance of spontaneous memory as a condition for art struck Proust, providing the missing link in his theory of literature. This revelation was to shape his writing of *Remembrance of Things Past* as he labored in his cork-lined Paris apartment.

Proust was physically unfit to serve during World War I, although the suffering of France affected him deeply. During the war, his life was more solitary than ever before, although he dined so frequently at a famous Paris hotel that he became known as "Marcel of the Ritz." Thus, the image of the dandy, the snob, the fop followed Proust throughout most of his life. Nevertheless, he had a huge coterie of loyal friends and servants and a reputation for courage (he once fought a duel with a libelous critic) and generosity. Before his death from asthma in 1922, he not only had been awarded the Prix Goncourt but also had received the recognition of his contemporaries as a genius.

ANALYSIS

Like Gustave Flaubert, Marcel Proust believed that of all literary forms, the novel most fully reveals the temperament of its writer. As George Painter's exhaustive biography of Proust demonstrates, there are innumerable, indeed seemingly endless, parallels between the lives of Marcel Proust and Marcel, the narrator of *Remembrance of Things Past*.

REMEMBRANCE OF THINGS PAST

While the novel reveals much of Proust's character and values, it is not an autobiography but a work of fiction in which the raw materials of personal experience and remembrance are transformed by the imagination into art of the highest order. Rather than yield to the temptation of a biographical reading of the novel, it is perhaps more profitable to concentrate on the development of the themes and to note the techniques that Proust employs to create his vision of humankind in their emotional, moral, and aesthetic worlds.

Like Dante and Honoré de Balzac before him, Proust creates a vast and teeming world, depicting the immense social changes that took place in French life between the end of the Franco-Prussian War in 1871 and the post-World War I era. While *Remembrance of Things Past* focuses on the wealthy bourgeois and nobility of Paris, it by no means excludes other classes. The detailed and sympathetic characterizations of Jupien the tailor, Françoise, and Aimé, the headwaiter at the Grand Hotel, testify to the social range of the novel. Given the work's considerable time span and its scope of social inquiry, it is not surprising that Proust is able to develop a variety of themes: the Dreyfus affair, homosexuality, the difficulties of love, the growth of the artist, the vanity of society, and so on. By doing this, Proust invests the worlds of Paris, Combray, and Balbec with solidity and seriousness. Each thematic concern is ultimately registered on the growing consciousness of the protagonist, Marcel; all themes are subordinated to the dominant thematic concern of the novel: Marcel's attempt to overcome the disappointments of love, the false social expectations and the faulty imaginings and appearances that separate him from reality. With the aid of memory, prompted involuntarily by physical stimuli, Marcel ultimately defeats time, and through art, he finds the joy that has eluded him in love and social life. It is difficult, therefore, to understand Wilson's characterization of the novel as "the gloomiest book ever written"; while Proust's world is obviously complex and borders on the tragic, the existence in it of a sensuous and moral art belies the charge of pessimism.

The need to give structure and unity to a work as thematically ambitious as *Remembrance of Things Past* was a major challenge for Proust. While Wilson may have been off the mark thematically, his observation that the novel's structure is symphonic, a series of shifting images with "multiplied associations," is accurate. In so describing Proust, Wilson, like other critics, emphasized Proust's debt to Symbolism specifically and Romanticism generally.

Proust's appreciation of introspection, his attentiveness to and enthusiasm for the natural world, his awareness of the power of the subjective and unconscious, and his use of image as symbol—all are variations on themes and techniques developed by nineteenth century French Romantics. Proust's affinity with the Symbolists was reinforced by his appreciation of the metaphysics of Henri Bergson, who was one of Proust's professors and a cousin by marriage. Although Proust denied any debt to Bergson, he, like Bergson, appreciated the role of intuition as a source of knowledge. Bergson also believed, as Wallace Fowlie has pointed out in his book *A Reading of Proust* (1964), that the capacity of an object to stimulate the memory lies in the individual himself, not in the object. By embracing the Symbolists and Bergson, Proust aligned himself clearly with those who resisted a purely scientific interpretation of reality.

Proust employs a variety of specific means to give shape to his world. Most important, perhaps, is the organization of *Remembrance of Things Past* into three major quests undertaken by the protagonist, Marcel. The first is the quest for love, a search that prompts much subjective analysis by the protagonist. In contrast, the second quest, Marcel's emergence into society, draws upon Proust's brilliant and often comic observations of both manners and morals. The quest for love begins with young Marcel's desperate desire for a goodnight kiss from his mother, a desire frustrated by Swann's call on his parents. Marcel's subsequent infatuations with Gilberte, the Duchess de Guermantes, and Albertine are paralleled by other, equally vain quests for love by Swann for Odette, Robert de Saint-Loup for Rachel, and Baron de Charlus for Morel. The quest for love is symbolized in part by Swann's Way, one of the two paths that leads young Marcel and his family from their home in Combray to the outside world. The other road, the Guermantes Way, symbolizes the quest for society that leads Marcel from the secure world of family, servants, and neighbors in Combray to the drawing room of Odette Swann and, later, to a higher echelon of society symbolized by the salon of the slightly déclassé "bluestocking," Madame de Villeparisis. From there, Marcel finds his way into the much sought-after world of the Duke and Duchess de Guermantes and ultimately to the most socially exalted milieu of all, the soirées given by Prince and Princess de Guermantes.

In the same way that Swann's Way and Guermantes Way are finally united when Swann's daughter marries a Guermantes, these two quests, one private, one public, come together in mutual disillusionment. What saves the novel from utter despair is the persistence of those things that are not defeated by time and human vanity: Marcel's memories of his grandmother's selflessness and love, his involuntary recollection of sensations that produced great happiness, his realization of the eternity that lies within art. Thus, failure in the first two quests allows for success in the third: Marcel's pursuit of a career as an artist. The quest for art, initially overshadowed by love and society, is hinted at, however, by the presence in the novel of three artists who, in spite of their foibles and miseries, have created enduring works of art: the novelist Bergotte, the painter Elstir, and the composer Vinteuil. Indeed, although the emphasis shifts from book to book, all three quests figure in each of the seven novels that together make up *Remembrance of Things Past*.

SWANN'S WAY

Swann's Way, the chronicle of Marcel's childhood, begins and ends with memories of the protagonist, the mature Marcel. The first memory, recounted in a section called "Overture," is preceded by a description of the disorientation and pleasure that come from awakening in a darkened room at night. This sensation is one that Marcel has learned to relish, because it leads him to recall other rooms, particularly those of Combray, his childhood home. Marcel recalls the particular evening when Swann called on his family. Wealthy, Jewish, suave, and sophisticated, Swann visits Marcel's family frequently when he is home from Paris. Swann's visit upsets Marcel because it interrupts the ritual of his mother's nightly kiss. In his room, young Marcel grows so desperate that he sends Françoise, the cook, to deliver a note to his mother. His mother does not come until Swann leaves, but Marcel's stern father suggests unexpectedly that she sleep in Marcel's room to comfort him.

The triumph of Marcel, touching yet disturbing in its power to manipulate, proves to be paradoxical. Even though he possesses his mother's attention, Marcel senses that such happiness, such a moment of unexpected success, is fleeting. "I knew that such a night could not be repeated." One function of this incident is clear: Marcel's quest for love has a most ambiguous beginning.

Immediately following the famous scene of the mother's kiss, Proust draws a crucial distinction between two types of memory. The first is voluntary, or recollection associated with intellect, "an exercise of the will." Voluntary memory is largely sterile and in vivid contrast to the sensations created by the second type, involuntary memory. Proust makes this distinction clear by recounting the episode of *la petite madeleine*, or little cake. The adult Marcel comes home on a winter day to tea and cakes. The crumbs in the spoon of tea give him exquisite pleasure, much to his surprise and delight. Initially puzzled by the sensation, Marcel suddenly recovers the memory: His Aunt Léonie had once given him tea and madeleines. An entire vision of forgotten elements of Combray surges over him. The incident is charming in itself, but it also anticipates a larger movement in the novel, Marcel's quest for the source of artistic inspiration.

Having resurrected memories of his youthful home in the madeleine incident, Proust logically moves to the next section, entitled "Combray." Here emerges Marcel's childhood as it is shaped by family, an occasional school friend such as the pugnacious Bloch, and his reading of novels, particularly the works of Bergotte, an acquaintance of Swann. While Proust has been accused of being careless, casual, and prolix, the Combray section indicates quite the opposite. The characters and the quest motifs and themes are introduced without diverting the reader's attention away from the immediate concern, the characterization of Marcel's early years. Like Charles Dickens, Proust creates characters that seem to have their own independent lives. The bedridden Aunt Léonie, for example, delights the reader with her quixotic pursuit of local gossip, yet her attachment to her sickroom clearly anticipates Marcel's own frequent retirements to his bed.

The Combray section also introduces the two "ways" that will influence Marcel's life, Swann's and Guermantes'. These two walks, the first represented by the lover Swann and the second by the socially prominent Duchess de Guermantes, will be the symbolic means by which Marcel will come to know the world outside Combray. While walking Swann's Way, Marcel first sees Swann's daughter, Gilberte, who will be the object of Marcel's first quest outside the confines of family. In an irony that is distinctly Proustian, Gilberte, standing under the pink hawthorns, makes an obscene gesture that to Marcel has the appearance of anger and rejection. The adult Marcel discovers that the reality was quite the opposite: Gilberte's youthful intentions were entirely sexual. This misreading of appearances emerges as one of the novel's central themes.

The Combray incidents are followed by what may seem an unlikely sequel, a novel within a novel entitled "Swann in Love." Although audacious technically, its position within the larger work is logical and effective. Swann's affair with Odette contributes to the whole in terms of both style and theme. Proust reveals first of all his flexibility in use of point of view. The entire episode is told by an omniscient narrator; Proust recognizes that there is no way that either the youthful or the adult Marcel could be privy to the history of Swann's romance. Focusing on the sophisticated Swann also allows Proust to characterize the social world of Paris that Marcel will someday pursue. Of particular interest is Proust's use of the Verdurins and their "little nucleus" of friends. Not only do they enlarge one's knowledge of the teeming social life of Paris, but also they form a comic, ironic backdrop for Swann's tender love. Comically vulgar, the Verdurins are on the bottom rung of the social ladder—bohemians, as Marcel's grandfather calls them. Yet Madame Verdurin will ultimately become much more than a backdrop; she will marry the Prince de Guermantes and prove herself to be the most vivid example of the immensity of the social change that occurs in the full novel's fifty-year time span. Another theme, similar in its social character, is also introduced in "Swann in Love." It occurs in a passing comment made by Oriane, the

Princess des Laumes, about Swann's being a Jew. While apparently irrelevant in the early part of *Remembrance of Things Past*, the question of anti-Semitism, raised by the Dreyfus affair, later divided France profoundly.

This section's title indicates the primary focus of "Swann in Love." Swann's obsession with Odette, replete with ironies and contradictions, foreshadows Marcel's own loves; Swann is indeed the archetype of the Proustian lover. Whether heterosexual or "inverted" (Proust's term for homosexual), the lover chooses as his object someone who at best only obliquely shares his values. Swann—a member of the Jockey Club, a friend of the Prince of Wales, a man whose eye is so sensitive that he sees reflections of Giotto's *Charity* in a kitchen maid, the very spiritual and artistic father of Marcel—is also a man who seeks after prostitutes. He is continually vulnerable to "the sight of healthy, abundant, rosy human flesh." Similarly, the elegant, manly Robert de Saint-Loup is obsessed with the plain, whorish Rachel, and the Baron de Charlus freely spends his social, moral, and emotional capital on the unscrupulous grandson of a valet, Morel. While Odette de Crécy is no ordinary courtesan, she nevertheless has little of Swann's sophistication and sensibility. Once Swann has possessed Odette physically, their love is composed of lies, infidelities, perhaps lesbianism on Odette's part, and jealousy and obsession on Swann's. Most significant, "this malady, which was Swann's love," will afflict Marcel as perniciously in his quest of Albertine.

A particularly brilliant scene, Swann attending a soirée at Madame de Sainte-Euverte's, illustrates both the function of Swann in the larger work and the tightly woven texture of Proust's art. Wishing to leave a drawing room—a room off-limits to Odette—Swann is irritated that he has been entrapped by the beginning of a musical piece. He soon recognizes a series of notes that proves to be a phrase from a sonata by the fictional composer Vinteuil, the same piece Swann had earlier called the national anthem of his love for Odette. Swann's experience as he listens to the piece foreshadows Marcel's most profound discoveries: involuntary memory as the source of revelation and disappointment in love. As he listens, Swann "could see it all: the snowy, curled petals of the chrysanthemum . . . the address 'Maison Dorée' embossed on the note paper . . . the frowning contraction of her eyebrows." From the moment he hears the sonata, Swann knows he can never revive his love for Odette.

Not only does Swann's epiphany, rooted in involuntary memory, foreshadow Marcel's in the final volume of the novel, but also it indicates how Proust develops a number of themes simultaneously. The party at Madame de Sainte-Euverte's is also fine social satire, one of Proust's major concerns. The important theme of music, represented by Vinteuil, is present. The works of Vinteuil will eventually play as large a role in Marcel's life as in Swann's. Most important, Swann is, as Vladimir Nabokov, in his *Lectures on Literature* (1980), calls him, "a kind of fancy mirror of the narrator himself," one who "sets the pattern." Significant, too, is the pervading sense of paradox and irony that attends Swann's realization of love gone stale. The scene unobtrusively knits together elements of plot and theme that preceded it, renders them with clarity in a fully realized present, and anticipates further enrichments of plot and theme to come. The scene does not conclude Swann's concern for Odette; their love goes through death throes described in images of disease and decay. As "Swann in Love" ends, it appears that Swann and Odette have separated permanently; as it turns out, however, only Swann's love has been lost.

Swann's Way concludes with a section entitled "Place-Names: The Name." The reader has reentered the world of Marcel's childhood, now set in Paris. Thematically, even in matters of plot, this last section is still clearly connected to "Swann in Love." Marcel wishes to travel; the names of Venice, Florence, and Balbec are magical to him. Because of his health, however, Marcel is forced to remain in Paris. While playing in the Champs-Elysées, he meets Gilberte, Odette, and Swann's daughter, the same girl he had seen in Combray. Initially, Gilberte is kind to Marcel; she gives him an agate marble and an essay by Bergotte on Jean Racine. Yet Gilberte's enthusiasm is in contrast to Marcel's, much as her mother's feelings had been for Swann. Marcel is aware that he loves alone, but he still maintains his keen interest for her parents. He tries to imitate Swann's mannerisms, and when Gilberte chooses not to be available, he watches the resplendent Odette walk along the Allée des Acacias. In this same locale twenty years later, the adult Marcel makes the closing observations of *Swann's Way*. On a somber November day, Marcel finds that "vulgarity and fatuity" have replaced the standards of elegance that Odette had set years before. More important, Marcel is led to reflect on memory and its relationship to reality: "The reality that I had known no longer existed." The sadness of Marcel as he feels the onslaught of fugitive time is not yet assuaged by the knowledge that time can, in fact, be regained with all of its color and truth. All he knows is that physical space, in this instance the Bois de Boulogne, does not contain the reality of the past. Marcel can remember Odette, but he experiences none of the ecstasy associated with involuntary memory. Thus, the melancholy tone of these closing pages indicates clearly that Marcel's goals of love, society, and an artistic vocation have not yet been achieved.

Within a Budding Grove

Even though Marcel's exact age is not stated, *Swann's Way* concerns itself generally with the years of Marcel's childhood, while *Within a Budding Grove* develops his adolescence. A sign of Marcel's increasing independence is his frequent visits to the drawing room of Madame Swann, whom Marcel's parents will not receive, despite their warm feelings for her husband. Thus, the first long chapter of *Within a Budding Grove* is entitled "Madame Swann at Home." The second, somewhat shorter section, "Place-Names: The Place," and the third and concluding chapter, "Seascape, with Frieze of Girls," depict Marcel's first venture away from his parents. Even though his grandmother accompanies him for reasons of health to the seaside hotel at Balbec, Marcel experiences considerable freedom. He mingles with the lower classes, young women, the members of the aristocratic Guermantes family, and the Impressionist painter Elstir (who, like the composer Vinteuil, is a composite of several real artists), all of whom contribute to his largely unconscious search for the real. Indeed, ap-

pearances still make their claim on Marcel, but new realities begin to make themselves felt.

In spite of *Within a Budding Grove*'s concentration on Marcel's life apart from parental influence, its first great scene occurs within the confines of the family; furthermore, it is one of the few scenes in which Marcel's father emerges with much clarity. The occasion is a small dinner for the Marquis de Norpois, a distinguished member of the Foreign Office (Marcel's father is Permanent Secretary there). While Norpois reappears frequently in later novels, his primary function at the dinner is to introduce subtly the themes that will find elaboration in subsequent scenes. Marcel's career as a writer, the major concern of *Remembrance of Things Past*, is first discussed openly at the dinner. Norpois champions the vocation of writer, an important gesture, because Marcel's father has opposed it. In the hands of Dickens, Norpois would be the archetype of the good uncle who intervenes on behalf of a young boy beset by an incompetent or hostile father figure.

While Proust's method of characterization does seek out the type in the individual, as Swann sees the Botticellian possibilities in Odette, the type is always fully rounded, almost to the point of contradicting the type. Françoise is the good, faithful servant, but her limitations are never ignored. Similarly, Swann is the connoisseur, yet, as Norpois points out, since his marriage to Odette he has at times played the parvenu. In the case of Norpois, while he promotes Marcel's writing career, he nearly cuts it short by agreeing with Marcel's falsely modest assertion that his first writing exercise was "childish scribbling." Norpois goes on to attack Marcel's beloved Bergotte, judging him precious and an "evil influence." In a manner typical of him, Proust makes twofold use of Norpois's literary remarks. They obviously frustrate and antagonize the sensitive Marcel; they also contain many of the objections that Proust's own novels met critically. Norpois particularly dislikes "all those Chinese puzzles of form," saying that "all these deliquescent mandarin subtleties seem to me to be quite futile." Ironically, when Marcel soon thereafter meets Bergotte at Odette's, he is immensely disappointed and recalls Norpois's assessment. Marcel's lofty vision of the novelist, inferred from his work, is mocked by Bergotte's disappointing physical qualities and his snobbery and ambition.

In addition to its effect on Marcel's writing career, Norpois's conversation reminds the reader of other topics and themes. Norpois's personal political credentials are established by his recollections of service to France under reactionary and radical governments; later he appears as the most reasonable of the anti-Dreyfusards. While Swann's Jewishness is not mentioned by Norpois, he does provide the missing exposition on Swann's marriage, and the reader is once again reminded of the love theme, which is reinforced by Norpois's insistence that Marcel be allowed to see the famous actress Berma perform as Phèdre in Jean Racine's great play. Norpois also plays a minor but important role in Marcel's growing social awareness; his influence extends from Odette's drawing room to the court of kings, yet he will not honor Marcel's simple, enthusiastic request that he mention his, Marcel's, name to Odette.

Before his journey to Balbec, Marcel does find admittance to Odette's salon. Marcel himself describes his time spent at Swann's house as a stage in his movement upward in society. Ironically, it was Marcel's quest for love, not society, that originally attracted him to Swann's. His first visit comes after Gilberte invites him to tea following his attack of asthma. He continues to call, but Odette takes more pleasure in his presence than does Gilberte. Finally, while coyly refusing to see Gilberte, Marcel remains faithful to Odette, among her chrysanthemums and coterie of bourgeois acquaintances. Marcel discontinues his visits when he learns another fact of love: Absence breeds forgetfulness. He still visits the Bois de Boulogne, knowing the exact time when Odette walks there, the very personification of Woman as she strolls with her mauve parasol, followed by Swann and his friends from the Jockey Club. This particular vision of Odette leads the adult Marcel to conclude that one's memories of "poetical sensations" are much greater than one's memory of suffering.

Two years pass before Marcel takes the 1:22 train to Balbec with his grandmother. The summer and fall Marcel passes there greatly increase his knowledge of society and, to a lesser extent, his knowledge of love. Although he longs to die when he first sees the unfamiliar room in the Grand Hotel, habit and the presence of Françoise and his grandmother soon make this new world bearable, even pleasurably exciting.

The much-desired world of society appears at first to be closed off to Marcel. He must resign himself to the presence of chattering, vulgar provincials and disdainful members of the local aristocracy. Circumstances, however, prove kind, and an accidental meeting between his grandmother and the Marquise de Villeparisis, her old schoolmate, slowly opens up a new world to Marcel. The Marquise is a member of the distinguished Guermantes family, and she proves to be an indispensable step in Marcel's movement to the very top of the social hierarchy. To demonstrate her fondness for Marcel, she takes him on carriage rides about the countryside. Proust identifies her closely with the arts; her family owns paintings by Titian, and her father entertained Stendhal. She herself will write a highly regarded memoir. She is also, unbeknown to Marcel, the Marquis de Norpois's lover. Madame de Villeparisis illustrates one of the central principles of Proust's world: A character's identity cannot be known at once; time will unfold its secrets, and the reader comes to see, as Nabokov has put it, that Proust's characters wear a series of masks.

Madame de Villeparisis also introduces Marcel to her nephews, two characters who figure prominently in the evolution of a variety of themes, including love and the analysis of society. Marcel's first impression of the handsome, elegant Robert, Marquis de Saint-Loup, is negative. His apparent insolence, however, masks a generosity that conquers both Marcel and his unpretentious, socially indifferent grandmother. The other, older nephew, Palamède, Baron de Charlus, wears an even more impenetrable mask. To characterize the Baron for Marcel, Robert relates an incident that illustrates both the Baron's virility and his hostility to inversion; Robert clearly is unaware that the Baron, who has stared fixedly at Marcel, is, in fact decidedly homosexual. Robert also points out with some family pride that the Baron, who moves with ease in the Faubourg Saint-Germain, the pinnacle of Parisian society, has a list at the Jockey Club of two hundred members to whom he would not permit himself to be introduced.

The Baron will play one of the central roles in Marcel's drama. His two major functions, furthering Marcel's social awareness and explicating the homosexual theme, are joined by a third: His formal social demeanor provides a vivid contrast to the crude behavior of Bloch, Marcel's Jewish friend. Part of Marcel's social education is his exposure to the Bloch family as well as to the Guermantes. Lest Proust's portrayal of the vulgarity of the Blochs be seen as anti-Semitic, however, one must recall that Proust's mother and her family, whom he loved and honored, were Jewish, as were many of his closest friends. As in his treatment of other minorities—ethnic, social, and sexual—Proust proves to be compassionate without indulging in apologies or sentimentality. No character would have been more offended by the Bloch family's lack of decorum than the Jewish Swann. Also, Robert's Jewish mistress, Rachel, while seen as manipulative, "had opened his mind to the invisible, had brought a serious element into his life, delicacy into his heart. . . ."

While Marcel finds pleasure in his new acquaintances at Balbec, his attention is most avidly focused on a band of young girls whom he sees about the town and countryside. He meets them through an unexpected source, the famous painter Elstir. Marcel's easy access to Elstir brings to mind one of the most frequent criticisms of the novel: The young, inexperienced Marcel makes a quick conquest of almost everyone he meets, from duchesses and novelists to lift boys. The reader's only direct clue to Marcel's charm is found in *The Guermantes Way*, when Marcel wittily entertains Robert's friends at the army town of Doncières. Marcel is usually passive both in tête-à-têtes and society. Elstir nevertheless takes Marcel seriously enough to deliver a stirring monologue on aesthetic matters and the nature of wisdom. Marcel, however, seems more concerned with the failure of a young girl, who occasionally visits Elstir's studio, to appear. Marcel does eventually meet this young girl, Albertine. His immediate response to her is distinctly Proustian: The real Albertine is less than the imagined one. Following an innocent courtship that thrives on games played in the sand dunes with a band of girls, Marcel chooses Albertine to be his love interest. Yet when Marcel makes advances toward her, she repulses them, and Marcel's initiation into the larger world of Balbec ends, as did *Swann's Way*, on a melancholy, cool note. The novel has, however, furthered Marcel's quest for love and prepared for his entry into the salons of Parisian society.

THE GUERMANTES WAY

The Guermantes Way begins with a mundane fact, but one crucial to the success of Marcel's dual quest for love and society. Marcel's family has moved to the Hôtel Guermantes, the Paris residence of the Duke and Duchess de Guermantes and Madame de Villeparisis; there, too, is Jupien's tailor shop. While it is conceivable that Marcel might have made his way into the most distinguished drawing rooms of Paris without this change, it clearly makes Proust's plotting easier, even though plot is, perhaps, comparatively a lesser concern in such an expansive, comprehensive work as *Remembrance of Things Past*. Proust's keen psychological analyses, his brilliant use of metaphors to give depth and clarity to his themes, his elegance of style, and his sense of comedy are his chief virtues. Perhaps of all the novels of Proust's epic, *The Guermantes Way* best illustrates the truth of such a proposition.

The key organizing principle of *The Guermantes Way* is a series of social engagements: matinees, dinners at restaurants, and evening parties. Their only interruption, by what might appear to be an incongruity, is the death of Marcel's grandmother. There is, however, a unity of action provided by Marcel's growing consciousness, fostered by his exposure to the world of the Guermantes. Once exposed, Marcel, relieved of his obsession with Oriane, the Duchess de Guermantes, states that "what troubled me now was the discovery that almost every house sheltered some unhappy person. . . . Quite half of the human race was in tears." He discovers the disparity between the romance that envelops a royal name and the reality of the royal person. Proust makes Marcel's disillusionment clearer by the use of metaphor. Marcel observes that each of my fellow guests at dinner, smothering the mysterious name under which I had only at a distance known and dreamed of them with a body and with a mind similar or inferior to those of all the people I knew, had given me the impression of flat vulgarity which the view on entering the Danish port of Elsinore would give to any passionate admirer of *Hamlet*.

Having met and conquered two of the members of the Guermantes family in Balbec, Madame de Villeparisis and Robert de Saint-Loup, Marcel, at the beginning of *The Guermantes Way*, sets his sights on Oriane, the beautiful Duchess de Guermantes. Marcel's own dreamlike state is reinforced by the magic of the great Berma's performance in Jean Racine's *Phèdre* (1677.) To Marcel's utter surprise, the Duchess acknowledges him with a wave of her hand. In comedy reminiscent of Dickens, Marcel thereafter stalks the Duchess, loitering in the streets in the hope of seeing her. When word reaches Marcel that his infatuation irritates the Duchess, he employs a new tactic: He goes to the military camp at Doncières to visit Robert de Saint-Loup, hoping to gain access to the Duchess through Robert's influence.

Even though Robert is unable to help Marcel, the rekindling of their friendship allows Proust the novelist to develop themes previously introduced. Robert's obsession with his mistress Rachel reminds the reader of Swann's relationship with Odette and anticipates both the Baron de Charlus's mad pursuit of Morel and, most important, Marcel's tortured relationship with Albertine. Even an apparently insignificant incident in which Robert strikes a homosexual is preparation for Robert's own sexual inversion later.

Robert's pursuit of his mistress brings him and Marcel back to Paris. Marcel is encouraged by his father to attend a matinee at Madame de Villeparisis'. While this occasion is of greater social significance than the gatherings Marcel had previously attended at Odette Swann's, it has limited status. Madame de Villeparisis, from the point of view of the Faubourg Saint-Germain, has been careless of her famous family name. She has married beneath her station, has had liaisons, and has associated herself closely with the academic and artistic worlds. Although the Duchess de Guermantes and the Baron de Charlus attend

the matinee, they do so out of family loyalty. The matinee, essentially comic in tone, focuses in part on the foibles of guests such as Legrandin, a shameless flatterer, and Marcel's boyhood friend, Bloch, who upsets a vase of apple blossoms. Few of Proust's scenes are as comic as that of Madame de Villeparisis pretending to be asleep when the humiliated Bloch comes to bid her farewell. The comic, however, is interwoven with themes of tragic potential, such as Norpois's discussion with Bloch about the Dreyfus Affair and the pervasive evidence of vicious snobbery. Most important, Marcel and the reader gain a clearer picture of the complexity of the Guermantes: Oriane, the Baron, and Madame de Marsantes, the mother of Robert. The Baron's comically indirect, elegant propositioning of Marcel as he leaves the matinee develops the homosexual theme and reveals Marcel's naïveté.

A hiatus of sorts follows Marcel's initiation into the world of the Guermantes. First, Marcel's grandmother dies. Having been convinced by an eminent physician, Dr. de Boulbon, that her ill health is psychosomatic, Marcel's grandmother follows his advice and accompanies Marcel to the Champs-Élysées. She rather suddenly interrupts their stroll to go into a public toilet. During the interim, Marcel talks to "la marquise," who attends the toilet, to which she refers as her "salon." Her conversation, coming so soon after the de Villeparisis matinee, is brutally satiric, as is Marcel's experience with a doctor, Professor E——, to whom he turns when it is apparent that the grandmother has suffered a stroke. Although he does examine her, Professor E—— is clearly more concerned with the mending of a buttonhole, a repair that is necessary before he calls on the Minister of Commerce. The protracted suffering of the grandmother and the devotion of Marcel's mother to her are set in stark contrast to the vanity, insinuations, and archness of the drawing room. Marcel will continue his social ascent, but the vision of his grandmother's love will provide a vivid contrast to the falseness of the *beau monde*.

Deeply touched by his grandmother's death, Marcel's attention nevertheless turns again to women. Although he successfully pursues a Madame de Stermaria, he is consoled by the reappearance of Albertine, finding that she no longer repulses his physical advances. Albertine's return coincides with a number of discoveries by Marcel. In spite of the kind of attention that Robert de Saint-Loup gives him, Marcel concludes that friendship is basically incompatible with the vocation of writing. Most important, he discovers that he has grown indifferent to the Duchess de Guermantes, as he had to Gilberte. This realization occurs ironically when Marcel receives an invitation from the Duchess to dine with her. Marcel's observations during the dinner, more than one hundred pages in length, are an excellent example of what Nabokov calls "Marcel the eavesdropper." Marcel's personality and concerns intrude little, if at all, in the description of the Guermantes at home. At the center is Oriane, the Duchess herself. One learns that as a young woman she was, by the Guermantes' standards, poor. What distinguished her was her beauty, her style, and her spirit: "She had had the audacity to say to the Russian Grand Duke: 'Well, Sir, I hear you would like to have Tolstoy murdered?'" In spite of her liberal views, she was most careful to marry well, and with the aid of her aunt, Madame de Villeparisis, she married the Prince des Laumes, the future Duke de Guermantes. Their marriage has scarcely been a happy one. The Duke is tight with money but profligate in his affection for other women. Yet the Duke admires his wife, particularly her sharp "Guermantes wit," which in reality often consists of terrible puns, poor imitations, cruel characterizations of her friends and family, and fatuous literary judgments. Marcel nevertheless finds something of value in the Faubourg Saint-Germain world that she represents. Like the peasants, the great noblemen still have a concern for the land, for history, for custom. In this way, they are superior to the bourgeoisie, who are interested only in money.

Although Marcel's social education is not yet complete, his evening with the Duchess does much to strip away the appearances and the magic of the world of names. Before the evening is out, however, Marcel will receive one more lesson. Invited by the Baron de Charlus to call on him after dinner, Marcel encounters a hostile Baron, who accuses Marcel

of ingratitude and tale-bearing. Marcel retaliates by trampling the Baron's new silk hat and begins his exit. The formerly imperious Baron seems sobered by Marcel's anger. A civilized conversation follows, one that reveals the Baron's quixotic intelligence and sensitivity, as well as his appreciation for his family. The scene, both comic and touching, reveals him in his fullness and has led Wilson to compare Proust's characterization of the Baron to William Shakespeare's characterization of Falstaff.

In the final scene of *The Guermantes Way*, Proust provides—as he had in the episode of the grandmother's death—a brilliant gloss on the artificiality and vacuity of the Guermantes' world. Marcel has received an invitation from the Princess de Guermantes, and being unsure of its authenticity, he goes to visit the Duke and Duchess upon their return to Paris. While he is there, Swann arrives with a photograph for a book he is writing on the knights of the Order of Malta. Oriane claims a great interest in Swann's project, but the Duke hurries her off to a dinner at a relative's. As they leave, Swann announces that he is dying. Although Swann is one of her oldest friends, the Duchess yields to her husband's demands that they leave for the dinner. The Duke tells Swann that he will outlive them all. The detail that fully reveals the cruelty of the Guermantes, however, is the Duke's concern for Oriane's forgotten red shoes. The Duke and his world chose to ignore whatever unpleasant reality discomforts them in favor of a dramatic appearance.

CITIES OF THE PLAIN

Cities of the Plain, a novel of brilliantly contrasted scenes, records the beginning of Marcel's descent into his own personal hell, the fuller description of which occurs in *The Captive* and *The Sweet Cheat Gone*. In *Cities of the Plain*, Marcel moves from the pinnacle of Parisian society, symbolized by the soirée given by the Prince and Princess de Guermantes, downward to the ridiculously comic Wednesdays at the Verdurins at La Raspelière. More significantly, Marcel himself reluctantly changes from detached observer to subjective sufferer because of the emergence of the phenomenon that dominates the novel: homosexuality.

One of the lingering criticisms of *Remembrance of Things Past* is that it gives excessive attention to the homosexual theme, thus distorting society as it was in Paris at the turn of the century. Some consider Proust's fascination with the subject merely self-indulgent; others, seeking to justify the theme, have called it a symbol of Original Sin or a symbol of the corruption and coming destruction of the aristocracy. Both the critics and Proust's defenders miss the point. Within the self-contained world of the larger novel, homosexuality functions primarily as an aesthetic device. Without its presence, there would be no Baron de Charlus, Proust's most brilliantly drawn character. Homosexuality also contributes to other major concerns of the novel, such as the characterization of much of the aristocracy, the love theme, and the education of the narrator. Without homosexuality, the central plot would not advance; had Albertine not mentioned her friendship with the homosexual woman who was the companion of Vinteuil's daughter, Marcel would not have urged her to come to Paris. One may further assume that the heterosexual Marcel's inability to find human love is directly connected to his ultimate quest for salvation in art. To see the function of homosexuality in terms of plot, theme, and characterization does not, however, negate its intrinsic interest. Like the characterization of the aristocracy and the descriptions of life in a provincial French town or sea resort, homosexuality resonates with the tragicomic complexity of human experience.

Cities of the Plain begins as an apparent extension of Marcel's pursuit of the world of the Guermantes. In a flashback, Marcel awaits the return of the Duke and Duchess de Guermantes to ask about the authenticity of an invitation he has received from the Princess de Guermantes. Marcel sees instead the Baron de Charlus meeting Jupien, the tailor. Although Marcel could scarcely be ignorant of the Baron's sexual proclivities, he is still surprised by the cooperation of Jupien in such matters. Marcel is, nevertheless, fascinated by the coquetry that takes place, and he uses an extended botanical metaphor comparing Jupien to an orchid and the Baron to a bee. The effect of the metaphor is to suggest that, while the encounter is unusual, it is in the larger scheme of things natural, "a

miracle." Jupien is just another member of the "human herbary" that intrigues Marcel, a "moral botanist." Samuel Beckett has noted the importance of Proust's use of "vegetal" images, stating,

> This preoccupation accompanies very naturally his complete indifference to moral values and human justices. Flowers and plants have no conscious will. They are shameless exposing their genitals. And so in a sense are Proust's men and women. . . .

While Beckett perhaps overstates the case, there is indeed no moral censure on young Marcel's part; neither is there a defense of homosexuality. Marcel concludes that homosexuals are essentially men-women and that in spite of the Baron's pretension of virility, he, in fact, has the sensibility of a woman. Marcel concludes that homosexuals are like "an Oriental colony, cultured, musical, malicious, which has certain charming qualities and intolerable defects." Proust's objective characterization of homosexuals is perfectly consistent with those of other minorities: Jews, aristocrats, artists, and so on. Thus, Marcel later says that, like his extremely moral grandmother, he also "enjoyed the diversity of other people without expecting anything of them or resenting anything that they did."

Yet there is another Marcel in *Cities of the Plain* who does not take such a sanguine view of humankind or homosexuality. The Marcel who captures the comedy, homosexual and otherwise, of the soirée at the Guermantes' (where the Baron shamelessly pursues two vapid brothers in the presence of their unwittingly cooperative mother) is quite different from the Marcel who returns to Balbec and discovers that he is not immune to the sting of "vice."

Marcel's return to Balbec with his mother marks a general movement toward a more somber, reflective, subjective protagonist. Upon reaching his old room at the Grand Hotel, Marcel takes off his boots, and involuntarily his memory returns to his grandmother. For the first time, he feels the effect of her death and learns from Françoise of the courage and sacrifice his grandmother concealed from him during their earlier stay at Balbec. His suffering diminishes, however, with Albertine's return to town. His comfort proves to be short-lived. While visiting a casino with Cottard, the doctor, Marcel sees Albertine dancing with Andrée. Cottard casually remarks that the two women are aroused. Unlike his detached response to the Baron de Charlus and Jupien, Marcel is deeply distressed by the possibility of a lesbian liaison between Albertine and Andrée. From this point on, *Cities of the Plain* develops the torturous relationship of Marcel and Albertine, a relationship that reveals the sometimes sadistic, paranoiac, and self-indulgent aspects of Marcel's character.

In *Cities of the Plain*, Proust does not yet entirely extricate Marcel and Albertine from the larger social fabric. Their physical but loveless affair grows within the context of life at the Grand Hotel and, more important, the Wednesdays at the Verdurins'. The "nucleus" that gathers around "The Mistress" has changed little since they first appeared in *Swann's Way*. If possible, they are even more ridiculously savage in their comedy. The evenings at La Raspelière are the supreme achievement of Proust's comedy. Whether it is the Faithful mistaking Meyerbeer for Claude Debussy, or Madame Cottard falling asleep, or the Baron de Charlus revealing his sexual proclivities by choosing strawberry juice rather than orangeade, the comedy is sublime. Madame Verdurin herself has become even more imperious and amoral. To her, the death of Deschampes the pianist is essentially a nuisance that threatens to spoil her first entertainment in her new country residence. Besides, she has a new protégé, the violinist Charles Morel. Morel, the grandson of Marcel's Uncle Adolphe's valet, emerges as one of Proust's greatest achievements in characterization. A fit companion for the Verdurins, Morel is utterly amoral, available either to men or women, entirely free of any loyalty, and he almost proves to be the Baron's nemesis. The Baron is so in love with Morel that he suffers the vulgarities and ignorance of the Verdurins and their circle in order to promote the young man's career and simply be in his presence. Like Odette and Albertine, Morel is one of those faithless creatures that ironically have the power to enslave a sensibility finer than their own. Morel's affair with the Baron is one panel in Proust's triptych of the vanity of human love.

In time, Marcel's jealousy and paranoia concerning Albertine lead him to resemble the Baron in his pursuit of Morel. At Balbec, however, Marcel's feelings are at best ambivalent. He is indeed possessive of Albertine and even jealous of her attention to his old friend Robert de Saint-Loup. So corrosive is the effect of this attachment on his moral behavior that he refuses to leave her alone with Saint-Loup in order to speak even briefly to Bloch's father. Yet Marcel still dreams of traveling, and he finally resolves that he will abandon her. Only when Marcel inadvertently discovers that Albertine is an old friend of the lover of Vinteuil's daughter does the specter of lesbianism rise up to shatter his resolution. It is scarcely the same detached Marcel, the moral botanist who watched Jupien lure the Baron, who announces to his mother that he will return to Paris and marry Albertine. While *The Guermantes Way* reveals Marcel's disillusionment in his quest for society, *Cities of the Plain* does the same for his quest for love. Salvation, if it exists it all, has thus far eluded Marcel.

THE CAPTIVE

Coupled with *The Sweet Cheat Gone, The Captive* has as its central concern Marcel's destructive relationship with the elusive Albertine. Although the love theme appears earlier, in the histories of Swann and Odette, Robert and Rachel, and the Baron de Charlus and Morel, it is in the painstaking treatment of Marcel's paranoid obsession with Albertine that Proust most fully explores the paradoxes of love. Wilson describes their relationship as "trying" at best: ". . . it is quite without tenderness, glamour, or romance." There is in it neither "idealism [nor] enjoyment." Yet this extended episode is crucial to the central concern of the novel: Marcel's discovery of his true vocation as an artist. Once love has proved itself impossible for Marcel, the only salvation is the world of art—as the final volume of *Remembrance of Things Past* will show.

Although *The Captive* includes one of Proust's most brilliant social scenes, the Verdurins' quarrel with the Baron de Charlus, it begins and ends with Marcel's life with Albertine. The novel opens with Marcel in his bedroom in Paris. As a number of critics have pointed out, the bedroom functions as one of the primary motifs in the work. Marcel's recurring bouts of ill health make his stays in bed, be it at Combray, Balbec, or Paris, credible; however, the emphasis in each instance is elsewhere. Consciously or not, Marcel's retirements represent a power struggle of sorts. His delicate health as a child guarantees the attention of his mother, and the famous scene at Combray where Marcel awaits and ultimately receives his mother's kiss represents an ambivalent victory for Marcel over his father. At his Balbec hotel room, the adolescent Marcel, although he is unaware of it, has a rival for his grandmother's attention: death itself. Again, Marcel temporarily wins the struggle. As an adult, Marcel once again retires to his bedroom and uses this withdrawal to imprison the third important woman in his life, Albertine. Her presence is in part a repetition of earlier experience. Marcel himself twice sees Albertine's kisses late at night as a reenactment of his mother's visit to his side after Swann had left that fateful night in *Swann's Way*. As was true with his mother and grandmother, Marcel has a rival for Albertine, her probable inclinations toward lesbianism.

It has been suggested that Albertine's presence in the home of Marcel's parents violates credibility. Bourgeois values would not have allowed it. Proust does, however, cover his tracks. First, Marcel's father is away on diplomatic business, and his indulgent mother is conveniently in Combray, attending a sick relative. Only the disapproving Françoise is present. Moreover, Marcel conceals Albertine's residency from friends. Most important, Marcel has never particularly adhered to social strictures, as is indicated by his moral indifference to the male citizens of Sodom and Gomorrah.

While Marcel the social observer is admirably tolerant, Marcel the lover has little to recommend him other than his lucid candor; why Albertine accepts Marcel's paranoia and jealousy as long as she does is not clear. Marcel's motives and behavior, on the other hand, are scrutinized uncompromisingly. Marcel tells Albertine that the doctor has ordered him to stay in bed. In truth, Marcel is so jealous of Albertine that he cannot bear to see her responses to other people in public. Thus, the tyrant Marcel permits Albertine to

go out only with Andrée or alone with the chauffeur, but he also asks both, in effect, to spy on her.

Marcel's desire for control over Albertine leads him to like her best when she is sleeping or just awakening. Marcel compares the waking Albertine to Eve come from the side of Adam—"astonished and submissive." So consuming is Marcel's jealousy that he finds he is less interested in Albertine's frequent intelligent comments than he is in some unguarded remark that will fuel his paranoia.

While his jealousy proves intensely painful to Marcel, he does find some pleasure in life with Albertine. He both admires and takes some credit for her intelligence. She does provide him physical titillation and satisfaction. His greatest pleasure seems to reside in his capacity simply to control her, to hold her captive. Whether he is choosing her clothing after consultation with the Duchess de Guermantes or begging her to return home from the Trocadéro, Marcel seeks to reduce Albertine to merely an instrument of his will. Marcel is fully conscious not only that his attachment to Albertine prevents him from traveling and working but also that he himself has become a captive to Albertine's lies and his own mania. Although unable to act on his knowledge, Marcel sees clearly that "I had clipped her wings, she had ceased to be a Victory, was a burdensome slave of whom I would fain have been rid."

The Captive does not develop Marcel's relationship with Albertine exclusively. Another love story, the Baron de Charlus's obsession with Morel, is also carried to a disastrous climax at the musical soirée held at the Verdurins. The humiliation of the imperious Baron at the hands of the Verdurins is but one of the important events that this brilliant scene develops. Its objectively cruel satire, directed toward the aristocrats and the members of the Verdurins' circle, provides a necessary contrast in tone and texture to the Albertine-Marcel story. The playing of Vinteuil's lost septet during the soirée also allows Marcel to consider questions crucial to his development as an artist.

In *The Captive*, the theme of the artist is like an underground stream that slowly makes its way to the surface. Marcel points out early in the novel that when he is not with the Duchess, he examines an album of Elstir's work, or one of Bergotte's books, or Vinteuil's sonata. Later, Marcel learns of Bergotte's death as he is viewing a Vermeer at an exhibition. Proust, anticipating *Time Regained*, suggests that the dead Bergotte's books, arranged three by three, are the symbol of his resurrection, his salvation. Marcel, while awaiting Albertine's return from the Trocadéro, plays Vinteuil's sonata. Fowlie points out that this scene is of primary importance in the transition of Marcel from lover to artist. After the sonata, Marcel plays a score of Richard Wagner's *Tristan und Isolde* (1859), and this arouses a number of questions in him. He admires the giants of the nineteenth century—Wagner, Honoré de Balzac, Victor Hugo—and their capacity to produce "Vulcan-like" massive works leaves Marcel unhappy and unsure whether a commitment to art is preferable to life as he leads it. At the Verdurins', Marcel hears Vinteuil's septet, and he realizes that Vinteuil's later work has been enriched by his love and suffering for his daughter. In this septet, Vinteuil, like Bergotte, has found a means of defeating time.

In contrast to the violet mist in which Vinteuil's immortal work is shrouded is the unheroic world of the Verdurins. The Baron's aristocratic guests ignore Madame Verdurin, and to get revenge, she poisons Morel's mind against the Baron. Even in this atmosphere of snobbery and viciousness, Proust avoids caricature. At evening's end, the Verdurins decide to provide anonymously for the financially broken Saniette, whom they have abused in the past. More dramatic, however, is the Queen of Naples, who returns to the Verdurins' for a misplaced fan and rather magnificently comes to the aid of the devastated Baron de Charlus. Thus, the major concerns that propel the previous novels—homosexuality, the development of the artist, the vanity of love, the emptiness of the aristocracy, the Janus-like nature of reality—are in this scene recapitulated seamlessly.

Marcel returns home to Albertine. They quarrel, and Marcel asks Albertine to leave. A reconciliation follows, but Marcel learns more disquieting facts about Albertine's past. Albertine herself grows restless, as symbolized by her violent opening of her window. When Marcel plans to end the relationship, Albertine ensures his continued bondage to jealousy by leaving him first. It would appear that Marcel's quest for love has reached its nadir. The descent, however, is not yet complete.

THE SWEET CHEAT GONE

The Sweet Cheat Gone, more than any of the novels that precede it, concerns itself with Marcel's loss of innocence. Proust emphasizes this theme by ending the novel with Marcel's return to the Combray of his childhood. There he finds the youthful object of his imagination and love, Gilberte, living in a fallen world. For Marcel, not only has Gilberte lost her appeal, but also her husband and his friend, Robert de Saint-Loup, seems stripped of nobility. Most poignant, the once beautiful Vivonne is now little more than "a meagre, ugly rivulet."

The novel begins with Marcel's desperate strategies to bring Albertine back to him. He recognizes the irony of seeking the return of one who afforded him mediocre pleasures while preventing him from realizing loftier goals. Alas, she had become a habit. No longer having Albertine about to lie to him, Marcel lies to himself. He persuades himself that her departure is an attempt to negotiate better terms. He therefore dispatches a letter telling Albertine that her departure is final, while Robert de Saint-Loup is sent to bribe Albertine's aunt. A second letter reveals an even baser Marcel; in it, he suggests that a Rolls-Royce and a yacht might be in the offing. The final communication, a telegram, asks Albertine to name her terms; all he wants is to hold her three times a week. So summarized, Marcel's actions are comic. The news of Albertine's death in a riding accident alters the tone, as does her last letter, in which she asks Marcel to take her back on any terms. Proust, however, makes no attempt to sentimentalize her death. There is a peculiar flatness in its description that undercuts any pronounced emotional response. The reader has known so little of Albertine that he is moved only by the irony of events.

The ironic tone is sustained in the treatment of Marcel's grief. The former captor is now enslaved by memory, and Marcel discovers that each season brings with it a new set of painful recollections. Temporarily affectionate memories of Albertine replace his former suspicions. Marcel feels guilt, as though he had murdered her. He deifies her, calls her "my sister, my child, my tender mistress." The exaggerated, unexpected sincerity of Marcel's grief once again approaches comedy. He begins to believe that Albertine is not dead and considers the possibility of immortality. Yet Marcel has at the same time commissioned Aimé, a former headwaiter at Balbec, to investigate Albertine's life at the resort; Aimé writes that Albertine had been an active lesbian. Aimé, on a second mission, discovers a laundress from whom Albertine had received profound pleasure, and Aimé believes the laundress's report because she has excited him sexually as well. Such revelations Marcel both believes and doubts. He continues his quest for the true Albertine, and while Andrée admits to having lesbian feelings, she denies any involvement with Albertine. Marcel is thus frustrated in his attempt to locate the one, the absolute Albertine. Instead, he discovers that memory crumbles, and the time will soon come when Albertine's room will be occupied by someone else.

Although Marcel's relationship with Albertine will surface again, the novel abandons it in favor of another and crueler kind of oblivion, which has taken place without Marcel's knowledge. Marcel is introduced in the drawing room of the Duchess de Guermantes to Mademoiselle de Forcheville, who is Gilberte Swann. While she had earlier recognized Marcel, Marcel had thought, indeed hoped, that she was a young woman of easy virtue whom Robert de Saint-Loup had once known. The return of Gilberte allows Proust to recall the aftermath of Swann's death. To everyone's surprise, Odette exhibited a long and sincere grief. She then married Forcheville, who in time adopted Gilberte. Gilberte has inherited an immense fortune from an uncle and has thus been received in aristocratic houses. Even the Duchess de Guermantes receives her, an event devoutly desired by Swann but denied to him during his life. Although Gilberte has inherited her father's tact and charm, she contributes to Swann's oblivion by addressing Forcheville as father, and soon no one mentions Swann's name in her presence. Her hypocrisy and snobbery are seen in her signature, "G. S. Forcheville." The Guermantes, whom Marcel now describes as "people whose lives have no purpose," aid in the destruction of Swann's memory. When Gilberte notices some Elstir sketches in the Guermantes' drawing room, the Duchess remarks that "some friends" recommended Elstir rather than embarrass Gilberte with the name of Swann.

While the scene serves the necessary function of reintroducing Gilberte to the plot, it also reveals the growth of Marcel, who no longer is enamored of names and rank. The concerted attempt to erase Swann's memory is particularly offensive to Marcel, because it was Swann who so unobtrusively provided a type of paternal authority for Marcel. In his affair with Albertine, Marcel constantly sees Swann's life with Odette as the prototype of love. Swann has also introduced Marcel to Bergotte and to an appreciation of Vinteuil. Had it not been for Swann's remarks about the Persian quality of the church at Balbec, Marcel believes, he might never have met Albertine or Elstir. Appropriately, the connoisseur of art, Swann, will himself be immortalized in the art of his aesthetic son, Marcel.

Albertine has not yet been forgotten either. Marcel speaks again with Andrée, from whom he receives "a terrible revelation." Andrée has lied previously about her lack of contact with Albertine; moreover, she tells Marcel that Albertine and Morel together enticed virginal girls into occasional orgiastic revels. Suggesting that while Albertine lived with Marcel she had reformed and looked to him to save her, Andrée further implies that Albertine's death was a suicide related to a lesbian scandal. The effect of Andrée's tales, however, is less than might be expected. Marcel no longer feels the need to believe in Albertine's innocence; so detached has he become that he now realizes that Albertine's lesbianism was perhaps a precondition for her frank and open manner, one that permitted their special camaraderie. Marcel realizes he will never know the truth about Albertine, and sorrow is finally replaced by exhaustion. Marcel knows that oblivion has made a conquest of him when, in Venice, he receives a telegram from Gilberte that at first appears to be from Albertinc. Even the possibility that Albertine is alive does not interest him.

Once the Albertine theme has reached its inevitable conclusion, Proust uses the closing pages of the novel to foreshadow the major concerns of the final volume, *Time Regained*. Foremost among them is the theme of time. While visiting Venice with his mother and an old friend, Madame Sazerat, Marcel sees Madame de Villeparisis seated with her old lover, Monsieur de Norpois. Time has grievously altered the Marquise; Madame Sazerat, whose father was ruined by a youthful affair with the noblewoman, can scarcely believe that the woman once "beautiful as an angel, wicked as a demon" is now "hunch backed, red-faced . . . hideous." A second theme, the social change brought by time, is contained in the news of two marriages: Gilberte to Robert de Saint-Loup and Jupien's niece to the nephew of Legrandin. In the union of Gilberte and Robert, Swann's Way and Guermantes Way unexpectedly come together. More startling is the story of Jupien's niece. Adopted by the Baron de Charlus and given a name, she dies shortly after her marriage to an impoverished member of the provincial aristocracy. Yet this young girl, enamored of and abused by Morel, through her death sends the royal houses of Europe into mourning. It is the same sense of irony and dramatic change that will permeate *Time Regained*.

The Sweet Cheat Gone concludes with a series of revelations that further strip away from Marcel any remaining romantic illusions. Gilberte's marriage to Robert is not a happy one; Robert appears to have inherited both his uncle's proclivities and his infatuation with Morel. Gilberte tries to make herself look like Rachel in a vain attempt to stop his infidelity, but she reaps only lies and melodramatic confessions of guilt. Marcel learns also that Gilberte's childhood gesture under the arch of hawthorns had been intentionally vulgar, a revelation that serves to reinforce one of Proust's central tenets. There is not a single Gilberte, but many Gilbertes: the little girl amid the hawthorns, the loving daughter of Swann, the snob, the suffering wife. What exists is not an absolute Gilberte but a series of Gilbertes relative to time and place. Even places fail to present an absolute image,

as Marcel's disappointment in his walks in Combray reveals. Innocence has been stripped away. The only quest left is the one for art.

The final installment of an ambitious and lengthy chronicle has a considerable number of tasks to perform. The reader nurtured on the nineteenth century novel expects to see the numerous loose threads of the plot knotted and the conflicts resolved. Themes must evolve, ripen, and produce; the characters that reflect such truths must complete their move from ignorance to greater knowledge. Most of all, there must be a sense of the conclusion's inevitability. Proust brilliantly fulfills such expectations in the final volume of *Remembrance of Things Past*. The matinee at the new mansion of the Prince and Princess de Guermantes allows Marcel to arrive at a knowledge that has eluded him previously in his various quests for society and love. Marcel, no longer young, himself victim of the onslaughts of time, discovers that, indeed, he is capable of the literary vocation that he had previously considered beyond his grasp. *Time Regained* is nothing less than a gallery of transformations. The guests at the matinee have aged so that Marcel first thinks he has come to a masquerade. French society itself has undergone a massive upheaval. Most significant, however, is the transformation in Marcel after he fortuitously steps on the uneven paving stones outside the Guermantes mansion.

TIME REGAINED

Time Regained begins in Combray, where Marcel lives among the shattered images of his youth. His own first love, Gilberte, now suffers from the homosexual infidelities of Marcel's dearest friend, Robert de Saint-Loup. In addition to these disappointments, a book given to Marcel by Gilberte, an unpublished *Journal* of the Goncourt brothers, convinces Marcel that he has no vocation in literature. A passage from the *Journal* describes an evening at the Verdurins. The description of Cottard and other members of the clan makes Marcel feel that he lacks the capacity to see and hear accurately. Also, if the Goncourts' work is genuine art, then art lies, for Marcel knows that the circle surrounding the Verdurins has little of the glamour that the Goncourts' account suggests. Although realistic in its detail, the passage has failed, because it has not penetrated the surface. Marcel recalls that Bergotte succeeded where the *Journal* fails, because he had the ability to become a mirror that reflected life accurately. His reading of the *Journal* leaves Marcel in a state of artistic depression, one that will not be relieved until he steps on the uneven stones.

The Goncourt *Journal* has a second function: Its description of society prepares the way for Marcel's return to the Paris of World War I. Although the war rages less than an hour away, Paris seems largely unaffected; the feud between Madame Verdurin and the Baron de Charlus continues. Although Madame Verdurin, with the aid of Morel's journalistic pieces, appears to have turned society against the supposedly pro-German Baron, he has lost none of his intellectual or sexual fervor. What the Baron dislikes about wartime France is its love of the hypocritical chauvinistic cant written by men such as Norpois and Brichot. The Baron, however, does find the soldiers attractive; indeed, when Marcel encounters him, he is following two Zouaves. By chance, Marcel also learns of the Baron's preference for the sexually bizarre. Jupien has come to operate a male brothel for the sake of the Baron's pleasures, among which is a whipping administered to him while he is chained to an iron bed. Robert de Saint-Loup also frequents Jupien's establishment, but the war has restored his old nobility: Robert dies when he returns to the front in order to cover the retreat of his men. Gilberte, in the meantime, is in Tansonville, and Marcel learns from her that the Méséglise Way of his childhood has been the scene of an eight-month battle in which 600,000 Germans have died.

The final scene in the novel comes several years after the war has ended. Marcel has returned to Paris from a sanatorium. He continues to regret his lack of talent for literature; even his desire to produce a great work is apparently dying. Having thus no reason to avoid society, banal as it is, he accepts the invitation of the Prince and Princess de Guermantes to a matinee. The afternoon produces two major surprises. First, Marcel discovers that the past can be profoundly recaptured, although involuntarily; then, he witnesses the shocking effect time has wrought on

the people he has known. His afternoon reaffirms his judgment that society has little to offer and that his one hope is to cheat death long enough to complete the work he now knows he must write.

Marcel's discoveries begin as he walks the last, short distance to the Guermantes' new mansion. He encounters an aged Baron de Charlus supported by Jupien. The Baron brings to Marcel's mind the image of great tragic figures such as Lear and Oedipus. In this accidental meeting, the larger spectacle of aging apparent at the matinee is anticipated. Filled with gloom, Marcel approaches the mansion, but, in avoiding a passing car, he trips against the uneven paving stones. Immediately, a happiness like that evoked by the madeleine his Aunt Léonie had fed him, the trees at Balbec, and the music of Vinteuil dispels his melancholy. He then remembers the experience that lies at the source of this pleasure: The uneven stones have produced the same sensation he experienced when he stood on similar stones in the baptistery of Saint Mark's. Once inside the Guermantes' mansion, Marcel continues to savor such memories: The sound of a spoon, the stiffness of a napkin invoke involuntary recollections. As Marcel relives the past, he is conscious of moving outside time.

Once cognizant of his ability to recapture past time, Marcel explores its relevance to creativity. In a profusion of brilliant, often aphoristic observations, Marcel indicates that the role of the artist is that of a translator of the impressions and sensations that lie within him into spiritual equivalencies. As Proust's own prose reveals, this transformation is accomplished primarily through the use of metaphor. Metaphor aids the artist in his search for the truths that lie obscured by conventional knowledge: "Through art alone are we able to emerge from ourselves, to know what another person sees of a universe which is not the same as our own. . . . " Unlike ordinary men, the artist understands that the images of daily life, the people one meets, are symbols waiting to be interpreted and read. As Wilson points out, Proust sees the role of the artist as prophetic and moral. Ideally, as Marcel states, "every reader is, while he is reading, the reader of his own self."

As Marcel savors his discoveries about the nature of art, he also perceives that Swann has indeed been his primary mentor and inspiration. Through Swann's influence, he has gone to Balbec and subsequently made the acquaintance of both the Guermanteses and Albertine. Marcel observes that even the Guermantes Way has emanated from Swann's Way, an idea reinforced when he meets Mademoiselle de Saint-Loup at the matinee. In this grand-daughter of Swann, the two ways have literally become one. This recollection of Swann also provides a smooth transition back to Marcel's immediate concern, the matinee. With irony characteristic of the novel as a whole, Marcel discovers, with something akin to horror, the destructive effect of time precisely at the moment that he conceives of a work that depends on memories existing outside time. Gathered at the Guermantes' are most of the personages—the "interwoven threads," as Marcel calls them—that have populated the novel: Bloch, Legrandin, Gilberte, Odette, the Baron, the Duke and Duchess de Guermantes, Morel, even Rachel, Robert de Saint-Loup's old mistress. Marcel discovers curious reversals and startling revelations: The Duchess de Guermantes now patronizes Rachel, whom she once had snubbed; the Duke, described as a "magnificent ruin," loves Odette; most shocking of all, the new Princess de Guermantes is Madame Verdurin. Marcel is struck by the vast change that has taken place in a society that he once considered stable, monumental, and without flux.

The vivid display of decay and cruelty that Marcel sees at the matinee, coupled with the news of the tragic death of the great actress, Berma, produces the appropriate effect on Marcel and the reader. The physical world, awash in the tide of time, is rendered absurd by the inevitability of suffering and death. For Marcel, the visceral knowledge of such a fact is the necessary spur to action. Rather than sink into despair, he sees that life can be restored to its "pristine shape" only within the confines of a book; he repeatedly insists that his purpose in writing such a work is that others may examine their own lives.

The end of *Remembrance of Things Past* is also its beginning. Marcel removes himself from society, and under the shadow of its own approaching death, he begins the work that will immortalize Swann, the Guermantes, Albertine, and himself. While the quests for love and society fail or lead to disappointment, the greater quest for immortality in art succeeds.

John K. Saunders

OTHER MAJOR WORKS

SHORT FICTION: *Les Plaisirs et les jours*, 1896 (*Pleasures and Regrets*, 1948).

NONFICTION: *Pastiches et mélanges*, 1919; *Chroniques*, 1927; *Contre Sainte-Beuve*, 1954 (wr. 1908; *By Way of Sainte-Beuve*, 1958).

TRANSLATIONS: *Le Bible d'Amiens*, 1904 (of John Ruskin's *The Bible of Amiens*); *Sésame et les lys*, 1906 (of Ruskin's *Sesame and Lilies*).

BIBLIOGRAPHY

Bloom, Harold, ed. *Marcel Proust*. New York: Chelsea House, 1987. Essays by Proust's most distinguished critics, including Germaine Brée, Samuel Beckett, and Walter Benjamin. There are essays on Proust's reading, on comparing him to James Joyce, and on his handling of time, narrative, and metaphor. Includes introduction, chronology, and bibliography.

_____. *Marcel Proust's "Remembrance of Things Past."* New York: Chelsea House, 1987. Overlaps somewhat with Bloom's other volume but contains important essays by Georges Bataille on "Proust and Evil" and by Georges Poulet on "Proustian Space." With an introduction, chronology, and bibliography.

Brady, Patrick. *Marcel Proust*. Boston: Twayne, 1977. A good introductory study, with chapters on voice, tone, selves, relationships, things, symbols, patterns, memories, and art. Includes chronology, notes, and an annotated bibliography.

Hodson, Leighton, ed. *Marcel Proust: The Critical Heritage*. New York: Routledge, 1989. Like other volumes in this series, this one carefully tracks the reception of the author's work in a thorough introduction, in contemporary reviews, and in later critical essays. Includes a bibliography.

Kilmartin, Terence. *A Reader's Guide to "Remembrance of Things Past."* New York: Random House, 1983. A very useful study guide, containing indexes of characters, persons, places, and themes.

Lamos, Colleen. *Deviant Modernism: Sexual and Textual Errancy in T. S. Eliot, James Joyce, and Marcel Proust.* Cambridge, England: Cambridge University Press, 1998. Examines *Remembrance of Things Past*, *Ulysses*, and Eliot's poetry. Focuses on sexual deviation and masculinity in the works.

Painter, George. *Proust: The Early Years.* Boston: Little, Brown, 1959. Renowned not only as a great biography of Proust but also as an exemplary work of biography in and of itself. Painter is noted for his extraordinary grasp of the autobiographical materials from which Proust's great novel evolved.

_____. *Proust: The Later Years.* Boston: Little, Brown, 1965. The second volume of Painter's distinguished biography.

White, Edmund. *Marcel Proust.* New York: Viking, 1999. An excellent, updated biography of Proust. Includes bibliographical references.

MANUEL PUIG

Born: General Villegas, Argentina; December 28, 1932
Died: Cuernavaca, Mexico; July 22, 1990

PRINCIPAL LONG FICTION

La traición de Rita Hayworth, 1968 (*Betrayed by Rita Hayworth*, 1971)
Boquitas pintadas, 1969 (*Heartbreak Tango*, 1973)
The Buenos Aires Affair: Novela policial, 1973 (*The Buenos Aires Affair: A Detective Novel*, 1976)
El beso de la mujer araña, 1976 (*Kiss of the Spider Woman*, 1979)
Pubis angelical, 1979 (English translation, 1986)

Maldición eterna a quien lea estas páginas, 1980 (*An Eternal Curse on the Reader of These Pages*, 1982)
Sangre de amor correspondido, 1982 (*Blood of Requited Love*, 1984)

OTHER LITERARY FORMS

Although he is best known for his novels, Manuel Puig was also an author of nonfiction and a screenwriter; his screenplays for his own *Boquitas pintadas* (1974) and for José Donoso's novel *El lugar sin límites* (1978) both won prizes at the San Sebastián Festival.

ACHIEVEMENTS

Puig established himself both as a Latin American novelist and as a writer capable of providing insight into contemporary American society. For many years, Puig was a highly mobile exile from Argentina, spending considerable stretches of time in New York and favoring other cosmopolitan centers, such as Rio de Janeiro. In the process, he became a cross-cultural writer, exploring such phenomena as the effects of mass communications and culture, the issues of changing gender roles and variant sexualities, and the need to establish new types of bonds in an impermanent and rapidly changing social environment.

In addition to the university audience that is likely to gravitate toward Latin American authors, Puig appeals to various subcultures in New York. Film enthusiasts are understandably drawn to this novelist, who used a storehouse of cinematic knowledge in his fiction. Film critic Andrew Sarris, among others, has directed his readers toward Puig's novels and followed Puig's career with interest. The growth of the gay people's liberation movement and the general interest in alternative sexualities also increased Puig's readership, and he, in turn, was willing to learn from this movement, with its stress on the validation of nonstandard sexual expression. The author was receptive to the idea that some readers would come to his works, lectures, and public readings specifically attracted by this content, and he discussed his thoughts about sexuality in the magazine *Christopher Street* and other gay forums. Puig also became a figure admired by another subculture, science-fiction readers and writers. This last-named group feels drawn not only to Puig's *Pubis Angelical*, with its unmistakable borrowings from science fiction, but also to the author's overall production, for its critique of culture and society.

Thus, Puig has reached an audience more diverse than the literary sophisticates who are the only audience for many experimental writers. His excellent relationships with cultural subgroups in the United States reveal his profound willingness to reach out to many types of readers, including the special enclaves that may be considered marginal or bizarre by the literary establishment.

BIOGRAPHY

Manuel Puig's early life, however confusing it may have been to him, provided him with excellent insight into the problems of mass-media saturation and contemporary uncertainties about sexuality and sex-role definition. As the author reported it, his almost daily filmgoing began before he had reached the age of four. The boy favored films with a strong element of glamour and fantasy, especially the extravagantly mounted musical comedies and dramas imported from the United States. His attention, he recalled, was directed almost exclusively to the female lead performers; male actors failed to provoke an empathetic response.

At the age of ten, Puig suffered a traumatic experience: an attempted homosexual rape. Because Puig chose to make public this very troubling incident in his early life, one may assume that it is associated with his later literary interest in showing the effects of formative experiences in the shaping of one's identity, particularly in the emergence of a conflicted or uneasy sense of one's sexual self.

Puig's hometown, General Villegas, was severely limited in its cultural and educational opportunities, but U.S. films provided continual reminders of the larger, cosmopolitan world. Puig's mother was an urban woman who had gone to the pampas to work in the provincial health services and ended up staying there and marrying a local man. This woman stood

(Jerry Bauer)

out from her surroundings in many ways; with her great passion for reading and filmgoing, she seems to have had a streak of Gustave Flaubert's Madame Bovary in her character. At any rate, the provincial's longing for a cosmopolitan environment became powerfully represented in Puig's first two novels.

A secondary factor in Puig's development was the disjunction between his Spanish-language environment and the English-language film world. The language used in Hollywood films, as conventionalized as it often is, cannot be considered representative of any spontaneously occurring form of expression, but Puig nevertheless identified the English language with Hollywood (indeed, as he later explained, it made him feel close to Hollywood), and he sought to bridge the gap between his world and the cinematic world by mastering English. The idea of English as the language of film persisted with Puig, to the extent that his first few writing efforts were film scripts in English. He was an active consultant in the translation of his novels into English, and he actually wrote the first version of *An Eternal Curse on the Reader of These Pages* in English, later composing a Spanish equivalent; the published English version of the novel was based upon both the unpublished English original and the Spanish "translation."

Puig's early career was marked by various unsuccessful attempts to find an outlet for his special love and knowledge of film and other popular forms. From 1955 to 1962, Puig sought to break into screenwriting and directing but was consistently unable to make progress in the film industry. A scholarship in 1957 to the Experimental Film Center permitted him to study filmmaking in Rome; later, he tried Spanish-language script work in Argentina, but he seemed to be insufficiently attuned to national realities. To become comfortable with an Argentine Spanish suitable for screenwriting, Puig worked at reproducing the voices he had heard around him in his hometown. The re-creation of these voices from a long-ago small-town world proved more absorbing than the task of screenwriting and allowed Puig to begin writing novels.

The sets of concerns referred to above are, essentially, the crucial issues of Puig's first two novels. In 1963, the restless Puig moved to New York, took a fairly undemanding job as an airline employee, and set about writing narrative, the literary form that would eventually prove his most successful medium. The author was soon able to obtain praise for his work, but it was 1968 before *Betrayed by Rita Hayworth* was published, and then without attaining a wide readership. *Heartbreak Tango* followed, as popular and readable as a soap opera, which it resembled. It drew readers to his earlier novel, and Puig became a celebrated feature of the Buenos Aires scene, which during those "boom" years tended to make celebrities of innovative writers.

In 1973, however, his third novel, *The Buenos Aires Affair*, was confiscated by authorities. After the impounding of the copies of this work, Puig published with the Barcelona firm of Seix Barral. Well established as a novelist with an international reputation, Puig traveled widely, spending considerable time in New York. He died in Mexico on July 22, 1990.

Analysis

Although Manuel Puig took pains to introduce new variants on his favored thematic issues and to seek new solutions to the formal problems of organizing a novel, he has tended to remain identified in many minds with his first work. The highly memorable title of this novel would seem to make actress Rita Hayworth a character in the plot, and, indeed, this implication is in a sense accurate, though the action takes place far from Hollywood.

Betrayed by Rita Hayworth

In *Betrayed by Rita Hayworth*, Hayworth and other luminaries of the late 1930's and early 1940's figure as vivid presences in the decidedly unglamorous lives of a group of small-town Argentine children growing into a troubled adolescence, continually turning to the films to supply satisfactions that are missing in their existence.

Betrayed by Rita Hayworth also introduced a type of character common throughout Puig's writings: the young person confused about sex. Here, the protagonist Toto is particularly prominent in this role. Toto's early stream-of-consciousness narratives reveal his inability to make the standard distinction between male and female; he identifies himself with Shirley Temple and his unreliable father with the treacherous Rita Hayworth. As is evident from the beginning, his uncertain notions about sexuality and sex roles are entwined with his popular-culture fantasy vision of life. The two themes come together in Toto's essay about the 1938 film *The Great Waltz*. Attempting to convey the film's ambience of a rapturous, waltz-mad Old Vienna, Toto inadvertently signals his conflict-filled view of sex. Among other things, he expresses the idea that heterosexual sex, even in the form of simple embracing and kissing, is physically harmful to women; he inserts his own element of voyeurism not found in the original film; and he dwells on the theme of insecurity about one's sexual attractiveness.

Betrayed by Rita Hayworth shows with extraordinary vividness the ability of a popular medium to bedazzle and distract consumers, particularly when audience members lack other sources of stimulation. Yet the novel cannot constitute simply a lovingly nostalgic evocation of a filmgoer's paradise, for Puig also offers a critique of popular culture. It becomes clear that his characters are suffering the effects of an acritical and unquestioning consumption of a mass-culture product.

As well as including material on the sexual lives of very young characters (both real and imaginary), this first novel was unusual enough in its approach to appear risky to publishers. The small, daring Buenos Aires firm of Jorge Álvarez launched the work but then was forced to close. Later, a more prestigious house, Editorial Sudamericana, reprinted it, but only after the publication of Puig's second novel, whose playfully nostalgic appeal convinced the public that Puig was readable. Although *Betrayed by Rita Hayworth* subsequently became a best-seller, it remains a difficult work to assess and to characterize. Perhaps most difficult of all the issues involved is that of establishing the work's relation to the phenomenon of popular culture.

Sudamericana's publicity for *Betrayed by Rita Hayworth* characterized the text as a "pop novel," certainly an attractive and catchy phrase. Along with the merrily kitsch cover, which showed a tawdry Art Deco fantasy vision of Hollywood-style glamour, the publicity surrounding the work suggested that Puig had produced either an item of pop culture or a denunciatory satire of the Hollywood culture. As Puig noted, these two options seem to account for most of the readings of his works, although neither is especially accurate. *Betrayed by Rita Hayworth*, for example, cannot be critically restricted to a mere part of pop culture, for the simple reason that it evinces complex new structures characteristic of the twentieth century novel. The narration is not undertaken by a recognizable and reliable narrative voice, as it typically is in the easy-to-read formula best-seller; rather, one must discover what is happening to the characters by extracting information from a variety of types of narration. These include a babble of neighborhood voices discussing the hero's birth and his mother's situation, extracts from a young girl's diary, diverse forms of stream-of-consciousness writing, a prize-winning school essay by the protagonist, letters, and other modes, all designed to look like transcriptions

from the flow of thought and language. Because the novel is so strikingly anomalous, with its paradoxical joining of sophisticated novelistic form and popular culture, it conveys the impression of a somewhat uneasy synthesis.

HEARTBREAK TANGO

Heartbreak Tango is much easier to read than its predecessor. It was an immediate best-seller when it appeared and, in effect, served to draw readers to Puig's more complex early novel. *Heartbreak Tango* takes the form of an old-fashioned installment novel, with each chapter revealing a new, tantalizing glimpse of a fairly intricate but banal plot. The reader is drawn along by two major lines of development: how a wondrously handsome young man of fairly good family came to an impoverished, tubercular end, and how the tense relations between a housemaid and her upwardly mobile seducer culminated in the latter's murder. Further interest comes from following the fates of three other young women: the handsome young rake's scheming sister; a local cattle baron's daughter, who rendezvouses with the rake while waiting to marry into the landed aristocracy; and another of the hero's conquests, an ambitious blonde who can never manage to rise above the lower middle class.

The characters, however sympathetic they may be at moments, are satirized for their obsession with status and standing. Puig warned against placing too great an emphasis on the satiric element. While well-educated urban readers might see the book as turning the members of the provincial middle class into figures of fun, such a reading fails to take into account the great amount of material dedicated to the exploration of Puig's twin themes of popular culture and concepts of sexuality.

One of the most telling indicators of the extent to which the media have saturated the culture is the language used by the characters to speak of their own lives. So enthralled are they by the commercially standardized language of sentimental and romantic films, advertising copy charged with mass-appeal allure, and other popular subgenres (song lyrics, sportscasting, "tearjerker" novels, and so on) that this language becomes second nature to them. The problem is the lack of correlation between their own existence and the rapturous, adventurous, or "macho" language they employ. The incongruity is especially acute in the area of courtship mores. The reader sees a small society in which both marriage and informal liaisons are heavily governed by questions of prestige and economic power, while the characters see love and sexuality through a haze of dreamily romantic or aggressively Don Juanesque phrases.

The presentation of popular culture in *Heartbreak Tango* is much more diverse than it is in *Betrayed by Rita Hayworth*. The characters, no longer children growing into adolescence, are young adults moving toward an early, disaffected middle age. Their patterns of pop-culture consumption reflect this shift. They have lost the child's ability to be enraptured by a film, and they turn to the cinema house as a meeting place, a distraction in which they indulge by ingrained habit. Concerned with presenting themselves impressively, they rely on advertising and magazine materials in order to master style. The artifacts of mass culture—photo albums, commercial art, decorative product packaging, dance-hall decor, and household bric-a-brac—surround them. They are living in the "golden age" of radio, and the airwaves are full of gimmicky programs, including variety shows, serial dramas, and musicals.

On one hand, the young people present the classic picture of "junk-culture addicts"; they show many signs of a virtual dependency on their pop culture. (One young woman, for example, cannot forgo her daily radio soap opera, even when a long-absent friend shows up at her house.) Yet despite this constant consumption of media, their satisfaction with it lessens. The rakish hero reports attending the cinema without feeling any interest in the film shown, while an observant heroine notices that her town is being shipped films that are too out-of-date to screen elsewhere. These expressions of ennui with the homogeneous mass media do not, however, entail a critical questioning of mass culture. The young people are not moved by their boredom and dissatisfaction with certain pop-culture artifacts to ask whether the massive standardization of this culture might be unwarranted and intellectually unhealthy. Nor is there an attempt to find alternative forms of diversion, for the young men and women remain fixed in their accustomed patterns.

The focus on sexuality is less concerned with individual cases than it is with the social codes that govern the expression of sexual feelings. The small-town young people try to satisfy various conflicting sets of standards. On the surface, the unmarried women are expected to remain chaste, while men are given more leeway, although they are required to satisfy conditions of respectability. Overlapping this Victorian standard, and at times in conflict with it, is the code of *machismo*, which demands of the young men a constant effort to conquer numbers of women, to cultivate a swaggering style, and to appear unconcerned with their own well-being. An additional set of factors has to do with the intense and widespread desire for upward mobility.

Apart from the inherent passion between the sexes, the desire for prestige is the most powerful force in determining the characters' involvements with one another. The Don Juanesque hero's sister continually schemes to link him with the cattleman's daughter and to steer him away from the blonde social climber, while the stockbroker seeks to guide his daughter toward a landowning customer. Meanwhile, the blonde attempts to minimize a loss of status incurred by an earlier seduction, hoping to charm her Casanova-lover into marriage. In a subplot, the hero masterminds the amorous life of a lower-class friend. Under this tutelage, the aspiring policeman seduces a servant, avoiding any lasting commitment that might impede his rise in society.

Of the various liaisons contracted during the novel, all are somehow colored by the dream of acquiring an advantageous match in marriage. The schemes uniformly come to nothing, for the hero dies without marrying any of his lovers; the wealthy landowner rejects the stockbroker's daughter, along with a shipment of diseased cattle; the policeman's brief enjoyment of middle-class status is ended by his spurned girlfriend's violence. In an ironic turnabout, the vision is realized only by the servant girl, who stands at the very bottom of this hierarchy. After being seduced, impregnated, and abandoned—even after murdering her lover—she somehow succeeds in obtaining for herself a stable and provident mate.

Puig is unmistakably critical of this scenario, in which sex and courtship are made part of the politics of class standing. He offers a condemnatory portrait of this system, making his attitude clear by portraying popular culture as stressing the acquisition of an impressive lover or spouse. (At the height of the cross-class tangle of sexual alliances, the local film-house is running a Hollywood film centered entirely on the concept of marrying for wealth and security.) The criticism is clear, but Puig has not begun to look at alternative arrangements that would remove sexuality from this very politicized framework. This missing factor does, however, appear in Puig's later work, when he turns to utopian speculations about the future of sex.

THE BUENOS AIRES AFFAIR

If Puig's first novel was substantially patterned after the modern "serious" novel and his second novel derived playfully from the serialized soap opera, his third work, *The Buenos Aires Affair*, offered a renovated version of the detective novel. Puig remained manifestly faithful to the idea of simplifying his novelistic form enough to allow easy reading, although this accessibility did not preclude subtlety and complexity.

The novel was confiscated in Buenos Aires and deemed obscene, although it contains little in the way of overwhelming erotic content. *The Buenos Aires Affair* would seem to have hit a sensitive spot because the pair of lovers, an art critic and an aspiring sculptress, clearly form a sadomasochistic team, and the man bears the burden of a very troubled homosexual past. In short, the theme of nonstandard sexuality, indirectly alluded to in the confusion of Toto in *Betrayed by Rita Hayworth*, now emerges as an overt theme.

The "affair" of the title refers to both a police case, in the sense of a mysterious set of circumstances requiring investigation, and a liaison between the protagonists. The two meanings of the word coalesce, for the police are called in to resolve an out-of-control situation between the lovers. The man, having lost his ability to keep his sexual expression

from interfering with society, has kidnapped his girlfriend and is holding her in bondage. This disruptive act, reported at the very beginning of the novel, eventually turns out to be merely the culmination of a torturous relationship that came to have such a grip on the hero that he was no longer able to refrain from destructive and self-destructive actions. The novel reconstructs the pressures that led this man, an educated and influential member of the arts community, to burst out in reckless, antisocial behavior. Intertwined is the story of the sculptress. The woman's history is less dramatic, for she does not succumb to any wild outbreak of deranged behavior; rather, she has gradually reached a point where she finds any purposeful action difficult to plan or execute, so that even her sculpting is largely the passive activity of presenting and "conceptualizing" found objects. A third direction in the novel's development is the unfolding of the events caused by the kidnapping. The police, far from solving the tangle of disturbing evidence, essentially go through various standard procedures until the hero brings the matter to an end by destroying himself in his panic; the ever-passive heroine is befriended by a sane, motherly neighbor woman. In effect, the total contribution of the authorities is to report as properly as possible on a set of circumstances that they can neither influence nor understand. If any detective work is accomplished, it is that performed by the reader in attempting to obtain some degree of insight into this disordered tale of unhappy sexual alliances and cultural fashions.

To provide an understanding of the protagonists' problems, Puig employs a number of narrative procedures that tend to place the characters on the psychiatric couch. Transcriptions of the hero's exchanges with his psychotherapist are included, as well as "case histories" of both the man and the woman. The histories of both characters' troubles are couched in a language of pseudoscientific objectivity, again evoking concepts of psychiatric investigation of the past.

In utilizing these "psychoanalytical" narratives, Puig would seem to be lampooning classical psychotherapy yet making use of its theories. The man's psychiatrist is, in effect, as confused and helpless as any layperson as he watches his patient display increasingly muddled thinking and erratic behavior. The woman, though not undergoing any type of psychiatric treatment that is directly presented to the reader, has recently fallen into the hands of the medical establishment as a result of her sudden inability to function, with similarly unhelpful results. It is worth remarking that the two people in the novel who are best able to counsel and soothe the frantic protagonists are simply laypersons who have a calm and stable outlook. The hero enters into a series of telephone exchanges with an older, tradition-steeped sculptress who, unlike the classically trained psychiatrist, is willing to speak to the disturbed man in commonsense terms. Her ability to carry on a sensible, reasonable conversation with the man stands out in a novel full of fatuous, jargon-filled talk. Reinforcing this theme that steady, ordinary people can function successfully as therapists is the appearance of the neighbor woman who, at the end, cares for the heroine. This neighbor, a young woman clearly satisfied with her husband and baby, asks the heroine as little as possible about the circumstances leading to her current beleaguered state, instead concentrating on getting her to rest and feel comfortable.

While the novel shows professional therapists being outdone by concerned laypersons, it is essentially favorable to the notion, heavily associated with psychiatry, that early-childhood experiences may underlie troubles faced in adulthood. At the same time, Puig is concerned with expanding the narrowly psychological and individualistic view of childhood development. He moves beyond the particular—the workings of the child's family—to look at factors that potentially affect all children reared in a particular society. The effects of mass media and culture are, once more, subjected to detailed scrutiny. The heroine, for example, carries a permanent sense of unease as a result of constantly being compared with the media-propagated images of perfect womanhood.

Her case history dwells upon her father's attempts to remake his daughter into a conventionally attractive, vivacious young woman and her resulting unhappiness over her failure to match this standard. The father's favored reading matter, the popular 1940's magazine *Rico tipo* (fancy guy), is singled out for particular denunciation for its tendency to promote a single image of acceptable femininity and to deride women who fail to adhere to this highly conventional pattern of attractiveness. Another spotlighted aspect of popular culture is the system of recreational clubs for young women. In *The Buenos Aires Affair*, these social organizations are seen as essentially concerned with questions of prestige and "connections." The heroine's childhood is further marred by her ambitious mother's attempts to attain upward mobility through this supposedly leisure-providing system.

In *The Buenos Aires Affair*, Puig is most critical of the distortion of artistic activity that allows conformity to the capitalist society's patterns of "product marketing." For example, although the hero is well read in the field of art criticism, he is seldom observed analyzing artistic work. His essential function is that of a publicist and impresario. His friends, with their incessant festival-going, see themselves as marketable commodities that must be kept in the art public's eye. In this unattractive panorama of self-packagers and self-promoters, only one exception stands out: the extraordinarily sane older woman who is able to counsel the troubled hero. All evidence points to her conscientious and principled practice of assemblage art; her steadfast and workmanlike approach strikes the art critic in his professional conscience. It is his realization that he has awarded a prize to his heavily "hyped," but inconsequential, sculptress-lover, rejecting the well-conceived work of the older woman, that precipitates his final round of deranged behavior.

Culture consumption as a search for prestige is another of the novel's motifs. An amusing example occurs on the night of the heroine's conception. Her parents have just seen a performance of a play by Eugene O'Neill that affords them theatergoing satisfaction, but they are inhibited in their later discussion of it by their extreme desire not to be "one-upped" by each other. Within the dynamics of this marriage, the wife can lay claim to some degree of superiority to her husband; while he tends to favor "easy reading" material, she has the time to maintain at least a superficial knowledge of the arts. The daughter continues this pattern of competence in the arts as a way of maintaining status. In addition, Puig points to the fact that the characters live in a mass-media culture by using excerpts from old Hollywood melodramas as epigraphs to the chapters. These film dialogues do not comment directly upon the issue treated in the chapter, but rather suggest a world in which the hyperbolic "Hollywoodization" of life situations has altered people's expectations about the drama, suspense, and romance they should find in their own lives.

The Buenos Aires Affair thus continues the examination of mass culture, but it is also a study in the attitudes and actions of fine-arts consumers. In earlier Puig novels, the characters can be seen as suffering from cultural deprivation, because of their lack of education, their isolation, or both. *The Buenos Aires Affair* presents characters who are of a cultural level comparable to that of an educated reader of novels; Puig thereby holds up a mirror to his reader which reflects criticism of the characters onto the reader himself. The heroine, Gladys, reads fashionable serious authors and spends time as a prizewinning, if docile and eager-to-please, art student. Her choices as a consumer of culture are typically those of a trend-conscious, informed viewer or reader, from a preference for starkly functional decor to her favorite television fare, relatively "classy" examples of Hollywood cinema. The hero is an influential art critic. What is amiss is their approach to culture. The heroine's artistic career offers an extreme example of a creator so uncertain of her own expression that she depends slavishly on the academic standards of competence that will win praise and awards for her. Leaving the structured world of the art school, she is unable to produce and becomes so distraught over her relation to art that even going to museums becomes unbearably painful.

If Gladys represents the constraints of academically institutionalized art, her lover reveals the same pattern in anti-establishment art. He is a leading figure on the experimentalist scene. His favored artists use approaches originally designed to defy and astound the art orthodoxy—found objects, assemblages, works with a strong random element, and so on. The creators of this work, however, are not rebels but dedicated careerists, obsessed with the notion of making a name for themselves. Among the ridiculous, petty actions attributed to this cliquish group, the worst is its treatment of Gladys. The woman is clearly going through a period of instability, but the avant-garde group chooses to perceive her as wildly innovative rather than unbalanced. Her debris sculptures, more pathological indications than works of art, are gaudily exploited as the last word in assemblage art. The group's disregard for the well-being of the disoriented woman at the center of all this promotional hoopla is the surest indictment of a type of high culture wholly dominated by the need to market and sell novelties to a jaded public.

The overall effect is to bring home the problem of passive cultural consumption and production by featuring characters and settings not likely to be far removed from the readers' own set of experiences. Particularly in Gladys, the bright, industrious young person who finds both modern culture and sex perpetually mind-boggling, Puig has created a figure capable of reflecting the reader's and the author's own difficulties amid the confusions of the current cultural scene.

The transition from the early, literarily complex Puig to the more accessible author of the later novels is not even. *Betrayed by Rita Hayworth* is set apart from the subsequent novels by its structural complexity and the amount of work the reader must perform to extract a sense of what is going on in the work. *Heartbreak Tango* was deliberately written for a broad audience, and Puig has expressed disappointment that the novel did not reach a wider public than it did. While the work does not require laborious reading, its commentary on the phenomenon of mass culture is by no means simplistic. *The Buenos Aires Affair*, relatively accessible despite a degree of narrative experimentation, introduced a new set of issues as Puig turned his critical scrutiny to the fine-arts culture, its consumers and practitioners, and the author's concern with nonstandard forms of sexuality.

KISS OF THE SPIDER WOMAN

Kiss of the Spider Woman, though a fascinating work in many respects, marks a certain repetition of themes and structures already familiar to Puig's readers. Without denigrating this work, one may describe it as lending itself less to critical consideration than do the previous works, for it appears designed for readers who are not literary analysts. To give only one example of this phenomenon, long citations from essays on homosexuality are included as footnotes, an inclusion having very little to do with the literary texture of the work and a great deal to do with Puig's desire to convey to lay readers a consciousness of this misunderstood phenomenon. The same process of "laicization"—of writing more and more for the reader who is not a literary specialist—was the most notable aspect of the evolution of Puig's writing after that time.

Puig accepted the courtship of such determinedly "lay" reader groups as science-fiction aficionados and cultural workers concerned with the presentation of alternatives in sexuality; at the same time, many academic readers were baffled by the evolution of Puig's work. It has yet to be determined whether Puig actually moved away from the typical high-culture, "literary" reader or whether this variety of reader simply learned new reading strategies to follow Puig.

Naomi Lindstrom

OTHER MAJOR WORKS

SCREENPLAYS: *Boquitas pintadas*, 1974; *El lugar sin límites*, 1978 (adaptation of José Donoso's novel).

BIBLIOGRAPHY

Bacarisse, Pamela. *Impossible Choices: The Implications of the Cultural References in the Novels of Manuel Puig*. Calgary, Alta.: University of Calgary Press, 1993. An excellent critical study of Puig's work. Includes bibliographical references and an index.

_____. *The Necessary Dream: A Study of the Novels of Manuel Puig*. Totowa, N.J.: Barnes & Noble, 1988. Chapters on the major novels. The introduction provides a useful overview of Puig's career and themes. Includes notes and bibliography.

Colas, Santiago. *Postmodernity in Latin America: The Argentine Paradigm*. Durham, N.C.: Duke University Press, 1994. Puig is discussed in this study of Argentine works, which also examines Julio Cortázar and Ricardo Piglia.

Kerr, Lucille. *Suspended Fictions: Reading Novels by Manuel Puig*. Urbana: University of Illinois Press, 1987. Chapters on each of Puig's major novels, exploring the themes of tradition, romance, popular culture, crime, sex, and the design of Puig's career. Contains detailed notes but no bibliography.

Lavers, Norman. *Pop Culture into Art: The Novels of Manuel Puig*. Columbia: University of Missouri Press, 1988. Lavers finds a close relationship between Puig's life and his literary themes. Biography, in this case, helps to explain the author's methods and themes.

Magnarelli, Sharon. *The Lost Rib: Female Characters in the Spanish-American Novel*. Toronto: Associated University Presses, 1985. In "Betrayed by the Cross-Stitch," Magnarelli provides a close reading and feminist analysis of *Betrayed by Rita Hayworth*.

Tittler, Jonathan. *Manuel Puig*. New York: Twayne, 1993. The best introduction to Puig. In addition to providing a useful survey of Puig's career in his introduction, Tittler devotes separate chapters to the novels. Chapter 7 discusses Puig's theatrical scripts, screenplays, and short stories. Includes detailed notes and an annotated bibliography.

Wheaton, Kathleen. "The Art of Fiction: Manuel Puig." *The Paris Review* 31 (Winter, 1989): 129-147. An intensive exploration of Puig's themes and techniques.

JAMES PURDY

Born: Near Fremont, Ohio; July 14, 1923

PRINCIPAL LONG FICTION

Malcolm, 1959

The Nephew, 1960

Cabot Wright Begins, 1964

Eustace Chisholm and the Works, 1967

Jeremy's Version, 1970
I Am Elijah Thrush, 1972
The House of the Solitary Maggot, 1974
In a Shallow Grave, 1976
Narrow Rooms, 1977
Mourners Below, 1981
On Glory's Course, 1984
In the Hollow of His Hand, 1986
Garments the Living Wear, 1989
Out with the Stars, 1992
Gertrude of Stony Island Avenue, 1997

OTHER LITERARY FORMS

In addition to his novels, James Purdy has written in a variety of genres, including poetry, the short story, and drama. The most important of these other works are *63: Dream Palace* (1956); *Color of Darkness: Eleven Stories and a Novella* (1957); *Children Is All* (1961), ten stories and two plays; and a volume of poetry, *The Running Sun* (1971).

ACHIEVEMENTS

Purdy is considered one of the most important of the postmodern American writers. Along with Thomas Pynchon, John Barth, and John Hawkes, Purdy is acknowledged as one of the best of the generation of post-Joycean experimental writers. He is a unique and powerful writer whose vision remains etched in the reader's mind. Like other postmodern writers, Purdy takes delight in experimenting with the texts and subtexts of a narrative and treats his themes with humor and irony. In essence, Purdy's characters are motivated by irrationality, his style is ornate and complex, and his themes are surreal; however, he is a writer whose works must be examined if the texture and ideas of the postmodern novel are to be appreciated.

BIOGRAPHY

James Otis Purdy was born on July 14, 1923, near Fremont, Ohio. He attended the University of Chicago and the University of Puebla in Mexico. Later, he worked as an interpreter in Spain, Latin America,

(Library of Congress)

and France. From 1949 until 1953, he taught at Lawrence College in Appleton, Wisconsin. In 1953, he decided to devote himself to writing full-time. Purdy received Guggenheim Fellowships in 1958 and 1962 and a Ford Fellowship in Drama in 1961. He took a teaching post at New York University and settled in Brooklyn Heights, New York.

ANALYSIS

Since James Purdy has been so hesitant to make public the details of his private life, it is impossible to correlate any of his works with his personal experiences. His works are hermetically sealed from his life and must be examined as entities in themselves. Purdy's themes, style, and ideas change, develop, and expand from novel to novel, so it is not possible to delineate any one particular aspect of his work that is found consistently throughout. Certain preoccupations, however, are found, in varying degrees, in most of his works, and certain characteristics that are typical of postmodern fiction.

The characters in Purdy's novels are bizarre, grotesque, and governed by abnormal impulses and desires. Purdy uses his characters for purposes of symbolic manipulation, rather than for the purpose of character development in the traditional sense. Many of his characters are physically and/or mentally mutilated: They are tattooed, wounded, stabbed, raped, and, in one case, crucified. One of the major characteristics of all of his novels is his use of "unreal" characters whose thinking processes are "nonrealistic."

A primary concern of Purdy is the relationship of children to their parents; most of his novels include a domineering phallic woman, the search for a father, and the interrelationships within a family matrix. Many of his characters are orphans, illegitimate children, or children who have been abandoned by their parents. Along with these motifs, Purdy is preoccupied with the idea of being "grown-up" or mature. Within the quest for a father figure, the idea of becoming mature is interwoven into the text, and within this framework Purdy usually parodies the search for identity and its resultant ambivalence.

The interplay of sex, love, and violence occurs frequently throughout his writing. Virtually no love between man and woman appears in Purdy's novels—the male/female relationships are either those of a prostitute and a man, or a man who rapes women. Purdy does include a number of homosexual affairs between men in his works, but these usually end in obsession and violence. In addition, many of the novels involve incest. Also interwoven in the stories are themes of tyranny, freedom, dominance, and obsessive love. Frequently, the female characters are aggressive and domineering, and often the male characters are passive and dominated. Many of the characters are attempting to find their "freedom" from dominance, but the nature of obsessive love does not permit this. Finally, in some manner or another, Purdy's novels all involve a writer within the narrative. In some books, this figure takes on more importance than in others; this device, typical of self-conscious "metafiction," serves to emphasize the autonomous reality of the fictive world.

MALCOLM

Many of the themes, motifs, and preoccupations of his subsequent novels are found in Purdy's first novel, *Malcolm*. The orphan motif that occurs so frequently in Purdy's works plays a vital part in *Malcolm*. Malcolm (no last name given), the reader is told, belongs nowhere and to nobody. His father has disappeared, and Malcolm's search for him forms the central psychological structure of the book. The fifteen-year-old Malcolm is sitting on a park bench outside of the hotel where he is staying when Mr. Cox, an astrologer, takes an interest in him. He gives Malcolm a series of addresses in order to interest him in "things," and the ensuing visits to the people who live at the respective addresses form the core of the action in the novel. Malcolm becomes a parody of the picaro, for instead of acting he is acted upon. His main concern is to find his father, but his actions are governed by the tyrannical Mr. Cox and his circle of friends.

Within Mr. Cox's circle are Madame Girard and Girard Girard, an eccentric billionaire. At one point in the novel, Malcolm is offered a chance to be Girard Girard's son, but Malcolm tells him he has only one father and Girard Girard cannot take his place. Later, after Malcolm marries Melba, a famous black singer, he believes that he sees his father at a restaurant. Malcolm follows this man into the restroom. The man, however, disclaims that he is Malcolm's father and throws Malcolm down, causing Malcolm to hit his head. After this incident, Malcolm, who has deteriorated physically since his marriage, becomes too weak to get out of bed and eventually dies.

Thus, in this first novel, Purdy reveals many of his recurring preoccupations. In addition to the orphan's search for the father (paralleling the search for identity), Purdy explores the topic of tyranny and the theme of the fatality of a loveless marriage. A concern with the maturation process is also found in *Malcolm*. Gus, one of Melba's former husbands, is chosen to help Malcolm mature before his marriage. Gus's solution to helping Malcolm "mature" is to have Malcolm tattooed and to have him visit a prostitute.

In *Malcolm*, the characters are constantly questioning the substantiality of their existence; they are two-dimensional, almost comic-book figures. Malcolm is given addresses, not names, and consequently, places and events take primacy over the development of the personality. Malcolm himself has no last name, and when he dies there is no corpse in his coffin. All that is left of Malcolm are three hundred pages of manuscript that he had written, which Madame Girard attempts to organize.

THE NEPHEW

In *The Nephew*, Purdy turns to the small town of Rainbow Center for his setting and tells a story that superficially resembles a slice of small-town life. Yet, underneath the seemingly placid exterior of Rainbow Center, as beneath the surface of the novel, much is happening. The text is surcharged with meanings, and the experience of reading this novel is similar to that of watching a film with the soundtrack slightly off.

The plot is simple and straightforward. Alma Mason and her brother Boyd receive news that their nephew, Cliff, is missing in action during the Korean War. Cliff, another of Purdy's orphans, had lived with the Masons. In order to alleviate some of the grief of his death, Alma decides to write a memorial honoring Cliff. The novel focuses on Alma's attempts to gather material for the writing of Cliff's memorial. During this process, she discovers many facets of Cliff's existence of which she had been unaware—particularly that Cliff had hated the town and that he had had a homosexual affair with Vernon—which lead her to some revelations about herself and her relationship to Boyd and others in the community.

One of Purdy's concerns that can be noted throughout the novel is the inadequacy of judging people by their actions and their words. Communication is always inadequate and misinterpreted. Alma never does finish her memorial to Cliff, another indication that one can never fully understand another person. By the end of the story, though, Alma does become much more tolerant in her attitude toward what she considers the foibles of others.

CABOT WRIGHT BEGINS

Like *The Nephew*, *Cabot Wright Begins* concerns the attempt to write about another person—in this case, a businessman-rapist named Cabot Wright. Instead of one narrative voice, as in *The Nephew*, many emerge in *Cabot Wright Begins*, and this blending and confusion of narrative voices further demonstrate the impossibility of learning the true story about another person.

Purdy's third novel is an extremely pessimistic indictment and extended meditation upon modern American culture. In *Cabot Wright Begins*, people are controlled by media-think, big business, and popular culture, and by all the superficial aspects of modern existence. Feelings, emotions, and actions are all superficial, and even the rape scenes involving Cabot Wright are narrated in a dispassionate manner—much like secondhand violence seen on television or in the cinema. People exist on the screen of the text, and their ability to function in normal human terms is questioned.

Cabot Wright, another orphan, is twenty-six years old during the time of the novel. He is a stockbroker turned rapist. Bernie Gladhart, a used-car salesman, has been cajoled by his wife into writing the great American novel and has decided that a life history of Cabot Wright would be the perfect subject matter. In fact, the tentative title of Bernie's novel is "Indelible Smudge," which indicates Purdy's judgment about American culture at this time. Princeton Keith, the owner of a large publishing house, however, has commissioned Zoe Bickle to write the story in terms of popular fiction. Through a skylight, Zoe literally falls upon Cabot Wright himself, and Cabot offers to help her ghostwrite his biography. In the process of turning his life into popular fiction, however, he becomes alienated from himself. To him, the story does not portray his real self.

Cabot Wright seems to symbolize the attempt of modern men and women to assert their identity through violence. Only through the act of rape can Cabot penetrate the surface of another, but even then he becomes increasingly alienated and less alive. For Cabot, there are no answers.

EUSTACE CHISHOLM AND THE WORKS

In *Eustace Chisholm and the Works*, Purdy presents his concept of the sacrificial, violent, and grotesque aspects of love. In many horrific scenes he shows the results of obsessional love. The story revolves around the homosexual love Daniel Hawes has for seventeen-year-old Amos Ratcliff. Amos, an illegitimate son, has been rejected by his father and has had incestuous relationships with his cousin (later revealed to be his mother). Daniel attempts to repress his feelings for Amos, but they finally become so overwhelming that he re-enlists in the army to escape. Instead of escaping, however, he permits his homosexual love for Amos to be brought to the surface and projected upon his commanding officer, Captain Stadger. During the affair between these two, Captain Stadger becomes increasingly more sadistic until finally he kills Daniel by disembowling him, then commits suicide. This incident is the first in a series of homosexual blood-sacrifices found in Purdy's novels.

Once again, as in all the previous works, there is an author involved in an attempt to write the story. In this case, Eustace Chisholm is the writer who is attempting to incorporate the story of Amos and Daniel within the context of a larger epic poem that he is writing.

JEREMY'S VERSION

Purdy's next novel, *Jeremy's Version*, was written as part 1 of a projected trilogy called *Sleepers in the Moon-Crowned Valleys*. Although Purdy had dealt with orphans, the search for a father figure, and interrelationships within families in his previous works, this was his first novel in which the family matrix formed the basis for the entire work.

Again, there is a writer—in this case, Jeremy Cready—narrating the story being told to him by Uncle Matt. The basic story (which actually occurred more than fifty years before) involves the battle of wills between two strong women, Elvira Summerlad and Winifred Fergus, a divorce case, and the interrelationships of the three sons with one another and with their mother and father. Elvira Summerlad and Wilders Fergus were married, much against the wishes of his sister, Winifred, who thought the marriage was doomed. In a sense, Winifred was right, because Wilders abandoned Elvira and their sons. Winifred, however, goes to Wilders and tells him that since his sons are almost grown, he is needed at home. When he arrives, Elvira starts divorce proceedings against him.

The basic conflict is between Elvira and Winifred for custody of the children. Wilders is indifferent to the whole affair. One of Purdy's major themes—that of the son confronting the father—occurs during the divorce proceedings, when the homosexual oldest son, Rick, confronts Wilders. Rick demands that Wilders tell him the reason for his existence since his father has never been around before to teach him—he has only had his mother, who, he claims, has emasculated him. After Elvira wins the divorce case, her second son, Jethro, attempts to shoot her, but Matt saves her and is wounded. A similar shooting scene, between mother and son, occurs again in *The House of the Solitary Maggot*.

I AM ELIJAH THRUSH

I Am Elijah Thrush is a dreamlike, ornate, and highly stylized book, populated with strange characters and filled with unusual events. More than any of Purdy's other novels, this book exists in the realm of allegory and symbols. Among the major characters are a famous mime, Elijah Thrush; his great-grandson, a mute, called the Bird of Heaven; Millicent De Frayne, a tyrannical old dowager who retains her youth by drinking the seminal fluid of young men; and Albert Peggs, the black memoirist who tells the story and who, himself, has a bizarre "habit." In addition, the novel incorporates many elements of mythology in a comic manner, suggesting the debasement of culture in modern America.

As in many of Purdy's previous novels, the plot in *I Am Elijah Thrush* involves a person (in this case, Albert Peggs) being hired by someone to write the story. Millicent De Frayne hires Albert to recount the story of Elijah Thrush. Once again, this story involves a clash of wills between two strong people—Millicent and Elijah. For more than fifty years, she has been trying to gain control of Elijah and marry him. Eventually, she succeeds by manipulating Albert, the Bird of Heaven, and Elijah onto her boat, where she finally marries him. Late in the novel, Albert's "habit" is discovered: He sustains the life of a golden eagle by permitting the eagle to feed upon him. At the wedding feast of Millicent and Elijah, the eagle is served as the entrée. After this incident, Albert "becomes" Elijah Thrush.

One of Purdy's major themes is that of confirming, or finding, an identity. In his novels, there is a plethora of name-changes, mistaken identities, disguises, masquerades, and other such motifs. The dreamlike structure of the narrative suggests that Albert Peggs is attempting to discover his identity by telling this story.

THE HOUSE OF THE SOLITARY MAGGOT

The House of the Solitary Maggot is part 2 of the series called *Sleepers in Moon-Crowned Valleys*. The story is reconstructed—this time on a tape recorder—by one of the characters, and, as in part 1 of the series, *Jeremy's Version*, the family matrix is the psychological focus in the novel. The story involves Mr. Skegg, the magnate (the "solitary maggot"); Lady Bythewaite; and their three illegitimate sons: Clarence, who is legally "acknowledged" by the father; Owen, who is "acknowledged" by the mother; and Aiken, who is not "acknowledged" by either parent until later in the book.

The novel takes place in a dying community called Prince's Crossing. Owen, the youngest son, hero-worships his brother Clarence, who goes to New York to become a famous silent-film star. After Clarence leaves, Owen turns to the other older brother, Aiken, whom he also worships. The two become inseparable. Aiken, who himself has no acknowledged father or mother, serves as a father figure to Owen, helping him "mature" by giving him his first shave and taking him to visit a prostitute. After visiting the whore, Owen loses his sight. Aiken, who has finally been acknowledged by Lady Bythewaite as her long-lost son, buys the Acres, the showplace of the community. When Clarence returns and refuses to accept Aiken as his brother, Aiken, whose pride is hurt, burns down the house and marries the prostitute. This marriage is a failure, and Aiken decides to leave.

Although Aiken has been estranged from Owen, he loves him obsessively. When Aiken goes to say good-bye to Owen and their mother, Owen shoots him. Lady Bythewaite, one of Purdy's typical strong-willed, castrating women, then shoots Owen. In another of Purdy's characteristically grotesque scenes,

Owen's eyeballs fall out and Aiken swallows them. While Aiken remains unconscious in the hospital, Clarence returns and wants to be acknowledged as Aiken's brother. When the unconscious Aiken cannot comply, Clarence slits his own throat. Eventually, Aiken comes to live with his mother. Mr. Skegg acknowledges him as his son and takes care of him in his illness. The story concludes with the death of Aiken, who, in a dreamlike sequence, tries to ride off on a horse with the dead Owen.

IN A SHALLOW GRAVE

The protagonist of Purdy's next novel, *In a Shallow Grave*, is Garnet Montrose, a war hero who has been so badly wounded that he is turned almost inside-out and is the color of mulberry juice. Garnet seeks "applicants" to take messages from him to the Widow Rance, whom he wishes to court, but the applicants are so appalled by Garnet's appearance that they cannot accept the job. Finally, Quintus, a black adolescent, shows up by accident at Garnet's house and accepts the position. Quintus's responsibilities are to read to Garnet and to rub his feet. Later, one Daventry shows up. Even though he is not an applicant, he takes the position of messenger to the Widow Rance. Within this narrative structure, Purdy pursues many of his recurring themes.

One of the primary scenes involves a communion among Garnet, Quintus, and Daventry. Garnet is about to have his property taken away, but Daventry says that he will save Garnet's land and property if Garnet will commune with him. Daventry takes his knife, slits open his chest, and the three of them drink his blood. Later, they discover that Garnet's property has been saved by the Veteran's Administration, who heard of his plight and paid the mortgage. The wounding and shedding of blood, along with the religious connotations of the scene, seem to indicate that language is inadequate for portraying emotions, that the only way to "love" another person is to shed blood for him.

Again, homosexual love appears in the novel, for Daventry and Garnet fall in love. They consummate their love in the dance hall where Garnet goes to dance by himself and relive the moments in the past when he was "normal." With Garnet's permission,

Daventry marries the Widow Rance, but on his wedding night, he is swept up by a strong wind, smashed against a tree, and killed.

NARROW ROOMS

Narrow Rooms is a story about the love-hate relationship between Roy Sturtevant (the renderer) and Sidney De Lakes. Roy Sturtevant had been in love with Sidney since the eighth grade, until Sidney slapped him publicly and humiliated him; from that time, Roy has been planning his revenge. The story opens after Sidney has returned from prison, where he served time for killing Brian McFee. He finds a job as keeper of Gareth Vaisey, who has been injured in a fall from a horse. Sidney and Gareth fall in love and have an affair, but Roy Sturtevant still exercises a strange power over them. In the central scene in the novel, after Roy and Sidney have a sexual encounter, Roy commands Sidney to crucify him on the barn door and then bring the body of Brian McFee to view the crucifixion. Roy, still alive, is taken down from the barn door and carried into the house. Sidney and Roy then pledge their love for each other, and Gareth, jealous, shoots them both. Subsequently, Gareth also dies. Though the subject matter of *Narrow Rooms* is largely sensational, the novel continues Purdy's exploration of the destructive nature of obsessive love.

MOURNERS BELOW

In *Mourners Below*, Purdy returns to the theme of hero-worship. Seventeen-year-old Duane Bledsoe is mourning the death of his two half-brothers, Justin and Douglas, who have been killed in the war. Eugene Bledsoe, the father, with whom Duane lives, is aloof and psychologically distant. The central episode in the novel occurs when Duane goes to a fancy-dress ball at the mansion of Estelle Dumont (who had been Justin's lover), and Estelle seduces him. After the ball, another of Purdy's rape scenes occurs when Duane is homosexually assaulted by two men along the roadside. During the brief affair between Duane and Estelle, Estelle conceives a child, also named Justin. At the end of the story, Duane is given the child to rear, and Eugene states that it is Duane's destiny to rear a son.

Although this novel incorporates many of Purdy's familiar conceptions, it appears to be much more optimistic about the human condition than his previous novels. For example, Eugene and Duane do become reconciled in many ways, and there are many indications that Duane will make a good parent for the child. Furthermore, many of the grotesque and sadistic aspects of love are absent in this book. The men and the women in the story are not the tyrannical types found in previous works; they exhibit much more normal motivation. *Mourners Below* seems to indicate a new phase in Purdy's development, for in this novel he emphasizes the hopeful qualities of love and human existence.

ON GLORY'S COURSE

The search for a lost son plays a crucial role in *On Glory's Course*. Adele Bevington, the main character in the novel, has had an illegitimate son taken away from her and placed for adoption. The rest of the novel revolves around her quest for her lost son. One of the wounded veterans living in Fonthill, the location of the novel, believes that he knows the identity of Adele's son—he is a soldier who has been gravely wounded in the war and is now residing at the Soldiers' Home, barely alive and unable to respond to any communication. Adele attempts to prove that this soldier, Moorbrook, is her son, but by the end of the novel, neither Adele nor the reader is certain about Moorbrook's identity. Once again, Purdy's recurring motif of the search for a father figure is woven into the text of the novel.

IN THE HOLLOW OF HIS HAND

In the Hollow of His Hand relates the kidnapping of a boy, Chad Coultas, by Decatur, a full-blooded Ojibwa Indian. Decatur is actually the father of the boy and wishes to rear him as an Indian; however, Lew Coultas, the man who has brought up Chad, wishes to recapture him and take him "home." The mother of Chad, Eva Lewis, had not even realized that Decatur was the father until he returned home from the military and began taking Chad on rides after school. She then remembered that she had, indeed, had a one-day affair with Decatur years before the action in the novel begins. During the attempt to find Chad, the town of Yellow Brook is awakened to its small-town foibles and provincial attitudes, and once again Purdy reveals the darker side of small-town life and values. This novel is darkly satiric and deals with Purdy's attempts to create an almost mythological construct of his obsession with the search for an identity within the context of the family. Yet *In the Hollow of His Hand* is also an extremely humorous novel, delving into the souls of small-town America and American culture.

GARMENTS THE LIVING WEAR

Set in Manhattan, *Garments the Living Wear* opens with Jared Wakeman, an actor and organizer of a theater group facing a desperate situation. Not only has his benefactor, Peg Shawbridge, almost run out of money, his actors have been decimated by acquired immunodeficiency syndrome (AIDS), which Purdy's characters refer to simply as the Plague. Even Des Cantrell, whom Jared refers to as his soul mate, shows the first signs of the illness. The situation radically changes when Edward Hennings, an aged financial wizard and Peg's former lover, arrives with his young androgynous bride, Estrallita. Edward desires Jared, luring him with the dual attractions of money for his theatrical endeavors and the mysterious Estrallita.

Purdy imbues the novel with an aura of myth and mystery as Edward seemingly cures Des. This atmosphere is reinforced by the appearance of Jonas Hakluyt, an ex-convict turned evangelist with messianic overtones. The novel combines humor and psychological realism, myth and magic, as Purdy's characters struggle to survive in a world where both people and events are unpredictable and reality is frequently overshadowed by illusion.

OUT WITH THE STARS

Out with the Stars revolves around a group of socially intertwined figures. Abner Blossom, with the support of his talented protégé, Val Sturgis, has emerged from his retirement to compose an opera based on a mysterious libretto that was found in a "parlor" where young men indulge in orgies. The libretto is based on the life of Cyrus Vane, a photographer who specialized in nude studies of young African American men. Vane's wife, Madame Petrovna, is bitterly opposed to production of the opera and will go to any lengths to stop it. A secondary theme in the novel deals with corruption and the loss of in-

nocence of Sturgis and his roommate, Hugh, as they drift deeper into the exotic world of Vane and Blossom. Purdy vividly explores both racial and sexual prejudice in *Out with the Stars*.

GERTRUDE OF STONY ISLAND AVENUE

In *Gertrude of Stony Island Avenue*, Carrie Kinsella, an elderly woman who has lived a dull and uneventful existence, attempts to understand the life and death of her daughter, Gertrude, a famous and flamboyant artist. During this search, she encounters a series of eccentric characters who influenced and were influenced by Gertrude. Purdy explores the nature of love and relationships as Carrie struggles to accept the fact that she and Gertrude failed to love one another. Like most of Purdy's novels, *Gertrude of Stony Island Avenue* presents a shadowy world full of pretense and ambiguity. Purdy's language and symbolism mirror this world which is often distorted, hiding more than it reveals.

Earl Paulus Murphy,
updated by Mary E. Mahony

OTHER MAJOR WORKS

SHORT FICTION: *Don't Call Me by My Right Name and Other Stories*, 1956; *63: Dream Palace*, 1956; *Color of Darkness: Eleven Stories and a Novella*, 1957; *The Candles of Your Eyes*, 1985; *The Candles of Your Eyes and Thirteen Other Stories*, 1987; *63, Dream Palace: Selected Stories, 1956-1987*, 1991.

PLAYS: *Mr. Cough Syrup and the Phantom Sex*, pb. 1960; *Wedding Finger*, pb. 1974; *Two Plays, pb. 1979* (includes *A Day After the Fair* and *True*); *Proud Flesh: Four Short Plays*, pb. 1980; *Scrap of Paper, and the Berry-Picker*, pb. 1981.

POETRY: *The Running Sun*, 1971; *Sunshine Is an Only Child*, 1973; *She Came out of the Mists of Morning*, 1975; *Lessons and Complaints*, 1978; *The Brooklyn Branding Parlors*, 1986.

MISCELLANEOUS: *Children Is All*, 1961 (10 stories and 2 plays); *An Oyster Is a Wealthy Beast*, 1967 (story and poems); *My Evening: A Story and Nine Poems*, 1968; *On the Rebound: A Story and Nine Poems*, 1970; *A Day After the Fair: A Collection of Plays and Stories*, 1977.

BIBLIOGRAPHY

Adams, Stephen D. *James Purdy*. New York: Barnes & Noble, 1976. Provides detailed interpretations of Purdy's early work, analyzing character, theme, style, and his distinctive use of symbol, placing him in the tradition of Herman Melville and Nathaniel Hawthorne.

Baldanza, Frank. "James Purdy on the Corruption of Innocents." *Contemporary Literature* 15 (Summer, 1974): 315-330. The recurring theme of "corruption" of an innocent, found throughout Purdy's works, receives critical discussion. The idea that the innocent enters into a corrupt and perhaps meaningless world is examined. A good introduction to the recurring motif of "innocence-corruption" found in Purdy.

Chudpack, Henry. *James Purdy*. Boston: Twayne, 1975. A good overview of Purdy's early works. Each of the early novels and works of short fiction is discussed in relationship to characters, plots, and themes. Contains a select bibliography and some additional notes.

Ladd, Jay L., comp. *James Purdy: A Bibliography*. Edited by Nels P. Highberg. Columbus: Ohio State University Libraries, 1999. A helpful tool for the student of Purdy. Includes an index.

Lane, Christopher. "Out with James Purdy: An Interview." *Critique* 40 (Fall, 1998): 71-89. Evaluates reasons for critical hostility to Purdy's writings. Presents Purdy's views on racial and sexual stereotyping, violence in art, and the effect of political correctness. Analyzes theme and subject, presenting real-life counterparts to characters in several novels.

Tanner, Tony. "Frames Without Pictures." In *City of Words: American Fiction, 1950-1970*. New York: Harper & Row, 1971. An excellent discussion of Purdy's early novels. The themes and concerns of these novels are examined and placed within the framework of postmodern American fiction. In particular, the paradoxical treatment of identity and meaning found in these novels is evaluated and analyzed.

Turnbaugh, Douglas Blair. "James Purdy: Playwright." *PAJ* 20 (May, 1998): 73-75. Discusses Purdy's international acclaim and publication history. Praises his uses of dialogue and vernacular in the novels. Critical evaluation of dramatizations of Purdy's novels, specifically focusing on the Public Broadcasting Service (PBS) distortion of *In a Shallow Grave*.

ALEXANDER PUSHKIN

Born: Moscow, Russia; June 6, 1799
Died: St. Petersburg, Russia; February 10, 1837

PRINCIPAL LONG FICTION

Arap Petra velikogo, 1828-1841 (*Peter the Great's Negro*, 1896)
Kirdzhali, 1834 (English translation, 1896)
Kapitanskaya dochka, 1836 (*The Captain's Daughter*, 1846)
Dubrovsky, 1841 (English translation, 1892)
Yegipetskiye nochi, 1841 (*Egyptian Nights*, 1896)
Istoriya sela Goryukhina, 1857 (*History of the Village of Goryukhino*, 1966)

OTHER LITERARY FORMS

Although Alexander Pushkin wrote in almost every genre a nineteenth century author could attempt, he was primarily a poet. In a literary career spanning twenty-four years, he published a rich and varied collection of verse. He wrote two important historical poems, three major comic poems, a half dozen verse narratives, four *skazki* (fairy tales in verse), and numerous lyric poems.

Pushkin's canon contains several dramatic works: *Boris Godunov* (1831; English translation, 1918) is a long play, written in the manner of William Shakespeare's historical plays, about a crucial period in Russian civilization, "The Time of Troubles." Four short plays make up Pushkin's "Little Tragedies": *Pir vo vryemya chumy* (1833; *The Feast in Time of the Plague*, 1925), *Motsart i Salyeri* (1832; *Mozart and Salieri*, 1920), *Skupoy rytsar* (1852; *The Covetous Knight*, 1925), and *Kamyenny gost* (1839; *The Stone*

Guest, 1936); each of these plays concentrates on a crucial moment in an individual's life. Though cast as drama, all five works are more lyric than theatrical; they are more intent on presenting character than on keeping the stage busy.

In addition to his long fiction, Pushkin wrote several short stories. The most famous and skillful of these works is *Pikovaya dama* (1834; *The Queen of Spades*, 1858), a story of greed, murder, and revenge set among the gaming tables of the aristocracy. Nearly as good are five stories collected as *Povesti Belkina* (1831; *Russian Romance*, 1875; better known as *The Tales of Belkin*, 1947): They depict, both comically and seriously, the life of the rural gentry and townspeople. Pushkin's research for his novel *The Captain's Daughter* provided him with materials for the nonfictional work *Istoriya Pugacheva* (1834; *The Pugachev Rebellion*, 1966).

Besides his published works, Pushkin wrote hundreds of letters to personal friends and fellow officials. The almost seven hundred surviving letters vividly chronicle both Pushkin's personal life and his literary development.

No complete, uniform, and authoritative English translation of Pushkin's work exists. Several volumes offer a selection of his verse, though translators agree that rendering Pushkin's lyricism is well nigh impossible. Translations that capture somewhat more of the original are readily available for Pushkin's plays and stories. *Alexander Pushkin: Complete Prose Fiction* (1983), translated and annotated by Paul Debreczeny, is a valuable edition for English-speaking readers. Pushkin's letters have been collected into a well-annotated edition by J. Thomas Shaw: *The Letters of Alexander Pushkin* (1963). The handiest compendium of Pushkin in all of his genres is still the Modern Library volume, *The Poems, Prose, and Plays of Pushkin*, edited by Avram Yarmolinsky and first published in 1936.

ACHIEVEMENTS

Pushkin is Russia's poet as Homer is Greece's, Dante is Italy's, and John Milton is England's. The nation mourned when he died,

and Nikolai Gogol, a writer of the next generation, called him a unique manifestation of the Russian spirit. Four decades later, Fyodor Dostoevski proclaimed Pushkin a prophetic phenomenon whose characters embodied the people Russians would become in the late 1800's. After the 1917 Revolution, Soviet scholars produced an extraordinary amount of research and criticism on Pushkin. Modern Russian readers still turn to Pushkin's poetry for a distillation of their hopes or fears and for its lyricism. Virtually every work is regarded as a classic by his admirers, and for once, the idolaters are mostly correct.

Unlike Russian writers of the previous century who imitated Western classicism and produced mostly pale reflections, Pushkin used European literary models to discover—or even to create—a literary Russia. When he began to write in the 1810's, Russian literature was at a turning point. For the previous sixty years, it had imitated the forms and themes of French classicism and English sentimentalism. A new sensibility was then sweeping Europe, the Romanticism of Johann Wolfgang von Goethe, George

(Library of Congress)

Gordon, Lord Byron, André-Marie Chénier, and Sir Walter Scott. Pushkin responded with amazing alacrity. Reading Pushkin's letters, one is struck by how aware he was of not only the literary currents of his own country but also those of the Continent.

Still, Pushkin brought into his country's literature places, characters, and themes unmistakably Russian. His reading of Byron inspired him to works as diverse as *Kavkazskiy plennik* (1822; *The Prisoner of the Caucasus*, 1895), which discovered primitive southern Russia as a backdrop, and *Evgeny Onegin* (1825-1832, 1833; *Eugene Onegin*, 1881), which delineated the upper-class soul in its sicknesses. His reading of Shakespeare and Scott led him to the presentation of Russian historical themes on a small scale of ordinary lives as well as on a grand scale of royal lives.

Pushkin's lyric verse, begun under the tutelage of Byron and Chénier, gradually grew freer as he experimented with the rhythms and rhymes of the Russian language as a tool for the recording of what it was like to live, love, and suffer as one who came of age in the 1820's. He gave folktales, proverbs, and native speech shelf space in literature's emporium. Whatever the genre or theme of the work, Pushkin's crowning achievement was his style. Though a contemporary of the great European Romantics, Pushkin owed more to their lean classical style than to their richness. His thoughts were always compressed, the scene or emotion always sketched with a few quick, apt words, the story told with pointed economy. The non-Russian reader, alas, misses what the average Russian reader loves him for most: the interplay of sensuous sound and simple sense.

One of Pushkin's classical features is his authorial objectivity. Unlike other Romantics, whose works are often autobiographical, Pushkin was not a confessional writer. Neither was he the distanced, detached, and "official" observer that the neoclassical poet was. His works are, more specifically, objective renderings—parables almost—of the emotional, psychological, and social life of the sensitive and intelligent contemporary Russian.

In this regard, Pushkin's long narratives (one work in verse and two in prose) may be most valuable to the non-Russian reader. *Eugene Onegin, Dubrovsky,*

and *The Captain's Daughter* form a useful introduction to the second half of Pushkin's life and career. They record in straightforward narratives the writer's hopes and fears for his society, both about the personal integrity of individuals and about society's path toward freedom and justice. In Pushkin's Russia, the burning question for individuals was the priorities of virtue (did individual love and honor outweigh obedience and social conformity?) and the burning question for the body politic was social progress (could it be achieved on the back of serfdom and autocracy?). Pushkin felt as if the answers were sometimes yes, sometimes no. In the latter moments, he seemed unsure whether to react to that realization with tears, laughter, or anger.

BIOGRAPHY

Alexander Sergeyevich Pushkin was born into a Moscow family that boasted a six-hundred-year lineage of nobility. Each parent contributed something to his makeup. From his mother, descended from an Abyssinian princeling who had served Peter the Great, Pushkin received his fierce, dark looks and a passionate nature. From his well-educated father, who wrote poetry, Pushkin inherited a love of literature and gained early access to a family library well stocked with European classics.

In 1811, Pushkin was one of thirty boys chosen for the first class of the *lycée* at Tsarskoe Selo, a new school designed to train administrators for Czar Alexander's government. Flourishing in a liberal arts curriculum, Pushkin rapidly became the poet among his peers and, by 1814, published his first poem. His work soon became known to established poets and to the literary societies that looked to Europe for literary models to make Russian writing as good as any in the world. Having seen their nation defeat Napoleon Bonaparte in 1815, young Russians were eager to match France culturally and to improve their country by importing European political ideals that would eliminate what liberal-thinking Russians thought were the twin cancers of their society: serfdom and autocracy.

Appointed to undemanding work in the Ministry of Foreign Affairs after graduation in 1817, Pushkin combined his literary and political fervors by writing poems like the ode "Vol'most': Oda" ("Ode to Freedom") with revolutionary themes. For three years, he pursued liberal ideals—and actresses of liberal virtue—until his poems attracted the attention of Saint Petersburg's military governor, who decided that the young firebrand needed the cooling discipline of service in remoter regions.

In 1820, Pushkin was officially transferred and unofficially exiled to southern Russia and spent time in the Crimea and the Caucasus before settling in Kishinev. Here Pushkin met young army officers who dreamed of political change and primitive tribesmen who lived fiercely and independently. These experiences, combined with his reading of the English Romantic poet Byron, helped Pushkin create several Romantic verse narratives about men who lived on the frontier of civilization and lived passionately according to their own wills. Pushkin would repeat throughout his career the pattern established here: Forced by circumstances into isolation, he would combine his own passionate apprehension of European literary fashions with distinctive Russian settings, characters, and themes.

In 1823, Pushkin secured a transfer to the Black Sea port of Odessa, but his reluctance to perform official duties and a letter expressing his atheist sentiments again earned for him official disapproval. He was dismissed from the service and sent to the family estate at Mikhailovskoe (three hundred safe miles from the capital), where his father, a local abbot, and the secret police could keep his political and religious views under surveillance. Once again cut off from society, Pushkin turned to literature, writing more verse and composing a play, *Boris Godunov*, modeled on Shakespeare's histories.

The exile at Mikhailovskoe kept Pushkin safe while a group of army officers—a few of them his friends, most of them readers of his revolutionary verse—led the unsuccessful Decembrist Revolt to block the accession of Nicholas I, presumed unsympathetic to Western reforms. At liberty, Pushkin's temperament might have led him to join the coup and thus to share the officers' fate of death or Siberian exile. By May of 1826, Pushkin, eager to leave exile

and hoping that Nicholas might prove progressive, petitioned for and received pardon. There was only one stipulation: Nicholas himself would censor Pushkin's writing.

For four years, Pushkin lived and worked in Saint Petersburg but accomplished little, writing only one poem and continuing *Eugene Onegin*, his magnum opus begun in 1823. In 1830, he determined to wed and successfully wooed the beautiful and younger Natalia Goncharov. The marriage seemed to settle Pushkin's adherence to Nicholas's regime: His wife's beauty made the couple in demand at palace balls; Pushkin reentered government service as a historiographer. Later, Nicholas appointed Pushkin to a court post, but the poet's fiercely independent and proud spirit did not allow easy mingling with aristocrats whose main political virtue was subservience.

In 1830, Pushkin began a period of intense creativity. Isolated for three autumn months at Boldino (far from Moscow and Saint Petersburg), Pushkin completed *Eugene Onegin*, wrote several short stories and plays, and composed verse. Returning to Saint Petersburg, he used the position of historiographer to research the peasant rebellion led by Yemelyan Pugachov in the 1770's, an uprising so destructive and traumatic that it halted the enlightened ideals of Catherine the Great and convinced subsequent czars that only iron-fisted rule prevented revolution from below. Another retreat to Boldino in the autumn of 1833 produced several works, including a history of the rebellion and the great poem *Medniy vsadnik* (1837; *The Bronze Horseman*, 1899). In 1836, Pushkin concluded six years of concentrated writing with a novel and a literary journal.

His uneasy relationship with Nicholas's court reached a critical point in late 1836 when an anonymous wit awarded Pushkin a diploma as a member in good standing of "The Order of Cuckolds," a reference to the flirtatious attentions by the young French officer Georges d'Anthès to Natalia. After two months of anger and hesitation, Pushkin issued the inevitable challenge to a duel that took place on January 29, 1837. Pushkin was shot first, was critically wounded, and died a week later.

ANALYSIS

Alexander Pushkin's three major works, *Eugene Onegin, Dubrovsky,* and *The Captain's Daughter,* reflect many dimensions of his literary achievement. They show his ability to adapt Western genres to a Russian context; they demonstrate his stylistic mastery that is simultaneously economical and rich. Finally, in their emotional variety, they chart Pushkin's attempts to reconcile himself to czarist society and politics.

Each of these three works owes a literary debt. *Eugene Onegin,* a novel in verse, takes its inspiration from Byron's *Childe Harold's Pilgrimage* (1812-1818) and *Don Juan* (1819-1824) but tempers their exuberance with characterization and scene setting from the eighteenth century novel of manners. *Dubrovsky* is kin to the robber tales of German Romanticism, which paint a heroic picture of an outlaw who is really more a self-willed outcast in opposition to social tyranny than an ordinary brigand. *The Captain's Daughter* is a historical novel in the manner of Sir Walter Scott, using the life of an ordinary participant to witness and to interpret some crucial national event. Pushkin's debt to foreign models is not surprising, because his letters show that he read practically everything, not only what was being produced in Russian but also what was being written in French, German, and English.

Like the greatest writers, Pushkin is a master of styles rather than a master of style. His long fictions are as varied as his whole corpus with its poems, plays, and folktales. *Eugene Onegin* is a complexly organized poem: There are eight chapters, each composed of at least 40 fourteen-line stanzas (389 stanzas all told), and each stanza follows a rigorous and formal rhyme scheme that disciplines a wealth of characterization, authorial commentary, and social observation into a coherent narrative. *Dubrovsky* is a quick-paced, dark-spirited, third-person narrative built around a stark contrast of justice and tyranny. *The Captain's Daughter* is a more leisured, romantic, first-person story in which youth and honor triumph over various obstacles.

The most interesting thing about Pushkin's three major long fictional works is the thematic course they chart. They all seek to depict life as led by members of the gentry, that social class which lives with one foot in the urban corridors of power and one in the rural paths of peasant-filled estates. No two of these works offer exactly the same perspective. *Eugene Onegin,* almost ten years in the writing during a crucial period of Pushkin's life, is the most complex and ambiguous work. No one emotion sums it up; by turns it is comic, satiric, pathetic, and tragic. *Dubrovsky* is an angry book, ruthless in its depiction of the petty tyrannies that infect the gentry with devastating effects. *The Captain's Daughter* shows murderous rebellion and government blindness but offers some small hope for the individual to steer between these twin disasters. Taking these works in order, the reader can trace Pushkin's diagnosis of the sickness of Russian society and his prescription for its remedy.

EUGENE ONEGIN

Eugene Onegin is a unique work. It is a product of the Romantic imagination that delighted in experimenting with literary conventions; it is a novel in verse, an attempt to mix the lyric insight of poetry with narrative's opportunity for social observation. Most other nineteenth century novels in verse failed, but Pushkin succeeded in writing both a powerful poem and an important work of fiction. To the Russian reader, sensitive to the nuances of tone and the play of imagery, *Eugene Onegin* is primarily a narrative poem. To the non-Russian reader who must rely upon translation, *Eugene Onegin* is more accessible as a lyric novel. Once past the first chapter (the least novel-like), in which Pushkin sketches the subtle strains of Negin's soul as molded by society, the reader of the translation begins an intriguing love story. Novel-like, this love story traces the evolution of a romance from a country estate to a city drawing room: It depicts both the private reveries of the lovers and their passionate, hurtful encounters, and evaluates their relationship as they understand it and as it mirrors the society at large.

Eugene Onegin is a fashionable young man of contemporary Saint Petersburg. His wealth and social status allow him to play the game he knows best: the seduction of beautiful women amid the endless round of teas, tête-à-têtes, and palace balls. An unbroken string of romantic conquests, however, makes him bored with life in general. At his uncle's death, Eugene inherits a country estate and retires to it. Here, he meets Vladimir Lensky, an eighteen-year-old who has all of Onegin's passionate nature but who has not yet had the chance to indulge it. All of Lensky's attention is directed toward Olga Larin, whom he loves romantically and for whom he writes poems. Through Lensky, Onegin meets Olga's sister Tatyana, an introspective and withdrawn girl who is convinced at first sight that Onegin is her destined lover. After several days of self-inflicted torment, knowing love only through novels, Tatyana writes Onegin a letter proclaiming her devotion. Two days later, he responds by lecturing her about the impossibility of anyone impressing his heart. Tatyana's spirit is crushed, but her love lives on.

Afterward, at Tatyana's name-day party, Onegin flirts outrageously with Olga, who unthinkingly enjoys his attentions. Vladimir does not enjoy them, suspecting his friend of trying to steal Olga's affection. He challenges Onegin to a duel that neither especially wants but that both know society demands when there is a woman in dispute. Onegin kills Vladimir and quickly departs on a foreign tour; Olga remains grief-stricken until another suitor replaces Vladimir; Tatyana haunts the house Onegin recently vacated, searching for a clue to his character, until her mother takes her to Moscow for the winter social season and a prospective husband.

When the story continues two years later, Tatyana is the wife of an army general. Onegin, returning to the social round, meets her and immediately falls in love. Making himself an intimate of the general's circle, Onegin dotes on Tatyana: helping with her cloak, opening doors for her, making constant small talk. Thoroughly infatuated but unsure of her feelings, Onegin writes her several letters professing his love. She grants him an interview at which she confesses that, although she still loves him, she rejects his love because she now has a wife's duty. She did not marry for love, she only married because the general was the least unattractive of bad choices, but she is determined to remain faithful to her role. The novel ends as the husband enters to reclaim Tatyana from a thunderstruck Onegin.

The story is told through a series of parallels and contrasts. The quick-paced, dissolute, and spiritually enervating life at Saint Petersburg contrasts with the tedious, controlled, and unimaginative life of the country. Tatyana's letter to Onegin and his reply (chapters 3 and 4) are ironically reversed in his letters to her and the subsequent interview (chapter 8). Tatyana's notions of sentimental love derive from her reading of eighteenth century novelists in the same degree that Onegin's spiritual lethargy is an imitation of nineteenth century Romantic angst. Lensky and Olga are more fulsome lovers than Tatyana and Onegin, yet their affection dies more quickly. Eugene dispatches the troublesome jealousy of Lensky with as little conscience as he dispatches the jejune affection of Tatyana.

Complicating the story is the presence of an obtrusive narrator. He has known Onegin, in fact, has shared many of his attitudes. Like Onegin, he has missed the possibility for real passion by playing at too many imitations of it. Like Onegin, the narrator has a sharp eye for the absurdities of those people who live the social pattern without sensing its limitations.

Eugene Onegin is the novel's protagonist, but he is not a hero. If anything, he is an early version of the traditional Russian antihero, the "superfluous man." A superfluous man is one who possesses the creature comforts his society can offer but who does not have any reason to possess them. The ultimate superfluous man is Ivan Goncharov's Oblomov, who thinks long and hard at trying to discover a reason that would get him up from the couch. Pushkin's Onegin is less extreme, but the times and his temperament have combined to drain him of real sensation and passion. Only when Tatyana is out of reach (is it because she is out of reach?) does Onegin think to discover some motivation for participating actively in life, once again taking charge of his existence and seeking to connect with another human soul. Too often Onegin is content to follow the code of his social class: live as lord of the estate but take more notice of neighbors than of management; maintain honor over a trifle even at the expense of a friend's life; if one's emotions run too high or too seriously, become a poet as an outlet.

Tatyana is better than Onegin: She lives an imaginative life that is at least honest, although she succumbs in the end to the same social code that grips Onegin. Though superstitious about omens that signal a true love, she is at least anxious to know something about Onegin. Though her visits to his unoccupied house originate in simplistic devotion, they do lead to insights about his character. Though she partakes of Saint Petersburg's fashionable whirl, she keeps aloof enough to remember her domestic commitment. On the outside, Tatyana is a lovely hoyden while Onegin is a work of fashion's art, but on the inside Tatyana draws two breaths and two heartbeats to every one of Eugene's.

The ending of the novel, in which Tatyana leaves the interview on her husband's arm while Onegin stands perplexed, is not a resolution. Though encouraged by friends to complete the story, Pushkin did not. Perhaps the tale ends appropriately as it stands, with the major characters etched in postures that represent their moral choices. Tatyana chooses sacrifice over happiness, and Eugene is doomed to pursue the unpursuable woman. The dramatic ending offers readers none of the traditional comforts by which characters are parceled out some share of contentment.

Dubrovsky

Dubrovsky is, like *Eugene Onegin*, an unfinished work. Unlike *Eugene Onegin*, it depicts oppression, violence, and death with only a few mitigating moments in which young love and honorable conduct win a momentary triumph. The story recounts the conversion of a young man, Vladimir Dubrovsky, from landowner to outlaw. Like Onegin, Dubrovsky is a member of the generation born about the turn of the century, but his family's relative poverty leaves little of the leisure allowed a young gallant of Saint Petersburg. The novel's theme is political rather than social: the tyranny of the landowning class.

The elderly Andrey Dubrovsky owns a few serfs and the village of Kistenyovka; he is a mild and appreciative master. The neighboring landowner Kirila Troyekurov owns a much larger estate and is known to tyrannize his serfs. Though Dubrovsky and Troyekurov served together in the army and had become friends, two minor disputes over hunting dogs and hunting rights blossom into a full-scale animosity. Unaccustomed to having his will challenged in anything, Troyekurov plots to take over Dubrovsky's estate by filing a highly technical lawsuit under the guidance of a cunning lawyer. When Troyekurov's claim prevails, Dubrovsky goes mad at this outrage against justice. Invalided at home, Dubrovsky summons his son Vladimir from army service back to the estate. Vladimir sets to work to regain the estate legally, but before he can accomplish it, Troyekurov drives the elder Dubrovsky into a fatal seizure by riding insolently into the courtyard of the mansion he will soon occupy. On the day of the funeral, Troyekurov sends officers to seize control of the estate and the village before young Vladimir can claim his inheritance.

Galled by this triumph of tyranny, young Vladimir Dubrovsky and his peasants lock the officials in the occupied mansion and set the building afire. Disappearing into the forest, Vladimir's band begins to terrorize the neighborhood: robbing travelers, seizing the mail, torching manor houses. The only estate to escape attack belongs, oddly enough, to Kirila Troyekurov.

Meanwhile, Troyekurov has hired a French tutor, Deforges, for his daughter Masha. He decides to have fun with the handsome young foreigner by locking him in a room with a hungry bear. Much to the sadistic landlord's surprise, the tutor pulls a gun from his pocket and shoots the bear. Deforges proves as charming as he does forearmed, and soon Masha is in love with him.

On a festival day, all the neighboring gentry gather for a party at Troyekurov's estate. One of them arrives late: Anton Pafnutyich, the lawyer who directed the suit against Vladimir and who was recently robbed by him. His story sets the guests to comparing tales about the notorious robber who steals with pomp and grace from only the richest of the local ruling class. Pafnutyich refuses to leave the safety of the estate and stays for the night in Deforges's room, only to discover that the tutor is actually Vladimir in disguise.

His identity now dangerously compromised, Vladimir plans to leave the estate after confessing his love to Masha, revealing his identity, and securing her promise that she will call for him if she ever needs assistance.

The promise seems superfluous until the next summer, when Troyekurov makes plans to marry Masha to his neighbor, Prince Vereysky. Twice Masha's age and driven to ennui and dissipation by unrestricted indulgence, Vereysky is a repugnant suitor in Masha's eyes, but her father insists on the marriage. Masha secures Vladimir's assistance in case she cannot talk her father out of his determination. She even writes a letter to Vereysky frankly avowing her repugnance, but it simply whets both his appetite and her father's to exert their authority. Forced to attend the wedding ceremony, Masha expects any minute to be rescued by Vladimir Dubrovsky, but he fails to appear before the priest pronounces the vows over bride and groom. Not until Vereysky's carriage is homeward bound does Dubrovsky appear; he seizes the Prince and pronounces Masha free, but she insists that like it or not, she is now a wife. Though wounded in the shoulder by a bullet and to the heart by her reply, Dubrovsky withdraws without hurting anyone or stealing a thing. In revenge, the authorities send soldiers to track Dubrovsky down. As they besiege his forest fortress, Dubrovsky escapes into the woods. The robberies and attacks on the local gentry cease, and Dubrovsky is rumored to have gone abroad.

Dubrovsky has all the plot conventions of late eighteenth, early nineteenth century robber fiction. Its hero is young, dashing, handsome, and no ordinary criminal. There is a maiden in distress who is, of course, his beloved. Her distress arises from the tyranny of a cruel parent and a lustful suitor. There is adventure, violence, and death in dark and unexpected places. Characters are little more than cardboard figures, for the emphasis is on a fast moving plot filled with dramatic confrontations of innocence and guile, good and evil.

What is sensational about *Dubrovsky* is its theme. Pushkin creates a rebellious hero who wins the reader's sympathy; Vladimir Dubrovsky is after all, like Robin Hood, on the side of justice and true love. In the Russia of Nicholas I, where even verbal dissent quickly caught official notice, such an ennobling of a man in opposition to the political system was an act of heresy. Yet in painting such a stark contrast between the tyranny of Troyekurov and the nobility of Dubrovsky, Pushkin seems to have written the story into a corner from which there is no escape. Commonly regarded as unfinished, *Dubrovsky* may have been abandoned where it stood because the author could think of no satisfactory conclusion. The heroine is cruelly married, the system has asserted an overwhelming power in defense of the local tyrant, and the pillaging by Dubrovsky's band is but an annoying hangnail on the strong fist of autocracy. Dubrovsky himself, as the manuscript ends, is in a hopeless situation. Like Eugene Onegin at the end of his novel, Vladimir Dubrovsky has lost his beloved to an older military man and has no means to extract any satisfying revenge to compensate for that loss. Pushkin wisely took leave of Onegin at that incomprehensible moment that Tatyana walks away with her husband. Similarly, Pushkin seems instinctively to have left Dubrovsky at that point because he has literally no future worth recounting; he is beaten. *Dubrovsky* may not be unfinished as much as it is unfinishable.

THE CAPTAIN'S DAUGHTER

Pushkin's final fictional work, *The Captain's Daughter*, offers thematic resolutions that *Dubrovsky* could not achieve. *The Captain's Daughter* is another tale of a young man of a gentry family who must oppose the system, but the hero of this novel is able to both fight for personal justice and remain (although with difficulty) in harmony with the political and social system. Perhaps by setting his story sixty years in the past, Pushkin was better able to see how an individual could control his own life and yet remain a part of society. The person who maintains his honor may in fact contribute to the betterment of the whole society.

The Captain's Daughter is set in the days of a peasant uprising, the Pugachov rebellion, which broke out in eastern Russia in the mid-1770's and was subdued in a few years after great difficulty by the armies of Catherine the Great. This uprising tempered Catherine's enthusiasm for bringing Western ways and ideas to Russia by showing precisely how fragile was the monarch's grip on the sprawling Russian landscape. Afterward, the Pugachov rebellion symbolized the autocracy's nightmare about the dangers that seethed under the surface of Russian civilization, that demanded constant vigilance; it was perhaps the one thing that made the ruling class reluctant to follow Europe's lead toward parliamentarian and constitutional government. In Nicholas I's Russia, where memories of the Decembrist coup were always fresh, to write about the Pugachov rebellion was practically to write about contemporary politics.

The Captain's Daughter tells how Peter Grinyov enters military service. Instead of sending his son Peter to elegant service with a Saint Petersburg battalion, the elder Grinyov, who is a believer in the old-fashioned values of sacrifice and hard work, has Peter assigned to a regiment on the eastern frontier of the empire at Orenburg. In disgust, Peter sets off with his faithful serf Savelyich and meets with two adventures along the way: An army veteran gets him drunk and cheats him at pool; a peasant saves Peter and Savelyich when they become lost in a snowstorm, and Peter repays the man with an expensive coat.

At Orenburg, Peter is assigned to a small outlying fort; he is only one of three regular army officers overseeing a ragtag battalion of local men. The second of the three is Shvabrin, a young dandy who has been exiled from Saint Petersburg for dueling. The third is the commandant of the fort, Captain Mironov, a somewhat comic figure who occasionally drills his troops in the distinctly unmilitary garb of nightshirt and nightcap. The only society for the three officers is provided by Mironov's wife, Vasilisa, and his maiden daughter Masha.

Rather quickly, Peter and Shvabrin become rivals for Masha and, in Saint Petersburg-like manner, engage in a duel. Peter is seriously wounded, but the injury turns out favorably because his convalescence requires the constant attention of Masha. This intimacy quickly leads the young people to confess their love for each other. Peter writes home for permission to wed Masha but receives a stinging and firm letter of refusal from his father.

As the unhappy lovers ponder their next move, the peasant rebellion led by Yemelyan Pugachov begins, and its main army approaches the mud-and-wood fort. The defenders are quickly overwhelmed. The captain is killed, Shvabrin goes over to the enemy, Masha goes into hiding, and Peter is spared execution because the rebel leader Pugachov is the same peasant to whom Peter generously gave his coat.

Returning to his own fortress at Orenberg, Peter eagerly counsels an attack in order to free Masha, but the commander is reluctant to stir from the city's safety. When Peter learns that Masha has been discovered and given to Shvabrin, he sets out alone to rescue her. Captured by rebel sentries, Peter is brought before Pugachov. Impressed by Peter's bravery and honesty, Pugachov decides to let the young man take Masha away. Escaping from the rebel camp, the lovers meet with a Russian detachment. Peter sends Masha to his family estate while he continues to serve against the rebels.

By the uprising's end, Masha has won the hearts of Peter's parents so that they no longer object to the marriage. Peter, however, is arrested on the charge of having helped the enemy. Unwilling to explain his movements back and forth between enemy camp and duty post in order to protect Masha, Peter risks court trial. Masha travels to Moscow to beg for mercy from the Empress herself. Telling her story to a woman she meets in the palace garden, Masha surprisingly discovers the next day that she had unknowingly spoken to Catherine herself. Catherine grants Peter pardon, and the lovers are free to wed.

In the character of Peter, Pushkin draws a composite of the young Russian of gentry class. Like others, Peter has to reconcile the conflicting claims of his European and Slavic heritages. It is not easy, because both heritages are mixtures of good and bad. The European inheritance has taught him to be an individual and to pursue Masha's love as a high good, but Europe is also the source of the dandyism and false honor represented by Shvabrin. The Slavic inheritance brings a high demand for loyalty to family and state, but its class structure hinges on oppression and cruelty. Peter tries to bring together the best of each heritage. He is a loyal subject of the Empress, but he is sensitive enough to the humanity of the rebel peasants to wish that reform would do away with those conditions that breed revolution.

Pushkin makes in political terms a daring parallel. Peter and Masha each undertake a solitary journey to save the other: Peter goes to Pugachov and Masha goes to Catherine. The monarchs behave remarkably alike: They detect the honesty and honor within the petitioner, which justifies granting mercy to an apparent enemy. For Pushkin to suggest that Pugachov was anything less than a madman or a devil's henchman or the epitome of betrayal was political heresy. While Peter never condones Pugachov's taking up arms, he is impressed by the leader's sincerity and—amid the expected horrors of the war—comparative humaneness.

Masha herself emerges an emblem of Russia. Like her country in the eighteenth century, poised between a Slavic past and a European future, the maidenly Masha is about to determine her future. Wisely, she rejects the superficial Western ways of Shvabrin in favor of the cultured but natural impulses of Peter. Endangered by rebellion, Masha's future hangs in the balance until she is rescued by the bravery, even fool-hardiness, of one who loves her. In turn, she repays love with love, risking public embarrassment to support the proposition that a man can talk to his country's enemy, even cooperate with him, and still be a patriot.

Peter's fate offers, then, a hope for autocratic, unchanging Russia. Horrified by the rapine and destruction, Peter is convinced that rebellion is no cure for what ails his country. Yet, he is living proof that ideals and manners can change for the better. Peter is less class-conscious than his father; he rejects the cronyism and immoral ways of the aristocratic soldier; he learns to see the humanity of the peasant beneath the rough exterior. Peter escapes the consequences of his new attitudes only because of Catherine's intervention. Still she does intervene, and she sees what a progressive monarch ought to see: Firm rule is not incompatible with individual integrity and public morality.

Set in the reign of one iron-fisted monarch, *The Captain's Daughter* speaks to another. It seeks to reassure Nicholas I that certain Western ideals (of love and personal honor) are not incompatible with traditional Russian virtues of obedience and loyalty. It suggests that a ruler can hasten national improvement by recognizing and cooperating with the heartfelt desire of others to improve the country. It reminds the monarch that statecraft is more than minding the jail so the prisoners do not escape. *The Captain's Daughter* is Pushkin's most positive fictional work because it suggests that although love will not overcome or solve all, love—personal and social—has a better chance than whatever is in second place to ameliorate the lot of the individual and consequently the nation.

Robert M. Otten

OTHER MAJOR WORKS

SHORT FICTION: *Povesti Belkina*, 1831 (*Russian Romance*, 1875; better known as *The Tales of Belkin*, 1947); *Pikovaya dama*, 1834 (*The Queen of Spades*, 1858).

PLAYS: *Boris Godunov*, wr. 1824-1825, pb. 1831 (English translation, 1918); *Skupoy rytsar*, wr. 1830, pr., pb. 1852 (*The Covetous Knight*, 1925); *Kamyenny gost*, wr. 1830, pb. 1839 (*The Stone Guest*, 1936); *Motsart i Salyeri*, pr., pb. 1832 (*Mozart and Salieri*, 1920); *Pir vo vryemya chumy*, pb. 1833 (*The Feast in Time of the Plague*, 1925); *Stseny iz rytsarskikh vryemem*, wr. 1835, pr., pb. 1937; *Rusalka*, pb. 1837 (*The Water Nymph*, 1924); *Little Tragedies*, pb. 1946 (includes *The Covetous Knight*, *The Stone Guest*, *Mozart and Salieri*, and *The Feast in Time of the Plague*).

POETRY: *Ruslan i Lyudmila*, 1820 (*Ruslan and Liudmila*, 1936); *Gavriiliada*, 1822 (*Gabriel: A Poem*, 1926); *Kavkazskiy plennik*, 1822 (*The Prisoner of the Caucasus*, 1895); *Bratya razboyniki*, 1824; *Evgeny Onegin*, 1825-1832, 1833 (*Eugene Onegin*, 1881); *Bakhchisaraiskiy fontan*, 1827 (*The Fountain of Bakhchisarai*, 1849); *Graf Nulin*, 1827 (*Count Nulin*, 1972); *Tsygany*, 1827 (*The Gypsies*, 1957); *Poltava*, 1829 (English translation, 1936); *Domik v Kolomne*, 1833 (*The Little House at Kolomna*, 1977); *Skazka o mertvoy tsarevne*, 1833 (*The Tale of the Dead Princess*, 1924); *Skazka o rybake ir rybke*, 1833 (*The Tale of the Fisherman and the Fish*, 1926); *Skazka o tsare Saltane*, 1833 (*The Tale of Tsar Saltan*, 1950); *Skazka o zolotom petushke*, 1834 (*The Tale of the Golden Cockerel*, 1918); *Medniy vsadnik*, 1837 (*The Bronze Horseman*, 1899); *Collected Narrative and Lyrical Poetry*, 1984; *Epigrams and Satirical Verse*, 1984.

NONFICTION: *Istoriya Pugacheva*, 1834 (*The Pugachev Rebellion*, 1966); *Puteshestviye v Arzrum*, 1836 (*A Journey to Arzrum*, 1974); *Dnevnik, 1833-1835*, 1923; *Pisma*, 1926-1935 (3 volumes); *The Letters of Alexander Pushkin*, 1963 (3 volumes); *Pisma poslednikh let 1834-1837*, 1969.

MISCELLANEOUS: *The Captain's Daughter and Other Tales*, 1933; *The Works of Alexander Pushkin*, 1936; *The Poems, Prose, and Plays of Pushkin*, 1936; *Polnoye sobraniye sochineniy*, 1937-1959 (17 volumes); *The Complete Prose Tales of Alexander Pushkin*, 1966; *Pushkin Threefold*, 1972; *A. S. Pushkin bez tsenzury*, 1972; *Polnoye sobraniye sochineniy*, 1977-1979 (10 volumes); *Alexander Pushkin: Complete Prose Fiction*, 1983.

BIBLIOGRAPHY

Debreczeny, Paul. *Social Functions of Literature: Alexander Pushkin and Russian Culture*. Stanford, Calif.: Stanford Univ. Press, 1997. Debreczeny divides his study into three parts: the first is devoted to selected readers' responses to Pushkin; the second explores the extent to which individual aesthetic responses are conditioned by their environment; the third concerns the mythic aura that developed around Pushkin's public persona.

Driver, Sam. *Pushkin: Literature and Social Ideas*. New York: Columbia Univ. Press, 1989. Driver examines, variously, Pushkin's politics, his aristocracy, his dandyism. A final chapter explores two unfinished Pushkin fragments, a Russian version of Edward Bulwer-Lytton's *Pelham* and a retelling of Tacitus's account of the death of Petronius Arbiter.

Muchnic, Helen. *Russian Writers Notes & Essays*. New York: Random House, 1971. Contains a succinct introductory essay on Pushkin's life and fiction.

Shaw, J. Thomas. *Pushkin's Poetics of the Unexpected: The Nonrhymed Lines in the Rhymed Poetry and the Rhymed Lines in the Nonrhymed Poetry*. Columbus, Ohio: Slavica Publishers, 1993. This is a highly specialized study of Pushkin's poetic technique that will be of most use to specialists.

Troyat, Henri. *Pushkin*. Trans. from the French by Nancy Amphoux. London: Allen & Unwin, 1974. This new edition of Troyat's biography of Pushkin—first published in the United States a decade earlier—reinstates material excised from the earlier edition. The last section of the book includes some new material relevant to Pushkin's duel and subsequent death.

BARBARA PYM
Mary Crampton

Born: Oswestry, England; June 2, 1913
Died: Oxford, England; January 11, 1980

PRINCIPAL LONG FICTION
Some Tame Gazelle, 1950
Excellent Women, 1952
Jane and Prudence, 1953
Less than Angels, 1955
A Glass of Blessings, 1958
No Fond Return of Love, 1961
Quartet in Autumn, 1977
The Sweet Dove Died, 1978
A Few Green Leaves, 1980
An Unsuitable Attachment, 1982
Crampton Hodnet, 1985
An Academic Question, 1986

OTHER LITERARY FORMS

In 1984, Hazel Holt and Hilary Pym published a one-volume edition of Barbara Pym's diaries and letters, entitled *A Very Private Eye: An Autobiography in Diaries and Letters*. In 1987, Holt edited a miscellany, *Civil to Strangers and Other Writings*, which contained mostly fiction but some nonfiction.

ACHIEVEMENTS

Pym was a writer of distinctive qualities who, having suffered discouragement and neglect for fifteen years, was rediscovered toward the end of her life, to take her rightful place as a novelist of considerable originality and force. Often compared favorably with Jane Austen's novels, Pym's are essentially those of a private, solitary individual, employing precise social observation, understatement, and gentle irony in an oblique approach to such universal themes as the underlying loneliness and frustrations of life, culture as a force for corruption, love thwarted or satisfied, and the power of the ordinary to sustain and protect the men and women who shelter themselves under it. Also like Austen, Pym has no illusions about herself and very few about other people: "I like to think that what I write gives pleasure and makes my readers smile, even laugh. But my novels are by no means only comedies as I try to reflect life as I see it."

The story of Pym's early achievements, her long enforced silence, and her remarkable rediscovery perhaps says more about the publishing world than about either her books or her readers. Between 1949 and 1961, while working as an editorial assistant at the International African Institute, Pym wrote a novel every two years. As each manuscript was finished, she sent it off to Jonathan Cape. Her first six novels established her style, were well received by reviewers, and enjoyed a following among library borrowers. *Excellent Women*, her most popular novel, sold a little more than six thousand copies.

Then, in 1963, Pym put her seventh novel, *An Unsuitable Attachment*, in the mail. A short time later, it was returned: Times, she was told, had changed. The "swinging sixties" had no place for her gently ironic comedies about unconventional middle-class people leading outwardly uneventful lives. "Novels like *An Unsuitable Attachment*, despite their qualities, are getting increasingly difficult to sell," wrote another publisher, while a third regretted that the novel was unsuitable for their list.

Being a woman of determination with a certain modest confidence in herself, Pym went to work on an eighth novel, *The Sweet Dove Died*, and she sent it off to Cape; it too came back. She adopted a pseudonym—"Tom Crampton"—because "it had a swinging air to it," but twenty publishers turned down the novel. Humiliated and frustrated, she began to feel not only that her new books were no good, but also that nothing she had ever written had been good. *No Fond Return of Love* was serialized by the British Broadcasting Corporation (BBC) and Portway Reprints reissued five others; her books retained their popularity among library borrowers; and Robert Smith published an appreciation of her work in the October, 1971, issue of *Ariel*—but despite these signs of the continuing appeal of her work, Pym could not find a publisher, and by the mid-1970's, her name appeared to have been forgotten.

A renaissance in Pym's fortunes came with startling suddenness in 1977, when, to celebrate three-quarters of a century of existence, *The Times Literary Supplement* invited a number of well-known writers to name the most over- and underrated novelists of the century. Both Philip Larkin and Lord David Cecil—for years staunch admirers of hers—selected Pym as having been too long neglected, the only living writer to be so distinguished in the poll. Larkin praised her "unique eye and ear for the small poignancies and comedies of everyday life." Cecil called her early books "the finest example of high comedy to have appeared in England" in the twentieth century.

The publicity surrounding the article, not surprisingly, had positive effects on Pym's reputation. Macmillan published her new novel, *Quartet in Autumn*, near the end of 1977; later it was shortlisted for the Booker Prize. Cape began to reissue her earlier books; Penguin and Granada planned a series of paperbacks; she was widely interviewed; finally, she appeared on "Desert Island Discs" as well as in a television film called "Tea with Miss Pym." *The Sweet Dove Died* was published in 1978, followed by her last novel, the posthumously published *A Few Green Leaves* (1980). The manuscript of *An Unsuitable Attachment* was found among her papers after her death and published in 1982 with an introduction written by Philip Larkin. A book was prepared from her diaries and short stories.

Pym's novels are distinguished by an unobtrusive but perfectly controlled style, a concern with ordinary people and ordinary events, and a constant aim to be readable, to entertain in a world that is uniquely her own. They are also distinguished by a low-key but nevertheless cutting treatment of assumptions of masculine superiority and other sexist notions—all this well in advance of the women's movement, and without the rhetoric which mars so much feminist fiction. Although hers is a closed world—what Robert Smith called "an enchanted world of small felicities and small mishaps"—it is also real and varied in theme and setting, with its own laws of human conduct and values, its peculiar humor and pathos. Middle-aged or elderly ladies, middle-aged or elderly gentlemen, civil servants, clergymen, anthropologists and other academics—these are the people about whom Pym develops her stories.

The world in which Pym's characters live, whether urban or provincial, is also a quiet world—evoked in such detail as to make the reader feel that the action could not possibly take place anywhere else. Taken together, her novels constitute that rare achievement: an independent fictional world, rooted in quotidian reality yet very much the creation of Barbara Pym. Central characters from one novel appear in passing or are briefly mentioned in another; delightful minor characters turn up in unexpected places. This pleasure of cross-references is characteristic of Pym's art, in which formal dexterity and a marvelous sense of humor harmonize with a modest but unembarrassed moral vision. "I prefer to write about the kind of things I have experienced," Pym said, "and to put into my novels the kind of details that amuse me in the hope that others will share in this."

Biography

Mary Crampton (Barbara Pym) was born on June 2, 1913, in Oswestry, Shropshire, a small English town on the border of Wales. Like many of her characters, she led a quiet but enjoyable life among middle-class people with an Anglican background. Her father, Frederick Crampton Pym, was a solicitor and sang in the choir; her mother, Irena (Thomas), was of half Welsh descent and played the organ.

Pym was given a good education (Huyton College, a boarding school near Liverpool; and St. Hilda's College, Oxford, from which she received a B.A., 1934, in English language and literature); saw some wartime service (Postal and Telegraph Censorship in Bristol, 1939, and the Women's Royal Naval Service in England and Italy, 1943-1946); and lived in various sections of London: Pimlico, Barnes, and Kilburn. She wrote down everything she saw in a series of little notebooks, and later "bottled it all up and reduced it, like making chutney."

In 1948, Pym began working at the International African Institute, first as a research assistant and later as an assistant editor of the journal *Africa*. She was given the job of preparing the research for publication, and regretted that more of the anthropologists did not turn their talents to the writing of fiction. In their work, she found many of the qualities that make a novelist: "accurate observation, detachment, even sympathy." Needed was a little more imagination, as well as "the leavening of irony and humour." Several of her novels draw on her years at the Institute to study the behavior patterns and rituals of a group of anthropologists. In *Less than Angels*, for example, she portrays an anthropologist and his female coworkers, gently mocking the high seriousness with which they pursue their research among primitive African tribes and the shameless jargon in which they converse. No doubt the narrator is speaking for Pym herself when she concludes: "And how much more comfortable it sometimes was to observe [life] from a distance, to look down from an upper window, as it were, as the anthropologists did."

Although her first novel did not appear until 1950, Pym began writing when she was a schoolgirl, and even completed a novel when she was sixteen. After leaving Oxford, she started to write seriously and finished two more novels, but did not succeed in getting them published. By then, however, her literary tastes were well set. Above all, she was addicted to novels. Anthony Trollope and Jane Austen were her favorite novelists, and she knew their works intimately; but she read all the fiction she could, and listed among her favorites Ivy Compton-Burnett, Anthony Powell, and Iris Murdoch. She was less tolerant of contemporary novels, and viewed popular and sentimental fiction with the critical eye of the satirist. Nowhere in her own fiction does the reader find the sentimental excesses and sensational unrealities of current popular fiction.

In 1971, Pym had a serious operation, and in 1974, she retired to live with her sister near Oxford. She died on January 11, 1980, at the age of sixty-six.

ANALYSIS

Like most novelists, Barbara Pym was interested above all in human nature, and for most of her life she trained both eye and ear upon the exploration of that subject in its many fascinating dimensions. Her first published novel, *Some Tame Gazelle*, sets the tone and subject for what is to come as she casts her specialist's eye on British lower-class and lower-middle-class life and focuses on the quiet domestic lives of a few people. At the center are two unmarried women who have decided that they will be happier living alone together. An all-pervasive influence of the Anglican church, numerous references to anthropology and English literature, the weakness of men, realism, and a sometimes devastatingly comic tone are among the many distinctive features of not only this early novel but the later ones as well. Much the same judgment may be made for two posthumously published novels: *Crampton Hodnet*, which she had written in the 1930's but never intended to publish, and *An Academic Question*, for which she had written two drafts (one in first person, another in third person) but abandoned to write *Quartet in Autumn*. In 1986, Hazel Holt published an amalgamation of the two drafts. In spite of their thin plots and shallow characterization, both novels contain Pym's characteristically sharp observations and lively dialogue among the minor characters, as well as her concern with the elderly. Considered together, in all twelve of her novels Pym communicates her vision in an engaging, entertaining, and readable way. Her wit, her sense of style, her devotion to language and its revelation of character, and the richness of her invention all compel respect and critical attention.

"In all of her writing," Philip Larkin has written of Pym, "I find a continual perceptive attention to detail which is a joy, and a steady background of rueful yet courageous acceptance of things." In this statement, Larkin points to perhaps the single most important technique—and theme—in Pym's work. *Excellent Women, A Glass of Blessings*, and *Quartet in Autumn* develop their effects, as indeed do all of Pym's twelve novels, by exploiting the comedy of contemporary manners. Like her anthropologists, whom she quietly mocks for their esoteric detachment, Pym scrupulously notes and records the frustrations, unfulfilled desires, boredom, and loneliness of "ordinary people, people who have no claim to fame whatsoever." The usual pattern for the heroine is either retrenchment into her own world or, as a result of interaction with others, self-realization. By representing intensively the small world most individuals inhabit, it is Pym's method to suggest the world as a whole as well.

Usually Pym appoints a heroine to comment on the intimate details of social behavior. In *Excellent Women*, the assignment falls to Mildred Lathbury, who, as an observer of life, expects "very little—nothing, almost." Typical of Pym's "excellent women," Mildred is preoccupied with order, stability, and routine, but her special interest centers on the lives and crises of those around her—including her new neighbors, Rockingham and Helena Napier; the vicar, Julian Malory; and the anthropologist, Everard Bone. Faced with Mildred's honesty, diffidence, and unpretentiousness, the crises are resolved happily.

In Pym's fifth novel, *A Glass of Blessings*, the heroine is Wilmet Forsyth, a young and leisured woman bored with her excessively sober civil-servant husband. Her near romances with a priest, her best friend's husband, and Piers Longridge (in whose friend Keith she discovers a rival) are only some of the pairings in this intricate drama of romantic errors. When the possibility of a love affair fails to materialize, Wilmet finds a different kind of consolation in religion.

Finally, Pym's antiheroic view of life is particularly obvious in her most somber work, *Quartet in Autumn*, the first of her novels to be published after fifteen years of silence. Whereas her earlier work was a small protest against everyday life, *Quartet in Au-*

tumn offered a formal protest against the conditions both of life itself and of certain sad civilities. The comedy is cold and the outlook is austere in this story of four people in late middle age who suffer from the same problem: loneliness. In its manipulation of the narrative among Edwin, Norman, Letty, and Marcia, the novel also represents Pym's greatest technical achievement.

Excellent Women

Excellent Women, described by one critic as the most "felicitous" of all of Pym's novels, explores the complications of being a spinster (and a religious one, at that) in the England of the 1950's. The setting is a run-down part of London near Victoria Station, but the very high Anglican Church of St. Mary's also provides the background for some of the events described. In the quiet comfort of this world, where everything is within walking distance and a new face is an occasion for speculation, the pleasantness and security of everyday life dominate. Only small crises—such as an argument between Winifred and Alegra over how to decorate the church altar—form the counterpoint to comfort. As the narrator says, "life was like that for most of us—the small unpleasantnesses rather than the great tragedies; the little useless longings rather than the great renunciations and dramatic love affairs of history or fiction."

Mildred Lathbury, the narrator, is representative of one of Pym's favorite character types: the "excellent woman." She lives very much as she did growing up in a country rectory, working part-time for the aid of impoverished gentlewomen and devoting herself to the work of the parish. As one who tends to get involved in other people's lives, she knows herself, she says, "capable of dealing with most of the stock situations or even the great moments of life—birth, marriage, death, the successful jumble sale, the garden fête spoilt by bad weather."

In all of Pym's novels, says Philip Larkin, "a small incident serves to set off a chain of modest happenings among interrelated groups of characters." In this instance, it is the entry into Mildred's life of Rockingham Napier. A flag lieutenant to an admiral, Rockingham has just returned from Italy, where he served his country by being charming to dull Wren

officers. His wife Helena, an anthropologist, does not welcome his return. Scornful of his easy charm and lack of serious purpose, she has become infatuated with another anthropologist, Everard Bone, her co-worker in Africa. As Helena pursues, however, Everard flees.

The reader depends upon Mildred for ironic commentary. Helena leaves her husband, who then departs for a cottage in the country. Excellent woman that she is, Mildred is invited by Rockingham to send him the Napier furniture, by Helena to get it back, by both to effect their reconciliation, and by Everard to read proof and make the index for his forthcoming book. Because the vicar, Julian Malory, needs to be protected from designing women and Everard needs her help with the book, it seems to Mildred that she may look forward to a "full life." Then she remembers Rockingham's smile and reads from Christina Rossetti: "Better by far you should forget and smile,/ Than that you should remember and be sad." "It was easy enough to read those lines and be glad at his smiling," she acknowledges, "but harder to tell myself there would never be any question of anything else." Still, Everard's affection is genuine, if undemonstrative—and not unmixed with a pragmatic desire to find a suitable typist, indexer, and all-around "helpmate"—and the reader is happy to learn, in a subsequent novel, that Mildred and Everard do indeed go on to wed.

Again set in the 1950's, town and country are contrasted in *A Glass of Blessings*, which Larkin regards as the "subtlest" of Pym's books. The novel opens in St. Luke's Church on the feast of its patron, the "beloved physician," as St. Paul called him. Celebrating the feast and her thirty-third birthday, Wilmet Forsyth, the narrator and heroine, is the well-to-do but aimless wife (subject to "useless little longings") of a typical Pym husband—hopelessly imperceptive, though well intentioned and reliable. Like Jane Austen's *Emma*, whom Pym has in mind throughout the novel, Wilmet is unused and spoiled. A beautiful woman, always exquisitely dressed, Wilmet is childless, idle, and snobbish. She is also utterly unknown to herself, unable to imagine another life, and afraid to risk herself, even on the London buses, certain that any disturbance will be disillusioning. Bored, without training for a career, despising routine, she plans "to take more part in the life of St. Luke's, to try to befriend Piers Longridge and perhaps even go to his classes."

Piers Longridge is a sour, moody homosexual, a fact Wilmet never quite seems to grasp until well into the novel. He has taken a seemingly useless degree and now teaches Portuguese in adult education classes. Believing that she might relieve his unhappiness, she forces herself on him, hoping for the grand passion of her life, another fact that she never really admits. Finally, in a scene of high comedy and bitter pain, exasperated by Wilmet's attentions and her naïveté, Piers confronts her with his secret lover, Keith, a male model, and accuses Wilmet of being incapable of affection. It is the first time anyone has told her anything near the truth, and in response, she says to Mary Beamish, "sometimes you discover that you aren't as nice as you thought you were—that you're in fact rather a horrid person, and that's humiliating somehow."

When she witnesses the courtship and marriage of Mary Beamish, an orphan and ex-Anglican nun, and Father Marius Lovejoy Ransome, Wilmet begins to perceive the possibilities of being useful in the parish and even of passion. After she finds out that Rodney has had an innocent flirtation with his secretary, Wilmet sees him differently, thinking, "I had always regarded Rodney as the kind of man who would never look at another woman. The fact that he could—and indeed had done so—ought to teach me something about myself, even if I was not quite sure what it was." The truth of it is that Wilmet has failed to recognize her society, including the parish of St. Luke's, for what it is—an erotic conclave of beauty and variety, both dangerous and enlivening. It is like George Herbert's "glass of blessings," full of the "world's riches"—"beautie . . . wisdome, honour, pleasure."

QUARTET IN AUTUMN

In her first six novels, Pym treats her characters with warm compassion and gentle irony. With *Quartet in Autumn*, however, her tone becomes harsher, more bitter, as she examines with bleak detachment the lonely rejection of the retired. Letty Crowe, another of Pym's excellent women, is sixty-five and faces retirement from the unspecified office job she has shared for many years with her colleagues, Marcia, Norman, and Edwin. For Letty, life in a rooming house is "a little sterile, perhaps even deprived." Retirement gives her a feeling of nothingness, as if she had never existed. During sleepless nights, her life unrolls before her, like that of a person drowning: forty years wasted looking for love. Images of dead leaves drifting to the pavement in autumn and being swept away recur throughout the novel. Indeed, Letty tries not to dwell on the image of herself lying among the autumnal leaves "to prepare for death when life became too much to be endured."

Her former colleagues are of no help to Letty. Norman is a scrawny, sardonic bachelor. Edwin is a widower preoccupied with "the soothing rhythms of the church's year." Marcia is gravely ill and at least slightly mad—collecting tins of food she never opens and milk bottles which she hoards in a shed. The only pleasures she knows are visits to the clinic for checkups and bus trips to look at the mansion of her adored surgeon. Incapable of thought, she is far more pathetic than Letty.

Unlike her colleagues, Letty does try to act bravely, reading books on sociology, participating in church activities, still caring for her hair and her dress. "She told herself, dutifully assuming the suggested attitude toward retirement, that life was still full of possibilities." At the close of the novel, she is, like Mildred and Wilmet, where she was at the beginning. Yet, at the slightest change in the routine of her eventless days, she courageously assures herself, "at least it made one realize that life still held infinite possibilities for change."

In *Excellent Women, A Glass of Blessings*, and *Quartet in Autumn*, Pym relies neither on violence nor on the bizarre. Nothing outwardly momentous happens, but the frustrations of a half dozen or more characters emerge clearly and poignantly. Some critics have felt that the narrowness of her life inevitably imposed limitations on her work. Beneath the calm surface of her novels, however, the events of the day do make an imprint—to a degree appropriate to the lives of ordinary middle-class people. Each novel is a miniature work of art, distinguished by an air of assurance, an easy but firm control of the material, and the economy of means to achieve it.

Dale Salwak

OTHER MAJOR WORKS

NONFICTION: *A Very Private Eye: An Autobiography in Diaries and Letters*, 1984.

MISCELLANEOUS: *Civil to Strangers and Other Writings*, 1987.

BIBLIOGRAPHY

Allen, Orphia Jane. *Barbara Pym: Writing a Life.* Metuchen, N.J.: Scarecrow Press, 1994. Part 1 discusses Pym's life and work; part 2 analyzes her novels; part 3 examines different critical approaches to her work and provides a bibliographical essay; part 4 provides a comprehensive primary and secondary bibliography. An extremely useful volume for both beginning students and advanced scholars.

Benet, Diana. *Something to Love: Barbara Pym's Novels.* Columbia: University of Missouri Press, 1986. Benet's fresh and insightful study examines Pym as "a chronicler of universal problems" whose focus—the many guises of love—moves, shapes, or disfigures all of her major characters. Includes an index.

Burkhart, Charles. *The Pleasure of Miss Pym.* Austin: University of Texas Press, 1987. A very readable discussion of Pym's life and autobiographical writings, as well as her fiction through *An Academic Question.* Focuses on her world view, the unique nature of her comedy, her religion, her place within the history of the novel, and her insights into male-female relationships. Includes photographs and an index.

Cotsell, Michael. *Barbara Pym.* New York: Macmillan, 1989. A cogent examination of all Pym's novels, paying particular attention to her characters' thoughts and feelings. Cotsell judges the novels to be "unabashedly romantic" and also considers Pym's sense of language, her unpublished writings, and her creative process. Includes an index.

Liddell, Robert. *A Mind at Ease: Barbara Pym and Her Novels.* London: Peter Owen, 1989. In this invaluable study, Liddell draws upon his fifty years of friendship with Pym to write a critical survey through *Crampton Hodnet.* Considers the attention she gave to her characters' domestic and emotional lives, examines the reasons for her revival in popularity, and guides the reader through her novels, explaining which ones are or are not successful and why. Also corrects errors by critics and dilutes the common misconception that Pym is a modern-day Jane Austen.

Long, Robert Emmet. *Barbara Pym.* New York: Frederick Ungar, 1986. A helpful treatment of Pym's first eleven novels, paying particular attention to her recurring themes and character types, her modes of social comedy and satire, and her pervasive concern with "unrealized" love and solitude. Finds that Jane Austen's dynamic English provincial world has reached a point of breakdown in Pym. Includes a chronology, notes, and an index.

Nardin, Jane. *Barbara Pym.* Boston: Twayne, 1985. An excellent introductory study of Pym's life and career, noting the origins and development of her themes, character types, and style. Contains a chronology, notes, a bibliography (listing primary and secondary sources), and an index.

Rossen, Janice, ed. *Independent Women: The Function of Gender in the Novels of Barbara Pym.* New York: St. Martin's Press, 1988. This collection of ten original essays seeks to test Pym's reputation by considering her craftsmanship, the literary influences on her work, and her special use of language. Includes biographical, historical, and feminist approaches to explore her unique creative process as it relates to events in her life. Notes and an index are provided.

_____. *The World of Barbara Pym.* New York: Macmillan, 1987. Focuses on twentieth century England as Pym saw, lived, satirized, and enjoyed it. Defines her significance within the framework of the modern British novel, traces her artistic development, explores interrelationships between her life and her fiction, and addresses broader themes regarding British culture in her work, such as spinsterhood, anthropology, English literature, the Anglican Church, and Oxford University. Notes and an index are provided.

Salwak, Dale, ed. *The Life and Work of Barbara Pym.* New York: Macmillan, 1987. Nineteen essays consider Pym's life and her novels, as well as her human and artistic achievements, from a variety of fresh perspectives. Includes notes and an index.

Snow, Lotus. *One Little Room an Everywhere: Barbara Pym's Novels.* Edited by Constance Hunting. Orono, Maine: Puckerbrush Press, 1987. In seven well-researched, clearly written chapters, Snow discusses Pym's interest in ordinary people and their mundane lives, her selection of character names, and her presentation of men and married women. Includes notes.

Weld, Annette. *Barbara Pym and the Novel of Manners.* New York: St. Martin's Press, 1992. Chapters on manners and comedy, poems, stories and radio scripts, the early novels, and her major fiction. Includes notes and bibliography.

Wyatt-Brown, Anne M. *Barbara Pym: A Critical Biography.* Columbia: University of Missouri Press, 1992. A fine narrative and analytical biography. See also the introduction: "Creativity and the Life Cycle." Includes notes and bibliography.

THOMAS PYNCHON

Born: Glen Cove, New York; May 8, 1937

PRINCIPAL LONG FICTION
V., 1963
The Crying of Lot 49, 1966
Gravity's Rainbow, 1973
Vineland, 1989
Mason and Dixon, 1997

OTHER LITERARY FORMS

Before his novels began to come out, Thomas Pynchon published a handful of short stories: "The

Small Rain" (1959), "Mortality and Mercy in Vienna" (1959), "Low-Lands" (1960), "Entropy" (1960), and "Under the Rose" (1961—an early version of chapter 3 of *V.*). With the exception of "Mortality and Mercy," these stories appear in the 1984 collection *Slow Learner,* which also includes "The Secret Integration," originally published in 1964. Two magazine publications, "The World (This One), the Flesh (Mrs. Oedipa Maas), and the Testament of Pierce Inverarity" (1965) and "The Shrink Flips" (1966), are excerpts from *The Crying of Lot 49.* Pynchon also published some pieces in *The New York Times Book Review,* including a 1984 meditation on distrust of technology ("Is It O.K. to Be a Luddite?"), a 1988 review of Gabriel García Márquez's *Love in the Time of Cholera,* and a 1993 sketch, "Nearer, My Couch, to Thee," on the sin of sloth (included in the collection *Deadly Sins,* by various hands). He penned introductions to a reissue of Richard Fariña's 1966 novel *Been Down So Long It Looks Like Up to Me* (1983), to a posthumous collection of writings by Donald Barthelme, *The Teachings of Don B.* (1992), and to a reissue of Jim Dodge's 1990 novel *Stone Junction* (1998). Pynchon also wrote liner notes for the albums *Spiked! The Music of Spike Jones* (1994) and *Nobody's Cool,* by the rock group Lotion (1995).

ACHIEVEMENTS

Among those contemporary novelists who enjoy both a popular and an academic following, Thomas Pynchon stands out as a virtual cult figure. His novels and stories stand up to the most rigorous critical analysis; they prove, like all great works of art, to be the product of a gifted sensibility and careful craftsmanship. At the same time, Dr. Samuel Johnson's "common reader" cheerfully wades through much abstruse matter because this author never fails to entertain—with bizarre plots, incandescent language, anarchic humor, and memorable characters.

Pynchon has an enormous, diverse, and fanatically loyal following. There are more than thirty books on his work, not to mention scholarly journals. Some of the fascination he holds for readers is derived from his reclusive habits. He refused to be interviewed, photographed, or otherwise made into a darling of the media. Thirty years after the publication of his first novel, it finally became known that Pynchon made his home in New York City.

Pynchon was honored with a number of literary awards. He received the William Faulkner Foundation Award for *V.*, the 1967 Rosenthal Foundation Award of the National Institute of Arts and Letters for *The Crying of Lot 49*, and the National Book Award for *Gravity's Rainbow* in 1974. Though the judging committee unanimously voted to award the Pulitzer Prize in fiction to Pynchon for *Gravity's Rainbow*, the committee was overruled by an advisory board which found the novel immoral and "turgid." The Howells Medal, awarded once every five years, was offered to Pynchon in 1975, but he declined it.

Pynchon occupies a place in the front rank of twentieth century American fiction writers, and more than one distinguished critic has declared him America's finest novelist.

BIOGRAPHY

Because of Thomas Ruggles Pynchon, Jr.'s passion for privacy, little is known about his life. His father was an industrial surveyor, and the family lived in Glen Cove, East Norwich, and Oyster Bay—all on Long Island in New York. His father, a Republican, eventually served as town supervisor of Oyster Bay. Pynchon was sixteen when he graduated from Oyster Bay High School in 1953. He was class salutatorian and winner of an award for the senior attaining the highest average in English. With a scholarship at Cornell University, he first majored in engineering physics but, though he was doing well academically, abandoned that curriculum after the first year. A year later, he decided to do a hitch in the Navy before completing his baccalaureate degree. He attended boot camp at Bainbridge, Maryland, and did advanced training as an electrician at Norfolk, Virginia. The two years in the Navy, partly spent in the Mediterranean, provided Pynchon with a number of comic situations and characters, which he has exploited in "Low-Lands," *V.*, *Gravity's Rainbow*, and *Mason and Dixon*. Pynchon finished at Cornell as an English major and was graduated in 1959. While at Cornell,

Pynchon took a class taught by Vladimir Nabokov; Nabokov's wife, Vera, who did her husband's grading, remembered Pynchon for his distinctive handwriting.

Pynchon lived briefly in Greenwich Village and in uptown Manhattan before taking a job with the Boeing Company and moving to Seattle. With Boeing for two and a half years (until September, 1962), he worked in the Minuteman Logistics Support Program and wrote for such intramural publications as "The Minuteman Field Service News" and *Aerospace Safety*. After leaving Boeing, he lived in California and Mexico and completed *V.*, which was published in 1963 and hailed as a major first novel.

Over the years Pynchon was rumored to be living in various places, including California, Mexico, and Oregon. In the late 1970's, he made a trip to England that mysteriously was noted in the national newsmagazines. For a long time the author eluded his pursuers, but in the 1980's he supplied a few tantalizing autobiographical facts in the introductory essays he wrote for his *Slow Learner* collection and for the 1983 Penguin reprint of *Been Down So Long It Looks Like Up to Me*, the 1966 novel by his Cornell classmate Richard Fariña.

In 1996, Nancy Jo Sales, writing for the magazine *New York*, traced Pynchon to the Manhattan apartment he shared with his wife, Melanie Jackson (also his agent), and their son. The following year a photograph taken by James Bone appeared in the London *Times Magazine*, and a camera crew from CNN taped Pynchon walking down a street. In these instances, Pynchon fought unsuccessfully to suppress publication or broadcast of his likeness.

ANALYSIS

The quest would seem to be the one indispensable element in the fiction of Thomas Pynchon, for each of his novels proves to be a modern-dress version of the search for some grail to revive the wasteland. Pynchon's characters seek knowledge that will make sense of their unanchored lives and their fragmented times; Pynchon hints that questing has a value irrespective of the authenticity of that for which one quests. The quest lends purpose to life, enabling one to function, to see life as worthwhile. At the same time, however, Pynchon invites his more privileged reader to recognize that the ordering principle thus projected is factitious. What is real is the gathering dissolution, the passing of human beings and whole civilizations. All attempts to discover or create order and system are doomed.

Even so, as Pynchon's career developed, one notes what may be a tendency to define some grail of his own, an inclination to search for a way out of the cul-de-sac of a metaphysics perhaps unduly in thrall to the principle of entropy (broadly defined as the gradual deterioriation of the universe caused by irreversible thermodynamic equalization). Pynchon's critics disagree sharply on this point. Some maintain that the intimation of counter-entropic orders in *The Crying of Lot 49* and *Gravity's Rainbow* is merely a hook by which to catch the unwary reader, a means of seducing him or her into system-making as delusive as that of any of Pynchon's characters. Other critics, unwilling to believe that Pynchon's frequently noted affinity with modern science has been frozen at a point attained some time in the 1950's, suspect that Pynchon means to hint at transcendental alternatives implicit in the vast mysteries of contemporary astronomy and particle physics.

Regardless of whether Pynchon is on a grail quest of his own (with all the propensity for mysticism that seems indispensable to such a quester), he continues to create intricate labyrinths in which readers experience the paranoia that also figures as a prominent theme in his work. Paranoia is the conviction that mighty conspiracies exist, that all things are connected "in spheres joyful or threatening about the central pulse of [one]self." Pynchon's protagonists come to believe in this infinite reticulation of conspiracy because it is preferable to the possibility that "nothing is connected to anything." Pynchon's readers, by the same token, encounter fictive structures that formally imitate the paranoid premise: All is connected in great, seamless webs of interdependent detail.

The dialectic between order and disorder is the dialectic between art and life, and it is with reference to this neglected commonplace that one should analyze

Pynchon's artifice. In art, traditionally, humanity lays claim—sometimes piously, sometimes impiously—to the divine prerogative of creation, the establishment of order where all before was without form and void. Pynchon gives evidence, since the almost nihilistic *V.*, of a fascination with the religious belief that there are "orders behind the visible," orders analogous to those found beneath the surface in works of art ostensibly reflecting life in all its chaotic aspects. *Gravity's Rainbow*, for example, strikes one at first as a complete mishmash, a welter of all-too-lifelike confusion, but one subsequently discovers it to be as finely crafted as James Joyce's *Ulysses* (1922) or *Finnegans Wake* (1939). Perhaps Pynchon can best be imagined like William Blake, William Butler Yeats, and D. H. Lawrence, as countering the smugness and complacency of a scientific age with a calculated antirationalism.

These remarks adumbrate the last major topoi in Pynchon's work—science and art. Pynchon knows and makes artistic use of science. He has, if nothing else, dispatched legions of humanists in search of information about modern physics, chemistry, engineering, and cartography—disciplines to which they had previously been indifferent. As suggested above, however, science serves vision, not the other way around. Pynchon's work does more than that of any other writer—scientific or literary—to reverse the widening "dissociation of sensibility" that poet T. S. Eliot noted as part of the intellectual landscape since the seventeenth century. In Pynchon, and in his readers to a remarkable extent, C. P. Snow's "two cultures" become one again.

V.

In his first novel, *V.*, Pynchon brilliantly interweaves two narratives, one in the present (mid-1950's), the other in the period 1880 to 1943. The historical narrative, presented obliquely, concerns an extraordinary woman who appears originally as Victoria Wren and subsequently under *noms de guerre* in which the letter *V* of the alphabet figures prominently: Veronica Manganese, Vera Meroving. This is V., who turns up whenever there is bloodshed in the course of the twentieth century. In 1898, for example, she appears at the periphery of the Fashoda crisis in

Egypt, and the following year she gravitates to Florence, where the spies of several nations are jockeying for position, engaging in what Pynchon calls "premilitary" activity. In 1913, she is in Paris, involved in a bloody theater riot which, like the crises in Egypt and Florence earlier, proves an earnest of World War I—a kind of fulfillment for V. in her early phase. When World War I ends with Western civilization intact, though permanently altered, V. begins to be involved with those elements that will figure in the more satisfying carnage of the century's real climacteric, World War II. In 1922, she is in German southwest Africa, where the massacre of the native Hereros reenacts the even greater massacre of two decades earlier and anticipates the really accomplished genocide in Europe between 1933 and 1945. On and off after 1918, she is on Malta, consorting with a group sympathetic to Mussolini and his Fascists. V. dies in an air raid on Malta in 1943—just as the tide turns against the Fascist cause with which she has become increasingly identified.

V.'s affinity with Fascism complements a decadent religiosity, and she comes to personify the drift to extinction of Western culture and of life itself. She gradually loses parts of her body and becomes more and more the sum of inanimate parts: false eye, false hair, false foot, false navel. She is a brilliant metaphor for entropy and the decline of civilization, and her baleful influence is projected in the novel's present in the decadence of the contemporary characters, most of whom are part of a group called the Whole Sick Crew. The Crew is exemplified by its newest member, the winsome schlemiel Benny Profane. Profane is incapable of love and emotional involvement; he is also perennially at war with inanimate objects. His dread of the inanimate suggests that he intuits the cultural situation as the century wanes. Though he is no thinker, he realizes that he and his fellows are Eliot's hollow men, on the way to their whimpering end. His inability to love is presented in comic terms—though fat, he is doted on by various desirable women, including the Maltese Paola Maijstral and the beautiful Rachel Owlglass. The failure is that of his entire circle, for though there is much sex among the Whole Sick Crew, there is no commit-

ment, no love, no hope. The one baby generated by all the sexual freedom is aborted.

The Whole Sick Crew is what Western civilization has become as a result of entropic processes that are utterly random and mindless. The meaninglessness of entropy is something difficult for the human mind to accept, however, and in Herbert Stencil, a marginal member of the Crew, Pynchon presents what becomes his standard character, a person who must discover conspiracy to deal with the fragmentation of life and culture. It is Stencil who does the mythmaking, the elevating of Victoria Wren from mere perverted adventuress to something awesome and as multifaceted as Robert Graves's White Goddess. Nor is Stencil alone, for the undeniable desire for connectedness is quintessentially human. It is also shared by the sophisticated reader, who flings himself or herself into the literary puzzle and becomes himself a Stencil, a quester for meaning in the convoluted plot of *V.* and in the identity of the mysterious personage who gives the novel its name. Pynchon's genius manifests itself in his ability to keep his readers suspended between his two mutually exclusive alternatives: that the clues to V.'s identity are the key to meaning and that V. is nothing more than a paranoid fantasy, the product of a mind that cannot deal with very much reality.

The fascination with which readers have responded to *V.* indicates that Pynchon is himself a brilliant mythmaker. Even after one has "solved" the mystery of V. and arrived at an enlightenment that Stencil explicitly rejects as a threat to his emotional and mental stability, one still finds the myth trenchant, moving, even terrifying. The decline of the West is a theme that one has encountered before, but never has one encountered it so cogently as in this woman who loves death and the inanimate. The real conspiracy, then, is an artistic one; the connectedness is that of the novel, the cabal between author and reader.

THE CRYING OF LOT 49

Pynchon's second novel, *The Crying of Lot 49*, seems slight between *V.* and *Gravity's Rainbow*, and Pynchon himself seems to consider it something of a potboiler. Some readers, however, believe it to be his most perfect work of art. It is the story of Oedipa Maas, who is named "executor, or she supposed executrix" of the estate of an ex-lover, the millionaire Pierce Inverarity. In carrying out her duties, she stumbles upon evidence of a conspiracy to circumvent the United States Postal Service. She discovers Tristero, a *sub rosa* postal system at war for centuries with all officially sanctioned postal services, first in the old world, then in the new. Tristero subsumes an extraordinary number of revolutionary or simply alienated groups. In its new-world phase, it seems to bring together all those within the American system who are disfranchised, disaffected, or disinherited—all those defrauded of the American Dream.

Oedipa, like Herbert Stencil, finds that the harder she looks, the more connections to Tristero she discovers, until the connections start revealing themselves in such number and variety that she begins to doubt her sanity. Oedipa's mental condition, in fact, becomes the book's central conundrum. She first confronts the question in a flashback early in the story. She recalls visiting a Mexico City art gallery with Pierce Inverarity and seeing a disturbing painting by Remedios Varo. In the painting, a group of girls are imprisoned at the top of a circular tower and made to embroider *el Manto Terrestre*—the earth mantle. The tapestry they create, extruded through the tower's windows, contains "all the other buildings and creatures, all the waves, ships and forests of the earth," for "the tapestry was the world." Oedipa recognizes in the painting a representation of the fact that she—like any other human being—is imprisoned mentally and perceptually in the tower of her individual consciousness. External reality, in other words, may be nothing more than what one weaves or embroiders in one's cranial tower. Oedipa weeps at human isolation. Later, tracking down the clues to Tristero (which seems coextensive with Inverarity's estate and enterprises), she cannot free herself from the suspicion that the proliferating connections she is discovering all have their throbbing ganglion in her own mind. She realizes that she is becoming a classic paranoid.

Though Pynchon does not resolve the question of Oedipa's sanity, he hints that becoming sensitized to the problems of twentieth century American culture (and to the horrors of the spiritual void contingent on certain twentieth century habits of mind) involves a necessary sacrifice of sanity or at least serenity. At the end, Oedipa is faced with a harrowing choice: Either she is insane, or Tristero—with its stupendous reticulation—really exists. When Oedipa attempts to rephrase the dilemma, she finds that the paranoia is somehow inescapable:

> There was either some Tristero beyond the appearance of the legacy America, or there was just America and if there was just America then it seemed the only way she could continue, and manage to be at all relevant to it, was as an alien, unfurrowed, assumed full circle into some paranoia.

Pynchon implies that Tristero, whatever its status as literal reality, is in effect a necessary fiction, a metaphor for the idea of an alternative to a closed system.

Oedipa's experiences are almost certainly an imaginative version of Pynchon's own. At the time of the novel, 1964, Oedipa is twenty-eight years old—the same age as Pynchon was in that year. Like Pynchon, she has attended Cornell and then gravitated to the West Coast. Like Pynchon, too, she comes to view herself as an "alien," unable to fit into the furrow of American success, prosperity, and complacency. Thus, one can read the novel as Pynchon's account of why he has gone underground. He has made common cause with America's disadvantaged; in all of his fiction, not to mention his article "A Journey into the Mind of Watts," one notes an obvious sympathy with minorities and something like loathing for the mechanisms of corporate greed responsible for the spoilage of the American landscape, both literal and psychic. *The Crying of Lot 49*, then, is a fictional hybrid of the spiritual autobiography—in the same tradition as St. Augustine's *Confessions* (397-401) and William Wordsworth's *The Prelude* (1850).

These speculations—the need for an alternative to a closed system, the hints of spiritual autobiography—are supported by Edward Mendelson's brilliant essay "The Sacred, the Profane, and *The Crying of Lot 49*" (the single most satisfying reading of the novel, this essay has been reprinted in Mendelson's

Pynchon: A Collection of Critical Essays, 1978). Mendelson points out the novel's high density of language with religious connotations; he argues that what Oedipa really searches for—and behind her twentieth century humankind—is a new species of revelation, a way out of the agnostic, positivistic cul-de-sac of contemporary rationalism. He also provides an explanation of the novel's odd title. "Lot 49" is a group of stamps—Tristero forgeries—to be sold as part of the settlement of Pierce Inverarity's estate. The novel ends as lot 49 is about to be "cried" or auctioned. Oedipa, present at the auction, expects to confront some representative of the mysterious Tristero, who will attempt to acquire the evidence of the secret organization's existence. Mendelson suggests that the number "49" refers obliquely to the forty-nine-day period between Easter and the descent of the Holy Spirit at Pentecost; the revelation that awaits Oedipa at the crying of lot 49 is symbolically the revelation awaited by the modern world, whose existence so tragically lacks a numinous dimension. Thus, Pynchon ends his novel on a note of expectation, a yearning for some restoration of mystery, some answer to what the narrator calls "the exitlessness, the absence of surprise to life" in the modern age.

GRAVITY'S RAINBOW

All of Pynchon's books are filled with bizarre characters and incidents, but *Gravity's Rainbow* is especially dense and demanding. The hero is Tyrone Slothrop, an American army lieutenant attached to an Allied intelligence unit in World War II. Slothrop's superiors become aware that the map of his sexual conquests (or his sexual fantasies; this is kept ambiguous) coincides with the distribution of German V-2 rockets falling on London. Significantly, the erection *precedes* the arrival of the rocket. This fact, which calls into question the usual mechanism of cause and effect (it complements the fact that the rocket, traveling faster than the speed of sound, is heard falling *after* it has exploded) is of central importance to the novel, for Pynchon means to pit two scientific models against each other. The older model, still seldom questioned, posits a mechanistic universe that operates according to the laws of cause and effect.

The character associated with this worldview is the sinister Dr. Pointsman, a diehard Pavlovian threatened by the new model, which posits a universe in which physical phenomena can be plotted and predicted only in terms of uncertainty and probability (Pynchon is on sound theoretical ground here; he is presenting the physics of Werner Heisenberg and Max Planck). The character who embraces the more up-to-date worldview is the sympathetic Roger Mexico, a statistician. Between these two, poor Slothrop—a kind of Everyman—tries to stay alive and if possible free. Pointsman and his minions concoct an experiment with Slothrop; they will provide him with the best information they have on the German rocket and then observe him closely for further revelations. Slothrop, aware that he is being used, goes AWOL to embark on a private quest to discover the truth of his personal destiny—and perhaps the destiny of his age as well.

Pynchon picks his historical moment carefully, for World War II was the moment when the technological world came of age. Technology offers humanity complete control of its environment and its destiny; techology offers something very like transcendence—or it offers annihilation. Pynchon's novel is a meditation on the choice, which is seen nowhere more clearly than in the new rocket technology. Will humanity use the rocket transcendentally, to go to the stars, or will people use it to destroy themselves? The answer has been taking shape since the German rocket scientists were sent east and west after World War II, and Pynchon concludes his great narrative with the split second before the ultimate cataclysm: The apocalyptic rocket plunges toward the "theatre" in which the film *Gravity's Rainbow* has unreeled before the reader. Critical opinion is split on the degree of bleakness in this ending. Figuratively, says Pynchon, the world is separated from its end only by "the last delta-t," the last infinitesimal unit of time and space between the rocket and its target. The delta-t, however, is a relative unit of measure. Modern human folly has indeed set in motion the process of his own destruction, but the process might still be arrested by a reordering of priorities, human and technological.

As for Slothrop, he simply fades away. Pynchon says he becomes "scattered," and the world reveals a characteristic aspect of Pynchon's genius. Just as Joyce forced religious and liturgical language to serve his aesthetic ends, Pynchon forces technological language to serve humanistic and spiritual ends. "Scattering," a trope from particle physics, refers to the dispersal of a beam of radiation, but it also evokes *sparagmos*, the ritual dismemberment and dispersal of the divine scapegoat. Slothrop has been associated all along with Orpheus, whose dismemberment became the basis of one of the many fertility cults in the Mediterranean and Near East. In a sense, Slothrop dies for the sins of the modern world, and his scattering coincides with the founding of the Counterforce, a group of enlightened, anarchic men and women devoted to reversing the technology of violence and death. The Counterforce, which has affinities with various countercultural movements waxing at the moment of this novel's composition, is not particularly powerful or effective, but it offers hope for a planet hurtling toward destruction.

After *Gravity's Rainbow*, Pynchon published no new fiction for seventeen years. During this period, the counterculture retreated as the forces of reaction, complacency, and materialism took over, and perhaps it was this frightening and disheartening development that was behind Pynchon's long silence. He may have abandoned a book or books that came to seem unattuned to the post-1960's *Zeitgeist*. Yet when the novelistic silence was at last broken, it was with a meditation on the historical polarization of the 1960's and the 1980's.

VINELAND

In his long-awaited fourth novel, *Vineland*, Pynchon returns to the California setting of *The Crying of Lot 49*. As in *V.*, Pynchon sets up a dual historical focus. He imagines characters in the present—the portentous year 1984—trying to come to terms with the period, twenty years earlier, when they and the whole country underwent a searing passage. Broadly, then, Pynchon here reflects on the direction the country's history has taken—from anarchic but healthy self-indulgence to neo-Puritan re-pression. These poles are visible in the People's Republic of Rock and Roll, with its ethic of freedom, pleasure, dope, music, and self-expression, and in the Nixonian and Reaganite reaction that put an end to the polymorphous perversity of the 1960's and ushered in the return to materialism and political conservatism.

The novel is structured—somewhat more loosely than is usual with Pynchon—around the quest of a girl named Prairie for the mother, Frenesi Gates, who abandoned her shortly after her birth. Prairie's father, Zoyd Wheeler, still loves Frenesi, as does the man with whom she was involved before him—the sinister Brock Vond, a federal agent who had used her to infiltrate and subvert PR[3] and other radical causes. Zoyd accepts his misery, but Vond will stop at nothing to get Frenesi back in his clutches—not even at kidnapping Prairie, who could be made into an instrument of renewed control. Also involved in the action are female Ninja Darryl Louise—DL—Chastain, an old friend of Frenesi, and DL's companion, the "karmic adjuster" Takeshi Fumimota, a kind of Zen private eye.

The centrality of Prairie, Frenesi, and DL, not to mention the narrational attention to Frenesi's mother and grandmother (Sasha Gates and Eula Traverse), make this essay Pynchon's first in feminist fiction. (Though a woman, V., was central to his first novel, it was really a parody of the kind of matriarchal vision associated with Robert Graves and the White Goddess.) It is in terms of this feminism that he is able in *Vineland* to move beyond the apocalyptic obsession that characterizes all three of his previous novels, as well as the stories "Mortality and Mercy in Vienna" and "Entropy." *Vineland* ends with a vision of familial harmony that is nothing less than mythic—an augury of what an America-wide family might be. Here the reader sees Prairie reunited with her mother and half-brother, as Zoyd and others are also integrated. Vond alone is excluded (his surname is an apocope of the Dutch word *vondeling*, a foundling—as if to hint at his inability to be integrated into family wholeness). The reunion of the Traverse-Becker clans, which seem to center in their women, is Pynchon's Vonnegut-like imagining of the millennium, the era of peace and harmony that ironically succeeds the apocalyptic disruptions everywhere expected in the novel.

Herein, too, is the meaning of Pynchon's setting, the imaginary community of Vineland that provides the novel with its title. Vineland is the name given to the American continent by the Vikings, its first European visitors, at the end of the first millennium. Pynchon's novel reminds American readers that their land has been known to history for one thousand years.

MASON AND DIXON

A more proximate past figures in *Mason and Dixon*. In this most massive of his novels, Pynchon ranges over the eighteenth century, with particular attention to the careers of Charles Mason and Jeremiah Dixon, who are sent by the Royal Society to the far corners of the earth to observe the 1761 and 1769 transits of Venus. Between these two assignments Mason and Dixon accept a commission to establish the much-contested boundary between Pennsylvania and Maryland. The central part of Pynchon's mammoth novel concerns this project, which occupies his protagonists from 1763 to 1767.

The dates are important: Mason and Dixon do their work on the very eve of the American Revolution. Pynchon looks at the America they traverse for the switching points of the great railroad called history. He sees colonial America as a place where Western civilization paused one last time before following its Faustian course toward more rationalism, greater dependence on technology, and the throwing out of spiritual babies with the bathwater of magic and superstition. The religious freedom it offered notwithstanding, America has always, Pynchon suggests, been a place of struggle between the spiritual and material energies of the West. By the latter part of the eighteenth century, with the Revolution in the offing, the secularizing tendencies of the Enlightenment (notably Deism) made America the conservator, merely, of a few "poor fragments of a Magic irreparably broken." No longer the setting of "a third Testament," the New World remained only sporadically the "object of hope that Miracles might yet occur, that God might yet return to Human affairs, that

all the wistful Fictions necessary to the childhood of a species might yet come true. . . ." Though aware that popular religion would always figure prominently in the moral economy of the emergent American nation, Pynchon suggests that some more genuine and legitimate spirituality was elbowed aside by the less-than-idealistic interests that fostered revolution (and he offers largely unflattering sketches of figures such as Founding Fathers Ben Franklin and George Washington). In the end, America became merely "one more hope in the realm of the Subjunctive, one more grasp at the last radiant whispers of the last bights of Robe-hem, billowing Æther-driven at the back of an ever-departing Deity." Pynchon seems, in *Mason and Dixon*, to reconceptualize the hallowed myth of a quest for religious freedom.

Indeed, he rewrites more than one archetypal American narrative. Thus he intimates, as in *The Crying of Lot 49*, some betrayal of the original American Dream; thus his protagonists, who twin the American Adam, must like so many of their literary predecessors decide whether to reenact the Fall. Pynchon also revisits the captivity narrative, with emphasis not on the godless savagery of the captors but on the nefarious scheming of the Europeans they serve. When American Indians kidnap Eliza Fields of Conestoga, they do so on behalf of evil Jesuits who seek to staff a bizarre convent-brothel called Las Viudas de Cristo: the Widows of Christ. Even more bizarre, perhaps, is Fields's escape with Captain Zhang, a Chinese Feng Shui master who objects to the severely rationalistic mensuration (and cartography) of the arch-Jesuit Padre Zarpazo.

Presently joining the crew of lumberjacks, roustabouts, and hangers-on accompanying Mason and Dixon, Zhang provides an important non-Western perspective on their project. "Boundaries," he declares, should "follow Nature—coast-lines, ridgetops, river-banks—so honoring the Dragon or *shan* within, from which the Land-Scape ever takes its form. To mark a right Line upon the Earth is to inflict upon the Dragon's very flesh a sword-slash, a long, perfect scar. . . ." Zhang characterizes the Visto (the unnaturally straight ten-yard-wide swath the surveyors cut through the wilderness) as a conductor of *Sha*, the "Bad Energy" that will bring in its train "Bad History." As Zhang subsequently observes, "Nothing will produce Bad History more directly or brutally, than drawing a Line, in particular a Right Line, the very Shape of Contempt, through the midst of a People—to create thus a Distinction betwixt 'em—'tis the first stroke—All else will follow as if predestin'd, unto War and Devastation." The American Civil War, half a century later, would validate Zhang's remark as prophecy.

Sir Francis Bacon, describing the Idols of the Theater, long ago recognized how received ways of knowing within a given historical period make certain kinds of thinking difficult, if not impossible. Mason, for example, aspires to membership in the Royal Society even as he desperately tries to believe that death—especially the death of his beloved wife Rebekah—is not final. Yet the scientific calling that he shares with Dixon affords little latitude for such hope. Pynchon ingeniously imagines his protagonists as imperfectly amphibious men of their age. Each struggles to reconcile a propensity for supernatural or magical thinking with professional obligations to the new, rationalist order. Whether in South Africa, on the island of St. Helena, in America, or at the North Cape, Dixon and Mason sense that they are the inconsequential pawns of forces indifferent or hostile to them. Servants of the powerful and remote Royal Society, the surveyors suffer from a paranoia somewhat different from the usual Pynchon article—or perhaps they simply show us, belatedly, the positive side of a putative psychopathology. Pynchon hints, that is, at something admirable, even redemptive, in the paranoia of his eighteenth century Rosencrantz and Guildenstern. Mason and Dixon resist the coercive intellectual forces of their age.

As brilliantly realized as that age is in these pages, Pynchon delights in anachronistic violation of his historical frame. At a number of points the reader realizes that some piece of elaborately rendered eighteenth century foolery actually mirrors a twentieth century counterpart, for Pynchon frequently circumvents historical constraint to offer droll glimpses of what America and American culture will become. Hilarious, lightly veiled allusions to Popeye, Daffy Duck, the Jolly Green Giant, and *Star Trek* abound, not to mention numerous clever periphrases of a later vernacular. There are no cheap shots here, only the occasional "inexpensive salvo." Characters do not get their backs up—they suffer "Thoracick Indignation." Those hoping to keep costs down are reminded that *prandium gratis non est* ("there's no such thing as a free lunch"). The reader smiles, too, at "teton dernier," "aviating swine," "coprophagously agrin," and (of Fenderbelly Bodine exposing his buttocks to a foe) "pygephanous."

Pynchon fills his pages with the imaginative conceits his readers have come to expect. There is, for example, a wonderful talking canine, the Learned English Dog. There is also a character who, at the full moon, turns into a were-beaver. An eighteenth century Valley Girl's every sentence features "as," rather than the "like" that would characterize the speech of her twentieth century sister. A chef with the punning name of Armand Allegre fends off the amorous attentions of a mechanical duck—part Daffy, part Frankenstein's Monster—invented by Jacques de Vaucanson. Such joking has its serious side: de Vaucanson's punch-card technology would be refined in the Jacquard loom and other automated weaving machines that played an important role in the Industrial Revolution, centerpiece of the Enlightenment. Subsequently, punch cards would play their role in the Age of Information.

In *Mason and Dixon*, then, Pynchon characterizes the eighteenth century as the moment in Western history when rationalism became a cultural juggernaut, crushing spiritual alternatives to Enlightenment thinking. As in *V.*, *Gravity's Rainbow*, and the 1984 essay "Is It O.K. to Be a Luddite?" the author focuses on the reification of Faustian appetite in scientific and technological advance, here symbolized in the profoundly unnatural Line that, arrowing its way into the mythic American West, consecrates the new world to reason—and to its abuses.

David Cowart

OTHER MAJOR WORKS

SHORT FICTION: *Slow Learner: Early Stories*, 1984.
NONFICTION: *Deadly Sins*, 1993.

BIBLIOGRAPHY

Berressem, Hanjo. *Pynchon's Poetics: Interfacing Theory and Text*. Urbana: University of Illinois Press, 1993. The most theoretically sophisticated treatment of Pynchon.

Chambers, Judith. *Thomas Pynchon*. New York: Twayne, 1992. A solid overview of Pynchon and his work, well suited to the student approaching Pynchon for the first time.

Cowart, David. *Thomas Pynchon: The Art of Allusion*. Carbondale: Southern Illinois University Press, 1980. This book contains some early biographical scourings, as well as an examination of Pynchon's use of art, cinema, music, and literature—especially as they define the pull in Pynchon between an "entropic" and a transcendental vision. Useful to beginning and advanced readers of Pynchon.

Grant, J. Kerry. *A Companion to "The Crying of Lot 49."* Athens: University of Georgia Press, 1994. Glosses allusions and major themes. Bibliographical references and index.

Green, Geoffrey, Donald J. Greiner, and Larry McCaffery, eds. *The Vineland Papers: Critical Takes on Pynchon's Novel*. Normal, Ill.: Dalkey Archive Press, 1994. First-rate essays and a *Vineland* bibliography by thirteen scholars, including N. Katherine Hayles, David Porush, Molly Hite, and Stacey Olster.

Hume, Kathryn. *Pynchon's Mythography: An Approach to "Gravity's Rainbow."* Carbondale: Southern Illinois University Press, 1987. A highly readable and important challenge to the critical argument that Pynchon, as postmodernist, relentlessly deconstructs myth.

Levine, George, and David Leverenz, eds. *Mindful Pleasures: Essays on Thomas Pynchon*. Boston: Little, Brown, 1976. Twelve important essays, by such critics as Richard Poirier, Tony Tanner, Edward Mendelson, and the editors themselves. Mathew Winston's biographical essay is especially useful for genealogical information.

McHoul, Alec, and David Wills. *Writing Pynchon: Strategies in Fictional Analysis*. Urbana: University of Illinois Press, 1990. An intriguing if not altogether successful reversal of the usual critical approach: The authors use Pynchon's writings as the theory by which to read Derrida.

Mendelson, Edward. *Pynchon: A Collection of Critical Essays*. Englewood Cliffs, N.J.: Prentice-Hall, 1978. Part of the reliable Twentieth-Century Views series, this collection contains fourteen essays and reviews, by such important critics as Tony Tanner, Frank Kermode, Richard Poirier, Paul Fussell, and Mendelson himself.

Newman, Robert D. *Understanding Thomas Pynchon*. Columbia: University of South Carolina Press, 1986. From a series aimed at readers seeking basic introductions, this book is a good starting place for the beginner.

Schaub, Thomas. *Pynchon: The Voice of Ambiguity*. Urbana: University of Illinois Press, 1981. A reliable account of how entropy and uncertainty figure in Pynchon. Includes discussion of Marshall McLuhan's influence on *The Crying of Lot 49* and the ironies attendant on Ivan Pavlov's role in *Gravity's Rainbow*. Places Pynchon in American literary tradition.

Slade, Joseph. *Thomas Pynchon*. New York: P. Lang, 1990. The first book on Pynchon (it originally appeared in 1974) and still one of the best, despite nearly thirty volumes of competition. A balanced and readable discussion, but especially strong on Pynchon's uses of science. Lack of an index reduces usefulness to the browser.

Tanner, Tony. *Thomas Pynchon*. London: Methuen, 1982. Tanner is one of Pynchon's most incisive—and earliest—critics. A short and readable introduction.

Weisenburger, Steven. *A "Gravity's Rainbow" Companion: Sources and Contexts for Pynchon's Novel*. Athens: University of Georgia Press, 1988. A superb and indispensable *vade mecum*.

R

FRANÇOIS RABELAIS

Born: La Devinière, near Chinon, France; c. 1494
Died: Paris, France; April, 1553

PRINCIPAL LONG FICTION

Pantagruel, 1532 (English translation, 1653)
Gargantua, 1534 (English translation, 1653)
Tiers Livre, 1546 (*Third Book*, 1693)
Le Quart Livre, incomplete 1548, complete 1552
    (*Fourth Book*, 1694)
Le Cinquième Livre, 1564 (*Fifth Book*, 1694)
Gargantua et Pantagruel (collective title for all of
    the above; *Gargantua and Pantagruel*, 1653-
    1694, 1929)

OTHER LITERARY FORMS

In preparation for his doctoral degree, François
Rabelais composed commentaries on the *Aphorisms*
of Hippocrates and the *Ars medicinalis* of Galen, in
editions of these works which Rabelais published in
1532. After his first trip to Rome, he edited a *Topographia antiquae Romae*, based on a work by Bar-
tolome Marliani, which was published by Sébastien
Gryphe in 1534. *La Sciomachie et festins* (simulated
combats and feasts), published in Lyons by Gryphe
in 1549, also refers to Rabelais's journeys. It is also
known that Rabelais composed poetry. Many of his
letters, especially letters from Rome, are available in
various editions.

ACHIEVEMENTS

With Rabelais, French literature entered into a
new phase. After the great medieval epics and romances of the twelfth and thirteenth centuries, there
had been a steady decline until the sixteenth century.
In France, the new learning brought about by the rediscovery of ancient Greek manuscripts, the invention of printing, and the great voyages of discovery
found its first expression in Rabelais. *Gargantua and
Pantagruel* breathes the spirit of enthusiasm, liberation, and discovery that inspired the rebirth of culture
and learning.

Nevertheless, there is in Rabelais much of the medieval. In fact, he chose as his inspiration a book popular at the time, *Grandes et inestimables cronicques
du grant et énorme géant Gargantua* (1532; great and
inestimable chronicles of the great and enormous giant Gargantua), based on the story of a giant associated with Merlin, Arthur, Morgan, and Mélusine.
Rabelais proposed a sequel in which he continued the
popular comic of the *cronicques*. He enriched his legend with notes on history, geography, local custom,
and theater; his is a Renaissance interpretation of a
medieval carnival.

The critic Jean Plattard notes that Rabelais maintained the medieval spirit of the farces and fabliaux
in his violent imagery, his vulgarity, and his preoccupation with sexual matters. At the same time, Rabe-

(Library of Congress)

lais introduced the spirit of the Renaissance with his rejection of Scholasticism, his confidence in antiquity, his faith in science, and his belief in human progress.

Rabelais did not write a novel in the modern sense of the word, nor did he intend to compose one. As Boulenger observes, Rabelais wanted to embroider a vast canvas both with fantasies and with scenes from real life; in his encyclopedic ambition, he was typical of the Renaissance. Rabelais's achievement lies above all in his style, in a remarkable exploitation of all the possibilities of language. His giants are polyglots, and so is their creator. He uses French and Latin with ease; he creates words in torrents. He is equally adept in dialect, patois, argot, and scientific terminology. Boulenger describes Rabelais's styles as "verbal intoxication in the dionysiac sense," yet when the occasion demands, as in the description of Badebec's death, Rabelais is a master of economy. The first French prose writer with genuine artistic talent and one of the greatest examples of the *esprit gaulois* found in the *Roman de Renart* (c. 1175-1205), the fabliaux, Molière, and Voltaire, Rabelais was truly a turning point in French literature.

BIOGRAPHY

Much of François Rabelais's biography is lost in obscurity, but modern scholars have established the principal events of his life. The date of Rabelais's birth, 1494, is still uncertain, but it is known that his father, Antoine, was a lawyer at the royal court of Chinon and was associated with the most enlightened men of his day. Rabelais spent his childhood at Chinon, especially at the family's country home, La Devinière, often mentioned in his works, and at Angers, his mother's birthplace. He was probably educated at the Benedictine abbey of Seuillé, evoked in Friar John's monastery in *Gargantua and Pantagruel.*

By 1521, Rabelais was a Franciscan monk at Fontenay-le-Comte in Bas Poitou; it was there that he met Pierre Amy, one of the outstanding Hellenists of the time, and entered into correspondence with the eminent French Hellenist Guillaume Budé. Rabelais translated some of Herodotus from Greek into Latin, and also contributed to André Tiraqueau's treatise on the laws of marriage, "De legibus connubialibus," echoes of which appear in book 3.

In 1523, the Greek books of the monastery were confiscated under orders from the Sorbonne, and shortly afterward Rabelais transferred to the Benedictines of Saint-Pierre-de-Maillezain, where he came into contact with the scholarly bishop Geoffroy d'Estissac. In 1527, Rabelais left the monastery and toured the same universities his Pantagruel visits in book 2. In 1532, he received his bachelor's degree in medicine from the University of Montpellier and assumed a post in Lyons, at that time the capital of the Renaissance. He also continued his classical commentaries and the same year published *Pantagruel,* censured by the Sorbonne for obscenity. Jean du Bellay, bishop of Paris, became Rabelais's protector in 1534, taking him to Rome as his personal physician. It was upon Rabelais's return that he published *Gargantua,* likewise censured because of its unfortunate coincidence with the Affair of the Placards.

Rabelais attempted briefly the life of a secular priest; by 1537, he was a doctor of medicine in Lyons. In 1541, he published a new edition of *Gargantua and Pantagruel,* with the attacks against the Sorbonne expurgated. The publication of book 3 in 1546 still provoked censure, as did that of the complete book 4 in 1552. His later days included more travel in Italy, especially with du Bellay. It is fairly certain that Rabelais died in Paris, at the beginning of April, 1553.

ANALYSIS

François Rabelais is universally regarded as one of the major figures in the Western literary tradition, in the company of Dante, Geoffrey Chaucer, William Shakespeare, and Miguel de Cervantes, yet he is more often praised than read. Indeed, in the judgment of the Soviet scholar Mikhail Bakhtin, "Of all the great writers of world literature, Rabelais is the least popular, the least understood and appreciated."

The difficulty of Rabelais, the quality that discourages many modern readers from making headway in his work, is not the strategic obscurity of a James Joyce or an Ezra Pound; rather, it resembles the difficulty that one experiences in "getting" a joke, the humor of which is not immediately apparent. To read Rabelais is essentially to laugh, but humor is notoriously elusive, dependent on a wide range of local cultural assumptions and linguistic practices and thus quick to be lost in time and in translation. Here, there is a comparison with Shakespeare: One vein of Shakespearean humor, closely related to the humor of Rabelais, is accessible to the modern reader only via scholarly explication of wordplay, allusions, implicit cultural assumptions, and so on, but Shakespeare remains highly readable even when many of his bawdy puns, for example, are entirely missed.

The difficulty in grasping the spirit of Rabelais's jokes, their underlying intent, is confirmed by ongoing critical debate. Even such a fundamental issue as Rabelais's attitude toward Christianity and the Church has been the subject of bitter controversy. Throughout *Gargantua and Pantagruel* there are frequent satiric jabs at the rites and institutions of the Church. While Rabelais ridicules monasticism and the Papacy, however, and while his parodies of Christian ritual could be deemed sacrilegious if not blasphemous, he stops short of the open atheism of the Enlightenment.

Critics such as Lefranc have argued that Rabelais was in fact a thoroughgoing rationalist who, unable to express his convictions openly, presented them in a humorous guise. According to such critics, Rabelais thus anticipated the skepticism of the Enlightenment. On the other hand, critics such as Lucien Febvre, who devoted a massive volume to a refutation of Lefranc, argue that Rabelais's satire was directed against institutional abuses of the Church, not against the heart of Christian belief.

Although such questions may never be definitively resolved, one helpful approach to Rabelais's humor is that of Bakhtin in *Rabelais and His World* (1968). Bakhtin places Rabelais in what he calls the carnival tradition, a tradition of folk humor with roots in the ancient past, encompassing such festivities as the Roman Saturnalia and still vital in the Middle Ages: "Celebrations of a carnival type represented a considerable part of the life of medieval men, even in the time given to them. Large medieval cities devoted an average of three months a year to these festivities."

Bakhtin suggests that it is Rabelais's indebtedness to this folk tradition, an expression of popular culture still largely unexplored by literary scholars, that accounts for the relative failure of modern readers to appreciate his work. In the carnival atmosphere, all of the sacred values of medieval society were travestied in a ritualistic manner—often with the full participation of the clergy. Thus, Rabelais's humor is characterized by the systematic inversion typical of carnival: parody, blasphemy, gross physical images, and so on.

By placing *Gargantua and Pantagruel* in this context, Bakhtin shifts the emphasis from an interpretation of Rabelais's values—that is, the personal beliefs informing his work—to the folk tradition of which his work was the supreme expression even as it marked the decisive break between the Renaissance and the Middle Ages.

GARGANTUA AND PANTAGRUEL

Rabelais's Renaissance spirit is nowhere more apparent than in his style, an overflowing fountain of verbal exuberance, a rich compound of slang, odd words, jargon of the various professions, interminable lists, and other heterogeneous elements. *Gargantua and Pantagruel* is full of puns difficult to translate: *service du vin/service divin* (the wine service/the divine service); Grandgousier's name, from *Que grand tu as (gosier)* (What a big gullet you have); or Epistemon, who has *la coupe têtée* (his chop headed off).

This exuberance is also evident in Rabelais's characterizations. Although he created types rather than flesh-and-blood people, his characters are unforgettable. Grandgousier, the progenitor of the illustrious family of giants, is the most shadowy. He appears as the noble lord, just and forgiving after the Picrocholine Wars and a good father to Gargantua. His son is curious, witty, garrulous, and loving. After the beginning of book 2, Grandgousier appears rarely, but always with concern for his son. Pantagruel, Gargantua's son, is the real hero of the story. After a well-delineated education, he becomes a kind lord, and his earlier wit changes to wisdom. Perhaps the best-portrayed characters are Friar John and Panurge. Friar John is the garrulous monk who always has something of the cloister about him; kind, generous, and witty, he enlivens all the adventures from the Picrocholine Wars to the voyage for the Divine Bottle. Panurge, the perpetual trickster and inventor of farces, changes his character in book 3 to that of a man caught in a dilemma: to marry or not to marry? To choose action or inaction? There are few female characters in *Gargantua and Pantagruel*; they are limited to Gargamelle, Grandgousier's wife, and Badebec, Gargantua's wife, who dies as she is giving birth to Pantagruel. Basically, the story is a very masculine one; as in the medieval farces, women are little more than bearers of children and objects of sexual desire.

GARGANTUA

Although published two years after *Pantagruel*, in 1534, *Gargantua* is known as book 1 because of its chronology. Gargantua is the father of Pantagruel, and the book tells of his miraculous birth, adolescence, education, and maturity. The prologue describes a *silenus*, a little box for rare drugs, which Rabelais compares to Socrates, and indeed to his own work: ugly from the outside but precious on the inside.

After Rabelais has made a Genesis-like presentation of Gargantua's genealogy, birth, and naming, the reader learns his first words: *à boire* (drink), symbolic of the thirst of the Renaissance man for the new learning. Much of book 1 is concerned with education; the critic Thomas M. Greene considers its essential theme to be the process of development in the young giant as he progresses from the "random equality of childhood experience . . . to poise and sophistication without losing his capacity for naïve joy." First educated in a haphazard manner by the Sophists, he is purged by Ponocrates and learns more by ear than by eye to integrate all activities— physical, mental, and spiritual—and grow from chaos to discipline and from ignorance to truth and justice.

A lengthy episode treats the wars between Picrochole, King of Lerné, and Grandgousier, Gargantua's father, a noble and peace-loving lord. Lefranc sees historical and biographical material in this unjust war, as it takes place around La Roche-Clamard, near

Seuillé, in Rabelais's native Chinon. As the war progresses, Friar John of the Funnels, the vibrant and impetuous monk, becomes Grandgousier's staunch ally. In the words and actions of Friar John, one finds some of Rabelais's finest satire of the monastic life he knew so well.

In recompense for his help in the war won by Grandgousier, Friar John receives the Abbey of Thélème, Rabelais's ideal for an elite community. This semiutopian monastery, modeled on the château of Bonnivet, admits both men and women of outstanding physical and moral traits, inviting them to spend their time in pursuit of culture and eventually to leave and marry. It is governed by only one rule: "Fay ce que voudras" (do what you wish). An enigmatic inscription in poetry concludes the book and invites the reader to continue the search for truth in the Renaissance spirit.

PANTAGRUEL

Book 2, *Pantagruel*, is the least coherent of the first four volumes. It reveals the author's unmistakable style and wit and gives promise of more adventures in the future. As in *Gargantua*, Rabelais traces the genealogy of Pantagruel in a burlesque parody of the Bible and Pliny the Elder's *Natural History* (77 C.E.), as he emphasizes his hero's gigantic appetite and prodigious strength. Because Pantagruel will later liberate himself and others from the bonds of ignorance, he frees himself as a child from the constraint of his cradle.

Education plays an important role here also, especially in chapter 8, in which Gargantua tells his son Pantagruel to become "an abyss of knowledge." Pantagruel also tours the famous universities of his day: Toulouse, a center of dance and fencing; Montepellier, noted for its wine; Avignon, for its women; Bourges, for its poor laws; and Angers, which he avoids because it is infested with the plague. He visits libraries, which Rabelais uses to satirize many spiritual texts and the immoral lives of those who read them.

In book 2, Pantagruel meets Panurge, who is to become his friend for life. Panurge is one of a long line of picaros; he introduces himself in many languages, a performance typical of his pranks, which, as Greene observes, "mingle in various measures humor, cunning, perversity, creative inspiration and malice." Rabelais describes Panurge as proper-looking, a bit of a lecher, always short of money (which he always finds by cunningly perpetrated larceny), and a perpetual trickster. His clever and often crude tricks form much of the wit of books 2 and 4.

In the courtly tradition, Panurge and Pantagruel go off to battle in Utopia, where Gargantua has been transferred by the fairy Morgue. Rabelais seems to return to the spirit of the *cronicques* as he ends his disjointed but highly original portrayal of the giants.

In contrast to the looseness of book 2, book 3 is the most unified of the entire series. In the prologue, Rabelais compares himself to Diogenes, who, though physically unfit for war, rolled his tub so as not to appear lazy. In the first six chapters, Panurge appears as the traditional spendthrift; having inherited an estate, he rapidly squanders his inheritance on feasting. In the remainder of the book, he engages in lengthy discussions on whether to marry. Many critics trace Rabelais's treatment of marriage and cuckoldry in book 3 to the medieval farces; others, such as Greene, see the search for truth and the importance of action as forming the real subject of the book.

Panurge consults various sources to resolve his dilemma: the *sortes vergilianae* (a book of Vergil opened at random), a fortune-teller, the poet Raminagrobis, the magician Herr Trippa. All give him the same response: If he marries, he will be cuckolded, beaten, and robbed. The theologian Hippothadée encourages him to choose someone like Solomon's "valiant woman"; the doctor Rondibilis tells him of woman's foibles; the philosopher Trouillogan has no definite answer. After a final consultation with the fool Triboulet, no more satisfactory than all the others, Pantagruel convinces Panurge to consult the Oracle of the Divine Bottle in Cathay. Thus, the stage is set for the adventures which occupy books 4 and 5.

In book 4, inspired by the accounts of navigation so prominent at the time, especially those of Jacques Cartier, Rabelais composed the travelogue or odyssey of his heroes—a fantastic account of imaginary places and allegorical people, filled with the marvelous and touching upon science fiction, such as the frozen words that melt and begin to speak. There are many realistic allusions to Rabelais's own day, such as the Decretals, the base of canonical jurisprudence; the officers of law and justice, portrayed in the Chicanous; and the wars between Protestants and Catholics, symbolized by the battle with the Andouilles.

Rabelais also satirizes perennial vices such as gluttony and its opposite, a sterile asceticism based on pride rather than on genuine piety. Panurge reassumes the character of the trickster and in a famous episode drowns the sheep of the avaricious merchant Dindenault. The travelers have not reached the Divine Bottle by the end of book 4, but Rabelais's imagination and invention are here at their height.

Originally published posthumously as *L'Isle sonante* in 1562, book 5 differs so radically from the preceding ones that critics today still question its authenticity; it is bitter, rambling, and far less creative than its predecessors. In it, the story of the navigation continues through many more fantastic islands.

The Isle Sonante (ringing island), with its perpetually clanging bells, is inhabited by birds that resemble men and women and whose names refer to the clergy and members of religious orders. The Chatsfourrés (furry cats) are the officers of the Parlement of Paris, who refused Michel de l'Hospital's proposal for an edict of toleration for the Protestants. The Apedeftes, or ignoramuses, are the tax collectors and clerks in the counting houses.

After many other such adventures, the travelers finally reach the Divine Bottle and admire the magnificent temple in which it is located. The priestess Bacbuc invites Panurge to hear the long-awaited pronouncement, which consists of one word: "Drink." The priestess has another word of wisdom: *in vino veritas* (in wine is truth). The enigmatic conclusion has as many interpretations as there are critics, for essentially it tells the reader to interpret his destiny for himself.

Irma M. Kashuba

OTHER MAJOR WORKS

NONFICTION: *La Sciomachie et festins*, 1549.

EDITED TEXTS: *Aphorisms*, 1532; *Ars medicinalis*, 1532; *Topographia antiquae Romae*, 1534.

MISCELLANEOUS: *Pantagruéline Prognostication*, 1532 (occasional verses and letters).

BIBLIOGRAPHY

Bakhtin, Mikhail. *Rabelais and His World*. Cambridge, Mass.: The M.I.T. Press, 1965. Recommended only for advanced students, this is a profound but difficult study by a renowned scholar and critic.

Bowen, Barbara C. *The Age of Bluff: Paradox and Ambiguity in Rabelais and Montaigne*. Urbana: University of Illinois Press, 1972. Concentrates on Rabelais's use of paradox, ambiguity, and shock.

_____. *Enter Rabelais, Laughing*. Nashville: Vanderbilt University Press, 1998. Each chapter is a different study of laughter: "literary," "humanist," the "comic lawyer," the "comic doctor." Includes notes and bibliography.

Carron, Jean-Claude, ed. *François Rabelais: Critical Assessments*. Baltimore: Johns Hopkins University Press, 1995. A selection and revision of papers delivered at a 1991 symposium at the University of California, Los Angeles.

Chesney, Elizabeth A., and Marcel Tetel. *Rabelais Revisited*. New York: Twayne, 1993. A good introduction to the novels, with an annotated bibliography of important studies on Rabelais. Examines relationships between men and women in the works.

Coleman, Dorothy Gabe. *Rabelais: A Critical Study in Prose Fiction*. Cambridge, England: Cambridge University Press, 1971. A meticulous analysis of Rabelais as a prose stylist and of the genres in which he wrote.

Frame, Donald M. *Francois Rabelais: A Study*. New York: Harcourt Brace Jovanovich, 1977. A detailed study of Rabelais's life and work, including several chapters on his major fiction and on topics such as obscenity, comedy, satire, fantasy, storytelling, giantism, humanism, evangelism, characters, fortunes. Includes detailed notes and annotated bibliography.

Greene, Thomas M. *Rabelais: A Study in Comic Courage*. Englewood Cliffs, N.J., 1970. Often cited as the best introductory study to Rabelais.

Keller, Abraham. *The Telling of Tales in Rabelais: Aspects of His Narrative Art*. Frankfurt am Main: Klosterman, 1963. A probing study that raises interesting and important critical questions. Keller provides articulate and persuasive analyses.

ANN RADCLIFFE

Born: London, England; July 9, 1764
Died: London, England; February 7, 1823

PRINCIPAL LONG FICTION

The Castles of Athlin and Dunbayne, 1789
A Sicilian Romance, 1790
The Romance of the Forest, 1791
The Mysteries of Udolpho, 1794
The Italian: Or, The Confessional of the Black Penitents, 1797
Gaston de Blondeville, 1826

OTHER LITERARY FORMS

In addition to her novels, Ann Radcliffe published *A Journey Made in the Summer of 1794 Through Holland and the Western Frontier of Germany* (1795). It recounts a continental journey made with her husband and includes copious observations of other tours to the English Lake District. The work became immediately popular, prompting a second edition that same year retitled *The Journeys of Mrs. Radcliffe*. Following a common practice of romance writers, Radcliffe interspersed the lengthy prose passages of her novels with her own verses or with those from famous poets. An anonymous compiler took the liberty of collecting and publishing her verses in an unauthorized edition entitled *The Poems of Ann Radcliffe* (1816). This slim volume was reissued in 1834 and 1845. Radcliffe's interest in versifying was increasingly evident when her husband, in arranging for the posthumous publication of *Gaston de Blondeville*, included with it a long metrical romance, *St. Alban's Abbey* (1826). Radcliffe also wrote an essay, "On the Supernatural in Poetry," which was published in *The New Monthly Magazine* (1826). The record of her literary achievement still remains available, as all of her novels and the poems are in print.

ACHIEVEMENTS

Mrs. Radcliffe's fame as a novelist today in no way compares to the popularity she enjoyed in the 1790's. With the publication of her third novel, *The Romance of the Forest*, this relatively unknown woman established herself as the best-selling writer of the period, receiving rave reviews from the critics and increasing demand for her works from circulating libraries.

Radcliffe's five gothic romances, published between 1789 and 1797, owed a portion of their motivation to Horace Walpole's *The Castle of Otranto* (1765) and two earlier gothic writers, Sophia Lee and Clara Reeve. The gothic tale reached its full development with Radcliffe's ability to manipulate the emotions of love and fear in such a manner as to provoke terror in her characters and readers alike. Though managing an effective use of the little understood complexities of the imagination, she offered her readers stereotyped plots, characters, and settings. Her disguises of foreign characters and lands were as thin as the supernatural illusions which often seemed anticlimactic in their emotional appeal. These weaknesses did not deter Radcliffe's public, who remained fascinated by her distinctive brand of romanticism, which combined the gloomy darkening vale of the more somber poets of the graveyard school, the extremes of imaginative sensibility (as in Henry Mackenzie's *The Man of Feeling*, 1771), and the medieval extravagance of the Ossianic poems of James Macpherson, as well as the pseudoarchaic fabrications of Thomas Chatterton's Rowley poems (1777).

Radcliffe nurtured this cult of melancholy, primitivism, sentimentalism, exoticism, and medievalism in her novels, becoming the epitome of the gothic genre to her contemporaries. *The Mysteries of Udolpho*, her best-known work, was satirized by Jane Austen in *Northanger Abbey* (1818) as representative of the entire mode. Her later importance was seen in a number of major Romantic writers who read her

romances in their childhood. Percy Bysshe Shelley's *Zastrozzi* (1810), an extravagant romance, was a youthful answer to the genre. Lord Byron's *Manfred* (1817) appears as a gothic villain committing spiritual murder in a landscape of "sublime solitudes." Matthew G. Lewis and Mary Wollstonecraft Shelley clearly benefited from Radcliffe's strengths as a novelist of suspense, mystery, and the picturesque. In America, Washington Irving's, Edgar Allan Poe's, and Nathaniel Hawthorne's tales of terror, along with Charles Brockden Brown's *Edgar Huntley* (1799), were suggested by Radcliffe's work.

As the most popular and perhaps most important novelist between the eighteenth century masters and Austen and Sir Walter Scott, Radcliffe continues to claim the attention of academicians. Psychological, feminist, folklorist, and the more traditional thematic studies have proved the strengths of her art. In 1980, Devendra P. Varma (*The Gothic Flame*, 1957) began serving as advisory editor for the Arno Press collection, *Gothic Studies and Dissertations*, which has published at least thirty-four texts dealing with Radcliffe's literary output; of those, fifteen discuss Radcliffe's novels at length. It is clear that there is at present a remarkable revival of interest in the gothic and in Radcliffe's work.

BIOGRAPHY

Mrs. Ann Radcliffe, *née* Ward, was born on July 9, 1764, in Holborn, a borough of central London, the only child of William Ward and Ann Oates Ward. Her father was a successful haberdasher who provided the family with a comfortable life, allowing Radcliffe access to a well-stocked library and the time to read the works of every important English author, as well as numerous popular romances.

This quiet, sheltered existence was enlivened by the visits of her wealthy and learned uncle, Thomas Bentley, who was the partner of Josiah Wedgwood, the potter. Bentley's London home was a center for the literati; there, among others, the pretty but shy girl met Mrs. Hester L. Thrale Piozzi, the friend and biographer of Samuel Johnson; Mrs. Elizabeth Montagu, "Queen of the Blue-Stocking Club"; and "Athenian" Stuart.

In 1772, Radcliffe joined her parents at Bath, where her father had opened a shop for the firm of Wedgwood and Bentley. She remained sequestered in this resort until her marriage to the young Oxford graduate, William Radcliffe, in 1788. William Radcliffe had first decided to become a law student at one of the Inns of Court but abandoned this for a career in journalism. The couple moved to London soon thereafter, where William subsequently became proprietor and editor of the *English Chronicle*. The marriage was happy but childless, and the couple's circle of friends were primarily literary, which added encouragement to William Radcliffe's argument that his wife should begin to write.

With her husband away on editorial business, Radcliffe spent the evenings writing without interruption. Her first book, *The Castles of Athlin and Dunbayne*, was unremarkable, but her next two novels established her reputation as a master of suspense and the supernatural. *A Sicilian Romance* and *The Romance of the Forest* attracted the public's voracious appetite for romances. Both works were translated into French and Italian, and numerous editions were published, as well as a dramatization of *The Romance of the Forest*, performed in 1794. Radcliffe's success culminated in the appearance of *The Mysteries of Udolpho*; her decision to rely less on external action and more on psychological conflict produced ecstatic reviews. The excitement created by the book threatened the relative solitude of the Radcliffes, but the publisher's unusually high offer of five hundred pounds freed them to travel extensively on the Continent.

In the summer of 1794, the Radcliffes journeyed through Holland and along the Rhine to the Swiss frontier. On returning to England, they proceeded north to the Lake District. While traveling, Radcliffe took complete notes concerning the picturesque landscape and included detailed political and economic accounts of the Low Countries and the Rhineland. These latter observations were probably contributed by her husband, though both Radcliffes found the devastation of the Napoleonic Wars appalling. In 1795, *A Journey Made in the Summer of 1794 Through Holland and the Western Frontier of Germany* appeared.

Radcliffe's interest in the human misery of these regions and the legends and superstitions of the great fortresses and Catholic churches of the Rhineland suggested her next work, *The Italian: Or, The Confessional of the Black Penitents*. As a romance of the Inquisition, it explored character motivation in great detail, while action became a method of dramatizing personalities and not a simple vehicle for movement from one adventure to another. *The Italian*, though not as popular as *The Mysteries of Udolpho*, was translated immediately into French and even badly dramatized at the Haymarket on August 15, 1797.

At the age of thirty-three, Radcliffe was at the height of her popularity; though she had never decided on writing as a potential source of income, her means by this time had become quite ample. With the deaths of her parents between 1798 and 1799, she found herself independently wealthy. Whether it was because of her secure financial condition or her displeasure with the cheap imitations of her novels, Radcliffe withdrew from the public domain and refrained from publishing any more works in her lifetime. Innumerable reports surfaced that she was suffering from a terminal illness, that the terrors of which she had written in her novels had driven her mad, or that she had mysteriously died. These reports were without substance; in fact, she wrote another novel, a metrical romance, and an extensive diary.

After her death, Radcliffe's husband found among her papers a novel, *Gaston de Blondeville*, which he arranged to have published. Written after Radcliffe's visit to the ruins of Kenilworth Castle in 1802, it came near to comparing with the historical romances of Scott but lost itself in a preoccupation with historical precision, leaving action and character to suffer from a lack of emphasis. The narrative poem, *St. Alban's Abbey*, appeared posthumously with this last novel; though Radcliffe had been offered an early opportunity for publication, she broke off negotiations with the publisher.

Content with retirement and relative obscurity, she wrote in her last years only diary entries concerning the places she and her husband had visited on their long journeys through the English countryside. From 1813 to 1816, she lived near Windsor and probably at this time began suffering from bouts of asthma. From all reports, she enjoyed the company of friends, maintained a ready wit and a sly humor, but insisted on delicacy and decorum in all things. Shortly before her final illness, she returned to London; she died there on February 7, 1823, in her sixtieth year. The "Udolpho woman" or "the Shakespeare of Romance Writers," as one contemporary reviewer called her, has achieved a secure place in the history of English literature.

ANALYSIS

The novels of Ann Radcliffe serve as a transition between the major English novelists of the eighteenth century and the first accomplished novelists of the nineteenth century. In the years between 1789 and 1797, her five novels established a style which profoundly affected English fiction for the next twenty-five years and had a considerable impact in translation as well. From the negligible first novel, *The Castles of Athlin and Dunbayne*, to the sophisticated romances, *The Mysteries of Udolpho* and *The Italian*, Mrs. Radcliffe demonstrated an ability to enrich the motives, methods, and machineries of each succeeding work. Manipulating the conventions of the gothic while introducing new thematic concerns and experiments with narrative techniques, Radcliffe became a master of her craft.

Improved control over the complex atmosphere of the gothic romance proved an early factor in her success. Radcliffe went beyond the traditional gothic devices of lurking ghosts and malevolent noblemen torturing innocent girls to an interest in natural description. This delight with nature's sublime scenery gave tone and color to her settings while emphasizing the heightened emotions and imagination that were produced in reaction to the landscape. A skillful use of numerous atmospheric factors such as sunsets, storms, winds, thunderclaps, and moonlight, intensified the romantic tendencies of her time.

A scene typifying the Radcliffe concept of landscape portraiture has a ruined castle in silhouette, arranged on a stern but majestic plain at nightfall. This view does not depend on precision of outline for effect but instead on an ominous vagueness, creating in the reader a queer mixture of pleasure and fear. Her delight in the architecture of massive proportions and in the picturesque derived in part from her reading of the nature poets and her study of the paintings of Claude Lorrain, Nicolas Poussin, and Salvator Rosa. She reflected a mid-eighteenth century English passion in cultivating an acute sensibility for discovering beauty where before it had not been perceived. While she made landscape in fiction a convention, it was her combining of beauty in horror and the horrible in the beautiful that reflected the Romantic shift away from order and reason toward emotion and imagination.

Radcliffe's novels rely not only on strategies of terror, but also on the psychology of feelings. The novels of sensibility of the past generation offered her alternatives to the gothic trappings made familiar in Horace Walpole's *The Castle of Otranto*; those gothic aspects now became linked to various emotional elements in a total effect. By drawing on the poetry of Thomas Gray and Edward Young or the fiction of Oliver Goldsmith and Henry Mackenzie, Radcliffe created a minority of characters with complex natures who not only exhibited melancholy and doubt, love and joy, but also hate and evil intentions. She was one of the first English novelists to subject her characters to psychological analysis.

Of particular psychological interest are Radcliffe's villains. Cruel, calculating, domineering, relentless, and selfish, they are more compelling than her virtuous characters. Since their passions are alien to the ordinary person, she dramatically explores the mysteries of their sinister attitudes. Radcliffe's villains resemble those created by the Elizabethan dramatists, and their descendants can be found in the works of the great Romantics, Byron and Shelley.

At her best, Radcliffe manifested strengths not seen in her first two novels nor in her last. Her first novel, *The Castles of Athlin and Dunbayne*, exhibits the most obvious borrowings, from sources as well known as *The Castle of Otranto* to numerous other gothic-historical and sentimental novels. Though immature, the work offers her characteristic sense of atmosphere with the marvelous dangers and mysteries of feudal Scotland depicted to full advantage. Its weaknesses become evident all too soon, however, as stock characters populate strained, often confused incidents while mouthing rather obvious parables about morality. Didacticism seems the motivating principle of the work; as David Durant observes in *Ann Radcliffe's Novels* (1980), "The characters are so controlled by didactic interests as to be faceless and without personality." The rigid obligations of *The Castles of Athlin and Dunbayne* to the morality of sentimental novels, the uniformity of a neoclassical prose style, and the repetitious, predictable action of the romance plot, trap Radcliffe into a mechanical performance.

A SICILIAN ROMANCE

Mrs. Radcliffe's second novel, *A Sicilian Romance*, has a new strategy, an emphasis on action and adventure while subordinating moral concerns. This approach, however, was not effective because of the obvious imbalance between the two methods, and characterization suffered before a mass of incident. The interest in fear was expanded throughout the tale as a long-suffering wife, imprisoned in the remote sections of a huge castle by a villainous nobleman (who has an attachment to a beautiful paramour), struggles helplessly until rescued, after much suspense, by her gentle daughter and the young girl's lover. The characters' shallowness is hidden by a chase sequence of overwhelming speed which prevents one from noticing their deficiencies. To dramatize the movement of plot, Radcliffe introduced numerous settings, offering the reader a complete vision of the Romantic landscape.

Though *A Sicilian Romance* lacks the sureness of technique of the later novels and remains a lesser product, it did establish Radcliffe's ingenuity and perseverance. It was followed by the three novels on which her reputation rests: *The Romance of the Forest*, *The Mysteries of Udolpho*, and *The Italian*. Radcliffe's last novel, the posthumous *Gaston de Blondeville*, which was probably never meant for publication, exhibits the worst faults of the two earliest romances. Lifeless characters abound in a narrative overloaded with tedious historical facts and devoid of any action. In reconstructing history, Radcliffe was influenced by Sir Walter Scott but clearly was out of her element in attempting to make history conform to her own preconceptions. The primary innovation was the in-

troduction of a real ghost to the love story. This specter, the apparition of a murdered knight demanding justice, stalks the grounds of Kenilworth Castle at the time of the reign of Henry III. Radcliffe detracts from this imposing supernatural figure when she resorts to explanations of incidents better left mysterious.

THE ROMANCE OF THE FOREST

With the publication of her third novel, *The Romance of the Forest*, Mrs. Radcliffe moved from apprenticeship to mastery. Her technique had advanced in at least two important elements: The chase with its multitude of settings is scaled down to an exacting series of dramas set among a few extended scenes, and characterization of the heroine is improved with the reduction of external action. Though suspense is extended rather illegitimately in order to produce a glorious final surprise, the novel is a genuine exploration of the realm of the unconscious. This remarkable advance into modern psychology gave life to the standard situations of Radcliffe's stories, allowing the reader to create his own private horrors.

Radcliffe's new emphasis on internal action makes her protagonist, Adeline, more credible than the stock romantic heroines whom she in many ways resembles. Adeline suffers from a nervous illness after mysteriously being thrust upon the LaMotte family, who themselves have only recently escaped, under curious circumstances, from Paris. Soon the group discovers a Gothic ruin, which contains the requisite underground room, rotten tapestries, blood stains, and a general aura of mystery.

Instead of the familiar chase scenes, a series of unified set-pieces portray the exploration of the ruin, the seduction of the heroine, and the execution of the hero. The entire plot depends upon the actions of a vicious but dominating sadist, the Marquis Phillipe de Montalt, and his conspiratorial agent, Pierre de LaMotte, against the unprotected Adeline. Because of the uncertainty of her birth, the sexual implications of this situation involve the risk of incest. Among contemporary readers, *The Romance of the Forest* became an immediate success, owing to its well-constructed narrative, the charm of its description of Romantic landscape, and a consummate handling of the principle of suspense.

THE MYSTERIES OF UDOLPHO

Mrs. Radcliffe's next novel, *The Mysteries of Udolpho*, remains her best-known work. The sublimity of her landscapes and the control which she demonstrates in this novel mark an important change from her earlier novels; Radcliffe's handling of action and character also reached new levels of subtlety and success, moving the novel a step beyond the rather strict conventions of the sentimental mode to one of psychological inquiry.

The period of the novel is the end of the sixteenth century. The principal scenes are laid in the gloomy enclave of the Castle of Udolpho, in the Italian Apennines, but many glances are directed toward the south of France—Gascony, Provence, and Languedoc—and the brightness of Venice is contrasted with the dark horrors of the Apennines. Emily St. Aubert, the beautiful daughter of a Gascon family, is the heroine; she is intelligent and extraordinarily accomplished in the fine arts. Though revealing all the tender sensibilities of the characters associated with a hundred sentimental tales, Emily emerges as a credible figure who seems aware of the connections between the scenery around her and the characters who inhabit it. As a painter, she sees and thinks of life as a series of pictures. As David Durant explains in *Ann Radcliffe's Novels* (1980), "She does not merely feel fright, but conjures up imaginary scenes which elicit it . . . scenery inhabits the inner life of the heroine, as well as locating her actions." A further element of Emily's characterization that adds to her credibility is her internalizing of the suspense produced by the action in the narrative. Her heightened sensibility reacts to fear and terror in an all-inclusive way; this acuteness of sensibility makes her easy prey for the villain, Signor Montoni. This sinister figure marries Emily's aunt for her money, and then conveys Emily and her unhappy aunt to the "vast and dreary" confines of the castle.

This impossible castle becomes a superbly appointed stage for the playing of the melodrama. As the melodrama has hopes of communicating a real sense of mystery, its action and characters remain subordinate to the environment, which pervades the entire texture of the work. Description of landscape is a major part of the book's concept, and Radcliffe pays homage to Salvator Rosa and Claude Lorrain in emphasizing pictorial detail. The somber exterior of the castle prepares the reader for the ineffable horrors that lie within the walls and adumbrates the importance of landscape and massive architecture in the novel.

There are certain shortcomings in Radcliffe's method: Landscape description strangles action; the visual aspects of the novel have been internalized; and the device of the chase over great stretches of land has been subordinated by mental recapitulation of past scenes—action becomes tableaux. This internal action is slow-moving, tortuously so in a novel of 300,000 words. Critics have also objected to Radcliffe's penchant for a rational explanation of every apparent supernatural phenomenon she has introduced; others, however, point out that Radcliffe's readers enjoyed terror only if they were never forced into surrendering themselves.

The Mysteries of Udolpho brought new energy to the picturesque, the sentimental, and the gothic novel. Radcliffe alternated effectively between the picturesque vagueness of the landscape and the castle's hall of terrors. Her deft handling of sexual feeling, shown as antagonism between Montoni and Emily, is characteristic of her refusal to acknowledge sex overtly except as a frightening nameless power. The artificial terror, heightened sensibility, and the pervading air of mystery produced a powerful effect on her readers, yet many felt cheated by her failure to satisfy fully the intense imaginative visions awakened by the book. These readers would have to wait for *The Italian*, probably Radcliffe's finest work and the high-water mark of gothic fiction.

THE ITALIAN

The unity, control, and concentration of *The Italian* display a superb talent. Mrs. Radcliffe's narrative technique is more sophisticated than at any previous time, particularly in the subtle revelation of the unreliability of feelings based on first impressions rather than on rational judgment. The dramatic pacing remains rigorous throughout and relatively free from digressions. The story's impulse depends upon the Marchesa di Vivaldi's refusal to allow her young son, Vincentio, to marry the heroine, Ellena di Rosalba, whose origins are in doubt. The Marchesa relies on the sinister machinations of her monk-confessor, Schedoni, who decides to murder Ellena. Radcliffe's antipathy to Roman Catholicism is evident in her account of the horrors of the Carmelite abbey and its order, including the labyrinthine vaults and gloomy corridors. A strange blend of fascination and disgust is evoked here and in the scenes of the trial in the halls of the Inquisition, the ruins of the Paluzzi, and in the prison of the Inquisition. Clearly, the gothic aspects of *The Italian* function as representations of a disordered and morally evil past.

The vividness continues through to the climax of the story, when Schedoni, dagger in hand, prepares to murder Ellena but hesitates when he recognizes the portrait miniature she wears. Believing the girl is his lost daughter, he tries to make amends for his crimes. Though the solution involves more complex developments, the excitement of the confrontation between these two figures remains exceptional. Ellena has been a paragon of virtue, displaying piety, sensibility, benevolence, constancy, and a love of nature. To this catalog, Radcliffe adds intelligence, courage, and ingenuity. As an idealized character, Ellena represents the strengths necessary to prevail in the Romantic conflict against external malign forces.

Schedoni, the devil/priest, is a figure of strong and dangerous sexual desire, associated, as is often the case in Radcliffe's work, with incest. Radcliffe counters the passivity and weakness of Ellena's virtues with this masculine version of desire—the lust of unregulated ambition. She describes him thus: "There was something terrible in his air, something almost superhuman. . . . His physiognomy . . . bore traces of many passions . . . his eyes were so piercing that they seemed to penetrate at a single glance into the hearts of men, and to read their most secret thoughts." His pride, greed, and loneliness combine to form a demonic figure vaguely suggesting John Milton's Satan.

Eino Railo, in *The Haunted Castle* (1964), believes *The Italian* and the central character, Father Schedoni, were created under the revivified Romantic impulse supplied by the tragic monastic figure in Matthew Gregory Lewis's *The Monk* (1796). According to Railo, the difference between Ambrosio and Schedoni is that the latter "is no longer a young and inexperienced saint preserved from temptations, but a person long hardened in the ways of crime and vice, alarmingly gifted and strenuous, hypocritical, unfeeling and merciless." Radcliffe was inspired by "Monk Lewis" to write a more impressive book than earlier conceived; her bias against sexual and sadistic impulses and toward heightened romantic effect win out in *The Italian*. While Ambrosio's passions remain tangled and confused by his need for immediate satisfaction and his lack of any lasting goal, Schedoni has well-defined goals for power, wealth, and status. His Machiavellian inclinations blend with pride, melancholy, mystery, and dignity, making him Radcliffe's most fully realized character. Her protest against *The Monk* created a story of tragic quality that goes beyond the conventional gothic paraphernalia and toward the psychological novel.

Mrs. Radcliffe remains the undisputed mistress of the gothic novel and a central figure in the gothic revival, beginning in the late 1950's, which has seen the resurrection of hordes of forgotten gothic novelists and their tales. The generous volume of Radcliffe criticism in recent decades has redefined her place in literary history, acknowledging the prodigious sweep of her influence. On first reading her works, one must remember to search behind the genteel exterior of the artistry to discover the special recesses of terror, subconscious conflict, and the psychology of feelings which played a major role in the evolution of dark Romanticism.

Paul J. deGategno

OTHER MAJOR WORKS

POETRY: *The Poems of Ann Radcliffe*, 1816; *St. Alban's Abbey*, 1826.

NONFICTION: *A Journey Made in the Summer of 1794 Through Holland and the Western Frontier of Germany*, 1795.

BIBLIOGRAPHY

Durant, David S. *Ann Radcliffe's Novels: Experiments in Setting*. Rev. ed. New York: Arno Press, 1980. Discovers a pattern of evolution in Radcliffe's novels from the sentimental *The Castles of Athlin and Dunbayne* to the historical *Gaston de Blondeville* that reflects the movement of eighteenth century British fiction and completes the transition between Fanny Burney's fiction and Sir Walter Scott's romances. This book still shows the shape of its original dissertation format, including footnotes: Nevertheless, it is one of the few easily accessible books on Radcliffe. Devotes six chapters to detailed analyses of her six novels, putting them in the context of their time and genre and illustrating their experimental styles.

Kiely, Robert. *The Romantic Novel in England*. Cambridge, Mass.: Harvard University Press, 1972. An important book on Romantic fiction, including Radcliffe's gothic romances, which analyzes in depth twelve Romantic novels to define the intellectual context of the era. Notes that concepts of reality were tested and changed by Romantic novels and that Edmund Burke's ideas of the sublime modified aesthetic forms. Radcliffe is given a prominent place in this general thesis and *The Mysteries of Udolpho* is analyzed in detail as the focus of her chapter. Her novel is shown as a progressive revelation that nature weakens beneath the power of human imagination to project itself upon nature, as her heroine is deprived of consolation from natural order. Finds a common drift toward death in most novels of this genre. Includes a set of notes and an index.

McIntyre, Clara Frances. *Ann Radcliffe in Relation to Her Time*. New Haven, Conn.: Yale University Press, 1920. Reprint. New York: Archon Books, 1970. A dated, but still useful, 104-page study of Radcliffe which reviews the facts of her life and surveys her work. Presents contemporary estimates of her novels, considers their sources, and lists translations and dramatizations of them. Argues that Radcliffe's main contribution is in her improvement of Horace Walpole's method of dramatic structure, demonstrated by an analysis of her structures and their influences on the structures of Sir Walter Scott, Mary Shelley, and others. Contains a bibliography which includes a list of references to magazines.

Miles, Robert. *Ann Radcliffe: The Great Enchantress*. Manchester: Manchester University Press, 1995. Explores the historical and aesthetic context of Radcliffe's fiction, with separate chapters on her early works and mature novels. Miles also considers Radcliffe's role as a woman writer and her place in society. Includes notes and bibliography.

Murray, E. B. *Ann Radcliffe*. New York: Twayne, 1972. Surveys Radcliffe's life, drawing from her *A Journey Made in the Summer of 1794 Through Holland and the Western Frontier of Germany* to illustrate her novels' geography. Examines the background of the gothic, with its supernatural elements, sentiment and sensibility, and sense of the sublime and the picturesque. Looks at Radcliffe's modern romance of medieval experience, *The Castles of Athlin and Dunbayne*; concentrates on the heroine's sufferings in *A Sicilian Romance*; examines the strengths in plot and atmosphere of *The Romance of the Forest*; views *The Mysteries of Udolpho* as her first successful synthesis of modern and medieval; and argues that *The Italian* is Radcliffe's best novel because it sustains the reader's interest. Provides an overview of Radcliffe's literary accomplishments and influence. Includes notes, a selected annotated bibliography, and an index.

Rogers, Deborah D., ed. *The Critical Response to Ann Radcliffe*. Westport, Conn.: Greenwood Press, 1994. A good selection of critical essays on Radcliffe. Includes bibliographical references and an index.

Smith, Nelson C. *The Art of the Gothic: Ann Radcliffe's Major Novels*. New York: Arno Press, 1980. Contains a valuable introduction which reviews the scholarship on Radcliffe between 1967 and 1980. Analyzes the ways Radcliffe developed the sophistication of her fiction from *The Castles of Athlin and Dunbayne* to *The Mysteries of Udolpho* and *The Italian* in a six-year period. Examines the nature of the gothic in order to focus on Radcliffe's heroines of sensibility. Notes a decline of didacticism in Radcliffe's fiction by isolating her heroes and villains for study. Analyzes the narrative techniques used to craft the gothic tale, and surveys the gothic writers who followed Radcliffe. Includes end notes for each chapter and a bibliography.

AYN RAND

Born: St. Petersburg, Russia; February 2, 1905
Died: New York, New York; March 6, 1982

PRINCIPAL LONG FICTION

We the Living, 1936
Anthem, 1938, rev. ed. 1946
The Fountainhead, 1943
Atlas Shrugged, 1957
The Early Ayn Rand: A Selection from Her Unpublished Fiction, 1984 (Leonard Peikoff, editor)

OTHER LITERARY FORMS

In addition to her three novels and one novelette, Ayn Rand published a play and several philosophical disquisitions. An early critique, *Hollywood: American Movie City*, was published in the Soviet Union in 1926 without Rand's permission.

ACHIEVEMENTS

Rand won the Volpe Cup at the Venice Film Festival in 1942 for the Italian motion-picture dramatization of *We the Living*, a novel about the failures of the Soviet system. The sole honorary degree, of doctor of humane letters, awarded to Rand by Lewis and Clark College in Portland, Oregon, in 1963 does not reflect the significance of her influence on America's philosophic and political-economic thought.

BIOGRAPHY

Alisa (Alice) Zinovievna Rosenbaum was born the eldest of three children into a Russian Jewish middle-class family in czarist Russia. When her father's pharmacy was nationalized following the Bolshevik Revolution of 1917, Alisa, who had been writing stories since she was nine, found a calling: She turned against collectivism, and she elevated individ-

ualism—personal, economic, political, and moral—into a philosophy that eventually attracted a large, occasionally distinguished, following. Early in her career she declared herself to be an atheist.

At the University of Petrograd (now St. Petersburg), Alisa studied philosophy, English, and history, graduating with highest honors in history in 1924. By then the works of French writers Victor Hugo and Edmond Rostand, and of Polish writer Henryk Sienkiewicz, had inspired her passion for the heroic and the ideal. Fyodor Dostoevski and Friedrich Nietzsche also left their mark.

Unhappy because the Soviet system was not moving in the direction of her republican ideals and because she had a dead-end job, Alisa accepted an invitation from relatives and went to Chicago in 1926. In the United States she restyled herself Ayn (the pronunciation rhymes with "mine") Rand and within a few months moved to Hollywood, California.

Working as a film extra, a file clerk, and a waitress and doing other odd jobs from 1926 to 1934, Rand perfected her language skills and became a screenwriter at various motion-picture studios. In 1937, she worked as an unpaid typist for Eli Jacques Kahn, a well-known New York architect, in preparation for her first major novel, *The Fountainhead*. Given her early experience in totalitarian Russia, Rand soon became known as the most driven of American anticommunists. She had acquired U.S. citizenship in 1931. In 1947, she appeared as a "friendly witness" before the House Committee on Un-American Activities (HUAC) during the period of the communist witch-hunts—an action she later admitted regretting. Along the way, in 1929, Rand married Charles Francis (Frank) O'Connor, a minor actor and amateur painter. He died in 1979.

After her major literary successes, Rand devoted herself exclusively to philosophizing, writing, and lecturing. She spoke on numerous Ivy League university campuses. She became a regular at the Ford Hall Forum and a columnist for the *Los Angeles Times*. She was coeditor or contributor to several philosophical publications. Rand was active in the Nathaniel Branden Institute, created to spread her philosophy of "objectivism," until her personal and professional break with Nathaniel and Barbara Branden in 1968. This triangular relationship had played an important part in Rand's life, for the Brandens formed the nucleus of a close group of followers, ironically known as "the collective."

In her seventies Rand, a chain smoker whose loaded cigarette holder had become a symbol of her persona, was diagnosed with lung cancer. She died in March, 1982, in the New York City apartment in which she had lived since 1951. Her wake was attended by hundreds, including Alan Greenspan, an early Rand devotee and later chairman of the Federal Reserve Board Bank. Philosopher Leonard Peikoff, Rand's intellectual and legal heir, was also present.

Rand's publications have sold well over twenty million copies in English and in translation even as literary critics generally dismissed her ideas as reactionary propaganda or pop philosophy. Rand was a paradox. She was a writer of romantic fiction whose ideas were often taken seriously, but she was also a controversial individualist and a contrarian who defied the moral, political, social, and aesthetic norms of her times.

ANALYSIS

In her two major works of fiction, Rand explicated her philosophy of objectivism in dramatic form. Thus, in *The Fountainhead* and especially in *Atlas Shrugged*, Rand argues that reality exists independent of human thought (objectively), that reason is the only viable method for understanding reality, that individuals should seek personal happiness and exist for their own sake and that of no other, and that individuals should not sacrifice themselves or be sacrificed by others. Furthermore, unrestricted laissez-faire capitalism is the political-economic system in which these principles can best flourish. Underlying this essence is the philosophy of unadulterated individualism, personal responsibility, the power of unsullied reason, and the importance of Rand's special kind of morality.

In her long fiction the philosopher-novelist spells out her concept of the exceptional individual as a heroic being and an "ideal man," with his happiness as the highest moral purpose in life, with productive

achievement the noblest activity, and reason the only absolute. Rand advocates minimal government intrusion and no initiation of physical force in human interactions. She represents such a system as enshrining the highest degree of morality and justice.

Because Rand also focuses on the denial of self-sacrifice and altruism, a staple of conventional morality and welfarism, she opposes both Christianity and communism. She finds it irrational to place the good of others ahead of one's own rational self-interest. Likewise, she denies mysticism but rather promotes the Aristotelian view that the world which individuals perceive is reality and there is no other. Both her major novels can be considered elitist and antidemocratic in that they extol the virtues of a few innovative, far-thinking individuals over the mediocre majority, which is either ignorant and uncaring or, even worse, actively striving to destroy the brilliant individuals of great ability. Besides disparaging mediocrity, Rand also decried the power of connections, conformity with what has been done before, a trend she found far too evident in the American wel-

(CORBIS/Oscar White)

fare state, and the intellectual bankruptcy she deemed it to have fostered.

Rand considered herself a practitioner of Romanticism, who was concerned with representing individuals "in whom certain human attributes are focused more sharply and consistently than in average human beings." Accordingly, in both these novels the characters of the heroes, sharply drawn, are idealized creations—not depictions of real individuals—who are in control of their own destinies despite major odds.

THE FOUNTAINHEAD

The Fountainhead is the story of Howard Roark, Rand's ideal man, an architect who has a vision of how buildings should really be designed. He is innovative and efficient; he also has a strong aesthetic sense and has integrity—in short, he is a man of principle and artistic individuality. Roark is contrasted with Peter Keating, a former classmate and fellow architect but a "second-hander," constantly replicating conventional styles since he has no originality of his own. He achieves a seeming success by manipulating others. Unlike Roark, whom he envies, Keating does not know who he really is.

Another of Roark's adversaries is Ellsworth Toohey. He writes a column for the *Banner*, arguing that architecture should reflect the art of the people. Gail Wynand is the *Banner*'s owner and newspaper magnate; he appreciates Roark's creativity but buckles under societal pressures, disregards his vision, and thereby engineers his own downfall as a worthy human being.

The love interest is embodied in Dominique Francon, the daughter of Guy Francon, the principal owner of the architectural firm that employs Peter Keating. She is a typical Rand heroine, a self-reliant idealist alienated by the shallow conventions of her day in interwar America and convinced that a life of principle is impossible in a world ruled by mediocrity. Her affair with Roark is motivated, not by physical or emotional passion, but by the recognition that he is a man of great worth. Along the way, in between and sometimes during other affairs, she marries Keating and then Wynand before finally becoming Mrs. Howard Roark. Dominique seems inconsistent in her ideals, attitudes, and critiques of architectural designs, but the inconsistencies are all part of her effort to spare Roark from ultimate destruction.

Roark, long professionally unsuccessful because he is unwilling to compromise the integrity of his creations, preferring not to work at all or to do menial tasks, eventually overcomes not only financial difficulties but also numerous intrigues by the likes of Keating. For instance, through the mean-spirited Toohey, Roark is assigned to build an interdenominational temple for a patron, Hopton Stoddard, a traditionalist who is abroad at the time. Toohey knows that Stoddard will hate Roark's radically innovative design. Roark makes the building's centerpiece Dominique's nude figure. Toohey incites public condemnation and persuades the patron to sue Roark for breach of contract. Stoddard wins the case, as Roark fails to defend himself in court.

Paradoxically, a friendship develops between Roark and Wynand, attracted to each other for different reasons. Wynand helps Roark in his defense at a second trial, which follows Roark's dynamiting a low-income housing project that Keating had commissioned. The latter had agreed not to alter Roark's design in any way in exchange for Roark's allowing Keating to claim credit for the former's innovative and cost-effective blueprint. When Keating fails to keep his promise and adulterates the design, Roark, with Dominique Francon's assistance, destroys the structure. The trial gives Roark the opportunity to spell out his—that is, Rand's—defense of ethical egoism and opposition to a world perishing from an "orgy of self-sacrifice" and conventional morality. After Roark's exoneration, Wynand commissions him to build the tallest skyscraper in New York City despite Wynand's losing Dominique to Roark.

Ultimately, *The Fountainhead* is a novel of ideas, of heroic characters who are the fountainhead of human progress and of their opposites, who live second-hand, second-rate lives and constantly seek social approval for their beliefs. The philosophy in the novel alternates with the action, and neither can be understood without the other.

ATLAS SHRUGGED

Rand's philosophy extolling the myth of absolute, rugged individualism and its relationship to society is most fully explicated in what proved to be her last work of fiction, several years in the making: the twelve-hundred-page *Atlas Shrugged*. In this novel, Rand tries to answer the question raised by one of her earlier heroes: "What would happen to the world without those who do, think, work, produce?" In this apocalyptic parable, it is John Galt of Twentieth Century Motors, a physicist, engineer, inventor, and philosopher, who is Rand's ideal man and leads the other "men of the mind" on a strike against the exploitation of the genuine creators of wealth by all the leeches and parasites—the nonproducers—whom they had been sustaining.

Rand's philosophy is played out through the stories of the four heroes, the authentic moneymakers. They are the Argentine Francisco d'Anconia, heir to the world's leading copper enterprise; the Scandinavian Ragnar Danneskjold, a onetime philosopher who turns pirate in order to steal wealth back from the looters and return it to the producers of legitimate values; Henry (Hank) Rearden, an American steel magnate and inventor of a metal better than steel; and finally, the other American, John Galt, who, with the others, stops the ideological motor of the world in a strike before rebuilding society. The heroine, rail heiress Dagny Taggart, wonders where the individuals of ability have gone.

Confronting them is an array of villains, manipulative appropriators, enemies of individualism and free enterprise, scabs, and moochers profiting from the achievements of the producers and united by their greed for unearned gains. Especially, there is Dr. Robert Stadler, the counterpart of Gail Wynand in *The Fountainhead*. Stadler, once the greatest physicist of his time, fully cognizant of the value of the human mind, fails to stand up for his principles. The progressive decay of James Taggart, Dagny's brother and the titular president of Taggart Transcontinental Railroad, parallels that of the society in which he lives.

In the novel, set some time in the vaguely defined future, America is following Europe down the long, hopeless path of socialism, government regulation, and a predatory state into a new Dark Age. The heroes join forces with other intelligent, freedom-loving leaders of commerce, industry, science, and philosophy to reverse the slide. They do this as Atlas may have done had he grown tired of holding the world on his shoulders without reward.

Eventually, the heroes repair to a secret Colorado mountain citadel, where they wait for their time to rebuild the decaying collectivist society whose end their "strike of the mind" against productive work is hastening. Galt, arrested and tortured by the looters but finally freed by the other heroes, delivers a thirty-five-thousand-word oration via a commandeered radio, epitomizing Rand's objectivism and views of the ideal man. Galt's (Rand's) philosophy then becomes that of the new society: "I swear by my life and my love of it that I will never live for the sake of another man, nor ask another man to live for mine." By the end of the novel, socialism has produced a bankrupt world pleading for the return of the men of the mind, who, after a confrontation with the parasites, start to rebuild society. *Atlas Shrugged* is Rand's most thorough exploration of the social ramifications of politics, economics, psychology, metaphysics, epistemology, aesthetics, religion, and ethics.

Peter B. Heller

OTHER MAJOR WORKS

PLAYS: *Night of January 16th,* pr. 1934 (also titled *Woman on Trial* and *Penthouse Legend*); *The Unconquered,* pb. 1940 (adapted from *We the Living*).

NONFICTION: *For the New Intellectual: The Philosophy of Ayn Rand,* 1961; *The Virtue of Selfishness: A New Concept of Egoism,* 1964; *Capitalism: The Unknown Ideal,* 1966; *Introduction to Objectivist Epistemology,* 1967, 2d enlarged ed., 1990 (Harry Binswanger and Leonard Peikoff, editors); *The Romantic Manifesto: A Philosophy of Literature,* 1969, rev. ed. 1971, 2d rev. ed. 1975; *The New Left: The Anti-Industrial Revolution,* 1971; *Philosophy: Who Needs It?,* 1982; *The Ayn Rand Lexicon: Objectivism from A to Z,* 1984 (Leonard Peikoff, editor); *The Voice of Reason: Essays in Objectivist Thought,* 1988 (Leonard Peikoff, editor); *The Ayn Rand Column,* 1991; *Letters of Ayn Rand,* 1995 (Michael S. Berliner, editor); *Journals of Ayn Rand,* 1997 (David Harriman, editor).

Miscellaneous: *The Objectivist Newsletter*, 1962-1965; *The Objectivist*, 1966-1971; *The Ayn Rand Letter*, 1971-1976.

Bibliography

Baker, James T. *Ayn Rand.* Boston: Twayne, 1987. An academic's brief but objective and highly readable treatment of the novelist's life and work, with a chronology, references, and bibliography.

Branden, Barbara. *The Passion of Ayn Rand.* Garden City, N.Y.: Doubleday, 1986. A provocative assessment, by one of her former inner circle, of Rand's life as an author, philosopher, and especially a woman with strong loves and hates. Includes photographs.

Branden, Nathaniel. *Judgment Day: My Years with Ayn Rand.* Boston: Houghton Mifflin, 1989. A personal account by Rand's disciple, organizer, spokesman, lover, and, ultimately, enemy. Includes photographs.

Gladstein, Mimi Reisel. *The Ayn Rand Companion.* Westport, Conn.: Greenwood Press, 1984. A compendium of the plots and major characters of Rand's fiction.

Rand, Ayn. *Journals of Ayn Rand.* Edited by David Harriman. New York: Penguin-Dutton, 1997. The author-philosopher's thoughts and feelings about her life and work, including a cavalcade of events and people. Foreword by her designated intellectual heir, Leonard Peikoff.

Sciabarra, Chris M. *Ayn Rand: The Russian Radical.* University Park: Pennsylvania State University Press, 1995. The evolution of the author as a philosopher, of her dialectics, and of her objectivism, beginning with her early years. Includes a bibliography and photographs.

Marjorie Kinnan Rawlings

Born: Washington, D.C.; August 8, 1896
Died: St. Augustine, Florida; December 14, 1953

Principal long fiction

Jacob's Ladder, 1931, 1940 (serial; in *When the Whippoorwill*), 1950 (book)
South Moon Under, 1933
Golden Apples, 1935
The Yearling, 1938
The Sojourner, 1953

Other literary forms

Although she is best known for one novel, *The Yearling*, Marjorie Kinnan Rawlings produced three other full-length novels and two novellas, the award-winning *Jacob's Ladder* and the undistinguished *Mountain Prelude*, which was serialized in 1947 in *The Saturday Evening Post* but never appeared in book form. She also wrote numerous shorter pieces for periodicals, beginning with a series of sketches about life in Cross Creek, Florida, which were printed in *Scribner's Magazine* under the title "Cracker Chidlings." During her lifetime Rawlings brought out only one book-length volume of short stories, *When the Whippoorwill* (1940). However, virtually all of the short fiction that she published in magazines was collected in Rodger L. Tarr's edition of *Short Stories by Marjorie Kinnan Rawlings* (1994). Rawlings was also the author of a notable autobiographical work, *Cross Creek* (1942), and an anecdotal cookbook, *Cross Creek Cookery* (1942). A children's book, *The Secret River*, was published posthumously in 1955. The author's versatility is evident in *The Marjorie Kinnan Rawlings Reader* (1956), edited by Julia Scribner Bigham. *Selected Letters of Marjorie Kinnan Rawlings* (1983) was edited by Gordon E. Bigelow and Laura V. Monti.

Achievements

During the 1930's and the 1940's, Marjorie Kinnan Rawlings's fiction was popular with the general public and acclaimed by critics. Her novella *Jacob's Ladder* placed second in the 1931 Scribner Prize Contest, and two of her short stories won O. Henry Awards, "Gal Young Un" in 1933 and "Black Secret" in 1946. Her first published novel, *South Moon Under*, was a Book-of-the-Month Club selection, as was *The Yearling*, which brought Rawlings a national rep-

(Library of Congress)

and unjustly neglected, along with the new emphasis on the relationship between human beings and the natural environment, resulted in the 1980's and the 1990's in an upsurge of interest in Rawlings, her novels, her short stories, and her compelling autobiography. Rawlings is now valued not only for her precision in describing a vanished way of life but also for her lyrical prose, her mystical feelings about nature, and her insistence that there are truly noble people who spend their lives in poverty and obscurity.

BIOGRAPHY

Marjorie Kinnan Rawlings was the older of two children born in Washington, D.C., to Ida May Traphagen Kinnan and Frank R. Kinnan, a patent attorney. Rawlings read widely and began writing early. By the time she was six, she was submitting stories to area newspapers. At age eleven, she won a two-dollar prize in a contest sponsored by the *Washington Post*; at fifteen, she placed second in *McCall's* Child Authorship Contest and saw her story published in that magazine.

Rawlings's father died in 1913, and the next year, the family moved to Madison, Wisconsin. That fall, Rawlings entered the University of Wisconsin, where she majored in English and was active in the college publications and in the drama society. As a junior, she was elected to Phi Beta Kappa. After graduation, she moved to New York City and worked for a year for the Young Women's Christian Association. In 1919 she married Charles A. Rawlings, Jr., a journalist whom she had met at the university, and they moved to his home town, Rochester, New York. During the next nine years, Rawlings wrote features for newspapers, advertising copy, and a syndicated column. However, all the short stories she submitted to magazines were rejected.

After visiting central Florida in 1928, the couple decided to move to the area. Purchasing an orange-grove property at Cross Creek, they settled down in their new home, and Rawlings began using Florida settings for her fiction. Within a year, she was a regular contributor to *Scribner's Magazine*, working closely with the influential editor Maxwell Perkins. Rawlings's first novel, *South Moon Under*, appeared

utation, a motion-picture contract, membership in the National Institute of Arts and Letters, and the 1939 Pulitzer Prize for fiction. Her autobiography *Cross Creek* was also a best-seller and a Book-of-the-Month Club selection.

After her death, however, Rawlings was remembered either as a local colorist or as the author of two books for children, *The Secret River*, which in 1956 was selected as a Newbery Honor Book, and *The Yearling*, which in 1963 won the Lewis Carroll Shelf Award. The classification of *The Yearling* as a children's book was ironic, since Rawlings had written it with Mark Twain's *The Adventures of Huckleberry Finn* (1884) in mind, intending to appeal at least as much to adults as to children.

The ongoing efforts of a few scholars to call attention to a writer they felt had been both misclassified in 1933. That same year, Charles and Marjorie were divorced.

For the next eight years, Rawlings lived alone at Cross Creek, ran her business and her household, and wrote short stories and two more novels, the disappointing *Golden Apples* and *The Yearling*. She enjoyed cooking and entertaining, going on outdoor expeditions, corresponding with interesting people, and visiting with her neighbors. One of her closest friends was Norton Sanford Baskin. In 1941, she married him and went to live at the Castle Warden Hotel in St. Augustine, which Baskin owned and managed. However, she continued to write stories and books about Cross Creek, including an autobiography entitled *Cross Creek* and an anecdotal cookbook, *Cross Creek Cookery*. Ironically, it was this autobiography, which critics consider one of her best, that cost the author four years of constant worry. In 1943, Zelma Cason filed a libel suit against Rawlings, based on the author's description of her in *Cross Creek*. The suit dragged on until 1947, when Rawlings was charged a nominal sum for damages.

Rawlings had decided that her next novel would have a different setting, upstate New York, where she spent her summers, as well as a more "serious" theme. Though it had been ten years in the making, *The Sojourner* lacked the vitality of the Florida works. Despite failing health, Rawlings now began research for a biography of her friend and fellow writer Ellen Glasgow. It would never be completed. On December 10, 1953, while Baskin and Rawlings were at their beach cottage, she suffered a cerebral hemorrhage. She died in the St. Augustine hospital on December 14 and was buried in the Antioch Cemetery at Island Grove, near Cross Creek.

ANALYSIS

Whether they first encounter *The Yearling* as children or as adults, few readers can remain dry-eyed during the scene at the end of the book when the young protagonist, Jody Baxter, is forced to kill his pet deer. However, that memorable episode is just one of many incidents in Rawlings's fiction that illustrate her uncompromisingly realistic view of life. Indeed, it is ironic that for so long Rawlings was thought of as a children's writer, for in fact her rural world is as grim as that of Victorian author Thomas Hardy. Penny Baxter, Jody's father, describes growing up as learning that life is hard, that human beings can be malicious, and that feelings of insecurity and desperate loneliness are just part of being human. Though Rawlings and many of her characters display a mystical appreciation of nature, she never permits us to forget that living in a natural environment means accepting ugliness as well as beauty, suffering as well as joy, and death as a part of the daily routine.

JACOB'S LADDER

The novella *Jacob's Ladder* is a moving story about two poor, young people from the Florida scrub. Florry Leddy and Martin, or Mart, meet one night at a dance and the next day run off together, less troubled about having to travel through a hurricane than by the possibility that Florry's abusive father Jo will awake from his drunken stupor and pursue them. Florry is sure that Mart will be kinder to her than Jo has been; her only regret is that she cannot take her dog Sport with her. Sadly, love and loss occur only too often during Florry's life with Mart. Every time she starts to feel secure in a new place, something happens, and they have to move on. Florry cannot stay near her baby's grave; she has to abandon her cat and later her pet raccoon; she even has to let her pet pig be butchered.

Florry knows that Mart is not to blame for what happens to them. After Florry comes down with malaria, the money he has saved from trapping is used for her medical care. His traps are seized by a creditor, who is noted for preying on customers in difficulty. Mart makes enough money fishing in the gulf to buy a boat and nets, but they are lost in a storm. He is doing well at moonshining until a spiteful neighbor informs on him, his still is smashed by revenue agents, and Mart is sentenced to thirty days of hard labor.

As critic Samuel I. Bellman pointed out, Rawlings took the title *Jacob's Ladder* from an old spiritual, which reiterates the idea of laying down one's burdens. When Mart reaches his breaking point, Florry takes up the burden he has carried for so long. The only place to which she has a claim, she tells him, is her old home, and that is where they will go. They make their way through another hurricane and reach the old cabin, which is in a sad state. Jo is made to understand that Mart and Florry are taking over, and the novella ends on a hopeful note.

SOUTH MOON UNDER

In *Jacob's Ladder*, Florry and Mart wandered from the piney woods and the Florida scrub to the Gulf Coast and back to the woods. By contrast, *South Moon Under* and *The Yearling* are set entirely in the "Big Scrub," a plateau bounded on the east by the St. John's River and on the west by the Ocklawaha. Before beginning *South Moon Under*, Rawlings spent several weeks in this wilderness area. Piety Fiddia, with whom she stayed, became the model for Piety Jacklin in the novel, and her moonshiner son became the character of Lant Jacklin.

Like Mart and Florry, old Lantry has had difficulty putting down roots, but he is propelled by fear. As he tells his daughter Piety, when he was making moonshine in North Carolina he killed a federal revenue agent, and he has been on the run ever since. However, the scrub is so remote, and his home there so isolated, that Lantry's worst fears are never realized. It is true that every season brings its own problems, drought or rain, insects or blight, but nevertheless Lantry and his family prosper. After his sons move on, Lantry persuades Piety to marry Willy Jacklin, who is a hard worker, if none too bright. Their son Lantry, or Lant, gives his grandfather great pleasure during the old man's last years. However, on his deathbed old Lantry once again succumbs to terror; only in death, it seems, can he escape from fear.

Old Lantry's story could be read simply as a morality tale. However, both in *Jacob's Ladder* and in *South Moon Under*, the author clearly sides with these hard-working, self-sufficient people who do not understand why there should be restrictions on such normal activities as hunting, fishing, whiskey-making, and letting livestock range freely, or why the government should constantly seek to block their efforts to support their families, even send them to prison, leaving those families destitute. As the fence-raising at the beginning of the novel illustrates, those who live in the Big Scrub rely on themselves and on each other, not on the government. One could almost justify Lant's killing his shiftless cousin Cleve as a service to the community, for Cleve is a spy and an informer, but in fact Lant was defending himself. Unlike Cleve's widow, who believes Lant and promptly marries him, outsiders would never understand. Like his grandfather, Lant will always have to live in fear of the law.

THE YEARLING

Although the setting for *The Yearling* is the same as that of *South Moon Under*, in this novel all of the action takes place within a single year, and instead of focusing on the conflict between two codes and two societies, *The Yearling* describes a boy's initiation into the natural world. It begins one April, with Jody Baxter so overwhelmed by nature's beauty that he cannot sleep; it ends the following April, with a revelation of nature's indifference. In all his hunting and fishing, Jody has never realized that the survival of one creature depends on the death of another. Then Jody's pet fawn Flag destroys the newly planted corn crop, and Penny tells his son the deer must be shot. Jody will never again view nature as he had the previous spring.

Now he knows too much, including the inevitability of loneliness, and only his father's understanding makes his discoveries endurable. Though, like young Jody, Rawlings responded to the breathtaking beauty of the Florida backwoods, she found even more to admire in many of the people who lived there. Her most memorable characters are those who, like Jody and Penny, have the courage to confront life and accept all that it holds for them, even the death of innocence.

Rosemary M. Canfield Reisman

OTHER MAJOR WORKS

SHORT FICTION: *When the Whippoorwill*, 1940; *Short Stories by Marjorie Kinnan Rawlings*, 1994 (Rodger L. Tarr, editor).

NONFICTION: *Cross Creek*, 1942 (sketches); *Cross Creek Cookery*, 1942; *Selected Letters of Marjorie Kinnan Rawlings*, 1983 (Gordon E. Bigelow and Laura V. Monti, editors).

CHILDREN'S LITERATURE: *The Secret River*, 1955.

MISCELLANEOUS: *The Marjorie Rawlings Reader*, 1956 (Julia Scribner Bigham, editor).

BIBLIOGRAPHY

Acton, Patricia Nassif. *Invasion of Privacy: The Cross Creek Trial of Marjorie Kinnan Rawlings*. Gainesville: University of Florida Press, 1988. A dramatic account of the legal battle between Rawlings and Zelma Cason. Includes notes, index, and illustrations.

Bellman, Samuel I. *Marjorie Kinnan Rawlings*. New York: Twayne, 1974. Stresses the analysis of Rawlings's works. Has copious notes, bibliography, and index.

Bigelow, Gordon E. *Frontier Eden: The Literary Career of Marjorie Kinnan Rawlings*. Gainesville: University of Florida Press, 1966. The first extensive study of Rawlings. Includes bibliographical checklist, chronology, drawings, photographs, and an index.

Morris, Rhonda. "Engendering Fictions: Rawlings and a Female Tradition of Southern Writing." *The Marjorie Kinnan Rawlings Journal of Florida Literature* 7 (1996): 27-39. Argues that though Rawlings used the male voice in order to be "taken seriously" by the establishment, her works reveal a feminist perspective. Well documented.

Parker, Idella, and Mary Keating. *Idella: Marjorie Rawlings' "Perfect Maid."* Gainesville: University Press of Florida, 1992. The employee described by Rawlings in *Cross Creek* as the "perfect maid" recalls her life with Rawlings and comments on the author's feelings about race. Includes photographs and index.

Silverthorne, Elizabeth. *Marjorie Kinnan Rawlings: Sojourner at Cross Creek*. Woodstock, N.Y.: Overlook, 1988. The standard biography, based on a close study of the author's papers, her unpublished works, and numerous interviews. Includes helpful list of reviews, illustrations, and index.

Tarr, Rodger L. *Marjorie Kinnan Rawlings: A Descriptive Bibliography*. Pittsburgh: University of Pittsburgh Press, 1996. Lists all of Rawlings's publications but very few secondary sources. Contains useful information about her film involvements.

ISHMAEL REED

Born: Chattanooga, Tennessee; February 22, 1938

PRINCIPAL LONG FICTION
The Free-Lance Pallbearers, 1967
Yellow Back Radio Broke-Down, 1969
Mumbo Jumbo, 1972
The Last Days of Louisiana Red, 1974
Flight to Canada, 1976
The Terrible Twos, 1982
Reckless Eyeballing, 1986
The Terrible Threes, 1989
Japanese by Spring, 1993

OTHER LITERARY FORMS

Ishmael Reed may be best known as a satirical novelist, but he also gained a reputation as a respected poet, essayist, and editor. His poetry collections, which include *Catechism of D Neoamerican Hoodoo Church* (1970), *Conjure: Selected Poems 1963-1970* (1972), *Chattanooga* (1973), *A Secretary to the Spirits* (1977), and *New and Collected Poems* (1988), established him as a major African American poet, and his poetry has been included in several important anthologies. In well-received collections of essays, including *Shrovetide in Old New Orleans* (1978), *God Made Alaska for the Indians* (1982), and *Writin' Is Fightin'* (1988), Reed forcefully presented his aesthetic and political theories. He also proved to be an important editor and publisher. *Nineteen Necromancers from Now* (1970) was a breakthrough anthology for several unknown black writers. *Yardbird Lives!* (1978), which Reed edited with novelist Al Young, includes essays, fiction, and graphics from the pages of the *Yardbird Reader*, an innovative periodical that published the work of minority writers and artists. Reed's most ambitious editing project resulted in *Calafia: The California Poetry* (1979), an effort to gather together the forgotten minority poetry of California's past.

ACHIEVEMENTS

Reed earned a place in the first rank of contemporary African American authors, but such recognition did not come immediately. Most established reviewers ignored Reed's first novel, *The Free-Lance Pallbearers*, and many of the reviews that were written dismissed the novel as offensive, childish, or self-absorbed. Although *Yellow Back Radio Broke-Down* was even less traditional than its predecessor, it received much more critical attention and became the center of considerable critical debate. Some reviewers attacked the novel as overly clever, bitter, or obscure, but many praised its imaginative satire and technical innovation. Moreover, the controversy over *Yellow Back Radio Broke-Down* stirred new interest in *The Free-Lance Pallbearers*. Reed's increasing acceptance as a major African American author was demonstrated when his third novel, *Mumbo Jumbo*, was reviewed on the front page of *The New York Times Review of Books*. Both *Mumbo Jumbo* and *Conjure*, a poetry collection published in the same year, were nominated for the National Book Award.

Subsequent novels maintained Reed's position in American letters. In 1975, Reed's *The Last Days of Louisiana Red* received the Rosenthal Foundation Award, and some reviewers viewed *Flight to Canada* as Reed's best novel. Yet his work proved consistently controversial. His novels have, for example, been called sexist, a critical accusation that is fueled by comparison of Reed's novels with the contemporary powerful fiction written by African American women such as Alice Walker and Toni Morrison. The charge of sexism is further encouraged by Reed's satirical attack on feminists in *Reckless Eyeballing*. Reed has also been called a reactionary by some critics because of his uncomplimentary portrayals of black revolutionaries. His fiction has been translated into three languages, and his poetry is included in *Poetry of the Negro, New Black Poetry, The Norton Anthology of Poetry*, and other anthologies. In 1998, Ishmael Reed was awarded the MacArthur "genius" fellowship. This is fitting recognition for a writer who consciously attempted to redefine American and African American literature.

BIOGRAPHY

The jacket notes to *Chattanooga* glibly recount Ishmael Scott Reed's life: "born in Chattanooga, Tennessee, grew up in Buffalo, New York, learned to write in New York City and wised up in Berkeley, California." Each residence played a crucial role in Reed's development.

Reed was born the son of Henry Lenoir and Thelma Coleman, but before he was two years old, his mother remarried, this time to autoworker Bennie Reed. When he was four years old, his mother moved the family to Buffalo, New York, where she found factory work. Reed was graduated from Buffalo's East High School in 1956 and began to attend Millard Fillmore College, the night division of the University of Buffalo, supporting himself by working in the Buffalo public library. A satirical short story, "Something Pure," which portrayed Christ's return as an advertising man, brought Reed the praise of an English professor and encouraged him to enroll in day classes. Reed attended the University of Buffalo until 1960, when he withdrew because of money problems and the social pressures that his financial

(James Lerager)

situation created. He married Priscilla Rose Thompson and moved into the notorious Talbert Mall Projects. The two years he spent there provided him with a painful but valuable experience of urban poverty and dependency. His daughter, Timothy Bret Reed, was also born there. During his last years in Buffalo, Reed wrote for the *Empire Star Weekly*, moderated a controversial radio program for station WVFO, and acted in several local stage productions.

From 1962 to 1967, Reed lived in New York City. As well as being involved with the Civil Rights movement and the Black Power movement, Reed served as editor of *Advance*, a weekly published in Newark, New Jersey. His work on the *Advance* was admired by Walter Bowart, and together they founded the *East Village Other*, one of the first and most successful "underground" newspapers. An early indication of Reed's commitment to encouraging the work of minority artists was his organization in 1965 of the American Festival of Negro Art.

In 1967, Reed moved to Berkeley, California, and began teaching at the University of California at Berkeley. In 1970, Reed and his first wife divorced (after years of separation), and he married Carla Blank. In 1971, with Al Young, Reed founded the Yardbird Publishing Company, which from 1971 to 1976 produced the *Yardbird Reader*, an innovative journal of ethnic writing and graphics. The Reed, Cannon, and Johnson Communications Company, which later became Ishmael Reed Books, was founded in 1973 and has published the work of William Demby, Bill Gunn, Mei Mei Bressenburge, and other ethnic writers. In 1976, Reed and Victor Cruz began the Before Columbus Foundation. In 1977, Ishmael Reed's daughter Tennessee was born, and he was denied tenure in the English department at the University of California at Berkeley. He continued to serve as a lecturer at Berkeley, however, and also taught at Yale, Harvard, Columbia, Dartmouth, and a number of other colleges and universities. In 1995, he was awarded an honorary doctorate in letters from the State University of New York at Buffalo.

Reed made important contributions as a poet, novelist, essayist, playwright, and as an editor and publisher. He stated that he considers himself a global writer, and his success at writing poetry in the African language of Yoruba and his study of Japanese language and culture for his novel *Japanese by Spring* support this assertion. He also extended his literary range to include plays, such as *The Preacher and the Rapper* (published in 1997), and jazz albums, such as *Conjure I* (1983) and *Conjure II* (1989), and he even completed a libretto and served as the executive producer for a cable television soap opera called *Personal Problems* (1981).

In the early 1990's, Reed was, perhaps, best known for his controversial essays on such issues as the Rodney King and O. J. Simpson trials and the U.S. Justice Clarence Thomas hearings, some of which were collected in *Airing Dirty Laundry* (1993). However, his most important contribution to American letters may well be his work as an editor and publisher for other ethnic writers. In all of his publishing ventures, Reed tries to expose readers to the work of Asian Americans, African Americans, Chicanos, and Native Americans in an effort to help build a truly representative and pluralistic national literature.

ANALYSIS

Ishmael Reed is consciously a part of the African American literary tradition that extends back to the first-person slave narratives, and the central purpose of his novels is to define a means of expressing the complexity of the African American experience in a manner distinct from the dominant literary tradition. Until the middle of the twentieth century, African American fiction, although enriched by the lyricism of Jean Toomer and Zora Neale Hurston, concentrated on realistic portrayals of black life and employed familiar narrative structures. This tendency toward social realism peaked with Richard Wright's *Native Son* (1940) and *Black Boy* (1945), but it was continued into the late twentieth century by authors such as James Baldwin. Reed belongs to a divergent tradition, inspired by Ralph Ellison's *Invisible Man* (1952), a countertradition that includes the work of Leon Forrest, Ernest Gaines, James Alan McPherson, Toni Morrison, and Alice Walker.

Believing that the means of expression is as important as the matter, Reed argues that the special qualities of the African American experience cannot be adequately communicated through traditional literary forms. Like Amiri Baraka, Reed believes that African American authors must "be estranged from the dominant culture," but Reed also wants to avoid being stifled by a similarly restrictive countertradition. In *Shrovetide in Old New Orleans*, Reed says that his art and criticism try to combat "the consciousness barrier erected by an alliance of Eastern-backed black pseudo-nationalists and white mundanists." Thus, Reed works against the stylistic limitations of the African American literary tradition as much as he works with them. Henry Louis Gates, Jr., compared Reed's fictional modifications of African American literary traditions to the African American folk custom of "signifying," maintaining that Reed's novels present an ongoing process of "rhetorical self-definition."

Although Reed's novels are primarily efforts to define an appropriate African American aesthetic, his fiction vividly portrays the particular social condition of black Americans. In his foreword to Elizabeth and Thomas Settle's *Ishmael Reed: A Primary and Secondary Bibliography* (1982), Reed expresses his bitterness over persistent racism and argues that the personal experience of racism that informs his art makes his work inaccessible and threatening to many readers: "I am a member of a class which has been cast to the bottom of the American caste system, and from those depths I write a vision which is still strange, often frightening, 'peculiar' and 'odd' to some, 'ill-considered' and unwelcome to many." Indeed, Ishmael seems to be an ironically appropriate name for this author of violent and darkly humorous attacks on American institutions and attitudes, for the sharpness and breadth of his satire sometimes make him appear to be a man whose hand is turned against all others. His novels portray corrupt power brokers and their black and white sycophants operating in a dehumanized and materialistic society characterized by its prefabricated and ethnocentric culture. Yet Reed's novels are not hopeless explications of injustice, for against the forces of repression and conformity he sets gifted individuals who escape the limitations of their sterile culture by courageously penetrating the illusions that bind them. Moreover, in contrast to

many white authors who are engaged in parallel metafictive experiments, Reed voices a confident belief that "print and words are not dead at all."

Reed's narrative technique combines the improvisational qualities of jazz with a documentary impulse to accumulate references and allusions. In his composite narratives, historical and fictional characters coexist in a fluid, anachronistic time. In an effort to translate the vitality and spontaneity of the oral, folk tradition into a literature that can form the basis for an alternative culture, Reed mixes colloquialisms and erudition in novels which are syncretized from a series of subtexts. The literary equivalent of scat singing, his stories-within-stories parody literary formulas and challenge the traditional limits of fiction.

Reed claims that his novels constitute "an art form with its own laws," but he does not mean to imply that his work is private, for these "laws" are founded on a careful but imaginative reinterpretation of the historical and mythological past. The lengthy bibliography appended to *Mumbo Jumbo* satirizes the documentary impulse of social realist authors, but it also underscores Reed's belief that his mature work demands scholarly research in order to be decoded. This artistic process of reinterpretation often requires the services of an interlocutor, a character who explicitly explains the events of the narrative in terms of the mythological past. Reed's novels describe a vision of an Osirian/Dionysian consciousness, a sensuous humanism that he presents as an appropriate cultural alternative for nonwhite Americans. His imaginative reconstructions of the American West, the Harlem Renaissance, the American Civil War, and contemporary U.S. politics, interwoven with ancient myths, non-European folk customs, and the formulas of popular culture, are liberating heresies meant to free readers from the intellectual domination of the Judeo-Christian tradition.

THE FREE-LANCE PALLBEARERS

Reed's first novel, *The Free-Lance Pallbearers*, takes place in a futuristic America called HARRY SAM: "A big not-to-be-believed out-of-sight, sometimes referred to as O-BOP-SHE-BANG or KLANG-A-LANG-A-DING-DONG." This crumbling and corrupt world is tyrannized by Sam himself, a vulgar fat man who lives in Sam's Motel on Sam's Island in the middle of the lethally polluted Black Bay that borders HARRY SAM. Sam, doomed by some terrifying gastrointestinal disorder, spends all of his time on the toilet, his filth pouring into the bay from several large statues of Rutherford B. Hayes.

The bulk of the novel, although framed and periodically informed by a jiving narrative voice, is narrated by Bukka Doopeyduk in a restrained, proper English that identifies his passive faith in the establishment. Doopeyduk is a dedicated adherent to the Nazarene Code, an orderly in a psychiatric hospital, a student at Harry Sam College, and a hapless victim. His comically futile efforts to play by the rules are defeated by the cynics, who manipulate the unjust system to their own advantage. In the end, Doopeyduk is disillusioned: He leads a successful attack on Sam's Island, uncovers the conspiracy that protects Sam's cannibalism, briefly dreams of becoming the black Sam, and is finally crucified.

The Free-Lance Pallbearers is a parody of the African American tradition of first-person, confessional narratives, a book the narrator describes as "growing up in soulsville first of three installments—or what it means to be a backstage darky." Reed's novel challenges the viability of this African American version of the *Bildungsroman*, in which a young protagonist undergoes a painful initiation into the darkness of the white world, a formula exemplified by Wright's *Black Boy* and James Baldwin's *Go Tell It on the Mountain* (1953). In fact, the novel suggests that African American authors' use of this European form is as disabling as Doopeyduk's adherence to the dictates of the Nazarene Code.

The novel is an unrestrained attack on U.S. politics. HARRY SAM, alternately referred to as "Nowhere" or "Now Here," is a dualistic vision of a United States that celebrates vacuous contemporaneity. The novel, an inversion of the Horatio Alger myth in the manner of Nathanael West, mercilessly displays American racism, but its focus is the corruptive potential of power. Sam is a grotesque version of Lyndon B. Johnson, famous for his bathroom interviews, and Sam's cannibalistic taste for children is an attack on Johnson's Vietnam policy. With *The Free-*

Lance Pallbearers, Reed destroys the presumptions of his society, but it is not until his later novels that he attempts to construct an alternative.

YELLOW BACK RADIO BROKE-DOWN

Yellow Back Radio Broke-Down is set in a fantastic version of the Wild West of popular literature. Reed's protagonist, the Loop Garoo Kid, is a proponent of artistic freedom and an accomplished Voodoo *houngan* who is in marked contrast to the continually victimized Doopeyduk. Armed with supernatural "connaissance" and aided by a white python and the hip, helicopter-flying Chief Showcase, the Kid battles the forces of realistic mimesis and political corruption. His villainous opponent is Drag Gibson, a degenerate cattle baron given to murdering his wives, who is called upon by the citizens of Yellow Back Radio to crush their rebellious children's effort "to create [their] own fictions."

Although *Yellow Back Radio Broke-Down* satirizes Americans' eagerness to suspend civil rights in response to student protests against the Vietnam War, its focus is literature, specifically the dialogue between realism and modernism. The Loop Garoo Kid matches Reed's description of the African American artist in *Nineteen Necromancers from Now*: "a conjurer who works JuJu upon his oppressors; a witch doctor who frees his fellow victims from the psychic attack launched by demons." Through the Loop Garoo Kid, Reed takes a stand for imagination, intelligence, and fantasy against rhetoric, violence, and sentimentality. This theme is made explicit in a debate with Bo Shmo, a "neo-social realist" who maintains that "all art must be for the end of liberating the masses," for the Kid says that a novel "can be anything it wants to be, a vaudeville show, the six o'clock news, the mumblings of wild men saddled by demons."

Reed exhibits his antirealist theory of fiction in *Yellow Back Radio Broke-Down* through his free use of time, characters, and language. The novel ranges from the eighteenth century to the present, combining historical events and cowboy myths with modern technology and cultural detritus. Reed's primary characters are comically exaggerated racial types: Drag Gibson represents the whites' depraved materialism, Chief Showcase represents the American Indian's spirituality, and the Loop Garoo Kid represents the African American's artistic soul. Reed explains the novel's title by suggesting that his book is the "dismantling of a genre done in an oral way like radio." "Yellow back" refers to the popular dime novels; "radio" refers to the novel's oral, discontinuous form; and a "broke-down" is a dismantling. Thus, Reed's first two novels assault America in an attempt to "dismantle" its cultural structure.

MUMBO JUMBO

In *Mumbo Jumbo*, Reed expands on the neohoodooism of the Loop Garoo Kid in order to create and define an African American aesthetic based on Voodoo, Egyptian mythology, and improvisational musical forms, an aesthetic to challenge the Judeo-Christian tradition, rationalism, and technology. Set in Harlem during the 1920's, *Mumbo Jumbo* is a tragicomical analysis of the Harlem Renaissance's failure to sustain its artistic promise. Reed's protagonist is PaPa LaBas, an aging hoodoo detective and cultural diagnostician, and LaBas's name, meaning "over there" in French, reveals that his purpose is to reconnect African Americans with their cultural heritage by reunifying the Text of Jes Grew, literally the Egyptian Book of Thoth. Reed takes the phrase Jes Grew from Harriet Beecher Stowe's Topsy and James Weldon Johnson's description of African American music's unscribed development, but in the novel, Jes Grew is a contagion, connected with the improvisational spirit of ragtime and jazz, that begins to spread across America in the 1920's. Jes Grew is an irrational force that threatens to overwhelm the dominant, repressive traditions of established culture. LaBas's efforts to unify and direct this unpredictable force are opposed by the Wallflower Order of the Knights Templar, an organization dedicated to neutralizing the power of Jes Grew in order to protect its privileged status. LaBas fails to reunify the text, a parallel to the dissipation of the Harlem Renaissance's artistic potential, but the failure is seen as temporary; the novel's indeterminate conclusion looks forward hopefully to a time when these artistic energies can be reignited.

The novel's title is double-edged. "Mumbo jumbo" is a racist, colonialist phrase used to describe the misunderstood customs and language of dark-skinned people, an approximation of some critics' description of Reed's unorthodox fictional method. Yet "mumbo jumbo" also refers to the power of imagination, the cultural alternative that can free African Americans. A text of and about texts, *Mumbo Jumbo* combines the formulas of detective fiction with the documentary paraphernalia of scholarship: footnotes, illustrations, and a bibliography. Thus, in the disclosure scene required of any good detective story, LaBas, acting the part of interlocutor, provides a lengthy and erudite explication of the development of Jes Grew that begins with a reinterpretation of the myth of Osiris. The parodic scholarship of *Mumbo Jumbo* undercuts the assumed primacy of the European tradition and implicitly argues that African American artists should attempt to discover their distinct cultural heritage.

THE LAST DAYS OF LOUISIANA RED

In *The Last Days of Louisiana Red*, LaBas returns as Reed's protagonist, but the novel abandons the parodic scholarship and high stylization of *Mumbo Jumbo*. Although LaBas again functions as a connection with a non-European tradition of history and myth, *The Last Days of Louisiana Red* is more traditionally structured than its predecessor. In the novel, LaBas solves the murder of Ed Yellings, the founder of the Solid Gumbo Works. Yellings's business is dedicated to combating the effects of Louisiana Red, literally a popular hot sauce but figuratively an evil state of mind that divides African Americans. Yelling's gumbo, like Reed's fiction, is a mixture of disparate elements, and it has a powerful curative effect. In fact, LaBas discovers that Yellings is murdered when he gets close to developing a gumbo that will cure heroin addiction.

In *The Last Days of Louisiana Red*, Reed is examining the self-destructive forces that divide the African American community so that its members fight one another "while above their heads . . . billionaires flew in custom-made jet planes." Reed shows how individuals' avarice leads them to conspire with the establishment, and he suggests that some of the most vocal and militant leaders are motivated by their egotistical need for power rather than by true concern for oppressed people. Set in Berkeley, California, *The Last Days of Louisiana Red* attacks the credibility of the black revolutionary movements that sprang up in the late 1960's and early 1970's.

FLIGHT TO CANADA

Flight to Canada, Reed's fifth novel, is set in an imaginatively redrawn Civil War South, and it describes the relationship between Arthur Swille, a tremendously wealthy Virginia planter who practices necrophilia, and an assortment of sociologically stereotyped slaves. The novel is presented as the slave narrative of Uncle Robin, the most loyal of Swille's possessions. Uncle Robin repeatedly tells Swille that the plantation is his idea of heaven, and he assures his master that he does not believe that Canada exists. Raven Quickskill, "the first one of Swille's slaves to read, the first to write, and the first to run away," is the author of Uncle Robin's story.

Like much of Reed's work, *Flight to Canada* is about the liberating power of art, but in *Flight to Canada*, Reed concentrates on the question of authorial control. All the characters struggle to maintain control of their stories. After escaping from the plantation, Quickskill writes a poem, "Flight to Canada," and his comical verse denunciation of Swille completes his liberation. In complaining of Quickskill's betrayal to Abraham Lincoln, Swille laments that his former bookkeeper uses literacy "like that old Voodoo." In a final assertion of authorial control and the power of the pen, Uncle Robin refuses to sell his story to Harriet Beecher Stowe, gives the rights to Quickskill, rewrites Swille's will, and inherits the plantation.

THE TERRIBLE TWOS

In *The Terrible Twos*, Reed uses a contemporary setting to attack Ronald Reagan's administration and the exploitative nature of the American economic system. In the novel, President Dean Clift, a former model, is a mindless figurehead manipulated by an oil cartel that has supplanted the real Santa Claus. Nance Saturday, another of Reed's African American detectives, sets out to discover Saint Nicholas's place of exile. The novel's title suggests that, in its second century, the United States is acting as selfishly and ir-

rationally as the proverbial two-year-old. The central theme is the manner in which a few avaricious people seek vast wealth at the expense of the majority of Americans.

RECKLESS EYEBALLING

Reckless Eyeballing takes place in the 1980's, and Reed employs a string of comically distorted characters to present the idea that the American literary environment is dominated by New York women and Jews. Although *Reckless Eyeballing* has been called sexist and anti-Semitic by some, Reed's target is a cultural establishment that creates and strengthens racial stereotypes, in particular the view of African American men as savage rapists. To make his point, however, he lampoons feminists, using the character Tremonisha Smarts, a female African American author who has written a novel of violence against women. Reed's satire is probably intended to remind readers of Alice Walker's *The Color Purple* (1982).

Because the novel's central subject is art and the limitations that society places on an artist, it is appropriate that Reed once again employs the technique of a story-within-a-story. Ian Ball, an unsuccessful African American playwright, is the novel's protagonist. In the novel, Ball tries to succeed by shamelessly placating the feminists in power. He writes "Reckless Eyeballing," a play in which a lynched man is posthumously tried for "raping" a woman with lecherous stares, but Ball, who often seems to speak for Reed, maintains his private, chauvinistic views throughout.

THE TERRIBLE THREES

The Terrible Threes, a sequel to *The Terrible Twos*, continues Reed's satirical attack on the contemporary capitalist system, which, he argues, puts the greatest economic burden on the least privileged. (Reed was also planning a third book in the series, *The Terrible Fours*.) In the first book, there appears a character named Black Peter—an assistant to St. Nicholas in European legend. This Black Peter is an imposter, however, a Rastafarian who studied and appropriated the legend for himself. In *The Terrible Threes*, the true Black Peter emerges to battle the false Peter but is distracted from his mission by the need to do good deeds. Black Peter becomes wildly popular because of these deeds, but a jealous St. Nick and concerned toy companies find a way to put Santa Claus back on top. Capitalism wins again.

JAPANESE BY SPRING

Japanese by Spring is postmodern satire. Like much of Reed's imaginative work, the book mixes fictional characters with "fictionalized" ones. Ishmael Reed himself is a character in the book, with his own name. The protagonist of *Japanese by Spring* is Benjamin "Chappie" Puttbutt, a teacher of English and literature at Oakland's Jack London College. Chappie dabbled in activist politics in the mid-1960's, but his only concern in the 1990's is receiving tenure and the perks that accompany it. He will put up with virtually anything, including racist insults from students, to avoid hurting his chances at tenure. As in many of Reed's books, Chappie is passive in the face of power at the beginning of his story. He is a middle-class black conservative, but only because the climate at Jack London demands it. Chappie is a chameleon who always matches his behavior to the ideology of his environment. However, when he is denied tenure and is about to be replaced by a feminist poet who is more flash than substance, Chappie's hidden anger begins to surface. Chappie has also been studying Japanese with a tutor named Dr. Yamato. This proves fortuitous when the Japanese buy Jack London and Dr. Yamato becomes the college president. Chappie suddenly finds himself in a position of power and gloats over those who denied him tenure. He soon finds, however, that his new bosses are the same as the old ones. Dr. Yamato is a tyrant and is eventually arrested by a group that includes Chappie's father, a two-star Air Force general. Dr. Yamato is released, though, and a surprised Chappie learns that there is an "invisible government" that truly controls the United States. Chappie has pierced some of his illusions, but there are others that he never penetrates, such as his blindness to his own opportunism.

The novel's conclusion moves away from Chappie's point of view to that of a fictionalized Ishmael Reed. This Reed skewers political correctness but also shows that the people who complain the most about it are often its greatest purveyors. Reed also lampoons American xenophobia, particularly toward Japan, but he does so in a balanced manner that does not gloss over Japanese faults. Ultimately, though, Reed uses *Japanese by Spring* as he used other novels before, to explore art and politics and the contradictions of America and race.

Carl Brucker, updated by Charles A. Gramlich

OTHER MAJOR WORKS

PLAY: *The Preacher and the Rapper*, pb. 1997.

POETRY: *Catechism of D Neoamerican Hoodoo Church*, 1970; *Conjure: Selected Poems, 1963-1970*, 1972; *Chattanooga*, 1973; *A Secretary to the Spirits*, 1977; *Cab Calloway Stands In for the Moon*, 1986; *New and Collected Poems*, 1988.

NONFICTION: *Shrovetide in Old New Orleans*, 1978; *God Made Alaska for the Indians*, 1982; *Writin' Is Fightin'*, 1988; *Airing Dirty Laundry*, 1993.

EDITED TEXTS: *Nineteen Necromancers from Now*, 1970; *Yardbird Lives!*, 1978 (with Al Young); *Calafia: The California Poetry*, 1979; *The Before Columbus Foundation Fiction Anthology: Selections from the American Book Awards, 1980-1990*, 1992 (with Kathryn Trueblood and Shawn Wong); *MultiAmerica: Essays on Cultural Wars and Cultural Peace*, 1997.

BIBLIOGRAPHY

Dick, Bruce, and Amritjit Singh, eds. *Conversations with Ishmael Reed*. Jackson: University Press of Mississippi, 1995. A collection of twenty-six interviews with Ishmael Reed, which cover the years 1968-1995. Includes one self-interview and a chronology of Reed's life.

Fabre, Michel. "Postmodern Rhetoric in Ishmael Reed's *Yellow Back Radio Broke-Down*." In *The Afro-American Novel Since 1960*, edited by Peter Bruck and Wolfgang Karrer. Amsterdam: Gruener, 1982. A valuable addition to the study of Reed regarding his postmodernism.

Fox, Robert Elliot. *Conscientious Sorcerers: The Black Post-Modern Fiction of LeRoi Jones/Amiri Baraka, Ishmael Reed, and Samuel R. Delaney*. New York: Greenwood Press, 1987. Situates Reed within both the tradition of black fiction and the self-conscious style of contemporary postmodernist fiction.

Gates, Henry Louis, Jr. *The Signifying Monkey: A Theory of Afro-American Literary Criticism.* New York: Oxford University Press, 1988. The section on Reed examines his fiction, especially the novel *Mumbo Jumbo*, as an extension of the tendency of black English to play deliberately with language.

Lee, A. Robert, ed. *Black Fiction: New Studies in the Afro-American Novel Since 1945.* New York: Barnes & Noble Books, 1980. Frank McConnell's essay on Reed uses a quotation about him from Thomas Pynchon's novel, *Gravity's Rainbow*, in order to speak broadly about parody in Reed's novels.

McGee, Patrick. *Ishmael Reed and the Ends of Race.* New York: St. Martin's Press, 1997. Looks at Reed's refusal to meet expectations associated traditionally with African American writers, and examines his use of satire and his antagonism toward political correctness.

Martin, Reginald. *Ishmael Reed and the New Black Aesthetic Critics.* New York: St. Martin's Press, 1988. A comprehensive and important look at Reed's work and theories in relation to the evolution of the black aesthetics movement.

The Review of Contemporary Fiction 4 (Summer, 1984). A special issue devoted to Reed. Especially important is an essay by James Lindroth, "From Krazy Kat to Hoodoo: Aesthetic Discourse in the Fiction of Ishmael Reed," and an interview with Reed by Reginald Martin.

ERICH MARIA REMARQUE
Erich Paul Remark

Born: Osnabrück, Germany; June 22, 1898
Died: Locarno, Switzerland; September 25, 1970

PRINCIPAL LONG FICTION
Die Traumbude, 1920
Station am Horizont, 1927-1928 (serial), 1998 (book)
Im Westen nichts Neues, 1929, 1968 (*All Quiet on the Western Front*, 1929, 1969)
Der Weg zurück, 1931 (*The Road Back*, 1931)
Drei Kameraden, 1938 (*Three Comrades*, 1937)
Liebe Deinen Nächsten, 1941 (*Flotsam*, 1941)
Arc de Triomphe, 1946 (*Arch of Triumph*, 1945)
Der Funke Leben, 1952 (*The Spark of Life*, 1952)
Zeit zu leben und Zeit zu sterben, 1954 (*A Time to Love and a Time to Die*, 1954)
Der schwarze Obelisk, 1956 (*The Black Obelisk*, 1957)
Der Himmel kennt keine Günstlinge, 1961 (*Heaven Has No Favorites*, 1961; also as *Bobby Deerfield*, 1961)
Die Nacht von Lissabon, 1962 (*The Night in Lisbon*, 1964)
Schatten im Paradies, 1971 (*Shadows in Paradise*, 1972)

OTHER LITERARY FORMS

Poetry, adventure stories, and articles by Erich Maria Remarque appeared in the 1920's in German newspapers and magazines before the young author had assumed his pen name, and the novel *Die Traumbude* was succeeded by *Station am Horizont*, a novel which appeared in installments in the journal *Sport im Bild*.

In the United States, several novels by Erich Maria Remarque reached mass circulation in magazines such as *Collier's* and *Good Housekeeping* before being published as single titles.

The film *The Other Love* (1947) was based on Remarque's unpublished story "Beyond," and the story "Der letzte Akt" (1955) was based on his screenplay of the book *Ten Days to Die* (1955) by Michael A. Musmanno, concerning the Nuremberg trials of Nazi war criminals. The film *On the Beach* (1959) contained dialogue adapted from Remarque's novel *Geborgtes Leben*, which appeared in the journal *Kristall* in 1959.

Questions of guilt and moral responsibility in wartime, dominant themes in Remarque's works, are treated also in the two-scene play *Die letzte Station*, which was produced in Germany in the 1950's and appeared in 1974 as *Full Circle*.

ACHIEVEMENTS

All Quiet on the Western Front is one of the world's most successful novels. Within months after its appearance in 1929, it was widely translated and distributed, and some four decades later its author observed that the work had been translated into almost fifty languages and had a circulation of twenty to thirty million copies, including so-called pirated editions. Only in the degree of its popularity, however, was this book exceptional among Remarque's works, for *Arch of Triumph* and *The Night in Lisbon* were also best-sellers, and more than half of his novels, as well as a short story, lent themselves to films.

Remarque's choice of subject matter explains the primary reason for his appeal. In his novels set against the background of the world wars, issues such as personal moral responsibility and military subordination, war guilt, and pacifism are treated from the perspective of the soldier. His novels set in the Weimar Republic depict the dislocation and disorientation of that era, a time of inflation, unemployment, and political unrest. Finally, his exile novels depict the fate of emigrants and exiles from Hitler's Third Reich.

The interest evoked by Remarque's choice of subject is heightened by a streamlined, uncomplicated style, which moves quickly and lends itself with an objective, semidocumentary tone to the excitement of automobile racing, the suspense of chase and pursuit, the stark horror of war, or the brutalities of a concentration camp. Consistent with the author's technique are characters drawn with such simplicity that they appear without betraying an insight into their internal lives or psychological motivations.

The ease with which Remarque's works can be read has influenced his critical reception in Germany, as has the magnitude of his commercial success. In Germany, his novels are classified as *Unterhaltungsliteratur* (entertainment literature), a rubric with pejo-

(Library of Congress)

rative aesthetic connotations. Nevertheless, critics are uneasy with such an evaluation, for the author's style is neither banal nor are moral issues trivialized in his work. Among readers not bound by critical predispositions, such as his English-language audience, for example, Remarque's work is more highly regarded.

BIOGRAPHY

Erich Maria Remarque was born Erich Paul Remark in Osnabrück, Germany, on June 22, 1898, the son of a bookbinder. While he was still a schoolboy, his life was interrupted by service in World War I. Like Paul Bäumer and Ludwig Bodmer, his personas in the novels *All Quiet on the Western Front* and *The Black Obelisk*, Remarque left the classroom to fight in the west, from which he returned with war injuries.

During the postwar years, Remarque tried his hand at various pursuits, including teaching, sales work, and automobile racing. As a journalist, he wrote articles on such subjects as automobiles, travel, and liquors, as well as poetry and prose. His novel *Die Traumbude* appeared in 1920.

Reverting to the original French spelling of his surname, the author assumed the name Remarque and in 1925 moved to Berlin, where his writing appeared in the metropolitan press during the Weimar Republic. In the same year, he married Jutta Ilse Zambona, from whom he was divorced only a few years later. In 1927 and 1928, the novel *Station am Horizont* appeared in installments in a popular magazine; generated by a sketch of 1924, "Das Rennen Vanderveldes," this work depicted an unhappy love affair played out against a background of horse racing and auto sports.

Remarque moved to Switzerland in the early 1930's, taking with him his considerable wealth and acquiring a luxurious villa on the Italian border in Tessin. The villa was located at Porto Ronco near Ascona on Laggo Maggiore, and Remarque maintained it all of his life. The conditions of the author's residence there and the voluntary nature of his absence from Germany were radically altered in 1933, when the Third Reich prohibited the publication and distribution of his work by consigning it to the blacklist for the crime of literary treason committed against the soldiers of World War I.

Three Comrades appeared in 1937 in the United States, and in 1938, it was published in German by the exile press Querido, in Holland. At that time, Remarque remarried his former wife in Saint Moritz. Deprived of his German citizenship, he was consigned to the fate of an estimated four hundred thousand emigrants from Nazi Germany, including some fifty thousand political and literary exiles. Many of them employed desperate means to flee an unknown fate, moving throughout the countries contiguous to Germany without legal status and therefore under the threat of apprehension by authorities of those professed democracies. Such a life in exile is the subject of *Flotsam*, a theme that would become familiar in Remarque's works.

The author himself remained luxuriously ensconced in Switzerland until 1939, at which time he departed for the United States and traveled to Hollywood to see acquaintances including Marlene Dietrich and members of the German exile community. Unlike other writers in exile, many of whom were unknown outside their native countries and therefore were forced to accept whatever work was available, Remarque enjoyed an international reputation. His fame, moreover, was matched by his wealth, which was augmented by the revenue from books, magazine serials, and several films. A film version of *The Road Back* in 1937 was followed by one of *Three Comrades* in 1938, the screenplay for the latter written by F. Scott Fitzgerald. The success of both was, however, dwarfed in 1930 by that of the film version of *All Quiet on the Western Front*, which won several Oscars and enjoyed long-term box-office success.

Remarque was joined in the United States by his wife shortly after his arrival there. This time the marital union was maintained until 1951; seven years later, Remarque married the film actress Paulette Goddard. Darkly handsome, a *bon vivant* and ladies' man, Remarque pursued his tastes for beautiful women, art (especially Impressionist works), and wines and liquors—interests shared by his characters (who, however, lack the financial means to enjoy them fully). These characters, moreover, have usually gained their knowledge of art in museums, during long hours of concealment from the police.

Arch of Triumph, in 1945, became Remarque's second great success, a novel of exile that reached several million copies in translation and remained in its popularity unrivaled by the author's succeeding four novels. In 1963, Remarque again successfully captured the imagination of his readers, and again with a best-selling novel, *The Night in Lisbon*. The threads of these works set in France and Portugal were then brought together in the posthumous novel *Shadows in Paradise*, which unfolds in the United States. Here, the exile Ross arrives from Lisbon last seen as the port of departure in *The Night in Lisbon*; Ravic, who lived through the last days in Paris before the outbreak of hostilities—as did the figures in *The Night in Lisbon*—returns from *Arch of Triumph*, now permitted in the United States to practice surgery once again.

During his later years, Remarque divided his time between New York City and the site of his villa in Switzerland; shortly after attaining United States citizenship, he returned to Germany in 1948 for the first time since he had emigrated. He made no attempt to regain that citizenship of which he had been deprived, and with some irony he notes the experience of the central figures in his last two novels upon their own postwar return to Germany. The man who, in *The Night in Lisbon*, has assumed the name Schwarz seeks to reestablish his identity at a time when hundreds of members of the master race were attempting to lose theirs; Ross in *Shadows in Paradise*, believing that war crimes should not go unpunished, is confronted by a wall of feigned ignorance and innocence regarding those who might be guilty.

Germany awarded Remarque a signal honor in 1967 by granting him the Great Service Cross of the Federal Republic. On September 25, 1970, he died in a hospital in Locarno, Switzerland, survived by his widow.

ANALYSIS

In *All Quiet on the Western Front*, the most famous novel by Erich Maria Remarque, the reader experiences events which, during World War I, from summer to fall, 1917, reduce a company of 150 men to only 32. Without purporting to be authentic, the account nevertheless compels credibility. The war is portrayed in a factual style with such immediacy and force that, however impartial, the report shocked Remarque's readership and provoked a strong pacifist response.

ALL QUIET ON THE WESTERN FRONT

One scene in the work is representative of many. It illustrates the undercurrent which awoke such a reaction and provides an insight into attitudes characteristic of Remarque's novels generally. When the teenage recruit Paul Bäumer takes refuge in a shell crater from which there is no retreat under fire, he finds himself unexpectedly forced to share the site with a Frenchman, whom he stabs. Forced to share cover with the corpse of his anonymous enemy during the long wait until the firing should cease, Bäumer familiarizes himself with the man's identity and background by examining his papers—those of a simple typesetter. Bäumer promises himself that he will thereafter support the man's family and oppose the war.

Such a scene, as well as the expressions of antimilitarism with which the work is rife, provoked a violent response from the political right, including public disturbances at the showing of the film version in Berlin in 1930. Zealots dedicated to avenging the perceived outrages perpetrated by the Treaty of Versailles were infuriated by the direct contradiction of National Socialist dogma: The defeat of the German army was portrayed not as the consequence of a perfidious "stab in the back" but as the result of an Allied advantage gained by fresher, more numerous troops with adequate matériel and support; Russians, a species relegated by National Socialist genetics to a subhuman order, behave in a more brotherly fashion to one another in captivity than do Germans to their comrades in arms.

Written in the style of the 1920's known as *Neue Sachlichkeit* (New Objectivity), *All Quiet on the Western Front* treats in simply constructed, precise, and quickly moving prose a theme current in the literature of that time. Coincidentally, it breaks sharply with another fashion then in vogue.

During the age of Bismarck and the kaisers, politics, society, and familial affairs were dominated by the authoritarian father figure, who brooked no dissent. A variant of this type was the tyrannical pedagogue, a familiar character in German literature since before the turn of the century. This figure intimidated his hapless subjects in an attempt to demean them and break their spirits; at the same time, however, he fostered a streak of antiauthoritarianism in the more hardy of them. In *All Quiet on the Western Front*, the attitudes engendered by such experiences are represented among boys who are marched out of the classroom as a body by their teacher to enlist for military service at the front. There, the teacher is succeeded by sergeants and other (interchangeable) figures of authority who provoke reactions of slavishness and insubordination known to the members of an entire generation.

All Quiet on the Western Front appeared during a time when works dealing with World War I enjoyed considerable popularity in Germany. Unlike Remarque's novel, however, most of these works presented a justification or rationalization, from the German point of view, of this terrible European tragedy. The fiction of Ernst Jünger, for example, glorifies the ennobling effects of war—its intensification of the manly virtues and the strength of the race.

Purporting to be "neither an accusation nor a confession" but rather a report on "a generation which was destroyed by the war even though it escaped the grenades," Remarque's work assumes the role of documentary journalism. No attempt is made, however, to preserve objective distance; the reader is induced to identify with Paul Bäumer and his comrades from the outset. Nineteen years old and neither men nor boys, the former classmates are tragically out of place at the front, members of a company whose numbers have been reduced from 150 to 80 in only two weeks. Daily encounters with death have endowed the adolescents with precious wisdom, cynicism regarding the pronouncements of the older generation, self-reliance, and a sense of camaraderie. The fate of their classmate Josef Behm conveyed a lesson for their generation. Behm had been reluctant to serve. Shot in the eyes during battle, he crawled around blindly, unable to find cover, and was picked off by gunfire—one of the first to be killed.

The message of the novel is written in the experience of Bäumer and his comrades. What has been learned in school is useless; the knowledge they need was never entrusted to them—for example, the trick of making fire from wet wood or the advantage gained by stabbing one's bayonet into the opponent's belly rather than into his ribs. The prospect of civilian life looms as a void upon the horizon. No occupational skills were learned in the military, and the resumption of study seems purposeless. The war has ruined men for everything. On leave from the front, Bäumer is unable to find his way about in the strange civilian world.

The impartiality conveyed by the objective tone of a military report is dispelled by the horror which the novel depicts. Thrust and parry, attack and counterattack follow mindlessly under a netlike arch of hand grenades as men forge forward over the trenches with spades and bayonets; wounded horses scream horribly until put to death after the last injured soldiers are retrieved. A wretched death is spread by poison gas, and even its survivors are nearly suffocated by repeated inhalation of nothing but their own warm breath under the gas mask. Young, inexperienced recruits, ignorant of the uses of cover or the sound of shells, appear, only to be immediately shot down in scene after scene.

Remarque's literary characters move quickly along the hazardous course that traces the path of their lives. *All Quiet on the Western Front* is composed of a number of episodes collected into chapters that illustrate how chance, ingenuity, and determination are employed by a handful of soldiers to prevail against peril. As the novel progresses, the number of men diminishes until, finally, only one remains, Paul Bäumer, who himself dies on a day when the military dispatch reports that on the western front all is quiet, or, more accurately that there is "nothing new" (*nichts neues*): That is, the killing continues unabated; another death is not extraordinary.

The precariousness of survival—and its importance—is illustrated by the role that ordinary, but essential, objects play. A soldier whose leg had been amputated leaves his much-envied boots to a comrade, and shortly before each man's death, the boots are passed symbolically to the next man until Bäumer dies with them on his feet as the last of the seven classmates.

Respite from continuous struggle to survive and from exposure to danger presents itself when eight men remove themselves from the chaos about them. Isolation from events and the passage of time is achieved as in a return to the womb. On patrol in an empty village under fire, the soldiers collect all the provisions found there—suckling pigs, wine and spirits, sausage, canned goods, tobacco, and mattresses—and occupy the cellar and first floor of an empty house. For two weeks, they luxuriate there with drink, piano and song, and various pastimes, on an island of self-indulgent contentment and oblivion amid the continuing holocaust.

ARCH OF TRIUMPH

The uncertainties and hazards of life and the exigencies of survival are revealed nowhere more markedly than in Remarque's exile novels, the most successful example of which is *Arch of Triumph*. The work provided a formula to which the author returned: France in 1939, when German aliens concealed themselves in a sordid world consisting of seedy hotels and illegal activities and counted themselves lucky as long as they could evade the authorities who sought them for deportation to Switzerland. The central figure is pursued by a Gestapo agent from his past, whom he murders; the murderer then recklessly compounds his danger by returning illegally to Germany before he is finally detained and interned by French authorities upon the outbreak of war.

As the novel contains certain factual episodes or themes that reappear in other works, so, too, it brings together in the characters a complex of personality traits that can be found elsewhere in Remarque's fiction. From the earliest sketches originates the woman who suffers from cancer: in *Arch of Triumph*, Kate Hegström; in *Shadows in Paradise*, Betty Stein. The disease assumes tragic significance when it is recognized as terminal in the case of Helen Baumann in *The Night in Lisbon*, as it is with her predecessor, Pat Hollmann, in *Three Comrades*. In *Arch of Triumph*, too, Joan Madou, will be found, beautiful and amoral, infatuated by the attention of men and a captive of their devotion; she is distinguished from Helen Baumann only by her possessiveness.

The protagonist of *Arch of Triumph* is the German exile Ravic, once a soldier on the western front with Bäumer, it is suggested; thereafter a respected chief surgeon; and now, as an alien, an illegal medical practitioner. When faith and ideals are no longer sacrosanct, he observes, everything becomes more sacred in a human way; one reveres the spark of life in its lowest living form.

The significance attributed to coincidence in *All Quiet on the Western Front*, where chance alone enables the soldier to survive, plays a no less weighty role in *Arch of Triumph*. Here it explains the fateful encounter of Ravic and Joan, as well as his subsequent deportation. Ravic's identity is established after he has been detained by the police as a witness, having passed a construction site as another pedestrian was injured there.

The couple's troubled love affair is threatened by

insurmountable barriers, and their reaction to these threats is typical of Remarque's characters. Permanently paralyzed by a revolver shot from another lover and suffering unbearable pain, Joan easily persuades Ravic to administer to her a fatal injection as a means to escape the fate that lies ahead of her. Ravic himself, interned by French authorities as an enemy alien after the outbreak of war, awaits his end fatalistically with the comfort and sustaining strength provided by the knowledge of poison hidden in a hollow locket on his person, the thought of which enabled him once before to survive the ordeal of imprisonment in a German concentration camp.

THE NIGHT IN LISBON

The Night in Lisbon unfolds in a flashback set in France immediately prior to and during the war, a time when illegal immigrants, once mathematics professors or doctors, turned to passport forgery or the sale of stockings or of their valued Impressionist paintings to survive. It is the tale of a German immigrant, Josef Schwarz, told to an acquaintance, who listens patiently in return for two tickets on a passenger ship leaving the last point of departure from occupied Europe. Schwarz and his wife, Helen, were fleeing across Europe in the attempt to escape to the United States when Helen suddenly died. Schwarz relinquishes those passports and visas for which the couple no longer has any use, thus enabling the listener and his wife to find refuge in America themselves.

The exile phenomenon is associated in Remarque's works with religious imagery, which in *The Night in Lisbon* reaches its most highly developed form. The refugees are compared to the Israelites who departed from Egypt through the Red Sea—behind them, the German army and the Gestapo; to both sides, French and Spanish police; before them, the promised land of Portugal. The path of flight from Belgium to the Pyrenees and the suffering endured thereon are called to mind by the *via dolorosa*, Christ's route by stations to the Cross; America appears as Mount Ararat, a refuge from the Nazi flood, to be reached by ark from Lisbon.

In Remarque's work, a character whose daily existence is not exposed to inordinate risk lives in a most self-indulgent manner—as, indeed, the author did himself. Occasionally a person finds a den of refuge for concealment, a capsule within which he can withdraw to isolate himself from the unrelenting dangers of life. Oblivious to the world without, he exists as in another dimension, surrendering himself to the primary physical pleasures, as do the eight men in *All Quiet on the Western Front.*

In *The Night in Lisbon*, Helen and Schwarz interrupt their frantic flight from the Germans and police across several national boundaries when they discover an unoccupied mansion in France. There the two isolate themselves in a self-contained never-never-land; with plentiful supplies of wine, potatoes, bread, honey, and firewood, they amuse themselves with abandoned masquerade costumes in a fool's paradise, undisturbed by the occasional drone of planes passing overhead.

When a central figure in Remarque's work sees his ultimate survival threatened by an insurmountable obstacle—such as cancer or the Gestapo—then he ends his own life, usually by poison, as in *Arch of Triumph.* The last days are played out with increasingly feverish enjoyment at an accelerating tempo to the discernibly approaching end. Helen's secret knowledge of her incurable malignant cancer heightens her frantic desire to enjoy herself, but the imminent threat of capture by the Germans, a prospect equivalent to death, requires an alternative sufficiently radical, and for this reason both Helen and Schwarz carry poison on their persons. The ultimate obstacle posed by Helen's terminal illness is surmounted by this means.

Remarque's individualism, his humanism, and his democratic instincts (however apolitical he was in practice) are the common threads that run throughout his work, linking *All Quiet on the Western Front* with his exile novels of the post-World War II years. It is, however, for a single book, his great novel of World War I, that Remarque will be remembered. In *All Quiet on the Western Front*, he gave voice to a lost generation—not metaphorically lost in the Paris of the 1920's but lost in battle by the hundreds of thousands.

Ward B. Lewis

OTHER MAJOR WORKS

PLAY: *Die letzte Station*, pr. 1956 (adapted by Peter Stone as *Full Circle*, 1974).

SCREENPLAY: *Der letzte Akt*, 1955.

BIBLIOGRAPHY

Barker, Christine R. and R. W. Last. *Erich Maria Remarque.* New York: Barnes & Noble, 1979. An excellent introduction to Remarque's career, this study covers all of his major fiction.

Firda, Richard Arthur. *"All Quiet on the Western Front": Literary Analysis and Cultural Context.* New York: Twayne, 1993. One of Twayne's masterwork studies, this is an excellent tool for students of the novel.

_____. *Erich Maria Remarque: A Thematic Analysis of His Novels.* New York: Peter Lang, 1988. Contains a good deal of helpful biographical material. Useful also for Firda's interpretation of the later novels.

Gilbert, Julie. *Opposite Attraction: The Lives of Erich Maria Remarque and Paulette Goddard.* New York: Pantheon, 1995. Although primarily a biography and love story, see chapter 1, "A German Youth." Gilbert also provides detailed notes and an excellent bibliography.

Owen, C. R. *Erich Maria Remarque: A Critical Bio-Bibliography.* Amsterdam: Rodopi, 1984. An excellent source for finding additional critical commentary on Remarque.

Taylor, Jr., Harley U. *Erich Maria Remarque: A Literary and Film Biography.* New York: Peter Lang, 1989. This very detailed study provides excellent background information on Remarque's family origins, his early years, military service, and the filming of *All Quiet on the Western Front.* There is a valuable bibliography of Remarque novels in German and English translation as well as a chronology, filmography, and index. Not as good on interpreting Remarque's fiction as Wagener and Barker.

Wagener, Hans. *Understanding Erich Maria Remarque.* Columbia: University of South Carolina Press, 1991. Separate chapters on all of Remarque's major work, interweaving biographical background with literary analysis. Includes a chronology, notes, and an excellent annotated bibliography.

MARY RENAULT
Mary Challans

Born: London, England; September 4, 1905
Died: Cape Town, South Africa; December 13, 1983

PRINCIPAL LONG FICTION

Purposes of Love, 1939 (pb. in U.S. as *Promise of Love*, 1940)
Kind Are Her Answers, 1940
The Friendly Young Ladies, 1944 (pb. in U.S. as *The Middle Mist*, 1945)
Return to Night, 1947
North Face, 1948
The Charioteer, 1953
The Last of the Wine, 1956
The King Must Die, 1958
The Bull from the Sea, 1962
The Mask of Apollo, 1966
Fire from Heaven, 1969
The Persian Boy, 1972
The Praise Singer, 1978
Funeral Games, 1981
The Alexander Trilogy, 1984 (includes *Fire from Heaven*, *The Persian Boy*, and *Funeral Games*)

OTHER LITERARY FORMS

All but two of Mary Renault's published works are novels. *The Lion in the Gateway: Heroic Battles of the Greeks and Persians at Marathon, Salamis, and Thermopylae* (1964) is a children's history of ancient Greek battles. *The Nature of Alexander* (1975) is a heavily documented biography placing the charismatic leader in the context of his time and customs, a book that also defines the two abiding preoccupations of Alexander's life and Renault's art. "Outward striving for honor," the Greek *to philotimo*, balances *arete*, the profound inward thirst for achieve-

ment knowingly made beautiful. Together, as Alexander himself wrote, they win immortality: "It is a lovely thing to live with courage,/ and die leaving an everlasting fame."

ACHIEVEMENTS

Critics praised Renault's first five novels, written and set around World War II, for their realism, psychological depth, and literary technique. In 1946, one year prior to its publication, *Return to Night* won the MGM Award, $150,000, then the world's largest literary prize. Although this novel was never made into a motion picture, the award brought Renault American acclaim, augmented later by the success of her Greek novels, but her work has never gained the academic attention it deserves. She received the National Association of Independent Schools Award in 1963 and the Silver Pen Award in 1971, and she was a Fellow of the Royal Society of Literature.

BIOGRAPHY

Mary Renault (the pen name of Mary Challans), a physician's daughter, was born on September 4, 1905, in London. At eight, she decided to become a writer, and she read English at St. Hugh's College, Oxford, from 1924 to 1927, where she preferred to study the Middle Ages, the setting of an attempted historical novel she destroyed after several rejections. She had once thought of teaching, but after graduation she entered nurses' training at Radcliffe Infirmary, Oxford, where she received her nursing degree in 1937. She dated her literary career from 1939, though she continued as a neurosurgical nurse at Radcliffe Infirmary throughout the war, writing in her off-duty hours. Her first novels were widely popular, but she claimed that "if her early novels were destroyed irrevocably, she would feel absolutely no loss" (Bernard F. Dick, *The Hellenism of Mary Renault*, 1972).

Renault's postwar travels in the eastern Mediterranean provided the impetus for a new literary phase marked by her immigration to South Africa in 1948. After this move, her exhaustive self-taught knowledge of ancient Greek history and philosophy made her a mesmerizing novelist able to re-create a lost world. In the estimation of Dick, Renault was "the only bona fide Hellenist in twentieth century fiction."

Renault remained a resident of South Africa until her death on December 13, 1983.

ANALYSIS

Mary Renault's novels celebrate and eulogize people's potential but transitory glory, a combination difficult for a world that has relinquished its acquaintance with the classics. Peter Wolfe regards Renault's first five novels as her literary apprenticeship, "1930's novels" marked by then-fashionable themes of political engagement and sexual liberation. Bernard F. Dick, her only other major commentator, believes her early fiction was influenced by the restrictive, pain-filled atmosphere of a World War II surgical hospital. Both are partly correct; Renault's early work deals with the individual's freedom from contemporary power structures and stifling social conventions.

Such topical concerns, however appealing to modern readers, are nevertheless peripheral to the core of Renault's art, the Platonism which she followed to the mythic depths in her later novels. When she began to write, Renault was already familiar with the Theory of Ideas developed in Plato's dialogues, wherein everything perceptible by human senses is imitative of changeless perfect Ideas beyond time and space. Each Idea corresponds to a class of earthly objects, all of which must inevitably change, leaving the Ideas the only objects of true knowledge in the universe. A transitory earthly object, however, may remind people of the Idea it represents. Plato theorized that before entering the body, the soul had encountered the infinite Ideas, and that once embodied, the soul might vaguely remember them. Renault often convincingly incorporates Plato's anamnesis, the doctrine that "learning is recollection," in her fiction. Plato also believed that human recognition of such natural truths as the mathematically perfect circle could lead people stepwise to the contemplation of Absolute Truth, which he equated with Absolute Goodness and Absolute Beauty. He taught that the immortal human soul may be reborn through metempsychosis, or transmigration, another concept found throughout Renault's work.

Renault's novels are also informed by Plato's theory of love as defined by Socrates in *The Symposium* (c. 388-368 B.C.E.): love is the desire for immortality through possession of or union with the Beautiful. Love manifests itself on its lowest levels by human sexuality, proceeds upward through intellectual achievement, and culminates in a mystical union of the soul with the Idea of Beauty. That Renault's heroes aspire to such union is their glory; that being mortal they must fail is the fate she eulogizes.

Plato, like most classical Greeks, allowed heterosexual love only the lowest rung on his ladder of love, as the necessary element for reproduction. Only the homosexual relationship was considered capable of inspiring the lifelong friendships which offered each partner the ideal of *arete*. All of Renault's novels illustrate some aspect of Platonic love; in the first, *Promise of Love*, she shows Vivian, a nurse, and Mic, who loves her because she resembles her brother Jan, achieving self-knowledge not through sexual passion but by affection, the ultimate stage of Platonic love, which at the close of the novel "recalls the true lover of [Plato's dialogue] the *Phaedrus* who is willing to sleep like a servant at the side of his beloved."

Renault's other early novels also have strong Platonic elements. *Kind Are Her Answers* foreshadows her interest in theater as mimetic form, Plato's first literary love, which she realized more fully in *The Mask of Apollo*. Her third novel, *The Middle Mist*, concludes with references to Plato's *Lysis*, his dialogue on friendship which claims that erotic satisfaction destroys *philia*, the more permanent nonphysical union promised by Platonic love, a theme to which Renault returned more successfully in *The Last of the Wine*. Renault attempted unconvincingly in *Return to Night* and *North Face* to state the *amor vincit omnia* tradition of "women's fiction" in mythological metaphors, and found that she had to develop a new fictional mode capable of expressing her archetypal themes with Platonic concepts.

THE CHARIOTEER

Not published in the United States until 1959 because of its forthright treatment of homosexuality, *The Charioteer* is the only Renault novel to incorporate a systematic development of Platonic philosophy as the vehicle for commentary on contemporary life. In the *Phaedrus* (c. 388-368 B.C.E.), Plato depicted reason as a charioteer who must balance the thrust of the white horse of honor against the unruly black horse of passion. The image unifies Renault's tale of Laurie Odell, wounded at Dunkirk, who must come to terms with his homosexuality. After his friendship with the sexually naïve conscientious objector Andrew Raines dissolves, Laurie finds a lifelong partner in Ralph Lanyon, who brought him back wounded after they had fought at Dunkirk. Laurie attains an equilibrium between the two conflicting halves of his nature in a Platonic denial of sexual excess. As Renault comments in the epilogue, a Greek device she favors, "Now their [the horses'] heads droop side by side till their long manes mingle; and when the charioteer falls silent they are reconciled for a night in sleep."

In the ideal Platonic pattern, the older man assumes a compassionate responsibility for the honor of the younger, altogether transcending physical attraction and cemented by shared courage in battle. Renault's efforts at an entirely convincing presentation of such friendship are hindered by the intolerance with which homosexual relationships are usually viewed in modern society and the often pathetic insecurity it forces upon them. Despite these handicaps, Renault sympathetically portrays Laurie as "a modern Hephaestus, or maimed artist," as Wolfe notes, a character who wins admiration through striving to heal his injured life and nature and make of them something lasting and beautiful.

From roots far deeper than Plato's philosophy, Renault developed the vital impulse of her eight Greek novels, her major literary achievement. Central is the duality of Apollo and Dionysus, names the Greeks gave to the forces of the mind and of the heart, gods whose realms the mythologist Walter Otto described in *Dionysus, Myth and Cult* (1965) as "sharply opposed" yet "in reality joined together by an eternal bond." In Greek myth, Zeus's archer son Apollo, wielder of the two-sided weapon of Truth, endowed people with the heavenly light called Art, by which he admonished humankind to self-knowledge and

moderation through his oracle at Delphi. Paradoxically, Apollo shared his temple and the festival year at Delphi with his mysterious brother Dionysus, god of overwhelming ecstasy, born of mortal woman and all-powerful Zeus, torn apart each year to rise again, offering both wine's solace and its madness to humankind. Thought and emotion were the two faces of the Greek coin of life—in Otto's words, "the eternal contrast between a restless, whirling life and a still, far-seeing spirit."

Each of Renault's Greek novels focuses on a crucial nexus of physical and spiritual existence in Greek history. The age of legendary heroes such as Theseus of Athens, subject of *The King Must Die* and *The Bull from the Sea*, was followed by the Trojan War, 1200 B.C.E., the stuff of classical epic and tragedy and the harbinger of Greece's Dark Age, when only Athens stood against the Dorian invasion. By the sixth century B.C.E., the setting of *The Praise Singer*, Athens, under the benevolent tyrant Pisistratus, had become the model *polis* of the Greek peninsula, building a democracy that repelled imperial Persia and fostered the world's greatest tragedies in their Dionysian festivals. *The Last of the Wine* treats the fall of Athens to Sparta in the Peloponnesian Wars, 404 B.C.E., torn by internal strife and bled by foreign expansion. The restored Athenian democracy of a half-century later is the milieu of *The Mask of Apollo*. Shortly after Plato's death, his pupil Aristotle taught a prince in Macedon who dreams of Homeric deeds in *Fire from Heaven*, accomplishes them in *The Persian Boy*, and leaves an empire to be shattered by lesser men in *Funeral Games*—Alexander the Great.

THE LAST OF THE WINE

The Last of the Wine, like most of Renault's Greek fiction, is ostensibly a memoir, a form favored by classical authors. Its fictional narrator, a young and "beautiful" Athenian knight named Alexias, endures the agonizing aftermath of Athens' ill-fated Sicilian venture under Alkibiades, the magnetic but flawed former student of Sokrates. With Lysis, the historical figure on whom Plato modeled his dialogue on ideal friendship, Alexias begins the idealistic attachment they learned together from Sokrates, but physical passion, handled with sensitivity by Renault, overcomes them, and they ruefully must compromise their ideal. Sacrificing his honor for Lysis during the famine caused by the Spartan siege of Athens, Alexias models for sculptors, at least one lascivious, to feed his wounded friend, and in the battle to restore Athenian democracy, Lysis falls gloriously with Alexias's name upon his lips.

The novel's title, an allusion to the Greek custom in which the wine remaining in a cup is tossed to form the initial of a lover's name, metaphorically represents Athens' abandonment of the ideals of its Golden Age. Renault poignantly shows Lysis, a gentleman athlete in pursuit of *philotimo*, the hero's struggle for outward glory to emulate his ideal, beaten sadistically in the Isthmian Games by a monstrous professional wrestler, just as Athenian democracy is becoming warped by politicians such as the vicious Kritias and the cold-blooded Anytos, who will help condemn Sokrates. Alkibiades' personal disaster, abandoning Athens for its Spartan enemies, is an exemplary case of a leader who cannot resist abusing his charismatic gifts.

The Greek ideal of democracy learned at Sokrates' side and based on individual *arete*, inward pursuit of honor, still allows Lysis a moral victory often overlooked in this splendidly elegiac novel of the death of an era. "Men are not born equal in themselves," Lysis tells Alexias over wine one evening in Samos, "a man who thinks himself as good as everyone else will be at no pains to grow better." Lysis fights and dies for "a City where I can find my equals and respect my betters . . . and where no one can tell me to swallow a lie because it is expedient." At the end of the novel, as he listens to the distorted minds of bureaucrats, Alexias remembers the lamps of Samos, the wine-cup on a table of polished wood, and Lysis's voice: "Must we forsake the love of excellence, then, till every citizen feels it alike?"

THE KING MUST DIE and THE BULL FROM THE SEA

Renault analyzes the ideal of kingship in *The King Must Die* and *The Bull from the Sea*. In the earlier novel, she traces Theseus's early life from Troezen and Eleusis, where with the bard Orpheus he es-

tablishes the Sacred Mysteries, to the labyrinthine palace of Crete, where he destroys the brutal son of King Minos, who oppresses Athens. In the second, she pursues Theseus's progressive rule in Athens through his abandonment of Ariadne to Dionysus's bloody cult and his capture of the Amazon Hippolyta to the great tragedy of his life, his fatal curse on their son Hippolytus. Stylistically more evocative of Homer's mighty simplicity than the Attic cadences of *The Last of the Wine*, Renault's Theseus novels treat kingship as a manifestation of the divine inner voice that chooses the moment of willing consent when the monarch sacrifices himself for his people.

Both novels discuss a past so dim that its events have become the raw material of myth. Theseus's birth meshes the earthly with the supernatural, since it results from the divinely inspired compassion of the Athenian King Aigios for the stricken land of Troezen; the reader is left, as is customary in Renault's fiction, to decide where history ends and metaphysics begins. Until his son's death, Theseus practices the lesson learned from his grandfather's ritual sacrifice of the King Horse, one of the shocking joys hidden in pain that opens much of Renault's fiction: "The consenting . . . the readiness is all. It washes heart and mind . . . and leaves them open to the god."

By closing himself to the speaking god, however, obeying not his reason but his emotional reaction to his wife Phaedra's false accusations of Hippolytus, Theseus is lost. Only two bright moments remain to him, an anamnetic dream of Marathon where he fights beside the Athenians defending their City, his name their stirring war cry; and a glimpse before he dies of the boy Achilles, "as springy and as brisk as noonday, his arm round a dark-haired friend." Prescient, Theseus watches tragedy in the making: "The god who sent him that blazing pride should not have added love to be burned upon it," but—consoled that his own reputation has become Achilles' "touchstone for a man"—Theseus for the last time consents to the god of the sea.

THE MASK OF APOLLO

By the mid-fourth century B.C.E., late in Plato's life, sophisticated Athenians had accepted the gods as metaphysical forces within the human personality. In *The Mask of Apollo*, Renault poses the primal duality of Apollo and Dionysus in Greek culture, the calm, farseeing force of reason and art balanced against the irresistible force of ecstasy. An old mask of Apollo, reputedly from the workshop of the Parthenon's architect Phidias, accompanies Renault's narrator Nikeratos through his successful acting career, the fascinating backdrop to the political career of Dion of Syracuse, Plato's noble friend, who might have become the ideal philosopher-king Plato postulated in *The Republic*.

Though Dion is a model soldier and a principled statesman, circumstances force him to abandon his philosophical ideals to save Syracuse from devastation. Renault parallels his fall with Nikeratos's performance in Euripides' *The Bacchae* (405 B.C.E.), the enigmatic masterpiece named for the followers of Dionysus. As he meditates before Apollo's mask, Nikeratos hears his own voice: "With *The Bacchae* he [Euripides] digs down far below, to some deep rift in the soul where our griefs begin. Take that play anywhere, even to men unborn who worship other gods or none, and it will teach them to know themselves."

Plato's tragedy, acted out by Dion, was the "deep rift" that made people unable to follow him with united minds and hearts: "No one would fight for Dion, when he gave, as his own soul saw it, his very life for justice." By serving Apollo and Dionysus equally, however, Nikeratos the artist earns his gifts, one a Platonic dream of acting in a strange revenge drama, speaking lines beside an open grave to a clean skull in his hand. Through his love for his protégé Thettalos, whom he frees for achievements he knows will be greater than his own, Nikeratos plays Achilles in Aeschylus's *The Myrmidons* in a performance viewed by Alexander, a boy for whom men will fight and die, "whether he is right or wrong," a prince who "will wander through the world . . . never knowing . . . that while he was still a child the thing he seeks slipped from the world, worn out and spent." Had he encountered Plato's Ideals, which he instinctively sought, Renault proposes as the curtain falls on *The Mask of Apollo*, the Alexander of history might have made the philosopher-king Plato's Dion never could have been; but Nikeratos observes that "no one will ever make a tragedy—and that is well, for one could not bear it—whose grief is that the principals never met."

FIRE FROM HEAVEN

Renault's Alexander grows from boy to king in *Fire from Heaven*, in which she abandons the memoir form for more objective narration, as though no single point of view could encompass Alexander's youthful ideals, fired by the blazing Homeric *philotimo* in Achilles' honor he learned at the epic-conscious Macedonian court. Modern archaeology supports Renault's conviction that Alexander deliberately patterned his actions, even his father Philip's funerary rites, upon the *Iliad* (c. 800 B.C.E.), which he read as though returning home, recognizing in his mutual love with Hephaistion the tragic bond of Achilles and Patroclus, the basis of the Western world's first, perhaps greatest, poem.

Arete, which cloaks the heavenly Idea of excellence in earthly beauty, came to Alexander less from Aristotle than through his instinctive attraction to Sokrates through Plato's works, which he read as a boy in Macedon. After defeating Thebes's Sacred Band at Cheironeia, where Philip's Macedonians secured the domination of all of Greece, Alexander stands "with surmise and regret" at Plato's tomb in Athens, listening to his disciple Xenokrates: "What he [Plato] had to teach could only be learned as fire is kindled, by the touch of the flame itself."

THE PERSIAN BOY

The novel in which Renault most precariously treats the question of homosexuality, *The Persian Boy*, is narrated by Bagoas, the handsome eunuch once King Darius's favorite and now the lover of Alexander. Renault's choice of Bagoas's point of view reflects her belief that Alexander was not corrupted by Persian luxury and imperial power, as many historians from classical times to the present have asserted, but that he sought to assimilate Eastern ways as a means of uniting his realm in spirit as well as military fact. Just as Alexander's "passionate capacity for affection" could allow him to accept affection wherever it was sincerely offered from the heart and yet remain wholly true to Bagoas's "victor now, forever," Hephaistion (who Renault feels is the most underrated man in history), Alexander felt "Macedon was my father's country. This is mine"—meaning the empire he had won for himself.

Renault believes that Alexander's eventual tragedy was that he was humanly unable to achieve equilibrium between his followers' personal devotion to him and their pragmatic selfish desires. Through Alexander's complex relationship with his dangerous mother Olympias, herself a devotee of Dionysus, Renault exemplifies the peril of neglecting the god of ecstasy basic to *The Bacchae*, in which Olympias herself had acted during Alexander's youth as a shocking challenge to Philip's authority. Toward the end of Alexander's own life, Dionysus's cruelty touches even him. Renault shows his purported deterioration as less his own fault than his men's when he must hold them by force as well as by love, even violating Macedon's dearest law, killing before their Assembly had condemned a man to death. The powerful god leads Alexander to excess; Bagoas sees that "his hunger grew by feeding." The Roman historian Arrian, following the memoir of Alexander's only faithful general Ptolemy, commented, "If there had been no other competition, he would have competed against himself."

Bagoas better than any also sees that "great anguish lies in wait for those who long too greatly." Alexander loses Hephaistion and with him nearly abandons his own senses, emerging only after his friend's funeral, in which he watches Thettalos, without Nikeratos for the first time, perform *The Myrmidons* one last time; " 'perhaps,' Bagoas thought, 'the last of the madness had been seared out of him by so much burning.'"

At the close of *The Persian Boy*, Renault notes in her Afterword, "When his [Alexander's] faults (those his own times did not account as virtues) have been considered . . . no other human being has attracted in his lifetime, from so many men, so fervent a devotion. Their reasons are worth examining." In her two novels of Alexander's life, Renault not only has examined the reasons, but also has brilliantly probed to the heart of one of the greatest human mysteries: how

one person can ask, as did Homer's Achilles, "now as things are, when the ministers of death stand by us/ In their thousands, which no man born to die can escape or even evade,/ Let us go."—and how other people, with all their hearts, can answer.

Such "true songs are still in the minds of men," according to the aged bard Simonides, narrator of *The Praise Singer*, recalling the "lyric years" when tragedy was being born of song and Athens was becoming the center of the earth. "We die twice when men forget," the ghosts of heroes seemed to tell him as a boy, and he has spent his life in "the bright and perilous gift of making others shine." In this novel, where Renault's heroic epitaph for *philotimo* and her noble elegy for people's hope of *arete* have given place to a gentler, less exalted nostalgia, she recognizes that "praising excellence, one serves the god within it." Renault also notes in her Afterword that "the blanket generalization 'absolute power corrupts absolutely' is a historical absurdity," and she demonstrates that the respected rule of Pisistratus, nominally a "tyrant," formed the solid foundation on which Pericles erected Athenian democracy, even presaging through a discredited seer "a lightning flash from Macedon."

In Alexander's time, Renault has remarked, "the issue was not whether, but how one made [war]." At his death, brought about at least in part by his self-destructive grief for Hephaistion, Alexander's generals embarked on a cannibalistic power struggle—only Ptolemy, his half-brother, emerging with any of the dignity Alexander had worn so easily in conquering his empire. Renault's *Funeral Games* is "the ancestral pattern of Macedonian tribal and familial struggles for his throne; except that Alexander had given them a world stage on which to do it."

FUNERAL GAMES

The most violent of Renault's Greek novels, *Funeral Games* contains a darkness that is alleviated only by flashes of Alexander reflected through the decency of the few who knew him best—Ptolemy; Bagoas; Queen Sisygambis, who looked upon Alexander, not Darius, as her son. In them, something of Alexander's flame lingers a little while, a heavenly light extinguished at last in the wreckage of his empire in human depravity which Alexander could not prevent nor Renault fail to record.

In her eight novels of ancient Greece, Renault far surpasses conventional historical fiction. She achieves a mythic dimension in her balance of Apollonian and Dionysian psychological forces and philosophical precision in her treatment of Platonic doctrines. Her style is adapted to the Greek literature of each period she delineates, Attic elegance for *The Last of the Wine* and *The Mask of Apollo*, Hellenic involution counterpoised against Alexander's Homeric simplicity of speech. Renault links all eight novels with a chain of works of art, a finely crafted touch the classical Greeks would have applauded: the great tragedies, *The Myrmidons* and *The Bacchae*, Polykleitos's sculpture of Hermes modeled on Alexias, and the bronze of the liberator Harmodios in Pisistratos's day all serve as shaping factors in the portrait of her ultimate hero, Alexander. Mastering time, space, and modern ignorance of the classical world, Renault captures the "sadness at the back of life" Virginia Woolf so aptly cited as the essence of Greek literature, the inevitable grieving awareness of people at the impassable gulf between their aspirations and their achievement. In the face of the eternal questions of existence, Renault's novels offer a direction in which to turn when, in Woolf's words, "we are sick of the vagueness, of the confusion, of the Christianity and its consolations, of our own age."

Mitzi M. Brunsdale

OTHER MAJOR WORKS

NONFICTION: *The Nature of Alexander*, 1975.

CHILDREN'S LITERATURE: *The Lion in the Gateway: Heroic Battles of the Greeks and Persians at Marathon, Salamis, and Thermopylae*, 1964.

BIBLIOGRAPHY

Burns, Landon C., Jr. "Men Are Only Men: The Novels of Mary Renault." *Critique: Studies in Modern Fiction* 4 (Winter, 1963): 102-121. A good, but limited, look at Renault's historical fiction. Burns examines character, theme, and use of classical myth in *The Last of the Wine, The King Must Die*, and *The Bull from the Sea*. Burns's careful study repeatedly stresses the high order of Renault's fiction.

Dick, Bernard F. *The Hellenism of Mary Renault*. Carbondale: Southern Illinois Press, 1972. An excellent introduction to Renault's work, examining her entire literary output through *Fire from Heaven*. Places Renault in the mainstream of fiction and applauds her as one of the most creative historical novelists of the century.

Sweetman, David. *Mary Renault: A Biography*. New York: Harcourt Brace, 1993. The first part explores Renault's life in England, including her education at Oxford. The second part describes her years in South Africa. A fascinating study of Renault's sexuality as it relates to her historical novels. Includes a bibliography.

Wolfe, Peter. *Mary Renault*. New York: Twayne, 1969. The first full-length examination of the writer, but limited through *The Mask of Apollo*. Wolfe's study is both a plea for Renault's recognition by the critics as an important twentieth century writer and a critical analysis of her work. He has high praise for most of her novels but dislikes *North Face* and *The Bull from the Sea*.

JEAN RHYS
Ella Gwendolen Rees Williams

Born: Roseau, Dominica Island, West Indies; August 24, 1894
Died: Exeter, England; May 14, 1979

PRINCIPAL LONG FICTION
Postures, 1928 (pb. in U.S. as *Quartet*, 1929)
After Leaving Mr. Mackenzie, 1930
Voyage in the Dark, 1934
Good Morning, Midnight, 1939
Wide Sargasso Sea, 1966

OTHER LITERARY FORMS

Though Jean Rhys is now primarily remembered for her novels, her first published book was a collection of short stories, *The Left Bank and Other Stories* (1927). As Ford Madox Ford pointed out in the preface to the collection, Rhys's heroines are geographically, psychologically, and emotionally of "the Left Bank," not only of Paris—though Rhys captured the Paris of the 1920's as well as anyone—but also of all of the cities of the world. They are underdogs, alone, betrayed, on the edge of poverty; they are women in a man's world.

Besides *The Left Bank*, Rhys published two other collections of stories: *Tigers Are Better-Looking* (1968) and *Sleep It Off, Lady* (1976). In 1987, *The Collected Short Stories* brought together her work in this genre. At her death, she left an essentially completed first section of an autobiography with Diana Athill, who had edited *Wide Sargasso Sea* and *Sleep It Off, Lady*. Athill published this section and a less complete second section as *Smile, Please: An Unfinished Autobiography* in 1979. A collection of letters was published in 1984.

Achievements

When *Wide Sargasso Sea*, her last novel, was published, Jean Rhys was described in *The New York Times* as the greatest living novelist. Such praise is overstated, but Rhys's fiction, long overlooked by academic critics, is undergoing a revival spurred by feminist studies. Rhys played a noteworthy role in the French Left Bank literary scene in the 1920's, and between 1927 and 1939, she published four substantial novels and a number of jewel-like short stories. Although she owes her current reputation in large measure to the rising interest in female writers and feminist themes, her work belongs more properly with the masters of literary impressionism: Joseph Conrad, Ford Madox Ford, Marcel Proust, and James Joyce. She began to publish her writing under the encouragement of her intimate friend Ford Madox Ford, and she continued to write in spite of falling out of favor with his circle. As prizes and honors came to her in her old age after the publication of *Wide Sargasso Sea*, it must have given her grim satisfaction to realize that she had attained entirely by her own efforts a position as a writer at least equal to that of her erstwhile friends.

Biography

Jean Rhys was born Ella Gwen Rees Williams in the West Indies on the island of Dominica in 1894, the daughter of a Welsh father and a part-Creole mother. English society classified her as "colored." Her child associates were often Creole, and she was surrounded by ideas peculiar to their culture, such as voodoo and witchcraft. At the same time, she attended a convent school and seriously considered the life of a nun. The colonial mentality was strong in Dominica, and the "proper" role for a well-bred young woman was sharply defined: passive, obedient, submissive.

In 1910, Rhys left Dominica and went to live in Cambridge, England, with her aunt, Clarice Rhys Williams. After a short term in a local school, she enrolled in the Royal Academy of Dramatic Art in London. Her father died soon after she arrived in England, and she found herself short of money. The transition from the West Indies to England must have been extremely painful for the sixteen-year-old girl: the climate harsh, the people cold, the social and economic situation threatening. Those who knew her as a young woman testified that she was strikingly beautiful. After a term at the Royal Academy of Dramatic Art, she toured as a minor actress or chorus girl with provincial theater troupes and did modeling. A young woman alone under these circumstances would have seen at first hand how male dominance and financial control in British society combined to exploit the female. Many of her stories and novels reflect scenes from her career on the stage, and most of them hinge on the theme of male exploitation of women through financial domination.

Near the end of World War I, Rhys married Jean Lenglet (alias Edouard de Neve), an adventurer who had served in the French Foreign Legion and who was probably employed by the French secret service during the war. The newlywed couple lived in Paris, constantly moving from one cheap hotel to another, although de Neve secured temporarily a position with the international mission administering Vienna. A son was born to them in 1919, but lived only three weeks. A daughter born in 1922 lived, but required special medical care. Rhys tried to earn a living in

Paris by modeling and writing. Pearl Adam, the wife of a correspondent for *The Times* of Paris, took an interest in some of her sketches and introduced her to Ford Madox Ford, then editor of *The Transatlantic Review*. Through him, she entered into the expatriate community of the early 1920's, meeting James Joyce, Ernest Hemingway, and other prominent writers. Shortly after Rhys met Ford in the autumn of 1924, her husband was sent to prison for illegal dealing in antiques. Ford was living at the time with the artist Stella Bowen. Rhys, penniless, moved in with them and soon formed an intimate relationship with Ford. A casual episode in Ford's generally messy life was something much more serious for the young woman; Rhys treats this affair in her first novel, *Quartet*. De Neve never forgave her for her involvement with Ford. After her divorce from de Neve, Rhys became closely involved with a literary agent, Leslie Tilden Smith. They were eventually married and lived together until his death in 1945. Subsequently, she married his cousin, Max Hamer, who later served time in prison for mismanagement of his firm's funds. Throughout the 1940's and 1950's, Rhys suffered greatly from poverty, poor health, and family problems. Her books were all out of print.

She was not, however, entirely forgotten. The actress Selma Vaz Diaz adapted a dramatic monologue from *Good Morning, Midnight* for stage use in 1949. Eight years later, the BBC's third program presented Selma Vaz Diaz's monologue, which received excellent notices. The publication of *Wide Sargasso Sea* in 1966 and the rapid growth of feminist studies led to a Rhys revival, and the reprinting of all her works followed.

ANALYSIS

Jean Rhys's first novel, *Quartet*, reflects closely her misadventures with Ford Madox Ford. The heroine, Marya Zelli, whose husband is in prison, moves in with the rich and respectable Hugh and Lois Heidler. Hugh becomes Marya's lover, while Lois punishes her with petty cruelties. The central figure is a woman alone, penniless, exploited, and an outsider. In her next novel, *After Leaving Mr. Mackenzie*, the central figure, Julia Martin, breaks off with her

rich lover, Mr. Mackenzie, and finds herself financially desperate. *Voyage in the Dark* tells the story of Anna Morgan, who arrives in England from the West Indies as an innocent young girl, has her first affair as a chorus girl, and descends through a series of shorter and shorter affairs to working for a masseuse. In *Good Morning, Midnight*, the alcoholic Sasha Jensen, penniless in Paris, remembers episodes from her past which have brought her to this sorry pass. All four of these novels show a female character subject to financial, sexual, and social domination by men and "respectable" society. In all cases, the heroine is passive, but "sentimental." The reader is interested in her feelings, rather than in her ideas and accomplishments. She is alienated economically from any opportunity to do meaningful and justly rewarding work. She is an alien socially, either from a foreign and despised colonial culture or from a marginally respectable social background. She is literally an alien or foreigner in Paris and London, which are cities of dreadful night for her. What the characters fear most is the final crushing alienation from their true identities, the reduction to some model or type imagined by a foreign man. They all face the choice of becoming someone's gamine, *garçonne*, or femme fatale, or of starving to death, and they all struggle against this loss of personal identity. After a silence of more than twenty years, Rhys returned to these same concerns in her masterpiece, *Wide Sargasso Sea*. While the four early novels are to a large degree autobiographical, *Wide Sargasso Sea* has a more literary origin, although it, too, reflects details from the author's personal life.

WIDE SARGASSO SEA

Wide Sargasso Sea requires a familiarity with Charlotte Brontë's *Jane Eyre* (1847). In Brontë's novel, Jane is prevented from marrying Rochester by the presence of a madwoman in the attic, his insane West Indian wife who finally perishes in the fire which she sets, burning Rochester's house and blinding him, but clearing the way for Jane to wed him. The madwoman in *Jane Eyre* is depicted entirely from the exterior. It is natural that the mad West Indian wife, when seen only through the eyes of her English rival and of Rochester, appears completely hideous and depraved. Indeed, when Jane first sees the madwoman in chapter 16 of the novel, she cannot tell whether it is a beast or a human being groveling on all fours. Like a hyena with bloated features, the madwoman attacks Rochester in this episode.

Wide Sargasso Sea is a sympathetic account of the life of Rochester's mad wife, ranging from her childhood in the West Indies, her Creole and Catholic background, and her courtship and married years with the deceitful Rochester, to her final descent into madness and captivity in England. Clearly, the predicament of the West Indian wife resembles that of Rhys herself in many ways. In order to present the alien wife's case, she has written a "counter-text," an extension of Brontë's novel filling in the "missing" testimony, the issues over which Brontë glosses.

Wide Sargasso Sea consists of two parts. Part 1 is narrated by the girl growing up in Jamaica who is destined to become Rochester's wife. The Emancipation Act has just been passed (the year of that imperial edict was 1833) and the blacks on the island are passing through a period of so-called apprenticeship which should lead to their complete freedom in 1837. This is a period of racial tension and anxiety for the privileged colonial community. Fear of black violence runs high, and no one knows exactly what will happen to the landholders once the blacks are emancipated. The girlish narrator lives in the interface between the privileged white colonists and the blacks. Although a child of landowners, she is impoverished, clinging to European notions of respectability, and in constant fear. She lives on the crumbling estate of her widowed mother. Her closest associate is Christophine, a Martinique *obeah* woman, or Voodoo witch. When her mother marries Mr. Mason, the family's lot improves temporarily, until the blacks revolt, burning their country home, Coulibri, and killing her half-witted brother. She then attends a repressive Catholic school in town, where her kindly colored "cousin" Sandi protects her from more hostile blacks.

Part 2 is narrated by the young Rochester on his honeymoon with his bride to her country home. Wherever appropriate, Rhys follows the details of Brontë's story. Rochester reveals that his marriage

was merely a financial arrangement. After an uneasy period of passion, Rochester's feelings for his bride begin to cool. He receives a letter of denunciation accusing her of misbehavior with Sandi and revealing that madness runs in the family. To counter Rochester's growing hostility, the young bride goes to her former companion, the *obeah* woman Christophine, for a love potion. The nature of the potion is that it can work for one night only. Nevertheless, she administers it to her husband. His love now dead, she is torn from her native land, transported to a cruel and loveless England, and maddeningly confined. Finally, she takes candle in hand to fire Rochester's house in suicidal destruction.

In Brontë's novel, the character of the mad wife is strangely blank, a vacant slot in the story. Her presence is essential, and she must be fearfully hateful, so that Jane Eyre has no qualms about taking her place in Rochester's arms, but the novel tells the reader almost nothing else about her. Rhys fills in this blank, fleshing out the character, making her live on a par with Jane herself. After all, Brontë tells the reader a great deal about Jane's painful childhood and education; why should Rhys not supply the equivalent information about her dark rival?

It is not unprecedented for a writer to develop a fiction from another writer's work. For example, T. H. White's *Mistress Masham's Repose* (1946) imagines that some of Jonathan Swift's Lilliputians were transported to England, escaped captivity, and established a thriving colony in an abandoned English garden, where they are discovered by an English schoolgirl. Her intrusion into their world is a paradigm of British colonial paternalism, finally overcome by the intelligence and good feeling of the girl. This charming story depends on Swift's fiction, but the relationship of White's work to Swift's is completely different from the relationship of Rhys's work to Brontë's. Rhys's fiction permanently alters one's understanding of *Jane Eyre*. Approaching Brontë's work after Rhys's, one is compelled to ask such questions as, "Why is Jane so uncritical of Rochester?" and, "How is Jane herself like the madwoman in the attic?" Rhys's fiction reaches into the past and alters Brontë's novel.

Rhys's approach in *Wide Sargasso Sea* was also influenced by Ford Madox Ford and, through Ford, Joseph Conrad. In the autumn of 1924, when Rhys first met Ford, he was writing *Joseph Conrad: A Personal Remembrance*. Some thirty years earlier, when Joseph Conrad was just beginning his career as a writer, his agent had introduced him to Ford in hopes that they could work in collaboration, since Conrad wrote English (a language he had adopted only as an adult) with great labor. Ford and Conrad produced *The Inheritors* (1901) and *Romance* (1903) as coauthors. During their years of association, Ford had some hand in the production of several works usually considered Conrad's sole effort, although it has never been clear to what degree Ford participated in the creation of the fiction of Conrad's middle period. About 1909, after Ford's disreputable ways had become increasingly offensive to Conrad's wife, the two men parted ways. Immediately after Conrad's death in 1924, however, Ford rushed into print his memoir of the famous author. His memoir of Conrad is fictionalized and hardly to be trusted as an account of their association in the 1890's, but it sheds a great deal of light on what Ford thought about writing fiction in 1924, when he was beginning his powerful Tietjens tetralogy and working for the first time with Rhys. Ford claimed that he and Conrad invented literary impressionism in English. Impressionist fiction characteristically employs limited and unreliable narration, follows a flow of associated ideas leaping freely in time and space, aims to render the impression of a scene vividly so as to make the reader see it as if it were before his eyes, and artfully selects and juxtaposes seemingly unrelated scenes and episodes so that the reader must construct the connections and relationships that make the story intelligible. These are the stylistic features of Rhys's fiction, as well as of Ford's *The Good Soldier* (1915), Conrad's *Heart of Darkness* (1902), Henry James's *The Turn of the Screw* (1898), and Joyce's *Ulysses* (1922).

An "affair"—the mainspring of the plot in an impressionist novel—is some shocking or puzzling event which has already occurred when the story begins. The reader knows what has happened, but he does not understand fully why and how it happened. The story proceeds in concentric rings of growing complication as the reader finds something he thought clear-cut becoming more and more intricate. In Conrad's *Lord Jim* (1900), the affair is the scandalous abandonment of the pilgrim ship by the English sailor. In *The Good Soldier*, it is the breakup of the central foursome, whose full infidelity and betrayal are revealed only gradually. Brontë's *Jane Eyre* provided Rhys with an impressionist "affair" in the scene in which the mad West Indian wife burns Rochester's house, blinding him and killing herself. Like Conrad's Marlow, the storyteller who sits on the veranda mulling over Jim's curious behavior, or *The Good Soldier*'s narrator Dowell musing about the strange behavior of Edward Ashburnham, Rhys takes up the affair of Rochester and reworks it into ever richer complications, making the initial judgments in *Jane Eyre* seem childishly oversimplified. "How can Jane simply register relief that the madwoman is burned out of her way? There must be more to the affair than that," the secondary fiction suggests.

One of the most important features of literary impressionism is the highly constructive activity which it demands of the reader. In a pointillist painting, small dots of primary colors are set side by side. At a certain distance from the canvas, these merge on the retina of the eye of the viewer into colors and shapes which are not, in fact, drawn on the canvas at all. The painting is constructed in the eyes of each viewer with greater luminosity than it would have were it drawn explicitly. In order to create such a shimmering haze in fiction, Ford advises the use of a limited point of view which gives the reader dislocated fragments of remembered experience. The reader must struggle constantly to fit these fragments into a coherent pattern. The tools for creating such a verbal collage are limited, "unreliable" narration, psychological time-shifts, and juxtaposition. Ford observes that two apparently unrelated events can be set side by side so that the reader will perceive their connection with far greater impact than if the author had stated such a connection openly. Ford advises the impressionist author to create a verbal collage by unexpected selection and juxtaposition, and *Wide Sargasso Sea* makes such juxtapositions on several levels. On the largest scale, *Wide Sargasso Sea* is juxtaposed with *Jane Eyre*, so that the two novels read together mean much more than when they are read independently. This increase of significance is what Ford called the "unearned increment" in impressionist art. Within *Wide Sargasso Sea*, part 1 (narrated by the West Indian bride) and part 2 (narrated by Rochester) likewise mean more in juxtaposition than when considered separately. Throughout the text, the flow of consciousness of the storytellers cunningly shifts in time to juxtapose details which mean more together than they would in isolation.

Because *Wide Sargasso Sea* demands a highly constructive reader, it is, like *The Good Soldier* or *Heart of Darkness*, an open fiction. When the reader completes *Jane Eyre*, the mystery of Rochester's house has been revealed and purged, the madwoman in the attic has been burned out, and Jane will live, the reader imagines, happily ever after. *Jane Eyre* taken in isolation is a closed fiction. Reading *Wide Sargasso Sea* in juxtaposition to *Jane Eyre*, however, opens the latter and poses questions which are more difficult to resolve: Is Jane likely to be the next woman in the attic? Why is a cripple a gratifying mate for Jane? At what price is her felicity purchased?

The *Doppelgänger*, twin, or shadow-character runs throughout Rhys's fiction. All of her characters seem to be split personalities. There is a public role, that of the approved "good girl," which each is expected to play, and there is the repressed, rebellious "bad girl" lurking inside. If the bad girl can be hidden, the character is rewarded with money, love, and social position. Yet the bad girl will sometimes put in an appearance, when the character drinks too much or gets excited or angry. When the dark girl appears, punishment follows, swift and sure. This is the case with Marya Zelli in *Quartet*, Julia Martin in *After Leaving Mr. Mackenzie*, Anna Morgan in *Voyage in the Dark*, and Sasha Jensen in *Good Morning, Midnight*. It is also the case in Brontë's *Jane Eyre*. The education of ane Eyre consists of repressing those dark, selfish impulses that Victorian society maintained "good little girls" should never feel. Jane succeeds in stamping out her "bad" self through a stiff British

education, discipline, and self-control. She kills her repressed identity, conforms to society's expectations, and gets her reward—a crippled husband and a burned-out house. Rhys revives the dark twin, shut up in the attic, the naughty, wild, dark, selfish, bestial female. She suggests that the struggle between repressed politeness and unrepressed self-interest is an ongoing process in which total repression means the death of a woman's identity.

Todd K. Bender

OTHER MAJOR WORKS

SHORT FICTION: *The Left Bank and Other Stories*, 1927; *Tigers Are Better-Looking*, 1968; *Sleep It Off, Lady*, 1976; *The Collected Short Stories*, 1987.

NONFICTION: *Smile Please: An Unfinished Autobiography*, 1979; *The Letters of Jean Rhys*, 1984 (also known as *Jean Rhys: Letters, 1931-1966*).

BIBLIOGRAPHY

Angier, Carole. *Jean Rhys: Life and Work*. Boston: Little, Brown, 1990. This biography grew out of Angier's brief 1985 critical study of Rhys's work. As it expanded into an account of her life, Angier felt obliged to jettison her chapters devoted to Rhys's short stories. What survived is a book that is broken into four parts: "Life, 1890-1927," "Work, 1928-1939," "The Lost Years, 1939-1966," and "The Lost Years, 1966-1979." Angier's lengthy book is a good introduction to the life, but it is—of necessity—a less than complete account of the work.

Benstock, Shari. *Women of the Left Bank: Paris, 1900-1940*. Austin: University of Texas Press, 1986. Discusses Rhys's work in the context of the Left Bank literary community. Rhys knew the members of the community but stood outside it, and Benstock demonstrates that Rhys's position as an outsider in life influenced her fiction.

Harrison, Nancy R. *Jean Rhys and the Novel as Women's Text*. Chapel Hill: University of North Carolina Press, 1988. Harrison is a feminist critic who argues that women tend to write, and respond to writing, in a different fashion from men. Women write in a way that invites the reader to join in the creation of the work; the author's activity of writing is stressed, and the work is not offered as a finished product. Analyzes *Voyage in the Dark* and *Wide Sargasso Sea* along these lines.

Malcolm, Cheryl Alexander, and David Malcolm. *Jean Rhys: A Study of the Short Fiction.* New York: Twayne, 1996. This book makes up for what Angier's biography—and most critical assessments of Rhys—lacks. After a section devoted to their assessment of Rhys's short fiction, the Malcolms provide a chapter on Rhys's views of herself—conveyed in excerpts from her letters and an interview—and conclude with a section that reprints a wide range of critical opinion about Rhys's fiction.

Staley, Thomas. *Jean Rhys: A Critical Study.* London: Macmillan, 1979. Probably most important for its first chapter, which gives an account of Rhys's life. Rhys has not been the subject of a full-length biography, and Staley's presentation of her life is the best available. Should be supplemented with Rhys's *Smile Please: An Unfinished Autobiography*, on which she was working at the time of her death in 1979.

ANNE RICE
Howard Allen Frances O'Brien

Born: New Orleans, Louisiana; October 4, 1941

PRINCIPAL LONG FICTION

Interview with the Vampire, 1976
The Feast of All Saints, 1979
Cry to Heaven, 1982
The Claiming of Sleeping Beauty, 1983 (as A. N. Roquelaure)
Beauty's Punishment, 1984 (as Roquelaure)
Beauty's Release: The Continued Erotic Adventures of Sleeping Beauty, 1985 (as Roquelaure; collective title for this volume and the previous two, *Sleeping Beauty Trilogy*)
Exit to Eden, 1985 (as Anne Rampling)
The Vampire Lestat, 1985

Belinda, 1986 (as Rampling)
The Queen of the Damned, 1988
The Mummy: Or, Ramses the Damned, 1989
The Witching Hour, 1990
The Tale of the Body Thief, 1992
Lasher: A Novel, 1993
Taltos: Lives of the Mayfair Witches, 1994
Memnoch the Devil, 1995 (together with *Interview with the Vampire, The Vampire Lestat, The Queen of the Damned*, and *The Tale of the Body Thief* also known by the collective title The Vampire Chronicles)
The Servant of the Bones, 1996
Violin, 1997
Pandora: New Tales of the Vampires, 1998
The Vampire Armand, 1998
Vittorio the Vampire: New Tales of the Vampires, 1999

OTHER LITERARY FORMS

Anne Rice is known primarily for her novels. In addition to her historical fiction and her well-known vampire and witch novel series, Rice published erotic novels. *The Claiming of Sleeping Beauty, Beauty's Punishment*, and *Beauty's Release: The Continued Erotic Adventures of Sleeping Beauty* appeared under the pseudonym A. N. Roquelaure, while Rice used the pen name Anne Rampling for *Exit to Eden* and *Belinda*. Rice also penned the screenplay for the film *Interview with the Vampire* (1994), based on her novel.

ACHIEVEMENTS

Anne Rice has experimented with several different literary genres and acquitted herself well in each: gothic horror, historical fiction, erotica, romance. The conventions of gothic fiction, however, best conform to Rice's obsessions with eroticism, androgyny, myth, and the nature of evil. Clearly, for critics and fans alike, the novels that constitute The Vampire Chronicles are her greatest achievement. Gothic horror, like all popular fiction, is customarily slighted by commentators, who peg it as nothing more than a barometer of its own time, devoid of resonance. Paradoxically perhaps, Rice's success grows out of her ability to revamp the vampire, to update the hoary ed-

(Victor Malafronte/Archive Photos)

ifice first built by Horace Walpole in 1765 in *The Castle of Otranto.* Yet she does more than merely put her archetypal hero, the vampire Lestat, in black leather on a motorcycle; she makes him, in all his selfishness and soul searching, emblematic of the waning days of the twentieth century. If horror can be defined as the sense that the world is on the verge of primeval chaos, Rice might be considered the novelist for the millennium.

BIOGRAPHY

Anne Rice—then named Howard Allen Frances O'Brien—was born on October 4, 1941, in New Orleans, Louisiana, to Howard O'Brien and Katherine Allen O'Brien. Howard O'Brien's reasons for bestowing his own name on his daughter remain obscure, but bearing a masculine name clearly had a profound effect on her. When she entered first grade,

the little girl christened herself Anne. The name stuck, as did a lifelong obsession with androgyny.

The exotic, decadent, intoxicating atmosphere of her hometown must also be counted among Anne Rice's early influences—as must her mother's alcoholism. As she approached puberty, Anne devoted much of her time to reading in a darkened bedroom to the increasingly incapacitated Katherine. It was there, perhaps, that Anne acquired an affinity for vampires. She would later recall how her mother first explained alcoholism as a "craving in the blood" and then asked her to say the rosary. Anne watched her mother alternate between wild exhilaration and collapse and finally waste away, her body drained by addiction and an inability to eat. When Katherine died in 1956, the nexus between blood, religion, and death must have taken root in her young daughter's psyche.

Anne's father remarried when she was sixteen, and, after Anne's sophomore year in high school, he moved the family to Richardson, Texas, where Anne met Stan Rice. Stan was a year younger than Anne, and at first he did not seem to share her romantic feelings about their relationship. It was not until after Anne graduated and moved away to San Francisco that Stan finally realized his feelings. They were married on October 14, 1961, when Anne was twenty.

The couple took up residence in the San Francisco Bay Area, where they would remain for the next twenty-seven years. Stan, a poet, completed his undergraduate education and began teaching creative writing. Anne, too, completed her B.A., majoring in political science. After receiving a master's degree in creative writing in 1972, she devoted herself full time to her writing career.

In the meanwhile, however, a momentous event had occurred in the Rices' lives. Their daughter, Michele, who was born in 1966, developed a rare form of leukemia and died two weeks before her sixth birthday. The trauma of this loss seems to have plunged Anne into depression. The old association between blood and death had returned to haunt her, but Rice fought off her demons by submersing herself in her writing. The result was her first published novel, *Interview with the Vampire.*

In 1978, the Rices had a son, Christopher, and a decade later they moved to New Orleans. With the proceeds of many best-selling books and the lucrative sale of film rights, Anne Rice purchased a mansion in the Garden District, which later became the setting of one of her novels and the scene of such memorable parties as the 1995 Memnoch Ball.

ANALYSIS

Rice discovered her strong suit early. Written in five weeks, *Interview with the Vampire* introduced the themes of compulsion, exoticism, and eroticism that would inform all her later works. Although she explored these themes against a wide variety of backdrops, it is her revival of the gothic—and of the vampire, in particular—that both brought her critical attention and transformed her into a popular cultural icon.

THE VAMPIRE CHRONICLES

Interview with the Vampire is the first of the books Anne Rice produced in her Vampire Chronicles series. The Vampire Chronicles shift back and forth in time, from the prevampire life of Lestat in eighteenth century rural France to his escapades in twentieth century New Orleans, and then, in *Memnoch the Devil*, to the time of the creation of heaven and hell.

Interview with the Vampire introduces Lestat through the narrative of Louis, a vampire Lestat has "made." Louis relates his story to Daniel, a young reporter. Even as Louis grieves for his mortal life, Daniel craves Louis's power and immortality. Daniel has to overcome his initial horror and skepticism before accepting the truth of what Louis says, but by the end of Louis's long story, Daniel is begging to be made a vampire, too. In *The Vampire Lestat*, Lestat relates his own version of his life. Lestat's narrative, like Louis's, is published as a book. (Indeed, Lestat has written his in order to correct several of Louis's errors.) Lestat, always a show-off, revels in publicity, and he uses the book to launch his career as a rock star. Like so many of Lestat's grand schemes, however, this plan crashes, ending when Lestat barely escapes his fellow vampires' murderous attack as they seek revenge for his unpardonable publication of a book that reveals their secrets.

In *The Queen of the Damned*, Lestat becomes the consort of Akasha, the Egyptian ruler who became the mother of all vampires when a demon wounded and invaded her body, giving her immortal life. Marius, an old Roman sage and vampire, has kept Akasha intact for over two thousand years, but it is Lestat's energetic wooing that brings her out of her long stupor. She revives determined to rid the world of men, whose violence has made them unfit to survive. Only a remnant will endure for breeding purposes, she declares. Having partaken of her blood and fallen deliriously in love with her, Lestat nevertheless struggles against her insane project. He is finally saved from Akasha's wrath by Maharet and Mekare, witches who are also twin sisters and who destroy Akasha.

In *The Tale of the Body Thief*, Lestat, suffering from ennui, succumbs to the temptations of a body thief, Raglan James. The body thief offers Lestat a day of adventure in a mortal body in exchange for his own. Stupidly, Lestat accepts, even paying James twenty million dollars for the privilege of enjoying one day of mortality. James then absconds with both the money and Lestat's body, which Lestat is able to repossess only with the help of David Talbot, head of the Talamasca, a society dedicated to investigating the occult. Lestat, who is in love with David, then makes the resistant David into a vampire.

In *Memnoch the Devil*, a terrified Lestat discovers that he is being stalked by Satan, who calls himself Memnoch because he does not regard himself as a rebel angel or as God's accuser. Memnoch invites Lestat to become his lieutenant—not to gather souls for hell, but to redeem those awaiting enlightenment and salvation. Memnoch's argument is that he is offering God a grander creation, a purer vision of humankind, than God himself has conceived. In the end, Lestat repudiates Memnoch, doubting the devil's word and wondering if what he has "seen" is only what he has imagined.

The Vampire Chronicles rejuvenate the conventions of gothic romance and the horror novel. Like earlier heroes, Lestat is a nobleman of surpassing courage and physical attractiveness. Indeed, the vampire elder, Magnus, makes him into a vampire because he has seen the handsome Lestat on the stage in Paris and admired his indomitable spirit. As in William Godwin's novel, *Caleb Williams* (1794), Lestat is an insatiably curious protagonist attached to an older hero who represents both good and evil. Lestat must know the origins of vampirism, and he must follow his desires regardless of the cost to himself and others.

Lestat's eroticism also partakes of the gothic tradition. Reflecting Anne Rice's abiding interest in androgyny, he finds himself attracted to both men and women, to the goddess Akasha, and to the head of the Talamasca, David Talbot. Deeply devoted to his mother, Gabrielle, he takes her as his vampire lover. Incestuous and homoerotic elements that are veiled or only hinted at in earlier gothic fiction explode in Rice's chronicles. Rice also succeeds in making gothicism contemporary by making Lestat into a rock star, thus underscoring parallels between the cult of celebrity and the allure of the vampire.

THE MAYFAIR WITCHES SERIES

Rice conceived the first installment of the Mayfair Witches cycle, *The Witching Hour*, in 1985 after concluding *The Vampire Lestat*. She had generated some new characters which she at first envisioned as playing parts in the next Vampire Chronicle. She soon reached the conclusion, however, that these characters—a family of witches and their presiding spirit—deserved an entirely separate book, one set in New Orleans.

The protagonist of *The Witching Hour*, Michael Curry, is a successful forty-eight-year-old businessman who has his life blighted by a near-death experience. After nearly drowning in San Francisco Bay, he is rescued by a mysterious woman in a passing boat. He then discovers that simply by touching objects and people with his hands he has access to other lives and events. His insights, however, are fragmentary—as is his memory of an encounter with otherworldly beings during his drowning episode, when he promised to fulfill a mission for them.

One of Michael's doctors puts him in touch with his rescuer, who Michael believes will help him understand what he is meant to do. When he meets Dr. Rowan Mayfair, a thirty-year-old blonde beauty and

a superb surgeon, Michael falls in love with her. Like Michael, Rowan is searching for answers. She has the power both to hurt and to heal people. She can stop a patient's bleeding simply by a laying on of hands; she can also cause a heart attack or stroke if she does not control her rage. Her obsession with saving people is her effort at self-redemption. Just as Michael hopes that touching Rowan and her boat will bring back his sense of mission, Rowan hopes that Michael will help reveal her past, which remains a mystery to her.

Rowan and Michael realize that their fates are linked to New Orleans, where as a boy Michael developed a fixation on a Garden District mansion that turns out to be Rowan's ancestral home. There he saw a spectral man, the Mayfairs' presiding spirit. Michael's intense memories of his childhood are connected, he is sure, with his near-death experience. When Rowan's birth mother dies, Rowan is visited by a spectral man, and she decides that she must return to the Crescent City.

Hovering around this couple is Aaron Lightner, an agent of the Talamasca. Through Aaron, Michael learns that Rowan is the descendant of a matriarchal family of witches that has fascinated the Talamasca for nearly three hundred years. A strong woman, Rowan believes she can destroy Lasher, the spectral man who has maddened the Mayfairs in an attempt to possess them. Like the others, however, Rowan loses control of Lasher, who invades the cells of the fetus growing within her and emerges as a powerful boy-man.

Rowan is rather like a female Dr. Faustus, determined to conquer the secrets of nature. She wants to heal, but the extremity of her desire cuts her off from her own humanity. Like Faust, she risks damnation. She is in thrall to her Mephistopheles, Lasher. When Michael playfully calls his lover Dr. Mayfair, the epithet suggests not only Dr. Faustus but also Dr. Frankenstein. Indeed, although Rowan finds Lasher's proposal that they create a super-race seductive, once their offspring is born, she plans to submit its cells to laboratory tests, thus reducing it to the status of a research subject.

In *Lasher*, the second installment in the series, Rowan has begun to help Lasher fulfill his desire. Together they have a girl child, Emaleth. The central revelation of the book is that the Mayfairs can, by interbreeding, produce a genetic aberration—a legendary race of nearly immortal giants known as Taltos, of which Lasher is a member. The Talamasca believe that Lasher is possessed of a unique genome, so when at the end of the book Michael Curry destroys him and Rowan does away with her demoniac girl child, it seems that Lasher's kind is no more.

However, *Taltos*, the third installment of the series, features another Taltos, Ashlar Templeton, an eccentric and reclusive billionaire toy maker. Ashlar's profession indicates that his nature is far more benign than Lasher's. Indeed, he more closely resembles Rice's vampires than his own protean kind. Unlike Lasher, he is not devoured by a need to propagate his supernatural breed; instead, he yearns—as much as Louis and, in his weaker moments, Lestat—for integration with humanity.

Lisa Paddock

OTHER MAJOR WORK

SCREENPLAY: *Interview with the Vampire*, 1994.

BIBLIOGRAPHY

Dickinson, Joy. *Haunted City: An Unauthorized Guide to the Magical, Magnificent New Orleans of Anne Rice.* New York: Citadel Press, 1995. Chapters on the city's Creole history, the French Quarter, the Garden District, the cemeteries and tombs, the churches, swamps, and plantations, and the nineteenth century milieu of Lestat.

Hoppenstand, Gary, and Ray B. Browne, eds. *The Gothic World of Anne Rice.* Bowling Green, Ohio: Bowling Green State University Press, 1996. Essays by the most important Rice critics on all aspects of her fiction: The Vampire Chronicles, the romances, and her stories of the supernatural.

Ramslund, Katherine, ed. *The Anne Rice Reader.* New York: Ballantine, 1997. Part 1 concentrates on interviews with Rice, her personal essays, and articles about her life and career. Part 2 focuses on literary critiques, assessing Rice's contribution to the literature about vampires, her relationship to the gothic tradition, the film of *Interview with the Vampire*, and her other horror novels.

_____. *Prism of the Night: A Biography of Anne Rice.* New York: Dutton, 1991. Written with her cooperation, this is the most complete source of information about Rice.

Roberts, Bette B. *Anne Rice.* New York: Twayne, 1994. A solid introductory study with chapters on Rice's life and art, her relationship to the gothic tradition, her vampire series, her historical novels, and her erotic fiction.

DOROTHY RICHARDSON

Born: Berkshire, England; May 17, 1873
Died: Beckenham, England; June 17, 1957

PRINCIPAL LONG FICTION

Pilgrimage, 1938, 1967 (includes *Pointed Roofs*, 1915)
Backwater, 1916
Honeycomb, 1917
The Tunnel, 1919
Interim, 1919
Deadlock, 1921
Revolving Lights, 1923
The Trap, 1925
Oberland, 1927
Dawn's Left Hand, 1931
Clear Horizon, 1935
Dimple Hill, 1938
March Moonlight, 1967

OTHER LITERARY FORMS

Dorothy Richardson's literary reputation rests on the single long novel *Pilgrimage*. She referred to the parts published under separate titles as "chapters," and they were the primary focus of her energy throughout her creative life. The first appeared in 1915; the last—unfinished and unrevised—was printed ten years after her death. Before 1915, she wrote some essays and reviews for obscure periodicals edited by friends and also two books growing out of her interest in the Quakers. She contributed descriptive sketches on Sussex life to the *Saturday Review* between 1908 and 1914. During the years writing *Pilgrimage*, Richardson did an enormous amount of miscellaneous writing to earn money—columns and essays in the *Dental Record* (1912-1922), film criticism, translations, articles on various subjects for periodicals including *Vanity Fair, Adelphi, Little Review*, and *Fortnightly Review*. She also wrote a few short stories, chiefly during the 1940's. None of this material has been collected. A detailed bibliography is included in *Dorothy Richardson: A Biography* by Gloria G. Fromm (1977).

ACHIEVEMENTS

The term "stream of consciousness," adapted from psychology, was first applied to literature in a 1918 review of Richardson's *Pointed Roofs, Backwater*, and *Honeycomb*. In the twentieth century, novels moved from outward experience to inner reality. The experiments that marked the change were made almost simultaneously by three writers unaware of one another's work: The first volume of Marcel Proust's *Remembrance of Things Past* appeared in 1913; James Joyce's *Portrait of the Artist as a Young Man* began serial publication in 1914; the manuscript of *Pointed Roofs* was finished in 1913.

Richardson was the first novelist in England to restrict the point of view entirely to the protagonist's consciousness, to take for content the experience of life at the moment of perception, and to record the development of a single character's mind and emotions without imposing any plot or structural pattern. Her place in literature (as opposed to literary history) has been less certain; some critics feel that her work is interesting only because it dates the emergence of a new technique. The absence of story and explanation make heavy demands on the reader. Since the protagonist's own limited understanding controls every word of the narrative, readers must also do the work of evaluating the experience in order to create meaning.

Richardson wrote what Virginia Woolf called "the psychological sentence of the feminine gender"; a sentence that expanded its limits and tampered with punctuation to convey the multiple nuances of a single moment. She deliberately rejected the description of events, which she thought was typical of male literature, in order to convey the subjective understanding that she believed was the reality of experience. The autobiographical basis of *Pilgrimage* was not known until 1963. Richardson, like her protagonist and like other women of her period, broke with the conventions of the past, sought to create her own being through self-awareness, and struggled to invent a form that would communicate a woman's expanding conscious life.

BIOGRAPHY

Dorothy Miller Richardson, born on May 17, 1873, was the third of four daughters. Her father, Charles Richardson, worked in the prosperous grocery business that his father had established, but he wanted to be a gentleman. He abandoned Nonconformity for the Church of England and, in 1874, sold the family business to live on investments. During Dorothy's childhood, periods of upper-middle-class luxury (a large house, servants, gardens, membership in a tennis club) alternated with moves arising from temporarily reduced circumstances.

Charles Richardson had hoped for a son, and he took Dorothy with him to lectures in Oxford and meetings of scientific associations. She was sent at age eleven to a private day school for the daughters of gentlemen. It was late enough in the century for the curriculum to emphasize academic subjects; her studies included logic and psychology. In 1890, realizing that her family's financial condition had become seriously straitened, Dorothy looked to the example of Charlotte Brontë and *Villette* (1853) and applied for a post as pupil-teacher in a German school. Six months in Hanover were followed by two years teaching in a North London private school and a brief spell as governess for a wealthy suburban family.

By the end of 1893, Charles Richardson was declared bankrupt; in 1895, two of Dorothy's sisters married. Her mother, Mary Richardson, was troubled by an unusually severe bout of the depression that had gripped her for several years. Dorothy took her mother to stay in lodgings near the sea and found that she required almost constant companionship and supervision. On November 30, 1895, while her daughter was out for a short walk in the fresh air, Mary Richardson committed suicide.

At the age of twenty-two, responsible for her own support and severely shaken by the past two years' events, Richardson moved to an attic room in a London lodging house and took a job as secretary and assistant to three Harley Street dentists. For young women at that time, such a step was unusual; by taking it Richardson evaded the restraint, protection, and religious supervision that made teaching an acceptable profession for young women of good family. The nineteenth century was drawing to a close and London was alive with new ideas. Richardson explored the city, made friends with women who worked in business offices, and lived on eggs and toast so that she could afford concert tickets.

Soon after moving to London, she was invited for a Saturday in the country by an old school friend, Amy Catherine Robbins, who had married her science instructor at London University—a man named H. G. Wells. He had just published *The Time Machine* (1895). Richardson was fascinated by Wells and by the people and ideas she encountered at his house but angered by his way of telling her what to do. She was aware that she stood outside the class system and between the Victorian and modern worlds. She was drawn both to picnics with cousins at Cambridge and to Anarchist and Fabian meetings. She sampled various churches (including Unitarian and Quaker) but refrained from committing herself to any group or cause.

In 1902, Richardson began contributing occasional articles and reviews to *Crank* and other magazines edited by a vegetarian friend. She refused a proposal from a respectable physician and broke her engagement to a Russian Jew, Benjamin Grad. Her friendship with Wells passed at some point into physical intimacy, but she continued to struggle against being overwhelmed by his ideas and personality. In 1906, finding herself pregnant, she brought the affair to an end; she looked forward to rearing the child on

her own and was distressed when she suffered a miscarriage.

Exhausted physically and mentally, Richardson left her dental job and went to Sussex to recover and think. In 1908, she began writing sketches for the *Saturday Review*. Then, as her fortieth year approached, she began deliberately searching for the form that would allow her to create what she called "a feminine equivalent of the current masculine realism."

Pointed Roofs was at first rejected by publishers. When it was published in 1915 it puzzled readers, distressed some reviewers, and failed to make money. Richardson persisted, however, on the course she had set, even while living an unsettled life in YWCA hostels and borrowed rooms and earning a minimal income by proofreading and by writing a monthly column for the *Dental Record*. In 1917, she married the artist Alan Odle, who was fifteen years younger than she and had been rejected for military service by a doctor who told him he had six months to live.

Richardson's books attracted some critical recognition in the years after World War I, but they never earned money; she was usually in debt to her publishers. She supported herself and Odle (who lived until 1948) and also coped with all the practical details of their life—housekeeping, paying taxes, writing checks, doing his business with publishers and exhibitors. The couple moved frequently, spending the off-season (when lodgings were less expensive) in Cornwall and going to rooms in London for the summer. During the early 1930's, Richardson took on the burden of five full-length translations from French and German. Returning to *Pilgrimage* and the state of mind in which it was begun became increasingly difficult for Richardson; the later volumes were weakened by extraliterary distractions and also by the psychological difficulty for the author in concluding the work that was based on her own life. The final segment, *March Moonlight*, was found unfinished among her papers after she died on June 17, 1957, at the age of eighty-four.

ANALYSIS

Pilgrimage is a quest; the protagonist, Miriam Henderson, seeks her self and, rejecting the old guideposts, makes her own path through life. The book remains a problem for many readers, although since 1915 most of Dorothy Richardson's technical devices have become familiar: unannounced transitions from third-person narration to the first person for interior monologue, shifts between present and past as experience evokes memory, disconnected phrases and images and fragmentary impressions representing the continuous nonverbal operations of the mind. Looking back on the period when she was trying to find a way to embody Miriam Henderson's experience, Richardson described her breakthrough as the realization that no one was *"there* to *describe* her." Impressed by Henry James's control of viewpoint, she went one step further. The narrator and the protagonist merge; the narrator knows, perceives, and expresses only what comes to Miriam's consciousness. Furthermore, the narrator does not speak to any imagined reader and therefore does not provide helpful explanations. The scenes and people are presented as they impinge on Miriam's awareness—thus the most familiar circumstances are likely to be undescribed and the most important people identified only by name, without the phrases that would place them or reveal their relationship to Miriam. Many readers are discouraged by the attempt to follow the book and make meaning of it; some are tempted to use Richardson's biography to find out what "really" happened and others prefer to read isolated sections without regard to sequence, responding to the feeling and imagery as if it were poetry. Because there is no narrative guidance, meaning is continually modified by the reader's own consciousness and by the extent of identification.

THE MIRIAM HENDERSON NOVELS

The first three titles show Miriam Henderson in the last stages of her girlhood and form the prelude to her London life. *Pointed Roofs* covers her experience in Hanover; in *Backwater*, she is resident teacher in a North London school and still drawn to the possibility of romance with a young man from her suburban circle; in *Honeycomb*, she briefly holds a post as governess before her sisters' weddings and her mother's death complete the disintegration of her girlhood family. *The Tunnel* begins Miriam's years in London and

introduces situations and characters that reappear in the next several volumes: the dental job, the room at Mrs. Bailey's lodging house, the new women Mag and Jan and the dependent woman Eleanor Dear, a visit to her school friend Alma who has married the writer Hypo Wilson. In *Interim*, Miriam perceives the difficulty of communicating her current thoughts and experiences to her sister and other old friends. *Deadlock* treats her acquaintance—growing into an engagement—with Michael Shatov. In *Revolving Lights*, she has decided not to marry Shatov and becomes increasingly involved with Hypo Wilson. *The Trap* shows her sharing a cramped flat with a spinster social worker and growing despondent about the isolation which, she realizes, she imposes on herself to avoid emotional entanglements. *Oberland* is a lyrical interlude about a holiday in Switzerland. In *Dawn's Left Hand*, Miriam has an affair with Hypo Wilson and an intense friendship with a young woman (Amabel) who becomes a radical suffragist. *Clear Horizon* concludes much of the practical and emotional business that has occupied Miriam for several years; she disentangles herself from Wilson, Shatov, and Amabel and prepares to leave London. In *Dimple Hill*, she lives on a farm owned by a Quaker family, absorbs their calm, and works at writing. *March Moonlight* rather hastily takes Miriam up to the point of meeting the artist who would become her husband and to the beginning of her work on a novel.

This summary of events is the barest framework. Life, for Miriam Henderson, exists not in events but in the responses that create her sense of awareness. The books are made up of relatively independent sections, each treating a single segment of experience or reflection. Because of the depth with which single moments are recorded, the overall narrative line is fragmentary. Despite *Pilgrimage*'s length, it embodies isolated spots of time. Frequently, neither narration nor the memories evoked by subsequent experience indicate what events may have taken place in the gaps between. Furthermore, the book concentrates on those moments important to Miriam's interior experience, and it leaves out the times when she acts without self-awareness—which may include significant actions that take place when Miriam is so engrossed by events that she does not engage in thought or reflection.

Richardson disliked the phrase "stream of consciousness" because it implies constant movement and change. She preferred the image of a pool—new impressions are added, and sometimes create ripples that spread over the previously accumulated consciousness. Thus, Miriam's interior monologue becomes steadily more complex as she grows older. Her consciousness widens and deepens; fragmentary phrases show her making connections with her earlier experiences and perceptions; her understanding of past events alters with later awareness. The earlier volumes have more sensory impression and direct emotion; later, as Miriam grows more self-aware, she has greater verbal skill and is more likely to analyze her responses. Because of her more sophisticated self-awareness, however, she also grows adept, in the later volumes, at suppressing impressions or fragments of self-knowledge that she does not want to admit to consciousness.

In many ways, Miriam is not likable—readers are sometimes put off by the need to share her mind for two thousand pages. In the early books, she is a self-preoccupied, narrow-minded adolescent, oppressively conscious of people's appearance and social class, annoyingly absorbed in wondering what they think about her, defensively judgmental. The wild swings in mood and the ebb and flow of her energies during the day appear to have little cause and to be unworthy of the attention she gives them. Most people, however, would appear unpleasantly selfish if their minds were open for inspection. Miriam creates her self by deliberate consciousness. The danger is that she tends to withdraw from experience in order to contemplate feeling.

PILGRIMAGE

The events of *Pilgrimage* span the decades at the turn of the century but, because of the interior focus, there is relatively little physical detail or explicit social history to create an objective picture of the era. Women's developing self-awareness, however, must be seen as one of the period's significant events. Miriam reflects the mental life of her times in her range of responses to religion, the books she reads, and the people, ideas, and movements she encounters.

A good deal of life's texture and even its choices take place at levels that are not verbalized. Richardson's first publisher described her work as "female imagism." Miriam responds particularly and constantly to the quality of light. Readers are also aware of her reaction to places, objects, and physical surroundings; ultimately, it is through mastering the emotional content of this response that she is able to discover what she needs to have in her life.

Another continuing thread is created by Miriam's thoughts about men, about men and women together, and about the roles of women in society. Her basic animosity toward men gives shape to a series of statements on their personal, emotional, social, and intellectual peculiarities that falls just short of a formal feminist analysis. Each possible romance, each rejected or forestalled proposal amounts to a choice of a way of life. The matter is, however, complicated by Miriam's sexual reticence. Even though she can talk about free love, she is not conscious—or perhaps will not permit herself to become conscious—of overt sexual urges or of physical attraction to men or to women. She struggles not to let her feeling for certain women lead her to be absorbed by their lives or roles. In *Backwater*, Miss Perne's religion is dangerously comfortable; Eleanor Dear's passive feminine helplessness forces Miriam to become her protector; Amabel's possessiveness is as stifling as Hypo Wilson's. At the end—in *March Moonlight*—there is a hint of emotional involvement with the unidentified "Jane." Struggling to know herself, Miriam is constantly faced with the problem of knowing other women.

POINTED ROOFS

Pointed Roofs comes close to being a structural whole—it begins with Miriam Henderson's journey to Hanover and ends with her return home six months later. She is on her first trip away from home, looking at new scenes, anxious about her ability to do her job and earn her wages, having her first taste of independence. Since Miriam is seventeen—and, as a Victorian daughter, a relatively innocent and sheltered seventeen—the reader often understands more than Miriam does and can interpret the incidents that develop her sense of who she is and where she fits in the world. Some of Miriam's reactions are cast in the form of mental letters home or imaginary conversations with her sisters, which provide a structured way to verbalize mental processes. Miriam pays attention to the sights and sounds and smells of Hanover because they are new, giving readers a sense of the physical setting absent in many of the later books.

Miriam's moods are typically adolescent. An incident or object can set off a homesick reverie or a bout of self-recrimination; the sound of music or the sight of rain on paving stones can create an inexpressible transport of joy. She is alternately rebellious and anxious for approval; she is glad to learn that her French roommate is Protestant (because she could not bear living with a Catholic), proud of the skill in logic that allows her to criticize the premises of a sermon, moved by the sound of hymns in German. She worries about her plainness, her intellectual deficiencies, her inability to get close to people. Observing class and cultural differences lets her begin to understand that she has unthinkingly absorbed many of her tastes and ideas; she starts to grow more deliberate. This portrait of Miriam at seventeen—which forms the essential background for the rest of *Pilgrimage*—is also interesting for its own sake.

Because the narrative is limited to Miriam's consciousness, the reader is able to supply interpretation. In one key scene, the middle-aged Pastor Lahmann, chaplain to the school, quotes a verse describing his ambition for "A little land, well-tilled,/ A little wife, well-willed" and then asks Miriam to take off her glasses so that he can see how nearsighted her eyes really are. Miriam, who is both furious at being "regarded as one of a world of little tame things to be summoned by little man to be well-willed wives" and warmed by the personal attention that makes her forget, for a moment, that she is a governess, is oblivious to the sexual implications of Pastor Lahmann's behavior, and cannot understand why the headmistress is angry when she walks in upon the scene. Although Miriam's consciousness will develop in subsequent volumes, her combination of receptivity to male attention, anger at male assumptions, and blindness to sexual nuance will remain.

DEADLOCK

Deadlock contains a greater proportion of direct internal monologue than the earlier books. Miriam has grown more articulate; she interprets her emotional states and examines the premises underlying her conflicts. During her first years in London, she had cherished the city for the independence it gave her. By such acts as smoking, eating alone in restaurants, and dressing without regard to fashion, she deliberately rejected Victorian womanhood. In *Honeycomb*, she refused a marriage that would have satisfied her craving for luxuries because she could not accept a subordinate role. In *Deadlock*, Miriam is faced by the loneliness that seems inextricably linked to independence. Her work has become drudgery because she no longer has the sense of a social relationship with her employer. A Christmas visit to her married sister reveals the distance that has grown betwen them; Miriam had not even realized that Harriet's marriage was unhappy.

Deadlock is shaped by the course of Miriam's relationship with Michael Shatov. The romance forces her conflicts to the surface. Shatov is a young Jew recently arrived from Russia; a lodger at Mrs. Bailey's arranges for Miriam to tutor him in English. As she shows Shatov London, tired scenes recapture their original freshness. Miriam is excited by her ability to formulate ideas when she argues about philosophy or works on a translation. Yet, although Miriam is buoyed by the joy of sharing her thoughts with another person, Shatov's continual presence comes between her and the life that was her own. Her love has a maternal quality: Though Shatov is only three years younger than Miriam, he is a foreigner and also, Miriam finds, rather impractical; she feels protective. She is also sexually reticent: Because she has despised traditional femininity, she does not know how to behave as the object of a courtship. The romance ends when Miriam deliberately engages Shatov in an argument that reveals his views of woman's limited nature. (The final scene restates the problem more concretely when Miriam visits an Englishwoman married to a Jewish man.) Beneath these specific difficulties lies the friction between Miriam's individualism and Shatov's tendency to see problems in the abstract—she talks about herself, he dwells on the future of the race. For Richardson, the conflict reflects the irreconcilable difference between masculine objectivity (or materialism) and feminine subjectivity. The images of darkness accumulate as Miriam realizes the extent of her deadlock; unable to be a woman in the sense that men see women, she seems to have no path out of loneliness and alienation.

DAWN'S LEFT HAND

Dawn's Left Hand is a prelude to the deliberate detachment and observation that would turn Miriam into a writer. *Oberland* (the preceding book) vibrates with the sensory detail of a two-week holiday in Switzerland that makes London complications seem far away; returning, Miriam sees people objectively even when she is with them. The transitions between third-person narrative and internal monologue are less noticeable; Miriam and the narrator have virtually merged. The visual content of scenes reveals their meaning. Miriam looks at pictorial relationships and examines gesture and tone for the nonverbal communications that, to women, are often more meaningful than words. (During the years that she worked on *Dawn's Left Hand*, Richardson wrote regularly about films—which were still silent—for the magazine *Close Up*.)

Images of light carry emotional and symbolic content throughout *Pilgrimage*. When Miriam visits Densley's medical office early in *Dawn's Left Hand*, the drawn shades are keeping out the light; she refuses his proposal—one last offer of conventional marriage—with a momentary wistfulness that is immediately replaced by a great sense of relief. She is increasingly aware of herself as an actor in the scenes of her life. Self-observation allows physical compositions to reveal power relationships: When Hypo Wilson comes into Miriam's room, she notices that he stands over her like a doctor, and when he embarks on a program of seduction to the music of Richard Wagner, she disputes his control by rearranging the chairs. On another occasion, in a hotel room, Miriam looks in the mirror to observe herself and Wilson. Her own position blocks the light and thus the scene is chilled even before she begins to see him as a pathetic naked male.

During the final stages of the Wilson affair, Miriam is increasingly preoccupied by a beautiful young woman—soon to be a radical suffragist—who pursues her ardently and pays homage to her as a woman in ways that bring home to Miriam the impossibility of real communion with men. Yet the deep commitment demanded by Amabel is frightening; her intense adoration forces Miriam into a role that threatens her independence more crucially than Hypo Wilson's overt attempts at domination. The advantage of being with people who interact only on superficial levels, Miriam realizes, is that she can retain her freedom.

MARCH MOONLIGHT

Although Richardson struggled to bring the events in *March Moonlight* up to 1912, the year that she began writing *Pilgrimage*, her form and subject virtually required the book to remain unconcluded. The narrative techniques of *March Moonlight* grow more deliberate; when Miriam begins to write, she thinks and sees differently and is aware of selecting and arranging details. Thus, the book's ending is only a middle: Miriam's sense of self would inevitably change as she reexamined and re-created her experiences in order to write novels. Once traditional formulas are rejected and *being* itself becomes the subject, there can be no ending; there is no epiphany, no coming of age, no final truth but rather a continuous process of self-making through self-awareness.

Sally Mitchell

OTHER MAJOR WORKS

NONFICTION: *The Quakers Past and Present*, 1914; *Gleanings from the Works of George Fox*, 1914; *John Austen and the Inseparables*, 1930.

BIBLIOGRAPHY

Bluemel, Kristin. *Experimenting on the Borders of Modernism: Dorothy Richardson's "Pilgrimage."* Athens: University of Georgia Press, 1997. The first chapter assesses Richardson and previous studies of her. Subsequent chapters explore Richardson's handling of gender, problems of the body, and science, and the author's quest for an ending to her long work. Includes notes and bibliography.

Fromm, Gloria G. *Dorothy Richardson: A Biography*. Champaign: University of Illinois Press, 1977. An objective biography, including previously inaccessible details, which could provide invaluable data to the literary analyst. Carefully draws distinctions between the events of Richardson's life and those of her fictional characters, but also identifies clear correlations between the two. Extensively researched and well written and supplemented by illustrations, chapter endnotes, a comprehensive bibliography, and an index.

Gevirtz, Susan. *Narrative's Journey: The Fiction and Film Writing of Dorothy Richardson*. New York: Peter Lang, 1996. A probing discussion of Richardson's aesthetic. This is a challenging study for advanced students. *Pilgrimage* receives detailed discussion throughout the book. Includes extensive bibliography not only on Richardson but also on feminist theory, literary and cultural theory, poetics and phenomenology, theology and spirituality, travel and travel theories, and narrative.

Radford, Jean. *Dorothy Richardson*. Bloomington: Indiana University Press, 1991. An excellent introductory study, with chapters on reading in *Pilgrimage*, the author's quest for form, London as a space for women, and Richardson as a feminist writer. Includes notes and bibliography.

Rosenberg, John. *Dorothy Richardson, the Genius They Forgot: A Critical Biography*. New York: Alfred A. Knopf, 1973. The strength of Rosenberg's biography lies in his scholarly credibility, as he aptly parallels events in *Pilgrimage* to Richardson's life. His concluding analysis of Richardson's pioneering impact upon the development of the novel, however, lacks the impact of his earlier writing. Contains both an index and an ample bibliography.

SAMUEL RICHARDSON

Born: Derbyshire, England; July 31 (?), 1689
Died: London, England; July 4, 1761

PRINCIPAL LONG FICTION

Pamela: Or, Virtue Rewarded, 1740-1741
Clarissa: Or, The History of a Young Lady, 1747-1748
Sir Charles Grandison, 1753-1754

OTHER LITERARY FORMS

In addition to the three novels on which his fame and reputation rest, Samuel Richardson's best-known work is a collection of fictitious letters which constitutes a kind of eighteenth century book of etiquette, social behavior, manners, and mores: *Letters Written to and for Particular Friends, on the Most Important Occasions* (1741), customarily referred to as *Familiar Letters*. It had been preceded, in 1733, by a handbook of instruction concerning the relationship between apprentices and master printers, which grew out of a letter Richardson had written to a nephew in 1731, *The Apprentice's Vade Mecum: Or, Young Man's Pocket Companion* (1733). Throughout his life, Richardson, like so many of his contemporaries, was a prolific letter-writer; notable selections of his correspondence include six volumes edited by his contemporary and early biographer, Anna L. Barbauld, the first of which was published in 1804, and his correspondence with Johannes Stinstra, the Dutch translator of his novels to whom Richardson had sent a considerably important amount of autobiographical material. Of only minor interest is Richardson's *A Collection of the Moral and Instructive Sentiments, Maxims, Cautions, and Reflexions, Contained in the Histories of Pamela, Clarissa, and Sir Charles Grandison*, published anonymously in 1755, a series of excerpts emphasizing his conviction that "instruction was a more important obligation to the novelist than entertainment."

ACHIEVEMENTS

Perhaps Richardson's most important contribution to the development of the novel was his concern for the nonexceptional problems of daily conduct, the relationships between men and women, and the specific class-and-caste distinctions of mid-eighteenth century England. He sought and found his material from life as he had observed and reflected upon it from childhood and youth as a member of the working class in a highly socially conscious society to his position as an increasingly successful and prosperous printer and publisher. He contemplated this material with passionate interest and recorded it with a kind of genius for verisimilitude that sets him apart from most of his predecessors. What one critic has called Richardson's "almost rabid concern for the details" of daily life and his continuing "enrichment and complication" of customary human relationship account in large measure for his enormous contemporary popularity: In *Pamela*, for example, the relationships between Pamela and Squire B. are so persistently grounded in the minutiae of ordinary life as to create a sense of reality seldom achieved in prose fiction prior to Richardson; at the same time, the outcome of the emotional and physical tugs-of-war between the two main characters and the happy outcome of all the intrigue, sensationalism, and huggermugger have about them the quality of conventional romantic love.

Richardson learned to *know* his characters, so intimately, so thoroughly, as to triumph over his prolixity, repetitiveness, moralizing, and sentimentality. Equally important was his development of the epistolary novel. Other writers had used letters as a story-telling device, but few if any of Richardson's predecessors had approximated his skill in recording the external events and incidents of a narrative along with the intimate and instant revelation of a character's thought and emotions in the process of their taking place, a method so flowing, so fluid, so flexible, as almost to anticipate the modern technique of stream of consciousness. Richardson's works, along with those of his three great contemporaries—Henry Fielding, Tobias Smollett, and Laurence Sterne— prepared the way for the great achievements of the nineteenth century English novel.

BIOGRAPHY

The exact date of Samuel Richardson's birth is uncertain, but he was born in Derbyshire, probably on July 31, 1689. His father was a joiner and, according to Richardson, a "good draughtsman" who "understood architecture" and whose ancestors had

(Library of Congress)

included several generations of small farmers in Surrey; of his mother, the second wife of Richardson *père*, little is known. The family returned to London, where Richardson may have attended the Merchant Taylor's School in 1701 and 1702, at which time his formal education ended. In 1706, he was apprenticed to the Stationers' Company, and in 1715, he became a "freeman" of the Company. He married his former employer's daughter, Martha Wilde, in November 23, 1721, set up his own business as a printer, was admitted to the Stationers' Company in 1722, and soon became what his major biographers—T. C. Duncan Eaves and Ben D. Kimpel—term a "prosperous and respected" tradesman. Six children, none of whom survived infancy or early childhood, preceded their mother's death in January, 1731. Two years later, on February 3, 1733, Richardson remarried, this time to Elizabeth Leake, also the daughter of a printer; four of their six children survived.

Richardson's career as an editor continued to prosper—among other distinctions, he was eventually awarded the lucrative contract to print the journals of the House of Commons—and by the mid-1730's, he had moved into a large house in Salisbury Court, where the family would live for the next two decades and where he would write the three novels on which his reputation rests.

For some time, two of Richardson's "particular friends," both of them London booksellers, had been urging him to compile a "little book . . . of familiar letters on the useful concerns of common life." An almost compulsive letter-writer since early childhood—before he was eleven he had written to an elderly widow, reprimanding her for her "uncharitable conduct"—Richardson began the undertaking, one letter of which was an actual account he had heard some years before, the story of a virtuous servant who eventually married her master. The recollection of the incident stimulated his imagination, and so, at the age of fifty, he temporarily abandoned the letters-project. In two months, writing as much as three thousand words a day, he completed the novel that, on November 6, 1739, without the author's name on the title page, was to explode upon the English scene:

Pamela: Or, Virtue Rewarded. In a Series of Familiar Letters from a beautiful Young Damsel, to her Parents. Now first published in order to cultivate the Principles of Virtue and Religion in the Minds of the Youth of both Sexes. A Narrative which has its Foundation in Truth and Nature; and at the same time that it agreeably entertains, by a Variety of Curious and affecting Incidents, is entirely divested of all those Images, which, in too many Pieces calculated for Amusement only, tend to inflame the Minds they should instruct.

Pamela was an instant success, going through five editions in less than a year and inspiring numerous burlesques, imitations, and parodies, including *An Apology for the Life of Mrs. Shamela Andrews* (1741, probably the work of Henry Fielding and the only parody of interest today) and serving as the impetus for Fielding's *The History of the Adventures of Joseph Andrews, and of His Friend Mr. Abraham Adams* (1742). *Pamela* was also dramatized in several forms and translated into German, French, and Dutch; its success, for the worse rather than the

better, led Richardson to write a sequel, centering on his heroine's life after her marriage.

Meanwhile, Richardson continued to combine the roles of successful and prosperous businessman and author. Exactly when he began the novel which was to be his masterpiece is uncertain—one of his biographers thinks he was considering it as early as 1741—but he had the concept of *Clarissa* "well in mind" before 1744, began the actual writing in the spring or summer of that year, and by November was ready to send parts of the manuscript to his old friend Aaron Hill. Unlike *Pamela, Clarissa* did not have its origins in "real life"; Clarissa and Miss Howe, Richardson insisted, were "entirely creatures of his fantasy." The novel, almost a million words in length, was three years in the writing, including two "thorough" revisions, and published in seven volumes between December 1, 1747, and December 7, 1748; a subsequent eight-volume edition, "with Letters & passages restored from the original manuscript," was published between 1749 and 1751.

Though *Clarissa* was somewhat less controversial than *Pamela*, its reception was tumultuous; among other things, the author was accused of indecency because of the dramatic fire scene, and Richardson took the charges seriously enough to write an eleven-page pamphlet defending it. Sarah Fielding wrote what has been called an "ambitious defense" of the novel, and her brother Henry, whose masterpiece *The History of Tom Jones, a Foundling* was published soon after the last volumes of *Clarissa* in 1749, lavishly praised Richardson's work, although Richardson's dislike of what he considered Fielding's improprieties, along with the opening sections of *Joseph Andrews* and Fielding's possible authorship of *Shamela*, made any friendship between the two impossible (indeed, their relationship—or, more accurately, the lack of it—reflects little credit on Richardson).

One of Richardson's closest friends, Lady Bradshaigh, had written him soon after publication of the fourth volume of *Clarissa*, entreating him not to let his heroine die, and subsequently urged him to write a "novel about a Good Man." How much this influenced Richardson, if at all, is purely conjectural, but early in 1750, he had begun what was to be his last novel. Despite his stated intention not to publish this "new work," the first six volumes of *Sir Charles Grandison* were published late in 1753 (November 13 and December 11), and the concluding volume on March 14, 1754. As had been the case with *Pamela* and *Clarissa*, Dutch, German, and French translations soon followed.

In his preface to *Sir Charles Grandison*, Richardson, in his guise as the "editor" of the manuscript, announced that after this third novel he would write no more. He had, however, been in the process of compiling a series of selections from his novels which was published in March, 1755, as *A Collection of the Moral and Instructive Sentiments, Maxims, Cautions, and Reflexions, Contained in the Histories of Pamela, Clarissa, and Sir Charles Grandison.* He continued to be active as a printer and to make minor revisions in his novels, particularly *Pamela*, but his "dislike to the pen" continued. During his last years, he devoted more and more time to his correspondence—since the early 1740's, he had kept copies of all or most of his letters—apparently with the idea of eventual publication. On June 28, 1761, he suffered a stroke that resulted in his death a few days later on July 4, 1761.

ANALYSIS

"Why, Sir, if you were to read Richardson for the story, your impatience would be so much fretted that you would hang yourself. But you must read him for the sentiment, and consider the story as only giving occasion to the sentiment." Samuel Johnson's comment is only partly relevant. As James E. Evans states in his introduction to Samuel Richardson's series of excerpts, the revival of Richardson's reputation in recent decades grows out of the assertion that he "remains a great writer in spite of his morality" and must be read "'for the story' (psychological realism and conscious artistry), because we no longer read 'for the sentiment.'"

Richardson himself stated quite clearly, in his prefaces to *Pamela* and *Clarissa*, and in his letters, that his purpose as an author was to depict "real life" and "in a manner probable, natural, and lively." At the same time, however, he wanted his books to be thought of as instruments of manners and morals intended to "teach great virtues." Fiction, he insisted, should be useful and instructive; it should edify readers of all ages, but particularly should be relevant and appealing to youth. Richardson observed with passionate interest and recorded with a genius for infinite detail the relationships between men and women; the concerns of daily life; and the particular class and caste distinctions of mid-eighteenth century England. This intense interest in the *usual* sets him apart from such predecessors as Daniel Defoe or the seventeenth century writers of prose romances. In all of his novels, and particularly, perhaps, in *Pamela*, the relationship between his main characters has about it the quality of traditional romantic love; at the same time, the novels are so realistically grounded in the accumulation of a mass of day-to-day realistic details as to create a remarkable sense of authenticity. Characteristic of this creation of the illusion of real life is the account, possibly apocryphal, of *Pamela*'s being read aloud by the local blacksmith to a small group of the village's inhabitants on the village green; finally, when Pamela's triumph by her marriage to Squire B. was assured, the villagers indulged in a spree of thanksgiving and merrymaking; it was *their* Pamela who had conquered.

Richardson, then, was both a conscious, self-avowed realist, and also an equally conscious, self-avowed teacher and moralist. This dualism permeates all three of his novels and is perhaps most apparent—and transparent—in *Pamela*. It is, indeed, Richardson's hallmark, and is the source both of his strength and weakness as a novelist.

PAMELA

Reduced to its simplest terms, the "story" or "plot" of the first volume of *Pamela* is too well known to warrant more than the briefest summary. The heroine, a young servant girl, is pursued by her master, Squire B., but maintains her virginity in spite of his repeated and ingenious efforts, until the would-be seducer, driven to desperation, marries her. Thus is Pamela's virtue rewarded. The continuation of the novel in volume 2, a decided letdown, is virtually plotless, highly repetitive, and highlighted only by Squire B.'s excursion into infidelity. Volumes 3 and 4, written partly because of Richardson's indignation with the various parodies of the first volume of *Pamela*, have even less to recommend them. Labeled as "virtually unreadable" by one modern commentator, even Richardson's most understanding critic-biographers, T. C. Duncan Eaves and Ben D. Kimpel, have dismissed them as "Richardson at his worst, pompous, proper, proud of himself, and above all dull."

Despite his frequent excursions into bathos and sentimentality, when he is not indulging in sermonizings on ethics and morality, the Richardson of the first volume of *Pamela* writes vigorously, effectively, and with keen insight and intimate understanding of his characters. *Pamela* contains many powerful scenes that linger long in the reader's memory: the intended rape scene, the sequence in which Pamela considers suicide, even parts of the marriage scene (preceded by some prodigious feats of letter-writing to her parents on the day prior to the wedding, from six o'clock in the morning, half an hour past eight o'clock, near three o'clock [ten pages], eight o'clock at night, until eleven o'clock the same night and following the marriage) are the work of a powerful writer with a keen sense for the dramatic.

In the final analysis, however, the novel succeeds or fails because of its characters, particularly and inevitably that of Pamela herself. From the opening letter in which she informs her parents that her mistress has died and Squire B., her mistress's son, has appeared on the scene, to the long sequence of her journal entries, until her final victory when her would be seducer, worn out and defeated in all his attempts to have her without marriage, capitulates and makes the "thrice-happy" Pamela his wife, she dominates the novel.

In effect, and seemingly quite beyond Richardson's conscious intent, Pamela is two quite different characters. On the one hand, she is the attractive and convincing young girl who informs her parents that her recently deceased mistress had left her three pairs of shoes that fit her perfectly, adding that "my lady had a very little foot"; or having been transferred to Squire B.'s Lincolnshire estate, laments that she lacks "the courage to stay, neither can I think to go."

On the other hand, she is at times a rather unconvincing puppet who thinks and talks in pious platitudes and values her "honesty" as a very valuable commodity, a character—in Joseph Wood Krutch's words— "so devoid of any delicacy of feeling as to be inevitably indecent."

Squire B. is less interesting than Pamela, and his efforts to seduce Pamela tend to become either boring or amusing. Her father, the Old Gaffer, who would disown his daughter "were she not honest," similarly frequently verges upon caricature, although one distinguished historian of the English novel finds him extremely convincing; and Lady Davers, Squire B.'s arrogant sister, tends to be more unbelievable than convincing, as do Pamela's captors, the odious Mrs. Jewkes and the equally repulsive Colbrand.

In spite of its shortcomings, *Pamela* cannot be dismissed, as one critic has commented, as "only a record of a peculiarly loathsome aspect of bourgeois morality." *Pamela* has great moments, scenes, and characters that pass the ultimate test of a work of fiction, that of *memorableness:* scenes that remain in the reader's consciousness long after many of the events have become blurred or dimmed. It is equally important historically: Among other things, its popularity helped prepare the way for better novelists and better novels, including what Arnold Bennett was to call the "greatest realistic novel in the world," Richardson's *Clarissa*.

CLARISSA

Unlike *Pamela, Clarissa* did not have its origins in "real life"; his characters, Richardson insisted, were "entirely creatures of his fantasy." He commenced the novel in the spring or summer of 1744; it was three years in the making, two of which were primarily devoted to revision (it has been said that when his old friend Aaron Hill misread *Clarissa*, Richardson devoted a year to revising the text for publication). Almost a million words in length, the plot of *Clarissa* is relatively simple. Clarissa Harlowe, daughter of well-to-do, middle-class parents with social aspirations, is urged by her family to marry a man, Solmes, whom she finds repulsive. At the same time, her sister Arabella is being courted by an aristocrat, Robert Lovelace. Lovelace, attracted and fascinated by

Clarissa, abandons his lukewarm courtship of Arabella and, after wounding the girl's brother in a duel, turns his attention to Clarissa, in spite of her family's objections. Clarissa lets herself be persuaded; she goes off with Lovelace, who imprisons her in a brothel, where he eventually drugs and rapes her; she finally escapes, refuses the contrite Lovelace's offers of marriage, and eventually dies. Lovelace, repentant and haunted by his evil act, is killed in a duel by Clarissa's cousin, Colonel Morden.

Counterpointing and contrasting with these two major characters are Anna Howe, Clarissa's closest friend and confidante, and John Belford, Lovelace's closest friend. Around these four are a number of contrasting minor characters, each of whom contributes to the minutely recorded series of events and climaxes, events which in their barest forms verge upon melodrama, and at times even farce. Even so, the novel in its totality is greater than the sum of its parts: It has about it the ultimate power of Greek tragedy, and Clarissa herself, like the major characters of Greek drama, rises above the occasionally melodramatic or improbable sequences to attain a stature not seen in English prose fiction before, and seldom surpassed since.

Much of the power and the drama of *Clarissa* grows out of the author's effective use of contrast—between Clarissa and Anna Howe; between Lovelace and Belford; and between the country life of the upper middle class and the dark, rank side of urban England. This and the richness and variety of incident redeem the sometimes improbable events and lapses into didacticism and give the novel a sense of reality larger than life itself.

In the final analysis, the great strength of the novel is the creation of its two main characters. Clarissa, with her pride and self-reliance, "so secure in her virtue," whose feelings of shame and self-hatred are such that she begs Lovelace "to send her to Bedlam or a private madhouse" (no less a master than Henry Fielding praised Clarissa's letter after the rape as "beyond anything I had ever read"), could have degenerated into bathos or caricature but instead attains a level of intensity and reality unique in the novel prior to 1740.

Though Clarissa dominates the novel, Richardson is almost as successful with Lovelace, despite the fact that in the early portions of the novel he seems for the most part like Squire B., just another Restoration rake. His transformation, following his violation of Clarissa, grows and deepens: "One day, I fancy," he reflects, "I shall hate myself on recollecting what I am about at this instant. But I must stay till then. We must all of us have something to repent of." Repent he does, after his terse letter announcing the consummation of the rape: "And now, Belford, I can go no further. The affair is over. Clarissa lives."

Belford, like the reader, is horror-stricken. By the rape, Lovelace has acted not as a man, but an animal, and his expiation is, in its own way, much more terrible than Clarissa's, who at times somewhat complacently contemplates her own innocence and eventual heavenly reward. Lovelace remains a haunted man ("sick of myself! sick of my remembrance of my vile act!") until his death in a duel with Colonel Morden, a death which is really a kind of suicide. The final scene of the novel, and Lovelace's last words, "Let this Expiate!," are among the most memorable of the entire novel, and Richardson's portrayal of a character soiled and tarnished, an eternally damaged soul, is unforgettable.

SIR CHARLES GRANDISON

As early as February, 1741, an anonymous correspondent had asked Richardson to write the "history of a Man, whose Life would be the path that we should follow." By the end of the decade, with *Pamela* and *Clarissa* behind him, and influenced by old friends, including Lady Bradshaigh, Richardson began thinking seriously about such a novel. Despite increasing ill health and the continuing demands of his business, he was soon immersed in the project, a novel designed to "present" the character of a "Good Man," and to show the influence such a character exerted "on society in general and his intimates in particular." Although he had at one time decided not to publish the novel during his lifetime, the first volumes of *Sir Charles Grandison* came out in 1753. Even before the seventh and last volume was in print the following year, some critics were stating their dissatisfaction with Sir Charles's "Unbelievable Perfection," a criticism Richardson repudiated in a concluding note to the last volume: "The Editor (that is, Richardson himself) thinks human nature has often, of late, been shown in a light too degrading; and he hopes from this series of letters it will be seen that characters may be good without being unnatural."

Subsequent critical opinion of the novel has varied widely, a few critics considering it Richardson's masterpiece, while many regard it as his least successful novel. *Sir Charles Grandison* differs dramatically from its predecessors in its concern with the English upper class and aristocracy, a world which Richardson freely acknowledged he had never known or understood: "How shall a man obscurely situated . . . pretend to describe and enter into characters in upper life?" In setting, too, the novel was a new departure, ranging as it does from England to Italy and including a large number of Italians, highlighted by Clementina, certainly the most memorable character in the novel. The conflict in Clementina's heart and soul, her subsequent refusal to marry Sir Charles because he is a Protestant, and her ensuing madness are as effective as anything Richardson ever wrote, and far more convincing than Sir Charles's rescue of Harriett Byron following her abduction by Sir Hargrove Pollexfen and their eventual marriage. Harriett, though not as interesting a character as either Pamela or Clarissa, shares with them one basic habit: She is an indefatigable letter writer, perhaps the most prolific in the history of English prose fiction, at times sleeping only two hours a night and, when not admiring Grandison from afar, writing letters to him (not uncharacteristic of her style is her appeal to the clergyman who is supposed to marry her to Sir Hargrove: "Worthy man . . . save a poor creature. I would not hurt a worm! I love everybody! Save me from violence!").

Sir Charles himself is similarly less interesting than either Squire B. or Lovelace, and it is difficult today for even the most sympathetic reader to find a great deal to admire in the man who is against masquerades, dresses neatly but not gaudily, is time and time again described as a "prince of the Almighty's creation," an "angel of a man," and "one of the finest dancers in England." Most of the other characters, including the Italians (with the notable exception of Clementina), are similarly either unconvincing or uninteresting, except for two small masterpieces of characterization: Aunt Nell, Grandison's maiden aunt; and Lord G., Charlotte Grandison's husband, a gentle and quiet man, in love with his temperamental wife, often hurt and bewildered by her sharp tongue and brusque actions.

Horace Walpole is said to have written off *Sir Charles Grandison* as a "romance as it would be spiritualized by a Methodist preacher"; and Lord Chesterfield also dismissed it, adding that whenever Richardson "goes, *ultra crepidem*, into high life, he grossly escapes the modes." On the other hand, Jane Austen specifically "singled . . . [it] out for special praise," and Richardson's major biographers believe that in *Sir Charles Grandison*, his "surface realism and his analysis of social situations are at their height."

Whatever his weaknesses, Richardson was one of the seminal influences in the development of the novel. His impact upon his contemporaries and their immediate successors was profound, not only in England but on the Continent as well, and eventually on the beginnings of the novel in the United States. He popularized the novel of manners as a major genre for several decades, and his use of the epistolary method added another dimension to the art of narrative. Though his novels have frequently suffered in comparison with those of his major contemporary, Henry Fielding, in recent years a renewed interest and appraisal of Richardson and his work have placed him securely in the ranks of the major English novelists.

William Peden

OTHER MAJOR WORKS

NONFICTION: *The Apprentice's Vade Mecum: Or, Young Man's Pocket Companion*, 1733; *Letters Written to and for Particular Friends, on the Most Important Occasions*, 1741; *A Collection of the Moral and Instructive Sentiments, Maxims, Cautions, and Reflections, Contained in the Histories of Pamela, Clarissa, and Sir Charles Grandison*, 1755; *The Correspondence of Samuel Richardson*, 1804 (Anna Barbauld, editor).

BIBLIOGRAPHY

Bloom, Harold, ed. *Samuel Richardson*. New York: Chelsea House, 1987. This collection reprints in order of their appearance what Bloom judges to be the best of modern criticism of Richardson. In addition to Bloom's own introduction, there are six essays devoted to *Clarissa* and two each to *Pamela* and *Sir Charles Grandison*. The book also includes a chronology of Richardson's life and a brief bibliography.

Brophy, Elizabeth Bergen. *Samuel Richardson: The Triumph of Craft*. Knoxville: University of Tennessee Press, 1974. Rejecting the notion that Richardson's unconscious produced great novels in spite of the author—a view held by even his most recent biographers—Brophy examines Richardson's statements about fiction in his letters and his prefaces and postscripts to his novels. Having determined his theories about fiction, Brophy then compares these ideas with Richardson's practice. Two short appendices discuss the novelist's "nervous complaint" and conclude that he probably suffered from Parkinson's disease.

Bueler, Lois E. *Clarissa's Plots*. London: Associated University Presses, 1994. Examines the themes in Richardson's seminal work. Includes bibliographical references and an index.

Doody, Margaret Anne. *A Natural Passion: A Study of the Novels of Samuel Richardson*. Oxford, England: Clarendon Press, 1974. Seeks the antecedents of Richardson's fiction in seventeenth and eighteenth century drama, romance, religious writing, thought, and art. Doody shows how Richardson transformed these materials into fiction probing "man's relation to himself and his fate."

Eaves, T. C. Duncan, and Ben D. Kimpel. *Samuel Richardson: A Biography*. Oxford, England: Clarendon Press, 1971. The definitive biography, based on fifteen years of research. Devotes three chapters to each of the novels and concludes with four excellent chapters on Richardson's personality, thoughts, reading, and achievements.

Golden, Morris. *Richardson's Characters*. Ann Arbor: University of Michigan Press, 1963. A psychological study of Richardson that sees in his characters aspects of himself. Suggests that while ostensibly Richardson supported morality, at least unconsciously he favored passion.

Kinkead-Weakes, Mark. *Samuel Richardson: Dramatic Novelist*. Ithaca, N.Y.: Cornell University Press, 1973. Seeking to understand Richardson's achievement and his appeal to nineteenth century writers such as Jane Austen and George Eliot, this study demonstrates Richardson's dramatic use of immediacy and explores the implications of his "writing to the moment."

McKillop, Alan Dugald. *Samuel Richardson, Printer and Novelist*. Chapel Hill: University of North Carolina Press, 1936. Long the standard biography, this study remains a good treatment of Richardson's life, which McKillop discusses in a lengthy appendix. The text itself focuses "on the origins, publication, and reception of" the three novels.

Myer, Valerie Grosvenor, ed. *Samuel Richardson: Passion and Prudence*. London: Vision Press, 1986. As in other collections of Richardson criticism, the majority of this volume's essays concern *Clarissa*, with one critical piece devoted to *Pamela* and one to *Sir Charles Grandison*. Myer also includes, in a section titled "The Sex's Champion," two essays on Richardson's influence. Unlike other collections of this type, Myer's book also contains a helpful index.

Watt, Ian. *The Rise of the Novel: Studies in Defoe, Richardson, and Fielding*. Berkeley: University of California Press, 1957. Contains excellent chapters on *Pamela* and *Clarissa*, praising the psychological depth of the characters. Analyzes Richardson's contribution to the development of English prose fiction and relates the novels to the social situation of their day.

Wolff, Cynthia Griffin. *Samuel Richardson and the Eighteenth-Century Puritan Character*. Hamden, Conn.: Archon Books, 1972. Examines Richardson's novels, especially *Clarissa*, as psychological and social studies, relating them to twentieth century psychology and eighteenth century Puritanism.

MORDECAI RICHLER

Born: Montreal, Canada; January 27, 1931

PRINCIPAL LONG FICTION

The Acrobats, 1954

Son of a Smaller Hero, 1955

A Choice of Enemies, 1957

The Apprenticeship of Duddy Kravitz, 1959

The Incomparable Atuk, 1963 (also known as *Stick Your Neck Out*)

Cocksure: A Novel, 1968

St. Urbain's Horseman, 1971

Joshua Then and Now, 1980

Solomon Gursky Was Here, 1989

Barney's Version, 1997

OTHER LITERARY FORMS

As a professional writer, spurning academic life for wider creative possibilities, Mordecai Richler is known for producing short stories, essays, articles, film scripts, television plays, and children's literature. Much of his work first appeared in prestigious magazines such as *The Atlantic Monthly*, *The New Yorker*, the *New Statesman*, and *Encounter*. Some of his individual stories, which would often become chapters in his novels, have been collected in *The Street: Stories* (1969). A children's book, *Jacob Two-Two Meets the Hooded Fang* (1975), and two novels, *Joshua Then and Now* and *The Apprenticeship of Duddy Kravitz*, have been made into motion pictures, the latter winning the Golden Bear Award at the Berlin Film Festival in 1974. Richler's screenplay for this film was also nominated for an Academy Award, and it won a Screenwriter's Guild of America Award.

ACHIEVEMENTS

Forsaking Canada for the more exciting atmosphere of Paris, Richler struggled with his work and lived in poor circumstances, publishing very few stories. Here, however, he met some significant figures of the new literary set who reacted favorably to his work; among them were Allen Ginsberg, Herbert

Gold, and Terry Southern. After returning to Canada for a short while, Richler finished his first novel, *The Acrobats*. As is so often the case with Canadian writers, Richler preferred to publish outside his own country, where he felt more appreciated. His first effort was accepted by André Deutsch in London. In later years, with his reputation secure, he decided to publish with the Canadian house McClelland and Stewart.

In order to make a living exclusively as a writer, Richler left Canada again. Still using his Canadian experience as the substance of his work, Richler was very productive in England, publishing stories and novels that met with much acclaim. Even his film scripts for *No Love for Johnnie* (1961), *Young and Willing* (1964), and *Life at the Top* (1965), which Richler considers inferior work for an often superficial medium, were positively reviewed. Richler twice won Canada's foremost literary prize, the Governor General's Award, for *Cocksure* and *St. Urbain's Horseman*. Although he achieved a certain notoriety for his searing portraits of Canadian life, he finally gained acceptance as one of Canada's most distinguished novelists.

BIOGRAPHY

Mordecai Richler was born in Montreal, Canada, in 1931, in the heart of the Jewish ghetto. His father was a junk dealer and his mother was a housewife who has recently written a book about her life. Her father was a rabbi whose influence ensured an orthodox household. By turning away from orthodoxy at a young age, however, Richler ran into trouble at home, which perhaps accounts for some of his perceptive but acerbic reflections on family life. To further compound his problems as a youth, his parents were divorced when he was thirteen. As a response to the breakdown at home, Richler joined a Zionist labor group called Habonim and dreamed of settling in Palestine. Only later did he go to Israel as a journalist.

In his adolescent years, Richler attended Baron Byng High School, a predominantly Jewish school even though it was part of the Protestant school system. In his stories and novels it is transformed into

Fletcher's Field High, and Richler peoples it with characters known to him as a schoolboy. After high school, Richler attended Sir George Williams University in Montreal (now Concordia University), since his grades were not good enough for McGill University. Although he returned to Sir George as writer-in-residence, the academic life did not appeal to him. He once remarked that "academe, like girls, whiskey, and literature, promised better than it paid." Rejecting a life of scholarship, Richler decided on the uncertain life of a freelance writer in Europe, where he could develop his own style and not merely put a stamp of approval on someone else's.

After living in Paris for two years, where he published his first story in a magazine called *Points* and got his first taste of expatriate life, Richler returned to Montreal. There he joined the Canadian Broadcasting Company for a short time, earning enough money to complete his first novel, *The Acrobats*. The novel aroused more attention in England than in Canada, which perhaps convinced him that the richer literary heritage there would fuel his talents. For the best part of twenty years, then, Richler lived in England, producing many novels, short stories, and film scripts.

Although Richler needed this geographical and cultural change to gain an ironic and critical distance in his work, he used his Canadian experience as the basis of his fiction; he has said that the first twenty years of a writer's life determine the character of his writing and inform his imaginative vision. Even after many years in England, Richler never felt sufficiently integrated into English society to capture the essence of that particular culture. Feeling himself an outsider in England and cut off from the social context of Canada, Richler returned in 1972 to settle with his wife and five children in Montreal.

ANALYSIS

In an article, "Why I Write," Mordecai Richler repeats the honest answer given by George Orwell to the same question: sheer egotism, aesthetic enthusiasm, political purposes, and historical impulse. These reasons, modified by Richler's unique perception, are clues to the form and content of his work.

Richler's egotistical desire to be talked about has, no doubt, been fulfilled, as he is the victim of attacks from both Jews and Protestants for what they consider to be unjust satirical portraits of their respective communities. He even said that to be a Jew and a Canadian is to emerge from the ghetto twice, as a sense of self-consciousness and envy pervades both societies. His satire, however, even when confined by the geography of Montreal, is more universal than some critics have assumed, and this element has enhanced his status as a significant writer. Although Richler never wanted to acquire the role of writer as personality (avoiding the talk-show circuit as much as possible and loathing being cast as the kind of figure Norman Mailer has become), his fierce attacks on provincialism, pretension, community arrogance, envy, and class economic superiority marked him as a highly visible, eccentric, and often vicious outsider.

While there is a great deal of harshness in Richler's writing, it is not merely personal vindictiveness,

(Christopher Morris)

but a narrative strategy of accurate observation informed by imagination; it is a grotesque comic style designed to emphasize the absurdity of the human condition and to mock those whose misdirected values merely cause suffering. In *The Acrobats*, Richler dissects a generation of hollow men who infest the corrupt world of Spain's festival time, in which a loss of belief is symbolized by *fallas*, empty wood and papier-mâché dolls. It is a nightmare world of confusion and fantasy which culminates in the death of antihero André Bennett. Without capturing the flavor and intensity of Ernest Hemingway's lost generation, Richler, in a limited way, sets the themes for his later novels by attacking all attitudes which he thinks are essentially destructive.

Richler admitted to a certain sense of guilt prompted by the discrepancy between his life at home facing a blank page and the memory of his father going to work in his junkyard in subzero weather. Perhaps this recognition of the severity of ordinary life gave him the focus of his work, the precisely observed but critically and ironically rendered life of the common man fighting circumstances greater than himself.

Richler's intelligence, however, does not allow him to glorify uncritically his protagonists. The tension between what is and what ought to be is always present; the result is a controlled realism balanced by a satirical distance which allows fantasy, nightmare, and a morally grounded sense of the ridiculous. As George Woodcock observed, Richler was influenced by the realism of André Malraux, Albert Camus, and Louis-Ferdinand Céline, but Richler himself praised Evelyn Waugh as the greatest novelist of his time, and there is in Richler's work much of the energy, sensibility, and bawdiness of American writers such as Philip Roth.

When Richler speaks of a political purpose, he follows Orwell's idea that a novelist should push the world in a certain direction, that in fact any serious novelist is therefore a moralist. Although many of his stories end tragically, there is still a sense that his characters exist not as victims of a cruel, impersonal fate, but as victims of their own and others' actions. The choices they make are important ones and often

lead to disaster when they are not based on a consistent moral viewpoint. Norman Price in *A Choice of Enemies* recognizes that choices are significant, but no longer has the courage to make the difficult ones that confront his modern generation. He ends up complacently accepting values from his friends. In *The Apprenticeship of Duddy Kravitz*, Richler succeeds in making Duddy a partially sympathetic character, often a victim of powerful people even more ruthless than he is, but Duddy, blinded by ambition, is the indirect cause of his friend Virgil's paralysis from a motor accident. In his enthusiasm for the direct, specific attack, however, Richler's moral position often seems diffuse or simply confusing. Two of his novels, *St. Urbain's Horseman* and *Joshua Then and Now*, manifest a more coherent intention which makes the satire even more meaningful.

Much of the force of Richler's work comes from his observation and memory of life in the Montreal ghetto of his youth. Even novels such as *Cocksure* and *The Acrobats* are distilled through the experience of the expatriate Canadian trying to make sense of a less provincial foreign world. Richler has said that he feels rooted in Montreal's St. Urbain Street, and because that was his time and place, he has elected to get it right. To this end, Richler often writes about the same characters from Fletcher's Field High School as they experience life at different stages of intellectual and emotional growth. A peripheral character such as Jake Hersh, for example, in *The Apprenticeship of Duddy Kravitz* and *The Street: Stories*, will become the focus of *St. Urbain's Horseman*.

THE APPRENTICESHIP OF DUDDY KRAVITZ

There is so much comic energy in *The Apprenticeship of Duddy Kravitz* that the reader can easily underestimate the social and moral implications of the work. Richler stated that to a certain extent the reader should sympathize with Duddy, who must rise above the poverty of the St. Urbain ghetto to challenge and defeat powerful manipulators such as Jerry Dingleman, the Boy Wonder. The ambiguity of Duddy's character creates a problem of moral focus, however, in that some of his victories are at the expense of truly kindhearted people, such as Virgil Roseboro and Yvette.

There are certainly many reasons for Duddy's aggressive, almost amoral behavior. His mother died when Duddy was very young, leaving him without the female stability he needed at the time. His father, Max the Hack, who drives a Montreal cab and pimps on the side, lets Duddy fend for himself, as most of his affection and attention went to the older son, Lenny. Duddy remembers that his father wrote many letters to Lenny when he worked at a resort, but Max refuses to write to Duddy. Max also encourages Lenny to go to medical school and is proud of his achievements; he makes it obvious that he expects little from Duddy and does not perceive the extent of Duddy's ambition nor his loyalty to his family. Duddy is also often humiliated by the affluent university students with whom he works as a waiter at the Hotel Lac des Sables. Irwin Shubert, for instance, considers Duddy a social inferior and, using a rigged roulette wheel, cheats him out of three hundred dollars.

Although eliciting sympathy by explaining Duddy's situation, Richler undercuts a completely sympathetic attitude toward Duddy by detailing the results of his actions. His exploitation of the other students of Fletcher's Field High School leads even his friend Jake Hersh to believe that he makes everything dirty. Duddy's schemes to make money are clever enough; he works out a system to steal hockey sticks from the Montreal Canadians, but he does not realize that the blame rests on the stick boy, who is trying to earn money through honest, hard work. More seriously, Duddy, through a cruel practical joke, is responsible for the death of Mrs. Macpherson, the wife of one of his teachers. Later, as he tries to make his dream of owning land come true, Duddy rejects his lover Yvette, causes the paralysis of his friend, Virgil, from whom he also steals money, and alienates his grandfather, Simcha, who cares for him more than anyone else.

Duddy's relationship with Simcha provides both the moral tone and the narrative drive of the novel. Simcha, a man trusted but not loved by the elders of the St. Urbain ghetto for his quiet, patient integrity, is loved by his favorite, Duddy. Like many others of his generation, Simcha feels the weight of the immigrant's fear of failure and instills Duddy with the idea that a man without land is a nobody. For Simcha, this cliché is a more complex concept associated with the traditional struggles of the Jews and presupposes a sense of responsibility. Duddy misinterprets the implications of his grandfather's advice and perceives it as being a practical imperative to be gained at any cost, involving himself in many schemes—from importing illegal pinball machines to filming bar mitzvahs with a bizarre, alcoholic documentary director—in order to purchase land for commercial development.

For a short time, Duddy's plans misfire; he goes bankrupt and is unable to pay for the land he wants so badly. Upon hearing that the Boy Wonder, the ghetto "miracle" who has escaped his environment by drug peddling and other corrupt means, covets the same land, Duddy forges checks in Virgil's name to get enough money to make the purchase. In a closing scene, Duddy brings his family to see his property. By coincidence, the Boy Wonder arrives, and Duddy drives him away with verbal abuse. His father is more impressed with this act of defiance than with Duddy's achievement, and later, among his circle of friends, Max begins to create a legend about Duddy in much the same way as he created the legend of the Boy Wonder. Although his victory has been effected by deceit and victimization, Duddy's behavior seems vindicated; he smiles in triumph, unaware that he continues only under the spell of a shared illusion. The reader is left elated to a certain extent at the defeat of the Boy Wonder, yet sobered by the figure of Simcha, crying in the car, after having been informed by Yvette of Duddy's method of acquiring the land.

ST. URBAIN'S HORSEMAN

Unlike Duddy Kravitz, whose life is defined by the wealth he acquires, Jake Hersh of *St. Urbain's Horseman* is defined by the exploits of his cousin, Joey, the "Horseman" of the title. In his quest for certainty and identity in a world of confusion and moral ambiguity, Jake chooses a dubious model of behavior which eventually becomes an obsession. Much of the comedy and much of the human drama in the book come from the discrepancy between Jake's illusions of the Horseman and the reality of his own life.

Richler experiments with a cinematic style of flashbacks and flash-forwards, not only to create a sense of suspense, but also to show the role memory plays in developing a character. It is obvious that Jake is involved in some sort of sex scandal which threatens his married and professional life. As the trial progresses, the narrative is punctuated by the events in Jake's life which have led him to this degradation. In his youth, he wanted to escape the St. Urbain ghetto and the provincial nature of Canada itself. Typically, however, he leaves Canada to escape boredom only to find it everywhere.

Although Jake's loving relationship with his wife offers the promise of real stability, Jake seems to believe that only his cousin Joey leads a meaningful life, fighting injustice wherever he can find it. Specifically, he thinks Joey is the lone avenger riding after Joseph Mengele, the feared *Doktor* of the Nazi extermination camps. At first, Joey is simply the black sheep of the Hersh family, leaving home at a young age and returning periodically to disrupt the mundane lives of his relatives. Jake, who is eleven years younger than Joey, perceives him to be a hero and dismisses the accusations that he is just a criminal taking advantage of others for his own gain. Uncle Abe even tells Jake that the famed Horseman is more likely to blackmail Mengele than kill him.

By adulthood, Jake's fantasies and nightmares about his cousin assume mythic proportions, and he incorporates this mythology into his daily concerns, measuring himself against the Horseman he has created. Jake's consequent search for Joey in Israel and Germany uncovers the grim reality of Joey's fraud, drug smuggling, and disastrous love affairs, but Jake only rationalizes his negative impression; he places the Horseman's quest for "justice" beyond the sphere of ordinary moral culpability or human responsibility.

Jake reasons that he is a product of his generation, conceived in the Depression. He and others like him lived through the Spanish Civil War, World War II, the Holocaust, Hiroshima, the Israeli War of Independence, McCarthyism, the Korean War, and finally the Vietnam War. They were always the wrong age to be involved; they were merely observers, moral bystanders who could protest and give advice, but who were fundamentally impotent. Jake wants answers to his plight, but feels even more alienated from the important issues of his time because he is a case history of the Jewish intellectual born into the Canadian working class. He finds his generation and its concerns trivial and peripheral, easily susceptible, in his thinking, to the guilt induced by the "injustice collectors"—the prison-camp survivors and the starvelings of Africa.

These issues, these betrayals of age, are contrasted with the more personal betrayals of life: Jake's father rejects his marriage to a non-Jew; Luke Scott decides to choose a British director instead of Jake, his best friend, for his first major script; Jenny dismisses Jake as a lover because he is too young; and Harry Stein implicates Jake in the rape of a young au pair girl. Jake is no more capable of understanding these events than the historical events of more significant import.

After the trial, in which Jake is found guilty of indecent assault and fined, he receives word that the Horseman has been killed in a plane crash while smuggling cigarettes. He retreats to his attic and finds a gun hidden in the Horseman's saddle. It fires only blanks, its efficacy as illusory as the Horseman's exploits. Upon discovering this, Jake seems to have returned to reality, but later in his nightmare, he dreams that he is the Horseman extracting gold fillings from Mengele's teeth with pliers. He wakes up and changes the Horseman's journal to read "presumed dead." The irony is that Jake will probably continue to search for certitude and will live a tolerable life based on illusion; he does not realize that the love of his wife is the stable point which will exist despite the illusion.

JOSHUA THEN AND NOW

There are many similarities between *St. Urbain's Horseman* and *Joshua Then and Now*: the time-schemes are not linear but shift backward and forward in a search for meaning which takes precedence over simple historical considerations; the characters are again graduates of Fletcher's Field High School who gain obvious material success, but who are not immune to even the minor ravages of time; the major issues of the world are always present, but private and personal issues dominate; and Joshua Shapiro, like Jake Hersh, tries to make sense of his own life in terms of facing the past. The important difference between the two novels is that Richler's attitude toward life in *Joshua Then and Now* is much more humane, and love is seen as the moral imperative that makes all other attitudes seem trivial.

Joshua Then and Now begins close to the present with Joshua in a cottage retreat suffering from multiple fractures incurred in a car accident. Because of hints of a sex scandal, he is guarded from the press by his father Reuben and his father-in-law, Senator Stephen Hornby. Joshua reads many letters from his fans and colleagues who have scorned him for what they think is his atrocious behavior, but he is able to put this criticism into perspective. He believes this public display of disapproval is what he deserves for the roguish behavior of his youth. Reflecting on his life, he now is able to see clearly what was of real importance.

Joshua's background seems almost surreal; certainly it is more colorful than the lives of his friends in St. Urbain. Joshua's aspiration to be a sportswriter derived from his father, Reuben, who was a Canadian boxing champion. After his retirement from the ring, Reuben became an enforcer for a gangster named Colucci. As a youngster, Joshua had to suffer both his father's long absences and the resentment of the neighborhood over Reuben's involvement with Colucci. Joshua's mother, Esther, is an eccentric who bewilders him even more than his father. At Joshua's bar mitzvah, Esther has too much to drink and decides to let the young boys see her perform as an exotic dancer. She shocks them with the explicitness of her movements and even lets them fondle her. Later in life, she gets involved in pornographic films and in running a massage parlor. It seems that Joshua's independent and sometimes improbable behavior is the logical result of his upbringing.

In trying to prolong his adolescence, Joshua becomes as ridiculous as his parents, and although his exploits seem harmless, they do have consequences; Joshua's fake letters about the novelist Iris Murdoch's homosexual activities, written to make money

at the expense of the University of Texas, end up being made public, to Joshua's disgrace. The pranks that he plays to gain revenge on his enemies—taking labels off Pinsky's valuable wine bottles, defacing Jonathan Coles's original painting, and planting illegal currency at Eli Seligson's house—conclude with Joshua's injuring himself in a high-speed car chase. For Joshua, at least, these episodes are a learning experience; they are stages on his way to maturity.

Joshua has many friends from his youth who still get together as the "Mackenzie King Memorial Society," the name being an ironic comment on a prime minister whom they consider a fraud. As successful as they are, however, in their middle age they are susceptible to law suits, tax-evasion inquiries, bypass operations, hair transplants, and cancer. The struggle for material wealth and its attainment now seem inadequate as values. More important is Joshua's involvement with the WASP, country-club circle. After marrying Pauline, Joshua is introduced to Jane and Jack Trimble and Pauline's brother Kevin. Joshua marries above his social class, but he takes a resentful and superior attitude to his wife's friends and relatives. He does as much as he can to sabotage a group that he believes has all the advantages. Through the years, however, he sees the disintegration of the Trimble marriage, the dashed hopes of the senator, and the death of Pauline's dependent brother, which precipitates her madness, and realizes that, even with their pretensions, they were only trying to survive.

The echoes of the past are most vividly sounded when Joshua returns to Ibiza, Spain, to confront Mueller, a German, who had disgraced him more than twenty-five years before. To gain revenge on Mueller, Joshua leaves his wife at a crucial time in her life, when she needs his comfort to fight off impending madness. In Spain, he notices remarkable changes: The friends he had are gone; many of his former haunts have been destroyed; the road to Almeria, the route of the retreating Republican army, is now dotted with hotels, condominiums, and commercial signs; and more significantly, Mueller is dead, a victim of cancer. To cleanse himself of the past, however, Joshua pays a price. His wife is institutionalized; then, after a prolonged stay at the hospital, she disappears. The novel ends with a loving reconciliation which suggests a change in Richler's perspective. Still on crutches as a result of his accident, Joshua recuperates at Hornby's cottage, accompanied by his children, the senator, and Reuben. In the final scene, Pauline returns, and Reuben sees Joshua in the vegetable garden without his cane, being supported by Pauline.

SOLOMON GURSKY WAS HERE

In *Solomon Gursky Was Here*, Richler creates his richest and most complex work, a 150-year chronicle of the ambitious and conniving Gursky family (loosely based on the real-life liquor kings of Montreal, the Bronfmans), weaving back and forth in time from the ill-fated Franklin Expedition in the Arctic to the political uncertainties of modern times. Beneath the surface of what is essentially a mystery story, a search for the elusive but seemingly ubiquitous Solomon Gursky, Richler examines the greed and corruption of society, the nature of the Jewish and Canadian people, mythological forces of the past, and the tenuous but compelling hold of love. Although uncompromising in his satirical portrait of the characters, Richler nevertheless alludes to the positive creative power of those who strive for understanding, however difficult the quest may be.

At the center of the novel stands writer Moses Berger, son of failed poet L. B. Berger, who has sold out to the Gurskys. Because of his father, Moses hears of Solomon Gursky at an early age and becomes obsessed with the almost mythical nature of this character. The alcoholic Moses, more a follower than the leader that his name suggests, investigates stories and documents and uncovers clues about why Solomon decided to resist the purely materialistic interests of his brothers Bernard, the ruthless businessman who has built his fortune by bootlegging, and Morrie, his unctious partner. Moses discovers that Solomon's enigmatic grandfather, Ephraim, was a criminal once imprisoned on Botany Bay, by incredible ingenuity the only survivor of the Franklin Expedition, a shaman of Eskimos who taught them Yiddish, and an energetic profligate perplexing in his moral ambiguity. Ephraim is, however, both a comic manifestation and a serious vital force of Judaism, instilling imagination and realism in Solomon, his spiritual heir.

Moses' search for the "real" Solomon, then, is an attempt to reclaim his past as a Jew and participate in the redemptive value of this figure, who takes on the mythic qualities of the raven that insinuates itself into a diversity of situations to provoke the apathetic and the misguided. Although Moses cannot quite verify all the incarnations of the mysterious Solomon, he suspects that Solomon has influenced many of the nobler acts that occur: the attempt to take over Bernard's McTavish distillery, the creation of the Israeli Air Force, and the success of the raid on Entebbe. By trying to restore order in his own life, through research and the dogged pursuit of the truth concerning Solomon, Moses begins to understand that honest engagement, not exploitation of life, is a source of value and meaning. No one is spared in Richler's caustic view, but some can glimpse hope, however concealed it may be.

BARNEY'S VERSION

In some respects, Moses' search for truth extends into *Barney's Version*, published almost a decade after *Solomon Gursky Was Here*. In this novel, though, Richler creates a character who risks becoming a parody not only of the author's earlier characters but also of the author himself. Barney Panofsky—"trash" television producer, lifelong Montrealer, and rabid hockey fan—is a man whose passions have often been too strong for his own good. Among other fiascoes, he drinks too much, smokes cigars obsessively, bungled three marriages, and potentially committed murder. His faults become an issue, however, only when he learns that Terry McIver, a friend from his youthful years in Paris, is about to publish an autobiography. Rightfully afraid of what Terry has to say about him, Barney immediately sets to penning his memoirs, his version of past events from which the novel's title is born.

The central action of *Barney's Version* is at turns poignant and hilarious. As expected, Barney recounts history much to his own benefit, including scorching depictions of his first two wives, a "martyred" feminist icon and a stereotypical Jewish princess. He rarely offers conscious insight into his own shortcomings and, in fact, often forgets or revises details of his life at its most crucial moments. Still, Barney manages to make his audience feel sympathy for him, especially in recalling his third botched marriage, to Miriam, a near-perfect woman, Barney's "heart's desire," and his likely soul mate. What ultimately emerges from Barney's memoir is a credible protagonist—foul-mouthed, hedonistic, sometimes oblivious, infrequently accepting blame—who manages to retain his desire for "true love" and for a creative outlet beyond the shallow commercialism of his television production company. As with Richler's other works, Barney becomes an enigmatic hero, tainted by his world experiences, yet still not devoid of hope.

Nevertheless, Barney's hope feels less substantial than the kind exhibited by characters in Richler's earlier fiction. One wonders if Barney truly longs for a better world, or simply for one in which people like Terry McIver do not threaten to reveal his secrets. This question is reinforced by the vitriol that Barney occasionally heaps on some of Richler's most familiar targets (feminists, Quebecer separatists, pretentious Jews, pseudointellectuals, vegetarians, antismoking zealots, and just about any other standard-bearer of political correctness). Despite the ongoing matter of whether Barney did or did not kill his former friend Boogie, the momentum of the novel sometimes feels less like a well-plotted story than a meandering path between Barney's occasional rants. Though unequivocally humorous, such tirades sometimes feel more like a lecture from Barney (or perhaps straight from Richler himself) in which the protagonist's own foibles are tragically overlooked in his attempt to decimate his targets.

Whether a narrow-minded curmudgeon or a keen social satirist, though, Barney does extend Richler's quirky vision of the world with undeniable force. Perhaps to request moderation from a writer like Richler is a mistake. His work has always been effective because of its raw power, its unsparing depiction of any character-type that happened to drift beneath the author's lens. Richler has been praised widely for the richness of his comic vision and for his keenly observed, unsentimental portrait of Montreal's inhab-

itants (Jew and non-Jew alike). Through an imaginative extension of this vision, Richler developed into a novelist of importance, with his message transcending the limited boundaries of St. Urbain Street to assume universal significance.

James C. MacDonald, updated by J. David Stevens

OTHER MAJOR WORKS

SHORT FICTION: *The Street: Stories*, 1969.

SCREENPLAYS: *No Love for Johnnie*, 1961 (with Nicholas Phipps); *Young and Willing*, 1964 (with Phipps); *Life at the Top*, 1965.

NONFICTION: *Hunting Tigers Under Glass: Essays and Reports*, 1968; *Shovelling Trouble*, 1972; *Notes on an Endangered Species and Others*, 1974; *The Great Comic Book Heroes and Other Essays*, 1978; *Home Sweet Home*, 1984; *Broadsides: Reviews and Opinions*, 1990; *Oh Canada! Oh Quebec!: Requiem for a Divided Country*, 1992; *This Year in Jerusalem*, 1994.

CHILDREN'S LITERATURE: *Jacob Two-Two Meets the Hooded Fang*, 1975; *Jacob Two-Two and the Dinosaur*, 1987; *Jacob Two-Two's First Spy Case*, 1997.

EDITED TEXTS: *Canadian Writing Today*, 1970; *Writers on World War II: An Anthology*, 1991.

BIBLIOGRAPHY

Benson, Eugene, and William Toye, eds. *The Oxford Companion to Canadian Literature*. Toronto: Oxford University Press, 1998. Provides further information on Richler's life and work as well as a solid cross-index to related writers and literary movements in Canada.

Craniford, Ada. *Fiction and Fact in Mordecai Richler's Novels*. Lewiston, N.Y.: E. Mellen Press, 1992. Addresses Judaism in Richler's fiction. Includes bibliographical references and index.

Darling, Michael, ed. *Perspectives on Mordecai Richler*. Toronto: ECW Press, 1986. A volume of essays devoted to reevaluating Richler's work using poststructuralist theory, close readings of individual texts, and innovative examinations of grammatical structure and symbolic patterns.

Dooley, D. J. *Moral Vision in the Canadian Novel*. Toronto: Clarke, Irwin, 1979. Discusses the artistic problem of Richler's attitude toward the character of Duddy Kravitz.

Khouri, Nadia. *Qui a peur de Mordecai Richler?* Montreal: Éditions Balzac, 1995. Explores Richler's views on Quebec-Ontario relations, Quebecer separatism, and Canadian nationalism.

McSweeney, Kerry. *Mordecai Richler and His Works.* Toronto: ECW Press, 1985. McSweeney argues that, with his increasing technical ability, Richler abandons a more passionate and darker vision of humanity.

Ramraj, Victor J. *Mordecai Richler.* Boston: Twayne, 1983. A comprehensive look at Richler's life and work, but short on detailed analysis.

Sheps, G. David, ed. *Mordecai Richler.* Toronto: McGraw-Hill Ryerson, 1971. A solid but standard collection of articles on Richler's work preceding his major achievements.

Woodcock, George, *Mordecai Richler.* Toronto: McClelland and Stewart, 1970. Presents a critical viewpoint emphasizing Richler's intellectual rather than intuitive approach to fiction. Also contains a brief biographical section.

CONRAD RICHTER

Born: Pine Grove, Pennsylvania; October 13, 1890
Died: Pine Grove, Pennsylvania; October 30, 1968

PRINCIPAL LONG FICTION

The Sea of Grass, 1936
The Trees, 1940
Tacey Cromwell, 1942
The Free Man, 1943
The Fields, 1946
Always Young and Fair, 1947
The Town, 1950
The Light in the Forest, 1953
The Lady, 1957
The Waters of Kronos, 1960
A Simple Honorable Man, 1962
The Grandfathers, 1964

The Awakening Land, 1966 (includes *The Trees*, *The Fields*, and *The Town*)
A Country of Strangers, 1966
The Aristocrat, 1968

OTHER LITERARY FORMS

Conrad Richter wrote fourteen novels, all of which were published by Knopf, but in addition to the longer fiction which Richter produced between 1937 and 1968, he also wrote short stories and a variety of nonfiction. He was nearly as prolific a short-story writer as he was a novelist, his earliest published story appearing in 1913. His first volume of collected short stories includes twelve stories under the title *Brothers of No Kin and Other Stories* (1924); nine more stories were collected in a volume entitled *Early Americana and Other Stories* (1936). Richter wrote short fiction throughout his career, producing more than thirty-one stories, most of which appeared in the *Saturday Evening Post*. Many of Richter's stories still remain uncollected, but a number were gathered in a collection entitled *The Rawhide Knot and Other Stories* (1978). Richter's nonfiction includes four book-length essays on his eclectic personal philosophy: *Human Vibrations* (1926); *Principles in Bio-Physics* (1927); *The Mountain on the Desert* (1955); and *A Philosophical Journey* (1955). Six of Richter's novels have been adapted for motion pictures and television, and Richter himself worked periodically as a writer for Metro-Goldwyn-Mayer in Hollywood between 1937 and 1950, but found that writing for motion pictures was not his forte. His continuing popularity as a writer is reflected by the fact that at present, nearly sixteen years after his death, ten of Richter's books are still in print, yet to date, his notebooks, correspondence, and other papers that would make for scholarly appreciation and analysis of his craft as a writer remain to be published.

ACHIEVEMENTS

Richter did not achieve widespread recognition during his long career as a writer despite the fact that he won the Pulitzer Prize for Fiction in 1951 for *The Town* and the National Book Award for Fiction in 1960 for *The Waters of Kronos*, beating out Harper

(Library of Congress)

Lee's *To Kill a Mockingbird* and John Updike's *Rabbit Run* among the competition. A reclusive man who spent much of his life in rural Pennsylvania and in the isolated mountains of New Mexico, Richter was not a colorful figure whose life drew attention to his work. Because much of his work appeared in serial form for popular and pulp magazines, he has been too hastily dismissed by academic critics. At his best, Richter is a historical novelist of the first rank. He recreates the past, not as a historian would, but rather, by reproducing the actualities of frontier experience which are conveyed by fidelity to details and local expression. When Richter's purposes as an artist are more fully understood, it seems certain that critical assessments of his work will acknowledge the judgment of the general reader, with whom Richter continues to be popular.

BIOGRAPHY

Conrad Michael Richter was born in Pine Grove, Pennsylvania, on October 13, 1890. The eldest of three sons of a Lutheran minister, he grew up in several small rural Pennsylvania towns where his father had congregations. He came from mixed German, French, and Scotch-Irish blood. One of his forebears served with George Washington's Continental Army and another fought as a Hessian mercenary for the British. His grandfather, uncle, and great-uncles were preachers. Richter was brought up in bucolic surroundings. and he passed a happy boyhood in a score of central and northern Pennsylvania villages. In 1906, he was graduated from Tremont High School and during the next three years took a number of odd jobs—clerking, driving teams, pitching hay, and working as a bank teller. His first permanent job was as a reporter for the Johnstown, Pennsylvania, *Journal*, which he began at nineteen. His first published story, entitled "How Tuck Went Home," was written in 1913 while he was living in Cleveland, Ohio. In 1914, a second story, "Brothers of No Kin," was awarded a twenty-five-dollar prize for being one of the best stories of the year. In 1915, Richter was married to Harvena Maria Achenbach. Taking his bride West to find his fortune in a silver mine venture at Cocur d'Alene, Idaho, he made a short sojourn as a speculator in the mine fields. After returning East, where a daughter was born in 1917, Richter started writing children's literature and published a periodical for juveniles called *Junior Magazine Book*. Meanwhile, his short stories had been appearing in magazines such as *Ladies' Home Journal* and *Saturday Review*.

Richter's early work as a newspaper reporter and editor influenced his literary style. His sparse method of expression was a product of his journalistic training, and the typical length of his novels is about two hundred pages. In lieu of formal education, Richter, like many self-taught people, became a voracious reader. In an interview, he said, "All my life I have been a reader and one of my joys as a boy and young man was a good book in which I could lose myself." His reading was eclectic, ranging from the adventure writer W. H. Hudson to scientific authors such as Michael Faraday and G. W. Crele, whose theories of chemistry and physics influence Richter's later philosophical works. Ralph Waldo Emerson, Henry David Thoreau, and John Burroughs also helped shape his idealistic views on nature. The most important influence on his own writing came, however, from Willa Cather, whose pioneer characters and Western backgrounds provided the model for much of Richter's fiction.

In his early short fiction, Richter used the formulas of the popular literature of the period, which still abided by the conventions of the genteel tradition. The typical tale revolved around stock plots such as a case of mistaken identity, a rich youth's rehabilitation through hardships shared with the common people, a city girl coming to terms with country life, and so on. As might be expected, these stories used cardboard characters and were tailored to readers' moral and social assumptions. Richter's first stories were self-admitted "potboilers" from which he only expected to get a bit of money for his family. During the period between 1917 and 1928, when Richter was engaged in hackwriting and publishing for a living, he started to develop his ideas on "psychoenergics," as he called his theory of human personality. This theoretical interest led to three works, *Human Vibration, Principles in Bio-Physics*, and a privately printed monograph called "Life Energy." These essays contained the germ of another book-length essay that he published twenty-eight years later as *The Mountain on the Desert*, his fullest attempt to articulate his personal philosophy.

In 1928, Richter's wife's illnesses caused a move to the Southwest, an event that would have a major effect on his career as a writer and mark a turning point in his life. What had started as a misfortune would turn out otherwise. Stimulated by the culture and climate of New Mexico, Richter published a second volume of stories, *Early Americana and Other Stories*, and his first novel, *The Sea of Grass*.

The writer's material was enlarged. He had always taken the ingredients of his fiction from family memories and observations; when he moved to New Mexico, as he later wrote in his unpublished *A Few Personal Notes*, "The backlog of my material still came from first sources, fine old-time men and women, chiefly from New Mexico and Arizona, Texas and Indiana territory, who lived through many of the early days. . . ."

In 1940, Richter published *The Trees*, the first volume of a trilogy that would be completed with *The Fields* in 1946 and *The Town* in 1950. After the publication of his southwestern novel *Tacey Cromwell* in 1942, Richter received his first literary award, the gold medal for literature given by the Society of Libraries of New York University. In 1944, an honorary Litt.D. degree was conferred upon him by Susquehanna University in recognition of a native son's attainments. During the decade of the 1940's, Richter also received the Ohio Library Medal Award for Literature.

In 1950, Richter returned to his native heath, Pine Grove, Pennsylvania, where he would remain for the rest of his life except for return trips to the Southwest, and winters in Florida. In 1951, Richter won the Pulitzer Prize in fiction for *The Town*. Although he wrote one more novel about the West, *The Lady*, most of Richter's remaining career was given over to the subjects with which he had started as a writer— the people and land of his birthplace. He completed his best-selling novel *The Light in the Forest* after his return home; like his later novel, *A Country of Strangers*, it was inspired by the beauty of the Eastern landscape and by the deeper sense of history one feels in the East. At the close of the 1950's, Richter was awarded his second honorary doctorate, this time by the university of his adopted state, New Mexico. In the early 1960's he completed two volumes of his projected Pennsylvania trilogy—*The Waters of Kronos* and *A Simple Honorable Man*. Richter won the National Book Award for the former; he was at work on the third volume of the trilogy when he died in 1968 at the age of seventy-eight. Since his death, two works have appeared: a novel, *The Aristocrat* and a book of stories, *The Rawhide Knot and Other Stories*.

ANALYSIS

Conrad Richter's qualities as a writer are partly described by the title of one of his late novels, *A Simple Honorable Man*. Although the book is about his father, the same terms might be used to characterize Richter's fiction, which is simple, concise, and concerned with basic virtues. Thus, it is something of a paradox that Richter's novels and stories are underpinned by a rather complex theory of human life and history, and that these philosophical, quasi-scientific ideas provide a conceptual framework over which the characters, plots, and settings of his fiction are stretched like a covering fabric. Another major tendency of Richter's fiction is that it is intensely autobiographical, deriving from family traditions and experience. In his youth, Richter heard stories of frontier experiences from relatives who had been pioneers themselves. It was his fascination with the way things had been and his conviction that he could inspire his readers to cope with modern problems by showing how ordinary people in the past had overcome the adversities of their frontier that prompted him to become a historical novelist.

Equally important to Richter's development as a novelist, however, were the quasi-scientific philosophical principles which he developed long before his first novel was published. Thus, Richter is unlike most writers in that his fiction does not represent the developing and unfolding of a philosophy, but rather the extension of a belief system that was essentially static after being established. This being the case, it is important to grasp some of the rudiments of Richter's philosophy before discussing his longer fiction, for his themes as a novelist grow out of his philosophical notions.

It must be pointed out that despite their would-be scientific titles and vocabulary (*Human Vibrations* and *Principles in Bio-Physics*), Richter's book-length essays lack the rigor of scientific methodology. At first glance, his theory of life seems to be based upon an odd merging of materialism and idealism. His first premise is that people function in response to bodily cellular vibrations or "vibes" which are regulated by the reserves of psychical or physical energy. If energy abounds, people are in harmony with life. The ultimate expression of human harmony is compassion for fellow humankind. Other signs are charity, fortitude, and the confidence to prevail against hardship, a sense of unity with nature, a tendency toward betterment in history, and a quest for freedom. On the other hand, if energy sources are low, there is a lack of harmony in life. Conflict with nature, with other

people, and with oneself all signify a deficiency of energy; other such manifestations are restless wandering, fruitless searching for intangibles, and historic change for the worse. Thus, as Richter explains it, human life and history are governed by mechanical laws.

Richter's second premise is based on what can best be described as quasi-scientific ideas. He holds that people respond in mind and body with "cellular energy" to outside stimuli. Activity causes the cells in one's body to overflow, revitalizing the weak cells. The process is like that of an electrical circuit in which there is a constant reenergizing while the operation continues. Therefore, constant use ensures a steady power source, whereas disuse can cause the source to decline and lose power. In human terms, mental and physical exertion stimulates the release of energy and speeds up "energy transfer" through the cell structure.

Like many American autodidacts, Richter combined Yankee know-how and practicality with the visions of the crank philosopher. His "bio-physics" serves as a point of departure for accurate historical fiction about the actualities of pioneer life. By Richter's own admission, much of what he produced before he moved to New Mexico in 1928 was hackwriting for the pulp magazines, but there, led to new literary subjects, he launched his career as a serious author with a series of stories and novels; inspired by the grand surroundings of his Western residence and informed by extensive research and the philosophical themes which would run through his subsequent fiction, he produced his first novel.

THE SEA OF GRASS

The Sea of Grass was well received on publication and is still highly regarded by readers and critics. The similarities between Richter's story of a strongwilled southwestern pioneer woman and Willa Cather's *A Lost Lady* (1923) were quickly noted. The central idea of *The Sea of Grass* was sounded in a short story entitled "Smoke over the Prairie," published two years earlier in the *Saturday Evening Post*. The novel is set in New Mexico during the last decades of the nineteenth century. It revolves around a feud between cattle ranchers, led by Colonel James

Brewton, who use the open grasslands for grazing and growing numbers of farmers, called "nesters" by the cattlemen, who are supported by Brice Chamberlain, a federal judge. A subplot concerns a love triangle between Brewton, his wife Lutie, and Chamberlain, which ends with the tragic death of the son of Brewton and Lutie, whose paternity is uncertain, since it is implied that Chamberlain might well have been the boy's father.

The major theme is the decline of the grasslands, a historic change for the worse. The story is narrated as a reminiscence by Hal Brewton, a nephew of Colonel Brewton. He tells the story of an era that has already passed and thus conveys an aura of nostalgia which Richter himself apparently felt for these bygone days. In fact, Hal Brewton is actually a persona for the author and reflects his attitudes toward events. For this reason, Hal remains a one-dimensional character, yet his role as narrator serves to create an objective view of the material. Hal is involved in the events he describes but not so closely as to have his judgment obscured. He is a boy when the story starts and is the town doctor when the story ends twenty-five years later. The first part of the book is devoted to Lutie, a lively and lovely belle from St. Louis, who comes to Salt Fork, New Mexico, to marry the cattle baron Jim Brewton. The "Colonel," as he is called, has a battle going on with the nesters because he believes that the dry lands are doomed to be blown away if they are plowed. The marriage results in three children, but Lutie grows tired of her life as a rancher's wife and simply walks out, staying away for fifteen years. She had left thinking that her lover Brice Chamberlain would come with her, but he remains to support the cause of the farmers.

The title of the book implies that it is a story about the land, and it is indeed, for the basic conflict of the novel arises from how the land will be used. Yet *The Sea of Grass* also introduces the typical Richter hero and heroine in Colonel and Lutie Brewton. The Colonel embodies the best combination of idealism and pragmatism, but he is not complex. He reflects the virtues Richter admires—integrity and courage; he exercises his control over his world with sure authority. Lutie, on the other hand, is the first in a line of female characters in Richter's fiction who are not in harmony with their existence, and who achieve maturity only through hardship and suffering. When she returns to the Southwest, she has finally learned that she needs the sense of fulfillment that comes from the exertion required to survive on the sea of grass. *The Sea of Grass* is ultimately a novel in which the triumph belongs to the earth, for it is the land itself that finally, through a drought, defeats the persistent nesters and subdues Lutie's willful romanticism when her son is destroyed by the violence of the Southwest. Although *The Sea of Grass* is a lasting achievement, it has some of Richter's characteristic flaws as well. There is a thinness to the writing that gives the impression of a screenplay or an extended short story rather than a fully realized novel, a charge leveled with even more justification against Richter's next novel, *Tacey Cromwell*.

TACEY CROMWELL

Tacey Cromwell was generally not as well received as *The Sea of Grass*, perhaps because the heroine is a prostitute and the hero a gambler. Recalling his Idaho experience, Richter sets the plot of *Tacey Cromwell* in a mining town called Bisbee; his treatment of this setting reflects extensive research concerning life in early Western mining towns. He shows the ethnic diversity of the miners and the pretensions of the leading townsmen, who have risen from humble origins to positions of wealth and power. The plot of the novel is built around the conflict between the rough-and-ready immigrants and the new rich ruling class in town. The narrator is again a small boy, Wickers Covington, who is both an observer and a partial participant in the action, about which he reminisces as he tells the story after the fact.

The book begins with the runaway boy Wickers escaping from an uncle in Kansas who has mistreated him. Changing his name to Nugget Oldaker, he heads to Socarro, New Mexico, where his half brother Gaye Oldaker is living. He finds his kinsman in a house of tolerance called the White Palace, which is ironically named, for it is a place of prostitution. His brother's mistress is a prostitute named Tacey Cromwell. Fearing that an upbringing in a bordello would prejudice the lad's morals, the couple moves away to give Nugget a decent home. They relocate in a mining town in Arizona, where they settle down and start the climb to success. Tacey and Gaye never marry, but they remain something of a team. She shows incredible altruism toward her former lover, even after he leaves her and takes the richest woman in town as his wife. Tacey's conversion to respectability is hastened by the adoption of two children of a neighbor killed in a mine accident. The good women of the town, however, take umbrage at the children being reared by even a reformed prostitute, and they bring legal action against Tacey, which results in her losing the children.

Undaunted by disappointment in love, community treachery, and sickness, Tacey starts a business as a dressmaker. At first she is boycotted by the priggish ladies, but one of her creations is worn at an annual ball by a lady who did not know or care about Tacey's reputation. The dress is a sensation, and her future as a dressmaker and designer is made overnight. Meanwhile, Gaye has been appointed territorial treasurer, a position he sought after being encouraged by Tacey. His wife, the haughty and puritanical Rudith Watrons, is drenched in a rainstorm that leads to a long illness and finally to her death. Nugget, who has grown up and become a mining engineer, returns to Bisbee, and one of the foster children taken from Tacey is restored to her. Thus, the novel ends with things returned to their original condition, but with the new harmony that hardship always hands to those who accept it in Richter's fictional worlds.

The novel also illustrates the conception of "westering," the process of evolution in which a region goes from frontier to community. Such a process, in Richter's conception, involves more than historical change. On the physiological and psychological levels, *Tacey Cromwell* depicts Richter's theory of altruism. Tacey's selfless assumption of guilt, both hers and her gambler-lover's, so that Gaye and his children might prosper, is close to the formula plot of the prostitute with a heart of gold used by Bret Harte in his Western fiction. Richter, however, has Tacey's sacrifice pay off, and she finally rises to respectability and eventual reunion with her lover and loved ones.

THE LADY

The Lady, Richter's ninth novel and his third with a southwestern setting, was published fifteen years later in 1957. *The Lady* was better received by the critics and evidences Richter's increased competence as a writer. It is a stronger novel because the central character, Doña Ellen Sessions, is more fully developed than Tacey Cromwell. The plot is partly based on an actual case, an unsolved New Mexico mystery of the frontier period, that involved the disappearance and probable murder of a judge and his young son. The conflict in this book centers on the struggle between Spanish American sheepherders and Anglo-American cattle ranchers. The story is told by a narrator named Jud, who tells of events which happened sixty years before, when he was a boy of ten. He, like the juvenile narrators of *The Sea of Grass* and *Tacey Cromwell*, is both a participant and a witness. Jud is taken in by his cousin, the Territorial Judge Albert Sessions, after his own father has abandoned him. The judge's wife is the charming and arrogant "Doña Lady Ellen," as she is styled because of her noble Spanish and English bloodlines. She is the mistress of a giant sheep spread, inherited from her parents. In addition to breeding and wealth, she has acquired skills as a horseback rider and markswoman. The villain of the piece is her brother-in-law, a mercenary and unethical lawyer, Snell Beasley. The violent feud that is the focus of the book is begun when Beasley drives a cattle herd through her ranch; there is shooting that results in the death of some of the cattlemen.

The chain of events that leads to the disappearance of Judge Sessions and his young son Wily is set in motion. Thinking Doña Ellen is now vulnerable, Snell Beasley sets out to destroy her completely. She is forced to sell her once great ranch, and it seems that her humiliation is complete, yet in the final scene of the novel, poetic justice is served. In a buggy race between Doña Ellen and Snell, there is an accident and her adversary is killed; thus, the heroine gets her revenge in a somewhat melodramatic ending. Her victory underscores Richter's central themes of endurance in the process of "westering" and the mystic bond between people and landscape. It is fitting that Richter's last book about his adopted Southwest should be concluded with a glorification of the land which had inspired him to write the type of fiction that would be his forte—historical romances.

THE TREES

While working on his southwestern novels, Richter began in the early 1940's his trilogy, titled *The Awakening Land* about the Pennsylvania-Ohio frontier, which was conceived from the first as a whole. The first novel of the trilogy, *The Trees*, is set in the late eighteenth and early nineteenth centuries; the novel unfolds the story of a typical pioneer family, the Luckett clan, whose frequent migrations through the great sea of woods that covers the Ohio Valley and the Allegheny mountains is the basis of the plot. In this novel, Richter vividly depicts the darkness of the forest floor as well as the moral darkness in the heart of people. The protagonist of *The Trees* is a "woods woman" named Sayward Luckett, a larger-than-life figure who is the focal character of the entire trilogy. She is married to Portius Wheeler, who, for reasons never explained, has abandoned his native New England, where he was educated as a lawyer, and has become a loutish and drunken backwoodsman. Although nearly all traces of culture and civilization have been erased from him by the time he is married to Sayward, she nevertheless prevents him from further decline, and he honors her by making a reformation.

In addition, *The Trees* tells how Sayward as a girl had wandered with her nomadic family, breaking away from that way of life to marry Portius and settle down. Richter intended that Sayward's experiences should reflect the whole pioneer experience of movement, settlement, and domestication. Using the span of one woman's life, the process of historical change in the Ohio Valley from hunters to farmers to town dwellers is reflected. Thus, like Richter's southwestern novels, *The Trees* traces social evolution; it also resembles his southwestern novels in being episodic, in having a strong heroine, and in its themes of hardship and endurance, ending in ultimate triumph. It differs most from the earlier books in that there is no boy-narrator; Richter's point of view is omniscient in the trilogy, and he uses more dialect in the dialogue. Further, in an effort to make his depiction of pioneer

life more convincing, he uses folktales and superstitions in order to reflect the primitive way of life on the frontier.

THE FIELDS

The final two volumes of the trilogy, *The Fields* and *The Town*, continue the portrait of Sayward and depict the conquering of the land through the process of civilization. *The Fields* tells of Sayward's ten children and her husband's affair with the local schoolmarm, who bears him an illegitimate daughter. Sayward is devastated by Portius's unfaithfulness, yet she recovers from this crushing experience when she hitches a pair of oxen to a plow and begins to till the fields. She sees in the great brutes' tolerance and strength and in the permanence of the earth a prescription for her own survival.

THE TOWN

The Town, though not any more successful artistically than the first two parts of the trilogy, was awarded the Pulitzer Prize in 1951, more for the entire series than for its concluding volume. *The Town*, which is set in pre-Civil War Ohio, deals mostly with the romance between Sayward's youngest son, Chancey, and her husband's illegitimate daughter, Rosa Tench. The love between the half brother and sister is marked by tragedy; she commits suicide following a balloon accident. The rest of the book completes Sayward's story. The conflict that fills out the plot is between mother and son: Sayward tries to make a pioneering man out of Chancey, but he refuses to accept her value system and goes off to edit a liberal newspaper in Cincinnati. The newspaper, which is supported by an unknown patron, publishes Chancey's socialist views, which are an affront to his mother. Just before her death, he learns that she was the secret benefactor who had supported his career over the years. Chancey has to reexamine his philosophy in the light of this revelation. He concludes that his mother's doctrine of hard work and self-reliance is a better one than his own. Thus, Sayward dies at eighty having won her last victory, rescuing her baby son from the heresy of socialism; the puritan faith in work of the older generation remains superior to modern liberal social theory.

Thus, in his trilogy, Richter brings full circle the

"westering" process in which wilderness gives way to farms and farms become towns—historic change for the better; that is the essence of the American experience. Yet as civilization conquers the wilderness, something is lost as well as gained. The frontier's hardships had tested people and honed their character. Modern Americans lack hardiness, vigor, and self-reliance, those qualities of mind and spirit which their ancestors had in abundance, as the heroine of his Ohio trilogy so amply shows.

Richter produced some half-dozen minor novels on various historical subjects and themes, but the major achievements of his later career are *The Waters of Kronos* and its sequel, *A Simple Honorable Man*, the first two volumes of a projected trilogy which he did not live to complete. The former is regarded as one of Richter's highest artistic successes and won wide critical acclaim, earning the National Book Award for 1960. The book is one of Richter's most autobiographical. His main character, a man named John Donner, resembles Richter himself; the character's parents are very much like his family as well. *The Waters of Kronos* is an almost mystical story in which John Donner, an ill and aged man, returns from the West to his Pennsylvania hometown, which is covered by a human-made lake, to visit the graves of his ancestors. At the cemetery, he meets an old man, who takes Donner down a steep hill where, to his incredulous eyes, he finds his town just as it looked sixty years ago. The remainder of the plot is a reexamination of the scenes of his childhood and a reunion with friends and relatives. The journey into the past enables him to learn that what he has always feared is not true—that the gap between his faith and that of his father is not as wide as he once thought. He discovers that he is his father's spiritual son. His final realization from his return to the past is that they have both worshiped the same god in different ways. Having come to terms with his father's god in his novel, Richter's next book shows how he gains further understanding of his parents as a person.

A SIMPLE HONORABLE MAN

A Simple Honorable Man describes the life of John Donner's father, Harry, who at age forty gives up a career in business for a lifetime of service to the Lutheran Church. Like *The Waters of Kronos*, this book is clearly autobiographical, but it is more than a nostalgic family history, for in this novel as in the previous one, Richter tries to come to grips with a number of philosophical problems. The novel emphasizes that the most important things in life are not social status, or power of office, or money, but altruistic service to others. Harry Donner's greatest satisfaction is not in putting money in the bank but in helping those who are in need.

The third volume of the trilogy, on which Richter was at work when he died, was intended to show, as the first two books had done, his reconciliation with his actual father, his final reconciliation with his spiritual father. The two volumes that he did complete are a fitting capstone to Richter's career as a writer. His personal struggles, reflected through those of the Donners, show him to be a man of spiritual and intellectual integrity. The order and lucidity of the narrative reveal his artistry; the restrained realism that characterizes his fiction mutes the sentimentality inherent in such materials, and even though dealing with personal subject of a moral nature, he never lapses into overt didacticism.

Except for *The Sea of Grass*, Richter's reputation will rest most firmly on the books written in the last stages of his career, especially *The Waters of Kronos*; nevertheless, he will probably continue to attract readers who admire exciting, concise, sometimes lyrical stories and novels about the early history of this country and the common people who experienced it.

Hallman B. Bryant

OTHER MAJOR WORKS

SHORT FICTION: *Brothers of No Kin and Other Stories*, 1924; *Early Americana and Other Stories*, 1936; *The Rawhide Knot and Other Stories*, 1978.

NONFICTION: *Human Vibrations*, 1926; *Principles in Bio-Physics*, 1927; *The Mountain on the Desert*, 1955; *A Philosophical Journey*, 1955.

BIBLIOGRAPHY

Barnes, Robert J. *Conrad Richter.* Austin, Tex.: Steck-Vaughn, 1968. A short and limited approach to Richter the writer. Opens with a brief biography and then follows with a survey of his fiction which used the Southwest as a setting—nine short stories out of seventy and three of his thirteen novels.

Edwards, Clifford D. *Conrad Richter's Ohio Trilogy.* Paris: Mouton, 1970. A good in-depth examination of Richter's Ohio Trilogy—*The Trees* (1940), *The Fields* (1946), and *The Town* (1950)—with a detailed analysis of the writer's philosophical and psychological themes.

Gaston, Edwin W., Jr. *Conrad Richter.* Rev. ed. Boston: Twayne, 1989. An excellent introduction to Richter, the man and the writer, and his work. Gaston scrutinizes Richter's life and philosophy as they resonate in all of his writings. Includes comprehensive notes, references, a bibliography, and an index.

Lahood, Marvin J. *Conrad Richter's America.* The Hague: Mouton, 1975. Lahood writes an appreciative, if not critical, summary of Richter's literary work. He avoids a chronological approach, devoting separate chapters to discussions of thematic subject matter.

Richter, Harvena. *Writing to Survive: The Private Notebooks of Conrad Richter.* Albuquerque: University of New Mexico Press, 1988. Richter's daughter offers an intimate look at personal notebooks by the writer dealing with the genesis of his literary work.

Alain Robbe-Grillet

Born: Brest, France; August 18, 1922

Principal long fiction

Les Gommes, 1953 (*The Erasers*, 1964)
Le Voyeur, 1955 (*The Voyeur*, 1958)
La Jalousie, 1957 (*Jealousy*, 1959)
Dans le labyrinthe, 1959 (*In the Labyrinth*, 1960)
La Maison de rendez-vous, 1965 (English translation, 1966)
Projet pour une révolution à New York, 1970 (*Project for a Revolution in New York*, 1972)

La Belle Captive, 1975 (René Magritte, illustrator; English translation, 1995)
Topologie d'une cité fantôme, 1976 (*Topology of a Phantom City*, 1977)
Souvenirs du triangle d'or, 1978 (*Recollections of the Golden Triangle*, 1984)
Un Régicide, 1978
Djinn, 1981 (English translation, 1982)
Le Miroir qui revient, 1984 (*Ghosts in the Mirror*, 1988)
Angélique: Ou, L'Enchantement, 1987
Les Derniers jours de Corinthe, 1994

Other literary forms

In addition to his novels, Alain Robbe-Grillet has written short fiction, nonfiction works on the New Novel, photo-essays, and screenplays.

Achievements

After the mid-1950's, Robbe-Grillet endeavored to explain and demonstrate what the innovative brand of fiction known as the *nouveau roman*, or New Novel, means. To him, the New Novel is a constantly evolving genre. Its form is not ready-made. Rather, it explores the human way of experiencing, understanding, and coping with the constantly changing realities of the age; it moves forward, beyond dogmas established for previous ages. The New Novel centers on individuals and their subjective reactions and relationships to the objects or things in the world around them. It reports humankind's limited experiences: how people see, feel, and imagine their lives. Thematic significance or meaning is given to objects or relationships only when they come into *temporary* existence with people. What Robbe-Grillet first called "supports"—thought-related objects and visual motifs representing part of a character's experience— were what T. S. Eliot called "objective correlatives." By using objects, people, and patterns of things as temporary objective correlatives, Robbe-Grillet achieves high levels of character-reader subjectivity. He forces the reader to collaborate in the work by connecting dislocated objects, experiences, and scenes and by accepting and understanding paradoxical similarities and themes.

With his first *ciné-roman* (film-novel), *L'Année dernière à Marienbad* 1961; (*Last Year at Marienbad,* 1962), Robbe-Grillet began a second career as a writer and director of several screenplays. Additionally, he helped establish the original *ciné-roman* as a genre distinct from either novel or film. Usually a simplified rendering of a script with stills from the film already made, Robbe-Grillet's film-novels contain imagery and story elements similar to those found in his novels, yet they are independently conceived and have a structural integrity uniquely their own.

In his second phase, in the 1960's and 1970's, Robbe-Grillet wrote his militant and sexually violent *Project for a Revolution in New York*. He also produced films with aberrant sexual behavior clearly depicted, such as *Trans-Europ-Express* (1967) and *Glissements progressifs du plaisir* (1974).

The three books that are termed Robbe-Grillet's "romanesques," *Le Miroir que revient*, 1984 (*Ghosts in the Mirror*, 1988); *Angélique: Ou, L'Enchantement* (Angelique: or, enchantment); and *Les Derniers jours de Corinthe* (last days of Corinthe), began a third cycle. Since these works integrate personal memories with artistic theories and invented obsessions, some critics have called them "autofictions" or "autobiographical fictions."

Robbe-Grillet is known in the United States as an iconoclastic breaker of traditions as well as for the novels *The Voyeur* and *Jealousy* and the film *Last Year at Marienbad*. None of these early works, however, offers more than a suggestion of the full extent of the experimentations of his third phase.

BIOGRAPHY

Alain Robbe-Grillet was born on August 18, 1922, in Brest, France. He studied at the Institut National Agronomique in 1941-1942. During the World War II German occupation of France, his Institut class was taken to a factory in Nuremberg and forced to work on lathes and milling machines. In 1943, ill with infectious rheumatism, he was sent for recovery to a French hospital. Later, he returned to the Institut, graduating in 1946. He also served as *charge de mission* with the Institut National des Statistiques, 1945-

(AP/Wide World Photos)

1948. From 1949 to 1951, he was an agronomist with the Institut des Fruits el Agrumes Coloniaux, traveling extensively in Morocco, Guinea, Guadeloupe, and Martinique. His novel *Un Régicide*, unpublished until 1978, was completed in 1949. Robbe-Grillet's second novel, *The Erasers*, was published in 1953 by Editions de Minuit in Paris. In 1955, he became a literary adviser to Minuit. In 1960, he accepted membership in the Television Programming Committee. During this decade he also married Catherine Rstakian (1957).

Robbe-Grillet and his literary work have received many honors. *The Voyeur* won the Prix des Critiques in 1955; the film *Last Year at Marienbad* won both the Prix du Lion d'or and the French Melies Prize. In 1964, he made his first trip to the United States for a lecture tour at several universities. Additionally, he was a term lecturer at New York University in 1972, 1975, and 1979; at University of California in 1978; at Columbia in 1989, and also at Washington University in St. Louis. In 1975, a ten-day colloquium on Robbe-Grillet was presented at Cerisy-la-Salle. He was guest of honor, in 1986, at the Writers' Week-Long Festival in New Zealand.

Robbe-Grillet was a center of critical controversy from the late 1950's onward. Few movements have sparked such acrimonious debates as his literary innovations. Notably controversial have been his depictions of women as victims, racism, and chauvinism, and his apparent fascination with sadomasochism. In 1974, when the film *Glissements progressifs du plaisir,* for which he wrote the screenplay, was shown in Italy, the theater was shut down; Robbe-Grillet was accused of being a pornographer. Conversely, in 1975, the French government accepted him into the French Legion of Honor.

ANALYSIS

The newcomer to the New Novel should read Alain Robbe-Grillet's books in the sequence in which they were written, because each work employs new elements developed in its predecessor. The temporal device of a stopped wristwatch in *The Erasers,* for example, parallels the suppression of a political investigator's childhood memory; the main character of *The Voyeur* is a wristwatch salesman who is obsessed with liquidating his timepieces while escaping apprehension for his crime; the narrator of *Jealousy* almost destroys his own and the reader's concept of time through his suspicion and obsessive fear.

Robbe-Grillet's narrators are characterized by their obsessions, ranging from an obsession to discover, to an obsession to remain undiscovered, to an obsession to disassemble time, and finally to suppressed and then blatant sexual obsessions. Aligning himself with Jean-Paul Sartre, who advised against the objective and the omniscient point of view, Robbe-Grillet's pronounced intention has been to produce a viewpoint that—like real, immediate experience—is entirely subjective, always taking place in the mind of an obsessive narrator. Thus, events from an over-imaginative, sometimes delirious point of view can

be shaped into a highly structured narration. Again, form is all-important.

THE ERASERS

Robbe-Grillet wrote a brief synopsis for the dust jacket of his first novel, *The Erasers.* He called the novel a conventional detective story involving a murder and a solution of the crime, but one in which the relationship between victim and detective becomes clear only as the story ends. Because of the narrative's symmetrical time structure—twenty-four hours, beginning and ending with a gunshot—everything that the detective realizes has happened takes place, the author explains, during the flight of the bullet. To reinforce this structure, the detective's wristwatch stops ticking for the same twenty-four-hour period and begins again when he kills the very man whose murderer he was supposed to find.

Prior to this moment of discovery, immediate recollection of past events and anticipation of future ones—as well as imagined scenes that are, in fact, hypothetical reconstructions of a falsely reported crime—combine to form the circular plot. During this time, the detective attempts to deal with his faltering mind by buying gum erasers from attractive female stationers. His inexplicable behavior eventually, at the final moment, brings to the surface of his subconscious mind a significant memory. The thoughts and views of the investigator are not the only ones the reader shares; the viewpoint shifts from detective to assassin, to the assassin's superior, to the local police chief, to the would-be victim. These shifting viewpoints create a severe narrative weakness: The reader is thus kept aware that whatever the psychological state of the detective may be, he is but one of several characters under the control of an omniscient intelligence.

The plot structure of *The Erasers* is a departure from the conventional dramatic form of Greek tragedy; Robbe-Grillet reshapes the familiar dramatic curve into a closed loop. Critics have identified elements common to both *The Erasers* and Sophocles' *Oedipus Rex* (c. 420 B.C.E.). Among them are the novel's five-act structure, the significance of the riddle of the sphinx, connective images, and most obviously the themes of patricide and incest. Yet this dramatic understructure also calls attention to the author's presence and fixed plan. Early critics suggested that the author had rejected plot in favor of the depiction of objects by protagonists whose view the reader shares. In fact, however, plot is very important to Robbe-Grillet. Plot is a formal element, and circular plot is more intricate than linear plot. With all the cycles observable in nature and human experience, it is the traditional plot line that appears unnatural and fragmented—an arc without closure.

THE VOYEUR

While in *The Erasers* a detective gropes toward discovery of a suppressed childhood memory, the lone viewpoint character of *The Voyeur*, Mathias, struggles to suppress the memory of his recent crime and thus his guilt. The viewpoint character is now on the other side of the law and normal thought. Eventually, the reader is able to determine what has taken place from the reappearances of objects that Mathias sees, remembers, or imagines.

The character Mathias has been compared to William Faulkner's Mink Snopes, but while Faulkner elevates the bad man Snopes, Robbe-Grillet coolly treats Mathias as a devious criminal whose furtive thoughts are also the reader's thoughts. Ultimately, the result of Mathias's suppression is what Robbe-Grillet labels "a void" in the narrative, a void that represents the unspeakable missing segment of the action that becomes obvious simply by its absence. Also, the void represents the obscenity that the reader may be unwilling to imagine, yet will imagine, thanks to meaningful objects observed.

Skulking about, the psychotic salesman supplies the novel's plot in the form of his movement, thinking ahead as he goes. He repeatedly anticipates his approaching business call at the home of the girl for whom he lusts. Having learned earlier that she is rumored to be promiscuous, he anticipates his reception—as a good salesman will—and the family's possible responses to his pitch; when near the end of part 1 he actually enters the house, the reader knows he is planning to do much more than pitch his wristwatches. Meanwhile, the suggestive objects he sees (knives, film posters depicting violence) and hears (sirens, the repeated slapping of water against rock),

as well as his preparations (he buys candy to lure the girl and cigarettes with which to torture her), build suspensefully toward the criminal acts the reader will not see but will know to have happened. These plot fragments, the views of a distorted, obsessive mind, gradually align until the sequence of events as they have really occurred becomes clear.

The title of the novel presents the reader with a puzzle: Which of the characters is the voyeur? Most analysts agree that it is not Mathias—he commits crimes separate from and in excess of Peeping Tomism. A more likely voyeur is young Julien Marek; Julien witnesses the rape and murder, but he seems willing to condone it, even to help cover it up by not reporting what he has seen and knows to be true, as if he is either ashamed to admit that he watched the crime without trying to stop it or is—through the guilt of his passivity—a collaborator. That the reader is the voyeur is a stronger possibility, and most likely the author's design, for the reader could not be involved more intimately. This participation of the reader operates through the narrator's view of certain objects and his repeated description of these objects. The reader-voyeur, then, collaborates both with Mathias and with his creator.

JEALOUSY

In *Jealousy*, events first imagined overlie events later realized, and objects seen overlie objects remembered. Driven by suspicion and fear, the narrator sees a montage of objects that represent recent, then immediate, then imagined future events. This use of montage in fiction comes directly from Gustave Flaubert, who compared his work to that of a composer of music, especially orchestrations, which are vast, complex montages of individual sounds. In such music and in *Jealousy*, form is part of the content. *Jealousy*'s narrator is not incoherent; the novel derives its dramatic energy from the narrator's attempts to restructure his experience. The narrator's stress provides the mainspring that powers his mental clock and the reader's sense of the time that constitutes the narrative.

Three characters form a typical love triangle: The narrator is the husband, who is jealous of "A." (his wife) and Franck, the neighboring husband whose own wife remains ill at home. The story takes place on a tropical plantation; that is, the story takes place in the mind of the jealous husband, who remains in the plantation house to sulk and suspect the worst, while A. and Franck take a trip together into town, returning very late, their relationship apparently less intimate than it had been. Within the story is a parallel text (the plot of a novel Franck has given A.) and several clockless time coordinates: various stages of a bridge that is being built near the house, the pruning and harvesting of banana trees, and shadows cast by columns of the veranda. A logistical reference point inside the house is the outline of a centipede squashed by Franck on the wall of the dining room. The image of the centipede forms a thematic and physical centrality to which the narrator repeatedly returns; it becomes the narrative's most visible objective correlative.

In *Jealousy* more than in his previous two novels, Robbe-Grillet placed the reader in the narrator-observer's mind to see exactly what he sees. The story *is* what is seen. The story's closure results from increased distance between the narrator and the reader as his worst fears recede. As the narrator's stress decreases, plot-related tension decreases. There has been no final resolution, only an end, however temporary, to the narrator's jealousy.

IN THE LABYRINTH

Unique among Robbe-Grillet's early novels, *In the Labyrinth* makes visible a narrator in the process of creating a narrative. He identifies himself by framing his narrative with personal pronouns: "I" is the first word of the story and "me" the last. The story's main events are as follows: A soldier has come to a strange city following a disorienting and controversial military retreat; determined to return the personal effects of a comrade in arms to an unidentified member of his family, the ill and feverish soldier tries unsuccessfully to find the meeting place, is helped on his way by a young boy and his mother, and is treated by a physician who later identifies himself as the narrator; but the soldier leaves the barracks to keep his rendezvous, is wounded by a motorcycle patrol, and eventually dies.

For the viewpoint character, the soldier, this city in which he finds himself is the labyrinth. Two other labyrinths are evident: the labyrinth of the novel-in-formation, through which the narrator progresses, imagining the experience of the soldier, and the labyrinth of the completed story, through which the reader must progress with object-related authorial guidance. The novel's form is at once all three labyrinths.

The narrator's methods of guiding the reader are also three: clockless time references, objects that interconnect events, and parallel scenes. Time references are established through description of snow accumulated on the street, the presence of darkness or daylight, and the growth of the soldier's beard. The reader is thereby able to locate linear events in nonlinear time. The second method of guiding the reader is the description, in precise geometric detail, of objects that interconnect events so that the reader can recognize these objects in the narrator's room and in the scenes the narrator imagines: Circles of light are cast by the narrator's lamp and by exterior street lamps, while marks in the surface dust of the room suggest marks in the snow outside, and the shape of a cross appears as a souvenir bayonet, a string tied around a box, the intersections of streets, hallways, and so forth.

The third way in which the narrator guides the reader through the labyrinth shows the narrator's imagination at work. One wall of his room is entirely curtained, suggesting a proscenium arch beyond which could be a stage or an audience. Also, an engraving hung on one wall of the narrator's room depicts a one-room café and shows three walls, the fourth being open to the viewer—the narrator, an audience of one, and all his readers. Present in the pictured café are doubles of objects and characters that will appear in the narrative: the boy who guides the soldier through the snow to his barrack room, the box tied with string that the soldier carries, the soldier seated at a table similar to a table in the narrator's room, the boy's mother working in the café as a waitress, and nondescript figures who will question the legitimacy of the soldier's retreat from battle. Thus, the reader in the labyrinth shares both the soldier's disoriented wandering and the narrator's creative exploration.

Although *In the Labyrinth* retains key elements of the author's continually evolving style, this novel is most striking in the visibility of its formation. In *The Voyeur*, imagined scenes occur in the mind of only one character but are related to his compulsion to escape, both mentally and physically. In *Jealousy*, the viewpoint character and the narrator are the same, and his obsessive emotions trigger imagined scenes. In *In the Labyrinth*, the narrator imagines everything except the room in which he sits, creating scenes deductively from objects at hand and a picture on the wall. These works represent Robbe-Grillet's early novels, and *In the Labyrinth* is the most important in terms of narrative invention and form.

La Maison de rendez-vous

The setting of *La Maison de rendez-vous* is the Blue Villa of Lady Ava in the British Crown Colony of Hong Kong. One of two principal characters, Lady Ava is the purveyor of entertainment, drugs, and women for a nebulous group of people, a sensual elite. Lady Ava's bordello replaces the solitary room of the narrator of *In the Labyrinth*; as the story's physical center, Blue Villa houses stage properties that are used to create narrative links with objects and events elsewhere.

Three principal devices are used to construct these links: statuary, the "freeze-frame," and the stage-curtain motif from *In the Labyrinth*. The statuary in the garden of Blue Villa is painted and life-size, and a variant of that statuary is a mannequin seen in a downtown store window; mannequins become a frequent device of Robbe-Grillet from this point on, allowing scene-doubling as well as character-doubling. The cinematic freeze-frame is used frequently in all Robbe-Grillet's fiction. This technique is used not merely to emphasize, as it usually is used in films, but also to signal the beginning of a new sequence of events, just as the onset of a new sequence of thoughts, in ordinary experience, often appears to be triggered by a personal gesture—stopping short and turning around, for example, or reaching for some object and seeing in startling detail for a frozen instant one's own outstretched hand. Robbe-Grillet uses street signs, posters, photographs, and engravings as thematic two-dimensional objects that trigger

turns of thought in a similar manner. The third device, at first the curtain covering the wall of the room of *In the Labyrinth*'s narrator, becomes in *La Maison de rendezvous* a real curtain and stage at Blue Villa, a stage on which are performed erotic tableaux whose actions connect via statuary and freeze-frames to scenes elsewhere in Hong Kong or on the mainland. Additional doublings are derived from two characters who are twins and from other characters who have alternate identities with similar names.

Analysts have balked at this novel because its plot has no clear purpose save the display of cinematic motifs that seem to have evolved from Robbe-Grillet's early novels and film work. Indeed, if one looks beyond this novel's sensual imagery and erotic content, beyond its visual structure and descriptive techniques, only the simplest story remains: In a locale of mystery and intrigue, an American client of Lady Ava wants to buy one of her employees—a young Eurasian woman whose fiancé either kills himself or is killed. Meanwhile, the American murders the drug vendor, who refuses to lend him money to buy the object of his lust, and when he returns to Blue Villa to steal his prize, he finds Lady Ava dying and the police awaiting him. The plot has been doubled too; a second story is to be found, parallel to the first.

To make appropriate an object-oriented narration of their subjective views, Robbe-Grillet employs characters who experience great physical stress and mental disunity: suppression, perversion, obsession, and feverish imaginings. In *La Maison de rendezvous*, he presents some of each as well as the effects of drugs. Some of these characters experience memory, imagination, and immediate existence indiscriminately—and that is how the first five novels are alike. An important difference between the first three novels and the two following is the presence of a narrator who forms the story as he goes along. In *La Maison de rendez-vous*, however, the second plot is provided by a second narrator, and it is the reader's challenge to find the two narrators.

Project for a Revolution in New York

Project for a Revolution in New York contains descriptive and formal elements that recall Robbe-

Grillet's early work: circular plot, parallel texts, object indicators of time or scene-shifting, and visual projections of the narrator's imagination. At one surrealistic juncture, a vacant city lot surrounded by a demolition fence and paved with flat stones suggestive of a chessboard contains props from other Robbe-Grillet fictions, objects that lie abandoned and waiting in the weeds to be discovered and pondered by the narrator. This device produces a cross-textual consciousness that interconnects the various novels like a composer's favorite elemental themes which are developed further in successive compositions. Playfully esoteric authorial intrusion also occurs during plot-related interrogative dialogues that double as lines of critical questioning about the worth and purpose of this novel; the reader who finds *Project for a Revolution in New York* revolting is thus anticipated. Yet by accepting these devices as viable narrative elements, the reader will recognize in this novel a startling coherence.

In *Project for a Revolution in New York*, a narrative viewpoint like that of *In the Labyrinth* and *La Maison de rendez-vous* becomes the vision of a character like Mathias of *The Voyeur*. This narrator does not enter the fiction; the fiction enters him—and the context is different. Whereas Mathias is sexually aberrant in a normal social setting, the narrator of *Project for a Revolution in New York* behaves normally within a peer group that is itself contained in an abnormal society. Abandoned buildings and the subways of the city are filled with a decadent revolutionary madness that culminates in politically motivated assaults on the young daughters of establishment families. This premise frees the willful cruelties of the Mathias figure, now a describer rather than a concealer of atrocity, who does not suppress, but reveals in detail, the gruesome machinations of members of the group.

Readers unacquainted with Robbe-Grillet's earlier novels will be surprised by the content as well as the form of *Project for a Revolution in New York*. Unlike *The Voyeur*, in which Mathias's crime occurs offstage to create the "void" better imagined by the reader, or *La Maison de rendez-vous*, in which sexual aberrance is largely suggestive, here violent sexual behavior is set forth in such a way that the reader need not imagine anything. Critical discussions about this work have related its content to sadistic themes of works now within the modern literary tradition and to archetypal literature containing mythic or acultural themes. Robbe-Grillet himself asserts a need for audience catharsis and here makes use of the masks and *deus ex machina* of Greek drama. He has used such elements before—*The Erasers* builds on plot elements from *Oedipus Rex*—but the fact remains that this novel describes cruel and deadly perversions performed by adult men on adolescent women. This device involves readers in a new way: The story's perverse content encourages the reader to see the characters and their actions metaphorically as social satire. The violence of the age, whether it be sexual, political, or civil, is pervasive yet habitually ignored. Shutting real violence out of view may ultimately create the absurd world of *Project for a Revolution in New York*, just as the novel's narrator creates a world of absurdities.

Topology of a Phantom City

In his 1954 essay "A Novel That Invents Itself," Robbe-Grillet refers to characters who "make themselves" and who, in turn, create their "own reality . . . a kind of living tissue, each cell of which sprouts and shapes its neighbors." The first narrative section of *Topology of a Phantom City* is entitled "In the Generative Cell." Although more than twenty years of writing separate the early statement from this 1975 novel, the connection remains fast. Underlying *Topology of a Phantom City* is the author's concept of cellular growth: Like life, fiction creates itself through a process of mitosis.

Robbe-Grillet consistently uses mathematical description to create the freeze-frame effect that usually signifies a shift of scene or viewpoint. At such a point in the narrative, objects are described in terms of their planes and angles, their shapes and configurations. The word "topology," moreover, is a mathematical term that refers to the properties of geometric forms that remain constant even when the forms change. In other words, topological elements carry over from one state of being to the next. Like *In the Labyrinth*, this story grows out of itself as the narrator discovers the final shape it should take. The narrator of *Topology of a Phantom City* begins his story by describing a single cell—a white room—that contains several young women who are being held captive. Some of the women are playing with tarot cards, and an illustrated notice of some kind is visible on one wall. From these stark details, the story grows, each scene a subdivision of the preceding scene, until the narrator has invented not only the lost city but also its recent history, its contemporary rebirth as a historical restoration, and an ancient mythology that includes timeless scenes of hermaphroditic ritual and tragic carnage. The phantom city thus grows backward from the single generative cell to its own mystical origin, while the novel grows forward into its ultimate form.

The narrative of *Topology of a Phantom City* has been reinforced with numerous cross-textual references. As in *Project for a Revolution in New York*, motifs from the author's other works appear in this text. The eye motif (now the eye of a camera) and parts of Mathias's bicycle from *The Voyeur* appear, for example, as do the mannequin and the iron bed from *Project for a Revolution in New York*. The narrator even refers overtly to the author's work, mentioning Lady Ava's Blue Villa and the eraser idea from the first novel. Extratextual references are also made: During one descriptive sequence, a character identified as D. H. and then as David H. photographs young women who assume sensual attitudes and mirrored poses that the reader may see in the photoessay entitled *Rêves de jeunes filles* (1971; *Dreams of a Young Girl*, 1971), a collaborative production of Robbe-Grillet and the photographer David Hamilton. Again and again, Robbe-Grillet, the author, superimposes his consciousness on that of his narrator and, through playful intrusions, refocuses the reader's attention on the inventive process, rather than on the product, of his narrative search.

Most obviously, the letter *V* carries blatant significance. The goddess Vanade (suggestive of a species of butterfly, a flying *vee*), the city of Vanadium, the obliteration of the inhabitants by gases from a volcano, the narrative attention given the words "David," "divan," "gravid," "vagina," and several more—all interconnect with triangular shapes such as the profile of the volcano, the city's wedge-shaped plaza, the pointed portico of the temple, the spread legs of sacrificial virgins, and so forth. Since *V* is also the Roman numeral five, many objects appear in this exact quantity, the symbolism of which is also significant: In occult numerology, the value five is located in the center of the human personality "cell," or matrix, representing feminine qualities traditionally exploited by men and—in medieval Christian symbol systems—the combined senses, thereby the corporeal life, the flesh. None of these references is subtly made, which is to say that the author repeatedly asserts what he is doing. He is generating a narrative, simultaneously inventing both content and form. The images he chooses are not symbolic allusions but cellular parts of the formal development, organic fictive growth.

DJINN

Robbe-Grillet's novel *Djinn* appears to be a transitional work. Gone are the erotic and the sadistic elements. Sly intertextual references have been replaced with wry and humorous ones, although the structure of this novel is far more complex than that of *In the Labyrinth*. Children are involved in the story not as objects but as clever protagonists who influence the narrator's method of telling and help lead him through an invisible labyrinth of his own making. *Djinn* is encoded with sudden shifts in viewpoint and verb tense that indicate the presence of double characters with double motives. There are also overtones of the Oedipus myth, with its psychological implications, but of the old, blind Oedipus at Colonus being led by a child.

Having written a French primer for intermediate language students (*Le Rendez-vous*, 1981), Robbe-Grillet employed the idea here as a framing device: A French teacher disappears, leaving behind a mysterious manuscript, the story of Simon Lecoeur and Djinn. Their narrative progresses with increasing intricacy as Simon's identity changes, by his own inclination and by the intrusion of an unclearly identified narrator who usurps both manuscript and viewpoint. Is Djinn male, female, or androgynous? The novel is a puzzle with pieces that are shaped alike: Simon is known to his students as Yann, spelled Ján; his young friend is named Jean, and Jean's sister is named Jeannie. Other Jeans and Jeannies surface, too. (A "djinn," or jinni, is a mythical Islamic spirit that can enter bodies at will for good or evil.) A novel that is this much a puzzle must be brief—128 pages—but its brevity heightens its complexity. Repeated readings lead to a fuller understanding of its manifold story; the structure of earlier works becomes clear by the second reading.

Autobiographical fiction

In the third phase of Alain Robbe-Grillet's career, *Ghosts in the Mirror*, *Angélique: Ou, L'Enchantement*, and *Les Derniers jours de Corinthe* present his autobiographical fiction. All three combine elements of fiction and nonfiction and so are difficult to classify. The first, *Ghosts in the Mirror*, includes details from his childhood memories, fantasies, commentaries on literary theory, history, and double versions of family and friends paired with fictional characters from his writings or borrowed from books and paintings. *Angélique* centers on the author's efforts to understand women, to respond to female critics and feminist charges of sexism, and to explore his own presentation of erotic themes.

Ghosts in the Mirror provides the oval mirror that the quasi-mythical Comte de Corinthe struggled to retrieve from the sea. Through this mirror's oval eye, the "I" of Robbe-Grillet, the sole narrator, directs or misdirects the readers while he spins his fictions. He describes his plot structure as a work progressing in a linear fashion through his life, from "critical essay to novel, from book to film, continually questioning," and including the sea and fear, two things giving theme or structure to previous works. His actual method, however, shows his usual scorn for traditions. An achronological approach dominates. Time sequences alter when dislocated descriptions, tangential ideas, critical theories, and subjective fantasies are incorporated where they neither belong nor seem to fit.

Robbe-Grillet's fictional characters reappear in fragmented or altered forms in these works. Angélique has many incarnations. She may be the living model for Violet or Jacqueline in *The Voyeur*. Other shifting images depict her, not only as Corinth's

fiancé but also as mysterious washerwomen fairies or even as a vampire bat. (This last pairs her with the author's mother, who shelters a bat in her blouse.) At her death, she becomes an Ophelia floating on the waters.

Cross-textual references to key objects and parallel scenes are again used as linking devices. Allusions to torn, blood-stained clothing and broken glass link related objects to previous sequences of sexual activity or interests to many scenes in *Angélique*. Childhood memories of Robbe-Grillet's red-curtained bedroom parallel one curtained room from *In the Labyrinth*. Robbe-Grille creates an imaginary, isolated white cell in which his fantasized captivity recalls women prisoners in another white room in *Topology of a Phantom City*. This depiction illustrates one of Robbe-Grillet's favorite concepts: generators, starting points for evolutionary growth. Here, Mersault's prison cell is a "generative cell" able to create its own cellular growth and shape other organic fictive growth such as the fantasy cell in *Ghosts in the Mirror*.

Another significant element is the sly, playful humor that surfaces. Repeatedly, Robbe-Grillet refocuses the reader's attention on the inventive process rather than on the product of his narrative search. In *Ghosts in the Mirror*, Robbe-Grillet admits, "I don't believe in truth," but he adds, "I'm not a truthful soul but nor do I tell lies." Further, according to Robbe-Grillet, "an author is a being without a face." If the author is writing his autobiography, not fiction, his query should be, "Who is Alain Robbe-Grillet?" rather than "Who was Henri de Corinthe?"—the first question in *Ghosts in the Mirror*. That confusing situation is at the heart of Robbe-Grillet's autofictions. Are these works fact or fiction? How much real biographical information does the author provide for the reader? Are his childhood memories real or false? In autobiography, a reader expects to discover more information about the author than has previously been known. Here, there are few documentable facts revealed that are not already known about Robbe-Grillet's personal and public life. The autofictions could be skillful and sly efforts to reject the familiar conventions of form by creating a new one. Indeed, without telling their readers, writers have been telling lies for centuries.

Joseph F. Battaglia, updated by Betsy P. Harfst

OTHER MAJOR WORKS

SHORT FICTION: *Instantanés*, 1962 (*Snapshots*, 1965).

SCREENPLAYS: *L'Année dernière à Marienbad*, 1961 (*Last Year at Marienbad*, 1962); *L'Immortelle*, 1963 (*The Immortal One*, 1971); *Trans-Europ Express*, 1967; *L'Homme qui ment*, 1968; *L'Éden et après*, 1970; *Glissements progressifs du plaisir*, 1974; *Le Jeu avec le feu*, 1975; *La Belle Captive*, 1983.

NONFICTION: *Pour un nouveau roman*, 1963 (criticism; *For a New Novel: Essays on Fiction*, 1965); *Rêves de jeunes filles*, 1971 (photographs by David Hamilton; *Dreams of a Young Girl*, 1971); *Les Demoiselles d'Hamilton*, 1972 (photographs by Hamilton; *Sisters*, 1973); *Le Rendez-vous*, 1981.

BIBLIOGRAPHY

Harger-Grinling, Virginia, and Tony Chadwick, eds. *Robbe-Grillet and the Fantastic*. Westport, Conn.: Greenwood Press, 1994. Analyses of Robbe-Grillet's work and experimental methods by critics and former students of Robbe-Grillet.

Hellerstein, Marjorie H. *Inventing the Real World: The Art of Alain Robbe-Grillet*. Selinsgrove, Pa.: Susquehanna University Press, 1998. Hellerstein studies the relationship to contemporary life in Robbe-Grillet's themes, motifs, and techniques. Extensive bibliography.

Ramsey, Raylene L. *The French New Autobiographies: Sarraute, Duras, and Robbe-Grillet*. Gainesville: University Press of Florida, 1996. Analyzes the genre of autobiographical fiction as practiced by three prominent French writers.

_____. *Robbe-Grillet and Modernity: Science, Sexuality, and Subversion*. Gainesville: University Press of Florida, 1992. Ramsey places Robbe-Grillet at the juncture of modern literary, artistic, and scientific developments.

Roland, Lillian Dunmars. *Women in Robbe-Grillet: A Study in Thematics and Diegetics*. New York: Peter Long, 1993. Views women's roles in the novels, in particular the ways they provide a variety of perspectives.

Stoltzfus, Ben. *Alain Robbe-Grillet*. Rutherford, N.J.: Fairleigh Dickinson University Press, 1985. Stoltzfus studies the differences between Robbe-Grillet's early and later novels. Stoltzfus also authored an earlier study, *Alain Robbe-Grillet and the New French Novel*, 1964.

ELIZABETH MADOX ROBERTS

Born: Perryville, Kentucky; October 30, 1881
Died: Orlando, Florida; March 13, 1941

PRINCIPAL LONG FICTION
The Time of Man, 1926
My Heart and My Flesh, 1927
Jingling in the Wind, 1928
The Great Meadow, 1930
A Buried Treasure, 1931
He Sent Forth a Raven, 1935
Black Is My Truelove's Hair, 1938

OTHER LITERARY FORMS

Before Elizabeth Madox Roberts was a novelist, she wrote poetry, including children's verse—facts which explain much about her work as a novelist—and she continued to produce some poetry throughout her career. Her first collection of verse, privately printed in 1915, was *In the Great Steep's Garden*, a pamphlet consisting of a few short poems accompanying photographs. A second collection of poetry, *Under the Tree*, appeared in 1922, published by Huebsch, Inc., which soon became The Viking Press, publisher of Roberts's subsequent work. A revised edition of *Under the Tree* appeared in 1930, and a third collection of Roberts's poetry, *Song in the Meadow*, came out in 1940.

In addition, Roberts wrote short stories, which, like her poetry, found a ready market in leading magazines of the day. Her short fiction was collected in

The Haunted Mirror (1932) and *Not by Strange Gods* (1941).

ACHIEVEMENTS

Roberts's reputation as a writer furnishes an interesting case study in literary fashions and critical evaluation. Few novelists have begun their careers to such popular and critical acclaim as Roberts achieved with *The Time of Man* in 1926, acclaim that was renewed and confirmed by *The Great Meadow* four years later. With the 1935 publication of *He Sent Forth a Raven*, however, Roberts's literary reputation went into a precipitous decline. By her death in 1941, it had struck bottom. Since then, there have been intermittent attempts, including several book-length studies, to resurrect her reputation, frequently with highly inflated praise. Claims that she is among the half dozen or so great American novelists of the twentieth century do her as much disservice as does the vague "regionalist" label which her special pleaders decry.

Perhaps as a result of her early success and her relative isolation in Kentucky, Roberts seems likewise to have overestimated her powers: With talents along the lines of a May Sarton, Roberts was apparently encouraged to think of herself as another William Faulkner, with a little Herman Melville and Thomas Mann thrown in for good measure. Her style, so often termed "poetic," achieves some fine effects indeed, but at immense cost to the narrative flow of her novels. Her style is allied to her narrative focus, almost invariably the novel's female protagonist, whose perceptions and sentiments are spun out at length while the reader waits for something to happen. Little does happen, except that the heroines take long walks. The effect is somewhat reminiscent of an agrarian Virginia Woolf. Perhaps the reader is treated to such a subjective focus because Roberts's protagonists, however different, are to some extent alter egos of their author, whose own comments blend imperceptibly into their observations. The results of all this are slow-moving and sometimes flimsy plots, dimly realized characters (except usually for the protagonist), loss of authorial perspective, and tedium. As if these results were not unhappy enough, Roberts also

(National Archives)

had trouble dealing with ideas and with the overall plans for her novels.

Despite all these limitations and failings, Roberts is due for, and deserving of, a revival. Most readers will find her lighter novels, *A Buried Treasure* and *Black Is My Truelove's Hair*, still entertaining, and *The Great Meadow* possesses some epic qualities. All of Roberts's novels involve significant themes, and all deal incidentally with significant social issues, such as economic conditions, racism, and sexism. In particular, both feminists and antifeminists will find much of interest in Roberts's depiction of her female protagonists, in her treatment of male-female relationships, and in Roberts's own biography.

BIOGRAPHY

Elizabeth Madox Roberts's life was marked by a few salient facts. Descended from early settlers of Kentucky, she was the second of eight children born to Mary Elizabeth Brent and Simpson Roberts, Confederate veteran, teacher, grocer, and occasional surveyor/engineer. Roberts lived most of her life in

Springfield, a small county-seat town on the south-western edge of the Kentucky Bluegrass. She attended high school in Covington, Kentucky (1896-1900), and college at the University of Chicago (1917-1921; Ph.D. with honors, English, 1921; David Blair Mc-Laughlin Prize for prose, Fiske Poetry Prize, president of Poetry Club, Phi Beta Kappa), beginning college at the age of thirty-one because limited finances and ill health delayed her. She suffered from poor health much of her life. From 1910 to 1916, she made various stays with a brother and a sister in Colorado, in part to recuperate from what was possibly tuberculosis. At the height of her literary career, she experienced severe headaches and a skin rash, both possibly nervous in origin. During her last years, when she wintered in Florida for her health, she suffered severely from Hodgkin's disease (cancer of the lymphatic system), the eventual cause of her death.

Because of her ill health and perhaps her own disposition, Roberts led a quiet personal life, at times almost reclusive. She never married, though she always enjoyed a circle of friends, including friends from her Chicago years whom she later wrote and sometimes visited. In a sense, she never left the family circle, building her own house onto her parents' Springfield home when she came into money from her writing. She also enjoyed contacts and visits with her brothers and sisters. At heart, she was a solitary, introspective individual who guarded her privacy, growing a hedge around her backyard garden. Besides reading and writing, her favorite activities included listening to music, gardening, sunbathing, and taking long walks into secluded areas of the countryside (from which she returned to make voluminous notes).

These conditions of Roberts's life exercised strong influences, both positive and negative, on her writing career. Her family's proud pioneer heritage not only stimulated her imagination but also encouraged her to paint an idyllic picture of Kentucky's past and present. The sleepy farming region around Springfield was also a rich source of material—indeed, her prime source—but at the same time it effectively isolated her from literary circles who might have served to encourage, temper, and appreciate her efforts. These functions were served briefly by her stay at the University of Chicago. Her heady experience of Chicago, where literary circles flourished both inside and outside the university, filled her with ideas and propelled her into sustained literary production, but perhaps this hothouse experience also encouraged her to overreach herself as a writer.

The effects of Roberts's cirucmscribed personal life can also be detected in her fiction, particularly in her efforts to depict character and to describe male-female relationships, possibly also in her habitual narrative focus. To a great extent, Roberts's fiction provides an ironic counterpoint to her personal life. In most of her novels, the main narrative interest is her heroines' search for identity, worked out through the rituals of courting and mating: Her heroines suffer their shipwrecks but eventually find safe harbor in marriage. The men in their lives are either grand-fatherly, brutish, bucolic, or childishly vengeful; the heroines get advice from the grandfatherly ones, are hurt by the brutish ones, and marry either the bucolic or childishly vengeful ones. Fathers are frequently possessive, obstructing their daughters from marriage; one can only wonder about Roberts's relationship with her father, who refused her money for college and then had her underfoot for the rest of his life. To Roberts's credit, it must be said that in her novels, men, however unpromising, are absolutely vital to the scheme of things.

On the other hand, too, if Roberts's personal life had been less circumscribed, she might not have taken up writing at all. Writing became her means of achieving identity—and against stronger odds than any of her heroines had to face. However sickly and easily demoralized Roberts might seem, she had a vein of iron in her character that also came out in her heroines and in her themes. Even Roberts's ill health furnished her with potent material. Her heroines frequently develop by means of long illnesses and convalescences, from which they emerge born again, like a butterfly from its pupa. It was perhaps toward such a rebirth that Roberts was aiming in her writing.

ANALYSIS

Although commentators on Elizabeth Madox Roberts like to describe her main theme in such terms as "the ordering of chaos" or "the triumph of spirit over matter," one need not be so high-minded and vague. A hardheaded Kentucky version of her major theme would be more specific: ownership of the land. This theme reflects an old, revered attitude in Kentucky, where in some parts even today one can be shot for trespassing. The theme also reflects an old, revered American (even Anglo-Saxon) attitude, a pioneer urge to settle and possess, if necessary by violence—an urge that today achieves its debased avatar in the mass media and advertising. In its gentler, more settled aspects, however, Roberts's theme embodies a Jeffersonian, agrarian vision of American democracy, the American Dream of independence through ownership of the land. The theme eventually embodies a more universal vision, a vision of harmony with the land, a realization, serenely accepted, that those who possess the land are also possessed by it. Unhappily, whether expressed by Roberts or by other American writers whose characters want to own chicken farms or raise rabbits, the theme is a poignant reminder that many Americans have in actuality been vagabonds, whether the pioneer variety or today's rootless variety. In this sense, then, the theme embodies an idyllic but unrealized American Dream; it was apparently Roberts's conviction, however, that this dream came very close to being realized in Kentucky.

In developing her theme, Roberts reveals the influence of her favorite philosopher, George Berkeley, the eighteenth century bishop who denied the existence of matter, holding that "things" exist only as "ideas" or "spirits" in the minds of God and people. Such a philosophy would seem, at first, to preclude any relationship with the land; on the contrary, it points to a divine immanence, to the spiritual nature of all "things," including the land. The philosophy also implies the worth of "subjective" truth, justifying Roberts's narrative focus on the lengthy observations of her protagonists. As a result of this focus, her novels are full of loving descriptions of the land, the flora and fauna, the weather. Held constantly before the reader, the land forms an immense backdrop or tableau against which human action is played out, a background so overwhelming at times that the char-

acters seem to emerge out of it and then sink back into it.

Because of their closeness to the land, many of Roberts's characters exhibit a sameness: Mostly simple farmers, their lives governed by the imperatives of the seasons, crops, animals, they identify with the soil in their talk and in their impulses. Rather inarticulate, they have a blood-knowledge of the earth that requires little discussion. The continuity of their lives with the land is also reflected in their impulses to create life, to mate and procreate. To Roberts, these characters represent an ideal, a settled state, though to her readers they might seem too bucolic to be interesting.

The state of health represented by such characters is what Roberts's protagonists aspire to and her maladjusted characters lack. Like the bucolic characters, Roberts's protagonists seek to mate and procreate. The protagonists do not achieve their aims easily, though, having to reenact the archtypal struggle of their pioneer ancestors before they reach a settled state. When misfortune frustrates their desires, they get back in touch with the earth through the simple therapies of raising chickens, growing a garden, sunbathing, or taking rides in the country. Some end up marrying farmers. Such is the ultimate salvation of Theodosia, the highbred protagonist of *My Heart and My Flesh*, whose alienation from the land is an index of her initial maladjustment. Other unhappy characters in Roberts's novels are similarly out of touch with the land, such as Stoner Drake in *He Sent Forth a Raven* and the evil Langtry in *Black Is My Truelove's Hair.*

These patterns of behavior exhibited by her characters are the prime means through which Roberts develops her theme, with examples of each pattern generally to be found in each of her novels. To some extent, however, each novel emphasizes a particular aspect of her theme, with *He Sent Forth a Raven* being Roberts's most ambitious effort to pull all her characteristic motifs together in a single work.

THE GREAT MEADOW

Although *The Great Meadow* was Roberts's fourth novel, it was apparently the first conceived. This is appropriate, since thematically *The Great Meadow* comes first among her novels. Set around the time of the American Revolution, it celebrates the early settlement of Kentucky, that other Eden, that paradise, that promised land. The epic qualities of this novel have led some commentators to compare it to Homer's *Odyssey* (c. 800 B.C.E.), though it could more appropriately be compared to Vergil's *Aeneid* (c. 29-19 B.C.E.). Like Latium, Kentucky has to be wrested from the "aborigines." The novel even has its epic heroine with a noble name, Diony, and noble progenitors, sturdy Pennsylvania Methodists and Quakers on her mother's side and Virginia Tidewater gentry on her father's. Diony is, in truth, the founder of "a new race," though before she marries and sets out for Kentucky, she has to get her father's permission (in typical fashion for Roberts's possessive fathers, he at first denies her).

After a slow start in Albemarle County, Virginia, the novel follows Diony, her husband, and a small party of settlers as they trek across the rugged Appalachians to Harrod's Fort, where they proceed to fight off the Native Americans and establish farms. The growth of their settlement corresponds to Diony's growth as a person, largely a development of awareness. A convinced Berkeleian who frequently quotes from the philosopher's works, she receives a real challenge to her beliefs when she is banged in the head with a tomahawk, but the tomahawk incident and the scalping of her mother-in-law are only smaller parts of the overall challenge represented by the alien wilderness. In the beginning, Diony had imagined God as a benevolent deity creating "a world out of chaos," but since everything which exists is a thought of God's, God must also have created the wilderness, where wolves howl and savages prowl. Unlike Daniel Boone—or for that matter the Native Americans—Diony cannot feel at home in the wilderness; instead, she must remake the wilderness into her vision of home, a vision of a settled, orderly, agrarian society where the land is "owned."

Although Diony clings stubbornly to her vision of order, the wilderness does make her more tolerant of disorder. Even before she leaves for Kentucky, she has a "wilderness marriage . . . without law" (performed by a Methodist minister). Later, her experiences of hardship and deprivation at Harrod's Fort lead her to observe that "men wanted law to live by" but that women and babies "followed a hidden law"—that is, a law based on concrete, immediate human needs. This frontier tradition of making do the best one can, without too much scrupling about moral and legal niceties, serves Diony well at the end of the novel. Her husband, Berk Jarvis, goes into the wilderness to seek revenge against the Native American, Blackfox, who has his mother's scalp. When Berk does not return in a year or so, he is presumed dead, and Diony marries Evan Muir, who had helped provide for her after Berk left. Then, three years after he left, Berk shows up. Faced with two husbands and a child by each, Diony exercises the frontier woman's option: She sends Evan away, takes Berk back, and then goes to bed for a good, sound sleep.

The same spirit of make-do morality also characterizes the settlers' relations with the Native Americans. Diony's mother, Polly, influenced by Quaker thought, not only opposes the slaveholding favored by the Tidewater gentry but also opposes taking land from the American Indians. At the dinner table where the men are enthusiastically discussing "the promise land" of Kentucky, Polly angrily announces that Kentucky "belongs to the Indians" and that white trespassers there will get "skulped." Quiet reigns while the men contemplate images of "battle, fire . . . rapine, plunder." These thoughts, however, dampen their enthusiasm only momentarily. Striking the table for emphasis, they argue that Kentucky, "a good country," belongs to those strong enough to take and hold it—that is, "the Long Knives." Later, the last term is revised to "civilized man." Apparently, the latter argument is the one Roberts favors, since the rest of her novel eulogizes the settlers' taking of Kentucky. For example, as Diony's party breaks through Cumberland Gap, Roberts describes them as marching forward, "without bigotry and without psalm-singing," to take "a new world for themselves . . . by the power of their courage, their order, and their endurance." Thus is a time-honored Kentucky tradition established.

If *The Great Meadow* celebrates the vision of this other Eden, *A Buried Treasure* and *Black Is My True-*

love's Hair celebrate the realization of the vision. Like all of Roberts's novels except *The Great Meadow*, they are set in early twentieth century Kentucky, roughly contemporaneous with the period of their composition. Both novels were expanded from shorter pieces and show the effects of padding and lengthening, but at the same time they are Roberts's most entertaining novels and exhibit, in its purest form, her theme of living on the land. Generally light and pleasant works, they depict a pastoral scene where the land is the source of happiness and renewal.

A BURIED TREASURE

A Buried Treasure differs from other novels in its comic tone and in its older protagonist, Philadelphia Blair. Philly's farmer husband, Andy, finds a pot of old gold and silver coins under a stump on their land, and the rest of the novel concerns their efforts to announce their find and at the same time protect it from thieves. The flimsy plot is complicated somewhat by Philly's machinations to slip away her cousin's daughter, Imogene (whose possessive father, Sam Cundy, will not let her wed), and marry her to Giles Wilson. In addition, a subplot, introducing experimentation with point of view and synchronous time, treats seventeen-year-old Ben Shepherd's search for his ancestors' graves. To a great extent, the whole novel is an extended pun on the meanings of "buried treasure." Ben Shepherd finds the graves of his ancestors, who naturally go all the way back to the pioneer settlers of Kentucky. Imogene marries her beau, a jolly young farmer who wears horseshoes. Philly becomes more aware of her deep love for Andy, particularly when he loans the widow Hester Trigg (who gives him cherry pie) two pearls that he got from the treasure pot and normally wears in a small sack tied around his lower abdomen. Both Philly and Andy become more aware of their love for the land, from whence the treasure pot came, put there perhaps by some ancestor. Despite an evil old hen that eats her own eggs, and the threat of two itinerant housepainters who are thieves, the novel ends happily in a communal ring dance out in the pasture under the moonlit sky of the summer solstice.

BLACK IS MY TRUELOVE'S HAIR

Compared to *A Buried Treasure, Black Is My Truelove's Hair* is somewhat less satisfactory. Its title drawn from an Appalachian ballad containing the line "I love the ground whereon he stands," *Black Is My Truelove's Hair* concerns a young woman, Dena Janes, who "loved too much" and whose first lover, the black-hearted Langtry, is untrue. A truck driver who brags that he has no home, Langtry takes Dena on the road, refuses to marry her, treats her brutally, and threatens to kill her if she ever loves another man. After six days, Dena flees home, walking most of the way. Beginning at this point (the affair with Langtry is told through brief flashbacks), the novel treats Dena's gradual rehabilitation in the rural community and her eventual engagement to marry the miller's son, Cam Elliot. Although received at first with leering remarks and invitations, Dena is not given the Hester Prynne treatment. Even on her way home from the Langtry affair, the distraught Dena maintains she has "a right to a life that makes good sense." Apparently the people of the community agree.

Dena restores herself with the help of time, a sympathetic sister, routine chores of gardening and tending animals, sunbathing, and the advice of the local oracle, the apple-grower Journeyman, who observes that Dena is like one of his overburdened apple trees, "destroyed by its own abundance." As Dena recovers, the passage of time is marked by great to-dos over a strayed gander and a lost thimble; these comic commotions are supposed to be highly symbolic, but to the reader they may seem merely silly. The reader is also likely to find the ending anticlimactic. The fearsome Langtry shows up, gun in hand, but when he chases Dena into Journeyman's moonlit orchard and views her abundance, he shoots to miss. The story is resolved when Journeyman appears, destroys the gun, and buries it in the earth, leaving Dena free to go her own way.

THE TIME OF MAN

While *The Great Meadow* and the pastoral novels emphasize the positive aspects of Roberts's theme, *The Time of Man* and her other novels emphasize negative aspects. Dealing with poor tenant farmers who move from place to place, *The Time of Man* shows the plight of people who live on the land but do not own it. They have, in effect, been reduced to beasts of burden. Laboring mainly for others, they receive only enough from their labors to ensure their continuing usefulness, their subsistence. Their inability to escape from this cycle probably means that their children will continue it.

Although Roberts's subject raises weighty social issues, suggesting a novel along the lines of John Steinbeck's *The Grapes of Wrath* (1939), *The Time of Man* is not a novel of social protest. Instead, with Roberts's narrative focus on the mind of her protagonist, *The Time of Man* is more a *Bildungsroman*, tracing the development of Ellen Chesser from a girl of fourteen to a woman in her mid-thirties.

The reader follows Ellen as she bounds about the woods and fields, joins a group of other teenagers, gets a boyfriend, loses her boyfriend, withdraws into her hurt, meets another man, marries him, has four children, is estranged from her husband when he is unfaithful, has a fifth child die, and is reconciled with her husband. In short, whatever her social status, Ellen's experience of life over a generation is typical of most people's; in this sense, then, her experience is representative of "the time of man"—experiences of beauty and love, disappointment and tragedy, all within the context of passing time. Her ability to hold her experiences within this context is the key to her appreciation of beauty and love and her endurance of disappointment and tragedy. This ability derives from her closeness to the land, her sense of the seasons and participation in the rhythms of the earth: her jaunts through the woods, her work in the fields and garden, her courtship and marriage, her children.

Ellen illustrates what the Native Americans knew—that one can live in harmony with the land without owning it. To this extent, the several moves she makes from farm to farm, first with her parents and then with her husband, are almost irrelevant. Still, Ellen is aware of the inequities and injustices of the landowner/tenant system, a carryover from slave plantations, with some landowners continuing to act as if they own their tenants. She is incensed when her husband, while she and the children starve, identifies with, even takes pride in, the richness and show of their arrogant landlord. Both she and her husband carry around a vision of having their own farm someday, in "some better country." Perhaps they are headed toward this vision when, at the end of the novel, after her husband has been wrongly accused of barnburning and run out of the country, they are on the road again.

Roberts's first novel, *The Time of Man* is judged by some critics to be her best. Her exposition of her heroine's mind and development is a consummate job, and the novel does include some recognition of social problems in "the great meadow" of Kentucky; many readers, however, will feel that Roberts dwells too long on Ellen's early years, so that the first part of the novel drags.

JINGLING IN THE WIND

Roberts's other novels could all be called "novels of maladjustment," since they all show, in one manner or another, people who are out of touch with the land. Of these, *Jingling in the Wind*, which includes Roberts's only depiction of an urban setting, presents the most extreme case. There is much that Roberts finds artificial, even bizarre, in the city, such as neon advertisements that usurp the stars. In short, *Jingling in the Wind*, sometimes described as a satiric fantasy, is an outright attack on many trends of modern civilization. The loose plot concerns a couple of rainmakers, Jeremy and Tulip, who give up their unnatural profession in order to marry and have children. Usually considered Roberts's worst novel, *Jingling in the Wind* is interesting for its contribution to her grand theme.

MY HEART AND MY FLESH

Another novel of maladjustment is *My Heart and My Flesh*, centering on Theodosia Bell, a neurasthenic product of the wealthy landowning class. In this Faulknerian work exhibiting the results of Southern decadence, the protagonist gradually loses everything which has insulated her from contact with the land—her wealth, her boyfriends, her home, her grandfather and sottish father, even her feelings of racial superiority (she discovers she is a half sister to three mulattoes in town, including one idiot). As a child, Theodosia is so out of place in the countryside that a pack of hounds attack her. As an adult, when disillusionment, poverty, and sickness have brought her down to earth, she moves in with the pack, even eats their food. Later she finds health and happiness by teaching in a country school, living in her pupils' homes, and marrying a farmer. Thus, the pattern of rebirth through contact with the land is perfectly illustrated by Theodosia.

HE SENT FORTH A RAVEN

Conversely, a negative example is provided by Stoner Drake, the monomaniacal old man in *He Sent Forth a Raven*. The title's biblical reference to Noah, who trusted in God, provides a lucid contrast to Drake's blasphemous behavior. When his second wife dies, Drake vows never to set foot on God's green earth again. His anger hardening into inflexible principle, he keeps his word, never venturing from the house and managing his farm from a rooftop observatory, summoning workers and family members with blasts on a hunting horn or conch shell. The blasts symbolize not only his pathetic defiance of God but also his alienation from other people and the land. To Drake, of course, they symbolize command, and in his house he is an absolute dictator.

His rancorous behavior is self-punishing, but it also takes a toll on the people around him. For example, he prevents his daughter, Martha, from entertaining suitors. When one finally ventures a polite visit as a guest, Drake confronts him and Martha with loud, vile charges of fornication. The young man leaves, and Martha, thunderstruck, falls into fever and delirium, temporarily losing her hearing; when after some weeks it returns, the first things she hears are "the loud horn and the screaming of the swine." She thereafter reconciles herself to being a spinster and to banking the fires at night (so the house will not catch fire and her father burn up with it).

Standing in contrast to Drake is his granddaughter Jocelle, the novel's heroine, who takes a lesson from her aunt's fate. Growing up in the house with Drake and Martha, Jocelle manages to live a relatively normal life because she is free to roam the fields, sometimes even beyond the range of the horn. Like all of Roberts's female protagonists, Jocelle does suffer her traumas, but she is strong enough to bounce back. For example, when she is raped by Walter, Drake's

nephew, Drake renews his ridiculous vow, but Jocelle eventually recovers from her shock. At the end of the novel, she is happily married and a mother, her husband the manager of the farm, while Drake sits before the fireplace and hardens into brittle senility, unable to remember the reason for his vow.

Harold Branam

OTHER MAJOR WORKS

SHORT FICTION: *The Haunted Mirror*, 1932; *Not by Strange Gods*, 1941.

POETRY: *In the Great Steep's Garden*, 1915; *Under the Tree*, 1922, 1930; *Song in the Meadow*, 1940.

BIBLIOGRAPHY

Adams, J. Donald. *The Shape of Books to Come*. New York: Viking Press, 1934. Adams was an early admirer of Roberts, and he compares her to Willa Cather and Ellen Glasgow. An interesting contemporary view of the novelist.

Auchincloss, Louis. *Pioneers and Caretakers: A Study of Nine American Women Novelists*. Minneapolis: University of Minnesota Press, 1965. Auchincloss offers a compact overview of the life and work of Roberts, whose best and most popular novel was her first, *The Time of Man*; she never wrote anything to equal it.

Campbell, Harry M., and Ruel E. Foster. *Elizabeth Madox Roberts: American Novelist*. Norman: University of Oklahoma Press, 1956. Full of information about Roberts's career, if somewhat dull to read.

McDowell, Frederick P. W. *Elizabeth Madox Roberts*. New York: Twayne, 1963. McDowell gives a useful critical overview of Roberts's works, including her poetry and short stories. Offers a short biography of her life, which was mostly spent in Springfield, Kentucky.

Rovit, Earl H. *Herald to Chaos: The Novels of Elizabeth Madox Roberts*. Lexington: University Press of Kentucky, 1960. A wonderful critique of Roberts's novels, probably the best one available. Rovit describes Roberts's style in a sensitive and perceptive manner and places her in the context of American, not simply Southern, literature.

Tate, Linda. "Elizabeth Madox Roberts: A Bibliographical Essay." *Resources for American Literary Study* 18 (1992): 22-43. A valuable addition to studies of Roberts's career and the history of her reputation.

ROMAIN ROLLAND

Born: Clamecy, France; January 29, 1866
Died: Vézelay, France; December 30, 1944

PRINCIPAL LONG FICTION

L'Aube, 1904
Le Matin, 1904
L'Adolescent, 1904
La Révolte, 1906-1907
La Foire sur la place, 1908
Antoinette, 1908
Dans la maison, 1909
Les Amies, 1910
Le Buisson ardent, 1911
La Nouvelle Journée, 1912 (previous 10 novels collectively known as *Jean-Christophe* [*John-Christopher*, 1910-1913, better known as *Jean-Christophe*, 1913])
Colas Breugnon: Bonhomme vit encore!, 1919 (*Colas Breugnon*, 1919)
Clérambault: Histoire d'une conscience libre pendant la guerre, 1920 (*Clerambault: The Story of an Independent Spirit During the War*, 1921, initially serialized as *L'Un contre tous*, 1917 [incomplete version])
Pierre et Luce, 1920 (*Pierre and Luce*, 1922)
L'Âme enchantée, 1922-1933 (*The Soul Enchanted*, 1925-1934)

OTHER LITERARY FORMS

In addition to his novels, Romain Rolland is known for his biographies, including *François Millet* (1902), which was published only in English; others are *Beethoven* (1903; English translation, 1907), *Michel-Ange* (1905), *La Vie de Michel-Ange* (1906; *The Life of Mi-*

chelangelo, 1912), *Haendel* (1910; *Handel*, 1916), *Vie de Tolstoï* (1911; *Tolstoy*, 1911), *Mahatma Gandhi* (1924; *Mahatma Gandhi: The Man Who Became One with the Universal Being*, 1924), *Essai sur la mystique et l'action de l'Inde vivante* (1929-1930; *Prophets of the New India*, 1930; includes *La Vie de Ramakrishna*, 1929 [*Ramakrishna*] and the two-volume *La Vie de Vivekananda et l'Évangile universel*, 1930 [*Vivekananda*]), and *Péguy* (1944, 2 volumes). Among his musicological works, *Goethe et Beethoven* (1927; *Goethe and Beethoven*, 1931) and the comprehensive work *Beethoven: Les Grandes Époques créatrices* (1928-1945)—part of which was translated as *Beethoven the Creator* (1929)—are of general interest. The genre which Rolland embraced initially, without much recognition, was drama. Rolland later grouped several of his plays into cycles. These are *Les Tragédies de la foi* (1913), consisting of his first published play, *Saint Louis* (1897), together with *Aërt* (1898) and *Le Triomphe de la raison* (1899), and the cycle *Théâtre de la révolution* (1909), originally consisting of *Les Loups* (1898; *The Wolves*, 1937), *Danton* (1900; English translation, 1918), and *Le Quatorze Juillet* (1902; *The Fourteenth of July*, 1918), and later including *Le Jeu de l'amour et de la mort* (1925; *The Game of Love and Death*, 1926), *Pâques fleuries* (1926; *Palm Sunday*, 1928), *Les Léonides* (1928), and *Robespierre* (1939). Editions which appeared during Rolland's lifetime show different or incomplete groupings. Among his other important writings for and about the theater are the satire *Liluli* (1919; English translation, 1920) and *Le Théâtre du peuple: Essai d'esthétique d'un théâtre nouveau* (1903; *The People's Theater*, 1918). Rolland was a prolific writer. Of his extensive correspondence, twenty-four volumes have been published since 1948 in the ongoing *Cahiers Romain Rolland*. Autobiographical works and published diaries include *Le Voyage intérieur* (1942; *The Journey Within*, 1947) and *L'Inde: Journal 1915-1943* (1949), as well as *Journal des années de guerre, 1914-1919* (1952). Rolland commanded international attention with his political, polemical, and pacifist writings. Among them are *Au-dessus de la mêlée* (1915; *Above the Battle*, 1916) and *Les Précurseurs* (1919), which reappeared together in *L'Esprit libre*

(1953). This collection of essays and open letters is essential for an understanding of Rolland's position within the post-World War I European intellectual elite.

ACHIEVEMENTS

Romain Rolland remained a relatively obscure figure until he was almost fifty years old. His education prepared him for a career in teaching the history of art and music, and he was on the faculty of the École Normale Supérieure and the Sorbonne until 1912 while maintaining a correspondence with various European intellectuals. Although Rolland had the support of some devoted friends, notably his former teacher Gabriel Monod and the aged German writer Malvida von Meysenbug, his early literary endeavors met with little success. In 1903, Charles-Pierre Péguy, his friend from the École Normale Supérieure with whom he shared both idealism and literary talent, published Rolland's work in his *Cahiers de la*

(The Nobel Foundation)

Quinzaine, which had a relatively small but international intellectual readership. In this periodical, the ten volumes of Rolland's novel *Jean-Christophe* appeared in segments dating from February 2, 1904, to October 20, 1912. These publications proved to be the foundation of his fame. In 1905, Rolland received the Vie Heureuse prize; in 1909, the award of the Légion d'Honneur; in 1913, the Grand Prix de la Littérature of the Académie Française; and in 1915, the Nobel Prize in Literature.

The basis of Rolland's philosophy was the achievement of a Pan-European unity and the social and intellectual emancipation of the masses through the efforts of an international elite—a goal which he perceived as attainable. His hopes were temporarily shattered by the outbreak of World War I and the ensuing spirit of nationalism and patriotism, which created political chasms between former friends. Some of Rolland's most polemical writings date from that period. He had, however, attained a faithful international following among the world's intellectual leaders. Among them were Albert Einstein, Maxim Gorky, Sigmund Freud, Richard Strauss, Ernst Bloch, and many others who honored him with contributions to the volume *Liber amicorum* (1926) for his sixtieth birthday. Although he favored the revolution in Russia, he decried the ensuing bloodshed that established the Communist regime. True progress, he claimed, could not be achieved by unprincipled means.

He then turned to the inspiration of Mahatma Gandhi's movement of passive resistance, which sought political freedom and self-government by nonviolent means. His vision of a Pan-European unity broadened to include an international humanist movement of global extent and the establishment of a European Shantiniketan, an international House of Friendship and Archives for pertinent publications of global interest and origin. He became disenchanted with the Indians when he perceived their lack of a sense of urgency. The rise of National Socialism, his marriage to the Russian Marie Koudachev in 1934, and a 1935 trip to the Soviet Union, where he visited Gorky, convinced him, in the face of the seeming impotence of the European alliance he had supported, that the international Communist movement offered the only alternative to Nazi Germany's power politics. He presided in absentia over the International Congress Against War and Fascism held in Amsterdam in 1932, refused the Goethe Prize offered him by Germany in 1933, and commenced writing polemical essays and open letters against Fascist propaganda in Germany and Italy. He watched the German invasion of France but died before the end of World War II.

While Rolland has been variously called a pacifist, an activist, a communist, an idealist, a humanist, a nationalist, a mystic, and a rationalist, he was, in effect, all of these. He is recognized for his undaunted attempts to promote the causes of peace and the brotherhood of humankind during the time of a war-torn Europe, for his desire to unite the world's intellectual elite to achieve these goals, for his belief in the ultimate prevalence of reason, and for his fiction that contains a didactic base for the dissemination of these beliefs.

BIOGRAPHY

Romain Edmé Paul-Émile Rolland was born at Clamecy (Nièvre), France, on January 29, 1866. His father, Émile, a fourth-generation notary, and his deeply religious and musically talented mother, Antoinette-Marie (née Courot), were financially secure and respected in the Burgundian borderland in which their families had lived since before the Revolution. One of his lasting early memories was the death of his younger sister Madeleine while the family was vacationing at Arcachon, near Bordeaux. The experience left the then five-year-old Rolland with a fear of death and a preoccupation with respiratory ailments. In later life, he included in his works images of suffocation, such as in the opening passages of *Beethoven*, and the frailty of his health, with which he struggled to the end of his life, contained a strong neurotic element.

To facilitate Rolland's schooling, the family moved to Paris in the fall of 1880. The impression he gained of the city, described in his *Mémoires et fragments du journal* (1956), is that of an unwholesome, immoral, feverish, sickening, godless abyss, breathing death and decay. The coarseness of literature,

vice on the streets, and the sexual brutality expressed by the young imbued him with a belief that this decadence foreshadowed the death of Western civilization, a theme which dominates the fifth (*La Foire sur la place*) and tenth (*La Nouvelle Journée*) volumes of his novel *Jean-Christophe*. After his years at the *lycée*, where he became friends with Paul Claudel and André Suarès, he studied art and music at the École Normale Supérieure from 1886 to 1889. The following two years he spent in Rome on an appointment to the École Française. While studying feverishly, he also fell passionately in love with a young woman, Sofia Guerrieri-Gonzaga, found a friend and confidante in the aged German writer Malvida von Meysenbug, who had enjoyed the friendship of Friedrich Nietzsche and Richard Wagner, and wrote his first plays: "Empédocle" (1890) remained a fragment; "Orsino" (1890) was finished but not published. The two years in Rome were to be among the happiest of his life. After his return to Paris, he married Clotilde Bréal, daughter of a philology professor, on October 31, 1892. This marriage lasted until May, 1901. During the years from 1892 to 1900, he wrote numerous plays which met with minimal success. Among them are *Les Baglioni* and *Niobé* (both written in 1892), *Caligula* (written in 1893), *Le Siège de Mantoue* (written in 1894), and *Savonarole* and *Jeanne de Pienne* (both written in 1896). His first published play was *Saint Louis*, and on May 3 and May 18, 1898, respectively, his *Aërt* and *The Wolves* were staged. In the meantime, he had also finished his dissertation in 1895 and had begun teaching the history of art at the École Normale Supérieure. Rolland's dramatic work contains a strong didactic element. Frequently based on historical figures or events, the protagonists often show a moral fortitude and spiritual strength that permits them to be emotionally "victorious" even in defeat. After outlining his ideas for a revitalization of the theater in *Le Théâtre du peuple*, he abandoned the dramatic genre for some time and turned to the production of novels and biographies.

The monumental work *Jean-Christophe*, its ten volumes written over a period of eight years, established Rolland as a writer. He wrote for and was acknowledged by an intellectual elite across Europe and beyond, among whom he developed a faithful following of friends. They were keenly aware of the political unrest which Rolland describes at the end of the novel as a smoldering fire ready to break into a full-fledged conflagration. After an automobile accident in October, 1910, which nearly killed him, he took two years' leave of absence from the Sorbonne, where he had been teaching since November, 1904, and he resigned altogether in 1912. Despite his political forebodings, news of the outbreak of World War I came as a surprise to him while he was vacationing with the American Helena Van Brugh De Kay in Switzerland. After the assassination of the Austrian Archduke Ferdinand, he decided to remain in this political refuge. From 1914 to 1915, he worked at the Agence Internationale des Prisonniers de Guerre. His political essays became increasingly scathing in their denunciation of the war and in their call for reason among the warring nations. His satire *Liluli*, unmasking the treachery of "illusion," had its conception in the early war years. In the spring of 1919, he wrote "Déclaration de l'indépendance de l'esprit," in which he blamed the intellectual elite for succumbing to petty nationalism and political party interests.

This led to a controversy with Henri Barbusse, who denounced "Rollandism" in *Light* (1919). In an open letter to Barbusse in *L'Art libre*, published in January, 1922, Rolland harshly denounced the doctrine of neo-Marxist Communism. By then, Rolland was an internationally known figure, had received several important awards for his work (including the Nobel Prize), and, after a brief return to France shortly before the death of his mother in 1919, had moved permanently to Switzerland, establishing himself, his father, and his sister in the Villa Olga in Villeneuve in 1922. His three shorter novels, *Colas Breugnon, Clerambault,* and *Pierre and Luce,* were followed here by another monumental novel divided into four books published in six volumes. *The Soul Enchanted,* published between 1922 and 1933, is feminist in its thrust and criticizes established social structures and concepts.

Having established contact with the Indian liberation movement, Rolland wrote Gandhi's biography and received a visit in June, 1926, from the Indian writer Ribindranath Tagore. Shortly after Gandhi visited Rolland in December, 1931, Rolland became disenchanted with the Indian philosophy. Although he was by then an old man, he was pervaded by a sense of urgency to combat the new global confrontation which he perceived gathering force. It was at this point that he turned to Communism's proclaimed international peace movement as an alternative to Fascism. In 1932, he accepted the presidency of the International Congress Against War and Fascism and became an honorary member of Leningrad's Academy of Sciences. Marie Koudachev, daughter of a Russian father and a French mother, became Rolland's second wife in the summer of 1934. A year later, he visited the Soviet Union and Gorky, returning convinced that the Russian Revolution had been a good thing.

Rolland continued his polemics against the National Socialist regime and against Benito Mussolini at every level. In 1938, he moved to Vézelay, only a short distance from his birthplace, and took up work, once more, on a play about the Revolution (*Robespierre*), on his *Mémoires et fragments du journal* (published unfinished, after his death), and on his last biography, *Péguy*. He also worked on the final volumes of *Beethoven: Les Grandes Époques créatrices*. Shortly after the publication of the autobiographical work *The Journey Within*, he became seriously ill and had three "visions" of a religious nature. Although he recovered sufficiently to continue working, his health remained precariously poor until his death on December 30, 1944.

ANALYSIS

The novel with which Romain Rolland established his fame, a work translated into numerous languages, was *Jean-Christophe*. Its inception dates at least to 1890—to the years in Rome and the friendship with Malvida von Meysenbug. She had, he insisted, "created" him, and he honored her memory in two of the novel's characters. With her, he also shared a veneration of Beethoven, on whom, according to Rolland, the protagonist is modeled. The hero, a great German musician, is forced by circumstance to live outside Germany in Paris, Italy, and Switzerland, and his experiences and perspectives are recounted and analyzed.

JEAN-CHRISTOPHE

While Rolland admits that the protagonist is not the historical Beethoven but a Beethoven of Rolland's own times, he also refers to the novel as the "history of my soul transposed into one greater than I." It is true that the parallels between Beethoven and Jean-Christophe are quickly exhausted and that many of Jean-Christophe's experiences and characteristics have their foundation in those of Rolland himself. Just as the novel's hero crosses the Rhine river, transcending in a symbolic gesture the boundaries between Germany and France, so Rolland attempted to overcome geographical and political barriers by uniting the intellectual elite of Europe's nations. The fifth book of *Jean-Christophe, La Foire sur la place*, not only shows Rolland's talents of critical evaluation but also is strongly reminiscent of his initial impression of Paris. Jean-Christophe finds the cultural life, particularly the world of theater and music, superficial and governed by the principles of economics; its representatives are without idealism, talent, or proficiency and merely court fame and money. Above the noise and the luxury, there is an all-pervasive smell of death and decay.

This, however, is only one side of France. Jean-Christophe finds the "real" France in his encounter with the "real" artist Olivier and his sister Antoinette. The distinction between what is the apparent and what is the true face of a nation is evident in his communication with European intellectuals from his early correspondence into the times of war: Germans per se are not the enemies of France but rather the nationalistic and corrupt elements in the German political hierarchy. The title of the fourth book, *La Révolte*, could accurately describe the action of the first nine. Jean-Christophe's mystical experience in book 9, *Le Buisson ardent*, where he claims defeat but is strengthened and encouraged by an indefinable but possibly divine being, is the upbeat prelude to the prophetic tenth book, *La Nouvelle Journée*. Conflict is eternal; thus, the river's mysterious voices echo Jean-Christophe's hope of resurrection in the death

scene and praise the "divine union" of love and hate, life and death.

Sigmund Freud, whom Rolland visited in Vienna in 1924, was intrigued by the water symbolism Rolland used in many of his works. In Rolland's personal symbolism, the river and the ocean are not merely conventional figures for the passage of life or the venture into eternity and death; they express the origin of religious energy. Others of the four elements of ancient philosophy (earth, air, fire, water) are also used frequently for dramatic value and symbolic interest. The storm or thunderstorm reveals to Jean-Christophe the nature of God in the third book, *L'Adolescent*, but it is an equally important and powerful motif in *Beethoven, The Life of Michelangelo*, and *Tolstoy*. Fire in the forest becomes a symbol in the tenth book of *Jean-Christophe* for the political chaos and destruction threatening Europe from all sides. Mystical experiences and visions clarify the path the protagonist is to take, as Rolland himself was guided by such phenomena. Finally, the motif of conflict and strife—central to *Jean-Christophe*—is apparent in almost every other work by Rolland. Rolland's protagonists are characteristically vanquished victors, suffering martyrs with a mission. Whether they preach the gospel of religious conviction or belief in that primal creative power many associate with God (*Saint Louis, Jean-Christophe*), the power of art (*Beethoven, The Life of Michelangelo*), or the doctrines of freedom, justice, and peace (*The Soul Enchanted, Clerambault, Pierre and Luce*), Rolland's heroes are aggressive spirits whose intellectual stamina overcomes their physical frailty. They single-handedly lead the fight against the world's iniquity and broadcast their message with the example of their death. To that extent, much of Rolland's fiction is didactic.

COLAS BREUGNON

A novel of a somewhat different character is *Colas Breugnon*. Revisiting his birthplace, Clamecy, Rolland was inspired in April, 1913, to sketch the robust, merry, occasionally malicious, always talkative people of his ancestral town. The novel was finished before the war but not published until after it. Perhaps because of its humorous style and the colorful and intriguing depiction of life in the provinces, *Colas Breugnon* is one of Rolland's most popular novels. Besides personifying the vitality and courage inherent in the local population, the character Colas Breugnon portrays some of the more somber aspects of existence. Rebuilding from the ravages of war, marrying a woman other than the one he loved, rearing sons with whom he is not compatible, protecting life and property from marauding soldiers, the carpenter grapples with crises and disappointments without losing his innate sense of humor. Rolland cannot resist adding a sprinkling of metaphysics in the guise of Breugnon's jovial philosophy: Every person, Breugnon declares, has twenty different persons within him, and thus a single god is insufficient. He believes in many gods, pagan and Christian, and within him they "all get along together very well, each with his job and his home."

CLERAMBAULT

Clerambault, published originally in 1917 in a serialized version under the title *L'Un contre tous*, appeared three years later in book form. Toward the end of 1916, Rolland spoke of his own "liberation" from the dominance of collective passions and the mysticism evident in *Jean-Christophe*, and of the subsequent maturation of his critical faculties. Clerambault, a member of the French middle class and an intellectual, undergoes a similar change in his emancipation from and criticism of the fanatic nationalism and anti-German hysteria during World War I. Initially, Clerambault questions the fervor of his son, Maxime, who perceives in the outbreak of war the rebirth of the Revolution: "Are you quite certain?" he asks him. His own patriotism is inflamed, however, while Maxime experiences a change of heart when confronted with the horrors of war at the front. When Maxime briefly returns home on furlough, Clerambault reads to his son hymns and marching songs which he has composed, expecting Maxime's approval. "Are you quite certain, father?" is Maxime's unspoken reaction, and he returns to the front and his death. When Clerambault recognizes that war is no solution to international conflict and that the mass hysteria fanned by fanatic patriots merely plays into the hands of unscrupulous politicians, he coura-

geously voices his opinion and, like Rolland himself, is branded as a traitor and pacifist. Like the Socialist leader Jean Jaurès, Clerambault is assassinated for his convictions. Rolland goes so far as to liken his protagonist to an apostle of Christ, whose agony reaches "the ends of the earth." The novel is a highly tendentious expression of Rolland's pacifism. Its theme is aptly stated in the introductory passage: Humanity is not served by those who betray their conscience, their intelligence, and their integrity in order to conform, but by those who oppose the misuse of power and rebel against an unjust authority, even if it leads to conflict with the majority.

THE SOUL ENCHANTED

Clerambault and its successor, *Pierre and Luce*, written under the vivid impressions left by World War I, were superseded by another monumental novel published in six volumes. *The Soul Enchanted* breathes the spirit of a new age of progress, hope, and emancipation. Like *Jean-Christophe*, it traces the emotional development of the protagonist through the battles of a lifetime; as in the earlier novel, the passage of time is symbolically connected to the image of the river—in conjunction with historical events, in Annette Rivière's name, and in the progressive intellectual and material emancipation she personifies, which Rolland perceived as a social phenomenon during his lifetime. Unlike *Jean-Christophe, The Soul Enchanted* has a female protagonist, renders a view of life's difficulties from the woman's perspective, and is frequently feminist in its approach. In a sense, Rolland's expressed desire, voiced as late as 1913, that he often "would have liked to be a woman," was fulfilled through the execution of this novel. His portrayal of Annette shows his penetrating insight into the social conditioning affecting women's self-perception, role modeling, and heterosexual relationships, as well as the political and materialistic consequences of these behavior patterns. Rarely has a male author so accurately portrayed woman on this dual level: her development in the context of external (social and material) influences, and in relation to her intellectual, emotional, and moral life. Annette is a woman of courage, strength, and motherliness who exhibits at the same time the instincts of a creature of nature.

Annette is the daughter of a Parisian architect. She is intelligent, educated, self-assured, and financially independent. Two occurrences drastically change the course of her future: She breaks her engagement to a promising young man of a wealthy family because she perceives that to be his wife means complete subordination to the point of self-abnegation, and she persists in her refusal to marry him even after she finds herself pregnant; after the death of her father, she loses her money through the unfortunate speculations of the curator. Annette's situation is considerably more traumatic than that of a lower-class girl in similar circumstances, for she has not been reared to compete for her daily bread in a world where hunger, poverty, illness, and unemployment are constant companions. Ostracized by the members of her social class because of her "immoral conduct" (she gives birth to a son and decides to rear him alone) and lacking marketable skills to earn a living, Annette experiences the full force of discrimination and prejudice against independent women. The novel follows Annette through the early stages of her new life, the building of a career, the joys and tribulations of motherhood, and the relative serenity of her mature years.

Rolland's purpose is not solely the depiction of the struggle for emancipation of France's women, although some sententious proclamations in the text certainly promote this cause. Male characters such as Philippe Villard are also engaged in a bitter struggle for survival. Rolland's protagonist is female because the difficulties encountered by the lower classes in general in a struggle for basic freedoms, rights, and equality are much more pronounced in that sex. Women, Rolland contends, are the last segment of the population still enslaved in the twentieth century. They have not yet recognized the advantage that lies in their numbers, they have not yet learned to organize their struggle on the model of Communism, and they are still fighting the primitive war on a one-to-one basis: not a struggle against fate or nature or the ruling class, but a war of worker against worker for the daily meager subsistence. The novel proclaims the need for a concerted effort in the manner of a class struggle to bring about change and the dawning of a new day of social equality.

The Soul Enchanted shows conflict as a necessary part of life, for it builds strength of character and is the foundation of great societies. Thus, Rolland returned in his mature years to an intellectually refined version of his earlier idealism, stripped of any religious overtones: "Peace is not the absence of war," he notes in *The Soul Enchanted*. "It is virtue born of the powers of the spirit."

Helene M. Kastinger Riley

OTHER MAJOR WORKS

PLAYS: *Saint Louis*, pb. 1897; *Aërt*, pr., pb. 1898; *Les Loups*, pb. 1898 (*The Wolves*, 1937); *Le Triomphe de la raison*, pr. 1899; *Danton*, pr., pb. 1900 (English translation, 1918); *Le Quatorze Juillet*, pr., pb. 1902 (*The Fourteenth of July*, 1918); *Le Temps viendra*, pb. 1903; *Théâtre de la révolution*, pb. 1909 (includes *Les Loups*, *Danton*, and *Le Quatorze Juillet*); *Les Tragédies de la foi*, pb. 1913 (includes *Saint Louis*, *Aërt*, and *Le Triomphe de la raison*); *Liluli*, pb. 1919 (English translation, 1920); *Le Jeu de l'amour et de la mort*, pb. 1925 (*The Game of Love and Death*, 1926); *Pâques fleuries*, pb. 1926 (*Palm Sunday*, 1928); *Les Léonides*, pb. 1928; *Robespierre*, pb. 1939.

NONFICTION: *François Millet*, 1902 (published only in English); *Beethoven*, 1903 (English translation, 1907); *Le Théâtre du peuple: Essai d'esthétique d'un théâtre nouveau*, 1903 (*The People's Theater*, 1918); *Michel-Ange*, 1905; *La Vie de Michel-Ange*, 1906 (*The Life of Michelangelo*, 1912); *Haendel*, 1910 (*Handel*, 1916); *Vie de Tolstoï*, 1911 (*Tolstoy*, 1911); *Au-dessus de la mêlée*, 1915 (*Above the Battle*, 1916); *Les Précurseurs*, 1919; *Mahatma Gandhi*, 1924 (*Mahatma Gandhi: The Man Who Became One with the Universal Being*, 1924); *Goethe et Beethoven*, 1927 (*Goethe and Beethoven*, 1931); *Beethoven: Les Grandes Époques créatrices*, 1928-1945 (partial translation *Beethoven the Creator*, 1929); *Essai sur la mystique et l'action de l'Inde vivante*, 1929-1930 (*Prophets of the New India*, 1930; includes *La Vie de Ramakrishna*, 1929 [*Ramakrishna*]; *La Vie de Vivekananda et l'Évangile universel*, 1930 [*Vivekananda*]); *Empédocle d'Agrigente, suivi de l'éclair de Spinoza*, 1931; *Quinze ans de combat, 1919-1934*, 1935 (*I*

Will Not Rest, 1936); *Compagnons de route, essais littéraires*, 1936; *Le Voyage intérieur*, 1942 (*The Journey Within*, 1947); *Péguy*, 1944 (2 volumes); *L'Inde: Journal 1915-1943*, 1949; *Journal des années de guerre, 1914-1919*, 1952; *L'Esprit libre*, 1953 (includes *Au-dessus de la mêlée* and *Les Précurseurs*); *Mémoires et fragments du journal*, 1956.

MISCELLANEOUS: *Cahiers Romain Rolland*, 1948-   .

BIBLIOGRAPHY

Fisher, David James. *Romain Rolland and the Politics of Intellectual Engagement*. Berkeley: University of California Press, 1988. Divided into sections on the turn-of-the-century idealist, his more ambiguous position in the 1920's, his involvement in left-wing politics in the 1930's, and a concluding chapter on "pessimism of the intelligence, optimism of the will." Includes detailed notes and bibliography.

Francis, R. A. *Romain Rolland*. Oxford: Berg, 1999. An excellent study of Rolland's life and influences on his art.

March, Harold. *Romain Rolland*. New York: Twayne, 1971. An introductory study, with chapters largely built around the places where Rolland lived and worked. Includes a chronology, notes, and bibliography.

Starr, William Thomas. *Romain Rolland and a World at War*. Evanston, Ill.: Northwestern University Press, 1956. Especially useful biographical material and an important corrective to Zweig

_____. *Romain Rolland: One Against All: A Biography*. The Hague: Mouton, 1971. Starr provides a study of Rolland based on his letters, his other writings, and the impressions of others. Starr argues that these strands cannot be separated in discussing Rolland. Includes a chronology and index.

Zweig, Stefan. *Romain Rolland: The Man and His Work*. New York: Thomas Seltzer, 1921. Zweig, a veteran biographer of many modern figures, provides a comprehensive, lively account, divided into Part I: Biographical; Part II: Early Work as Dramatists; Part III: The Heroic Biographies; Part IV: *Jean Christophe*; Part V: Intermezzo Scherzo; Part VI: The Conscience of Europe. This structure is meant to capture the complexity of a public intellectual, political activist, and major literary figure. Zweig, a friend of Rolland, tends to eulogize his subject.

HENRY ROTH

Born: Tysmenica, Galicia, Austro-Hungarian Empire (now in Ukraine); February 8, 1906
Died: Albuquerque, New Mexico; October 13, 1995

PRINCIPAL LONG FICTION

Call It Sleep, 1934
Mercy of a Rude Stream, 1994-1998 (includes *A Star Shines over Mt. Morris Park*, 1994; *A Diving Rock on the Hudson*, 1995; *From Bondage*, 1996; and *Requiem for Harlem*, 1998)

OTHER LITERARY FORMS

In addition to his novels, Henry Roth wrote a number of essays, short stories, and fragments that editor Mario Materassi collected and published in 1987 as *Shifting Landscape: A Composite, 1925-1987*.

ACHIEVEMENTS

With *Call It Sleep*, Henry Roth created a masterpiece of American Jewish fiction and a classic novel of immigration, one that brilliantly adapts the insights associated with Austrian psychoanalyst Sigmund Freud and the techniques associated with Irish writer James Joyce in order to recount the traumatic experiences of an impressionable young foreigner in New York City. However, it was not until thirty years after its publication that the book began to be widely read, studied, and admired. Discouraged by neglect of his first novel, Roth abandoned the literary life and did not return to writing novels until a prodigious burst of creativity in his final years yielded 3,200 manuscript pages of disturbing autobiographical fiction, the tetralogy titled *Mercy of a Rude Stream*, half of which appeared after the author's death at eighty-nine. The sixty-year gap between publication of *Call It Sleep*, in 1934, and *A Star Shines over Mt. Morris Park*, the first volume of the tetralogy, in 1994, represents the most remarkable instance in American literary history of writer's block and late artistic renewal.

BIOGRAPHY

Like David Schearl, the young protagonist of *Call It Sleep*, Henry Roth was born in the Galician region of the Austro-Hungarian Empire but was brought to New York City when only two. Like many other working-class Jewish immigrants, the Roths settled on the lower East Side of Manhattan but later relocated to Harlem. Roth manifested talent with a story in the student magazine of New York's public City College. Eda Lou Walton, a professor at New York University who befriended Roth and encouraged him to write, became his mentor and lover. Eventually, Roth moved into her Greenwich Village apartment, where he wrote *Call It Sleep*. Though Walton helped him find a publisher, the Depression year 1934 was not propitious for a literary debut, and, though the book received favorable reviews, its publisher, Robert O. Ballou, was forced into bankruptcy.

Roth began a second novel but, convinced that it was unworthy of the Marxist ideals he then set for himself, he abandoned both it and the cosmopolitan ferment of New York. He married Muriel Parker, a composer he had met at the Yaddo artists' colony, and moved with her to rural Maine. Abandoning her own musical aspirations, Muriel supported him and their two sons by teaching school, while Roth helped by chopping wood, selling maple syrup, fighting forest fires, tutoring Latin and math, and serving as an attendant at a mental hospital. For most of a decade, he raised and slaughtered geese and ducks.

In 1964, *Call It Sleep* was rediscovered, and, at the age of fifty-eight, its obscure au-

thor suddenly found himself famous. Roth was plagued by persistent questions about his current projects. In 1968, after an abortive effort to write a novel set during the Spanish Inquisition, he and Muriel moved to Albuquerque, New Mexico. After Muriel's death in 1990, Roth attempted suicide but survived to complete his last great literary task at eighty-nine. Despite agonizing rheumatoid arthritis, he managed to produce an enormous autobiographical fictional sequence, one that revisited its author's strained relationship with his abusive, embittered father and incestuous relationships with his sister and his cousin. Upon Roth's death in 1995, two of the four volumes of *Mercy of a Rude Stream* had been published, while the final two appeared posthumously, in 1996 and 1998, respectively. Enough material remained for two additional volumes, but Roth's publisher, St. Martin's Press, determined that they fell outside the *Mercy of a Rude Stream* cycle and remained uncertain about when or whether they would be published.

ANALYSIS

For much of the twentieth century, Henry Roth, the novelist who vanished for sixty years after a stun-

(Harvey Wang)

ning debut, seemed a gloss on writer F. Scott Fitzgerald's quip that American lives lack second acts. Yet his long life offers enough acts to please the most garrulous of playwrights and challenge the most assiduous of biographers. He is at once salutatorian and valedictorian of twentieth century America, a contemporary of both William Faulkner and Don DeLillo. His pioneering use of stream of consciousness captured a newly urbanized, industrialized society undergoing massive transformation, but Roth survived into a very different era to write his own requiem.

In retrospect, *Call It Sleep* seems so unequivocally a major artistic achievement that it is difficult to understand why it was neglected for thirty years. However, in 1934 American culture lacked a category for American Jewish literature. By 1964, Roth fulfilled the need to anoint a worthy ancestor to Saul Bellow, Bernard Malamud, and Philip Roth, to legitimate a newly canonized tradition. It was only after ethnicity became a crucial issue in American society that Roth's novel could be appreciated for its pioneering embodiment of multiculturalism and multilingualism.

Mercy of a Rude Stream is of a different order of accomplishment than *Call It Sleep*. The fictional sequence that Roth created in his final years is of compelling interest to those fascinated by a tormented author's representation of his own compulsions and his desperate attempt to find closure. If Roth's virtuosic first novel appeared ahead of its time, his parting tetralogy was a throwback—a fictional sequence that not only is set in the 1920's but also employs the naturalistic style common to that era. From *Call It Sleep* to *Requiem for Harlem*, Roth's frustrated literary career is itself the most remarkable narrative he created.

CALL IT SLEEP

Call It Sleep begins in May, 1907, with the arrival by ship from Europe of two-year-old David Schearl and his mother Genya. They are met at Ellis Island by David's father, Albert, a surly, abusive man who is embittered by disappointment. Albert is forever falling out with fellow workers and forced to seek new employment, as a printer and then as a milkman. The family moves from modest lodgings in Brooklyn's Brownsville neighborhood to a crowded tenement on the lower East Side of Manhattan. Roth's book focuses on young David's troubling experiences during the years 1911-1913, as a stranger in a strange land. *Call It Sleep* is a coming-of-age novel about a hypersensitive Jewish boy who is forced to cope alone with the mysteries of sex, religion, and love.

After a brief prologue recounting David's arrival in America, Roth organizes his story into four sections, each defined by a dominant image: "The Cellar," "The Picture," "The Coal," and "The Rail." What might otherwise seem casual details are magnified by refraction through the mind of an anxious child. Roth's use of stream of consciousness intensifies the sense of an unformed mind trying to assimilate the varied sensations that assault it. The family apartment is a haven for David, as long as his father, who even doubts his paternity of the boy, is not home and his doting mother can lavish her affections on him. When David ventures out into the clamorous streets, he encounters threats, from both rats and humans.

At the cheder, the drab religious school where Jewish boys are given rote instruction in a Hebrew Bible they cannot understand, David is confused and inspired by Isaiah's account of the angel with a burning coal. Eavesdropping on a conversation between his mother and her sister Bertha, he misconstrues an explanation for why Genya, disgraced after being jilted by a Gentile, married Albert. When Leo, an older Polish boy, persuades David to introduce him to his cousin Esther, David is overwhelmed by incredulity and guilt over the sexual liberties that Leo takes. Fleeing his brutal father, David is shocked into unconsciouness after touching the live rail of a street car. Faced, like the reader, with sensory overload, David might as well call it sleep, embracing temporary oblivion as restoration after a long, disorienting day.

To explore the tensions among Albert, Genya, and David, a clanging family triangle rife with resentments and recriminations, Roth appropriates the theories of Sigmund Freud, particularly in describing the powerful Oedipal bond between mother and son as well as the almost patricidal strife between Albert and David. The authority of James Joyce asserts itself, not only in the fact that Roth's account of David Schearl, a surrogate for the author himself, is in effect another portrait of the artist as a young man but also in his lavish use of stream of consciousness and his meticulous deployment of recurrent imagery.

During the two decades surrounding the turn of the twentieth century, massive, unprecedented migration from eastern and southern Europe was radically reshaping American society, and, more effectively than any other novel, *Call It Sleep* records the traumas experienced when the Old World met the New. Many of Roth's immigrants are inspired by the American Dream of enlarged opportunity, while others are repulsed by an urban nightmare. Call *it*, too, *sleep*. Though the Schearls are Polish Jews, the eclectic slum in which they live also serves as home to immigrants and natives from many other backgrounds. Not the least of Roth's accomplishments is his success at rendering the diversity of David's environs. Yiddish is the first language of the Schearls, but English, German, Hebrew, Italian, and Polish are also spoken, in varying registers, by characters in the story. In a novel designed for an anglophonic reader, it would be misleading and demeaning to put fractured English into the mouths or minds of fluent Yiddish speakers when they are assumed to be using their native language. Instead, Roth fashions English prose supple enough to represent the varying speech and thoughts of those who speak and think in other tongues.

Call It Sleep is significant for reflecting a momentous phenomenon that transformed the United States but was ignored by many of Roth's literary contemporaries. In its vivid rendition of a child's-eye view, its dramatic exposure of family tensions, and its creation of a rich linguistic texture, Roth's first novel is an artistic triumph.

MERCY OF A RUDE STREAM

Though they were published separately and can be read independently and autonomously, the four novels that constitute *Mercy of a Rude Stream* are best understood together, as a single narrative sequence. The entire tetralogy follows the coming of age of Ira Stigman, a Jewish emigrant to New York,

from 1914, when he is eight years old, until 1927, when he is twenty-one and a senior at City College. Despite the change in names and the addition of a younger sister, Minnie, Ira seems largely an extension of David Schearl from *Call It Sleep*. He is also a thinly disguised version of Roth himself. The autobiographical basis of the books is made even more apparent by interpolated sections in which an older Ira, an ailing octogenarian author living in Albuquerque, addresses his word processor, calling it "Ecclesias." He comments on his own renewed, belated efforts at writing fiction. Ira as author poses the question that most readers will raise about Roth himself—why, approaching death, does he struggle to record such lacerating memories?

In narrating his story, Ira forces himself to revisit an unhappy childhood and adolescence, in which he and his mother Leah are terrorized by his psychotic father Chaim. When the family moves from the lower East Side to a largely Irish neighborhood in East Harlem, Ira feels rudely wrenched out of an organic, nurturing Jewish community. He recalls the painful details of broken friendships and of his public disgrace when he was expelled from high school for stealing fountain pens. The most agonizing recollections—and the element that has drawn the most attention to Roth's final books—concern Ira's sexual transgressions. The second volume, *A Diving Rock on the Hudson*, offers the startling revelation that, beginning when he was sixteen and she was fourteen, Ira regularly, furtively committed incest with his sister Minnie. He also maintained covert sexual relations with his younger cousin Stella. Recollections of incest continue through volumes 3 and 4 and fuel the author's suicidal self-loathing. The older Ira longs to die but feels compelled to tell his story first, as though narration might bring purgation and even redemption.

Unlike the bravura *Call It Sleep*, much of *Mercy of a Rude Stream* is written in undistinguished prose that is at best serviceable in evoking working-class, urban life during and after World War I. Ira offers details of jobs he held, including stock boy in an upscale food store, soda peddler in Yankee Stadium and the Polo Grounds, and salesman in a candy shop. His sentimental education is very much connected to his intellectual one, and, though his grades are mediocre, Ira thrives in college. Publication of a short story in the student magazine awakens literary ambitions; his friendship with affluent Larry Gordon enlarges Ira's life beyond his own squalid situation. He begins to acquire social graces and to strike on ideas. Ira becomes inebriated with reading, particularly after Edith Welles, the professor who was Larry's lover, becomes Ira's mentor and lover. Edith, who is modeled after Roth's own Eda Lou Walton, introduces Ira to the most influential books and people of New York's bohemian culture. In the final pages of the cycle's final book, *Requiem for Harlem*, Ira bids farewell to his dysfunctional, debilitating family and his loathsome sexual compulsions by moving down to Greenwich Village to live with Edith. The apprentice artist is finally ready to write a novel very much like *Call It Sleep*. Finally, after disburdening himself of excruciating secrets, the eighty-nine-year-old Roth finished writing and prepared at last to call it sleep.

Steven G. Kellman

OTHER MAJOR WORKS

SHORT FICTION: "Broker," 1938; "Somebody Always Grabs the Purple," 1940; "Petey and Yorsee and Mario," 1956; "At Times in Flight," 1959 (parable); "The Dun Dakotas," 1960 (parable).

MISCELLANEOUS: *Shifting Landscape: A Composite, 1925-1987*, 1987 (Mario Materassi, editor).

BIBLIOGRAPHY

Buelens, Gert. "The Multi-Voiced Basis of Henry Roth's Literary Success in *Call It Sleep*." In *Cultural Difference and the Literary Text: Pluralism and the Limits of Authenticity in North American Literatures*, edited by Winfried Siemerling and Katrin Schwenk. Iowa City: University of Iowa Press, 1996. A study of Roth's first novel, the ways in which he represents different languages and voices.

Lyons, Bonnie. *Henry Roth: The Man and His Work*. New York: Cooper Square, 1976. The first book-length study of Roth's early work, it also includes an interview and some biographical information.

Sokoloff, Naomi B. *Imagining the Child in Modern Jewish Fiction*. Baltimore: The Johns Hopkins University Press, 1992. Roth's David Schearl is linked to representations of the child by other Jewish writers, including Sholom Aleichem, Hayim Nachman Bialik, Jerzy Kosinski, Aharon Appelfeld, David Grossman, A. B. Yehoshua, and Cynthia Ozick.

Walden, Daniel, ed. *Studies in American Jewish Literature* 5, no. 1 (Spring, 1979). A special issue of this journal devoted to essays on Roth. Includes a bibliography and an interview with the author.

Wirth-Nesher, Hana, ed. *New Essays on "Call It Sleep."* New York: Cambridge University Press, 1996. A collection of some of the most engaging and useful analyses of Roth's first novel.

_____

PHILIP ROTH

Born: Newark, New Jersey; March 19, 1933

PRINCIPAL LONG FICTION

Letting Go, 1962
When She Was Good, 1967
Portnoy's Complaint, 1969
Our Gang, 1971
The Breast, 1972, revised 1980
The Great American Novel, 1973
My Life as a Man, 1974
The Professor of Desire, 1977
The Ghost Writer, 1979
Zuckerman Unbound, 1981
The Anatomy Lesson, 1983
Zuckerman Bound, 1985 (includes *The Ghost Writer, Zuckerman Unbound, The Anatomy Lesson*, and *Epilogue: The Prague Orgy*)
The Counterlife, 1986
Deception, 1990
Operation Shylock: A Confession, 1993
Sabbath's Theater, 1995
American Pastoral, 1997
I Married a Communist, 1998

OTHER LITERARY FORMS

Five of Philip Roth's short stories are collected along with his novella *Goodbye, Columbus* in a volume bearing that title (1959). A number of his essays, interviews, and autobiographical pieces appear in *Reading Myself and Others* (1975). An unproduced screenplay, *The Great American Pastime*, was anthologized in 1968, and two of his works, *Goodbye, Columbus* and *Portnoy's Complaint*, have been made into films by others. In 1975, Roth began editing a series called Writers from the Other Europe for Penguin Books, to which he contributed several introductions. *The Facts: A Novelist's Autobiography* appeared in 1988. *Patrimony*, a memoir of his father's life, was published in 1991.

ACHIEVEMENTS

Philip Roth emerged as a leading Jewish American writer when his first published book, *Goodbye, Columbus*, won the National Book Award in 1960. Many of his subsequent works involved Jewish characters and specifically Jewish American dilemmas; novels such as *Portnoy's Complaint*, *The Counterlife*, and *Operation Shylock*, in particular, involve characters struggling to reconcile their desires to be fully American during the age of American triumphalism with their deeply ingrained sense of separateness. More than a touch of local color, his depictions of Jewish communities form a base from which to spin— and unspin—national and personal narratives. Along with contemporary writers such as John Barth and Norman Rush, Roth created some of American literature's most memorable and most self-conscious storytellers, the angst-ridden Alexander Portnoy, the irrepressible Nathan Zuckerman, and the outwardly controlled, inwardly crumbling Swede Levov.

Roth's special concern in his work is the relationship between a writer and his subject, which is often closely drawn from his own personal life. His fictional accounts of smothering Jewish mothers, harried Jewish fathers, and illicit love affairs involving Jews in his early work made him notorious among the conservative Jewish establishment during the 1970's. Subsequent depictions of family relationships bearing a close resemblance to his own drew fire from his

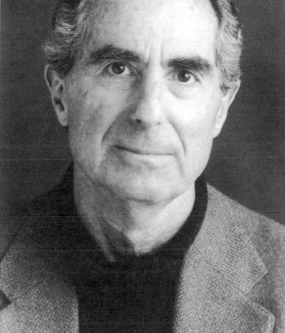

(Nancy Crampton)

ex-wife Claire Bloom, among others. In his later work, Roth brilliantly presented the fascinating relationship between fiction and autobiography, using fictional surrogates, such as Nathan Zuckerman, to explore what he called "counterlives," or the proliferation of possible lives one single person might have lived.

Throughout his fiction, Roth exhibits the abilities of a master comedian. His ear is arguably the best of any contemporary writer, capturing the spoken voice in a wide variety of accents, intonations, and cadences, but his facility with dialogue sometimes leads critics to miss the serious undercurrents of his work. Roth's fiction covers a variety of satiric modes, from the social (*Portnoy's Complaint*) to the political (*Our Gang*) to the literary and academic (*The Professor of Desire*). Whatever mode he adopts, he presents the objects of his satire or comedy in vivid and compelling fashion. Once referred to as preeminently a social realist (as in *Goodbye, Columbus*), he has transcended that mode successfully in such works as *The Counterlife* and

Deception, which show him, as ever, both a consummate craftsman and a tireless experimenter with his medium.

Roth won numerous prestigious awards for his work, including the National Book Critics Circle Award for *Patrimony*, the PEN/Faulkner Award for *Operation Shylock*, the National Book Award for *Sabbath's Theater*, and the Pulitzer Prize for *American Pastoral*.

BIOGRAPHY

Born in the Weequahic section of Newark, New Jersey, on March 19, 1933, Philip Roth learned very early what it was like to grow up Jewish in a lower-middle-class neighborhood of a large metropolitan area. His parents were Beth Finkel and Herman Roth, a salesman for the Metropolitan Life Insurance Company. After he was graduated from Weequahic High School in 1950, Roth worked for a while at the Newark Public Library and attended Newark College of Rutgers University. A year later, he transferred to Bucknell University. Although the family could ill afford the expense of a private college, Herman Roth determined that if his son wanted to go there, he would go. At Bucknell, Roth began writing stories and edited the school's literary magazine. He also had his first love affairs, from which he drew incidents (fictionally transformed, of course) for his subsequent novels. He received his B.A. in English, magna cum laude, in 1954, and he accepted a teaching fellowship at the University of Chicago for graduate work in English.

After receiving his M.A. in English from Chicago, Roth enlisted in the United States Army, but a back injury suffered during basic training resulted in an early discharge. He returned to Chicago to pursue doctoral studies in English but continued writing short stories, which had begun to get published as early as the fall of 1954 in small literary journals such as the *Chicago Review* and *Epoch*. Several of his stories were anthologized in Martha Foley's *Best American Short Stories* and in *The O. Henry Prize Stories*. These awards, the success of his first published volume, *Goodbye, Columbus*, a Houghton Mifflin Literary Fellowship, and a Guggenheim Fellowship persuaded Roth to abandon graduate work in English for a career as a creative writer.

While a graduate student and instructor at the University of Chicago, Roth met and later married his first wife, Margaret Martinson Williams. The relationship was never a happy one, and after a few years they separated, Margaret steadfastly refusing to agree to a divorce. Meanwhile, they spent one year of their marriage (1960) at the Writers' Workshop at the University of Iowa, where Philip served on the faculty. After his first full-length novel, *Letting Go*, was published in 1962, he became writer-in-residence at Princeton University. He later taught English literature at the University of Pennsylvania. His experiences as an academic provided much material for novels, many of which have a university setting or are otherwise peopled by academics.

The publication of *Portnoy's Complaint* in 1969, a year after his estranged wife was killed in an automobile accident, launched Roth's greatest notoriety, especially among the conservative Jewish community in America, and assured his fame as a novelist. He became an increasingly prolific writer, spending part of the year in his Connecticut home and part in London in an apartment near his writing studio. For years he shared his life with the British stage and screen actress Claire Bloom, whom he married in April, 1990. Their difficult relationship and 1995 divorce became a subject of Bloom's memoir, *Leaving a Doll's House*, and received fictionalized treatment in Roth's 1998 novel, *I Married a Communist*.

ANALYSIS

While his early works clearly show the influence of his literary idols—Henry James, Leo Tolstoy, Gustave Flaubert, Thomas Wolfe, and Theodore Dreiser—Philip Roth came into his own as a novelist beginning with *Portnoy's Complaint*, which reveals a unique voice in American literature. His subsequent development parallels his growing interest in other Continental writers, such as Anton Chekhov, Franz Kafka, Fyodor Dostoevski, and particularly contemporary writers such as Milan Kundera, whom Roth assisted in getting his works published in America. Roth's first novels are set squarely in his native land:

in Newark, where he was born and reared; in the great Midwest, where he went to graduate school; and in New York and Philadelphia, where he lived, wrote, and taught literature at several universities. The protagonists of his later fiction travel abroad to Western and Eastern Europe and as far as Hong Kong. Roth's development as a novelist is thus the development, in part, of a growing cosmopolitanism along with a deepening interest in basic human concerns and predicaments.

Chief among those predicaments is the endless struggle between the id and the superego or, in less Freudian terms, between the drive for sensual gratification and the drive for moral uprightness. On the one hand, pulling at his protagonists (all but one of whom are men) is the powerful desire for sexual conquest; on the other is the almost equally powerful desire to lead a morally self-fulfilling and decent life. These drives, conflicting at almost every turn, nearly tear his protagonists apart. Even when, as at the end of *The Professor of Desire*, David Kepesh believes that he has at least achieved a reasonable equilibrium and found peace, a nagging unease enters the picture, upsetting his contentment and providing a presentiment of doom.

Indeed, Roth's heroes, if one can apply that term to such unlikely characters, all seem doomed in one way or another. Their pervasive sense of disaster, however, does not destroy Roth's comedy; it deepens it. The sense of the absurd, of the incongruities of human experience, also pervades Roth's novels and is the source of much rich humor. Moreover, his protagonists usually are fully self-aware; they understand their predicaments with uncommon self-perception, if (more often than not) they are utterly baffled in trying to find a solution to or resolution of their dilemmas. Again, their awareness and frustration combine to make the reader laugh, though the reader must be careful not to let the laughter obscure or nullify the compassion that is also the character's due.

LETTING GO

Roth's first full-length novel, *Letting Go*, sets out all these themes and influences. The principal character, Gabe Wallach, is the educated, sophisticated young son of well-off middle-aged Easterners, who

after a brief stint in the army pursues graduate studies in the Midwest. His mother has recently died, leaving her son with a heavy moral burden: not to interfere in the lives of others as she, regretfully, has done. It is a legacy Gabe finds almost impossible to live up to, until the very end, after he has nearly ruined the lives of several people close to him. Before that, he succeeds, however, in remaining aloof from his widower father, who is lonely and adrift and tries to persuade Gabe to return home. This is Gabe's only success, however, as eventually his father meets and marries a widow who helps him rediscover life's pleasures.

Meanwhile, Gabe has his affairs, none of which works out happily, and his friendships, especially with Paul and Libby Herz, whom he meets during graduate school in Iowa. Paul is a hardworking, highly principled young man who married Libby while they were still undergraduates at Cornell. Their mixed marriage—Paul is Jewish, Libby Catholic—is mainly the result of Paul's misguided sense of devotion and responsibility. Although the passion has long since gone out of their relationship, owing to Libby's poor health and neurotic disposition, Paul remains loyal. Together, they struggle with financial and other problems, including opposition from both sets of parents.

Gabe's life and the Herzes' intersect at various points, invariably with well-intentioned but almost disastrous consequences. At Iowa, Gabe tries to befriend the couple, offers various forms of assistance to them, and finds an unusual attractiveness in Libby, which culminates in little more than a kiss. Their affair, such as it is, focuses partly on Henry James's novel *The Portrait of a Lady* (1880-1881), which Gabe lends to Paul; Libby reads the book, finding in it the last letter Gabe's mother had written him when she lay dying. Both the novel and the letter help to form a bond between Gabe and Libby that endures. Later, when Gabe is teaching at the University of Chicago, their relationship resumes when Gabe helps Paul get a job in his department.

Through Martha Reganhart, with whom Gabe has begun to live, Gabe finds someone who is willing to let her unborn baby be adopted by the Herzes. Paul and Libby have wanted a child and nearly had one, but poverty-stricken as they were, Paul persuaded

Libby to have an abortion. The incidents surrounding that event are both comical and dreadful. Afterward, Libby's health never becomes robust enough for her to risk conceiving another child; hence, they hope to adopt one. The circumstances of trying to adopt a baby involve episodes best referred to as "deadly farce," including several in which Gabe intervenes on their behalf. At the same time, Gabe's relationship with Martha, a divorcee with two young children, deepens and then falls apart, largely the result of his inability to make a full and lasting commitment.

Gabe and Paul thus represent contrasting studies in personality. At the end, Gabe finally learns to "let go," the lesson his mother tried to teach him from her deathbed, but letting go for him means abandoning lover, friends, family, and career to become a wanderer in Europe, whence he writes Libby a final letter. Forwarded many times, an invitation to her adopted daughter's first birthday party arrives with no other message in it. This Gabe takes as "an invitation to be forgiven" for his nearly catastrophic interference in their lives. Gabe, however, feels unable to accept forgiveness—not yet, anyway. He is not "off the hook," he says, and does not want to be let off it, not until he can make some sense of the "larger hook" he feels he is still on.

The larger hook on which Roth's later protagonists wriggle is precisely the dilemma between commitment and freedom that they all experience. Thus, Alexander Portnoy finds himself torn between his desire to maintain his position as New York's Assistant Commissioner for Human Opportunity, a job of considerable responsibility as well as prestige, and his desire to enjoy the full sexual freedoms heralded by the 1960's. For a while he seems to manage both, until his affair with Mary Jane Reed develops into something else—Mary Jane's wish to get married. Her sexual adroitness—she is called "the Monkey"—has kept them together for more than a year, but this demand for full commitment proves too much for Alex, who abandons her in Athens during a trip to Europe in which they have experienced the ultimate of their sexual adventures. Alex flees to Israel, the land of his forefathers, only to find that when he tries to make love there he is impotent. The experience

drives him to seek help from Dr. Otto Spielvogel, a New York psychiatrist.

The novel, in fact, is told as a series of confessions, or therapy sessions, and derives its title from the name Dr. Spielvogel gives to his patient's illness. "Portnoy's Complaint" is "a disorder in which strongly felt ethical and altruistic impulses are perpetually warring with extreme sexual longings, often of a perverse nature." The symptoms of the illness, Spielvogel believes, can be traced to the mother-child relationship, and indeed Portnoy's boyhood has been fraught with problems, often hilarious ones as he recounts them, occasioned by his stereotypical Jewish mother. Sophie Portnoy is a domineering, overprotective mother who frequently drives her young son to distraction, as he tries in vain to understand her demands upon him and her suffocating affection. Jack Portnoy, his father, long-suffering (mostly from constipation) and hardworking, seems unable to mitigate the family relationship, exacerbating Alex's quandary. No wonder he grows up as he does, afflicted with the dilemma, or the condition, Dr. Spielvogel describes. By the end of the novel, after the long unfolding of his tales of woe, all Alex hears from his therapist is, "Now vee may perhaps to begin. Yes?"

In a sense, that *is* just the beginning. Roth tried hard to progress further in his next "family" novel, *My Life as a Man*, which took him years to write. Meanwhile, he wrote the pre-Watergate Nixon satire *Our Gang* and the satirical burlesque of American culture *The Great American Novel*, which takes the great American pastime, baseball, as its focus and its vehicle. Yet it was the fictionalized account of his marriage—or rather, the affair which turned into marriage through a masterful trick—that really preoccupied Roth in the years following *Portnoy's Complaint*. Roth invents not one fictional surrogate but two: Peter Tarnopol, a writer, and Tarnopol's own fictional surrogate, Nathan Zuckerman. The two "useful fictions" that precede "My True Story," or the novel proper, are Roth's early experiments with "counterlives" developed at greater length and complexity in his finest novel, *The Counterlife*. They provide alternative, "possible" accounts of Peter Tarnopol's early life—and, through Tarnopol's, Roth's.

Peter's problem is trying to discover how he ever got involved with Maureen, his wife of ten years, from whom he is finally separated but who refuses to grant him a divorce. Related to this problem is the current one he experiences with his beautiful and dutiful lover, Susan Seabury McCall, a young widow who provides Peter with apparently everything he wants; however, she is essentially too submissive, too dull. One part of Tarnopol misses the excitement—no, the frenzy—that Maureen brought into his life, while another part hates it. Though it does not follow a strict chronological sequence, the novel becomes an account of his experience first with Maureen, then with Susan, whom he finally also leaves and determines to give up, despite her attempted suicide. Writing the novel in guarded solitude at an artist's colony called Quahsay, Tarnopol retrospectively tries to understand his plight.

THE BREAST

The Breast is another novel written during this period when Roth was trying to compose *My Life as a Man*. This book is the sequel to *The Professor of Desire*, written a few years later. Like Portnoy, Zuckerman, and Tarnopol, Kepesh is a nice Jewish young man brought up by caring parents in a sheltered Jewish environment, who early in life experiences the pleasures of emancipation and of the flesh, first as a Fulbright scholar living in London, then as a graduate student at Stanford University. Like Tarnopol, he becomes the victim of a femme fatale, a woman who, like Maureen, has "lived." Helen Baird is a striking beauty, but more than her beauty, her experience living abroad as the lover of a Hong Kong millionaire attracts Kepesh. They become lovers and later, disastrously, husband and wife. Gradually, Kepesh sinks into the condition of becoming Helen's servant, if not slave, until she flees once more to Hong Kong, hoping to reunite with her erstwhile lover. He will not have her, and David must rescue her, but in the process he becomes aware that their life together is over, and they get divorced.

David now moves back to New York, where he gets a job teaching comparative literature, meets Claire, a young schoolteacher, and falls in love with her. During this period he undergoes psychotherapy

to "demythologize" his marriage to Helen; Dr. Klinger becomes Claire's advocate against David's brooding over Helen. During this period also, David's mother dies, and like Gabe Wallach in *Letting Go*, Kepesh has a widowed father on his hands. Yet the elder Mr. Kepesh is by no means as demanding as Dr. Wallach; on the contrary, he is delighted with his son's liaison with Claire (as he was not with the marriage to Helen) and hopes that they will marry. The novel ends as the young couple along with the elder Mr. Kepesh and a friend of his, a concentration camp survivor, spend a weekend in a bungalow in the Catskills, not far from where David grew up, and where he now ponders his future. He seems to have everything he wants or needs, but somehow he feels dissatisfied, anxious, afraid that ennui will set in and destroy everything or that some other disaster will overtake them.

It does, but the disaster is hardly anything that David Allen Kepesh anticipates. About a year later, as his lovemaking with Claire has almost ceased, he turns into a six-foot, 155-pound breast. In *The Breast*, Roth partly follows Franz Kafka's "The Metamorphosis" (1915), an obvious, but not exact, source for this novella. Unlike Kafka, Roth tells the story from Kepesh's point of view, using the first-person narrator to convey something of the real anguish Kepesh feels and his amazement at his condition. If he was beset by a dilemma at the end of *The Professor of Desire*, his bafflement there is nothing to what he experiences now. Despite the aid and comfort that everyone—Claire, his father, Dr. Klinger—tries to give him, he remains at the end as bitterly confused and disturbed as ever, thoroughly unreconciled to his lot except as he vainly tries to persuade everyone that what has happened has not happened, that it is all a bad dream from which eventually he will awake, or that he has simply gone mad.

THE GHOST WRITER

Roth's next novels form a trilogy to which he appends an epilogue, all under the title of *Zuckerman Bound*. Again, Roth borrows from autobiography to write his fiction, his own "counterlife." In *The Ghost Writer*, the first of the series which make up this portrait novel, Nathan Zuckerman is at the beginning of a promising career as a writer. He has published a few short stories and is now staying at an artist's colony (Quahsay again), trying to write more. Since he is not far from the home of E. I. Lonoff, a writer he much admires, he visits and is welcomed by the older writer and his wife. Zuckerman is surprised by them in many ways: first by Lonoff's austere life as a writer, spent endlessly turning his sentences around, and then by Hope Lonoff's conviction that her husband would be better off without her. By birth and upbringing far different from him—she is a New England Yankee as opposed to his immigrant origins—she is temperamentally unsuited to the kind of life they have led for many years. She is convinced, moreover, that Lonoff would be better off living with a younger woman, like Amy Bellette, a former student from the nearby women's college where Lonoff teaches, who obviously adores him. Lonoff refuses, however, to entertain any such thoughts of abandoning Hope or realizing his fantasy of living abroad in a villa in Italy with a younger woman.

Nathan is persuaded to stay the night, especially after meeting Amy Bellette, who is also staying there on a brief visit. Nathan has his own fantasy that evening, that Amy is really Anne Frank, author of the famous diary, who has miraculously survived death camps. They fall in love, get married, and thus show his parents and other relatives that, despite what they may think from some of his stories, he is a good Jewish man, the worthy husband of the famous Jewish heroine. As a tribute to Roth's skill as a writer, the account of Amy's survival is quite credible; moreover, it shows Roth's understanding of compassion for the suffering in the death camps. At the same time, it supports Nathan Zuckerman's qualifications as a writer, justifying Lonoff's praise and encouragement of the young man.

ZUCKERMAN UNBOUND

Lonoff's belief in Nathan is borne out in *Zuckerman Unbound*, the second novel in the trilogy. By now Zuckerman is the author of several novels, including the notorious *Carnovsky*. This novel is to Zuckerman what *Portnoy's Complaint* was to Philip Roth, and *Zuckerman Bound* recounts experiences similar to those Roth must have had, such as the no-

toriety that involved mistaking his fictional characters for his real mother and father. Zuckerman is accosted in the streets, on the telephone, and apparently everywhere he goes by people who think they know him because they mistake his confessional novel for actual autobiography. Yet fiction and autobiography are at best distant relatives; for example, unlike Zuckerman's father, who is extremely upset by his son's novel and turns on him at his death, Roth's parents remained proud of their son's accomplishments and never took offense at what he wrote, notwithstanding the uproar in the Jewish community.

Zuckerman is beset by would-be hangers-on, such as Alvin Pepler, the Jewish marine, once a quiz-show winner but deprived of full fame by a scam reminiscent of the Charles Van Doren scandal. Zuckerman's brief affair (actually, no more than a one-night stand) with the Irish actress Caesara O'Shea is a comic treatment of the adventures attributed to Roth by columnists such as Leonard Lyons, who insisted he was romantically involved with Barbra Streisand, though actually Roth at that time had not so much as met her. Finally, Zuckerman's trip to Miami with his brother, Henry, which ends with their estrangement on the way home after their father dies of a stroke, is totally different from actual events in Roth's life. All these incidents are, after all, "counterlives," imaginative renderings of what might have or could have happened, not what did.

THE ANATOMY LESSON

Similarly, in *The Anatomy Lesson*, the third novel in the series, Roth borrows from incidents in his own life but fictionalizes them so that no one-to-one equivalence can be made. Now, some years later, Zuckerman is afflicted with a strange ailment that causes him intense pain, from which he gets temporary relief only from vodka or Percodan. He can no longer write, but four different women tend to his other needs, including his sexual ones. Among them are a young Finch College student, who also works as his secretary; his financial adviser's wife; an artist in Vermont who occasionally descends from her mountaintop to visit; and a Polish émigrée, whom Zuckerman meets at a trichological clinic (in addition to everything else, Zuckerman is losing his hair).

In despair of his life and his calling, Zuckerman decides to give up writing and become a doctor. He flies to Chicago, where he hopes his old friend and classmate, Bobby Freytag, will help him get admitted to medical school. En route on the plane and later from the airport, Zuckerman impersonates Milton Appel, a literary critic modeled on Irving Howe, who early praised Roth's work and then turned against it. In this impersonation, however, Zuckerman pretends that Appel is a pornography king, editor and publisher of *Lickety Split* and an impresario of houses of pleasure. The impersonation is triggered by Appel's appeal, delivered through an intermediary, to Zuckerman to write an op ed article on behalf of Israel.

Zuckerman as the porn king Appel provides plenty of material for those who like to see Roth as antifeminist but who thereby miss the point of his fiction. It is a tour de force, a persona adopting a persona—miles away from the real Roth. At his office in the hospital, Bobby Freytag reminisces with Zuckerman for a bit and then tries to talk him out of his scheme. Only the next day when, under the influence of too much Percodan and vodka, Zuckerman falls and fractures his jaw, does the healing begin, in soul as well as body. Zuckerman learns what real pain and loss are, as he walks the corridors of the hospital watched over by his friend, who also weans him from his drug addiction. At the end, Zuckerman is a chastened and more altruistic individual, though still deluded into thinking he could change into a radically different person.

THE PRAGUE ORGY

The epilogue, *The Prague Orgy*, shows Zuckerman not as a doctor but as a famous novelist undertaking an altruistic mission on behalf of an émigré Czech writer whose father had written some excellent, unpublished stories in Yiddish. Unfortunately, the Czech's estranged wife holds the stories but will not release them. Zuckerman manages to fetch them without having to sleep with her, despite her pleas, but the stories are immediately confiscated by the police, who then escort him out of the country (this is pre-1989 Czechoslovakia). Zuckerman thus learns to accept his limitations and to become reconciled to them. He accepts that he will not become "trans-formed into a cultural eminence elevated by the literary deeds he performs."

THE COUNTERLIFE

In *The Counterlife*, Nathan and his brother are briefly reunited, mainly so that Roth can explore alternative versions of a fate that first befalls one and then the other. The plot thus doubles back on itself more than once and is too complex for summary treatment. Despite its complexity, the novel is not difficult to follow and is full of surprises that intellectually stimulate as they also amuse the reader. Particularly interesting are the episodes in Israel, where Henry has fled to start a new life, bringing Nathan after him to discover what is going on. Much is going on, including a considerable amount of discussion from characters on the political left and right, with Nathan clearly in the middle. The latter part of the novel finds Nathan in London, married to an English divorcee with a child and trying to come to grips with British anti-Semitism, including some in his wife's family. Throughout the novel, Roth implicitly and sometimes explicitly raises questions about the nature of fiction and the characters that inhabit it.

He does so, too, in *Deception*, though in that novel, written almost entirely in dialogue, the experiment takes on a different form. Here, Roth drops his surrogate, Nathan Zuckerman; his main character, present in all the dialogue, is called Philip, who also happens to be a novelist who has written about a character named Zuckerman. Thus Roth seems here to speak in his own voice, though of course he does not, quite: He merely makes the partition separating him from his characters that much thinner, almost to the point of transparency, as when he takes on the critics who claim that when he writes fiction, he does autobiography, and vice versa. The novel is filled with discussions between "Philip" and his lover, who proves to be the woman Nathan married in *The Counterlife*; thus, much of the talk is naturally about fiction.

SABBATH'S THEATER

Roth turned away briefly from his various author personas to write the wickedly funny *Sabbath's Theater*, a novel about an aging pornographic puppeteer obsessed with death and socially proscribed forms of sex. Mickey Sabbath's perverse confessions and the absurd situations Sabbath creates for himself may remind some of Roth's early novel *Portnoy's Complaint*. Yet whereas Alexander Portnoy was tortured by his conflicting desires to be a model American and to satisfy his sexual longings, there is no such conflict in Sabbath. He revels in his capacity to break bourgeois mores, becoming a *cause célèbre* for First-Amendment defenders in the 1950's, when running his randy street theater resulted in his arrest. Since that time, he has lived in a small New England town teaching college drama, until he is forced to resign for sexually harassing female students. Now he is locked in an acrimonious marriage with his wife Roseanna, a recovering alcoholic, and mourning the death of his sexually adventurous mistress, Drenka. If *Portnoy's Complaint* revolved around Portnoy's confessions, *Sabbath's Theater* revolves around Sabbath's unapologetic reveling in nastiness. Through Sabbath's repellent diatribes against the Japanese, women, and self-help groups, Roth draws a figure for whom readers will find little sympathy. Because Sabbath himself seems so thoroughly jaded, many critics have decried the novel's sentimental turn toward Sabbath's past, into the death of his much admired brother in World War II and the resulting demise of his mother, to contextualize Sabbath's bitterness.

AMERICAN PASTORAL

Roth portrays another bitter and obsessed character in *American Pastoral*, but in this novel the stakes are higher and the perspective a degree removed. Merry Levov is the stuttering teenage daughter of a beauty queen and a successful assimilated American Jew. She grows up in a prosperous New Jersey suburb in a loving home, the center of her father Swede's ideal, his "American pastoral." Then life changes. Merry's protests against the Vietnam War turn into ever more violent, clichéd complaints against American imperialism, capitalism, bourgeois complacency, and, finally, her family's own success story. She bombs the town's post office, killing a well-loved doctor and challenging her father's understanding of his life and his country. The story is told through her father's tortured pursuit of both his daughter and the reasons for her rage. Roth deftly weaves social criti-

cism into this compelling story for an insightful depiction of an entire generation blindsided by the great upheavals of the 1960's. Zuckerman reappears to interpret Swede Levov's story as an epic clash between the American innocent pursuing upward mobility and the return of the repressed violence inherent in that American Dream. Merry Levov, Zuckerman says, "transports him out of the longed-for American pastoral and into everything that is its antithesis and its enemy, into the fury, the violence, and the desperation of the counterpastoral—into the indigenous American berserk."

I MARRIED A COMMUNIST

Just as ambitious as *American Pastoral*, Roth's next book, *I Married a Communist*, takes the 1950's as its historical backdrop. Nathan Zuckerman again acts partly as interpreter and partly as scribe, this time to his former high school teacher, Murray Ringold. Murray tells the story of his brother Ira, a radio actor who was blacklisted during the era of McCarthyism. Ira becomes a populist hero to many, including young Nathan, until his actress wife, exasperated by Ira's repeated betrayals with other women, exposes him by publishing a tell-all book, *I Married a Communist*. The book destroys not only Ira's heroic profile but also his career, for he becomes blacklisted. The plot once again alludes to events in Roth's own life, particularly to his divorce from Claire Bloom. Like the character Eve Frame, Bloom had a talented teenage daughter who caused friction in the marriage. Also like Eve Frame, Bloom published a memoir in which she, like Roth in several of his novels, exposed intimate details of their personal life. Ira's unthinking acceptance of the Communist Party and his subsequent devolution into an angry, bitter cynic give this political novel a decidedly conservative overtone.

Surveying the corpus of Roth's longer fiction, one may conclude that he is a novelist who rarely repeats himself, even as he reworks ideas, issues, and dilemmas or reintroduces characters and locales. This is the essence of the "counterlife" motif that was present in Roth's work from the start but became explicit only later on.

Jay L. Halio, updated by Julie Husband

OTHER MAJOR WORKS

SHORT FICTION: *Goodbye, Columbus and Five Short Stories*, 1959.

NONFICTION: *Reading Myself and Others*, 1975, expanded 1985; *The Facts: A Novelist's Autobiography*, 1988; *Patrimony: A True Story*, 1991.

BIBLIOGRAPHY

Cooper, Alan. *Philip Roth and the Jews*. Albany: State University of New York Press, 1996. Part of the SUNY series in modern Jewish literature and culture, this work examines Judaism in literature and Roth's handling of Jewish characters. Includes bibliographical references and an index.

Halio, Jay L. *Philip Roth Revisited*. New York: Twayne, 1992. This solid overview is excellent for the beginning student of Roth. Replaces the 1978 Twayne edition, with much biographical and critical data.

Jones, Judith Paterson, and Guinevera A. Nance. *Philip Roth*. New York: Frederick Ungar, 1981. This slim volume traces three themes throughout Roth's work: the "good" Jewish child's struggle to free him- or herself from parental coercion and guilt, the "conflict between high-minded moral responsibility and sensuous self-assertion," and the absurdities of contemporary American society, which elicit satirical treatment from the novelist. Each essay contains discrete sections devoted to individual novels and is very accessible.

McDaniel, John M. *The Fiction of Philip Roth*. Haddonfield, N.J.: Haddonfield House, 1974. An early review of Roth's work, the volume's concern with the "Jewish question" and "fictional hero types" may seem dated, but it is valuable for its close reading of Roth's early stories.

Milbauer, Asher Z., and Donald G. Watson, eds. *Reading Philip Roth*. New York: St. Martin's Press, 1988. Borrowing its title from Roth's own collection of essays, this book begins with an informative interview with Roth and includes essays by writers such as Roth's friends Aharon Appelfeld and Milan Kundera. Most of the volume, however, contains fairly heavy readings of Roth's fiction by European and American critics such as Clive Sinclair, Martin Green, Sam B. Girgus, Donald Gartiganer, and Hana Wirth-Nesher. Indexed, but no bibliography.

Pinsker, Sanford. *The Comedy That "Hoits": An Essay on the Fiction of Philip Roth*. Columbia: University of Missouri Press, 1975. A witty, learned, and perceptive short book on Roth by a Jewish scholar who understands the language and structure of Roth's novels exceptionally well. No index or bibliography, but secondary references are footnoted.

_____, ed. *Critical Essays on Philip Roth*. Boston: G. K. Hall, 1982. An outstanding collection of some of the best essays and reviews on Roth. It includes excellent essays by Mark Schechner, Sarah Blacher Cohen, and Morton Levitt, a personal memoir by Theodore Solotaroff, and the famous attack by Irving Howe called "Philip Roth Reconsidered." Contains an index but no bibliography.

Rodgers, Bernard F., Jr. *Philip Roth*. Boston: Twayne, 1978. This solid critical study by Roth's bibliographer contains a wealth of biographical and other information, along with clear and perceptive readings of the novels. Fully annotated and indexed, it also contains a "Select Bibliography" of both primary and secondary sources.

SUSANNA ROWSON

Born: Portsmouth, England; 1762
Died: Boston, Massachusetts; March 2, 1824

PRINCIPAL LONG FICTION

Victoria, 1786
The Inquisitor: Or, Invisible Rambler, 1788
Mary: Or, The Test of Honour, 1789
Charlotte: A Tale of Truth, 1791 (published in the United States as *Charlotte Temple*, 1797)
Mentoria: Or, The Young Lady's Friend, 1791
The Fille de Chambre, 1792 (better known as *Rebecca: Or, The Fille de Chambre*, 1814)
Trials of the Human Heart, 1795

Reuben and Rachel: Or, Tales of Old Times, 1798
Sarah: Or, The Exemplary Wife, 1813
Charlotte's Daughter: Or, The Three Orphans,
    1828

OTHER LITERARY FORMS

Susanna Rowson was a prolific, well-rounded writer. Besides her ten works of long fiction, she produced three volumes of poetry: *Poems on Various Subjects* (1788), *A Trip to Parnassus* (1788), and *Miscellaneous Poems* (1804). Between 1794 and 1797, she wrote about seven dramatic works, most of which were probably performed but not published; the most popular of these was *Slaves in Algiers: Or, A Struggle for Freedom* (1794). She also composed the lyrics for numerous songs and contributed to the production of at least two periodicals: the *Boston Weekly Magazine*, for which she wrote articles on a

(Library of Congress)

wide range of subjects and apparently also served as editor between 1802 and 1805; and the *New England Galaxy*, which was founded in 1817 and for which Rowson wrote chiefly religious and devotional prose pieces. Finally, she wrote and had published six pedagogical works: *An Abridgement of Universal Geography* (1805), *A Spelling Dictionary* (1807), *A Present for Young Ladies* (1811), *Youth's First Step in Geography* (1818), *Exercises in History* (1822), and *Biblical Dialogues* (1822).

ACHIEVEMENTS

Opinions of Rowson's achievements as a novelist have fluctuated widely since the nineteenth century. Earlier critics were high in their praises of the moral tendency of her work and her storytelling skills, while later estimates have tended to disparage both and to find her writing limited and ordinary.

Among the handful of Americans who wrote novels in the late eighteenth century, Rowson was both the most prolific and most coherent. As Dorothy Weil has shown, a well-developed system of aims and values emerges from all of Rowson's writings and gives her work notable unity and breadth. In particular, as Weil has demonstrated, Rowson's belief in the equality of the sexes and her concern with feminist issues and positive goals for women deserve wider recognition than they have received. In other respects, Rowson's novels are typical of the novelist's theory and practice in newly independent America and are interesting and revealing as a window on the nature of fiction in the late eighteenth century.

BIOGRAPHY

Susanna Haswell Rowson's remarkably full, active life began in Portsmouth, England, where she was born in 1762. Her mother died shortly after, and Rowson's first visit to America occurred when her father settled and married in Massachusetts and, in 1767, brought his daughter to join him, his new wife, and his three stepsons. Some of Rowson's experiences during this visit, including a shipwreck, appear later in *Rebecca*. By 1778, she was back in England, her father's apparently doubtful loyalty having led the fledgling American government first to confiscate his property and intern his family and him and then return them to England.

Rowson's initiative and independence soon revealed themselves. By the time she was in her twenties, she had secured a position as governess in the family of the Duchess of Devonshire, beginning a life of service through teaching and writing; she also helped her father gain a pension, and she began publishing her fiction and poetry.

Rowson was twenty-four when her first novel, *Victoria*, appeared in London in 1786. The work's subtitle, a sign of her aims and interests as a novelist, declared that *Victoria* was "calculated to improve the morals of the female sex, by impressing them with a just sense of the merits of filial piety." Later in 1786, she married William Rowson, and though he was apparently an ineffectual person, they shared an interest in music and theater and remained married for thirty-eight years.

Between Rowson's marriage and her immigration to America in 1793, she wrote prolifically, publishing five novels and two books of verse. In 1792, following the failure of her husband's hardware business, the couple, along with Rowson's sister-in-law Charlotte, decided to join a theater company and tour the British Isles. The decision was fateful, because in 1793 they were seen by Thomas Wignell, an American who was recruiting players for the theater he was about to open in Philadelphia. Wignell took them to America in 1793, and thus began Rowson's American period, during which she blossomed both as a performer and as an educator amd moralist who attempted to serve others through many activities, including novel writing.

Rowson published her four-volume novel, *Trials of the Human Heart*, in 1795, and continued acting and writing in the theater until 1797. Then, once again, she turned her life and her career of service in a new direction. She opened a Young Ladies' Academy in Boston in 1797. Starting with only one pupil, she had one hundred and a waiting list within a year. She continued to instruct young women in her school until 1822, but she also continued to do so through her writing. She published the novels *Reuben and Rachel* and *Sarah* as well as another book of poetry,

various songs and odes, and a theatrical piece. Her major works, however, were the six pedagogical books she wrote and published between 1805 and 1822 for use in her school.

All of this got done even as Rowson found time and energy for rearing several adopted children and for supporting church and charity, which included holding the presidency of Boston's Fatherless and Widow's Society. When she died on March 2, 1824, Rowson left in manuscript her final work, *Charlotte's Daughter*, the sequel to *Charlotte*; it was published posthumously in 1828.

ANALYSIS

Benjamin Franklin certainly had neither women nor novelists foremost in his mind when he published his "Information for Those Who Would Remove to America" in 1782. Yet Susanna Rowson, who would remove to America a little more than a decade later, was exactly the sort of migrant Franklin would have wanted. America, he said, required useful members of society rather than persons "doing nothing of value, but living idly on the labour of others." Citizens of the new nation "do not inquire concerning a stranger, *what is he?* but *what can he do?* If he has any useful art, he is welcome; and if he exercises it and behaves well, he will be respected by all that know him."

Rowson understood the kind of labor Franklin meant, and the years she spent in America as writer and educator show that she cared about becoming a useful, respected member of society. Doing this as a novelist was no easy task, for while fiction might be popular among young readers, the "common verdict with respect to novels," as Noah Webster expressed it in 1788, was that "some of them are useful, many of them pernicious, and most of them trifling."

Rowson responded by producing novels that consistently stress Franklin's service ideal, especially for the young women she saw herself addressing. "We are not sent into the world to pass through it in indolence," says one of Rowson's wise widows to the heroine of *Trials of the Human Heart*. "Life which is not serviceable to our fellow creatures is not acceptable to our Creator."

Such was the ideal that Rowson held up to the women for whom she wrote and that she herself sought to embody by writing novels that would be an honor to herself and a benefit to society. For many modern readers and writers of fiction, there may well be something objectionable about regarding novel writing as akin to useful arts of the kind Franklin mentions with approval in his prospectus—farming, carpentry, tanning, weaving, shoemaking, and the like—but Rowson and a few other scrupulous early American novelists were in effect trying to do just that: produce fiction that would be of direct, lasting benefit to its readers by helping them live happy, fulfilled lives.

Rowson's novels typically exhibit a clear moral purpose and an unmistakable connection between virtue and happiness. The strong didactic element which modern readers may find distasteful in Rowson and her contemporaries was in fact the essential finishing touch for many early American novelists. Of what use, these writers might have said, was an uncultivated field or undeveloped talent? Almost from the outset, Rowson stressed that the moral purpose of her fiction and the well-being of her readers were more important to her than financial or critical success.

Rowson realized, of course, that there were too many novels which were either trifling or pernicious, as Webster said, and did their readers no good. Her awareness was sharp enough that in *The Inquisitor* she offers a detailed summary of what she considered a typical "Modern Novel." To Rowson, the problem with such novels was that they were more likely to harm than improve the reader, mislead rather than enlighten. They tended to encourage vice and error by showing that they lead to happiness rather than suffering, thus making them attractive instead of repugnant to the unwary reader. Novels such as these, and writers such as Jean Jacques Rousseau and Johann Wilhelm von Goethe, were said to misuse the power of fiction by ennobling errant behavior such as suicide or adultery and charming the reader into accepting and even living by untruths made too attractive.

For Rowson and her contemporaries, fiction was never to make error noble and vice fascinating, deluding the reader and ultimately causing her unhappiness; it should have exactly the opposite psychological effect. Rowson would have agreed with what Columbia College student Daniel Tompkins, in 1794, called fiction's "true design and intent." Novels, he wrote in his journal, "are representations of men and things qualified to excite to the love of virtue and the detestation of vice." Such novels used the power of narrative and the feelings and imaginations of readers to move the reader away from vicious behavior and toward that which was virtuous and rewarding. As Rowson describes this process in her preface to *Trials of the Human Heart*, she hopes to "awaken in the bosoms of . . . youthful readers a thorough detestation of vice, and a spirited emulation to embrace and follow the precepts of Piety, Truth, and Virtue."

At the heart of Rowson's novels, then, is her concern with what she likes to call the "true felicity" of her readers and her belief that virtue leads to happiness as surely as vice and error do not. In changing the reader for the better, the novels seek to be both moral and affective. They work through the feelings and imagination and end in well-rooted, satisfying behavior. A closer look at three representative novels of Rowson's will show how she tried to achieve these results.

CHARLOTTE

As Dorothy Weil observes in her study of Rowson, *In Defense of Women* (1976), *Charlotte* (entitled *Charlotte Temple* in the American edition of 1797) is one of the wonders of American literature, primarily because of its immediate and long-lasting popularity. It was widely read upon its publication in America in 1797—about twenty-five thousand copies sold shortly after it appeared—and by the middle of the nineteenth century it had become the most frequently published popular novel in America. By 1905, it had gone through as many as two hundred editions, and in 1932, in his bibliographical study of Rowson, R. W. G. Vail claimed that more people had read *Charlotte* than any other work of fiction printed in America. Fueled by the novel's popularity, legends about the real-life identities of its main characters have flourished. In New York City's Trinity Churchyard, the grave of Charlotte Stanley, supposedly the model for the novel's heroine, now bears a slab with the inscription "Charlotte Temple."

The novel is also a revealing example of one kind of narrative by which Rowson tried to affect her readers as useful fiction was supposed to do. She does this by relating and having her readers imaginatively participate in one of the eighteenth century's favorite plots: the story of the causes and consequences of youthful error and delusion in which the heroine herself, and thus the reader, learns by bitter experience to love virtue and hate vice. Rowson also presents the heroine's learning process in a moral context of clearly stated values, thereby insuring that the nature of virtue and vice is well defined throughout.

The main events of the novel are easily summarized. Charlotte Temple is a fifteen-year-old student at a boarding school in Chichester, England; the year is 1774. One day, she meets Lieutenant Montraville, who, finding Charlotte attractive and eventually deciding that he loves her, persuades her to see him and then to accompany him to America. Although she doubts herself the moment she decides to go, Charlotte nevertheless leaves her friends and her parents behind and, in the company of her lover, his deceitful friend Belcour, and her evil teacher Madmoiselle La Rue, sails to America. Once there, Montraville falls in love with another woman even as Belcour deceives him into believing that Charlotte has been unfaithful; Montraville abandons her, though she is now pregnant with his child. Virtually alone and friendless, Charlotte has her baby and dies just after her distracted father has finally located her. Montraville kills Belcour in a duel and lives out his days married to the woman he loves but still sad and remorseful over his part in Charlotte's ruin. La Rue later dies in misery brought on by her life of dissipation.

This is the grisly narrative that Rowson attempts to make useful and instructive to the "young and thoughtless of the fair sex." She does this first by anchoring the events of the story in a context of contrasting values. In a novel designed to make virtue lovely and vice and error detestable, the reader should be very certain just what virtue and its opposites are. Among the important good people offered as attractive examples of the life of virtue are Char-

lotte's parents and Mrs. Beauchamp, her only real friend in America. These characters are distinguished by that active service to others that Rowson valued so highly. Each possesses a feeling heart and a generous hand, and each knows the exquisite satisfaction of comforting less fortunate fellow creatures. Moreover, these characters have given up fast-paced city life in favor of the simple, contented rural existence that befits men and women of feeling.

In contrast to such characters are the novel's bad people, especially La Rue and Belcour, who represent the false pleasures and values of selfishness. These clear contrasts between virtue and vice are established early in the novel and are regularly reinforced by a narrator who both relates and freely comments on the story. "Oh, my dear girls, for to such only am I writing," she says at one point in a typical utterance, "listen not to the voice of love unless sanctioned by parental approbation . . . pray for fortitude to resist the impulse of inclination when it runs counter to the precepts of religion and virtue."

The secret of fiction's power to further the happiness of readers lay not in static commentary and contrast, however, as much as in *process*—the learning process which the feeling reader would go through by participating imaginatively in the experience of the novel's heroine, Charlotte Temple. She is a poor deluded child who must learn by adversity that virtue leads to happiness, vice to misery. The novel is thus a psychological history of the causes and effects of error and vice, with Charlotte starting the novel as "an innocent artless girl" and ending "a poor forsaken wanderer" suffering "extreme agitation of mind" and "total deprivation of reason" as a result of her mistakes.

Rowson tries to show that Charlotte's basic problem is her inability to resist an impulse when it runs counter to the precepts of religion and virtue. Despite the fact that she was reared by exemplary parents, Charlotte falls, and she does so, Rowson shows, because she allows herself to come under the influence of bad people who disable her power to resist dangerous, delusive inclinations in herself—just what was said to happen to weak, unwary readers of pernicious novels. Charlotte thus ends as "the hapless victim of imprudence and evil counsellors," the "poor girl by thoughtless passion led astray."

Like bad novels, the evil counsellors who overwhelm Charlotte's discretion and good sense are capable of using appearances—particularly the power of language and dress—to disable and deceive. A sorceress possessed of the "art of Circe," La Rue convinces Charlotte to meet, and later to continue seeing Montraville against her own better judgment. Thus does Charlotte "forsake the paths of virtue, for those of vice and folly." Eloping to America with Montraville, becoming pregnant and then left abandoned "to die with want and misery in a strange land," the very opposite of a useful and respectable member of society, Charlotte is "held up as an object of terror, to prevent us from falling into guilty errors." The reader, Rowson would hope, sees and feels that deviation from virtue is "an object of detestation," and vice and error themselves as detestable as their opposites, embodied in happy characters, are desirable. The ideal reader is the "reader of sensibility" who will "acutely feel the woes of Charlotte" and therefore behave so as to avoid them.

MENTORIA

Implicit in *Charlotte* is a pattern for a second type of useful novel which Rowson employed in *Mentoria*. As noted, the third-person narrator of *Charlotte* both relates and comments on the tale, making sure her readers understand its moral import and learn from it. In *Mentoria*, the nameless, wholly reliable preceptress of *Charlotte* becomes the story's main character. Her name is Helena Askham, and, in a series of letters to Lady Winworth's three daughters for whom she earlier was governess, Helena dispenses stories and lessons based on her own experience, which are designed to instruct young women on subjects of concern to them.

Like Charlotte, Helena combines humble origins with a good education. Unlike Charlotte, she is strong enough to resist impulses which run counter to the precepts of religion and virtue. She is able to do so because, sensitive and feeling though she is, she is also "endowed with discernment and sense far superior to the generality of young women of her age."

She shows her mettle early on when, placed in a situation very much like Charlotte's with Montraville, she is courted by Lady Winworth's son. Unlike Charlotte, who allowed the rhetoric and appearance of La Rue and Montraville to disable her judgment and excite errant, delusive hopes, Helena displays the control of feeling and pleasing inclination that is the mark of Rowson's strong women, and that enables her to stifle her rising passion for her suitor and reject him. Later, he does in fact marry someone closer to him in rank and fortune, and so does Helena, until her husband's death leaves her free to become governess and then mentor to the three Winworth children.

As this wise widow, a woman who, like the narrator of *Charlotte*, combines sensibility with strong good sense, Helena becomes the central character of *Mentoria*. The several stories she relates, therefore, are meant to do what the single story of Charlotte did: Use the power of narrative as a memorable, striking means of instruction for young women, a way of making "a lasting impression on the minds of fair readers" and thereby of advancing their happiness.

For example, the life of Helena's friend Louisa Railton is offered as "a model by which every young woman who wishes to promote her own felicity, will regulate her conduct." The beauty of the virtue of filial piety is illustrated by Louisa's choosing, after her mother's death, "a low roofed mansion, scanty meals, and attendance on a sick peevish father, to the lofty apartments, plenteous table, and variety of amusements she might have enjoyed with Lady Mary," her rich relative. She thereby gains, however, "a contented happy mind, [and] serenity dwelt in her heart and cheerfulness beamed in her eyes. . . . She lived beloved by all and died universally regretted." Made desirable and attractive, and distinguished as in *Charlotte* from its selfish opposite, the virtue of filial devotion should impress the reader and prompt her to imitation. As Helena writes her pupils, "Be wise, my dear children, follow Louisa's example, so shall your lives be happy and your last moments peace." Helena continues to deal similarly with such topics as friendship, reputation, love, pleasure, and marriage, using the force of the striking instance to impress readers with the felicity of the virtuous life and the miseries of vice and error.

TRIALS OF THE HUMAN HEART

In *Trials of the Human Heart*, Rowson demonstrates a third type of "useful fiction." Her aim is to achieve the same effect as before—"to awaken in the bosoms of my youthful readers," as she says in the novel's preface, "a thorough detestation of vice, and a spirited emulation, to embrace and follow the precepts of Piety, Truth and Virtue." Like *Charlotte, Trials of the Human Heart* is a story of adolescent initiation, but rather than involving the reader in the misfortunes of a heroine such as Charlotte whose imprudence is her undoing, Rowson offers the character of Meriel Howard, who is the undeserving victim of the cruelty or caprice of others and as a result suffers through what one character calls "some of the heaviest trials to which the human heart is incident"—four volumes' worth, in fact, related through letters exchanged among the characters.

Like other Rowson heroines, Meriel is artless and innocent at the start—having indeed spent much of her childhood in a convent—and she possesses a generous heart as well. As she writes her convent friend Celia, "I am weak as an infant, whenever a scene of distress or happiness meets my eye; I have a tear of sympathy for the one, and a smile of gratulation for the other." Thus endowed, Meriel leaves the convent and enters a world that ends up causing her far more distress than happiness.

The first incidents of the novel, when Meriel is about sixteen, are typical of the pattern of disappointed expectation that repeats itself in Meriel's life and occasions her learning and uttering many lessons about life. On her way home to Bristol, she thinks about the coming reunion with her parents, whom she has not seen for most of her childhood. "I pictured them to myself, as very amiable old people—and, in fancy, felt their embraces and kissed off the tears of joy I saw falling from their eyes." What she finds instead is a "suffering saint" of a mother, her settled melancholy the result of living with a husband who is cruel and unfeeling and a son notable for "frigid coldness." Meriel soon discovers that her father—who much later in the novel turns out *not* to be

her father—is a freethinker and a hypocritical villain, concealing under the "mask of integrity and honour every vice which can disgrace human nature." Indeed, it was because of her father's vitiated morals that Meriel was originally placed in a convent. She now finds him ardently pursuing an adulterous affair; after she succeeds in breaking that up, she herself becomes the object of his amorous attention, an event one character describes as "too dreadful, too shocking to human nature, to wear even the face of probability."

Soon after, Meriel reflects that she no doubt has many more trials yet to endure, and she is absolutely right. In one episode after another, she—like her counterpart Rebecca, the heroine of the novel of the same name—attracts the compromising notice rather than the solicitude of married men and the venom rather than the pity of other women. As Meriel remarks later, looking back over her life, "how hard is my fate. Possessed as I am of a heart moulded to compassion, glowing with universal affection toward my fellow creatures, I am constantly thrown among people, whose every feeling is absorbed in self."

For Meriel as for the reader of this and virtually every other Rowson novel, the purpose of the heroine's experiences is to teach about truth and error—what Meriel calls the "useful lessons taught me in the school of adversity." Born to be the sport of fortune, Meriel learns that "this is a sad—very sad world to live in.—For if we love anything we are sure to lose it." The truly important lesson, however, follows on this. Having so painfully discovered the error of her innocent belief that "every heart glowed with humanity, friendship and sincerity toward each other," Meriel periodically entertains the opposite error. "What a world this is," she writes to her enviably placid convent friend. "Were it not impious, I could wish I had never entered it."

Despair is indeed impious, and the heroine, like the reader, learns that such feelings run counter to the precepts of religion and virtue. Unlike Charlotte, however, Meriel is capable of pulling back from harmful vice and error. The proper response to misfortune is, first, to bear up under it; one's duty, as

Meriel says, is "to submit without repining, to the will of Him, who never lays on his creatures the rod of affliction but for some wise purpose." Second, one must serve, not retreat: "We are not sent into the world to pass through it in indolence," Meriel is told. "Remember, that life which is not in some measure serviceable to our fellow creatures, is not acceptable to our Creator." As Meriel and the reader learn, the suicidal response in any form is never appropriate. At the end of the novel, Meriel anticipates a happy marriage and hopes both to deserve and preserve her good fortune "by exerting the abilities with which I am amply endowed to chear the desponding heart, sooth the afflicted spirits and soften the bed of pain."

Like other Rowson heroines, Meriel has found the secret of happiness. For her readers, Rowson wanted nothing less. Living happily in the real world of human folly and disappointment is the ideal which her many novels and her own varied life embody. To have found so many ways to demonstrate that ideal is surely a tribute to her strength and her inventiveness.

Michael Lowenstein

OTHER MAJOR WORKS

PLAYS: *Slaves in Algiers: Or, A Struggle for Freedom*, pr., pb. 1794; *The Female Patriot*, pr. 1795; *The Volunteers*, pr., pb. 1795; *Americans in England*, pb. 1796, pr. 1979 (revised as *The Columbian Daughter*).

POETRY: *Poems on Various Subjects*, 1788; *A Trip to Parnassus*, 1788; *Miscellaneous Poems*, 1804.

NONFICTION: *An Abridgement of Universal Geography*, 1805; *A Spelling Dictionary*, 1807; *A Present for Young Ladies*, 1811; *Youth's First Step in Geography*, 1818; *Exercises in History*, 1822; *Biblical Dialogues*, 1822.

BIBLIOGRAPHY

Davidson, Cathy N. *Revolution and the Word: The Rise of the Novel in America*. New York: Oxford University Press, 1986. Davidson's superb interdisciplinary study of the eighteenth century "reading revolution" highlights commonplace responses to the extraordinarily popular *Charlotte Temple* and analyzes Rowson's complex characterization of the villain Montraville. Argues that Rowson's plots of "sexual crime and feminine punishment" expose society's double standard of justice. Rowson's other novels are briefly discussed.

Fielder, Leslie A. *Love and Death in the American Novel*. Rev. ed. New York: Stein & Day, 1966. Although a classic study of the novel, Fiedler defines sentimentalism and specifically *Charlotte Temple* as "not literature" and "completely a woman's book"; he is equally mean-spirited in his denigration of Rowson's literary skills. The study has minor use for placing Rowson in the literary context of "Prototypes and Early Adaptations."

Loshe, Lillie Deming. *The Early American Novel*. New York: Columbia University Press, 1907. Significant biographical details support Loshe's contention that Rowson relied upon personal experience for many of her themes. This study is of most value, however, for placing Rowson's work in the context of the early sentimental novel: Unlike most authors of "domestic melodrama," Rowson developed realistic rather than romantic plots.

Spengemann, William C. *The Adventurous Muse: The Poets of American Fiction, 1789-1900*. New Haven, Conn.: Yale University Press, 1977. Spengemann argues that *Charlotte Temple* is a "pure" example of "the spirit of domesticity." Although he criticizes the emotionalism of Rowson's characterizations and her extravagant style, Spengemann acknowledges the value Rowson placed on factuality. Most useful for its discussion of the distinguishing features of American "domestic romances."

Stern, Julia A. *The Plight of Feeling: Sympathy and Dissent in the Early American Novel*. Chicago: University of Chicago Press, 1997. Studies *Charlotte Temple*, Hannah Webster Foster's *Coquette*, and Charles Brockden Brown's *Ormond*.

Vail, R. W. G. *Susanna Haswell Rowson, the Author of "Charlotte Temple": A Bibliographical Study*. Worcester, Mass.: American Antiquarian Society, 1933. Vail's comprehensive bibliography of Rowson's writings includes not only standard lists of editions of her various novels but also such delightfully unusual features as the parts Rowson portrayed as an actress and auction records that attest to her continuing popularity among collectors. Brief biographical essays arc also included.

Weil, Dorothy. *In Defense of Women: Susanna Rowson (1762-1824)*. University Park: Pennsylvania State University Press, 1976. An astute analysis of Rowson's literary aspirations and accomplishments and of her extensive concern for the religious, moral, and intellectual education of young women. Weil's text incorporates extensive excerpts from rarely published works by Rowson and includes an excellent bibliography of primary and secondary sources.

(Jerry Bauer)

SALMAN RUSHDIE

Born: Bombay, India; June 19, 1947

PRINCIPAL LONG FICTION

Grimus, 1975

Midnight's Children, 1981

Shame, 1983

The Satanic Verses, 1988

Haroun and the Sea of Stories, 1990 (fable)

The Moor's Last Sigh, 1995

The Ground Beneath Her Feet, 1999

OTHER LITERARY FORMS

The Jaguar Smile: A Nicaraguan Journey (1987) is a book of travel and political observations, written following Salman Rushdie's visit to Nicaragua in July, 1986, as guest of the Sandinista Association of Cultural Workers. Rushdie has also published several short stories; the best known is "The Prophet's Hair," which appeared originally in the *London Review of Books* in 1981 and has been reprinted in *The Penguin Book of Modern British Short Stories* (1987). A fable in the style of *The Arabian Nights' Entertainments*, *Haroun and the Sea of Stories* was published in 1990, and a collection of short stories, *East, West: Stories* (1994), included "The Prophet's Hair" and the dazzling "At the Auction of the Ruby Slippers."

ACHIEVEMENTS

Though furor and indignation followed publication of each Rushdie novel, each also received critical praise and rave reviews. *Midnight's Children* won the James Tait Black Memorial Prize, the English Speaking Union Literature Award, and the Booker Prize; it has been translated into twelve languages. Though *Shame* was banned in Pakistan, as *Midnight's Children* had been in India, it too received critical plaudits for its seriocomic portrait of Pakistani life. No writer since English satirist Jonathan Swift has aroused as much ire from so many sources, notwithstanding the notoriety of *The Satanic Verses*, which won the Whitbread Award as best novel of 1988. On February 14, 1989, the Ayatollah Ruhollah Musavi Khomeini, the fundamentalist spiritual leader of Iran, issued a *fatwa* (a proclamation concerning a matter of Muslim faith) that called for Rushdie's death as an enemy of Islam and sanctioned similar reprisals against those who published or distributed the book.

Rushdie's novels, actually modern picaresques, explore the tragicomic results of lost identity; they portray in exuberant, highly inventive, satirical style what he considers the consequences of living in cultures that have become mixed, distorted, and diluted through combinations of expediency, political ineptitude, and exploitive religion.

BIOGRAPHY

Ahmed Salman Rushdie was born in Bombay, India, on June 19, 1947, less than two months before the end of the British Raj. His father, Anis Ahmed Rushdie, and his mother, Negin Butt Rushdie, were Muslims with ties to the region that would become Pakistan. The family did not at first join the Muslim exodus to Pakistan that began after partition in September, 1947. Even so, they became increasingly aware of their minority status as Muslims in a predominantly Hindu state.

Though the Rushdies were nominally Muslim, they also identified with India and with Great Britain. Rushdie's father had been educated in England, at the University of Cambridge, and had determined to rear his son and three daughters to appreciate their multicultural background. As a result, Rushdie had, from boyhood, access to a variety of works in his father's library. It became a recurring argument between father and son, however, that the boy did not make adequate use of this wealth of books. His private reading during boyhood was generally limited to an English translation of the *The Arabian Nights' Entertainments* (or *One Thousand Nights and a Night*). His mother, considered "keeper of the family stories," regaled young Rushdie and his sisters with a wealth of anecdotes on family history; he remembered them all, and would adapt many of them in his writings.

Rushdie was sent to the Cathedral and John Connon School, a British-administered primary school with Anglican affiliation located in Bombay. As his sister Sameen recalls, "he mopped up all the prizes," was not very adapt at games, read extensively in both serious and popular literature and loved both American B films and Hindu hit films. In 1961, at the age

of thirteen, he was sent to the prestigious Rugby public school in England. At Rugby, however, although the masters were generally fair-minded, Rushdie felt alienated from his classmates, the "old boys" from British established families, who subjected him to cruel pranks. Rushdie compensated for the pranks and racial taunts by excelling at debates, appearing in theatrical productions, and thriving in academic areas, winning the Queen's Medal for history and securing (but refusing) a scholarship at Balliol College, Oxford.

In 1964, the Rushdie family had emigrated to Karachi, Pakistan, and while Rushdie was not enthusiastic about returning to England, he had been offered a scholarship at his father's university, King's College, Cambridge, and amidst the India-Pakistan war in 1965, his father literally pushed him onto an airplane for the United Kingdom. Rushdie's attitude toward his father was often argumentative, and there was a serious rupture in their relationship when he entered Cambridge. Shortly before the elder Rushdie's death in 1987, there was a rapprochement between the two men.

At Cambridge, Rushdie decided to read for a degree in history, and eventually attained a 2.2 (that is, "second rate") degree, but he thrived in the social atmosphere of the mid-1960's. "It was a very good time to be at Cambridge," he said. "I ceased to be a conservative snob under the influence of the Vietnam War and dope." He continued his involvement in theater, and upon his graduation in 1968, he attempted to work in the entertainment industry in Pakistan, found censorship was inescapable, and returned to London where he worked in amateur theatricals and supported himself as a copywriter at the J. Walter Thompson advertising agency. He had already begun to think of himself as a writer, however, and he completed a never-published novel in 1971, *The Book of the Pir*, which he described as "post-Joycean and sub-Joycean."

Grimus was Rushdie's first published novel, written while he was still working irregularly in advertising to provide an income. It was a commercial failure and never was published in the United States, but it was favorably reviewed in London's *The Times Liter-*

ary Supplement (January 21, 1975), and it attracted notice and the beginnings of an audience for Rushdie. It took several short stories and five years before Rushdie produced *Midnight's Children*.

Midnight's Children won rave reviews on both sides of the Atlantic, but it also offended a great many people, among them the family of Indira Gandhi, then Prime Minister of India. Rushdie made a public apology for the cutting satirical references to her and specific members of her family, but he made no changes in subsequent editions of the book. The affair was exacerbated by the fact that Rushdie's accusations coincided with the Indian army's assault on the Golden Temple of the Sikh Muslims. The assassination of Mrs. Gandhi in 1984 brought a tragic end to this series of events.

Having offended large numbers of Indians with *Midnight's Children*, Rushdie published *Shame*, his portrayal of the blood feuds that led to the deposing and execution of Pakistan's prime minister Zulfikar Ali Bhutto by his former protégé, Muhammad Zia al-Haq. The same pattern followed publication of this novel, but this time Rushdie had offended the Pakistanis, India's enemies. Again there were great commercial success and critical plaudits, but *Shame*, which Rushdie called *Midnight's Children's* "antisequel," was denied publication in Pakistan just as *Midnight's Children* had been banned in India.

By 1985 Rushdie was sought after by every major publisher. Viking Penguin offered him an advance of $850,000 for rights to his work then in progress, leading to a rancorous break with Liz Calder, an old friend trying to establish her own publishing firm. Everyone in publishing circles knew that the new book would cause a sensation, but no one, not even Rushdie, could have known that *The Satanic Verses* would make him a marked man. After February 14, 1989, with the Khomeini decree of death on his head, Rushdie's life came to resemble the plots of his novels. The threat of assassination forced him to close his London home and go into hiding. Viking Penguin received thousands of threatening letters. Bookstores that did not remove *The Satanic Verses* from their shelves were threatened with bombings. There were riots in Bombay; at least five people were killed and

dozens injured in Islamabad, Pakistan; two Muslim leaders were killed in Brussels, Belgium, after they expressed opposition to censoring the book. Two bookstores in Berkeley, California, were firebombed, and a bomb blast in London, which killed the terrorist who had placed the bomb, was attributed to the anti-Rushdie campaign. Rushdie's Japanese translator was murdered, his Italian translator was wounded in a knife attack, and his Norwegian publisher was almost killed in a shooting.

Although some members of the British political establishment expressed a personal distaste for Rushdie, and authors such as John le Carré and Roald Dahl (who called him a "dangerous opportunist") claimed that Rushdie deserved his predicament, Scotland Yard was assigned the task of protecting him. His wife, the American novelist Marianne Wiggins (Rushdie's first marriage to the English publicist Clarissa Luard ended in divorce in 1985), joined Rushdie as he was moved from one safe house to another, but shortly after he went into hiding, they separated, and a year later they were divorced. Writers such as William Styron, Milan Kundera, and Norman Mailer called upon the governments of democratic nations to exert pressure on Iran, and, without making his position public, horror writer Stephen King insisted that any book chain that gave in to threats and removed Rushdie's books from their shelves would have to remove King's as well. In 1990, Rushdie issued a statement that he had "converted" to Islam to show "people who viewed me as some kind of enemy that I wasn't one," but he realized that he had acted out of "despair and disorientation" and "made strenuous steps to get out of the false position."

When Rushdie made a secret trip to the United States in 1992, the Bush administration avoided contact with him, but in 1993 he was able to arrange a brief meeting in the White House with President Bill Clinton. The British government of Prime Minister John Major was more supportive, albeit discreetly, than its predecessor. In the third year of his concealment, Rushdie began to write again, remarking "If I can't write, then, in a way, the attack has been successful." His fable *Haroun and the Sea of Stories*, written as a means of speaking to his son Zafar, whom he could not contact while in hiding, was published in 1990, and a collection of short fiction, *East, West*, was released in 1994. After five years of labor, *The Moor's Last Sigh* was published in 1995. During the mid-1990's, Rushdie appeared in public with greater frequency, unannounced but usually greeted with considerable enthusiasm, and was active in encouraging international resistance to the *fatwa*. In 1998, some more moderate members of the Iranian government moved toward a withdrawal of the *fatwa*, but Rushdie's safety was still not entirely guaranteed, and he remained cautious in terms of his movements at the end of the twentieth century.

ANALYSIS

Many Western readers, ignorant of Islam and Hinduism, the 1947 partition of the Indian subcontinent and the creation of Pakistan, the India-Pakistan war of 1965, and the Pakistani civil war of 1974, may tend to read Salman Rushdie's novels as bizarre entertainments. This is unfortunate, since each is a picaresque allegory into which the author has inserted details from his own life in order to prove that myth is history, today is yesterday, and the life of one person is integral to the history of nations. Rushdie masks events here and there and relentlessly mixes Persian and Hindu myths, but the hiatus in logic that this method creates is merely to prove his contention that an Anglo-Indian-Pakistani is a person with a hole in the body, a vital place in which there is a haunting void.

MIDNIGHT'S CHILDREN

Midnight's Children is Rushdie's allegorical picaresque on the history of the modern state of India. Its narrator, Saleem Sinai, is one of those whose birth coincided with the hour and day India achieved independence: midnight, August 15, 1947. He and many others, including Jawaharlal Nehru, India's first prime minister, considered that these "midnight's children" were singled out, privileged by the hopeful hour at which they began their lives. Saleem discovers that he does indeed have special powers; he can, in his mind, summon all the other children born during the midnight hour of August 15, 1947, and when a boy he does so nightly, establishing the "Midnight Children's Conference," a forum he hopes will augur well for organizing the leaders of the new state.

Saleem's family is prosperous; they reside in one of Bombay's more affluent sections on an estate of homes once owned by an Englishman, William Methwold, who left India on the very day the Raj ended. Through a bizarre series of events (an accident at school that reveals that his blood type corresponds to neither parent and the subsequent confession of Mary Pereira, a nurse who had worked at the hospital at which Saleem was born), Saleem's family discovers that Mary had intentionally switched children, giving the Sinais a child of one of Bombay's poorest families. Only Saleem, through his telepathic powers, knows that the Sinais's real son, reared as a street urchin named Shiva, is actually an illegitimate child of the Englishman Methwold. Though the Sinais make no attempt to locate their own boy and do accept Saleem as their own, Saleem recognizes Shiva as his nemesis and realizes that Shiva may well destroy him.

All the children of midnight have some special talent or ability by virtue of their time and date of birth: Saleem's telepathic skills, Shiva's extraordinarily strong knees (which he uses to kill the Indian street entertainer he believes is his father), and the abilities of Parvati-the-witch, who seeks to use her talents only for good. All the children become caught up in the political machinations that follow upon India's independence and the creation of Pakistan. Saleem's family, aware that they are part of India's unwanted Muslim minority, emigrate to Pakistan. This event, plus the fact that Saleem no longer wishes to have any contact with Shiva, the rightful heir of the Sinais, ends Saleem's nightly summonings of the Midnight Children's Conference. Once in Pakistan, Saleem discovers that his telepathic powers do not work. He tries, instead, to develop his exceptional powers of smell, utilizing his huge nose to smell danger, injustice, unhappiness, poverty, and other elements of Pakistani life.

Saleem and his family become caught up in Pakistan's 1965 war with India. His former countrymen become his enemies, and all of his family are killed in the war, except his sister, who has taken the name

Jamila Singer and become famous as a singer of patriotic songs. When the east wing of Pakistan secedes in 1973 and declares itself the independent state of Bangladesh, Saleem enlists in Pakistan's canine patrol, the Cutia, performing the function of a dog to sniff out traitors. Pakistan's devastating loss in the war leaves Saleem without a country. Ultimately, it is Parvati-the-witch who uses her magic to make him disappear and return him to India.

Saleem marries Parvati but is unable to consummate the marriage. Whenever he tries to do so, he sees the decaying face of Jamila, the woman who had been reared as his sister. Saleem had loved Jamila, but also had come to recognize that their nominal brother-sister relationship would not allow her to be his. Out of frustration, Parvati takes Shiva, now a major in India's army, as her lover. She gives birth to his child, named Aadam, whom Saleem acknowledges as his own son.

Shiva, the destroyer, supervises the slum clearance project that not only eliminates the Bombay quarter in which the magicians had lived but also kills Parvati and many of her magician colleagues who had refused to leave their homes. Saleem is one of those arrested and brought to Benares, the town of the widows. Here he is imprisoned, forced by Shiva to name and identify the skills of the children of midnight, and released only after having been forcibly sterilized. Oddly, those arrested as a result of Saleem's information do not blame him; they, too, are sterilized.

Much more happens in *Midnight's Children*. The novel is structured as a family history that reaches back to Saleem's grandparents and describes the political circumstances in India after World War I, through World War II and the end of the Raj, to the war with Pakistan and the Pakistani civil war. It is also highly mythic. Sinai, the surname of the narrator, masks the name of the Arabian philosopher Avicenna (Abu ʿAli al-Husain ibn ʿAbd-Allah ibn Sina; 980-1037), who saw the emanations of God's presence in the cosmos as a series of triads of mind, body, and soul. The triads appear in the three generations of Sinais who appear in the novel, but the three religions of India—Hinduism, Islam, and Christian-

ity—which also appear, do nothing to reverse the downward course of India's fortunes after 1947. Sin is the ancient moon god of Hadhramut, who acting at a distance can influence the tides of the world. He is represented by the letter *S* and is as sinuous as the snake. Appropriately, Saleem discovers his son Aadam in the care of a master snake charmer, Picture Singh. Sinai is both the place of revelation, of commandments and the golden calf, and the desert of barrenness and infertility that is Rushdie's view of modern India.

Saleem's nose resembles the trunk of the elephant deity, Kali, who is the god of literature, and the huge ears of Saleem's son Aadam carry the motif into India's future. Shiva is the Hindu god of destruction and reproduction, a member of the trinity that includes Brama and Vishnu. The closing chapters of the novel find Saleem the manager of a Bombay pickle factory owned by his former nurse, Mary Pereira, the woman who had originally exchanged him for the true son of the Sinais, underscoring the motif of absurd continuity, pickled history, and Saleem's huge nose, which is called a cucumber as often as it is an elephant's trunk.

The most savage satire of the book is reserved for Indira Gandhi, daughter of Nehru and, until her 1984 assassination, Prime Minister of India. Rushdie repeatedly cites the famous newspaper photograph in which her hair was white on one side, black on the other to symbolize hypocrisy. He ridicules Sanjay Gandhi, her son, now also dead, as the mastermind of India's slum clearance and birth-control plans. Specific members of Gandhi's cabinet appear in the novel with appendages to their titles, such as "Minister for Railroads and Bribery." Gandhi's campaign slogan "Indira is India, and India is Indira," which Rushdie often quotes in these contexts, thus becomes a dire prophecy. It is little wonder that distribution of *Midnight's Children*, published during India's state of national emergency, was prohibited. The novel also made Rushdie persona non grata in the country of his birth.

SHAME

Shame is what Rushdie called his "antisequel" to *Midnight's Children*. It has picaresque and seriocomic elements that resemble those of the earlier novel, but its characters are Pakistanis, members of the power elite that had its historical counterpart in the circle of deposed prime minister Zulfikar Ali Bhutto and Bhutto's protégé, the man who engineered the coup and Bhutto's trial and execution, Muhammad Zia al-Haq. *Shame* created as much consternation in Pakistan as *Midnight's Children* had in India, with precisely the same result: The novel was banned in Pakistan, and Rushdie was considered subversive.

The title of *Shame* derives from the Urdu word *Sharam*, and it contains an encyclopedia of nuance the English barely suggests: embarrassment, discomfiture, indecency, immodesty, and the sense of unfulfilled promise. Rushdie thus explores here themes that are similar to those of his first novel. All the characters experience shame in one or another of these forms, as well as some its converse, shamelessness.

Shame also maintains the highly mythic, literary tone of *Midnight's Children*. Its unprepossessing hero is evocatively named Omar Khayyám Shakil, a paunchy doctor of great promise with the name of the Persian poet known for the twelfth century *Rubáiyát*, the erotic lyric poems, imitated in English by Edward FitzGerald in 1859. Rushdie's Omar is born in a crumbling house called Nishapur (also the town of the historical poet's birth), once the mansion of an Englishman, Colonel Arthur Greenfield, in a Pakistani backwater identified only as "Q," but perhaps Quetta.

The circumstances of Omar's birth are ambiguous. He has three mothers: Chhunni, Munnee, and Bunny Shakil. These three sisters all consider him their son, and none discloses which of them actually gave him birth; nor will they disclose the name of his father, though the reader learns that he is an Englishman. Omar's situation is thus a metaphor of the mixed cultural legacy Rushdie often describes. Indeed, Rushdie often speaks of himself as a man with three mothers: India, Pakistan, and England. The house in which Omar is reared is a labyrinth, a relic of the British Raj; its corridors lead to rooms unoccupied for generations, and Omar, who in his early boyhood is prohibited from leaving the house at any

time, is frightened out of his wits when he ventures too far and sees that the water-seeking roots of a tree have punctured the house's outer walls. All of this is Rushdie's metaphorical description of the state of mind of a person with mixed and hostile origins: alienated, loveless, relentlessly, fearfully traversing the labyrinth of the mind, and feeling shame. Omar's only glimpse of the world outside Nishapur is through his telescope, appropriately since the poet for whom he was named was also an astronomer.

The novel is filled with a wealth of characters whose backgrounds are similarly symbolic and complex. Rushdie draws them together both through family relationships and through their individually shameful actions as well as their capacity to feel shame. For example, Bilquìs Kemal Hyder is a woman reared in Bombay, India, by her father, Mahound "the Woman" Kemal, owner of a motion-picture theater. The epithet regularly applied to her father is simultaneously an indication of his motherly solicitude for his daughter and a jibe at his having lost his masculinity by assuming the burden of child rearing. After her father dies in a terrorist bomb blast that also destroys his theater, Bilquìs is rescued by Raza "Razor Guts" Hyder, Rushdie's version of Zia al-Haq, an ambitious young military officer who takes her as his bride and returns to the family home in Karachi, Pakistan, the country created by partition of the Indian subcontinent. Thrust into an uncompromisingly Muslim environment, she finds herself shamed when she is unable to bear Hyder a son. Of their two daughters, Sufiya Zinobia Hyder and Naveed "Good News" Hyder, the first is perpetually childlike, the result of a mistreated case of meningitis. Bilquìs and Hyder's second daughter, "Good News," atones for her mother's relative infertility by bearing twenty-seven children.

The focus of *Shame* is the rise to power of Omar's companion in dissipation, Iskander "Isky" Harappa, based on Zulfikar Ali Bhutto. Isky gives up drinking and womanizing in middle age, adopts the veneer of a devout Muslim, and seizes power after the loss of Pakistan's east wing. For a time he remains popular, assisted by his beautiful unmarried daughter, Arjumand "Virgin Ironpants" Harappa, Rushdie's satiric depiction of prime minister Benazir Bhutto. Isky's wife, Rani Humayun Hyder, remains out of the lime- light on the family's isolated estate, and weaves shawls that document all of her husband's acts of shame—a twist on the Penelope motif of Homer's *Odyssey* (c. 800 B.C.E.). By the time Isky is hanged in a military coup, Rani has completed eighteen of them. (Rushdie enumerates the details of each in an angry excursus modeled on a Homeric epic catalog.)

When Hyder seizes power, he encourages the trial and conviction of Isky Harappa. A curious combina- tion of circumstances causes Harappa's death, and Hyder orders the corpse hanged, ostensibly carrying out the court's sentence of execution. Hyder's in- creasing concern is, however, the deviant behavior of his daughter Sufiya Zinobia. Though well past twenty, she has the mental age of less than ten. Hyder accepts Omar Shakil's offer to marry her, made out of shame for his past womanizing and Platonic love for the young woman whose life he had saved. Sufiya Zinobia is, however, aware that some act about which she knows nothing regularly accompanies marriage. She twice escapes from the Hyder house, where she is literally imprisoned (recalling Shakil's own im- prisonment in youth), allows herself to be raped at random by street-walking men, then decapitates the men who have raped her. The villagers who discover these decapitated corpses create the legend of a wild white panther to explain the murders, but Hyder knows that his daughter is the killer and fears that she will eventually decapitate him.

When Hyder's downfall appears imminent, he, his wife Bilquìs, and Shakil escape to the closed man- sion of Shakil's youth, and Shakil's three mothers give them sanctuary. Shakil quickly realizes, how- ever, that the three old women plan to kill Hyder in reprisal for his having ordered the death of their younger son, Babar Shakil, for his terrorist involve- ments. This they do, though not before the accidental death of Bilquìs. Shakil dies soon thereafter, shot by Talvar Ulhaq, Hyder's son-in-law and former state police chief. The pantherlike figure of Sufiya Zino- bia observes the carnage, with Harappa's daughter Arjumand hovering as a vision of a future of "a new cycle of shamelessness."

Rushdie's point, developed through these and other complexities of plot, is that shame and shame- lessness develop through religious and political fail- ure; the images of Islam and Pakistan that he invokes are filled with parricide and cruelty, but never genu- ine and simple love. That those who destroy one an- other are related by family as well as national ties merely compounds the tragedy and the shame. Rushdie's Pakistan is presented as "a failure of the dreaming mind."

THE SATANIC VERSES

The Satanic Verses is Rushdie's strongest indict- ment of politicized religion, mixed cultural identity, and insensitive, arbitrary officialdom. Its tone is al- legorical, picaresque, satiric, and irreverent. Those who know details concerning the founding of Islam, British politics, and contemporary London will rec- ognize the objections made to the book; those un- aware of these particulars will likely be puzzled by the novel's character and chronological shifts and may even wonder why it has caused such conster- nation.

The novel begins with an explosion, a passenger airplane destroyed by a terrorist bomb as it flies over the English Channel. Only two passengers survive: Gibreel Farishta and Saladin Chamcha, two actors of Indian origin. Miraculously, they float to earth un- harmed. Farishta, whose first name is that of the an- gel Gabriel, has made his reputation playing Krishna, Gautama Buddha, Hanuman, and other Indian deities in films known as "theologicals." Chamcha, a com- plete Anglophile, has achieved fame by doing com- mercial voice-overs in England, though his face is unknown to his admiring audience. With this as background, Rushdie establishes the figure of the an- gel Gibreel (in Islam associated with bringing Al- lah's call to Muhammad) and the apparently diaboli- cal Chamcha, who has traded his ethnic identity for a pseudo-British veneer.

When they land, Chamcha discovers that he has grown horns under his very English bowler, as well as cloven hooves and a huge phallus—this despite his mild demeanor, elegant manners, and proper British appearance. Farishta (whose surname means "sweet") finds that he has a halo, despite his being an unconscionable womanizer. His very trip to England was a pursuit of Alleluia Cone, the British "ice queen" of Polish refugee parents. Cone is an internationally famous mountain climber who had conquered Mount Everest. Rushdie thus mixes the imagery of good and evil, angel and demon; this is an exponential motif of the entire novel. It follows that the British police arrest Chamcha as an illegal immigrant and brutalize him terribly. Farishta, however, because of his angelic appearance, remains free, having charmed the police and having refused to identify Chamcha.

The narrative then abruptly shifts to introduce Mahound, a blasphemous name for Muhammad, the founder of Islam. Edmund Spenser used the name Mahound in *The Faerie Queene* (1590, 1596) to represent a heathen idol reserved for oaths sworn by the wicked. Rushdie's Mahound profanely recreates Muhammad's call from Allah through the angel Gabriel. Mahound, like Muhammad, is a businessman; he climbs Mount Cone and looks down upon the city of sand that Rushdie calls Jahilia, a fictive town that corresponds to Mecca. Mahound's pursuit of his destiny on Mount Cone corresponds to Gibreel's pursuit of mountain climber Alleluia Cone; his dreamfilled sleeps as he awaits the angel Gibreel resemble the trancelike seizures, ever increasing in severity, of Gibreel Farishta.

Mahound's companions are described as the scum of Jahilia (Muhammad's were former slaves), and Rushdie puckishly names one of them "Salman." They have the habit, dangerous in a city built entirely of sand, of constantly washing themselves (a parody of Muslim ritual purification). The twelve whores of Jahilia (which means "ignorance" or "darkness"), reminiscent of Muhammad's twelve wives and known as "Mothers of the Believers," reside in a brothel called the Curtain. Translated as *hejab*, this can be associated with the curtainlike veil worn by pious Muslim women.

Abu Simbel, the name of the village flooded in the 1960's when Egypt constructed the Aswan High Dam, is the name given here to the ruler of Jahilia, a city also endangered by water. Because he recognizes Mahound as a threat to his power, Abu Simbel offers him a deal. If Mahound's Allah will accept a mere three of Jahilia's 360 deities into the new monotheistic religion, he will recognize it and give Mahound a seat on the ruling council. It will not be much of a compromise, Abu Simbel insists, since Mahound's religion already recognizes Gibreel as the voice of Allah and Shaitan (Satan) as the spirit the Quran records would not bow before Adam.

Mahound decides to compromise. He climbs Cone Mountain, consults with his Gibreel, then returns to Jahilia to announce the new verses: "Have you thought upon Lat and Uzza, and Manat, the third, the other? . . . They are the exalted birds, and their intercession is desired indeed." These are the so-called Satan-inspired inclusions of the goddesses of motherhood (Lat), beauty and love (Uzza), and fate (Manat) as daughters of Allah, which the Quran rejects as heresy. Mahound later publicly recants this heretical insertion and flees to Yathrib (the ancient name for Medina), corresponding to the historical account of the *hegira*, Muhammad's flight from Mecca to Medina. Gibreel reappears to announce: "It was me both times, baba, me first and second also me." One can draw implications that Islam was founded by rationalizing good and evil, that its founder was both a sincere mystic and a power-hungry entrepreneur, and that Gibreel, an actor who specializes in impersonating deities, had given at least one bravura performance that changed history.

Rushdie goes on to recount a masked sardonic version of the holy war to establish Islam, continuing to blur the distinction between ancient and modern times. A bearded, turbaned imam in exile in London (which he considers Sodom) is in exile from his homeland, called Desh. When a revolution begins in Desh and overthrows the corrupt empress, named Ayesha (ironically also the name of Muhammad's favorite wife), Gibreel (perhaps the angel, perhaps the actor Farishta, perhaps one and the same) flies the imam to Desh on his back in time to see the carnage. This episode can be interpreted as the recall to Iran of the Ayatollah Khomeini, in exile near Paris until the overthrow of the Shah. When the revolution succeeds, Ayesha metamorphoses into the mother goddess, Al-Lat, she whom Mahound had falsely named a daughter of Allah in the satanic verses.

In a parallel sequence, an epileptic peasant girl, also named Ayesha, arouses the lust of a landowner named Mirza Saeed, whose wife is dying of breast cancer. As Moses led the Israelites out of Egypt, so Ayesha, who declares that her husband the archangel Gibreel has told her to do so, leads the entire village, including Saeed's wife, on a pilgrimage by foot to Mecca. She declares that the Arabian Sea will open to admit them (recalling the parting of the Red Sea in Exodus); butterflies mark their privileged status, and they are Ayesha's only food (recalling the manna of the Israelites). All that the unbelievers see as they watch the pilgrims is their disappearance into the Arabian Sea. The implication remains that Ayesha parts the sea for those who believe; to everyone else, the entire enterprise ends as a cult suicide. This motif emphasizes the novel's focus on migration, which Rushdie claims is its central subject.

Much more happens in *The Satanic Verses*. London, called "Ellowen Deeowen" by Farishta, is beset by ethnic antagonisms. Its police and most whites are brutal racists; its Indians are rogues or displaced mystics. Still, nothing in Rushdie's novel is what it appears to be, and that is his point. Empires and religions alike arise from a combination of noble and sordid motives. It is impossible to admire or hate anything unreservedly; there is evil even in that which appears absolutely good, and, conversely, one can explain evil in terms of good gone awry. Such relativism is hardly new, but the notoriety *The Satanic Verses* has received has obscured the author's point. What is clear is that *The Satanic Verses* is the logical sequel to ideas Rushdie began to develop in *Midnight's Children* and *Shame*, as well as an allegory that strains narrative and religious sensibilities to the breaking point.

THE MOOR'S LAST SIGH

As a kind of permanent immigrant, a man who can neither return to a home country (India) nor feel really at home in any other land, Rushdie has, as Henry Louis Gates, Jr., said, presented a "vision of migrancy as the very condition of cultural modernity." A crucial aspect of this aesthetic position, however, has been an intense examination of the various homelands that formed—and continued to inform—the intellectual, spiritual, and political components of Rushdie's psychological being. Whereas *Midnight's Children* and *Shame* focused on India and Pakistan at specific, contemporary moments in their postcolonial history, *The Moor's Last Sigh* is an attempt to account for and understand the origins and evolution of the complex cultural matrix that Rushdie refers to as "Mother India." Its narrative combines the overall structure of the classic nineteenth century novel, projecting the epic sweep of history with an episodic linkage of individual incidents and characters akin to the picaresque; it is also similar to Eastern story-cycles.

The Moor of the title is Moraes Zogoiby, son of Aurora Da Gama, whose lineage is Indian Muslim, and Abraham Zogoiby, whose ancestors include Muslim and Jewish exiles who were banished from Spain in 1492. Through the course of the novel, Moraes tells the story of his family from the mid-nineteenth century to the present (the 1990's), where he, the lone survivor, has returned to Spain to continue a frustrating quest for his mother's legacy: the Moorish paintings that may reveal the essential truth and meaning of his life. This intricate, swirling mix of history, myth, legend, personal feuds, ethnic rivalries, and disappointed love is both the story of a man trying to make some sense of his life and of his fascinating, driven family. It is also the saga of a country with a long past, an interim as a semisubjugated colonial entity, and a turbulent, troubled present. While much of the narrative is written with the kind of vivid, detailed realism that is one of the marks of Rushdie's style—an abundance of descriptive images and evocative details—there are frequent infusions of mystic moments, almost hallucinatory states of being, apparent intrusions of the supernatural, and other features of a Magical Realism, which contribute to a larger dimension than a historic record. This is especially apparent in the presentation of Aurora Zogoiby as a symbol for India itself, an equivalent to the *Mother India* (the name of a 1957 film, the year of Moraes's birth) that represents all of the clashing, tempestuous qualities exerting an immense emotional pull on its inhabitants. It is also apparent in Moraes's (meaning Rushdie's) exhilarated response to and evocation of the city of Bombay, an urban masculine complement to the more pastoral, and historically traditional, feminine motherland.

Moraes states early in the novel that his account is one of regret, "a last sigh for a lost world" and the world which he re-creates or reimagines is a rich fusion of cultures, a hybrid set in sharp contrast to what Rushdie calls "the fundamentalist, totalized explanation of the world" which he has challenged throughout his work. The novel begins in the region of Cochin, where the West (Europe) and the East (India) met and mingled for the first time. It was the central site of the pepper crop, and among other extended metaphors that are threaded through the novel, spice—the source of the Da Gama family wealth—stands for passionate love. The shift from commerce in the spice trade to the contemporary economics of currency and technology underscores the separation of the human from its most significant strengths and is one of the primary causes of the downward course that the Da Gama line takes.

For Rushdie, love begins as an irresistible rush of physical feeling that overwhelms the senses but then is complicated by the circumstances of family, ambition, and cultural forces beyond individual control. While Moraes maintains that "defeated love would still be love," Rushdie has observed that "the central story of Aurora and Abraham in the book is a story of what happens when love dies." Moraes struggles to fill the "dreadful vortex" of its absence, and though his life in retrospect reveals his failure in all the realms where love matters (nation, parents, partner), his efforts to understand love's power and to use it in accordance with a set of human values redeem his failure.

The loss of Moraes's family foundation due to love's blindness and treachery is balanced by the restoring capacity of the love for a place and by the invigorating experience of artistic consciousness as a means of illumination. *The Moor's Last Sigh* is a paen to a special place, the vanishing (perhaps never existent) India of Rushdie's heart's core, the "romantic myth of a plural, hybrid nation" which he lovingly describes in Aurora's paintings.

A sense of loss permeates the narrative, as Moraes's three sisters, his treacherous lover Uma Sarasvati (possibly based on Marianne Wiggins), many acquaintances, and various semiadversaries die prematurely. Adding to this loss are his estrangement from his parents and his separation from the places he has known as home. As a compensation of sorts, India continues to glow in Moraes's mind, rendered indelibly in Rushdie's verbal paintings. It is the unifying concept for what Rushdie calls "the four anchors of the soul," which he lists as "place, language, people, customs." The sheer size of the India that Rushdie constructs, in addition to a palimpsest of its layers, makes it an elusive, almost chimerical country. *The Moor's Last Sigh*, laced with loss, disappointment, frustration, and anger, is not a pessimistic vision of existence, because even when place, peoples, and customs are removed, language remains, and Moraes—who exhibits all of the verbal virtuosity that is a feature of Rushdie's style—utilizes the powers of language in the service of truth, to his last breath.

Robert J. Forman, updated by Leon Lewis

OTHER MAJOR WORKS

SHORT FICTION: *East, West: Stories*, 1994.

NONFICTION: *The Jaguar Smile: A Nicaraguan Journey*, 1987; *Imaginary Homelands: Essays and Criticism, 1981-1991*, 1991.

BIBLIOGRAPHY

Afzal-Khan, Fawzia. *Cultural Imperialism and the Indo-English Novel: Genre and Ideology in R. K. Narayan, Anita Desai, Kamala Markandaya, and Salman Rushdie*. University Park: Pennyslvania State University Press, 1993. An academic study of the relationship of ideology to imaginative fiction in four Indian novelists writing in English. The section on Rushdie shows how he "debunks myth" in examining postcolonial society to develop "liberation strategies."

Appignanesi, Lisa, and Sara Maitland, eds. *The Rushdie File*. Syracuse, N.Y.: Syracuse University Press, 1990. A survey of critical reaction to *The Satanic Verses*. Contains a chronology of events following the novel's publication, extracts from several interviews with Rushdie, the text of the Khomeini *fatwa*, reprints of representative articles from Europe and the United States, and a series of reflections on religion, censorship, Islam, toleration, and the relation between truth and fiction.

Hamilton, Ian. "The First Life of Salman Rushdie." *The New Yorker*, December 25, 1995, 89-113. An excellent, illuminating presentation of Rushdie's life before the *fatwa*, written with Rushdie's assistance and including accounts from interviews with many of Rushdie's friends and peers.

Harrison, James. *Salman Rushdie*. New York: Twayne, 1992. A good introductory overview, providing a basic biography and a discussion of the historical context from which Rushdie's work emerges.

Mortimer, Edward. "*Satanic Verses*: The Aftermath." *The New York Times Book Review*, July 22, 1990, 3, 25. A discussion of the right to publish offensive literature. Mortimer concludes that genius and literary worth can mitigate such offense and allow publication. Mortimer believes that *The Satanic Verses* is, indeed, a work of genius and not, as some have claimed, an unreadable novel published to provoke controversy. He does, however, suggest that an author's self-imposed censorship has its place in the writing of fiction.

Pipes, Daniel. *The Rushdie Affair: The Novel, the Ayatollah, and the West*. New York: Birch Lane Press/Carol Publishing Group, 1990. This volume also recounts the controversy attending publication of *The Satanic Verses*, though it examines the question from the Muslim point of view. It suggests that the valid arguments of many against

publication were lost in the wake of the Khomeini *fatwa* that decreed Rushdie's death, in effect giving credence to the wild Muslim stereotype held by many Westerners. It also contains information on the historical founding of Islam, which will be helpful to readers of *The Satanic Verses* who are without this background.

Rushdie, Salman. "Salman Rushdie." Interview by John Haffenden. In *Novelists in Interview*, edited by John Haffenden. New York: Methuen, 1985. Conducted following the success and controversy of *Shame*, this interview concentrates on Rushdie's background and contains insights into his early life in Bombay and Karachi, his schooling at Rugby School and Kings College, Cambridge, and his experiences as actor, advertising copywriter, and aspiring author.

Taneja, G. R., and R. K. Dhawan, eds. *The Novels of Salman Rushdie*. New Delhi: Indian Society for Commonwealth Studies, 1992. A wide-ranging compilation of essays by contributors from the Indian subcontinent, covering all of Rushdie's writing through 1992 except *The Satanic Verses*. Provides a perspective beyond the criticism of Anglo-American authors.

Weatherby, W. J. *Salman Rushdie: Sentenced to Death*. New York: Carroll & Graf, 1990. A sensationally written biography of Rushdie that focuses on his difficulties with his family (particularly his father) and his disputes with publishers and agents, fellow writers, and wives. It offers an essentially negative portrait of a brilliant but insecure and ruthlessly ambitious man.

S

ANTOINE DE SAINT-EXUPÉRY

Born: Lyons, France; June 29, 1900
Died: near Corsica; July 31, 1944

PRINCIPAL LONG FICTION

Courrier sud, 1929 (*Southern Mail*, 1933)
Vol de nuit, 1931 (*Night Flight*, 1932)
Pilote de guerre, 1942 (*Flight to Arras*, 1942)

OTHER LITERARY FORMS

An original and accomplished prose stylist, Antoine de Saint-Exupéry published his first two or three volumes as novels before arriving at his definitive literary form, a combination of essay, memoir, fable, and prose poem that is difficult to classify. To this latter category belong his best-known volumes: an autobiography in the form of a novel, *Terre des hommes* (1939; *Wind, Sand and Stars*, 1939); the posthumously published *Citadelle* (1948; *The Wisdom of the Sands*, 1950), consisting of philosophical observations and reflections; and *Le Petit Prince* (1943; *The Little Prince*, 1943), which, published with the author's own watercolor illustrations, has since become an international children's classic.

ACHIEVEMENTS

Saint-Exupéry drew critical attention early in his short life as perhaps the only pioneer aviator with the soul and talent of a poet. Although several other pilots, including Charles Lindbergh himself, had attempted to record on paper their impressions and reflections from the air, only "Saint-Ex," as his friends came to call him, had the literary skill and sensitivity to produce documents, at first fictionalized, that proved to be of lasting value. Since his plane disappeared off the coast of Corsica, presumably shot down by German fighters, Saint-Exupéry's writing has suffered somewhat from both critical and general neglect, perhaps in part because air travel has long since become commonplace. His style, however, remains as fresh and thought-provoking as when his works were first published. Reflective, unobtrusively "classical" in style, and showing erudition lightly worn, Saint-Exupéry's works appear destined to survive and to be remembered long after they have outlived their "historical" or documentary value.

Both at home and abroad, Saint-Exupéry is perhaps best remembered as the author of *The Little Prince*, a substantial prose work written and destined for children but one that has found a wide and appreciative audience among adults as well. Perhaps best summarized as an illustrated parable of relativity, or at least of relative importance (thereby recapitulating the author's major contributions as a writer-pilot), *The Little Prince* ostensibly recalls the author's chance encounter, while stranded in the desert, with the child-prince and sole inhabitant of the distant asteroid B-612. *The Little Prince* is emphatically not a work of science fiction, even in juvenile form: Harking back to the venerable literary tradition of the imaginary voyage, exemplified by such eighteenth century masterpieces as Charles de Montesquieu's *Persian Letters* (1721), Voltaire's *Micromegas* (1752), and Jonathan Swift's *Gulliver's Travels* (1726), *The Little Prince* invites the reader, young or old, to suspend his or her preconceived judgments and view the universe through the oddly perceptive eyes of the ingenuous prince. Somewhat marred for today's audience (even among the young) by a certain preciosity and triteness of expression, *The Little Prince* has nevertheless earned the stature of a true classic in the genre, thanks to the genuine wisdom and mature insight only half-concealed among its hundred-odd pages.

BIOGRAPHY

Scion of an old, distinguished, and noble Limousin family, Antoine-Marie-Roger de Saint-Exupéry was born in Lyons on June 29, 1900. It might reasonably be said of him, and without insult, that he was surely among the most successful failures of his generation, having experienced severe setbacks in most of his attempted ventures, including aviation. Only his writing career appears to have developed and prospered without undue incident, yet few who knew him in his youth would have foreseen that he would become a writer. A notoriously poor student, Saint-Exupéry failed his entrance examination to the French École Navale (naval academy) and tried thereafter to apply himself to architecture, as he had earlier attempted music. Tempted by aviation ever since his first flight, as a passenger at about the age of twelve, "Saint-Ex" had the good fortune to emerge from his required military service some ten years later as a pilot-officer. Dissuaded from a career in aviation by the family of the woman to whom he was then betrothed, Saint-Exupéry obligingly turned to office work, spending most of his free time in the air. By 1925, he had begun to write about aviation for trade periodicals; the following year, he was engaged by Latécoère's aviation company, initially as a test pilot and soon thereafter to fly the mail between France and her African colonies.

Following the success of *Southern Mail*, which is based upon his African experiences, Saint-Exupéry at last received a diploma in naval aviation and removed to South America, where he was placed in charge of airmail service for the government of Argentina. Soon after writing and publishing *Night Flight* in 1931, Saint-Exupéry found himself in charge of a new, reorganized mail route between France and South America; earlier in the same year, he had married Consuelo Suncin de Sandoval, widow of an Argentine journalist. Throughout the 1930's, despite documentably modest abilities as a pilot, Saint-Exupéry continued his attempt to forge new territories through the air; although frequently lost or injured, or both, he continued to draw comfort and perseverance from the simple fact of his survival, frequently eulogizing fallen aviators less fortunate than he.

To his credit, Saint-Exupéry established several new mail routes before deciding, in 1937, to cover the Spanish Civil War as a journalist; later in that year, however, he was seriously injured in his attempt to forge yet another air route, between New York and Tierra del Fuego. Commissioned a captain of air service during the "phony war" of 1939-1940, Saint-Exupéry repaired soon thereafter to New York, where he conducted experiments on jet propulsion and worked on his manuscripts while awaiting the opportunity for further military service. In May, 1943, he rejoined his former squadron, by then under United States command, in North Africa. Hampered by advancing age and the cumulative result of his injuries, Saint-Exupéry was frequently discouraged from flying but chose to ignore the advice of superior officers, both French and American. On July 31, 1944, already well past the limit of flights that had been grudgingly allowed him, he took off from Corsica on "one last" reconnaissance flight over the Alps. At the time of his disappearance, returning toward Corsica, he was

(National Archives)

wearing the "oak leaves" of a major in the United States Army Air Corps.

ANALYSIS

"The airplane," wrote Antoine de Saint-Exupéry in *Wind, Sand and Stars*, ". . . has helped us to discover the true face of the earth; for centuries, the roads had kept us fooled. . . ." Throughout his career, at first in fictionalized narrative, later in such extended lyric essays as *Wind, Sand and Stars* and *The Wisdom of the Sands*, Saint-Exupéry would exploit the still rare perspective of the aviator for his memorable insights into life, death, and the human condition. Regardless of the original "packaging," Saint-Exupéry's work is, in fact, all of a piece, with little distinction visible between his mature essays and those earlier works initially conceived and marketed as novels. As W. M. Frohock observes, Saint-Exupéry's novels are indeed quite alike in theme and content: "An aviator is aloft in his plane exposed to danger by the very fact of flight itself, while another man, familiar with all the dangers the first is exposed to, anxiously awaits the outcome of the ordeal." *Southern Mail*, Saint-Exupéry's first published book, is the most novelistic of the lot, with a strong and memorable romantic subplot; thereafter, the stuff of adventure itself sufficed for the telling of a tale.

Characterization in Saint-Exupéry's fiction, although always plausible, depends primarily upon basic human responses to the combined stimuli of discovery and danger, tending toward Ernest Hemingway's proclaimed ideal of "grace under pressure." Even more important, however, is the lucidity apparently made possible by flight; in Saint-Exupéry's strongest passages, solitude and altitude combine to form an epiphanic wisdom. From several thousand feet in the air, people and their buildings appear small indeed, the differences among them likewise diminished. Perceptive observations abound in Saint-Exupéry's work, both fictional and otherwise; the pilot's lucidity, once obtained, serves him admirably on the ground as well as in the air. One of his best-realized and most memorable reflections occurs at the end of *Wind, Sand and Stars*, as the author recalls a recent train trip across Eastern Europe. Wandering from one end of his train to the other, Saint-Exupéry found himself walking through a third-class car filled with recently displaced laborers on their way back from France. On their faces, he claims, he could plainly read the dehumanizing effects of brutal, mindless work. Fixing his eyes on one particularly brutalized couple, he tries to reconstruct in his mind a time when either man or wife might have been attractive or might have found each other so. Unfortunately, he muses, "there is no gardener for men," who grow up and grow old as they must, without cultivation. As the author muses, his gaze falls at last upon a promising-looking little boy, asleep between his parents. For want of proper attention, the boy will doubtless soon become as dehumanized as they are, to society's ultimate loss. Looking around the car, he concludes, "It is as if, in each of these people, Mozart had been assassinated."

SOUTHERN MAIL

In his earliest published works, Saint-Exupéry intersperses his reflections with enough plot and characterization that the books might reasonably be classified as novels. *Southern Mail*, eventually successfully filmed, presents the career and eventual death of the airmail pilot Jacques Bernis against the background of his feelings for Geneviève Herlin, a married woman two years his senior with whom he has apparently been in love since adolescence. Narrated by a nameless friend and fellow pilot who has known Geneviève as long as Bernis has, *Southern Mail* derives considerable effect from descriptions of Geneviève's troubled marriage and the death of her young son. The main function of such background, however, is to deepen the portrayal of Bernis as a man, not merely as a pilot; included also are brief glimpses of his and the narrator's youth, together with mention of the books that both boys were obliged to read in school. The challenge of aviation is thus related through the lives of two exemplary individuals who have chosen to accept it; the narrator, meanwhile, is careful to reveal somewhat less about himself than he does about Bernis.

In *Southern Mail*, Saint-Exupéry experiments frequently with narrative voice, seeking and occasionally finding the singular viewpoint of his later efforts. Couched initially in the first-person plural "we," suggesting the fraternity of fliers, the narration thereafter alternates between third-person exposition and first-person recollection, with occasional shifts into the second person as the narrator speaks directly to Bernis. Throughout his work, even after abandoning the novel form, Saint-Exupéry continued the practice of second-person narrative, addressing himself to fellow pilots both living and dead. Unlike the younger novelist Michel Butor, who, in *A Change of Heart* (1957), sought to revolutionize the genre through the use of second-person narration, Saint-Exupéry adopted the form quite naturally and unobtrusively, avoiding many of the pitfalls of omniscience commonly associated with asides or with abrupt changes in narrative voice. The author's style, for all of its classical correctness and even elegance, is unfailingly natural in its effect, as if the author were inviting the reader to peer over his shoulder as he searches for the most appropriate figure of speech.

NIGHT FLIGHT

Night Flight, based upon the author's flight and management experience in South America, retains the structure and pacing of a novel while dispensing with many of the conventions employed in *Southern Mail*. Fabien's bride of six weeks admires his body while he sleeps and fears for his safety in the air, but far less is seen of her than of Geneviève Herlin in the earlier novel. In keeping with the author's recent experience, the ground manager Rivière rivals or exceeds in importance the pilot Fabien, yet little is revealed of him beyond the limits of his job. Narrated entirely in the third person, *Night Flight* focuses primarily upon the challenge of flying the mail over long stretches of treacherous and often hostile territory. As in *Southern Mail*, Saint-Exupéry derives some of his appeal from the exotic setting of his narrative; his main concern, however, is the one later spelled out in *Wind, Sand and Stars*: "The earth teaches us more about ourselves than do any books, because it resists us. Man discovers himself by measuring himself against an obstacle." The airplane, he maintains, serves the pilot as a useful tool toward the discovery of universal truth, much as a plow serves the farmer toward the same end. Throughout *Night Flight*, the elemental struggle of people against the

elements recapitulates in each life the whole of human history, including the discovery of fire and the invention of the wheel.

As Frohock points out, however, the vast majority of images in *Night Flight* are marine in origin, harking back to humankind's age-old struggle against the sea. To be sure, Saint-Exupéry did not single-handedly invent the use of marine imagery applied to aviation. In the early days of powered flight, common wisdom would refer as easily to "airships" as to "horseless carriages," and to the pilot of an airborne "vessel" as its "captain." Frohock is correct, however, in noting Saint-Exupéry's fondness, at times almost obsessive, for nautical simile and metaphor, conceding that the author's use of his imagery is highly skillful, never forced or hackneyed. The notion of night flight, indeed, readily suggests the solitude and dangers of sea voyage; as Frohock observes, the pilot flying without instruments loses his sense of horizon at night and is likely to confuse ground lights with stars. The author's sustained use of marine imagery, however, appears more firmly established in his own mind than in its supposed referent, causing Frohock to conclude that Saint-Exupéry was, in fact, neither a novelist nor even an essayist but rather a poet who happened to express himself in prose, occasionally labeling his product as novels.

WIND, SAND AND STARS

With *Wind, Sand and Stars*, Saint-Exupéry abandoned all pretense of attempting a novel, writing candidly and anecdotally in his own person. Part memoir, part speculative essay, *Wind, Sand and Stars* is nevertheless among the most successful and rewarding of his works, combining valuable insights with equally valuable eyewitness documentation. Somewhat more convincing in his own right than any of his previous fictionalized characters, Saint-Exupéry revisits, with fresh eyes and narrative voice, much of the same territory covered in the novels, recalling the thrills, dangers, and challenges of pioneer air travel. Among his more memorable recollections is one of being stranded in the Sahara after a forced landing early in 1936, an incident that would later form the basis of his speculative children's fantasy *The Little Prince*. Too personal and discursive to approach philosophy, *Wind, Sand and Stars* nevertheless quite literally reaches toward new heights in the reflective essay form, with well-phrased ideas that remain challenging and valid long after powered flight has ceased to be a novelty.

Following his service as a military aviator before the fall of France in 1940, Saint-Exupéry wrote of his experience in *Flight to Arras*, a tightly written memoir that often resembles a novel, even though the names of its characters have not been changed from those of the real-life persons on whom they are modeled. Typically, *Flight to Arras* is rich in reflection and imagery; unlike *Wind, Sand and Stars*, however, Saint-Exupéry's war narrative is neatly structured, with a beginning, a middle, and an end. *The Little Prince*, published in the following year, is perhaps the most openly "creative" of the author's published works, ostensibly re-creating a vision that occurred to him in his delirium while he was stranded in the desert. In thought and theme, however, *The Little Prince* hardly differs from those of Saint-Exupéry's works originally intended for an adult audience. The posthumously published *The Wisdom of the Sands*, on which the author had begun work as early as 1936, is an extended speculative essay couched in a prose so dense and "poetic" that it often appears deliberately obscure. Perhaps indirectly influenced by Surrealism as by other post-Symbolist experiments in poetry, the work falls short of the philosophical statement toward which Saint-Exupéry seems to be striving and remains, even for his staunchest supporters, a difficult and baffling text.

It is difficult to say what direction Saint-Exupéry's work might have taken had he survived World War II to behold the nuclear age. The obscurity of *The Wisdom of the Sands* suggests strongly that, in any case, his best and most effective writing was probably behind him. By the end of World War II, moreover, aviation was long past the pioneer stage, and there were fewer potential readers who had not experienced air travel in some form. His early works, however, remain unchallenged for what they were and are: well-phrased expressions and illustrations of indomitable human dignity, rendered timeless by the observer's innate sense of poetry. As Frohock wryly observes of

Saint-Exupéry, "A survey of his imagery does not reveal a novelist. But a poet, even in the 1930's, did not need to be a novelist."

David B. Parsell

OTHER MAJOR WORKS

SHORT FICTION: *Le Petit Prince*, 1943 (*The Little Prince*, 1943).

NONFICTION: *Terre des hommes*, 1939 (autobiography in novel form; *Wind, Sand and Stars*, 1939); *Citadelle*, 1948 (philosophical observations and reflections; *The Wisdom of the Sands*, 1950).

BIBLIOGRAPHY

Breaux, Adele. *Saint-Exupéry in America, 1942-1943: A Memoir.* Madison, N.J.: Fairleigh Dickinson University Press, 1971. See Chapter 5, *The Little Prince.*

Capestany, Edward J. *The Dialectic of "The Little Prince."* Lanham, Md.: University Press of America, 1982. A searching study of Saint-Exupéry's use of myth. There is a chapter by chapter analysis, along with notes.

Higgins, James E. *"The Little Prince": A Reverie of Substance.* New York: Twayne, 1996. Divided in literary and historical context (including the book's critical reception) and a reading (emphasizing the "eye of innocence," "the landscape of metaphor," explorations of the spirit and of responsibility. There is an appendix on approaches to teaching the novel as well as notes and an annotated bibliography.

Robinson, Joy D. Marie. *Antoine de Saint-Exupéry.* Boston: Twayne, 1984. Chapter 1 discusses Saint-Exupéry's childhood, chapter 2 his student and soldier years, chapter 3 his career as an aviator, with subsequent chapters following the development of both his life and writing. Includes chronology, notes, and an annotated bibliography. This is perhaps the best book to consult for the beginning student of Saint-Exupery, since it is an unusually thorough study.

Schiff, Stacy. *Saint-Exupéry.* New York: Knopf, 1995. Contains considerably new material on Saint-Exupéry's life and career, especially his experience as a war pilot. Drawing on extensive interviews, Schiff considers the relationship between Saint-Exupéry the aviator and writer. Includes very detailed notes and bibliography.

J. D. SALINGER

Born: New York, New York; January 1, 1919

PRINCIPAL LONG FICTION

The Catcher in the Rye, 1951

OTHER LITERARY FORMS

Little, Brown and Company has published three collections of J. D. Salinger's short fiction: *Nine Stories* (1953), *Franny and Zooey* (1961), and *Raise High the Roof Beam, Carpenters, and Seymour: An Introduction* (1963). An unauthorized paperback collection of his stories in two volumes, apparently published by an unidentified source in Berkeley, California, *The Complete Uncollected Short Stories of J. D. Salinger*, was issued in 1974. It provoked Salinger's first public statement in some years, denouncing the collection, which was suppressed by the copyright holders. There has been one film adaptation of his work, produced by Samuel Goldwyn and adapted by Julius J. and Phillip G. Epstein from Salinger's "Uncle Wiggily in Connecticut," renamed *My Foolish Heart* (1950) and starring Susan Hayward and Dana Andrews. Salinger was so upset by the screen version that he banned all further adaptations of his work into any other medium.

ACHIEVEMENTS

In the post-World War II years, Salinger was unanimously acclaimed by both literate American youth and the critical establishment. His only novel has sold steadily since its publication, and it not only still generates high sales but also generates intense discussion as to its appropriateness for classroom use. Although he is not a prolific writer, Salinger's popularity in terms of both sales and critical articles

and books written about him has continued unabated since the early 1950's.

The Catcher in the Rye is one of the most widely read and influential postwar novels, and it entered the culture as a statement of youth's view of the complex world. The novel has been translated into German, Italian, Japanese, Norwegian, Swedish, French, Dutch, Danish, Hebrew, Czechoslovakian, Yugoslavian, and Russian, and has been highly successful. In Russia, possession of a copy of *The Catcher in the Rye* became something of a status symbol for young intellectuals. Although there have been problems in translating the particularly American idiom into foreign languages, the story touches a nerve that cuts across cultural and global lines. The novel has also been favorably compared to Mark Twain's *The Adventures of Huckleberry Finn* (1884) in terms of its portrayal of the "phoniness" of society, the coming of

(National Archives)

age of a young man, and its use of colloquial language.

Salinger's reputation, paradoxically, has been aided by his refusal to give interviews or to be seen in public. Critics and magazine writers have pursued him relentlessly, trying to discover his thoughts, concerns, and approaches to literature and writing.

BIOGRAPHY

Jerome David Salinger was born in New York, New York, on January 1, 1919, the second child and only son of Sol and Miriam (Jillich) Salinger, although details on Salinger and his parents' life is clouded. Salinger's father was born in Cleveland, Ohio, and has been noted as being the son of a rabbi, but he drifted far enough away from orthodox Judaism to become a successful importer of hams and to marry a Gentile, the Scotch Irish Marie Jillich, who changed her name soon after to Miriam to fit in better with her husband's family. During J. D.'s early years the Salingers moved several times, to increasingly affluent neighborhoods.

Salinger attended schools on Manhattan's upper West Side, doing satisfactory work in all subjects except arithmetic. He probably spent most of his summers in New England camps like most sons of upper-middle-class New York families; he was voted the "most popular actor" in the summer of 1930 at Camp Wigwam in Harrison, Maine. When he reached high school age, he was placed in Manhattan's famed McBurney School, a private institution, where he was manager of the fencing team, a reporter on the *McBurnean,* and an actor in two plays; however, he flunked out after one year. In September of 1934, his father enrolled him at Valley Forge Military Academy in Pennsylvania.

During his two years at Valley Forge, Salinger did satisfactory, but undistinguished, work. He belonged to the Glee Club, the Aviation Club, the French Club, the Non-Commissioned Officers' Club, and the Mask and Spur, a dramatic organization. He also served as literary editor of the yearbook, *Crossed Sabres,* during his senior year. He is credited with writing a three-stanza poetic tribute to the academy that has since been set to music and is sung by the cadets at

their last formation before graduation. Although not yet the recluse that he would later become, Salinger began to write short stories at that time, usually working by flashlight under his blankets after "lights out." Astonishingly, he also appeared interested in a career in the motion-picture business, as either a producer or a supplier of story material. He graduated in June of 1936.

It is unclear what Salinger did after graduation, but he enrolled at least for the summer session of 1937 at Washington Square College in New York. Salinger, in one of his rare interviews, mentioned that he spent some time in Vienna, Austria, and Poland learning German and the details of the ham importing business; it is not clear if his father accompanied him or not, but his trip probably occurred before Adolf Hitler's Anschluss, possibly in the fall of 1937.

On his return, Salinger enrolled at Ursinus College, a coeducational institution sponsored by the Evangelical and Reformed Church at Collegeville, Pennsylvania, not far from Valley Forge. Although he remained only one semester, he wrote a humorous and critical column, "The Skipped Diploma," for the *Ursinus Weekly.* He returned to New York and enrolled in Whit Burnett's famous course in short-story writing at Columbia University. It has been noted that Burnett was not at first impressed with the quiet boy who made no comments in class and seemed more interested in playwriting. Yet Salinger's first story, "The Young Folks," was impressive enough to be published in the March, 1940, issue of *Story,* edited by Burnett.

After publishing in a magazine famous for discovering new talent, Salinger spent another year writing without success until, at age twenty-two, he broke into the well-paying mass circulation magazines with a "short, short story" in *Collier's* and a "satire" in *Esquire*; he even had a story accepted by *The New Yorker,* which delayed publication of "Slight Rebellion off Madison," until after the war. This story proved to be one of the forerunners to *The Catcher in the Rye.*

During 1941, he worked as an entertainer on the Swedish liner MS *Kungsholm.* Upon his return to the

United States, he wrote to the military adjunct at Valley Forge, Colonel Milton G. Baker, to see if there was some way that he could get into the service, even though he had been classified as 1-B because of a slight cardiac condition. After Selective Service standards were lowered in 1942, Salinger was inducted and attended the Officers, First Sergeants, and Instructors School of the Signal Corps. He also reportedly corrected papers in a ground school for aviation cadets. He applied for Officers' Candidate School but was transferred to the Air Service Command in Dayton, Ohio, and wrote publicity releases. Finally, at the end of 1943, he was transferred to the Counter-Intelligence Corps. He also conducted a long correspondence with Eugene O'Neill's daughter Oona (later the last Mrs. Charles Chaplin).

He continued to write whenever he found the opportunity, publishing again in *Collier's*, *Story*, and at last in the well-paying and highly celebrated *Saturday Evening Post*. One of the *Saturday Evening Post* stories marks the first mention of the character Holden Caulfield. Salinger also sent Whit Burnett two hundred dollars from his earnings from the "slicks" to be used to encourage young writers and be applied to future writing contests for college undergraduates, such as the one won by Norman Mailer in 1941.

After training in Tiverton, Devonshire, he joined the American Fourth Division and landed on Utah Beach five hours after the initial assault wave on D-Day. He served with the Division through five European campaigns as a special agent responsible for security of the Twelfth Infantry Regiment. There is an unsupported story that Salinger had an audience with author and war correspondent Ernest Hemingway, who shot off the head of a chicken either to impress Salinger or to demonstrate the effectiveness of a German Luger. This incident has been used to explain why Salinger has written about Hemingway in a bad light in his stories and has Holden Caulfied in *The Catcher in the Rye* detest Hemingway's *A Farewell to Arms* (1929). There are also reports that during the war Salinger married a French woman, Sylvia, who was a doctor, possibly a psychiatrist. The two returned together to the United States after the war, according to biographer Ian Hamilton, but the mar-

riage, which took place in September, 1945, lasted only eight months.

After the war, Salinger decided to make a living by selling stories to the so-called "slicks," publishing again in the *Saturday Evening Post* and *Collier's*, which issued "I'm Crazy" in its Christmas issue. "I'm Crazy" featured the long-delayed debut of Holden Caulfield, who had been mentioned as missing in action in several of Salinger's wartime stories. *Mademoiselle*, *Good Housekeeping*, and *Cosmopolitan* also published Salinger's work. *Cosmopolitan* featured a short novelette, "The Inverted Forest," an involved, obscure allegory of an artist, his possible muses, and his fate. During part of this period, Salinger lived with his parents but also kept a Greenwich Village apartment to entertain various young women. He also, supposedly, began to develop an interest in Zen Buddhism that is illustrated in his stories following publication of *The Catcher in the Rye*, especially the Glass family saga, but there is no suggestion that he actually converted to Buddhism.

After the disastrous film version of "Uncle Wiggily in Connecticut" and stories in *Harper's* and *World Review*, he settled down with a contract to produce stories solely for *The New Yorker* and thereafter published exclusively for that magazine. At that time, Salinger was also his most public: He lived in Tarrytown, New York, and even visited a short-story class at Sarah Lawrence College. Although he seemed to enjoy the conversation and interaction, he never repeated it. It was during that period that he decided to avoid all public appearances and concentrate his efforts on writing.

The Catcher in the Rye finally made its appearance on July 16, 1951, although years earlier Salinger submitted, had accepted, and then withdrew a much shorter version. It was not the immediate hit that time suggests, but it did gain Salinger enormous critical praise and respect. The novel was successful enough to cause Salinger to have his picture removed from the dust jacket of the third edition and all subsequent editions; annoyed by the letters, autograph seekers, and interviewers that sought him, he apparently sailed to Europe to keep his composure and avoid publicity.

In 1952 Salinger settled in Cornish, New Hampshire, a small town across the Connecticut River from Windsor, Vermont. His first house in Cornish was a small saltbox on ninety acres with no furnace, no electricity, and no running water. In 1953, Salinger met his future wife, Claire Douglas, in Manchester, Vermont. The daughter of a well-known British art critic, she was then a nineteen-year-old Radcliffe student. During his first two years in Cornish, Salinger fraternized with high school students in the area, attended their basketball games, and entertained them in his home. In November of 1953 he granted Shirley Blaney an interview for the high school page of the Claremont, New Hampshire, *Daily Eagle*. He became upset when the interview was printed prominently on the editorial page of the paper instead. Thereafter he ceased entertaining area students and built a fence around his home.

In January, 1955, he returned to print in *The New Yorker* with the publication of "Franny," the first of the Glass Family series that occupied all of his forthcoming stories. He supposedly dedicated it to his new bride, whom he married in Barnard, Vermont, on February 17, 1955. On December 10 of that year, the Salingers became the parents of their first child, Margaret Ann; on February 13, 1960, his only son, Matthew, was born. Afterward, Salinger concentrated his efforts on rearing his family and documenting the Glass family. Little was heard or read from Salinger after the 1965 publication of "Hapworth 16, 1924" in *The New Yorker*. He was divorced from his wife in November, 1967.

The reclusive Salinger, dubbed "the Greta Garbo of American letters" by *People Weekly* in reference to another famous but hermitic figure, was thrust into the media limelight in the mid-1980's because of disputes over the content of a biography being published by Ian Hamilton. Thwarted in his quest for an interview with Salinger, Hamilton had nevertheless found two valuable, and hitherto untapped, research sources: collections of Salinger letters in Princeton University's Firestone Library and the library of the University of Texas. Galleys of Hamilton's book were slipped to Salinger by a book dealer in 1986, and Salinger immediately protested the use of his unpublished letters. Attempts at compromise failed, and Salinger filed suit against Hamilton and his publisher, Random House. Eventually, a U.S. Court of Appeals ruling decreed that the letters were indeed Salinger's property and could not be quoted, or even paraphrased, without his permission. The Supreme Court declined to hear an appeal, and Salinger returned to his seclusion. Hamilton's book *In Search of J. D. Salinger*, minus the content of the letters but filled out with a detailed account of the controversy, was finally published in 1988.

ANALYSIS

J. D. Salinger's characters are always extremely sensitive young people who are trapped between two dimensions of the world: love and "squalor." The central problem in most of his fiction is not finding a bridge between these two worlds but bringing some sort of indiscriminate love into the world of squalor: to find a haven where love can triumph and flourish. Some characters, such as the young, mixed-up Holden Caulfield, adopt indiscriminate love to aid them in their journey through the world of squalor, while others, such as Seymour Glass, achieve a sort of perfect love, or satori, and are destroyed, in Seymour's case by a bullet through his head. Each of these characters is metropolitan in outlook and situation and is introverted: Their battles are private wars of spirit, not outward conflicts with society. The characters' minds struggle to make sense of the dichotomy between love and squalor, often reaching a quiet peace and transcending their situation through a small act.

Frederick L. Gwynn and Joseph L. Blotner, in *The Fiction of J. D. Salinger* (1958), offer an analysis of Salinger that claims he is the first writer in Western fiction to present transcendental mysticism in a satiric mode, or simply to present religious ideas satirically. Although much has been made of Salinger's Zen Buddhism, the stories do not seem to be about applying Buddhist principles to modern life, nor do they present a clear and coherent statement of what these principles entail or signify. Holden Caulfied does not react as a Buddhist would, nor does he seek consolation from Buddhism. The Glass family may mention Buddhism, but because of their acquaintance with all religions and their high intelligence and hyperkinetic thirst for knowledge, Salinger suggests they they have picked and chosen aspects from various religions and created a composite of them all. If anything, Salinger's characters seem to move toward a "perfect" Christian ideology—indiscriminate love.

The normality of the characters in Salinger's stories is a primary attraction for readers. Holden Caulfield is no better or no worse than any young high school boy; he is merely a bit more articulate and honest in his appraisals, more open with his feelings. Even though the Glasses are brilliant, they are not cerebral or distanced from the reader because of their brilliance; and all the characters live in the same world and environment as the readers do. Their moments of pain and delight are the same as the readers', but Salinger's characters articulate these moments more naturally and completely.

Another element that draws readers into Salinger's world is his use of satire. The satire not only touches upon the characters' descriptions and reactions to the world but also touches on the characters themselves. Holden Caulfield's confrontation with Maurice, the brawny Edmont Hotel elevator operator/pimp, shows not only the ridiculousness of the antagonist but also Holden's stupidity for attempting to reason with him. Even if he does not realize it, Holden does many of the things that he tells readers he hates. He is critical enough, however, to realize that these things are wrong.

All of Salinger's work has also a strong focus on the family; it is held as an ideal, a refuge, and a raft of love amid a sea of squalor. Although the family does not provide the haven that Salinger suggests it might, it is through coming home that the characters flourish, not by running away. Holden Caulfield, in *The Catcher in the Rye*, never realistically considers running away, for he realizes that flight cannot help him. At the critical moment his family may not be ready to grant him the salvation that he needs, but it is his only security. If the world is a place of squalor, perhaps it is only through perfect love within the family unit that an individual can find some kind of salvation. It is important to notice that the family unit is never satirized in Salinger's fiction.

THE CATCHER IN THE RYE

The basic story of *The Catcher in the Rye* follows the adventures of sixteen-year-old Holden Caulfield, an independent, self-indulgent, idealistic, and sentimental figure of adolescent rebellion, during a forty-eight-hour period after he has been expelled from Pencey Prep, the latest of three expulsions for Holden. After confrontations with some fellow students at Pencey, Holden goes to New York City, his hometown, to rest before facing his parents. During the trip he tries to renew some old acquaintances, attempts to woo three out-of-towners, hires a prostitute named Sunny, and copes with recurring headaches. Eventually, after two meetings with his younger sister, Phoebe, he returns home. At the beginning of the novel he has told us that he is in California recovering from an illness and that he is reconciled with his family. The entire story of Holden's exploits comes to us through a first-person narration, one which contains youthful phrasing and profanity and has many digressions, but one which has a mesmerizing flow to it.

Holden Caulfield is a confused sixteen-year-old, no better and no worse than his peers, except that he is slightly introverted, a little sensitive, and willing to express his feelings openly. His story can be seen as a typical growing process. As he approaches and is ready to cross the threshold into adulthood, he begins to get nervous and worried. His body has grown, but his emotional state has not. He is gawky, clumsy, and not totally in control of his body. He seeks to find some consolation, some help during this difficult time but finds no one. The school cannot help him, his peers seem oblivious to his plight, his parents are too concerned with other problems (his mother's nerves and his father's business activities as a corporate lawyer). His girlfriend, Sally Hayes, who has a penchant for using the word "grand" and whom Holden calls the "queen of the phonies," is no help, and his favorite teacher, Mr. Antolini, merely lectures him drunkenly. The only people with whom he can communicate are the two young boys at the museum, the girl with the skates at the park, and his younger sister Phoebe. All of them are children, who cannot help him in his growing pains but remind him of a simpler time, one to which he wishes he could return. Eventually, he does cross the threshold (his fainting in the museum) and realizes that his worries were unfounded. He has survived. At the end of the book, Holden seems ready to reintegrate himself into society and accept the responsibilities of adulthood.

Through Holden's picaresque journeys through New York City, he grows spiritually. He slowly begins to recognize the "phoniness" around him and the squalor that constantly presses down on him. Although he castigates himself for doing some of the phony things, lying especially, Holden does realize that what he is doing is incorrect: This understanding sets him above his fellows; he knows what he is doing. Holden never hurts anyone in any significant way; his lies are small and harmless. Conversely, the phony world also spins lies, but they are dangerous since they harm people. For example, Holden mentions that Pencey advertises that it molds youth, but it does not. He is angry with motion pictures because they offer false ideals and hopes. Yet, his lies help a mother think better of her son. Like Huck Finn, he lies to get along, but not to hurt, and also like Huck, he tries to do good. Near the end of the novel Holden dreams of fleeing civilization and building a cabin out west, something which belies his earlier man-about-town conduct.

By the end of the book, Holden has accepted a new position—an undiscriminating love for all humanity. He even expresses that he misses all the people who did wrong to him. Although not a Christ figure, Holden does acquire a Christlike position—perfect love of all humankind, good and evil. He is not mature enough to know what to do with this love, but he is mature enough to accept it. In this world, realizing what is squalor and what is good and loving it all is the first step in achieving identity and humanity: Compassion is what Holden learns.

Recalling all the suffering and pain that he has witnessed, Holden develops a profound sense of the human condition and accepts Christ's ultimate commandment. In the passage regarding Holden's argument with his Quaker friend Arthur Childs, Holden argues that Judas is not in hell because Jesus would have had the compassion and love not to condemn Judas to hell. Also, Jesus did not have time to analyze who would be perfect for his Disciples; thus, they were not perfect and would have condemned Judas if they had had the chance. In this discussion, Holden points out his own dilemma, not having time to analyze his decisions, and his belief in the perfect love that he embraces at the end of the book. Although not a would-be saint, Holden does become a fuller human being through his experiences.

The title symbol of the novel comes from Holden's misreading of a line from a song of Robert Burns. Holden's wish, as expressed to his sister, is to be a catcher in the rye, one standing beneath a cliff waiting to catch any child who falls over it: He seeks to spare children the pain of growing up and facing the world of squalor. He also hopes to provide some useful, sincere activity in the world. The catcher-in-the-rye job is one that Holden realizes is impractical in the world as it is. Only by facing the world and loving it indiscriminately can anyone live fully within it and have any hope of changing it.

In the novel, Holden is also constantly preoccupied with death. He worries about the ducks in Central Park's lagoon freezing in winter, about Egyptian mummies, and about his dead brother Allie. He cries to Allie not to let him disappear. This symbolizes Holden's wish not to disappear into society as another cog in the great machine, and his desire not to lose what little of himself he feels that he has. To Holden, the change from childhood to adulthood is a kind of death, a death he fears because of his conviction that he will become other than he is. This fear proves groundless by the end of the book. His name also provides a clue: Holden—hold on. His quest is to hold on to his adolescent self and to save other children from the pain of growth. His quest fails, but his compassion and the growth of his humanity provide him with better alternatives.

Regarding sex, Holden tends to be puritanical. His trouble lies in the fact that he begins to feel sorry for the girls he dates, and he has too much compassion for them to defile their supposed virtue. This problem ties in with his compassion: He tries to see people as they are and not as types. He looks quickly and may make rash judgments, but once he talks to or acquaints himself with someone, he sees him or her as an individual. His mentioning of the boring boy he knew in school who could whistle better than anyone is the perfect example: Holden cannot help but confront people as individuals. Again, this shows his growing compassion and indiscriminate love. He sympathizes with the girl's position, which is a very mature quality for a teenager. At Pencey, for example, he wants to protect a childhood friend named Jane Gallagher from Ward Stradlater, remembering that she always kept her kings in the back row in checker games and never used them.

The Catcher in the Rye also reflects the art of a maturing author. Although there is no indication that Holden will become a novelist, there are clues scattered throughout the novel that he has an artistic sensibility. His sensitivity, his compassion, his powers of observation, and his references to himself as an exhibitionist are several such clues.

Later, Salinger more fully develops the contrast between squalor and love in the world and reintroduces various elements of his Caulfield family saga in his grand design of charting the story of the Glass family. The compassion, the satire, the heights of perfect love, the love of the family unit, and the use of brilliant conversational language that characterized Salinger's great novel, *The Catcher in the Rye*, will continue to set his fiction apart.

Domenic Bruni,
updated by James Norman O'Neill

OTHER MAJOR WORKS

SHORT FICTION: *Nine Stories*, 1953; *Franny and Zooey*, 1961; *Raise High the Roof Beam, Carpenters, and Seymour: An Introduction*, 1963.

BIBLIOGRAPHY

Belcher, William F., and James W. Lee, eds. *J. D. Salinger and the Critics*. Belmont, Calif.: Wadsworth, 1962. This collection of critical essays could function as a casebook for Salinger study. Part 1 contains thirteen essays exclusively on *The Catcher in the Rye*; the smaller part 2 covers his stories and contains general studies. Suggests topics for essays and includes a bibliography.

French, Warren. *J. D. Salinger, Revisited*. New York: Twayne, 1988. This revision offers a detailed introduction to Salinger and analyzes all of his work. Includes an annotated bibliography and a thorough chronology.

Gwynn, Frederick L., and Joseph L. Blotner. *The Fiction of J. D. Salinger*. Pittsburgh, Pa.: University of Pittsburgh Press, 1958. This tiny book provides capsule introductions to Salinger's fiction and is most useful in its discussion of his early stories. Contains a short bibliography.

Laser, Marvin, and Norman Furman, eds. *Studies in J. D. Salinger: Reviews, Essays, and Critiques of "The Catcher in the Rye" and Other Fiction*. New York: Odyssey Press, 1963. Although the collection concentrates on *The Catcher in the Rye*, it includes four explications of "For Esmé—with Love and Squalor," a section on censorship of *The Catcher in the Rye*, some negative evaluations of Salinger's work, and some suggested writing topics.

Lundquist, James. *J. D. Salinger*. New York: Frederick Ungar, 1979. Discusses Salinger's work as exhibiting four stages of development: alienation resulting from World War II, isolation ended through "Zen-inspired awakening," Zen art applied to the short story, and philosophical experimentation. Especially strong on Salinger's later work, the book also contains an exhaustive bibliography.

Maynard, Joyce. *At Home in the World: A Memoir*. New York: Picador USA, 1998. This memoir reveals many details of Salinger's private life, which he struggled to suppress. Best source for biographical information.

Pinsker, Sanford. *"The Catcher in the Rye": Innocence Under Pressure*. New York: Twayne, 1993. Argues that *The Catcher in the Rye* has affinities with several great American novels told by a retrospective first-person narrator and that it is perhaps the best portrait of a sixteen-year-old American boy ever written.

Salzman, Jack, ed. *New Essays on "The Catcher in the Rye."* Cambridge, England: Cambridge University Press, 1991. Has an introduction, a selected bibliography, and five essays on the novel. The essays deal with the book's subliminal war features, its narrator and audience, its cultural codes, its spirit of protest, and its themes of love and death.

GEORGE SAND
Amandine-Aurore-Lucile Dupin, Baronne Dudevant

Born: Paris, France; July 1, 1804
Died: Nohant, France; June 8, 1876

PRINCIPAL LONG FICTION

Indiana, 1832 (English translation, 1833)
Valentine, 1832 (English translation, 1902)
Lélia, 1833, 1839 (English translation, 1978)
Mauprat, 1837 (English translation, 1870)
Spiridion, 1839 (English translation, 1842)
Le Compagnon du tour de France, 1840 (*The Companion of the Tour of France*, 1976; also as *The Journeyman Joiner*, 1847)
Consuelo, 1842-1843 (English translation, 1846)
La Comtesse de Rudolstadt, 1843-1844 (*The Countess of Rudolstadt*, 1847)
Jeanne, 1844
Le Meunier d'Angibault, 1845 (*The Miller of Angibault*, 1847)
Lucrezia Floriani, 1846
La Mare au diable, 1846 (*The Devil's Pool*, 1929; also as *The Enchanted Lake*, 1850)
Le Péché de M. Antoine, 1847 (*The Sin of Monsieur Antoine*, 1900)
La Petite Fadette, 1848-1849 (*Fanchon the Cricket*, 1864; also as *Little Fadette*, 1850)
François le champi, 1850 (*Francis the Waif*, 1889)
Les Maîtres sonneurs, 1853 (*The Bagpipers*, 1890)
Elle et lui, 1859 (*She and He*, 1902)
Le Marquis de Villemer, 1861 (*The Marquis of Villemer*, 1871)
La Ville noire, 1861

Mademoiselle la Quintinie, 1863
Mademoiselle Merquem, 1868 (English translation, 1868)
Historic and Romantic Novels, 1900-1902 (20 volumes)

OTHER LITERARY FORMS

George Sand, who was famous during her lifetime primarily as a novelist, earned a living for many years as a journalist. Some of her essays on art, literature, politics, and social questions are collected in two posthumous volumes, *Questions d'art et de littérature* (1878) and *Questions politiques et sociales* (1879). Her twenty-volume autobiography, *Histoire de ma vie* (1854-1855; *History of My Life*, 1901), is considered by some to be her masterpiece. Georges Lubin produced an excellent annotated edition of this work and other autobiographical writings for Gallimard in 1970. Other important nonfictional works include *Lettres d'un voyageur* (1837; *Letters of a Traveller*, 1847), *Lettres à Marcie* (1837), and *Un Hiver à Majorque* (1841). Sand's plays were published in five volumes in 1877. She wrote more than nineteen thousand letters and was called by André Maurois "the best French epistolary writer." Since 1964, Lubin has devoted himself to a new edition of Sand's letters, many of which were unpublished or published in truncated form. The fifteenth volume was published in 1981, and the series is projected to include twenty-five volumes. Thanks to Lubin's tireless diligence, Sand scholars will soon have the material they need to analyze her work.

ACHIEVEMENTS

To her contemporaries, George Sand was a great novelist and a fallen woman. The controversy surrounding her life continued into the twenty-first century. Until the late 1980's, scholars neglected her enormous production of literary works to concentrate on biographical quarrels. Sand was recognized as a major novelist by Honoré de Balzac, Ivan Turgenev, Victor Hugo, and Henry James. She was widely read in the United States and Great Britain, where she influenced writers such as the Brontë sisters and George Eliot. In Russia, where political treatises were banned, her novels passed on progressive ideas and inspired political thinkers such as Mikhail Bakunin as well as novelists such as Fyodor Dostoevski, Gustave Flaubert called Sand "My Dear Master," and Marcel Proust's most poignant childhood memories involved his mother reading Sand's rustic novels to him. This picture of Sand's pastoral or rustic novels persists in France today, where the average reader considers her a writer of sentimental stories for children. Because of this image, she has been attacked by political liberals who accuse her of supporting the status quo with her tales of happy peasants. Scholars, on the other hand, regard her rustic novels as the perfection of a literary genre. To the nineteenth century public, Sand's novels calling for the emancipation of women (and men) from arranged marriages, equality between the sexes, and education for women seemed outrageously feminist. Her novel *Lélia* shocked readers by its explicit analysis of female sexuality. Twentieth century feminists, however, point to the limits of Sand's feminism, especially to her opposition to the participation of women in political affairs, for she felt that women should be educated before they were given the right to vote. Because of the volume of Sand's work and the speed at which she was forced to write to support her family, her artistic circle, and her charitable contributions, the quality of her fiction is uneven, yet literary critics admire her fluid style and her techniques of psychological analysis. All agree in considering *Mauprat, Consuelo,* and the rustic novels as powerful masterpieces.

BIOGRAPHY

George Sand was born Amandine-Aurore-Lucile Dupin in Paris on July 1, 1804, to parents who had been married scarcely a month. Her father, Maurice Dupin, was a descendant through bastard lines of the King of Poland, Augustus the Strong, and her mother, Sophie Delaborde, was a camp follower and the daughter of a Paris bird-seller. Thus, from the beginning, Sand was exposed to the class struggle. When she was four years old, her father was killed in a fall from a horse; three years later, her mother gave up custody of her to her aristocratic maternal grandmother, who brought her up as a lady at her country estate of Nohant in the Berry region. Sand neverthe-

less reached out to her mother in Paris and the working class she represented.

In 1817, Sand returned to Paris, where she entered the Couvent des Anglaises for her education. In 1820, she returned to the country while her grandmother attempted to arrange a suitable marriage for her; Sand preferred to read books and ride horses. After the death of her grandmother in 1821, Sand returned to Paris to live with her mother. This arrangement proved unsatisfactory because of her mother's violent temper, and the girl sought refuge at the country estate of her father's friends, the Roëttiers. Through the Roëttiers, she met Casimir François Dudevant, the illegitimate but recognized son of a baron; she married Dudevant in 1822.

At first, the couple seemed happy enough, but after the birth of their son Maurice in 1823, their incompatibility became evident. A second child, Solange, was born in 1828. After a fight with her husband, Sand arranged to spend half of each year in Paris, where Dudevant would send her an allowance from the revenues of her land. In 1831, she left for Paris to live with Jules Sandeau, a law student who

(Library of Congress)

aspired to become a writer. To supplement her meager pension, Sand obtained a job writing for *Le Figaro*, a newspaper run by Hyacinthe de Latouche, an acquaintance from Berry. In collaboration with Sandeau, Sand wrote several short stories and at least one novel, which was signed "J. Sand." When Sand wrote *Indiana* alone at Nohant and returned to Paris to publish it, de Latouche suggested that she keep the name "Sand" and choose another Christian name. She chose "Georges" (soon anglicized to George) because it seemed to her to be typical of the Berry region. *Indiana*, the first novel signed "George Sand," was published in 1832. More than seventy others were to follow.

In 1833, Sand fell in love with the poet Alfred de Musset and left with him for Venice, the city that all the Romantic writers dreamed of visiting. There they both fell ill. Following several violent incidents resulting from Musset's overindulgence in wine and women, they agreed to separate. When Musset's illness recurred, Sand nursed him faithfully but fell in love with his Italian doctor, Pietro Pagello. Barely restored to health, Musset returned to Paris while Sand and Pagello stayed in Italy. Sand addressed much of her correspondence in *Letters of a Traveller* to Musset in Paris. In 1834, she returned to Paris with Pagello but neglected him, feeling herself drawn again to Musset. Musset wrote some of his most famous poems about this relationship and analyzed it in his *La Confession d'un enfant du siècle* (1836; *The Confession of a Child of the Century*, 1892). After Musset's death, in 1857, Sand reevaluated their adventure in *She and He*.

After many painful scenes, Sand finally broke with Musset in 1835. Later that year, she met and fell in love with the Republican lawyer Michel de Bourges. When she returned to Nohant, she had a definitive fight with her husband and sued for a legal separation, since divorce did not exist in France at that time. De Bourges acted as her lawyer.

In 1838, Sand began a relationship with Frédéric Chopin, whom she met through a mutual friend, Franz Liszt. For nine years, Sand was Chopin's mother, mistress, and nurse, protecting him and enabling him to write some of his best music. The most famous

event in their years together was the ill-fated trip they took with Sand's children to Majorca in the winter of 1838-1839, which she described in *Un Hiver à Majorque*. Most literary critics agree that Sand was satirizing her relationship with Chopin in her novel *Lucrezia Floriani*. Sand and Chopin separated in 1847, disagreeing over the marriage of her daughter Solange to the sculptor Jean-Baptiste Auguste Clésinger.

In 1848, Sand returned to Paris as soon as she received word that the monarchy had been overthrown. She wrote most of the official bulletins for the new Republican government, which included many of her old friends. When the Republicans were arrested in May, Sand took refuge at Nohant. Although she continued to intercede with the Emperor Napoleon III for her friends, Sand has been accused of turning her back on the Revolution to write bourgeois pastoral novels.

After 1848, Sand spent more time at Nohant than in Paris, but she returned to Paris often, frequently for the openings of her plays. From 1850 to 1865, Alexandre Manceau, an engraver and a friend of her son Maurice (who was an artist, a pupil of Eugène Delacroix), was Sand's private secretary and lover. In 1864, Manceau bought a small house near Paris, where they lived in order to leave Nohant to Maurice and his new wife, Lina, the daughter of the engraver Luigi Calamatta, an old friend of Sand. After Manceau's death from tuberculosis in 1865, Sand traveled, lived in Paris, visited Flaubert at Croisset, and went to the Ardennes region to document a novel, but she considered Nohant her home again. There, she received Flaubert and Turgenev as well as other friends. She died at Nohant of a painful intestinal blockage on June 8, 1876.

ANALYSIS

Faced with the enormous number of George Sand's novels, literary critics quickly moved to divide them into categories. The traditional categories include feminist novels, socialistic novels, and rustic novels. While this oversimplification is inaccurate, it does help the reader to identify the major themes that recur in most of her novels.

VALENTINE

Valentine is a good example of the critics' dilemma. The novel recounts a love story of a married noblewoman and an educated peasant which ends tragically with the death of the lovers. The plot is a Romantic one, both in the sense of "a love story" and in the literary-historical sense of the term, for it contains several of the essential themes of French Romanticism: the passing of time, the passing of love with time, and a search for the meaning of the universe beyond the limits of human life. In *Valentine*, Sand's Bénédict is a melancholy, meditative person who resembles Chateaubriand's René. He is killed accidentally by a jealous husband, but Valentine, the heroine, dies from sorrow soon after his death. At first reading, the novel seems to be primarily Romantic, yet Valentine's fruitless attempts to find personal happiness and satisfaction, despite her financially arranged marriage and her indifferent and absent husband, suggest classification among the feminist novels. The beautiful descriptions of the Berry countryside and details of the daily life of the peasants are characteristic of her rustic novels. The love affair between two people of different social classes suggests classification as a socialistic novel. The conclusion is obvious: Most of Sand's novels contain Romantic elements, Romanesque elements, feminist elements, rustic elements, and socialist elements.

The novels that contain the highest percentage of feminist elements are the early ones. Clearly, Sand's unhappy personal experiences were reflected in novels such as *Indiana*, in which the heroine leaves her despotic husband, is betrayed by her lover, and ultimately finds happiness with her cousin, who serves as a father figure for her and becomes her lover on a lush tropical island in a primitive paradise that owes something to Jean-Jacques Rousseau and Jacques-Henri Bernardin de Saint-Pierre. Sand's feminist novel *par excellence* is *Lélia*, which reinterprets the metaphysical dilemma of the Romantic hero in feminine terms.

Sand's socialistic novels are generally less successful artistically than her work in other genres, perhaps because her theoretical digressions are not well integrated into the plots. One exception, *The Companion of the Tour of France*, was reedited by the University Press of Grenoble in the late 1980's and then began to receive long-overdue critical attention. In addition to its story of the love between the lady of a manor and a carpenter-artist, the novel contains a study of secret trade guilds and a portrait of the daily life of workers—a class that was neglected by Balzac in *The Human Comedy* (1829-1848). *The Miller of Angibault* is also a successful socialistic novel, but it contains many elements of the rustic novels as well. *The Sin of Monsieur Antoine* and *La Ville noire* expose the problems of factory workers, making Sand the only French novelist before Émile Zola to analyze seriously the effects of the Industrial Revolution.

SAND'S RUSTIC NOVELS

Sand's experiments with the rustic novel began with *Jeanne*, whose peasant heroine is compared to Joan of Arc and Napoleon. In this novel, Sand attempted to make her peasants speak the Berry dialect. Later, she decided that *Jeanne* was a failure because the language of the peasants clashed with the more polished language of the narrator. In her later rustic novels such as *The Devil's Pool, Fanchon the Cricket, Francis the Waif*, and *The Bagpipers*, she resolved this problem in two ways. First, she began to fashion a clear, simple language for her characters that was halfway between the Berry dialect and the French her middle-class readers expected; the best example of this technique is found in *The Devil's Pool*. Her second strategy was to use a peasant as narrator; the best example of this technique is found in *The Bagpipers*.

In the rustic novels, Sand saw herself as an intermediary between Paris and Nohant, between bourgeois and peasant. She hoped to bring about a reconciliation between the two by portraying the best qualities of the country folk to make them acceptable to urban readers. She did not, however, neglect the very real problems of rural life. Her peasants are often hungry and overworked, but they have a noble character that enables them to conquer all obstacles and a resourcefulness that comes from living in harmony with nature.

Sand never claimed to be a realist, even though she documented her novels carefully. There are realistic elements in her psychological analyses, in her landscapes, and in her portrayal of the everyday life of workers and peasants. Nevertheless, what counted for Sand, as she states in the introduction to *The Devil's Pool*, was "ideal truth" rather than "a slice of life." She wanted to inspire readers to live up to their potential, in contrast to the productions of the realist and naturalist schools, which, she felt, depressed people by showing the ugly side of life. In her autobiography, she quotes Balzac as saying to her, "You search for man as he should be, while I take him as he is. Believe me, we are both right."

LÉLIA

Lélia is a flawed masterpiece. Its lyric tone and mystical examination of God, love, the universe, and the nature of truth make it both a profound philosophical work and a difficult novel for most readers. The characters tend toward allegory: Lélia represents doubt, according to a document published in *Sketches and Hints* (1926); Trenmor, expiation and stoicism; Sténio, poetry and credulity; Magnus, superstition and repressed desire; and Pulchérie, the senses (as opposed to the mind or soul). They also represent different aspects of Sand's own personality. She wrote in *Journal intime* (1926; *The Intimate Journal*, 1929), which was published with *Sketches and Hints*, "Magnus is my childhood; Sténio, my youth; Lélia is my maturity; Trenmor will perhaps be my old age. All these types have been in me."

When Sand published *Lélia* in 1832, it had a *succès de scandale*. A novel by a woman treating explicitly the problem of female frigidity, briefly touching on lesbianism, and creating a superior heroine to rival melancholy Romantic heroes (Chateaubriand's René, Étienne de Senancour's Obermann, Johann Wolfgang von Goethe's Werther, and Benjamin Constant's Adolphe) was more than even Paris was prepared to accept. Yet Sand's passionate cry of suffering was so revealing that Musset and many of her contemporaries called her "Lélia."

Sand, who ordinarily did not rewrite novels, rewrote *Lélia*, cutting out the sexually explicit passages and transforming its profoundly skeptical and pessimistic tone into a more positive and progressive one. The second version, published in 1839, was chosen by the author to be included in an edition of her complete works. After that, the 1832 edition disappeared from view until André Maurois entitled his 1952 biography *Lélia: Ou, La Vie de George Sand* (*Lélia: The Life of George Sand*, 1953). Maurois asserted that the first *Lélia* was, with *Indiana* and *Consuelo*, one of Sand's finest novels and artistically superior to the 1839 version. In 1960, Pierre Reboul published the text of the 1832 *Lélia*, and scholars now generally agree with Maurois. Östen Södergård published a comparison of the two editions in 1962 and showed how and why Sand changed her novel.

In the first *Lélia*, the heroine is presented to the reader as seen from afar by the young poet Sténio, who worships and fears her. The question the first part of the novel asks is whether Lélia will be able to love Sténio. Trenmor, a rehabilitated gambler resigned to a calm philosophical life, says no. Lélia is older and wiser than Sténio and so frustrated by unsatisfying love affairs that she is no longer capable of physical love. She proposes a more spiritual love, but the poet insists that ideal love unites the senses with the spirit. After many vain power struggles, Lélia leaves Sténio with her courtesan-sister Pulchérie, with whom he makes love, believing her to be Lélia. In this way, Lélia hopes to teach him that sensual love is unreliable. Instead, Sténio, disillusioned by the experience, decides that pleasure alone is real and throws himself into debauchery. Finally, he drowns himself in a lake; while Lélia weeps over his body, she is strangled by Magnus, a priest who has become an atheist and has been driven insane by his desire for Lélia. At the end, Lélia and Sténio, the lovers who could not agree on earth, are united as stars in Heaven; and the philosopher Trenmor continues his pilgrimage alone.

The love story at the center of *Lélia* is less important than Lélia's desperate search for God, herself, and truth—what Maria Espinosa, the translator of the original version of *Lélia* into English, calls the "spiritual odyssey" of Lélia and, of course, of Sand herself. Lélia searches for a man who is perfect, like God; not finding one, she makes a god of the man she loves. When she realizes her mistake, it is too late for her ever to obtain the fresh, pure love of which she dreams. She has lived too much without enjoyment, and her fantasies surpass any possible realization. This makes her doubt God and hate herself while she is filled with a burning and insatiable physical desire. Seeking relief in a year's voluntary claustration, Lélia waits in vain to achieve the stoic resignation of Trenmor, who is emotionally dead. Since, for her, physical love represents a submission of the woman to the man, she finds it distasteful and tries to solve her dilemma by taking the dominant male role in love scenes. For this reason, she treats Sténio like her son and loves him most when he is passive—sleeping or dead. Unable to find a solution to her problems, Lélia is finally content to be killed by Magnus.

In the 1839 version, Lélia becomes a nun who teaches girls how to resist men and reforms the Church. Trenmor becomes a reformed murderer and acquires a secret identity as Valmarina, a benefactor of the poor and needy as well as the head of a mystico-political secret society somewhat like the Italina Carbonaros. Even though Lélia dies in disgrace at the end of the second version, the reader feels that she will be vindicated. Thus, both Trenmor and Lélia find meaningful things to do with their lives as Sand passes from Romantic pessimism to preach active reform of society.

MAUPRAT

The reader who finds the lyric and philosophical passages of *Lélia* long and painful will be enchanted by *Mauprat*. The latter, a more traditional novel, combines the beautiful exterior scenes of Sand's rustic novels with a historical adventure story of the type written by Sir Walter Scott or Alexandre Dumas, *pére*. Political and philosophical reflections are carefully woven into the fabric of the work so as not to impede the swift movement of the plot toward its suspense-filled conclusion—for *Mauprat* also contains a detective story. These disparate elements are skillfully united to form a *Bildungsroman*. The central focus of the novel is the education of Bernard de Mauprat, that is, the transformation of a wild barbarian interested only in sensual gratification into a sensitive, loving, and cultured man. This transformation is the work of Bernard's cousin Edmée, who uses his love for her to force him to change.

From the outside, Edmée seems to resemble Lélia. She is cold and proud; she dominates Bernard and treats him like her son. Yet Edmée is not frigid; she merely appears that way because she suppresses her own desire for Bernard and patiently waits for him to become her equal, emotionally and morally, before she agrees to marry him. Meanwhile, like Sand herself, Edmée carries a knife to commit suicide if necessary to protect her virtue.

Bernard, who was taken at age seven by his grandfather Tristan de Mauprat to a disintegrating castle, grew up in an atmosphere of violence and crime as his marauding uncles filled the countryside with terror, re-creating in the eighteenth century their family's feudal domination of the peasants. Bernard's slow progress from this life of darkness to the light of civilization begins when Edmée de Mauprat, the sole heir of the respectable younger branch of the family, loses her way in the forest and is captured by the evil uncles. She convinces Bernard, who only wants to make love to her, to rescue her and flee from the castle with her. In order to do this, she promises Bernard that she will belong to no other man before him.

This solemn promise shapes the future of both the young people. Bernard, who is seeking only instant physical gratification, slowly and painfully discovers that Edmée will withhold this from him for many years, while he, like the medieval knight, is forced to overcome obstacles to merit her love. Chivalrous motifs are reinforced by a young man named Arthur, who serves as Bernard's friend and guide in the American Revolution, explaining to him what he must do to earn the favors of the fair maiden. The medieval knight had to conquer dragons (exterior enemies) while Bernard must conquer his own savage nature. For Edmée, on the other hand, this promise to make love is tantamount to a promise of marriage.

Sand states in her preface to *Mauprat* that the trauma of the legal separation from her husband made her begin to reflect upon the dream of an ideal marriage and an eternal love; thus, Bernard de Mauprat, who narrates his story at the age of eighty, tells his listeners that he loved only one woman in his entire life, before his marriage, during his marriage, and after her death. This is certainly a strong response to Sand's contemporaries, who criticized her for attacking the institution of marriage.

As the love story gives unity to the plot, the theme of the perfectibility of humankind forms the center of the philosophical framework of the novel. Here, Sand is undoubtedly following one of her first mentors, Rousseau. In a sense, Edmée is like Julie in Rousseau's *Eloise: Or, A Series of Original Letters* (1761; also as *Julie: Or, The New Eloise*, 1968), who moves from a passionate lover, Saint-Preux, to a reasonable husband, Wolmar, creating a utopia out of her farm. The major difference is that Sand unites Saint-Preux and Wolmar to form one character, Bernard. Edmée does create a utopia with the aid of Patience, an old hermit who gives up his solitary lifestyle to help Edmée build a life of dignity and honor for the peasants. Bernard and Edmée are happy to give up their wealth with the arrival of the French Revolution, which they see as a step toward a more equitable society.

In *Mauprat*, Sand uses the medieval trappings, the plot of an adventure story, and the psychological developments of a love story to interest her reader in the essential message—that the human race can improve with education. This progressive theme signals Sand's own movement toward a more optimistic view of the world.

CONSUELO

Consuelo and its sequel, *The Countess of Rudolstadt*, form, like *Mauprat*, a *Bildungsroman*. This time, however, the person who learns and grows by overcoming obstacles is a woman. *Consuelo*, considered by many to be Sand's masterpiece, has been called France's answer to Goethe's saga of Wilhelm Meister. The novel is set in the eighteenth century, in Venice, Bohemia, Vienna, and Berlin—for Consuelo is a talented singer, born in Spain of a Gypsy mother, who travels in Europe perfecting her voice and developing her career. The character is roughly based on Pauline Garcia Viardot, a close friend of Sand; as a prototype of the Romantic artist, Consuelo also shares many traits with Sand herself. Consuelo has the misfortune of being ugly until she is transformed by her music. As Béatrice Didier points out in "*Consuelo* et la création féminine," her ugliness may not

be a disadvantage after all, because it saves her from easy success and venal protectors, enabling her to keep her independence and grow in her art.

The *Bildungsroman* operates on three levels as Consuelo follows an artistic itinerary which leads to becoming a composer, a political itinerary that makes her aware of the evils of despotism and dedicated to helping the poor and suffering, and a spiritual itinerary that culminates in her initiation into the secret society of the Invisibles, who work to correct social injustice. Consuelo's artistic voyage begins when the famous maestro Porpora agrees to give the poor girl free music lessons in Venice. After Porpora teaches her the fundamentals of her art, Consuelo becomes an opera star. At this point, Porpora feels he must warn her to beware of men—both would-be protectors such as Count Justiani and would-be lovers such as Anzoletto, her childhood friend. Porpora persuades Consuelo to devote her life to art and sends her off to the Castle of the Giants in Bohemia to give music lessons to the young Baroness Amélie.

In this castle, which has all the subterranean passageways and mysteries of the gothic novel, Consuelo meets Albert de Rudolstadt, Amélie's cousin, who is subject to temporary mental disorders during which he imagines that he is the reincarnation of the Prince Podiebrand or the Hussite hero Jean Ziska. He plays violin music that has a magical influence on Consuelo. Albert and his deranged peasant friend Zdenko teach her the history of Bohemia and its suffering under political and religious oppression. They introduce her to folk music and begin her initiation into the occult. After saving Albert's life by carrying him through secret underground passages, tunnels, and wells, Consuelo becomes ill and is nursed back to health by Albert, who falls in love with her. She refuses to marry him and leaves the castle for Vienna to pursue her study of music.

On the trip to Vienna, Consuelo dresses up like a man to protect herself. This loss of female identity gives her a freedom that helps her develop as an artist. She accidentally meets young Joseph Haydn, who accompanies her on the long trip on foot. As a result of this journey, she learns about war, despotism, and the oppression of the peasants. In Vienna, she finds Porpora again and learns about tyranny from Maria Theresa.

As she is leaving Vienna for Berlin, Consuelo receives a message that Albert is dying. She rushes to the Rudolstadt castle and agrees to marry him *in extremis*. After his death, she renounces his wealth and title and continues on to Berlin, where she is imprisoned by Frederick the Great for conspiracy. In prison, she discovers the joys of musical composition and memorizes her creations, moving even closer to traditional folk music. She is freed from prison by the Invisibles, who take her to a palace where she studies their mysteries and decides to become a member of their secret society. She falls in love with her mysterious rescuer Liverani, only to discover that Albert is still alive and an Invisible. Forced to choose between love and duty, Consuelo follows her higher instincts and chooses Albert, who reveals that he is Liverani. After her initiation into the Invisibles, which takes place in another castle, with the symbolic name of Castle of the Grail, the marriage of Consuelo and Albert is renewed.

In the epilogue, the reader learns that the Invisibles have been forced underground, that Consuelo has lost her voice and Albert, his reason. She has become a composer writing music for Albert's poems. They wander with their children through the countryside, bringing hope to the poor and needy. Thus, Consuelo is as poor at the end of the novel as she was at the beginning, but she has become the "Good Goddess of Poverty." She has fulfilled her artistic destiny by becoming a creator—a complete Romantic artist. She has fulfilled her political and spiritual destiny by helping the needy. Finally, she has fulfilled her destiny as a woman by uniting physical and spiritual love in her relationship with Albert. She is the whole woman Lélia wanted to be. She lives up to her name "Consuelo" by bringing "consolation" to those around her.

The religious and political philosophy of Albert and the Invisibles, which Consuelo adopts at the end of the novel, was inspired by Pierre Leroux, a Socialist thinker whom Sand admired. In *Consuelo*, the Invisibles base their doctrine on a belief in absolute equality between sexes and classes. They also pro-claim the right of the people to participate as fully as the priests in religious sacraments. Their motto, The Cup to the People, refers to the communion chalice. This desire to reform the Catholic church was a constant preoccupation of Sand, best expressed in *Spiridion*, which develops a religious philosophy of history. Parallel to her desire to reform the Church is her desire to reform society, which finds in *Consuelo* its most complete expression.

This novel, which is epic in scope, has been called a novel of initiation as well as a *Bildungsroman*. Because of its length, it is a challenge to most modern readers. Its beautiful landscapes, fascinating characters, and exciting plot, however, reward readers for their perseverance.

THE DEVIL'S POOL

If *Consuelo* can be likened to an epic poem, *The Devil's Pool* is more like a folk song. Considered the perfect example of Sand's rustic novels, it is short, simple, and tightly structured. The novel has only two major characters, Germain, a thirty-year-old widower with three children, and Marie, a poverty-stricken sixteen-year-old girl. The title of the novel leads one to think that the occult might play as large a role in this novel as in *Consuelo*. Actually, the Devil's Pool, which forms the center of the narrative structure, is magic only because it makes people lose their way in the forest at night. Marie and Germain, accompanied by Germain's oldest child, Pierre, lose their way near this pool and there discover the truth about themselves—that they love each other. The major theme of the novel is thus quasi-biblical: "Those who think they are lost are found," or "One finds one's way by losing it."

The conflict in the plot arises from the fact that Germain must remarry to ensure the economic viability of the family unit, although at first he has no desire to do so. Marie is considered an unfit wife for him because of her youth and poverty. In the forest, however, she shows her true character—she is provident, attuned to nature, and clever at caring for children. After Germain recognizes her special gifts, he still has to persuade the elders of his family that she is an appropriate bride for him. Until the end of the story, he is uncertain whether Marie returns his love.

The ideological basis of this novel springs from Rousseau's theories about the purity of country life and the corruption of the cities. Germain and Marie, the innocent country people, find their opposites in the vain, materialistic Cathérine Guérin, a widow whom Germain was supposed to marry, and the Farmer of Ormeaux, the licentious master who attempts to seduce Marie. It is important to note that they are both members of the middle class as well as inhabitants of a village. Sand's vision of the country, however, is more than simply an ideological construct. She grew up in the country, and her portraits of the peasants of Berry have done much to preserve the language and folklore that were beginning to disappear.

There is an innate conflict in the rustic novels between Sand's desire to conserve and preserve a disappearing way of life and her avowed purpose of reforming society by promoting understanding between the bourgeois and the peasant. Her rustic novels have been read for one hundred years as tributes to the status quo and have been used by the French educational system to keep people in their place. This is clearly not what Sand intended when she wrote in the introduction to *The Devil's Pool*, "It is necessary for Lazarus to leave his dungheap so that the poor will no longer rejoice in the death of the rich. It is necessary that all be happy so that the happiness of the few may not be criminal and cursed by God." In this introduction, Sand explains that the novel was inspired by an engraving by Hans Holbein the Younger showing death as the only recompense for a life of hard labor in the fields. Sand believed that nineteenth century laborers should have life rather than death as a reward and that inequities should be rectified on earth rather than in Heaven. In this way, *The Devil's Pool* joins the technical perfection of a new genre of novel with an expansion of Sand's constant concern for the suffering of humanity.

Lucy M. Schwartz

OTHER MAJOR WORKS

SHORT FICTION: *Contes d'une grand'mère*, 1873, 1876 (*Tales of a Grandmother*, 1930).

PLAYS: *Théâtre complet de George Sand*, pb. 1877 (5 volumes).

NONFICTION: *Lettres à Marcie*, 1837; *Lettres d'un voyageur*, 1837 (*Letters of a Traveller*, 1847); *Un Hiver à Majorque*, 1841; *Histoire de ma vie*, 1854-1855 (20 volumes; *History of My Life*, 1901); *Questions d'art et de littérature*, 1878; *Questions politiques et sociales*, 1879; *Letters*, 1896 (9 volumes); *Journal intime*, 1926 (*The Intimate Journal*, 1929); *Sketches and Hints*, 1926; *Correspondance*, 1964-1981 (15 volumes); *Oeuvres autobiographiques*, 1970-1971 (2 volumes).

MISCELLANEOUS: *Works*, 1887 (38 volumes).

BIBLIOGRAPHY

Atwood, William G. *The Lioness and the Little One: The Liaison of George Sand and Frédéric Chopin*. New York: Columbia University Press, 1980. A careful scholarly account of a part of Sand's life and career that has often been distorted and sensationalized.

Cate, Curtis. *George Sand*. Boston: Little, Brown, 1975. A sound, comprehensive biography. See the preface for a discussion of Maurois's classic biography and the fluctations of Sand's reputation.

Crecelius, Kathryn J. *Family Romances: George Sand's Early Novels*. Bloomington: Indiana University Press, 1987. An informative study, with chapters on Sand's handling of heroic romance and bourgeois realism, her role as woman artist, with separate chapters on *Lélia*, *Mauprat*, and *Valentine*. Includes very detailed notes but no bibliography.

Danahy, Michael. *The Feminization of the Novel*. Gainesville: University of Florida Press, 1991. Studies novels by Sand (*Fanchon the Cricket*), Gustave Flaubert, and Madame de La Fayette.

Dickenson, Donna. *George Sand: A Brave Man—The Most Womanly Woman*. New York: Berg, 1988. Focuses on Sand's sexuality, feminism, improvisatory work and personality, and daring Byronic career. Includes chronology, detailed notes, and an annotated bibliography. One of the few book-length introductory studies in English of Sand.

George Sand Papers, Conference Proceedings, 1976, University Center for Cultural and Intercultural

Studies, Hofstra University. New York: AMS Press, 1976. A wide range of studies on Sand relevance, her career in Paris, her use of social protest in her early work, her feminism, her view of Honoré de Balzac, her reputation among Russian writers, and other topics.

Maurois, André. *Lélia: The Life of George Sand.* New York: Harper & Brothers, 1953. A classic biography by one of the genre's most renowned practitioners. Less scholarly than Cate, but written with verve and a sure grasp of both the subject and her period.

Powell, David A. *George Sand.* Boston: Twayne, 1990. An excellent introduction to the life and works of Sand. Includes bibliographical references and an index.

(D.C. Public Library)

WILLIAM SAROYAN

Born: Fresno, California; August 31, 1908
Died: Fresno, California; May 18, 1981

PRINCIPAL LONG FICTION

The Human Comedy, 1943
The Adventures of Wesley Jackson, 1946
Rock Wagram, 1951
Tracy's Tiger, 1951
The Laughing Matter, 1953 (reprinted as *The Secret Story,* 1954)
Mama I Love You, 1956
Papa You're Crazy, 1957
Boys and Girls Together, 1963
One Day in the Afternoon of the World, 1964

OTHER LITERARY FORMS

Despite his many novels, William Saroyan is more famous for his work in the short story, the drama, and autobiography. Each of these areas received emphasis at different stages in his career. In the 1930's, he made a spectacular literary debut with an avalanche of brilliant, exuberant, and unorthodox short stories. Major early collections were *The Dar-*

ing Young Man on the Flying Trapeze and Other Stories (1934), *Inhale and Exhale* (1936), *Three Times Three* (1936), and *Love, Here Is My Hat and Other Short Romances* (1938). *My Name Is Aram* (1940), a group of stories detailing the experiences of Aram Garoghlanian growing up in a small California town, marks the culmination of his short-story artistry.

Most of Saroyan's plays and his productions on Broadway were concentrated in the years between 1939 and 1942. *My Heart's in the Highlands* was produced by the Group Theatre in April, 1939. His second major production, *The Time of Your Life* (1939), was awarded both the Pulitzer Prize and the New York Drama Critics' Circle Award and is still considered Saroyan's best play. *Hello Out There* (1941), a one-act play, is also regarded as a fine drama.

In 1951, Saroyan and Ross Bagdasarian published a popular song, "Come On-a My House." Saroyan also wrote several television plays, including an adaptation of *The Time of Your Life.* Starting with *The Bicycle*

Rider in Beverly Hills (1952), Saroyan composed extensive memoirs, including *Here Comes, There Goes, You Know Who* (1961), *Not Dying* (1963), *Days of Life and Death and Escape to the Moon* (1970), *Places Where I've Done Time* (1972), *Sons Come and Go, Mothers Hang in Forever* (1976), *Chance Meetings* (1978), and *Obituaries* (1979).

ACHIEVEMENTS

A thorough evaluation of Saroyan's achievement as a writer has yet to be made. By the age of twenty, he had already decided his role in life was to be that of a professional writer, and throughout his remaining fifty years he dedicated himself to that vocation, publishing voluminously in all literary forms, with the exception of poetry. The sheer bulk of his work and his admission that much of it was done merely to earn money have worked against him. Further, his frequent arguments with his critics and his increasingly difficult personality left him with few strong critical advocates.

Saroyan's lasting literary achievement is in the area of the short story, where he expanded the genre by linking narrative form to the essay and infusing his work with a highly individual vision of poetic intensity. Many of his stories feature a character modeled on Saroyan, a writer-persona who, though often obsessed with his own ideas and feelings, is vitally alive to the world of his immediate experience. Several of the most successful stories concern childhood experiences in an ethnic, small-town environment modeled on Saroyan's Fresno. Saroyan impressed his early readers with his rediscovery of the wondrous in the texture of ordinary American life. *The Saroyan Special: Selected Stories* (1948) is a collection of his best stories. *My Name Is Aram* delineates with some beautiful character portraits Saroyan's sense of the poetic interplay of values in the ethnic community.

Saroyan's plays oppose the vitality of personality and individual dreams to the force of social institutions and the threats of war. In their sense of improvised movement, his plays were a deliberate challenge to the strictly plotted productions of the commercial theater.

Starting in the mid-1940's, Saroyan turned his attention to longer fiction, writing over the next two decades a series of novels concerned with marriage and divorce. Apparently inspired by his own experiences, the books become increasingly skeptical about romantic love and reflect Saroyan's growing cynicism about the man-woman relationship while retaining his fondness for the charm of childhood.

Saroyan's longer fiction grows gradually out of those short stories concerned with growing up in a small town. *My Name Is Aram*, a story collection moving toward novelistic unity, leads directly to *The Human Comedy*, where Saroyan finally succeeds in making a novel out of his childhood material. While *The Adventures of Wesley Jackson* must be regarded as a failed attempt to write in the picaresque mode, *Rock Wagram* is a surprisingly mature handling of the thematic scope provided by the novel form. Whereas *The Adventures of Wesley Jackson* presents marriage as an idyllic goal for the solitary man, *Rock Wagram* focuses on the crushing effect of the title character's failed marriage. Several shorter book-length works—*Tracy's Tiger, Mama I Love You*, and *Papa You're Crazy*—seem more tied to Saroyan's earlier material in their confinement to the perspectives of childhood and youth and, for the most part, are limited in theme and story situations. Saroyan's other novels—*The Laughing Matter, Boys and Girls Together*, and *One Day in the Afternoon of the World*—are deliberate forays into social areas where relationships are often intense and events are somber in their finality. Like *Rock Wagram*, each of these books centers on a male's struggle with marriage, death, and divorce. The last novel, *One Day in the Afternoon of the World*, features a character who at last seems to have acquired the wisdom to deal with such personal crises. Though his longer fictions are professionally wrought, Saroyan's achievements in the novel form are limited.

The mood of the later novels is picked up and carried to greater extremes in Saroyan's memoirs, a series whose loose formats encourage the author to reveal, often in free associations, his deep anxiety about his relationship to his society. Saroyan's memoirs, generally his weakest works, become increasingly preoccupied with death, the significance of his literary achievements, and with his struggle to ward off a bitterness that he occasionally admits but wants to deny.

BIOGRAPHY

So much of William Saroyan's work—especially his fiction—is drawn from the circumstances of his life that it has a biographical dimension. He was born in 1908, in Fresno, California, the city where he died on May 18, 1981. The child of Armenian immigrants, he faced his first hardship when, at his father's death in 1911, he was placed for four years in the Fred Finch orphanage in Oakland. During these years, his mother worked in San Francisco as a maid, finally gathering the money to move back to a house in Fresno with her four children. Here Saroyan lived from age seven to seventeen, learning Armenian, acquiring an irreverence for the town's chief social institutions, the church and the school, and working as a newspaper boy and as a telegraph messenger to help support the family. At fifteen, he left school permanently to work at his Uncle Aram's vineyards. In 1926, he left Fresno, first to go to Los Angeles, then, after a brief time in the National Guard, to move to San Francisco, where he tried a number of jobs, eventually becoming at nineteen, the manager of a Postal Telegraph branch office. In 1928, determined to make his fortune as a writer, he made his first trip to New York. He returned to San Francisco the following year, somewhat discouraged by his lack of success. In the early 1930's, however, he began to write story after story, culminating with his decision in January, 1934, to write one story a day for the whole month. That year, *Story* published "The Daring Young Man on the Flying Trapeze," and suddenly Saroyan stories were appearing in many of the top periodicals. His first book of stories was published that year, and the following year he had enough money to make an ethnic return, a trip to Soviet Armenia.

Except for a few months in 1936 spent working on motion pictures at the Paramount lot, Saroyan spent the majority of the 1930's in San Francisco. By 1939, he had shifted his activities to drama, writing and producing plays on Broadway. After *The Time of Your Life* won both the New York Drama Critics' Circle Award for the best play of 1939 to 1940 and the Pulitzer Prize, Saroyan made headlines by rejecting the Pulitzer on the grounds that he was opposed to prizes in the arts and to patronage. More controversy followed when he wrote *The Human Comedy* as a screenplay for Metro-Goldwin-Mayer, then argued about directing the film and tried to buy his work back for twenty thousand dollars, more than he was paid for it. At that time he was also, in a letter to *The New York Times*, publicly denouncing the Broadway theater.

Even though he had pacificist sympathies, Saroyan was inducted into the United States Army in October, 1942, serving until 1945. His most traumatic experience in the 1940's, however, was his marriage to Carol Marcus, which lasted from 1943 to 1949, and which was resumed briefly from 1951 to 1953, before a final divorce. The couple had two children, Aram and Lucy.

In the 1950's, Saroyan began to write more long fiction, much of it dealing with marital difficulties. In addition, in 1951, he was the coauthor of a hit song, "Come On-a My House," and in the late 1950's, he began writing television plays. From 1952 to 1959, he lived in a Malibu beach house, an environment which encouraged him to work very steadily. During this time, he lived a less public existence and, feeling monetary pressure because of his gambling and his huge income tax debt, he increasingly developed a reputation as a difficult personality.

In 1960, after some travel about the world, he settled in a modest apartment at 74 Rue Taitbout, Paris. The following year he was briefly a writer-in-residence at Purdue University. By 1962, he had arranged to buy two adjacent houses in Fresno and thereafter alternated living between Fresno and Paris. He spent most of the last fifteen years of his life working on various volumes of memoirs. Five days before his death he called the Associated Press to give this statement: "Everybody has got to die, but I have always believed an exception would be made in my case. Now what?" After much success (much money earned by writing, much money lost by gambling), much international travel, much controversy, much fame, and much obscurity, William Saroyan died of cancer in his hometown, Fresno, in 1981.

ANALYSIS

William Saroyan's work habits were a major determinant (for better or worse) of his unique literary effects. He regarded writing as work, something that required disciplined effort, but also as an activity whose chief characteristic was the free play of the mind. As he explained his practice, Saroyan would often give himself assignments, a story or a chapter a day (or so many hours of writing), but would seldom work from a detailed organizational plan. Uncomfortable with mulling over possible styles, attitudes, narrative directions, he would often prefer to plunge into writing, fueled by coffee and cigarettes, hoping that whatever got down on paper would inspire the story to "take off on its own." Whatever relationships would be worked out would be those of deep structure, drawn from his inner being rather than from rhetoric. At times he would begin with a "theory" or abstract idea. (For example, the theory stated at the end of "War" is that hatred and ugliness exist in the heart of everyone.) The act of writing itself was to clarify and refine the idea for the writer. In "Myself upon the Earth," the writer's own situation, his dead father, and his attitudes toward the world begin to weave into the free connections that substitute for a conventional plot. Thematically, the apparently undisciplined becomes the true discipline as the dedication expressed in an attitude toward life—toward humanity is transformed through the narration into a dedication to art.

There are obvious difficulties with this method of composition. "The Man with His Heart in the Highlands" begins in the course of its improvisation to split in two; when Saroyan puts it into the form of a full-length play, the theme of the importance of acceptance in forming the new American community is finally seen as a basic articulation in the material. Saroyan also acknowledged revision as an important stage in the writing process, but much of his work suffers from a lack of objectivity, the ability to see his own work clearly and revise it accordingly.

While the act of writing was for Saroyan both a kind of thinking and a performance, the materials of his art were usually the materials of his life. Much in the manner of Thomas Wolfe (an early influence), Saroyan's fiction was often drawn directly from his experience. A letter to Calouste Gulbenkian (in *Letters from 74 Rue Taitbout*, 1969) shows how Saroyan drew in detail on his external experience and his frame of mind for most of the content of "The Assyrian." Writing, he came to believe, was connected with "noticing" life and with the sense that life itself was theatrical. Although Saroyan acknowledged that the process of writing had to discover form in its materials and that the writer had to be transformed into a character framed by his art, the sense of witnessed scene and character in his best work lends a necessary solidity to his creative exuberance.

The favorite writer-personas in Saroyan's early fiction were poet-philosophers in the manner of Walt Whitman; American wiseguys (the young grown suddenly smarter about the ways of the world than their elders); or combinations of the two. His later long fiction featured the writer as a veteran of life, sometimes bitter but with his own philosophic resignation, a mode of stoic humility about what he might be able to accomplish. Saroyan's typical themes—the advocacy of love and a condemnation of war and violence—are less important than the way in which he plays the narrator (usually a writer) against the narrator's circumstances. In the most deep-seated manifestation of this paradigm—the ethnic boy responding to his American environment—Saroyan associates the ethnic self in the ethnic community with naturalness, lack of self-consciousness, true being, and dignity of person. The American environment, while it promises opportunity with its training and its competitive games, also has institutions which seem to specialize in modes of restriction, punishment, and prejudice.

The ethnic responds to his environment with a complex involvement and detachment. On the one hand, he is willing, even eager, to be assimilated; on the other hand, however, he is always aware of a kind of existence that has no adequately defined relationship to the American world of conventional social fact. The ethnic's psychological relationship to the world recalls Whitman's democratic paradox of people being intensely individual and at the same time like everyone else. In Saroyan's fiction, there is at times an emphasis on the individual's alienation—as when the protagonist in "The Daring Young Man on the Flying Trapeze" feels "somehow he had ventured upon the wrong earth" and the central character in "1,2,3,4,5,6,7,8" feels the room he is living in is not a part of him and wants a home, "a place in which to return to himself." Invariably, however, the ethnic family and its small-town environment expand quite naturally for Saroyan into a version of the democratic family of people.

This sense of communal home, however, is not easily preserved—as Saroyan's novels with their marital catastrophes and lonely protagonists repeatedly demonstrate. From the beginning, the fate of Saroyan's ethnic was complicated by the fact that his deepest allegiance was to a national community that no longer existed. In an early story, "Seventy Thousand Assyrians," the Assyrian states, "I was born in the old country, but I want to get over it . . . everything is washed up over there." Though Saroyan could be sympathetic to such practicality, he tried to achieve, often with a deliberate naïveté, a poetic point of view that would embrace both existence in the old community of family values (which was a basic part of his being) and existence in the practical new world (which offered the only opportunity for becoming).

From the perspective of Saroyan's writer-persona, the world outside is continually new, funny, sometimes strange, often wonderful, a place of innocent relationships and suspended judgments. A recurring situation in his work has someone who is apprehended for theft trying to explain that he is not guilty because his value system is different from that of his accusers. On the one hand, Saroyan believes in an attitude of joyful acceptance: Here he sees man "on the threshold of an order of himself which must find human reality a very simple unavoidable majesty and joy, with all its complications and failures." On the other hand, he imagines, like Whitman, a more somber mystic vision based on "the joyous sameness of life and death." In this mysterious crucible, life is

fate, perhaps only glimpsed fully when "drawing to the edge of full death every person is restored to innocence—to have lived was not his fault." Saroyan's basic impulse is to preserve, recapture, and restore the innocence that the world has lost that state of being which sees experience only as a fantastic fate which serves ultimately to redeem the primal self.

MY NAME IS ARAM

Like Sherwood Anderson's *Winesburg, Ohio* (1919) and William Faulkner's *The Unvanquished* (1938), *My Name Is Aram* is a book that falls midway between short-story collection and novel. The stories are separate and distinct, but they all concern the small-town experiences of the same boy, Aram, with his Armenian relatives. There is little sense of sequence but rather an accumulated manifestation of the potential wisdom in this world. Saroyan emphasizes the preservation of innocence, the warding off of the absolute element in the values of the adult culture. Aram and his friends turn social rituals into human games, and in the course of their experiences demonstrate that the many social failures in these stories have really two constituents, the innocent immediacy of the experience (its essential value) and the cultural "truths" and judgments applied to it. Through vital participation in their world, Aram and his friends begin to negotiate its preconceived ideas.

THE HUMAN COMEDY

The setting, the characters, and the young man's perspective which predominate in *The Human Comedy* all have their sources in Saroyan short stories. The background is World War II, and the California small town has accordingly become "the home front." In the book's basic drama, the innocence in this environment—its vulnerable children, young people, and women and its emotional closeness—must come to terms with death and its finalities.

Within the context of the small-town milieu, the novel focuses primarily on the Macauley family and most often on Homer Macauley, a fourteen-year-old telegraph messenger boy. As Homer delivers telegrams announcing the deaths of soldiers, he finds himself getting caught up psychologically in the shock of the family reactions. On his first such delivery, to Rosa Sandoval, the woman responds with an eerie, calm hysteria in which she confuses Homer with her dead son and begins to think of both as little boys. Feeling at first both compassion and an urge to flee, Homer gradually arrives at an awareness of the meaning of death. With the help of his mother (whose husband has recently died), he fights through feelings of loneliness and isolation toward the idea that death and change afford perspectives for redeeming the values of innocence, love, and life itself.

The ideal of the community dominates the book. The novel implies in its moments of crisis and healing—Homer becoming briefly transformed into the son of another woman; Tobey taking the place of the dead Marcus in the Macauley family—that humankind is a single family. Though the fact of death and the awareness of death are constant threats to the individual, the book, as the allusions to Homer's *Odyssey* (c. 800 B.C.E.) imply, is about to return home, the coming back from the ugly realities of the outside world to the love and security which humankind can provide.

The book seems intent on assuring its readers that despite economic tribulations, the discontent of restless desire, the anxiety connected with competition, and the confining tendency of its institutions, the community is an active, positive force. A working out in the rhythms of experience of the differences between people—age, sex, degrees of formality—invariably shows positive contrasts. The many relationships Homer has with older people are all thematically active ingredients for dramatizing the closeness of the community. *The Human Comedy* insists—perhaps too facilely at times—on the capacity of the American community to regulate the experience of life and the encounter with death.

THE ADVENTURES OF WESLEY JACKSON

The Adventures of Wesley Jackson may be Saroyan's worst novel. It is marred by two closely related problems, an uncertain grasp of form and a confusion about its issues. Saroyan's indiscriminate use of his own military experience takes the novel hopelessly out of control. Evidently attempting to give himself ample latitude with the novel form, Saroyan chose to employ the picaresque form, referring in his comments on the novel to Mark Twain's *The Adventures of Huckleberry Finn* (1884). Unfortunately, Wesley is much too introverted to be an effective picaro of any kind. He is intended to be a nonconformist, but, except for a few anti-Army establishment opinions, his personal idealism and prosaic earnestness only serve to make him seem as remote from the realities of Army life as from the realities of war. Lacking a feeling for the actual operations of the Army, the book meanders haphazardly from the bureaucratic to the personal, from one location to another, from family concerns to writing ambitions, succeeding finally in giving the impression of an Army journal rather than a picaresque novel.

At times the book develops an antiwar theme; at times the theme seems to be the pettiness of the Army bureaucracy. No one theme, however, is developed consistently. Wesley's self-absorbed narration does provide some shaping by turning the officers into bad fathers (cruel figures of authority), the women into sympathetic (though vague) images, and his fellow soldiers into boys, sometimes naughty but basically innocent. In sporadic, almost desultory, fashion the first part of the book features Wesley's search for his father, the essentially good man who has been displaced and ignored by organized society. The last part of the book becomes concerned with Wesley's search for a son (actually a search for a woman to bear him a son). Were Wesley's narration less limited, less egotistical, these thematic threads might have made firmer connections.

ROCK WAGRAM

The split structure of *Rock Wagram*—approximately half the novel taking place in September, 1942, and half in February, 1950—emphasizes the drive of Rock Wagram (pronounced Vah-GRAM) to be married to Ann Ford and his resultant puzzled desperation when that marriage fails. The chronological gap, by omitting the marriage and Rock's military experience, accents the negative quality of this part of his life. Yet by leaving out the specific difficulties that are so much a part of his later depression, the novel makes Rock's psychology a problematic frame for understanding events instead of using the events of the past to put his psychology in an understandable perspective. At times, the failure of the marriage seems explained by Ann's frivolous, lying character. At other times, the failure seems to grow out of Rock's ethnic assumption that people must become involved in a family existence.

Rock Wagram explores the tensions between people as individuals and people as social animals. In his motion-picture career, Rock has become successful as an individual star, but his acquaintance with Ann Ford kindles his memories of certain values from his Armenian background, particularly the notion that a man is not complete until he had founded his own family, been husband to his wife, father to his children. Unhappily for him, Ann turns out to be like so many other characters whose departures from their true natures disturb him; her lies signify to him that she is refusing to be herself, hoping for something better. Earlier Rock has met a series of males rebelling against their heritage: Paul Key, the Hollywood producer who hates being a Jew; Sam Schwartz, Paul's nephew, who devotes himself to becoming the image of success; and Craig Adams, the completely assimilated Armenian. Although these men are denying both their heritage and their own individuality, they are better adapted to the world of casual social relationships than he, and the book raises doubts about the possibilities of a deeply authentic existence.

Rock chooses to see his life—and the life of man—as involving continual adjustment to a Shavian life force, a power which, once he begins to perceive it through his Armenian ethnic environment, becomes his ultimate guide to true being. To get in tune with this force, he tries to be uninhibited in his social relationships, to go with the flow of events, to pay attention to his circumstances and to the people he is with, and to be, as he puts it, "a good witness" to his own experience and to his world.

Part of Rock's effort to live in terms of true being is a half-conscious cultivation of strategies toward death. His reaction to the death of his brother Haig is rage; at the death of his friend Paul Key, he affects a Hemingwayesque stoicism; and to his mother's death, he responds by plunging deeply and intensely into his subjective nature. In spite of all attempts to come to terms with the reality of death, he seems at last depressed, left with a sense of being part not only

of a dying culture but also of a dying world. As he goes back to acting at the end of the narrative, his feeling for his art is one of obligation rather than enthusiasm for an individualized expression of himself. Yet, as the humor in his last statement indicates, he is finally not without hope in probing his lonely situation for its satisfactions.

THE LAUGHING MATTER

The laughter of *The Laughing Matter* is that of black comedy. From the time Swan Nazarenus announces to her husband that she is pregnant with another man's child, *The Laughing Matter* moves powerfully but erratically toward what seems an almost self-indulgently gruesome ending. The story line is captive to the emotional tensions and explosions of Evan Nazarenus as he attempts to sort out a future direction for himself, Swan, and their two children, Red and Eva. As he resorts successively to drink, violence, a return to family harmony, an abortion, and more violence, the problem-pregnancy tends to be obscured by his confusing attempts at solution. Since his personality is never clarified in the characterization, and since he often gives the impression of running aimlessly about the countryside, Evan becomes progressively less sympathetic in his shifting relationship to people and events.

The accompaniment to the mad rhapsody of his behavior is more carefully controlled. The children are innocent victims, becoming increasingly aware that something is wrong and even acting out some of the tensions themselves. The Walzes, a neighbor couple, have their own fights, and Evan's brother, Dade, who has, after years of domestic turbulence, lost his family entirely, conveniently defines one possible outcome.

Complicating the question of what to do is the issue of who is to blame. In one scene between Evan and Dade, the two brothers—who often speak in an old-country tongue—review their ethnic fate as heads of families, Evan wondering what they as males have done wrong. Evan debates whether he ought to be more feminine, more kindly, or strive to retain his masculine pride in the face of what may be an essential challenge to his person. His solution, the abortion, is less an act of harsh morality (as he later views it) than the result of a desire to begin again, to regain a kind of innocence by reversing events.

The ironies and the deaths pile up so rapidly at the conclusion that they achieve only a blurred effect. The fact that so much violence results from simple ignorance begins to make the characters comic rather than tragic, and this may have been the prompting behind Saroyan's title. When Evan accuses the wrong man as the adulterer (pushing the poor lonely man toward suicide), and when he shoots and kills his brother Dade under the mistaken notion that they have been responsible for Swan's death from abortion, Evan seems more the incompetent than the grief-stricken victim. His own death in an auto accident may have been meant to suggest that the whole chain of events was merely a series of accidents, but this must be weighed against the remarks of the doctor who explains to Dade that Swan committed suicide and that she had evidently had a strong death wish for several years. For all its masculine madness, this book begins and ends by pointing an accusing finger at the woman.

BOYS AND GIRLS TOGETHER

Boys and Girls Together is a realistic study of a husband-wife relationship that moves with an understated satire toward black humor. The husband, Dick, is a writer who finds that his current domestic relationship has made it impossible for him to work, thus heaping financial strain upon his already turbulent marriage to Daisy. In the course of their sporadic fighting, the couple discovers greater and greater depths of incompatibility. Dick comes to the conclusion that she is ignorant, trivial, and selfish; Daisy accuses him of being egotistical and immature. Were it not for the two children (Johnny, five, and Rosey, two and a half), the writer, who is a family man, would undoubtedly leave.

As this account of a few days in their lives demonstrates, what keeps the marriage together is their socializing with other couples. The slight story line follows the meeting of Dick and Daisy with two other couples for a few days of fun in San Francisco. Though only casual friends, all the couples have common characteristics: In each instance, the husband has achieved prominence in the arts; in each

case, the husband is many years older than the wife; and in each instance, the difference in age seems part of the strain on the marriage. Before all six can get together, the oldest husband, Leander, dies of a heart attack, an episode witnessed by Oscar Bard (the actor) and his wife, and by Leander's wife Lucretia. Dick and Daisy arrive soon after the attack and seem generally ineffective in preventing the scene from sliding from seriousness to farce. Dick eventually begins to act as satiric observer, commenting on Oscar's egotistical discomfort and on Lucretia's performance as grieving widow. The scene has its climax in Oscar's long speech on the difficulties of their kind of marriage. While he begins by pointing out realistically that the women they have married are not for them, he finally comes to the conclusion that it is sexual attraction that gives the necessary life to all partners in such marriages and which makes them continue to put up with each other. Dick does not disagree. Soon the survivors are planning a trip to Reno as another distraction from the harsh realities around them. Earlier, Dick had resented it when his wife teased him about being a fool for sex. In the last part of the novel, his understated satiric vision outlines them all as characters in a sexual farce.

If all of William Saroyan's writing can be regarded as his attempt to understand and define his position in the world, his long fiction must be seen as his deliberate recognition of the crueler circumstances in that world—death, the failure of love, divorce, the recalcitrant details of life itself. His own marital troubles undoubtedly inspired the novels of the 1950's and 1960's with their fragmented families, and while the intently masculine perspective in these books reveals a serious but virtually unexamined reverence for love and marriage, it also demonstrates the author's own very personal irritation with wives. In nearly all of his novels, the formal problem tends to be the male protagonist's varied reactions to his situation. In *Rock Wagram* and *The Laughing Matter*, Saroyan is successful in focusing these reactions by means of intense emotional pressures, but his confusion about final blame for the marital breakdown makes a fictional closure difficult. With *Papa You're Crazy* and *Mama I Love You*, he moves to the detachment of the child's point of view but is still uncertain about the extent to which the world's facts ought to—and must—impinge on the individual family member. (To what degree, for example, does the particular existence of the parent doom or mold the life of the child?) In *Boys and Girls Together* and *One Day in the Afternoon of the World*, Saroyan gets mixed results from mining the attitudes of his male protagonists for a perspective that would be both a consistent and legitimate interpretation of their marital situations. In Saroyan's long fiction, as well as in his other writing, both his strengths and his weaknesses derive from his insistent emotional presence.

Walter Shear

OTHER MAJOR WORKS

SHORT FICTION: *The Daring Young Man on the Flying Trapeze and Other Stories*, 1934; *Inhale and Exhale*, 1936; *Three Times Three*, 1936; *The Gay and Melancholy Flux: Short Stories*, 1937; *Little Children*, 1937; *Love, Here Is My Hat and Other Short Romances*, 1938; *The Trouble with Tigers*, 1938; *Three Fragments and a Story*, 1939; *Peace, It's Wonderful*, 1939; *My Name Is Aram*, 1940; *Saroyan's Fables*, 1941; *The Insurance Salesman and Other Stories*, 1941; *Forty-eight Saroyan Stories*, 1942; *Some Day I'll Be a Millionaire: Thirty-four More Great Stories*, 1944; *Dear Baby*, 1944; *The Saroyan Special: Selected Stories*, 1948; *The Fiscal Hoboes*, 1949; *The Assyrian and Other Stories*, 1950; *The Whole Voyald and Other Stories*, 1956; *William Saroyan Reader*, 1958; *Love*, 1959; *After Thirty Years: The Daring Young Man on the Flying Trapeze*, 1964; *Best Stories of William Saroyan*, 1964; *The Tooth and My Father*, 1974.

PLAYS: *The Hungerers: A Short Play*, pb. 1939; *My Heart's in the Highlands*, pr., pb. 1939; *The Time of Your Life*, pr., pb. 1939 (also includes essays); *Love's Old Sweet Song*, pr., pb. 1940; *Three Plays: My Heart's in the Highlands, The Time of Your Life, Love's Old Sweet Song*, pb. 1940; *Subway Circus*, pb. 1940; *The Ping-Pong Game*, pb. 1940 (one act); *The Beautiful People*, pr. 1940; *The Great American Goof*, pr. 1940; *Across the Board on Tomorrow Morning*, pr., pb. 1941; *Three Plays: The Beautiful People, Sweeney in the Trees, Across the Board on Tomorrow Morning*, pb. 1941; *Hello Out There*, pr. 1941 (one act); *Jim Dandy*, pr., pb. 1941; *Razzle Dazzle*, pb. 1942 (collection); *Talking to You*, pr., pb. 1942; *Get Away Old Man*, pr. 1943; *Sam Ego's House*, pr. 1947; *A Decent Birth, a Happy Funeral*, pb. 1949; *Don't Go Away Mad*, pr., pb. 1949; *The Slaughter of the Innocents*, pb. 1952; *The Cave Dwellers*, pr. 1957; *Once Around the Block*, pb. 1959; *Sam the Highest Jumper of Them All: Or, The London Comedy*, pr. 1960; *Settled Out of Court*, pr. 1960; *The Dogs: Or, The Paris Comedy and Two Other Plays*, pb. 1969.

NONFICTION: *Harlem as Seen by Hirschfield*, 1941; *Hilltop Russians in San Francisco*, 1941; *Why Abstract?*, 1945 (with Henry Miller and Hilaire Hiler); *The Twin Adventures: The Adventures of William Saroyan*, 1950; *The Bicycle Rider in Beverly Hills*, 1952; *Here Comes, There Goes, You Know Who*, 1961; *A Note on Hilaire Hiler*, 1962; *Not Dying*, 1963; *Short Drive, Sweet Chariot*, 1966; *Look at Us: Let's See: Here We Are*, 1967; *I Used to Believe I Had Forever: Now I'm Not So Sure*, 1968; *Letters from 74 Rue Taitbout*, 1969; *Days of Life and Death and Escape to the Moon*, 1970; *Places Where I've Done Time*, 1972; *Sons Come and Go, Mothers Hang in Forever*, 1976; *Chance Meetings*, 1978; *Obituaries*, 1979; *Births*, 1983.

CHILDREN'S LITERATURE: *Me*, 1963; *Horsey Gorsey and the Frog*, 1968.

MISCELLANEOUS: *My Name Is Saroyan*, 1983 (stories, verse, play fragments, and memoirs).

BIBLIOGRAPHY

Balakian, Nona. *The World of William Saroyan*. Lewisburg, Ohio: Bucknell University Press, 1998. Balakian, formerly a staff writer for *The New York Times Book Review*, knew Saroyan personally in his last years, and her observations of him color her assessment of his later works. She viewed it as her mission to resurrect his reputation and restore him among the finest of twentieth century American writers. Traces his evolution from ethnic writer to master of the short story, to playwright, and finally to existentialist.

Calonne, David Stephen. *William Saroyan: My Real Work Is Being*. Chapel Hill: University of North Carolina Press, 1983. A good introduction to Saroyan's work. Calonne balances his examination of Saroyan's short stories, plays, novels, memoirs, and essays. Includes excellent notes, a bibliography, and an index.

Foster, Edward Halsey. *William Saroyan: A Study of the Short Fiction*. New York: Twayne, 1991. This volume separates into three parts. The first is devoted to Foster's assessment of Saroyan's career as a short-story writer, the second focuses on Saroyan himself—and reprints an interview with the writer as well as several of his nonfiction pieces—and the third reprints essays on Saroyan written by other critics.

Keyishian, Harry, ed. *Critical Essays on William Saroyan*. New York: G. K. Hall & Co., 1995. Like other volumes in this series, this book includes contemporaneous reviews, outstanding extant criticism, and original commissioned essays. In addition to a preface by Keyishian and a substantial introduction to Saroyan and his critics by Alice K. Barter, the volume contains valuable new comparative studies of Saroyan and Walt Whitman and of Saroyan and Gertrude Stein.

Lee, Lawrence, and Barry Gifford. *Saroyan: A Biography*. New York: Harper & Row, 1984. A vivid biography of Saroyan that concentrates on the writer. Its unusual three-part structure opens at the height of his career (1940-1950), shifts to his roots and early literary struggles (1908-1939), and concludes with his last years (1950-1981).

MAY SARTON

Born: Wondelgem, Belgium; May 3, 1912
Died: York, Maine; July 16, 1995

PRINCIPAL LONG FICTION
The Single Hound, 1938
The Bridge of Years, 1946
Shadow of a Man, 1950
A Shower of Summer Days, 1952
Faithful Are the Wounds, 1955
The Birth of a Grandfather, 1957
The Fur Person: The Story of a Cat, 1957
The Small Room, 1961
Joanna and Ulysses, 1963
Mrs. Stevens Hears the Mermaids Singing, 1965
Miss Pickthorn and Mr. Hare: A Fable, 1966
The Poet and the Donkey, 1969
Kinds of Love, 1970
As We Are Now, 1973
Crucial Conversations, 1975
A Reckoning, 1978
Anger, 1982
The Magnificent Spinster, 1985
The Education of Harriet Hatfield, 1989

OTHER LITERARY FORMS

A poet as well as a novelist, May Sarton published a considerable number of volumes of verse. Her *Collected Poems, 1930-1973* appeared in 1974. She also wrote a fable, *Miss Pickthorn and Mr. Hare*; an animal fantasy story, *The Fur Person: The Story of a Cat*; several volumes of autobiography, including *I Knew a Phoenix: Sketches for an Autobiography* (1959), *Plant Dreaming Deep* (1968), and *A World of Light: Portraits and Celebrations* (1976); and several journals of her life in Nelson, New Hampshire, and York, Maine.

ACHIEVEMENTS

It was after World War II, with the novel *The Bridge of Years* and the poems collected in *The Lion and the Rose* (1948), that Sarton's reputation began to grow. Her novels met with a mixed response from critics and reviewers, sometimes condemned for awkward or imprecise style, an odd charge against a practicing poet. Even Carolyn Heilbrun, Sarton's defender, admits that confusing shifts of viewpoint occur in her fiction. On the other hand, Sarton's honesty in presenting human problems, seeing them from varied perspectives, has generally been acknowledged. In some ways, novels such as *Mrs. Stevens Hears the Mermaids Singing* and *Crucial*

Conversations are dramatized debates about art, feminine culture, interpersonal relationships, tradition, and memory. Sarton was also accused of sentimentality and preciousness, and she tried to shift her style to a more direct, less self-conscious one after the early 1970's, perhaps answering critics of *Mrs. Stevens Hears the Mermaids Singing*, who saw it as too arch, too knowing. She tended to take current issues or fashions such as the Vietnam War, death-and-dying, feminine consciousness, and Jungian psychology as material for her novels. Autobiographical material frequently enters into her fiction, particular characters being reinvoked in various works and especially types such as authoritarian women, supportive women, and rebellious young people.

Sarton complained of the lack of serious critical scrutiny of her work and expressed disappointment as well at her failure to achieve a large popular success. She has been stereotyped as a woman's writer, presumably creating slick plot situations, overdramatic dialogue, and conventional characters in romantic duos or trios. Some of these charges are true; she herself, noting the difficulty of supporting herself by her work even as late as the 1970's, although she was a prolific and well-established writer, spoke of the difficulties of being a single woman writer not sustained by a family or a religious community. Nevertheless, she affirmed the possibility of self-renewal, commenting: "I believe that eventually my work will be seen as a whole, all the poems and all the novels, as the expression of a vision of life which, though unfashionable all the way, has validity." The surge of interest in her work at the end of the twentieth century, particularly among feminist scholars, would seem to confirm Sarton's hopes.

BIOGRAPHY

May Sarton was born Eléanore Marie Sarton in Wondelgem, Belgium, on May 3, 1912. Her mother, Mabel Elwes Sarton, a designer who worked at Maison Dangette, Brussels, was a determined craftsperson and an uncompromising seeker of high standards. Her father, George Sarton, pampered by his Belgian upper-middle-class family after losing his mother early, was an active socialist who did mathe-

(Gabriel Amadeus Cooney)

matical studies at the University of Brussels before settling into his life's work as a major historian of science; he founded the leading journal in the field, *Isis*, in 1912. He was a methodical scholar who even after his day's scholarly labors would make notes in the evening concerning recent research by other scholars. May's mother compromised her talents for her husband's career, but Mrs. Sarton's gift of "refashioning things magically" inspired her daughter's own verbal artistry.

One close friend of her mother was Céline Dangotte Limbosch or "Mamie," whose home near Brussels Sarton has recalled as the one place in the world which would not change and whose traits appear in the heroine of *The Bridge of Years*. Her husband, Raumond Limbosch, a poet who never published his poems, also figures in that novel as a philosopher.

Sarton's earliest years were spent in Belgium, but with the coming of World War I, the family fled to England. In 1915, the Sartons went to America, staying briefly in New York before settling in Washington, where the Carnegie Institute gave support to Mr. Sarton's projected history of science. May's mother founded Belgart, specializing in handmade fashion apparel. May's father's somewhat informal appointment at Harvard University led the family to Cambridge, Massachusetts, in 1918. There, young May attended Shady Hill School, a Spartan institution run by an educational innovator, Mrs. Ernest Hocking, wife of a well-known philosopher, who combined the study of philosophy with poetry. Miss Edgett, an imaginative math teacher, inspired Sarton to be a poet, but Sarton also received encouragement from a family friend in Cambridge, Edith Forbes Kennedy. Edith was the inspiration for a character, Willa MacPherson, in *Mrs. Stevens Hears the Mermaids Singing*, whose friendship and encouragement push young Hilary Stevens along on her poetic career. School plays also awakened Sarton's interest in drama.

In 1919, the family briefly returned to settle their affairs in Belgium. For a short time, Sarton attended the Institute Belge de Culture Française, which she later attended for a year at age twelve. The institute was presided over by Marie Closset, who published poetry as "Jean Dominique," and two other women. Literature was taught from great works, and memorization was required. Sarton spent that year with the Limbosches while her parents were in Beirut so that her father could learn Arabic for his research. The literary atmosphere and general culture which she encountered there influenced Sarton greatly.

A 1926 graduate of Cambridge Latin High School, Sarton recalled attending Boston Repertory Theater, reading poems with friends, and feeling revolutionary about Henrik Ibsen during these years. Her parents had settled into Channing Place, Cambridge, which was the center of Sarton's life until her parents' deaths. Sarton spent two years wanting to be an actress, doing summer stock in Gloucester before joining Eva LeGallienne's Civic Repertory Theater in 1929. She spent three years with the theater company; from 1931 to 1932, Sarton was in Paris working as director of the company's apprentices. While in Paris, she became friends with Aurélian-Marie Lugné-Poë, a founder of Théâtre de L'Œuvre, a theater which brought many new plays to France. Lugné-Poë appears as a director in *The Bridge of Years*. Although he thought Sarton had more talent as a writer, he was willing to help her improve her acting skills. Their unsuccessful romantic relationship par-

allels that which occurs in *A Shower of Summer Days*, whose heroine goes to a country home in Ireland to overcome a love affair.

When LeGallienne ran out of money, Sarton, together with Eleanor Flexner and Kappo Phelan, kept the Apprentices Theater going, settling in Dublin, New Hampshire, and appearing elsewhere on tour. That venture failed after two years, a considerable shock for Sarton which turned her in the direction of writing fiction. In the following year, she wrote several short stories, none of which sold. In June, 1936, she went to Cornwall, England, first staying with Charles Singer, the historian of science, and then moving to London. She met Elizabeth Bowen, who was to become a friend over the next several decades and was the subject of passionate feelings; Juliette and Julian Huxley, at whose apartment over the London Zoo she spent a month; and Virginia Woolf. She also met James Stephens, the Irish poet, and became a particular friend of S. S. Koteliansky, editor and mentor of various writers, including Katharine Mansfield. From 1936 to 1940, Sarton visited Belgium each spring, and for decades she could not decide whether she was European or American. She began writing poetry at the age of twenty-six. Needing funds and having no settled career, she returned to the United States in 1939 to read her poetry at various colleges. Despite feeling "the inward disturbance of exile," she felt the love and friendship of many different people.

During the years of World War II, she worked for the Office of War Information in the film department. In 1943, she set up poetry readings at the New York Public Library to provide cultural experience for wartime workers. She returned to England in 1944 to visit her friend Elizabeth Bowen, who also visited Sarton whenever she was in the United States. With *The Bridge of Years*, Sarton's novel-writing began again in earnest. Novels and other fiction and volumes of poetry have appeared at close intervals since. Her early poetry won her the Gold Rose for Poetry and the Edward Bland Memorial Prize (1945).

Sarton supported herself by teaching, serving as Briggs-Copeland instructor in composition at Harvard from 1950 to 1952, poet-in-residence at Bryn

Mawr from 1953 to 1954, and lecturing on poetry at Harvard, the University of Iowa, the University of Chicago, Colorado College for Women, and Wellesley and Beloit colleges. In 1953, she met Louise Bogan, whose calm and order she valued considerably, though Bogan, poetry editor of *The New Yorker*, did little to forward Sarton's career. Other novels appearing in the early 1950's earned Sarton a Guggenheim Fellowship from 1954 to 1955. Her reputation had grown with *A Shower of Summer Days*, though the critical reception, as with later novels, was mixed.

The Birth of a Grandfather came at a turning point in Sarton's life: Her mother had died in 1950 after a long illness and her father died quite suddenly in 1956. The family home in Cambridge was sold, and Sarton moved in October, 1958, to an old house equipped with a barn and thirty-six acres in Nelson, New Hampshire, a small village. *The Small Room*, a novel dealing with women training women as intellectual disciples in the atmosphere of a small women's college, was written there. It also introduced a lesbian love affair between Carryl Cope, a brilliant but flinty scholar, and Olive Hunt, a benefactor of the college. *Mrs. Stevens Hears the Mermaids Singing*, which was written at a time of gloom because of worries over her financial situation, was at first refused publication because it depicted a lesbian affair, and the publishers required excisions before the book was accepted.

Kinds of Love, As We Are Now, Crucial Conversations, and *A Reckoning* explore various marital or amatory dilemmas along with the problem of being feminine and an artist. During this period, Sarton settled briefly in Ogunquit, Maine, and then in York, Maine, in an old house on the coast, writing further volumes of poetry, autobiographical sketches, and journals. Her love for animals is reflected in *The Fur Person*, a story about a gentleman cat's adventures.

Sarton's career reflected her conviction that "art must become the primary motivation for love is never going to fulfill in the usual sense." Increasingly, she took her stand as feminist: "We [women] have to be ourselves." Her own sexual orientation seems to have grown partly out of her isolation as a woman and a writer and her sense that marriage and family would detract from her creativity. She died in Maine in 1995.

ANALYSIS

The Bridge of Years is, perhaps, Sarton's most complex work. This is partly because the prototypes of the main characters were close to Sarton's own experience and the themes were motivated by intellectual friendships established in Europe prior to World War II.

THE BRIDGE OF YEARS

Based upon Sarton's student years in Belgium and memories of her own family, *The Bridge of Years* centers on a Belgian family, Paul and Melanie Duchesne, and their three daughters, during four segments of their lives. These periods, besides accounting for personal growth in the major characters, also demarcate the stages of political change after World War I: optimism in the immediate postwar period; the decline of public morale and search for political solutions to the Depression of the 1930's; the fear of renewed European conflict attendant upon the rise of Hitler; and the outbreak of that conflict as liberal, humanitarian values come under attack with World War II.

Melaine Duchesne, a designer of furniture, a stickler for fine craftsmanship, a courageous and optimistic woman whose country home is a model of stability, is based upon Sarton's mother and her longtime friend, Céline Limbosch. Paul, the temperamental philosopher who cannot express his thoughts, is partly based on Raymond Limbosch and partly on George Sarton, May's father, especially in his need for an ordered existence and exact routine. Paul's breakthrough into true philosophical statement under the pressure of the war is, as much as anything, Sarton's own search for authentic expression. Her father's leftist socialism and critical intelligence are reflected in Pierre Poiret, the university-student son of close friends of the Duchesnes'. The immemorial Bo Bo, the stiff but protective Teutonic nursemaid, is a portrait of Sarton's childhood governess.

Of the daughters, Colette, the youngest, is the poet, a romanticist living in a fairy world, Sarton's view of herself as a child. Solange, who becomes a veterinarian, has the patient skill with animals that Sarton herself possessed. The eldest daughter, Françoise, with her long affection for Jacques Croll, a fatigued soldier from World War I, believes that art is everything, turning herself inward when Jacques, maneuvered by Melanie, marries a local girl. Françoise feels compromised when Jacques tips her a wink as he walks down the church aisle with his bride. Her resulting emotional breakdown, and the awareness that art cannot be everything when "life [is] lived near the point of conflict," reflect Sarton's own emotional turmoil in the 1930's as she sought to become an artist.

Paul Duchesne's skepticism about the perfectibility of the human spirit is tempered by his German friend, the intellectual Gerhard Schmidt, who sees the need for individual effort to resist tyranny. After escaping from his homeland during Hitler's purge of intellectuals, he goes to fight with the Loyalists in Spain while his son, Hans, hypnotized by the Nazis, becomes a stormtrooper. This opposition of father and son is repeated in the case of Emile Poiret, a pious Catholic floral illustrator with a sense of cosmic presence in things, and his antireligious son, Pierre. The novel presents facets of the European response to the breakdown of democratic civilization in the 1920's and 1930's and, at a more personal level, reflects the idea that some persons must extend themselves in love if civilization is to continue.

THE BIRTH OF A GRANDFATHER

The question of who one is, especially in the context of generations and of change, was a continuing concern of Sarton. It is presented through the dramatic, carefully staged scenes of *The Birth of a Grandfather*, in which the omniscient author moves among the characters, heightening the effect by the questions which they ask themselves. The interior speculation is in the style of Henry James, though the consciousness attributed to a given character does not always seem consistent with his personality or inner life. This novel begins at the Maine island retreat of the wealthy and established Wyeth family. Tom Dorgan, a Boston Irish Catholic, is romantically involved with Betsy Wyeth, Frances and Sprig Wyeth's daughter. In contrast to these young lovers, Lucy, Frances's sister, is undergoing a divorce. It is Frances, the major character, and her husband, Sprig, from the middle-aged generation, whose painful readjustment to marriage and to age form the basis of the plot.

The older generation includes Uncle Joe, an urbane retired diplomat, Aunt Jane, a wise old woman capable of immersing herself in others, and Gran-Quan, Sprig's father, a man consumed by dramatic self-pity over the death of his wife and constantly supported by his sister, Jane. The Wyeths' son, Caleb, is reluctantly in the heart of family matters, biding his time until he gains independence from them. Appropriately enough, a major scene is the family's Fourth of July celebration on a nearby island. The fireworks are, for Frances, like moments of purity amid darkness, but they also herald the sudden death of Aunt Jane and the breaking up of Gran-Quan's private world and descent into insanity. Betsy and Caleb see their parents in new ways: Frances represents human frailty, and Sprig is seen as one sheltered from the pains of life.

The second part of the novel, "Ice Age," set in Cambridge, Massachusetts, shows the threat that tension and obligation bring to family unity. Tom and Betsy have married, and a child is on the way. This potentially joyful event threatens Sprig, who cannot accept the loss of direction in his life, which has settled into traditional philanthropy and conservation of the family wealth. By contrast, his friend Bill Waterford, who treats life with saving grace, calmly announces his impending death from cancer. Bill's life has had a sense of purpose. Two dinner scenes set forth two perspectives: In one, Hester, Sprig's sister, sees Sprig and Frances trying vainly to avert the emotional threat of Caleb's demand to be allowed to go alone to Greece for a year. In another, Tom Dorgan, innocently holding forth on the coming prospect of family life, exacerbates the conflict of generations, but he also sees that the Wyeths can admit to being wrong and remain loyal to each other. Caleb puts aside his immediate demand for independence, recognizing his father's own imprisonment in his reticence and sense of responsibility.

Coming to terms with Caleb leaves Sprig uncertain about his love for his wife, and a visit to Bill provokes the question of what real life is. Bill's wife, Nora, warns him that one may fail to exercise one's talents out of fear of freedom and power, a question which Sarton explored in various ways in probing the nature of the artist. Caleb's destination, Greece, awakens other echoes in Sprig, reminding him of the Greek scholarship for which he had once wished; Sprig then realizes his potential for continued growth.

In the third part, the grandfather is reborn, both in the sheer physical sense of the new grandchild and in meeting the meaning of his own life. Sprig must surrender his friendship with Bill, and he must test his own talent, no longer relying on Bill's support. Frances wonders whether she has not turned self-detachment into a prison; the answer comes with the realization that birth and death, the march of ongoing generations, has significance. This insight strikes her when, while visiting Bill, she encounters his nearly exhausted wife, Nora; a seemingly unsuitable marriage has worked because Bill was able to give of himself. Upon the departure of Caleb, to whom Sprig has given financial independence so that Caleb may try what he has wanted, Sprig himself turns to translating Greek plays as a self-imposed test. He acknowledges also that he has loved himself rather than Caleb in their relationship. With new honesty and willingness to assume self-defined responsibility, Sprig reconnects to the exuberance of his youth. He and Frances reaffirm their faithfulness, and love wins out as absolute value.

Sarton uses imagistic motifs such as the current in the Charles River or the isles of Greece to suggest important ideas in the novel. The shifting omniscient viewpoint highlights dramatic intensities, but it is used at times without strong motivation or without a careful build-up of character. It also can turn into undisguised narrative commentary. Moral implications do come through in catchwords such as "escape" and "freedom," which reverberate through the novel. Occasionally, moral judgements become banal. The novel has shown Sprig's life as empty of personal demands upon himself and his resistance to his children as a fearful reaction to his own aging, but the moral tends to blunt the focus.

MRS. STEVENS HEARS THE MERMAIDS SINGING

Coming roughly at the middle of Sarton's career, *Mrs. Stevens Hears the Mermaids Singing* is the author's most intense study of the feminine artist. Here, too, the style received mixed reviews, one critic praising the music of the prose, another objecting to the fussiness and humorlessness of the writing. What one critic found to be a well-done presentation of the mystery of the creative impulse, a second found to be "an embarrassing probing of art" and "acute self-consciousness," and a third found the novel's characters "musechasers who believe themselves to be delicate vessels of talent." Carolyn Heilburn, in noting that the novel deals with the poet Hilary Stevens's escape from the passivity of a feminine destiny, sees Sarton as aware that "the real artist is not the fantasy creature imagined by women trapped in domesticity." Art comes, as Hilary insists, at the expense of every human being, the self and the self's ties with other people.

The plot interweaves Hilary's initiation of Mar Hemmer, a potential poet recovering from an intense relationship with a man, with her reveries as she is being interviewed about her own poetic development. Mar, despite his lack of emotional proportion, helps her to see her own life in perspective. Married to an unstable war veteran in England, Hilary began to write poetry after his sudden death. An intellectual friend, Willa MacPherson, encourages her to continue writing poetry and provides one night of passionate sexual exploration. Another friend, however, creates self-doubt, which Hilary identifies with the masculine force in herself. She knows that she can preserve her artistry only by caring about life, which does not necessarily mean sparing others from pain. As Hilary later points out to Mar, poetry and feeling are connected only if the poet understands that "true feeling justifies whatever it may cost." One cannot be anesthetized against the pain of life.

Philippa Munn, Hilary's proper girlhood governess with whom she is infatuated, plays the role which Sarton's own teachers did in her youth. Poetry diffuses sensuality, Hilary learns; it creates a moment of revelation, not simply of indulgence. As Hilary's wise physician tells her as she lies in the hospital recovering from a breakdown over her husband's death, she must write poems about objects and about a person to whom she can fasten herself deeply, but she should not confuse love for someone with poetry. Poetry can become "passionate decorum" in which love is presented as a mystique; what gives strength to poems is form.

Mrs. Stevens Hears the Mermaids Singing mixes the Platonic tradition of poet as maker whose creations surpass his own conscious understanding with an Aristotelian stress on the formal artifact which has its own laws of being and is autonomous. The notion of the poet as rapt by emotional experience lies also within the Platonic tradition of poetry as ecstasy. The events making up the life of Hilary Stevens have parallels with Sarton's own life, and the novel is a justification of that life. The presentation of the poet as a solitary individual misunderstood by the world also reflects Sarton's romanticism.

A RECKONING

As the heroine of *A Reckoning*, Laura Spelman, resident of an upper-middle-class Boston suburb, faces terminal cancer, she interprets her growing "death-wish" as a return to the Jungian "house of gathering." It is a world of timeless personages; Sarton had been reading Jung before writing the book. She had also become more concerned with feminism and more open about lesbianism. As Laura is alienated from her own body, she works to resolve her unexamined passions by assessing her life. She comes, according to one critic, to an "understanding of life as an amalgam of human relationships, culture, and the natural world."

The novel also shows Harriet Moors, a budding novelist and lesbian, trying to put her life into art, an issue complicated by the opposition of her lover to any fiction that might hint at the truth of their liaison. It seems that not only marriage but also a binding lesbian attachment is fatal to art: Harriet Moors will have to suffer the loss of her lover as the price of continuing with her art.

Laura has to sort out her feelings for her mother, Sybille, a woman of dazzling power whose beauty and charm have oppressed her daughters. Jo, Laura's sister, after her mother had interrupted Jo's passion

for a woman, had fled into the sterile intellectuality of academic life. Daphne, Laura's other sister, has become insecure and emotionally dependent. Laura has found escape in marriage. The destructive Sybille is a less flattering version of Céline Limbosch, of whom Sarton has said that she forced friends into decisions they did not wish to make and attacked their authentic being. Even in her senility in a nursing home, Sybille is someone about whom her daughter treads warily. Earlier in her life, Laura had had an intense friendship with Ella; the reader may strain, in fact, to realize it was a lesbian affair. Harriet Moors's visits for advice on her novel rekindles in Laura her memories of Ella. She comes to realize that if love is painful, then art is mutilating. Yet in dying, Laura finds positive answers in music and in poetry. The final reckoning is instigated by Laura's warm and helpful Aunt Minna, whose reading aloud to Laura forces her to consider that "journey into being a woman" and what women are meant to be. Women are locked away from one another in a man's world, she decides. Marriage may be normal destiny, but for those living intensely, a mystical friendship is the hope—of women for women, of men for men. Sybille, according to Ella, feared "the tenderness of communion."

Laura's loss of lonely autonomy is convincingly presented, but the master image, that of weaving a pattern, is imposed rather than dramatized. Ella's appearance at the end does not really complete the final weaving of the pattern by mystical friendship; the scene reminds the reader of sentimental fiction often found in women's magazines. Clearly, too many issues have come within the compass of the heroine's last months. Death may force its victims to focus their lives and aspirations, but the last days of Laura Spelman are not deeply and plausibly linked to her life as a married woman and parent or even to her efforts to approach art. As in *Mrs. Stevens Hears the Mermaids Singing*, reminiscence plays a key role. Whole scenes are recalled in dramatic form, but the very selectivity of memory and its often self-serving quality may raise questions about the honesty and sheer structural relationship between what Laura recalls and what she really was—a Boston upper-middle-class housewife with delusions of creativity, the kind of thing against which Sarton herself warned. Finally, the linkage of femininity and artistic creation is sidetracked by the lesbian issue. *A Reckoning* lacks the strengths of Sarton's best work: thematic depth, balanced characters, organic use of imagery, adequate plot development, and motivated action.

Roger E. Wiehe

OTHER MAJOR WORKS

PLAY: *The Underground River*, pb. 1947.

POETRY: *Encounter in April*, 1937; *Inner Landscape*, 1939; *The Lion and the Rose*, 1948; *The Land of Silence and Other Poems*, 1953; *In Time Like Air*, 1958; *Cloud, Stone, Sun, Vine: Poems, Selected and New*, 1961; *A Private Mythology*, 1966; *As Does New Hampshire and Other Poems*, 1967; *A Grain of Mustard Seed: New Poems*, 1971; *A Durable Fire: New Poems*, 1972; *Collected Poems, 1930-1973*, 1974; *Selected Poems of May Sarton*, 1978; *Halfway to Silence*, 1980; *Letters from Maine*, 1984; *The Silence Now*, 1989; *Collected Poems, 1930-1993*, 1993; *Coming into Eighty*, 1994.

NONFICTION: *I Knew a Phoenix: Sketches for an Autobiography*, 1959; *Plant Dreaming Deep*, 1968; *Journal of a Solitude*, 1973; *A World of Light: Portraits and Celebrations*, 1976; *The House by the Sea*, 1977; *Writings on Writing*, 1980; *Recovering: A Journal*, 1980; *At Seventy: A Journal*, 1984; *After the Stroke: A Journal*, 1988; *Honey in the Hive: Judith Matlock, 1898-1982*, 1988; *Endgame: A Journal of the Seventy-ninth Year*, 1992; *Encore: A Journal of the Eightieth Year*, 1993; *At Eighty-two*, 1996.

CHILDREN'S LITERATURE: *Punch's Secret*, 1974; *A Walk Through the Woods*, 1976.

MISCELLANEOUS: *Sarton Selected: An Anthology of the Journals, Novels, and Poems of May Sarton*, 1991 (Bradford Dudley Daziel, editor); *May Sarton: Among the Usual Days*, 1993 (Susan Sherman, editor); *From May Sarton's Well*, 1994 (edited by Edith Royce Schade).

BIBLIOGRAPHY

Bloin, L. P. *May Sarton: A Bibliography*. Metuchen, N.J.: Scarecrow Press, 1978. In two parts, the first listing Sarton's poetry, novels, nonfiction, essays, and articles. The second part lists secondary sources, including book reviews. A conscientious compilation of sources that is most useful to the Sarton scholar. The author acknowledges Sarton's assistance in putting together this work.

Curley, Dorothy N., Maurice Kramer, and Elaine F. Kramer, eds. *Modern American Literature*. 4 vols. 4th ed. New York: Ungar, 1969-1976. A collection of reviews and criticisms of Sarton's poems and novels, the latest entry being 1967. Includes criticism on *Mrs. Stevens Hears the Mermaids Singing*, considered an important book and which the author says was most difficult to write. The supplement has reviews on Sarton's *Collected Poems*.

Evans, Elizabeth. *May Sarton, Revisited*. Rev. ed. Boston: Twayne, 1989. In this volume in Twayne's United States Authors series, Evans upholds Sarton as a writer who speaks for women, insisting they claim their own identity; hence, her increasing popularity among feminists. An interesting addition to this somewhat standard criticism is an appendix of letters of Sarton's to her editor while writing *Mrs. Stevens Hears the Mermaids Singing*. Selected bibliography.

Grumbach, Doris. "The Long Solitude of May Sarton." *The New Republic* 170 (June 8, 1974): 31-32. Grumbach draws together Sarton's philosophy, in particular the serenity of her writing in the face of her declared "traumas." Noting that critics have often ignored Sarton, Grumbach says: "Hers has been a durable fire . . . her small room seems to make most male critics uncomfortable." An article well worth reading.

Peters, Margot. *May Sarton: A Biography*. New York: Knopf, 1997. The first full-length biographical treatment of this most autobiographical of writers. After her death in 1995, there was an upsurge of interest in Sarton, and this book certainly contributes to her legacy. Peters herself is fair in her assessment of Sarton: clear about why this woman inspired such a devoted following among readers and equally straightforward about her uncertainty concerning the literary value of much of Sarton's work.

Sibley, Agnes. *May Sarton*. New York: Twayne, 1972. Obviously a must for criticism on Sarton, because there is so little of book-length size written about her—despite her prodigious output. This study discusses Sarton's poems, from *Encounter in April* in 1937 to *A Durable Fire*, published in 1972. Sibley has grouped novels under two themes that she considers relevant to Sarton: "detachment" for the early novels and "communion" for the later ones.

Swartzlander, Susan, and Marilyn R. Mumford, eds. *That Great Sanity: Critical Essays on May Sarton*. Ann Arbor: University of Michigan Press, 1992. Thoughtful essays on Sarton's works. Includes bibliographical references and an index.

JEAN-PAUL SARTRE

Born: Paris, France; June 21, 1905
Died: Paris, France; April 15, 1980

PRINCIPAL LONG FICTION

La Nausée, 1938 (*Nausea*, 1949)
L'Âge de raison, 1945 (*The Age of Reason*, 1947)
Le Sursis, 1945 (*The Reprieve*, 1947)
La Mort dans l'âme, 1949 (*Troubled Sleep*, 1950;
  also known as *Iron in the Soul*)(previous 3 novels collectively known as *Les Chemins de la liberté*, in English *The Roads to Freedom*)

OTHER LITERARY FORMS

Around the time that he published *Nausea*, Jean-Paul Sartre drew considerable attention as a promising writer of short fiction with the stories collected in *Le Mur* (1939; *The Wall and Other Stories*, 1948). Trained as a philosopher, Sartre went on to define and develop his concept of existentialism in *L'Être et le néant* (1943; *Being and Nothingness*, 1956), turning also to the theater with such famous plays as *Les Mouches* (1943; *The Flies*, 1946), *Huis clos* (1944; *No Exit*, 1946), and *Les Mains sales* (1948; *Dirty Hands*, 1948), in which the basic tenets of his

thought are brilliantly executed and easily grasped. He is known also for essays and reviews collected in several volumes of the journal *Situations*, as well as for psychological criticism of such authors as Charles Baudelaire, Gustave Flaubert, and Jean Genet. In 1964, he published a partial autobiography, *Les Mots* (*The Words*, 1964).

ACHIEVEMENTS

For students and readers of long fiction, Sartre is perhaps most notable as the author of *Nausea*, an unsettling and groundbreaking work that has exercised considerable influence over developments in the novel during the postwar era. His later efforts in the genre—the unfinished tetralogy *Roads to Freedom*—are viewed less charitably by most of his commentators, who would contend that Sartre had by that time turned his finest efforts toward the drama. Henri Peyre, however, argues that Sartre's later novels have simply been obscured by the sensational publicity afforded his plays and other writings. In any event, Sartre himself appears to have lost interest in the writing of fiction, preferring such alternative forms as the essays on Baudelaire and Flaubert, discussed by Joseph Halpern in his useful volume *Critical Fictions* (1976). Notwithstanding, Sartre's influence on fiction, both long and short, has been considerable. In 1964, Sartre was awarded the Nobel Prize in Literature, which he declined to accept.

BIOGRAPHY

Born in Paris in 1905, Jean-Paul Sartre grew up in a book-filled, if fatherless, household. Sartre was a brilliant student, and his secondary schooling at the time-honored Lycée Henri IV was followed by competitive admission to the École Normale Supérieure. Although he failed his first attempt at the likewise competitive *agrégation*, or teaching credential, before successfully retaking it in 1929, Sartre had opted early for a life of the mind and had written at least one novel (later destroyed for want of a publisher) while still in his teens. He had also made the acquaintance of Simone de Beauvoir, a fellow philosophy student who would remain his companion for life, even as both rejected as "inauthentic" the "bour-

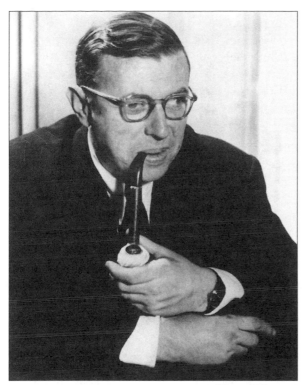

(Library of Congress)

geois" institution of marriage. During the 1930's, Sartre taught philosophy in *lycées* at Le Havre and elsewhere, traveling during vacations with the help of a small inheritance, before settling into the life of the professional writer and thinker as author of *The Wall and Other Stories* and *Nausea*.

Briefly incarcerated by the Germans as a prisoner of war in 1940 and 1941, Sartre was nevertheless able to pursue his literary and philosophical work during the Occupation with a minimum of interference. As founding editor of the liberal periodical *Les Temps modernes* (ironically named for the 1936 Charles Chaplin film *Modern Times*, which both he and Beauvoir admired), Sartre became perhaps the most frequently quoted spokesman of the intellectual French Left, even as he "kept his options open" and refrained from the ultimate commitment of membership in the Communist Party. As the leading proponent of existentialism, Sartre also attracted the attention of the print and broadcast media, achieving during the postwar years celebrity status as existentialism was widely discussed and misinterpreted,

seen by many commentators as the immediate ancestor of such phenomena as the Beat Generation. His plays, meanwhile, shone brightly as the strongest and most durable of his creative efforts, performed worldwide before increasingly appreciative audiences.

During his later years, Sartre traveled widely and, when in Paris, spent most of his time and energy on his psychobiographical study of Flaubert, *L'Idiot de la famille: Gustave Flaubert, 1821-1857* (1971-1972; partial translation, *The Family Idiot: Gustave Flaubert, 1821-1857*, 1981, 1987), a massive work conceived in much the same spirit as his earlier studies of Baudelaire and Jean Genet. Sartre died in Paris on April 15, 1980.

ANALYSIS

Hailed in the immediate prewar years as a rising master of prose fiction, Jean-Paul Sartre soon deserted the form and would leave unfinished the fourth and final volume of *The Roads to Freedom*, originally announced as a tetralogy. As it turned out, his creative talents were perhaps indeed better suited to the theater; encouraged by the eminent director Charles Dullin (1885-1949), Sartre, between 1943 and 1959, turned out eight original plays, fully half of which survived him and are still included in the world's repertory. Unlike his onetime friend and colleague Albert Camus (1913-1960), who repeatedly tried and failed to apply his gifts to the stage, Sartre possessed a particularly dramatic imagination that proved especially well suited to the exposition even of the most difficult philosophical concepts originally expounded in his essays. To be sure, a number of his concepts found their earliest, albeit undeveloped, expression in *Nausea* and in the stories to be collected in *The Wall and Other Stories*; nevertheless, Sartre found fiction a comparatively inefficient vehicle for the communication of his ideas.

NAUSEA

Completed as early as 1936 under the working title of "Melancholia" (inspired by Albrecht Dürer's engraving *Melancholia I*, 1514), *Nausea* proved to be as unconventional in content as it was apparently conventional in form. Cast in the more or less familiar format of a diary discovered after the death (or disappearance) of its author, a convention in turn derived from the time-honored epistolary form, Sartre's first novel bodied forth a disoriented, disorienting vision of the world as perceived through the eyes of its rapidly changing protagonist and narrator: Antoine Roquentin, a thirty-year-old historian and former teacher, finds himself suddenly overcome by the sensation of his own existence, a sensation that soon evokes in him the nausea of the book's eventual, publisher-selected title. Overwhelmed by the evident contingency of his own being, Roquentin soon senses the same contingency in others, and in inanimate objects as well: In one memorable scene, Roquentin watches and describes his own hand as if it were a monstrous creature quite divorced from his existence, a beached crab with hair; in another scene, a glass of beer appears to be spying on him. His eventual and perhaps inevitable conclusion is that he is superfluous (*de trop*), a quality shared by most of the things and people around him.

Had Sartre limited *Nausea* to Roquentin's record of the changes taking place in his own mind, the book might well have been dismissed as an inventive simulacrum of a psychological case history. What assures the viability and power of *Nausea* is the nature and aptness of Roquentin's powers of observation, powers that alternately feed on and are fed by the operations of his mind. Even without the record of Roquentin's depression, *Nausea* might well have earned a respectable place in French literary history as a rare work of biting yet perceptive social satire in which few conditions of life are spared. To his credit, Sartre in *Nausea* repeatedly manages portraits that closely approach caricature yet stop short of straining the reader's credulity.

Trained as a historian, Roquentin is perhaps well chosen as an observer, yet not even he is presented wholly without satire. Dissatisfied with teaching, able to survive (if barely) on a small but regular unearned income, Roquentin probably is superfluous, at least by certain people's standards; in 1932, when he begins his journal, he has been working for some three years on the study of one Marquis de Rollebon, a minor survivor of the French Revolution whose descendants have willed the Marquis' papers to the city

of Bouville (Mudville, equated by most of Sartre's commentators with the port city of Le Havre). Roquentin's daily work at the public library of Bouville has exposed him to a small but highly memorable cast of characters, including the Corsican librarian and especially the Self-taught Man (*l'autodidacte*), a drab civil servant and World War I veteran who spends all of his free time in the library, attempting to educate himself by reading all of the books in alphabetical order, as filed under the author's name: "He has passed brutally from the study of coeleopterae to the quantum theory," observes Roquentin, "from a work on Tamerlaine to a Catholic pamphlet against Darwinism, he has never been disconcerted for an instant." Later in the novel, the Self-taught Man will emerge as a deeply committed if somewhat fuzzy-minded Socialist not unlike those satirized around the same time by George Orwell in Britain; Roquentin, decreasingly proud (or even certain) of his own humanity, will turn a deaf ear to his acquaintance's declarations of predigested humanism. In a brief scene near the end of the book, the Self-taught Man stands cruelly revealed and judged as a barely repressed pederast, permanently expelled by the Corsican from the library that has come to represent his entire life. The greater part of Sartre's satire and Roquentin's scorn is reserved for the bourgeois "city fathers," however, whose portraits hang proudly on the walls of the civic museum—"les salauds," Roquentin calls them, using a term perhaps best rendered into English as "the bastards." For Sartre, as for Roquentin, the *salauds* are perhaps the most superfluous of all, born into a system which was set in place by their ancestors and which they themselves accept without question even as they perpetuate it; such individuals were to serve as models for Sartre's diatribes against inauthentic or "received" behavior. Roquentin, perversely fascinated by one portrait of particularly fearsome aspect, makes no secret of his pleasure upon learning that the man portrayed stood barely five feet tall.

Inevitably, Roquentin abandons his work on the life and career of Monsieur de Rollebon, having long since begun to suspect its futility. A brief visit to Paris and his former girlfriend, Anny, yields little more of consequence; Anny, a second-rate actress apparently addicted to striking poses, freely announces that she has become another man's "kept woman" and that, moreover, she is about to leave the country. Roquentin notes with some satisfaction that Anny has grown quite fat and wonders, between the lines of his journal, why he ever lent his collusion to her endless poses and "game-playing." With love thus discredited, Roquentin then moves on to the oddly Proustian conclusion that art alone offers a possible clue to life's meaning, if any, and a potential cure for his "nausea." Perhaps, he thinks, he might have found more meaning in life if he had written a novel. In any case, it is now too late, and the journal trails off into nothingness.

Throughout the diary, to be sure, Roquentin's only solace against his disquieting revelations has come through art, *authentic* art as opposed to the commissioned excrescences on display in the Bouville museum. A particular favorite is a jazz tune that he first heard on the lips of American soldiers during 1917, now preserved on a record on the jukebox in the Railwaymen's Café. As he continues his journal, the record grows in importance until, toward the end, Roquentin conjures up a vision of a Jewish musician and a black woman vocalist, who in less than five minutes of recorded playing time have achieved their immortality. The song, initially associated in Roquentin's mind with Anny, has long since acquired an authentic life of its own; by then, however, Roquentin has tacitly rejected the option of creative salvation for himself. Instead, he simply disappears, leaving the diary behind.

From the 1940's onward, it was customary to read *Nausea* in the reflected light of Sartre's subsequent efforts, finding Roquentin's memoirs complete illustration of such Sartrean categories as "essence," "existence," "anguish," and "bad faith." As James Arnold and other scholars have shown, however, the novel originally conceived as "Melancholia" represents a somewhat earlier stage in the evolution of Sartre's thinking, and such examples as there are (such as the implicit "bad faith" of the *salauds*) must be seen as prototypical rather than exemplary; those in search of specific illustrations might be better ad-

vised to consider such plays as *The Flies, No Exit*, or *Dirty Hands*. To be sure, Sartre's particular concept of "existence" receives its first exposition in *Nausea*, as Roquentin discovers and explores the "unjustified" fact of his being in all of its contingency; the "nausea" that overwhelms him as a result might likewise be interpreted as an early manifestation of the state later described as *angoisse* (anguish). Still *Nausea* demands to be read and appreciated as an independent work of art rather than as an existentialist manifesto. As Arnold has pointed out, moreover, the novel is also rich in autobiographical elements, however skillfully reworked and transposed; the character of Anny, for example, was drawn quite closely from life, in the person of an artist-actress with whom a very young Sartre once believed himself to be in love and whose perennial posing provided him with an invaluable object lesson in the "art" of inauthentic behavior. Like "The Wall" and its companion stories, *Nausea* must thus be seen, regardless of its thought-provoking "content," above all as a work of literary art.

It was not until well after *Nausea*, during the wartime and postwar years, that Sartre would truly emerge as an original and provocative thinker. His ideas, afforded scholarly and rather ponderous exposition in *Being and Nothingness*, soon gained widespread exposure through his plays, particularly *The Flies* and *No Exit*, as well as in essays and columns initially published in *Les Temps modernes*. Soon a coherent existentialist attitude began to emerge, roughly delineated as follows: Of all beings, Sartre maintains, only the "human animal" is capable of *creating* itself through continual, fully conscious acts of *choice*; at birth, people share *essence* with rocks, plants, and other animals, but they must then proceed toward a uniquely human *existence* of their own choosing. Those who refuse to choose, or to accept responsibility for choices already made, are guilty of "bad faith" (*mauvaise foi*) in renouncing their potential "existence" (*pour-soi*) for a subhuman fixed "essence" (*en-soi*) that is tantamount to death. Indeed, as the godless prefigured hell of *No Exit* makes abundantly clear, those who reject the "anguish" of perpetual free choice for the illusory comfort of self-applied "labels" are in fact already dead to the world. Only after real, physical death should it be possible to draw the bottom line, to add up the total of a human life; until that time, any effort to complete the phrase "I am . . ." with a predicate, adjective, or noun identifies the speaker as a person "in love with death," one who has forsaken the unique human privilege and potential of existence. Sartre applies this theory with particular clarity in his *Réflexions sur la question juive* (1946; *Anti-Semite and Jew*, 1948), in which bigotry is portrayed not as an "opinion" or "reaction" but rather as a "passion," a predisposition which antedates its object. Bigots, Sartre maintains, are at bottom terrified of their own freedom, of their own capacity for change; they have therefore opted, in conscious or unconscious bad faith, for the fixed essence of a position that they perceive as self-protective: Refusing to consider the possibility that the world is simply ill-made, they choose to blame all of its ills on a particular minority—Jews, blacks, or Arabs, for example. "If the Jew did not exist," concludes Sartre with the persuasion of simple logic, "the anti-Semite would have to invent him."

As Hazel E. Barnes has pointed out, much of Sartre's argument against anti-Semitism, and against bigotry in general, was outlined in the prewar novella "L'Enfance d'un chef" ("Childhood of a Boss"), the longest of the tales collected in *The Wall and Other Stories*. Frequently too broad in its satire of bourgeois mentality and morality to be thoroughly credible, "Childhood of a Boss" nevertheless announces, even more clearly than *Nausea*, the provocative blend of philosophy, psychology, and politics that would become characteristic of Sartre's mature output: The life of Lucien Fleurier is a life lived almost totally in bad faith, including a constant search for comforting, self-applied labels and dilettantish flirtation with the artistic "fads" of the time, most notably Surrealism. Insecure from his earliest childhood onward, Lucien constantly seeks to hide behind something larger and stronger than himself, ultimately finding refuge in Fascist anti-Semitism. Haunted also by suspicions of his latent homosexuality, he relates to women only insofar as he can "objectify" them, to be objectified by them in his turn. In the end, Lucien is so strength-ened by his reactionary politics as to have crystallized into the archetypal, unbending capitalist "boss" of the title, not unlike the *salauds* of Bouville.

THE ROADS TO FREEDOM

In the projected tetralogy *The Roads to Freedom*, begun around the same time as *Being and Nothingness* and the early plays, Sartre endeavors to illustrate his developing philosophy through the lives of several continuing characters, most of whom are fortunately drawn less close to caricature than the hapless Lucien Fleurier. Although narration throughout is in the objective, "affectless" third person, the apparent central character in the three published novels is one Mathieu Delarue, a disaffected intellectual in his thirties who resembles Sartre even more than does Antoine Roquentin. The first volume, ironically entitled *The Age of Reason*, deals mainly with Mathieu's efforts to secure an abortion for his unloved and unlovely live-in mistress, Marcelle; only at the end, having met with odd opposition from unexpected quarters, will Mathieu ruefully conclude that he has at last reached "the age of reason." Among the more intriguing characters of *The Age of Reason* and its sequels is Mathieu's friend Daniel, an avowed homosexual who nevertheless cherishes his clandestine friendship with Marcelle and refuses Mathieu a loan for the abortion, claiming that he does not have the money when in fact he does. A protracted earlier scene has shown Daniel contemplating suicide, planning first to drown his three beloved cats in order to be free of his last responsibilities; unable to kill the cats, he will likewise lack the nerve to carry out his projected self-annihilation. At the end of *The Age of Reason*, he will astound the reader and his fellow characters alike by choosing to marry Marcelle, ostensibly to assure her unborn child a home and father but also, and perhaps more likely, to lock himself into a situation in which he will be condemned to feel false, deserving of contempt as well.

For Barnes, Daniel is perhaps the archetypal character in existentialist fiction, defined not by heredity or environment, as in the traditional novel, but rather, simply by choice. As Barnes points out, nothing is revealed of Daniel's parentage, childhood, or early sexual encounters; Daniel is shown only *in situa*, defining himself (however negatively) through continuous and conscious acts of choice. It is Daniel's *choice* to be reviled and hateful, for whatever unknown reasons. Like Lucien Fleurier—although with far greater lucidity, reflecting the subsequent evolution of Sartre's thought—Daniel is so terrified of his potential freedom that he repeatedly uses that freedom to turn himself into a detestable object, a walking testimonial to the negative effects of bad faith. Mathieu, in turn, "has discovered his freedom but does not know what to do with it." Less interesting as a character than is Daniel, although perhaps equally complex, Mathieu functions throughout the existing trilogy less as protagonist than as catalyst, a common acquaintance shared by the variety of characters portrayed. Toward the end of the third novel of the series, *Troubled Sleep*, which portrays the end of the "phony war" and the start of the Vichy regime, Mathieu falls in battle and is apparently left for dead, his "central" position being assumed by the committed Communist Brunet; from Sartre's descriptions of the projected fourth volume, however, as well as from excerpts from it published in *Les Temps modernes* during 1949, it was clear that Mathieu would survive his wounds and that Daniel, perhaps too predictably, would collaborate with Occupation forces.

As in *Nausea*, Sartre in *The Roads to Freedom* proves to be a keen observer of human nature, as well as a social satirist of no mean talent; among his more skillful portraits are those of Mathieu's brother Jacques, a successful lawyer (who in turn will refuse to lend Mathieu the abortion money) and Jacques's wife, Odette, an intelligent but bored (and boring) bourgeoise. By the early 1940's, however, social satire had lost ground in relative importance to the development of Sartre's philosophical and political attitudes; diverting though the social portraiture may be, it is clear throughout *The Roads to Freedom* that what really matters are the *choices* facing, and made by, each of the characters, whether consciously or unconsciously. As early as 1939, Sartre had addressed himself as a critic to the delineation of character in fiction, calling for a clear-cut distinction between exposition and "advocacy" on the part of a supposedly ominiscient narrator, berating François Mauriac, in particular, for assuming a "godlike" attitude in denying his characters their "freedom." "God is no novelist," Sartre opined in a now-famous statement, "and neither is François Mauriac." In *The Roads to Freedom*, Sartre appears to have been quite determined to allow his characters their freedom, even at the cost of plausibility; taking care to preserve their integrity by denying his personages the customary justifications of heredity and/or environment, Sartre frequently strains the reader's credulity by asking him or her to accept the validity of a voluntary, seemingly unmotivated action, a practice perhaps derived from André Gide's earlier concept of the *acte gratuit*, or unmotivated gesture, exemplified in the murder of Fleurissoire in *Lafcadio's Adventures* (1914). Perhaps not surprisingly, Sartre's ideas received considerably more credible and effective presentation in his plays, in which actors could accomplish the necessary mediation between text and audience; one is reminded, in particular, of Electra's sudden but thoroughly plausible recourse to bad faith in *The Flies*. In all of Sartre's published fiction, perhaps the best illustration of his developing theories is to be found in his story "The Wall," narrated throughout by an unprivileged first-person narrator from inside a situation that threatens him with imminent extinction; that Pablo survives to tell the tale at all is surely among the greater, and more skillfully managed, ironies in all modern fiction. In the longer form, however, Sartre proved somewhat less skillful at bridging the gap between theory and practice; indeed, few of his commentators expressed any real surprise when his tetralogy was left unfinished.

With or without the support of Sartre's unfolding existentialism, *The Roads to Freedom* appears not to have stood the test of time. However carefully observed, the disaffected, often marginal characters of the trilogy seem unlikely to capture or maintain the reader's interest, perhaps least of all in what might have become of them in the projected fourth volume. Of the existing volumes, *The Reprieve* has perhaps deservedly received the greatest critical attention, owing mainly to Sartre's skillful experiments with time and simultaneity, a technique admittedly borrowed from the cinema by way of John Dos Passos. On balance, however, Sartre was doubtless well advised to turn his talents elsewhere.

David B. Parsell

OTHER MAJOR WORKS

SHORT FICTION: *Le Mur*, 1939 (*The Wall and Other Stories*, 1948).

PLAYS: *Les Mouches*, pr., pb. 1943 (*The Flies*, 1946); *Huis clos*, pr. 1944 (*In Camera*, 1946, better known as *No Exit*, 1947); *Morts sans sépulture*, pr., pb. 1946 (*The Victors*, 1948); *La Putain respectueuse*, pr., pb. 1946 (*The Respectful Prostitute*, 1947); *Les Jeux sont faits*, pr., pb. 1947 (*The Chips Are Down*, 1948); *Les Mains sales*, pr., pb. 1948 (*Dirty Hands*, 1949); *Le Diable et le Bon Dieu*, pr. 1951 (*The Devil and the Good Lord*, 1953); *Kean: Ou, Désordre et génie*, pb. 1952 (adaptation of Alexandre Dumas, *père*'s play; *Kean: Or, Disorder and Genius*, 1954); *Nekrassov*, pr. 1955 (English translation, 1956); *Les Séquestrés d'Altona*, pr. 1959 (*The Condemned of Altona*, 1960); *Les Troyennes*, 1965 (adaptation of Euripides' play; *The Trojan Women*, 1967).

NONFICTION: *L'Imagination*, 1936 (*Imagination: A Psychological Critique*, 1962); *Esquisse d'une théorie des émotions*, 1939 (*The Emotions: Outline of a Theory*, 1948); *L'Imaginaire: Psychologie phénoménologique de l'imagination*, 1940 (*The Psychology of Imagination*, 1948); *L'Être et le néant*, 1943 (*Being and Nothingness*, 1956); *L'Existentialisme est un Humanisme*, 1946 (*Existentialism*, 1947; also as *Existentialism and Humanism*, 1948); *Réflexions sur la question juive*, 1946 (*Anti-Semite and Jew*, 1948); *Baudelaire*, 1947 (English translation, 1950); *Qu'est-ce que la littérature?*, 1947 (*What Is Literature?*, 1949); *Situations I-X*, 1947-1975 (10 volumes; partial trans. 1965-1977); *Saint-Genet: Comédien et martyr*, 1952 (*Saint Genet: Actor and Martyr*, 1963); *Critique de la raison dialectique, précédé de question de méthode*, 1960 (*Search for a Method*, 1963); *Critique de la raison dialectique, I: Théorie des ensembles pratiques*, 1960 (*Critique of Dialectical Reason, I: Theory of Practical Ensembles*, 1976); *Les Mots*, 1964 (*The Words*, 1964);

L'Idiot de la famille: Gustave Flaubert, 1821-1857, 1971-1972 (3 volumes; partial trans. *The Family Idiot: Gustave Flaubert, 1821-1857*, 1981, 1987); *Un Théâtre de situations*, 1973 (*Sartre on Theater*, 1976); *Les Carnets de la drôle de guerre*, 1983 (*The War Diaries of Jean-Paul Sartre: November, 1939-March, 1940*, 1984); *Le scénario Freud*, 1984 (*The Freud Scenario*, 1985).

BIBLIOGRAPHY

Aronson, Ronald, and Adrian van den Hoven. *Sartre Alive*. Detroit: Wayne State University Press, 1991. Sections on Sartre's continuing political relevance, rethinking his political and philosophical thought, his fiction and biography, his relationship with de Beauvoir and other writers, and concluding assessments of his career. Aronson and van den Hoven provide a judicious and well-informed introduction.

Brosman, Catharine. *Jean-Paul Sartre*. Boston: Twayne, 1983. Begins with a chapter on Sartre's biography and then one on his philosophy through 1945. Chapters 2 and 3 deal with his early and later fiction. Includes chronology, notes, and an annotated bibliography.

Hill, Charles G. *Jean-Paul Sartre: Freedom and Commitment*. New York: Peter Lang, 1992. Discusses Sartre's quest for freedom and authentic actions as well as his recognition of the ambiguities of commitment. See especially chapter 2, on *Nausea*. Includes chronology, notes, and bibliography.

Kellman, Steven G. *The Self-Begetting Novel*. New York: Columbia University Press, 1980. See the chapter on *Nausea*.

Kern, Edith, ed. *Sartre: A Collection of Critical Essays*. Englewood Cliffs, N.J.: Prentice-Hall, 1963. See especially the first section on Sartre's fiction. Also includes essays on the other genres in which he wrote, a chronology, and a bibliography.

Masters, Brian. *Sartre: A Study*. Totowa, N.J.: Rowman and Littlefield, 1970. A short but wide-ranging critical study, with a biographical note and bibliography. Somewhat hampered by the lack of an index.

Thody, Philip. *Jean-Paul Sartre: A Literary and Political Study.* New York: Macmillan, 1960. See part 1, devoted to Sartre's fiction. Other chapters explore his theory of literature and politics. Includes notes and bibliography.

DOROTHY L. SAYERS

Born: Oxford, England; June 13, 1893
Died: Witham, England; December 17, 1957

PRINCIPAL LONG FICTION

Whose Body?, 1923
Clouds of Witness, 1926
Unnatural Death, 1927 (also as *The Dawson Pedigree*)
Lord Peter Views the Body, 1928
The Unpleasantness at the Bellona Club, 1928
The Documents in the Case, 1930 (with Robert Eustace)
Strong Poison, 1930
The Five Red Herrings, 1931 (also known as *Suspicious Characters*)
The Floating Admiral, 1931 (with others)
Have His Carcase, 1932
Ask a Policeman, 1933 (with others)
Murder Must Advertise, 1933
The Nine Tailors, 1934
Gaudy Night, 1935
Six Against the Yard, 1936 (with others; also known as *Six Against Scotland Yard*)
Busman's Honeymoon, 1937
Double Death: A Murder Story, 1939 (with others)
The Scoop, and Behind the Scenes, 1983 (with others)
Crime on the Coast, and No Flowers by Request, 1984 (with others)

OTHER LITERARY FORMS

In addition to the twelve detective novels that brought her fame, Dorothy L. Sayers wrote short stories, poetry, essays, and plays, and distinguished herself as a translator and scholar of medieval French and Italian literature. Although she began her career as a poet, with Basil Blackwell bringing out collections of her verse in 1916 and 1918, Sayers primarily wrote fiction from 1920 until the late 1930's, after which she focused on radio and stage plays and a verse translation of Dante. She also edited a landmark anthology of detective fiction, *Great Short Stories of Detection, Mystery, and Horror* (1928-1934; also known as *The Omnibus of Crime*).

Outside of her fiction, the essence of Sayers's mind and art can be found in *The Mind of the Maker* (1941), a treatise on aesthetics that is one of the most illuminating inquiries into the creative process ever written; in her essays on Dante; and in two religious dramas, *The Zeal of Thy House* (1937), a verse play written for the Canterbury Festival that dramatizes Sayers's attitude toward work, and *The Man Born to Be King*, a monumental series of radio plays first broadcast amidst controversy in 1941-1942, which takes up what Sayers regarded as the most exciting of mysteries: the drama of Christ's life and death, the drama in which God is both victim and hero. Of her

(Library of Congress)

many essays, the 1946 collection *Unpopular Opinions* and the 1947 *Creed or Chaos?* provide a good sampling of the acumen, wit, and originality with which Sayers attacked a variety of subjects, including religion, feminism, and learning.

In 1972, James Sandoe edited *Lord Peter*, a collection of all the Wimsey stories. Two other collections, both published during Sayers's lifetime (*Hangman's Holiday*, 1933, and *In the Teeth of the Evidence and Other Stories*, 1939), include non-Wimsey stories. At her death, Sayers left unfinished her translation of Dante's *Cantica III: Paradise*, which was completed by her friend and colleague Barbara Reynolds and published posthumously in 1962 as the final volume in the Penguin Classics edition of Dante that Sayers had begun in 1944. An unpublished fragment of an additional novel, called *Thrones, Dominations* and apparently abandoned by Sayers in the 1940's, was also left unfinished, as was her projected critical/biographical study of Wilkie Collins. This last fragment was published in 1977. From 1973 to 1977, the British Broadcasting Corporation (BBC) produced excellent adaptations of five of the Wimsey novels for television, thus creating a new audience for Sayers's work.

ACHIEVEMENTS

One of the chief pleasures for readers of Dorothy Sayers is the companionship of one of fiction's great creations, Lord Peter Wimsey, that extraordinarily English gentleman, cosmopolite, detective/scholar. Although the Wimsey novels were created primarily to make money, his characterization demonstrates that his creator was a serious, skillful writer. As the novels follow Wimsey elegantly through murder, mayhem, and madness, he grows from an enchanting caricature into a fully realized human being. The solver of mysteries thus becomes increasingly enigmatic himself. Wimsey's growth parallels Sayers's artistic development, which is appropriate, since she announced that her books were to be more like mainstream novels than the cardboard world of ordinary detective fiction.

Lord Peter is something of a descendant of P. G. Wodehouse's Bertie Wooster, and at times he emulates Conan Doyle's Sherlock Holmes, but in Wimsey, Sayers essentially created an original. Sayers's novels integrate elements of earlier detective fiction—especially the grasp of psychological torment typified by Joseph Sheridan Le Fanu and the fine delineation of manners exemplified in Wilkie Collins—with subjects one would expect from a medieval scholar: virtue, corruption, justice, punishment, suffering, redemption, time, and death. The hallmarks of her art—erudition, wit, precision, and moral passion—provoke admiration in some readers and dislike in others.

Sayers's novels are filled with wordplay that irritates those who cannot decipher it and delights those who can. Her names are wonderful puns (Wimsey, Vane, Freke, de Vine, Snoot, Venables), her dialogue is embedded with literary allusions and double entendres in English, French, and Latin, and her plots are spun from biblical texts and English poetry. Reading a Sayers novel, then, is both a formidable challenge and an endless reward. Hers are among the few detective novels that not only bear rereading, but actually demand it, and Sayers enjoys a readership spanning several generations. To know Sayers's novels is to know her time and place as well as this brilliant, eccentric, and ebullient artist could make them known. Because of her exquisite language, her skill at delineating character, and her fundamentally serious mind, Sayers's detective fiction also largely transcends the limits of its time and genre. Certainly this is true of novels such as *Strong Poison, The Nine Tailors, Gaudy Night*, and *Busman's Honeymoon*, books which did much toward making the detective novel part of serious English fiction.

BIOGRAPHY

Dorothy Leigh Sayers was born on June 13, 1893, in the Choir House of Christ Church College, Oxford, where her father, the Reverend Henry Sayers, was Headmaster. Mr. Sayers's family came from County Tipperary, Ireland; his wife, the former Helen Mary Leigh, was a member of the old landed English family that also produced Percival Leigh, a noted contributor to the humor magazine *Punch*. Sayers's biographer, James Brabazon, postulates that her preference for the Leigh side of the family caused her to insist upon including her middle initial in her name; whatever the reason, the writer wished to be known as Dorothy L. Sayers.

When Sayers was four, her father left Oxford to accept the living of Bluntisham-cum-Earith in Huntingdonshire, on the southern edge of the Fens, those bleak expanses of drained marshland in eastern England. The contrast between Oxford and the rectory at Bluntisham was great, especially as the new home isolated the family and its only child. Sayers's fine education in Latin, English, French, history, and mathematics was conducted at the rectory until she was almost sixteen, when she was sent to study at the Godolphin School, Salisbury, where she seems to have been quite unhappy. Several of her happiest years followed this experience, however, when she won the Gilchrist Scholarship in Modern Languages and went up to Somerville College, Oxford, in 1912. At Somerville, Sayers enjoyed the congenial company of other extraordinary women and men and made some lasting friends, including Muriel St. Clare Byrne. Although women were not granted Oxford degrees during Sayers's time at Somerville, the University's statutes were changed in 1920, and Sayers was among the first group of women to receive Oxford degrees in that year (she had taken first honors in her examination in 1915).

Following her undergraduate days, Sayers did various kinds of work for several years: first, as poetry editor for Blackwell's in Oxford from 1916 to 1918, then as a schoolmistress in France in 1919, and finally in London, where she worked as a freelance editor and as an advertising copywriter for Benson's, England's largest advertising agency. At Benson's, Sayers helped create "The Mustard Club," a phenomenally successful campaign for Colman's mustard. Around 1920, when Sayers's mind was focused not only upon finding suitable employment but also upon surviving economically, the character of Lord Peter Wimsey was miraculously born, and Sayers's first novel, *Whose Body?*, introduced him to the world in 1923.

These early years in London were scarred by two bitterly disappointing love affairs, one of which left Sayers with a child, born in 1924. The novelist married Oswald Atherton Fleming, a Scottish journalist,

in 1926, and shortly thereafter assumed financial responsibility for him as he became ill and ceased working several years after their marriage. Perhaps these pressures encouraged Sayers to keep turning out the increasingly successful Wimsey novels.

By the end of the 1930's, however, Sayers was in a position to "finish Lord Peter off" by marrying him to Harriet Vane, the detective novelist who first appeared in *Strong Poison* and who, like Wimsey, reflected part of Sayers's personality. After the Wimsey novels, Sayers was free to do the kind of writing she had always wanted to do: manifestly serious work such as religious dramas and a translation of Dante that would occupy most of her time from 1944 to 1957. While working on these demanding projects and writing incisive essays on a wide range of issues, Sayers also became something of a public figure, playing the role of social critic and Christian apologist with great brilliance and panache.

On December 17, 1957, Sayers died of an apparent stroke while alone in the house that she had shared with Fleming from 1928 until his death in 1950. Although she left an unpublished autobiographical fragment, "My Edwardian Childhood," much of Sayers's life is reflected in her novels, which depict the Oxford of her college days (*Gaudy Night*), the Fen wastes of her girlhood (*The Nine Tailors*), and the excitement and confusion of the London she knew as a young writer (*Murder Must Advertise*). Excellent though much of her other work is, Sayers will probably be remembered primarily for her novels.

ANALYSIS

If one should wish to know England as it was between the two world wars—how it was in its customs, among its different classes, and in its different regions, how it regarded itself and the world, what weaknesses festered, what strengths endured—there is no better place to learn its soul or to revel in its singular delights and peccadilloes than in the novels of Dorothy L. Sayers. When Harriet Vane marries Peter Wimsey in *Busman's Honeymoon*, she happily realizes that she has "married England," revealing that Sayers herself recognized the symbolic import of her hero. As a survivor of World War I, a war that decimated a generation of young Englishmen and left their society reeling, Wimsey represents England's fragile link with a glorious past and its tenuous hold on the difficult present. His bouts of "nerves" and persistent nightmares dramatize the lasting effects of this "War to End All Wars," while his noble attempts at making a meaningful life represent the difficult task of re-creating life from the rubble.

Sayers's England encompasses tiny villages unchanged for centuries (*Busman's Honeymoon*), the golden-spired colleges of Oxford (*Gaudy Night*), the "gloom and gleam" of London (*Murder Must Advertise*), the deceptive calm of the southern seacoast (*Have His Carcase*), the brooding Fens (*The Nine Tailors*), and the primitive north counties (*Clouds of Witness*). The novelist ranges throughout this varied landscape with some constants: Accompanied by his indefatigable "man," Bunter (who is Jeeves transformed), Lord Peter reasons his way through all but one mystery (he is absent from *The Documents in the Case*). Through Wimsey's well-wrought consciousness, Sayers maintains a certain *Weltanschauung* that seems a peculiar blend of mathematical rigor and lush, witty, insightful language.

Carolyn Heilbrun's praise for Sayers's special blend of "murder and manners" points out to an understanding of both the novelist's appeal and her place in English fiction: Sayers is an inheritor not only of the more literary branch of detective fiction, but also of the older comedy-of-manners tradition. She can reveal a character, time, or place in a bit of dialogue or one remark. From a brief sentence, for example, the reader knows the Duchess of Denver: "She was a long-necked, long-backed woman, who disciplined herself and her children." A short speech summarizes all *The Unpleasantness at the Bellona Club*, revealing not only a character but also the values and condition of his world:

> Look at all the disturbance there has been lately. Police and reporters—and then Penberthy blowing his brains out in the library. And the coal's all slate. . . . These things never happened before the War—and great heavens! William! Look at this wine! . . . Corked? Yes, I should think it *was* corked! My God! I don't know what's come to this club!

The character upon whom Sayers lavishes most of her considerable talent is Lord Peter. Although it is possible, as some of her critics have said, that Sayers created Wimsey, the perfect mate for an intellectual woman, because actual men had disappointed her, the psychobiographical approach can explain only part of her novels' motivation or meaning. In Wimsey, Sayers dramatizes some significant human problems, including the predicament of the "Lost Generation," the necessity of every person's having a "proper job," and the imperative synthesis of forces that are often perceived as opposites, but which are really complementary: intellect and emotion, good and evil, male and female. When viewed in these terms, Sayers's fictional world fits naturally into the entire cosmos of her creation, because it deals with some of the very subjects she addressed in other, more patently serious forms.

It is appropriate to speak of all Sayers's work as one, for, as she concludes in *The Mind of the Maker*, "the sum of all the work is related to the mind [of the artist] itself, which made it, controls it, and relates it to its own creative personality." From beginning to end, Sayers's work investigates the possibility of creative action; for her the creative act consists of establishing equilibrium among competing powers, of drawing together disparate, even warring elements. Of course, since she writes detective novels, Sayers focuses upon the opposite of creative action in the crimes of her villains, crimes that destroy life, property, sanity, peace. Wimsey, who solves the mysteries and thereby makes a life from destruction, is the creative actor.

The Mind of the Maker argues that there is a discoverable moral law, higher than any other, that governs the universe. In a way, Sayers's novels attempt to discover or reveal this universal moral law, which in its most superficial form is reflected in civil codes. This process of moral discovery, however, becomes increasingly complex and ambiguous; if Sayers's subjects are constant, her understanding of them deepens as her art matures. Since Sayers's artistic maturation parallels her hero's development, a comparison of how Wimsey functions in the early and late novels will elucidate both the consistency and the change that mark Sayers's fiction.

WHOSE BODY?

The most striking quality of *Whose Body?* as a first novel is the deftness with which it presents Sayers's hero and his world. In its opening pages, the reader gets to know Lord Peter Wimsey, the dashing man-about-town and collector of rare books (which, amazingly, he seems to read). Keen of mind and quick of tongue, like an exotic bird chirping in a formal English garden that, perhaps, conceals a jolly corpse or two, he is a remarkable personage at birth. Wimsey is also quite marvelously a wealthy man who knows how to spend both his time and his money; his elegant apartment's only acknowledged lack is a harpsichord for his accomplished renditions of Domenico Scarlatti. The product of an older England marked by civility, restraint, and order, Wimsey is accompanied in his first tale by two challengers to his wits and position: his valet, Bunter, and the middle-class Inspector Parker of Scotland Yard, who will make sure that Wimsey never nods during fourteen years of fictional sleuthing. Even his mother, the delightfully balmy Duchess of Denver, is introduced here, and the reader quickly guesses from their relationship that Sayers is interested in how men and women coexist in this world. The Dowager Duchess and her son are as different in appearance as they are similar in character, the narrator remarks, thus signaling that the superficial differences between men and women often conceal more important similarities. Wimsey and his entourage enter the world nearly complete, and their creator has a firm grasp of character, dialogue, and the mystery plot from the beginning of her career.

The theme of *Whose Body?* plants the seeds of one of Sayers's ever-flourishing ideas. Her first and perhaps most horrid villain, Sir Julian Freke, suffers from one of the great problems facing modern people: the disassociation from mind and heart that often renders "civilized" people incapable of moral behavior. The great surgeon Freke, who is aptly named because he is a freakish half-human, denies the importance of intangibles such as the conscience, which he considers akin to the vermiform appendix. With this perfectly criminal attitude, Freke coolly kills and dissects an old competitor, ironically from one of the oldest, least rational of motives, jealousy and revenge. Freke therefore demonstrates Sayers's point: that people, as creatures of both intellect and passion, must struggle to understand and balance both if moral action is to be possible. Freke, the dissector of life, destroys; the destruction he causes awaits the truly healing powers of a creative mind.

The somewhat surprising link between moral action and detective work is suggested by Wimsey, who observes that anyone can get away with murder by keeping people from "associatin' their ideas," adding that people usually do not connect the parts of their experience. The good detective, however, must study the fragments of human life and synthesize the relevant data. This synthesis, the product of imagination and feeling as well as reason, reveals not only "who did it," but how, and why. Thus, according to Sayers's own definitions, her detective pursues moral action in his very sleuthing, not only in its final effects of punishment for the criminal and retribution for society. Wimsey's detective method typifies this creative synthesis by incorporating different aspects of a rich experience: poetry, science, history, psychology, haberdashery, weather reports. When Wimsey finally realizes that Freke is the murderer, he remembers "not one thing, nor another thing, nor a logical succession of things, but everything—the whole thing, perfect and complete . . . as if he stood outside the world and saw it suspended in infinitely dimensional space." In this moment, Wimsey is not merely a successful detective, he is a creator, his mind flashing with godlike insight into human life. The story has moved, therefore, from destruction to creation because disparate aspects of life have been drawn together.

Freke's failure as a human being is exemplified in his failure as a physician, just as Wimsey's successful life is instanced in the skillful performance of his "job," his compulsive "hobby of sleuthing." More than a hobby, detection is actually Wimsey's "proper job." In a crucial discussion with Inspector Parker, Wimsey admits to feeling guilty about doing detective work for fun, but the perceptive Parker warns him that, as a basically responsible person for whom life is really more than a game, he will eventually have to come to terms with the seriousness of his actions. What is clear to the reader at this point is that Wimsey, an English aristocrat displaced by social change and scarred by World War I, is at least carving out a life that is socially useful while it is personally gratifying. He is not simply feeding the Duke of Denver's peacocks.

If Wimsey seems almost too perfect in the early novels, Sayers redeems him from that state by slowly revealing the finite, flawed, and very human man within the sparkling exterior. To make this revelation, she has to create a woman capable of challenging him, which she does in the character of Harriet Vane. By the time he appears in *The Nine Tailors*, Wimsey is less of a god and more of a human being. After all, the great lover has been humiliatingly unsuccessful in wooing Harriet Vane, whom he saved from the hangman four years earlier in *Strong Poison*. The beginning of *The Nine Tailors* finds Wimsey, the supersleuth, wandering about the Fens, that bleak terrain of Sayers's childhood, muttering about the misery of having one's car break down on a wintery evening and dreaming of hot muffins. When offered shelter at the rectory of Fenchurch St. Paul, the great connoisseur of haute cuisine is delighted with tea and oxtail stew. The greatest change in Wimsey's character and in Sayers's fiction, however, is evidenced in the novel's richer, more subtle structure, and in its newly complex view of crime and punishment, of good and evil.

The Nine Tailors

Indicative of Sayers's increasing subtlety, *The Nine Tailors* is as much a metaphysical meditation on time and change as it is a murder mystery; there is not even a corpse until Part 2. In place of Lord Peter's jolly but rather macabre singing of "We insist upon a [dead] body in a bath" (in *Whose Body?*), *The Nine Tailors* resonates with the sound of church bells and an explication of campanology (bell or change-ringing). The bells at Fenchurch St. Paul, which are rung for both weddings and funerals, seem ambiguously to stand for both life and death, good and evil. The whole question of good versus evil is quite complicted here, for unlike the wholly innocent victim of the cold-blooded murder in *Whose Body?*, the man killed here is probably the worst person in the book,

and he is accidentally killed by the ringing of holy bells. Locked in the church's bell chamber as a precaution by someone who knows of his criminal past, Geoffrey Deacon is killed by the intense sound of the bells, and ultimately by the hands of every man who unwittingly pulls a bell rope that New Year's Eve. This group includes Wimsey, who just happens to be there because of several coincidences.

Although Deacon perhaps deserves to die, not only for his jewel robbery but also because of a generally dishonorable life, his death forces Wimsey to reexamine himself and his motives. In ringing the changes, Wimsey thought he was simply following a set of mathematical permutations to a neat conclusion; in reality, he was taking a man's life. This greatly sobers the old puzzle-solver, who has always had some qualms about attacking life as a game. Indeed, Wimsey's role in Deacon's death is but an exaggerated version of the detective's role in any mystery: He causes the villain or criminal to come to justice, which usually means death. Wimsey cannot ignore the consequences of his actions in *The Nine Tailors*, because they are direct, obvious, and significant in human terms. He voices his concern about the morality of all his "meddling" to the rector, who assures him that everyone must "follow the truth," on the assumption that this path will lead invariably if somewhat indirectly to God, who has "all the facts" in the great case of life. Thus, it is impossible to be too curious, to probe too far, to ask too many questions, even though some answers or consequences may be painful.

In this great novel, Wimsey actually experiences the central Christian paradox, that of good coming from evil or of the two being inextricably linked. The mystery is over when he realizes, in a grisly pun, that Deacon's killers are already hanged, since they are the very bells in the church's tower. As one of the inscriptions on this ancient church says, the nine tailors, or the nine peals, "make a man," suggesting that the bells not only signify a man when they toll his passing, but also stand as timeless, disinterested judges of human behavior. The dead man, Deacon, mocked honorable work in his thievery, and thus began the cycle of destruction that ends in his own death, a death which ironically leads to Wimsey's discovery or creative act. From evil thus confronted and comprehended, good may grow. Mr. Venables, the rector, wittily pricks Wimsey with the irony that "there's always something that lies behind a mystery . . . a solution of some kind." For Wimsey, as for Sayers, even the solution to a mystery leads to further mysteries; the answer to the mystery of Deacon's death leads to a more subtle inquiry into one of the essential mysteries of life: how to determine responsibility or meaning for human action. In this paradoxical world, victims may be villians and right action is often based in error, chance, or even transgression.

Wimsey leaves this complex novel with greater insight into himself and the ambiguous nature of life; he is, therefore, finally ready to come to terms with the greatest mystery of his life, Harriet Vane, who is also about ready to accept his inquiry. In *Gaudy Night*, Wimsey reaches his fulfillment, a fulfillment that is expressed in terms of resolving the conflict between man and woman, between intellect and emotion, and between good and evil. In fact, Wimsey's fulfillment represents the culmination of Sayers's search for a resolution of these forces. The novel's subject is also one of Sayers's oldest: the moral imperative for every person to do good work that is well done, and the terrible consequences of not doing so. All of these ideas come into play in this subtle novel, which is on one level the mystery of the "Shrewsbury Poison Pen" and on another, more important one, an unusual and profound love story. Reflecting the subtlety and delicacy with which Sayers spins her tale, there is not even a death in this book; the psychological violence caused by the Poison Pen is alarming, but here evil is banal, and all the more powerful for being so.

GAUDY NIGHT

Gaudy Night takes place at Oxford, which held happy memories for Sayers as the place of her birth and formal education, and the entire novel is a paean to that golden-spired city. Harriet Vane goes to Oxford to attend the Shrewsbury Gaudy, an annual spring homecoming celebration, where she has the opportunity to judge her old classmates and teachers in terms of how well they, as women, have been able to

live meaningful lives. Shrewsbury is obviously a fictional version of Somerville, Sayers's college, and just as clearly Vane, a famous detective novelist who is wrestling with the question of "woman's work" and with the problem of rendering reality in fiction, is to some extent Sayers, the self-conscious artist. Having been pursued by Wimsey for five frustrating years, Vane finally accepts him at the end of *Gaudy Night*. She accepts him because the experiences in this book teach her three interrelated things: that Wimsey, as an extraordinary man, will not prevent her from doing her "proper job," a consequence she feared from any relationship with a man; that men and women can live together and not destroy each other, but create a good life; and therefore, that there can be an alliance between the "intellect and the flesh." Vane's discoveries in this novel thus signal the solution of problems that had preoccupied Sayers throughout her career.

Vane learns all of these things through Wimsey's unraveling of the mystery of the Poison Pen, who is a woman frightfully flawed because she has never been able to strike a balance between the intellect and the flesh, and therefore has never done her proper job. Annie Wilson, the Poison Pen who creates so much confusion and instills so much fear in the intellectual women of Shrewsbury, is the victim of sentimentality and a radically disassociated sensibility; she hates all learning because her dead husband was punished long ago for academic dishonesty. Ironically, Harriet Vane suffers from the same problem, but in its other manifestation; she begins the novel capable of trusting only the intellect, and fears any bonds of the flesh or heart. When she finally sees that neither the sentimentality of Annie nor the hyperintellectualism of Shrewsbury can solve the "problem of life," Harriet realizes that it is only through balancing intellect and passion that creative or truly human action is possible.

Wimsey, who solves the mystery because he is able to bring these forces into equilibrium and to acknowledge the potency of both, is rendered acceptable to Vane because of this ability. Her new willingness to admit her feelings reveals to her what Sayers's readers had known for a long time: She loves Wimsey. The man she loves has changed, too.

He is no longer an unattainable paragon who sees good and evil as discrete and life as a game, but a middle-aged man who fears rejection and death, who is idiotically vain about his hands, and who, to Harriet's surprise, looks as vulnerable as anyone else when he falls asleep: the man behind the monocle. All of this does not argue that Wimsey is less extraordinary than he was; in fact, perhaps what is most extraordinary about him now is that he seems a real person—flawed, finite, vulnerable—who is yet capable of that rare thing, creative action. Indeed, his very life seems a work of art.

BUSMAN'S HONEYMOON

Wimsey and Vane finally embark upon marriage, that most mundane and mysterious of journeys, in *Busman's Honeymoon*, the final novel that Sayers aptly called a "love story with detective interruptions": The detective novelist had moved that far from the formula. In the closing scene of this last novel, Wimsey admits that his new wife is "his corner," the place where he can hide from a hostile, confusing world and shed tears for the murderer whose execution he caused. This is not the Wimsey who blithely dashed about in the early novels, treating criminals as fair game in an intellectual hunting expedition, but it is the man he could have become after fourteen years of living, suffering, and reflecting. Indeed, it was a masterful stroke for Sayers to create Harriet Vane, a woman who could match Wimsey's wits and passions, because through her and through his loving her, the reader can learn the most intimate facts of this once-distant hero. If a man is to cry in front of anyone, that witness should most likely be his wife, especially if she is an extraordinary person who understands his tears. The early Wimsey may have been the kind of man that an intellectual woman would imagine for a mate, but the mature Wimsey is one with whom she could actually live. The fragment of a later novel called *Thrones, Dominations* indicates that the Wimsey-Vane marriage was just this workable.

Finally, the marriage of Wimsey and Vane symbolizes the paradoxical and joyful truth of good coming out of evil, for if Harriet had not been falsely accused of murder, they would never have met. She quiets Wimsey in one of his familiar periods of pain-

ful self-scrutiny about his "meddling" by reminding him that, if he had never meddled, she would probably be dead. The point seems clear: that human action has consequences, many of which are unforeseen and some painful, but all necessary for life. It is not difficult to imagine a novelist with this vision moving on shortly to the drama of Christ's crucifixion and resurrection, nor even the next step, her study and translation of that great narrative of good and evil, desire and fulfillment, mortality and eternity, Dante's *The Divine Comedy* (c. 1320). Indeed, all of Sayers's work is of a piece, creating that massive unity in diversity by which she defined true art.

Catherine Kenney

OTHER MAJOR WORKS

SHORT FICTION: *Hangman's Holiday*, 1933; *In the Teeth of the Evidence and Other Stories*, 1939; *Lord Peter*, 1972 (James Sandoe, editor); *Striding Folly*, 1972.

PLAYS: *Busman's Honeymoon*, pr. 1937 (with Muriel St. Clare Byrne); *The Zeal of Thy House*, pr., pb. 1937; *The Devil to Pay, Being the Famous Play of John Faustus*, pr., pb. 1939; *Love All*, pr. 1940; *The Just Vengeance*, pr., pb. 1946; *The Emperor Constantine*, pr. 1951 (revised as *Christ's Emperor*, 1952).

RADIO PLAY: *The Man Born to Be King: A Play-Cycle on the Life of Our Lord and Saviour Jesus Christ*, pr. 1941-1942.

POETRY: *Op 1*, 1916; *Catholic Tales and Christian Songs*, 1918; *Lord, I Thank Thee—*, 1943; *The Story of Adam and Christ*, 1955.

NONFICTION: *The Greatest Drama Ever Staged*, 1938; *Strong Meat*, 1939; *Begin Here: A War-Time Essay*, 1940; *Creed or Chaos?*, 1940; *The Mysterious English*, 1941; *The Mind of the Maker*, 1941; *Why Work?*, 1942; *The Other Six Deadly Sins*, 1943; *Unpopular Opinions*, 1946; *Making Sense of the Universe*, 1946; *Creed or Chaos? and Other Essays in Popular Theology*, 1947; *The Lost Tools of Learning*, 1948; *The Days of Christ's Coming*, 1953, revised 1960; *The Story of Easter*, 1955; *The Story of Noah's Ark*, 1955; *Introductory Papers on Dante*, 1957; *Further Papers on Dante*, 1957; *The Poetry of Search and the Poetry of Statement, and Other Posthumous*

Essays on Literature, Religion, and Language, 1963; *Christian Letters to a Post-Christian World*, 1969; *Are Women Human?*, 1971; *A Matter of Eternity*, 1973; *Wilkie Collins: A Critical and Biographical Study*, 1977 (E. R. Gregory, editor).

CHILDREN'S LITERATURE: *Even the Parrot: Exemplary Conversations for Enlightened Children*, 1944.

TRANSLATIONS: *Tristan in Brittany*, 1929 (Thomas the Troubadour); *The Heart of Stone, Being the Four Canzoni of the "Pietra" Group*, 1946 (Dante); *The Comedy of Dante Alighieri the Florentine*, 1949-1962 (Cantica III with Barbara Reynolds); *The Song of Roland*, 1957.

EDITED TEXTS: *Oxford Poetry 1917*, 1918 (with Wilfred R. Childe and Thomas W. Earp); *Oxford Poetry 1918*, 1918 (with Earp and E. F. A. Geach); *Oxford Poetry 1919*, 1919 (with Earp and Siegfried Sassoon); *Great Short Stories of Detection, Mystery, and Horror*, 1928-1934 (also known as *The Omnibus of Crime*); *Tales of Detection*, 1936.

BIBLIOGRAPHY

Brabazon, James. *Dorothy L. Sayers: A Biography.* New York: Charles Scribner's Sons, 1981. The "authorized" biography based upon Sayers's private papers, containing an introduction by her only son, Anthony Fleming. Brabazon shows that Sayers's real desire was to be remembered as an author of poetry and religious dramas and as a translator of Dante.

Coomes, David. *Dorothy L. Sayers: A Careless Rage for Life.* New York: Lion Publishing, 1992. Coomes concentrates on reconciling the author of religious tracts with the detective novelist, thereby providing a portrayal of a more "complex Sayers." He draws heavily on her papers at Wheaton College. Brief notes, no bibliography.

Dale, Alzina, ed. *Dorothy L. Sayers: The Centenary Celebration.* New York: Walker, 1993. Memoirs and essays situating Sayers in the history of detective fiction. Includes a brief biography and annotated bibliography.

Gaillard, Dawson. *Dorothy L. Sayers.* New York: Frederick Ungar, 1981. In a brief 123 pages, Dawson tries to establish a link between Sayers's de-tective fiction and her other literary works. One chapter is devoted to her short stories, four to her mystery novels, and a sixth to a summary of Sayers's literary virtues.

Hall, Trevor H. *Dorothy L. Sayers: Nine Literary Studies.* Hamden, Conn.: Archon Books, 1980. In nine critical essays, Hall discusses the connection between Sayers's creation, Lord Peter Wimsey, and Arthur Conan Doyle's creation, Sherlock Holmes. Hall also speculates in some detail on the influence of Sayers's husband, Atherton Fleming, on her writing.

Scott-Giles, Charles Wilfrid. *The Wimsey Family: A Fragmentary History from Correspondence with Dorothy Sayers.* New York: Harper & Row, 1977. Scott-Giles, an expert on heraldry, creates a family history and biography for Sayers's most memorable creation, Lord Peter Wimsey. Illustrations include the Wimsey family coat of arms, designed by Sayers.

Youngberg, Ruth Tanis. *Dorothy L. Sayers: A Reference Guide.* Boston: G. K. Hall, 1982. An extensive guide to 942 English-language reviews, articles, books, introductions, and addresses published between 1917 and 1981. The annotations are designed to provide information, rather than criticism, to allow the reader to evaluate the particular item's usefulness.

SIR WALTER SCOTT

Born: Edinburgh, Scotland; August 15, 1771
Died: Abbotsford, Scotland; September 21, 1832

PRINCIPAL LONG FICTION
Waverley: Or, 'Tis Sixty Years Since, 1814
Guy Mannering, 1815
The Antiquary, 1816
The Black Dwarf, 1816
Old Mortality, 1816
Rob Roy, 1817
The Heart of Midlothian, 1818

The Bride of Lammermoor, 1819
A Legend of Montrose, 1819
Ivanhoe, 1819
The Monastery, 1820
The Abbot, 1820
Kenilworth, 1821
The Pirate, 1821
The Fortunes of Nigel, 1822
Peveril of the Peak, 1823
Quentin Durward, 1823
St. Ronan's Well, 1823
Redgauntlet, 1824
The Betrothed, 1825
The Talisman, 1825
Woodstock, 1826
The Fair Maid of Perth, 1828
Anne of Geierstein, 1829
Count Robert of Paris, 1831
Castle Dangerous, 1831
The Siege of Malta, 1976

(Library of Congress)

OTHER LITERARY FORMS

Sir Walter Scott's first published work was a translation of two ballads by Gottfried August Bürger, which appeared anonymously in 1796. In 1799, he published a translation of Johann Wolfgang von Goethe's 1773 drama *Götz von Berlichingen with the Iron Hand.* In 1802, the first two volumes of *Minstrelsy of the Scottish Border* appeared, followed by the third volume in 1803. This was a collection of popular ballads, annotated and often emended and "improved" with a freedom no modern editor woud allow himself. A fascination with his country's past, formed in his early years and lasting all his life, led him to preserve these ballads, the products of a folk culture that was disappearing. In 1805 came *The Lay of the Last Minstrel,* the first of the series of long narrative poems that made Scott the most widely read poet of the day. It was followed by *Marmion: A Tale of Flodden Field* (1808). *The Lady of the Lake* (1810) brought him to the height of his popularity as a poet. The later poems were less successful and he was gradually eclipsed by Lord Byron. In 1813, he completed the manuscript of a novel he had laid aside in 1805. This was *Waverley,* which appeared anony-

mously in 1814. (Scott did not publicly admit authorship of his novels until 1827.) It created a sensation and launched him on the series that remained his chief occupation until the end of his life. Other important works were his editions of Dryden (1808) and of Swift (1814), a series of lives of the English novelists completed in 1824, and *The Life of Napoleon Buonaparte,* begun in 1825 and published in nine volumes in 1827. *Chronicles of the Canongate* (1827) is composed of three short stories: "The Highland Widow," "The Two Drovers," and "The Surgeon's Daughter."

ACHIEVEMENTS

The central achievement of Scott's busy career is the series of novels that is conventionally designated by the title of the first of them. The sheer bulk of the Waverley novels is in itself impressive, as is the range of the settings they present. For example, *Ivanhoe* is set in twelfth century England, *The Talisman* in the Holy Land of the Third Crusade, *Quentin Durward* in fifteenth century France, *The Abbot* in the Scotland of Queen Mary, *Kenilworth* in the reign of Elizabeth, and *The Fortunes of Nigel* in that of

James I. In spite of his wide reading, tenacious memory, and active imagination, Scott was not able to deal convincingly with so many different periods. Moreover, he worked rapidly and sometimes carelessly, under the pressures of financial necessity and, in later years, failing health. Some of the novels are tedious and wooden, mechanical in their plots and stilted in their dialogue. Scott himself was aware of their flaws and he sometimes spoke and wrote slightingly of them.

Yet most readers find that even the weaker novels have good things in them, and the best of them have a narrative sweep and a dramatic vividness that render their flaws unimportant. The best of them, by common consent, are those set in Scotland as far back as the latter part of the reign of Charles II. When he attempted to go further back, he was less successful, but in such novels as the four discussed below—*Waverley, Old Mortality, Rob Roy,* and *The Heart of Midlothian*—Scott's sense of history is strong. They are among the most impressive treatments of his great theme, the conflict between the old and the new, between Jacobite and Hanoverian, between the heroic, traditional, feudal values of the Tory Highlands and the progressive commercial interests of the Whig Lowlands, between stability and change. Though some of the other novels offer historical conflict of a comparable kind (*Ivanhoe* and *Quentin Durward,* for example), the Scottish novels present the conflict with particular insight and force and convey a strong sense of the good on both sides of it. Scott values the dying heroic tradition even as he recognizes the benefits that change brings. Earlier writers had mined the past to satisfy a market for the exotic, the strange, or the merely quaint. Scott saw the past in significant relation to the present and created characters clearly shaped by the social, economic, religious, and political forces of their time, thus providing his readers with the first fictions that can properly be called historical novels.

BIOGRAPHY

An important factor in the vividness of the Scottish novels was the strong oral tradition to which Sir Walter Scott had access from his early childhood. After a bout with polio in his second year, he was sent away from Edinburgh to his paternal grandfather's house at Sandyknowe in the Border country, in the hope that the climate would improve his health. It did, and though he remained lame for the rest of his life, his boyhood was an active one. In this region from which his ancestors had sprung, he heard stories of Border raids, Jacobite risings, and religious struggles from people for whom the past survived in a living tradition. Throughout his life he added to his fund of anecdotes, and his notes to the novels show how very often incidents in them are founded on actual events which he had learned about from the participants themselves or from their more immediate descendants.

Scott's father was a lawyer, and in 1786, having attended Edinburgh High School and Edinburgh University, Scott became an apprentice in his father's office. In 1792, he was admitted to the bar, and all his life he combined legal and literary activities. After losing his first love, Williamina Belsches, to a banker, he married Charlotte Carpenter in 1798. In 1805, he entered into a secret partnership with the printer James Ballantyne, and four years later they formed a publishing firm. This firm ran into financial difficulties, and in 1813, Scott escaped ruin only through the intervention of another publisher, Archibald Constable. Scott continued to overextend himself. In 1811, he had bought a farm on the Tweed at a place he named Abbotsford, and in the years that followed he wrote furiously to provide funds for building a splendid house and buying additional land. His ambition was to live the life of a laird. In 1826, the financial collapse of Constable and Ballantyne ruined Scott. In his last years, he worked tirelessly to pay his creditors. The effort told on his health, and he died in 1832, at the age of sixty-one. The debts were finally cleared after his death by the sale of his copyrights.

ANALYSIS

Waverley displays, at the start of Sir Walter Scott's career as a novelist, many of the features that were to prove typical of his best work. In the Jacobite rebellion of 1745, he saw an instance of the conflict between the older feudal and chivalric order, strongly colored with heroic and "romantic" elements, and the newer order of more practical and realistic concerns which had already begun to supplant it. His focus is not on the great public figures whose fates are at stake, and this too is typical. The Pretender, Prince Charles Edward, is not introduced until the novel is more than half over, and most of the major events of this phase of his career are only alluded to, not presented directly. He is shown almost exclusively in his dealings with the fictional character for whom the novel is named, and largely through his eyes.

WAVERLEY

Edward Waverley, like so many of Scott's heroes, is a predominantly passive character who finds himself caught between opposing forces and "wavering" between his loyalty to the House of Hanover, and the attractions of the Stuart cause. Though his father Hoccupies a post in the Whig ministry, he has been reared by his uncle Sir Everard, a Tory who had supported the earlier Jacobite rebellion of 1715, though not so actively as to incur reprisals when it was put down. His father's connections procure Edward a commission in King George's army, and he is posted to Scotland. Shortly after arriving, he makes an extended visit to his uncle's Jacobite friend, the Baron of Bradwardine, and his daughter Rose. When a Highland raider, Donald Bean Lean, steals several of the Baron's cows, Waverley goes into the Highlands in the company of a follower of Fergus MacIvor, a chieftain who has the influence to secure the return of the cows. Waverley is impressed by Fergus and infatuated with his sister Flora. They are both confirmed Jacobites preparing to declare for the Pretender upon his arrival in Scotland.

As a result of Waverley's protracted absence and of a mutiny among the small band of men from his family estate who had followed him into the army, Waverley is declared absent without leave and superseded in his office. By coincidence, his father also loses his government position. Waverley's resentment at this twofold insult to his family by the Hanoverian government is heightened when, on a journey to Edinburgh to clear himself, he is arrested. Rescued by Donald Bean Lean, he is later brought to Edinburgh (now in the hands of the Jacobites), meets the

Pretender, and is won over to his cause. He takes part in the Jacobite victory at Preston, but is separated from Fergus's troop in a skirmish at Clifton, in which Fergus is captured. After a period in hiding, Waverley is pardoned, through the good offices of Colonel Talbot, whom he had saved from death and taken prisoner at Preston. Fergus is executed for treason.

Objections to *Waverley* usually center on the character of the hero, whom Scott himself called "a sneaking piece of imbecility." Certainly it is possible to be impatient with his lack of self-awareness, and the frequency with which he is acted upon rather than acting puts him often in a less than heroic light. Waverley, however, is not intended to be a romantic hero, and his susceptibility to external influence is necessary to enable Scott to show within a single character the conflict between the two forces that compose the novel's theme. For most of the book, Scott's view of the hero is ironic, emphasizing his failings. There is, for example, his vanity. One of the things that reconciles his Jacobite Aunt Rachel to his serving in the Hanoverian army is the fact that he is becoming infatuated with a local girl. Scott mocks Waverley's feelings, first by giving their object the inelegant name of Cecilia Stubbs, and then by telling the reader that on Waverley's last Sunday at the parish church he is too preoccupied with his own dashing appearance in his new uniform to notice the care with which Miss Stubbs has arrayed herself. The complement of this detail occurs later in the novel when Waverley, having joined the Jacobites, puts on Highland dress for the first time, and one of Fergus's followers remarks that he is "majoring yonder afore the muckle pier-glass." More seriously, the memory of "the inferior figure which he had made among the officers of his regiment," resulting from his inability to keep his mind on detail and routine, contributes to his decision to change sides.

In addition to exposing his vanity, Scott often undercuts Waverley's Romantic view of experience. On finding himself for the first time in the Highlands, he muses over "the full romance of his situation." It occurs to him that "the only circumstance which assorted ill with the rest, was the cause of his journey—the Baron's milk cows! this degrading incident he kept in the background." If, instead of deploring Waverley's inadequacy as a romantic hero, one attends to the irony with which Scott undercuts his fascination with romance and heroism, one will be better prepared for the author's reluctant dismissal of heroic virtues at the end of the novel. Waverley's character is perfectly appropriate to one who will survive into the new age, an age in which the dashing but destructive energies of Fergus have no place.

The real problem with the character is not his passivity or his ordinariness, but Scott's occasional failure to dramatize certain features of his personality, as opposed to merely making assertions about them. On two occasions he is credited with remarkable conversational powers, but no sample of them is given. During Waverley's period in hiding, Scott declares, "he acquired a more complete mastery of a spirit tamed by adversity, than his former experience had given him," but there is no demonstration of this "mastery." These flaws, however, hardly justify dismissing the characterization as a failure. The eagerness of Waverley's response to the new scenes and experiences he encounters, the growth of his resentment against the established government and his conversion to Jacobitism, his delayed recognition of his love for Rose, the cooling of his regard for Fergus as he comes to see the chieftain's selfishness and then the reawakening of that regard when Fergus is in danger—all these phases of his development are convincingly presented. Moreover, there are a few scenes where he shows real firmness (for example, his confrontation with Fergus when he has been shot at by one of Fergus's men), and several where he displays active generosity.

This said, one may concede that Waverley remains a rather slender figure to carry the weight of a novel of this length. He does not have to, however, for Scott surrounds him with a number of vivid characters from a wide range of classes and backgrounds. It is chiefly through their speech that he makes his characters live. The dialogue is not consistently successful: The bright small talk between Fergus and Flora can be downright dreadful, and some of the language of the other upper-class characters is stiff. The speech of most of the secondary characters, however, is convincing, and the dialect writing is particularly effcctive. Scott's most important contribution here is the achievement of a wide variety of tones in dialect speech. Before Scott, dialect was almost exclusively a comic device, but he was able to write dialect in different keys all the way up to the tragic. The best evidence of this is the scene in which Fergus and his follower Evan Dhu Maccombich are condemned to death. When Evan Dhu offers his life and the lives of five others in exchange for his chieftain's freedom, volunteering to go and fetch the five others himself, laughter breaks out in the courtroom. In a speech that loses nothing in dignity by being couched in dialect, Evan Dhu rebukes the audience and then proudly rejects the judge's invitation to plead for grace, preferring to share his chieftain's fate.

Fergus is perhaps the most interesting of the major characters. He possesses throughout the capacity to surprise the reader. Scott prepares the reader carefully for his first appearance. Waverley first hears of him in chapter 15 as an extorter of blackmail or protection money and is surprised to learn that he is nevertheless considered a gentleman. When he is introduced several chapters later, the reader discovers that this feudal leader of a troop of half-savage Highlandmen is a polished and literate individual with a very good French education. He is clearly fond of his sister, and yet quite prepared to exploit her as bait to draw Waverley into the Jacobite ranks. In the early part of the novel, the emphasis is on his courage, his hospitality, and his ability to inspire loyalty, and he is for the most part an attractive figure.

Gradually, however, both Waverley and the reader come to view him more critically. It grows increasingly clear that his commitment to the Jacobite cause is founded on self-interest. On learning that Prince Charles Edward is encouraging Bradwardine to leave his estate to Rose instead of to a distant male relative, he attempts to make the Prince promote his marriage to Rose. When the Princc refuses, he is furious, later saying that he could at that moment have sold himself to the devil or King George, "whichever offered the dearest revenge" (chap. 53). Yet as the Jacobite fortunes ebb, his generosity returns, and for the first time he attempts to use his influence over Waverley for the latter's good, telling him there is no dishonor in his extricating himself from the now certain wreck of their cause and urging him to marry Rose: "She loves you, and I believe you love her, though, perhaps, you have not found it out, for you are not celebrated for knowing your own mind very pointedly." He refuses to allow Waverley to witness his execution, and, by a generous deception regarding the hour at which it is to take place, he spares his sister the pain of a final interview. As he strides out of his cell, it is he who is supporting Waverley.

Throughout the novel, the portrait of Fergus is sharpened by a number of contrasts, explicit and implicit, between him and other characters. The contrast with Waverley is obviously central. There is also a contrast between him and his sister. While Fergus's Jacobitism is tinged with self-interest and he sometimes resorts to duplicity to advance the cause, Flora's devotion to the Stuarts is absolutely pure. She cannot reconcile herself to her brother's dealing with a thief of Donald Bean Lean's stripe even in the interest of the cause, and she resists his wish that she encourage Waverley's infatuation with her in order to win him to their side. Fergus's preoccupation with the more practical aspects of the campaign is set against Bradwardine's comically pedantic concern with form and ceremony in the question of whether and how to exercise his hereditary privilege of drawing off the king's boots. Yet Bradwardine's old-fashioned loyalty lacks all taint of self-interest, and, though he has been largely a comic figure, he behaves after the failure of the rebellion with a gallant fortitude comparable to that of Fergus. In the latter part of the novel, a new character enters to serve as Fergus's complete antithesis. Colonel Talbot, who supplants him in guiding Waverley's fate, differs from Fergus on practically every count—political affiliation, disinterested generosity, attitude toward women, and even age.

Several other characters are paired in contrast. Flora's strength of character, heroic bent, intellectual accomplishments, and striking beauty are repeatedly contrasted with the less remarkable gifts of the placid and domestic Rose. Sir Everard Waverley and his brother Richard are opposite numbers in all respects.

When Waverley is arrested on his way to Edinburgh, Melville and Morton, the magistrate and the clergyman who hear his defense, take differing views of his case. One of Fergus's henchmen, Callum Beg, commits a crime for his master when he attempts to shoot Waverley, while Humphry Houghton, one of Waverley's followers, involves himself in a conspiracy and mutiny. Both are carrying out what they mistakenly believe to be their masters' wishes, and they receive differing treatment for their actions.

This network of contrasts contributes much to the unity of a novel that is sometimes criticized as loosely structured. Scott's general preface to the 1829 edition of the whole series lends credence to this charge: "The tale of Waverley was put together with so little care, that I cannot boast of having sketched any distinct plan of the work. The whole adventures of Waverley, in his movements up and down the country with the Highland cateran Bean Lean, are managed without much skill." Whatever Scott meant by this, it cannot really be said that the book is loosely plotted. A glance at the retrospective explanations contained in chapters 31 and 65 will remind any reader of the great number of details that at first looked unimportant but that turn out to be essential to the mechanics of the plot. Such after-the-fact explanations may be technically awkward, and they may lay Scott open to the charge of unnecessary mystification in the episodes leading up to them, but they certainly evidence some careful planning.

It is rather for excessive reliance on coincidence that the plot can be criticized. The retrospective explanations just mentioned make some of these appear less unreasonable and incredible, but there are still a great many of them, and this is true of all Scott's novels. Also, the pace of the narrative is at times uncertain. Although the opening chapters describing Waverley's education are important to an understanding of the character, they make an undeniably slow beginning, and some of the set pieces retard the narrative flow.

In spite of its flaws, however, the novel is sustained by its central theme of the process of historical change and by Scott's ability to do justice to both sides in the conflict. Part of him responded strongly to the gallant romance of the Jacobite and to the love of tradition behind it. At the same time, he realized that the world had passed all that by. As Waverley himself points out, there have been four monarchs since James II was deposed, and the divine right absolutism for which the Stuarts stood would have sorted ill with the political and economic realities of the mid-eighteenth century. So Fergus is executed, his head is stuck up over the Scotch gate, and the Edinburgh youth whom Waverley has engaged as a valet comments, "It's a great pity of Evan Dhu, who was a very weel-meaning, good-natured man, to be a Hielandman; and indeed so was [Fergus MacIvor] too, for that matter, when he wasna in ane o' his tirrivies [tantrums]." In a snatch of dialogue, the heroic perspective is replaced by one more down-to-earth and commonplace. The threat to the prevailing order that the rebellion represented is already diminishing in importance in the popular view. To the common man secure in the established order, the energies that burned in Fergus amount to no more than "tirrivies."

OLD MORTALITY

Old Mortality deals with an earlier rebellion, one in which the issue is religious. Charles II had won the support of the Scottish Presbyterians by subscribing to the Solemn League and Covenant, which provided for the establishment of Presbyterianism as the state religion in Scotland and in England and Ireland as well. After the Restoration, however, Charles sought to impose episcopacy on Scotland, and the Covenanters were persecuted for their resistance to the bishops. In 1679, the assassination of the Archbishop of St. Andrews by a small party of Covenanters led by John Balfour of Burley sparked a gathering of insurgents who managed at Drumclog to defeat the Cavalier forces, under John Graham of Claverhouse, that were sent against them. A few weeks later, however, the Covenanters, divided by moderate and extremist factions, were routed at Bothwell Bridge by an army commanded by the Duke of Monmouth. The novel's title is the nickname of an old man who travels through Scotland refurbishing the markers on the graves of the martyred Covenanters.

Out of these events, Scott built one of his starkest and swiftest plots. Once again he portrays a hero caught between conflicting forces. Just after the Archbishop's murder, Henry Morton gives shelter to Burley because Burley and his father had been comrades-in-arms and Burley had saved the elder Morton's life. Henry Morton's moderate principles lead him to condemn the murder, but he also deplores the oppression that provoked it, and Burley hopes that he will eventually take up arms with the Covenanters. Morton is, however, drawn to the Cavalier side by his love for Edith Bellenden (one of Scott's more pallid heroines) and by his friendship for her granduncle.

Morton receives some firsthand experience of the oppressive measures of the Cavaliers when he is arrested for harboring the fugitive Burley and is brought before Claverhouse. This figure is Burley's opposite number, rather as Talbot is Fergus MacIvor's in *Waverley*, except that Talbot is wholly admirable while Claverhouse is a more complex character. Like Burley, Claverhouse sees in Morton qualities of courage and leadership that could be valuable to the rebels. He is about to have him executed when one of his subordinates, Lord Evandale, intervenes. Evandale is a suitor of Edith, and at her request he generously asks Claverhouse to spare his rival's life. Morton is carried along as a prisoner with Claverhouse's troops, and when they are defeated by the Covenanters at Drumclog, he is set free. Under Burley's auspices, he is given a high post in the rebel army.

In this phase of the novel, Morton shows himself a much more active hero than Waverley. He quickly repays his debt to Evandale by saving his life in the rout of the loyalist forces, and he does so again in a later chapter, when Evandale has become Burley's prisoner. He plays a prominent part in the Covenanters' attempts to take Glasgow. He draws up a statement of the rebels' grievances and presents it to Monmouth just before the battle of Bothwell Bridge, and even though the Covenanters obstinately refuse the terms he secures, he does not defect, but instead fights heroically in the battle that ensues.

In spite of the vigor with which Morton fulfills his commitment to the Presbyterians, they distrust him, and Scott sharply dramatizes their ignorance, factiousness, bigotry, and cruelty. He also exposes the unscrupulous streak in Burley's enthusiasm. This zealot is convinced that the most barbaric cruelties and the rankest deceptions are justified by his cause. He is surrounded by a gallery of fanatics, of whom the most horrifying is the insane preacher Habbakuk Mucklewrath. In flight after the defeat at Bothwell Bridge, Morton and his servant Cuddie stumble upon a group of Covenanting leaders in an isolated farmhouse at Drumshinnel. They have been praying for guidance, and the arrival of Morton, whom they irrationally regard as the cause of their defeat, convinces them that God has sent him to them as a sacrifice. They conduct a kind of trial, though the verdict of death is never in doubt. It is the Sabbath, however, and they are unwilling to execute him before midnight. Eventually, Mucklewrath jumps up to put the clock ahead, crying, "As the sun went back on the dial ten degrees for intimating the recovery of holy Hezekiah, so shall it now go forward, that the wicked may be taken away from among the people, and the Covenant established in its purity."

This display of the Covenanters' fanaticism is the complement of the earlier trial before Claverhouse, in which Morton was threatened with the arbitrary cruelty of the Cavalier side. Ironically, it is Claverhouse who now arrives to save Morton. (He has been led to the farmhouse by Cuddie, who had been allowed to escape.) Most of the Covenanters are slaughtered. Riding back to Edinburgh in the custody of his rescuers, Morton is divided between horror at Claverhouse's habitual cold indifference to bloodshed and admiration for his urbanity and his valor. Claverhouse admits that he is as much a fanatic as Durley but adds, "There is a difference, I trust, between the blood of learned and reverend prelates and scholars, of gallant soldiers and noble gentlemen, and the red puddle that stagnates in the veins of psalm-singing mechanics, crack-brained demagogues, and sullen boors." Scott counters this assessment in the very next chapter by showing the fortitude of one of the Covenanting leaders, Ephraim MacBriar, as he is brutally tortured and then condemned to death. The reader may also recall that it was prolonged imprisonment by the Cavaliers that drove Mucklewrath insane. As in *Waverley*, Scott sees both sides objectively.

Morton is sentenced to exile, and there is a gap of ten years in the narrative. In 1689, when the Glorious Revolution has put William and Mary on the throne, Morton is free to return to Scotland. Edith is on the point, finally, of accepting marriage to Evandale. Claverhouse, loyal to the Stuarts, is now ironically a rebel in his turn. He is killed in the battle of Killecrankie, but his army is victorious. He had once said to Morton, "When I think of death . . . as a thing worth thinking of, it is in the hope of pressing one day some well-fought and hard-won field of battle, and dying with the shout of victory in my ear—*that* would be worth dying for, and more, it would be worth having lived for!" The rather too crowded closing pages describe the deaths of Burley and Lord Evandale.

The novel displays Scott's dramatic gifts at their best. Though the language of Morton, Edith, and Evandale is sometimes stiff, the dialogue of the rest of the characters is vigorous and precisely adjusted to their various stations and backgrounds, and the language of the Covenanters, loaded with scriptural allusions, idioms, and rhythms, constitutes a particularly remarkable achievement. In addition to the characters already discussed, three others stand out. One is Sergeant Bothwell, who is descended from an illegitimate son of James VI and resents his failure to attain preferment. He is one of the novel's chief embodiments of the bullying oppression and extortion to which the Covenanters are subjected, but he is also capable of the courtesy and bravery that he regards as incumbent on one of his blood. Another is Mause Headrigg, whose compulsive declarations of her extreme Presbyterian principles are always ill-timed, to the chagrin of her pragmatic son Cuddie, who has no ambition to become a martyred Covenanter. The third is Jenny Dennison, Edith's maid. Like her mistress, Jenny has a suitor on each side of the conflict, and Scott thus creates a comic parallel to the Morton-Edith-Evandale triangle. She chooses Morton's servant Cuddie over her other suitor, a soldier in the Cavalier army, and this match foreshadows the eventual union of Edith and Morton. Jenny, however, has more vitality, resourcefulness, and charm than her mistress. She has been criticized for trying to promote Edith's marriage to the wealthy Evandale with a view to securing the future of herself, her husband, and their children. One can admit this fault and go on to point out that it is related to the success of the characterization. The most convincing characters in *Old Mortality* are those in whom Scott reveals a mixture of motivations or a blending of admirable with deplorable traits.

ROB ROY

Rob Roy is probably the least successful of the four novels considered here. It resembles *Waverley* in that it takes a young Englishman into the Highlands during a Jacobite rising, this time that of 1715. Like Edward Waverley, Frank Osbaldistone has a romantic and poetical turn and responds eagerly to the unfamiliar world of the Highlands. Like Waverley, he has a touch of vanity and of obstinacy in his temper. Like Waverley, he is slow to understand his feelings for the heroine. That he is not as slow as Waverley was to realize that he loved Rose may be attributed to two factors: There is only one possible object for Frank's affections, not two; and that object, Diana Vernon, bears a much closer similarity to Flora, who captivated Waverley immediately, than to Rose.

Frank Osbaldistone, however, is a less interesting hero than Waverley, largely because he does not experience any serious internal conflict. In spite of his love for Diana, a committed Jacobite, he never considers supporting the Pretender. His conflicts are all external. Having angered his father by refusing to follow him into trade, Frank is sent to stay with his uncle's family in Northumberland, to be replaced in the firm by one of his cousins. Though it is understandable that his father should turn to a nephew when his son has disappointed him, it is not clear what point he has in sending Frank to Osbaldistone Hall. Frank's uncle and five of his cousins are boors with no interests beyond hunting and drinking. The sixth son, Rashleigh, is clever, villainous, ugly, and lame. He is the one chosen to take Frank's place in the firm. He had been tutor to Diana, who is his cousin on his mother's side, but had attempted to seduce her, and she has since kept him at a distance. Nevertheless, their common Jacobite sympathies remain a bond between them. Rashleigh, resenting Di-

ana's obvious liking for Frank and smarting under an insult from him, forms a plan that will ruin the Osbaldistone firm and at the same time hasten the rising of the clans in support of the Pretender. The financial details of this scheme are not clear, and it therefore lacks credibility. This flaw in the plot is fairly serious because in *Rob Roy* commercial activity has considerable thematic importance.

Once in London, Rashleigh wins his uncle's confidence and then absconds with certain crucial documents. Frank's task is to follow him to Glasgow and then into the Highlands to recover them. It is in fact not Frank but Diana Vernon's father (whose identity is a mystery to Frank and the reader until the end of the book) who gets the documents back, and this in spite of the fact that he is also a Jacobite and might thus be expected to further rather than thwart Rashleigh's plot. Punishment comes to Rashleigh not from Frank but from the Highland chieftain Rob Roy. Rashleigh turns traitor to the Jacobites, and, after the failure of the rebellion, he arranges the arrest of Diana and her father. In the process of rescuing them, Rob Roy kills Rashleigh.

Thus, though Frank is a party to his fair share of adventures, he is too often merely a party rather than the chief actor, even though he is clearly meant to be the hero. Although Rob Roy appears at practically every crisis of the story, those appearances are intermittent, and the crises mark stages in the experience of Frank. Everything, down to the use of Frank as first-person narrator, points to him as the central character. (Everything, that is, except the title, but a writer with Scott's sense of what sells would hardly call a book *Osbaldistone*.) At too many crucial points, however, Rob Roy displaces Frank as the focus of the reader's interest. Though their relationship may appear to resemble that of Waverley and Fergus or of Morton and Burley, Morton and even Waverley are more active characters than Frank and thus are never eclipsed by Burley and Fergus to the extent that Frank is by Rob Roy. This seems to be largely a result of the bonds that unite Fergus with Waverley and Morton with Burley in a common enterprise for much of their respective stories. The cause shared by each pair of characters makes it possible for each pair to share the spotlight, so to speak, against a common background without compromising the novel's unity. Rob Roy and Frank, by contrast, do not act together in a public cause, since Frank is not a Jacobite. Furthermore, the distance between them is emphasized in the early part of the novel by the fact that, though he takes action several times in Frank's behalf, Rob Roy's identity is unknown to Frank until the novel is half over. In short, the plot keeps these characters separate as Waverley is not kept separate from Fergus nor Morton from Burley, and as a result the novel seems marred by a divided focus.

There is also a failure to unify the public and the private themes as convincingly as in the other two novels. The vagueness of the link between the ruin of the Osbaldistone firm and the rising of the clans has already been noted. A related problem is the absence of specificity about Diana Vernon's Jacobite activities. A wary reader will recognize Scott's irony in having Frank respond to an early warning about Diana with the words, "Pshaw, a Jacobite?—is that all?" There is, however, a lack of concrete detail about her role in the conspiracy. This is perhaps inevitable, given the first-person point of view and the fact that Diana keeps Frank out of the secret of the conspiracy, but it weakens the characterization of the heroine. In contrast, Flora MacIvor's political obsession is fully convincing. Diana is perhaps not meant to seem as much a fanatic as Flora, yet she too has sacrificed all personal inclination to the cause—or to her father's will. At the end of the novel, the reader learns that her father has been a central figure in the conspiracy and has often stayed at Osbaldistone Hall in the disguise of a priest, and that Rashleigh's hold over Diana resulted from his having penetrated her father's disguise. This is a fairly dramatic situation, but the reader is, so to speak, asked to do the dramatizing for himself in retrospect. The specifics about Diana's part in the conspiracy are too little too late.

Since Sir Frederick Vernon has no identity for the reader until the closing pages, he can never be more than a minor figure. Yet to him, Scott assigns the account of the actual rebellion. In the penultimate chapter, the rebellion and its collapse are perfunctorily described by Sir Frederick in less than two pages.

This is a signal failure to unify the personal and historical dimensions. Instead of the climax that it should have been, the 1715 rising seems almost an afterthought.

There is, however, a good deal of effective characterization in the novel. Diana Vernon is probably the most attractive and interesting of Scott's heroines. She is well educated, strong-minded, outspoken, aggressive, and witty. She may not quite hold her own in the company to which critical opinion sometimes promotes her, the company of William Shakespeare's Beatrice and Jane Austen's Elizabeth Bennett, but the dialogue Scott gives her does indeed amply express intelligence and vitality. If there is one false note, it is Scott's finally allowing her to marry Frank, but one's reservations may be qualified by the consideration that Frank seems politically almost neutral. If he does not support the Stuarts, he is not in the debt of Hanover either. It is not quite as if Flora MacIvor had married Edward Waverley.

Diana first appears before Frank on horseback wearing "what was then somewhat unusual, a coat, vest, and hat, resembling those of a man, which fashion has since called a riding-habit." Scott several times underlines her firm and forthright behavior by comparing it to a man's. There is a much stronger masculine streak in the only other important female character in this book which has just four speaking roles for women. Rob Roy's wife Helen is a virago capable of ambushing a British troop with only a small band and of cold-bloodedly ordering the drowning of a hostage. She should have been a powerful figure, but the language she speaks is impossibly bookish and rhetorical, an objection which is not sufficiently answered by Scott's later remarking that her "wild, elevated, and poetical" style is caused by the fact that she is translating from Gaelic into English, "which she had acquired as we do learned tongues."

The characterization of Rob Roy himself is on the whole successful, despite a certain lack of impact in his first few appearances, during which a reader who has skipped Scott's unusually cumbersome prefatory material may not even realize that this is the titular character. He gains added weight by being the chief embodiment of one side of the novel's main thematic conflict. The focus of the novel is not on the Jacobite-Hanoverian struggle but on the related but distinguishable conflict between the half-barbaric feudal life of the Highland clans and the modern commercial world of trade. Rob Roy is an outlaw relying on blackmail to support himself and his followers, who acknowledge no leader but him. Their way of life breeds narrow loyalties (a point emphasized also by the judge in the trial of Fergus MacIvor). Helen MacGregor cannot "bide the sight o' a kindly Scot, if he come frae the Lowlands, far less of an Inglisher." The clansmen are a threat to peace and order because rebellion and disorder are conditions far more likely to improve their lot. As Rob Roy says of the expected uprising, "Let it come . . . and if the world is turned upside down, why, honest men have the better chance to cut bread out of it."

Rob Roy is contrasted with the Glasgow weaver and magistrate Bailie Nichol Jarvie. A business associate of the Osbaldistone firm, he accompanies Frank in his pursuit of Rashleigh. Scott makes Rob Roy and Jarvie kinsmen in order to point out the contrasts between them more sharply. These contrasts are most clearly drawn in two fine scenes, one in the Glasgow jail midway through the novel and the other near the end. In the latter scene, when Bailie Nichol Jarvie deplores the ignorance of Rob Roy's sons, the Highlander boasts, "Hamish can bring down a black-cock when he's on the wing wi' a single bullet, and Rob can drive a dirk through a twa-inch board." Jarvie retorts, "Sae muckle the waur for them baith! . . . An they ken naething better than that, they had better no ken that neither." Rob Roy scorns his kinsman's offer to take his sons as apprentices: "My sons weavers! . . . I wad see every loom in Glasgow, beam, traddles, and shuttles, burnt in hell-fire sooner!" Shortly afterward, however, he admits to Frank that he is troubled at the thought of his sons "living their father's life." That kind of life in fact remained possible for only about three more decades, for after the rising of 1745, the rule of law was extended into the Highlands and the power of the clans was permanently broken.

That defeat in effect completed the Union of England and Scotland that had been established in 1707. In chapter 27, when Andrew Fairservice, Frank's servant, speaks disparagingly of the Union, Jarvie sternly rebukes him:

> Whisht, sir—whisht! it's ill-scraped tongues like yours, that make mischief atween neighbourhoods and nations. . . . I say, Let Glasgow flourish! . . . judiciously and elegantly putten round the town's arms, by way of by-word—Now, since St. Mungo catched herrings in the Clyde, what was ever like to gar [make] us flourish like the sugar and tobacco trade? Will ony body tell me that, and grumble at the treaty that opened us a road westawa' yonder?

Jarvie expresses Scott's own sense of the benefits that the growing commercial activity of the eighteenth century had brought to Scotland. Emotionally, he admired the romantic and adventurous character of Rob Roy's way of life, but his reason put him finally on the Bailie's side. Jarvie states the theme in terms of honor versus credit: "I maun hear naething about honour—we ken naething here but about credit. Honour is a homicide and a bloodspiller, that gangs about making frays in the street; but Credit is a decent honest man, that sits at hame and makes the pat play [pot boil]" (chap. 26).

THE HEART OF MIDLOTHIAN

The Heart of Midlothian is regarded by many as Scott's best work. In addition to the familiar virtues of a fully realized specific historical milieu and a large cast of characters from a variety of social levels who create themselves through the dialogue, the novel has for its heroine one of the common people, with whom Scott's powers of characterization were at their surest, and it has a truly serious ethical theme in the heroine's refusal to lie to save the life of her younger sister. Jeanie Dean's dilemma enables Scott to examine the relation of the law to justice and to mercy.

The novel opens with an extended presentation of an actual historical event, the Porteous riots in Edinburgh in 1736. Immediately after the execution of a smuggler named Wilson, John Porteous, Captain of the City Guard, reacts to a minor disturbance among the spectators by needlessly ordering his troop to fire upon the crowd. Several people are killed, and Porteous is sentenced to be hanged. On the very day set for his execution, he is reprieved by Queen Caroline. That night a mob storms the prison, the Tolbooth (to which the novel's title is a reference). Porteous is dragged out and hanged.

In Scott's version, the mob is led by George Robertson, an accomplice of Wilson, who would have died along with him had Wilson not generously made possible his escape. Robertson has another reason besides revenge on Porteous for breaking into the Tolbooth. In the prison is Effie Deans, who has been seduced by him and has borne his child. She is to stand trial under a statute which stipulates that if a woman conceals her pregnancy and then can neither produce the infant nor prove that it died a natural death, she shall be presumed to have murdered it and shall suffer the death penalty. Once inside the prison, Robertson seeks her out and urges her to make her escape in the confusion, but she refuses. (One wonders why he did not remove her forcibly, but evidently he has his hands full directing Porteous's fate.) The next night, Robertson summons Effie's sister Jeanie to a remote spot and tells her that the case can be removed from under the statute if Effie is found to have communicated her condition to anyone. Jeanie refuses to lie about her sister's having done this, and she repeats her refusal in an affecting interview with Effie just before the trial. When Effie is condemned to death, Jeanie travels on foot all the way from Edinburgh to London, wins the support of the Duke of Argyle, and persuades Queen Caroline to pardon her sister. A few days after Effie is released, she elopes with Robertson

At this point the novel is in effect finished, or nearly so, but Scott added a fourth volume to stretch the book to the length for which he had contracted. In it, the Duke of Argyle arranges for Jeanie, her new husband Reuben Butler (a clergyman), and her father to remove to a remote part of Scotland under his protection. This pastoral coda contrasts too strongly with the tone of the rest of the novel, and there is an unfortunate emphasis on the material blessings showered on Jeanie that rather qualifies one's sense of the disinterested heroism of her achievement. The closing chapters are, to be sure, tied to the main plot by

the reappearance of Effie and her husband and by the discovery of their son, now a member of a small gang of bandits. Robertson is killed in an encounter with this gang, probably by his own son. There is an interesting variation on the novel's central situation, for the son, probably actually guilty of unnatural murder as his mother Effie was not, escapes when Jeanie goes to the room where he is confined and in her compassion loosens his painfully tight bonds. If this repetition of the novel's central event, Jeanie's saving a prisoner from execution, is aesthetically interesting, it is nevertheless ethically problematic, for the youth is a lawless individual who shows no compunction at what he has done and who does not hesitate, once Jeanie has loosened his bonds, to endanger her life by setting a fire in order to effect his escape. Jeanie's mercy seems in this case ill-judged.

It is the first three volumes that contain the most effective probing of the relation of the law to justice and to mercy. Scott contrasts a number of characters, each of whom stands in a different relation to the law. Wilson is a criminal justly condemned for smuggling, but his last offense is the generous one of saving a life by enabling his young accomplice to escape, and it wins him the sympathy of the populace and sets him in sharp contrast to the enforcer of the law, the Captain of the City Guard. Porteous's excessive zeal in the performance of his office leads to the loss of life and earns him the hatred of the populace when he gives the order to fire upon the crowd. His callousness is also shown by his earlier refusal to loosen Wilson's painfully tight handcuffs on the way to the execution, pointing out that all his pain will soon be at an end.

Among the mob that punishes Porteous, Robertson is concerned to preserve order because he wishes to stress the justice of their action, yet in his own person he has much to fear from justice. He is, moreover, clearly moved more by a desire for revenge than by a true concern for justice, and also, as has already been noted, he has in Effie Deans an ulterior motive for storming the Tolbooth.

Of all the prisoners the novel describes, Effie is in the worst plight, since she is entirely innocent of the crime she is charged with and since the statute does not even require that a crime be proved to have occurred. Moreover, she is in a sense to suffer for the guilt of others, for the government wishes to make an example of her because of the increasing frequency of child murder. Also, the Queen's anger at the response to the pardon of Porteous makes a royal pardon for Effie unlikely. Her situation is rendered more hopeless by these two factors that in strict justice have no bearing on her case.

Effie is linked with Wilson in that he and she have both sacrificed themselves for Robertson. Effie staunchly refuses to reveal her seducer's identity, even when she is "offered a commutation and alleviation of her punishment, and even a free pardon, if she would confess what she knew of her lover." In her desire to protect Robertson, she goes so far as to withhold all information concerning Meg Murdockson, the woman to whom Robertson had sent her when her child was due.

Robertson clearly does not deserve her generosity (nor Wilson's, for that matter). He is completely selfish. Effie is not the first girl he has abused. Meg Murdockson had long been a servant in his family, and he had seduced her daughter Madge. When her mother put Madge's infant out of the way so it would not pose an obstacle to Madge's finding a husband, Madge lost her wits. She is one of a number of pathetic simpletons who wander through Scott's novels, a company that includes David Gellatley in *Waverley* and Goose Gibbie in *Old Mortality*. Robertson's guilt in Madge's case has far-reaching consequences, for it is anger at the prospect of Effie's taking her daughter's place that moves Meg Murdockson to spirit away Effie's infant and later to attempt to waylay Jeanie on her journey to London.

Robertson's real name is Staunton. He has been among other things an actor, and this is appropriate, for, besides being selfish, he is the rankest hypocrite. In the scene where he confronts Jeanie to explain how she can save her sister, he heaps blame on himself liberally, but it is all empty gesture and rhetoric. He expects someone else to solve the problem. Jeanie is to save Effie by telling a lie when he could do it by surrendering himself and telling the truth. When Effie has finally been sentenced, then indeed he leaps

on his horse with the intention of securing her reprieve by giving himself up as the leader of the Porteous mob, but his horse loses its footing and Staunton is thrown and severly injured. Jeanie learns of this on her journey to London when, by a remarkable coincidence, she meets him in his father's house, where he is recuperating. He authorizes her to trade his life for that of her sister, but only if her own unsupported plea is refused.

When Effie is reprieved and Staunton marries her, he becomes an actor in good earnest, and so does she. Sir George and Lady Staunton live for years in fear that their past will be discovered, and his unhappiness is much aggravated by the fact that they are childless. A series of coincidences reveals that their son is not dead, but is part of a small gang of bandits in the very vicinity where Jeanie and her family now live. When Staunton arrives in search of him and is killed, Jeanie prepares the body for burial. She discovers "from the crucifix, the beads, and the shirt of hair which he wore next his person, that his sense of guilt had induced him to receive the dogmata of a religion, which pretends, by the maceration of the body, to expiate the crimes of the soul" (chap. 52). The verb *pretends* conveys Scott's view of the appropriateness of Staunton's conversion to Roman Catholicism.

Jeanie Deans, in contrast, is firmly anchored in her father's rigid Presbyterianism and has a horror of every kind of pretense or falsehood. Her principles prevent her from lying to save Effie, but her generosity enables her to accomplish what all of Staunton's empty heroics are powerless to achieve. It is interesting to consider a misunderstanding that arises between Jeanie and her father, David Deans, regarding her testifying at Effie's trial. Deans is a Cameronian, the strictest kind of Scottish Presbyterian, and his memory goes back to the battle of Bothwell Bridge and the persecutions that followed it. He is doubtful of the propriety of even appearing in court, since doing so might seem to constitute an acknowledgement of a government that has abandoned the Solemn League and Covenant and that exercises what he regards as undue influence over the Kirk. Though Deans has never before hesitated to tell anyone what to do, in the present case he says to himself, "My daughter Jean may have a light in this subject that is hid frae my auld een—it is laid on her conscience, and not on mine—If she hath freedom to gang before this judicatory, and hold up her hand for this poor cast-away, surely I will not say she steppeth over her bounds" (chap. 18). The inconsistency is too touching and too clearly rooted in his love for Effie to be called hypocrisy. It is another instance of the conflict between principles of conduct and emotional claims, and it enriches the character and underlines his relation to the central theme.

When he attempts to convey to Jeanie his resolution of his scruples, she, who has no thought of refusing to appear in court, takes it that he is encouraging her to give false testimony. The misunderstanding increases her sense of isolation and lack of support and thus makes her behavior all the more heroic.

The heroic impact of the journey itself is marred somewhat by the melodramatic events with which Scott seeks to enliven it. The lurid coloring is overdone in the scene of Jeanie's captivity at the hands of Meg, Madge, and two underworld cronies of theirs (to whom the old woman is known as Mother Blood). Scott is more successful when he modulates into comedy in the scene in which the demented Madge, in the absence of Meg and the others, leads Jeanie to a nearby village and then into church, where Madge's fantastic behavior causes her captive considerable embarrassment. The tension between the comic elements here and the very real danger of Jeanie's situation makes a strong effect. Shortly afterward, however, the tone shifts back to melodrama with the coincidental meeting with the convalescent Staunton, and the dramatic temperature drops during one of those retrospective narratives which Scott's complex plotting often forced on him.

The climactic confrontation with the Queen is very well done. Oddly enough, although Scott often had trouble finding a convincingly natural mode of utterance for his invented characters of the upper class, for actual historical figures he often succeeded in writing dialogue that is elevated without being stilted, polished without being wooden. Such is the language of Prince Charles Edward in *Waverley*, of

Claverhouse in *Old Mortality*, and of Queen Caroline here.

The psychology of the Queen and her language are noteworthy. Jeanie's simple plea is effective, but it is not, or not only, emotional considerations that cause the Queen to grant the pardon. Even her response to Jeanie's main speech—"This is eloquence"—suggests objective evaluation of the speech more than emotional assent, and Scott keeps the scene well clear of sentimentality by a persistent emphasis on the political factors in the Queen's decision. She is divided between resentment of the Scots for their response to her pardoning of Porteous and her inclination to remain on good terms with Jeanie's sponsor, the Duke of Argyle. Even though he is at present out of favor, her policy is based on the principle that political allies may become opponents and opponents may again become allies. Another element in the scene is her complex attitude toward Lady Suffolk, also present at the interview. The Queen has so arranged matters that Suffolk is both her chief confidante and the King's mistress. After inadvertently making a remark that the Queen construes as a reflection on herself, Jeanie rights herself with a chance reference to "the stool of repentance," the punishment in Scotland "for light life and conversation, and for breaking the seventh command." The Queen is amused at the obvious embarrassment of "her good Suffolk."

The novel as a whole indicates that although the law is an absolute necessity, it can never do more than approximate justice because it is made and administered by human beings. It is ironically the generous instincts of Effie (in protecting Staunton) and the uncompromising honesty of Jeanie that make Effie the victim of a law which, it is repeatedly suggested, is a bad law because it exacts punishment in cases where there may have been no crime. It seems unjust too that the strict enforcement in the present instance is caused by factors external to Effie's case, the rise in child murder and the royal anger over the Porteous affair. Moreover, the author tends to place the human agents who enforce the law in an unflattering light. Porteous abuses the authority vested in him. The Doomster, or executioner, is a kind of untouchable who inspires horror in everyone when he makes his ritual appearance at Effie's sentencing. Ratcliffe, a thief four times condemned to the gallows, is the only prisoner besides Effie who rejects the opportunity to escape when the mob breaks into the Tolbooth. His reason is that he wants the post of underturnkey. The authorities actually grant this audacious request after considering how valuable his knowledge of the underworld is likely to prove. Scott provides a striking emblem of the amount of practical compromise involved in the enforcing of the law when he shows Ratcliffe and Sharpitlaw, the superintendent of police, at the start of the interview in which they bargain over Ratcliffe's request: "They sate for five minutes silent, on opposite sides of a small table, and looked fixedly at each other, with a sharp, knowing, and alert cast of countenance, not unmingled with an inclination to laugh."

The scene with the Queen indicates that the prerogative of mercy that is intended to mitigate the sternness of the law or correct miscarriages of justice is likewise governed by considerations of policy and expediency. The outcome of that scene, however, shows that the gap between ideal justice on the one hand, and policy or expediency on the other, can be bridged by the selfless exertions of someone motivated simply by love.

Although the four novels discussed here are likely to appear on anyone's list of the best of Scott, they are by no means the only ones worthy of a modern reader's attention. *The Antiquary, The Bride of Lammermoor, A Legend of Montrose,* and *Woodstock* have all found advocates among modern critics. There is also a very successful third panel in what might be called the Jacobite triptych that includes *Waverley* and *Rob Roy: Redgauntlet,* set in the 1760's, describes the last throes of the Jacobite movement. In addition to a plot full of intrigue, it is noteworthy for its combination of letters and journals with third-person narration and for autobiographical elements in the main characters of Alan Fairford and Darsie Latimer. Obviously Scott will never again have the huge audience he enjoyed throughout the nineteenth century, but he is more than merely a chapter in literary history. In addition to establishing the genre of

the historical novel and influencing nineteenth century historiography, he wrote several novels that can be judged major achievements by any but the most narrow and rigid criteria.

John Michael Walsh

OTHER MAJOR WORKS

SHORT FICTION: *Chronicles of the Canongate,* 1827.

PLAYS: *Halidon Hill,* pb. 1822; *Macduff's Cross,* pb. 1823; *The Doom of Devorgoil,* pb. 1830; *Auchindrane: Or, The Ayrshire Tragedy,* pr., pb. 1830.

POETRY: *The Eve of Saint John: A Border Ballad,* 1800; *The Lay of the Last Minstrel,* 1805; *Ballads and Lyrical Pieces,* 1806; *Marmion: A Tale of Flodden Field,* 1808; *The Lady of the Lake,* 1810; *The Vision of Don Roderick,* 1811; *Rokeby,* 1813; *The Bridal of Triermain: Or, The Vale of St. John, in Three Cantos,* 1813; *The Lord of the Isles,* 1815; *The Field of Waterloo,* 1815; *The Ettrick Garland: Being Two Excellent New Songs,* 1815 (with James Hogg); *Harold the Dauntless,* 1817.

NONFICTION: *The Life and Works of John Dryden,* 1808; *The Life of Jonathan Swift,* 1814; *Lives of the Novelists,* 1825; *The Life of Napoleon Buonaparte: Emperor of the French, with a Preliminary View of the French Revolution,* 1827.

TRANSLATIONS: *The Chase, and William and Helen: Two Ballads from the German of Gottfried Augustus Bürger,* 1796; *Goetz von Berlichingen,* 1799 (Johann Wolfgang von Goethe).

EDITED TEXTS: *Minstrelsy of the Scottish Border,* 1802-1803 (3 volumes); *A Collection of Scarce and Valuable Tracts,* 1809-1815 (13 volumes); *Chronological Notes of Scottish Affairs from the Diary of Lord Fountainhall,* 1822.

BIBLIOGRAPHY

Crawford, Thomas. *Scott.* Rev. ed. Edinburgh: Scottish Academic Press, 1982. A revision and elaboration of Crawford's widely acclaimed study of Scott. Examines Scott's work as a poet, balladist, and novelist in a compact style.

Daiches, David. *Sir Walter Scott and His World.* London: Thames and Hudson, 1971. A well-written account of Scott, generously illustrated. Contains much valuable information in a readable style by an eminent scholar of Scott.

deGategno, Paul J. *Ivanhoe: The Mask of Chivalry.* New York: Twayne, 1994. This volume of the Twayne Masterwork Series follows the series format, placing the novel in literary and historical context before it is given a particular reading. DeGategno's reading emphasizes the novel's pertinence to its own time and its importance as a reflection of Scott's society. But then, interestingly, deGategno concludes his book with a selection of his students' responses to *Ivanhoe.* This book provides a good general introduction to one of Scott's most compelling and long-lived works.

Hart, Francis R. *Scott's Novels: The Plotting of Historical Survival.* Charlottesville: University of Virginia Press, 1966. A survey of Scott's novels, generally favorable and emphasizing the author's diversity.

Humphrey, Richard. *Waverley.* Cambridge, England: Cambridge University Press, 1993. This short volume also provides a useful introduction to a seminal Scott novel. Humphrey divides his analysis of the novel into four parts: "Scott's changing world and the making of *Waverley,*" "*Waverley* as story," "*Waverley* as history," and "*Waverley* as initiator"—by which he means that the novel provided a model not only for subsequent Scott works, but also for novels written by many other writers. An interesting appendix contains contemporary accounts of the Battle of Prestonpans.

Johnson, Edgar. *Sir Walter Scott: The Great Unknown.* 2 vols. New York: Macmillan, 1970. Now considered the definitive biography of Scott, replacing John Gibson Lockhart's. Johnson has used the many sources and information available on Scott to present an accurate portrayal of the author. A must for the serious Scott scholar.

Lauber, John. *Sir Walter Scott.* Rev. ed. Boston: Twayne, 1989. A good introduction to Scott, ideal for the beginning student or new reader of Scott. Rather than concentrating on the *Waverley* novels, takes a "sampling" of Scott's finest works. Contains a useful bibliography.

MARY LEE SETTLE

Born: Charleston, West Virginia; July 29, 1918

PRINCIPAL LONG FICTION

The Love Eaters, 1954
The Kiss of Kin, 1955
O Beulah Land, 1956
Know Nothing, 1960
Fight Night on a Sweet Saturday, 1964
The Clam Shell, 1971
Prisons, 1973
Blood Tie, 1977
The Scapegoat, 1980
The Killing Ground, 1982 (revision of *Fight Night on a Sweet Saturday*)
Celebration, 1986
Charley Bland, 1989
Choices, 1995

OTHER LITERARY FORMS

In addition to her novels, Mary Lee Settle has written several nonfiction books. Her juvenile works, *The Story of Flight* (1967) and *Water World* (1984), the latter being a parallel history of humanity's exploration of the sea, are not as significant as her autobiographical *All the Brave Promises: Memories of Aircraft Woman Second Class 2146391* (1966) or her historical study *The Scopes Trial: The State of Tennessee vs. John Thomas Scopes* (1972). *All the Brave Promises* describes her experiences as an American volunteer in the Women's Auxiliary Air Force of the Royal Air Force (RAF) in 1942 and 1943. *The Scopes Trial*, like *All the Brave Promises*, deals with human responses to a historical confrontation. *Addie* (1998) examines her life as it is framed by her ancestors, including her grandmother, Addie Tompkins.

ACHIEVEMENTS

As late as 1978, when she won the National Book Award in Fiction for *Blood Tie*, critics were calling Settle an "unknown" writer. With the earlier publication of four of her historical novels, some of them had praised her for research-based realism, resulting in works more respectable than the typically lurid products of that genre. Critics, however, found her complexity sometimes confusing, pointing out the changes in point of view, the flashforwards and flashbacks, and sometimes the assumption that the reader knew the history of her characters as well as the writer did. There was a lack of agreement as to whether her characters were well developed. After the completion of the Beulah Quintet in 1982 (*O Beulah Land, Know Nothing, Prisons, The Scapegoat, The Killing Ground*), however, critics recognized the depth and scope of her vision, arguing that Settle's structural complexity was justified by her aim: to present the truth about human relationships in their historical context. To her early champions, among them Malcolm Cowley and George Garrett, were added numerous other reviewers, who saw evidence of her considerable talent in her contemporary works as well as in the historical novels. To them, the award for *Blood Tie* was a belated recognition, rather than an unexpected one. When *Celebration* was published, Settle received praise, rather than blame, for her stylistic and technical feats, and she was no longer faulted for her characterization. With such articles as that by Peggy Bach in the October, 1984, *The Southern Review*, Settle's reputation was established as a skillful, serious writer, whose approach to her material is necessitated if she is to document her own search and that of her characters for, in Bach's words, "their own personal past and the taproot that was cut."

BIOGRAPHY

Mary Lee Settle was born in Charleston, West Virginia, on July 29, 1918. She attended Sweet Briar College from 1936 to 1938. An aspiring actress, during the winter of 1938-1939 she worked as a model for several major modeling houses. In the summer of 1939 she married an Englishman, the father of her only son, Christopher. After the war broke out, he joined the Canadian army, and they separated, divorcing in 1946. After serving in the RAF Women's Auxiliary Air Force during World War II, she became a freelance writer and journalist, working briefly as an editor for *Harper's Bazaar* and later as English correspondent for *Flair*. After writing several plays,

still unpublished, she turned to fiction, publishing her first novel in 1954. She was awarded Guggenheim Fellowships in 1957-1958 and in 1959-1960. In 1965 her play *Juana La Loca* was given an Off-Broadway production. After *Blood Tie*, Settle founded the now-prestigious PEN/Faulkner Award for Fiction, raising funds to ensure that it would aid other writers. During that time she also waged a battle against cancer. In 1987 she converted to Roman Catholicism. She has lived in Italy, Greece, England, and Turkey as well as in the United States and has sometimes has supported herself by working at various jobs, including teaching and journalism. Her husband, writer and historian William Tazewell, settled in Charlottesville, Virginia, where Settle took a teaching job at Georgetown University. The University of South Carolina Press bought Settle's entire backlist, which it planned to reissue with new introductions by the author.

ANALYSIS

Whether her works are set in the present or in the past, in Europe or in West Virginia, Mary Lee Settle's preoccupations are always the same: the quest for freedom and the pursuit of love in a threatening, changing social environment. Like a Greek dramatist, she employs a background of ordinary people, who ignore the issues and the dangers of their time and place, who accept their intellectual and social prisons, blindly assuming that all is for the best, no matter what persons or what ideals they betray. In contrast to this chorus are a few exceptional people who are incapable of that blind and easy acceptance. Whatever the social cost, they insist on honesty. Whatever the political and economic cost, they seek freedom. Their ideals are ultimately democratic, for they will not judge others by narrow social standards or limit their associations by social formulas. Because they are uncompromising, they are destined to be misunderstood, ridiculed, deserted, even betrayed, but they may also be followed, admired, and loved.

Settle's novels fall into three categories: the southern novels, such as her first two published works, *The Love Eaters* and *The Kiss of Kin*, as well as *The Clam Shell* and *Charley Bland*; the Beulah Quintet, five historical novels published between 1956 and 1982, out of chronological order; and the European novels, the award-winning *Blood Tie*, set in contemporary Turkey, and *Celebration*, set in London but tracing the past lives of its characters to Kurdistan, Hong Kong, and Africa. Before *Celebration*, Settle had finally concluded the Beulah Quintet with *The Killing Ground*, which brought her several families into the present. In *Celebration*, although her characters deal with their past, they find redemption. More than any of her other works, *Celebration* moves joyfully into the future, symbolized by the central section, in which the characters of the work gather to watch the moon walk.

THE LOVE EATERS

The Love Eaters is set in Canona, West Virginia, among the Country Club people who will appear again in the final novel of the quintet, *The Killing Ground*—Anne Randolph Potter, for example, the drawling Virginian, and her "real American" husband George Potter. The men work, talk, and drink; the women decorate their homes, plan community projects, talk, and drink. With her fine ear for dialogue. Settle captures their sterile lives by carefully recording that talk, the beauty-shop gossip blaring under the hair dryers, the brief exchanges between husbands and wives, mothers and daughters, men in the Country Club locker-room. The marriages in Canona have become the routine relationships of people who live politely in the same house, like the Potters and their friends the Dodds, Jim and Martha. Because she was tired of the meaningless talk, Martha married Jim, and when she feels alone in their silent home, she reminds herself that she got exactly what she wanted. What Jim himself wanted was a quiet routine; knowing this, Martha has not even permitted herself to bear him a child.

The bored women of the Canona Country Club have brightened their lives by organizing an acting company, and it is through this venture that one of the two disrupting forces in *The Love Eaters* comes to Canona. As the novel opens, the itinerant director Hamilton Sacks descends from the train, accompanied by his devoted mother. Sacks is a physical and emotional cripple, who delights in "playing" the people he meets as if he were playing to an audience, as indeed he is, and who has no sense of moral responsi-

bility for the effect that his wicked hints may have on their lives.

The second disrupting force comes, ironically, through the placid Jim Dodd. Through a letter, he has learned the whereabouts of the son whom he had by a previous marriage, about whom he had never told his childless present wife. With the arrival of charming, slender, handsome, and above all, lovable Selby Dodd in Canona, the lives of Jim and Martha are changed forever.

In Settle's modern version of Seneca's *Phaedra* (c. 40-55 C.E.), the passion of a menopausal woman, trapped in the aimless days and nights of a society which thinks in stereotypes and in a marriage whose value has been its placid silence, is no more surprising than the fact that George Potter keeps the local beautician as his mistress. Martha's upcountry old mother is familiar with the yearnings of middle-aged women, familiar enough to warn that infatuations with young men, while not surprising, are generally unwise. Martha is not the only one who is taken with Selby Dodd, who, as Hamilton comments, lives on love and, without exerting himself, attracts women of all ages, as well as men such as Hamilton; Martha's contemporary Anne Randolph Potter and her seventeen-year-old daughter Sally Bee Potter vie for Selby from the first time they meet him. There is, then, very little shock in speculations about Martha's feelings. It is Martha herself who inflicts the punishment upon herself, and her emphasis is not on the immorality of incestuous feelings or fear of a heroic husband—for neither moral rectitude nor heroism is common in Canona society—but on her own need for Selby's physical and emotional love. As Hippolytus, Selby is neither morally outraged nor committed to a young princess. He trifles with Sally Bee Potter under the same rules which she observes in teasing him, but no love is involved, for Selby, like Hamilton, is too narcissistic to love anyone but himself and too opportunistic to be troubled by morality. Because his long-range plans include acquiring as much of Jim's property as possible, however, Selby cannot afford to risk angering Jim, and his pose must remain that of loving son and considerate stepson.

The differences between the traditional tragic

characters in this account of a stepmother's passion for her stepson and Settle's characters, who lack the tragic stature and the rigid moral sense of those in the earlier versions of the story, indicate the diminished standards of modern society, which imprisons its members within patterns which have no moral dimension, but merely the force of mindless custom. At the end of the novel, Martha at least briefly takes responsibility for Selby's death, but instead of dying, she loses her mind. Jim, too, escapes from reality; having made his dead son into a hero, he waits for Martha to become her old self.

THE KISS OF KIN

In *The Kiss of Kin*, the imprisoning society is a southern family, brought together for a funeral. Into this society comes Abraham Passmore, summoned to claim his inheritance and determined also to discover the wrong which his father's people once did to his mother. By the end of the novel, Abraham has forced the members of the family to admit the truth, but it is obvious that they will not therefore become honest. Only the cousin who leaves with him has been forced by the day's events to reject the family, as well as her similarly dishonest Yankee lover, in order to find her own freedom.

While entertaining, *The Kiss of Kin* is too clearly an adaptation of the light comedy which Settle had first written. Like *The Love Eaters*, it was skillfully constructed, hilariously satirical, accurate in dialogue; avoiding authorial comment, it depends upon dramatic scenes and upon the meditations of the few sensitive characters to comment upon the society which is its target. At this point, Settle made an important turn in her literary career. She produced the first of the Beulah Quintet novels, which plunged into the historical past to find the roots of that southern society realized in her first two novels.

Settle's first two historical novels were written in chronological order. *O Beulah Land* is set in what was later to be West Virginia at the time of the French and Indian War; *Know Nothing*, in the 1840's and 1850's. It is significant that both of these novels take place just before a momentous historic event—in the first case, the American Revolution; in the second, the Civil War. In both of them, exceptional people understand the issues of their time and respond heroically. Others either insist on living in a changeless world, clinging to a familiar pattern, or blindly refuse to admit that change is inevitable.

O BEULAH LAND

In *O Beulah Land*, a massacre results from the insistence of two English men, at opposite ends of the social scale, that the New World pattern is no different from the old. "Squire" Josiah Devotion Raglan steals, as he did in England; the arrogant British commander is rude, as he could afford to be in England. Unfortunately, the American Indians, whose tomahawk is stolen and whose pride is offended, are not governed by Old World rules, and the massacre is the outcome. Significantly, Hannah Bridewell, a transported prostitute and thief, survives captivity by the American Indians and reaches safety in the arms of a frontiersman, Jeremiah Catlett. Adapting to the New World, they create a marriage outside the church, which has not yet come to the wilderness, and later defend their home by the justifiable murder of the blackmailing Squire, who once again has miscalculated in the New World.

In the Lacey family, Settle again contrasts the selfish and the blind with those perceptive, freedom-loving individuals who refuse to enslave themselves to an old pattern. Sally Lacey, the spoiled, pretentious wife of Jonathan Lacey, refuses to adapt to frontier life. Failing in her lifelong crusade to make over her homely neighbors, Sally at last goes mad. In contrast, the printer Jarcey Pentacost has lost his shop rather than tailor his efforts to the values of a community already stagnating; for him, the frontier means freedom.

KNOW NOTHING

In *Know Nothing*, although the historical background is very different, the descendants of the characters in *O Beulah Land* must choose between enslavement to older patterns, which no longer suit the changing country, and emerging new patterns. Another Sally Lacey and her husband, Brandon, must move west because the plantation economic system has failed them. Unable to adapt, Brandon kills himself and Sally retreats permanently into the contemplation of her heredity. Other casualties of inherited patterns are Johnny Catlett, who cannot escape from his role as slaveowner and finally as Confederate officer; Lewis Catlett, the prisoner of his religious obsession, whose abolitionism, the result of his mother's influence, has in it no grain of compassion; Melinda Lacey and Sara Lacey, both trapped in miserable marriages from which, in a society which does not permit divorce, only death can release them. Already in *Know Nothing*, the same kind of social prisons from which American immigrants escaped have been established in the New World, and the quest for freedom has become more and more difficult.

FIGHT NIGHT ON A SWEET SATURDAY

In 1964, Viking Press published *Fight Night on a Sweet Saturday*, which was to have been the concluding work in the "Beulah Trilogy." In that book, Hannah McKarkle, who is named for the heroic Hannah of *O Beulah Land*, comes to Canona, West Virginia, originally to see her brother and then to investigate his death. During her visit, she begins to explore the past of her family and of her region, thus, in a sense, becoming Mary Lee Settle herself. Unfortunately, the publishers so cut *Fight Night on a Sweet Saturday* that Settle found the relationships obscured. Eventually, she was to add two volumes to the Beulah works, *Prisons* and *The Scapegoat*, and to rewrite *Fight Night on a Sweet Saturday*, which was published as *The Killing Ground*.

PRISONS

Still pursuing the democratic ideal, Settle returned to Great Britain, where she tracked down a chance reference to John Lilburne, the leader of a group of radicals, a number of whom were executed by the forces of Cromwell, who were averse to the "Leveling" principles of true egalitarians. It is the story of one of these executed radicals which Settle tells in her seventeenth century novel *Prisons*, which becomes the first novel in the Beulah Quintet, viewed chronologically. Its hero, the brave, idealistic Johnny Church, enmeshed in amoral public policy, refuses to save his own life by becoming Oliver Cromwell's agent among the men who see Johnny as a natural leader. It is the descendants of Johnny Church, both literal and spiritual, who continue to fight for freedom in Settle's historical and contemporary novels.

THE CLAM SHELL

Meanwhile, Settle had published another novel set in the contemporary South, *The Clam Shell*, which is set among the same Country Club set as *The Love Eaters*. In Canona in 1966, Anne Randolph Potter, "Plain" George Potter, and their friends are involved in their usual rituals. This time, however, the disrupting influence is one of their own friends, the woman protagonist, who watches them watching football, drinking, and reminiscing. Unlike Martha Dodd, she learned young that she was unable to fit the mold of her friends in Canona, just as she could not fit the mold of the Virginia finishing school to which she was sent. Musing on her youth, remembering her unjust treatment at the finishing school, she realizes that she has long ago ceased wishing to be accepted by mindless, restrictive upper-class Virginia or West Virginia society. Like Abraham Passmore, she is content to be an honest exile.

In literary quality, *The Clam Shell* is one of Settle's less effective novels. Satirical and often angry, it divides its characters into two groups: those who understand life and those who, from dullness or from choice, choose not to understand but, instead, to persecute those who do.

After this simplistic novel came one of Settle's best, *Blood Tie*, a contemporary work set on a Turkish island. The protagonist—idealistic, innocent Ariadne—has come to Ceramos to recover from a mid-life divorce. There she becomes acquainted with a group of expatriates, the sensationalist Basil, a German archaeologist, a Jewish bar owner, a wealthy American girl, and the CIA agent Frank Proctor. None of the expatriates understands the language well enough to realize the disapproval, the contempt, and the ridicule with which they are viewed by the natives. Nor have the expatriates any idea of the intrigue with which they are surrounded. The archaeologist, for example, does not guess that a hunted university student is hiding in the sacred caverns which he cannot find. As the Turks manipulate the expatriates for gain, the expatriates utilize one another and the Turks for the sensations they seek. Through the corruption walks Ariadne, mothering the spoiled American girl and the mute Turkish child, struggling with her sense of rejection and with her own troublesome sexuality, unintentionally shocking the Turks, who misinterpret her actions. When she and the other expatriates at last leave the island, the Chief of Police praises her because of all the visitors only Ariadne tried to see the Turks as individuals, rather than as background figures in an exotic environment. Although Ariadne does not know it, she has made a difference to the troubled, mute child, for at last he is able to speak.

THE SCAPEGOAT

In *The Scapegoat*, published only three years after *Blood Tie*, Settle again created complex characters who have a moral sense. Foolish, innocent, and idealistic though they may be, such individuals do provide some hope for the future. Like its predecessors in the series, *The Scapegoat* takes place at a time of confrontation, on a single day, June 7, 1912, when the hostility between British mine owners and their hired thugs, on one hand, and the mines with their union leaders, on the other, results in armed conflict. In the middle of the conflict are the mine owners, Beverley and Ann Eldridge Lacey, who hope to keep their mine, their home, and their friendships apart from the approaching violence. Ironically, the idealism of their daughter Lily Ellen Lacey, home from college, leads directly to the violence. Her friendship with a young striker is exploited to inflame both the strikebreakers and the strikers. As the day develops, basically good people do evil. To save her son, Lily's friend sacrifices a new immigrant, the "scapegoat" of the title; to help the friend escape, Lily and Beverley take advantage of the death of the scapegoat, thus in a sense participating in the guilt.

In her later books, however, Settle is dealing more realistically with guilt, seemingly recognizing that in this world every act is tainted. Rather than expecting her exceptional characters to be flawless and fully cognizant of the situation in which they are placed, Settle is more compassionate toward the well meaning, even if, like Lily, they unintentionally play into the hands of clearly evil forces. Granted, ignorance cannot exempt one from guilt. Lily's service as a nurse in World War I, which results in her death, is a course deliberately chosen because she must take the responsibility for her tragic blindness. Yet in her later works, Settle castigates fewer characters for their blindness and permits more of them the possibility of redemption.

THE KILLING GROUND

In her final volume of the Beulah Quintet, *The Killing Ground*, Settle's writer Hannah McKarkle sums up what she has learned of history. In clash after clash, people struggle for freedom. Often, as Johnny Church learned in the English Civil War, as the Laceys saw in the American mine wars, both sides in a confrontation seek power, and it is a third group which must struggle for real freedom. Whatever its pretensions, every society is made up of many who are blind, often for their own comfort, and of many who, though perceptive, are unprincipled. Because of that convenient or deliberate blindness, the rebels, the seekers for freedom, must always struggle, first to see the truth, then, and only then, to act upon it.

Because critics are now becoming aware of Settle's themes, they can justify the shifts in point of view and the movements back and forth in time which make her work difficult. In *The Scapegoat*, for example, Settle tells her story through the eyes of several different characters, whose testimony, weighed and judged by the reader, can add up to objective truth. Similarly, in *Blood Tie*, the mutual misunderstandings between the Turkish and the expatriate populations are dramatized by frequent changes in point of view, often revealing opposite interpretations of events and statements. Thus, the thematic emphasis on the pursuit of truth is exemplified by Settle's own method of revealing the truth.

Moreover, because as William Faulkner believed, the truth of any one moment involves the past of an individual, a community, a people, and because the human mind never lives purely in present consciousness, Settle's frequent shifts in time are also a technical expression of a thematic emphasis. In a comic novel such as *The Kiss of Kin*, the thrust of the work is toward the revelation of a single element in the past, and therefore the dramatic technique is effective. In a complicated novel such as *The Killing Ground* or *Blood Tie*, however, in which characters attempt to understand the present while always being conscious of the past, the shifts in time are both effective and thematically necessary.

CELEBRATION

Settle's increasing technical mastery and her developing theme of redemption are both evident in *Celebration*. The six chapters of the novel alternate between London and three distant areas where various characters once lived: Kurdistan, Hong Kong, and Africa. The process through which the main characters must go is that of the mass: an honest facing of the past, the acceptance of guilt, repentance, redemption, and joy. Each of the characters has crossed what Settle terms "the Styx," directly confronting death and despair. For Teresa Cerrutti, it was the death of her husband in Malakastan, followed by her own surgery for cancer. For Noel, Lord Atherton, it was a disastrous encounter with a Chinese lover in Hong Kong. For Ewen Stuart McLeod, it was the betrayal by his uncle, who trapped him in an unsavory African expedition and involved him in the murder of innocent people.

The movement toward a joyful future is suggested in the fourth of Settle's chapters, when her major characters and their friends together watch the moon landing, which is an affirmation of humankind's possibilities. That chapter, however, is followed by the darkest account in the novel, Ewen's African adventure, revealing humanity at its treacherous, murderous worst. Ewen's life was saved by the black Roman Catholic priest, Pius Deng, who is also now in London, one of the friends.

In the final chapter, there is a celebration of death and of life. The priest is killed by London muggers, but as the guilt-stricken youngest of them comments, he died in a state of grace. Furthermore, the commitment for which he had hoped, the marriage of Ewen and Teresa, concludes the novel. Under the influence of the saintly Pius and through their ever-increasing love for one another, the London friends have made the Styx not a river of death, but one of life.

CHARLEY BLAND

In *Charley Bland*, Settle returns once more to the class tensions between the Country Club people and the intellectual, both surrounded by the poor of Appalachia, this time in the decades just after World War II. Characters in the novel suggest ghosts of Settle's own biography as well as their counterparts in *The Love Eaters* and *The Clam Shell*. In fact, some of them are the same characters. Also as in *The Clam Shell*, the central figure, a young novelist, finds herself drawn back into the world of small-town society, only to learn that she can never be part of that world again. Her life in postwar England and France has expanded her vision so far that she and the Country Clubbers no longer speak the same language.

Like other of Settle's characters, she is shaped by her origins as the daughter of a well-to-do mine owner. Thus, although her father once lost his money and although she has long felt freed from any obligations to her remote, unloving mother, when her mother tries to arrange a match between her daughter and the eligible Charley Bland, she feels powerless to resist the arrangements. Bland's family have always been both friends and rivals of her own, and Bland himself is almost a southern stereotype—the irresistibly charming bachelor, a "devil with women" whose only flaw appears to be that he drinks too much.

The intended love affair occurs, and the narrator finds herself moving into old patterns of social life she thought she had left long before. Yet even as she enjoys the romance, she recognizes that Charley Bland is more deeply flawed than he first appeared, partly because his alcoholism is much more serious than anyone admits and partly because he has no intention of defying his mother, who intends to use him as her protector and her source of entertainment as long as she lives. The narrator is only one in his long series of romances. At the same time, the narrator gradually realizes that the people she used to know intend to freeze her out of their world. It is a world she is ready to leave again but which she will leave with great pain because she loves its mountains and hollows, its seasons, and the language of its people.

CHOICES

Choices takes the form of a memoir of Melinda Kregg Dunston, who looks back on the eighty-two years of her life to examine the choices that have shaped it. They have been the choices of one whose compassion has always moved her to support the oppressed, first through her Red Cross work in support of striking coal miners (the source of her family's wealth), later her fight against Fascism in Spain in 1937, and later still in her involvement in the Civil Rights movement. These are issues that engaged Settle's own passions as an unapologetic liberal in a conservative community. The dangers involved in responding to those passions have the power to give people a heightened recognition of the beauty and fragility of life; this novel dramatizes the potency of the choices a person such as Dunston can make.

In her works, Mary Lee Settle has always stressed the need for personal honesty, for emotional and political freedom, and for a democratic acceptance of others on an individual basis. In her early southern novels, she emphasizes the stagnant, snobbish, superficial society which broke the weak and drove the strong into exile. In the Beulah Quintet and in the European novels, however, while still castigating the cruel, the selfish, and the blind, Settle increasingly emphasized the possibility of expiation or of redemption. As her imagination has moved backward in time and outward in space, her sense of human possibilities has intensified. With *Celebration*, she seems to have expressed an honest hope for those who are willing to face life with honesty and courage; with that novel, she has also almost faultlessly synthesized her matter and her manner.

Rosemary M. Canfield Reisman,
updated by Ann D. Garbett

OTHER MAJOR WORKS

PLAY: *Juana la Loca*, pr. 1965.

NONFICTION: *All the Brave Promises: Memories of Aircraft Woman Second Class 2146391*, 1966; *The Scopes Trial: The State of Tennessee vs. John Thomas Scopes*, 1972; *Turkish Reflections: A Biography of a Place*, 1991 (with an introduction by Jan Morris); *Addie*, 1998.

CHILDREN'S LITERATURE: *The Story of Flight*, 1967; *Water World*, 1984.

BIBLIOGRAPHY

Bach, Peggy. "The Searching Voice and Vision of Mary Lee Settle." *Southern Review* 20 (October, 1984): 842-850. After outlining the various critical assessments of Settle's work, Bach supports her own insistence that it can hardly be rated too highly. In the Beulah Quintet, Settle has traced a family through three hundred years of history, showing how desperately even people beginning fresh in a new land need to have a sense of their past.

Galligan, Edward L. "The Novels of Mary Lee Settle." *The Sewanee Review* 104 (Summer, 1996): 413-422. Galligan begins with a discussion of *Choices*, viewing it in the context of Settle's other fiction and the history of her time. He goes on to offer a general view of her fiction, focusing on her variety and unpredictability in order to undergird his argument that she is worthy of a serious place in American letters.

Garrett, George. *Understanding Mary Lee Settle*. Columbia: University of South Carolina Press, 1988. Garrett is one of Settle's most prolific analysts; in this work he offers an overview of her oeuvre, including sympathetic discussions of her major fiction, with special attention to the Beulah Quintet. He also devotes chapters to *Blood Tie*, *Celebration*, and some of her nonfiction.

Joyner, Nancy Carol. "Mary Lee Settle's Connections: Class and Clothes in the Beulah Quintet." In *Women Writers of the Contemporary South*, edited by Peggy Whitman Prenshaw. Jackson: University Press of Mississippi, 1984. Stresses the theme of social rigidity and social injustice in Settle's Beulah Quintet. In these five books, which range across two continents and through three centuries, Joyner sees the repeated emphasis on class consciousness and family connections, which help to perpetuate wrongs, generation after generation, even in the supposedly classless New World. An interesting, if somewhat limited, approach.

Rosenberg, Brian. *Mary Lee Settle's Beulah Quintet: The Price of Freedom*. Baton Rouge: Louisiana State University Press, 1991. Rosenberg examines the Quintet as a single fiction instead of a series of related novels, seeing it as a grand-scale work which uses the history of West Virginia as a paradigm of the history of the United

States. He also examines the history of the novels' critical reception and the injustice of labelling the novels historical romances.

Settle, Mary Lee. Interview by Wendy Smith. *Publishers Weekly* 230 (October 10, 1986): 73-74. This interview was prompted by the growing recognition of Settle's stature as a novelist, indicated by the paperback reissues of a number of her works. Her comments about her writing methods and her perception of the American experience, as well as her clear statement of purpose, are extremely revealing.

Speer, Jean Haskell. "Montani Semper Liberi: Mary Lee Settle and the Myths of Appalachia." In *Southern Women Writers: The New Generation.* Tuscaloosa: University of Alabama Press, 1990. Speer contends that in the Beulah Quintet one of Settle's purposes was to debunk such myths as the assumption that there is a single, easily defined Appalachian culture whose people are both ignorant and innocent. This essay argues that Settle's realistic fiction has done much to define the real Appalachia for her readers.

Stephens, Mariflo. "Mary Lee Settle: The Lioness in Winter." *The Virginia Quarterly Review* 74 (Fall, 1996): 581-589. Novelist Stephens records her acquaintance with Settle, including material about Settle's life, politics, and writing. Stephens believes that politics inspired a negative review of *Choices.*

MARY WOLLSTONECRAFT SHELLEY

Born: London, England; August 30, 1797
Died: London, England; February 1, 1851

PRINCIPAL LONG FICTION

Frankenstein, 1818
Valperga: Or, The Life of Castruccio, Prince of Lucca, 1823
The Last Man, 1826
The Fortunes of Perkin Warbeck, 1830
Lodore, 1835
Falkner, 1837

OTHER LITERARY FORMS

Mary Shelley was a prolific writer, forced into copiousness by economic necessity. Punished by Sir Timothy Shelley, her husband Percy Bysshe Shelley's father, for her violation of his moral codes with his son, Mary Shelley was denied access to the Shelley estate for a long time after her husband's death. Her own father, William Godwin, was eternally in debt himself and spared her none of his troubles. Far from helping her, Godwin threw his own financial woes in her lap. It fell to Mary to support her son by writing, in addition to her novels, a plethora of short stories and some scholarly materials. The stories were mainly available to the public in a popular annual publication called the *Keepsake,* a book intended for gift-giving. Her stories were firmly entrenched in the popular gothic tradition, bearing such titles as "A Tale of Passion," "Ferdinand Eboli," "The Evil Eye," and "The Bride of Modern Italy." Her scholarly work included contributions to *The Lives of the Most Eminent Literary and Scientific Men* in *Lardner's Cabinet Encyclopedia* (1838). She attempted to write about the lives of both her father and her husband, although her efforts were never completed. She wrote magazine articles of literary criticism and reviews of operas, an art form that filled her with delight. She wrote two travel books, *History of a Six Weeks' Tour Through a Part of France, Switzerland, Germany, and Holland* (1817) and *Rambles in Germany and Italy* (1844). Shelley edited two posthumous editions of her husband's poetry (1824 and 1839), and she wrote several poetic dramas: *Manfred,* now lost, *Proserpine* (1922), and *Midas* (1922). She wrote a handful of poems, most of which were published in *Keepsake.*

ACHIEVEMENTS

Shelley's literary reputation rests solely on her first novel, *Frankenstein.* Her six other novels, which are of uneven quality, are very difficult indeed to find, even in the largest libraries. Nevertheless, Mary Shelley lays claim to a dazzling array of accomplishments. First, she is credited with the creation of modern science fiction. All subsequent tales of the brilliant but doomed scientist, the sympathetic but horrible monster, both in high and mass culture, owe their lives to her. Even Hollywood's dream factory owes her an imaginative and economic debt it can never repay.

Second, the English tradition is indebted to her for a reconsideration of the Romantic movement by one of its central participants. In her brilliant *Frankenstein* fantasy, Mary Shelley questions many of the basic tenets of the Romantic rebellion: the Romantic faith in people's blissful relationship to nature, the belief that evil resides only in the dead hand of social tradition, and the Romantic delight in death as a lover and restorer.

Finally, she created one of the great literary fictions of the dialogue with the self. The troubled relationship between Dr. Frankenstein and his monster is one of the foundations of the literary tradition of "the double," doubtless the mother of all the doubles in Charles Dickens, Robert Louis Stevenson, and even in Arthur Conan Doyle and Joseph Conrad.

Biography

Mary Shelley, born Mary Wollstonecraft Godwin, lived the life of a great romantic heroine at the heart of the Romantic movement. She was the daughter of the brilliant feminist Mary Wollstonecraft and the equally distinguished man of letters, William Godwin. Born of two parents who vociferously opposed marriage, she was the occasion of their nuptials. Her mother died ten days after she was born, and her father had to marry for the second time in four years to provide a mother for his infant daughter. He chose a rather conventional widow, Mary Jane Clairmont, who had two children of her own, Jane and Charles.

In her childhood, Mary Shelley suffered the torments of being reared by a somewhat unsympathetic stepmother; later, she led the daughter of this extremely middle-class woman into a life of notoriety. The separation traumas in her early years indelibly marked Mary Shelley's imagination: Almost all of her protagonists are either orphaned or abandoned by their parents.

(Library of Congress)

Mary Shelley's stormy early years led, in 1812 and until 1814, to her removal to sympathetic "foster parents," the Baxters of Dundee. There, on May 5, 1814, when she was seventeen years old, she met Percy Bysshe Shelley, who was then married to his first wife, Harriet. By March 6, 1815, Mary had eloped with Shelley, given birth to a daughter by him, and suffered the death of the baby. By December 29, 1816, the couple had been to Switzerland and back, had another child, William, and had been married, Harriet having committed suicide. Mary Shelley was then nineteen years old.

By the next year, Mary's stepsister, Jane Clairmont, who called herself Claire Clairmont, had had a baby daughter by Lord Byron, while Mary was working on *Frankenstein*, and Mary herself had given birth to another child, Clara.

The network of intimates among the Shelley circle rapidly increased to include many literati and artists. These included, among others, Leigh and Marrianne Hunt, Thomas Love Peacock, Thomas Jefferson Hogg, and John Polidori. The letters and diaries of the Shelleys from this period offer a view of life speeded up and intensified, life at the nerve's edge.

While the Shelleys were touring Switzerland and Italy, they sent frantic communications to their friends, asking for financial help. Mary issued frequent requests for purchases of clothing and household items such as thread. There were also legal matters to be taken care of concerning publishing, Shelley's estate, and the custody of his children from his previous marriage.

The leaves of the letters and diaries are filled with urgent fears for the safety of the Shelley children and the difficulties of what was in effect an exile necessitated by the Shelleys' unorthodox style of life. In 1818, Clara Shelley died, barely a year old, and in 1819, William Shelley died at the age of three. Five months later, a son, Percy Florence, was born, the only child of the Shelleys to grow to maturity.

In 1822, Mary Shelley's flamboyant life reached its point of desolation. Percy Shelley, while sailing with his close friend Edward Williams, in his boat *Ariel*, drowned in the Gulf of Spezia. Mary's letters and diaries of the time clearly reveal her anguish, her exhaustion, and her despair. Her speeding merry-go-round suddenly and violently stopped.

Literary historians find themselves in debate over this point in Mary Shelley's life. Her letters and diaries record unambiguous desolation, and yet many scholars have found indications that Percy Shelley was about to leave her for Jane Williams, the wife of the friend with whom he drowned. There is also some suspicion that Mary's stepsister had recently given birth to a baby by Percy Shelley, a rumor that Mary Shelley denied. Because of Percy Shelley's mercurial nature, such speculations are at least conceivable. Against them stands Mary's diary, a purely private diary, which suggests that she would have no reason to whitewash her marriage among its confidential pages.

Mary's tragedy did not prompt warmth and help from her estranged father-in-law. He refused to support his grandson, Percy Florence, unless Mary gave the child to a guardian to be chosen by him. This she would not do, and she was rewarded for her persistence. Her son became heir to the Shelley estate

when Harriet Shelley's son died in 1826. After the death, Mary's son became Lord Shelley. Just as important, however, was the warm relationship that he maintained with Mary until her death. Mary Shelley's life ended in the tranquil sunshine of family affection. Her son married happily and had healthy children. Mary seems to have befriended her daughter-in-law, and, at the last, believed herself to be a truly fortunate woman.

ANALYSIS

Mary Shelley's six novels are written in the gothic tradition. They deal with extreme emotions, exalted speech, the hideous plight of virgins, the awful abuses of charismatic villains, and picturesque ruins. The sins of the past weigh heavily on their plot structures, and often include previously unsuspected relationships.

Shelley does not find much use for the anti-Catholicism of much gothic fiction. Her nuns and priests, while sometimes troublesome, are not evil, and tend to appear in the short stories rather than in the novels. She avoids references to the supernatural so common in the genre and tends instead toward a modern kind of psychological gothic and futuristic fantasy. Like many gothic writers, she dwells on morbid imagery, particularly in *Frankenstein* and *The Last Man*. Graphic descriptions of the plague in the latter novel revolted the reading public which had avidly digested the grotesqueries of Matthew Gregory Lewis's *The Monk* (1796).

With the exception of *Frankenstein*, Shelley's novels were written and published after the death of her husband; with the exception of *Frankenstein*, they appear to be attempting to work out the sense of desolation and abandonment that she felt after his death. In most of her novels, Shelley creates men and particularly women who resign themselves to the pain and anguish of deep loss through the eternal hope of love in its widest and most encompassing sense. Reconciliation became Shelley's preponderant literary theme.

FRANKENSTEIN

Frankenstein is Shelley's greatest literary achievement in every way. In it, she not only calls into the world one of the most powerful literary images in the English tradition, the idealistic scientist Victor Frankenstein and his ironically abominable creation, but also, for the one and only time, she employs a narrative structure of daring complexity and originality.

The structure of *Frankenstein* is similar to a set of Chinese boxes, of narratives within narratives. The narrative frame is composed of the letters of an arctic explorer, Robert Walton, to his sister, Mrs. Saville, in England. Within the letters is the narrative of Victor Frankenstein, and within his narrative, at first, and then at the end within Walton's narrative, is the first-hand account of the monster himself. Walton communicates to England thirdhand then secondhand accounts of the monster's thoroughly unbelievable existence. Here, it would seem, is the seminal point of Joseph Conrad's much later fiction, *Heart of Darkness* (1902): the communication to England of the denied undercurrents of reality and England's ambiguous reception of that intelligence. In *Frankenstein* as in *Heart of Darkness*, the suggestion is rather strong that England cannot or will not absorb this stunning new perception of reality. Just as Kurtz's fiancée almost a century later cannot imagine Kurtz's "horror," so Mrs. Saville's silence, the absence of her replies, suggests that Walton's stunning discovery has fallen on deaf ears.

The novel begins with Walton, isolated from his society at the North Pole, attempting to achieve glory. He prowls the frozen north "to accomplish some great purpose"; instead, he finds an almost dead Victor Frankenstein, who tells him a story which, in this setting, becomes a parable for Walton. Frankenstein, too, has isolated himself from society to fulfill his great expectations, and he has reaped the whirlwind.

Frankenstein tells Walton of his perfect early family life, one of complete kindness and solicitude. It is a scene across which never a shadow falls. Out of this perfection, Victor rises to find a way of conquering death and ridding himself and humankind of the ultimate shadow, the only shadow in his perfect middle-class life. Like a man possessed, Frankenstein forges ahead, fabricating a full, male, human body from the choicest corpse parts he can gather. He animates the creature and suddenly is overwhelmed by the wrongness of what he has done. In his success, he finds utter defeat. The reanimated corpse evokes only disgust in him. He abandons it in its vulnerable, newborn state and refuses to take any responsibility for it.

From that day, his life is dogged by tragedy. One by one, all his loved ones are destroyed by the monster, who at last explains that he wanted only to love his creator but that his adoration turned to murderous hate in his creator's rejection of him. Ultimately, Frankenstein feels that he must destroy the monster or, at the very least, die trying. He succeeds at both. After Frankenstein's death in the presence of Walton—the only man other than Frankenstein to witness the monster and live—the monster mourns the greatness that could have been and leaves Walton with the intention of hurling himself onto Frankenstein's funeral pyre.

The critical task regarding this fascinating work has been to identify what it is that Frankenstein has done that has merited the punishment which followed. Is the monster a kind of retribution for people's arrogant attempt to possess the secrets of life and death, as in the expulsion from Eden? Is it the wrath of the gods visited on people for stealing the celestial fire, as in the Prometheus legend, a favorite fiction of Percy Shelley? Or is this a rather modern vision of the self-destructiveness involved in the idealistic denial of the dark side of human reality? Is this a criticism of Romantic optimism, of the denial of the reality of evil except as the utterly disposable dead hand of tradition? The mystery endures because critics have suggested all these possibilities; critics have even suggested a biographical reading of the work. Some have suggested that Victor Frankenstein is Shelley's shrewd insight into her husband's self-deceived, uncritical belief in the power of his own intelligence and in his destined greatness.

VALPERGA

Valperga, Shelley's second novel, has a fairy-tale aura of witches, princes, maidens in distress, castles, and prophecies. The author uses all these fantasy apparatuses, but actually deflates it as being part of the fantasy lives of the characters which they impose on a fully logical and pragmatic reality. The novel pits Castruccio, the Prince of Lucca, a worldly, Napoleonic conquerer, against the lost love of his youth, the beautiful and spiritual Euthanasia. Castruccio's one goal is power and military dominion, and since he is enormously capable and charismatic, not to mention lucky, he is successful. Nevertheless, that he gains the world at the price of his soul is clearly the central point of the novel.

To gain worldly sway, he must destroy Valperga, the ancestral home of his love, Euthanasia. He must also turn Italy into an armed camp which teems with death and in which the soft virtues of love and family cannot endure. His lust for power raises to predominance the most deceitful and treacherous human beings because it is they who function best in the context of raw, morally unjustified power.

In the midst of all this, Castruccio, unwilling to recognize his limits, endeavors to control all. He wants to continue his aggrandizing ways and have the love of Euthanasia. Indeed, he wants to marry her. She reveals her undying love for him, but will only yield to it if he yields his worldly goals, which he will not do. As his actions become more threatening to her concept of a moral universe, Euthanasia finds that she must join the conspirators against him. She and her cohorts are betrayed, and all are put to death, with the exception of Euthanasia. Instead, Castruccio exiles her to Sicily. En route, her ship sinks, and she perishes with all aboard. Castruccio dies some years later, fighting one of his endless wars for power. The vision of the novel is that only pain and suffering can come from a world obsessed with power.

Surely the name Euthanasia is a remarkable choice for the novel's heroine. Its meaning in Shelley's time was "an easy death"; it did not refer to the policy of purposefully terminating suffering as it does today. Euthanasia's death is the best one in the story because she dies with a pure heart, never having soiled herself with hurtful actions for the purpose of self-gain. Possibly, the import of Shelley's choice is that all that one can hope for in the flawed, Hobbesian world of *Valperga* is the best death possible, as no good life can be imagined. It is probable that this bleak vision is at least obliquely connected with the comparatively recent trauma of Percy Shelley's death and Mary Shelley's grief and desolation.

THE LAST MAN

The degenerating spiral of human history is the central vision of *The Last Man*. Set in the radically distant future of the twenty-first century, this novel begins with a flourishing civilization and ends with the entire population of the world, save one man, decimated by the plague. Lionel Verney, the last man of the title, has nothing to anticipate except an endless journey from one desolate city to another. All the treasures of man are his and his alone; all the great libraries and coffers open only to him. All that is denied to him—forever, it seems—is human companionship.

The novel begins before Lionel Verney's birth. It is a flashback narrated by Lionel himself, the only first-person narrator possible in this novel. Lionel describes his father as his father had been described to him, as a man of imagination and charm but lacking in judgment. He was a favorite of the king, but was forced out of the king's life by the king's new wife, a Marie Antoinette figure. The new queen, depicted as an arrogant snob, disapproves of Verney's father and effects his estrangement from the king by working on her husband's gullible nature.

Verney's father, in ostracized shame, seeks refuge in the country, where he marries a simple, innocent cottage girl and thus begets Lionel and his sister Perdita. Verney's father can never, however, reconcile himself to his loss of status and dies a broken man. His wife soon follows, and Lionel and Perdita live like wild creatures until chance brings the king's son, Adrian, into their path. Their friendship succeeds where the aborted friendship of their fathers failed, despite the continued disapproval of the queen.

What is remarkable to the modern reader is that Shelley, having set her story two hundred years in the future, does not project a technologically changed environment. She projects instead the same rural, agrarian, hand-and animal-driven society in which she lived. What does change, however, is the political system. The political system of *The Last Man* is a republican monarchy. Kings are elected, but not at regular intervals. The bulk of the novel concerns the power plays by which various factions intend to capture the throne by election rather than by war.

Adrian and Lionel are endlessly involved with a dashing, Byronic figure named Lord Raymond, who cannot decide whether he wants life in a cottage with Perdita, or life at the top. Ultimately, Raymond, like the protagonist of *Valperga*, wants to have both. He marries Perdita and gives up all pretensions to power, but then returns with her to rule the land. Power does not make him or his wife happy.

Despite the sublimation of the power process into an electoral system, the rage for power remains destructive, degenerating finally into war. The plague which appears and irrevocably destroys humankind is merely an extension of the plague of people's will to power. Not only Raymond and Perdita, but also their innocent children, Lionel's wife, Iris, and Adrian's sister, who stayed home to eschew worldly aspirations, are destroyed. No one is immune.

Lionel's survival carries with it a suggestion of his responsibility in the tragedy of humankind. His final exile in a sea of books and pictures suggests that those who commit themselves solely to knowledge and art have failed to deal with the central issues of life. In simply abdicating the marketplace to such as Lord Raymond, the cultivators of the mind have abandoned humanity. Through Lionel, they reap a bitter reward, but perhaps the implication is that it is a just reward for their failure to connect with their fellow human beings.

A number of critics consider *The Last Man* to be Mary Shelley's best work after *Frankenstein*. Like *Frankenstein*, this novel rather grimly deals with the relationship between knowledge and evil. Its greatest drawback for modern audiences, however, is its unfortunate tendency to inflated dialogue. Every sentence uttered is a florid and theatrical speech. The bloated characterizations obscure the line of Shelley's inventive satire of people's lemminglike rush to the sea of power.

THE FORTUNES OF PERKIN WARBECK

The Fortunes of Perkin Warbeck attempts to chronicle the last, futile struggles of the House of York in the Wars of the Roses. Perkin Warbeck was a historical character who claimed to be Richard, the son of Edward IV of England. Most scholars believe that Richard died in the tower with his brother Edward; Perkin Warbeck claimed to be that child. Warbeck said that he had survived the tower, assumed another identity, and intended to reclaim the usurped throne held by Henry VII.

Shelley's novel assumes that Perkin was indeed Richard and documents his cheerless history from his childhood to his execution in manhood by Henry VII. The novel attempts to explore once more man's fruitless quest for power and glory. Richard is an intelligent, virtuous young man who finds true companionship even in his outcast state, and the love of a number of women, each different, utterly committed, and true. He is unable, however, to forsake the dream of conquest and live simply. As he presses onward to claim the throne, he suffers a series of crushing losses, not one of which will he yield to as a revelation of the wrongheadedness of his quest. His rush toward the throne achieves only the death of innocent persons. When he is executed at the end of the novel, his wife Katherine is given the last words. She needs to find a way of continuing to live without him. She is urged by his adherents to forsake the world, and for his sake to live a reclusive life. Although Katherine appears only briefly in the interminable scenes of war and the grandiose verbiage through which the reader must trudge, her appearance at the end of the novel and her refusal to forsake the world in her grief are the most impressive moments in the work.

In refusing to retreat from the world, Katherine commits herself to the only true value in the novel, love, a value which all the senseless suffering of Richard's quest could not destroy. Katherine, as the widow of the gentle but misguided warrior, becomes a metaphor for the endurance of love in a world that has its heart set on everything but love. Her final, gracious words are a relaxing change from the glory-seeking bombast of the action, "Permit this to be, unblamed—permit a heart whose sufferings have been and are, so many and so bitter, to reap what joy it can from the strong necessity it feels to be sympathized with—to love." Once again, Shelley's basic idea is an enthralling one, but her execution of her plan includes a grandiose superfluity of expression and incident.

LODORE

Lodore and Shelley's last novel, *Falkner*, form a kind of reconciliation couplet to end her exploration of loss and desolation. Reward for persistence in loving through the trials of death and social obliquy is her final vision. In *Lodore*, an extremely long parade of fatal misunderstandings, the central image is the recovery of a lost mother. The novel begins veiled in mystery. Lord Lodore has exiled himself and his fairylike, delicate daughter, Ethel, to the forests of Illinois in far-off America. Lord Lodore is without his wife, who has done something unnamed and perhaps unnameable to provoke this unusual separation. Reunion with her is the central action of the plot.

Lord Lodore is a perfect gentleman amid the cloddish but honest American settlers. His one goal is to produce the perfect maiden in his daughter, Ethel. Father and daughter are entirely devoted to each other. A series of flashback chapters reveal that Lady Lodore, very much the junior of Lord Lodore, had been overly influenced by her mother, who had insinuated herself between husband and wife and alienated her daughter's affections from Lord Lodore. Lord and Lady Lodore lived what life they had together always on the brink of rapproachement, but utterly confounded by the wiles of the mother-in-law, who managed to distort communicated sentiments to turn husband and wife away from each other, finally effecting a radical separation that neither Lord nor Lady Lodore wanted.

The American idyll ends for Ethel and her father when Ethel is about fifteen years old. The unwanted attentions of a suitor threaten Ethel's perfect life, and her father moves his household once more. Lodore thinks of reestablishing the bond with his estranged wife but is killed in a duel hours before departing for England. His last thoughts of reconciliation are buried with him, because the only extant will is one recorded years ago when he vindictively made Lady Lodore's inheritance dependent on her never seeing Ethel again. Ethel returns to England shaken and abandoned, but not to her mother. Instead, she lives with Lodore's maiden sister.

Ethel is wooed and won by a gentleman, Edward Villiers, coincidentally one of the few witnesses to her father's death and many years older than herself. The marriage of this truly loving couple is threatened because Edward, reared in luxury, is in reduced financial circumstances owing to the irresponsibility of his father, one of the few truly despicable characters in the novel.

Much suffering ensues, during which Edward and Ethel endeavor to straighten out priorities: Which is more important, love or money? Should they part to give Ethel a chance at a more comfortable life, or should they endure poverty for love? They choose love, but Edward is taken to debtor's prison, Ethel standing by for the conjugal visits that the prison system permits.

Through a series of chance encounters, Lady Lodore, now a seemingly shallow woman of fashion, becomes aware of Ethel's needs and of her need to be a mother to the young woman. Telling no one but her lawyer what she intends, she impoverishes herself to release Edward from prison and to set the couple up appropriately. She then removes herself to a humble country existence, anticipating the blessings of martyrdom. She is, however, discovered, the mother and daughter are reunited, and Lady Lodore is even offered an advantageous marriage to a rich former suitor who originally was kept from her by the machinations of his sisters.

Lodore includes many particulars that are close to the biographical details of the author's life: the penury and social trials of her marriage to Shelley, the financial irresponsibility of her father, and the loss of her mother. Shelley's familiarity with her material appears to have dissolved the grandiose pretensions of the previous novels, which may have sprung from her distance from their exotic settings and situations. *Lodore* has the force of life despite its melodramatic plot. If it were more widely available, it would be a rich source of interest for historians and literary scholars. It contains an interesting image of America as envisioned by the early nineteenth century European. It also contains a wealth of interest for students of women's literature.

FALKNER

If *Lodore* offers a happy ending with the return of a long-lost mother, then *Falkner* finds contentment in the restoration of an estranged father. Here, the father is not the biological parent, but a father figure, Rupert Falkner. The plot is a characteristic tangle of gothic convolutions involving old secrets and sins, obdurate Catholic families, and the pure love of a young girl.

The delightful Elizabeth Raby is orphaned at the age of six under severe circumstances. Because her fragile, lovely parents were complete strangers to the little town in Cornwall to which they had come, their death left Elizabeth at the mercy of their landlady. The landlady is poor, and Elizabeth is a financial burden. The landlady keeps her only because she suspects that the now decimated, strange little family has noble connections. Thus begins a typical Shelley fiction—with abandonment, innocence, and loss of love.

The plot is set in motion by a mysterious stranger who identifies himself as "John Falkner." Falkner undertakes the guardianship of Elizabeth, not only because of her charm, but also because of an unfinished letter found in the family cottage. This letter connects Elizabeth's mother to one "Alithea." The reader comes to learn that Falkner was Alithea's lover, that he carries the guilt of her ruin and death since Alithea was a married woman, and that her husband continues to bear his wife's seducer a vindictive grudge. Happily, for the moment, Alithea's husband believes that the seducer was surnamed Rupert. Alithea's husband was and is an unsuitable mate for a sensitive woman, and the marriage was one from which any woman would have wanted to flee. Alithea's infraction was only against the letter of the marriage bond, not its spirit.

The vindictive husband has conceived a hatred for Alithea's son, Gerard, on account of Alithea's connection with "Rupert." Elizabeth, Falkner's ward, coincidentally meets and forms an attachment to Gerard. Falkner repeatedly attempts to separate them because of his guilty feelings. Their attachment blooms into a love which cannot be denied, and Falkner is forced to confess all to Gerard after the boy saves Falkner's life. He is the infamous Rupert, Rupert Falkner.

With the revelation comes the separation of Elizabeth and Gerard, she to stand loyally with Falkner, he to defend his father's honor. For the first time in his life, Gerard finds himself on his father's side, but familiarity breeds contempt. Gerard wants to fight a manly duel for honor, while his father wants to crush Falkner for economic gain in the legal system. Gerard finds this an inexcusable pettiness on his father's part. He then joins Elizabeth to defend Falkner in court. To do this, they will need to go to America to bring back a crucial witness, but the witness arrives and saves them the voyage: Falkner is acquitted. The legal acquittal is also metaphorical: In comparison with the ugly sins of greed, the sins of passion are pardonable.

Elizabeth, the reader knows, is also the product of an elopement in defiance of family, a sin of passion. The proud Catholic family which once spurned her decides to acknowledge Elizabeth. Gerard and Elizabeth, both wealthy and in their proper social position, marry. Falkner will have a home with them in perpetuity.

Once again, Shelley's fictional involvement in the domestic sphere tones down her customary floridity and affords the reader fascinating insights into the thinking of the daughter of an early feminist, who was indeed an independent woman herself. It can only clarify history to know that such a woman as Mary Shelley can write in her final novel that her heroine's studies included not only the "masculine" pursuits of abstract knowledge, but also needlework and "the careful inculcation of habits and order . . . without which every woman must be unhappy—and, to a certain degree, unsexed."

Martha Nochimson

OTHER MAJOR WORKS

SHORT FICTION: *Mary Shelley: Collected Tales and Stories*, 1976.

PLAYS: *Proserpine*, pb. 1922; *Midas*, pb. 1922.

NONFICTION: *History of a Six Weeks' Tour Through a Part of France, Switzerland, Germany, and Holland*, 1817; *Lardner's Cabinet Cyclopaedia*, 1838 (Numbers 63, 71, 96); *Rambles in Germany and Italy*, 1844; *The Letters of Mary Shelley*, 1980 (2 volumes; Betty T. Bennett, editor).

BIBLIOGRAPHY

Baldick, Chris. *In "Frankenstein"'s Shadow: Myth, Monstrosity, and Nineteenth-Century Writing.* Oxford, England: Clarendon Press, 1987. Baldick analyzes the structure of modern myth as it has adapted and misread Shelley's novel until the film version of 1931. Focuses on Shelley's novel as itself a monster, which is assembled, speaks, and escapes like its protagonist. Also examines transformations in E. T. A. Hoffmann, Nathaniel Hawthorne, Herman Melville, and Elizabeth Gaskell; links *Frankenstein* to Thomas Carlyle, Charles Dickens, and Karl Marx; and traces the novel's influence on late Victorian stories of mad scientists, H. G. Wells, Joseph Conrad, and D. H. Lawrence. The last chapter argues that literary realism is itself a result of *Frankenstein*'s shadow. Includes footnotes, five illustrations, an appendix summarizing the novel's plot, and an index.

Forry, Steven Earl. *Hideous Progenies: Dramatizations of "Frankenstein" from Mary Shelley to the Present.* Philadelphia: University of Pennsylvania Press, 1990. Examines the influence of Shelley's novel on the history of theater and cinema from 1832 to 1930, discussing in great detail the popularization of the story until it became an enduring myth. After an introduction to the prevailing theater in London from 1823 to 1832, Forry studies the various Victorian adaptations of the novel from 1832 to 1900 and its revivals in twentieth century drama and cinema from 1900 to 1930. Provides the texts of seven dramatic adaptations of *Frankenstein*, from Richard Brinsley Peake's 1823 *Presumption* to John Lloyd Balderston's 1930 *Frankenstein*. Contains thirty-one illustrations, a list of ninety-six dramatizations from 1821 to 1986, an appendix with the music from *Vampire's Victim* (1887), a bibliography, and an index.

Kiely, Robert. *The Romantic Novel in England.* Cambridge, Mass.: Harvard University Press, 1972. An important book on Romantic prose fiction, including Shelley's gothic romances, which analyzes in depth twelve Romantic novels to define the intellectual context of the era. Notes that concepts of reality were tested and changed by Romantic novels and Edmund Burke's ideas of the sublime modified aesthetic forms. Shelley makes a significant contribution to this general thesis, and *Frankenstein* is analyzed in detail. Examines the story as a tragedy of suffering and superiority, in which a nightmarish experience carries moral themes. Finds a common drift toward death in most novels of this genre. Includes a set of notes and an index.

Mellor, Anne K. *Mary Shelley: Her Life, Her Fiction, Her Monsters.* London: Methuen, 1988. An important book which argues against trends of analysis which subordinate Shelley to her husband Percy Bysshe Shelley. Extends feminist and psychoanalytic criticism of *Frankenstein* to include all of Shelley's life and work, arguing that her stories are creations of the family she never enjoyed. The strength of her stories is their expression of her ambivalent desire for and criticism of the bourgeois family as an exploitation of property and women by a patriarchal ideology. Establishes Shelley's need for family, her feminist critique of science, and her analysis of the relationship between fathers and daughters. Includes eight illustrative plates, a chronology, ample notes, a bibliography, and an index.

Nitchie, Elizabeth. *Mary Shelley: Author of "Frankenstein."* New Brunswick, N.J.: Rutgers University Press, 1953. This critical biography evaluates Shelley in her own right in the milieu of people and places she knew. Assesses Shelley's temperament and talent, discussing her faults and strengths. Follows her life and career, from her earliest appearance as a self-conscious girl with a critical mind to her widowhood when she wrote largely forgotten works. Although primarily a biography, contains valuable comments on her writings, seen as art and as expressions of her life. A bibliography, an index, and six appendices, including a chronology, a list of works, a note on the unpublished novella *Mathilda*, the stage history of *Frankenstein*, and some unpublished poems, are provided.

Smith, Johanna M. *Mary Shelley.* New York: Twayne, 1996. This good introductory volume on Mary Shelley opens with a chapter devoted to her biography, then divides Shelley's works into categories. Separate chapters consider science fiction (including *Frankenstein*), historical fiction, domestic-sentimental fiction, literary biography and criticism, and travel narratives. More descriptive than analytical, this overview of Shelley's career is most accessible. A selected bibliography includes both primary and secondary sources.

Spark, Muriel. *Mary Shelley*. London: Constable, 1988. A revision of Spark's *Child of Light* (Essex, England: Tower Bridge, 1951) which reassesses the view that Shelley craved respectability after her husband's death. Spark skillfully narrates Shelley's life and then analyzes her writings. Argues that Shelley's pessimism was the consequence of her rationalist upbringing by William Godwin, but that she possessed an inner tranquility with which she created her novels. Concentrates on *Frankenstein* as the end of gothic fiction for its rational exposé of gothic mystery, on *The Last Man* as an expression of Shelley's feeling of solitude, and on *The Fortunes of Perkin Warbeck* as her challenge to learn from Sir Walter Scott's Waverley novels. Contains eight pages of illustrations, a selected bibliography, and an index.

(Library of Congress)

Oni srazhalis za rodinu, 1943-1944 (serial), 1971 (book; *They Fought for Their Country*, 1959)
Sud'ba cheloveka, 1956-1957 (novella; *The Fate of a Man*, 1958)

OTHER LITERARY FORMS

Mikhail Sholokhov's early collections of short stories were published in 1926 as *Donskiye rasskazy* and in the same year as *Lazorevaya Step*. In 1931, *Lazorevaya Step* was expanded to include *Donskiye rasskazy* and translated in 1961 as *Tales from the Don*. His short stories form volume 1 of his complete works, *Sobranie sochinenii* (1956-1960), which were first published in Moscow in eight volumes; war stories and essays form volume 8. They are also available in English as *One Man's Destiny and Other Stories, Articles and Sketches, 1923-1963* (1967) and *At the Bidding of the Heart: Essays, Sketches, Speeches, Papers* (1973).

MIKHAIL SHOLOKHOV

Born: Kruzhilino, Russia; May 24, 1905
Died: Kruzhilino, U.S.S.R.; February 21, 1984

PRINCIPAL LONG FICTION

Tikhii Don, 1928-1940 (partial translation *And Quiet Flows the Don*, 1934, also as *The Don Flows Home to the Sea*, 1940 complete translation *The Silent Don*, 1942, also as *And Quiet Flows the Don*, 1967)

Podnyataya tselina, 1932, 1960 (translation of volume 1 *Virgin Soil Upturned*, 1935, also as *Seeds of Tomorrow*, 1935 translation of volume 2 *Harvest on the Don*, 1960 complete translation *Virgin Soil Upturned*, 1979)

ACHIEVEMENTS

The author of the greatest novel to be published in the Soviet Union, *The Silent Don*, Sholokhov occupies a unique place in Soviet literature. He has been compared to Leo Tolstoy in his creation of a national epic, to Fyodor Dostoevski in his portrayal of Grigorii Melekhov, to Nikolai Gogol and Anton Chekhov in his evocations of the steppe. In 1965, he was permitted by the Soviet authorities to receive the Nobel Prize in Literature, a privilege denied to Boris Pasternak, who wrote a more profoundly philosophical novel. In addition, Sholokhov held numerous positions of honor in the Communist Party and the Union of Soviet Writers. He won the Stalin and Lenin prizes for literature (1941, 1960) and received honorary degrees from Western and Soviet universities.

In his two major works, *The Silent Don* and *Virgin Soil Upturned*, Sholokhov succeeds in bringing to life the Cossack world that he knew so well. Shrouded in legends, scorned for their barbarity, the Cossacks were little known to the Russians and totally unknown to Western readers. Sholokhov speaks in their dialect, clothes his characters in colorful Cossack traditions, and arms the soldiers with a spirit of courage and adventure. Part 1 of *The Silent Don* in particular and much of *Virgin Soil Upturned* shows them in their daily occupations, their celebrations and their interaction, much in their colorful and often crude language. Through his fictitious characters, all modeled on his own friends and acquaintances, the image of a people emerges.

Particularly in *The Silent Don*, Sholokhov skillfully combined Socialist Realism and art. Officially promulgated in 1934, Socialist Realism requires that literature serve the ideals of the Communist Party and portray a positive Soviet citizen. Early Soviet critics—with the exception of Aleksandr Serafimovich and Maxim Gorky—could not understand that *The Silent Don*, with its vacillating hero and its objective portrayal of both Reds and Whites, was a true proletarian novel, and they tried desperately to block its publication. Eventually, however, the critics accepted it because it showed the triumph of the Revolution through suffering and violence on both sides. Yet it was the artistic qualities of the novel, already evident in Sholokhov's early short stories, and to be continued in *Virgin Soil Upturned*, that won millions of readers in the Soviet Union and abroad. The hu-

manness of suffering, the tenderness of love, and the uncertainty of truth touched them, and as of 1980 more than seventy-nine million copies of his works had been sold in 974 editions.

It was not without difficulty that Sholokhov acquired this reputation. Particularly in *The Silent Don*, the censors mercilessly changed and deleted some of his most brilliant passages. Joseph Stalin asked that the hero of *The Silent Don*, Grigorii Melekhov, accept Communism, but Sholokhov refused, saying that this was against the artistic conception of the work. Although *Virgin Soil Upturned* received less criticism, the death of Davydov was a concession to Stalin's wishes, since Sholokhov had planned a suicide. Yet the changes imposed on Sholokhov or accepted by him did not dim the original ideas that he had researched and reflected on painstakingly from 1925 to 1940 for *The Silent Don*, and from 1930 to 1960 for *Virgin Soil Upturned*. Outspoken like his Cossack hero Grigorii, Sholokhov says that an artist must follow his heart. He did not hesitate to criticize the inefficiency of the Soviet system and to express the depth of human suffering that accompanied the Revolution. On the other hand, as a dutiful Communist, he said that one's heart must follow the Party. This was a difficult reconciliation, yet Sholokhov seems to have effected it more successfully than any other writer in the Soviet Union.

It should be noted, however, that ever since the publication of the first part of *The Silent Don*, Sholokhov's authorship of this masterwork, which clearly stands above the rest of his production, has been questioned. Among those to raise this charge is Aleksandr Solzhenitsyn, who believes that the actual author was a Cossack officer named Fyodor Krykov, who had written several books about the Don region before his death in the Civil War. This charge against Sholokhov has yet to be conclusively proved or disproved.

BIOGRAPHY

Born on May 24, 1905, in the Cossack village of Kruzhilino near Veshenskaya, Mikhail Aleksandrovich Sholokhov was himself not a true Cossack. His father, Aleksandr Mikhailovich, did not marry his mother, Anastasiya Danilovna Chernikova, until 1912, when Sholokhov's birth was legitimized, and the Cossack status he had held from his mother's first husband was abrogated. Nevertheless, he grew up in the customs and traditions of the Cossack world that he was later to convey with such realism to his readers. His early education in his native village was minimal when he left for a year in Moscow in 1914. Financial reasons precluded his continuing, but he was subsequently enrolled in an eight-year *gymnasium* in Boguchar. The German invasion of 1918 marked the end of his formal education but did not interrupt his love of reading and writing.

In the years between 1918 and 1922, he worked for the new Soviet regime in many capacities, especially grain-requisitioning, and wrote plays for young people. His home was in an area controlled by the Whites. He saw much violence, participated in it himself, and was twice at the point of being killed. This experience is reflected especially in the violence and objectivity of *The Silent Don*, where Grigorii broods confusedly on the injustices committed by both sides.

In 1922, Sholokhov married Maria Petrovna Gromoslavskaya, the daughter of a well-to-do and long-established Cossack family. She was to prove an ideal "comrade" for him and became the mother of his four children. The couple moved to Moscow, where Sholokhov began his first serious commitment to literature. He published a number of short stories, uneven in literary value but extremely popular. In their vividness of language, diversity of speech, and lively dialogue, they anticipate the achievements of his mature fiction. Never at home in the capital, or in any city, Sholokhov returned to Kruzhilino in 1924.

Sholokhov began working on his masterpiece, *The Silent Don*, in 1925, amid innumerable difficulties with the censors. It was only the intercession of Aleksandr Serafimovich, editor of the monthly *Oktyabr'*, that permitted publication of the initial segment of the novel. Serafimovich's support, however, did not prevent the many attacks on the novel and on Sholokhov himself, who was first accused of plagiarism in 1929-1930. Later, Gorky's intervention, and ultimately Stalin's, permitted him to com-

plete publication of the novel. Sholokhov worked on *The Silent Don* almost constantly from 1925 to 1930, the most productive years of his career. He interrupted *The Silent Don* in 1930 to begin *Virgin Soil Upturned*. In 1932, he gained admission into the Communist Party, and in 1934 he was elected to the presidium of the Union of Soviet Writers. He visited Sweden, Denmark, Britain, and France as a representative of the Writers' Union. His success did not prevent him from speaking out fearlessly against the bureaucracy, which ultimately placed him in a dangerous position, especially in 1938, when he narrowly escaped liquidation. His personal friendship with Stalin saved him, and he always remained loyal to his friend, even after Stalin's death.

During World War II, in which he experienced much personal suffering, including the loss of his manuscripts, Sholokhov became a war correspondent. His writings as such are not his best; nevertheless, after the war he devoted himself mainly to journalism, with the exception of volume 2 of *Virgin Soil Upturned*; *They Fought for Their Country*, an unfinished novel in a war setting; and a very successful novella, *The Fate of a Man*. In the postwar era, he enjoyed an unparalleled success in the Soviet Union, receiving many prizes, the most notable of which was the Nobel Prize in Literature in 1965. He became a staunch defender of Party policies, attacking such dissidents as Pasternak, Solzhenitsyn, Yuli Daniel, and Andrei Sinyavsky, all of whom are superior to him as writers. Typical of his attacks on the West was an invective against the President of the United States, Harry S Truman.

Until his death in 1984, Sholokhov lived in the village where he was born, hunting and fishing, traveling widely in Europe, the United States, and Japan, and enjoying his substantial wealth and international reputation.

ANALYSIS

The critic Herman Ermolaev has observed that Mikhail Sholokhov's art embraces the epic, the dramatic, the comic, and the lyric; to this one might justly add the tragic, at least in *The Silent Don*. Helen Muchnic, for example, sees in the character of Grigorii the fatal flaw that marks the heroes of Greek tragedy: Grigorii is doomed by his failure to recognize the greatness of Bolshevism. His error lies in his independence. Like Oedipus, Grigorii cannot *not* know the truth, but unlike Sophocles' hero, Sholokhov's is destined never to know clearly. Even Soviet critics noted the tragic element in *The Silent Don*, and in 1940, Boris Emelyanov compared *The Silent Don* to Aeschylus's *The Persians* (472 B.C.E.), since both were written from the viewpoint of the vanquished. *The Silent Don* is of epic proportions because of its length and its scope in time (1912-1922) at a crucial period in history, World War I and the Soviet Revolution. It was serialized in *Oktyabr'* and *Novy mir* from 1928 to 1940. Volume 1 was published by Moskovskii Rabochii in 1928, volume 2 in 1929; Khudozhestvennaya Literatura published volumes 3 and 4 in 1933 and 1940 respectively.

THE SILENT DON

The novel is the story of the fall of a people seen through some of its most representative families: Melekhov, Korshunov, and Koshevoi in particular. Often compared to Tolstoy's *War and Peace* (1865-1869), *The Silent Don* unfolds a vast panorama of people and world-shaking events, and 1917 is to Sholokhov what 1812 was to Tolstoy. Yet Sholokhov is no Tolstoy. He lacks Tolstoy's depth of vision, moral intensity, and psychological analysis. Sholokhov's choice of a secluded and anachronistic prerevolutionary society places *The Silent Don* in the category of the primitive and popular epics, as David Stewart demonstrates through his analysis of action, character, language, and meaning in the novel.

Early in his career, Sholokhov was attracted to the theater, and thus it is not surprising that in both of his novels dialogue and action are of extreme importance. Sholokhov uses lively and spirited conversation, filled with dialectical and sometimes crude Cossack expressions, and often incorrect Russian. In fact, the major part of the novels is dialogue rather than narrative, and important events come to light through the characters rather than through the author. Sholokhov does not write reflective philosophical works. Grigorii Melekhov's search for truth is less evident in his thoughts than in his actions, as he vac-

illates constantly between Red and White, and between his wife Natalia and his mistress Aksinia. Collectivization is not a well-thought-out plan in *Virgin Soil Upturned* but rather a process that occurs because each farmer moves in that direction.

Both people and nature are actors in Sholokhov's works, and he moves effortlessly and harmoniously from one to the other. The poetic evocations of nature that make up at least one-fourth of *The Silent Don* and a good part, though less, of *Virgin Soil Upturned* show Sholokhov's lyric mastery at its height. Most are placed at strategic positions, such as the beginning and end of chapters, and convey the union of people with nature. In somewhat pantheistic exultation, Sholokhov rejoices with nature in its cycle of birth, death, and resurrection. As one might expect from the titles of his novels, the Don mirrors human hopes and sorrows. Sholokhov's books convey the feel of the earth—the Russian soil—and evoke the rhythm of nature.

Nature is frequently associated with love in Sholokhov's fiction. Ermolaev, who has studied the role of nature in Sholokhov, identifies floral blooming with Aksinia; Easter, the spring, and rain, with Natalia. In Grigorii and Aksinia, one finds perhaps the tenderest love story in Soviet literature. Their passionate and fatal love recalls Anna Karenina or Dmitri Karamazov. As with Sholokhov's poetic lyricism, his love stories are close to the earth and show the deep bond of human beings with nature. The tenderness of maternal love also plays an important role in Sholokhov's works, as seen in the tender farewell of Ilinichna for her dead son Piotra, and contrasts sharply with the brutality and violence of war.

Sholokhov's humorous vein is more evident in *Virgin Soil Upturned* but is not absent from *The Silent Don*, where one might cite Panteleimon Melekhov's wit. *Virgin Soil Upturned* abounds in comic characters and scenes: Shchukar's endless stories, the exuberance of the induction into the Party, the initial reactions to collectivization at the village meetings. Sholokhov's dialogue is brisk and witty; his colloquial and dialectical language, always appropriate to the speaker, lightens the heavy subject and makes both novels highly readable.

Indeed, Sholokhov's style is brisk and light; the chapters, composed of short vignettes, leave the reader momentarily in suspense, for Sholokhov knows where to break his tale. His rapid transitions from humor to violence, from love to war, from nature to humanity, show the all-encompassing unity of life and the complexity of the Revolution and its effects. He shows the stark reality of war, the atrocities of both Reds and Whites, and humankind's inhumanity to others. On the other hand, he portrays the tenderness of love and the exultation of nature, as in his beautiful apostrophe to the steppe that rivals Gogol. He works in a linear manner, without flashbacks or foreshadowing, much in the tradition of the nineteenth century or indeed the ancient and medieval epic. He portrays life and love, the endless rhythm of birth and death, as seen in one great epoch, the Soviet Revolution.

The Silent Don was first conceived as an epic of the Don and of the role of the Don Cossacks in the Revolution, and Sholokhov projected the title "Donshchina," later abandoning it because of its archaic allusions. The story begins in 1912 and ends in 1922. It shows the peaceful agrarian life of the Don Cossacks in the small village of Tatarsk. The domineering patriarch Panteleimon Melekhov and his independent and passionate son Grigorii clash often, especially in regard to Grigorii's liaison with the bewitching Aksinia. Neither the father's wrath and the arranged marriage with the beautiful and virtuous Natalia Korshunova, daughter of the prosperous Miron, nor the abuse by Aksinia's husband, Stepan Ashtakov, can break the liaison. The two lovers, defying all convention, finally choose to live together as hired help on the estate of Listnitsky.

The calm of the Cossack existence, broken only by such outbursts of passion, is shattered by mobilization in Tatarsk in 1914. Grigorii is called into battle, where his attraction and repulsion toward killing and violence are first evident. The war provides Grigorii's first contact with Bolshevism, for which he also feels both an attraction and repulsion. On leave in Tatarsk because of a wound, he learns of Aksinia's unfaithfulness and returns to his wife, who later gives birth to twins.

Like World War I, the Revolution is portrayed through the eyes of the soldiers and villagers and evoked through images of nature: "Above blood-soaked White Russia, the stars wept mournfully." The desertion of the troops, Kornilov's arrest, and the fall of Kerensky are moments of confusion to the Don Cossack soldiers. Grigorii embraces Bolshevism and becomes an officer but is incapable of the cold dedication exemplified by Bunchuk, whose brief idyll with the Jew Anna Pogudko softens the drama, and by Mishka Koshevoi, Grigorii's former friend and henceforth implacable enemy.

When Grigorii joins the Whites, his position becomes more dangerous. The violence grows more senseless and immediate, with victims such as Miron Korshunov and Piotra Melekhov, the latter killed by Mishka Koshevoi. Family tragedies also cloud Grigorii's existence and confuse his values. His sister-in-law, Daria, commits suicide; his wife, Natalia, dies as the result of an abortion after learning of Grigorii's return to Aksinia; his father dies of typhus. Parallel to Grigorii's uncertainty is Mishka's advance in the Soviet ranks and in coldheartedness. Even his marriage to Grigorii's sister Dunia does not dull his determination to kill Grigorii, which the reader surmises will occur when Grigorii returns home, having lost Aksinia to a stray bullet. Only his son Mishatka remains, and the implacable march of history will destroy the unwilling Grigorii, born to greatness at a point in history when only conformity can save him.

In 1930, Sholokhov interrupted his work on *The Silent Don* to address a contemporary problem: collectivization. He published part 1 of *Virgin Soil Upturned* in 1932, practically without any censorship difficulties. Part 2 was not completed until 1960 and is radically different in spirit. This novel is much more concentrated in scope, since it covers only the period between 1930 and 1932, has fewer characters, and is confined to the small Cossack village of Gremyachy Log. Although it does not have the epic sweep of *The Silent Don*, it is an on-the-spot documentary of a crucial phase in Soviet history.

VIRGIN SOIL UPTURNED

Also unlike *The Silent Don*, *Virgin Soil Upturned* has no main tragic character. Stewart observes that the heroes are dissolved by the Party, so that the real hero is perhaps the collective people at Gremyachy Log. The logical hero is Siemion Davydov, a former factory worker and sailor, who was mobilized in 1930 to organize collective farms. He becomes chairman at Gremyachy Log and manifests the zeal and inefficiency typical of early Soviet leaders. He is a colorless but not unlikable character. His death at the end of part 2 is far less tragic than Grigorii's return to Tatarsk. Although he shows his human side in his love affairs with Nagulnov's former wife, Lukeria, and with a gentle, shy seventeen-year-old, Varia Kharlamova, he is not convincing as a lover.

Siemon's associate, the passionate and impulsive Makar Nagulnov, secretary of the Gremyachy Log Party nucleus and still secretly in love with his former wife, is more attractive. Even better portrayed is Andrei Razmiotov, chairman of the village Soviet. His one passion is his deceased wife, Yevdokia, and the novel ends as he visits her grave and wistfully mourns her absence. Stewart, however, regards Kondrat Maidannikov as the novel's most convincing character: A "middling Cossack," Kondrat joins the collective farm because he believes in it, yet his instincts draw him to his own property. He does not join the Party until he has reflected carefully. In his simplicity, he is the most philosophical and intellectually convinced Communist in the novel.

The plot of the story is simple: the gradual conversion of the village to the collective farm. The beginning reflects Sholokhov's portrayal of violence and brutality, as entire kulak families are deported. Although collectivization is presented as voluntary, those who withdraw after reading Stalin's pronouncement are left with no animals and inferior land. The end of part 1 is indecisive though promising. In part 2, collectivization is complete, and a revolt is suppressed. Thus, this volume becomes mainly a series of sketches and stories, mostly in a humorous vein. It seems to be the work of a writer who has totally accepted Party policies, writing about an accomplished fact no longer questioned.

Actually Sholokhov's best creative period ended before World War II, and part 2, written in 1960, weakens what promised to be a powerful, though limited, novel. Nevertheless, Sholokhov's treatment of collectivization has not been surpassed, and his wit and lyricism make *Virgin Soil Upturned* a valuable contribution to literature.

Irma M. Kashuba

OTHER MAJOR WORKS

SHORT FICTION: *Donskiye rasskazy*, 1926; *Lazorevaya Step*, 1926, 1931 (1931 edition includes *Donskiye rasskazy*; *Tales from the Don*, 1961); *Early Stories*, 1966.

MISCELLANEOUS: *Sobranie sochinenii*, 1956-1960 (8 volumes); *One Man's Destiny and Other Stories, Articles and Sketches, 1923-1963*, 1967; *At the Bidding of the Heart: Essays, Sketches, Speeches, Papers*, 1973.

BIBLIOGRAPHY

Ermolaev, Herman. *Mikhail Sholokhov and His Art.* Princeton, N.J.: Princeton University Press, 1982. A study of Sholokhov's life and art, philosophy of life, handling of style and structure, with a separate chapter on the historical sources of *The Quiet Don*, and another on the question of plagiarism. Includes maps, tables (of similes), notes, and bibliography.

Klimenko, Michael. *The World of Young Sholokhov: Vision of Violence.* North Quincy, Mass: The Christopher Publishing House, 1972. The introduction discusses the Sholokhov canon as well as the man and his critics. Other chapters explore the genesis of his novels, his vision of life, his heroes, and his treatment of revolution. Includes a bibliography.

Medvedev, Roy. *Problems in the Literary Biography of Mikhail Sholokhov.* Cambridge, England: Cambridge University Press, 1977. A piercing examining of *The Quiet Don*, exploring the issue of Sholokhov's authorship and how it poses problems for his literary biography This is an indispensable study carried out by one of Russia's great scholars.

Murphy, A. B., V.P. Butt, and H. Ermolaev. *Sholokhov's "Tikhii Don": A Commentary in Two Volumes.* Birmingham, England: Department of Russian Language and Literature, the University of

Birmingham, 1997. An excellent study of *The Silent Don*.

Price, Robert F. *Mixail Soloxov in Yugoslavia: Reception and Literary Impact*. Boulder: East European Quarterly, 1973. Although most of this study is irrelevant to beginning students, see chapter two for a useful discussion of critics' reactions to Sholokhov (here given a Yugoslav spelling).

Stewart, D.H. *Mikhail Sholokhov: A Critical Introduction*. Ann Arbor: University of Michigan Press, 1967. The book to begin with in a study of Sholokhov. Chapter 1 discusses the author "cossack work"; chapter 2 his early fiction; chapter 3 the origins and direction of *The Quiet Don*; chapter 4 *The Quiet Don* as epic; chapter 5 *Virgin Soil Upturned*. Stewart also includes an appendix on Sholokhov's career and another on the novel's translation into English. There are also helpful notes and a bibliographical essay.

(The Nobel Foundation)

HENRYK SIENKIEWICZ

Born: Wola Okrzejska, Poland; May 5, 1846
Died: Vevey, Switzerland; November 15, 1916

PRINCIPAL LONG FICTION

Na marne, 1872 (*In Vain*, 1899)

Szkice węglem, 1877

Ogniem i mieczem, 1884 (*With Fire and Sword: An Historical Novel of Poland and Russia*, 1890)

Potop, 1886 (*The Deluge: An Historical Novel of Poland, Sweden, and Russia*, 1891)

Pan Wołodyjowski, 1887-1888 (*Pan Michael: An Historical Novel of Poland, the Ukraine, and Turkey*, 1893)

Bez dogmatu, 1891 (*Without Dogma*, 1893)

Rodzina Połanieckich, 1895 (*Children of the Soil*, 1895)

Quo vadis, 1896 (*Quo Vadis: A Narrative of the Time of Nero*, 1896)

Krzyżacy, 1900 (*The Knights of the Cross*, 1900; also as *The Teutonic Knights*, 1943)

Na polu chwały, 1903-1905 (*On the Field of Glory*, 1906)

W pustyni i w puszczy, 1911 (*In Desert and Wilderness*, 1912)

Dzieła, 1948-1955 (60 volumes)

OTHER LITERARY FORMS

There can be no doubt that it was Henryk Sienkiewicz's success as an author of historical novels that led the Swedish Academy to select him as the recipient of the Nobel Prize in Literature in 1905. Yet he was at the same time a prolific writer of short stories, many of which continue to be ranked among the finest ever written in the Polish language. One of his masterworks in this genre is entitled "Janko myzikant" (1879; "Yanko the Musician," 1893). In this story, a young peasant boy named Yanko is so obsessed with the beauty of music that he is unable to resist the temptation of stealing a violin from the manor house of the local squire. When caught, he is beaten so severely that he dies. The underlying irony of this tale stems from the fact that those who lived in the manor house considered themselves to be patrons of the arts and frequently traveled to Italy for the purpose of discovering and assisting young artists.

Equally popular is "Latarnik" (1882; "The Lighthouse Keeper of Aspinwall," 1893), whose plot centers on the fate of an aged Polish exile who finally succeeds in being hired as a lighthouse keeper on the island of Aspinwall near the Panama Canal Zone. One day he receives a parcel of Polish books that includes a copy of Adam Mickiewicz's *Pan Tadeusz* (1917). He becomes so engrossed while reading this patriotic national epic that he forgets to light the beacon and, having caused a ship to run aground, is fired for his negligence. As is the case with most of Sienkiewicz's short stories, those two works were first published in periodicals and subsequently incorporated into editions of his collected works, the first of which appeared while he was still in his early thirties. For this reason, the numerous collections of his short stories in English translation have no Polish-language counterparts as such and were actually gathered together under one cover in accordance with the personal preferences of the individual translators themselves.

Throughout his adult life, Sienkiewicz was an inveterate traveler, and there are two journals written during his trips abroad that are still capable of holding the contemporary reader's attention. The first of these is entitled *Listy z podróży do Ameryki* (1876-1878, serial; 1896, book; *Portrait of America*, 1959). These letters, arising from a journey to America, were commissioned by a Polish periodical and record Sienkiewicz's firsthand impressions of the United States—chiefly of New York City, the Plains states, and California. The Polish author's views are, it should be noted, far more balanced than those to be found in Charles Dickens's *American Notes* (1842), in which life in the United States is depicted in largely negative terms. Later in his career, Sienkiewicz traveled throughout East Africa and wrote *Listy z Afryki* (1891; letters from Africa). In these reports from Africa, the role of European colonization is judged to be generally beneficial for the indigenous peoples, but Sienkiewicz is highly critical of the Arabs, who ruthlessly exploited the native populace in this region. Both the American and the African journals are, in short, valuable historical records pertaining to everyday life in a bygone era.

ACHIEVEMENTS

Sienkiewicz is both a literary and a political phenomenon in his homeland. In order to appreciate the twofold significance of his major novels, it is necessary to recall the troubled state of Polish national life throughout the nineteenth century. Poland had been partitioned by Russia, Prussia, and Austria during the latter part of the eighteenth century and had completely disappeared from the map of Europe. The largest portion of Poland, including Warsaw itself, came under the control of the Russians, and Sienkiewicz was destined to spend his entire life as an involuntary subject of the Czar. Two full-scale insurrections against the Russians, the first occurring in 1831 and the second in 1863, ended in defeat, and their failure served only to intensify the oppressive policies of the czarist officials. Both of these revolts were largely inspired by Romantic idealists. After the debacle of 1863, the Polish intelligentsia appeared to wash its collective hands of the doctrines of Romanticism and rapidly embraced the scientifically oriented philosophy of positivism as the best solution to the problems confronting the nation. The adherents of positivism in Poland openly abandoned the quixotic quest for national independence by means of political conspiracy and armed insurrection and focused their energies on promoting organic economic development in the various Polish territories as well as on expanding educational opportunities available to the masses. The transition from Romanticism to positivism signaled a rejection of the feudal values cherished by the landowning gentry and the adoption of the ideals of capitalism championed by the middle class.

For the positivists, writers had a moral obligation to tackle contemporary social problems in their works, and Sienkiewicz's early writings were duly composed in accordance with this stricture. Before long, however, his own ancestral heritage and aristocratic temperament came to the fore, and in 1882 he began work on a historical trilogy whose aim was to dramatize Polish military exploits of the seventeenth century. The first volume bears the title *With Fire and Sword*; the other two are *The Deluge* and *Pan Michael*. These three novels are collectively designated the "Trilogia" (trilogy). Sienkiewicz's decision to write about the seventeenth century stemmed from his desire to depict a period in Polish history during which the country successfully defended its national existence against the attacks launched by a combination of powerful enemies. Unlike the positivists, who tended to dwell on the failures of Poland's ruling classes, Sienkiewicz chose to emphasize the valorous feats achieved by Polish arms. The inspirational intent of the author was explicitly acknowledged in the brief postscript to the final volume of the trilogy, in which he asserts that the entire series was written "for the sake of the strengthening of hearts." Public response to these novels was so enthusiastic that sentiment for the cause of Polish independence increased immeasurably throughout the land, and Sienkiewicz soon found himself regarded as his nation's foremost champion, both at home and abroad.

After the publication of the trilogy, Sienkiewicz wrote a pair of moderately successful novels on contemporary themes and then went on to compose two additional historical novels of major stature. The first deals with the persecution of Christians in Rome during the reign of the Emperor Nero and is entitled *Quo Vadis*. It soon became an international best-seller of unprecedented magnitude and remains Sienkiewicz's most popular novel among the reading public outside the author's native land. In the second of these works, Sienkiewicz returns to the annals of Polish history and depicts Poland's struggle against an aggressive military order of Teutonic monks who are ultimately defeated in the year 1410 at the Battle of Greenwold. This novel bears the title *The Knights of the Cross*. Most Polish critics consider it to be superior to *Quo Vadis* in terms of literary merit, and a few even go as far as to prefer it to the trilogy itself. In 1905, Sienkiewicz was awarded the Nobel Prize in Literature, and he took the occasion to thank the members of the Swedish Academy for recognizing the fact that Poland, though physically enslaved, lived on in spiri-

tual freedom. The abiding popularity of his works in present-day Poland is ample testimony that Sienkiewicz is still capable of strengthening the hearts of his countrymen, as he did during his own lifetime.

BIOGRAPHY

Henryk Sienkiewicz's paternal ancestors were Lithuanian Tartars who had traditionally followed a military vocation. His great-grandfather, Michael, was baptized in 1740 and subsequently admitted to the ranks of the gentry (*Szlachta*) in 1775 through an act of the national diet by way of recognition of the family's military service on behalf of the Polish Commonwealth. Despite this honor, he and his descendants continued to remain impoverished. His own father, Józef, managed to advance himself both socially and financially in 1843 by marrying Stefania Cieciszowska, a young woman from a well-established household of landowners who were generally conceded to be members of the aristocracy. Sienkiewicz was born on May 5, 1846, on an estate that belonged to his mother's parents. This estate (as well as the nearby village) was named Wola Okrzejska and was located near Siedlice, a city in Russian-occupied Poland approximately fifty miles to the east of Warsaw. Sienkiewicz had one brother and four sisters, and when he was nine years old, his parents purchased an estate of their own in the province of Mazovia. A few years later, they sold the estate and bought an apartment house in the Warsaw suburb of Praga in order to supplement their modest financial resources from rental payments made by the tenants. They also hoped to give their children the educational advantage of attending schools in the city that had once been the nation's capital.

Sienkiewicz became an avid reader quite early in life. While still at Wola Okrzejska, he immersed himself in popular Romantic poetry extolling the virtues of gallant knights and fair ladies and thus acquired an abiding affection for the institution of chivalry. He also developed an intense desire to travel through reading Daniel Defoe's *Robinson Crusoe* (1719) and Johann Rudolph Wyss's *The Swiss Family Robinson* (1812-1827) and even dreamed of settling on an uninhabited island once he grew up. During the time that he attended secondary school in Warsaw, he frequently neglected his studies to read the historical romances of Sir Walter Scott and Alexandre Dumas, *père*. Except for the areas of literature and history, Sienkiewicz's scholastic achievements were relatively modest. Despite his aptitude for literary and historical studies, however, he never seriously considered becoming a writer during his adolescent years.

When the time arrived for him to matriculate at the newly founded University of Warsaw, then called Szkoła Główna (Central Academy), he readily acceded to his mother's wishes and entered the Faculty of Law in 1866. Soon after, he switched to medicine and finally to history and literature. Students at the University of Warsaw in those years were imbued with a philosophy known as positivism, which was based on the ideas espoused by the French thinker Auguste Comte (1789-1857), and Sienkiewicz himself soon became a confirmed, if only transient, adherent of this social doctrine. Unable to obtain much financial assistance from his parents, Sienkiewicz was obliged to earn funds through employment as a private tutor while still working toward a degree. For reasons that are still unclear, Sienkiewicz terminated his studies at the University of Warsaw in 1871 without bothering to take the final examinations and abruptly embarked on a career as a freelance writer and journalist.

Within a year, Sienkiewicz was finding success in his new career. His first novel, *In Vain*, dealt with student life and was serialized in a biweekly periodical. At about the same time, he became a feature writer for a newspaper named *Gazeta Polska* and contributed numerous sketches, literary essays, and reviews to its *feuilleton* section. On assignment for *Gazeta Polska*, he went to Vienna in 1873. In the following year, he undertook longer trips abroad, to Obstend and Paris, for personal motives. Upon returning to Warsaw in 1875, Sienkiewicz became acquainted with the famous Polish actress Helena Modjeska and her circle of friends. It was within this circle that the utopian idea of founding a Polish Socialist community in California was first proposed. Both Sienkiewicz and Modjeska had personal reasons for wishing to leave Poland—an unhappy love affair on his part

and a weariness with the backstage intrigues of the theater world on hers. The worsening political situation in Poland, moreover, made the prospect of leaving the country doubly attractive. When their plan was made public, the *Gazeta Polska* commissioned Sienkiewicz to write a series of articles devoted to his impressions of the New World. He therefore set out in advance of the main party, which was to include Modjeska and her husband as well as her teenage son from a previous marriage.

Less than a month after he left Liverpool for New York, Sienkiewicz had crossed the continent and arrived in San Francisco on March 16, 1876. After a brief stay, he moved on to Southern California and eventually chose a site near Anaheim as the best location for the colony. Modjeska and her small party arrived in September, 1876. The project ran into difficulties almost immediately, owing largely to the group's collective inexperience with the methods of farming, and was abandoned after only a few months. Modjeska thereupon decided to resume her former vocation. Unlike Sienkiewicz, she chose to remain abroad and managed to have a successful stage career in the United States as well as in Great Britain, where she fulfilled her lifelong ambition to play Shakespearean roles in English in the Bard's own country. Her son, Ralph Modjeski, went on to become one of the foremost bridge engineers in the United States and culminated his career by serving as the chairman of the board of consulting engineers for the San Francisco-Oakland Bay Bridge that was completed in 1936.

After a lengthy sojourn in France and Italy, Sienkiewicz returned to Poland in April, 1879, and gradually assumed his activities as a journalist. The two years spent in the United States were by no means unproductive with respect to his literary development. His impressions of the United States were published in *Gazeta Polska* on a regular basis from 1876 to 1877. In addition, the American experience provided Sienkiewicz with the material for a number of short stories whose locale is the American West—most of which, however, were written after his return to Europe. While still in California, he also wrote a group of satiric sketches about rural life in Poland that was originally published in installments by the *Gazeta Polska* and that now constitutes the novel entitled *Szkice węglem* (charcoal sketches). Inspired by the tenets of positivism, this work depicts events in a benighted Polish village whose plight, the author intimates, stems ultimately from the indifference of the local gentry toward the welfare of the peasants, whose recent emancipation has left them totally unprepared to cope with the ensuing changes in their way of life. A clear signal that Sienkiewicz was already turning away from the doctrines of positivism may, however, be seen in the short story called "Niewola Tatarska" (1880; "Tartar Captivity," 1897). Here he offers his readers a chivalric account of life in the Old Polish Commonwealth that ran counter to the negative assessments of the positivist historians and their allies in the literary establishment. Critical disapproval notwithstanding, the general public was delighted.

On August 18, 1881, Sienkiewicz married an attractive young lady named Maria Szetkiewicz who was known to have a tubercular condition. Despite the chronic illness of his wife, he was to find great happiness in this brief marriage. A son, Henryk Józef, was born in July, 1882; a daughter, Jadwiga, in December, 1883. Maria's health took a sudden turn for the worse shortly thereafter, and she died on October 19, 1885. Throughout this entire period, so full of joy and sorrow, Sienkiewicz somehow managed to maintain a productive professional life both as a journalist and as a writer of fiction. Not long after his marriage, he accepted an appointment as editor of a newly founded Warsaw daily called *Słowo*. At the same time, he engaged in extensive historical research in preparation for writing a series of three novels based on the military upheavals in seventeenth century Poland. The project was to take him six years to complete.

With Fire and Sword, the first volume in the trilogy, was published in installments in *Słowo* as well as in the Krakow newspaper *Czas*. Sienkiewicz was thus able to reach readers in both the Russian and the Austrian occupied areas of Poland. The next two volumes, *The Deluge* and *Pan Michael*, were serialized simultaneously, not only in Warsaw and Krakow but

also in Poznan—the largest city in the Polish territories annexed by Germany. There it was published by *Dziennik Poznański*. This arrangement had the advantage of allowing the author to receive three separate royalty payments. When subsequently published in book form, each of these works became a bestseller. Now that he had become the most popular writer in Poland, Sienkiewicz resigned the post of editor for *Słowo* in 1887.

In his next two novels, Sienkiewicz returned to the contemporary scene. The first, *Without Dogma*, constitutes an attack on *fin de siècle* decadence. The novel is written in diary form, and its hero is a highly cultivated aristocrat who is completely unproductive and purposeless, owing to his intellectual incapacity to believe in anything whatsoever. The second novel, *Children of the Soil*, is considerably more positive in tone. Its protagonist, a member of a family named Polaniecki, is a philistine businessman of noble ancestry who, despite his numerous shortcomings, manages to advance the welfare of his own family as well as that of his countrymen.

Both of these novels were received more warmly abroad than in Poland. Polish readers apparently desired additional historical romances from the undisputed master of this genre, and Sienkiewicz duly responded to the public's wishes with his next novel. Its topic, however, caught his readers by surprise. Instead of another work based on Polish history, Sienkiewicz chose to re-create the events surrounding the persecution of Christians in Rome during the reign of the emperor Nero. He did, however, return to the realm of Polish history in his succeeding novel, a work published in 1900 whose title has been variously translated as *The Knights of the Cross* and *The Teutonic Knights*. Like the trilogy itself, each of these historical novels proved to be enormously successful with the readership in Poland. *Quo Vadis*, moreover, went on to become an unprecedented international favorite and was eventually translated into more than thirty different languages.

Sienkiewicz's devoted admirers looked forward to honoring him on the twenty-fifth anniversary of his literary debut. Strictly speaking, this commemoration should have taken place in 1898, but Sienkiewicz himself requested that it be postponed until 1900 so that it would not interfere with the centennial celebrations to be held in homage of the poet Adam Mickiewicz, who was born in 1798. On the occasion of his own jubilee, Sienkiewicz was presented with a small estate which was purchased from donations made by the public at large. The estate, called Oblegorek, was situated approximately one hundred miles due south of Warsaw near the city of Kielce.

On May 5, 1904, Sienkiewicz married a distant relative named Maria Babska, who was herself a writer. The marriage seems to have been contracted in a spirit of deep friendship rather than one of passionate love, but the arrangement provided Sienkiewicz with a comfortable domestic environment. In the following year, the Swedish Academy selected him to be the recipient of the Nobel Prize in Literature. It is, however, ironic that at the time he became a Nobel laureate, his creative powers were already on the wane. Although he continued to write, his only true success thereafter was a work of children's literature entitled *In Desert and Wilderness*, in which an English girl and a Polish boy, having been abducted from their parents, undergo an unending chain of adventures in Egypt and the Sudan.

The outbreak of World War I interrupted Sienkiewicz's work on a novel dealing with the fate of the Polish legions that formed an important part of the Grande Armée of Napoleon during the ill-fated invasion of Russia in 1812. Moving from Oblegorek to Vevey in neutral Switzerland, Sienkiewicz abandoned his literary activities in order to serve as chairman of the Central Swiss Committee for Victims of War in Poland. This organization, whose chief sponsor was the Polish pianist and composer Ignacy Jan Paderewski, succeeded in raising large sums of money to alleviate the suffering of their compatriots back in war-torn Poland. On November 15, 1916, Sienkiewicz died of arteriosclerosis and thus was denied the privilege of witnessing the restoration of Polish independence in the aftermath of the Allied victory over the Central Powers in 1918. In the fall of 1924, however, his ashes were transferred from Switzerland to Poland and interred in the crypt of Saint John's Cathedral in Warsaw. This church, although subsequently rebuilt, was totally destroyed by the Germans in the fall of 1944 as part of their punitive demolition of the city of Warsaw after the failure of the uprising of the Polish Home Army. Even though Poland subsequently fell under Communist domination, Sienkiewicz continues to remain one of the official cultural heroes of his nation, and the dissemination of his writings is actively promoted today throughout the People's Republic of Poland.

ANALYSIS

Some degree of familiarity with Polish history is essential for an appreciation of Henryk Sienkiewicz's *The Knights of the Cross* and the three novels that form the trilogy. Most translators of these works have, accordingly, provided extensive historical introductions for the benefit of the uninitiated reader. With respect to *The Knights of the Cross*, the most useful introduction is surely the one written by Alicia Tyszkiewicz to accompany the translation which she published in 1943 under the title *The Teutonic Knights*. Those about to embark on a reading of this work in any one of its various translations may also find an exceptionally clear survey of medieval Polish history in the third chapter of James Michener's bestselling novel *Poland* (1983).

THE KNIGHTS OF THE CROSS

Because of the wedge-shaped black crosses embroidered on their white mantles, the members of the Order of Teutonic Knights were always referred to by the Poles as *krzyżacy*, or Knights of the Cross. (The term *krzyżacy* is derived from *krzyż*, the Polish word for "cross," and its literal meaning is "those of the cross.") This order was founded in Palestine around 1190, during the Third Crusade. Thirty-five years after its founding, it was formally invited by Duke Conrad of Mazovia, in an act of utter folly, to settle along the eastern shores of the Baltic Sea. Its official mission was to subdue a heathen people called the Prussians, who were closely related to the Lithuanians both culturally and linguistically. The Teutonic Knights succeeded in subduing the Prussian tribes within fifty years, chiefly by following a policy of extermination, and then sought to expand their realm at the expense of the Lithuanians under the pretext of spreading Christianity to this still-pagan people. They also turned on their Polish hosts, despite the fact that Poland had already converted to Christianity in the tenth century. An alliance between the Kingdom of Poland and the Grand Duchy of Lithuania was clearly in the interests of both countries, and in 1386 the Polish Queen Jadwiga and the Lithuanian Grand Duke Jagiełło were wed. Both nations were thus joined in a personal union. As one of the conditions for his elevation to the Polish throne, Jagiełło agreed to abandon paganism and to impose Christianity on his Lithuanian subjects.

The inevitable confrontation with the Teutonic Knights occurred on the morning of July 15, 1410, when a combined force of 46,000 Poles, Lithuanians, and assorted allies joined battle with 32,000 of the enemy on the fields near the little village of Grunwald in East Prussia. By day's end, half of the Teutonic Knights lay dead and the other half were in captivity. Although the Order continued to exist until it was secularized in the aftermath of the Protestant Reformation, its power to expand had been effectively checked. The victory of Poland and Lithuania at Grunwald was the subject of one of the most famous historical paintings by the Polish artist Jan Matejko (1838-1893). How deeply the crushing defeat of the Teutonic Order continued to rankle the sensitivity of the Germans over the succeeding centuries may be inferred from the concerted effort made by the Nazis to locate the whereabouts of this huge canvas after their conquest of Poland in September, 1939.

Prior to this date, Matejko's painting had been the centerpiece of the collection housed in the Polish National Art Museum in Warsaw. Fearing for its destruction at the hands of the Germans, the curator had the canvas removed from its frame and rolled up so that it could fit into a crate made of solid oak. This crate was then placed in a concrete vault five feet underground at a secret location in eastern Poland. The German authorities offered a reward of two million Reichsmarks (a sum equivalent to $750,000 in terms of the currency exchange rates in effect at that time) as well as safe passage out of Poland to a neutral country to anyone who would reveal the location of Matejko's painting. Today the Grunwald picture is on permanent display in the fortified medieval castle at Marienburg that was built by the Teutonic Knights to serve as their central administrative headquarters. Marienburg, moreover, reverted to its previous Polish name of Malbork at the end of World War II.

Sienkiewicz's *The Knights of the Cross* has the Battle of Grunwald as its climax and may be considered the literary counterpart of Matejko's renowned historical canvas. Parts of the book were, in fact, read publicly by Sienkiewicz himself while standing beside the painting that had been his constant inspiration in the course of writing the novel. In addition to presenting a graphic description of the battle itself, Sienkiewicz offers his readers a brilliant pageant of medieval society as it existed in northeastern Europe around 1400. The cast of characters is predominantly fictive, but there are a few historical figures in the novel. King Jagiełło and Queen Jadwiga, however, play relatively minor roles. The historical figures and the fictive characters, it should be noted, function independently of each other for the most part. Neither of these groups plays a significant role in determining the fortunes of the other.

The fictive plot which runs parallel to the historical events described in the novel centers on a young Polish knight, Zbyszko, and his relationship with two women. He falls in love with a delicate beauty named Danusia and marries her. At the same time, he maintains a strong friendship with Jagienka, a warrior maiden who is very much like him in terms of robust health and vivacious demeanor. Danusia, who happens to be the daughter of the powerful Polish magnate Jurand, is kidnapped by members of the Teutonic Order shortly after her marriage to Zbyszki in an attempt to wrest political concessions from her father. While in captivity, Danusia is mistreated to such a degree that she dies directly following her rescue by Zbyszko. After a long period of mourning, Zbyszko decides to marry Jagienka, who really should have been his first choice in matrimony from the outset. As for Jurand himself, he, too, falls into the clutches of the Teutonic Knights and is subjected to bestial treatment. Sometime after his release, his erstwhile tormentors become his prisoners. Instead of avenging himself by retaliating in kind, Jurand chooses to pardon them. In this way, Sienkiewicz is underscoring his belief that the Polish gentry had more affinity with the ideals of Christianity than did the monks belonging to the Order of the Teutonic Knights. The degree of haughtiness, cruelty, and lust for power attributed to the Teutonic Knights by Sienkiewicz might once have appeared somewhat excessive, but the traumatic events that occurred in Poland and in much of Eastern Europe in the course of World War II have done much to enhance the plausibility of his portrayal.

The alliance between the Kingdom of Poland and the Grand Duchy of Lithuania that made the victory at the Battle of Grunwald possible was to continue over the next two centuries, despite many periods of acute political tension. In 1569, moreover, the two countries agreed to a charter, known as the Union of Lublin, that united them in a single political entity called the Polish Commonwealth. The Commonwealth was a multinational state whose territories extended from the Baltic Sea in the north to the Black Sea in the south. In addition to incorporating the Poles and the Lithuanians within its borders, the Commonwealth comprised large numbers of Byelorussians, Ukrainians, Cossacks, and Tartars. The viability of such an oddly constituted state was put to the test in the seventeenth century through a series of domestic insurrections and foreign invasions, and it is these trials that furnish the historical background for the works that form Sienkiewicz's trilogy.

The central event in each of these three novels involves the heroic defense of a Polish city that is under siege by the enemy. The historical incidents depicted in the trilogy span a period of approximately twenty-five years. Each novel covers a different war and takes place in a different part of the Commonwealth. The first volume, *With Fire and Sword*, deals with the Cossack rebellion in the Ukraine between the years 1647 and 1649. The second volume, *The Deluge*, tells the story of the Swedish attempt to add Poland to the personal domain of the Swedish king, Charles Gustavus, in the mid-1660's. The third volume, *Pan Michael*, although beginning with the year 1669, focuses on the struggles with the Turks and the

Tartars during the years 1672 and 1673. Many of the characters that are introduced in *With Fire and Sword* reappear in the successive novels of the trilogy. Some personages that make their first appearance in *The Deluge* are, likewise, carried over into the plot of *Pan Michael*. A major character in one novel may be demoted to playing a minor role in another, and the reverse may also occur. The fictive and the historical figures in the trilogy, it should be noted, interact far more than is the case in *The Knights of the Cross*.

WITH FIRE AND SWORD

The historical events that constitute the narrative framework of Sienkiewicz's *With Fire and Sword* occurred in the course of the Polish-Cossack wars that were waged on the steppes of the Ukraine. Under the inspired leadership of Bohdan Chmielnicki, the Cossacks initially scored a number of impressive victories over Polish forces. The long-suffering Ukrainian peasants, sensing an opportunity to throw off the yoke of foreign oppression, joined the Cossacks and began a savage massacre of Polish landowners and Catholic clergy. Jews also perished by the tens of thousands, because they usually served as administrators and overseers on the Polish estates.

Retribution on the part of Poland came in the person of a powerful prince named Jarema Wiśniowiecki, whose army checked the advances of the Cossacks and restored Polish authority over large sections of the Ukraine. Both Chmielnicki and Prince Jarema play major roles in the plot of *With Fire and Sword*. As portrayed in the novel, the Polish commander is a man of noble character whose courage and patriotism are largely responsible for his nation's triumph over the Cossacks and their Tartar auxiliaries. Sienkiewicz does, however, permit this hero's virtue to be tested. As a result of his military successes in the Ukraine, Prince Jarema soon found himself in a position to make the entire region subservient to his personal rule and was sorely tempted to sacrifice his country's interests for the sake of his own private ambitions. Midway through the novel, Prince Jarema engages in a debate with his conscience that takes the form of a lengthy monologue which he delivers while kneeling beneath a crucifix during a nocturnal prayer vigil. As dawn breaks, he resolves to remain loyal to the Commonwealth, even though he disapproves of many of its policies pertaining to the suppression of the insurrection in the Ukraine.

Despite the prominence of the historical figures in *With Fire and Sword*, they do not overshadow the fictive characters and their private adventures. The most memorable fictive personality in the novel is an old warrior named Zagloba, whose droll appearance and ribald speech have led critics to categorize him as the Polish Falstaff. Zagloba's antics provide much welcome comic relief in a novel filled with grim scenes. The chief nonfactual narrative involves a love triangle. Jan Skrzetuski, an adjutant of Prince Jarema, falls in love with an orphaned princess named Helena. The two soon agree to marry, but a Cossack officer named Bogun abducts Helena in the hope of persuading her to become his own bride. She is eventually rescued by Jan's loyal retainer Jendzian. Before the two lovers can be reunited, however, the city of Zbaraż is besieged by thousands of Cossacks and Tartars. Prince Jarema is in charge of the small Polish garrison within the city and finally decides to let Jan make an attempt to slip through enemy lines in order to summon aid from the Polish king, Jan Kazimierz. The royal army is duly dispatched, and the heroic defenders of Zbaraż are at last relieved after having withstood the determined attacks of Chmielnicki's troops for more than six weeks.

The decisive victory over the Cossacks did not occur until two years later, at the Battle of Beresteczko (1651), and Sienkiewicz skips over the intervening period to give his readers an account of this crucial confrontation in the final chapter of the novel. Bogun is among the Cossack prisoners who are taken at Beresteczko, and Prince Jarema turns him over to Jan for punishment. Jan, who married Helena after the siege of Zbaraż had been lifted, chooses to be magnanimous in victory and pardons the Cossack officer.

THE DELUGE

The next two novels in the trilogy have a narrative structure similar to that employed in *With Fire and Sword*. Both feature fictive love triangles in which the heroine is first abducted and then rescued. The chief historical figure in *The Deluge* is a Polish het-

man named Stefan Czarniecki, whose tireless energy and soldierly talent contributed greatly to the ultimate expulsion of the Swedish invaders from the territory of the Commonwealth. He did not, however, participate in the key military engagement of the Swedish-Polish conflict: namely, the defense of the fortified Pauline monastery of Jasna Góra (Bright Hill). Jasna Góra, which is located within the city of Czestochowa, was founded in 1382. Two years later, it came into possession of an icon depicting the Virgin Mary and the infant Jesus that is reputed to have been painted by Saint Luke the Evangelist. (This work is now referred to as the Black Madonna because of the dark hue that distinguishes the face and hands of each subject.) When the Polish garrison within the monastery put up a heroic defense and finally forced the Swedes to lift the siege and depart, the credit for this signal victory was assigned to the miraculous powers of the icon itself. Believing themselves to be under the special protection of the Virgin Mary, the Polish people took heart and rallied to the nation's cause.

PAN MICHAEL

In contrast, the siege of Kamieniec that is depicted in the closing chapters of *Pan Michael* ends in a defeat for the Polish defenders and a triumph for the Turkish invaders. The eponymous hero of the novel is a fictive personage named Pan Michael Wołodyjowski. (The designation "Pan" is a polite form of address in Polish that is analogous to the use of "Mister" and "Sir" in English.) Rather than surrender to the Turks, he chooses to perish in the ruins of the city when it is finally overrun. The novel, nevertheless, ends on a positive note, because among those who attend the ceremony accompanying Pan Michael's interment in a nearby monastery church is the hetman Jan Sobieski, the future king of Poland who was destined to lead a contingent of twenty thousand Polish soldiers to fight against the Turkish forces that were besieging the city of Vienna in the summer of 1683. Sienkiewicz himself was later to write a novel with Jan Sobieski as its protagonist, entitled *On the Field of Glory*. This novel proved to be a great disappointment to almost everyone, for Sienkiewicz inexplicably failed to depict the victory at Vienna and chose to restrict himself to relating events that occurred during the winter of 1682-1683.

QUO VADIS

Quo Vadis, like the other historical novels by Sienkiewicz, has a cast of fictive and historical personages. This time, however, the non-Polish reader is on familiar ground with respect to the historical background, because the work is set in ancient Rome circa A.D. 64. Among the well-known figures are the Apostles Peter and Paul as well as Nero and Petronius. Petronius was the author of the Satyricon (first century A.D.) and enjoyed the reputation of being the arbiter of elegance throughout Rome. He was also a great favorite of the Emperor Nero, who made him the director of entertainment at his court. It is his fictive nephew, Vinicius, who falls in love with a foreign princess named Lygia. (Her name indicates that she belongs to the tribe known as the Lygians, who inhabited the heartland of Poland in ancient times.) Lygia, it soon becomes known, is a member of the clandestine Christian community in Rome. Vinicius makes several attempts to obtain Lygia's sexual favors by force, but he is foiled each time by Christians who take it upon themselves to watch out for Lygia's welfare. As he gets to know the Christians and their doctrines better, Vinicius finds himself gradually transformed into an adherent of the teachings of Jesus. Now that they share a common faith, Lygia agrees to marry Vinicius. The couple's plans, however, are interrupted by the persecution of Christians that began in the aftermath of the fire which destroyed Rome.

Nero decides to put Rome to the torch in the hope that this personal experience with catastrophe will enable him to compose an immortal epic poem celebrating the city's destruction. In order to divert suspicion from himself, he subsequently accuses the Christians of having set the fires and has them hunted down all over Rome. Petronius does his best to dissuade the Emperor, but to no avail. Both Saint Peter and Saint Paul are to become martyrs on the same day. At first, Saint Peter attempts to escape the persecutions that are decimating his followers by fleeing from Rome along the Appian Way. Before long, he sees a radiant figure coming toward him whom he recognizes as Jesus and asks, "Quo vadis, Domine?" ("Where are you

going, Master?"). Jesus replies, "If you desert my people, I am going to Rome to be crucified a second time." Thoroughly ashamed of his moral weakness, Saint Peter turns about and retraces his steps. Back in Rome, he himself is crucified. Lygia, for her part, narrowly escapes martyrdom. After being arrested and imprisoned, she is stripped of her clothing and tied to the back of a huge bull that is released into the arena. Her faithful servant, a giant named Ursus, manages to break the bull's neck with his bare hands. The spectators are so overwhelmed by the feat that they insist on freedom for both Lygia and Ursus. Lygia then joins Vinicius in an escape to Sicily. Having lost the favor of Nero for his defense of the Christians, Petronius is obliged to commit suicide at the request of Nero—an act which he performs with great style at a banquet held in his home. Sienkiewicz concludes the novel with a brief epilogue in which Nero's own suicide is depicted in a manner that underscores the cowardly nature of the Emperor.

All of Sienkiewicz's historical novels are primarily works in which action is stressed at the expense of psychological development of character. The fact that each of them was first serialized in a periodical greatly influenced the structure of the narrative, for Sienkiewicz felt obliged to conclude every installment with an episode that kept the reader in suspense. The historical accuracy of these works has been the subject of considerable debate. Some historians defend their accuracy; others find fault with it. No one, however, has ever accused Sienkiewicz of failing to research his topic thoroughly or of neglecting to include sufficient data within the novels themselves. More important is the fact that Sienkiewicz possessed the narrative skills and the stylistic gifts needed to create works which quicken the spirit and comfort the heart.

Victor Anthony Rudowski

OTHER MAJOR WORKS

SHORT FICTION: *Yanko the Musician and Other Stories*, 1893 (includes "Yanko the Musician" and "The Lighthouse Keeper of Aspinwall"); *Lillian Morris and Other Stories*, 1894; *Hania*, 1897 (includes "Tartar Captivity"); *Let Us Follow Him and*

Other Stories, 1898; *For Daily Bread and Other Stories*, 1898; *Sielanka: A Forest Picture and Other Stories*, 1898; *Life and Death and Other Stories*, 1904; *Tales*, 1931; *Western Septet: Seven Stories of the American West*, 1973.

NONFICTION: *Listy z Afryki*, 1891; *Listy z podróży do Ameryki*, 1876-1878 (serial), 1896 (book; *Portrait of America*, 1959).

BIBLIOGRAPHY

Coleman, Arthur Prudden and Marion Moor Coleman. *Wanderers Twain: Modjeska and Sienkiewicz: A View From California*. Chesire, Conn.: Cherry Hill Books, 1964. A useful study of the trip Henry Sienkiewicz and Helena Modjeska made to Anaheim, California, in 1876. Most useful for the student of Sienkiewicz's fiction are the early chapters on his early years in Poland.

Giergielewicz, Mieczyslaw. *Henryk Sienkiewicz*. New York: Twayne, 1968. This introductory volume properly begins with a section on historical background, since Sienkiewicz's fiction is tied so closely to the fate of Poland and of Central Europe in the eighteenth and nineteenth centuries. There are also chapters on his life, his experience as a journalist, his tales, and his epic novels. Includes a chronology, notes, and an annotated bibliography.

_____. *Henryk Sienkiewicz: A Biography*. New York: Hippocrene, 1991. An excellent source for information on Sienkiewicz's life and times.

Krzyanowski, Jerzy R. "Sienkiewicz's Trilogy in America." *The Polish Review* 41 (1996): 337-49. A good example of well informed scholarship on Sienkiewicz's fiction.

Lednicki, Waclaw. *Henryk Sienkiewicz: A Retrospective Synthesis*. The Hague: Mouton, 1960. Lednicki met the novelist on several occasions and uses his personal experience of the author to provide insightful and well balanced comments on Sienkiewicz's significance.

Modjeska, Helena. *Memories and Impressions: An Autobiography*. New York: Macmillan, 1910. The actress who accompanied Sienkiewicz to Anaheim, California. She also knew the novelist in Warsaw, and she provides insight into his character and literary sensibility.

Phelps, William Lyon. *Essays on Modern Novelists*. New York: Macmillan, 1910. Although brief, Phelps's essay on Sienkiewicz is an excellent place to begin for an assessment of the novelist's place in world literature.

LESLIE MARMON SILKO

Born: Albuquerque, New Mexico; March 5, 1948

PRINCIPAL LONG FICTION
Ceremony, 1977
Almanac of the Dead, 1991
Gardens in the Dunes, 1999

OTHER LITERARY FORMS

Leslie Marmon Silko's first published book, *Laguna Woman* (1974), is a collection of poems. Her earliest published works were short stories, published in magazines, most of which were later included in *Storyteller* (1981). This book defies genre classification by including short fiction, poetry, retellings of traditional stories, and family photographs, all linked by passages of commentary and memoir. Her interest in images interacting with words led Silko to produce a film in 1980 with Dennis Carr entitled *Estoyehmuut and the Gunnadeyah* (Arrowboy and the Destroyers). In shooting the film at Laguna, New Mexico, using pueblo residents and elders instead of professional actors, Silko documented a time and place that no longer exist.

Silko's nonfiction works include *The Delicacy and Strength of Lace: Letters Between Leslie Marmon Silko and James Wright* (1986; edited by Ann Wright), and *Yellow Woman and a Beauty of the Spirit: Essays on Native American Life Today* (1996), a collection of essays. In *Sacred Water: Narratives and Pictures* (1993), she self-published her essay on water interwoven with her Polaroid photographs. The first edition was hand sewn and glued by Silko; a subsequent edition was conventionally bound.

ACHIEVEMENTS

The publication of Silko's first novel, *Ceremony*, along with N. Scott Momaday's winning of the 1969 Pulitzer Prize for *House Made of Dawn*, marked the beginning of a surge in publishing by Native American authors—the "Native American renaissance" of the late 1960's and early 1970's. Yet just as her works defy genre classification, Silko transcends the category of Native American writer. Her earlier works draw heavily on her own experiences and the traditional stories of Laguna Pueblo; later works move beyond the pueblo while maintaining a strong connection with the Southwest and with traditional and autobiographical materials. Her first two novels, *Ceremony* and *Almanac of the Dead*, are experimental in form, testing the limits of the novel as a genre and format. Indeed, Silko once said that she loves working in the novel form because its flexibility imposes so few limitations on the writer. Her third novel, *Gardens in the Dunes*, adheres more closely to conventional novel form, but like the previous two, it is highly political, reflecting Silko's activism.

Her books, particularly *Ceremony* and *Storyteller*, are widely taught in colleges and universities; her short fiction and poetry are widely anthologized. Her works have been translated into Italian and German and are popular internationally, both in translation and in the original English.

Silko's works in fiction, nonfiction, and poetry earned her a National Endowment for the Arts (NEA) Discover Grant (1971), *The Chicago Review* Poetry Award (1974), the Pushcart Prize for Poetry (1977); a MacArthur Prize Fellowship (1981); the *Boston Globe* prize for nonfiction (1986); a New Mexico Endowment for the Humanities "Living Cultural Treasure" Award (1988); and a Lila Wallace *Reader's Digest* Fund Writers Award (1991). Her story "Lullaby" was selected as one of twenty best short stories of 1975.

BIOGRAPHY

Leslie Marmon Silko was born to Leland (Lee) Howard Marmon and Mary Virginia Leslie in 1948. Her extended mixed-heritage family (Laguna, Mexican, white) had a rich history of tribal leadership and a rich tradition of storytelling. Growing up at Laguna Pueblo, Silko rode horses, hunted, and was free to explore the land of her ancestors, land that was inextricably tied to the traditional stories told by her aunts and grandmother.

In 1964 she entered the University of New Mexico. In 1966, she married Richard Chapman and gave birth to Robert William Chapman. During her sophomore year, she took a creative writing class. Despite the success of a short story written for that class, "The Man to Send Rainclouds," which was published first in *New Mexico Quarterly* and then in Kenneth Rosen's anthology of Native American writing as the title piece, Silko did not yet see herself primarily as a writer. After receiving her B.A. in 1969, she entered the University of New Mexico law school in the American Indian Law Fellowship program. During the same year, she separated from and eventually divorced Chapman.

In 1971, she left law school. Convinced that the American justice system was inherently unjust, and believing that her own role was to call attention to this injustice by telling stories, she entered graduate school in English at the University of New Mexico. She soon left to teach at Navajo Community College. During the same year, she married John Silko (whom she would also later divorce) and gave birth to her second child, Cazimir Silko.

Leaving the Southwest for the first time, Silko moved with her husband and children to Ketchikan, Alaska, in 1973. The impact of the Alaskan landscape and climate can be seen in her short story "Storyteller," written during this time, and it resurfaces in *Almanac of the Dead*. She also began writing *Ceremony* while in Alaska, re-creating her beloved southwestern landscape.

Silko returned to Laguna for a short time before moving to Tucson in 1978, where she taught at the University of Arizona. She eventually settled on a ranch outside Tucson, enjoying the physical labor of ranch life. In 1981, the year in which *Storyteller* was published, Silko was awarded the MacArthur Prize Fellowship. Sometimes called the "genius award," the MacArthur Prize provided five years of financial support, allowing her, for the first time, to devote all of her efforts to writing. While writing *Almanac of the Dead*, she became incensed about Arizona politics, leading her to paint a mural of a snake with political graffiti on the outside wall of her Stone Avenue office. Though later owners painted over the mural, it was well received by the people of the neighborhood and was important both in helping Silko (who describes herself as a "frustrated painter") to overcome writer's block and to develop further her technique of combining images with words. After the publication of *Almanac of the Dead* in 1991, Silko's desire for independence from the publishing world and her experiments with photography (in part inspired by her father, a professional photographer) led her to self-publish *Sacred Water: Narratives and Pictures*.

ANALYSIS

Leslie Marmon Silko once stated that she tries to write a very different book every time. Indeed, her novels are as different from one another as they are from her books in other genres. Despite such diversity, however, Silko's novels share certain common traits. All draw heavily on her personal experiences, but they are not conventionally autobiographical. Although only *Ceremony* deals exclusively with Native American themes and characters, Native American themes and characters are central in the other two novels as well.

Silko was so attuned to the political situation in northern Mexico that, in *Almanac of the Dead*, published two years before the Zapatista uprising in Chiapas, her description of an uprising in northern Mexico seems prophetic. Silko's work makes use of her eclectic reading on topics as diverse as the Gnostic gospels and orchid collecting.

Silko uses very little dialogue, yet her characters are richly drawn through the use of an omniscient narrator who reveals their inner thoughts and reactions. Her descriptions are vivid and detailed. Though predominantly serious, all of Silko's novels display her wry, ironic sense of humor. An important recurring theme in all of Silko's novels is the conflict between the "destroyers," those whose disregard for the land leads them to exploit it and its people for profit, and those who are in touch with and respect the land. Although those in touch with the land are usually the

indigenous people who have not separated themselves from nature, indigenous people can be destroyers, and whites can be in touch with the land.

CEREMONY

In *Ceremony*, Tayo, a young veteran of mixed Laguna and white ancestry, returns from World War II with what would now be called post-traumatic stress syndrome. When the Veterans Administration hospital sends him home to the pueblo uncured, his family asks the tribal healer, old Ku'oosh, to perform the traditional ceremony for reincorporating warriors into the community. The ceremony is only partially successful; Tayo is still deeply disturbed, blaming himself for his cousin and friend Rocky's death and turning to alcohol along with a group of friends who are also veterans. After a fight with his friend Emo, Tayo is sent back to the V.A. hospital, but his treatment is no more successful than it was the first time.

Betonie, a Navajo medicine man who uses unconventional methods, is more successful. He conducts a Navajo healing ceremony for Tayo that sets him on the road to recovery. When Tayo leaves, Betonie says that to complete the ceremony Tayo must recover the spotted cattle that Tayo and his Uncle Josiah had planned to raise but that had presumably wandered off in Tayo's absence after Josiah died. Tayo discovers that the cattle were stolen by white ranchers and realizes that he had believed the lie that only Indians and Mexicans stole because whites did not need to steal. With the help of Ts'eh, a mysterious woman who turns out to be the spirit of the sacred mountain, Tayo takes the cattle home.

Meanwhile, Emo has become one of the destroyers, a participant in witchery, and he convinces the rest of the group to cooperate in his plan to kill Tayo. Warned by Ts'eh, Tayo is able to resist the witchery. He returns home and tells his story to the elders in the kiva, who recognize Ts'eh as the spirit who brings rain and healing to their drought-stricken land. Tayo's separation from his community, in part caused by the war but also caused by his rejection as an illegitimate "half-breed," was symptomatic of a larger rift in the community. His healing demonstrates that things must change, that the new must be incorporated into the old, and that the "half-breed" can act as a mediator between the old traditions and the new world. Much of *Ceremony* is told in flashbacks. Traditional Laguna stories are woven throughout, set off from the text. The language is lyrical, and the message is of healing and conciliation.

ALMANAC OF THE DEAD

When Silko read from this novel at the time of its publication, she announced, "This book attempts to crush linear time." It succeeds by repeatedly shifting time frames. Silko interweaves an enormous cast of characters involved in multiple subplots. They tell the story, in an indeterminate time in the not-too-distant future, of a spontaneous uprising across the Americas of dispossessed indigenous people who move throughout the novel toward an apocalyptic convergence on Tucson, Arizona.

Lecha and Zeta are twins, mixed-blood Yaquis, who have been given pieces of an old Mayan book (the almanac of the title). Unlike the Mayan Codices, this book has stayed in the hands of the people. As they work to transcribe the pieces, they discover that the Mayans foretold the coming of the white European invaders—and foretold their demise as well. Seese, a young white woman whose baby has been kidnapped, consults Lecha, who is a psychic, and stays to work for her. Sterling, an old man who is exiled for revealing tribal secrets, also comes to work at the twins' ranch.

Other characters include Allegria, a mercenary architect, and her husband, Menardo, who live near Mexico City; the Tucson branch of the Blue family, mafiosi who dominate the Tucson real estate market; the Indian twin brothers Tacho and Wacah, who embody the mysterious power of twins and lead the people north toward Tucson; and Marxist Mexican revolutionaries Angelita (La Escapia) and El Feo. Their stories intertwine as they converge on Tucson, where the Barefoot Hopi warns that the familiar way of life on earth will end unless the destroyers change their ways and respect the earth. "Eco-warriors" to the north threaten a suicide bombing of a dam. The novel ends as all are poised on the brink of revolution.

GARDENS IN THE DUNES

In an unpublished interview, Silko described her third novel as "full of flowers and light." Set in the time immediately following the stock market crash of 1893, *Gardens in the Dunes* tells the story of Indigo and Sister Salt. The young sisters are the last of the Sand Lizards, a fictional tribe based loosely on the Colorado River tribes that were wiped out around the beginning of the twentieth century. After a Ghost Dance they are attending is raided by the police, the girls are separated from their mother as they flee. Later, their grandmother dies and Indigo is captured by the police. She is sent to boarding school in Riverside.

There she is befriended by Hattie and Edward, a wealthy couple who live near the school. Before marrying Edward, Hattie attended Harvard University until her unconventional thesis proposal on the Gnostic gospels was rejected. Edward is a professional plant collector who sells rare specimens to wealthy buyers. They take Indigo along on their European trip during the school's summer break. Indigo sees the Jesus of the European churches as another manifestation of Wovoka, the prophet of the Ghost Dance. Edward's scheme to steal citron cuttings fails; Hattie, disgusted by his greed, divorces him and vows to help Indigo find her family.

Meanwhile, Sister Salt is befriended by Big Candy, who fathers her baby, the "little black grandfather." When Big Candy's preoccupation with wealth causes him to neglect Sister Salt and the baby, she and the Chemehuevi twins leave to farm land that the twins acquired from an aunt. The sisters are reunited, returning to the old gardens. Indigo plants the seeds and bulbs she collected on her journey, mixing the impractical but beautiful flowers with the traditional food crops. As in earlier works, Silko emphasizes the need to live in harmony with the land, the dangers of capitalism, and the need to use the new along with the old.

Robin Payne Cohen

OTHER MAJOR WORKS

SHORT FICTION: *Yellow Woman*, 1993.

PLAY: *Lullaby*, pr. 1976 (with Frank Chin).

POETRY: *Laguna Woman*, 1974.

NONFICTION: *The Delicacy and Strength of Lace: Letters Between Leslie Marmon Silko and James*

Wright, 1986; *Sacred Water: Narratives and Pictures*, 1993; *Yellow Woman and a Beauty of the Spirit: Essays on Native American Life Today*, 1996.

MISCELLANEOUS: *Storyteller*, 1981 (includes prose and poetry).

BIBLIOGRAPHY

Allen, Paula Gunn. *The Sacred Hoop: Recovering the Feminine in American Indian Traditions*. Boston: Beacon Press, 1986. In the chapter entitled "The Feminine Landscape of Leslie Marmon Silko's *Ceremony*," Allen traces the traditional origins of the novel's female characters, illuminating their symbolism.

Coltelli, Laura. *Winged Words*. Lincoln: University of Nebraska Press, 1990. A collection of interviews with Native American authors. The interview with Silko gives insight into her experiences and influences in writing *Almanac of the Dead* in addition to reviewing her earlier work.

Owens, Louis. *Other Destinies: Understanding the American Indian Novel*. Norman: University of Oklahoma Press, 1992. 167-191. In the chapter entitled "The Very Essence of Our Lives: Leslie Silko's Webs of Identity," Owens analyzes *Ceremony* as a search for identity through memory and returning home.

Salyer, Greg. *Leslie Marmon Silko*. New York: Twayne, 1997. A useful overview of Silko's life and work prior to *Gardens in the Dunes*. Good chronology and bibliography.

Studies in American Indian Literatures (*SAIL*) 2, no. 10. Fall, 1998. Special issue on *Almanac of the Dead*. Includes excellent essays as well as Ellen Arnold's interview, in which Silko discusses *Gardens in the Dunes*.

IGNAZIO SILONE
Secondo Tranquilli

Born: Pescina dei Marsi, Italy; May 1, 1900
Died: Geneva, Switzerland; August 22, 1978

PRINCIPAL LONG FICTION

Fontamara, 1930, 1933, rev. 1958 (English translation, 1934, rev. 1960)
Pane e vino, 1937, rev. 1955 (as *Vino e pane*; first pb. as *Brot und Wein*, 1936; *Bread and Wine*, 1936, rev. 1962)
Il seme sotto la neve, 1942 (first pb. as *Der Samen unterm Schnee*, 1941; *The Seed Beneath the Snow*, 1942)
Una manciata di more, 1952 (*A Handful of Blackberries*, 1953)
Il segreto di Luca, 1956 (*The Secret of Luca*, 1958)
La volpe e le camelie, 1960 (*The Fox and the Camellias*, 1961)

OTHER LITERARY FORMS

While known primarily for his novels, Ignazio Silone also wrote short stories, sketches, essays, and plays. The essays and plays are considered to be among his finest works. Silone's essays are, for the most part, autobiographical in character and apologetic in tone. His most famous essay, "Uscita di sicurezza" ("Emergency Exit," which first appeared in English in 1949), was published in Italian in 1951. The essay recounts the author's personal odyssey from early allegiance to the Communist Party, through his opposition to the Fascist regime in Italy and eventual exile in Switzerland, to a dramatic break with the Italian Socialist Party in the years following the reestablishment of democracy. Despite its intention to defend the author's controversial political stances, the essay is free of polemical rhetoric and is distinguished by the simple and direct manner of expression which marks the style of Silone's novels as well. This essay also appeared in 1965 in a collection with the same name.

The plays, though they often employ the same themes as the novels, lack their dramatic intensity and complex symbolic development. *La scuola dei dittatori* (1938; *The School for Dictators*, 1938), a satire, seems foreign to the usual tone of Silone's work. *Ed egli si nascose* (1944; *And He Did Hide Himself*, 1946), which elaborates a single strand of the plot of the novel *Bread and Wine*, falls short of the latter work's rendering of the complexities of human relationships. *L'avventura di un povero cris-*

tiano (1968; *The Story of a Humble Christian*, 1971), the last work of the Silone canon, comes closest to realizing the dramatic promise of its form. This may perhaps be explained by the extraordinary traits of its hero, Pope Celestine V, whose unprecedented gesture of renouncing his position makes him a particularly engaging and enigmatic figure. Silone has used the inherently intriguing features of his central character to great advantage in this, his final play. Yet all of his plays seem less than perfectly suited to the demands of theatrical production and may with some justice be accurately described as prose narratives cast in dialogue form.

One of the most notable features of Silone's fiction is his near-indifference to the technical experimentation that has characterized much of twentieth century European fiction. He confessed that during the earlier years of his literary career, he was little interested in aesthetics, and he has been widely criticized on this point, yet a study of the entire corpus of his works reveals that he was increasingly concerned with the formal demands of his art, a fact exemplified by his decision to revise and reissue versions of three of his earlier novels in the 1960's. Silone often spoke of his novels as parables, a term which is well suited to the simplicity and clarity with which they present their themes and ideas. On balance, Silone's novels represent triumph of literary realism in an age that seems all too anxious to abandon this traditional perspective. His novels insist on the coordination of simple story, believable characters, and symbolic meaning. Perhaps the literary credo that lies behind this amalgam is suggested by the sentiments of the aged priest Don Benedetto in *Bread and Wine*. Truth, he remarks, always appears simple and crude when compared to the elegant veneer of hypocrisy. In these terms, Silone has consistently chosen the way of truth for his novels.

ACHIEVEMENTS

The most curious fact of Silone's literary reputation is that he has been highly regarded almost everywhere except in his native Italy. He received the honorary degree of doctor of letters from Yale, Toulouse, and Warwick universities and was a member of the

(Library of Congress)

French Légion d'Honneur, yet Silone has been severely criticized on both literary and political grounds by his countrymen.

Silone's political commitments and his devotion to literary realism place him at odds with the main currents of twentieth century Italian literature. Turning his back to the models of aestheticism, eroticism, and Hermetism, which have to a great extent dominated modern letters in Italy, he was determined to make of literature a means to awaken the social conscience of his contemporaries. Such an aim is likely to stir opposition and controversy, for it often requires touching the raw nerves of national pride. Silone's writings reflect an era of economic distress, political repression and instability, and military failure. Further, Silone was dedicated to examining the causes, effects, and remedies of this chaotic social scene through a vision of rural Italian life. This vision, with its constant reference to Abruzzi mountain villages, is anything but an appeal to the glory of twentieth century Italian culture: Silone's characters embody values antithetical to urban industrialized Italy. In this sense, he would seem to be quite reactionary, yet he does not propose a return to an idyllic past. The humble people of the land who populate his fiction are sometimes backward and unimaginative, and their dependence upon the past is often portrayed as a tremendous handicap. The fidelity to a simple code of compassion and personal integrity, which appealed so strongly to Silone, found its fullest expression in those characters that lived close to the land. The virtues of the Silone hero, be it Bernardo Viola, Pietro Spina, or Luca Sabatini, point not toward the past but toward a timeless world where, by a difficult and even dangerous sort of ascesis, the trials of life in an imperfect world may be endured if not overcome.

The choice of peasants to portray this set of values, the *cafoni* of the author's native Abruzzi, met with resistance from Italian literati; in a similar way, Silone's disavowal of political parties cost him the support of many partisan readers. By remaining faithful to his own understanding of the terms of an ageless and universal struggle for human dignity, Silone effectively abdicated the claim to literary ingenuity and political propriety which his own culture expected of him, yet the success with which he fashioned his universal message from the most provincial details of Italian life is indicated precisely by the acclaim given Silone outside his own land, where, though the *cafoni* he wrote about were total strangers, they were nevertheless recognized as authentic representations of heroic resistance to adverse fate and human injustice. It is this particularized portrayal of humankind's resilience and indomitability that constitutes Silone's greatest achievement.

BIOGRAPHY

Born Secondo Tranquilli in a village of the rugged Abruzzi region of central Italy, Ignazio Silone (a pseudonym he later used to protect his family from Fascist persecution) could never totally separate the image of its rugged topography from his view of human destiny. Again and again its mountains and valleys, as well as the harshness of life this terrain breeds, serve as the background for the struggles of his characters. The Abruzzi was a link between the medieval origins and the modern dilemmas of Italian culture, and the course of Silone's own life runs parallel to the region's emergence from a religious past into a secular and politicized present.

Partly because of poor health in his youth, Silone was educated close to home in religious schools, and though thoughts of entering the priesthood were abandoned rather early, he seems never to have forgotten the lessons of faith which were no doubt inculcated during this period of his life. He later referred to his commitment to Socialist causes as a matter of "faith," and the roots of this secular *via fidei* can be traced to the era of World War I, when Silone became the secretary of a syndicalist peasant movement, the Federation of Land Workers of the Abruzzi. The year 1917 found him in Rome, where he was again associated with liberal causes through his selection as secretary of the Socialist Youth of Rome. His career as political journalist began with editorial duties on the Socialist weekly *Avanguardia* in 1918, and by 1921, he was respected enough to be chosen as a delegate to the conference in Moscow which organized the Italian Communist Party. During the 1920's, Silone was a member of the Central Committee of the Italian Communist Party, but in 1930, he broke ties with the Party, feeling that its dogmatism and its dependence on Moscow's directives compromised the ideals he held for social reform in Italy. In the same year, three warrants for his arrest were issued by the Fascist Special Tribunal, and Silone fled to Switzerland, where he lived until the autumn of 1944, after the fall of the Fascists.

In these years of exile, Silone wrote a number of cultural and political essays, a play, and three novels, including what is perhaps his most famous work, *Bread and Wine*. Upon his return to Italy, he served as a member of the Italian Constituent Assembly from 1946 to 1948 and as a member of the Executive Committee of the Italian Socialist Party until 1947. In addition, he founded and edited the liberal journal *Tempo presente*. Silone's outspoken criticism of the postwar Italian Communist Party and its leader, Palmiro Togliatti, earned for him the wrath of many Italian intellectuals.

Having finally left the Italian Socialist Party, Silone maintained an independent political stance through the Cold War years, one that again put him at odds with other "committed" European writers. The Soviet invasion of Hungary in 1956 moved Silone to condemn both the Soviets and the Americans, the latter for failing to come to the aid of the Hungarian people. On this issue, he clashed sharply with Jean-Paul Sartre, and the two were never fully reconciled. Silone's fierce independence in political issues and in response to current affairs won for him no friends among Italian intellectuals, who sought, with considerable success, to exclude Silone from his country's political life after 1950. These same years of enforced isolation produced two highly acclaimed novels, *A Handful of Blackberries* and *The Secret of Luca*, as well as writings that eventually would appear in *Uscita di sicurezza* (1965; *Emergency Exit*, 1968), a retrospective volume of essays (which includes the previously released "Emergency Exit") on the writer's experiences before and during the Fascist years.

Judging by the tone of the works written in this latter phase of his literary career, Silone seems to have accepted his exclusion from public life with equanimity. There is a quiet dignity in both his public pronouncements and his writing which is impressive, a dignity not unlike that exhibited by many of the humble inhabitants of the Abruzzi who fill the pages of his fiction. Like Pope Celestine V in Silone's final work, the author appears to have been resigned to paying a price for fidelity to his own principles and beliefs.

The final measure of Silone's separation from the world of politics and public intellectual life is suggested by the poverty and the obscurity in which he died. His cremation was attended only by his wife of thirty-four years, Darina, by a single friend from Italy, and by a handful of consular officials and journalists.

Analysis

Although the literary canon of Ignazio Silone may be divided into several fairly distinct phases or periods, a number of themes and motifs serve to unite his works into a single vision of life. One of the most obvious of these is the use of Abruzzi villages as the setting for his fiction. A second common element is a fascination with the idea of the hero as a solitary figure who must strive to restore communion with his fellow human beings. Yet another may be found in the persistent motif of the hero's return to his native region, an experience that triggers a flood of ambivalent emotion in more than one Silone character. Finally, the symbolic role of women and the emphasis accorded to acts of self-sacrifice and renunciation also help to unify Silone's works. Taken together, these elements create a peculiarly Silonean frame of reference in which the vicissitudes of history and circumstance test the capacity of the human spirit to endure and prevail.

Fontamara

Fontamara, Silone's first novel, portrays the injustices suffered by a mountain village at the hands of the Fascist state. In one sense, the entire village is the hero of this work, with its collective sorrows and bewilderment serving as the focal point of the action. While the emphasis rests on this common tragedy, the novel also reveals its author's interest in the reactions of individuals caught up in the aggregate patterns of human fate. Thus, the fortunes of the village of Fontamara are interwoven with the private destiny of one of its sons, Bernardo Viola. Viola's hopes for a better life, a life enriched by love and freedom from poverty, are dashed on the rocks of the times in which he lives. Having journeyed to Rome to seek his fortune, Viola is betrayed by the false promise of urban life under Fascism and, upon hearing of the death of the woman he loves in Fontamara, he confesses to crimes he has not committed in order to allow a young revolutionary to go free.

Viola's personal sacrifice, though certainly noble, is less than redemptive as far as Fontamara is concerned. The young revolutionary who has been freed because of Viola's sacrifice makes his way to Fontamara and sets up a clandestine newspaper, which the villagers decide to call *What Must We Do?* When the authorities trace the paper to Fontamara, the village is attacked and many of its inhabitants murdered by Fascist militiamen. The few survivors are described at the end of the novel as asking the same question which had served as the title for their newspaper: "What can we do?" The novel thus closes on a highly ambiguous note, for the villagers' query is never answered. This ambiguity deepens the tragedy which befalls the village and Viola, who ends his own life in a jail cell. *Fontamara* thus portrays the defeat of human hope on both the collective and the individual level. It seems content with alerting its readers to the dangers of Fascism and to the tragic triumph of history over human desire. The bleakness of *Fontamara* presents a challenge to Silone's basic faith in the resilience of the human spirit, and it was only in his later works that he could clearly respond to the haunting question with which this early text ends.

BREAD AND WINE

In *Bread and Wine*, his second novel, Silone discovered resources upon which he could draw for the remainder of his literary career. These resources were both thematic and technical: The title of the novel suggests the power latent in the communion of humankind and the dynamics of literary symbols which point beyond the present moment to a better future.

Pietro Spina, the novel's hero, returns in disguise to his native Italy from exile in Belgium. Because he is still a hunted man, Spina assumes the identity of a priest and calls himself Paolo Spada. As a "priest" of the secular gospel of brotherhood and social reform, Spina feels himself bonded to the lives of the humble rural folk through breaking bread and drinking wine with them. As the plot progresses, the terms of this secular eucharist become more and more explicit, until in the episode of the funeral meal for a young Socialist, Luigi Murica, who has been killed by the Fascist authorities, the full meaning of the novel's title is revealed. The many grapes needed to make wine and the ears of grain necessary for the production of bread speak of the merging of individual human lives into a common identity. It is the strength of this new corporate identity that provides the hope that beyond the present misery lies a brighter future.

This dominant theme is even hinted at by the novel's time scheme, a span of approximately nine months, to which the period needed for the matura-

tion of grapes and grain and that alloted for human gestation correspond. The motif of gestation applies to subtle changes undergone by Spina himself during the novel. The limitations of his devotion to political principle are suggested by the hero's growing interest in people rather than in doctrine and by the episode of the apparent suicide of the embittered revolutionary Uliva in Rome. For belief in causes, Silone substitutes a compassion rooted in the experience of human solidarity. Lest the novel seem blindly optimistic, however, the fate of the old Don Benedetto, priest and teacher of Spina, is included. Don Benedetto attempts to maintain his faith and personal integrity in the face of the progressive corruption of Church and State and is finally murdered when he drinks poisoned sacramental wine while saying Mass. The figurative implications of the old priest's death mitigate the hope inspired by the novel's central image of communion by reminding the reader that wine also symbolizes blood, sorrow, and death.

In the novel's two most prominent women, Bianchina Girasole and Christina Colamartini, Silone presents both the two sides of human nature, body and soul, and a dual vision of Italy dominated by Fascism. Bianchina, a rural girl who eventually becomes a prostitute in Rome, represents the physical degradation endured by the oppressed Italian people. Christina, the daughter of an aristocratic old family, is devoured by wolves after following Spina into the mountains as he tried to escape capture by government authorities; her fate represents the death of the human spirit under Fascism. At the close of the novel, then, the promise of human solidarity suggested by the image of communion is imperiled. Spina's flight to the mountains may be read as an allusion to Moses on the mountain or Christ at Golgotha, but in fact the text of *Bread and Wine* is silent concerning his fate. This ambiguous closure, though it recalls the end of *Fontamara*, also transcends it, for Spina, unlike Viola, is still alive and thus may return to reestablish his communion with the peasants of the Abruzzi. For this reason, and for many others, *Bread and Wine* is a more satisfying and affirmative novel than *Fontamara*.

The Seed Beneath the Snow

The Seed Beneath the Snow is designed as a sequel to the message of *Bread and Wine*. It picks up the thread of Pietro Spina's story but does not address the question of what happened to him after his flight to the mountains. The reader knows only that Spina has survived and is searching for a means by which the promise of human solidarity may be sustained. As in the previous novel, the direction of this hope is implied by the metaphor of its title. The respect for the earth and agrarian life, which is implicit in Silone's earlier fiction, evolves into a complex reverence in *The Seed Beneath the Snow*. In addition to Spina, this novel focuses on two figures, each of whom is rather extraordinary. The first is "Aunt" Euremia, a strange old woman whose supposed wealth is coveted by the inhabitants of the village where she lives. She is a skewed version of Silone's image of Italy as woman, and her sexual indeterminacy suggests again the distorted nature of this nation under Fascism. The "wealth" of Euremia consists of chests full of her own excrement, which may be taken as another sign of the corruption of Italian culture.

The second figure is the village deaf-mute, Infante, whom Spina tries to teach to speak. The first word he attempts to have Infante pronounce is "manure," which provides a curious link with the figure of Euremia. In dedicating himself to Infante, Spina suppresses his love for Donna Faustina. This sacrifice seems to come to naught when Infante, who has murdered his own brutal father, must flee the village to avoid arrest. In one final, dramatic gesture of self-sacrifice, Spina himself confesses to the crime, and the novel ends with the police leading him away. The grand hope with which the novel began has thus been reduced to a single gesture of sacrifice, the value of which is at best questionable.

The "seed" of new life does not bear the sort of fruit that the reader might have expected from *The Seed Beneath the Snow*, but it does anticipate Silone's later interest in gratuitous gestures of self-sacrifice, which stand at the center of works such as *The Secret of Luca* and *The Story of a Humble Christian*. In a sense, *The Seed Beneath the Snow* brings to a close that phase of Silone's thought which emphasized a radical reordering of individual lives and of society according to the prophetic hope for political reform. Hereafter, Silone's hope is more circumscribed, focusing on gestures of the individual rather than grand movements which seek to change society as a whole.

A Handful of Blackberries

A Handful of Blackberries, published more than a decade after the appearance of *The Seed Beneath the Snow*, reveals the contours of Silone's new priorities. Its hero, Rocco de Donatis, returns to his native Abruzzi and becomes a leader in the local Communist Party. He gradually loses faith in its promises, however, as did the author himself at one point in his life, and turns instead to the twin virtues of love and endurance, the first exemplified by the refugee Jewess Stella, whom he marries, and the second by the figure of the old peasant Lazzaro. Lazzaro, whose name associates him with the Lazarus who was raised from death in the Bible, represents the new life, which has been the object of the quest of Silone's heroes since the novel *Bread and Wine*.

Metaphorically, Lazzaro is associated with that bread which sustains human hope, for he is at one point in the novel compared to a cart loaded with wheat in a starving village. In him, symbolically, the reader may see the fruit of the seed planted in the Pietro Spina novels. The figure of Lazzaro is also the embodied answer to the question posed at the end of *Fontamara*. What must be done is to root oneself in the enduring virtues of the earth itself, in its serene endurance and fruitfulness, drawing from it a sustenance more real than that provided by any commitment to abstract political ideals. The emblem of this simple manner of living is found in the novel's title: The handful of blackberries suggests a humble rural meal rather than a sacramental feast of bread and wine, and the modulated symbolic overtones of this new image are in keeping with the character of the final phase of Silone's works. Rocco de Donatis has adopted the virtues of Lazzaro's life as the novel ends; he is shown passing his days quietly in the company of friends while serving in a movement whose goal is to improve the lot of farm laborers. The same rhythms of provincial life, which seemed tantamount to imprisonment in *Fontamara*, lend to life its true worth in *A Handful of Blackberries*. Such is the transformation of thought that distinguishes Silone's final works.

THE SECRET OF LUCA

The culmination of the evolution of Silone's vision of life may be observed in his last major novel, *The Secret of Luca*. The plot of the novel centers on Andrea Cipriani, a young man recently released from prison after serving twelve years for anti-Fascist activities, and his attempt to understand the aged Luca Sabatini, who has also been released from prison after having spent forty years there for a crime he did not commit.

Both men return to the mountain village of Cisterna, and Cipriani begins his search for the truth behind Luca's refusal to testify in his own defense at his trial years earlier. The only other villager who seems at all concerned about Luca is the priest Don Serafino. The rest of the people seem to resent the old convict's very presence. Luca's secret involves his devotion to a woman whom he could never possess, and his suffering stems from his steadfast refusal to compromise her reputation. Here again is the act of gratuitous self-sacrifice, an act akin to Pietro Spina's confession to Infante's crime in *The Seed Beneath the Snow* and to Bernardo Viola's confession for the sake of the young revolutionary in *Fontamara*. Yet Luca's motives are purer than those of his precursors by just so much as love is superior to despair and desperation. In this novel, Silone seems to discern beauty and truth in two contradictory modes of human existence: the integrity of love and the enigma of sacrifice. In the case of Luca, these forms of truth intersect. The old man's virtue stands as a mute rebuke to the selfishness and pettiness of his fellow villagers, and they smart from it.

Luca stands as an emblem of the power of renunciation to purify the human spirit; in him, the reader can glimpse some of Silone's own willingness to sacrifice public acclaim to remain true to his principles in the latter part of his career. With Luca, as with Lazzaro in *A Handful of Blackberries*, Silone accomplished what he could not do with Pietro Spina, the hero of the first phase of his literary vision. These older men seem to have returned from the mountain having seen the promised land of social justice and

human dignity, which seems to have eluded Spina. They realize, as perhaps Spina did not, that the kingdom sought by the Silone hero, like the Kingdom of God in the Gospel of Luke, lies within the human spirit. The heroes of Silone's final works possess quiet and determined spirits, and these spirits produce the seeds of virtue that may be planted in the lives of those who recognize the Lucas and Lazzaros of this world. In this way only, spirit by spirit, can the field of human society bear the long-awaited harvest of brotherhood, which was the central concern of Silone's life and art.

REVISIONS

No discussion of Silone's writing would be complete without reference to the author's revision of his first three novels some twenty years after their original dates of publication. Silone commented that he wished to render these novels more enduring works of art by deleting elements which he felt in retrospect to be too subjective or dated. This impulse bears witness to Silone's development as an artist. The changes made in his works preserve their original thematic emphases for the most part. The structure of *Bread and Wine* is changed by the division of its plot into twenty-nine short chapters instead of the twelve of the earlier version, but the effect on the action is minimal. Of greater import is the suppression of the murder of the old priest Don Benedetto, a modification that relieves the darkened atmosphere of the novel's final chapters. The revisions of *Fontamara* and *A Seed Beneath the Snow* are of similar character and effect.

Perhaps the most suggestive remark contained in the author's "Note on the Revision of *Bread and Wine*" is the one dealing with the reversal of the words of the title from *Pane e vino* in 1937 to *Vino e pane* in 1955. Silone states that it is his impression that wine plays a larger role than bread in the new version of his novel. While his words may be taken in a number of ways, they certainly point to the author's sensitivity to the symbolic import of his writing. One possible reading of his emphasis on wine is that while *pane* could easily summon up thoughts of collectivist worker and peasant slogans from the 1930's, *vino* may more readily suggest the cup of personal destiny from which every human being must drink alone. Hence, Silone may be alluding once more to ascendency of the solitary hero in his later work.

Be this as it may, the author's note to the revised version of *Fontamara* contains a passage in which he compares himself to certain monks in the Middle Ages who spent their whole lives painting the figure of Christ over and over again. Like these monks, Silone's portrait of humankind becomes more delicate and finely detailed with each successive canvas. This devotion is another dimension of Silone's personal integrity. Never satisfied with seeing life darkly in the mirror of art, he constantly strove to create an image of truth beheld face-to-face.

Paul Reichardt

OTHER MAJOR WORKS

SHORT FICTION: *Mr. Aristotle*, 1935.

PLAYS: *La scuola dei dittatori*, pb. 1938 (*The School for Dictators*, 1938); *Ed egli si nascose*, pb. 1944 (*And He Did Hide Himself*, 1946); *L'avventura di un povero cristiano*, pb. 1968 (*The Story of a Humble Christian*, 1971).

NONFICTION: *Uscita di sicurezza*, 1965 (essays; *Emergency Exit*, 1968).

BIBLIOGRAPHY

Krieger, Murray. *The Tragic Vision: Variations on a Theme in Literary Interpretation*. New York: Holt, Rinehart and Winston, 1960. See chapter 3, section 2, "Ignazio Silone: The Failure of the Secular Christ." This a probing study of *Bread and Wine*.

Lewis, R. W. B. *The Picaresque Saint*. New York: Lipponcott, 1956. Contains one of the most perceptive and succinct essays on Silone.

Mooney, Harry J., Jr., and Thomas F. Staley, eds. *The Shapeless God: Essays on Modern Fiction*. Pittsburgh: University of Pittsburgh Press, 1968. See chapter 2, "Ignazio Silone and the Pseudonyms of God." This is chiefly a study of *Bread and Wine*, but there are illuminating references to Silone's other novels as well.

Origo, Iris. *A Need to Testify: Portraits of Lauro de Bosis, Ruth Draper, Gaetano Salvemini, Ignazio Silone and an Essay on Biography*. New York: Harcourt Brace Jovanovich, 1984. A penetrating portrait of the writer by a distinguished biographer. Includes notes but no bibliography.

Scott, Nathan A, Jr. *Rehearsals of Discomposure: Alienation and Reconciliation in Modern Literature: Franz Kafka, Ignazio Silone, D. H. Lawrence, T. S. Eliot*. New York: Columbia University Press, 1952. In "Ignazio Silone: Novelist of the Revolutionary Sensibility," Scott offers a wide-ranging overview of his fiction in the context of European literature.

Slonim, Marc. Afterword to *Bread and Wine*, by Ignazio Silone. New York: New American Library, 1963. A useful introduction to the novel, explaining the circumstances in which it was written, analyzing its characters, the author's politics, and Silone's artistic achievement.

GEORGES SIMENON

Born: Liège, Belgium; February 13, 1903
Died: Lausanne, Switzerland; September 4, 1989

PRINCIPAL LONG FICTION

Pietr-le-Letton, 1931 (*The Strange Case of Peter the Left*, 1933; also known as *Maigret and the Enigmatic Lett*, 1963)

M. Gallet, décédé, 1931 (*The Death of Monsieur Gallet*, 1932; also known as *Maigret Stonewalled*, 1963)

Le Pendu de Saint-Pholien, 1931 (*The Crime of Inspector Maigret*, 1933; also known as *Maigret and the Hundred Gibbets*, 1963)

Le Charretier de la "Providence," 1931 (*The Crime at Lock 14*, 1934; also known as *Maigret Meets a Milord*, 1963)

La Tête d'un homme, 1931 (*A Battle of Nerves*, 1939)

Le Chien jaune, 1931 (*A Face for a Clue*, 1939; also known as *Maigret and the Yellow Dog*, 1987)

La Nuit du carrefour, 1931 (*The Crossroad Murders*, 1933; also known as *Maigret at the Crossroads*, 1964)

Un Crime en Hollande, 1931 (*A Crime in Holland*, 1940)

Au rendez-vous des terreneuves, 1931 (*The Sailors' Rendezvous*, 1940)

La Danseuse du Gai-Moulin, 1931 (*At the "Gai-Moulin,"* 1940)

La Guinguette à deux sous, 1931 (*The Guinguette by the Seine*, 1940)

Le Relais d'Alsace, 1931 (*The Man from Everywhere*, 1941)

Le Passager du "Polarlys," 1932 (*The Mystery of the "Polarlys,"* 1942; also known as *Danger at Sea*, 1954)

Le Port des brumes, 1932 (*Death of a Harbour Master*, 1941)

L'Ombre chinoise, 1932 (*The Shadow in the Courtyard*, 1934; also known as *Maigret Mystified*, 1964)

L'Affaire Saint-Fiacre, 1932 (*The Saint-Fiacre Affair*, 1940; also known as *Maigret Goes Home*, 1967)

Chez les Flamands, 1932 (*The Flemish Shop*, 1940)

Le Fou de Bergerac, 1932 (*The Madman of Bergerac*, 1940)

Liberty Bar, 1932 (English translation, 1940)

L'Écluse numéro un, 1932 (*The Lock at Charenton*, 1941)

Les Gens d'en face, 1933 (*The Window over the Way*, 1951)

La Maison du canal, 1933 (*The House by the Canal*, 1948)

Les Fiançailles de M. Hire, 1933 (*Mr. Hire's Engagement*, 1956)

Le Coup de lune, 1933 (*Tropic Moon*, 1942)

Le Haut Mal, 1933 (*The Woman in the Gray House*, 1942)

L'Homme de Londres, 1934 (*Newhaven-Dieppe*, 1942)

Le Locataire, 1934 (*The Lodger*, 1943)

Les Suicidés, 1934 (*One Way Out*, 1943)

Maigret, 1934 (*Maigret Returns*, 1941)

Quartier Nègre, 1935

Les Demoiselles de Concarneau, 1936 (*The Breton Sisters*, 1943)

Faubourg, 1937 (*Home Town*, 1944)

Le Blanc à lunettes, 1937 (*Talatala*, 1943)

L'Assassin, 1937 (*The Murderer*, 1949)

Chemin sans issue, 1938 (*Blind Alley*, 1946)

L'Homme qui regardait passer les trains, 1938 (*The Man Who Watched the Trains Go By*, 1945)

Monsieur la Souris, 1938 (*The Mouse*, 1950)

Les Inconnus dans la maison, 1940 (*Strangers in the House*, 1951)

Il pleut, bergère . . . , 1941 (*Black Rain*, 1949)

Le Voyageur de la Toussaint, 1941 (*Strange Inheritance*, 1950)

La Veuve Couderc, 1942 (*Ticket of Leave*, 1954; also known as *The Widow*, 1955)

Oncle Charles s'est enfermé, 1942 (*Uncle Charles Has Locked Himself In*, 1987)

L'Aîné des Ferchaux, 1945 (*Magnet of Doom*, 1948)

La Fuite de Monsieur Monde, 1945 (*Monsieur Monde Vanishes*, 1967)

Le Clan des Ostendais, 1947 (*The Ostenders*, 1952)

Lettre à mon juge, 1947 (*Act of Passion*, 1952)

Maigret à New York, 1947 (*Maigret in New York's Underworld*, 1955)

La Neige était sale, 1948 (*The Snow Was Black*, 1950; also known as *The Stain in the Snow*, 1953)

Les Vacances de Maigret, 1948 (*Maigret on Holiday*, 1950; also known as *No Vacation for Maigret*, 1953)

Maigret et son mort, 1948 (*Maigret's Special Murder*, 1964)

Pedigree, 1948 (English translation, 1962)

La Première Enquête de Maigret, 1949 (*Maigret's First Case*, 1958)

Mon Ami Maigret, 1949 (*My Friend Maigret*, 1956)

Le Fond de la bouteille, 1949 (*The Bottom of the Bottle*, 1954)

Les Fantômes du chapelier, 1949 (*The Hatter's Ghosts*, 1956)

Les Quatre Jours du pauvre homme, 1949 (*Four Days in a Lifetime*, 1953)

Les Volets verts, 1950 (*The Heart of a Man*, 1951)

Maigret et la vieille dame, 1950 (*Maigret and the Old Lady*, 1958)

L'Amie de Mme Maigret, 1950 (*Madame Maigret's Own Case*, 1959; also known as *Madame Maigret's Friend*, 1960)

Les Mémoires de Maigret, 1951 (*Maigret's Memoirs*, 1963)

Maigret au "Picratt's," 1951 (*Maigret in Montmartre,* 1954)

Maigret en meublé, 1951 (*Maigret Takes a Room,* 1960)

Maigret et la grande perche, 1951 (*Maigret and the Burglar's Wife,* 1969)

Une Vie comme neuve, 1951 (*A New Lease on Life,* 1963)

Maigret, Lognon, et les gangsters, 1952 (*Inspector Maigret and the Killers,* 1954; also known as *Maigret and the Gangsters,* 1974)

Le Révolver de Maigret, 1952 (*Maigret's Revolver,* 1956)

Maigret et l'homme du banc, 1953 (*Maigret and the Man on the Bench,* 1975)

Maigret a peur, 1953 (*Maigret Afraid,* 1961)

Maigret se trompe, 1953 (*Maigret's Mistake,* 1954)

Antoine et Julie, 1953 (*The Magician,* 1955)

Feux rouges, 1953 (*The Hitchhiker,* 1955)

Crime impuni, 1954 (*The Fugitive,* 1955)

Le Grand Bob, 1954 (*Big Bob,* 1954)

Les Témoins, 1954 (*The Witnesses,* 1956)

Maigret à l'école, 1954 (*Maigret Goes to School,* 1957)

Maigret et la jeune morte, 1954 (*Maigret and the Dead Girl,* 1955)

Maigret chez le ministre, 1954 (*Maigret and the Calame Report,* 1969)

Maigret et le corps sans tête, 1955 (*Maigret and the Headless Corpse,* 1967)

Maigret tend un piège, 1955 (*Maigret Sets a Trap,* 1965)

Les Complices, 1955 (*The Accomplices,* 1964)

En cas de malheur, 1956 (*In Case of Emergency,* 1958)

Un Échec de Maigret, 1956 (*Maigret's Failure,* 1962)

Maigret s'amuse, 1957 (*Maigret's Little Joke,* 1957)

Maigret voyage, 1958 (*Maigret and the Millionaires,* 1974)

Les Scrupules de Maigret, 1958 (*Maigret Has Scruples,* 1959)

Dimanche, 1958 (*Sunday,* 1960)

Maigret et les témoins récalcitrants, 1959 (*Maigret and the Reluctant Witnesses,* 1959)

Une Confidence de Maigret, 1959 (*Maigret Has Doubts,* 1968)

Maigret aux assises, 1960 (*Maigret in Court,* 1961)

Maigret et les vieillards, 1960 (*Maigret in Society,* 1962)

L'Ours en peluche, 1960 (*Teddy Bear,* 1971)

Betty, 1961 (English translation, 1975)

Le Train, 1961 (*The Train,* 1964)

Maigret et le voleur paresseux, 1961 (*Maigret and the Lazy Burglar,* 1963)

Maigret et les braves gens, 1962 (*Maigret and the Black Sheep,* 1976)

Maigret et le client du samedi, 1962 (*Maigret and the Saturday Caller,* 1964)

La Porte, 1962 (*The Door,* 1964)

Les Anneaux de Bicêtre, 1963 (*The Patient,* 1963; also known as *The Bells of Bicêtre,* 1964)

Maigret et le clochard, 1963 (*Maigret and the Bum,* 1973)

La Colère de Maigret, 1963 (*Maigret Loses His Temper,* 1964)

Maigret et le fantôme, 1964 (*Maigret and the Apparition,* 1975)

Maigret se défend, 1964 (*Maigret on the Defensive,* 1966)

La Chambre bleue, 1964 (*The Blue Room,* 1964)

Le Petit Saint, 1965 (*The Little Saint,* 1965)

La Patience de Maigret, 1965 (*The Patience of Maigret,* 1966)

Maigret et l'affaire Nahour, 1966 (*Maigret and the Nahour Case,* 1967)

Le Confessional, 1966 (*The Confessional,* 1968)

La Mort d'Auguste, 1966 (*The Old Man Dies,* 1967)

Le Chat, 1967 (*The Cat,* 1967)

Le Voleur de Maigret, 1967 (*Maigret's Pickpocket,* 1968)

Maigret à Vichy, 1968 (*Maigret in Vichy,* 1969)

Maigret hésite, 1968 (*Maigret Hesitates,* 1970)

L'Ami de l'enfance de Maigret, 1968 (*Maigret's Boyhood Friend,* 1970)

La Prison, 1968 (*The Prison,* 1969)

La Main, 1968 (*The Man on the Bench in the Barn,* 1970)

Novembre, 1969 (*November*, 1970)

Maigret et le tueur, 1969 (*Maigret and the Killer*, 1971)

Maigret et le marchand de vin, 1970 (*Maigret and the Wine Merchant*, 1971)

La Folle de Maigret, 1970 (*Maigret and the Madwoman*, 1972)

Maigret et l'homme tout seul, 1971 (*Maigret and the Loner*, 1975)

Maigret et l'indicateur, 1971 (*Maigret and the Informer*, 1972)

La Disparition d'Odile, 1971 (*The Disappearance of Odile*, 1972)

La Cage de verre, 1971 (*The Glass Cage*, 1973)

Les Innocents, 1972 (*The Innocents*, 1973)

Maigret et Monsieur Charles, 1972 (*Maigret and Monsieur Charles*, 1973)

OTHER LITERARY FORMS

Georges Simenon is known primarily for his fiction. Throughout his career as novelist, however, he frequently displayed mastery of shorter forms as well, both with and without the presence of his famous Inspector Maigret. Originally published for the most part in periodicals, his short stories and novellas have been collected in such volumes as *Les Dossiers de l'Agence O* (1943), *Nouvelles exotiques* (1944), and in English translation as well. In his late thirties, erroneously informed by his doctors that he had but a short time to live, Simenon began writing his autobiography as a memoir for his infant son. At the urging of the eminent novelist André Gide (1869-1951), he soon thereafter abandoned the project, incorporating its best portions into the novel *Pedigree*, published in 1948. After publicly renouncing the practice of fiction shortly before his seventieth birthday, Simenon published his recollections in *Mémoires intimes* (1981; *Intimate Memoirs*, 1984).

ACHIEVEMENTS

Simenon is among the most prolific fiction writers of his generation. During fifty years (1922-1972) of sustained creative activity, he published upward of three hundred novels under his own name, exclusive of lesser efforts for which he employed a variety of pseudonyms. Although best known for his novels featuring Inspector Maigret of the Paris police, Simenon in fact published more titles *outside* the detective genre and was justly acclaimed both in France and abroad for his keen analysis of human character in mainstream fiction.

Simenon was a gifted student of human nature and a born raconteur whose keen powers of observation, linked to a highly retentive memory, have furnished the world with a vast array of memorable characters both within and outside the mystery genre. Incredibly, the sheer quantity of Simenon's work had little, if any, negative effect upon its quality; throughout most of his career, Simenon was taken seriously, as a "serious" novelist, by general readers and critics alike.

Heir apparent to the tradition of French naturalism that flourished a quarter of a century before his birth through the works of Émile Zola, Guy de Maupassant, and Edmond and Jules de Goncourt, Simenon brought the best features of naturalism into the twentieth century. Unlike some other novelists and playwrights of his own generation, who pretended to "psychological realism" by parroting forth, as if undigested, the latest insights of Sigmund Freud and

(Archive Photos)

Carl Jung, Simenon evolved throughout his career a mode of psychological observation and recording that is all the more credible, and convincing, for its lack of cant or visible erudition. In most of his novels, Simenon appears to be suggesting that it is unnecessary to read Freud or Jung to gain an understanding of the criminal or psychotic mind, that all one need do is observe one's peers closely, with understanding and compassion. Maigret, among the most convincing and memorable of modern fictional detectives, is an "instinctive" psychologist who solves many initially baffling murders by focusing his attention upon the victim, attempting to figure out what he or she might have done to invite violent death. In the non-Maigret novels, it is Simenon himself, as unseen and frequently omniscient narrator, who portrays apparently "normal" characters driven to sudden crime and violence by inevitable forces which they themselves can barely comprehend, if at all. Seldom, in either type of novel, does the action appear forced or the characters' behavior unconvincing—a fault that hampers, if only infrequently, even the finest narratives of Zola and Maupassant.

It can be argued that Simenon's Maigret has contributed as much to the development of the mystery novel as did Sherlock Holmes himself, implicitly awarding to psychology the role in detection that Arthur Conan Doyle, writing a half century earlier, had attributed to the then-innovative scientific method. To Simenon and Maigret, as to their contemporary readers, it is usually more important (as well as entertaining) to understand *why* a crime was committed than precisely *how* it was done. Of perhaps equal importance is Simenon's role in helping to create, through his Maigret novels, a subgenre of detective fiction known as the "police procedural," by now widely read and written the world over.

Departing from the frequently romantic private detective whose dazzling insights make law officers look like buffoons, Simenon and his many followers in the subgenre focus instead upon the grueling routines of police work itself, featuring career detectives whose profiles often fall far short of the heroic. Maigret is a case in point—a portly, balding, dedicated civil servant in late middle age with a durable, affectionate, but unfortunately childless marriage. Assisted in his many investigations by a recurring cast of subordinates and his voluble physician friend, Pardon, Maigret puts in long and frequently fruitless hours in his efforts to look at and through the crime to the mind of the criminal. Among the least judgmental of fictional detectives, Maigret has on occasion come to "understand" the crime so well that he either lets the criminal go free or agrees to testify in his defense.

At the risk of belaboring the obvious, it is perhaps appropriate to observe that the main difference between Simenon's Maigret novels and his "mainstream" works (by far the larger part of his production) is that in the latter, Maigret does not appear. Without Maigret's avuncular presence to tie up the loose ends of the characters' lives, the loose ends remain untied—with frequently disastrous results. As Lucille Becker observes, the

> reassuring presence of Maigret . . . convinces us that there is an order, a structure, and a meaning to life. In the other novels, there is no Maigret to whom the protagonist can confess, there is no one to understand or with whom to communicate, leaving him immured in his solitude, stifled and suffocated by repressed confessions.

Indeed, the usual and highly credible atmosphere is one of utter solitude, alienation, and estrangement in which the characters, fully comprehensible to the author and hence to the reader, are just as fully incomprehensible to one another. Among twentieth century French novelists, perhaps only the Nobelist François Mauriac—a possible source for some of Simenon's novelistic predicaments—has rendered as convincingly as Simenon the heart-wrenching predicaments of cross-purposes and unheard cries for help that often reverberate through life and love. In Mauriac's fictional universe, however, there is always the promise, secured only by the author's personal religious faith, of a better life to come in the next world. In those of Simenon's novels without Maigret, by contrast, hell on earth is most often simply hell. In his own defense, Simenon argues with some justice that the novel, in the twentieth century, fulfills much the same function that tragedy did for the ancient Greeks. People's destiny is played out in a repeated dialogue between author and audience, the one compelled to exorcise inner demons and the other to see its best hopes and worst fears replicated in the characters' behavior. Once the reader is thus reassured—presumably by a catharsis similar to that emerging, in Aristotle's view, from the viewing of a classical tragedy—he will be able to address himself to life with renewed vigor, aware of his limitations but better suited to savor the sights, sounds, and smells of everyday life.

Among literary critics, Simenon was most often reproached, like Zola before him, for his lack of literary style. Advised early in his career by the novelist Colette, then serving as one of his editors, to pare his work down to the barest essentials, Simenon soon perceived that his most effective style was one that favored the literal over the figurative, the concrete over the abstract. Over the years, that decision served him well, especially in the creation of plausible atmospheres in which to place his often hapless characters.

BIOGRAPHY

Born in 1903 in Liège, the elder of two brothers, Georges-Joseph-Christian Simenon enjoyed an urban childhood sufficiently middle-class that he recalled being disgruntled when his mother felt herself obliged to take in boarders in order to make ends meet. The failing health of his father, an insurance clerk, obliged the young Simenon to cut short his formal education and join the work force at about age sixteen. After false starts as apprentice to a pastry cook and subsequently as a sales clerk, Simenon found steady work as a journalist at a still-precocious age and thereafter earned his living through writing, either as a journalist or as a secretary-speechwriter. Married in 1923 to Régine Renchon, Simenon later in that year began selling short stories to newspapers and soon expanded to the novel as well, publishing more than two hundred potboilers under various pseudonyms between 1925 and 1934, by which time his own name, thanks in part to Maigret, was beginning to assure brisk sales.

According to Becker, Simenon originally attempted the detective novel "as a bridge between the popular potboilers he had been writing and the more serious literary efforts to which he aspired but for which he did not consider himself ready." His proposal accepted by the publisher Fayard, Simenon contracted in 1929 to write eighteen Maigret novels, which in time would expand to eighty-three in addition to shorter Maigret adventures. Curiously, Simenon's talent and fame as a mainstream novelist developed almost simultaneously with his reputation as a mystery writer, with several examples of each type of novel published annually throughout the 1930's to generally good sales and reviews.

In the mid-1930's, Simenon traveled extensively throughout the world; the "exotic" novels resulting from these voyages are justly famous among readers and scholars, although they constitute a small fraction of his literary output and depend more heavily upon character than upon atmosphere for their overall effect. Soon after the outbreak of World War II, already involved in refugee relief work, Simenon began writing his memoirs in the erroneous belief that he was soon to die of a respiratory ailment; after revision, those memoirs would form the basis of the major novel *Pedigree*, completed during 1943 but not published until five years later. Toward the end of the hostilities, Simenon traveled extensively in North America and met the Canadian Denise Ouimet, who, after his divorce in 1950, would become his second wife. Residing first in Arizona, Simenon settled in northern Connecticut following his marriage to Ouimet; there he would write a number of his best-remembered novels, many with American settings and characters.

After returning to Europe in 1955, Simenon spent most of his time in the Lausanne area of Switzerland, where he was to die in 1989. Around 1972, Simenon renounced the writing of fiction, preferring instead to record on tape the most salient excerpts of his photographic memory. In 1981, he published his massive autobiography, *Intimate Memoirs*, notable for its sensational disclosures with regard to his unconventional sex life and his obsession with the suicide of his daughter, Marie-Jo. Despite its self-advertised candor, it is a strangely unrevealing work; Simenon the man remains elusive.

ANALYSIS

Named by the highly regarded André Gide as the greatest modern French novelist, Georges Simenon indeed compiled an enviable record of achievement, producing a body of work equally remarkable for its quality as for its quantity. The apprenticeship he served in writing his so-called potboilers appears to have served him well, allowing him to write fluently while maintaining rigorous standards of content and characterization. Simenon's demonstrated proficiency in the mystery genre alone would no doubt suffice to secure his position in the history of modern letters; nevertheless, he further confirmed his reputation with a solid list of mainstream titles valued for their psychological insights.

Simenon's prodigious accomplishment may be explained, at least to a point, by acknowledging that his fictional universe remains essentially the same regardless of whether Maigret is involved in the action; in both types of novel, the true protagonists are hounded, uncommunicative creatures with little more than the most marginal knowledge of what makes them behave as they do. The main difference, as Becker has observed, lies in the thoughtful, reconciling presence of Maigret, who functions almost as a psychoanalyst in "solving" the mystery of behavior to the satisfaction of characters and readers alike; in the mainstream novels, the characters remain in their own private hells, understood (if at all) only by the narrator and his reader. Rarely, and then with remarkable effect, does Simenon surprise the reader with his conclusions; even then, as elsewhere in Simenon's novels, the denouement soon appears inevitable, amply prepared for by what he has revealed of the characters' makeup and motivations.

THE MAIGRET NOVELS

By his own admission, Simenon "discovered" Maigret at a time when, still unsure of his skills as a novelist, he was seeking a viewpoint character who could move about in space and time as the conventional narrator (or novelist) could not; eventually, he settled upon a policeman as ideally suited to his needs and proposed the Maigret series, initially planned for eighteen volumes. The result, by now almost legendary, was one of the most durable characters in the history of detective fiction, further established by his omnipresent pipe, his childless wife, and cold meals ordered "to go" during the late-night hours from the obliging Brasserie Dauphine. Modeled upon Simenon's own pensive, easygoing father, Maigret is on occasion so appealing that he makes the prospect of crime seem nearly attractive to the reader. In 1975, the eminent playwright Jean Anouilh paid indirect homage to Maigret with *L'Arrestation*, in which an aging gangster, mortally wounded in a motor accident, is fortunate enough, in his final moments, to have his entire life explained to him by an even older inspector, who has devoted his own career to studying the gangster's lifestyle and habits. Habitual criminals are, however, rather rare quarry for Maigret; more commonly, the crimes with which he deals are perpetrated by inhabitual offenders, seemingly normal people suddenly propelled toward violence by an accumulation of privation or resentment.

Maigret's murderers frequently kill for love or for its cherished memory. In *Maigret and the Loner*, one of Simenon's later Maigret adventures, more than twenty years elapse before a lovesick painter avenges his girlfriend's murder with the apparently gratuitous killing of his erstwhile rival, who has since become a homeless derelict. To Maigret, as to his creator, the painter could not possibly have behaved otherwise, his crime having long since been predetermined. Indeed, Maigret solves easily half of his initially baffling mysteries by reconstructing the life of the victim, in search of signs of irregularity or stress that could have engendered violence. Simenon himself has claimed, upon study of the evidence, that "there are at least eight crimes in ten in which the victim shares to a great extent the responsibility of the murderer." Similar cases abound throughout Maigret's career, from nagging spouses and sadistic lovers to the "public enemy" Fumal in *Maigret's Failure*, who himself victimized so many people that Maigret is hard put to choose among them as he reluctantly searches for Fumal's killer.

Occasionally, as in *Maigret Sets a Trap*, the identity of the murderer is known early in the novel, lacking only Maigret's deductive analysis to render the case against him (or her) conclusive. Identified by a police "plant" and hemmed in by circumstantial evidence, the admittedly unlikely mass murderer, a mild-mannered interior decorator named Moncin, eludes conviction only because an additional, identical murder was committed after he was taken into custody. As Maigret, following a hunch, delves deeper into Moncin's life and career, he finds a spoiled and highly intelligent man dominated by his wife and mother, who compete ceaselessly for top billing in his life. Either woman, Maigret reasons, would have had both motive and capacity to commit the "decoy" murder; in fact, it was the wife who did it, thus scoring a final, irrefutable "point" against her husband's mother.

STRANGERS IN THE HOUSE

Generally similar in theme and subject matter to the novels featuring Maigret, Simenon's mainstream titles likewise abound in ill-adjusted characters who live in quiet desperation, occasionally bursting out in violence. The expository method employed is frequently similar to that of the detective novel, with one or more characters attempting to solve the mystery in their lives. A case in point is that of Loursat in *Strangers in the House*, an intriguing novel perhaps even more timely in the twenty-first century than when it first appeared. A once-promising attorney, Loursat has responded to his wife's desertion by hiding out for years, bottle in hand, in the sanctuary of his personal library. A gunshot and the discovery of a body in his attic one night forces his attention to the fact that his adolescent daughter, Nicole, who lives in the same house but whom he has seen only at mealtimes, is in fact the leader of a housebreaking ring and that their accumulated loot is stored in Loursat's own attic. The dead man proves to have been a criminal who was blackmailing Nicole's band. Nicole's lover, Émile Manu, a poor young man who proves a convenient but innocent suspect, is arrested. As Loursat—his professional instincts and sense of justice awakened from long dormancy by what he knows is an unjust arrest—attempts to track down the real killer, he proceeds as well toward a long-overdue assessment of his own strengths and weaknesses; in time, Loursat discovers the true murderer and obtains Manu's freedom, proceeding thereafter to resume the life and career that he had abandoned years earlier.

UNCLE CHARLES HAS LOCKED HIMSELF IN

Such happy endings are rare in Simenon's work; more frequently, the self-knowledge reached through deduction is then used for self-serving means, with little prospect of true liberation. Such is the case in *Uncle Charles Has Locked Himself In*, in which deduction leads a petty embezzler toward the even greater satisfaction of "invisible" blackmail.

Mild-mannered and unprepossessing, like many of the criminals ferreted out by Maigret, "Uncle" Charles Dupeux has for years nursed a grudge against his overbearing employer and brother-in-law, Henri, occasionally feeding that grudge with small thefts which, carefully managed, have grown into a considerable fortune; presumably, he will one day make his "break," supported by the embezzled nest egg. Before that can happen, however, Charles discovers that Henri is being blackmailed, and with good cause: Henri, although not legally responsible for his late partner's early death, in fact conspired to bring it about. Armed with this knowledge, Charles retreats to the attic, where he keeps his hoard of stock certificates, trying to decide how best to use what he has learned. To Henri's consternation, he refuses a generous offer for his silence, knowing that Henri does not even suspect him of embezzlement. Instead, Charles prefers "the revenge of the underdog"—to hold over Henri's detested head the potential threat of exposure and thus avenge himself, albeit in secret, for what he regards as years of exploitation.

THE WITNESSES

Yet another of Simenon's memorable character studies is *The Witnesses*, which recalls the Maigret series as it carefully considers the often fragile foundations of justice. *The Witnesses* presents the tale of two men, the judge and the accused, and of circumstances which might, on occasion, be assessed as "circumstantial evidence." Little but the judicial bench, indeed, separates Judge Lhomond from Lambert in the dock; both men have notoriously bad marriages and have lately been prone to irregular behavior. As Lhomond successfully enjoins his jury to allow for "reasonable doubt" in Lambert's case, he is sure that the man would be convicted were not he, Lhomond, sitting on the bench that day.

TROPIC MOON

Simenon's exotic novels of the 1930's, although few in number, contain some of his best-remembered insights and descriptions; as elsewhere in his work, however, the setting is of interest to Simenon almost solely for its effects upon human behavior. Joseph Timar, the ill-starred protagonist of *Tropic Moon*, arrives in the Congo only to find that the company that hired him is about to go bankrupt, that his job lies ten days upriver, and that his predecessor is still in place, having threatened to kill anyone who might be sent in to replace him. Soon thereafter, somewhat corrupted by an older woman of his acquaintance, Timar goes more than a little mad; aboard the ship that has been sent to fetch him home, he confidently declares that "there is no such place as Africa."

QUARTIER NÈGRE

Hardly more fortunate is the engineer Dupuche of *Quartier Nègre*, who, like Timar, discovers upon arriving at the site of a new job that his position has been abolished as a result of the firm's bankruptcy. Set in Panama, *Quartier Nègre* is perhaps even richer in atmosphere than *Tropic Moon*. In any case, both novels resulted in lawsuits against Simenon by residents of the Congo and Panama, respectively, who considered themselves ill-represented in his works. Unlike Timar, Dupuche never leaves the tropics. Necessarily separated from his wife, who finds employment while he does not, Dupuche gradually but definitively goes native, residing in a tumbledown shack with his black mistress and their several children until he eventually dies, still young, of a tropical disease. Somewhat more fortunate is Ferdinand Graux, the title character of *Talatala*, who survives both the heat and his infatuation with a wanton Englishwoman long enough to rebuild his life and career with the help of his wife, Emmeline.

PEDIGREE

Unique among Simenon's many works outside the detective genre is the novel *Pedigree*, successfully mined by many of his critics in search of clues to his life and technique. Covering scarcely sixteen years in the life of Simenon's alter ego Roger Mamelin, *Pedigree* memorably chronicles the sights, sounds, and smells of Liège during the author's youth, adding unforgettable portraits of "Roger's" parents, aunts, and uncles. Implicit throughout the novel is the author's satiric attack upon his German-descended mother and her representation of the lower-middle class, which would sooner starve than eat the cheap, abundant food favored by "peasants." Included as well are detailed portraits of his mother's boarders, many of whom had already appeared, or would soon appear, with slight fictional disguise, in Simenon's novels. Of Roger's parents, the ailing father is by far the more wise and sympathetic, if less forceful and therefore less significant; later, in *Lettre à ma mère* (1974; *Letter to My Mother*, 1976), the septuagenarian Simenon would give even fuller vent to his resentment of his mother. In any case, it is clear from *Pedigree* that were it not for the influence of his mother, Simenon would never have had the determination and perseverance to become a writer and that without his father, he would never have acquired the patience, skill, and compassion that made his work as successful as it is.

SUNDAY

Among Simenon's later novels, *Sunday* is one of the most memorable and impressive, rivaled perhaps only by *The Old Man Dies*. As befits its title, the events of the novel take place on a particular Sunday, the day that Émile, an accomplished chef, has selected in advance for the murder of his wife, Berthe, who is also his employer. Impotent in marriage, released from his affliction only in the arms of a wild and uncultured young waitress, Émile remains unaware of his abiding dependence upon the domineering Berthe. So great, in fact, is Berthe's hold upon Émile that when he learns that she has outsmarted him, feeding to his young mistress the poisoned lunch intended for herself, he meekly heeds her suggestion that he is already late for the regional soccer match. By the time he returns, all traces of the girl and his act will be gone, and everything will be restored to order.

THE OLD MAN DIES

In *The Old Man Dies*, similarly concerned with the running of a restaurant, the heir apparent, Antoine, is portrayed initially as an unsympathetic character, only to divide with his brothers, upon their father's death, a supposed "legacy" that is in fact wholly composed of his own funds. The true legacy, implies Simenon, is the restaurant itself, a business long since spurned by Antoine's brothers.

Simenon still stands virtually unchallenged in the territory that he claimed as his own between the two world wars. Faulted by some observers for his essentially negative, deterministic view of human nature and by others for his implied derogation of women and marriage, Simenon nevertheless remains among the most accomplished observers and chroniclers of his generation, his own legacy a challenge to any aspiring successors.

David B. Parsell

OTHER MAJOR WORKS

SHORT FICTION: *Les Dossiers de L'Agence O*, 1943; *Nouvelles exotiques*, 1944; *Les Nouvelles Enquêtes de Maigret*, 1944 (*The Short Cases of Inspector Maigret*, 1959).

NONFICTION: *Le Roman de l'homme*, 1958 (*The Novel of Man*, 1964); *Quand j'étais vieux*, 1970 (*When I Was Old*, 1971); *Lettre à ma mère*, 1974 (*Letter to My Mother*, 1976); *Mémoires intimes*, 1981 (*Intimate Memoirs*, 1984).

BIBLIOGRAPHY

Assouline, Pierre. *Simenon: A Biography*. Translated by Jon Rothschild. New York: Knopf, 1997. A good reference for biographical information on Simenon.

Becker, Lucille Frackman. *Georges Simenon*. Boston: Twayne, 1977. An informative introductory study, with chapters on Simenon's family background; the creation of Maigret; his handling of basic themes, especially solitude and alienation; and his understanding of the art of the novel. Includes chronology, notes, and an annotated bibliography.

Bresler, Fenton. *The Mystery of Georges Simenon*. Toronto: General Publishing, 1983. A well-written biography that gives a strong sense of Simenon's roots and the development of his career.

Collins, Carvel. "The Art of Fiction IX: Georges Simenon." *The Paris Review* 9 (Summer, 1993): 71-90. A comprehensive interview with the author about his career and his fictional methods.

Eskin, Stanley. *Simenon: A Critical Biography*. Jefferson, N.C.: McFarland, 1987. More scholarly than Bresler, Eskin provides a meticulous narrative and analysis of Simenon's work. His notes and bibliography are very detailed and helpful.

Franck, Frederick. *Simenon's Paris*. New York: Dial, 1970. While this is basically a book of illustrations of Paris, a good deal is revealed about the way Simenon chose locations for his fiction.

Gill, Brendan. "Profiles: Out of the Dark." *The New Yorker*, January 24, 1953, 35-45. A succinct biographical and critical profile by an astute essayist.

Marnham, Patrick. *The Man Who Wasn't Maigret: A Portrait of Georges Simenon*. London: Bloomsbury, 1992. An excellent study of Simenon's life and times. Includes bibliographical references and an index.

Raymond, John. *Simenon in Court*. New York: Harcourt Brace and World, 1968. An excellent overview of Simenon's fiction, as valuable as Becker's introductory study.

Rolo, Charles J., ed. *New World Writing*. New York: The New American Library of World Literature, 1952. Contains an authoritative study of the mystery story, concentrating on the problem of evil. This is also a study of the hero in Simenon and Mickey Spillane.

WILLIAM GILMORE SIMMS

Born: Charleston, South Carolina; April 17, 1806
Died: Charleston, South Carolina; June 11, 1870

PRINCIPAL LONG FICTION

Martin Faber: The Story of a Criminal, 1833
Guy Rivers: A Tale of Georgia, 1834

The Yemassee: A Romance of Carolina, 1835

The Partisan: A Tale of the Revolution, 1835

Mellichampe: A Legend of the Santee, 1836

Richard Hurdis: Or, The Avenger of Blood, a Tale of Alabama, 1838

Pelayo: A Story of the Goth, 1838

The Damsel of Darien, 1839

Border Beagles: A Tale of Mississippi, 1840

The Kinsmen: Or, The Black Riders of the Congaree, 1841 (revised as *The Scout*, 1854)

Confession: Or, The Blind Heart, 1841

Beauchampe: Or, The Kentucky Tragedy, a Tale of Passion, 1842

Helen Halsey: Or, The Swamp State of Conelachita, a Tale of the Borders, 1845

Count Julian: Or, The Last Days of the Goth, a Historical Romance, 1845

Katharine Walton: Or, The Rebel of Dorchester, 1851

The Sword and the Distaff: Or, "Fair, Fat and Forty," 1852 (revised as *Woodcraft*, 1854

Vasconselos: A Romance of the New World, 1853

The Forayers: Or, The Raid of the Dog-Days, 1855

Eutaw: A Sequel to the Forayers, 1856

Charlemont: Or, The Pride of the Village, 1856

The Cassique of Kiawah: A Colonial Romance, 1859

OTHER LITERARY FORMS

William Gilmore Simms wrote extensively in all major literary genres. He began as a poet and achieved his first widespread fame in the northern United States with his long poetic work *Atalantis: A Story of the Sea* (1832). Although he continued to write and publish his verse throughout his lifetime, and, indeed, felt himself to be a good poet, his reputation has never rested on his poetic abilities. Still, his poetry is not without interest, for Simms often reveals a sharp eye for natural detail in his descriptions, especially of the Southern landscape. His accomplishments as a writer of short fiction only began to be appreciated in the late twentieth century. His emphasis on realism can be seen in such works as "The Hireling and the Slave," and his wonderful command of folk humor can be found in such literary "tall tales" as "Bald-Head Bill Bauldy" and "How Sharp Snaffles Got His Capital and Wife." Longer stories such as "Paddy McGann" contain further elements of the tall tale and folklore. Simms was not a good dramatist; he wrote a number of aborted plays and, in the case of *Pelayo*, adapted a failed drama into novel form. His best play is considered to be *Michael Bonham: Or, The Fall of Bexar, A Tale of Texas* (1852), which deals with the Texas war for independence.

In his nonfiction works, Simms often turned to the history of the South. Of his four major biographies, two—*The Life of Francis Marion* (1844) and *The Life of Nathanael Greene* (1849)—grew out of his abiding interest in the Revolutionary War in the South; both men also appeared as characters in his novels. His historical writings include *The History of South Carolina* (1840), a general history of the state, beginning with its settlement; *South-Carolina in the Revolutionary War* (1853), which concentrated on

(Archive Photos)

that part of the state's history which he so often used in his fiction; and his contemporary account of the Civil War, *Sack and Destruction of the City of Columbia, S.C.* (1865), an inspired example of reporting. Although Simms was not always accurate or unbiased, he was a surprisingly good historian. He collected sources throughout his life, made use of private recollections and memories, and today his work provides a storehouse of information often overlooked by more standard historical works. Simms's combination of the factual and the imaginative in his historical romances is one of his strongest and most appealing traits.

ACHIEVEMENTS

Although during his lifetime William Gilmore Simms's popularity as a novelist ranked second only to that of James Fenimore Cooper, his reputation steadily diminished after his death, so that by the turn of the century he was little more than a footnote in literary histories. With the University of South Carolina Press publications of *The Letters of William Gilmore Simms* (1952-1956; five volumes, Mary C. Simms Oliphant, editor) and the first volumes of *The Centennial Edition of the Writings of William Gilmore Simms* (1969-1975; sixteen volumes, John C. Guilds and James B. Meriwether, editors), however, there has been a growing interest in his work. Still, the fact remains that Simms's contributions to the development of American literature in the first half of the nineteenth century have been much underrated. Put simply, Simms was the most important antebellum Southern man of letters. He created a body of work that is awesome in size and scope. More than eighty separate volumes were published during his life, and ongoing research is uncovering more of his writings hidden in forgotten periodicals or under various pseudonyms.

When, in 1832, Simms first traveled to New York City, he was determined to establish himself as a writer of national importance. He made the necessary publishing connections and paid homage to the leading Northern literary figures. The publication of his poetic work *Atalantis* in that year was enthusiastically received, but it and his short novel *Martin*

Faber, published the following year, were still apprenticeship pieces which followed patterns set down by others. With *Guy Rivers*, *The Yemassee*, and *The Partisan*, Simms not only staked out his own literary territory but also publicly placed himself in competition on a national level. Simms was an ardent supporter of the idea that America must produce its own unique brand of writing, inspired by its own land and people and experiences. Simms's own interest lay in the South, but, as he explained in the preface to *The Wigwam and the Cabin* (1845), by mastering sectional material, the writer could still be of national importance, since no single writer could adequately depict the country as a whole.

It was in his commitment to the South that Simms achieved his greatness. He saw the South as a land of exciting potential. He loved its rawness as well as its manners, its violence as well as its vitality. Its heritage was rich, he felt, but largely unknown to people both inside and outside the region. Thus, Simms, with his passion for history and folklore, set out to reveal this past to Southerners and Northerners alike, to correct the historical picture he found so lacking. In his romances, he helped to define the popular image of the South from precolonial times up to the American Civil War. The Northerner, Simms maintained, had no right to feel superior to his Southern brethren, but the Southerner had all too often been remiss in preserving and appreciating his own heritage.

As the political disputes between North and South intensified, Simms became a protector of a way of life he felt was being threatened. In this time of trouble, he maintained that the past held lessons for the present: The courageous spirit of the pioneer and the partisan soldier could still inspire, the inherent nobility of the manor-born ladies and gentlemen could still instruct. Thus, Simms's tales of an earlier era, marked by characters of indomitable strength, could be seen as examples for his own time.

The sheer quantity of Simms's work remains staggering and his overall achievement approaches the heroic. Although he sometimes bemoaned the lack of appreciation and support he received in the South, most of his contemporaries, despite occasional carping, freely awarded him the laurels of leadership. A less courageous and confident person would never have faced the challenges that Simms invited. Before the war, he sought, through his own example, to impart a sense of dignity to the Southern artist. For the five years he lived after the war, he struggled to rekindle the pride of a defeated people, in the midst of his own great personal tragedy. As a critic and an editor, as a poet and a writer of fiction, he worked at first with energy and enthusiasm, later out of a kind of desperation against the inevitable, but he never stinted in his devotion to art and to a world which came to lie in ruins around him.

BIOGRAPHY

William Gilmore Simms was born in Charleston, South Carolina, on April 17, 1806, the second son and only surviving child of William Gilmore and Harriet Ann Augusta Singleton Simms. Simms's father came from Ireland after the American Revolution and established a successful mercantile business in Charleston. His mother's family, the Singletons, had lived in the port city for generations. Her grandfather, Thomas Singleton, was one of the Charleston citizens arrested by the British authorities during their occupation and, despite his advanced age, sent in exile to St. Augustine; her father, John Singleton, had fought as a soldier on the side of the patriots. Simms's mother died in 1808, and shortly thereafter, his father, grief-stricken at the loss of his wife, left Charleston to journey westward, placing his only child in the care of his late wife's mother, Mrs. Jacob Gates (she had remarried in 1800 after the death of John Singleton in 1799). The elder Simms went on to lead what must have seemed an incredibly exciting life to his impressionable son; the boy heard tales of his father's fighting under Andrew Jackson in the Indian Wars in Florida and later at the Battle of New Orleans in the War of 1812 before settling in Mississippi, then the edge of the frontier. Thus, Simms the boy grew up surrounded by legends and dreams of almost mythical characters—the Revolutionary War heroes on the Singleton side of the family, and the pioneer-soldier he saw in his own father. Both romantic threads would run throughout Simms's writings. In addition, growing up in historic Charleston

allowed him to visit sites of Revolutionary incidents in and near the city. His unflagging interest in history (especially that of South Carolina but also of foreign lands) provided a foundation for his wilder imagination, and his writings would always contain a solid understructure of fact.

Although tradition has held that Simms grew up in genteel poverty in Charleston, feeling ostracized by that aristocratic city's more prominent citizens, his father had, in fact, left him substantial property holdings, and Simms was recognized early for his achievements. Still, it is equally clear that Simms was sensitive to slight—at least partly because of boyhood loneliness after the loss of his immediate family—and his enormous artistic energy no doubt fed on this partial uncertainty.

In 1812, at the age of six, Simms began school in Charleston. He entered the College of Charleston when he was ten, and at twelve he began work in a local apothecary shop. He was already writing poetry and drama. By the age of sixteen, he had published verse in a Charleston newspaper; at seventeen he was editing a juvenile periodical, the first of many editorships he would undertake in his lifetime. The next year, 1824 to 1825, Simms spent with his father in Mississippi. Together they ranged into the wilderness, where Simms met and carefully observed the types of frontiersmen (rascals and rogues among them) and Native Americans which would people his romances.

When Simms returned to Charleston in 1825, he set about establishing himself as a writer. His first volume of verse, *Monody on the Death of Gen. Charles Cotesworth Pinckney* (1825), made him a prominent local talent. In 1826, he married Anna Malcolm Giles. The next year Simms was admitted to the bar and published his second and third volumes of poetry. In 1828, he became editor of the *Southern Literary Gazette*; in 1829, his fourth volume of verse appeared, and his fifth followed in 1830. Also in 1830, he became copartner in the Charleston *City Gazette*; in this role he figured as a leading opponent to the Nullification Movement which was dividing South Carolina into two very fractious parties. Simms's opposition brought him into serious disfavor with many important citizens, and it was an experience which he would remember with a mixture of anger and regret.

The year 1832 was a decisive one for Simms. His wife, Anna, died in February. Overtaxed by emotional and professional demands, Simms gave up his legal practice (never a foremost interest), sold the *City Gazette*, and journeyed to New York City, determined to make his way in earnest as a literary man. In New York, he formed what was to be a lifelong friendship with James Lawson. Simms would use Lawson's home as his northern base until the Civil War finally intervened; Lawson would be among the first to help Simms in the dark days after the war as well. With Lawson's encouragement and advice, Simms published his sixth volume of poetry, *Atalantis*, in 1832. When it proved extremely popular with the Northern audience, Simms followed it with his first novel, *Martin Faber*, and his first collection of short fiction, *The Book of My Lady*, both in 1833. With the publication of *Guy Rivers* in 1834 and of *The Partisan* and *The Yemassee* in 1835, Simms had announced his literary directions, as these three books were the first of his Border, Revolutionary, and Colonial romances, respectively.

The next twenty or so years were generally good ones for Simms. In 1836, he married Chevillette Eliza Roach, the daughter of a prominent land owner in South Carolina. As part of his marriage inheritance, Simms obtained "Woodlands" plantation, which became his most prized retreat, an emblem of all he saw best in the Southern way of life. The demands of his lifestyle made it necessary that Simms publish as much and as often as possible, but because of the laxity of copyright laws he often received far less than he was due for what he did write. Simms would travel to New York about once a year to confer with his publishers (for a time new works by Simms came out annually) and to visit old friends. He enjoyed his growing reputation as spokesman for the South. Although he was always interested in politics and acted as an informal adviser to a number of political leaders in South Carolina, he served only one term in government, as a member of the South Carolina House of Representatives from 1844 to

1846. His most notable literary position during this time was as editor of *The Southern Quarterly Review* from 1849 to 1854.

Beginning in the 1850's, Simms became a leading and increasingly strident voice in the call for Southern secession from the Union and in the defense of slavery. Unfortunately, he is too often remembered for the attitudes struck in these pronouncements, so at odds with modern understanding, at the expense of his more important creative works. As a public figure, Simms attracted the opprobrium aimed at the South as war became inevitable. His 1856 lecture tour of the North on the role of the South in the American Revolution had to be cut short when Simms enraged his audiences with his vigorous and even pugnacious arguments against the Union stand. He welcomed the final break and was confident of Southern victory, but as the war progressed, he came to see the specter of defeat.

The last years of Simms's life were tragic. In 1862, "Woodlands" was partially burned but was rebuilt through the subscriptions of appreciative South Carolinians. In 1863, his second wife died, a devastating blow to Simms, who had also lost nine of his children. In 1865, "Woodlands" was again set ablaze, this time by stragglers from General Sherman's army. Simms lost in this conflagration his private library of ten thousand volumes, considered to be the finest in the South at the time. During the five years remaining to him after the war, Simms worked as never before, as editor of two newspapers—the Columbia *Phoenix* and the *Daily South Carolinian*—and as the author of still more poems, addresses, short fiction, and serialized novels. Despite his own almost inconceivable losses, Simms did what he could to bring about the resurrection of his land and people. When he died on June 11, 1870, a world and a way of life had clearly passed with him.

ANALYSIS

As early as 1835, in the preface to *The Yemassee*, William Gilmore Simms attempted to define his goals as a writer. He distinguished his full-length fiction as "romances" rather than novels. Following definitions already in vogue, Simms described the novel as picturing ordinary people in everyday situations, both domestic and common. These works he traced to Samuel Richardson and Henry Fielding. The "romance," on the other hand, he saw as the modern-day equivalent to the ancient epic, drawing its inspiration and power from both drama and poetry. The romance (as practiced by writers such as Sir Walter Scott, Edward Bulwer-Lytton, and James Fenimore Cooper) was of "loftier origins" than the novel. Its characters were individuals caught up in extraordinary, uncertain, even improbable events. As Simms saw it, the writer of a romance was not as bound by strict logic as was the novelist; indeed, the romancer's ingenuity in plotting was often a strong point in the work. As critics have pointed out, a number of Simms's supposed literary sins—stock characters, absurd resolutions, inflated dialogue—resulted from the Romantic tradition in which he worked rather than from a lack of art or skill.

To categorize Simms simply as a writer of romances is, however, somewhat misleading, and more recent studies have emphasized the strong sense of realism that is found in his work. During his lifetime, Simms was regularly accused of exceeding the bounds of propriety. He answered these objections on numerous occasions. In his "Advertisement" to *Mellichampe*, for example, he insisted that his purpose was to "adhere as closely as possible, to the features and the attributes of real life." Thus, although he endeavored to invest his stories with noble characters involved in stirring adventures, he wished to write neither "a fairy tale, [n]or a tale in which none but the colors of the rose and rainbow shall predominate."

This sense of realism, which must have seemed uncouth in Simms's own time, has come to be recognized as one of his strongest traits. He was clearly influenced by the "realism" of the legends and frontier tales of his youth and in the writings of the southern and southwestern humorists. Augustus Baldwin Longstreet's *Georgia Scenes* was published in 1835, the same year as *The Yemassee* and *The Partisan*. (Simms would himself write several brilliant "tall tales" such as "Bald-Head Bill Bauldy" and "How Sharp Snaffles Got His Capital and Wife.") Simms's sense of realism did not apply only to "low" charac-

ters and their exploits, however, as has often been implied. Simms would modify the nobility, the wisdom, even the courage of his "model characters," his aristocrats, if the story warranted it. His heroes could learn, could fail, could grow; and his villains were often surprisingly complex, capable of unexpected decency and courageous deeds.

Underlying all of Simms's romances was a strong awareness of history, of what had actually happened at the time and place about which he wrote. Simms felt free to bend fact to the demands of art, but not to misrepresent the essential truth of the situation. The *facts* of history, he said, standing by themselves, carried little weight, but the artist—the creative writer—by giving *shape* to the facts, could give them life and meaning. Thus, it is the writer who is the true historian, and it was as an "artist-historian" that Simms wrote most of his romances.

As all commentators on Simms like to point out (and as Simms himself was aware), he usually wrote too rapidly and carelessly. He simply produced too much for the good of his own reputation. His faults are often glaring, but they are usually the result of haste and little or no revision. Simms could write with clarity and precision, but he could also sacrifice both for blood and thunder. Simms was a storyteller, and his books, for all their length, keep a steady pace. When he turned his hand to psychological interpretations of characters, when he tried to "analyze the heart," he often did so with the concomitant loss of energy and drive. In his best works, however, he was able to combine complexity of character with a compelling story.

Simms's Revolutionary War novels

Simms wrote eight romances dealing with the Revolutionary War in the South, and as a group they represent his best work. The novels cover the period from 1775, when the first open warfare began, to 1783, when the British abandoned Charleston and the soldiers returned home to a new and difficult way of life. The internal chronology of the novels does not correspond to the sequence of their composition. "Joscelyn: A Tale of the Revolution," which was meant to be the "opening scene" in Simms's "grand drama" of the South's seven-year war of Revolution, was one of the very last works he wrote, and the only one of the eight never to appear in book form during his lifetime. It appears as volume 16 of *The Centennial Edition of the Writings of William Gilmore Simms*. "Joscelyn" is set around the Georgia-South Carolina border and describes the early conflicts between those who joined in the growing freedom movement and those who remained loyal to the crown. It also shows that people on both sides of the issue could be motivated by cruelty as well as courage, by selfishness as well as honor.

THE PARTISAN, MELLICHAMPE, and KATHARINE WALTON

The three novels *The Partisan, Mellichampe*, and *Katharine Walton* were conceived of by Simms as a trilogy, with developing characters and overlapping plots, although each was also meant to stand as an independent work. These books cover the events of 1780, following the fall of Charleston to the British. *The Partisan* is a big, sprawling book which Simms later described as a "ground-plan," a setting of the stage for the works to come. It introduces numerous characters, both historical—Francis Marion, Lord Cornwallis, Sir Banastre Tarleton, Horatio Gates, Baron de Kalb—and fictional—Major Robert Singleton, Colonel Richard Walton, his daughter Katharine, Lieutenant Porgy—who return in later works in the series. *The Partisan*'s story lines include the development of Marion's guerrilla forces in the swamps of South Carolina, the growth of love between Singleton and Katharine Walton, and the agony of Colonel Walton's decision to align himself with the rebel cause. The novel closes with a detailed description and analysis of the Battle of Camden (August, 1780), wherein Gates and the Southern Continental Army were soundly defeated by Cornwallis. *Mellichampe* is set in the fall of 1780. It put less emphasis on the large historical picture and was more clearly intended as a work of fiction, although here again the "facts" of the war are not forgotten. In *Mellichampe*, Simms expands his description of Marion's role in the war, develops several minor characters found in *The Partisan*, and illustrates the "excesses of patriotism" and the necessity of honor in times of conflict. The third book of this trilogy, *Katharine Walton*, again takes up

the story of Colonel Walton, his daughter, and Robert Singleton. It is set largely in Charleston during the last months of 1780 and describes the social life and attempts at rebellion in the captured city at this very trying time.

THE SCOUT

The next in the series is *The Scout*, which moves into the central region of South Carolina. It is, in some ways, the most "romantic" and melodramatic of the novels. Its plot of feuding brothers and mysterious outriders is heavy with conventions, but in its description of the marauding outlaw bands which terrorized the back country and in its discussion of Nathanael Greene's siege of the British fort at Ninety-Six (upstate South Carolina) in the summer of 1781, *The Scout* is an impressive and absorbing story.

The Forayers and *Eutaw*, which were first conceived as one book, follow the retreat of the British from Ninety-Six to Charleston and present the events leading to the climactic battle at Eutaw Springs, South Carolina, in September, 1781, which effectively ended British rule in the state, although the battle itself was a draw.

WOODCRAFT

The last of the Revolutionary War novels is *Woodcraft*, which begins in December, 1782, after the British evacuation. Its theme is the readjustment of soldiers to domestic life, and its main character is Lieutenant Porgy, the wastrel aristocrat soldier whom many feel to be Simms's most successful character. Porgy appears in five of the eight novels, but his most important role is in *Woodcraft*. Basically a comic character (Porgy is often compared to William Shakespeare's Falstaff, although such comparisons rarely go beyond surface descriptions), this fat soldier confronts the challenges of peace after the adventures of war. Born of the landed gentry, Porgy is known to have wasted his inheritance as a young man, and despite his courage and wit, he is not one of Simms's noble heroes. He is, however, among the most likable and (with reservations) the most admirable of Simms's characters, and it is his mood of reconciliation (after one final battle) and acceptance that presides over this last book. Some critics hold

Woodcraft to be Simms's best work (although *The Forayers* and *Eutaw* might be better choices), and it certainly shows Simms at his most relaxed and amiable.

GUY RIVERS

Commonly listed under the category of Simms's Border Romances are *Guy Rivers, Richard Hurdis, Border Beagles, Beauchampe, Helen Halsey, Charlemont,* "Voltmeier: Or, The Mountain Men," and "The Cub of the Panther." These works lack the specific historical overview of the Revolutionary War novels—they are closer to Simms's own time and are not as likely to be built around identifiable events—but they do give excellent descriptions of the frontier of the Old South—the customs, speech patterns, and lifestyle of settlers, outlaws, and adventurers. The first of these, *Guy Rivers,* was Simms's first full-length novel as well. Set in the mountainous region of Georgia, where gold was being mined in the early 1800's, the story centers on the conflict between Guy Rivers, a notorious outlaw (though once a respected lawyer) and Ralph Colleton, a young South Carolinian whose own frustrations with love and family have led him to the frontier. There he meets Mark Forrester, a native of the region who helps Ralph in his "natural" education. Colleton foreshadows such later Simms heroes as Robert Singleton, Ernest Mellichampe, and Willie Sinclair (in *The Forayers* and *Eutaw*), while Forrester anticipates Thumbscrew Witherspoon in *Mellichampe* and Supple Jack Bannister in *The Scout,* woodsmen who teach the young aristocrats the need for clear thinking and honorable actions. Rivers is the melodramatic villain of the type that would chew the scenery and threaten feminine virtue in a number of Simms's works: Barsfield in *Mellichampe,* Edward Conway in *The Scout,* Captain Inglehardt in *The Forayers* and *Eutaw.*

RICHARD HURDIS

Richard Hurdis, the second of the Border novels, is perhaps the best of them. Set in Alabama, the story is loosely based on the outrages of John Murrell and his outlaw gang which roamed throughout Alabama and Mississippi. Simms apparently had met witnesses to or even participants in some of this gang's doings while visiting his father in Mississippi as a boy. The plot is somewhat similar to that of *The Scout.* In each novel, two brothers—one virtuous and one criminally inclined—find themselves at odds; both books are concerned with the attempts to bring outlaw bands to justice. In a sense, *Border Beagles* is a continuation of *Richard Hurdis*; a tale of bandits on the Mississippi frontier, it is generally considered a less effective story than its predecessor.

BEAUCHAMPE

Beauchampe was Simms's retelling of the notorious Beauchampe-Sharpe "Kentucky tragedy," a murder case in which Beauchampe killed Warham Sharpe, the seducer of Margaret Cooper, whom Beauchampe had married. In 1856, Simms returned to this story in *Charlemont,* which detailed the events leading up to the "tragedy" in *Beauchampe.* Thus, *Beauchampe,* although published first, was, in Simms's words, the "sequel" to *Charlemont.* Simms's last two Border romances were both published in magazines in 1869, at the very end of his life. "Voltmeier" was published again in 1969 as volume 1 of *The Centennial Edition of the Writings of William Gilmore Simms.* "Voltmeier" and "The Cub of the Panther" were drawn from Simms's personal observations and experiences during trips into the mountainous regions of North Carolina, and they contain some of his best writing.

THE YEMASSEE

Simms dealt with the settling of South Carolina in the early eighteenth century in two important works, *The Yemassee* and *The Cassique of Kiawah.* *The Yemassee* was Simms's most popular novel, and, because of its American Indian theme, was immediately compared to the works of Cooper. The novel described the 1715 Yemassee Indian War against the colonists. Simms's tale concentrates on two main characters: Governor Charles Craven (a historical figure), who takes the disguise of Gabriel Harrison for much of the book, and Sanutee, the chief of the Yemassee. Simms illustrates Sanutee's problem with sympathy and understanding—the Native American had originally welcomed the settlers and then found himself and his tribe threatened by them—but the novel finally argues in favor of the whites and the advanced civilization they bring with them. Despite *The Yemassee*'s popularity—it is still the work for which

Simms is best remembered—the novel is not as impressive as *The Cassique of Kiawah*, a much later and more mature work, which deals with similar material but has received little critical attention. It has been argued that Simms's picture of the American Indian was more realistic than Cooper's. He avoided the idea of the "noble savage," but often imbued his Native Americans with traits of courage and dignity. In addition to these two novels, Simms used colonial and American Indian material in several of his shorter works found in *Carl Werner* (1838) and *The Wigwam and the Cabin*.

Simms's interest in European history, especially in Spanish history, dated back to his childhood and formed the basis for four foreign romances. *Pelayo* had been conceived when Simms was seventeen as a drama on the conquest of Spain by the Moors. The play was never performed, and the material later grew into a novel. *Count Julian* was the sequel to *Pelayo*, but its publication was delayed for a number of years because its manuscript was lost for a time. *The Damsel of Darien* was inspired by the adventures of explorer Vasco Núñez de Balboa, while *Vasconselos* concerned itself with Hernando de Soto's explorations in the New World. Most critics and readers would agree that these works are among Simms's weakest.

MARTIN FABER

Simms's first novel was *Martin Faber: The Story of a Criminal*. It recounts the first-person confessions of the title character, who has seduced and murdered one girl and married another, whom he then begins to suspect of adultery. Faber tells his story in prison, just before his execution. The book is a short and emotional work, and it was quickly linked to William Godwin's *Things as They Are: Or, The Adventures of Caleb Williams* (1794), although its antecedents could also be found in numerous gothic romances. Simms returned to this type of story in *Confession: Or, The Blind Heart*, which, in his introduction, Simms linked to Godwin. *Confession* was the reworking of an idea Simms had played with as a younger writer. He explained that he had forgotten the work before he found the manuscript by accident years later. As he reread it, he was "led away" by the

psychological aspects of the tale. *Confession* tells of Edward Clifford, a young lawyer who is consumed by jealousy of his wife. Convinced of the worst, Clifford kills the entirely virtuous woman; when he later discovers the truth, he condemns himself to a life of wandering and self-recrimination. The similarities to Shakespeare's *Othello* (1604) are obvious, although Simms maintained that the materials were "gathered from fact."

The same interests in crime, guilt, and retribution are found throughout his other works—he was always intrigued by the psychological complexities of sinners and criminals—and it could be argued that *Beauchampe* and *Charlemont* might better be placed in this group than among the Border tales. These psychological novels, however, are not the works for which Simms is remembered. Although his constantly inquiring imagination was stirred by these situations, he was the master of scope and action rather than the kind of close analysis these topics demanded. The twists and entanglements of plot which could be overridden in his more sweeping works became all too obvious when related at a slower, more concentrated pace.

In his lasting works, Simms's long undervalued contribution to America's literary heritage is clearly evident. His was the voice of the South—the maker of its romances, the singer of its legends, the keeper of its history, and the defender of its traditions. More than any other writer, he embodied his time and place: its grandeur, its courage, and its wrongheadedness.

Edwin T. Arnold III

OTHER MAJOR WORKS

SHORT FICTION: *The Book of My Lady*, 1833; *Carl Werner*, 1838; *The Wigwam and the Cabin*, 1845; *Southward Ho!*, 1854.

PLAY: *Michael Bonham: Or, The Fall of Bexar, A Tale of Texas*, pb. 1852.

POETRY: *Monody on the Death of Gen. Charles Cotesworth Pinckney*, 1825; *Early Lays*, 1827; *Lyrical and Other Poems*, 1827; *The Vision of Cortes*, 1929; *The Tri-Color*, 1830; *Atalantis: A Story of the Sea*, 1832; *Areytos: Or, Songs of the South*, 1846;

Poems Descriptive, Dramatic, Legendary and Contemplative, 1853.

NONFICTION: *The History of South Carolina*, 1840; *The Geography of South Carolina*, 1843; *The Life of Francis Marion*, 1844; *Views and Reviews in American Literature, History and Fiction*, 1845; *The Life of Captain John Smith*, 1846; *The Life of Chevalier Bayard*, 1847; *The Life of Nathanael Greene*, 1849; *The Lily and the Totem: Or, The Huguenots in Florida*, 1850; *South-Carolina in the Revolutionary War*, 1853; *Sack and Destruction of the City of Columbia, S.C.*, 1865; *The Letters of William Gilmore Simms*, 1952-1956 (5 volumes; Mary C. Simms Oliphant, editor).

MISCELLANEOUS: *The Centennial Edition of the Writings of William Gilmore Simms*, 1969-1975 (16 volumes; John C. Guilds and James B. Meriwether, editors).

BIBLIOGRAPHY

Guilds, John Caldwell. *Long Years of Neglect: The Work and Reputation of William Gilmore Simms*. Fayetteville: University of Arkansas Press, 1988. This collection brings together a dozen essays, some rather scholarly, though many suitable for the high school student. In addition to useful articles, offers a reproduction of an oil portrait of Simms.

_____, ed. *Simms: A Literary Life*. Fayetteville: University of Arkansas Press, 1992. The first critical biography of Simms to appear in one hundred years, Guilds's book proceeds in a chronological fashion and emphasizes Simms's accomplishments as a novelist. Five appendices include a chart of birth and death dates for Simms's fifteen children; the will of Nash Roach, Simms's father-in-law, bequeathing the bulk of his estate to Simms and Chevillette Roach Simms, his wife; a letter written by Simms to the United States Congress in support of an international copyright bill; two elegies published in Charleston periodicals after Simms's death; and a useful list of Simms's writings appearing in book form.

Parks, Edd Winfield. *William Gilmore Simms as Literary Critic*. Athens: University of Georgia Press, 1961. Though the focus of this book is narrow—

Simms's reviews and literary essays—it offers some insight into his creative works.

Wakelyn, Jon L. *The Politics of a Literary Man: William Gilmore Simms*. Westport, Conn.: Greenwood Press, 1973. Although he mostly explores the political aspects of Simms and his writings, Wakelyn now and then contributes literary insights. Contains an extensive bibliography and a photograph of Simms.

Watson, Charles S. *From Nationalism to Secessionism: The Changing Fiction of William Gilmore Simms*. Westport, Conn.: Greenwood Press, 1993. Examines the political and social views of this Southern author. Includes bibliographical references and an index.

Wimsatt, Mary Ann. *The Major Fiction of William Gilmore Simms*. Baton Rouge: Louisiana State University Press, 1989. Though its discussions sometimes rise above the high school and undergraduate level, this is the most lavishly illustrated book on Simms available, with fourteen pages of pictures, maps, and photographs of Simms and the people and places associated with him.

CLAUDE SIMON

Born: Tananarive, Madagascar; October 10, 1913

PRINCIPAL LONG FICTION

Le Tricheur, 1945
Gulliver, 1952
Le Sacre du printemps, 1954
Le Vent: Tentative de restitution d'un rétable baroque, 1957 (*The Wind: Attempted Restoration of a Baroque Altarpiece*, 1959)
L'Herbe, 1958 (*The Grass*, 1960)
La Route des Flandres, 1960 (*The Flanders Road*, 1961)
Le Palace, 1962 (*The Palace*, 1963)
Histoire, 1967 (English translation, 1968)
La Bataille de Pharsale, 1969 (*The Battle of Pharsalus*, 1971)

Les Corps conducteurs, 1971 (*Conducting Bodies*, 1974)
Triptyque, 1973 (*Triptych*, 1976)
Leçon de choses, 1975 (*The World About Us*, 1983)
Les Géorgiques, 1981 (*The Georgics*, 1989)
L'Acacia, 1989 (*The Acacia*, 1991)
Le Jardin des plantes, 1997

OTHER LITERARY FORMS

In addition to his novels, Claude Simon has published *La Corde raide* (1947; the tightrope), a journal containing various impressions of the Spanish Civil War and World War II as well as reflections upon painting and writing; *Orion aveugle* (1970; blind Orion), an art edition that includes portions of his novel *Conducting Bodies* along with reproductions of several paintings mentioned in the text; and *Femmes* (1966; women), a series of commentaries on paintings by Joan Miró.

ACHIEVEMENTS

One of the foremost members of a group of avant-garde writers in France usually designated by the term New Novelists, Claude Simon has successfully merged critical theory with the practice of writing. In so doing, he has extended the limits of the novel while at the same time elaborating a unique fictional universe. He has referred to his novels as a "field of investigation"; that is to say, he has constantly experimented with new modes of narrative discourse, not with a particular and ultimate form in mind but as a means of exploring diverse perspectives on the relationship between reality and its representation. By conceiving of the novel as production rather than product, by refusing to allow the text to become transparent and self-erasing as it progresses toward an inevitable resolution—as tends to be the case in the traditional, realistic novel—Simon has obliged readers to change their habits. His novels require an active participation by the reader in the shaping of the text.

Unlike some of the New Novelists, Simon has not reduced the novel to an arid linguistic game or a treatise on narrative technique. His works, no matter how experimental, are never mere pretexts for the founding of a new science of the novel. He has been able to

(The Nobel Foundation)

combine brilliantly his aesthetic preoccupations with themes and images that probe the nature of the human condition and exert a compelling attraction upon those readers who are willing to undergo the demanding apprenticeship that his novels require.

The protagonists of Simon's fictional universe find that once the complacent order of their everyday lives is disrupted, they are forced to confront fundamental questions regarding the human condition and the role of language in shaping, or distorting, their comprehension of reality and, ultimately, of their own identity. Simon's doubt about the ability of words to seize the nature of experience gives rise to a literary language that can be extraordinarily rich, sensual, and evocative. This flow of language tends to create its own order out of the chaos of existence. Although Simon's audience will perforce be a limited one, drawn largely from the university, he has provided these "happy few" with compelling insights into the character of existence and the process of fiction-making. For his efforts, he was granted the Nobel Prize in Literature in 1985.

BIOGRAPHY

Claude Simon was born on October 10, 1913, in Tananarive, the capital city of the island of Madagascar, then a French possession. He left Madagascar at a young age and spent his childhood in Perpignan, a small city in the eastern Pyrenees. His father, an army officer, was killed in World War I. In 1924, Simon entered the Lycée Stanislas in Paris, where he completed his secondary education. He decided to prepare himself for a career as a painter and studied under André Lhôte.

As a young man traveling in Europe during the 1930's, Simon found himself in Spain at the time of the Civil War and participated in the conflict on the Republican side. At the beginning of World War II, he was drafted into a cavalry regiment. In May, 1940, he took part in the Battle of the Meuse, in which France suffered a crushing defeat. He was captured by the Germans and placed in a prisoner-of-war camp, from which he escaped in November, 1940. Thereafter he lived in Paris, spending part of his time in the Perpignan region, where he was once a wine grower.

Although he began writing in the early 1940's, Simon did not publish his first novel, _Le Tricheur_, until 1945. In 1960, he received the Prix de l'Express for _The Flanders Road_ and in 1967 the Prix Médicis for _Histoire_. In 1963, his only theatrical work, _La Séparation_, based upon _The Grass_, was produced in Paris but met with little success. Simon won the Nobel Prize in Literature in 1985.

After 1985, Simon published photographic collections, autobiographical novels, and a work of nonfiction based on a writer's conference, _L'Invitation_ (1987; _The Invitation_, 1991), whose themes are taken up in the 1997 novel _Le Jardin des plantes_. In interviews, Simon said that he preferred to think of his novels as reflections of a lived reality, rather than as direct transcriptions of a life. He continued to write, collect art, and live in Paris for most of the year and in Perpignan in the summers.

ANALYSIS

Most of Claude Simon's critics divide the evolution of his novels into three principal phases: an initial period, consisting largely of traditional novels and ending with two transitional works, _The Wind_ and _The Grass_; a middle period, commencing with _The Flanders Road_ and concluding with _Conducting Bodies_; and a third period, beginning with _Triptych_, which includes _The Georgics_. These divisions, although somewhat arbitrary, are based upon Simon's developing formal concerns.

Thematically, there is considerable unity among Simon's novels. Indeed, it is this thematic material, with its psychological, social, and cultural richness, that—combined with Simon's experimentation with the novelistic form—separates him from other New Novelists whose works often serve as pretexts for the demonstration of a particular theory of novel writing. Simon's novels are not confined within a prison of solipsistic self-reflection that reduces all the elements of fiction to metaphors of its own creation.

At the heart of Simon's universe lies a fundamental "absurdity"—a tension between the inherent disorder of reality and those means by which the human consciousness attempts to impose a logic and coherence upon it. War, sexual desire, and, to a lesser extent, avarice are the violent forces that tend to shatter the specious order of everyday existence and thus reveal its underlying chaos. Simon's vision of reality is pessimistic: Matter is in a constant state of mutation; the passage of time ineluctably undermines human activity; history seems to mock the human desire for progress, for it offers only patterns of cyclic repetition that reduce human beings to actors playing out predetermined roles; eroticism becomes a means of provisionally escaping from time and history.

A crucial aspect of the absurdity of the human condition lies in the attempt to discern the reality of experience and hence establish a definitive identity. The intrusion of human consciousness into the world results in the transformation of perceptions into images. No sooner does a given perception take place than it becomes a mental image, stripped of its original spatiotemporal coordinates and shaped by and connected with other images by a variety of associative processes. Thus, if knowledge of the real is essentially subjective, a creative representation, the self becomes an imaginary construct. A crucial complication arises from the use of language as a tool of discovery. For Simon, there is an inevitable "slippage" between word and thing. Experience is filtered through the order of language and thus becomes the material of fiction.

Simon's early novels differ from those of his middle and recent periods in that their largely traditional plot structure, character development, and language create a coherence that is not consonant with Simon's view of reality—style and vision are not integrated. With *The Wind* and notably the novels of his middle period, *The Flanders Road*, *The Palace*, *Histoire*, *The Battle of Pharsalus*, and *Conducting Bodies*, the central narrative consciousness becomes aware not only of the nature of experience, such as Simon depicts it, but also of the inadequacy of the means by which one attempts to seize its reality and that of the self immersed in it. This awareness naturally converges with the search for new forms by the novelist. Thus, one finds in these novels, among other characteristics, the dissolution of chronology and plot, the fragmentation of character, and an unstable narrative perspective. These novels are also marked, to varying degrees, by the proliferation of language: an abundance of descriptive terms to circumscribe a given phenomenon, syntactic dislocation to accommodate various associative links as well as appositions and rectifications, frequent use of the present participle to detemporalize actions and transform them into states. The inevitable generation of fictions transforms the novel into a mode of knowledge. Other media are frequently used to put into sharper relief the illusory movement of the text. Frequent references to paintings and other kinds of "stills" as well as to the cinema reflect upon the nature of that movement through the animation of the isolated, static image. Like the optical illusion created by the movement of frames in a film, a painting or postcard is narrated and is transformed into a text with its complex web of associations. This process has been compared to the reconstruction of a fossil, where a few bare bones may evoke an entire epoch. Other literary texts may also serve as part of

the cultural inventory by which fictions are generated and in which the narrative consciousness attempts to locate itself.

In the phase of Simon's writing that comprises *Triptych*, *The World About Us*, and *The Georgics*, the central narrative consciousness disappears and is replaced by the text constituting itself as tissue through the interweaving of several stories. The proliferating language of Simon's middle phase gives way to more coherently structured intersecting sequences which serve as elements of a particular story as well as associative junction linking one story to another.

Simon's departure from traditional modes of narration has resulted in the need for a more active participation by the reader, who must create (rewrite), through the process of reading, those patterns and structures that are suggested by the text. Only through this difficult but ultimately rewarding participation can the reader share with the writer the conception of the novel as a means of exploring the shifting, complex relationships between self, world, and word.

THE WIND

Although *The Wind: Attempted Restoration of a Baroque Altarpiece* bears many resemblances to Simon's earlier, more traditional fiction, it poses, both thematically and stylistically, several of the questions regarding narrative perspective, temporality, the elusive nature of reality, and the structuring role of language that would henceforth preoccupy the author.

The novel's title refers to the ceaselessly blowing wind that characterizes the climate of the unnamed town in southern France where the events of the novel take place. More than a simple indication of local color, the wind functions as a metaphor of the destructive passage of time—its ceaseless activity, its erosive power, its effect of intermingling disparate elements. Its pervasive presence underlines the transitoriness of the characters' lives and their futile attempts to impose a coherence upon reality. The novel's subtitle adumbrates the narrator's failure to adequately restore the past. The notion of an altarpiece suggests that the reconstitution in question will be an artistic endeavor that will leave the past still mysterious and even mystical. One can apply the term "baroque" to the sort of fiction that Simon produces in *The Wind* and also in his later novels. In this context, one can think of the baroque as the dynamic tension that exists between product and production, between the completed work of art as an illusion and the processes that engendered it and which tend to undermine that illusion.

The mysterious past that the anonymous narrator of the novel attempts to restore has as its locus the protagonist of the story, Antoine Montès. He is a thirty-five-year-old man whose development seems to have been arrested during his childhood. Like Fyodor Dostoevski's Prince Myshkin in *Idiot* (1868; *The Idiot*, 1887), a novel to which *The Wind* is indebted, Montès is an innocent, an almost saintlike figure to whom people are mysteriously attracted. He is incapable of comprehending the complex and sometimes sinister events that swirl around him and for which his presence acts as a catalyst. The naïveté of Montès makes it even more difficult for the narrator to reconstitute the story of what transpired during the seven months that Montès had recently spent in the town.

Montès returns to the town where he was conceived in order to claim his deceased father's estate—a valuable but rather dilapidated farm. Montès arrives in town as an obvious eccentric. His shabby, ill-fitting clothes are covered by an even shabbier, stained raincoat. Around his neck hangs an expensive camera—he is a photographer by profession—and he carries with him a worn leather briefcase stuffed with documents and letters of various sorts.

He quickly discovers that claiming his inheritance is more difficult than he had expected. The resident steward of the property ties up the estate in litigation. Montès is compelled to spend most of his time in legal affairs and is forced to take a room in a seedy hotel. There he falls in love with a maid named Rose— if love is indeed the term one can apply to the curious affection he feels for the woman. Rose lives with a gypsy boxer named Jep, who has fathered her two children. Montès's involvement with Rose is further complicated when he discovers that she is concealing the loot from a jewel theft in which Jep was involved. She is persuaded to give the jewels to Montès for safekeeping, an act that leads to her death. She is

stabbed by Jep, who in turn is shot dead by the police.

Also living at the hotel is a traveling salesman named Maurice. He tries in vain to obtain the jewelry and is forced to settle for attempted blackmail. He steals a letter written to Montès by his young cousin Cécile. The letter asks for a rendezvous with Montès, whom Cécile, having broken her engagement, is apparently attempting to seduce so she can get a share of the property. Cécile's sister Hélène snatches the letter from Maurice before he can extort money from her father, Montès's uncle, a gentleman farmer living in a crumbling house, surrounded by the portraits of his illustrious military forebears.

With Rose dead, her two daughters in an orphanage, and the case against the steward lost, Montès is obliged to sell the property and leave town. Once his disturbing presence is removed, the town resumes its former patterns of existence as if nothing had ever happened. Rose is replaced by another maid, Cécile returns to her fiancé, the steward occupies the farm. The narrator is left behind, as it were, to try to piece together what has taken place. He begins to suspect that the melodrama he has established in his attempt to reconstitute the past is but an illusion, based, in part, upon his inherent desire to give an order and coherence to events and personalities that would by their very nature otherwise elude him. He is also aware that his means of ordering the past— language—is suspect. He compares language to a thick sauce by means of which one holds together the disparate components of a dish and renders them edible. The logic of grammar and syntax restructures and domesticates reality. The disparity between the order of language and the disorder of reality is also manifested in certain stylistic traits that in later novels, particularly in *The Flanders Road*, would become characteristic of Simon's writing. Among them one can note a proliferation of descriptive terms used to "capture" a given phenomenon and the frequent use of the temporally indeterminate present participle.

THE FLANDERS ROAD

The publication of *The Flanders Road* placed Simon in the first ranks of the New Novelists, bringing him the critical attention he had hitherto not enjoyed.

It remains the best known of his novels. The protagonist of the novel is a young man named Georges. As a soldier in World War II, he is a victim of the rout of the French army by vastly superior German forces. His cavalry unit is decimated, and its leader, Captain de Reixach, Georges's aristocratic cousin, is killed. Georges is captured and placed in a German prisoner-of-war camp along with two of his comrades, Blum, a Jew suffering from tuberculosis, and Iglésia, a jockey formerly in the employ of de Reixach. Two years after the end of the war, Georges has a brief affair with Corinne, de Reixach's beautiful wife, now remarried. During the course of a night of lovemaking in a hotel room, Georges, his memory stimulated by the presence of Corinne, attempts to recapture the events of the war and, in so doing, determine his own identity.

Two questions emerge as leitmotifs in Georges's search for the past. One concerns the circumstances of de Reixach's death. Was he simply a casualty of the war, surprised in a German ambush, or had he sought to expose himself to death after having discovered that his wife had been unfaithful with Iglésia? The second question is more fundamental, encompassing the doubt about the Captain's death and the whole of Georges's enterprise: "How do we know?"

Georges is faced with the problem of separating fact from fantasy. He must somehow reconstitute his perceptions of the war, such as they took place at the time, freeing them from the network of mental images in which they are bound. Furthermore, he must in some way also find a language that will not transform his experiences into fictions. This search upon which Georges has embarked can result only in failure.

War reveals to Georges the tyranny of time and history. In a previous novel, *The Grass*, Simon compared the process of history to the continuous showing of a film—the same pattern of events returning at regular intervals. In *The Flanders Road*, the story of a de Reixach ancestor who served as a general in one of the revolutionary armies exemplifies this view of history as cyclic. He reputedly shot himself, perhaps as a result of a disastrous military defeat—all wars resemble one another—perhaps as a result of discov-

ering his wife's adultery with one of his domestics. History would, then, have made de Reixach one of its victims—he had but to act out his role. This kind of repetition also blurs the reality of any specific event, which comes to mirror countless similar occurrences.

The nature of time is conveyed through the central symbol of the novel, the horse. Simon described the shape of the novel as taking the form of an ace of clubs that one draws with a continuous line, passing through the same point three times. That point is represented in the novel by a decomposing horse on the side of the road, slowly sinking into the mud of Flanders so that—its matter transmuted—it will, in turn, nourish the grass that will sustain other horses. Georges envies the horse, for it has escaped from time and history.

He seeks an analogous escape in his lovemaking with Corinne. He compares her to an Earth Mother in whose womb he wishes to be engulfed. Eroticism, however, offers but a temporary "death," a brief moment of ecstasy during which the individual self in time is dissolved and merges with the Other. Georges's search for oblivion in Corinne's body marks his frustration at his inability to seize the reality of her person. During his imprisonment, he and his two comrades fantasized about Corinne, thereby transforming her into a mythical creature. Now, in the presence of the actual woman, he is unable to separate truth from invention and thereby determine the real cause of de Reixach's death. Ultimately, the text itself becomes the locus of desire as Georges seeks meaning through the textualization of his memories.

Georges's father, apparently a professor of literature, comes from an illiterate peasant family and, as befits that background, puts enormous faith in the magical power of language to capture reality. Georges does not share his father's confidence in language. He sees language as an instrument that distorts reality, transforming it into fictions and imposing a specious order upon it. As for the self, it is fragmented in the stories that language tells about it. Moreover, as Georges perceives, langage is incapable of arresting time—as soon as it is evoked, the present slips into the past and becomes yet another memory. He depicts language as a solitary voice that is drowned out by the sound of horses' hoofbeats—the inexorable passage of time.

The style of *The Flanders Road* reflects Georges's inability to resolve the questions he has raised and thus objectively recall the past. Its most salient feature is its dense flow of proliferating observations and images. In the attempt by the narrating consciousness to capture reality adequately, each perception or event becomes surrounded by words that attempt to circumscribe it. Parenthetical statements, appositions, and rectifications abound, as well as such qualifiers as "perhaps" and "doubtless." Traditional punctuation and paragraph and chapter divisions fail to segment the narration logically and, in so doing, manifest their artificiality. Words branch in a variety of directions, linking diverse subjects and moments—most notable in this regard is the constant shifting between the vocabulary of riding and that of sexual activity. One finds in the text—and it is a trait already discernible in *The Wind*—an unusually high frequency of present participles. These forms, which carry no mark of duration and person, create a mythical present, transforming activities into states. They suggest in their accumulation, and hence detachment from the subject, that the protagonist is not the shaper of events but the medium or theater through which they pass.

The reader participates both in the urgency of Georges's quest for truth and in the processes by which language transforms reality. In the absence of chronology and other guides that permit the reader of the traditional novel to recognize the ultimate meaning of what is related and organize its disclosure, the reader of *The Flanders Road* is obligated to discover in his or her rewriting of the text the multiple possibilities of meaning that can emerge from the chaos of Georges's defeat.

THE BATTLE OF PHARSALUS

In *The Battle of Pharsalus*, Simon plunges his readers into an inter- and intratextual battle. Only fragments of plots, characters, and settings remain to remind one that it is the varied assemblages of these elements and not their sustained development within a dramatic structure that constitutes the substance and interest of this novel. These assemblages yield possible meanings that are unstable and dissolve into other structures. Each signified, thus constructed and deconstructed, occasions a signifier that will tend toward yet another signified.

The last part of the novel contains a section in which the reader discovers the narrator in his room—though one is not certain of that identification—surrounded by a number of objects, a kind of inventory, which may have served to arouse the narrator's imagination and memory. Among them are a Larousse dictionary (an encyclopedia as well as a lexicon—the second section of the novel is entitled "Lexicon"), a frieze depicting a battle from antiquity, and a pack of Gauloise cigarettes with its emblem of a winged helmet. The predominant color of the objects in the room is yellow. From the window of the room, one can see railroad tracks and agricultural machinery. All of these elements will appear in multiple variations in the text. Present as well, but only in the narrator's mind, are a variety of literary texts and paintings. The later, mostly of battle scenes, are by such famous artists as Nicolas Poussin, Caravaggio, Piero della Francesca, and Pieter Brueghel the Elder. More important will be the presence in the novel of two literary texts, among others: Paul Valéry's "Le Cimetière marin" (1920; "The Graveyard by the Sea") and Marcel Proust's *À la recherche du temps perdu* (1913-1927; *Remembrance of Things Past*, 1922-1931).

The specific historical reference in the novel's title is to the site in Thessaly where Caesar defeated Pompey in 48 B.C.E. In 1897, the same locality served as a battleground in a war between Greece and Turkey. The narrator visits the battlefield, only to find there a soccer game between some Greek boys (another kind of battle) and, nearby, the rusting hulk of a McCormick thresher-combine.

To evoke one war, such as the one between Caesar and Pompey, is, for Simon, to evoke all wars. References to the Spanish Civil War and World War II amplify the theme of history's lack of progress, despite the inexorable corruption of time. The image of a Greek—or Roman—warrior appears frequently in the novel, and the arms he bears proliferate in metonymic variations—javelins, swords, lances, arrows.

There will be sexual warriors as well, brandishing their "spears"; *Pharsalus*, the reader is reminded, contains the letters *p-h-a-l-u-s*. Contrasted with the weapons of war is the McCormick thresher-combine, the modern plowshare into which the soldiers' swords might be beaten.

The violence of war is played against the violence of sex. The text indicates a sexual relationship between the narrator and a model, who apparently consorts with other men and may be another aspect of the Corinne of *The Flanders Road*. His jealousy is given full expression when, having discovered his mistress in bed with another man, he is left to hammer on her locked door in frustration. The story of Swann and Odette in *Remembrance of Things Past* is the intertextual counterpoint to the narrator's love affair. Just as the relationship between Charles Swann and Odette served as a negative model for that of the protagonist Marcel with Albertine, the narrator's uncle, named Charles, has preceded his nephew in having an unhappy relationship with his mistress. Marcel eventually rejected love for art and withdrew from the world to write his novel. The narrator seems to have followed the same path, only to generate a novel that lacks the spatial, temporal, and psychological coherence of Proust's. One might say that Simon himself has come to grips with Proust—as perhaps all French novelists must—by reinscribing the Proustian material within a radically different text.

The poem by Valéry provides an equally rich pretext for Simon. One of the principal themes of "The Graveyard by the Sea" is the opposition between mobility and immobility, an opposition whose variants are change versus stasis, creation versus meditation. The "play" between mobility and immobility appears in Simon's numerous references to paintings as well as to photographs and postcards. They become generators of texts as, through language, they are given a temporality and movement. That movement is illusory, obtained through the magic of narration. The Valéry poem contains references to Zeno of Elea, the Greek philosopher, who, in a number of paradoxes concerning the flight of an arrow and a race between Achilles and a tortoise, maintained the impossibility of movement. Achilles, an ancient warrior, is one

of the elements from the Valéry poem that Simon recirculates in his text. Another crucial element from Valéry's poem is the image of the doves, which in the original text represent white sailing ships. They reemerge as pigeons in Simon's novel and are linked to flight of various sorts—the feathered arrows of war, the soaring of memory and imagination that will be inscribed by the pen, once a quill feather.

The thresher-combine can be interpreted as a metaphor of the novel's creative processes. It serves, as a quotation from philosopher Martin Heidegger indicates, as a demonstration of utensility; it points to the intrusion of human consciousness in the world as a means to accomplish a task. The delving of the narrator's mind into the mass of language and culture produces a novel that functions like the machine once did: It harvests that which has been generated by diverse linguistic mechanisms and binds together, if only provisionally, otherwise disparate elements. A precarious but fruitful tension is maintained between proliferating growth and its threshing-combining. One might cite as an example of this tension the presence of the color yellow, so dominant in *The Battle of Pharsalus*. The color traditionally symbolizes jealousy and, in a larger sense, the anarchy of love. It links, among other elements, a lance, pubic hair, an old woman, and the sun. Its phonic combinations, as Jean Ricardou has demonstrated in *Pour une théorie du nouveau roman* (1971; for a theory of the new novel), will associate *nuage* (cloud), *nue* (naked), *Jeanne* (the name of Joan of Arc), and *âne* (donkey). This sort of generative wordplay serves as the novel's most striking stylistic trait.

Once again, Simon asks his reader to become an ever more active reader-writer, to become part of the act of literary production. The letter *O* that designates the narrator suggests that the novel has an empty center of meaning, that it is concerned with those combinatory processes by which possible meanings are posited.

TRIPTYCH

Triptych takes its title from a term used to describe a painting that is divided into three panels, usually conveying some sort of narrative content, such as episodes from the life of a saint. Simon's novel also contains three panels, three principal narrative sequences, but—unlike the sort of painting from which the title is derived—the three stories in question are not inherently related. They merge into one another through the complex web of associations that progressively link them.

The three principal stories can be easily summarized. One story deals with two young boys who forsake their fishing, as well as a young child left in their care, in order to spy on a couple making love in a barn. A second story portrays a bridegroom who, while celebrating with his friends in a tavern, winds up behind the store, making love to the barmaid. The third story is set in the Riviera, where a middle-aged woman—perhaps an older Corinne—languishes in her hotel room. In exchange for sexual favors, she obtains the liberation of her son, who has been arrested for possession of drugs.

Each story has a different cast of characters and takes place in a different location—the first in a rural area, the second on the outskirts of a city, the third on the Mediterranean coast. As he would do in his later novels, *The World About Us* and *The Georgics*, Simon transforms these separate stories into a text. The word "text" is related to "textile"; it is a fabric of interwoven threads. In the traditional novel, the process of interweaving remains hidden and the threads all belong to the same basic design, the patterning of a single story, but such is not the case in *Triptych*. There is no longer, as there was in Simon's previous novels, a localized narrative consciousness. In *Triptych*, the changes of narrative perspective and the switching from one story to another must be ascribed to the associative powers of language to shape the overall text.

In *Triptych*, as in many of Simon's novels, there is a "play" between narrative movement and the static image that may have served as its point of departure. The action of the boys observing the couple in the barn can be linked to an engraving showing a similar scene that is hanging in the hotel room. The woman in the hotel room, lying partially nude in bed, can be found on a strip of film the two boys scrutinize; she is also the subject of a motion picture that is being filmed as well as of a film that is being shown in a lo-

cal theater that was once a barn. The scene between the bridegroom and the barmaid may be the subject of the novel the woman on the Riviera is reading and can also be found in a film poster. There is a fourth thread in the novel, not so prominent as the principal three, which deals with the performance of a clown in a circus and which seems to derive from a poster affixed to the wall of the barn in which the couple is making love. Given the presence of generators of one story in another story, the novel suggests a set of interlocking mirror images in which any sense of the real tends to disappear.

A shifting from one story to another, frequently within the same sentence, may cause virtually any image to accumulate multiple associations and transcend whatever meaning it may have had within a particular story frame. A rabbit killed and skinned by a peasant woman can be linked to various nude bodies. Its death throes recall and anticipate erotic activity, as do its rose and purple colors. The removal of its eyes can be connected with broader thematic concerns—seeing and not seeing. Sounds, colors, objects of varying sorts, actions, gestures may all function within such multiple contexts.

The clown's performance suggests a parodic counterpoint to what is taking place in the three principal panels. His actions and gestures mimic the violence and the lust that are present in the other stories. His painted mask, his costume, his offering of himself as a spectacle, all serve to make the reader reflect upon the illusions of reality that the text creates.

A crucial image in *Triptych*, one that can be found in several of Simon's novels, but without the same emphasis, is the film camera. Not only does the novel deal explicitly with the making and viewing of a film, but many of the descriptions, particularly the country setting in which the story of the two young voyeurs takes place, are depicted from various camera angles, with considerable attention also paid to lighting and color. The pervasive presence of the camera accentuates certain elements of Simon's literary medium: the significance of perspective, the absence of psychological commentary, the use of sequential contiguity to replace overt plotting, and the irregular movement of the narrative.

THE ACACIA

The Acacia draws once again on World War I and World War II, and the story is knit together in the narrator's mind as he remembers his family's history. There are allusions to 1880 as well as to the 1980's. Simon's narrator participates in world history at the same time as he remembers his own personal history. Images of the bloodletting of the two world wars dominate the novel, particularly the ill-fated cavalry under attack by German tanks at Meuse in Belgium. As in *The Flanders Road* and *Histoire*, the author juxtaposes individual memories to create a collection of disparate characters, events, and scenes. Many of the same techniques are used: suppression of punctuation, page-long sentences with parenthetical statements within parenthetical statements, and sequencing of scenes and memories by association. However, with this novel, Simon becomes increasingly autobiographical. As he said in an interview with the French newspaper *Libération* in 1989, "in comparison with books like *Histoire* or *La Route des Flandres*, the fictional element has completely disappeared."

In *The Acacia*, Simon's father and mother appear; the father is an officer who dies in World War I, the mother, with son in tow, is in search of her dead husband's resting place. Simon's own experience at Meuse in 1940 parallels the war experience of the dead father-officer. *The Acacia*, as well as *Le Jardin des Plantes*, uses literary collage and juxtaposition. Collage is never far from the readers' minds when reading Simon, as he was trained as an artist and has written about art, painted, and photographed for much of his life.

LE JARDIN DES PLANTES

Indeed, in *Le Jardin des Plantes*, works of art are simply listed in isolated fragments among the collage-memories of the narrator. Yet the works of art do not dominate the fragmented narrative; instead, Simon once again draws on both old and newer memories to create the image of a life filled with the most diverse and varied experiences: having brief surgery on his lung, being in the cavalry at Meuse, participating in a writer's conference in Russia in the 1980's, making love, attending chapel as an adolescent, having an interview with a beady-eyed and uncomprehending journalist. What unites all the memories is the narrator-author; yet chronology is destroyed and a kind of temporal chaos pervades the novel. Simon not only juxtaposes memories but also uses an inventive typography: The page is split, with two competing or contemporaneous memories facing each other across a strip of white paper.

For example, Simon juxtaposes the memory of an army camp where he shaved once a week with the associated memory of going to a barbershop. The two memories are twenty or thirty years apart in real time, but they are linked by association. *Le Jardin des plantes*, like its namesake botanical garden with its myriad species of plant life, is a vast compendium of a lifetime of memories that remain uncatalogued, linked by triggering associative words or images. It is perhaps one of the best examples in any language of how memory and the mind work. Linear narrative is abandoned in favor of psychological truth. The single unifying factor is the writer's life experience.

Alain Robbe-Grillet, probably the best-known practitioner of the New Novel, states in *Pour un nouveau roman* (1963; *For a New Novel*, 1966) that "all literary revolutions are made in the name of realism." Changing concepts of reality, he maintains, require concomitant changes in the literary forms with which that reality is represented. The evolution of Simon's novels reveals their author's commitment to this continuing revolution. An integral part of Simon's exploration of the novel, his "field of investigation," has been the changing role of the reader. The latter has been transformed from a relatively passive recipient of a disturbing but fascinating vision of the human condition into a cocreator of that vision, a participant both in the narrative of an adventure and in the adventure of a narrative.

Philip H. Solomon, updated by Margaret Krausse

OTHER MAJOR WORKS

PLAY: *La Séparation*, pr. 1963.

NONFICTION: *La Corde raide*, 1947 (journal); *Femmes*, 1966 (commentaries on painting by Joan Miró); *Orion aveugle*, 1970 (portions of *Conducting*

Bodies and paintings); *La Chevelure de Bérénice*, 1983; *Discours de Stockholm*, 1986 (Nobel Prize speech); *L'Invitation*, 1987 (*The Invitation*, 1991).

BIBLIOGRAPHY

Birn, Randi, and Karen Gould, eds. *Orion Blinded: Essays on Claude Simon*. London: Associated University Presses, 1981. Brings together fifteen critics on Simon, plus an interview with the novelist. Concentrates on groupings of essays on Simon's worldview, different critical approaches, studies of evil, and links between Simon and Latin American fiction in the 1970's.

Britton, Celia, ed. *Claude Simon*. New York: Longman Publishing, 1993. A collection of articles, from 1959 to 1982. Britton has selected diverse critics who address questions of perception and memory, textual space, bricolage, intertextuality, the subject, and the problem of the referent; she covers all approaches in an extended introduction to the articles.

Duffy, Jean H. *Reading Between the Lines: Claude Simon and the Visual Arts*. Liverpool, England: Liverpool University Press, 1998. An illustrated study that explores and analyzes the relation between Simon's fiction and the visual and plastic arts. Duffy analyzes such artists as Jean Dubuffet and Paul Cézanne in connection with Simon's frequent statements about painting and the role of art in his novels. Excellent bibliography of both works on the visual arts and on Simon, including extended list of interviews and short pieces by him for newspapers.

Fletcher, John. *Claude Simon and Fiction Now*. London: Calder and Boyars, 1974. British critic assesses Simon's novels in the context of modernism. Fletcher provides a study of Simonian themes and compares him to other modernists after World War II. He concludes with a chapter on humanism, tragedy, and the avant-garde.

Gould, Karen. *Claude Simon's Mythic Muse*. Columbia, S.C.: French Literature Publications Company, 1979. Gould provides an exhaustive study of mythic and mythological themes as inspiration for Simon's novels.

Jimenez-Fajardo, Salvador. *Claude Simon*. Boston: Twayne, 1975. This early study examines Simon's novels through *Triptych*. Situates the novelist in the tradition of Marcel Proust and William Faulkner; examines the themes of Eros, death, memory, and representation.

Loubère, J. A. E. *The Novels of Claude Simon*. Ithaca: Cornell University Press, 1975. Eclectic, broadly based introduction to Simon's fiction that focuses on formal approach; Loubère relies frequently on Simon's statements about his fiction.

Ricardou, Jean. *Claude Simon: Colloque de Cérisy*. Paris: Union Générale d'Éditions, 1975. Collection of presentations at Cérisy-la-Salle conference. The preeminent critic of the French New Novel views Simon through a formal, linguistic lens.

Sykes, Stuart. *Les Romans de Claude Simon*. Paris: Minuit, 1979. Sykes, like Loubère, is a pioneer in Simonian criticism. He concentrates on the spatial and structural dimensions in the novels to 1979.

UPTON SINCLAIR

Born: Baltimore, Maryland; September 20, 1878
Died: Bound Brook, New Jersey; November 25, 1968

PRINCIPAL LONG FICTION

Springtime and Harvest, 1901
Prince Hagen, 1903
The Journal of Arthur Stirling, 1903
Manassas, 1904 (revised as *Theirs Be the Guilt*, 1959)
The Jungle, 1906
A Captain of Industry, 1906
The Overman, 1907
The Metropolis, 1908
The Moneychangers, 1908
Samuel the Seeker, 1910
Love's Pilgrimage, 1911
Sylvia, 1913
Sylvia's Marriage, 1914
King Coal, 1917

Jimmie Higgins, 1919
100%, 1920
They Call Me Carpenter, 1922
Oil! A Novel, 1927
Boston, 1928
Mountain City, 1930
Roman Holiday, 1931
The Wet Parade, 1931
Co-op, 1936
The Flivver King, 1937
No Pasaran!, 1937
Little Steel, 1938
Our Lady, 1938
World's End, 1940
Between Two Worlds, 1941
Dragon's Teeth, 1942
Wide Is the Gate, 1943
Presidential Agent, 1944
Dragon Harvest, 1945
A World to Win, 1946
Presidential Mission, 1947
One Clear Call, 1948
O Shepherd, Speak!, 1949
Another Pamela: Or, Virtue Still Rewarded, 1950
The Return of Lanny Budd, 1953
What Didymus Did, 1954
It Happened to Didymus, 1958
Affectionately Eve, 1961

(Library of Congress)

OTHER LITERARY FORMS

Between 1901 and 1961, Upton Sinclair wrote or rewrote more than forty novels, but in addition to his longer fiction, Sinclair also wrote and published a massive amount of nonfiction, including pamphlets, analyses of diverse subjects, memoirs, twelve plays, and letters by the thousands. The bibliography of his works is testimony to his amazing fluency, but no one who is so prolific can escape being uneven, and this is indeed the case with Sinclair. His career, which spanned more than six decades, was unified in one respect, however, for both his fiction and his nonfiction were devoted to a single aim—the achievement of social justice. Everything that he wrote was written primarily as a means to attain the end he sought, bettering the conditions of life for all people. Thus,

much of what Sinclair produced is not belletristic in any full sense, but propaganda to spread his ideas about politics and economics. In books such as *The Industrial Republic* (1907), he tries to explain how socialism will be arrived at by a natural process in America; the theory is based on the premise that social revolutions are bound to be benevolent. During the period following World War I to the onset of the Depression, most of Sinclair's writing was nonfiction. In a number of books, which he called his Dead Hand series, an ironic allusion to Adam Smith's "Invisible Hand" of laissez-faire economics, Sinclair deals with the destructive influence of capitalism on numerous American institutions: *The Profits of Religion* (1918) treats the abuses of institutional religions, showing how the established church supports the ruling classes in exchange for economic advantages; *The Brass Check: A Study in American*

Journalism (1919) details the operation of class bias in American journalism; *The Goose-Step: A Study of American Education* (1923) reveals higher education's lackeylike relationship to capitalism, fostered by grants and endowments made to the universities by wealthy families and industry. In *The Goslings: A Study of the American Schools* (1924), the same kind of servile relationship with the capitalist status quo is exposed as existing in elementary and high schools, and in *Mammonart* (1925), Sinclair shows how artists and writers down through history have been duped into serving oppressive economic and political power structures. Not even William Shakespeare, Fyodor Dostoevski, or Joseph Conrad were their own men according to Sinclair's ideological criticism. Although the Dead Hand series is flawed by an excess of socialist polemics, Sinclair did an extensive amount of research to produce each book, and though the case is overstated, there is a grain of truth in his analysis of the all-pervasive influence of the economic and political structure of America on those areas that should be most independent of such pressure—the Church, the press, the educational system, the arts.

Of more interest to the general reader are Sinclair's autobiographical works *American Outpost: A Book of Reminiscences* (1932) and *The Autobiography of Upton Sinclair* (1962), which updates his life for the thirty years intervening between the two books. In his accounts of his life, Sinclair reveals himself to be an honest but self-centered idealist. He chronicles his victories and defeats through childhood, youth, and marriage as the educational experiences of a genius; he offers in generally positive and optimistic terms his lifelong belief in progress and his hatred of social inequality and social exploitation.

ACHIEVEMENTS

Sinclair's literary remains weighed in at eight tons when being collected for donation to Indiana University Library. Of modern American writers, he is among the most widely translated, his works having been translated into forty-seven languages in thirty-nine countries, yet his literary reputation steadily declined after the 1940's, despite the fact that *The Jun-*

gle was still widely read in high school and college classrooms. Moreover, Sinclair himself has historical importance for the role he played in the American radical movement.

Sinclair's recurring theme as a novelist was class conflict, the exploitation of the poor by the rich, of labor by management, of the have-nots by the haves. With few exceptions, the rich are depicted as useless, extravagant, and unprincipled, while the poor are essentially noble characters who are the victims of capitalistic society. Sinclair's literary method, which came to be called "muckraking," was intended to expose the evils of such a society. Apart from *The Jungle*, which is the best-known example of this genre, there is the Lanny Budd series—ten historical novels that trace the history of the world from 1913 to 1946. *Dragon's Teeth*, the third in the series, won the Pulitzer Prize for Fiction in 1942 by virtue of its vivid portrayal of conditions in Nazi-dominated Europe. In addition to these, the most widely read of Sinclair's novels, he produced novels on almost every topic of then-current social history, including coal strikes in Colorado in *King Coal*, exploitation by the oil industry in California in *The Wet Parade*, and the legal injustices of the Sacco-Vanzetti case in *Boston*. All of Sinclair's fiction was aimed at the middle-class liberal, whom he hoped to convert to his idealistic vision of a fellowship of labor. Sinclair was thus a spokesman for the progressive era of American history; a chronic protester and iconoclast, he tried to stir the conscience of his nation and to cause change. In only one case, *The Jungle*, was he successful in prompting the desired changes through legislation. As a propagandist writing in the spirit of Thomas Paine and in the idiom of Karl Marx, Sinclair made a permanent impact by what he said, if not by how he wrote, and to this day, he still serves as one of the chief interpreters of American society to other nations.

BIOGRAPHY

Upton Beall Sinclair was born in Baltimore, Maryland, but reared in New York. Finishing high school at the age of twelve, he was too young for college and had to wait until he was fourteen before he could enter the City College of New York. While an undergraduate, he helped support himself by writing stories and jokes for pulp magazines. In one span of a few weeks, he turned out fifty-six thousand words, an incredible feat even for a prolific prodigy such as Sinclair. In 1898, after taking his B.A. from CCNY, Sinclair enrolled as a special student in the Graduate School of Columbia University, but withdrew after a professor told him, "you don't know anything about writing." In 1900, Sinclair married Meta Fuller and began work on his first novel, *Springtime and Harvest*, which was written in Canada. Shortly afterward, in 1902, he joined the Socialist Party. The reception of his early fiction gave him little critical encouragement and no cash of which to speak. His first four novels brought him less than one thousand dollars, and the threat of poverty put a strain on his marriage. In 1905, Sinclair, with Jack London, formed the Intercollegiate Socialist Society, an indication of his growing political radicalism.

Sinclair's first fame came with his fifth novel, *The Jungle*; he was even invited to the White House by President Theodore Roosevelt to discuss the book. With the thirty thousand dollars that *The Jungle* earned for him, Sinclair founded a utopian community, Helicon Colony, in New Jersey. In 1907, an arsonist burned down the colony and Sinclair's fortune with it. This was the first actual persecution that Sinclair had experienced for professing unpopular views. In private life, he faced further difficulties; his wife divorced him in 1911; he remarried in 1913 and moved West with his new wife, Mary Kimbrough, in 1915. Continuing to write at a furious pace, Sinclair became a publisher during World War I with the *Upton Sinclair Magazine*. He also issued a series of tracts on the effects of capitalism, objecting to its effects on education, art, journalism, and literature.

Not all of Sinclair's energies went into writing. He was instrumental in creating The League for Industrial Democracy and the American Civil Liberties Union. Three times he ran for the California state legislature and three times for governor, usually on the Socialist Party ticket but also as a Democrat. In *I, Governor of California and How I Ended Poverty* (1933), he set forth his platform, "End Poverty in

California" or "E.P.I.C.," which explained the Depression as a result of private ownership and the economic insanity of limited production. His ideas found a large degree of public acceptance in the early days of the New Deal, and he came close to being elected despite the mudslinging of his opponent. Some critics believe that the chief reason for Sinclair's decline as a novelist was his involvement in electoral politics in the 1930's. His novels of that decade are about specific political situations. *The Flivver King* attacks Ford Motor Company and makes a case for labor unions. "Little Steel" is a story about the organization of steel-mill owners against unions. "Pasaram!" is another short story from the 1930's about the brave fight in the Spanish Civil War against right-wing dictators.

During World War II, Sinclair began the historical record of his times in the Lanny Budd series. The novels in this ten-book series show the metamorphosis of the hero, Lanny, from an espouser of socialist causes to an anti-Communist, a change that reflected Sinclair's own changed sympathies.

By the decade of the 1950's, Sinclair had entered semiretirement, during which he nevertheless managed to expand his autobiography and finish six books, including a clever parody of Samuel Richardson's epistolary novel *Pamela* (1740-1741), entitled *Another Pamela*, and a biography of Jesus. In these years, Sinclair finally settled his quarrel with the status quo. In his old age, he came to approve of the American establishment's foot-dragging on civil rights and supported American intervention in Vietnam. The old radical had, like so many before him, softened his position.

ANALYSIS

Upton Sinclair was a prodigy as a writer and wrote with great fluency and consequent unevenness. For him, the essential purpose of literature was to expose social evils and promote change; his end as a writer was the improvement of the condition of humankind. Thus, his literary reputation is not really germane to what he was trying to do as a writer. His fiction has more relevance when it is regarded in a political and historical light rather than as literature per se. As the social and economic issues of his time recede into history, so does interest in those books that were simply propaganda.

Although Sinclair was regarded as a literary rebel for his iconoclastic attacks on America's economic, intellectual, and political institutions, he was not in any way an avant-garde writer in terms of style and structure. His subject was society rather than the individual human consciousness. It is necessary in any analysis of Sinclair's fiction to admit at once the defects in his writing. Most of it is journalistic in quality rather than belletristic. In fact, he deliberately wrote against the genteel tradition in American letters. Sinclair employed his rhetoric for practical results rather than to achieve poetic effects. His polemics were couched in fictional form because he believed the novel was a particularly effective medium for his idealistic radicalism.

Sinclair's first four novels were produced between 1900 and 1904. These early works were awkward but full of passionate idealism. In *Prince Hagen* and *The Overman*, which were written before Sinclair discovered socialism, there is already a conflict between the pure-minded and the corrupt oppressors, but no solutions for the problems are proposed. The ideology of socialism provided him with solutions, although Sinclair was not a traditional Socialist; to him, socialism was the purest expression of the American Dream. He did not see himself as an overthrower of American values, but as a writer who was helping his fellow citizens return to a vision of human alliance.

MANASSAS

Prior to *Manassas*, Sinclair's fiction had been based on personal experience. In this novel about the Civil War, a young southerner, Alan Montague, the son of a Mississippi plantation owner, becomes a supporter of abolition. The protagonist is present at many historic moments—the raid at Harper's Ferry, the bombardment of Fort Sumter—and encounters many historical figures, such as Abraham Lincoln, Jefferson Davis, Frederick Douglass, and John Brown. *Manassas* differed from Sinclair's early books in that it was more realistic and objective. As a work of art, however, *Manassas* is not remarkable. The plot is often an inert review of historical facts, the character-

izations are shallow, and the story is too filled with coincidence to be plausible. Despite its flaws, *Manassas* marked a turning point in Sinclair's career. In this novel, he revealed attitudes that pointed toward his development as a writer of exposés.

THE JUNGLE

In 1904, Sinclair was asked by the editor of *The Appeal*, a radical paper, to write a novel about wage slavery and the oppressive conditions of industrial workers which would show that their plight was analogous to that of the black in the Old South. Responding to this offer, Sinclair spent two months in the meat-packing houses of Chicago talking to the workers; he visited the plants also as an official tourist, and in disguise as a worker. The impressions and information Sinclair gathered from this experience were extremely distressing to him. His personal reaction to the corruption he saw was outrage; it is his identification with the exploited workers and his naturalistic descriptions of the oppressive industrial conditions that make *The Jungle* so gripping.

As Sinclair explains in his memoirs, *American Outpost*, he returned to his farm in New Jersey after he had collected his data on the meat-packing industry in Chicago and started writing the novel on Christmas Day, completing it in the summer of 1905 after less than six months' work. Although it was published in serial form as it was being written, Sinclair had trouble finding a publisher for the book; it was refused by five houses before Doubleday & Company took it after their lawyers made a careful investigation to avoid any possible libel suits. When *The Jungle* was published in February, 1906, the public was horrified, not by the novel's account of the conditions of the workers as Sinclair and his socialist friends expected, but by the naturalistic descriptions of the slaughterhouses and the evidence of criminal negligence in meat inspection. *The Jungle*, like most of Sinclair's fiction, straddles genres; it is partly a novel and partly exposé journalism. Sinclair's purpose in writing the book was to protest the exploitation of the workers and to recommend socialism as a corrective ideology to capitalism; the revelations of unsanitary packing-plant procedures were only a means to those ends. Hardly a dozen pages of this long novel are explicitly concerned with the repugnant details of the slaughterhouse, yet what remains in the reader's mind long after the plot line and thematic intentions fade are the scenes of grinding up poisoned rats, children's fingers, and carcasses of steers condemned as tubercular for canning meats; and the rendering of hogs dead of cholera for a fine grade of lard. Most dramatic of all, however, was Sinclair's report that the men who served in the cooking room occasionally fell into the boiling vats and were returned to the world transubstantiated into Durham's Pure Leaf Lard. The vividness of the author's descriptions had two effects: The first was an immediate drop in meat sales across America and Europe; the second was a summons to the White House to detail the abuses in the meat industry to President Theodore Roosevelt. The outraged public brought pressure to bear on politicians, and Congress enacted the Federal Pure Food and Drug Act of 1906.

The sensational revelations of *The Jungle* have drawn attention from the book's literary qualities. *The Jungle* has been compared to the polemical late works of Leo Tolstoy and to the naturalistic fiction of Émile Zola because of its pessimistic determinism. The setting is the grim slums of Chicago and the gory stockyards. The novel tells the story of a group of recent Lithuanian immigrants who have been lured to America from their old-world villages with promise of high wages.

Jurgis Rudkus, the novel's principal character, comes to the stockyard district, along with several of his friends and relatives, expecting to realize the American Dream, little aware that they have entered a jungle. Unable to speak English, the immigrants are exploited by almost everyone in power—the politicians, the police, the landlords, and the "Beef Trust" bosses. Jurgis has to pay his foreman part of his low salary to keep his job. He is cheated by a crooked real-estate agent, who sells him a house with a hidden clause which allows the mortgage company to foreclose on Jurgis. After losing his house, Jurgis and his family are afflicted with misery. His job is taken away after he is blacklisted; he serves a jail term for slugging his wife's lascivious boss, who has compromised her honor. In turn, his father dies of disease,

his wife and infant son die in childbirth, and finally, he loses his last son in a drowning accident. Jurgis is left without anything; alone and in ill health, he is a broken man. He becomes a hobo, a petty criminal, and a strike-breaking scab—the lowest form of degradation for him.

In his extremity, Jurgis for the first time reflects upon how unjustly he has been treated by society, which he begins to regard as his enemy, but his views are inchoate. One day, by chance he hears a Socialist speak. The lecture transforms his conception of the world; socialism is like a revelation, for now there is a way by which the workers of the world can win respect. With Jurgis's conversion, the novel as a narrative ends for all practical purposes. The last chapters are devoted to socialist propaganda and socioeconomic analysis. The optimistic conclusion of the novel contrasts sharply with the pessimistic naturalism of the first chapters. Ironically, and to Sinclair's disappointment, the appeal to socialism and the protest against wage slavery did not win the hearts and minds of his audience, but his realistic portrayal of conditions in the meatpacking industry (as he once remarked) surely turned the stomach of the nation.

The Jungle will never be placed in the first rank of American fiction because of its mixture of fictional and journalistic elements, its unresolved contradictions in theme, and its melodramatic plot and bifurcated structure. Sinclair tried to do too many things at once, and he was only partially successful. Most readers think that the true significance of Sinclair's achievement in *The Jungle* lies in the uncensored presentation of the conditions of working-class life. Only Stephen Crane in *Maggie: A Girl of the Streets* (1893) had dealt with slum subjects with such integrity, and Sinclair had no models to follow in depicting this strata of society. In his firsthand observations and deep compassion for the oppressed, he was breaking new ground for literary treatment, which Theodore Dreiser would follow to different purposes.

THE METROPOLIS, THE MONEYCHANGERS, and LOVE'S PILGRIMAGE

Following the success of *The Jungle* was difficult for Sinclair. He spent the next eight years trying to repeat what he had done with his first and best "muckraking" book. He produced a number of novels focused on specific problems, but at the other end of the social scale. *The Metropolis* is an exposé of conspicuous consumption among upper-class New York socialites. It is a poor book by Sinclair's own admission and is remarkable only for the absence of socialistic sermons by the author. Sinclair, like F. Scott Fitzgerald, apparently believed that money sets the very wealthy quite apart from the rest of society, but, rather than seeking rapport with his wealthy characters, as Fitzgerald did, Sinclair hoped to reform them. Another novel of this period, *The Money Changers*, is a story of the machinations of a high financier, obviously patterned on J. P. Morgan; the story tells of the exploits of Dan Waterman, the elderly head of the Steel Trust, who creates a panic on Wall Street purely for personal revenge against a rival steel magnate. Although *The Money Changers* is not very good fiction, it does have an interesting premise, suggesting a connection between sexual desire and the drive for financial power.

Another novel of this period that deserves mention for its subject is *Love's Pilgrimage*; neofeminist in theme, this work examines the pressures on Sinclair's own marriage because of his male insensitivity to his wife's personal, sexual, and intellectual needs. The novel is also interesting for the insight it offers into Sinclair's personality, for he implies that the divorce his first wife sought was deserved because he prudishly withheld from sexual relations on the theory that it would decrease his creative energy.

King Coal

In 1914, Sinclair was remarried and living in California. The transition in his life resulted in a change in his writing. In the West, Sinclair was drawn back to the problems of the proletariat by labor strife in the Colorado coal mines. As a result of the attempt by the United Mine Workers to organize the miners, the governor of Colorado had called up the state militia to break up strikes. In 1914, in the town of Ludlow, National Guard troops fired into a camp of strikers and their families, killing eleven women and two children. This shocking event outraged Sinclair as nothing had since he had witnessed the brutal conditions of the stockyards.

Following the methods he had used to collect background material for *The Jungle*, he went to Colorado, visited the miners and their families, and talked with the mining officials and labor leaders. His direct contact with the working-class people stirred his emotions and gave him a more realistic point of departure for his next novel, *King Coal*, than any he had employed since *The Jungle*. In fact, *King Coal* was an attempt to repeat the same sort of muckraking performance that had succeeded so well in the former case. Unfortunately for Sinclair, *King Coal* did not create the response aroused by *The Jungle*, a fact largely resulting from the lag time in the publication of the novel. When *King Coal* appeared in 1917, the events in Ludlow were three years old and yesterday's news. America had just entered World War I, and the nation's mind was on "doughboys" rather than on coal miners.

The poor reception of *King Coal* was a great disappointment to Sinclair, because he knew he had produced the kind of novel he wrote best. *King Coal*, while not as powerful as *The Jungle*, has the rhetorical strength and the factual validity of the earlier book. Sinclair tells the story of a rich young man named Hal Warner, who impersonates a coal miner in order to investigate working conditions in the western coal camps. He becomes a union sympathizer and labor agitator after he becomes convinced that the mine owners are denying the miners their legal rights and are cheating them out of their wages by rigged scales. After witnessing the futility of getting justice for working men inside the legal system, the miners go on a wildcat strike. Hal convinces his coworkers to join the union, and the novel ends with the lines drawn between labor and management while Hal returns to college, vowing to continue his fight for the working people of America.

Although *King Coal* is not as powerful in its naturalistic details as *The Jungle* and lacks the pessimistic determinism of that novel, it is in the opinion of most critics Sinclair's second-best effort at muckraking. If very few Americans responded to Sinclair's account of the dangers of cave-ins, coal dust, and explosions, this result may be because they were never exposed to such perils, whereas all were subject to health hazards as a result of unsanitary food processing. For this reason, the exposé of negligence in Chicago meat-packing plants had a much more profound and practical effect than the exposé of the inhuman conditions in the coal camps of Colorado.

OIL! A NOVEL and BOSTON

Between World War I and the start of the Depression, Sinclair wrote two remarkable novels based on topical social or political situations. *Oil! A Novel* delves into the Tea Pot Dome and other oil scandals of the Harding administration, and thus has considerable historical significance as well as being one of Sinclair's most readable books. *Boston*, on the other hand, represents Sinclair's best use of a contemporary event for fictional purposes. This novel enfolds the drama of the Sacco-Vanzetti case, but it also encompasses the whole of Boston's society, suggesting that the city itself was responsible for what happened in this tragic case. The central character is again from the upper classes, an elderly Back Bay aristocrat, Cornelia Thornwell, wife to a governor. Full of vitality and intelligence, she thinks that she has spent her life as an artificial adornment to a great family. She determines late in life to emancipate herself from the mores and manners of the mansion and moves out to board with the Brini family, who are honest Italian mill hands, and starts to earn her own living in a factory.

At this point, Vanzetti enters the story. During a strike in the mill, he plays an important role in keeping up the workers' spirits. He also prevents them from organizing, because as an anarchist, Vanzetti did not support unions. Afterward, Vanzetti and his friend Sacco are marked as "anarchist wops" by the police. They are picked up as suspects in a payroll robbery, and in the midst of the deportation mania of the postwar period, the city's reason and sense of justice are beclouded. The courts, judge, jury, and prosecutor seem determined to make the foreigners pay—if not for the crime, then for their politics. The climax of the novel comes when the cogs of justice bring the proletarian saints, Vanzetti and Sacco, to the electric chair with many doubts about their guilt still lingering.

Through a blending of fact and fiction, Sinclair is able to record a complex and tragic story of social injustice, although the story of the runaway grandmother does get lost in the final pages as the historical facts dominate the plot. As a novel, the two-volume *Boston* is too long except for readers with some special interest in the Sacco-Vanzetti case. As usual, Sinclair was writing for a mass audience, and the novel employs many stock characters and a melodramatic plot; furthermore, a statement of socialist doctrine forms a coda to the novel. Sinclair does, however, create a convincing portrait of Vanzetti. It is in Sinclair's account of the death of this man of dignity and intelligence that the novel gains its greatest power.

THE LANNY BUDD SERIES

The major literary effort of Sinclair's career was launched just before the outbreak of World War II: a ten-novel series offering a fictionalized history of the Western world in the first half of the twentieth century. The series is unified by its central character, Lanny Budd, and is known collectively by his name. One of the Lanny Budd novels, *Dragon's Teeth*, won for Sinclair a Pulitzer Prize in 1943. A chronicle of Germany's slide into Nazism, *Dragon's Teeth* is a scrupulous study of the fateful years between 1930 and 1934 and reflects an extensive research effort on Sinclair's part. In fact, several critics claimed that if the book were stripped of its fictional ingredient, it might well serve as a history text.

Sinclair creates an air of impending doom as he shows how quickly Europe was led to the abyss. His protagonist, Lanny Budd, is a neutral observer traveling the Continent with his millionaire wife, Irma, who is especially obtuse about economics, politics, and national traits. She is a foil to the sensitive and intelligent Lanny, who is aware of the coming crisis. Irma and her upper-class female friends refuse to believe that their smug routine of bridge and dinner parties will be disrupted. The reader in 1942 received these opinions with a great deal of dramatic irony. Meanwhile, Lanny grows increasingly concerned about the absence of morality in the political climate of Germany. Lanny has rather improbable meetings with the bigwigs of the Nazi regime. He goes hunting with Hermann Göring, has cocktails with Joseph Goebbels, and a discussion with Adolf Hitler about the Jewish question. His interest in this topic is not merely academic, since his sister is married to one of Germany's most prominent Jews. The Jews in Germany, however, are like Irma's circle; they refuse to face the realities of Nazism. The novel ends with Lanny's contriving to help his brother-in-law escape the dragon's teeth of the Nazi menace, closing the story on an exciting climax, somewhat like that of a cliffhanger film of the 1940's.

Sinclair continued the adventures of Lanny Budd, interweaving fiction with fact as he related the sequence of world events in *World's End*, which covers the years 1913 to 1919; *Between Two Worlds* deals with the events between the Versailles Treaty and the stock market crash of 1929; the author then covers the Nazi "Blood Purge" of 1934 to the Spanish Civil War in *Wide Is the Gate*; the annexation of Austria, the invasion of Czechoslovakia, and the Munich pact in *Presidential Agent*; the fall of France in *Dragon Harvest*; and America's entry into the war in *A World to Win*. The years of Allied setbacks, 1941-1943, are covered in *Presidential Mission; One Clear Call* and *O Shepherd, Speak!* deal with the Normandy Invasion and the defeat of the German military machine; and in the sequel to the series, *The Return of Lanny Budd*, Sinclair brings events up to 1949 and the onset of the Cold War between the United States and the Soviet Union.

As a whole, this group of novels is interesting, in part simply because the series surveys a dramatic period of history in considerable detail. Throughout the series, Sinclair's careful research is evident, but the popularity of these novels was also a result of their appeal to patriotism. America's role as the savior of civilization is increasingly emphasized in the later novels in the series. During this period, Sinclair's confidence that progress was represented by socialism and communism was shaken by the example of the Soviet Union. Like so many early twentieth century political radicals, he became an anti-Communist in the 1950's.

Sinclair was a propagandist first and a novelist second, if propaganda is defined as an "effort directed systematically toward the gaining of support for an opinion or course of action." He wrote millions of words trying to change, improve, or expose oppressive conditions. Because Sinclair so obviously used literature for ulterior purposes and because he was so prolific, serious critics have unduly neglected him; on the other hand, he has been overrated by those foreign critics who delight in finding indictments of America by an American writer. As time puts Sinclair's contribution to American literature into perspective, it seems certain that he will never be regarded as a great novelist, but he will fairly be judged an honest, courageous, and original writer.

Hallman B. Bryant

OTHER MAJOR WORKS

PLAYS: *Plays of Protest*, pb. 1912; *Hell: A Verse Drama and Photo-Play*, pb. 1923; *The Millennium*, pb. 1924; *The Pot Boiler*, pb. 1924; *Singing Jailbirds*, pb. 1924; *Bill Porter*, pb. 1925; *Wally for Queen!*, pb. 1936; *Marie Antoinette*, pb. 1939; *A Giant's Strength*, pr., pb. 1948.

NONFICTION: *Our Bourgeois Literature*, 1904; *The Industrial Republic*, 1907; *The Fasting Cure*, 1911; *The Profits of Religion*, 1918; *The Brass Check: A Study in American Journalism*, 1919; *The Book of Life, Mind, and Body*, 1921; *The Goose-Step: A Study of American Education*, 1923; *The Goslings: A Study of the American Schools*, 1924; *Mammonart*, 1925; *Letters to Judd*, 1925; *Money Writes!*, 1927; *Mental Radio*, 1930; *American Outpost: A Book of Reminiscences*, 1932; *I, Governor of California and How I Ended Poverty*, 1933; *The Way Out—What Lies Ahead for America?*, 1933; *The EPIC Plan for California*, 1934; *What God Means to Me*, 1936; *Terror in Russia: Two Views*, 1938; *Expect No Peace!*, 1939; *A Personal Jesus*, 1952; *The Cup of Fury*, 1956; *My Lifetime in Letters*, 1960; *The Autobiography of Upton Sinclair*, 1962.

CHILDREN'S LITERATURE: *The Gnomobile: A Gnice Gnew Gnarrative with Gnonsense, but Gnothing Gnaughty*, 1936.

BIBLIOGRAPHY

Colburn, David R., and George E. Pozzetta, eds. *Reform and Reformers in the Progressive Era*. Westport, Conn.: Greenwood Press, 1983. An essay by Judson Grenier examines Sinclair's position as a muckraker and his role in inspiring Progressive reforms. Unlike other journalistic writers, Sinclair was personally and ideologically committed.

Dell, Floyd. *Upton Sinclair: A Study in Social Protest.* New York: AMS Press, 1970. Dell's treatment of Sinclair's career analyzes the apparent discrepancy between his literary position in the United States and throughout the rest of the world. Personal incidents and psychological insights are intertwined with evaluations and interpretations of specific works. Contains a bibliography of out-of-print books and an index.

Harris, Leon. *Upton Sinclair: American Rebel.* New York: Thomas Y. Crowell, 1975. This biography traces Sinclair's rise from obscurity to fame, with his subsequent decline in popularity. The text provides interesting information regarding source materials for some of his novels. A section of photographs, extensive notes, a list of Sinclair's books, and an index complete the book.

Herms, Dieter, ed. *Upton Sinclair: Literature and Social Reform.* New York: Peter Lang, 1990. This is a collection of papers from the Upton Sinclair World Conference of July, 1988, at the University of Bremen. Includes bibliographical references.

Mookerjee, R. N. *Art for Social Justice: The Major Novels of Upton Sinclair.* Metuchen, N.J.: Scarecrow, 1988. Mookerjee, a critic of writers of the 1930's, provides a reevaluation of *The Jungle, King Coal, Oil! A Novel, Boston,* and the Lanny Budd series. This slender volume is a valid reminder of the pioneering role of Sinclair in the "documentary novel." Contains a good selected bibliography.

Scott, Ivan. *Upton Sinclair: The Forgotten Socialist.* Lewiston: Edwin Mellen Press, 1997. See especially chapters 1 and 2, "The Formation of Genius" and "*The Jungle.*" In his introduction, Scott makes a good case for Sinclair's importance. A sound scholarly biography, drawing extensively on the Sinclair collection at Lilly Library, the University of Indiana.

Yoder, Jon A. *Upton Sinclair.* New York: Frederick Ungar, 1975. Like some other critics, Yoder attributes Sinclair's "meager reputation" in part to his socialist views. Five chapters in this slim volume examine various facets of the novelist's life and career. A chronology, notes, a bibliography, and an index supplement the text.

ISAAC BASHEVIS SINGER

Born: Leoncin, Poland; July 14 or November 21, 1904
Died: Surfside, Florida; July 24, 1991

PRINCIPAL LONG FICTION

Der Sotn in Gorey, 1935 (*Satan in Goray,* 1955)
Di Familye Mushkat, 1950 (*The Family Moskat,* 1950)
Der Hoyf, 1953-1955 (*The Manor,* 1967, and *The Estate,* 1969)
Shotns baym Hodson, 1957-1958 (*Shadows on the Hudson,* 1998)
Der Kuntsnmakher fun Lublin, 1958-1959 (*The Magician of Lublin,* 1960)
Der Knekht, 1961 (*The Slave,* 1962)
Sonim, de Geshichte fun a Liebe, 1966 (*Enemies: A Love Story,* 1972)
Neshome Ekspeditsyes, 1974 (*Shosha,* 1978)
Der Bal-Tshuve, 1974 (*The Penitent,* 1983)
Reaches of Heaven: A Story of the Baal Shem Tov, 1980
Der Kenig vun di Felder, 1988 (*The King of the Fields,* 1988)
Scum, 1991
The Certificate, 1992
Meshugah, 1994

OTHER LITERARY FORMS

The first work that Isaac Bashevis Singer published when he moved to the United States was the novel known as "Messiah the Sinner," which was serialized in 1936 but was never published as a book. It was serialized in three Yiddish daily papers: *Der Vorwärts* (the *Jewish Daily Forward,* in New York), the *Warshanahaint* (in Warsaw), and the *Pariser Haint* (in Paris). Singer himself considered this work a "complete failure" and never attempted to translate it. In addition to his novels, Singer wrote memoirs, *Mayn Tatn's Bes-din Shtub* (1956; *In My Father's Court*, 1966), *A Little Boy in Search of God* (1976), *A Young Man in Search of Love* (1978), and *Lost in America* (1980); more than one hundred stories; and numerous books for children. He wrote two works on Hasidism, one in collaboration with the artist Ira Moskowitz entitled *The Hasidim* (1973). His Yiddish translations of works by such noted authors as Stefen Zweig, Knut Hamsun, Erich Maria Remarque, and Thomas Mann are well regarded, as are his many literary essays and reviews. Several of Singer's short stories have been adapted as plays; "Yentl der Yeshive Bocher" ("Yentl, the Yeshiva Boy"), which was written in Yiddish in the 1950's, became a Broadway play in 1975 and a film (*Yentl*) in 1983.

ACHIEVEMENTS

Singer has been acclaimed by some critics as a genius and referred to by others as one of the greatest writers of the modern world. In the aftermath of the Holocaust, which resulted in the obliteration of central and eastern European Jewry, the works of Isaac Bashevis Singer stand as monuments to a vibrant and vital world. Singer's writing does not idolize this community: He depicts it in its totality, in its full humanity. His people are saints and sinners, believers and heretics, fools and scholars, avaricious merchants and ineffectual rabbis, patient wives and termagants. His imaginative world includes demons, elves, dybbuks, and magicians, mystical figures from a lost folk culture. However, Singer's fiction does more than recall a world destroyed by the Holocaust. The power of his work, while remaining thoroughly Jewish, transcends the boundaries of cultural and religious ethnicity to raise questions about life that have been translatable across the changing contexts of twentieth century thought.

Singer's works are written in Yiddish, the language of the shtetl—the eastern European village or town. For Singer, Yiddish is more than the vernacular of the people of the central and eastern European Jewish community. It is, as he stated in his Nobel Prize lecture, "the wise and humble language of us

(The Nobel Foundation)

all, the idiom of a frightened and hopeful humanity." His Yiddish reflects the influence of three languages, Yiddish, Hebrew, and Aramaic, and contains frequent allusions to rabbinic and Talmudic lore. The richness of his prose and its texture, pace, and rhythm are not easy to capture in translation. Singer worked with his translators and participated in the editing. All of his major works first appeared in serial form in the *Forward* (originally a daily, the *Jewish Daily Forward*, then a weekly) prior to their translation and rendition into book form except for his first novel, *Satan in Goray*, which was serialized in the magazine *Globus* in Warsaw in 1934.

One of the outstanding characteristics of Singer's tales is his use of demoniac imagery. This motif does not represent a love of the bizarre, the occult, or the gothic, although Singer is interested in these aspects.

His demons figuratively portray the evil side of human nature; moreover, Singer believed that supernatural powers—both good and evil—do exist, and he affirmed his ultimate faith in Providence.

Singer's vision is optimistic when it concerns cosmic matters but pessimistic in dealing with humanity. He differs from his Yiddish literary contemporaries or predecessors in that most have been secularists who relinquished the past in favor of the Enlightenment. Most Yiddish writers after the 1940's portrayed an idealized and sentimental view of the shtetl. Singer could not accept this tradition. He maintains that the greatest gift of God is freedom of choice. Where there is no evil, there is also no freedom. He is aware that good does not always triumph, so his Jews are not all good. His characters share the traits and illusions of all humankind.

Singer is a supreme storyteller. For him, the suspense, the adventure, the age-old pleasures of narrative are paramount. He leaves explanations and interpretations to his readers and critics. Singer achieved a popular success unusual for a writer of his distinction: His works have become best-sellers and have been translated into fifty-eight languages. He won the National Book Award twice and Newberry Awards three times, and he was awarded the Nobel Prize in Literature in 1978. A number of his works have been dramatized and widely performed; some have also been made into motion pictures. He was an engaging and popular figure on the campuses of colleges and universities and a favorite of interviewers; he served as writer-in-residence at Oberlin College, at the University of California, and at Bard College. In 1989, the American Academy and Institute of Arts and Letters bestowed on Singer its highest award, its Gold Medal.

BIOGRAPHY

Isaac Bashevis Singer was born in Leoncin, Poland. There has long been some uncertainty as to the date of his birth; In *Isaac Bashevis Singer: The Magician of West Eighty-sixth Street* (1979), biographer Paul Kresh quotes Singer as stating that November 21 was, as far as he knew, "more or less" the actual date of his birth. For many years, however, he had celebrated July 14 because his parents had told him that was his birthday to cheer him up after they moved.

He was the third child in a family of four siblings, who included an older sister, Hinde Esther, an older brother, Israel Joshua, and a younger brother, Moishe. His parents were Pinchas Mendel Singer, a Hasidic rabbi from Tomoszov, and Bathsheba Zylberman, the daughter of the *Mitnagid*—the opposing sect—rabbi of Bilgoray. The couple seemed to be mismatched. Pinchas Mendel, a gentle, pious, spiritual man, was an ardent follower of Hasidism. Bathsheba, a learned, strong-minded woman, was a rationalist and a pragmatist. Israel Joshua, eleven years Singer's senior, inherited his mother's rationalism; Moishe, two years Singer's junior, inherited his father's piety. The confluence of parental legacies—the mysticism of Singer's father and the rationalism of his mother—was Singer's inheritance, reflected in the tensions of his fictive characters: conflicts between the heart and the head, the sacred and the profane, the spiritual and the secular.

Four years after Singer's birth, the family moved to Warsaw, to an apartment on Krochmalna Street. Rabbi Pinchas Mendel became the rabbi of Krochmalna Street, and the Singer home served as its *bet din*, or rabbinic court. Singer's memoirs *In My Father's Court* and *A Day of Pleasure: Stories of a Boy Growing Up in Warsaw* (1969) and the novels *Shosha* and "Yarme and Kayle" (serialized in the *Forward* in 1977 but never published in book form) re-create the intricate life that existed on this cobblestoned shtetl street, a "literary goldmine" to which Singer regularly returns.

In 1917, World War I forced Singer, his mother, and his younger brother to flee the city. They went to Bilgoray, where they stayed for four years. The visit was crucial in his development as a writer. The village of Bilgoray, far removed from the bustle of cosmopolitan Warsaw, appeared to be untouched by modernity. Young Singer witnessed old-world spirituality unblemished by the encroaching Enlightenment. This experience remained with him as an eternal reminder of his rootedness—indeed, humankind's rootedness—in the past, in history, in that which transcends human nature. Bilgoray plays an important role in many of his works; Singer once said that he could never have written *Satan in Goray* without having been there. In Bilgoray, he studied the Talmud and modern Hebrew, which in turn he taught in private homes. He also studied the Kabbalah, read the works of philosopher Baruch Spinoza, and studied German and Polish. He became immersed in the rural Hasidic folk culture that would permeate his work.

In 1921, Singer entered a rabbinical seminary in Warsaw. He remained for a year and then went back to Bilgoray and supported himself by teaching Hebrew. Shortly afterward, he joined his parents in Dzikow, a shtetl close to Bilgoray, where his father had accepted a position as a rabbi. He found this village stifling and depressing, and he was delighted when his older brother, who was coeditor of the *Literarische Bleter*, offered him a job as proofreader for the journal. In 1923, Singer moved back to Warsaw to take up this new position. His family was settled in Dzikow, and he never saw his mother or younger brother again.

Singer's brother Israel Joshua was also a writer and served as Singer's mentor. He was the person who exerted the greatest influence on the young Singer, encouraging him when he began to write and instructing him in the rules of good storytelling. Although Isaac was given to mysticism, Israel Joshua was a realist who became part of the Jewish Enlightenment, the *Haskalai*, which was overtaking the shtetl at the beginning of the twentieth century. This situation had caused friction in the Singer home, especially with their father, who was a traditionalist. Joshua—no one called him by his first name—moved out of the house, becoming an artist and then a writer. Singer often visited his brother and discovered, in his studio, a whole new world. He describes the experience of going from his father's house to his brother's studio in *In My Father's Court*, saying: "It is just one step from the study house to sexuality and back again. Both phases of human existence have continued to interest me." Through his brother, he was introduced to secular literature. Singer lived, for the most part, in his brother's literary shadow. He used pseudonyms for his early writings; some stories were

signed "Isaac Bashevis" (a form of his mother's first name in Yiddish) to distinguish his works from those of Joshua, while some were signed "Isaac Warshawsky" ("man of Warsaw").

In 1925, Singer made his fiction debut in Yiddish with a short story, "Oyf der elter" (in old age), which won a prize in *Literarishe bleter*'s literary contest. It was published under the pseudonym "Tse." In 1935, it was reprinted in the *Jewish Daily Forward*. His second published story, "Nerot" (candles), appeared in 1925 in *Ha-yon*. In 1932, Singer edited, with Aaron Zeitlin, a magazine called *Globus*, which printed several of Singer's short stories and in 1933 serialized his first novel, *Satan in Goray*, which was published in book form by the Warsaw PEN Club in 1935. In these early years, Singer also began a series of translations into Yiddish, which by 1935 included Hamsun's *Pan* and *Victoria*, Remarque's *All Quiet on the Western Front*, and Mann's *The Magic Mountain*.

Singer fell in love with Runya, the mother of his only child, Israel, who was born in 1929, the year of Singer's father's death. Runya was an avid communist and wanted to live in Russia. She and Singer quarreled heatedly, frequently about political issues. Runya finally took their child and left for Russia in 1934. She was expelled shortly thereafter and went to join her mother in Palestine. Once settled there, she sent their son to Kibbutz Bet Alpha. He changed his name to Israel Zamir—the Hebrew equivalent of Singer. Singer did not see his son until 1955, when Zamir decided to visit his father; this episode is described in the short story "The Son" in the collection *A Friend of Kafka and Other Stories* (1970).

Joshua Singer emigrated to the United States with his family in 1933 and found a job on the Yiddish daily, the *Jewish Daily Forward*. He urged his brother to do likewise. With the shadow of Adolf Hitler extending over most of Europe, Singer did not need much coaxing, and in 1935 he followed his brother. He never returned to Poland. Singer's acclimation to America was difficult. English was a strange language to him, and Yiddish, his mother tongue and his literary language, did not seem to have a future in America. *Lost in America* records this transitional period. He reviewed plays for the *Jewish Daily For-*

ward but could not resume his writing. At the urgings of his Warsaw friend Aaron Zeitlin, he completed a novel, begun in Warsaw, known as "Messiah the Sinner." It was not a success.

In 1937, Singer met Alma Haimann Wasserman at a summer resort in the Catskill Mountains in New York State. She had emigrated from Germany the previous year. Theirs was an attraction with "telepathic qualities," Singer would reminisce in his later years. They married on February 14, 1940. For many years, Alma supported Singer's writing by working in sales positions in New York department stores. She tended to all their financial concerns and served as one of his translators.

The "greatest misfortune" of his life, according to Singer, was the death of his brother Joshua in 1944. In the dedication to the English version of *The Family Moskat*, he extols his brother as his "spiritual father and master." Singer's family sagas, *The Family Moskat*, *The Manor*, and *The Estate*, are efforts to emulate his brother's work; critics agree that they do not represent the best of Isaac Bashevis Singer and are not typical of his work. However, these novels do present a historical overview of Jewish life in Poland, beginning with the Polish uprising of 1863 in *The Manor* and culminating in the catastrophe of the Holocaust during World War II in *The Family Moskat*.

In 1943, *Satan in Goray and Other Tales* was published in New York in Yiddish, and in the mid-1940's Singer's fiction began appearing regularly. In 1945, "Gimpel Tam" ("Gimpel the Fool"), perhaps Singer's most famous story, was published in *Yidisher kemfe*. In the 1950's a range of Singer's work—long and short novels, a novella, and a collection of short-stories—was brought before an English-speaking public. The May, 1953, publication of "Gimpel the Fool," translated by Saul Bellow in the *Partisan Review*, was a crucial breakthrough for Singer. Thereafter, his work appeared widely in English in magazines such as the *Partisan Review*, *Commentary*, *The New Yorker*, *Harper's*, and *Esquire*. In 1960 Singer began his long affiliation with the publishing house of Farrar Straus Giroux. With the publication by *The New Yorker* of "The Slaughterer" in 1967, later collected in *The Seance and Other Stories*, Singer began his exclusive associ-ation with that magazine that lasted until his death.

At the suggestion of a friend, Elizabeth Shub, Singer started writing children's books; the first, *Zlateh the Goat and Other Stories*, appeared in 1966. He published more than fifteen books for children. Singer's books for children are not written with the left hand; indeed, the format is particularly congenial to certain aspects of his genius. His children's books have been extremely popular and have won numerous prizes; they have been translated into a dozen languages in addition to the standard English, French, Spanish, Japanese, and Hebrew. Singer worked with a variety of translators, including his wife, Alma, and his nephew, Joseph.

ANALYSIS

An oft-quoted line from Isaac Bashevis Singer's story "Gimpel Tam" ("Gimpel the Fool") epitomizes his theory of fiction and his worldview: "No doubt the world is entirely an imaginary world, but it is only once removed from the real world." His approach to his material is both imaginative and historical. Sometimes these strains run concurrently; at other times, one is subdued by the other. Through his use of the supernatural, he imaginatively portrays the Jewish community from the seventeenth to the twentieth century.

Singer's concern is not only with Jewish destiny but also with the destiny of any individual. He believes that the soul is a battleground for good and evil impulses. His use of the fantastic suggests the tenuous line between reality and fiction; it also provides what Singer termed a "spiritual stenography" of human behavior. He suggests that the perversions in which humans engage are otherworldly, that people are not always in control of their actions. Although individuals have freedom of choice, this freedom may be illusory because the forces of evil, if allowed to prevail, can be stronger than the forces of good. Ultimately, however, a desire for good can triumph if people can exert all their efforts to that end. The struggle between good and evil, between the spiritual and sensual, supplies the tension in his works. Singer contends that humankind cannot be separated from its passions; they are one and the same. His early novels, especially *Satan in Goray* and *The Magician of Lublin*, illustrate the problem of passions ruling the individual. Singer's solution to human problems is a return to one's ancestral heritage.

SATAN IN GORAY

Singer's first novel, *Satan in Goray*, written while he was still in Poland, is a gothic tale, commingling the historical with the phantasmagoric, the mysticism of Hasidism with the influences of Fyodor Dostoevski and Edgar Allan Poe, the sacred with the profane. The work is historical, contemporary, and prophetic. Its vision is dark, its tone harsh, and it deals with eternal conflicts: between good and evil, between predestination and freedom of choice.

Two historical events constitute the background of this novel: The first is the Cossack rebellion (1648-1649) led by Bogdan Chmielnicki against the Polish landowners, which resulted in the destruction of 100,000 Jews. This was a period of Jewish history remembered for its tremendous loss of life and for its acts of absolute barbarism, surpassed only by the Holocaust of World War II. The second is the messianic movement known as Shabbeteanism, after its originator Shabbetai Zvi (1626-1676). Historically, these movements converged when Shabbetai Zvi, in Smyrna, Turkey, proclaimed himself messiah in the year 1648, the time of the Chmielnicki massacres.

For Singer, however, historical events are important only in their effects upon individuals. His interest, at all times, lies with the passions that govern individuals and engage them in a continuous struggle. In this early work, Singer presents the shtetl of Goray in the aftermath of the Chmielnicki pogrom and indicates how the spiritual decline of the community is related to its physical destruction. The action of the novel takes place in the year 1666 as the survivors of the massacre move back to Goray and attempt to resume their lives. The village, however, cannot be resuscitated. Its people are maimed; its leaders are ineffectual; all are vulnerable. Singer focuses on what happens to people during a time of utmost vulnerability. He presents a good but misguided community, easily led astray by promises of redemption and the cessation of their earthly travails. The community has suffered much, and its prospects for the future

are bleak. Its roads and its earth are drenched with the blood of recently murdered people. Life appears meaningless. The inhabitants move about sluggishly. It would seem that the guardian of Israel slumbers, while her adversaries are on the alert.

The work is divided into two parts. The first deals with the struggle between good and evil as represented by the opposing factions within the community. Rabbi Benish Ashkenazi, the spiritual leader of this enervated community, one of its last survivors to return, represents the forces of good within the shtetl. His is the voice of traditionalism. He was a strong leader before the events of 1648. He did not allow the study of the Kabbala, with its promise of messianic redemption and with the asceticism of its adherents. At present, he can resume certain rabbinic functions within the community, he can deal with legal matters, but he cannot handle the spiritual and social problems of the villagers. He cannot control the dissension within his family; likewise, he cannot control the growing dissension in Goray. In both situations, he retreats into his own chambers and ultimately is concerned only with his own salvation. Meanwhile, rumors of the new messiah have filtered into the secluded village, injecting into it a vitality heretofore absent, resurrecting the shtetl as only messianism can. It is, however, a destructive messianism, one which must be preceded by absolute evil, an abrogation of societal restraints, an immersion in sexual perversity and religious heresy. Part 1 ends with the rabbi's leaving town, after being wounded in a battle with Satan, because he does not want to be buried in Goray. He fears that the evil which has overtaken Goray will contaminate even the dead.

Part 2 concerns the spiritual decline of the community through lack of leadership and perversions of the Law in the name of Shabbeteanism. The battle has been lost. Once the rabbi leaves, total chaos ensues. Part 2 begins with Rechele's marriage to an impotent ascetic—who is also a believer in Shabbeteanism—and ends with her death, after the dybbuk (a form of Satanic possession) in her body was exorcised. In the interim, the community gets a new leader, Reb Gedaliya, an emissary who proclaims the news of the crowning of the messiah. He is a ritual slaughterer by trade, a charlatan by profession. One of Singer's many perverted religious functionaries, his lust for blood is exceeded only by his lust for Rechele, who is the innocent victim of life's misfortunes. Gedaliya persuades the community that its redemption can take place only upon the abandonment of traditional Jewish life. Singer vividly portrays the manner in which the community loses sight of the relationship between traditional Judaism and redemption and the depths of moral turpitude into which it has plunged. Ultimately, evil—the dybbuk—is exorcised, together with the remaining Shabbeteans, and good returns to Goray. The novel ends in the spirit of a morality tale with these words: "Let none attempt to force the Lord. . . . The Messiah will come in God's own time."

Satan in Goray is a bleak tale in which the forces of good and evil fight for the human soul; humankind, maimed, vulnerable, and misguided, easily succumbs to the passions of lust and perversity. Critics have seen this work as adumbrating events that were soon to take place in Europe. The strength of this early novel lies in its use of demonology and the supernatural, which became a distinctive feature of Singer's fiction.

THE MAGICIAN OF LUBLIN

Written in 1958, serialized in 1959, and published in English in 1960, *The Magician of Lublin* also deals with human passions, but it is not overcast with the gloom of past events. It reflects an expansiveness often missing in Singer's works. Its focus is not on the Jewish community itself but on the individual in a timeless context. Singer's magician-protagonist is well cast. On a literal level, he is representative of the artist. On a symbolic level, every person may be seen as a magician, living life, like Yasha Mazur, the novel's protagonist, "as if walking the tightrope merely inches from disaster." The variegated personality of the hero, "religious and heretical, good and evil, false and sincere," and the lack of dates in the work lend themselves to a symbolic interpretation. Singer focuses on the single individual and the choices he or she makes. In *Satan in Goray*, historical events negate options. In *The Magician of Lublin*, Singer removes the encumbrances of history and allows his hero to make conscious decisions that determine the progress of his life.

Yasha Mazur is a complex person, vital, exuberant, intense—above all, a man with a personal destiny. Unlike Jacob, the protagonist of *The Slave*, for example, who is a good person, motivated to do right no matter what the circumstances are, Yasha has an intricate personality. It engages him constantly in a struggle of opposing forces. In *Satan in Goray*, the opposing forces are presented as two distinct elements within the community. The triumph of one necessitates the removal of the other. When evil was victorious, Rabbi Benish Ashkenazi had to leave Goray. In *The Magician of Lublin*, however, these forces exist within the individual, enduring aspects of human nature. Yasha Mazur's entire life is a battle. He can never conquer the evil drive. He can only negotiate with it, appease it, or in some other way deal with it, so that it remains dormant. He never knows, however, when it will awaken to begin another round.

Yasha Mazur was reared in a pious Jewish home, studied the Talmud until his father died—his mother died when he was seven—and then joined the circus. He maintains a home in Lublin with his wife, Esther, but roams the Polish countryside as a "circus performer and hypnotist." As an artist or magician, he moves in various worlds, assumes various guises or personalities, and has a different mistress in each world. He aspires to higher things: He is a successful artist and would like to perform in Warsaw, in the summer theater of the prestigious Saxony Gardens. He is barred from doing so because he is Jewish. The closest he comes to achieving this goal is at the apartment of the middle-class Gentile Emilia, located on a street opposite the Saxony Gardens. Yasha's relationship with Emilia focuses the tensions of the work. He thinks he is in love with her, but she refuses the role of mistress. She wants to be his wife. To marry her, Yasha would have to divorce Esther, convert to Christianity, and procure great wealth to maintain the façade he has established in his courting of Emilia. These are formidable decisions that will determine his future.

Singer establishes the dichotomy of predestination and free will early in the work in the contrasting attitudes toward life represented by Yasha and his wife. Esther is a religious woman, married twenty years to Yasha; they have no children. Her entire life consists of making a home for a husband who returns to it only on holidays. She loves him but regrets, at times, not having married someone more stable. The thought of changing her life, however, never crosses her mind. She is a strong believer in Providence and accepts her fate as a lonely woman.

Yasha, although he says that "everything is fate," realizes that he shapes his own destiny in all his choices. He is a magician who consorts with thieves, but he refuses to use his powers for evil purposes. He will not become a thief. When he finally attempts it, out of a desperate need to support Emilia, he fails and injures himself. The man who is so agile that he can walk a tightrope to the awe of his audience becomes a shlemiel and bungles a simple act of burglary. Although he is Jewish by birth, he is a nonbeliever—or says he is—by choice. He does not pray, because God does not answer the prayers of his supplicants: his "gifts" are "plagues, famines, poverty, and pogroms." Nevertheless, to become a Christian for Emilia is a difficult choice for him. He is a libertine, yet he considers the institution of marriage sacred and cannot easily make the decision to break up his home for his new infatuation. He is faced with the dilemma of choosing "between his religion and the cross, between Esther and Emilia, between honesty and crime." These choices will "seal his destiny." He finally chooses to remain with his own religion and decides also that traditionalism is more meaningful than assimilationism.

Yasha is aware that life is the most powerful seductress. He returns to his home and builds for himself a doorless brick prison which frees him from temptation and allows him to meditate on his past actions, yet he discovers that as long as he is alive, he cannot shut out the world. As an artist or a magician, he went out into the world, succumbing to carnal pleasures, drinking, eating, loving unrestrainedly. Having come to the realization that "there must be discipline," he undergoes the transformation from sinner to saint. As an ascetic, in the confines of his self-imposed banishment, considered by all a "holy man,"

the world comes to him. Even his past love writes him a letter. Yasha's imprisonment has been only partially successful. He has turned his intense feelings in another direction, moving from the sensual to the spiritual. In this work, Singer suggests that people cannot escape their essence: They and their passions are one. *The Magician of Lublin* presents a positive outlook even though it concludes (as does Singer's novel *Shosha*) in a dark cell or room.

ENEMIES: A LOVE STORY

Singer's novels *Enemies* and *Shosha* directly address the most tragic time of Jewish history, the Holocaust. *Enemies*, ironically subtitled *A Love Story*, is Singer's only novel set in the United States; it deals specifically with survivors of the Holocaust. In *Shosha*, Singer returns for another nostalgic look at the destroyed world in which he grew up and attempts to capture the spirit of his people as the perimeters of death close in on them.

Like *The Magician of Lublin*, *Enemies* is written on two levels. It fills a gap in Singer's canon. Until this work, Singer's literary aim was to re-create the destroyed world of eastern European Jewry, to present the pulsating life that existed specifically in his native Poland. *Enemies* acknowledges the destruction of his fictive world and deals with problems confronting those who survived. In a note that precedes the work, Singer asserts that although he has lived with survivors for years, this work is in no way typical of the Holocaust experience. The novel presents the "exceptional case," he says, unique to an individual who is a victim both of his own personality and of his persecutors. Certainly, this can be said of all victims, and the novel, despite his abjuration, is a moving depiction of the varied problems many survivors have encountered. Singer's note cautions the reader against a rigorous historical interpretation. The Holocaust serves as a framework within which Singer presents his perennial concern: humankind battling its adversaries in the dark of night, in the fashion of Jacob and the angel. In the biblical narrative, Jacob is not overcome; he walks away, at daybreak, limping but unvanquished. Singer's hero also walks away, but not as a victor.

Enemies bears a similarity to *Satan in Goray* both

in its focus on an individual who lives a tormented life, burdened with the knowledge of the tragic destruction of all that is meaningful to him, and in its use of the supernatural. In this work, the spiritual powers that represent the forces of good and evil also reflect a movement away from traditionalism. In addition, they indicate the extent to which the characters, through their previous experiences, have lost touch with reality. *Enemies* also has affinities with *The Magician of Lublin*: The multiple personalities of the protagonist are reflected in his relationships with three strikingly different women.

Enemies is a ghostly story. Herman Broder, the protagonist, is defined through his actions in the Holocaust. He spent those years hiding in a hayloft and has acquired a negative identity in the Holocaust's aftermath. Now, as a survivor, he is psychologically warped and socially maimed. He lacks the courage to commit suicide, hides behind schizophrenia to "deaden" his consciousness, and assumes the guise of a demon. In New York, Broder becomes a ghostwriter for a rabbi. He shuns contact with others to preserve his anonymity and lives a life of haunting duplicity with his second wife and his mistress. The tensions in his spiritual juggling act are intensified by the appearance of his wife from the Old World—he had assumed her to be dead. Ultimately, he disappears, vanishing like a ghost.

The work is divided into three parts. Part 1 establishes the diverse personalities of Herman Broder, "a fraud, a transgressor—a hypocrite," as he sees himself, and the complications they create. Broder's current life in New York is eclipsed by the terrifying experiences of his past. He lives in Brooklyn with his second wife, Yadwiga, the Polish woman who worked for his family before the war and who hid him in a hayloft during the Nazi occupation. He married her in gratitude for saving his life, but his relationship with her is deceitful. She does not know about his professional life or about his mentally disturbed mistress, Masha, who shares with him her experience of the Holocaust. He spends as much time with Masha as he does with Yadwiga, always telling Yadwiga that, as a book salesman, he must go out of town to sell books.

The tangled web of Broder's relationships is further complicated when his first wife, Tamara, who has survived being shot twice—one bullet still lodged within her—comes to New York and seeks him out. Part 1 ends with an additional complication when Masha claims to be pregnant and Broder promises to marry her.

Part 2 attempts a resolution of the problems. Through Broder's conversations with Masha and Tamara, much of the Holocaust experience is recreated. Like Elie Wiesel and other writers of the Holocaust, Singer points out that the full enormity of the Holocaust can never be expressed, because words are inadequate to the task. That which is related, however, is extremely powerful. Singer deals with the theological, social, and philosophical problems, both individual and universal, that confront humankind in coming to terms with the Holocaust. While presenting the myriad issues with which survivors have been faced—equivocal attitudes toward faith, a missing spouse who turns up after the other has remarried, disorientation in a new environment, reestablishing an identity that was nonexistent for a time, relating to people as human beings within a society rather than as individuals competing for survival—Singer indicates that the individual is also his or her own victim, governed by passions he or she cannot or will not control. Broder would not have married Yadwiga if he had thought that Tamara were alive. Now, however, he wants to hold on to all three women. They satisfy different needs: Yadwiga cares for him and worships him with a childlike simplicity; Masha fulfills his sexual desires and fires his imagination with her nightlong storytelling; Tamara is his wife, to whom he feels committed.

When the intricacies of his life seem overwhelming, he resorts to traditionalism as a life-sustaining measure, yet he cannot maintain his resolve to be a good Jew. He is a weak person by nature, and the impact of the Holocaust has left him without a will, without the power to make meaningful choices and decisions. He is, as he tells Tamara, a "corpse." His only alternative is to vanish. Herman Broder joins Singer's other eternal wanderers, the most famous of whom is Gimpel the Fool. The epilogue, in an almost

Darwinian statement, attests the insignificance of the individual in the larger scheme of things by confirming Herman Broder's disappearance and suggesting that life nevertheless continues for those who can battle their enemies successfully.

SHOSHA

Shosha is narrated in the first person, unusual in Singer's novels that have been translated into English. Originally appearing in the *Forward* under the title *Neshome Ekspeditsyes* (soul expeditions) in 1974, it is considered a fictionalized and expanded version of the memoir *A Young Man in Search of Love*, which appeared almost simultaneously in 1978. A beautifully wrought work, it is one of the most poignant of all of Singer's novels. Set in Poland in the 1930's, the novel portrays the plight of the Jewish community, overcast with the gloom of the Nazi invasion, yet it brims with the lives, loves, and hopes of its characters. It combines realism with humor and pathos. It is another nostalgic glance at a decimated world, but it is not a gloomy work. It is, as the Yiddish title indicates, the journey of the author's soul, in an affectionate tribute to the vitality of the shtetl, and stands in defiance of his statement at the end of the work: "Time is a book whose pages you can turn forward, not back." *Shosha* presents a marvelous picture of Warsaw before the war, focusing on its Yiddish cultural and intellectual life, its writers, artists, philosophers, actors, critics, and dilettantes, as well as its simple people. Within this historical framework, Singer presents his protagonist's life in Poland at the time of greatest stress, a time when Jewish life and culture were disintegrating.

In *Shosha*, the conflict between good and evil which animates all of Singer's works takes the form of the relationship between victim and persecutor. All of the characters are concerned with their immediate gratification. They arouse the reader's sympathy because they become victims of their own blindness and naïveté. In their determination to live normally, they love, argue, philosophize, celebrate holidays. They write plays about dybbuks and talk about dybbuks within themselves. They do not recognize the external evil, the phantom which surrounds them or pursues them.

The first part of the novel charts the circular movement of the protagonist as he attempts to reestablish a sense of belonging, transporting the reader to the halcyon days of the narrator's childhood and moving forward to the period preceding the destruction of the shtetl by Hitler. The ancestors of the protagonist, Aaron Greidinger, have lived in Poland for seven hundred years. Krochmalna Street, already familiar to Singer's public through his memoir *In My Father's Court*, not only is a place housing his father's judiciary but also is the scene of the narrator's first love, for Shosha—his neighbor, his playmate, his first audience—who believes and trusts him implicitly and unconditionally.

The work delineates the maturation of the narrator, as the serenity of his youthful universe is quickly replaced by the turmoil of world events with their disquieting effect upon the Jews of Poland. The first twenty years of his life pass rapidly as he moves from Krochmalna Street and attempts to define himself as a writer. In Warsaw, the Writers' Club becomes the focal point for the intellectuals, much as the synagogue was the focal point of the traditional Jewish community. It is through the people whom he meets at the Writers' Club that Aaron Greidinger works out his role as writer and lover.

Greidinger's destiny and identity are intimately bound to his youth on Krochmalna Street, and after twenty years, he returns to the area and visits Shosha and her mother. He is amazed that Shosha has changed only slightly during the years: She and Greidinger are the same age, but she looks like a child. Greidinger falls in love with her immediately. He explains to Betty Slonim, the Yiddish actress from America for whom he is writing a play, that he sees himself in Shosha. Shosha represents the naïveté and gentleness of his childhood, a phase of his life that he wants to recapture and repossess. She is Krochmalna Street. She is the shtetl. She is the traditionalism that refuses to keep in step with modernity but is beautiful nevertheless. She also represents the sources of his creativity, the childlike wonder which Singer the writer still possesses in old age. Part 1 ends with Greidinger's movement back in time, his failure as a playwright, his proposal to Shosha, and his spending most of his time in the small apartment on Krochmalna Street as the political situation worsens for the Jews in Poland.

Part 2 develops the protagonist's affirmation of his unity with his people. It is Yom Kippur, a day of judgment and reckoning for all Jews. The war is getting closer, Poles are more outspoken in their anti-Semitism, and Greidinger spends the day with Shosha, fasting. He marries Shosha two months later during the festival of Hanukkah. By doing so, he forgoes the opportunity to leave Warsaw before the Germans enter. He will not forsake Shosha, knowing that she could not survive by herself during these times. His writing career has improved; he is writing novels that have been accepted by his publisher. Part 2 concludes with the war imminent but with everyone presenting reasons for not leaving Warsaw prior to the German invasion. The epilogue ties the loose ends together. It takes place thirteen years later, during Greidinger's trip to Israel, where he meets his Warsaw friend, Haiml. While seated in the dark, each tells the story of what happened to his family, his friends, and how he escaped. Shosha died, as expected, because in her fragility, she could not keep ahead of the march of malevolence pursuing her and overtaking Europe.

THE KING OF THE FIELDS

Singer's last novel to be published before his death in 1991 was *The King of the Fields*, set in prehistoric Poland, a violent, animalistic place where tribes of cave-dwelling hunters struggle against Poles who cultivate the land. Singer seems to have dipped into a nightmare world so embedded in the past as to be unrelated to the present, yet the hellish qualities of this Stone Age Poland and the brutality of its inhabitants conjure up the Poland of the Holocaust—a wilderness of corruption, a wasteland for humanity.

SCUM

Scum, written in the late 1960's and published in English the year of Singer's death, re-creates the pre-Holocaust Warsaw at the beginning of the twentieth century. Max Barabander, a thief turned businessman, returns to Singer's famous Krochmalna Street after decades in Argentina. His son has died, and his grieving wife ignores him; he has become impotent. His journey backward to Krochmalna Street is his attempt to journey toward renewed health, or at least

toward a new life. He becomes involved both with the Shmuel Smetena, the central figure in Krochmalna Street mobster activities, and with a saintly rabbi whose daughter, Tsirele, he wants to marry. He poses as a grieving widower to win Tsirele while working with Shmuel Smetena's mistress on a scheme to seduce unsuspecting young women and ship them off to an Argentinian brothel. The project has a restorative effect on Max's virility, but when the web of lies he must weave begins to unravel, he is exposed as bereft of moral character, one for whom life—his or another's—is devoid of meaning. His only dreams are of "shady deals." *Scum* is Singer's version of the underworld; the literal underworld of gangsters mirrors the underworld of demons and dybbuks that make no appearance in this novel. When human beings are such scum, there seems to be no need for the Evil One.

THE CERTIFICATE

The Certificate, serialized in the *Forward* in 1967, was published posthumously in 1992. Its protagonist, David Bendinger, an eighteen-year-old would-be writer, arrives in Warsaw in 1922 with an unfinished novel, an essay on Spinoza and the Kabbala, and a collection of prose poems. Like so many of Singer's males, David soon finds himself involved with three women: Sonya, his old girlfriend; Minna, a woman whom he agrees to marry in order to obtain immigration papers for Palestine; and Edusha, his Marxist landlady. Like the youthful Singer, whom he resembles, David turns every event, no matter how seemingly insignificant, into an occasion for philosophical musing. Unlike Max Barabander of *Scum*, David Bendinger dreams of more than shady deals, and he believes that those around him have worth. No matter how complicated his life becomes, he dreams of writing and he thinks of God.

MESHUGAH

Meshugah, which means crazy, was first called *Lost Souls*, a title that connects this novel with *Shosha*, which was first called *Neshome Ekspeditsyes* (soul expeditions). Serialized in the *Forward* in the early 1980's and appearing in English in 1994, the novel brings Aaron Greidinger, the protagonist of *Shosha*, into a post-Holocaustal 1950's setting. This most

Singer-like character is a Polish exile who serializes novels in Yiddish for the *Forward*. While Aaron has his series of women, his primary mate, Miriam Zalkind, who is writing her dissertation on his work, juggles her own set of men. All are "lost souls" harboring memories of the Holocaust, mourning loved ones, contemplating suicide. Aaron discovers that the real truth of human suffering defies the power of writing—the world is meshugah.

SHADOWS ON THE HUDSON

Shadows on the Hudson was originally serialized in Yiddish twice a week in the *Forward* between January, 1957, and January, 1958. Singer had long wanted this novel to be published in English, but the project was undertaken only years after his death. It is set in the 1940's in Manhattan, and the lives of its characters are, like those in *Meshugah*, overshadowed by the Holocaust. As bleak as *Scum* but without its sordid underworld, *Shadows on the Hudson* deals with characters who strive for some sense and meaning in a world that continuously trips them up. Hertz Dovid Grein rotates between wife, mistress, and lover, always yearning for the one who is not there. His lover, Anna, juggles him along with her first and second husbands. His mistress, Esther, marries another, divorces, flees with Grein, and, in turn, flees him.

In the second part of this three-part novel, these chaotic couplings seem to be headed for resolution in a return to the past and traditional values. Grein returns home to his wife and to orthodoxy, Anna returns to her first husband, Esther marries, and even Anna's long-widowed father marries and has a son. The hope that a retreat from the secular will result in a return to meaning is demolished in part 3, however, when the new couplings are undone and the newborn child is recognized as severely retarded. The shadows of the Holocaust stretch over the Hudson and into the future. What saves this novel, and much of Singer's fiction, from a darkness too intense to bear is his extraordinary ability to create comic situations from the bleakest of moments. Whether caricaturing secondary characters or rendering outlandish a protagonist's rationalization of his or her latest sexual exploit, Singer's comic touch lightens his vision. Except in a few novels such as *Scum* and *The King of the Fields*, there is a redemptive quality in the very need his characters display for meaning and for love.

Singer occupies a unique place in the literary world. His works transcend the barriers of age, education, and culture, and they appeal to all peoples. Singer was a chronicler, historian, spiritualist, and moralist, and his writings are informed by a deep compassion for men and women who are, after all, only human. Singer may admit to a pessimistic view of humankind, but it is a sympathetic rather than a cynical pessimism. Throughout the darkness of his presentation, there flickers a spark of faith in the basic goodness of humankind, the promise of a universal and eternal light.

L. H. Goldman, updated by Grace Farrell

OTHER MAJOR WORKS

SHORT FICTION: *Gimpel the Fool and Other Stories*, 1957; *The Spinoza of Market Street*, 1961; *Short Friday and Other Stories*, 1964; *The Séance and Other Stories*, 1968; *A Friend of Kafka and Other Stories*, 1970; *A Crown of Feathers and Other Stories*, 1973; *Passions and Other Stories*, 1975; *Old Love*, 1979; *The Collected Stories*, 1982; *The Image and Other Stories*, 1985; *The Death of Methuselah and Other Stories*, 1988.

PLAYS: *The Mirror*, pr. 1973; *Yentl, the Yeshiva Boy*, pr. 1974 (with Leah Napolin); *Shlemiel the First*, pr. 1974; *Teibele and Her Demon*, pr. 1978.

NONFICTION: *Mayn Tatn's Bes-din Shtub*, 1956 (*In My Father's Court*, 1966); *The Hasidim*, 1973 (with Ira Moskowitz); *A Little Boy in Search of God*, 1976; *A Young Man in Search of Love*, 1978; *Lost in America*, 1980.

CHILDREN'S LITERATURE: *Zlateh the Goat and Other Stories*, 1966; *The Fearsome Inn*, 1967; *Mazel and Shlimazel: Or, The Milk of a Lioness*, 1967; *When Shlemiel Went to Warsaw and Other Stories*, 1968; *A Day of Pleasure: Stories of a Boy Growing Up in Warsaw*, 1969; *Elijah the Slave*, 1970; *Joseph and Koza: Or, The Sacrifice to the Vistula*, 1970; *Alone in the Wild Forest*, 1971; *The Topsy-Turvy Emperor of China*, 1971; *The Wicked City*, 1972; *The Fools of Chelm and Their History*, 1973; *Why Noah*

Chose the Dove, 1974; *A Tale of Three Wishes*, 1975; *Naftali the Storyteller and His Horse, Sus, and Other Stories*, 1976; *The Power of Light: Eight Stories*, 1980; *The Golem*, 1982; *Stories for Children*, 1984.

BIBLIOGRAPHY

Alexander, Edward. *Isaac Bashevis Singer*. New York: Twayne, 1980. An incisive book-length introduction to Singer's life and work that provides a useful starting point for further study.

Allentuck, Marcia, ed. *The Achievement of Isaac Bashevis Singer*. Carbondale: University of Southern Illinois, 1969. Includes Edwin Gittleman's brilliant analysis, "Singer's Apocalyptic Town: *Satan in Goray*," as well as studies of *The Family Moskat*, *The Magician of Lublin*, *The Manor*, and *The Slave*. Also looks at several short stories, including "Gimpel the Fool" and "The Spinoza of Market Street." Eli Katz's contribution discusses Singer's deviation from the Yiddish literary tradition.

Buchen, Irving H. *Isaac Bashevis Singer and the Eternal Past*. New York: New York University Press, 1968. Buchen maintains that to place either Singer's Yiddish traditions or his modernist connections in the foreground is to distort the whole, which serves as a crucible for the meeting of the ancient and the modern. Singer's demons serve as the point at which the unconscious and the cosmic meet.

Farrell, Grace, ed. *Critical Essays on Isaac Bashevis Singer*. New York: G. K. Hall, 1996. An extensive introduction to Singer's critical reception and the issues that have preoccupied him and his critics. Collects both contemporary reviews and a wide range of essays, including Leslie Fiedler's "I. B. Singer: Or, The American-ness of the American Jewish Writer."

_____. *From Exile to Redemption: The Fiction of Isaac Bashevis Singer*. Carbondale: Southern Illinois University Press, 1987. A study of the Kabbalic subtexts of Singer's fiction, especially its concern with the linguistic nature of reality and its connection with humankind's yearning for wholeness and exile from meaning.

_____. *Isaac Bashevis Singer: Conversations.*

Jackson: University Press of Mississippi, 1992. A collection of interviews with Singer that reveal the connections among his philosophy of life, his perspective on literature, and his mode of living.

Hadda, Janet. *Isaac Bashevis Singer: A Life*. New York: Oxford University Press, 1997. An generally unflattering biography of Singer. Hadda, both a Yiddish scholar and psychoanalyst, portrays Singer as cold, selfish, and even sometimes cruel in his personal relationships.

Kresh, Paul. *Isaac Bashevis Singer: The Magician of West 86th Street*. New York: Dial Press, 1979. A biography that includes many quotations and anecdotes, some relayed in a seemingly day-by-day manner. Kresh attempts to clarify details of the publishing history of Singer's work. Photographs, index, and bibliography.

Malin, Irving, ed. *Critical Views of Isaac Bashevis Singer*. New York: New York University Press, 1969. Malin's book reprints essays, reviews, and interviews published throughout the 1960's; includes a valuable bibliography.

Zamir, Israel. *Journey to My Father, Isaac Bashevis Singer*. New York: Arcade, 1995. A lively memoir by Singer's only child that paints a complex portrait of the writer.

JOSEF ŠKVORECKÝ

Born: Náchod, Czechoslovakia; September 27, 1924

PRINCIPAL LONG FICTION
Zbabělci, 1958 (*The Cowards*, 1970)
Legenda Emöke, 1963 (*Emöke*, 1977)
Bassaxofon, 1967 (*The Bass Saxophone*, 1977)
Konec nylonoveho véku, 1967
Farářův konec, 1969 (with Evald Schorm)
Lvíče, 1969 (*Miss Silver's Past*, 1974)
Tankový prapor, 1969 (*The Republic of Whores: A Fragment from the Time of the Cults*, 1993)
Mirákl: Politická detectivka, 1972 (*The Miracle Game*, 1991)

Prima sezóna, 1975 (*The Swell Season: A Text on
    the Most Important Things in Life*, 1982)
Konec poručíka Borůvky, 1975 (*The End of Lieu-
    tenant Boruvka*, 1989)
Příběh inženýra lidských duší, 1977 (*The Engineer
    of Human Souls: An Entertainment on the Old
    Themes of Life, Women, Fate, Dreams, the Work-
    ing Class, Secret Agents, Love, and Death*, 1984)
Návrat poručíka Borůvky, 1981 (*The Return of
    Lieutenant Boruvka*, 1990)
Scherzo capriccioso: Veselý sen o Dvořákovi, 1983
    (*Dvořák in Love: A Light-Hearted Dream*,
    1986)
Nevěsta z Texasu, 1992 (*The Bride of Texas*, 1995)

OTHER LITERARY FORMS

Josef Škvorecký published books on jazz, such as
Talkin' Moscow Blues (1988), and films, such as *All
the Bright Young Men and Women: A Personal History of the Czech Cinema* (1971). He is also known
for publications concerning literature and politics.

ACHIEVEMENTS

During the Communist-dominated regime in
Czechoslovakia, Škvorecký did not receive proper
recognition for his achievements, except for the
Writers' Union Annual Award for *Konec nylonoveho
véku* in 1967. Ironically, in 1990, Czech president
Václav Havel awarded the Order of the White Lion,
the Czech Republic's highest award for foreigners,
to Josef Škvorecký and his wife, the former singer
and actress Zdena Salivarová, for their promotion of
Czech literature through their publishing firm. Most
appreciation for Škvorecký's work as a writer came
from his adopted home in Canada and from the United
States. In 1980 the University of Oklahoma awarded
him the Neustadt International Prize for Literature.
He received the Canadian Governor General's Award
for best fiction in English, the first translation so honored, for *The Engineer of Human Souls* in 1985.

Beyond the official prizes, Škvorecký won recognition for his promotion of Czech literature. His early
novels defied the Soviet insistence on Socialist Realism, and his creation of character Danny Smiricky
provided Czechoslovaks with an often comic anti-

hero, one clever enough to exist under authoritarian
rule. Škvorecký's supple use of the Czech language
subverts the empty Communist slogans ponderously
translated into Czech. He is a highly visible champion of Czech literature in speeches and written commentary, serving as a bridge between the cultures of
his native and adopted countries.

BIOGRAPHY

Much of Škvorecký's life can be learned by reading his fiction: Significant events are recalled in several works. While he was attending the local gymnasium from 1935 to 1943, he developed his lifelong
appreciation for jazz and began his study of English, reading American authors in translation. During the Nazi occupation, he was a forced laborer in a
Messerschmitt factory, an experience which is described in *The Cowards* and *The Engineer of Human
Souls*. He earned a Ph.D. in philosophy from Charles
University in Prague in 1951. His writing career
started auspiciously; he won a university prize for his
short stories. He taught at a girls' school in Horice
(described in *The Miracle Game*) for a year, and in
1951, he was inducted into the army, serving two
years in a tank division.

By 1948 he was a member of the Prague "underground" group of writers and artists, reacting against
the Soviet occupation and control of Czechoslovakia,
which took place in 1945. Between 1948 and 1949 he
worked on his first novel, *The Cowards*, which was
not published for ten years. He abandoned *Konec
nylonoveho véku* during this time; it was unpublished
but perhaps privately circulated because of the oppressive censorship of the Soviet regime. Although
The Cowards was popularly received in 1958, the
book was banned, and Škvorecký lost his post as dep-
uty editor-in-chief of the magazine *Světová Literatura*. Škvorecký, however, had established himself as
a worthy essayist, critic, and translator, particularly
of modern American literature giants Ernest Hemingway, John Steinbeck, and William Faulkner.

With the arrival of the Soviet tanks in 1968,
Škvorecký and his wife, Zdena, whom he had married in 1957, emigrated to Canada. The Škvoreckýs
settled in Toronto, where Škvorecký joined the faculty

of the University of Toronto as a writer-in-residence and a member of the English department. In 1971 the Škvoreckýs founded Sixty-Eight Publishers, a conduit for the publications of Czech literature, including Škvorecký's own works. Now free to devote himself to writing, Škvorecký began an amazingly productive period. He also began to broadcast for the U.S. government-run radio network Voice of America, not only speaking about Czech literature but also reviewing publications by British and American writers. No longer just a symbol of dissidence, he emerged as a significant figure in international literature.

ANALYSIS

Škvorecký deliberately challenges readers by creating a complex structure for his novels. He shifts episodes, conversations, and images around, then groups them to give some meaning to the individual's struggle to rise above the confusion of modern life. Švorecký deliberately places incidents and characters at random to keep readers alert. His fragmentation gives emphasis to the term "postmodern." It is an oversimplification to dismiss him as just an autobiographical novelist. The Danny Smiricky novels may echo some important episodes in Škvorecký's life, but Škvorecký clearly states the artist's right to embellish, to embroider, to transpose.

Above all, Škvorecký brings a special humor to his writing; he once commented that he never intended to write satire, but he found himself producing fiction "indistinguishable" from it. He enjoys playing with language, a fact that is best appreciated by those who can read his original Czech. Perhaps his most successful use of humor is in his creation of a pertinent incident that is often inherently comic and demonstrates a theme or idea. This is evidenced in *The Engineer of Human Souls*, with Škvorecký's description of the arrival of a paranoid messenger carrying a banned book into Toronto Union Station to deliver it to an unfamiliar receiver, Danny. The whole passage can be extracted from the novel and used as a short story with an obvious theme: the difference between the East and the West.

Škvorecký's novels are novels of ideas; they are neither didactic nor propagandistic. He faced criticism for not championing the reformers and ideologies made popular during the Prague Spring of 1968, but he purposefully created an apolitical hero in Danny, who does not espouse one truth over others. Again, Škvorecký challenges readers not only to construct his novels but also to examine critically their own thinking.

THE MIRACLE GAME

The Miracle Game is an excellent example of Škvorecký's method of writing, as it spans a twenty-year period while avoiding a linear chronology. The novel involves crucial years in Czechoslovak history, from the Soviet occupation to the Prague Spring. In it, Škvorecký satirizes the authoritarian control over the Czechoslovaks, particularly Danny Smiricky's fellow artists. Danny is a jazz-loving adolescent, a member of the tank corps, and a mature writer of innocuous musical comedies. Danny is distracted from ideological warfare. He is on the fringe of the writers' groups and manages to view the "intellectuals" from an "inferior" perspective. One of the miracles of the book's title is the Prague Spring itself, but Danny does not side with any new, strong position, and he prefers to watch disputes from the sidelines. Škvorecký does not miss the opportunity for satire, particularly at the writers' conference, featuring delegates who actively support Socialist Realism, the Communists' view of "good" literature. The satire against authoritarianism is also evident in the hilarious episode of the matriculation exams for the students at Danny's school.

If the Prague Spring represents a Marxist miracle, the Roman Catholic Church, the other dominant force in Czechoslovakia, can boast of a miracle of its own. A statue of Saint Joseph in a remote chapel moves during morning mass, apparently bowing, possibly toward the West. In the search for the truth about the miracle, the novel borrows from Škvorecký's detective fiction. Was the statue's movement a scheme to undermine the Church? Did Father Doufal, the priest saying mass at the time, "manufacture" the miracle, as the authorities claimed? Was another culprit involved? For more than twenty years the veracity of the miracle is debated. After an inspiring visit to a sanatorium, Danny seems close to learning the solution; the "answer," when revealed, however, is ambiguous. The cynical Danny cannot make the leap of faith needed to accept the apparent truth. Readers are forced to make their own choice.

THE ENGINEER OF HUMAN SOULS

The declaration (often attributed to Soviet leader Joseph Stalin) that a writer must be the "engineer" directing humanity toward acceptance of Marxist ideology almost demands Škvorecký's satire. Not only is Škvorecký conscious of the artist's independence, but also he questions the right of any entity to impose its version of truth on the rest of society. This premise echoes throughout Škvorecký's fiction and is brought to fruition in this, the richest of his novels of ideas.

The book is the fifth and last in the saga of Danny Smiricky, but it is not merely a sequel to *The Miracle Game*. Danny is safely ensconced as a faculty member at the University of Toronto, still apolitical, still passive, more reflective—a modern hero caught between the past and the need to adapt to a new culture. He still defies rules and annoys political ideologues, never losing his sense of humor.

The fragmentation of the novel is eased by naming the seven chapters for some of Škvorecký's favorite authors: Edgar Allan Poe, Nathaniel Hawthorne, Mark Twain, Stephen Crane, F. Scott Fitzgerald, Joseph Conrad, and H. P. Lovecraft. They are featured on Danny's syllabus for his course, and allusions to their work lend substance to the narrative. Readers are again amused as Danny challenges his students with solemn declarations of Conrad's prescience in detecting the evils of communist dominance in the figure of Mr. Kurtz in *Heart of Darkness* (1902). Škvorecký, however, does not skirt the agony of the past; old friends Benno, Prema, Vrata die, and another former friend languishes in Israel. The letters written to Danny over twenty-five years are the richest of the fragments that comprise the novel; they underscore Danny's greatest skill—listening.

Characters may move rapidly through the narrative, but they leave a resonant impact, especially the earnest publisher, Mrs. Santner, the predatory Dotty, and the homesick Veronika. Danny's old and new friends remind readers that Škvorecký writes for two audiences, Czechs and North Americans. Though Škvorecký (and Danny) cannot return to the past, as Veronika did, he must make peace with the present.

DVOŘÁK IN LOVE

Beginning with the title of the book, *Dvořák in Love* presents the reader with challenges that are often unsettling. The Czech title, *Scherzo capriccioso*, was deemed too obscure for readers, but the English translation is misleading. As a scherzo, the book should yield a sprightly transition of time and place, but even these characteristics are denied in the reader's confrontation of numerous characters and incidents. Škvorecký omits a unifier—a first-person narrator—and thus places the burden of assembly on the reader.

Most editions of the work provide a chronology of Antonín Dvořák's life, signaling that Škvorecký is not producing the traditional biographical novel. By not entering Dvořák's consciousness, Škvorecký simplifies the process of introducing a contradictory, complex character, an earthy genius; Dvořák is viewed only externally. The apparently plotless novel actually focuses on three love triangles, Dvořák's love for Josephine Čermáková and for her sister Anna, whom he later married; his devotion to Josephine despite her marriage to Count Kounic; and Dvořák's daughter's attraction to two suitors.

Škvorecký helps to link parts of the novel with poetic devices, such as imagery and symbolism; above all, he uses music as a running thread. An amber field, a circling butterfly, and a reference to Dvořák's famous *Stabat mater* introduce the novel. Echoes of these devices resound to the last pages. The focus on America and its music is another theme: Dvořák is lured to New York to direct the National Conservatory of Music, meeting music critic James Huneker, black violinist Will Marion Cook, and Harry T. Burleigh, who brought spirituals to the concert stage. As American music inspired Dvořák, he, in turn, affected jazz and, by extension, even influenced popular pianist George Gershwin's music. The novel is both scherzo and elegy, Škvorecký's tribute to a fellow artist and countryman.

THE BRIDE OF TEXAS

Although it may seem unusual for a Czech émigré to focus on a segment of American history in a novel,

Škvorecký became intrigued with his discovery of the records of Czechoslovak soldiers who had fought in the Union Army during the Civil War. Most of the characters are real, but Škvorecký uses dramatic license to add some significant fictional characters. Most of the Czechoslovak soldiers are real émigrés who served under General William Tecumseh Sherman; Škvorecký places them in one division, allowing for exchanges of stories and a camaraderie based on a common language. They are distinguished by their reasons for leaving home; most were beckoned by the promise of freedom and economic opportunity. Škvorecký views the war from their point of view, but he defends Sherman's intensity in the afterword, because he was impressed with Sherman's efforts to end the war.

Škvorecký introduces a semifictional character, Lorraine Tracy, a writer of romances and friend of General Ambrose Burnside, to examine the general's role in the prosecution of Copperhead Clement Vallandigham. Tracy, an abolitionist, provides insight into the slavery issue, with the help of her black maid Jasmine. The central fictional characters are Cyril Toupelik and his sister Lida, who fled Moravia. Lida, the bride of the title, represents the materialistic desire for a new life with her determination to marry a rich husband. Cyril is an idealist, determined to locate and marry the slave Dinah.

While Škvorecký employs a common structural pattern of assembling flashbacks, anecdotes, and other narratives, he introduces a poetic strain in his descriptive prose, marked with the stately repetition of such phrases as "turpentine forest on fire."

Škvorecký manages to make the novel a tribute to his past and present: Czechoslovak history as viewed through the difficulties of Czechs dominated by Austria and Hungary and their own upper classes, as well as an appreciation of America for giving Czechs refuge and an opportunity to succeed.

Elizabeth R. Nelson

OTHER MAJOR WORKS

SHORT FICTION: *Smutek poručíka Borůvky*, 1966 (*The Mournful Demeanour of Lieutenant Boruvka*, 1973); *Hříchy pro pátera Knoxe*, 1973 (*Sins for Fa-*ther *Knox*, 1988); *Povídky tenorsaxofonisty*, 1993 (*The Tenor Saxophonist's Story*, 1997).

NONFICTION: *O nich—o nás*, 1968; *All the Bright Young Men and Women: A Personal History of the Czech Cinema*, 1971; *Jiří Menzel and the History of the "Closely Watched Trains,"* 1982; *Talkin' Moscow Blues*, 1988; *Headed for the Blues: A Memoir*, 1996.

BIBLIOGRAPHY

Kalish, Jana. *Josef Škvorecký: A Checklist.* Toronto: University of Toronto Library, 1986. Extremely helpful but limited to pre-1986 subject matter.

O'Brien, John, ed. "Special Issue: Mario Vargas Llosa and Josef Škvorecký." *The Review of Contemporary Fiction* 17, no. 1 (Spring, 1997): 78-158. Contains brief but perceptive essays, a limited select bibliography, an interview with and a previously unpublished short story by Škvorecký, and two essays on *The Bride of Texas*.

Solecki, Sam, ed. *The Achievement of Josef Škvorecký.* Toronto: University of Toronto Press, 1994. Concentrates on the major works and includes an essay on the literary scandal surrounding the publication of *The Cowards*. Extensive bibliography.

_____. *Prague Blues: The Fiction of Josef Škvorecký.* Toronto: ECW Press, 1990. The best starting point for a study of Škvorecký. Solecki has an appreciation of Škvorecký's work and is extremely perceptive. Includes a good bibliography.

Trensky, Paul I. *The Fiction of Josef Škvorecký.* New York: St. Martin's Press, 1991. A good perspective on the earlier works, with additional comments on the detective stories.

JANE SMILEY

Born: Los Angeles, California; September 26, 1949

PRINCIPAL LONG FICTION
Barn Blind, 1980
At Paradise Gate, 1981
Duplicate Keys, 1984

The Greenlanders, 1988
A Thousand Acres, 1991
Moo, 1995
The All-True Travels and Adventures of Lidie Newton, 1998

OTHER LITERARY FORMS

In addition to her novels and novellas, Jane Smiley is the author of several short stories and numerous nonfiction essays. Her stories have appeared in *The Atlantic Monthly*, and five are included in *The Age of Grief: A Novella and Stories* (1987). The most notable of her nonfiction essays, "Say It Ain't So, Huck: Second Thoughts on Mark Twain's 'Masterpiece'" (*Harper's*, January, 1996), produced a storm of controversy when Smiley questioned the primacy of Mark Twain's *The Adventures of Huckleberry Finn* (1884) in American fiction, arguing that critics have been evasive about the racism present in Twain's work and that Harriet Beecher Stowe's *Uncle Tom's Cabin* (1852) offers a franker and more open approach to racism. Other nonfiction work includes a series of essays titled *Catskill Crafts: Artisans of the Catskill Mountains* (1988).

ACHIEVEMENTS

Jane Smiley is a prolific writer with three O. Henry Awards (1982, 1985, and 1988) to her credit.

The Age of Grief received a nomination for the National Book Critics Circle Award in 1987. *A Thousand Acres* garnered prestigious literary prizes, including the Pulitzer Prize for Fiction, the National Book Critics Circle Award, the Midland Authors Award, and the Heartland Prize, all in 1992. The film adaptation of *A Thousand Acres* was released in September, 1997. Smiley enjoyed other prestigious honors, such as a Fulbright Fellowhip, which took her to study in Iceland (1976-1977). She is twice the recipient of fellowships from the National Endowment for the Arts (1978, 1987). Critics generally praise Smiley for her fine craftsmanship, psychological subtlety, and competence in handling complex and varied historical, sociological, and scholarly issues.

BIOGRAPHY

Although Jane Smiley writes extensively and convincingly about the American rural landscape and agricultural themes, she grew up a city girl in St. Louis, Missouri, among gifted writers and storytellers. Her mother, Frances Nuelle (Graves) Smiley, held a newspaper job, and her father, James La Verne Smiley, was a West Point graduate and career military man. Smiley attributes much of her literary success to the fact that she grew up in a family that loved to tell its own history; listening to this history engendered in Smiley a lifelong fascination with character motives and plots.

Smiley attended Vassar College, from which she received her B.A. in 1971. The rest of her education was completed at the University of Iowa, including her M.F.A., her M. A., and her Ph.D. Her career began humbly as a worker in a teddy-bear factory, but at Iowa State University, she rapidly progressed from an assistant professor in 1981 to a distinguished professor in 1992. Smiley retired from teaching in 1996 and settled in northern California, where she could pursue writing fulltime and enjoy horseback riding. Her third husband, Mark Mortensen, and three children, Phoebe Silag, Lucy Silag, and Axel James Mortensen, constitute her family.

(Stephen Mortensen)

At six feet, two inches, Jane Smiley is affectionately known as the tallest woman in American fiction. Perhaps her height contributes to the fact that she is not easily intimidated. Rather, she is plainspoken and, by her own admission, sometimes "too hard to take." Although she considered teaching at other colleges, her immense self-confidence and lack of conformity proved off-putting to prospective employers. At Iowa State, though, she enjoyed prodigious popularity among faculty and students alike. Students flocked to her creative-writing class, where she refrained from either criticism or praise, regarding each student's work as a mode for educational analysis.

ANALYSIS

The hallmark of Jane Smiley's work is variety: She has written a mystery (*Duplicate Keys*), an epic (*The Greenlanders*), a tragedy (*A Thousand Acres*), a comedy (*Moo*), and a romance (*The All-True Travels and Adventures of Lidie Newton*). All her works, with the exception of a few short stories, are consistent in craftsmanship, meticulous attention to detail, and evidence of careful, scholarly research. Certain themes do recur, such as the relationship between power and love, the ecological consequences of farming with chemicals, the successes and failures of capitalism, and simple human fallibility. Smiley consistently refuses to offer tidy solutions to complex human conflicts; her characters move gradually toward the light but receive no moments of blinding epiphany. Her vision can best be described as tragicomic: Her most tragic tales have moments of biting humor, and her most comic tales contain a melancholic strain.

THE NOVELLAS

Some of Jane Smiley's finest work can be found in her three novellas: *The Age of Grief*, *Ordinary Love*, and *Good Will*. All these works are finely crafted stories of family life and marriage. The novella, with its compactness and intensity, seems to be the ideal form for Smiley's rich talent for examining the psychological subtleties of ordinary human life. Without the encumbrances of subplots and multiple characters, Smiley is able to do what she does best: examine one theme deeply and meditatively. A theme shared by these novellas is that human fallibility prevents us from achieving our visions of marital and family bliss. Dave and Dana, the couple in *The Age of Grief*, seem to have everything that would make a marriage happy—love (at least at the beginning of their marriage), a successful joint dental practice, an equitable arrangement for childcare, and even good looks. Their marriage survives an extramarital affair, which neither of the two openly acknowledges or seems to understand. Dave, the narrator, is left with little more knowledge of his marriage than he had before; he is even perplexed about exactly what marriage is, other than something too small to contain the complexities of two individuals. *Ordinary Love* and *Good Will*, which were published together, are intended to be paired novellas, one from the point of view of a mother, and one from the point of view of a father. Smiley sees one of these narratives as essentially masculine, with its linear plot, and one as essentially feminine, with a plot that relies upon revealing that which is hidden. *Ordinary Love* is the story of a woman who helped create and then destroy a perfect family. The protagonist, a middle-aged woman, reveals an extramarital affair that destroyed the marriage to her children's father, only to have her children (now adults) almost vengefully reveal tales of physical abuse, abandonment, and sexually inappropriate behavior suffered in the presence of their father.

Good Will is the story of a man who created his own eden on a Pennsylvania farm. His family also seems perfect in this idyllic setting, where he and his wife grow their own food, make their own clothes, and rely upon bartering their trades and services rather than earning money to accumulate worldly goods. However, Bob Miller, the protagonist, is intent upon creating his world, including his wife and son, in his own image, a vision that history tells us must fail. This and *Ordinary Love* are rooted in the theme that fulfillment of desire does not necessarily bring human happiness.

A THOUSAND ACRES

Of all Smiley's novels, *A Thousand Acres* has enjoyed the greatest literary and popular acclaim, not only receiving a Pulitzer Prize and the National Book

Critics Circle Award, but also remaining on *The New York Times* paperback best-seller list for twenty-nine weeks. The literary appeal of this novel is due in part to its plot, a feminist revision of William Shakespeare's drama *King Lear* (1605-1606). Its popular appeal may be attributed to America's greater awareness of sexual-abuse issues. Motivated by the question of what could have caused King Lear's daughters to feel such anger, Smiley chooses to retell this classical tragedy through the eyes of one of his daughters. *A Thousand Acres* is set on a farm in Zebulon County, Iowa, with Lawrence Cook and his three daughters: Ginny, Rose, and Caroline. Ginny and Rose correspond to the characters of Lear's "evil" older daughters, Goneril and Regan, whereas Caroline plays the part of Lear's "good" youngest daughter, Cordelia. True to the *King Lear* plot, Lawrence Cook proposes to divide his kingdom, a one-thousand-acre farm, between his three daughters. The two oldest daughters, farm wives themselves, accept, while the youngest daughter, a lawyer living in Des Moines, refuses. A nearby farmer, Harold Clark, takes the part of the Earl of Gloucester, with his two rivalrous sons, Loren and Jess. After the land transaction takes place, Lawrence Cook apparently goes mad (although he could be faking insanity to get his land back); Harold Clark loses his eyesight in a farm chemical accident; Ginny and Rose commit adultery with the same man, Jess Clark; and Ginny tries unsuccessfully to poison Rose. Although Smiley's retelling of Shakespeare's tragedy may rob King Lear of his majesty, as Christopher Lehmann-Haupt complains, she more than adequately restores the dignity of women silenced by incest and patriarchal suppression.

The story is narrated from the point of view of Ginny Cook Smith, a woman who, in the beginning, caters to her father's every whim without ever offering her own opinion. Rose is no less servile than Ginny, but she is more visibly angry. Smiley allows the subplot of this *King Lear* story to unfold gradually, not revealing the issue of incest until at least halfway through the novel. Suddenly Ginny's self-conscious physical awkwardness and Rose's vitriolic anger begin to make sense, when Rose reveals her

memory of their father having sex with both of them. Ginny at first denies Rose's revelation, having completely repressed this horrific childhood memory. Ironically, as Ginny makes the bed that her lover, Jess, will sleep in—her own childhood bed—she begins to recalls bits and pieces of this incestuous relationship, for example, the balding spot on her father's head and the way that his knees forced hers apart. Ginny, knowing that she cannot bear to recall this memory in full, consciously chooses not to, but Rose dwells on the memory, determined until her dying day not to forgive the unforgivable.

A second theme, poisoning, is closely allied with the theme of incest. The women of Zebulon County have been poisoned by agricultural chemicals used as either pesticides or fertilizers. Three women—Ginny and Rose's mother, Jess Clark's mother, and Rose herself—succumb to cancer. Ginny is rendered infertile, suffering five miscarriages as a result of drinking the well water. When Ginny discovers that Rose has stolen her lover, Jess Clark, she devises an elaborate scheme to poison Rose with hemlock-laced sausages, determined that Rose should die from her own gluttonous appetites. Ginny's scheme is thwarted with Rose's conversion to vegetarianism, but on another level, Rose is already poisoned by her hatred and inability to forgive her father. Smiley never suggests that Rose should forgive her father; nevertheless, Rose's lack of the ability to forgive clearly poisons all her relationships, including her relationship with Ginny.

Moo

Smiley, who enjoys experimenting with different genres, decided that she would write two novels with agricultural themes: a tragedy set on a farm (*A Thousand Acres*) and a comedy set at a university (*Moo*). The midwestern university setting of *Moo* is suspiciously similar to Iowa State University, where Smiley taught for fifteen years, but she denies having used Iowa State directly as a model. *Moo* is a satire of academic life, with a rich array of characters, including administrators, faculty members, students, a secretary, a governor, and a few community members. Most notable of these characters are Lionel Gift, a corrupt distinguished professor whose goal is to profit from gold mining beneath the last remaining virgin cloud forest in the Western Hemisphere; Arlen Martin, a Texas billionaire who conspires with Dr. Gift; Mrs. Walker, a lesbian secretary with amazing powers to subvert university finances for what she considers worthy projects; Tim Monohan, a self-centered writer who thinks that his talents are wasted at Moo U.; Cecilia Sanchez, a woman from Los Angeles with Costa Rican roots, who, unable to adjust to life in the Midwest, develops an insatiable passion for Chairman X, a Marxist vegetarian and Dr. Gift's sworn enemy; Helen Levy, a language professor who abandons her academic ambitions for the sensual pleasures of cooking, gardening, and sex; Loren Stroop, a paranoid farmer-inventor, who actually does invent a machine that may save the university; Orville T. Early, the governor, who remains an offstage but menacingly stupid presence with his constant schemes for budgetary cuts; and finally, Earl Butz, a hog who must carry not only his seven-hundred-pound weight but also the weight of the central metaphor of the novel. Hidden away near the center of the university, Earl Butz is an expensive agricultural experiment with the sole purpose of seeing just how big a hog might grow if allowed to eat continuously. Like Earl Butz, many of these characters are single-mindedly pursuing one greed or another, whether it is greed for food, sex, power, fame, or money.

Smiley sees *Moo* as a "slippery slope" novel that warns us what can happen when there is not a clear separation between the university and the corporate world. The university becomes corrupt and loses its educational focus, supporting only profit-making research and technical education. Land-grant universities are especially culpable, with their support of the destructive tendencies of large-scale agriculture. Some critics are disappointed with Smiley's refusal to cut the university down to size, but most critics are pleased with the gentleness of this satire. Clearly, Jane Smiley loves the university too much to engage in any really vicious satirical attacks. The university is composed of people, and these people are as people are everywhere: fallible, needy, sometimes sad, and often comical or absurd.

Nancy E. Sherrod

OTHER MAJOR WORKS

SHORT FICTION: *The Age of Grief: A Novella and Stories*, 1987; *"Ordinary Love" and "Good Will": Two Novellas*, 1989.

NONFICTION: *Catskill Crafts: Artisans of the Catskill Mountains*, 1988.

BIBLIOGRAPHY

Carden, Mary Paniccia. "Remembering/Engendering the Heartland: Sexed Language, Embodied Space, and America's Foundational Fictions in Jane Smiley's *A Thousand Acres.*" *Frontiers: A Journal of Women's Studies* 18, no. 2 (1997): 181-202. An examination of how Smiley challenges agrarian ideologies that serve to silence women.

Leslie, Marina. "Incest, Incorporation, and King Lear in Jane Smiley's *A Thousand Acres.*" *College English* 60, no. 1 (January, 1998): 31-50. Scholarly comparison of *King Lear* and *A Thousand Acres*, with an emphasis on Shakespearean criticism that recognizes incest themes in *King Lear.*

Olson, Catherine Cowen. "You Are What You Eat: Food and Power in Jane Smiley's *A Thousand Acres.*" *Midwest Quarterly* 40, no. 1 (1998): 21-33. Shows how food reflects Ginny's rebellion or submission under patriarchal rule in *A Thousand Acres.*

Sheldon, Barbara H. *Daughters and Fathers in Feminist Novels.* New York: P. Lang, 1997. Examines *A Thousand Acres* and novels by Gail Godwin, Mary Gordon, and other feminist writers.

TOBIAS SMOLLETT

Born: Dalquhurn, Scotland; March 19, 1721 (baptized)
Died: Antignano, Italy; September 17, 1771

PRINCIPAL LONG FICTION

The Adventures of Roderick Random, 1748
The Adventures of Peregrine Pickle: In Which Are Included Memoirs of a Lady of Quality, 1751

The Adventures of Ferdinand, Count Fathom, 1753
The Adventures of Sir Launcelot Greaves, 1760-
 1761
The Expedition of Humphry Clinker, 1771

OTHER LITERARY FORMS

Tobias Smollett combined his medical practice with an active and varied career as a man of letters. His earliest, though unsuccessful, effort was as a playwright with *The Regicide: Or, James the First of Scotland, a Tragedy* (1749), published by subscription a full ten years after fruitless attempts at having it staged in London. Two other disappointments followed with his inability to secure a production for *Alceste* (1748-1749), a combination of opera, tragedy, and masque, and with the rejection of his first comedy, *The Absent Man* (1751), which was never produced or published. Both of these works have now been lost. His only success on the stage came finally with *The Reprisal: Or, The Tars of Old England* (1757), a comedy; this farce was produced by David Garrick at the Theatre Royal, Drury Lane.

Smollett's deep moral energy surfaced in two early verse satires, "Advice: A Satire" (1746) and its sequel, "Reproof: A Satire" (1747); these rather weak poems were printed together in 1748. Smollett's poetry includes a number of odes and lyrics, but his best poem remains "The Tears of Scotland." Written in 1746, it celebrates the unwavering independence of the Scots, who had been crushed by English troops at the Battle of Culloden.

As Smollett's literary career grew, his hackwork for publishers increased with translations. His most popular work among these projects was *A Complete History of England* (1757-1758) and its sequel, *Continuation of the Complete History of England* (1760-1765). He took great pride in his achievements as a historian and as a historical editor of *A Compendium of Authentic and Entertaining Voyages* (1756). A diversity of interests from medicine to politics prompted the writing of numerous pamphlets and essays. *An Essay on the External Use of Water* (1752) was a farsighted proposal for the improvement of public hygiene at Bath that caused a furor among the resort's staff and patrons.

(CORBIS/Bettmann)

Though his health was rapidly deteriorating from overwork, Smollett completed a thirty-five-volume edition of *The Works of M. de Voltaire* (1761-1774). In the hope that a warm climate would improve his health, he traveled to France and Italy, and on returning to England he published *Travels Through France and Italy* (1766). His didactic observations instructed his readers to accept England, for all its faults, as the best nation for securing happiness on earth. His last nonfiction works were *The Present State of All Nations* (1768-1769) and the political satire *The History and Adventures of an Atom* (1749, 1769). Lewis M. Knapp offers the best modern edition of the *Letters of Tobias Smollett* (1970).

ACHIEVEMENTS

Smollett cannot be said to have added dignity to the art of the novel in the manner of Henry Fielding's imitation of the epic, nor can it be argued that he gave form to the genre as did Samuel Richardson, yet the eighteenth century novel cannot be discussed without giving full attention to Smollett's stylistic virtuosity and satiric intent.

Smollett successfully challenged Richardson's and Fielding's substantial popular reputation by providing "familiar scenes in an uncommon and amusing point of view." In *The Adventures of Roderick Random* (commonly known as *Roderick Random*), his first novel, he displayed a thorough understanding of the distinction between the novel and the romance, of which Samuel Johnson would speak in *The Rambler* essays (1750-1752). Borrowing from Latin comedy and Elizabethan drama, Smollett created caricatures of human beings with the dexterity of William Hogarth and Thomas Rowlandson. Though his characters lack the psychological depth of Richardson's, they possess breathtaking energy and evocative power.

Only in the late twentieth century did Smollett's role in the development of the English novel become fully appreciated. Criticism of that time emphasized the wrongheadedness of viewing Smollett's satiric energy as a deviation from Fielding's epic ambitions for the novel. Instead, Smollett is seen at the beginning of another tradition. Sir Walter Scott and Charles Dickens both valued Smollett's work; Dickens acknowledged his debt to Smollett's picaresque realism and comic characterization in *Pickwick Papers* (1836-1837). Among modern novelists, the savage comedy of writers as various as Evelyn Waugh and Joseph Heller is in Smollett's tradition rather than that of Fielding or Richardson.

Smollett's works continue to provoke critical inquiry. Eight books and numerous dissertations have appeared in the last two decades, as well as many articles. The Oxford English Novels series has published all five of his novels, and the University of Delaware has begun to publish its *Bicentennial Edition of the Works of Tobias Smollett*, under the editorship of O. M. Brack, with *The Expedition of Humphry Clinker* (commonly known as *Humphry Clinker*) appearing in 1979.

BIOGRAPHY

Tobias George Smollett was born at Dalquhurn, Dumbartonshire, in western Scotland, and baptized on March 19, 1721. He was the son of Archibald Smollett, a lawyer, who suffered from ill health, and Barbara Cunningham Smollett, a woman of taste and elegance but no fortune. Smollett's grandfather, of whom the boy was especially proud, had been knighted by King William in 1698 and had become an influential member of the landed gentry as a local Whig statesman. When Smollett's father died only two years after his son's birth, the family suffered from lack of money.

Smollett's education, for all of his family's financial deterioration, was of superior quality though erratic. He entered Dumbarton Grammar School in 1728, remaining for five years, and received the traditional grounding in the classics. His matriculation to Glasgow University (though officially unrecorded) was interrupted when he became a Glasgow surgeon's apprentice while still attending university medical lectures. In the fall of 1739, Smollett was released from his apprenticeship to go to London; now eighteen, he had some reputation as a writer of earthy satires and doggerel. While traveling to London, Smollett carried the manuscript of a tragedy, *The Regicide*, which, he soon realized, would provide no entrée for him with the London theater managers. He is described at this time as "attractive, entertaining as a *raconteur*, and blessed with self-assurance." His future as a London man of letters uncertain, Smollett received advice from a number of Scottish physicians suggesting he continue practicing medicine. On March 10, 1740, he received a medical warrant from the Navy Board and embarked on the HMS *Chichester* as a surgeon's second mate.

The author's naval experience, material used later for *Roderick Random*, began during the outbreak of war with Spain and continued through the bloody Carthagena, West Indies, expedition of 1741. Smollett returned to England in 1742, but was drawn back to Jamaica, where he resided until 1744. While living on the island, he met the daughter of an established family of planters, the Lassells; he married Anne Lassells in 1743. She is described as an affectionate and beautiful woman, in her early twenties, of considerable fortune.

Smollett, on the advice of her family, returned to London alone, where he set up a practice as a surgeon on Downing Street in May, 1744. Having never lost hope of a literary career, he worked on improving his fluency in Spanish and then began translating Miguel de Cervantes's *Don Quixote de la Mancha* (1605, 1615), which was published in 1755. The years from 1747 to 1750 were marked by considerable literary activity, numerous changes in residence, various trips abroad, a widening circle of acquaintances, and the birth of his only child, Elizabeth, in 1747.

In January, 1748, *Roderick Random* was published; this was followed by the impressive translations of Alain Le Sage and Cervantes, and in 1749, *The Regicide* was printed. The success of *Roderick Random* was instantaneous and prolonged, with sixty-five hundred copies sold in twenty-two months; it was to rival the popularity of Fielding's *Joseph Andrews* (1742). The success of *Roderick Random*, which was written in less than six months, became a kind of revenge on the theater managers of London. During this period, Smollett made plans to produce *Alceste*, his opera (George Frideric Handel was contracted for the music), but this effort was to fail; only a lyric from this work survives. His comedy *The Absent Man* was submitted to David Garrick but not accepted; Smollett's failure at drama was a continuing source of frustration throughout his career.

In June, 1750, Smollett purchased his medical degree from Marischal College, Aberdeen, and in the same month moved his family to Chelsea, a fashionable London suburb. It became an ideal home for him, where both his medical practice and his writing flourished; he remained there for thirteen years until forced abroad by his health in 1763. It was in Chelsea that he wrote *The Adventures of Peregrine Pickle* (commonly known as *Peregrine Pickle*), a work of nearly 330,000 words composed at top speed in anticipation of a trip to Paris. On February 25, 1751, his second novel was published to laudatory reviews and wide popularity.

Smollett's involvement with various periodicals began during the 1750's, first as a book reviewer for the *Monthly Review* and later as editor and proprietor of the *Critical Review*. Smollett joined Oliver Goldsmith in launching the *British Magazine* (the *Monthly Repository* beginning in 1760), remaining as coeditor

until 1763. With a final venture, Smollett gained public notoriety and untold enemies by agreeing to write the *Briton*, a political effort in support of Lord Bute's ministry. Of Smollett's various journalistic efforts, only the work in the *Critical Review* is exceptional; as a literary periodical, it remains one of the most significant of the last half of the eighteenth century.

In the early 1750's, Smollett was driving himself in order to escape debt. Publishing a medical paper, *An Essay on the External Use of Water*, brought him little money, and in February, 1753, his third novel, *The Adventures of Ferdinand, Count Fathom* (commonly known as *Ferdinand, Count Fathom*), was published with poor financial results. The book attracted few readers, and Smollett was forced to borrow money and to supplement his medical fees with further hackwork. The years of hack writing began in earnest with *A Complete History of England*, a translation of Voltaire's writings, a geographical reference work, and several digests of travel. The period from 1756 to 1763 destroyed Smollett's health, but his reputation as a critic and a successful writer became unquestioned. Unfortunately, this frantic production hardly kept him from debtor's prison. Returning to the novel in the *British Magazine*, Smollett published "the first considerable English novel ever to be published serially"—*The Adventures of Sir Launcelot Greaves* (commonly known as *Sir Launcelot Greaves*). In monthly installments from January, 1760, to December, 1761, the novel gave the six-penny periodical substantial popularity.

In the midst of this literary hard labor, Smollett was imprisoned for three months, having been convicted of libeling an Admiral Knowles in an article in the *Critical Review*. On his release in early 1761, Smollett continued fulfilling his contracts with certain booksellers but also traveled extensively, possibly to Dublin, even though troubled by asthma and tuberculosis. In addition to these difficulties, his spirit was nearly broken by the illness and death of his daughter in April, 1763. This final shock caused him to cut all his London ties and move his family to the Continent, hoping to calm his wife and cure his ailments in the mild climate of the south of France and Italy. He spent two years abroad, returning to England in July, 1765; the literary result of his tour was *Travels Through France and Italy*. Though ill health plagued him, he sought for the third time a consulship but was rejected; in 1768 he left England for the last time.

Arriving in Pisa, Italy, Smollett visited with friends at the university, finally settling at his country villa in Antignano, near Leghorn, in the spring of 1770, where he completed his masterpiece, *Humphry Clinker*. Immediately following its publication, he received the rave notices of friends and critics concerning the novel, but he had little time to enjoy the praise. On September 17, 1771, he died from an acute intestinal infection and was buried at the English cemetery at Leghorn.

ANALYSIS

Tobias Smollett is not only a great comic novelist; he is also a morally exhilarating one—a serious satirist of the brutality, squalor, and hideous corruption of humankind. His definite moral purposes are firmly grounded in the archetypal topic of all novelists—people's unceasing battle for survival in the war between the forces of good and evil. Smollett insists that people defy "the selfishness, envy, malice, and base indifference of mankind"; in such a struggle, the hero will ultimately prevail and will be rewarded for his or her fortitude.

RODERICK RANDOM

The principal theme of Smollett's first novel, *Roderick Random*, is the arbitrariness of success and failure in a world dominated by injustice and dishonesty. Smollett's decision to use realistic detail as a guise for his satire produces a lively and inventive work; moreover, the hero, Roderick, is not a mere picaro nor a passive fool but an intent satiric observer "who recognizes, reacts, and rebukes." The novel is organized in a three-part structure. The initial stage reveals Roderick's numerous trials as a young man; he loses his innocence during the years of poverty in Scotland, of failure in London, and of brutal experience in the Navy. The middle of the narrative embodies "the lessons of adversity" as the hero declines into near collapse. In a final brief section, Roderick recovers his physical and moral equilibrium and pro-

motes the simple human values of friendship, love, and trust as the only viable bases for a satisfying existence.

Roderick's problem is both to gain knowledge of the world and to assimilate that knowledge. M. A. Goldberg, in *Smollett and the Scottish School* (1959), finds that "at first his responses are dictated by his indignation, by passions . . . eventually, he learns . . . to govern the emotions with reason." The struggle between these two forces is central to an understanding of eighteenth century England and its literature. In Smollett's first novel, good sense seems a sufficient defense against the sordid viciousness of the world. Good sense, however, can only be achieved, or learned, when the hero can control his pride and passionate nature, which are inextricably linked. Equilibrium, an orderly existence, arises paradoxically from the ashes of his random adventures. This understanding develops as the hero pursues the happiness he thinks he deserves but can never fully attain; as a good empiricist, Roderick gathers knowledge from each reversal, finally achieving a "tranquility of love" with the prudent Narcissa.

In *Roderick Random*, the hero's search for happiness differs significantly from the quest of the traditional picaro. While gaining an education and suffering the rebukes of others, Roderick remains good and effectual, unlike Don Quixote, who is powerless against cruelty. Roderick's youthful ferocity contributes to the practicality of the satire. Smollett's approach to correcting the ills of society is to allow no attack or insult to go unavenged. A thorough whipping of a bully or the verbal punishment of a pedant lifts the book beyond the picaresque and advances it past the formal verse satire. The center of the satiric discussion implicates the surroundings and not the hero, thus permitting Smollett to offer a long list of evil, self-centered figures who provide an excellent contrast to the goodness and charity of the ill-served protagonist. Only his faithful servant, Strap; his uncle, Tom Bowling; and the maid, Narcissa, join him in opposing his neglectful grandfather, the scoundrel Vicar Shuffle, the tyrannical Captain Oakum, the dandiacal Captain Whiffle, and the rapacious Lord Strutwell.

The last section of the novel provides the hero with the riches of his long quest: family, wealth, and love. The moral of the adventures follows as Roderick's recently discovered father "blesses God for the adversity I had undergone," affirming that his son's intellectual, moral, and physical abilities had been improved "for all the duties and enjoyments of life, much better than any education which affluence could bestow." The felicity of this final chapter provides a conventional ending, but the crucial point is that Roderick, having completed a rigorous education in the distinctions between appearance and reality, is now deserving of these rewards.

PEREGRINE PICKLE

The protagonist of Smollett's long second novel, *Peregrine Pickle*, reminds one of Roderick in every aspect, except that Peregrine is an Englishman, not a Scot. The supporting players are improved; among the novel's outstanding comic creations are Commodore Hawser Trunnion and the spinster, Grizzle Pickle. Often described as the best picaresque novel in English, *Peregrine Pickle* satirizes the upper classes of mid-eighteenth century England. Rufus Putney argues in "The Plan of *Peregrine Pickle*" (1945) that Smollett "meant to write a satire on the affectations and meannesses, the follies and vices that flourished among the upper classes in order that his readers might learn with Peregrine the emptiness of titles, the sordidness of avarice, the triviality of wealth and honors, and the folly of misguided ambition."

The novel begins by sketching Peregrine's social and emotional background and introducing other principal characters. Following this introductory section, Smollett's protagonist describes his adolescence and education at Winchester and Oxford, where he becomes addicted to coarse practical jokes and to satisfying his overbearing pride. Here the hero meets Emilia, a beautiful orphan with whom he falls in love; because of his capricious nature, however, he cannot remain long with her. Having become alienated from his parents, Peregrine departs on the Grand Tour with the best wishes of his guardian, Trunnion.

Peregrine returns from France an unprincipled, arrogant rogue whose every action supports his vanity. After numerous incidents including the death of Trunnion and his replacement with the eccentric Cadwallader Crabtree as Peregrine's mentor, the hero tests the virtue of Emilia and is rebuffed. The remainder of the novel observes the long distress, the eventual imprisonment, and the final rehabilitation of the protagonist, who by now is convinced of the fraud and folly of the world. As Putney mentions, only after matriculating to the "school of adversity," which reduces his pride and vanity, can Peregrine hope to achieve wealth, marry his true love, triumph over his enemies, and retire to the country. Adversity teaches him to distinguish between the complex vices of the urban sophisticates and the simpler but more substantial pleasures of generosity and love in a rural retreat. Despite its picaresque vigor and satisfactory resolution, the novel suffers from a confusion of purposes: Peregrine's arrogance undermines the credibility of his role as a satirist of high society. Thus, Smollett's satiric intentions are blunted by his aspirations to a novel of character.

FERDINAND, COUNT FATHOM

Ferdinand, Count Fathom is remembered today for its dedication, in which Smollett gives his famous definition of the novel, and for its place as the first important eighteenth century work to propose terror as a subject for a novel. In *The Novels of Tobias Smollett* (1971), Paul-Gabriel Boucé finds that the major defect of the novel is the author's "mixture of genres, without any transition brought about by unfolding of the story or the evolution of the characters." Fathom's dark cynicism informs the majority of the work, with the last ten chapters unraveling into a weak melodrama; nevertheless, Smollett's satire remains effective as a bitter denunciation of the hypocrisy and violence of elegant society. As an early contribution to the literature of terror, the novel probes the emotions of a young, virtuous girl who undergoes isolation, deprivation, and sadistic brutality at the hands of a rapacious creature. The figure of Fathom is used to undercut sentimental conventions and show their uselessness when civilized norms are forgotten.

SIR LAUNCELOT GREAVES

Sir Launcelot Greaves completed serialization in December, 1761, and was published as a book in

March, 1762. Because of its serial publication, the novel's structure suffers from the frequent contrivance of artificial suspense. Recent criticism, however, has pointed to an underlying thematic unity based upon a series of variations on the theme of madness, with minute investigation into the physical, psychological, and moral aspects of the disorder. Greaves, the quixotic hero, launches a noble crusade for reform. His hopeless demand that a corrupted world listen to reason embraces Smollett's social idealism. If moral intention were the only measure of a novel's worth, then the didactic power of *Sir Launcelot Greaves* would guarantee its success; unfortunately, the delicate balance of the genre remains disordered by the force of an overobvious moral preoccupation.

HUMPHRY CLINKER

Smollett's last novel, *Humphry Clinker*, appeared in the bookstalls on June 15, 1771; Smollett had written the three volumes over a five-year period. It is his masterpiece, and it remains among the great English novels. The work was inspired by the epistles of Christopher Anstey's witty and popular *New Bath Guide* (1766). Using the epistolary method instead of the travel narrative of the early novels, Smollett characterizes his correspondents by means of their wonderfully individual letter-writing styles. Old Matthew Bramble of Brambleton Hall, Wales, travels with his household through Gloucester, Bath, London, Scarborough, Edinburgh, Cameron (Smollett country), Glasgow, Manchester, and home again. Squire Bramble suffers various physical complaints, and his ill health makes him sensitive to the social ills surrounding him on his journey. Bramble searches for a recovery but finds himself becoming worse, not better, yet his compassionate nature remains undiminished. The journey was begun so that Bramble might distract his young niece, Lydia Melford, from a strolling actor named Wilson. The party also includes Tabitha, his aging, narrow-minded, old-maid sister; her malapropic maid, Winifred Jenkins, the classic example of the illiterate servant; and the modishly cynical nephew, Jery. En route, they adopt, much to Tabitha's delight, a Scottish veteran of American Indian warfare, Obadiah Lismahago. Soon, they add Humphry

Clinker to the party as a new footman; he turns out to be the natural son of Matthew.

There are three major plots to develop, and numerous minor episodes, all of which hinge upon the characteristic picaresque device of the journey; Smollett exchanged the rogue hero for a group of picaros—Bramble and nephew Jery—who analyze and observe society. Through careful stages in letter after letter, Matthew's character is revealed to the reader, who learns to trust him as a reliable observer of society's foibles; in this respect *Humphry Clinker* is much stronger than *Peregrine Pickle*, where the satire was blunted by the protagonist's unreliability.

Smollett's satire strikes not individuals but categories of people and assorted social institutions; in particular *Humphry Clinker* is an exposé of the false attitudes and disordered life of the eighteenth century *nouveaux riches*. His conservative political views are displayed in Bramble's rages against an unrestricted press, politically biased juries, and the ignorance of the mob, and, as in *Peregrine Pickle*, he contrasts the folly and depravity of urban life with idealized pictures of the country.

Smollett's achievement in *Humphry Clinker* depends on his skillful use of the picaresque and epistolary traditions. His last novel is also distinguished by a warmth and tolerance not found to such a degree in his earlier works. Bramble's cynicism never becomes obnoxious to the reader; the brutality of Roderick is muted here. Smollett allows his hero to accept human society, despite "the racket and dissipation." Finally, for all his burlesque of Samuel Richardson's epistolary method, Smollett's characterization of Lydia has a depth and intensity that raises her above mere romantic convention.

In contrast to many critical reports, *Humphry Clinker* ends on a buoyant note of pure happiness, a happiness which fulfills the eighteenth century dictum of conformity to the universal order. Smollett's novels embrace moral and virtuous methods for pursuing one's goals. Passions and reason must remain in balance, and within this harmony, nature and art can moderate the demands of vice and folly.

Paul J. deGategno

OTHER MAJOR WORKS

PLAYS: *The Regicide: Or, James the First of Scotland, a Tragedy*, pb. 1749; *The Reprisal: Or, The Tars of Old England*, pr. 1757.

NONFICTION: *The History and Adventures of an Atom*, 1749, 1769; *An Essay on the External Use of Water*, 1752; *A Compendium of Authentic and Entertaining Voyages*, 1756; *A Complete History of England*, 1757-1758; *Continuation of the Complete History of England*, 1760-1765; *Travels Through France and Italy*, 1766; *The Present State of All Nations*, 1768-1769; *Letters of Tobias Smollett*, 1970 (Lewis M. Knapp, editor).

TRANSLATIONS: *The Adventures of Gil Blas of Santillane*, 1748 (Alain René Le Sage); *The History and Adventures of the Renowned Don Quixote*, 1755 (Miguel de Cervantes); *The Works of M. de Voltaire*, 1761-1774 (35 volumes); *The Adventures of Telemachus, the Son of Ulysses*, 1776 (François de Salignac de La Mothe-Fénelon).

BIBLIOGRAPHY

Bold, Alan, ed. *Smollett: Author of the First Distinction*. New York: Barnes & Noble Books, 1982. Contains four essays dealing with general issues and five concentrating on each of Smollett's major novels. Indexed.

Boucé, Paul-Gabriel. *The Novels of Tobias Smollett*. Translated by Antonia White. London: Longman, 1976. A slightly abridged version of the 1971 French study. Includes a biographical sketch, chapters on the major novels, and good discussions of Smollett's realism and comic devices. Contains a chronologically arranged bibliography of secondary works from 1928 to 1975.

Bulckaen, Denise. *A Dictionary of Characters in Tobias Smollett*. Nancy, France: Presses Universitaires de Nancy, 1993. An extremely useful way of keeping track of the plethora of characters in Smollett's fiction. Each character is identified; chapter and page number of the character's first appearance are also cited. There is also an index of the main categories of characters.

Grant, Damian. *Tobias Smollett: A Study in Style*. Totowa, N.J.: Rowman & Littlefield, 1977. As the title suggests, Grant ignores questions of realism and moral purpose to concentrate on what he regards as Smollett's three styles: comic, passionate, and, to a lesser extent, lyrical.

Knapp, Lewis Mansfield. *Tobias Smollett: Doctor of Men and Manners*. Princeton, N.J.: Princeton University Press, 1949. The standard life, sympathetic and detailed, but with little critical analysis of the works.

Rousseau, G. S. *Tobias Smollett: Essays of Two Decades*. Edinburgh: T. & T. Clark, 1982. Collects fifteen previously published essays and reviews on such topics as Smollett as letter writer and his role in various medical controversies of his day. Makes a good case, *inter alia*, for not regarding Smollett's novels as picaresques.

Rousseau, G. S., and Paul-Gabriel Boucé, eds. *Tobias Smollett: Bicentennial Essays Presented to Lewis M. Knapp*. New York: Oxford University Press, 1971. Includes ten essays that examine all aspects of Smollett's writings, including his voluminous, oft-neglected histories. The index allows for cross-references.

Spector, Robert D. *Smollett's Women: A Study in an Eighteenth-Century Masculine Sensibility*. Westport, Conn.: Greenwood Press, 1994. Organized differently from most books on Smollett, with chapters on society, personality, and literary tradition; heroines, fallen women, and women as victims; and the comic and the grotesque. Includes notes and bibliography.

_____. *Tobias George Smollett*. 1968. Rev. ed. Boston: Twayne, 1989. The first chapter of the book quickly surveys Smollett's minor works. The rest of the book is a consideration of his novels. Contains a useful annotated bibliography of secondary criticism.

Wagoner, Mary. *Tobias Smollett*. New York: Garland, 1984. Provides an extensive list of editions of Smollett's works as well as an annotated bibliography of secondary material. Arranged by subject (for example, "Biographies and Biographical Material" and "The Expedition of Humphry Clinker") and therefore easy to use for locating criticism on a specific topic.

C. P. SNOW

Born: Leicester, England; October 15, 1905
Died: London, England; July 1, 1980

PRINCIPAL LONG FICTION

Death Under Sail, 1932, 1959
New Lives for Old, 1933
The Search, 1934, 1958
Strangers and Brothers series (includes *Strangers
    and Brothers*, 1940 [reissued as *George
    Passant*, 1972])
The Light and the Dark, 1947
Time of Hope, 1949
The Masters, 1951
The New Men, 1954
Homecomings, 1956 (pb. in U.S. as *Homecoming*)
The Conscience of the Rich, 1958
The Affair, 1960
Corridors of Power, 1964
The Sleep of Reason, 1968
Last Things, 1970
The Malcontents, 1972
In Their Wisdom, 1974
A Coat of Varnish, 1979

OTHER LITERARY FORMS

Reflecting his various careers and interests, C. P.
Snow published, in addition to his novels, a number
of books, including the literary biographies *Trollope:
His Life and Art* (1975) and *The Realists* (1978), as
well as many reviews and articles. He had some inter-
est in the drama, encouraging the staging of his novels
The Affair, The New Men, and *The Masters*, writing a
full-length play, *A View over the Bridge*, produced in
London in 1950, and collaborating with his wife,
Pamela Hansford Johnson, on six one-act plays pub-
lished in 1951: *Spare the Rod, The Pigeon with the
Silver Foot, Her Best Foot Forward, The Supper
Dance, To Murder Mrs. Mortimer*, and *Family Party*.

ACHIEVEMENTS

As a man, Snow's accomplishments were many
and varied; as a novelist his achievement was more

limited, and yet (*ars longa*, public life frequently
breva) probably more long lasting. Snow the scientist
and Snow the public figure cannot, however, be divorced from Snow the writer. Just as his novels drew
upon his experiences in his nonliterary careers, so
were his sociopolitical ideas presented in his novels.
Yet, there is less of the details of "doing" science,
less of the specificity of the public life than one
might have expected from Snow's background had he
been more of a naturalistic novelist, and there is less
ideological content than might have been anticipated
from one with Snow's strong views had he been more
of a propagandist.

Snow was, rather, a realistic novelist, using his
particular knowledge, background, and political ideology not primarily for their own sake, but in the service of his art. This art was conventional, relatively
old-fashioned. Snow had limited patience with James
Joyce and the literary avant-garde. As a *roman-
fleuve, Strangers and Brothers* has a few interesting
features, but it certainly lacks the subtlety that Snow
admired in Marcel Proust. Snow did little to advance
novelistic techniques; his own craftsmanship shows
scant development over the course of a long writing
career. His style has frequently been described as dull
or pedestrian; Edmund Wilson found his novels "unreadable."

Snow implicitly defended his own style in discussing Anthony Trollope's, praising his predecessor
for using language that was often intentionally made
flat in order to be clear. Snow's style is certainly
more serviceable than inspired. His imagery is limited and repetitious. Unity and impact are achieved
through the recurrence of a limited number of images, such as those of lighted windows and rivers, but
the impact is gained at the expense of a degree of monotony.

If Snow's style and imagery are little more than
adequate, his plot construction is only somewhat
more skillful. Unlike Trollope, whom Snow admired
and to whom he has frequently been compared, Snow
uses plots that are usually suspenseful; one reads his
books partly to see how they will come out. This element of suspense, going back to his first published
novel, a "whodunit," no doubt helps explain his hav-

ing attracted a fairly wide and loyal audience, many of whom were not regular readers of novels. Snow's plots, however, are seldom particularly ingenious or original; essentially, they are a means to the revelation of character.

It is in characterization that Snow's prime virtue as a novelist lies; yet his characterizations excel only within certain limits. These limits arise from his subject matter. As has been frequently noted, Snow is particularly effective in dealing with "man in committee." This focus, related to the election, by thirteen Fellows, of a new head of their college, is central to Snow's most highly praised novel, *The Masters*. A similar focus is present in a number of his other novels, most strongly in *The Affair*. The men operate in committees because of the nature of their work—they are professionals involved in their careers, as academics, businessmen, scientists, civil servants. This *work*—not the physical labor described in a "proletarian novel" but the work of "The New Men," the professional, bureaucratic, technological, managerial classes—is presented with knowledgeable detail to be found in hardly any other novelist. Snow's work, in effect, filled a vacuum.

Snow filled another vacuum in his treatment of love and sex. While these topics have hardly been ignored by novelists, Snow's consideration of the social dimensions of a love affair or a marriage—the effect, for example, of a particular passion upon a man's career, such as Jago's protective love, in *The Masters*, for his wife—is rare, if not unique, among modern novelists, especially as, in Snow, the passion per se, however important, is never (not even in *Time of Hope*) the central concern.

This concern is character; the conditions of work, the politicking in committee, the impact of love—all these are used to reveal character in action. Thus, Snow is fundamentally a very traditional novelist, even though his distinctive reputation rests upon his having been a kind of contemporary social psychologist, carefully observing particular segments of modern society. While he is likely to continue to be read for some time for the picture of parts of society that his special experience allowed him to present, he may well still be read when this picture, encrusted by

time, is of only historical interest. If, as seems likely, his novels do so survive, it will be because, while dealing with the time-bound particulars of their age, they were able to rise to an understanding of fundamental human motivation and thus to enjoy the longevity of true art.

BIOGRAPHY

Charles Percy Snow was born on October 15, 1905, in the Midland city of Leicester, the second of four sons. His background was similar to that of his fictional persona, Lewis Eliot. Snow's family had risen to the lower levels of the middle class; his father worked as a clerk in a shoe factory. Like Eliot's father, who led a choir, Snow's father played the organ in church; when he was no longer able to do so, he died soon after, at the age of eighty-four.

In school, Snow specialized in science; after graduation he worked as a laboratory assistant while he prepared for the examination which won him a scholarship, in 1925, at the University College of Leicester. He was graduated, in 1927, with First Class Honors in chemistry and received a grant that allowed him to proceed to a Master of Science degree in physics in 1928. Subsequently, he gained a scholarship to Cambridge, where he entered Christ's College as a research student in physics, published a paper on the infrared investigation of molecular structure, and, in 1930, received a Ph.D. and was elected a Fellow of Christ's College, a post he held until 1950, serving as Tutor from 1935 until 1945.

Like the fictional Lewis Eliot, whose law career hinged upon doing well in examinations and receiving scholarships, Snow must have worked hard (as did the hero of *The Search*) and must have been driven by ambition. His lifelong friend William Cooper (H. S. Hoff) has written novels about the life of the young people in Leicester in which the young Snow appears in fictional form; this work helps confirm the autobiographical quality of Snow's *Time of Hope*. Snow himself suggests the autobiographical aspect of *The Conscience of the Rich*, writing that when he was "very poor and very young," he "was taken up by one of the rich patrician Anglo-Jewish families."

Just as Lewis Eliot changes careers, and as the narrator of *The Search* turns from science to writing, Snow also did not rest in the comfort of being a rising young scientific don. He later wrote that since eighteen or so he knew that he wanted to be a writer, and while an undergraduate he wrote a novel, never published, called *Youth Searching*. He had gone into science because it offered a practical possibility for a poor boy. Although he did good scientific work at Cambridge and published some significant papers, according to William Cooper in *C. P. Snow* (1959), when some of Snow's scientific research went wrong through oversight, he abandoned scientific experimentation and turned more to his writing.

Snow had already published his first novel, *Death Under Sail*, a detective story, in 1932; he looked on it as practice for his later, more serious fiction. The next year he published *New Lives for Old*, combining his interest in science and politics in a work of science fiction. Worried that it would hurt his scientific career, he published this novel anonymously; it has never been reprinted. The first of his "serious" novels, *The Search*, appeared in 1934; like the Lewis Eliot series, it had a significant autobiographical element.

Snow did not move away from science to a complete commitment to literature at this time; rather, he became involved in administration, starting at his college. In 1939, he was appointed to a committee of the Royal Society that was organizing scientists for the war effort. This position led to a career in civil service; during World War II, he worked with the Ministry of Labour, being responsible for scientific personnel; after the war, he recruited scientists for government service. Beginning in 1944, he was associated with the English Electric Company, becoming a member of its Board of Directors in 1947. He was a Civil Service Commissioner from 1945 until 1960.

Snow's public life led to public honors; in 1943 he was made a Commander of the British Empire; in 1957 he was knighted. In 1964, when the Labour Party resumed power, Snow, making a decision different from Lewis Eliot's, was made a life peer, Baron Snow, of the City of Leicester and served for two years as parliamentary secretary of the Ministry of Technology.

During these years of public service, Snow was, of course, also living a personal life. He married the novelist Pamela Hansford Johnson in 1950. Like Margaret Davidson in the *Strangers and Brothers* series, she had been previously married, and like Lewis Eliot, Snow became a stepfather before having a son of his own, Philip Hansford Snow, born in 1952. Lady Snow has written autobiographically; her accounts are especially interesting in suggesting the similarities and differences between her children and the fictional children presented, especially in *Last Things*, by Snow.

Both the public and the personal sides of Snow's life were reflected in the *Strangers and Brothers* series, the idea for which occurred to him, he wrote, on January 1, 1935, while he was in France. It is difficult to determine the degree to which the whole series was worked out in advance. It would seem that Snow developed early certain controlling themes, such as "possessive love" and the idea of the "resonance" of experience upon the narrator, Lewis Eliot, while remaining flexible regarding the number and nature of the volumes that would make up the series. The first volume, *Strangers and Brothers*, which was to give the title to the whole series, appeared in 1940. It was followed in 1947 by *The Light and the Dark*. The subsequent nine volumes of the series appeared at roughly two-year intervals. They continued to draw directly upon his own life, including his eye operations, his cardiac arrest, his interest in the Moors murder case, and his experience in parliament.

The course of Snow's simultaneous literary and public careers brought him increased recognition and honors, including numerous honorary degrees, and appointment as rector of the University of St. Andrews, Scotland. (Like Lewis Eliot, he postponed the first of his eye operations in order to attend this academic installation.) They also involved him in notable controversy, the most famous resulting from his Cambridge lectures in 1959, later published as *The Two Cultures and the Scientific Revolution*. Snow's position, which included a criticism of intellectuals' general lack of understanding of modern science, provoked much discussion and a strong attack, renewed in 1961 by the noted Cambridge literary critic,

F. R. Leavis. In 1960, Snow, while on one of his trips to the United States, stirred up another controversy by his lectures at Harvard. In those lectures, he criticized some of the military-scientific decisions made by Winston Churchill's government during World War II.

In his later years, Snow continued to speak out on public policies. He remained a controversial figure, but he gradually acquired the image of an elderly, liberal sage, even if his sagacity was frequently questioned by both the political Left and Right. Following the completion of the *Strangers and Brothers* series, he revised it for an "Omnibus Edition" and continued his writing, publishing *The Malcontents, In Their Wisdom*, and ending his career, as he began it, with a detective story (of sorts), *A Coat of Varnish*. His remarkably full life ended on July 1, 1980.

Analysis

Characterization is the foundation of Snow's fiction. While theme and idea, as one might expect from a writer as political and *engagé* as was C. P. Snow, are important to his work, and while plot is nearly always a major source of interest, character is fundamental. It was his special approach to characterization, at once limited and complex, that allowed him to employ theme and plot, as well as style and imagery, in its service and which made certain subject matter particularly appropriate. Consequently, his works have their own distinctive and satisfying unity.

In his study of Anthony Trollope, a writer whom he valued highly and with whom he identified in a number of ways, Snow speaks interestingly of characterization. He defines character as persona, distinguishes it from inherent, individual nature, and considers personality to be a fusion of nature and character. These distinctions are certainly relevant to Snow's own work. His starting interest is in "characters," that is, an individual's personal qualities that are conditioned by, and expressed in, social experience. Yet, recognizing that this "character" interacts with "nature," Snow, in attempting to represent a rounded picture of "personality," must demonstrate the interaction. His fiction, then, is simultaneously concerned with showing people their "character" in social situations, indicating their "nature" or personal

psychology, and presenting the interplay of the two, the social character and the private nature. All people have, in differing proportions, both a private and a social side to their personalities; all are both strangers and brothers.

Given this approach, it is not difficult to understand why Snow dealt frequently with "man in committee," or why he balanced this social material with presentation of individual passions, such as Lewis Eliot's for Sheila. Work and careers, seen in relation to individual "nature" and love and sex, were the two poles to which his subject matter flowed. As the social side of personality developed, Snow was able to suggest its changing formation. One observes, for example, Walter Luke's evolution from a brash young scientist to Lord Luke of Salcombe; his persona, but not his basic nature, changes with the years. Because an individual's "nature" is inherent (like his or her physiology), it is taken as a *donnée*, and its effects are dealt with. It is, for example, a given fact that Roy Calvert is a kind of "manic-depressive"; the reader discovers what the results of this nature will be, both for Calvert himself and for those with whom he interacts.

It was convenient for Snow that this approach to character was quite appropriate to the type of plotting that he apparently preferred. Most of his novels pose a question: "What will Martin decide?" "Who will be elected master?" "Will Roger Quaife succeed?" The reader, in attempting to anticipate the answer, and Snow, in providing and justifying it, must consider the personalities involved. This consideration requires some understanding of the characters' public personae, their social interactions, and their private passions. Plot, a strong element in its own right, is based on character.

Imagery also consistently reinforces Snow's binocular view of personality. The light of brotherhood wages a never-ending Manichaean conflict with the dark of private estrangement. Windows may be lit, inviting people to "come home" to social involvement, but they often walk the dark streets, locked out in their lonely individuality.

Much of Snow's style also reflects his view of personality. E. A. Levenston, in a careful study of Snow's sentence structure (*ES*, 1974), has noticed the prevalence of qualifying "interrupters." Many of these are a result of Snow's comparing the particular to the general, one person's qualities to many people's. Expressions such as "very few men, George least of all" or "Roy was not a snob, no man was less so," run throughout his work.

Thus, Snow was consistent in his craft. If this consistency imposed some limitations on his achievements, it also provided a valuable unity to his whole literary corpus.

DEATH UNDER SAIL

For reasons that he later described as "obscure," Snow "signalled" that he intended to abandon his scientific career by writing "a stylised, artificial detective story very much in the manner of the day." *Death Under Sail* is a competent example of this form; it remains quite readable and in some ways foreshadows his more significant work. Told in the first person (curiously, for a book by a twenty-six-year-old, the narrator is sixty-three), it employs light and dark and also water imagery; it includes a political discussion regarding class society being justified through the ranks of the elite being open to talent; and it is concerned with friendship and the "generation gap." More important, the plot hinges on character. While the novel's characterization is relatively superficial, it involves both social character, as seen in the interaction of a small group (the narrator, the detective, and the suspects), and the individual psychology of concealed motives. It is thus typical of Snow's novels, most of which have the element of a suspense story based on the two sides, public and private, of personality.

NEW LIVES FOR OLD

Snow's second published novel, *New Lives for Old*, is the weakest of his whole canon, but it is not without its virtues. The story involves the discovery of a rejuvenating process and the subsequent questions of whether the process will be suppressed, its effects on the love lives of some of the characters, and the political implications of the discovery. These three questions are not well unified; instead of integrating the love interest and the politics, in this one instance Snow treats them as essentially separate stories, at the expense of both. The love story in the

middle section becomes tedious; in the last section of the book Snow, atypically, lets a political interest stifle the story. The first part of the book, however, is fairly successful. Here, the plot is related to character, social interactions, private motivations, and moral decisions. Snow is doing what he does best. The falling-off of the work after its relatively effective beginning, however, justifies his decision not to have it reprinted; it is now a difficult book to obtain.

THE SEARCH

His third published novel, *The Search*, was slightly revised and reprinted twenty-four years after its first appearance. It is generally superior to the first two novels and more easily related to the *Strangers and Brothers* series, especially *Time of Hope* and *Homecoming*. Although Snow warns the reader, in his preface to the 1958 edition, that the book's narrator and protagonist, Arthur Miles, is "not much like" Snow himself, clearly there is an autobiographical element in the story of a poor boy's using his talent, determination, and scholarships to make a career in science, later to abandon it to turn to writing. The book was praised for its accurate picture of what it is like to be a scientist; in fact, very little scientific activity per se is present. Rather, professional concerns, ambitions, the relation between love and career, and the decisions made by men in committees constitute the basic material of the book. The protagonist might just as easily be a barrister as a scientist. Indeed, *The Search*, while a worthwhile book in its own right, can be seen as a trying out of the material that Snow was to go on to develop in his series. The defects of *The Search* result primarily from attempting to try out too much at once; the book's construction becomes somewhat confused. The virtues arise from Snow's basing his work on personal experience; he employed, more thoroughly than in his first two published novels, his skill in showing the interconnections of the personal and public aspects of personality.

The favorable reception given to *The Search* certainly encouraged Snow to continue his career as a novelist; within a year of its publication, he conceived of the series on which his reputation rests. He must have made various plans for the series as a whole; the first volume, however, did not appear until 1940, six years after *The Search*. Writing a *roman-fleuve*, as opposed to a series of individual novels, presents an author with certain problems and various opportunities. While Snow avoided some of the pitfalls, such as narrative inconsistency, he failed to take advantage of some of the potentialities of the form. The overall pattern of this series is more blurred than it need have been. This is indicated by the order in which the books were published; it is not the essentially chronological order of the "Omnibus Edition," published after the series was concluded. While this authorial rearrangement must be accepted, the fact that Snow did not originally insist on it suggests a certain random quality to the series' organization as first conceived of and executed. Furthermore, proposed systems of classification of the books within the series—as, for example, novels of "observed experience" and of "direct experience," or novels dealing with individuals, groups, or a mixture of both—while useful, fail to make clear a compelling pattern.

Indeed, the individual volumes of the series, with the possible exception of the final *Last Things*, stand on their own and easily can be enjoyed separately. That is not to say that nothing is gained by reading them all in the order that they appear in the "Omnibus Edition." As compared, however, to a work such as Anthony Powell's *roman-fleuve, A Dance to the Music of Time* (1951-1975), *Strangers and Brothers* fails to develop the potential cumulative effect of a series.

The series form does allow the overlapping of incident and the "resonance" between events as seen and felt by the narrator, Lewis Eliot. Snow has an interesting concept here but he does too little with it. The reader does not, as in some of the novels of Joyce Cary, see the same events through different eyes; rather, one is given different accounts by a relatively consistent Eliot. The result is that events described for the second time sometimes bore the reader; at other times the reader feels cheated by the inadequacy of the first account. Only occasionally does the technique work well, as, for example, in the two accounts, in *The Light and the Dark* and *The Masters*, of Roy Calvert's giving of a self-damning

paper to Winslow. The first account omits material in order to focus on Calvert; subsequently, as one learns of the larger implications of the act, it takes on new meaning.

THE STRANGERS AND BROTHERS SERIES

More obvious benefits of a series novel are present in *Strangers and Brothers*; the reader observes more characters, over a longer period of time, than would normally be possible in a single volume. Snow, however, possibly in the interest of verisimilitude, does relatively little with his opportunity. Roy Calvert is killed off, George Passant's change is not traced; one does see more of Martin Eliot and Francis Getliffe, but their developments, such as they are, have little drama. There is little in Snow corresponding to the surprises that Powell gives the reader when, for example, his villain, Widmerpool, makes one of his sudden appearances. Only quite rarely does Snow make effective use of surprise, as when the elderly Hector Rose is found to have acquired a younger, sexy wife.

The time span of the series does, however, allow Snow to present the succession of generations, and he does a fine job of suggesting how childhood experiences affect parents as they react to their own children and their friends' children. The parents' point of view is an important part of human experience, infrequently treated in fiction; here again, in presenting parental love, Snow effectively filled a vacuum.

A more fundamental aspect of the *roman-fleuve* is the development of the narrator. Lewis Eliot does change, both in his attitudes and in his style, becoming more ironic in the later volumes. Looking back on earlier events, such as his support of Jago in *The Masters*, he recognizes his errors. While Eliot's development adds interest to the whole series, it would be difficult to maintain that this interest is central.

There are two final aspects of a series novel that make *Strangers and Brothers* something other than eleven separate books—repetition and thematic development. The former is a two-edged device. Any reader of the whole series will be struck by the frequent repetition of certain phrases, sententious remarks, images, and tricks of style, and can readily assemble a list. Are the values of the repetition—

interesting variations on a theme and a sense of continuity—greater than the drawback—monotony? In Snow's case, it is something of a tossup. On balance, although many readers may be inclined to say "Oh no! Not another lighted window," the recurring images of light and darkness do form a pattern that unifies the series and reinforces its themes.

Finally, there is theme. Snow himself, in a note preceding *The Conscience of the Rich*, indicated the importance of recurring themes, including "possessive love" and love of, and renunciation of, power. The list could be easily expanded; as has been indicated, the title of the series itself points to a fundamental thematic concern. By seeing these various themes dramatized through different characters in differing circumstances, and learning Lewis Eliot's reactions, the reader certainly gains a perspective that would be impossible in a single volume. Thematic perspective, then, provides the most convincing justification for Snow's series. It is a sufficient justification; the whole is greater than the sum of the parts. That Snow's strength lay more in characterization than thematic presentation may account for the occasional failures of the series.

A brief discussion of three of the eleven novels of the series may serve to suggest aspects of the volumes considered as individual works. *Time of Hope* is both an early novel and one that focuses upon Lewis Eliot; *The Masters*, generally the most highly regarded of the series, is from the middle period and has a "collective hero"; *Corridors of Power*, a later novel, centers on a protagonist other than Eliot.

TIME OF HOPE

Time of Hope was the third volume in the series; in terms of internal chronology, however, it comes first, dealing with the years 1914 to 1933, during which Lewis Eliot matures from a boy of nine to an established barrister, involved in an "impossible" marriage. Strongly unified by its plot, it is perhaps the most emotionally moving volume of the whole series, and one of the more successful.

Indicative of Snow's central concern for the interconnections of the public and private aspects of character, the title refers to both the hope for a better society that Lewis Eliot shares with George Passant's group, and the hero's private ambitions. Asked what he wants from life, Eliot, in a phrase he returns to much later in the series, replies that he wants to see a better world, spend his life not unknown, and gain love.

The suspense in the novel is based on the question of whether Eliot will succeed, whether he will at least be started on the road to realizing these hopes. The conflict and tension behind this question provide the angst that contrasts to the hope. The book begins with a "homecoming," dreaded by the young Eliot. (In a clear parallel with Marcel Proust, Snow picks this up at the start of the very last volume of the series.) Just as he had reason to fear this first homecoming, Eliot later dreads subsequent returns to the woman he manages to marry. Eliot's success is mingled with failure. Through a combination of his "nature," which gives him the drive to struggle, and his social "character," which wins him the help of George Passant, Eliot's "personality" wins through on the public level: He succeeds in becoming a barrister. On the personal level, however, while he "succeeds" in marrying Sheila, his possessive love evokes no response; his marriage is personally disastrous and a handicap to his career.

Snow in *Time of Hope* thus successfully utilizes his approach to character and his recurring themes in a self-contained story, but one which also prepares for subsequent volumes. His techniques in this volume are typical of the series: The imagery of light and darkness prevails; secondary characters, such as Herbert Getliffe, the barrister under whom Eliot trains, are well drawn; the "nature" of a major character is presented as a *donneé*. Not being shown what makes her the strange person she is, one must take Sheila's problems as given. Fortunately for the story, it is easier to do so than to accept Roy Calvert's inherent depression in *The Light and the Dark*. As a *Bildungsroman*, *Time of Hope* is more conventional than the majority of the volumes in the series. Consequently, it is both one of the more satisfactory of Snow's novels and one of the less distinctively interesting.

THE MASTERS

While *Time of Hope* has a clear protagonist, *The Masters*, the first volume in the revised series, has no one hero. Snow is particularly good at dealing with interactions within a group, and *The Masters* has been the most highly regarded of his novels. The title refers to two "masters" or heads of a college; after the first one dies, a new one must be elected. It is on this election, involving the votes of thirteen Fellows of the college, that the plot centers. The election comes down to two candidates, Jago and Crawford. While Lewis Eliot, now one of the Fellows, supports Jago, and while the reader's sympathies are involved on this side, Snow is careful to avoid making the choice one between good and evil. There are very few outright villains in Snow's novels, and Crawford is certainly not one. Politically on the left, but personally not so well suited for the mastership, he is contrasted to Jago, whom Eliot finds less appealing politically but much more appealing as a man. Thus, the issue is essentially between personal "nature" and public "character." The different Fellows line up on this basis, thereby reflecting their own natures and characters; their ultimate votes demonstrate the balance of these two aspects of "personality."

Interestingly, given Snow's famous dispute, following the publication of the *The Masters*, over "the two cultures," the literary and the scientific, one might see Jago, a scholar of English literature, as the humanists' candidate, and Crawford, a member of the Royal Society, as the scientists'. Snow, opposed to the split between the "cultures," does not have the Fellows vote on the basis of this split. Walter Luke, a scientist, judges by nature and sticks with Jago. Francis Getliffe, also a scientist, although recognizing Jago's virtues, is motivated by "public" principle and supports Crawford. Eustace Pilbrow, a literary scholar, agrees with Getliffe. Nightingale, another scientist, jealous of Crawford's professional success, initially supports Jago. Paradoxically, Despard-Smith, because he identifies with Jago, supports Crawford.

Having established the initial lineup of votes, Snow skillfully shows the interactions of motives that cause some of them to shift. One particularly important consideration is the question of Jago's wife; her character, thought to be unsuitable for that of a Master's spouse, becomes an issue in the election. The personal issue here involves another form of "posses-

sive love" and sets up a "resonance" for Eliot, who is ambivalently trapped in his marriage to Sheila. Snow handles the development of the plot and the suspense leading to the election quite effectively. In bringing so many insightful changes on the interactions of the personalities within a small group, Snow wrote what may be his own masterpiece.

In the later volumes of the series, Eliot moves from college to national and international political maneuvers; the implications are that there is not that much difference. Nevertheless, the "Tolstoyan" view of history—that individuals are secondary to the larger forces of history, which is explicitly mentioned more than once in the series—is more pronounced in the later volumes. Snow suggests that with other people, probably the same policies would be carried out, the same forces would operate. Thus, the *mechanisms* of politics are of primary interest, but to understand them, one must understand the people who work and are worked by them. As Snow once said, one must understand how the world "ticks" if one is to change it for the better.

CORRIDORS OF POWER

Corridors of Power, the ninth volume in the series, gives the reader a picture of how the high-level decision making that he also described in *The New Men* and questioned in *Science and Government* (1961) does operate. However deterministic its underlying historical philosophy, the novel supports the statement of one of its characters that what is important is how something is done, who it is done by, and when it is done.

The story centers on Roger Quaife, a politician committed to an "enlightened" view of the use of atomic weapons. Once again, one sees both the public and private side of a protagonist, the "nature" and "character" that interact to form Quaife's "personality"; again, however, the nature is essentially a *donneé*—Quaife is to be taken as found. Ostensibly happy in his marriage, Quaife has a mistress; she is a factor, although not a decisive one, in his political career. Snow is quite good at showing the interactions of career considerations and more personal feelings within the triangle composed of Quaife, his wife Caro, and his mistress Ellen. Sex is seen as a *rela-*

tionship, social as well as emotional and physical. In order to present this relationship, however, verisimilitude must be stretched a bit, because Lewis Eliot, the narrator, has to be in places and hear confidences from which one would expect him to be barred. Not only does Eliot learn much about private lives, but also he is rather surprisingly ubiquitous at political councils. Here, in describing some of the behind-the-scenes maneuvers, Snow is quite effective, as he is with the presentation of secondary characters, such as the member of Parliament, "Sammikins," and the important civil servant, Hector Rose.

After the completion and revision of the *Strangers and Brothers* series, Snow not only worked on biographical studies—*Trollope* (1975), The Realists (1978), *The Physicists* (1981)—but also continued his novel writing. Although the final volume in the series, *Last Things*, was diffuse in plotting, he returned, in his final novels, to the use of a strong plot line. Both *The Malcontents* and *A Coat of Varnish* are forms of the "whodunit," and *In Their Wisdom*, like *The Sleep of Reason*, maintains the reader's interest in the outcome of a law case.

THE MALCONTENTS

The Malcontents received generally poor reviews. It does have obvious weaknesses; the dialogue, usually one of Snow's stronger points, is somewhat unconvincing. Well attuned to the talk of his cohorts, Snow's ear for the speech of contemporary youth was less acute. A more serious defect is related to the mystery-story requirement of providing a goodly number of suspects. Too many characters are introduced at the beginning; the reader has an initial problem in differentiating them, and the book gets off to a slow start. Once the story is underway, however, the narrative interest is strong. It involves the interaction of a group of seven young people, planning to take action against the establishment. One of them is known to be an informer. Typically for a Snow novel, to appreciate fully the narrative one must consider the formative aspects of each individual's personality. Class background, family relations, ideological positions, and love interests all enter in. Diffused through seven characters, however, Snow's analysis of these factors is somewhat superficial, with the ex-

ception of Stephen Freer, whose relationship to the older generation is presented with sensitivity. An underlying sympathy for the ends, if not the means, of the young radicals informs much of the book. This sympathy, while somewhat Olympian, avoids being patronizing and becomes one of the novel's virtues.

IN THEIR WISDOM

In Their Wisdom is a more successful work. Again, to develop narrative interest, a problem is posed. In this instance, it involves an argument over a will and the results of a trial over the disputed legacy. Just as the reader's sympathy is involved, in *The Masters*, on Jago's side, here there is no question of whom to support in the contest. Julian, a selfish and opportunistic young man, is Snow's closest approach to a clear villain. By simplifying some of the characters, Snow is able to devote more attention to the others. Jenny is particularly interesting, different from characters in Snow's earlier books. In showing her life of genteel poverty and the effect upon her of the trial and its outcome, Snow once again effectively intertwines the personal and the public. Although it devotes an excessive amount of space to the House of Lords, *In Their Wisdom* is one of Snow's more successful novels.

A COAT OF VARNISH

His last novel, *A Coat of Varnish*, was a return to the detective-story genre of his first book. A less pure example of this genre than *Death Under Sail*, however, it is somewhat unsatisfactorily considered simply as a mystery. The title refers to a line within the book, to the effect that civilization is a thin coat of varnish over barbarism, a notion relevant also to *The Sleep of Reason*. A fairly interesting cast of characters is introduced, but none of them is treated with the depth of analysis of which Snow was capable. Here, character is secondary to plot, and plot itself is used to comment on society. To try to work out who is guilty, one must understand motives: money, sex, and power. In understanding these motives, one gains, Snow expects, an understanding of society. Although this is one of Snow's weaker novels, certainly not ending his career triumphantly, it does manage a degree of fulfillment of the Horatian formula, to delight and to instruct.

Perhaps one should ask for no more. Throughout his career as a novelist, Snow, although with varying degrees of success, never failed to provide a number of intelligent readers with these twin satisfactions. This may not put him in the ranks of a Leo Tolstoy or a Proust; it is, nevertheless, no small accomplishment.

William B. Stone

OTHER MAJOR WORKS

PLAYS: *A View over the Bridge*, pr. 1950; *The Supper Dance*, pb. 1951 (with Pamela Hansford Johnson); *Family Party*, pb. 1951 (with Johnson); *Spare the Rod*, pb. 1951 (with Johnson); *To Murder Mrs. Mortimer*, pb. 1951 (with Johnson); *The Pigeon with the Silver Foot*, pb. 1951 (with Johnson); *Her Best Foot Forward*, pb. 1951 (with Johnson); *The Public Prosecutor*, pr. 1967 (with Johnson; adaptation).

NONFICTION: *Richard Aldington: An Appreciation*, 1938; *Writers and Readers of the Soviet Union*, 1943; *The Two Cultures and the Scientific Revolution*, 1959 (revised as *Two Cultures and a Second Look*, 1964); *The Moral Un-Neutrality of Science*, 1961; *Science and Government*, 1961; *A Postscript to Science and Government*, 1962; *Magnanimity*, 1962; *C. P. Snow: A Spectrum, Science, Criticism, Fiction*, 1963; *Variety of Men*, 1967; *The State of Siege*, 1969; *Public Affairs*, 1971; *Trollope: His Life and Art*, 1975; *The Realists*, 1978; *The Physicists*, 1981.

BIBLIOGRAPHY

De la Mothe, John. *C. P. Snow and the Struggle of Modernity*. Austin: University of Texas Press, 1992. Chapters on Snow's view of literature, science, and the modern mind and his career as writer and public intellectual. Includes extensive notes and bibliography.

Karl, Frederick S. *C. P. Snow: The Politics of Conscience*. Carbondale: Southern Illinois University Press, 1963. A generally useful study of Snow that analyzes his novels up to and including *The Affair*. Some of the statements about him are misleading, however, and should be read with caution.

Ramanathan, Suguna. *The Novels of C. P. Snow: A Critical Introduction*. London: Macmillan, 1978. A fresh, sympathetic assessment of Snow that dis-

cusses all of his novels save his two earliest works, *Death Under Sail* and *New Lives for Old*. Notes Snow's "imaginative impulse," his understanding of the changing social scene in England over a span of fifty years, and the gradual change in his outlook from hopefulness to doom. Upholds Snow as being free from fanaticism. A recommended reading.

Shusterman, David. *C. P. Snow*. Rev. ed. Boston: Twayne, 1991. A competent, compact study of Snow, including his early life, the controversies surrounding his nonfiction, and his literary output. Contains an in-depth analysis of the *Strangers and Brothers* series of novels, noting their interest apart from their literary value. Includes a chronology and a select bibliography.

Snow, C. P. *C. P. Snow: A Spectrum, Science, Criticism, Fiction*. Edited by Stanley Weintraub. New York: Charles Scribner's Sons, 1963. A useful introduction to Snow's life and works. The commentary covers many aspects of his fiction, criticism, and writings on science.

Thale, Jerome. *C. P. Snow*. New York: Charles Scribner's Sons, 1965. Considered an excellent secondary source on Snow that is both readable and informative. Presents Snow's work up to and including 1964. Discusses his nonfiction writings, among which are his two controversial works, *The Two Cultures and the Scientific Revolution* and *Science and Government*.

ALEKSANDR SOLZHENITSYN

Born: Kislovodsk, U.S.S.R.; December 11, 1918

PRINCIPAL LONG FICTION

Odin den' Ivana Denisovicha, 1962 (novella; *One Day in the Life of Ivan Denisovich*, 1963)
Rakovy korpus, 1968 (*Cancer Ward*, 1968)
V kruge pervom, 1968 (*The First Circle*, 1968)
Avgust chetyrnadtsatogo, 1971 (*August 1914*, 1972)
Lenin v Tsyurikhe, 1975 (*Lenin in Zurich*, 1976)

Krasnoe koleso (includes *Avgust chetyrnadtsatogo*, expanded version, 1983 [*The Red Wheel*, 1989]; *Oktiabr' shestnadtsatogo*, 1984 [*October 1916*, 1999]; *Mart semnadtsatogo*, 1986-1988; *Aprel' semnadtsatogo*, 1991)

OTHER LITERARY FORMS

Although Aleksandr Solzhenitsyn's reputation rests largely on his long prose works, this prolific writer sought to experiment in numerous genres. The short story "Matryona's House" is an excellent example of Solzhenitsyn's attention to detail as well as his reverence for old Russian values as exemplified by the peasant woman Matryona and her home. In addition to his short stories, in 1964 Solzhenitsyn published *Etyudy i krokhotnye rasskazy*, a collection of prose poems (translated in *Stories and Prose Poems by Alexander Solzhenitsyn*, 1971), each of which generally conveys a single message by focusing on a solitary image. Solzhenitsyn also composed the long poem *Prusskie nochi* (1974; *Prussian Nights*, 1977), which he committed to paper only after his release from prison. Drama, as well, interested Solzhenitsyn from his early years as a writer. His dramatic trilogy was written between 1951 and 1954, but the plays were never published or staged in the Soviet Union. Solzhenitsyn's eagerness to experiment with different genres and to mesh them makes him an unusually interesting writer. Fairy tales, film scenarios, drama, poetry, and prose are continually found interwoven in Solzhenitsyn's works. A particularly striking example of his desire to mix genres is his history of the Stalinist labor camps, *Arkhipelag GULag, 1918-1956: Opyt khudozhestvennogo issledovaniya* (1973-1975; *The Gulag Archipelago, 1918-1956: An Experiment in Literary Investigation*, 1974-1978).

ACHIEVEMENTS

The publication of Solzhenitsyn's first work, *One Day in the Life of Ivan Denisovich*—in Russian in 1962 and in English in 1963—sent shock waves throughout both the East and the West. Suddenly a new voice was heard in the Soviet Union, shattering the long, oppressive decades of silence and revealing forbidden truths of Stalinist society. In his preface to

(The Nobel Foundation)

One Day in the Life of Ivan Denisovich, Aleksandr Tvardovsky, an established Soviet poet and editor of the journal *Novy mir*, notes that the talent of the young writer is as extraordinary as his subject matter. Tvardovsky states that *One Day in the Life of Ivan Denisovich* is a work of art. The decision to make this comment is revealing, for, from the outset, it has been difficult, if not impossible, for readers both in the East and in the West to evaluate Solzhenitsyn as an artist apart from his political views. Solzhenitsyn became a symbol of hope. Born after the Revolution, educated in the Soviet system, and tempered by war and the Stalinist camps, he was in every sense a Soviet man. With the publication of *One Day in the Life of Ivan Denisovich*, he also became a Soviet writer published in the Soviet Union—a writer who, through the actions and words of a simple peasant, unmasked decades of terror and tyranny.

Solzhenitsyn's focus on the peasant in *One Day in the Life of Ivan Denisovich* and in the short story "Matryona's House" contributed to the tremendous upsurge and success of the village theme in contemporary Soviet literature. "Village prose," as the movement has been called, treating the concerns of the Soviet Union's vast rural population, represents one of the dominant and interesting trends in the 1960's and 1970's. Solzhenitsyn's initial success undoubtedly encouraged other writers to turn to such subjects as a means of speaking the truth, a means of "acceptable" protest.

The nomination of Solzhenitsyn for the Lenin Prize in 1964 demonstrates the height of popularity and prestige that the author attained in his own country. Although he was not to receive his country's highest literary honor, six years later, in 1970, he was accorded worldwide recognition as the Nobel laureate in literature. In his Nobel lecture, Solzhenitsyn stressed the writer's responsibility to the truth, a responsibility that he has taken seriously. Solzhenitsyn has taken it upon himself to record—in both his fiction and his nonfiction works—events which would otherwise be lost to the world. His history of the Stalinist camps (*The Gulag Archipelago*) as well as his writings on the prerevolutionary politics of Russia (such as *August 1914*, *Lenin in Zurich*, and *October 1916*) and on the workings of the Soviet literary machine (*Bodalsya telyonok s dubom* [1975; *The Oak and the Calf*, 1980]) will serve as historical sources for future generations. Solzhenitsyn's works had been translated into more than forty languages only ten years after his first publication. Popularity and politics aside, Solzhenitsyn will be remembered as a master of Russian prose whose works are among the finest of the twentieth century. His preoccupation with the profound issues confronting humankind and his search for a literary means to express these themes mark him as a great writer.

Biography

Aleksandr Isayevich Solzhenitsyn was born in Kislovodsk, a city in the north Caucasus, on December 11, 1918, one year after the Russian Revolution. His father, whose studies at the university were interrupted by World War I, died in a hunting accident six months before his son was born. Solzhenitsyn's mother, Taisiya Zakharovna Shcherbak, worked as an office clerk throughout Solzhenitsyn's childhood, earning very little money. In 1924, Solzhenitsyn and his mother moved to Rostov-on-Don, a city at that time of nearly a quarter million people. Because of financial considerations and the poor health of his mother, Solzhenitsyn was to continue his education there until he was graduated in 1941 from the University of Rostov-on-Don, specializing in mathematics and physics. From an early age, Solzhenitsyn dreamed of being a writer. Having displayed a natural talent for math and finding no adequate literary institution in Rostov-on-Don, however, Solzhenitsyn studied mathematics and physics. Nevertheless, in 1939, Solzhenitsyn decided to pursue his literary interests and began a two-year correspondence course in literature at the Moscow Institute of History, Philosophy, and Literature while continuing his studies in mathematics and physics. He finished this course of study in 1940, the same year that he married Natal'ya Alekseyevna Reshetovskaya (the apparent prototype of Nadya in *The First Circle*). Reshetovskaya, a specialist in physical chemistry and biochemistry, taught at the Agriculture Institute in Rostov-on-Don. On October 18, 1941, Solzhenitsyn was drafted; he hardly saw his wife for the next fifteen years.

Solzhenitsyn served in the army in various capacities, working his way up to battery commander. He was a decorated and inspiring leader, but his army duty was cut short in February, 1945, when he was summoned into his commanding officer's quarters and arrested. The charges, as was typical throughout the Stalinist era, were not made clear to Solzhenitsyn at that time. Later, he determined that he had been arrested for oblique, derogatory remarks concerning Stalin and his mismanagement of the war, which he had made in a personal journal and in a letter to a friend. Upon his arrest, he was taken to the Lubyanka, the notorious prison in Moscow. On July 7, 1945, after four months of interrogation, he was sentenced in his absence to eight years of hard labor. Solzhenitsyn's novella *One Day in the Life of Ivan*

Denisovich, his novel *The First Circle*, and his multi-volume work *The Gulag Archipelago* are all based on his firsthand experience of the Stalinist labor camps. He, like countless other Soviet citizens, was sentenced, under Section 58 of the Soviet penal code, for counterrevolutionary crimes. Solzhenitsyn spent the beginning of his term at Butyrka, a Moscow prison, laying parquet floors, as does Nerzhin, Solzhenitsyn's protagonist of *The First Circle*. Later in 1946, because of his training in mathematics and physics, he was transferred to a *sharashka* (a prison where scientists work on special projects for the state) very similar to the one depicted in *The First Circle*. After one year in the *sharashka*, Solzhenitsyn was sent to a labor camp in northern Kazakhstan. During his stay there, a tumor was removed; the prisoner was not told that it was malignant.

In February, 1953, Solzhenitsyn was released from prison only to enter perpetual exile (a common Stalinist practice) in Kok-Terek, Kazakhstan. There, Solzhenitsyn taught mathematics until his health deteriorated so severely that, in 1954, he was permitted to travel to Tashkent for treatment. In Tashkent, he was admitted to a clinic where he was treated for cancer and where he gathered material for his novel *Cancer Ward*. After his treatment, he returned to Kok-Terek to teach and began working on the play *Olen'i shalashovka* (1968; *The Love Girl and the Innocent*, 1969; also as *Respublika truda*) as well as *The First Circle*. In June, 1956, as a result of the "thaw" that followed Stalin's death in 1953, Solzhenitsyn was released from exile, and he moved to Ryazan, where he taught physics and mathematics until the end of 1962. In Ryazan, he saw his wife for the first time in many years. She had remarried and had two children from her second marriage. In that same year, Reshetovskaya left her second husband and reunited with Solzhenitsyn.

Solzhenitsyn and his wife stayed in Ryazan, where they both taught and where Solzhenitsyn continued to write in secret. In 1961, upon hearing Aleksandr Tvardovsky's speech to the Twenty-second Party Congress, in which he called for writers to tell the whole truth, Solzhenitsyn, in a bold move, sent his novella *One Day in the Life of Ivan Denisovich* to Tvar-

dovsky's then-liberal journal *Novy mir* (new world). The literary battles waged for the publication of this work and subsequent works by Solzhenitsyn are documented by the author in *The Oak and the Calf* and in Vladimir Lakshin's *Solzhenitsyn, Tvardovsky, and "Novy Mir"* (1980). The response to the novel made Solzhenitsyn an immediate celebrity, and he was nominated for the Lenin Prize in 1964. The political tide was beginning to turn, however, and with it the possibilities for the future publication of Solzhenitsyn's works.

At this time, Solzhenitsyn's unpublished works were already being circulated in *samizdat* (a self-publishing underground network for literary, philosophical, and political works) and were being smuggled abroad. In 1964, his prose poems appeared in the West German journal *Grani* (facets). By 1966, when Solzhenitsyn's "Zakhar-the-Pouch" appeared in the Soviet press, the political and artistic tensions were further intensified by the highly publicized trials of Andrei Sinyavsky and Yuli Daniel. That same year, permission to publish *Cancer Ward* in the Soviet Union was denied. Finally in 1968, both *The First Circle* and *Cancer Ward* were published in the West without authorization from Solzhenitsyn.

The following year, Solzhenitsyn was expelled from the Soviet Writers Union, a fatal blow to his career in the Soviet Union, for without membership, publication there was impossible. The situation was quite serious in 1970, when Solzhenitsyn was awarded the Nobel Prize in Literature. The author did not travel to Sweden to accept the prize at that time for fear that he would not be allowed to return to his country. From that point on, Solzhenitsyn, recognizing the impossibility of publication within his own country, authorized the publication of some of his works abroad. Personal attacks as well as attacks from the Soviet press continued to mount, and in 1974, after ignoring two summons from the State Prosecutor's Office, Solzhenitsyn was arrested and taken to Lefortovo prison. There he was interrogated, charged with treason, and placed on a plane. Only upon landing was he informed that he had been exiled. Six weeks later, Solzhenitsyn was joined in Zurich by his second wife, Natal'ya Svetlova (he had divorced Reshetovskaya in 1973), their three sons, and his stepson.

In October of 1974, the United States Senate conferred honorary citizenship upon Solzhenitsyn (an honor bestowed only twice before—to the Marquis de Lafayette and Sir Winston Churchill). He soon settled in Vermont, where he continued to write, deliver occasional lectures, and promote the publication of materials dealing with the Soviet Union.

Living by choice in his Vermont isolation, Solzhenitsyn turned his attention to the past, writing historical works centered on the early twentieth century. His antipathy toward his adopted country was matched only by his lack of contact with his native land and his failure to stay in touch with the evolution of that complex country. He eventually returned to Russia in 1994, a few years after the collapse of the Soviet Union. Somewhat to his surprise, instead of revisiting the land of the evil gulags and oppressed but saintly people, Solzhenitsyn arrived in a consumerized, highly commercial country striving to compete in European and global contexts. The gulags were remembered only by the oldest and were largely dismissed as uninteresting by the young. Irony had dealt Russian history a new blow by reinstating Russian Orthodoxy and removing secular saintliness—including the monastic, agrarian ideals propounded by Solzhenitsyn, Russia's self-conscious prophet.

Undaunted by his lack of popularity, Solzhenitsyn continued to pursue his platform with the support of many respectable nationalist factions. Although his television talk show lasted only for a few months, until objections to his verbosity and unwillingness to listen prevailed, he tried to reach out to Russians of the post-Soviet era, propounding his ideals of a special Slavic nationality and its mission in the world.

Analysis

Aleksandr Solzhenitsyn and his novels are better appreciated and understood when the author's vision of himself as a writer is taken into consideration; he believes that a great writer must also be a prophet of his or her country. In this tradition of the great Russian novelists Leo Tolstoy and Fyodor Dostoevski, Solzhenitsyn seeks to discover a place for the individual in history and in art. To Solzhenitsyn, art, history, life, and people continually interact, forming a single pulsing wave that creates a new, vibrant, and oftentimes disturbing vision of reality and the future. From his first publication, *One Day in the Life of Ivan Denisovich*, to his cycle of historical novels, *Krasnoe koleso*, Solzhenitsyn concentrates on people's ability to survive with dignity in an environment that is fundamentally inhumane. Whatever the situation of his hero or heroine—whether in a Stalinist prison camp, a hospital, the army, or exile—Solzhenitsyn demands from his protagonist a certain moral integrity, a code of behavior that separates him or her from those who have forsaken their humanity. It is the ability or inability to adhere to this code that renders the protagonist triumphant or tragic.

Given the importance of the interrelationship of history, art, and life in Solzhenitsyn's works, it is not surprising that the author is often preoccupied with the larger issues confronting humanity. For the most part, Solzhenitsyn's novels are concerned less with action and plot than with ideas and ethical motivation. Radically different characters are thrown together into artificial environments, usually state institutions, which are separated from society as a whole and are governed by laws and codes of behavior that are equally estranged from society. Such institutions serve as a means of bringing together and equalizing people who would normally not have contact with one another; previous status and education become meaningless. Physical survival itself is usually at issue—for prisoners and soldiers struggle for food, patients for treatment, and "free" people for continued freedom and integrity. For Solzhenitsyn, however, physical survival is not the only issue, or even the primary one. Several of his characters, including Alyosha in *One Day in the Life of Ivan Denisovich* and Nerzhin in *The First Circle*, actually welcome the prison camp experience, for they find the time in camp to be conducive to reflection on fundamental questions.

Nerzhin, like many of the other *zeks* (prisoners in the Stalinist camps), is also aware that in prison, in contrast to the "free" Stalinist society, one is allowed a greater opportunity to speak one's mind, to debate issues freely and openly, and to come to terms with the society and state that have imprisoned him or her. The freedom that some of the prisoners enjoy, the freedom that the ill-fated patients experience in the *Cancer Ward*, is the freedom encountered by those who have nothing left to lose. As the author indicates through one of the prisoners in *The First Circle*, society has no hold over a person once it has taken everything from him or her. Solzhenitsyn repeatedly returns to the theme of materialism as a source of manipulation and a potential evil in people's lives. According to Solzhenitsyn, a person who maintains material ties can never entirely be free, and therefore his or her integrity can always be questioned and tested. Worldly possessions per se are not evil, nor is the desire to possess them, nor does Solzhenitsyn condemn those who do have or desire them. The author is skeptical of their value, however, and ultimately holds humankind's conscience as its single treasured possession. Neither home nor family nor friends are worth betraying that most valuable trust— for people have only one conscience.

Solzhenitsyn's insistence on integrity extends beyond the life of the individual. Solzhenitsyn asserts that since a person has only one conscience, he or she must not allow that conscience to be compromised on a personal level, by justifying personal actions or the actions of the state by insisting that the end, no matter how noble, justifies the means. This single observation is the foundation of Solzhenitsyn's attack upon the Soviet state. A brilliant, perfect Communist future is not motivation or justification enough for a secretive, censor-ridden socialist state, not in Stalin's time or in the author's lifetime. In Solzhenitsyn's view, corrupt means cannot produce a pure end.

Detractors of Solzhenitsyn in both the East and the West have claimed that he is too political and generally unconcerned with stylistic matters. Given the life and the times of the man, these objections fail to be particularly persuasive. Solzhenitsyn's language is rich and textured, and both a glossary (Vera Carpovich, *Solzhenitsyn's Peculiar Vocabulary*, 1976) and a dictionary (Meyer Galler, *Soviet Prison Camp Speech*, 1972) of his language have been produced. Prison slang, camp jargon, political slogans,

colloquialisms, and neologisms all mesh in Solzhenitsyn's text. His attention to language is often voiced by his characters, such as Ignatich in "Matryona's House" or Sologdin in *The First Circle*, and his prose is sprinkled with Russian proverbs and folk sayings that often summarize or counteract lengthy philosophical debates. A further indication of his concern for language can be seen in his insistence on commissioning new translations of many of his works, which were originally issued in hurried translations to meet the worldwide demand for them.

On another stylistic level, Solzhenitsyn employs two narrative techniques which enhance his focus on the exchange of ideas and debate as a means of attaining truth: *erlebte rede*, or quasi-direct discourse, and polyphony. Quasi-direct discourse involves the merging of two or more voices, one of these voices usually being that of a third-person narrator and the other the voice of the character depicted. Through this device, Solzhenitsyn draws the reader as close as possible to the thoughts, perceptions, and emotions of the character, without interrupting the narrative by either direct or indirect speech. Similarly, polyphony, a term introduced by the Soviet critic Mikhail Bakhtin in regard to Dostoevski's narrative and structural technique and a term that Solzhenitsyn himself has applied to his own novels, is employed in order to present more empathetically a character's point of view. Polyphony allows each character in turn to take center stage and present his or her views either directly or through quasi-direct discourse; thus, throughout the novel, the narrative focus continually shifts from character to character. The third-person omniscient narrator serves as a linking device, seemingly allowing the debates to continue among the characters alone.

In addition to these literary techniques, Solzhenitsyn's prose, particularly in *The First Circle*, is permeated with irony and satire. A master of hyperbole and understatement, Solzhenitsyn is at his best when caricaturing historical figures, such as Lenin and Stalin, to name but two. Solzhenitsyn further deepens the irony by underscoring small physical and verbal gestures of his targets. The target need not be as powerful as Lenin or Stalin to draw the author's fire, and there are touches of self-irony which provide a corrective to Solzhenitsyn's occasionally sanctimonious tone.

ONE DAY IN THE LIFE OF IVAN DENISOVICH

Not all of Solzhenitsyn's works are dependent on irony and satire. *One Day in the Life of Ivan Denisovich* is striking for its restraint, verbal economy, and controlled tone. This *povest'*, or novella, was originally conceived by the author in 1950-1951 while he was in the Ekibastuzskiy prison. The original draft, written in 1959 and entitled "One Day in the Life of a Zek," was significantly revised, politically muffled, and submitted to *Novy mir*.

Set in a labor camp in Siberia, *One Day in the Life of Ivan Denisovich* traces an ordinary day in the life of a prisoner. The author reveals through a third-person narrator the stark, grim world of the *zek* in meticulous detail, including the daily rituals—the searches, the bedchecks, the meals—as well as the general rules and regulations that govern his daily existence—little clothing, little contact with the outside world, little time to himself. Every detail of Ivan Denisovich's day resounds in the vast, cold emptiness of this remote camp. As Georg Lukács indicates in his book *Solzhenitsyn* (1969), "camp life is represented as a permanent condition"; into this permanent condition is thrust a common person, who quietly and simply reveals the essence of retaining one's dignity in a hopeless, inhumane environment.

Uncharacteristic of Solzhenitsyn's works, the tone of *One Day in the Life of Ivan Denisovich* is reserved, solemn, and dignified; irony only occasionally surfaces. The tone is probably somewhat attributable to the editing of Tvardovsky, whose language is felt here. Throughout the work, which is uninterrupted by chapter breaks, the focus remains on Ivan Denisovich and the passage of this one day. Secondary characters are introduced only insofar as they touch his day, and flashbacks and background information are provided only to deepen the reader's understanding of Ivan Denisovich's present situation. Unlike Solzhenitsyn's later novels, which focus largely on an institution's impact on many different individuals, *One Day in the Life of Ivan Denisovich* focuses on one man. Criticism of the camps is perceived by the reader, who

slowly observes and absorbs the daily steps of this man. Only after Solzhenitsyn has revealed the drudgery of that one day, one almost happy day, does he place it in its context, simply stating that "there were three thousand six hundred and fifty-three days like this in his sentence, from reveille to lights out. The three extra ones were because of leap year."

CANCER WARD

Unlike its predecessor, *Cancer Ward* directly reveals the constant intense emotional pressure of its characters and its themes. Solzhenitsyn fixed upon the idea of writing this novel at his discharge from the Tashkent clinic in 1955. The author did not begin writing the novel until 1963 and only after a two-year hiatus returned to serious work on *Cancer Ward*. In 1966, having finished the first part of the work, Solzhenitsyn submitted it to the journal *Novy mir*; it was rejected by the censor. Meanwhile, Solzhenitsyn completed the novel, which soon began to circulate in *samizdat*. Eventually, *Cancer Ward* was smuggled to the West and published, first in excerpts and later in its entirety. It was never published in the Soviet Union.

On the surface, *Cancer Ward* depicts the lives of the doctors, patients, and staff of a cancer clinic. The two protagonists of the novel, Pavel Rusanov and Oleg Kostoglotov, are socially and politically polar opposites: the former a member of the Communist Party, well established, living a comfortable life with a wife and a family; the latter, a former prisoner who arrives at the hospital with no one and nothing. Because of the cancer that has afflicted them both, they find themselves in the same ward with an equally diverse group of patients. The novel is largely plotless and focuses on the contrasting attitudes of the patients in regard to the institutions, their treatment, and life and death, as well as other philosophical and political issues.

The one plot line which runs through the novel centers on Kostoglotov, who, having been imprisoned and consequently deprived of female companionship for years, becomes an avid "skirt-chaser," pursuing both his doctor, Vera Gangart, who ironically falls victim to the very cancer in which she specializes, and a young medical student, Zoya. Kostoglotov throughout the novel continually objects to the secrecy that surrounds his treatment and demands that he has a right to know. In a twist characteristic of Solzhenitsyn, Zoya informs Kostoglotov that the X-ray treatment that he is receiving will temporarily render him impotent. This serves as another reminder to Kostoglotov that, as in prison, his fate, his manhood, and in fact his life are beyond his control and in the hands of yet another institution. Throughout *Cancer Ward*, the abuses, idiocies, and tragedies of Soviet medical care are revealed, as terminally ill patients are released believing they are cured, patients are misdiagnosed, and the hospitals prove to be poorly staffed and supplied.

Unfortunately, *Cancer Ward* suffers from its near-absence of plot, its heavy-handed dialogues and debates, and its lack of focus, either upon a genuine protagonist or upon an all-encompassing theme. Little sympathy is felt for Rusanov, a Party member, or Kostoglotov, despite the fact that he has been unjustly imprisoned and a victim of cancer. Kostoglotov is generally impatient, intolerant, and at times completely insensitive to others. Nevertheless, he does grow in the course of the novel. In a discussion with Shulubin, another patient in the ward, Kostoglotov dismisses Shulubin's warning that happiness is elusive and only a mirage, but when he is finally dismissed from the clinic, Kostoglotov, wandering the streets free from prison and free from cancer, realizes that an appetite can be more easily stimulated than satisfied. By the conclusion of the work, Kostoglotov understands Shulubin's warning and abandons his dreams of love with Vera and Zoya.

Despite the work's significant shortcomings, there are scenes in the novel which remain unforgettable for their sensitivity and poetry. One such scene is between the two adolescents Dyomka and Asya. Dyomka is to lose his leg; Asya, a breast. Asya, a seventeen-year-old, worries about her appearance in a swimsuit and her future with men, lamenting that no man will ever touch her breast. In an act of both hope and despair, Asya asks Dyomka to kiss her breast before, as the narrator observes, it is removed and thrown into the trash. Throughout the novel, compassion, sensitivity, poetry, and philosophy are shamelessly interrupted by

the reality of the cancer ward. The sharp contrast between the human spirit of hope and the ominous presence of death and destruction in the form of cancer simultaneously underscores the fragility of human existence and the immortality of the human spirit. It is this spirit that is admired and celebrated in this novel and that is also a feature of Solzhenitsyn's finest work, *The First Circle*.

THE FIRST CIRCLE

The First Circle, like *Cancer Ward*, is largely autobiographical, based in this case on Solzhenitsyn's experiences in the *sharashka*. The author began writing the novel while in exile in Kok-Terek in 1955. Between 1955 and 1958, Solzhenitsyn wrote three redactions of the novel, none of which has survived. After 1962, he wrote four additional redactions of the novel, the last of which appeared in 1978. The novel was first published abroad in 1968 and, like *Cancer Ward*, was never published in the Soviet Union. The 1978 redaction differs from the sixth redaction (the edition used for all foreign translations) largely in the addition of nine chapters. The discussion below is based on the sixth redaction.

The First Circle masterfully combines all of Solzhenitsyn's finest assets as a writer. It is by far the most artistic of his novels, drawing heavily on literary allusions and abounding with literary devices. The title itself is a reference to Dante's *La divina commedia* (c. 1320; *The Divine Comedy*), alluding to the first circle of Hell, the circle designated for pagan scholars, philosophers, and enlightened people, where the pain and the suffering of Hell are greatly diminished. The *sharashka*, as Lev Rubin indicates in the chapter "Dante's Idea" (chapter headings are particularly revealing in this novel), is the first circle of the Stalinist camps. Unlike Ivan Denisovich, who is in a hard-labor camp, the *zeks* in the *sharashka* have adequate food and livable working conditions. Thus, the *zeks* inhabiting the *sharashka* have a great deal to lose, for if they do not conform to the rules governing the *sharashka*, they may fall from the first circle into the lower depths of the Stalinist camps.

Three of the four protagonists of the novel, Gleb Nerzhin, Lev Rubin, and Dmitri Sologdin, face a decision which may endanger their continued stay at the *sharashka*. Each must decide if he is willing to work on a scientific project which may result in the imprisonment of other citizens or, if he is to retain his integrity, refuse to work on the project and consequently endanger his own life. Thus, the debates and discussions that permeate this novel are well motivated, playing a significant role in revealing the character and philosophies of these prisoners while drawing the reader deeply into their lives and minds. The tension of the novel arises as the reader attempts to determine whether a prisoner will act in accordance with his conscience. Placed in a similar situation, Innokenty Volodin, a free man and the fourth protagonist of the novel, decides to risk imprisonment by warning a fellow citizen that he may be in danger. Volodin decides to follow his conscience in the first chapter of the novel; in his case, suspense depends on the questions of whether he will be caught and punished for his actions and whether he will continue to endorse the decision that he has made.

The First Circle is a novel of characters and choices; the choices which must be made by nearly all the characters, primary and secondary, are of compelling interest to the reader, for each choice functions as an echo of another person's choice. The overall impact of nearly every character (free and imprisoned) faced with a life-threatening decision based upon moral issues vividly demonstrates the inescapable terror of the time. Furthermore, the multidimensional aspects of this novel—the wide range of characters from virtually every social stratum, the numerous plots, the use of polyphony, the shifting to and from radically different settings, the views of peasant and philosopher, the plethora of literary allusions, the incredible richness of the language—show the sophistication and remarkable depth of the author.

AUGUST 1914

Solzhenitsyn's historical works were first seen with the publication of *August 1914* in the West in Russian in 1971 and its English translation in 1972. This book was a greatly shortened variant of the intended whole book, and it was met with general perplexity. Paralleling the "literary experimentation" style of his nonfiction work *The Gulag Archipelago* (published in English 1974-1978), Solzhenitsyn casts his figures as embodiments of historical situations and ethical issues. Whereas in *The Gulag Archipelago* he wrote from personal experience, in *August 1914* he tries to reconstruct a past of which he was not a part, with varying results. The book's chapter on Lenin, deliberately withheld from publication in the first edition, was published separately in Paris in 1975 as *Lenin v Tsyurikhe* and translated in 1976 as *Lenin in Zurich*. Solzhenitsyn had expanded and reworked it after his 1974 exile. Many other chapters were written and added in 1976 and 1977.

KRASNOE KOLESO

August 1914 was republished in English in 1989, this time in its entirety. It was identified as a section, or "knot," of Solzhenitsyn's historical series *Krasnoe koleso* (words that translate into English as "the red wheel"). Confusingly, this version was published under the title *The Red Wheel* rather than *August 1914*. By the time of the 1989 translation, Solzhenitsyn had published two more knots of *Krasnoe koleso* in Russian, *Oktiabr' shestnadtsatogo* (1984; translated as *October 1916* in 1999) and *Mart semnadtsatogo* (1986-1988). A fourth knot, *Aprel' semnadtsatogo*, appeared in 1991. That same year the Soviet Union collapsed. The "evil empire" that had formed the fulcrum for the critical leverage of Solzhenitsyn's prose was gone, and Solzhenitsyn became a prophet without a cause. The work, while historical in nature and presumably impervious to the vagaries of political change, settled into Russian literary history almost like an anachronism. It had a very limited readership.

The structure of the work was intended to reveal the nature of Russia's history as Solzhenitsyn believed it to be. Unlike the first publication (*August 1914*), *The Red Wheel* and *Krasnoe koleso* as a whole used a framework composed of "knots," nodes at which historical events are compressed. Solzhenitsyn's philosophy, responding to Tolstoy's from *War and Peace* (1865-1869), conforms to the proposition that history is not so much shaped by great people as by all people striving to make the proper ethical choices when forced to take a part in significant events. However, Tolstoy's ideas are revealed in the narration; Solzhenitsyn uses narrative structure instead of describing the idea, leaving the narration in large measure beyond the ordinary means of artistic forms. His intention was to reveal the "full column" of historical actors, yet such a structure tends to obscure history at the same time that it loses literary form through diffusion of the plot.

Solzhenitsyn had created an enormous role for himself as a prophet of Russian history with his first novella, *One Day in the Life of Ivan Denisovich.* In his later life, history granted him only a piece of the past. *Krasnoe koleso* fell outside the interest of the Russian readership it was intended to instruct. Moreover, Solzhenitsyn's ambitions and personal interests came under hostile scrutiny by the Russian literati, who questioned his motivation for returning to Russia in 1994. However, Solzhenitsyn remained unmoved by the criticism and continued to work as before, motivated from within, defiant of the exterior world.

Suzan K. Burks, updated by Christine D. Tomei

OTHER MAJOR WORKS

SHORT FICTION: *Dlya pol'zy dela,* 1963 (*For the Good of the Cause,* 1964); *Dva rasskaza: Sluchay na stantsii Krechetovka i Matryonin dvor,* 1963 (*We Never Make Mistakes,* 1963); *Krokhotnye rasskazy,* 1970; *Rasskazy,* 1990.

PLAYS: *Olen'i shalashovka,* pb. 1968 (*The Love Girl and the Innocent,* 1969; also known as *Respublika truda*); *Svecha na vetru,* pb. 1968 (*Candle in the Wind,* 1973); *Dramaticheskaya trilogiya-1945: Pir pobediteley,* pb. 1981 (*Victory Celebrations,* 1983); *Plenniki,* pb. 1981 (*Prisoners,* 1983).

SCREENPLAYS: *Znayut istinu tanki,* 1981; *Tuneyadets,* 1981.

POETRY: *Etyudy i krokhotnye rasskazy,* 1964 (trans. in *Stories and Prose Poems by Alexander Solzhenitsyn,* 1971); *Prusskie nochi,* 1974 (*Prussian Nights,* 1977).

NONFICTION: *Les Droits de l'écrivain,* 1969; *Nobelevskaya lektsiya po literature 1970 goda,* 1972 (*The Nobel Lecture,* 1973); *A Lenten Letter to Pimen, Patriarch of All Russia,* 1972; *Solzhenitsyn: A Pictorial Autobiography,* 1972; *Arkhipelag GULag, 1918-*
1956: Opyt khudozhestvennogo issledovaniya, 1973-1975 (*The Gulag Archipelago, 1918-1956: An Experiment in Literary Investigation,* 1974-1978); *Iz-pod glyb,* 1974 (*From Under the Rubble,* 1975); *Pis'mo vozhdyam Sovetskogo Soyuza,* 1974 (*Letter to Soviet Leaders,* 1974); *Bodalsya telyonok s dubom,* 1975 (*The Oak and the Calf,* 1980); *Amerikanskiye rechi,* 1975; *Warning to the West,* 1976; *East and West,* 1980; *The Mortal Danger: How Misconceptions About Russia Imperil America,* 1980; *Kak nam obustroit' Rossiiu?: Posil'nye soobrazheniia,* 1990 (*Rebuilding Russia: Reflections and Tentative Proposals,* 1991); *Russkii vopros,* 1994 (*The Russian Question: At the End of the Twentieth Century,* 1994); *Invisible Allies,* 1995.

MISCELLANEOUS: *Sochineniya,* 1966; *Stories and Prose Poems by Alexander Solzhenitsyn,* 1971; *Six Etudes by Aleksandr Solzhenitsyn,* 1971; *Mir i nasiliye,* 1974; *Sobranie sochinenii,* 1978-1983 (10 volumes); *Izbrannoe,* 1991.

BIBLIOGRAPHY

Dunlop, John B., et al., eds. *Aleksandr Solzhenitsyn: Critical Essays and Biographical Materials.* New York: Collier, 1975. An excellent collection of essays on Solzhenitsyn's early work, perhaps the best collection in English, by a host of major writers, including Czesław Miłosz, and Heinrich Böll.

_____. *Solzhenitsyn in Exile: Critical Essays and Documentary Materials.* Stanford, Calif.: Hoover Institution, 1985. A solid collection of articles on all aspects of Solzhenitsyn's work.

Lakshin, Vladislav. *Solzhenitsyn, Tvardovsky, and "Novyi Mir."* New York: Oxford University Press, 1980. Lakshin presents an insider's view of the publication history of *A Day in the Life of Ivan Denisovich,* involving Aleksandr Tvardovsky, a poet and the editor of the journal *Novyi Mir.*

Moody, Christopher. *Solzhenitsyn.* New York: Barnes and Noble Books, 1976. Moody provides an essentially negative view of Solzhenitsyn's literary works to 1975 that represents an alternative to the generally favorable reception of his early work.

Scammell, Michael. *Solzhenitsyn: A Biography.* New York: Norton, 1984. A meticulously researched,

exhaustive, and even-handed study of Solzhenitsyn's life that explores its importance to his
works.

_____, ed. *The Solzhenitsyn Files*. Chicago: Edi-
tion q, 1995. A carefully edited documentation of
Solzhenitsyn's struggles with Soviet literary and
political authorities.

Thomas, D. M. *Alexander Solzhenitsyn: A Century in
His Life*. New York: St. Martin's Press, 1998. An
imaginative, well-documented, and at times com-
bative biography of Solzhenitsyn. It includes discussion of his return to Russia in 1994.

WOLE SOYINKA

Born: Ijebu Isara, near Abeokuta, Nigeria; July 13,
1934

PRINCIPAL LONG FICTION

The Interpreters, 1965
Season of Anomy, 1973

OTHER LITERARY FORMS

Wole Soyinka is best known as a dramatist. He
has written more than twenty plays in various modes,
including *The Swamp Dwellers* (1958), *The Lion and
the Jewel* (1959), *A Dance of the Forests* (1960),
Madmen and Specialists (1970, revised 1971), and
Death and the King's Horseman (1975). He is also a
director and filmmaker He has published several collections of poetry, including *Idanre and Other Poems*
(1967), *A Shuttle in the Crypt* (1972), and *Mandela's
Earth and Other Poems* (1988), and the long poem
Ogun Abibiman (1976). His nonfiction prose includes impressive books of criticism such as *Myth,
Literature, and the African World* (1976) and *Art, Dialogue, and Outrage* (1988). His autobiographical
works examine various aspects of his life experiences: his prison years in *"The Man Died"* (1972),
his early life in *Aké: The Years of Childhood* (1981),
and the influence of his father in *Ìsarà: A Voyage
Around "Essay"* (1989). In addition, he has trans-

lated the Yoruba novel *Ogboju Ode Ninu Igbo Irunmale*, by D. O. Fagunwa, as *Forest of a Thousand
Daemons: A Hunter's Saga* (1968).

ACHIEVEMENTS

Soyinka is perhaps the most talented and versatile
writer to have emerged during the literary flower-
ing in Africa beginning in the 1950's. He is, without
doubt, the finest dramatist; he is also an accomplished
poet and has written two novels so experimental that
critics are not yet sure what to make of them. While
tapping numerous twentieth century fictional devices,
the novels are based on his own cultural heritage,
combining ritual, myth, comedy, and hard realism in
a new configuration. He draws from the Yoruba mythology of his native region but makes contact with a
larger public by frequent references and parallels to
myths and literatures of other cultures. Not only his
literary achievements but also his championing of individual freedoms have gained for him recognition
both in his native Nigeria and abroad. He has received numerous awards, including first prize at the
Dakar Negro Arts Festival in 1960, the John Whiting
Drama Prize in 1966, the Jock Campbell Award for
Fiction in 1968, and the Nobel Prize in Literature in
1986.

BIOGRAPHY

Akinwande Oluwole Soyinka was born July 13,
1934, at Abeokuta, in western Nigeria. A Yoruba by
birth, he studied Yoruba mythology and theology and
made it the basis of his literary themes. His formal
education, however, was British. He attended primary and secondary schools in Abeokuta and Ibadan,
began his undergraduate work at University College,
Ibadan, and received his bachelor of arts degree with
honors in English (1957) at the University of Leeds.
He would continue to be associated with various universities throughout his academic and literary career,
holding lectureships, delivering papers at academic
meetings, and publishing critical reviews and articles. His career as a dramatist began at Leeds and
continued with his establishment of acting companies in Lagos and Ibadan. Aside from the theater and
his own literary endeavors, he has been a political ac-

tivist; the Nigerian authorities detained him in prison during the Biafran War, from August, 1967, to October, 1969. Individual freedom and social responsibility are themes in his earliest work, but his commitment to social justice became even more intense after his prison experiences and the Nigerian atrocities during the war.

After winning the Nobel Prize in 1986, Soyinka received the honorary title of Order of Commander of the Federal Republic of Nigeria. Yet just a few years later, in 1994, he was forced to flee the country, when his criticism of the new military dictator General Sani Abacha made him once again a target for political imprisonment. Tension had been rising in Nigeria after the military annulled the democratic elections of 1993, and when Soyinka's vocal opposition group learned that he was soon to be arrested, he was forced into exile. In the following years Soyinka held appointments at both Harvard and Emory universities in the United States while continuing his biting criticism of Abacha, as evidenced in the 1996 publication of *The Open Sore of a Continent*, a political tract that exposes the abuses of Abacha's regime. This work led in 1997 to Abacha's transparently false treason charges against Soyinka for allegedly participating in a series of bombings across Nigeria. Not until Abacha's death in 1998 was Soyinka able to return to Nigeria, and then only after Abacha's successor dropped the treason charges and openly courted Soyinka and other exiled dissidents to come home.

ANALYSIS

Like other novelists in Africa during the years just before and after independence, Wole Soyinka faced the question of ethnic and cultural identity. The now notorious negritude movement, begun in the 1930's, had attempted to promote a pan-African identity by distinguishing between two mentalities: the rational, methodical, categorical tendency of the industrialized Westerner and the emotional spontaneity of the African still in tune with the rhythms of nature. Many, including Soyinka, came to see this definition as a sign of cultural dependency—the African described by contrast to the dominant European culture. In his most famous remark on the subject, Soyinka

declared that "the tiger does not proclaim his tigretude!" Soyinka presumably meant that Africans need not be defensive about their identity; at any rate, Soyinka has proclaimed unabashedly, in all of his works, including his two novels, the indigenous source of his themes and inspiration.

As Soyinka makes clear in his book of criticism *Myth, Literature, and the African World*, his own cultural heritage is Yoruba. Drawing from its fascinating and complex mythology, Soyinka concentrates on two central events. One is the disintegration of primal oneness, which he calls Orisa-nla. In the beginning, only Orisa-nla existed, with his servant Akunda; in a moment of revolution or treachery, depending upon the point of view, Akunda rolled a boulder down the back of Orisa-nla, shattering him into the fragments that became the human race and the gods of the Yoruba pantheon; god and humanity were thence-

(The Nobel Foundation)

forth separated from one another. Among these individuated gods, two stand out, Obatala and Ogun, as aspects of the original oneness. Soyinka uses human representations of them both in his novels. Obatala appears as the titular leader of a traditional community. While not actively pursuing the rejuvenation of society, he tries to hold things together: "He is the embodiment of the suffering spirit of man, uncomplaining, agonised, full of the redemptive qualities of endurance and martyrdom." Soyinka also includes a third human figure in the novels, a woman, who appears as the fertility principle inherent in Orisa-nla and promises continuity.

The most important god for Soyinka, however, is Ogun, whose story is central to the plots in the two novels and whose complex character makes him the most complete symbol of the original oneness. Most simply, he is the god of creation and destruction, and he is incarnate in humankind. After the original disintegration, Ogun took upon himself the task of entering the abyss that separated humankind from the gods and of building a bridge across the primeval gulf to reunite them. To accomplish this task, he had to "die," to risk total disintegration of the personality (thus repeating the original fragmentation) and to reintegrate himself through an act of the will. Ogun's success was his grand triumph that humanity must strive to emulate. Ogun's cautionary tale does not, however, end here. At the call of human beings, he reluctantly descended to aid them, but his gift of "Promethean" fire—Ogun is the god of the forge—gave humankind the power of destruction as well as creation. During his sojourn among people, Ogun, as god of wine and of war, then experienced his most shameful moment, the massacre in battle, while in a drunken rage, of both friends and enemies. This destructive power of the will repeated the drunken act of Akunda and symbolizes the ever-present threat of humankind's own destructiveness. It is especially Ogun's personality and social roles that provide for Soyinka a rationale for contemporary events. Ogun's story proclaims the will as the crucial ethical faculty, individual heroism as the dynamic factor in social change, and the communal function of the heroic act as its sanction.

THE INTERPRETERS

Soyinka's first novel, *The Interpreters*, is a dark comedy. The settings are the capital city of Lagos, the university city of Ibadan, and the surrounding lagoons, at a time soon after Nigeria's independence, in the early 1960's. Soyinka presents a directionless society seen mainly through the eyes of a few university-educated observers who have just returned from abroad to take up their roles, which they have yet truly to discover, in the new state. What they see is an assortment of professional people holding on to or seeking status and power; their attractive public image is but a disguised sleaziness, a combination of Old World corruption and Victorian hypocrisy. Moving through this structured society are various lost people seeking stability: an American black homosexual, an evangelical preacher, a thief, and occasional transients from outside Africa. The novel traces the lives of the five interpreters—Egbo, Sagoe, Kola, Sekoni, and Bandele—as they get in touch with themselves and their society. What sets them apart, in particular, is their refusal to accept wholesale imported Western values and mores, as well as a vague sense that an indigenous worldview should mold the new state. The problem is to get in touch with it and revive it. Soyinka does not offer any hope of immediate success.

Of all the interpreters, Egbo and Sekoni are most closely associated with the Ogun experience. Sagoe, Kola, and Bandele do not share the risky heroism of Ogun's nature but seem closer to the passive, suffering attitude of the god Obatala, though it is difficult and undesirable to make such identifications with any allegorical rigidity. Sagoe, the newspaper reporter whose experiences give insight into the corrupt practices of business and politics and into the religious void of modern Nigeria, suffers in the first part of the novel from inebriation and a morning hangover. He has developed an absurd philosophy of Voidancy, a solipsistic return to original oneness, a passive loss of identity. A recurring childhood memory perpetuates a Western, Manichean split between divine and human nature. He finally agrees to abandon his philosophy and commit himself to his fiancé, Dehinwa, but Sagoe never displays any deep internal struggle. Kola is a painter who is intellectually aware of Yoruba tradition; he spends several months finishing his huge canvas, a symbolic representation of the Yoruba pantheon using contemporary models. Kola gradually recognizes his own inadequacy as an artist—Ogun is Soyinka's divine symbol of the true artist—and is almost ready to accept his role as simply a teacher of art. The painting itself would suggest, at least in the eyes of Egbo, an inadequate conception of human struggle and redemption. Kola presents Ogun (Egbo) not in his creative role as architect of order but as a drunken murderer. Bandele is the clearest image of the god Obatala. Throughout the novel, he tries to mediate among the various interpreters and to judge and encourage ethical behavior. He also tries to live a life of compromise, to prevent a complete split between the intellectuals and the rest of society. In the end, he continues his role of judge—as the traditional Oba—but strikes out at the society itself, ensuring a split, as he sarcastically accuses the hypocritical professional class of burying its own children.

Soyinka measures human character against divine behavior after the original fragmentation. Only Ogun, among all the gods, risked the loss of individuation in the abyss of transition. Egbo, the grandson and heir of a village chief, is on the edge of the abyss. The novel places two choices before him: between the power and privileges of the Osa chiefdom and a life in a modern state, and between a sensuous life with Simi, a nationally famous and beautiful courtesan, and a New World university student, a feminist rebel pregnant with his child. While he has not made either choice definitively at the end of the novel, he leans toward contemporary demands. Such a commitment would be a denial of African heritage as superficially perceived but an assertion of it in essential terms. The university student is herself a heroine, defying artificial conventions of the day and committed to her child and to her education in spite of bitter rejection by the professional elite. She is also the only person with whom Egbo has shared his religious commitment to the Yoruba gods; their night of love takes place in his sacred retreat under the bridge crossing the Ogun River. Egbo has at least three initiation ex-

periences, all sexual, described as symbolic leaps into the abyss of death and rebirth: twice during his first night with Simi and once during his more mature "venturing" with the unnamed student girl. By the end of the novel, he knows, though he has not yet made the decision, that "he could not hold her merely as an idyllic fantasy, for the day rose large enough and he was again overwhelmed by her power of will."

While Egbo's Ogun experience is still on the level of "idyllic fantasy," Sekoni's has a degree of fulfillment and a tragic finality. Like Egbo, at the beginning of the novel he perceives the sacred through physical reality. Egbo calls the fleshy black dancer at the Club Cabana "the exaltation of the Black Immanent." For Sekoni, she is a symbol of the original oneness: It would be profane, he says in his stuttering excitement, "t-t-to bring her in c-c-conflict." In moments of inspiration, as he comes into contact with spiritual reality, his language breaks down and his stuttering increases. Sekoni's first profession is engineering. His dream is to harness the powers of nature. A flashback has him returning home aboard ship, imagining the ocean as "a deafening waterfall defying human will," and his creative fingers as shapers of bridges, hospitals, derricks, and railroads. The sea, however, proves to be too strong; the bureaucracy at home gives him a desk job and then allows him to build a rural power plant only to have it condemned by an expatriate expert. The failure drives him insane. When he is released from the mental hospital, he goes on a pilgrimage to Jerusalem (not to Mecca, as his devout Muslim father would have wished), and by putting his fingers through the broken walls of the city, he has a mystical experience. Soyinka's description of it suggests an identification between the Jewish and the African diaspora, the disintegration of traditional community, and, by implication, a repetition of the original fragmentation of Orisa-nla. Sekoni returns to Nigeria as an inspired artist. His one great work, a sculpture which he calls *The Wrestler*, seems a race against time. Using Bandele as a model and a rough incident with a bouncer at the Club Cabana as the inspiration, Sekoni depicts what appears to be Ogun just beginning to relax after subduing the forces of chaos in the abyss. Kola admires and envies

Sekoni's genius, his ability to create "that something which hits you foully in the stomach."

When Ogun grants such powers, however, he demands a sacrifice in return. In a symbolic scene, with obvious mythological references and a typical Soyinka setting, Sekoni dies in an automobile accident during a raging storm, near a bridge that spans a precipice. As god of the forge, Ogun is associated with automobiles and bridges and with the metal that draws down lightning from the heavens. On that chaotic night, the "dome" of heaven "cracked," and, like Ogun in the abyss, Sekoni loses his identity, literally, except as he survives in his sculpture. His death leaves the other interpreters drained of energy, searching desperately for a myth that will convince them of rebirth. That Sekoni is not reborn seems to provoke estrangement. At the end, the four remaining interpreters are no longer a close-knit group: They experience "a night of severance, every man . . . going his way." The Ogun paradigm would suggest that, since everyone is an incarnation of Ogun, the interpreters are facing the transition experience.

SEASON OF ANOMY

Like *The Interpreters*, *Season of Anomy* has as its major theme the reestablishment of cultural and spiritual continuity. Bandele's searing rebuke of his peers, that they are burying their own children, applies even literally to the generation in power in Soyinka's second novel. The ruling Cartel (a conglomerate of business, political, and military leaders) use their positions to exploit the country (a fictionalized Nigeria) and to intimidate, suppress, and massacre in order to maintain control. The novel's main antagonist is the innocuous-appearing community of Aiyéró, headed by the wise Pa Ahime, which perpetuates the traditional African values of community and harmony with nature. Ahime resembles the Obatala personality in his passive, suffering role as priest. Beneath his surface calm dwell "doubts upon doubts, thicker than the night" about African ideals ever overcoming the forces of exploitation. He himself, however, does not struggle actively against the forces outside the community. The conflict in the novel begins when Ofeyi, the novel's protagonist and the Ogun personality in its artistic, creative aspect, goes

out into the larger world to combat the Cartel. Ofeyi is at first a propagandist jingle writer for the Cocoa Corporation, an ally of the Cartel; under the influence of Ahime and his own vision of a new Africa, however, he uses his position to undermine the corporation, until he has to resign under fire. The novel, then, presents a conflict between these two forces, creation and destruction, but the plot is a tracing of Ofeyi's growing commitment to his cause, his debate in particular over using either peaceful or military means, his eventual acceptance of violence, and his personal and communal quest for Iriyise, his mistress, whom Soyinka develops as a goddess of fertility, an aspect of Orisa-nla, who gave birth to the Yoruba pantheon. Ofeyi travels into the center of the Cartel's massacres in order to rescue Iriyise from the enemy prison and carry her, though comatose, safely back to the refuge of Aiyéró.

While the novel often operates on a realistic level—with its vivid pictures of war, for example—its language is infused with ritual and myth. Ofeyi's actions take on a ritualistic meaning and, as in ritual and myth, detailed, causal explanations are not always forthcoming. The novel does not follow a clear chronological line; it oscillates between the communal life in Aiyéró and the outside world and between the inner life of Ofeyi, his memories and reflections, and public action. The novel tries to make sense of the chaotic events through which Ofeyi moves. It judges the Cartel according to traditional values and myths. In particular, it condemns an exploitation that forgets the obligation of one generation to another. Ofeyi's subversive jingles accuse the Cocoa Corporation of milking the country dry: "They drained the nectar, peeled the gold/ The trees were bled prematurely old/ Nor green nor gold remained for the next generation." The proverb that defines the Cartel, one of its own choosing, damns it: "The child who swears his mother will not sleep, he must also pass a sleepless night." The mother (the Cartel), accusing the child of the crime, fails to acknowledge that the child is restless and screams for attention because the mother has not been nurturing him. The Cartel fails in its function of ensuring continuity from one generation to the next. Aiyéró, on the other hand, through its rituals and myths, maintains the three necessary connections, between generations, between the living and the dead, and between gods and humanity. Aiyéró is not a pastoral paradise; it has a reputation for its boatbuilding, uses hydroelectric power, and manufactures guns. Soyinka's notion of the idyllic community is not backward. Still, its communal ideal suggests strongly its allegorical representation of the divine world attempting to reestablish ties with the fragmented human race to achieve wholeness.

Ogun's transitional journey is the paradigm for the novel's plot and theme. Individual scenes and incidents reinforce the idea. Ofeyi's main concern is whether his actions will make any impact on history: whether the attempt to create order out of chaos is hopeless and whether his own personal contribution will soon be covered in obscurity. When he is still debating his role, sitting in a canoe on the pond that the people of Aiyéró use as a retreat for reflection, Ofeyi watches the wake quickly disappear as the waters resume their calm cover. Even "this simple rite of passage," he says, seems a meaningless challenge. Beneath the pond are centuries of history— "Slaves, gold, oil. The old wars"—and his efforts seem doomed to join them. The oil could be a promise for the future; like Ogun, Ofeyi regards resources as the raw materials of creativity. As he contemplates the Cartel's exploitation of them, he determines, through an act of the will, that victory requires "only the rightful challenger."

The novel's central symbol of the new Nigeria, as conceived by Ahime and Ofeyi, is the dam at Shage, which will, when completed, span the river into Cross-river, the region most antagonistic to Aiyéró's ideas and known for its xenophobia. Mainly Aiyéró men, living outside their native community, are engaged on the project, and Ofeyi, as ideologue, has been its inspiration. It, like Iriyise's dance performed for the workers on the construction site, celebrates the harmonious creation of power—hydroelectric power— out of natural forces. Later, however, after the Cartel has begun to react to the initiatives of the Aiyéró men and has begun to repress them, Ofeyi passes by Shage Dam on the way to Cross-river. The site is abandoned, the dam only partially finished, and dead bodies—perhaps the men of Aiyéró—lie floating in the artificial lake. The Cartel has begun its massacres. When Ofeyi first sees the crane with its rope suspended over the lake, he recalls a similar scene in Scotland and remembers his reaction to the unfinished bridge there. It seemed to him then that all unfinished things were sublime—a Western romantic notion to which he had clung until this day at Shage Dam. Now he reevaluates that experience, according to the myth of his own culture: "It all remained unfinished, and not sublime." Ofeyi as the Ogun personality cannot accept the chaos of the abyss as the end of the creative effort. The goal must be to restore order, not aesthetically admire the incomprehensible.

When Ofeyi arrives at the bridge that will carry him into Cross-river, he, like Egbo in *The Interpreters*, bathes himself in the purifying waters. Unlike Egbo, however, he then takes the final plunge into the abyss. He enters Cross-river in search of Iriyise. As he experiences at first hand the horrors of war, he moves deeper and deeper into enemy territory and ends in Temoko Prison. He is there not because he is forced to be but because he wills to be. In the final symbolic act of the abyss, he is knocked unconscious, loses his "individuation," and then wills himself back to life. This unrealistic mythical event accompanies his simultaneous rescue of Iriyise from the prison. Their return to Aiyéró with Ahime and Demakin (the warrior aspect of Ogun) means a temporary defeat for society but a victory for Ofeyi, whose will has overcome the recurring temptation of passivity.

A common complaint against Soyinka, in spite of the high acclaim he receives for his artistry and his patriotism, is his failure to speak realistically to the issues confronting African societies. Not only does his complex, allusive style encourage elitism, but his characters also are intellectuals whose problems and solutions have little direct relationship to the larger society. Whereas Western audiences, especially critics, might be attracted to such a highly individualistic aesthetic, African readers and critics might wish for a voice that is closer to their pitch, that seems to echo their complaints.

Certainly, many would wish fervently that one

who is perhaps the most talented literary figure on the continent could use his gift to effect real and visible change. Nevertheless, three things must be said about Soyinka as an African spokesman. First, his novels have as their underlying theme the freedom of the individual and the use of that freedom in the interests of society. Second, he insists on African roots and traditional African concepts as rationales and sanctions for human behavior. Finally, Soyinka does not indulge in experimentation for its own sake, nor does he employ fiction merely as a medium for presenting the tensions of contemporary conflict; rather, by incorporating ritual and myth in his novels, he seeks to suggest the very communal sense that must ultimately hold the society together.

Thomas Banks, updated by Harland W. Jones III

OTHER MAJOR WORKS

PLAYS: *The Swamp Dwellers*, pr. 1958; *The Lion and the Jewel*, pr. 1959; *The Invention*, pr. 1959 (one act); *The Trials of Brother Jero*, pr. 1960; *A Dance of the Forests*, pr. 1960; *Camwood on the Leaves*, pr. 1960 (radio play); *The Strong Breed*, pb. 1963; *Three Plays*, pb. 1963; *Five Plays*, pb. 1964; *Kongi's Harvest*, pr. 1964; *The Road*, pr., pb. 1965; *Madmen and Specialists*, pr. 1970 (revised pr., pb. 1971); *Jero's Metamorphosis*, pb. 1973; *The Bacchae*, pr., pb. 1973 (adaptation of Euripides' play); *Collected Plays*, pb. 1973, 1974 (2 volumes); *Death and the King's Horseman*, pb. 1975; *Opera Wonyosi*, pr. 1977 (adaptation of Bertolt Brecht's play *The Three-Penny Opera*); *A Play of Giants*, pr., pb. 1984; *Six Plays*, pb. 1984; *Requiem for a Futurologist*, pb. 1985; *A Scourge of Hyacinths*, 1991 (pr. on radio); *From Zia, with Love*, pr., pb. 1992; *"The Trials of Brother Jero" and "The Strong Breed": Two Plays*, pb. 1992; *"From Zia, with Love" and "A Scourge of Hyacinths,"* pb. 1992; *The Beatification of Area Boy: A Lagosian Kaleidoscope*, pb. 1995.

POETRY: *Idanre and Other Poems*, 1967; *Poems from Prison*, 1969; *A Shuttle in the Crypt*, 1972; *Ogun Abibiman*, 1976; *Mandela's Earth and Other Poems*, 1988.

NONFICTION: *"The Man Died": Prison Notes of Wole Soyinka*, 1972 (autobiography); *Myth, Litera-*

ture, and the African World, 1976; *Aké: The Years of Childhood*, 1981 (autobiography); *Art, Dialogue, and Outrage*, 1988; *Ìsarà: A Voyage Around "Essay,"* 1989; *The Credo of Being and Nothingness*, 1991; *Wole Soyinka on "Identity,"* 1992; *Orisha Liberated the Mind: Wole Soyinka in Conversation with Ulli Beier on Yoruba Religion*, 1992; *"Death and the Kings' Horseman": A Conversation Between Wole Soyinka and Ulli Beier*, 1993; *Ibadan: The Penkelemes Years: A Memoir, 1946-1965*, 1994; *The Beautification of Area Boy: A Lagosian Kaleidoscope*, 1995; *The Open Sore of a Continent: A Personal Narrative of the Nigerian Crisis*, 1996; *The Burden of Memory, the Muse of Forgiveness*, 1999.

TRANSLATION: *Forest of a Thousand Daemons: A Hunter's Saga*, 1968 (of D. O. Fagunwa's novel *Ogboju Ode Ninu Igbo Irunmale*).

BIBLIOGRAPHY

Adelugba, Dapo, ed. *Before Our Very Eyes: Tribute to Wole Soyinka*. Ibadan, Nigeria: Spectrum, 1987. This collection of sixteen essays is divided into two parts, the first part consisting of ten personal tributes and the second of six analytical essays. Brian Crow's essay on Soyinka's romanticism is particularly useful.

Gibbs, James, ed. *Critical Perspectives on Wole Soyinka*. London: Heinemann, 1981. Wide-ranging anthology of essays that touch on all aspects of Soyinka's art. Includes a subtle essay by Mark Kinkead-Weekes on *The Interpreters*.

_____, ed. *Research on African Literatures* 14, no. 1 (Spring, 1983). Special issue on Wole Soyinka. The best of the handful of journal issues devoted entirely to Soyinka. Does not address the long fiction directly, however.

Jones, Eldred Durosimi. *The Writing of Wole Soyinka*. Rev. ed. London: Heinemann, 1988. For years, the standard general introduction to Soyinka's work and still a useful resource. Contains lucid analysis of all the major works and helpful information about Soyinka's background.

Lindfors, Bernth, and James Gibbs, eds. *Research on Wole Soyinka*. Trenton, N.J.: Africa World, 1992. Comprehensive bibliography of works dealing with Soyinka, including primary and secondary works and reviews. A valuable source for Soyinka scholars.

Maja-Pearce, Adewale. *Wole Soyinka: An Appraisal*. Ibadan, Nigeria: Heinemann, 1994. Diverse collection of essays published in honor of Soyinka's sixtieth birthday. Includes articles by fellow novelists Nadine Gordimer and Wilson Harris, as well as a penetrating critique of Soyinka's critical writings by Kwam Anthony Appiah. Also reprints Soyinka's Nobel Prize speech, "This Past Must Address Its Present."

Wright, Derek. *Wole Soyinka Revisited*. New York: Twayne, 1993. Extremely valuable, wide-ranging study of Soyinka's entire oeuvre. Early chapters focus on the Yoruba context of Soyinka's work and include a valuable glossary of Yoruba terms. A later chapter deals directly with the novels, reading them together as an attempted (though flawed) progression from ritual to reality.

(Jerry Bauer)

MURIEL SPARK

Born: Edinburgh, Scotland; February 1, 1918

PRINCIPAL LONG FICTION
The Comforters, 1957
Robinson, 1958
Memento Mori, 1959
The Ballad of Peckham Rye, 1960
The Bachelors, 1960
The Prime of Miss Jean Brodie, 1961
The Girls of Slender Means, 1963
The Mandelbaum Gate, 1965
The Public Image, 1968
The Driver's Seat, 1970
Not to Disturb, 1971
The Hothouse by the East River, 1973
The Abbess of Crewe: A Modern Morality Tale, 1974

The Takeover, 1976
Territorial Rights, 1979
Loitering with Intent, 1981
The Only Problem, 1984
A Far Cry from Kensington, 1988
Symposium, 1990
The Novels of Muriel Spark, 1995
Reality and Dreams, 1996

OTHER LITERARY FORMS

In addition to her novels, Muriel Spark produced a sizable amount of work in the genres of poetry, the short story, drama, biography, and criticism. Her volumes of poetry include *The Fanfarlo and Other Verse* (1952) and *Collected Poems I* (1967). Her first collection of short stories, entitled *The Go-Away Bird and Other Stories*, appeared in 1958, followed by *Collected Stories I* (1967) and *The Stories of Muriel Spark* (1985). *Voices at Play*, a collection of short stories and radio plays, appeared in 1961, and a play, *Doctors of Philosophy*, was first performed in London in 1962 and published in 1963. Spark's literary partnership with Derek Stanford resulted in their editing *Tribute to Wordsworth* (1950), a collection of essays on the centenary of the poet's death, and *My Best Mary: The Selected Letters of Mary Shelley* (1953). Spark and Stanford also edited *Letters of John Henry Newman* (1957). Spark produced a study of Mary Shelley, *Child of Light: A Reassessment of Mary Wollstonecraft Shelley* (1951, revised as *Mary Shelley*, 1987), and of *John Masefield* (1953). Spark also edited *The Brontë Letters* (1954; pb. in U.S. as *The Letters of the Brontës: A Selection*, 1954).

ACHIEVEMENTS

Critical opinion about Spark's status as a novelist is sharply divided. In general, her work is less highly valued by American critics; Frederick Karl, for example, dismissed her work as being "light to the point of froth" and said that it has "virtually no content." English critics such as Frank Kermode, Malcolm Bradbury, and David Lodge, on the other hand, would consider Spark a major contemporary novelist. Kermode complimented her on being "obsessed" with novelistic form, called *The Mandelbaum Gate* a work of "profound virtuosity," and considered her to be a "difficult and important artist." Bradbury, who regarded Spark as an "interesting, and a very amusing, novelist" from the beginning of her career, later added his assessment that she is also a "very high stylist" whose work in the novella shows a precision and economy of form and style. In a reassessment of *The Prime of Miss Jean Brodie*, Lodge commented on the complex structure of the novel and Spark's successful experimentation with authorial omniscience.

Spark is known for being able to combine popular success with critical acclaim. In 1951, she received her first literary award, the *Observer* Story Prize for the Christmas story "The Seraph and the Zambesi." A radio drama based on *The Ballad of Peckham Rye* won the Italia Prize in 1962, and in the same year she was named Fellow of the Royal Society of Literature. In 1965, Spark received the prestigious James Tait Black Memorial Prize for Fiction for the *The Mandelbaum Gate*. Spark earned the Order of the British Empire in 1967.

BIOGRAPHY

Muriel Sarah Spark was born in Edinburgh, Scotland, on February 1, 1918, of a Jewish father, Bernard Camberg, and an English mother, Sarah Uezzell Camberg. She attended James Gillespie's School for Girls in Edinburgh, an experience that later formed the background for *The Prime of Miss Jean Brodie*. She lived in Edinburgh until 1937, when she married S. O. Spark and moved to Africa. During the next two years she gave birth to her son, Robin, and divorced Spark, who had become abusive and was showing signs of mental illness. She moved into an apartment with a young widow and her child and wrote poems and plays while waiting for the long process of her divorce to conclude. Her life in Rhodesia and South Africa provided background material for some of her earliest successful short stories, such as "The Portobello Road" and "The Seraph and the Zambesi." The onset of World War II interfered with her plans to return to Scotland, and she worked at a number of jobs before managing to book a passage home in 1944; because there were travel restrictions for children, her son was unable to join her for a year and a half.

During her sojourn as young divorcee awaiting the arrival of her child, she moved to London to find work, and she lived at the Helena Club, which had been endowed by Princess Helena, the daughter of Queen Victoria, for "ladies from good families of modest means who are obliged to pursue an occupation in London." Spark's experiences at the Helena Club with other young women earning a living in a big city became the background for her novel *The Girls of Slender Means*.

From 1944 to 1946, she worked in the Political Intelligence Department of the British Foreign Office, an experience she later drew upon when writing *The Hothouse by the East River*. Her interest in poetry led to her serving as General Secretary of the Poetry Society in London from 1947 to 1949 and as editor of the *Poetry Review*; in 1949, she introduced a short-lived journal entitled *Forum Stories and Poems.* In the 1950's, she began a successful career as a critic and editor which included books on William Wordsworth, Mary Shelley, Emily Brontë, John Masefield, and John Henry Newman, publishing several of these works with her literary partner and friend Derek Stanford.

The major turning point in Spark's career as a writer occurred in 1954, when she converted to Roman Catholicism. Brought up in the Presbyterian religion, she said that she had "no clear beliefs at all" until 1952, when she became "an Anglican intellectually speaking," although she did not formally join the Anglican Church until late in 1953. The Church of England was, however, a halfway house for Spark, who was an Anglo-Catholic for only nine months before her conversion to Roman Catholicism. She believed that the writings of John Henry Newman were an important factor in her move to the Catholic Church. Her conversion initially caused her a great deal of emotional suffering, and she said that her mind was, for a period of time, "far too crowded with ideas, all teeming in disorder." This feeling of mental chaos gave way later to what she called "a complete reorganization" of her mind that enabled her to begin writing fiction. Several persons encouraged her to produce a novel, among them Graham Greene and Macmillan and Company, which was looking for new writers at the time; the result was *The Comforters.*

In 1961, Spark traveled to Jerusalem to research the background for *The Mandelbaum Gate,* and in 1964 she moved from her home in London to New York. She lived for less than a year in an apartment close to the United Nations Building, a location that later became the setting for *The Hothouse by the East River.* In 1967, she was awarded the Order of the British Empire and left England to settle in Italy. In 1982, after fifteen years in Rome, she moved to Tuscany.

ANALYSIS

Muriel Spark frequently used the word "minor" to describe her achievement as a novelist, a term which, in her vocabulary, is not as derogatory as it may at first appear. Believing that the artist is by definition a

"minor public servant," Spark claimed that she chose to write "minor novels deliberately." This characterization of the artist and of her own intentions as a writer reflects her concerns about the novel as a form and the creative process in general, issues which are present throughout her work. She admitted that while writing her first novel, *The Comforters,* she had difficulty resigning herself to the fact that she was writing a novel, a genre which, in her opinion, was a "lazy way of writing poetry." For Spark at that time, poetry was the only true literature, while the novel was an "inferior way of writing" whose "aesthetic validity" was very much in doubt. Although she apparently revised her earlier low estimation of the novel, she said that she always considered herself a poet rather than a novelist and believed that her novels are "the novels of a poet."

Spark's distrust of the novel form also results from her suspicions about fiction's relationship to truth; she said that she was interested in "absolute truth" and that fiction is a "kind of parable" from which a "kind of truth" emerges which should not be confused with fact. The truth that the novel can embody is similar to her definition of "legend" in *Emily Brontë: Her Life and Work.* Speaking of the literary legends that surround a writer such as Emily Brontë, she said that these stories, though not literally true, are "the repository of a vital aspect of truth" which should be accorded respect in their own right. It is imperative, however, for writers and readers to discriminate among types of truth and between life and art, a discrimination that Charmian Colston, the aged novelist in *Memento Mori,* is capable of making. She tells another character that "the art of fiction is very like the practice of deception," and, when asked if the practice of deception in life is also an art, replies, "In life . . . everything is different. Everything is in the Providence of God." Spark, who was careful to maintain this distinction in her statements about her work, described her own novels as a "pack of lies."

Caroline Rose in *The Comforters,* who shares this distrust of fiction, struggles against being a character in a novel because she resents being manipulated by the novelist. At one point, she describes the author of the fiction as an "unknown, possibly sinister being."

The writer's "sinister" nature results from his or her ability to create fictions that are imaginative versions and extensions of the truth rather than the truth itself; perhaps more important, the novelist deprives his or her characters of their free will and independence. As Patricia Stubbs observed, Spark perceives a parallel between God and the novelist, and the act of creating fiction is, in a sense, "dabbling in the devil's work."

As a result, Spark's novels are filled with would-be artists and artist-figures, people who attempt to create fictions in real life and consequently bring about discord and mischief. In *The Prime of Miss Jean Brodie*, Miss Brodie begins to view the people around her as characters in a story she is creating and attempts to bring about sexual pairings and heroic deeds in her self-made "plot" with disastrous results. Both Alec Warner in *Memento Mori* and Dougal Douglas in *The Ballad of Peckham Rye* are involved in "research" into the lives of the people around them; Douglas carries his curiosity about others a step further, fictionalizing an autobiography for an actress and later becoming the author of "a lot of cock-eyed books." In two later novels, *The Public Image* and *Territorial Rights*, fictions are devised even more consciously—and are potentially more dangerous. In *The Public Image*, film actress Annabel Christopher is, for the most part, merely the product of a clever publicity campaign with its accompanying lies, distortions, and omissions. After her husband's suicide, she becomes the victim of his well-planned attempt to destroy her career, for he has left behind a group of letters that would impugn her sexual morality and destroy her carefully devised "public image." In *Territorial Rights*, Robert Leaver stages his own kidnapping and sends threatening letters filled with truth and lies to his family and friends. In addition, he leaves fragments of a "novel" he is supposedly writing that contain a sensational mixture of fact and fiction which could hurt many of the people around him. Just as these characters are guilty of trying to manipulate reality by inserting carefully constructed "fictions" into the lives of real people, Sir Quentin Oliver in *Loitering with Intent* overtly plagiarizes a fictional model to accomplish his ends. After reading Fleur Talbot's novel *Warrender Chase*,

he begins to orchestrate the lives of the members of the Autobiographical Association according to its plot, an action which causes Fleur to complain that "He's trying to live out my story."

The ubiquitous "listening devices" and spying present in Spark's fiction are another aspect of her fascination with the process of creating fictions. Dougal Douglas, the artist-to-be, sells tape recorders to African witch doctors; the Abbey in *The Abbess of Crewe* is bugged; and Curran in *Territorial Rights* has a sudden moment of paranoia in a restaurant when he wonders if his fellow diners are all spies armed with "eavesdropping devices." As the servants in *Not to Disturb* realize, recording and preserving experience allows the person doing the recording to alter, and, in a sense, to create reality. Armed with tape recorders and cameras, they are busy creating their own version of the events of an evening that culminates in the deaths of the Baron and Baroness Klopstock and their secretary; the servants are artist-figures, manipulating the plot of the story which they will soon sell to the public media. Spark sees the novelist, like the "typing ghost" who plagues Caroline Rose in *The Comforters*, as an eavesdropper who spies upon his characters and then manipulates their actions in order to create a fiction; and she peoples her novels with characters who are also engaged in this process.

Because Spark is so intent upon acknowledging her fiction as fiction, most of her novels are consciously artificial in both form and content. She never had a desire to be a realistic novelist or to write the "long novel"; she said she grew bored writing her only lengthy novel, *The Mandelbaum Gate*, because of its length. Rather, she claimed to speak in a "kind of shorthand" in which the narrative voice is curiously impersonal. Not surprisingly, in several novels, among them *Not to Disturb* and *The Driver's Seat*, she experimented with her own version of the New Novel. In Spark's fiction, however, unlike that of many of the antinovelists, all details, no matter how arbitrary they at first appear, are ultimately significant. In fact, a word that appears throughout her statements about fiction and in her novels is "economy." In *The Takeover*, the narrator mentions the "intuitive artistic sense of economy" that characterizes the creative person, and Spark emphasized her belief that the artist should carefully select only the most appropriate details in order to create meaning.

At the same time, holding the belief that it is "bad manners to inflict emotional involvement on the reader," in her novels the narrator's witty detachment from the subject matter signifies Spark's goal of creating art that remains distanced from the human suffering it presents. Literature, according to her, should not continue to sympathize with the victims of violence and tyranny; art should instead abandon sentimental depictions of the human condition so that it can "ruthlessly mock" the forces which cause the individual to suffer. It is Spark's belief that art needs "less emotion and more intelligence" and should aspire to become an art of satire and ridicule. The world, for Spark, is essentially absurd, and "the rhetoric of our time should persuade us to contemplate the ridiculous nature of the reality before us, and teach us to mock it."

THE COMFORTERS

Spark's first novel, *The Comforters*, reflects the two pivotal experiences of her life: her conversion to Roman Catholicism and her change as a writer from poet to novelist. Spark said that in order to overcome her aesthetic skepticism about the novel form, it was necessary for her "to write a novel about somebody writing a novel." In addition, she believed that *The Comforters* is a result of the "complete reorganization" of her mind that followed her conversion and that its theme is "a convert and a kind of psychic upheaval." Caroline Rose, the novel's central character, is in the process of coming to terms with both these issues. A recent convert to Catholicism who dislikes many of her fellow Catholics, Caroline is writing a book called *Form in the Modern Novel* and trying to understand why she has begun to overhear a disembodied "novelist," complete with typewriter, who is writing a novel about her and her friends.

The Comforters is about the battle between the author and her characters, a battle in which Caroline struggles to preserve her free will in the face of the novelist's desire to control the events of the story. Caroline finds the experience of being "written into"

someone else's narrative painful, just as her friend Laurence Manders protests that "I dislike being a character in your novel" when he discovers that Caroline is writing fiction that includes the story of their relationship. Caroline believes that it is her "duty" to "hold up the action" of the novel, to "spoil" it, and she asserts her right to make her own decisions, finding, however, that this is usually impossible; the predetermined "plot" of the novelist prevails.

Caroline remains unaware, however, that she in turn is capable of affecting the novel as it is being written. The narrator admits that Caroline's "remarks" continue to interfere with the book and that she does not realize her "constant influence" on the story's development. From Caroline's perspective, she has only partial knowledge of the plot, and she complains that the voices she overhears only give her "small crazy fragments" of a novel in which there may be other characters whom she does not know. In this sense, Caroline is a surrogate for Spark the novelist, a character who "discovers" the plot, as does its creator, while it is being written. As a result, *The Comforters* concludes with Caroline leaving London to write a novel which apparently will be *The Comforters*.

Spark would appear to be working out both the technique and the morality of writing fiction in her first novel. Caroline's fascination with "form in the modern novel" is also Spark's fascination, and Spark writes a story about the problems involved in writing a story: *The Comforters* is about the struggle between the novelist's will to impose form and the continued growth and development of the characters, who begin to become independent entities in the narrative, insisting upon the right to break free of the restraints of plot and situation. One of the reasons Caroline Rose gives for opposing the novelist is that Caroline "happens to be a Christian"; Spark, as a Catholic, is uneasy with the idea of the novelist "playing God" and depriving her characters of choice.

The Comforters is also about Catholicism and the recent convert's attempts to find an identity as a Catholic. Georgina Hogg, the Catholic in the novel whom Caroline particularly despises, symbolizes Caroline's (and Spark's) reservations about individual Catholics. These reservations are not, it should be emphasized, about Catholicism as a religion. Rather, Mrs. Hogg represents a Catholicism which, in the hands of a certain type of individual, becomes simply dogma. Mrs. Hogg, who lacks insight or any true feeling about her religion, uses her sense of self-righteousness to impinge upon the people around her. In the novel, she is called a "sneak," a "subtle tyrant," and a "moral blackmailer," and she is indeed guilty of all these accusations. At one point in the story, Caroline decides that Mrs. Hogg is "not a real-life character . . . merely a gargoyle"; she is so lacking in identity that she literally "disappears" when there are no other people around to perceive her existence. As several characters observe, Georgina Hogg "has no private life," a phrase which ironically underscores her lack of substance as a character and a Catholic.

Mrs. Hogg's lack of identity is a major theme of the novel, and a problem which several other characters share. Helena Manders, when she has a sudden sense of how "exhilarating" it is to be herself, actually perceives her personality as belonging to someone else. Eleanor Hogarth, as Caroline realizes, has completely lost contact with her true personality because she has for so long been satisfied with mimicking others, adopting other roles to play. Caroline's auditory hallucinations are another aspect of this problem, for she feels that her free will as an individual is being taken from her: Is she Caroline Rose, or simply a character in someone else's novel? At the same time, she is obsessed with the identity of what she calls the "typing ghost," at one point making a list entitled *"Possible identity"* which speculates about who the typist-novelist may be—Satan, a hermaphrodite, a woman, or a Holy Soul in Purgatory.

The characters' lack of identity is related to their isolation and inability to communicate with one another. "Is the world," asks Caroline, "a lunatic asylum then? Are we all courteous maniacs discreetly making allowances for everyone else's derangement?" Although she rejects this idea, *The Comforters* certainly depicts a world in which individuals search for an identity while remaining locked into a very subjective set of preconceptions about everything external to them. The way out of this trap, at

least for Caroline, is to write a novel, the novel which Spark has actually written. *The Comforters* represents Spark's successful confrontation with and resolution of the issues of Catholicism, creativity, and the novel as a genre. Her interest in the novel as a form and the process of creating fictions has continued throughout her career as a novelist.

THE PRIME OF MISS JEAN BRODIE

In an interview, Spark said that the eponymous protagonist of *The Prime of Miss Jean Brodie* represents "completely unrealised potentialities," a descriptive phrase which reflects the same ambiguity with which she is treated in the novel. The story of an Edinburgh schoolmistress and her effects on the lives of six of her pupils, *The Prime of Miss Jean Brodie* concentrates on the relationship between Jean Brodie and Sandy Stranger, the student who eventually "betrays" her. Like many other characters in Spark's fiction, Miss Brodie begins to confuse fact and fiction, and it is when Sandy perceives that her teacher has decided that Rose Stanley must begin an affair with art teacher Teddy Lloyd that Sandy realizes that Jean Brodie is no longer playing a game or advancing a theory: "Miss Brodie meant it." As David Lodge notes in his article on the novel in *The Novelist at the Crossroads* (1971), Sandy and Jenny intuitively understand when their fiction, a made-up correspondence between Miss Brodie and music teacher Gordon Lowther, should be buried and forgotten; unlike her students, Jean Brodie does not know when fantasies should be discarded.

In addition to seeing herself as an artist-figure who can manipulate the lives of her students and lovers, Jean Brodie is also guilty, in Sandy's eyes, of serious religious and political errors. Although she has not turned to religion at the time, a very young Sandy is frightened by her vision of all the "Brodie set" in a line headed by their teacher "in unified compliance to the destiny of Miss Brodie, as if God had willed them to birth for that purpose." Later, Sandy is horrified to discover that her former teacher "thinks she is Providence" and that she can see the beginning and the end of all "stories." Jean Brodie's lack of guilt over any of her actions results from her assurance that "God was on her side"; she elects herself to grace with an "exotic suicidal enchantment" which drives her to the excesses that eventually result in her forced retirement. Jean Brodie's view of herself as "above the common moral code," a phrase she applies to Rose, her chosen surrogate for an affair with Teddy Lloyd, is related to her political views as well. An early admirer of Italian Premier Benito Mussolini and German Chancellor Adolf Hitler whom Sandy later characterizes as a "born fascist," she sees herself as dutybound to shape the personalities and the destinies of the young girls around her. "You are mine," she says to her "set," whom she has chosen to receive what she calls the "fruits of her prime," which will remain with the girls "always," a prophecy which is partially true.

The complexity of *The Prime of Miss Jean Brodie* lies in the fact that Jean Brodie is not simply a villainous character who oversteps her bounds as a teacher and begins to exert a potentially corruptive force on the young people entrusted to her. Although she flirts with Fascism (after the war she calls Hitler "rather naughty"), she at the same time encourages a fierce individualism in her chosen students, who, as the headmistress of the Marcia Blaine School for Girls sadly learns, are totally lacking in "team spirit." She makes good her promise to "put old heads on young shoulders" and creates the "capacity for enthusiasm" for knowledge that remains with several of her students for life. The lecture to her girls on her theory of education—"It means a leading out. To me education is a leading out of what is already there in the pupil's soul. . . . Never let it be said that I put ideas into your heads"—is, like the portrait of Jean Brodie that Spark presents in the novel, open to several interpretations. Although in the later years of her prime, Miss Brodie *does* attempt to put "ideas" into the girls' heads, at the same time she bequeaths to her students a knowledge of and sensitivity to art, culture, and ideas that would have been impossible in a more conventional educational situation.

Just as *The Prime of Miss Jean Brodie* is about "unrealised potentialities," Miss Brodie also communicates to her students a knowledge of the unlimited potential inherent in all experience. In her late thirties, Jenny Gray has an experience that reawakens a memory of her "sense of the hidden possibility in

all things" that she felt as an eleven-year-old student under the tutelage of Jean Brodie. More important, however, is the teacher's influence on Sandy Stranger. In his book on Spark, Derek Stanford said that "Truth, for Muriel Spark, implies rejection," and Sandy laments in the novel that she has had nothing, particularly in the religious realm, to react against or reject. Jean Brodie finally provides this catalyst, and Sandy's decision to "put a stop" to her results from a variety of reasons: her moral indignation over Miss Brodie's "plans" for Rose and Joyce Emily, sexual jealousy of Teddy Lloyd's continued infatuation with her teacher, and her awakening sense of Christian morals.

As an adult, however, Sandy acknowledges that Jean Brodie was her most important formative influence and in a sense responsible for the course her life has taken. Her conversion to Catholicism and taking of the veil are the result of her affair with Teddy Lloyd, an affair she instigates in order to subvert Jean Brodie's plans. Although Spark does not indicate the exact subject of the psychological treatise that has made Sandy famous, other than the fact that it concerns the nature of "moral perception," its title, "The Transfiguration of the Commonplace," reveals that it in some way deals with the mind's ability to alter everyday reality. Clearly, this topic owes a debt to Jean Brodie's communication to her students of the endless "possibilities" that surrounded them and is a reflection of Jean Brodie's constantly changing nature in the novel. The narrator observes that, unlike her colleagues, Miss Brodie is in a "state of fluctuating development"; like her students, her "nature was growing under their eyes, as the girls themselves were under formation." One element of Jean Brodie's "prime" is her nonstatic personality, and the problem, of course, is the direction in which the changes take place. As the narrator notes, "the principles governing the end of her prime would have astonished herself at the beginning of it."

In *The Prime of Miss Jean Brodie*, Spark is at the height of her powers as a novelist, and nowhere else in her fiction is she more in control of her subject. The "flash-forwards" which occur throughout the novel cause the reader to concentrate on the characters' mo-

tivations and interrelationships rather than on any intricacies of the plot, and Spark makes use of the principle of "economy" that she so values on almost every
page, providing only the most telling details of the
story while refraining, for the most part, from any
authorial interpretation. In fact, the idea of economy is
an important thematic element in the book. Sandy is
first fascinated by the economy of Jean Brodie's fusing
her tales of her dead lover, Hugh, with her current associations with Gordon Lowther and Teddy Lloyd, and
later she is angered and intrigued by the economy of
the art teacher's paintings, which make Jean Brodie's
students resemble their teacher. When Sandy betrays
Miss Brodie to the headmistress, she uses this principle after concluding that "where there was a choice of
various courses the most economical was the best."
Both in form and style, *The Prime of Miss Jean Brodie*
shows Spark utilizing her own "intuitive artistic sense
of economy."

THE DRIVER'S SEAT

In *The Driver's Seat*, Spark writes her revisionist
version of the New Novel. She said that she dis-
agreed with the philosophical tenets of the antinovel,
and she adopted many of its techniques to prove the
invalidity of its philosophy. Although *The Driver's
Seat* initially appears to be filled with randomly chosen, objectively described phenomena, ultimately the
novel denies the entire concept of contingency. As
Frank Kermode states in *The Sense of an Ending*
(1966), Spark's fiction is not about any kind of "brutal
chaos" but rather presents a "radically non-contingent
reality to be dealt with in purely novelistic terms."
Every event, every description becomes, in the light
of the ending of *The Driver's Seat*, significant.

The novel concerns a young woman named Lise
who leaves her home in northern Europe to travel
south. Spark carefully fails to specify which cities are
involved in order to create the same impersonal,
anonymous air in the novel that characterizes Lise's
world in general. The purpose of her journey is to
find a man to murder her, and in this story Spark in-
verts the typical thriller: The "victim" relentlessly
stalks her murderer and finally "forces" him to act.
Lise, who has abandoned the sterile loneliness of
her former existence symbolized by her apartment,

which "looks as if it were uninhabited," takes control
of her life for the first time and decides to take the
most dramatic final step possible. In the opening
scene, she shouts at a salesgirl who attempts to sell
her a dress made of nonstaining fabric because, having already decided that she is to be stabbed to death,
she wishes for clothing that will provide the more lurid touch of bloodstains. At the conclusion of the
scene, Lise again shouts at the salesgirl "with a look
of satisfaction at her own dominance over the situation," and the remainder of the novel is about Lise's
carefully planned murder and the trail of information
and clues she leaves for Interpol all across Europe.

Unlike Caroline Rose in *The Comforters*, whose
response to being a character in a novel is to write a
novel about characters in a novel, Lise actually
wrests control of the plot from the narrator, who is
forced to admit ignorance of her thoughts and intentions. "Who knows her thoughts? Who can tell?"
asks the narrator, who is even unsure as to whether or
not Lise tints her hair or the reason she attracts so
much attention. As a result, the narrator is forced to
give only external information, but this information
is, as the reader begins to realize, all pertinent to the
outcome of the novel. Only at the conclusion, after
Lise's death, does the narrator seem privy to the interior knowledge accessible to the omniscient author.

One of the most important themes in *The Driver's
Seat* is, as in many other Spark novels, the inability
of people to communicate with one another. In the
majority of the conversations, no logical connections
are made between the participants, who remain isolated in their own worlds of obsessional concerns. It
would even appear that the more sane the individual,
the less likely it is that any communication can take
place. Instead, it is the more psychotic characters
who are capable of nonverbal, intuitive understanding. Lise realizes immediately, as does Richard, that
he is the man who is capable of murdering her, and
he initially avoids any conversation with her. The
three men who do converse with her, Bill, Carlos, and
the sickly looking man on the plane, are not, as she
phrases it, "her type"; this is because they attempt to
communicate verbally with her. As Lise says of the
salesman in the department store, "Not my man at

all. He tried to get familiar with me. . . . The one I'm looking for will recognize me right away for the woman I am, have no fear of that." The verb "sense," which is used several times in the novel, signifies the subterranean, psychotic apprehension of other people that is the only perception taking place in *The Driver's Seat*.

Although most of Mrs. Friedke's conversations with Lise have the same illogical, uncommunicative structure that characterizes the other dialogues, she does momentarily enter Lise's realm of supernatural perception. She buys a paper knife for her nephew Richard similar to the one Lise decides against purchasing at the beginning of her journey, and this gift becomes the weapon Richard uses to murder Lise. She also prophetically insists that "you and my nephew are meant for each other . . . my dear, you are the person for my nephew." It is at this point that Lise reveals how she will recognize the man for whom she is searching.

In a phrase that tells a great deal about her past life, she says that she will know him not as a feeling of "presence" but as a "lack of absence." Malcolm Bradbury, in his essay on Spark in *Possibilities: Essays on the State of the Novel* (1973), says that Spark's fiction "conveys significant absences, a feeling of omission, and so has considerable resemblances to a good deal of contemporary art, including the *nouveau roman*." Lise's search for a "lack of absence" is a statement about the emptiness and lack of meaning in her own existence and the type of novel Spark has chosen to write about her: The form of the antinovel is used to comment both on the psychosis of the main character and the failure of the New Novel to deal with the ultimate significance of phenomena. In the New Novel, the present tense frequently signifies the meaninglessness and ephemerality of events; in *The Driver's Seat*, the present tense is used to create a world of terrifying inevitability in which the smallest details become integral elements in Lise's carefully plotted death.

Spark called *The Driver's Seat* "a study, in a way, of self-destruction" but also admitted that the novel was impossible for her to describe. She said that she became so frightened while writing the story that she

was forced to enter a hospital in order to complete it. The fear the novel inspired in her—and many readers—cannot be explained simply by Lise's self-destructiveness; Lise's decision to assert herself, to play god with her life independent of any control by the novelist or a higher power, also contributes to the frightening dimension of the novel. Spark, who expressed a belief that "events are providentially ordered," creates a character who decides to *become* providence and the author of her own story; unlike Jean Brodie, who mistakenly thinks she can see the "beginning and the end" of all stories, Lise successfully orchestrates the novel's conclusion.

LOITERING WITH INTENT

In *Loitering with Intent*, Spark's heroine, novelist Fleur Talbot, frequently quotes from Benvenuto Cellini's *The Autobiography of Benvenuto Cellini* (wr. 1558-1562): "All men . . . who have done anything of merit, or which verily has a semblance of merit . . . should write the tale of their life with their own hand." *Loitering with Intent* is the fictional autobiography of its "author," Fleur Talbot, and a meditation by Spark on her own career as a novelist; it is, in addition, a meditation on the creative process and the relationship between fiction and autobiography. Spark shows that she has come a long way from her early distrust of the novel: *Loitering with Intent* is a paean to the artistic, fiction-making sensibility. Although the habitual tension between life and art and the danger of confusing the two are still present in this novel, Spark firmly comes down on the side of art, defending it against individuals who would seek to "steal" its myth and pervert its truth.

Fleur Talbot frequently comments on "how wonderful it is to be an artist and a woman in the twentieth century." At the conclusion, she admits that she has been "loitering with intent"; that is, she has used her observations about the people and events around her as fictional material, taking joy in both the comic and tragic occurrences in the lives of the individuals who become characters in her own "autobiography." "I rejoiced in seeing people as they were," she says, and the word "rejoice" occurs many times in the novel as Fleur repeatedly uses Cellini's phrase, saying that she "went on her way rejoicing." In her later life she is accused by her friend Dottie of "wriggling out of real life," but Fleur makes no apologies for the way in which she handles the relationship between her life and her creativity; instead, *Loitering with Intent* calls into question the use "real" people make of the fictions of others.

Fleur becomes the secretary of Sir Quentin Oliver, head of the spurious Autobiographical Association he has formed in order to bring people together to compose their memoirs. Like the character of Warrender Chase in the novel Fleur is in the process of completing, Sir Quentin begins to exert a devastating influence on the Association's members, psychologically manipulating them not for blackmailing purposes but for the enjoyment of pure power. Instead of encouraging them to fictionalize their autobiographies, as Fleur attempts to do, Sir Quentin begins to fictionalize their lives with tragic results. Fleur says that

I was sure . . . that Sir Quentin was pumping something artificial into their real lives instead of on paper. Presented fictionally, one could have done something authentic with that poor material. But the inducing them to express themselves in life resulted in falsity.

Fiction, when acknowledged as fiction, can help the individual to comprehend reality more clearly, as Fleur notes when she tells a friend that she will have to write several more chapters of *Warrender Chase* before she will be able to understand the events of the Autobiographical Association. In the same way, she says that one can better know one's friends if they are imaginatively pictured in various situations. Sir Quentin, however, inserts "fictions," frequently stories and events taken from Fleur's novel, into the lives of the Association's members.

The relationship between Sir Quentin and Fleur symbolizes the battle between life and art that is waged in *Loitering with Intent*, for Fleur accuses him of "using, stealing" her myth, "appropriating the spirit" of her legend, and trying to "live out the story" she creates in *Warrender Chase*. Although she believes that it is wrong for Sir Quentin to take her "creation" from her, she in turn believes that he may well be a creation of hers, particularly when he be-

gins to resemble her character Warrender Chase as the story progresses. She takes pride in saying that she could almost "have invented" Sir Quentin and that at times she feels as if she *has* invented him; in fact, this feeling so persists that she begins to wonder if it is Warrender Chase who is the "real man" on whom she has partly based the fictional character of Sir Quentin. From Fleur's point of view, this kind of inversion of life and art is necessary and productive for the artistic process and is not dangerous because it results in a bona fide fiction that acknowledges itself as fiction; Sir Quentin's appropriation of her "myth," however, is dangerous because he refuses to acknowledge the fictiveness of his creation. One irony of this situation is editor Revisson Doe's refusal to publish *Warrender Chase* because it too closely resembles the activities of the Autobiographical Association: Sir Quentin's literal and figurative theft of Fleur's novel almost results in its never becoming a work of art available to the public.

The relationship between life and art has another dimension in *Loitering with Intent*. In this novel, Spark is also concerned with the psychic potential of the artist, the ability of the creative imagination to foresee the future in the process of creating fictions. Just as Fleur remarks that writing a novel or imagining her friends in fictional situations helps her to understand them better, so does the artist often predict the future while constructing a work of art. At the end of the novel, Dottie admits that Fleur had "foreseen it all" in *Warrender Chase*, and the events of *Loitering with Intent* do bear an eerie resemblance to the plot of Fleur's first novel. In her book on Emily Brontë, Spark said that "Poetic experience is . . . such that it may be prophetic." In *Loitering with Intent*, Fleur uses reality as raw material for her novel, while Sir Quentin attempts to use art to tamper with the lives of real people; at another level, however, Fleur's poetic imagination perceives and creates future events.

Loitering with Intent also permits Spark to look back on her life as a novelist and defend many of her fictional techniques. Fleur's philosophy of art is, to a great degree, Spark's philosophy, and Fleur's descriptions and explanations of her craft could easily be addressed by Spark directly to her readers. Like

Spark, Fleur is a believer in economy in art, observing "how little one needs . . . to convey the lot, and how a lot of words . . . can convey so little." Fleur does not believe in authorial statements about the motives of her characters, or in being "completely frank" with the reader; in fact, "complete frankness is not a quality that favours art." She defends herself against the charge of writing novels that are called "exaggerated" by critics and states that her fiction presents "aspects of realism." The novel, she believes, is not a documentary transcription of reality but should always seek to transform its subject. "I'm an artist, not a reporter," she informs her readers.

Fleur also answers the critics who in the past have accused Spark of treating her material in a flippantly detached manner. She says that she treats the story of Warrender Chase with a "light and heartless hand" which is her method when giving a "perfectly serious account of things" because to act differently would be hypocritical: "It seems to me a sort of hypocrisy for a writer to pretend to be undergoing tragic experiences when obviously one is sitting in relative comfort with a pen and paper or before a typewriter." At one point in the novel, Spark even challenges the "quality" of her readers, having her narrator remark that she hopes the readers of her novels are of "good quality" because "I wouldn't like to think of anyone cheap reading my books."

The most significant theme of *Loitering with Intent*, however, is joy: the joy the artist takes in the everyday reality that contributes to the imaginative act, and the euphoria the artist feels in the act of creation. Spark has indeed traveled a great distance from her early suspicions of the fiction-making process and of the novel as form.

THE ONLY PROBLEM

In her three novels after *Loitering with Intent*—*The Only Problem*, *A Far Cry from Kensington*, and *Symposium*—Spark continued to play variations of her characteristic themes. *The Only Problem* centers on the problem of evil: How can a just God "condone the unspeakable sufferings of the world"? Spark's protagonist, Harvey Gotham, an eccentric Canadian millionaire, wrestles with this question in a treatise on the Book of Job. Harvey's study is repeatedly in-terrupted as a consequence of the escapades of his young wife, Effie, who joins a terrorist group, kills a French policeman, and is herself eventually shot and killed by the police during a raid on a terrorist hide-out. The intrusion of these events helps Harvey to appreciate the ultimate inscrutability of the human condition. Here again Spark celebrates the fiction-making process: In contrast to scholars who attempt to rationalize Job's story or abstract the philosophical issues from it, Harvey recognizes the unique power to the story itself. Spark's novel is thus a "commentary" on Job that remains true to the spirit of the original.

A FAR CRY FROM KENSINGTON

A Far Cry from Kensington, like *Loitering with Intent*, draws on Spark's experiences in postwar London. *A Far Cry from Kensington* is a retrospective first-person narrative; from the vantage point of the 1980's, the narrator recalls events that took place in 1954 and 1955. She was then in her late twenties, a war widow who had married at age eighteen a man whom she had met only a month before. Throughout the narrative other characters address her as Mrs. Hawkins (her married name), rather than by her given name, and she is regarded as a reliable confidante—in part, she suggests, because she was then rather fat. As Mrs. Hawkins loses weight, she acquires a first name, Nancy, and gradually becomes Nancy in her own eyes and those of others. Some of her neighbors and office peers worry that she is ill and wasting away, especially the superstitious war refugee Wanda, who believes there is a curse on her. The medical student, William, who lives in the flat next to Nancy, begins to see her as a woman, not merely as a confidant and a doer of good works. Nancy and William begin an affair and ultimately get married.

As Mrs. Hawkins loses weight and gains a personal life of her own, she is less willing to fill the needs of others. She says to the reader,

My advice to any woman who earns the reputation of being capable, is not to demonstrate her ability too much. You give advice; you say, do this, do that, I think I've got you a job, don't worry, leave it to me. All that, and in the end you feel spooky, empty, haunted.

And if you then want to wriggle out of so much responsibility, the people around you are outraged. You have stepped out of your role. It makes them furious.

Spark shows how the transformation of Mrs. Nancy Hawkins evokes resentment from those around her for services not rendered, services others never should have expected.

The backdrop of the story is the London publishing scene, especially its dubious fringe. The narrator's encounters with a variety of publishers and literary hangers-on are deftly sketched; also figuring in the plot are devotees of "radionics," a pseudoscience employing a device similar to Wilhelm Reich's orgone box. In particular, Mrs. Hawkins jousts with a hack writer and an adept of radionics, Hector Bartlett, whom she dubs a *pisseur de copie*. Initially, this conflict might seem to be merely a matter of aesthetics, and Bartlett—with his absurd pretensions and truly awful writing—merely a figure of comedy, yet he is shown to be an agent of evil, responsible for the death of a troubled woman. Unsettled by this mixture of nostalgia and satire, light comedy and metaphysical probing, the reader is never allowed to become comfortable. Evidently, this is Spark's intention.

Symposium

Symposium, focusing on a dinner party in Islington, offers a similarly unsettling mixture, for which the reader is duly prepared by an epigraph from Plato's *Symposium* that suggests the interdependence of comedy and tragedy. *Symposium* features an omniscient narrator who tells of the robbery of two of the dinner guests prior to the beginning of the main story, then injects flashbacks and parallel happenings, as the dinner, which constitutes the body of the story, progresses. Spark's technique owes something to that used by Virginia Woolf in *Mrs. Dalloway* (1925); her juxtaposition of a gala dinner party and a murder that is occurring simultaneously also remind the reader of W. H. Auden's 1939 poem, "Musée des Beaux Arts."

At the beginning of the novel, many characters are introduced and described; some prove to be unimportant and are never mentioned again. Spark seems to be deliberately confusing the reader by obscuring the main focus of the novel, perhaps in imitation of real-life events, in which often the most important elements are initially obscure and only become clear with time. Neither the guests nor those who serve them are what they seem. The butler and his attractive young assistant, an American graduate student who has been employed by several of the guests and is admired for working his way through school, are in a burglary ring that observes houses and files away conversations spoken at society parties about valuable possessions. Among the guests are a newly married young couple; the bride is a fresh, appealing Scottish girl who is so innocent and kind she appears to be too good for this world. In time the reader will come to see this young lady in a different light.

As *Symposium* progresses, the plot grows denser and darker, although an overlay of superficial dinner conversation pervades the novel. There is talk of the "evil eye" (reminiscent of the occult machinations of Hector Bartlett in *A Far Cry from Kensington*). The concept is absurd, and yet as the narrative develops there is evidence that one of the women present at the party genuinely possesses this maleficent power. In this novel, more than ever, Spark manipulates her characters with detachment: The reader is always aware that this is a performance. Yet if Spark's novels are coolly ironic entertainments, they are also oblique parables that explore with obsessive persistence the nature of evil.

Angela Hague,
updated by Isabel Bonnyman Stanley

Other major works

SHORT FICTION: *The Go-Away Bird and Other Stories*, 1958; *Voices at Play*, 1961 (with radio plays); *Collected Stories I*, 1967; *The Stories of Muriel Spark*, 1985; *Open to the Public: New and Collected Stories*, 1997.

PLAY: *Doctors of Philosophy*, pr. 1962.

POETRY: *The Fanfarlo and Other Verse*, 1952; *Collected Poems I*, 1967.

NONFICTION: *Child of Light: A Reassessment of Mary Wollstonecraft Shelley*, 1951 (rev. as *Mary Shelley*, 1987); *Emily Brontë: Her Life and Work*, 1953 (with Derek Stanford); *John Masefield*, 1953; *Curriculum Vitae*, 1992 (autobiography).

CHILDREN'S LITERATURE: *The Very Fine Clock*, 1968.

EDITED TEXTS: *Tribute to Wordsworth*, 1950 (with Derek Stanford); *My Best Mary: The Selected Letters of Mary Shelley*, 1953 (with Stanford); *The Brontë Letters*, 1954 (pb. in U.S. as *The Letters of the Brontës: A Selection*, 1954); *Letters of John Henry Newman*, 1957 (with Stanford).

BIBLIOGRAPHY

Montgomery, Benilde. "Spark and Newman: Jean Brodie Reconsidered." *Twentieth Century Literature* 43 (Spring, 1997): 94-106. An insightful study of the influence of John Henry Newman on the tension between Jean Brodie and Sandy Stranger in *The Prime of Miss Jean Brodie*, arguably Spark's most enduring novel.

Page, Norman. *Muriel Spark*. New York: St. Martin's Press, 1990. Part of the Modern Novelists series, this book contains biographical information, criticism, and interpretation of Spark and her works. Includes bibliography and index.

Randisi, Jennifer Lynn. *On Her Way Rejoicing: The Fiction of Muriel Spark*. Washington, D.C.: Catholic University of America Press, 1991. A good view of Spark's fiction that both updates and complements earlier studies.

Richmond, Velma Bourgeois. *Muriel Spark*. New York: Frederick Ungar, 1984. A valuable resource on Spark that includes commentary on her plays. Chapter 8, "The Darkening Vision," gives sound interpretations of *The Driver's Seat*, *The Public Image*, and *Not to Disturb*.

Walker, Dorothea. *Muriel Spark*. Boston: Twayne, 1988. An informative study on the main themes of Spark's work, with emphasis given to the wit and humor of her characters. The extensive bibliography is particularly helpful.

Whittaker, Ruth. *The Faith and Fiction of Muriel Spark*. New York: St. Martin's Press, 1982. A definitive look at Spark and the relationship between the secular and the divine in her work. This scholarly study, with its extensive bibliography, is a fine source for reference and critical material on Spark.

CHRISTINA STEAD

Born: Rockdale, Australia; July 17, 1902
Died: Sydney, Australia; March 31, 1983

PRINCIPAL LONG FICTION
Seven Poor Men of Sydney, 1934
The Beauties and Furies, 1936
House of All Nations, 1938
The Man Who Loved Children, 1940, 1965
For Love Alone, 1944
Letty Fox: Her Luck, 1946
A Little Tea, A Little Chat, 1948
The People with the Dogs, 1952
Dark Places of the Heart, 1966 (pb. in England as *Cotters' England*, 1966)
The Little Hotel, 1973
Miss Herbert: The Suburban Wife, 1976
I'm Dying Laughing: The Humourist, 1986

(Kimberly Dawson Kurnizki)

OTHER LITERARY FORMS

Christina Stead began her career with a volume of short stories, *The Salzburg Tales* (1934), and she has contributed short stories to both literary and popular magazines. A posthumous collection, *Ocean of Story: The Uncollected Short Stories of Christina Stead*, was published in 1985. Her volume *The Puzzleheaded Girl* (1967) is a collection of four novellas. Her other literary output includes reviews and translations of several novels from the French. She also edited two anthologies of short stories, one with her husband William Blake.

ACHIEVEMENTS

Stead is considered to be in the first rank of Australian novelists; in 1974, she received Australia's Patrick White Award. One of Stead's novels, *The Man Who Loved Children*, received special critical acclaim. Stead resisted critics' attempts to represent her as a feminist writer, but she has received attention from feminist critics for her depiction of women constricted by their social roles.

BIOGRAPHY

Christina Ellen Stead's parents were David George Stead, a naturalist and fisheries economist, and Ellen Butters Stead, who died of a perforated appendix when Christina was two years old. David Stead then married Ada Gibbons, a society woman, and they had six children to whom Stead became big sister. Stead trained at the Sydney Teachers College, where she became a demonstrator in experimental psychology. As a public school teacher, she taught abnormal children and administered psychological tests in the schools. Stead suffered voice strain, however, and she later saw it as a symptom of her being unfit for the work. Like Teresa Hawkins in *For Love Alone*, Stead studied typing and shorthand to embark on a business career. In 1928, she left Sydney, sailing on the *Oronsay* for England. In London and Paris, she worked as a grain clerk and a bank clerk, experiences that became background for her novel about finance, *House of All Nations*. By that time, Stead had met the economist and writer William Blake (born William Blech), whom she married in 1952. Stead settled in the United States from 1937 to 1946, publishing several novels and working for a time as a writer with Metro-Goldwyn-Mayer in Hollywood. At the end of World War II, Stead returned to Europe with Blake, living in various places on the Continent and returning to England when she feared that she was losing her feel for the English language. In 1968, Stead's husband died, and a few years later, in 1974, she returned to live with one of her brothers in Australia. She died in Sydney on March 31, 1983, at the age of eighty.

ANALYSIS

Christina Stead was preeminently a novelist of character. She identified herself as a psychological writer, involved with the drama of the person. Her stories develop out of the dynamics of characters asserting their human energy and vigor and developing their wills. Stead established personality and communicated its energy and vitality through her creation of a distinctive language for each character. This individuating language is explored in the characters' dialogues with one another (Sam Pollit talking his fantastic baby talk to his children), in their interior monologues (Teresa Hawkins, walking miles to and from work, meditating on her need to find a life beyond the surface social conventions), and in letters (the letter to Letty Fox from her former lover, who wants his money back after she has had an abortion). The language establishes the sense of an individual person with obsessions and characteristic blindnesses. One gets to know the quality of the mind through the texture of the language. Christopher Ricks expressed Stead's accomplishment by saying that she re-creates the way people talk to themselves "in the privacy of [their] skulls." His phrase gives the sense of how intimately and deeply the language belongs to the person: It is in the skull and the bone.

In her novel *Letty Fox*, Stead has Letty sum up her adventures to date by saying, "On s'engage et puis on voit." The statement (roughly translated as "one gets involved and then one sees") is an existentialist one that reconciles what critics see as two forces in Stead's fiction: a preoccupation with character that links her to nineteenth century novelists, and an analysis of social, psychological, and economic structures behind individual lives that links Stead to her contemporaries.

The phrase "On s'engage et puis on voit" also sums up Stead's method. First, she immerses the reader in the particular atmosphere of the character's mind and world; only then does she lead the reader to see a significance behind the individual passion. The phrase implies that one cannot see clearly by being disengaged, looking down on the human spectacle with the detachment of an objective physical scientist. Instead, one must become part of that experience, seeing it as a participant, in order to understand its reality. Some of the constant preoccupations of Stead's characters include family, love, marriage, money, and individual power.

THE MAN WHO LOVED CHILDREN

Stead's masterpiece, as critics agree, is the larger-than-life depiction of a family, *The Man Who Loved Children*. Out of print for twenty-five years, the book enjoyed a second life because of a partly laudatory review by the poet Randall Jarrell that was included as an introduction when the novel was reissued in 1965. *The Man Who Loved Children* immerses its readers in the life of the Pollit family, in its swarming, buzzing intimacy. The father, Sam Pollit, is a garrulous idealist who advocates eugenics for the unfit but who fantasizes for himself babies of every race and a harem of wives who would serve his domestic comfort. On the surface, Sam's passions are his humanitarian ideals and his love for his children, but his underlying passion is what Geoffrey Chaucer said women's was—his own way or his own will. Sam is an egotistical child himself; he sees only what he wants to see. His characteristic talk is his overblown, high-sounding rhetoric expressing schemes to right the world and the fanciful, punning baby talk, whining and wheedling, that he uses with the children.

Henny, wife to Sam and stepmother to Louisa, is Sam's compulsive antagonist, worn down with childbearing and the struggle to manage the overextended household. Henny's passion is to survive, to fight dirt and debt and the intermittent sexuality that involves her in continual childbearing. Henny's characteristic talk is insult and denunciation, castigating with

graphic details and metaphors the revolting sights, sounds, smells, tastes, and touches that assault her. Stead emphasizes Henny's eyes in descriptions of the fierce eyeballs in her sockets and her mouth in descriptions of her incessantly drinking tea and mouthing insults.

Stead's way of explaining the unbridgeable gap between the minds and sensibilities of the marriage partners is to say that they have no words in common. Sam's abstraction can never communicate with Henny's particularity. They have no words that they understand mutually, and so for most of the book the two characters communicate with each other only through messages relayed by the children or by terse notes concerning household necessities. In spite of that essential gap, a sixth child is conceived and born to the couple during the novel, and the resources of the household are further strained, finally to the breaking point.

What brings the family to destruction is a complex of causes, many of which are fundamentally economic. The death of David Collyer, Henny's once rich father, is a blow to the family's fortunes. The family loses its home, and Henny's creditors no longer expect that her father will pay her debts. Collyer's death also leaves Sam without a political base in his government job, and Sam's enemies move to oust him. The money crisis is intensified by Sam's refusal to fight for his job. Instead, he retires to their new ramshackle home to do repairs and to play with the children. Sam grandly waits to be exonerated, while Henny struggles to keep the family fed and clothed.

Another cause of the breakup of the family is the birth of Sam and Henny's newest baby. Part of the trouble is economic: The new child means more expenses when Henny had promised her money-conscious eldest son Ernie that there would be no more children. The birth also brings an anonymous letter charging falsely that the child is not Sam's because Sam has been away in Malaya for several months. The letter, filled with spite, probably has been sent by one of Henny's disappointed creditors, but it exacerbates the mutual resentment of the couple and drives them closer and closer to serious violence against each other. (The pregnancy has not only invaded Henny's body and multiplied her worries, but it has also cost her her lover, who deserts her when he hears of the pregnancy. Henny is more than ever in Sam's power.)

A pivotal character in the fierce struggle between the parents is Louisa, oldest daughter of Sam and stepdaughter of Henny. Louisa's emergence from childhood upsets the hierarchy of the household. The man who "loved children" does not love them when they question his authority and threaten his position as "Sam the Bold," leader of the band of merry children. In retaliation, Sam calls Louisa names from "Loogoobrious" to "Bluebeak." In disputing Sam's ability to make it rain (his cosmic power), Louisa and Ernie—who is quick to jump in with what he has learned in school about evaporation—introduce norms from the world outside the family.

By the end of the novel, the family tears itself apart. Sam is unconsciously comparing himself to Christ and seeing Nature as his bride, while he says that women are "cussed" and need to be "run" and that he will send Henny away and keep the children. When Louisa asks for freedom to be sent to her dead mother's relatives in Harper's Ferry, Sam says that he will never let her leave, that she must not get married but must stay and help him with the children and his work. The quarreling between the parents increases until Louisa thinks that they will kill each other. The quarrels become physical battles, and Henny screams to the children to save her from their father. In despair, Ernie makes a dummy out of his clothes and hangs himself in effigy. Sam teases and humiliates the children, insisting that they stay up all night and help him boil down a marlin, an image that is reminiscent of Henny with its staring eye, deep in its socket, and its wound in its vitals.

Louisa sees the two parents as passionate and selfish, inexorably destroying each other and the children, completely absorbed in their "eternal married hate." To save the children, Louisa considers poisoning both parents. Sam provides both the rationale, that the unfit should make room for the fit, and the means, cyanide that he ghoulishly describes as the bringer of death. Louisa succeeds in getting the grains of cyanide into only one large cup of tea when Henny

notices what she has done and drinks it, exonerating Louisa and saying "damn you all." Even with Henny dead and Louisa's confession of her plan and its outcome, Sam refuses to believe her and refuses to let her go. Louisa's only escape is to run away, thus seizing her freedom.

The power of the novel derives partly from the archetypal nature of the conflicts—between parents and children for independence; between man and woman, each for his or her own truth and identity; and between parents for their children, their objects of greatest value. The power also results from the particularity of the characterization, the metaphors that Stead employs to communicate the nature of each family member, and the astounding sense of individual language mirroring opposed sensibilities.

LETTY FOX and FOR LOVE ALONE

The epigraph to another Stead novel, *Letty Fox: Her Luck*, says that one can get experience only through foolishness and blunders. The method that Letty follows in her adventures puts her in the stream of picaresque heroes; the novel's subtitle, "her luck," makes more sense with reference to the notion of a submission to experience, to one's fate, than it does with reference to the common meaning of "luck" as "good fortune." Letty's "luck" is that she survives and learns something about the ways of the world.

Stead once said that in *For Love Alone*, the novel that preceded *Letty Fox*, she wrote about a young girl of no social background, who tries to learn about love, and that readers did not understand the story. Thus, in *Letty Fox*, she gave American readers a story that they could understand: the story of a modern American girl searching for love and trying to obtain status through marriage.

In both novels, the social structure tells young women that they have no valid identity except through the men they marry. In *For Love Alone*, Teresa Hawkins, like her friends, fears becoming an old maid. Even though Letty Fox has had a series of lovers and a series of responsible, interesting jobs, she does not feel validated without the security of marriage.

This firmly held conventional belief is belied by Letty's own family situation. Her beloved father Solander has a mistress, Persia, with whom he has lived faithfully for many years. The family women wonder how Persia can hold Solander without a paper and without a child. On the other hand, Mathilde, Letty's mother, has the marriage title but little else. She has three daughters—Letty, Jacky, and the much younger Andrea, conceived in a late reconciliation attempt—but Persia has Solander.

Like the picaresque hero, on her own, Letty learns the ways of the world. She truly loves Luke Adams, who tantalizes her with pretended concern for her youth and innocence and fans her fascination with him. She lives for a summer with a married man and has an abortion for which she must repay him. Originally confused by Lucy Headlong's interest in her, Letty refuses a lesbian affair with her. Letty sees a range of choices in the lives of the women around her: from her sister Jacky, in love with an elderly scientist, to her younger sister Andrea, sharing the early maternal experience of her friend.

Letty wants the security of marriage, but the men she knows do not want to make serious commitments. In *For Love Alone*, Teresa remarks on the short season for the husband hunt, with no time for work or extended study. In the marriage market for the comparatively long season of seven years, Letty does not catch a husband, even when her vicious cousin Edwige does.

Except in the matter of marriage, Letty trusts her own responses and takes credit for her own integrity. When her lover Cornelius is about to leave her for his mistress in Europe and his wife, Letty faces him with the truth of relationships from a woman's point of view. She tells Cornelius that she has ambition and looks. She works for men, and she is their friend. She suffers without crying for help and takes responsibility for her life. Yet she sees men run after worthless, shiftless women and honor the formality of marriage when there is no substance to their relationships with them. All these facts might be just part of the injustice of the world, but Cornelius and many other men Letty knows also expect that she should be their lover and yet admit that there is no love involved but only a relationship of mutual convenience. Like the British poet William Blake, Letty sees prostitution as an invention of men who have tried to depersonalize the

most intimate relationship between people. Letty affirms the reality of the sexual experience in its intimacy and its bonding.

With all her clear sight and all her independence, however, Letty does not feel safe and validated until she is married to her longtime friend Bill Van Week. Ironically, Letty marries Bill when he has been disinherited by his millionaire father, so the security Letty attains is not financial. In summing up her life to date, Letty does not claim total honesty, but—like a typical picaresque hero—she does claim grit. She says that with her marriage, her journey has begun. Here Stead limits the awareness of her character. At the end of the novel, Letty says that marriage gives her not social position but self-respect. In this retreat, Letty joins the social mainstream but denies her individual past experience. Self-respect is not an award; it is not issued like a diploma or a license. Letty, who may stand up very well to the practical problems of real life with Bill, is by no means liberated, and her awareness is finally limited.

DARK PLACES OF THE HEART

Published in Britain as *Cotters' England*, *Dark Places of the Heart* is an exploration of the influence of Nellie Cotter Cook on the people around her—her family, friends, and acquaintances. A central concern is the relationship between Nellie and her brother Tom, a jealous relationship with which Nellie seems obsessed. Like Michael and Catherine Baguenault, the brother-sister pair in *Seven Poor Men of Sydney*, Nellie and Tom seem too close to each other, too intimately attuned to each other's sensibilities. In their battles, Nellie calls Tom a man out of a mirror, who weaves women into his life and then eats their hearts away. Tom calls Nellie a spider, who tries to suspend a whole human being on a spindly thread of sympathy. Tom also criticizes Nellie's bent for soul-saving, saying that it gets people into trouble.

The motif of hunger and starvation runs through the novel. When Tom brings a chicken to the family home in Bridgehead, no one in the family knows how to cook it. When George goes away to Italy, he writes that Nellie should buy cookery books, a suggestion that she scorns. Seemingly exhibiting a strange kind of hunger, Nellie craves followers who will make her destiny. Nellie and Tom's battles often center on Tom's relationships with women, which precipitate a tug-of-war between Nellie and Tom for the love of the woman in question. Many allusions and incidents in the novel suggest that Nellie's interest is lesbian. Nellie begins her luring of these women by demanding their friendship and, ultimately, by forcing them to prove their loyalty through death. Such demands literalize the existentialist definition of love, that the lover puts the beloved beyond the value of the world and his or her life, making that beloved the standard of value, the absolute. The demand is messianic, and in this novel the cost is the suicide of Caroline Wooler, after her witnessing what seems to be a lesbian orgy. Caroline climbs a building under construction and jumps to her death.

Nellie views Caroline's death as a personal triumph. At the end of the novel, with her husband dead, Nellie goes with the window-washer Walter to a temple, a "Nabob villa," where she explores "problems of the unknowable." Like Sam Pollit, who at his worst compared himself to Christ, Nellie Cook is drawn finally to outright mysticism, an interest that combines, in Nellie's case at least, a fascination with death, a craving for a high destiny, and an uncontrollable urge to manipulate other people. It seems that for Stead, the "dark places of the heart" make people dissatisfied with their humanity.

Kate Begnal

OTHER MAJOR WORKS

SHORT FICTION: *The Salzburg Tales*, 1934; *The Puzzleheaded Girl*, 1967; *Ocean of Story: The Uncollected Short Stories of Christina Stead*, 1985.

TRANSLATIONS: *Colour of Asia*, 1955 (of Fernand Gignon); *The Candid Killer*, 1956 (of Jean Giltène); *In Balloon and Bathyscaphe*, 1956 (of August Piccard).

EDITED TEXTS: *Modern Women in Love*, 1945 (with William Blake); *Great Stories of the South Sea Islands*, 1956.

BIBLIOGRAPHY

Brydon, Diana. *Christina Stead*. London: Macmillan, 1987. While admitting that she has presented Stead's work from an essentially feminist perspective, Brydon qualifies this stance by examining Stead's fiction as about both sexes in varied social relationships. Provides a thorough examination of all the novels and includes a chapter entitled "Stead and Her Critics," which throws interesting light on Stead's critical reception. Also contains an extensive secondary bibliography.

Gardiner, Judith Kegan. *Rhys, Stead, Lessing, and the Politics of Empathy*. Bloomington: Indiana University Press, 1986. Recommended for advanced students. Gardiner explores feminist themes in the context of psychoanalytic language and of contemporary literary theory, which some readers will find difficult to comprehend.

Jarrell, Randall. "An Unread Book." Introduction to *The Man Who Loved Children*, by Christina Stead. New York: Holt, Rinehart and Winston, 1965. This first serious and thorough critical examination of Stead's work incorporates many of the themes on which subsequent critics enlarge. Jarrell, a distinguished American poet, praises the novel for its record of a family, its inventive style, and its account of the artist's development: He predicts that the novel, which first appeared in 1940, will be widely read and appreciated by future audiences in this new edition.

Lidoff, Joan. *Christina Stead*. New York: Frederick Ungar, 1982. The earliest full reading of Stead's fiction from a feminist perspective, this book concentrates on *The Man Who Loved Children* and *For Love Alone*. Examines what Lidoff calls Stead's "domestic gothic" and how this technique reveals the long suppressed rage of women. Also examines Stead's characters as wanderers, more fearful of a patriarchal home than of homelessness. Includes an interview, a chronology, and an extensive secondary bibliography.

Ross, Robert L. "Christina Stead's Encounter with 'The True Reader': The Origin and Outgrowth of Randall Jarrell's Introduction to *The Man Who Loved Children*." In *Perspectives on Australia*, edited by Dave Oliphant. Austin: University of Texas Press, 1989. Relies entirely on fifty years of correspondence between Stead and Stanley

Burnshaw, her New York editor and friend. Outlines Stead's literary career, focusing on the republication of *The Man Who Loved Children* in 1965, with an introduction by the American poet Randall Jarrell. Shows, through her letters, the great delight Stead took in Jarrell's introduction, which she considered the impetus for her novel's rediscovery. Also tells of her reaction to sudden fame after years of literary oblivion and recounts the unhappy period following her husband's death.

Rowley, Hazel. *Christina Stead: A Biography.* New York: H. Holt, 1994. A good study of Stead's life and times. Includes bibliographical references and an index.

Sheridan, Susan. *Christina Stead.* Bloomington: Indiana University Press, 1988. While conceding that Stead disclaimed feminism and always insisted that she was not a feminist writer, Sheridan creates a dialogue between Stead's major novels and contemporary feminist literary theory. Intends not to argue that Stead's work is feminist, but to uncover feminist themes in it. The study rejects other critical approaches that place the novels in the naturalistic or international tradition.

Williams, Chris. *Christina Stead: A Life of Letters.* Melbourne: McPhee Gribble, 1989. This admirable and first full-length biography of Stead depends in large part on unpublished materials, including Stead's letters and early drafts of stories, and on interviews with friends and family members. Provides a detailed account of her childhood in Australia and stresses the importance of men in Stead's life, including her father, who was the model for the main character in *The Man Who Loved Children*, and her husband, William Blake, on whom she depended for stability. Concludes with a record of her final years, after Blake's death, during which she battled against loneliness and alcoholism and was unable to write.

Yelin, Louise. *From the Margins of Empire: Christina Stead, Doris Lessing, Nadine Gordimer.* Ithaca, N.Y.: Cornell University Press, 1998. Examines the political and social views of the three authors and the themes of imperialism and decolonization.

WALLACE STEGNER

Born: Lake Mills, Iowa; February 18, 1909
Died: Santa Fe, New Mexico; April 13, 1993

PRINCIPAL LONG FICTION
Remembering Laughter, 1937
The Potter's House, 1938
On a Darkling Plain, 1940
Fire and Ice, 1941
The Big Rock Candy Mountain, 1943
Second Growth, 1947
The Preacher and the Slave, 1950
A Shooting Star, 1961
All the Little Live Things, 1967
Angle of Repose, 1971
The Spectator Bird, 1976
Recapitulation, 1979
Joe Hill, 1980
Crossing to Safety, 1987

OTHER LITERARY FORMS

Wallace Stegner also published two collections of short fiction, *The Women on the Wall* (1950) and *The City of the Living and Other Stories* (1956); two biographies, *Beyond the Hundredth Meridian: John Wesley Powell and the Second Opening of the West* (1954) and *The Uneasy Chair: A Biography of Bernard De Voto* (1974); a collection of critical essays, *The Writer in America* (1951); a historical monograph, *The Gathering of Zion: The Story of the Mormon Trail* (1964); and two volumes of personal essays on the Western experience. *Wolf Willow: A History, a Story, and a Memory of the Last Plains Frontier* (1962) and *The Sound of Mountain Water* (1969). Stegner also published a number of edited works, both nonfiction and fiction.

ACHIEVEMENTS

Stegner would have three distinct audiences after the start of his career: the popular magazine audience, readers interested in modern American literature, and a regional audience interested in the culture and history of the American West. From the 1930's,

(Library of Congress)

Arts and Letters, and he was awarded fellowships by Phi Beta Kappa, the Huntington Library, The Center for Advanced Studies in the Behavioral Sciences, and the Guggenheim, Rockefeller, and Wintergreen Foundations. In 1937, he won the Little, Brown Novelette Prize for *Remembering Laughter*. He also won the O. Henry Memorial Award for short stories in 1942, 1948, and 1950, and in 1971 he won the Pulitzer Prize for Fiction for his *Angle of Repose*. Other awards for his work include the Houghton Mifflin Life-in-America Award in 1945 and the Commonwealth Club Gold Medal in 1968. In 1981, he became the first recipient of the Robert Kirsch Award for Life Achievement in the *Los Angeles Times* Book Awards.

As a master of narrative technique and a respected literary craftsman, Stegner had the opportunity to influence many young writers associated with the Stanford University Creative Writing Program, where he taught from 1945 to 1971, including Eugene Burdick, one of the authors of *The Ugly American* (1958), Ken Kesey, and Thomas McGuane. His own theory of literature is rather traditional and appears in his only extended piece of criticism, *The Writer in America*. The creative process, he believed, is basically the imposition of form upon personal experience. The committed writer must discipline himself to the difficult work of creation, choosing significant images from the insignificant and selecting significant actions for his characters. The writer must change the disorderliness of memory into symmetry without violating his readers' sense of what is true to life.

he published seventy-two short stories, with fifty of them appearing in such magazines as *Harper's, Mademoiselle, Collier's, Cosmopolitan, Esquire, Redbook, The Atlantic Monthly, The Inter-Mountain Review,* and the *Virginia Quarterly*. Bernard De Voto, Van Wyck Brooks, and Sinclair Lewis recognized his talent early, and De Voto was instrumental in encouraging Stegner to continue writing. Stegner enjoyed a solid critical reputation as a regional American writer concerned largely with the problems and themes of the western American experience.

He also won numerous honors throughout his career. He was elected to the American Academy of Arts and Sciences and the National Academy of

BIOGRAPHY

Wallace Earle Stegner was born on February 18, 1909, in Lake Mills, Iowa, the second son of George and Hilda Paulson Stegner. He was descended from Norwegian farmers on his mother's side and unknown ancestors on his father's side. His father was a drifter and a resourceful gambler—a searcher for the main chance, the big bonanza. In Stegner's early years, the family moved often, following his father's dream of striking it rich, from Grand Forks, North Dakota, to Bellingham, Washington, to Redmond, Oregon, to East End, Saskatchewan, where they lived from 1914 to 1921. East End left him with memories of people and landscapes that played an important role in *The Big Rock Candy Mountain*. The family moved in 1921 to Salt Lake City, Utah, where Stegner attended high school and began college. Here, Stegner went through the pains of adolescence and, although not himself a Mormon, developed a strong attachment to the land and a sympathy for Mormon culture and values, which are reflected in his later books such as *Mormon Country* (1942), *The Gathering of Zion*, and *Recapitulation*.

From 1925 to 1930, Stegner attended the University of Utah, where he balanced his interest in girls and his studies with a job selling rugs and linoleum in the family business of a close friend. By a fortunate chance, he studied freshman English with Vardis Fisher, then a budding novelist, and Fisher helped stimulate Stegner's growing interest in creative writing. In 1930, he entered the graduate program at the University of Iowa, completing his M.A. in 1932 and completing his Ph.D. in 1935 with a dissertation on the Utah naturalist Clarence Dutton, entitled "Clarence Edward Dutton: Geologist and Man of Letters," later revised and published as *Clarence Edward Dutton: An Appraisal* by the University of Utah in 1936. This work fed his interest in the history of the American West and the life of the explorer John Wesley Powell, the subject of his *Beyond the Hundredth Meridian*. Teaching English and creative writing occupied him for several years, beginning with a one-year stint at tiny Augustana College in Illinois in 1934. Next, he went to the University of Utah until 1937, moving from there to teach freshman English at the University of Wisconsin for two years. He also taught at the Bread Loaf School of English in Vermont for several summers and enjoyed the friendship of Rob-

ert Frost, Bernard De Voto, and Theodore Morrison. In 1940, he accepted a part-time position at Harvard University in the English writing program. There, during the Depression, he was involved in literary debates between the literary left, led by F. O. Matthiessen, and the conservative De Voto.

In 1945, Stegner accepted a professorship in creative writing at Stanford University, where he remained for twenty-six years until his retirement in 1971. The Stanford years were his most productive; he produced a total of thirteen books in this period. In 1950, he made an around-the-world lecture tour, researched his family's past in Saskatchewan and Norway, and spent much of the year as writer-in-residence at the American Academy in Rome. He was also an active environmentalist long before ecology became fashionable. During the Kennedy administration, he served as assistant to the secretary of the interior (1961) and as a member of the National Parks Advisory Board (1962).

ANALYSIS

Wallace Stegner was a regional writer in the best sense. His settings, his characters, and his plots derive from the Western experience, but his primary concern is with the meaning of that experience. Geographically, Stegner's region runs from Minnesota and Grand Forks, North Dakota, through Utah and northern Colorado. It is the country where Stegner lived and experienced his youth. Scenes from this region appear frequently in his novels. East End, Saskatchewan, the place of his early boyhood, appears as Whitemud, Saskatchewan, in *The Big Rock Candy Mountain*, along with Grand Forks and Lake Mills, Iowa, his birthplace. Salt Lake City figures prominently in *Recapitulation* and *The Preacher and the Slave*, the story of Joe Hill, a union martyr. *Wolf Willow*, furthermore, is historical fiction, a kind of history of East End, Saskatchewan, where he spent his early boyhood, and *On a Darkling Plain* is the story of a much decorated and seriously wounded veteran of World War I who withdraws from society in an isolated shack on the plains outside of East End.

In a much larger sense, Stegner is concerned with

the spiritual West—the West as an idea or a consciousness—and with the significance of the Western values and traditions. He is also concerned with the basic American cultural conflict between East and West and with the importance of frontier values in American history. Bo Mason, modeled after Stegner's father, the abusive head of the Mason family in *The Big Rock Candy Mountain*, is an atavism, a character who may have been at home in the early frontier, who searches for the elusive pot of gold—the main chance of the Western myth. Never content with domestic life or with stability, Bo Mason, like George Stegner, moves his family from town to town always looking for an easy fortune. As a man of mixed qualities—fierce pride, resourcefulness, self-reliance, and a short, violent temper—he is ill at ease in the postfrontier West, always chafing at the stability of community and family ties. He continually pursues the old Western myth of isolated individualism that preceded twentieth century domestication of the region. He might have made a good mountain man. Stegner stresses his impact on his family and community and shows the reader the basic tragedy of this frontier type trapped in a patterned world without easy bonanzas.

In *Angle of Repose*, Stegner explores the conflict between the values of self-reliance, impermanence, and Western optimism and the Eastern sense of culture, stability, and tradition. In a way, this is the basic conflict between Ralph Waldo Emerson's party of hope (the West) and the party of the past (the East). He also explores the idea of community as a concept alien to the Western myth. Indeed, community as the close-knit cooperation between individuals is shown in Stegner's work as the thing that ended the frontier. In *The Big Rock Candy Mountain* and in *Recapitulation*, there is a longing for community and a pervasive feeling that the Mason family is always outside the culture in which it exists, particularly in Utah, where Mormon culture is portrayed as innocent, solid, stable, and, as a result, attractive. Mormon life is characterized by the absence of frontier individualism and by a belief in permanence and group experience, an anomaly in the Western experience.

The Big Rock Candy Mountain

A third major concern throughout Stegner's work is his own identity and the meaning of Western identity. Bruce Mason in *The Big Rock Candy Mountain* is much concerned with his relationship as an adolescent to the Utah culture and its sense of community.

The Big Rock Candy Mountain, Stegner's fifth novel, is an obviously autobiographical account of his childhood and adolescence. A family saga, the novel follows the history of the rootless Mason family as it follows the dreams of Bo Mason, a thinly disguised version of Stegner's father, as he leads them to Grand Forks, North Dakota, to the lumber camps of Washington, then back to Iowa and up to Whitemud, Saskatchewan, and finally to Salt Lake City and Reno. Family identity problems are played out against the backdrop of an increasingly civilized and domesticated West against which the self-reliant and short-tempered character of Bo Mason stands out in stark relief. His qualities, which might have had virtues in the early settlement of the West, create family tensions and trauma that cause Bruce Mason (Stegner) to develop a hatred for his father only partially tempered by a grudging respect. Bo Mason relentlessly pursues the American Dream and the Western myth of easy success rooted in the early frontier: He endlessly pursues the Big Rock Candy Mountain.

Throughout this odyssey, the family longs for stability and community, for a place to develop roots. Even in Salt Lake City, where Bruce spends his adolescence, Bo keeps the family changing houses to hide his bootlegging business during the Prohibition period. His activities in the midst of puritanical Mormon culture only highlight the contrast between the Masons and the dominant community. Even in his later years, Bo pursues his dream in Reno by operating a gambling house.

Stegner vividly illustrates how this rootless wandering affects family members. Else, Bo's wife, representing the feminine, domesticating impulse, is a saintly character—long-suffering, gentle, and protective of her two sons. She longs for a home with permanence but never finds it. Her initial good nature and mild optimism eventually give way to pessimism as resettlements continue. Three of the family members die: Else is destroyed by cancer; Chet, the other son, who is defeated by both marriage and career, dies young of pneumonia; and Bo, with all his dreams shattered and involved with a cheap whore after Else's death, shoots himself. Only Bruce is left to make sense of his family's experiences, and he attempts to understand his place in the family saga as he strives to generalize his family's history. In the final philosophical and meditative chapters, Stegner tries to link Bruce (and therefore himself) to history, to some sense of continuity and tradition. His family history, with its crudeness and tensions, is made to represent the history of the frontier West with its similar tensions and rough edges. Bruce, who long sought solace and identity in books, excels in school and finally follows the civilized but ironic path of going to law school at the University of Minnesota. He has, finally, reached a higher level of culture than his family ever attained. *The Big Rock Candy Mountain* has achieved a reputation as a classic of American regionalism, while it also deals with broader national themes and myths.

ANGLE OF REPOSE

Angle of Repose, published in 1971 and awarded the Pulitzer Prize for Fiction, is regarded by many critics as Stegner's most finely crafted novel. The metaphoric title is a mining and geological term designating the slope at which rocks cease to fall, the angle of rest. Stegner uses it to apply to the last thirty years of the marriage of Susan Burling and Oliver Ward, two opposite personalities, after their often chaotic early married years. This ambitious work, covering four generations, is a fictionalized biography of the turn-of-the-century writer and illustrator Mary Hallock Foote (1847-1930) and her marriage to Arthur De Wint Foote, an idealistic pioneer and self-educated mining engineer.

Lyman Ward, the narrator, was reared by his grandparents Susan Burling Ward and Oliver Ward, fictionalized versions of the Footes, and is a retired history professor from Berkeley who was crippled in middle age by a progressively arthritic condition. He has been transformed by the disease into a grotesque creature who loses first his leg and then his wife Ellen, who runs off with the surgeon who amputated

Lyman's leg. Bitter and disillusioned by his wife's behavior and his son Rodman's radical idealism and contempt for the past, he retires to Grass Valley, California, to write his grandparents' biography. Here, he is assisted by Shelly Hawkes, a Berkeley dropout who shares Rodman's attitude toward history.

As he reads through his grandparents' correspondence, he simultaneously recounts the development of their marriage and discovers the dynamics of their personalities. Susan Ward, cultured, educated in the East, and artistically talented, marries Oliver Ward, an idealistic mining engineer, her second choice for a husband. Without having resolved her disappointment at his lack of culture and appreciation for the arts, she marries him and begins two decades of following him through the West as he looks for professional and financial success in the unstable mining industry. The years in New Almaden, California, Leadville, Colorado, Michoacán, Mexico, and southern Idaho increasingly wear Susan down, despite brief interludes of stability and the frequent company of other Eastern scientists and engineers during her Western exile.

In Boise Canyon, Idaho, as Oliver's grand irrigation project falls apart, Susan falls into infidelity with Frank Sargent, Oliver's colorful assistant, and steals away to the countryside under the pretext of taking five-year-old Agnes Ward for a walk. Soon, Agnes's body is found floating in a nearby canal, and the day after her funeral, Frank Sargent commits suicide. Suspecting the worst, Oliver leaves his wife for two years until persuaded to return. For the remaining fifty years of their marriage, Oliver treats her with a kind silence and lack of physical affection, never truly forgiving her. Lyman learns that his grandparents' angle of repose was not the real thing, not a time of harmony but a cold truce full of human weakness. His naïve image of his grandparents based on childhood memories is undercut as he comes to understand them in a more sophisticated way. He learns to respect their strength and complexity.

Lyman's discoveries are all the more poignant because of the similarities between his grandparents' experience and his own relationship with an unfaithful wife who has broken trust, and who, it is implied, will seek a reconciliation. As in *The Big Rock Candy Mountain*, the two main characters symbolize two conflicting impulses in the settlement of the West—Oliver, the dreamer and idealist, pursuing his vision of success in a world with few amenities, and Susan, the finely cultured Easterner, yearning for stability and society. Lyman discovers links between his family's past and present and encounters universals of history such as suffering and infidelity which are more poignant to him because he discovers them in his own family history. Finally, the novel suggests that frontier values and the civilizing impulses need their own angle of repose. In essence, American experience had not yet reached its angle of rest; frontier and domestic values lie instead in a kind of uneasy truce.

RECAPITULATION

A continuation of the family saga played out in *The Big Rock Candy Mountain*, *Recapitulation*, published in 1979, is the moving drama of Bruce Mason's return to Salt Lake City to face his past. Toward the end of a successful career as a diplomat in the United States Foreign Service, Mason returns to the scene of his turbulent adolescence and the death of his family to attend his maiden aunt's funeral. Upon his arrival at the funeral home, the attendant presents him with a message to call Joe Mulder, his best friend in high school and in college at the University of Utah. Bruce was virtually a member of Joe's family for three years during the time when his father's bootlegging business threatened to jeopardize his social life.

Bruce remembers the 1920's and his adolescence before the stock market crash. Trying to find himself, he slowly remembers the time when he was an outsider in Mormon country, a time when he found many of the values that sustained him after the death of his family. Well-liked in high school by his teachers, Bruce was also picked on by the bigger boys and the less able students and acutely embarrassed by the family's house, which doubled as a speakeasy. His first major romance, with Nola, a Mormon country girl who was half American Indian, led to his first sexual encounter. Bruce was infatuated with her but knew her intellectual limits—that ideas put her to sleep and art bored her. Throughout the narrative, he recounts the disintegration of his family during his adolescence.

Stegner stresses Bruce's close relationship with Joe Mulder, but Bruce is emotionally incapable of meeting Joe because he hates being treated as "The Ambassador," a visiting dignitary—a title that would only exaggerate the changes and losses of the past forty-five years. In a sense, he finds that he cannot go home again. He would have nothing in common with Joe except memories of adolescent love affairs and youthful myths. Their past could never be altered or renewed.

A second major theme in *Recapitulation* is the need to belong to some larger community. The Mormon sense of community, whatever its intellectual failings, is viewed nostalgically. Bruce envies the close-knit families of his friends. Nola's family, for example, seems like a tribe, a culture unto itself full of unspoken values and understandings. His decision to attend law school in Minnesota irrevocably removes him from Nola, Utah, and his adolescence, and ultimately from his chance to belong. When he returns to Utah, he is in the later stages of a successful but lonely adult life. His first job out of law school was in Saudi Arabia—a place without available women. He finally becomes a Middle Eastern specialist and a permanent bachelor.

Stegner ends the novel with Bruce, lonely, nostalgic, and emotionally incomplete, unable to make contact with Joe Mulder and with his past in a satisfying way. Even though the act of thinking through his past has served him therapeutically, he will continue as a diplomat, making formal contacts with people, living in the surface world of protocol, unable to connect emotionally with people. As the last of his family, he is a solitary figure, a man of deep feelings which he is unable to express. He is, finally, a man who has partially tamed the frontier restlessness and anger of his father and risen above his family's self-destructive tendencies. Still, Bruce carries on the family's feeling of rootlessness, in a more formal, acceptable way. In the Foreign Service, he never develops roots and is shifted from one diplomatic post to another. In a more formal sense than his father, Bruce is still a drifter. Stegner ends the novel fittingly with Bruce Mason being called back to the diplomatic service as United States Representative to an important OPEC meeting in Caracas, Venezuela, reluctantly pulled away from his efforts to understand his past.

CROSSING TO SAFETY

Crossing to Safety introduces a new set of characters but also is about coming to terms with the past. Larry and Sally Morgan are a young couple who have moved to Madison, Wisconsin, because Larry has been given a teaching post for a year at the university there. Almost magically, they meet a personable young couple like themselves, Sid and Charity Lang, who also turn out to be very generous. In these Depression days, security is the most sought-after item, and all the young academics vie furiously for tenure. Yet, the Langs (though engaged as furiously in the contest as any) bestow on the Morgans a friendship rare in this backbiting atmosphere—wholehearted, sincere, and giving. Envy and jealousy are not part of their emotional makeup, though they do have their problems. Charity comes from an academic household (her father is a professor), and she wants the same for her family, including a professorship for her husband, who, however, really wants only to write poetry.

Stegner's portrayal of this lifelong friendship is neither idealistic nor blind. He reveals the human sides to his characters, keeping this paragon of *amicitia* from being falsely perfect. The ups and downs of their lives are relayed through flashback: Larry and Sally have come to visit the Langs because Charity is dying from cancer. Larry and Sally's life has not been without tragedy either: The summer after bearing their first child, Sally contracts polio and is permanently disabled.

Ultimately, Larry becomes a successful writer, while Sid never becomes successful either as an academic or as a poet. Belying her name—for she is a strong personality at best, harsh and unyielding at worst—Charity never really forgives Sid for his failure. Yet, Stegner concentrates on the love these people have for one another through thick and thin, creating a compelling story without resorting to tricks of

subterfuge or violence to sustain the reader's interest. Stegner's great strength lies in knowing people; he knows their quirks and foibles so well that they come alive on the page without being demeaned or caricatured. In addition, his feeling for mood and setting are twin talents that infuse his writing with life, placing Stegner firmly on the short list of great American novelists.

Richard H. Dillman

OTHER MAJOR WORKS

SHORT FICTION: *The Women on the Wall*, 1950; *The City of the Living and Other Stories*, 1956; *Collected Stories of Wallace Stegner*, 1990.

NONFICTION: *Mormon Country*, 1942; *One Nation*, 1945 (with the editors of *Look*); *Look at America: The Central Northwest*, 1947; *The Writer in America*, 1951; *Beyond the Hundredth Meridian: John Wesley Powell and the Second Opening of the West*, 1954; *Wolf Willow: A History, a Story, and a Memory of the Last Plains Frontier*, 1962; *The Gathering of Zion: The Story of the Mormon Trail*, 1964; *The Sound of Mountain Water*, 1969; *The Uneasy Chair: A Biography of Bernard De Voto*, 1974; *Ansel Adams: Images 1923-1974*, 1974; *One Way to Spell Man*, 1982; *The American West as Living Space*, 1987; *On the Teaching of Creative Writing: Responses to a Series of Questions*, 1988 (Edward Connery Lathem, editor); *Where the Bluebird Sings to the Lemonade Springs: Living and Writing in the West*, 1992.

EDITED TEXTS: *An Exposition Workshop*, 1939; *Readings for Citizens at War*, 1941; *Stanford Short Stories, 1946*, 1947 (with Richard Scowcroft); *The Writer's Art: A Collection of Short Stories*, 1950 (with Scowcroft and Boris Ilyin); *This Is Dinosaur: The Echo Park and Its Magic Rivers*, 1955; *The Exploration of the Colorado River of the West*, 1957; *Great American Short Stories*, 1957 (with Mary Stegner); *Selected American Prose: The Realistic Movement*, 1958; *Report on the Lands of the Arid Region of the United States*, 1962; *Modern Composition*, 1964 (4 volumes); *The American Novel: From Cooper to Faulkner*, 1965; *Twenty Years of Stanford Short Stories*, 1966; *The Letters of Bernard De Voto*, 1975.

BIBLIOGRAPHY

Arthur, Anthony, ed. *Critical Essays on Wallace Stegner*. Boston: G. K. Hall, 1982. Two sections divided into reviews and articles and essays. Includes treatments of several Stegner novels, especially *The Big Rock Candy Mountain* and *Angle of Repose*, and of his use of Western history. Includes an interview with Stegner and an introductory essay. No bibliography.

Benson, Jackson J. *Wallace Stegner: His Life and Work*. New York: Viking, 1996. An excellent study of Stegner's Westerns, along with biographical information. Includes an index.

Burrows, Russell. "Wallace Stegner's Version of Pastoral." *Western American Literature* 25 (May, 1990): 15-25. In this article, Burrows discusses the importance of the topic of ecology in Stegner's fiction. The article includes some discussion of *Crossing to Safety*, but a more in-depth review (by Jackson J. Benson) of that book follows Burrows's article. Includes reference notes and a bibliography.

Lipson, Eden Ross. "Back to Work After Bora-Bora." *The New York Times Book Review* 92 (September 20, 1987): 14. This interview with Stegner includes his reflections on writing *Crossing to Safety* as well as a discussion of that novel.

Meine, Curt, ed. *Wallace Stegner and the Continental Vision: Essays on Literature, History, and Landscape*. Washington, D.C.: Island Press, 1997. This is a collection of essays presented at a May, 1996, symposium in Madison, Wisconsin.

Mosher, Howard Frank. "The Mastery of Wallace Stegner." *The Washington Post*, October 4, 1987. This review of *Crossing to Safety* includes some biographical information on Stegner as well as an in-depth discussion of the novel.

Robinson, Forrest Glen, and Margaret G. Robinson. *Wallace Stegner*. Boston: Twayne, 1977. Part of Twayne's United States Authors series, this volume provides a brief chronology of personal and professional events in Stegner's life and some general biographical information. After a discussion of his work, there are primary and secondary bibliographies and an index.

GERTRUDE STEIN

Born: Allegheny, Pennsylvania; February 3, 1874
Died: Neuilly-sur-Seine, France; July 27, 1946

PRINCIPAL LONG FICTION

Three Lives, 1909
The Making of Americans, 1925
Lucy Church Amiably, 1930
A Long Gay Book, 1932
Ida, a Novel, 1941
Brewsie and Willie, 1946
Blood on the Dining-Room Floor, 1948
Things as They Are, 1950 (later as *Quod Erat Demonstrandum*)
Mrs. Reynolds and Five Earlier Novelettes, 1931-1942, 1952
A Novel of Thank You, 1958

OTHER LITERARY FORMS

Any attempt to separate Gertrude Stein's novels from her other kinds of writing must be highly arbitrary. Stein thought the novel to be a failed literary form in the twentieth century, claiming that no real novels had been written after Marcel Proust, even including her own novelistic efforts in this assessment. For this and other reasons, it might be claimed that few, if any, of Stein's works are novels in any traditional sense. In fact, very few of Stein's more than six hundred titles in more than forty books can be adequately classified into any traditional literary forms. Her philosophy of composition was so idiosyncratic, her prose style so seemingly nonrational, that her writing bears little resemblance to whatever genre it purports to represent. Depending on one's definition of the novel, Stein wrote anywhere between six and twelve novels, ranging in length from less than one hundred to 925 pages. The problem is that none of Stein's "novels" has a plot in any conventional sense, that few have conventionally developed and sustained characters, and that several seem almost exclusively autobiographical, more diaries and daybooks than anything else. It is not any easier to categorize her other pieces of writing, most of which are radically *sui generis*. If references to literary forms are made very loosely, Stein's work can be divided into novels, autobiographies, portraits, poems, lectures, operas, plays, and explanations. Other than her novels, her best-known works are *The Autobiography of Alice B. Toklas* (1933); *Tender Buttons* (1914); *Four Saints in Three Acts* (1934); *Lectures in America* (1935); *Everybody's Autobiography* (1937); and *Portraits and Prayers*, 1934.

ACHIEVEMENTS

Whether towering or crouching, Stein is ubiquitous in contemporary literature. A child of the nineteenth century who staunchly adhered to many of its values halfway through the twentieth, she nevertheless dedicated her creative life to the destruction of nineteenth century concepts of artistic order and purpose. In her own words, she set out to do nothing less than to kill a century, to lay the old ways of literary convention to rest. She later boasted that "the most serious thinking about the na-

(AP/Wide World Photos)

ture of literature in the twentieth century has been done by a woman," and her claim has great merit. During the course of her career, Stein finally managed to convince almost everyone that there was indeed some point, if not profundity, in her aggressively enigmatic style. The ridicule and parody that frustrated so much of her early work had turned to grudging tolerance or outright lionizing by 1934, when Stein made her triumphant American lecture tour; for the last fifteen or so years of her life, she was published even if her editor had not the vaguest idea of what she was doing (as Bennett Cerf later admitted he had not). On the most concrete level, Stein's distinctive prose style is remarkably significant even when its philosophical dimensions are ignored. William Gass has observed, Stein "did more

with sentences, and understood them better, than any writer ever has."

More important was Stein's influence on other leaders in the development of modernism. As a student of William James and as a friend of Alfred North Whitehead and Pablo Picasso, Stein lived at the center of the philosophical and artistic revolutions of the twentieth century. She was the natural emblem for modernism, and in her person, career, and legend, many of its salient issues converged. In the light of more recent developments in the novel and in literary theory, it has also been argued that Stein was the first postmodernist, the first writer to claim openly that the instance of language is itself as important as the reality to which it refers. Among major writers, Ernest Hemingway was most obviously influenced by his association with her, but her genius was freely acknowledged by F. Scott Fitzgerald, Sherwood Anderson, and Thornton Wilder. William Saroyan explained her influence most directly when he asserted that no American writer could keep from coming under it, a sentiment reluctantly echoed by Edmund Wilson in *Axel's Castle* (1931), even before Stein's great popular success in the mid-1930's.

BIOGRAPHY

Gertrude Stein was born on February 3, 1874, in Allegheny, Pennsylvania, but she was seven before her family settled into permanent residence in Oakland, California, the city she was later to describe as having "no there there." Her birth itself was contingent on the deaths of two of her five brothers and sisters: her parents had decided to have only five children, and only after two children had died in infancy were Gertrude and her older brother, Leo, conceived. Identity was to become one of the central preoccupations of her writing career, and the tenuous nature of her own birth greatly influenced that concern.

Stein's early years were comfortably bourgeois and uneventful. Her father, a vice president of the Union Street Municipal Railway System in San Francisco, was authoritarian, moody, and aggressive, but vacillating, and he may have helped foster her sense of independence, but he undoubtedly left her annoyed by him in particular and by fatherhood in general. Her mother barely figured in her life at all: A pale, withdrawn, ineffectual woman, she left most of the rearing of her children to governesses. By the time Stein was seventeen, both parents had died and she had grown even closer to her immediate older brother, Leo. In 1893, she entered Harvard Annex (renamed Radcliffe College the following year), thus rejoining Leo, who was a student at Harvard. There, Stein studied with William James and Hugo Munsterberg and became involved in research in psychology. Together with the great influence exerted on her thinking by William James, this early work in psychology was to provide her with both a subject and a style that would continue in many forms throughout her career. She was awarded her A.B. by Harvard in 1898, almost a year after she had entered medical school at The Johns Hopkins University. Her interest in medicine rapidly waned, and she left Johns Hopkins in 1901, failing four courses in her final semester.

After leaving medical school, Stein spent two years moving back and forth between Europe and America. During that time, she was involved in an agonizing love affair with another young woman student at Johns Hopkins, May Bookstaver. The affair was painfully complicated, first by Stein's naïveté, then by the presence of a more sophisticated rival for May's love, Mabel Haynes. The resulting lover's triangle led Stein, in an effort to understand May, to begin formulating the theories of personality that dominated her early writing. The frustration and eventual despair of this lesbian relationship profoundly influenced Stein's view of the psychology of personality and of love. Most directly, Stein's troubled affair with May Bookstaver provided her with many, if not most, of the concerns of three of her books, *Quod Erat Demonstrandum*, *The Making of Americans*, and *Three Lives*, the first two of which she began while living in New York in the winter of 1903.

After a brief stay in New York, she lived with Leo, first in Bloomsbury in London, and then, beginning in 1903, in Paris at 27 rue de Fleurus, the address she was to make so well known to the world. In Paris, Gertrude and Leo became more and more interested in painting, buying works by new artists such as Henri Matisse and Picasso. Leo's preference was for works by Matisse, while Gertrude favored the more experimental works of Picasso, marking the beginning of a distancing process that would lead to Leo's complete separation from his sister in 1913. Leo was bright and opinionated, and fancied himself by far the greater creative talent of the two, but his brilliance and energy never produced any creative or significant critical work, and he grew to resent both his sister's independent thinking and her emerging ability to write. Later in his life, he would dismiss Gertrude as "dumb," her writing as "nonsense."

In 1907, Stein met another young American woman in Paris, Alice Toklas, and Alice began to displace Leo as the most important personal influence in Gertrude's life. Alice learned to type so she could transcribe Stein's handwritten manuscripts, beginning with portions of *The Making of Americans* in 1908. In 1909, Alice moved in with Gertrude and Leo at 27 rue de Fleurus, and by 1913, Alice had replaced Leo as Gertrude's companion and as the manager of her household. Stein later referred to her relationship with Alice as a "marriage," and few, if any, personal relationships have ever influenced a literary career so profoundly. Apart from providing Stein with the persona for her best-known work, *The Autobiography of Alice B. Toklas*, Alice typed, criticized, and valiantly worked to publish all of Stein's work for the rest of her career and for the twenty years that Alice lived after Stein's death. While it is doubtful that Alice was directly responsible for any of Stein's writing, her influence on its composition and on Stein's life was tremendous.

Gertrude and Alice spent the first months of World War I in England as houseguests of Alfred North Whitehead, returning to Paris briefly in 1914, then spending more than a year in Spain. They joined the war effort in 1917 when Stein ordered a Ford motor van from America for use as a supply truck for the American Fund for French Wounded, an acquisition which began Stein's lifelong fascination with automobiles, particularly with Fords. She and Alice drove this van, named "Auntie," until the war ended, work for which she was later awarded the Medaille de la Reconnaissance Française.

Modernism had burst on the American consciousness when the Armory Show opened in New York in 1913, and this show, which had confronted Americans with the first cubist paintings, also led to the association in the public mind of Stein's writing with this shockingly new art, particularly since Stein's first periodical publications had been "Matisse" and "Picasso" in *Camera Work*, the year before. Stein's mammoth, 925-page novel, *The Making of Americans*, was published in 1925, and in 1926, she lectured at Oxford and Cambridge, attempting to explain her idiosyncratic writing style. Her "landscape" novel, *Lucy Church Amiably*, appeared in 1930, but it was in 1933, with the publication of the best-selling *The Autobiography of Alice B. Toklas*, that Stein first captured the public's interest. She became front page news the fol-

lowing year when her opera *Four Saints in Three Acts* was first performed and when she embarked on a nationwide lecture tour, later described in *Everybody's Autobiography* and *Lectures in America*.

Stein and Toklas spent World War II in Bilignin and then in Culoz, France. Although Stein and Toklas were both Jewish, they were never persecuted by occupying forces, owing in part to the influence of Bernard Fay, an early admirer of Stein's work who directed the Bibliothèque Nationale for the Vichy regime. When, after the war, Fay was sentenced to life imprisonment for his Vichy activities, Stein was one of his few defenders. That her art collection survived Nazi occupation virtually intact can only have been through Fay's intercession. During the war, Stein finished another novel, *Mrs. Reynolds* (unpublished), and *Wars I Have Seen* (1945), an autobiographical work. Her novel *Brewsie and Willie*, a series of conversations among American soldiers, was published in 1946.

Stein died following an operation for cancer in the American Hospital in Neuilly-sur-Seine, France, on July 27, 1946. While Alice Toklas's account of Stein's last words may be apocryphal, it certainly is in keeping with the spirit of her life. As Alice later reconstructed their last conversation, Stein had asked her "What is the answer?" Then, when Alice remained silent, Stein added, "In that case, what is the question?"

ANALYSIS

While Gertrude Stein's persistence finally earned her access to readers, it could never guarantee her readers who would or could take her strange writing seriously. As a result, more confusing and contradictory information surrounds her career than that of any other twentieth century writer of comparable reputation. Usually responding in any of four basic ways, readers and critics alike seemed to view her as (1) a literary charlatan of the P. T. Barnum ilk, interested in publicity or money rather than in art; (2) something of a naïve child-woman incapable of comprehending the world around her; (3) a fiery-eyed literary revolutionary, den mother of the avant-garde; or (4) an ageless repository of wisdom and genius. Ultimately, the reader's acceptance or rejection of these various categories will greatly determine his or her response to Stein's writing, which forces the reader to make as many cognitive choices as does that of any major writer.

Stein's many explanations of her writing further complicate its interpretation: Even her "explanations" frustrate as much as they reveal, explicitly setting her up in cognitive competition with her reader, a competition suggested by her favorite cryptogram, which works out to read: "I understand you undertake to overthrow my undertaking." Stein proposes a rhetoric not of misunderstanding, but of antiunderstanding; that is, her "explanations" usually argue precisely against the desirability of explaining.

As Stein bluntly put the matter, "understanding is a very dull occupation." "Understanding" has a special denotation for Stein, sometimes meaning as little as "paying attention to" or "reading." "To understand a thing means to be in contact with that thing," she proclaimed. Central to her mistrust of explanations and interpretations was Stein's often anguished belief that her thoughts could never really be matched to anyone else's. She was deeply troubled by this doubt as she wrote *The Making of Americans*, referring in that work to "the complete realization that no one can believe as you do about anything" as "complete disillusionment in living." Starting from this assumption that no one can ever really understand what someone else says or writes because of the inherent ambiguity of language, Stein not only decided to force her readers to confront that ambiguity but also claimed it as a primary virtue of her writing. She announced triumphantly that "if you have vitality enough of knowing enough of what you mean, somebody and sometimes a great many will have to realize that you know what you mean and so they will agree that you mean what you know, which is as near as anybody can come to understanding any one." Stein's focus here is on relationships or process rather than on product—on the act of trying to become one with, rather than focusing on the ultimate result of that act.

Stein's thinking about understanding manifests itself in a number of distinctive ways in her writing, as do her theories of perception and of human psychology. Moreover, during the nearly fifty years of her writing career, her style developed in many related but perceptibly different stages, such as her "cubist" or her "cinema" phases. As a result, no single analysis can do more than describe the primary concerns and features of one of her stylistic periods. There are, however, three central concerns that underlie and at least partially account for all the stages in the development of her style. These concerns are with the value of individual words, with repetition as the basic rhythm of existence, and with the related concept of "movement" in writing. Her articulations of these central concerns all run counter to her reader's expectations about the purpose and function of language and of literature. Her writing surprised her readers in much the same way that her penchant for playing only the black keys on a piano surprised and frustrated all but the most patient of her listeners.

One of Stein's goals was to return full meaning, value, and particularity to the words she used. "I took individual words and thought about them until I got their weight and volume complete and put them next to another word," she explained of seemingly nonsense phrases such as "toasted Susie is my ice cream," or "mouse and mountain and a quiver, a quaint statue and pain in an exterior and silence more silence louder shows salmon a mischief intender." This sort of paratactic juxtaposition of seemingly unrelated words rarely occurs in Stein's novels but represents a problem for her reader in many other ways in her writing. She frequently chose to stress or focus on a part or aspect of the object of her description that the reader normally does not consider. The "things" Stein saw and wrote of were not the "things" with which readers are familiar: Where another observer might see a coin balanced on its edge, Stein might choose either of the descriptive extremes of seeing it literally as a thin rectangle, or figuratively as the essence of money. Characteristically, her most opaque parataxis refers to essences or processes rather than to objects or static concepts.

A related quirk in Stein's style results from her intellectual or emotional attachment to particular words and phrases at certain stages of her career. As she admitted in *The Making of Americans*,

> To be using a new word in my writing is to me a very difficult thing. . . . Using a word I have not yet been using in my writing is to me a very difficult and a peculiar feeling. Sometimes I am using a new one, sometimes I feel a new meaning in an old one, sometimes I like one I am very fond of that one that has many meanings many ways of being used to make different meanings to everyone.

Stein said she had learned from Paul Cézanne that everything in a painting was related to everything else and that each part of the painting was of equal importance—a blade of grass as important to the composition of the painting as a tree. She attempted to apply these two principles to the composition of her sentences, taking special delight in using normally "overlooked" words, arguing that articles, prepositions, and conjunctions—the transitive elements in grammar—are just as important and more interesting than substantives such as nouns and verbs. Her reassessment both of the value of words and of the conventions of description resulted in what Michael J. Hoffman in *The Development of Abstractionism in the Writings of Gertrude Stein* (1965) has described as Stein's "abstractionism." It also resulted in her including in her writing totally unexpected information in perplexingly paratactic word-strings.

A second constant in Stein's style is the pronounced repetition of words, phrases, and sentences, with no change or with only incremental progressions of sounds or associations. Works such as *The Making of Americans* and *Three Lives* contain long passages in which each sentence is a light variation on some core phrase, with great repetition of words even within a single sentence. Stein termed this phenomenon "insistence" rather than repetition, citing her former teacher, William James, as her philosophical authority. James's argument in his *The Principles of Psychology* (1890) that one must think of the identical recurrence of a fact in a fresh manner remarkably resembles Stein's contention that "in expressing anything there can be no repetition because the essence of that expression is insistence, and if you insist you must each time use emphasis and if you use emphasis it is not possible while anybody is alive that they should use exactly the same emphasis." Repetition or insistence is perhaps the central aspect of what has been called Stein's "cinema style," based on her claim that in writing *The Making of Americans* she was "doing what the cinema was doing." She added that her writing in that book was "like a cinema picture made up of succession and each moment having its own emphasis that is its own difference and so there was the moving and the existence of each moment as it was in me."

Stein's discussion of "what the cinema was doing" appears in her *Lectures in America* and also suggests the third basic concern of her writing: movement. By "movement," she referred not to the movement of a message to its conclusion or the movement of a plot or narrative, but to "the essence of its going" of her prose, a timeless continuous present in the never-ending motion of consciousness. Stein also credits Cézanne with discovering this concern, "a feeling of movement inside the painting not a painting of a thing moving but the thing painted having inside it the existence of moving." She seemed to understand Cézanne's achievement in terms of William James's model of consciousness as an ever-flowing stream of thought. Accordingly, she used her writing not to record a scene or object or idea (products of thought), but to try to capture the sense of the process of perceiving such things. Stein's subject is almost always really two things at once: whatever attracted her attention—caught her eye, entered her ear, or crossed her mind—and the mobile nature of reality, particularly as it is perceived by human consciousness. In fact, Stein was usually more concerned with the nature of her own perception and with that of her reader than she was with its objects. She wanted to escape the conventions of linguistic representation, arbitrary arrangements similar to the "rules" for perspective in painting, and to present "something moving as moving is not as moving should be." As confusing as her resulting efforts sometimes are, her concern with motion makes sense as an attempt to mimic or evoke the nature of consciousness as she understood it.

From James at Harvard and possibly from Henri Bergson in Paris, Stein had learned that the best model for human consciousness was one that stressed the processual, ever-flowing nature of experience.

She added to this belief her assumption that the essence of any subject could only be perceived and should only be represented through its motion, echoing Bergson's claim that "reality is mobility." Unfortunately, this belief led her writing into one of its many paradoxes: She could only attempt to represent the continuous stream of experience through the segmented, inherently sequential nature of language. Streams flow; words do not. Instead, they proceed one by one, like the cars pulled by a train engine. While James would certainly have objected to Stein's sequential cinema model as an approximation of the stream of consciousness, her motion-obsessed writing probably suggests the flow of consciousness as well as does any literary style.

QUOD ERAT DEMONSTRANDUM

Written in 1903, but put out of her mind until 1932 and not published until 1950, Stein's *Quod Erat Demonstrandum* (first published as *Things as They Are*) is her most conventional novel. Its sentences employ no unexpected syntax or diction, its central concerns are clear, its time scheme is linear, and its characters are conventionally drawn. If anything, Stein's style in this first novel is markedly old-fashioned, including highly formal sentences that frequently sport balanced serial constructions. "Adele vehemently and with much picturesque vividness explained her views and theories of manners, people and things, in all of which she was steadily opposed by Helen who differed fundamentally in all her convictions, aspirations and illusions." While its conventional style (crudely reminiscent of that of Henry James) is completely unlike that of any other Stein novel, *Quod Erat Demonstrandum* is a very significant work for the consideration of Stein's career. Apart from convincingly refuting the suspicion of some of her detractors that Stein was incapable of rational writing, this book establishes her preoccupation with psychological typecasting and vaguely hints at the importance of repetition in her thinking and writing.

Quod Erat Demonstrandum charts the growth, turbulence, and eventual dissolution of the relationships among three young women: Adele, the book's central consciousness, an obviously autobiographical figure; Helen Thomas, the object of Adele's love; and Mabel Neathe, Adele's calculating rival for Helen's affection. These three characters closely parallel Stein, May Bookstaver, and Mabel Haynes, and the story of their relationship is the story of Stein's first, agonizing love affair. While the novel follows these three young women for three years, not much happens. Most of the book relates conversations and correspondence between Adele and Helen, showing Adele's torment first from her not yet understood desire for Helen, then from her growing realization that she is losing Helen to Mabel. Of principal interest to the reader is Stein's self-characterization in her portrayal of Adele.

THREE LIVES

Three Lives is easily Stein's best-known and most respected piece of fiction. Technically three novellas, this work is unified by its three subjects, by its central concern with the nature of consciousness, and by its attempt to blend colloquial idioms with Stein's emerging style, here based largely on her understanding of Cézanne's principles of composition, particularly that "one thing was as important as another thing." "The Good Anna," "Melanctha," and "The Gentle Lena" are the three sections of this work. Anna and Lena are poor German immigrants who patiently work as servants in Bridgepoint, Baltimore; Melanctha is a young black woman who discovers sexuality and love, then turns from a frustrating relationship with a sincere young black doctor to a dissipative affair with a gambler. Because all three women are essentially victimized by their surroundings and die at the end of their stories, this work is deterministic in the naturalist tradition, but *Three Lives* marks the transition from naturalism to modernism as Stein departs from nineteenth century literary conventions. She abandons conventional syntax to try to follow the movement of a consciousness rather than of events, and she develops a new narrative style only partially tied to linear chronology. The result is an interior narrative of consciousness in which Stein's prose style serves as the primary carrier of knowledge. Through the rhythms of her characters' speech and the rhythms of her narration, Stein gives her reader a sense of the basic rhythms of consciousness for these three women—what Stein would elsewhere refer to as their "bottom natures."

Possibly Stein's most widely celebrated piece of writing, "Melanctha" recasts the anguishing love triangle of *Quod Erat Demonstrandum* into the conflict between Melanctha and Jeff Campbell, whose inherently conflicting "bottom natures" or personality types parallel the conflict between Helen and Adele in the earlier work. "Melanctha" has been praised by Richard Wright, among others, as one of the first realistic and sympathetic renderings of black life by a white American author, but Melanctha's race is actually incidental to Stein's central concerns with finding a style to express the rhythms of personality and the frustrating cycles of love.

THE MAKING OF AMERICANS

Although it was not published until 1925, Stein's *The Making of Americans* occupied her as early as 1903 and was in fact begun before *Quod Erat Demonstrandum* and *Three Lives*. This mammoth novel began as a description of the creation of Americans from a representative immigrant family: "The old people in a new world, the new people made out of the old, that is the story that I mean to tell, for that is what really is and what I really know." Stein's projected family chronicle soon lost its original focus, becoming first a history of everyone, then a study of character types rather than of characters. Leon Katz, who has worked with this book more than has anyone else, calls it "a massive description of the psychological landscape of human being in its totality." Although the book ostensibly continues to follow events in the lives of two central families, the Herslands and the Dehnings, its real concern is almost always both larger and smaller, ranging from Stein's questions about her own life and identity to questions about the various personality types of all of humanity. As Richard Bridgman suggests, this is "an improvised work of no identifiable genre in which the creator learned by doing," one "full of momentary wonders and botched long-range schemes, lyrical outbursts and anguished confessions." Accordingly, Bridgman concludes that *The Making of Americans* is best thought of "not as a fictional narrative nor a philosophic tract, but as a drama of self-education."

In a way, the book chronicles the "making" of Gertrude Stein, presenting a phenomenology of her mind as it works its way through personal problems toward the distinctive "cinema style."

Underlying a great part of the writing in this book is Stein's belief that human personality consists of variations on a few basic "bottom natures" or kinds of identity that can be perceived through a character's repeated actions. "There are then many things every one has in them that come out of them in the repeating everything living have always in them, repeating with a little changing just enough to make of each one an individual being, to make of each repeating an individual thing that gives to such a one a feeling of themselves inside them." There are two basic personality types, "dependent independent" and "independent dependent," polarities identified in part by the way the person fights: the first kind by resisting, the second by attacking. Concerns with character-typing dominate the book's first two sections, "The Dehnings and the Herslands" and "Martha Hersland" (the character most closely modeled on Stein's own life), while the third section, "Alfred and Julia Hersland," contains mostly digressions about contemporary matters in Stein's life. The fourth section, "David Hersland," becomes a meditation on the nature of aging and death ("He was dead when he was at the beginning of being in middle living."), and the final section, "History of a Family's Progress," is—even for Stein—an incredibly abstract and repetitive series of reflections on the concerns that had given rise to the novel. This final section contains no names, referring only to "some," "any," "every," or "very many."

Stein later described her efforts in this book as an attempt "to do what the cinema was doing"; that is, to give a sense of motion and life through a series of highly repetitive statements, each statement only an incremental change from the preceding one, like frames in a strip of film. One of the main effects of this technique is to freeze all action into a "continuous present." Not only do Stein's sentences exist in overlapping clusters, depending more for their meaning on their relationships to one another than on individual semantic content, but also her verbs in *The Making of Americans* are almost exclusively present participles, suspending all action in the present progressive tense. "The business of Art," Stein later explained, "is to live in the actual present, that is the complete actual present." As a result, while *The Making of Americans* does ostensibly present a history of four generations of the Hersland family, there exists in it little or no sense of the passage of time. Instead, the book presents a sense of "existence suspended in time," a self-contained world existing quite independently of the "real world," a basic modernist goal that has also become one of the hallmarks of postmodernism.

A 416-page version, abridged by Stein, was published in 1934 but has not been accepted by Stein scholars as adequately representative of the longer work. For all its difficulty, *The Making of Americans* is one of modernism's seminal works and an invaluable key to Stein's literary career.

LUCY CHURCH AMIABLY

Described by its author as "a novel of Romantic beauty and nature and which Looks Like an Engraving," *Lucy Church Amiably* shares many characteristics with Stein's best-known play, *Four Saints in Three Acts*, and with the several works she called "geographies." The book was Stein's response to the area around Belley, France, where she and Alice spent many summers. Stein's title plays on the existence of the church in a nearby village, Lucey. As Richard Bridgman has observed, Lucy Church refers throughout the book to both that church and to a woman who resembles a relaxed Gertrude Stein. As Bridgman also notes, "the book is essentially a long, lyric diary," with Stein including in it information about the geography, residents, and flora of the surrounding area. This information appears, however, in Stein's distinctive paratactic style:

> In this story there is to be not only white black tea colour and vestiges of their bankruptcy but also well wishing and outlined and melodious and with a will and much of it to be sure with their only arrangement certainly for this for the time of which when by the way what is the difference between fixed.

This novel can perhaps best be thought of as a pastoral and elegiac meditation on the nature of place.

THE WORLD IS ROUND and IDA, A NOVEL

In 1939, Stein's novel for children, *The World Is Round*, was published, with illustrations by Clement Hurd. The book focuses on a series of events in the lives of a nine-year-old girl, Rose, and her cousin, Willie. These events are more enigmatic than dramatic but seem to move both children through several kinds of initiations. Identity worries both Rose and Willie ("Would she have been Rose if her name had not been Rose and would she have been Rose if she had been a twin"), as does the contrast between the uncertainties of their lives and the advertised verities of existence, emblemized by the "roundness" of the world. Comprising both the children's meditations and their songs, the book is, for Stein, relatively conventional. Although its sentences are highly repetitive and rhythmic, they present a compelling view of a child's consciousness, and Stein scholars agree on the importance and success of this little-known work.

Originally intended as "a novel about publicity," *Ida, a Novel* expands many of the concerns of *The World Is Round*, extending them from Ida's birth well into her adult life. As is true of all of Stein's novels, there is not anything resembling a plot, and many of the things that happen in Ida's life are surrealistically dreamlike. "Funny things" keep happening to the young Ida, and while the nature of these things is never explained, most of them seem to involve men. Frequently, these men have nothing at all to do with her, or they only glance at her, but Ida sees them as vaguely threatening, and insofar as her novel can be said to have a central concern, it is with certain problems of sexuality. Although Stein later described Ida as having been based on the Duchess of Windsor, this connection is only superficial, and Ida is better seen as another in the long line of Stein's autobiographical characters.

BREWSIE AND WILLIE

Stein's novel *Brewsie and Willie* redirected her revolutionary spirit from literary to social and economic problems. In this series of conversations among American soldiers and nurses awaiting redeployment from France to the United States after World War II, Stein pessimistically considered the future of her native land. Stein had long held that the United States was "the oldest country in the world" because it had been the first to enter the twentieth century. By 1945, she felt that America had grown "old like a man of fifty," and that its tired, middle-aged economic system had become stale and repressive. In *Brewsie and Willie*, she describes that economic system as "industrialism," portraying a stultifying cycle of depleting raw materials for overproduction and installment buying. This cycle also locked the worker into "job thinking," making of him a kind of automaton, tied to his job, locked into debt, and, worst of all, robbed of freedom of thought. Through conversations involving Brewsie (Stein's spokesman), Willie, and several other soldiers and nurses, Stein portrays an apprehensive generation of young Americans who see the potential dangers of postwar America but who fear they do not "have the guts to make a noise" about them. These conversations cover a wide range of subjects, from a comparison of French and American baby carriages to the tentative suggestion that the American system must be torn down before "pioneering" will again be possible.

Stein makes little or no effort in this book to differentiate the voices of her speakers, but she does rather amazingly blend her own voice with those of the soldiers. The result is a style that is characteristically Stein's but that also has the rhythm and the randomness of overheard conversation. Often overlooked, *Brewsie and Willie* is one of the most remarkable documents in Stein's writing career.

However idiosyncratic Stein's writing may seem, it must be remembered that a very strong case can be made for its substantial philosophical underpinnings. To her way of thinking, language could refuse few things to Stein, and the limitations of language were exactly what she refused to accept. She bent the language to the very uses that process philosophers such as James and Bergson and Whitehead feared it could not be put. Her stubborn emphasis on the individual word—particularly on transitive elements—her insistent use of repetition, and her ever-present preoccupation with the essential motion of words were all part of Stein's monumental struggle with a language she felt was not accurately used to reflect the way people perceive reality or the motion of reality it-

self. In a narrow but profound sense, she is the most serious realist in literary history. Stein was not a philosopher—her magpie eclecticism, associational flights, and thundering *ex cathedra* pronouncements ill-suited her for systematic explanation—but in her writing a wealth of philosophy appears.

Brooks Landon

OTHER MAJOR WORKS

PLAYS: *Geography and Plays*, pb. 1922; *Operas and Plays*, pb. 1932; *Four Saints in Three Acts*, pr., pb. 1934; *In Savoy: Or, Yes Is for a Very Young Man (A Play of the Resistance in France)*, pr., pb. 1946; *The Mother of Us All*, pr. 1947; *Last Operas and Plays*, pb. 1949; *In a Garden: An Opera in One Act*, pb. 1951; *Lucretia Borgia*, pb. 1968; *Selected Operas and Plays*, pb. 1970.

POETRY: *Tender Buttons: Objects, Food, Rooms*, 1914; *Two (Hitherto Unpublished) Poems*, 1948; *Bee Time Vine and Other Pieces: 1913-1927*, 1953; *Stanzas in Meditation and Other Poems: 1929-1933*, 1956.

NONFICTION: *The Autobiography of Alice B. Toklas*, 1933; *Matisse, Picasso, and Gertrude Stein, with Two Shorter Stories*, 1933; *Portraits and Prayers*, 1934; *Lectures in America*, 1935; *Narration: Four Lectures*, 1935; *The Geographical History of America*, 1936; *Everybody's Autobiography*, 1937; *Picasso*, 1938; *What Are Masterpieces*, 1940; *Wars I Have Seen*, 1945; *Reflections on the Atomic Bomb*, 1973; *How Writing Is Written*, 1974.

CHILDREN'S LITERATURE: *The World Is Round*, 1939.

BIBLIOGRAPHY

Bowers, Jane Palatini. *Gertrude Stein*. New York: St. Martin's Press, 1993. A succinct, feminist-oriented introduction to Stein, with separate chapters on *The Making of Americans* and *Tender Buttons* and on her plays. Includes notes and bibliography.

Bridgman, Richard. *Gertrude Stein in Pieces*. New York: Oxford University Press, 1970. Still an indispensable source, this was the first book to look critically at the whole Stein canon and to analyze its genesis. Bridgman remains immune from the many statements Stein made to explain her own work and arrives at honest and independent—if not always completely acceptable—judgments.

Doane, Janice L. *Silence and Narrative: The Early Novels of Gertrude Stein*. Westport, Conn.: Greenwood Press, 1986. Strong on the development of Stein's unique narrative voice with its focus on the speech of working-class women. Demonstrates Stein's sensitivity to nuance.

Hoffman, Michael J., ed. *Critical Essays on Gertrude Stein*. Boston: G. K. Hall, 1986. The most current collection of writing on Stein, representing varied points of view. A good starting point for beginners.

_____. *Gertrude Stein*. Boston: Twayne, 1976. A useful book with strong analyses of Stein's writing and interesting sidelights on its production and its relationship to the avant-garde movements of the period. Especially strong on cubist influences.

Kellner, Bruce, ed. *A Gertrude Stein Companion*. New York: Greenwood Press, 1988. Kellner supplies a helpful introduction on how to read Stein. The volume includes a study of Stein and literary tradition, her manuscripts, and her various styles, and biographical sketches of her friends and enemies. Provides an annotated bibliography of criticism.

Knapp, Bettina K. *Gertrude Stein*. New York: Ungar, 1990. A short introductory study, with useful chapters on her verbal portraits, *Tender Buttons*, her plays, and her use of fact and fiction. Includes chronology, notes, and bibliography.

Mellow, James R. *Charmed Circle: Gertrude Stein and Company*. New York: Praeger, 1974. A deeply felt and pleasing illustrated book by one of Stein's scholarly admirers. Contains interesting, detailed discussions of her writing, her family background and relationships, her association with artists and writers in Paris over fifty years, and her enduring relationship with Alice B. Toklas.

Neuman, Shirley, and Ira B. Nadel, eds. *Gertrude Stein and the Making of Literature*. Boston: Northeastern University Press, 1988. Offers some of the most current feminist readings of Stein, clarifying the innovations that originated with Stein and had a sweeping influence on later writers including Ernest Hemingway, Ford Madox Ford, and Sherwood Anderson.

Steiner, Wendy. *Exact Resemblance to Exact Resemblance*. New Haven, Conn.: Yale University Press, 1978. Perhaps the best book available for linking Stein's modernism to her interest in and study of psychology and philosophy.

JOHN STEINBECK

Born: Salinas, California; February 27, 1902
Died: New York, New York; December 20, 1968

PRINCIPAL LONG FICTION
Cup of Gold, 1929
The Pastures of Heaven, 1932
To a God Unknown, 1933
Tortilla Flat, 1935
In Dubious Battle, 1936
The Red Pony, 1937, 1938, 1945
Of Mice and Men, 1937
The Grapes of Wrath, 1939
The Moon Is Down, 1942
Cannery Row, 1945
The Pearl, 1945 (serial), 1947 (book)
The Wayward Bus, 1947
Burning Bright, 1950
East of Eden, 1952
Sweet Thursday, 1954
The Short Reign of Pippen IV, 1957
The Winter of Our Discontent, 1961

OTHER LITERARY FORMS
In addition to his seventeen novels, John Steinbeck published a story collection, *The Long Valley* (1938), and a few other uncollected or separately printed stories. His modern English translations of Sir Thomas Malory's Arthurian tales were published posthumously in 1976. Three plays he adapted from

his novels were published as well as performed on Broadway: *Of Mice and Men* (1937), *The Moon Is Down* (1942), and *Burning Bright* (1951). Three of the six film treatments or screenplays he wrote—*The Forgotten Village* (1941), *A Medal for Benny* (1945), and *Viva Zapata!* (1952)—have been published; the other three also were produced as films—*Lifeboat* (1944), *The Pearl* (1945), and *The Red Pony* (1949), the latter two adapted from his own novels. His nonfiction was voluminous, and much of it remains uncollected. The more important nonfiction books include *Sea of Cortez* (1941, with Edward F. Ricketts), *Bombs Away* (1942), *A Russian Journal* (1948, with Robert Capa), *Once There Was a War* (1958), *Travels with Charley: In Search of America* (1962), *America and Americans* (1966), *Journal of a Novel* (1969), and *Steinbeck: A Life in Letters* (1975; Elaine Steinbeck and Robert Wallsten, editors).

(AP/Wide World Photos)

ACHIEVEMENTS

From the publication of his first bestseller, *Tortilla Flat*, in 1935, Steinbeck was a popular and widely respected American writer. His three earlier novels were virtually ignored, but the five books of fiction published between 1935 and 1939 made him the most important literary spokesman for the Depression decade. *In Dubious Battle, The Red Pony,* and *Of Mice and Men* established him as a serious writer, and his master work, *The Grapes of Wrath*, confirmed him as a major talent. During these years, his popular and critical success rivaled that of any of his contemporaries.

Although his immense popularity, public recognition, and the impressive sales of his works persisted throughout his career, Steinbeck's critical success waned after *The Grapes of Wrath*, reaching a nadir at his death in 1968, despite his Nobel Prize in Literature in 1962. During World War II, his development as a novelist faltered for many reasons, and Steinbeck

never recovered his artistic momentum. Even *East of Eden*, the work he thought his masterpiece, proved a critical failure although a popular success. Since his death, Steinbeck remains widely read, both in America and abroad, while his critical reputation has enjoyed a modest revival. Undoubtedly the appreciation of his considerable talents will continue to develop, as few writers have better celebrated the American Dream or traced the dark lineaments of the American nightmare.

BIOGRAPHY

John Ernst Steinbeck was born on February 27, 1902, in Salinas, California. The time and place of his birth are important because Steinbeck matured as an artist in his early thirties during the darkest days of the

Depression, and his most important fictions are set in his beloved Salinas Valley. In one sense, Steinbeck's location in time and place may have made him a particularly American artist. Born just after the closing of the frontier, Steinbeck grew up with a frustrated modern America and witnessed the most notable failure of the American Dream in the Depression. He was a writer who inherited the great tradition of the American Renaissance of the nineteenth century and who was forced to reshape it in terms of the historical and literary imperatives of twentieth century modernism. Steinbeck's family background evidenced this strongly American identity. His paternal grandfather, John Adolph Steinbeck, emigrated from Germany, settling in California after serving in the Civil War. His mother's father, Samuel Hamilton, sailed around Cape Horn from northern Ireland, finally immigrating to the Salinas Valley. John Ernst Steinbeck and Olive Hamilton were the first-generation descendants of sturdy, successful, and Americanized immigrant farm families. They met and married in 1890, settling in Salinas, where the father was prominent in local business and government, and the mother stayed home to rear their four children—three daughters and a son, the third child named for his father. The Steinbecks were refined, intelligent, and ambitious people who lived a quiet middle-class life in the small agricultural service town of Salinas.

Steinbeck seems to have enjoyed a happy childhood, and in fact he often asserted that he did. His father made enough money to indulge him in a small way, even to buy him a red pony. His mother encouraged him to read and to write, providing him with the classics of English and American literature. At school, he proved a popular and successful student and was elected president of his senior class.

After graduation from Salinas High School in 1919, Steinbeck enrolled at Stanford University. His subsequent history belies the picture of the happy, normal young man. He was soon in academic difficulties and dropped out of college several times to work on ranches in the Salinas Valley and observe "real life." His interests were varied, but he settled on novel-writing as his ambition, despite his family's insistence that he prepare for a more prosaic ca-

reer. This traumatic rejection of middle-class values would prove a major force in shaping Steinbeck's fiction, both his social protest novels and his lighter entertainments such as *Cannery Row.*

Leaving Stanford without a degree in 1925, Steinbeck sojourned in New York for several months, where he worked as a laborer, a newspaper reporter, and a freelance writer. Disillusioned in all his abortive pursuits, Steinbeck returned to California, where a job as winter caretaker of a lodge at Lake Tahoe provided the time to finish his first novel, *Cup of Gold.* The novel, a romance concerned with the Caribbean pirate Henry Morgan, was published by a small press directly before the crash of 1929, and it earned the young writer little recognition and even less money. In 1930, he married Carol Henning and moved with her to Los Angeles and later to Pacific Grove, a seaside resort near Monterey, where he lived in his parents' summer house. Still supported by his family and his wife, the ambitious young writer produced the manuscripts of several novels.

A friend, Edward F. (Ed) Ricketts, a marine biologist trained at the University of Chicago, encouraged Steinbeck to treat his material more objectively. Under Rickett's influence, Steinbeck modified his earlier commitment to satire, allegory, and Romanticism and turned to modern accounts of the Salinas Valley. Steinbeck's next two novels, *The Pastures of Heaven* and *To a God Unknown,* are both set in the Valley, but both still were marked by excessive sentimentality and symbolism. Both were virtually ignored by the public and the critics. Steinbeck's short fiction, however, began to receive recognition; for example, his story "The Murder" was selected as an O. Henry Prize story in 1934.

Tortilla Flat, a droll tale of Monterey's Mexican quarter, established Steinbeck as a popular and critical success in 1935. (Unfortunately, his parents died just before he achieved his first real success.) The novel's sales provided money to pay his debts, to travel to Mexico, and to continue writing seriously. His next novel, *In Dubious Battle,* established him as a serious literary artist and began the period of his greatest success, both critical and popular. This harshly realistic strike novel followed directions established in stories such as "The Raid," influenced by the realistic impulse of American literature in the 1930's. Succeeding publications quickly confirmed this development in his fiction. His short novels *The Red Pony* and *Of Mice and Men* followed in 1937, his story collection *The Long Valley* in 1938, and his epic of the "Okie" migration to California, *The Grapes of Wrath*, in 1939. His own play version of *Of Mice and Men* won the Drama Critics Circle Award in 1938, and *The Grapes of Wrath* received the Pulitzer Prize in 1940. Steinbeck had become one of the most popular and respected writers in the country, a spokesman for an entire culture.

In 1941, Pearl Harbor changed the direction of American culture and of John Steinbeck's literary development. During the war years, he seemed in a holding pattern, trying to adjust to his phenomenal success while absorbing the cataclysmic events around him. Steinbeck's career stalled for many reasons. He left the California subjects and realistic style of his finest novels, and he was unable to come to terms with a world at war, though he served for a few months as a front-line correspondent. Personal developments paralleled these literary ones. Steinbeck divorced his first wife and married Gwen Conger, a young Hollywood starlet; no doubt she influenced his decision to move from California to New York. Steinbeck began to write with an eye on Broadway and Hollywood.

Steinbeck was forty-three when World War II ended in 1945; he died in 1968 at the age of sixty-six. Over those twenty-three years, Steinbeck was extremely productive, winning considerable acclaim—most notably, the Nobel Prize in Literature in 1962. Yet the most important part of his career was finished. The war had changed the direction of his artistic development, and Steinbeck seemed powerless to reverse his decline.

Again, his personal life mirrored his literary difficulties. Although Gwen Conger presented him with his only children—Tom, born in 1944, and John, born in 1946—they were divorced in 1948. Like his first divorce, this one was bitter and expensive. In the same year, his mentor Ricketts was killed in a car accident. Steinbeck traveled extensively, devoting himself to film and nonfiction projects. In 1950, he married Elaine Scott, establishing a supportive relationship that allowed him to finish his epic Salinas Valley novel *East of Eden*.

Steinbeck tried again and again to write his way back to the artistic success of his earlier years, notably in *The Wayward Bus*, but his commercial success kept getting in the way. *East of Eden*, Steinbeck's major postwar novel, attempted another California epic to match the grandeur of *The Grapes of Wrath*. Although the book was a blockbuster best-seller, it was an artistic and critical failure. Steinbeck himself seemed to recognize his own decline, and in his last years he virtually abandoned fiction for journalism.

Of his last novels, only *The Winter of Our Discontent* transcends mere entertainment, and it does not have the literary structures to match its serious themes. Despite the popularity of nonfiction such as *Travels with Charley*, despite awards such as the Nobel Prize and the United States Medal of Freedom, despite his personal friendship with President Lyndon Johnson as a supporter of Vietnam, Steinbeck was only the shell of the great writer of the 1930's. He died in New York City on December 20, 1968.

ANALYSIS

John Steinbeck remains a writer of the 1930's, perhaps *the* American writer of the 1930's. Although his first novel, *Cup of Gold*, was published in 1929, its derivative "Lost Generation" posturing gives little indication of the masterpiece he would publish at the end of the next decade, *The Grapes of Wrath*. Steinbeck developed from a Romantic, imitative, often sentimental apprentice to a realistic, objective, and accomplished novelist in only a decade. The reasons for this change can be found in the interplay between a sensitive writer and his cultural background.

A writer of great talent, sensitivity, and imagination, John Steinbeck entered into the mood of the country in the late 1930's with an extraordinary responsiveness. The Depression had elicited a reevaluation of American culture, a reassessment of the American Dream: a harsh realism of observation balanced by a warm emphasis on human dignity. Literature and the other arts joined social, economic, and political thought in contrasting traditional American ideals with the bleak reality of breadlines and shanty-towns. Perhaps the major symbol of dislocation was the Dust Bowl; the American garden became a waste-land from which its dispossessed farmers fled. The arts in the 1930's focused on these harsh images and tried to find in them the human dimensions which promised a new beginning.

The proletarian novel, documentary photography, and the documentary film stemmed from similar im-pulses; the radical novel put more emphasis on the inhuman conditions of the dislocated, while the films made more of the promising possibilities for a new day. Painting, music, and theater all responded to a new humanistic and realistic thrust. The best balance was struck by documentary photographers and film-makers: Dorothea Lange, Walker Evans, and Arthur Rothstein in photography; Pare Lorentz, Willard Van Dyke, and Herbert Kline in film. As a novelist, Stein-beck shared this documentary impulse, and it refined his art.

IN DUBIOUS BATTLE

In Dubious Battle tells the harsh story of a violent agricultural strike in the "Torgas Valley" from the viewpoint of two Communist agitators. Careful and objective in his handling of the material, the mature Steinbeck provided almost a factual case study of a strike. In a letter, he indicated that this was his con-scious intention:

> I had an idea that I was going to write the autobiogra-phy of a Communist. Then Miss McIntosh [his agent] suggested I reduce it to fiction. There lay the trouble. I had planned to write a journalistic account of a strike. But as I thought of it as fiction the thing got bigger and bigger . . . I have used a small strike in an orchard val-ley as the symbol of man's eternal, bitter warfare with himself.

For the first time, Steinbeck was able to combine his ambition to write great moral literature with his de-sire to chronicle his time and place.

Significantly, the novel takes its title from John Milton's *Paradise Lost* (1667, 1674) in which the phrase is used to describe the struggle between God and Satan, but it takes its subject from the news-papers and newsreels of the 1930's. The underly-ing structure demonstrates the universal struggle of good and evil, of human greed and selfishness versus human generosity and idealism. Jim, the protagonist killed at the conclusion, is obviously a Christ fig-ure, an individual who has sacrificed himself for the group. Here, Steinbeck needs no overblown symbolic actions to support his theme. He lets his contempo-rary story tell itself realistically and in documentary fashion. In a letter, he describes his method in the novel: "I wanted to be merely a recording conscious-ness, judging nothing, simply putting down the thing." This objective, dispassionate, almost documentary realism separates *In Dubious Battle* from his earlier fiction and announces the beginning of Steinbeck's major period.

OF MICE AND MEN

Of Mice and Men was written in 1935 and 1936 and first published as a novel in 1937 at the height of the Depression. Steinbeck constructed the book around dramatic scenes so that he could easily re-write it for the stage, which he did with the help of George S. Kaufmann. The play opened late in 1937, with Wallace Ford as George and Broderick Craw-ford as Lennie. A film version, directed by Lewis Milestone, appeared in 1939. The success of the play and film spurred sales of the novel and created a wide audience for Steinbeck's next book, *The Grapes of Wrath*.

Like his classic story of the "Okie" migration from the Dust Bowl to the promised land of Califor-nia, *Of Mice and Men* is a dramatic presentation of the persistence of the American Dream and the trag-edy of its failure. His characters are the little people, the uncommon "common people," disoriented and dispossessed by modern life yet still yearning for a little piece of land, that little particle of the Jefferso-nian ideal. Lennie is the symbol of this visceral, inar-ticulate land-hunger, while George becomes the poet of this romantic vision. How their dream blossoms and then dies is Steinbeck's dramatic subject; how their fate represents that of America in the 1930's and after becomes his theme. His title, an allusion to the Scottish poet Robert Burns, suggests that the best laid plans "of mice and men often gang a-gley"; so the American vision had gone astray in the Depression decade Steinbeck documented so movingly and realistically.

THE RED PONY

The Red Pony involves the maturation of Jody Tiflin, a boy of about ten when the action opens. The time is about 1910, and the setting is the Tiflin ranch in the Salinas Valley, where Jody lives with his father, Carl, his mother, Ruth, and the hired hand, a middle-aged cowboy named Billy Buck. From time to time, they are visited by Jody's grandfather, a venerable old man who led one of the first wagon trains to California. "The Gift," the first section of the novel, concerns Jody's red pony, which he names Gabilan, after the nearby mountain range. The pony soon becomes a symbol of the boy's growing maturity and his developing knowledge of the natural world. Later, he carelessly leaves the pony out in the rain, and it takes cold and dies, despite Billy Buck's efforts to save it. Thus Jody learns of nature's cruel indifference to human wishes.

In the second part, "The Great Mountains," the Tiflin ranch is visited by a former resident, Gitano, an aged Chicano laborer reared in the now vanished hacienda. Old Gitano has come home to die. In a debate that recalls Robert Frost's poem "The Death of the Hired Man," Carl persuades Ruth that they cannot take Old Gitano in, but—as in Frost's poem—their dialogue proves pointless. Stealing a broken-down nag significantly named Easter, the old man rides off into the mountains to die in dignity. Again, Jody is faced with the complex, harsh reality of adult life.

In "The Promise," the third section, Jody learns more of nature's ambiguous promises when his father has one of the mares put to stud to give the boy another colt. The birth is complicated, however, and Billy Buck must kill the mare to save the colt, demonstrating that life and death are inextricably intertwined. The final section, "The Leader of the People," ends the sequence with another vision of death and change. Jody's grandfather comes to visit, retelling his time-worn stories of the great wagon crossing. Carl Tiflin cruelly hurts the old man by revealing that none of them except Jody is really interested in

these repetitious tales. The grandfather realizes that Carl is right, but later he tells Jody that the adventurous stories were not the point, but that his message was "Westering" itself. For the grandfather, "Westering" was the source of American identity. With the close of the frontier, "Westering" has ended, and the rugged Westerners have been replaced by petty landholders such as Carl Tiflin and aging cowboys such as Billy Buck. In his grandfather's ramblings, Jody discovers a sense of mature purpose, and by the conclusion of the sequence, he too can hope to be a leader of the people.

The Red Pony traces Jody's initiation into adult life with both realism and sensitivity, a balance which Steinbeck did not always achieve. The vision of the characters caught up in the harsh world of nature is balanced by their deep human concerns and commitments. The evocation of the ranch setting in its vital beauty is matched only in the author's finest works, such as *Of Mice and Men*. Steinbeck's symbols grow naturally out of this setting, and nothing in the story-sequence seems forced into a symbolic pattern, as in his later works. In its depiction of an American variation on a universal experience, *The Red Pony* deserves comparison with the finest of modern American fiction, especially with initiation tales such as William Faulkner's *The Bear* (1942) and Ernest Hemingway's Nick Adams stories.

Responding to a variety of social and artistic influences, Steinbeck's writing had evolved toward documentary realism throughout the 1930's. In fiction, this development is especially clear in *In Dubious Battle, Of Mice and Men*, and *The Long Valley*. Even more obvious was the movement of his nonfiction toward a committed documentation of the social ills plaguing America during the Depression decade. Steinbeck's newspaper and magazine writing offered detailed accounts of social problems, particularly the plight of migrant agricultural workers in California's fertile valleys. The culmination of this development was *Their Blood Is Strong* (1938), a compilation of reports originally written for the *San Francisco News* and published with additional text by Steinbeck and photographs by Dorothea Lange originally made for the Farm Security Administration.

THE GRAPES OF WRATH

It is significant that Steinbeck first conceived of *The Grapes of Wrath* as just such a documentary book. In March, 1938, Steinbeck went into the California valleys with a *Life* magazine photographer to make a record of the harsh conditions in the migrant camps. The reality he encountered seemed too significant for nonfiction, however, and Steinbeck began to reshape this material as a novel, an epic novel.

Although his first tentative attempts at fictionalizing the situation in the agricultural valleys were heavily satiric, as indicated by the early title *L'Affaire Lettuceberg*, Steinbeck soon realized that the Okie migration was the stuff of an American epic. Reworking his material, adding to it by research in government agency files and by more journeys into the camps and along the migrant routes, Steinbeck evolved his vision. A grand design emerged; he would follow one family from the Oklahoma Dust Bowl to California. Perhaps this methodology was suggested by the sociological case histories of the day, perhaps by the haunted faces of individual families that stared back at him as he researched in Farm Security Administration files.

In discussing his plans for his later documentary film, *The Forgotten Village* (1941), Steinbeck remarked that most documentaries concerned large groups of people but that audiences could identify better with individuals. In *The Grapes of Wrath*, he made one family representative of general conditions. The larger groups and problems he treated in short interchapters which generalized the issues particularized in the Joad family. Perhaps the grand themes of change and movement were suggested by the documentary films of Pare Lorentz (later a personal friend), *The Plow That Broke the Plains* (1936) and *The River* (1938), with their panoramic geographical and historical visions. Drawing an archetypal theme from Sir Thomas Malory, John Bunyan, John Milton, and the Bible—the ultimate source of his pervasive religious symbolism—Steinbeck made the journey of the Joads into an allegorical pilgrimage as well as a desperate race along Route 66. During this journey, the Joad family disintegrates, but the larger human family emerges. Tom Joad makes a pilgrim's progress from a narrow, pessimistic view to a transcendental vision of American possibilities. The novel ends on a note of hope for a new American Dream.

The Grapes of Wrath was a sensational best-seller from the beginning. Published to generally favorable reviews in March, 1939, it was selling at the rate of more than twenty-five hundred copies a day two months later. Controversy helped spur sales. As a semidocumentary, its factual basis was subject to close scrutiny, and many critics challenged Steinbeck's material. Oklahomans resented the presentation of the Joads as typical of the state (many still do), while Californians disapproved of the depiction of their state's leading industry. The book was attacked, banned, burned—but everywhere it was read. Even in the migrant camps, it was considered an accurate picture of the conditions experienced there. Some 430,000 copies were sold in a year, and in 1940, the novel received the Pulitzer Prize and the Award of the American Booksellers Association (later the National Book Award). Naturally, all the excitement attracted the attention of Hollywood, in spite of the fact that the controversy over the novel seemed to preclude a film version, or at least a faithful film version. Nevertheless, Darryl F. Zanuck produced and John Ford directed a faithful adaptation starring Henry Fonda in 1940; the film, like the novel, has become a classic, and it gave Steinbeck's vision of America in the 1930's even wider currency.

Indeed, Steinbeck's best work was filmic in the best sense of that word—visual, realistic, objective. These qualities nicely balanced the allegorical and romantic strains inherent in his earlier fiction. During World War II, however, his work, much to its detriment, began to cater to the film industry. In fact, much of his postwar writing seems to have found its inspiration in Hollywood versions of his work. His own screen adaptation of an earlier story, *The Red Pony*, proves a sentimentalized reproduction of the original. Still, he was occasionally capable of recapturing his earlier vision, particularly in his works about Mexico—*The Pearl* and *Viva Zapata!*

THE PEARL

Mexico always had been an important symbolic place for Steinbeck. As a native Californian, he had been aware of his state's Mexican heritage. Even as a boy, he sought out Chicano companions, fascinated by their unconcern for the pieties of WASP culture; he also befriended Mexican fieldhands at the ranches where he worked during his college summers. Later, his first literary success, *Tortilla Flat*, grew from his involvement with the *paisanos* of Monterey, people who would today be called Chicanos.

For Steinbeck, Mexico was everything modern America was not; it possessed a primitive vitality, a harsh simplicity, and a romantic beauty—all of which are found in *The Pearl*. Mexico exhibits the same qualities in the works of other modern writers such as Malcolm Lowry, Aldous Huxley, Graham Greene, Hart Crane, and Katherine Anne Porter. All of them lived and worked there for some time, contrasting the traditional culture they discovered in Mexico with the emptiness of the modern world. Steinbeck also was fascinated by a Mexico still alive with social concern. The continued extension of the Revolution into the countryside had been his subject in *The Forgotten Village*, and it would be developed further in *Viva Zapata!* For Steinbeck, Mexico represented the purity of artistic and social purposes that he had lost after World War II.

This sense of the writer's personal involvement energizes *The Pearl*, making it Steinbeck's best work of fiction in the years following the success of *The Grapes of Wrath*. At the beginning of the novella, the storyteller states: "If this story is a parable, perhaps everyone takes his own meaning from it and reads his own life into it." The critics have read Steinbeck's short novel in a number of ways, but strangely enough, they have not considered it as a parable of the author's own career in the postwar period. Much like Ernest Hemingway's *The Old Man and the Sea* (1952), *The Pearl* uses the life of a simple fisherman to investigate symbolically an aging artist's difficult maturation.

Steinbeck was presented with the tale during his Sea of Cortez expedition in 1940. In his log, he recounts "an event which happened at La Paz in recent years." The story matches the basic outline of *The Pearl*, though Steinbeck made several major changes, changes significant in an autobiographical sense. In the original, the Mexican fisherman was a devil-may-care bachelor; in *The Pearl*, he becomes the sober young husband and father, Kino. Steinbeck himself had just become a father for the first time when he wrote the novella, and this change provides a clue to the autobiographical nature of the parable. The original bachelor thought the pearl a key to easy living; Kino sees it creating a better way of life for the people through an education for his baby son, Coyotito. If the child could read and write, then he could set his family and his people free from the social and economic bondage in which they toil. Kino is ignorant of the dangers of wealth, and *The Pearl* is the tale of how he matures by coming to understand them. Steinbeck, too, matured from his youthful innocence as he felt the pressures of success.

As in his best fiction of the 1930's Steinbeck fuses his universal allegory with documentary realism. Perhaps planning ahead for a screenplay, Steinbeck's prose in the novel often takes a cinematic point of view. Scenes are presented in terms of establishing shots, medium views, and close-ups. In particular, Steinbeck carefully examines the natural setting, often visually contrasting human behavior with natural phenomena. As in his best fiction, his naturalistic vision is inherent in the movement of his story; there is no extraneous philosophizing.

Steinbeck's characters in *The Pearl* are real people in a real world, but they are also universal types. Kino, the fisherman named for an early Jesuit explorer, Juana, his wife, and Coyotito, their baby, are almost an archetypal family, like the Holy Family in a medieval morality play. Kino's aspirations are the same universal drives to better himself and his family that took the Okies to the California valleys. Like the Joads, this symbolic family must struggle at once against an indifferent natural order and a corrupt social order. Unfortunately, aside from the screenplay of *Viva Zapata!*, Steinbeck would never again achieve the fusion of parable and realism which energizes *The Pearl*.

In his Nobel Prize speech of 1962, Steinbeck indicated what he tried to accomplish in his work:

The ancient commission of the writer has not changed. He is charged with exposing our many grievous faults and failures, with dredging up to the light our dark and dangerous dreams, for the purpose of improvement.

No writer has better exposed the dark underside of the American Dream, but few writers have so successfully celebrated the great hope symbolized in that dream—the hope of human development. Steinbeck's best fictions picture a paradise lost but also posit a future paradise to be regained. In spite of his faults and failures, John Steinbeck's best literary works demonstrate a greatness of heart and mind found only rarely in modern American literature.

Joseph R. Millichap

OTHER MAJOR WORKS

SHORT FICTION: *Saint Katy the Virgin*, 1936; *The Long Valley*, 1938.

PLAYS: *Of Mice and Men*, pr., pb. 1937; *The Moon Is Down*, pr. 1942; *Burning Bright*, pb. 1951.

SCREENPLAYS: *The Forgotten Village*, 1941; *Lifeboat*, 1944; *A Medal for Benny*, 1945; *The Pearl*, 1945; *The Red Pony*, 1949; *Viva Zapata!*, 1952.

NONFICTION: *Their Blood Is Strong*, 1938; *The Forgotten Village*, 1941; *Sea of Cortez*, 1941 (with Edward F. Ricketts); *Bombs Away*, 1942; *A Russian Journal*, 1948 (with Robert Capa); *Once There Was a War*, 1958; *Travels with Charley: In Search of America*, 1962; *Letters to Alicia*, 1965; *America and Americans*, 1966; *Journal of a Novel*, 1969; *Steinbeck: A Life in Letters*, 1975 (Elaine Steinbeck and Robert Wallsten, editors).

TRANSLATION: *The Acts of King Arthur and His Noble Knights*, 1976.

BIBLIOGRAPHY

DeMott, Robert J., ed. *Steinbeck's Typewriter: Essays on His Art*. Troy, N.Y.: Whitston, 1996. A good collection of criticism of Steinbeck. Includes bibliographical references and an index.

French, Warren. *John Steinbeck's Fiction Revisited*. New York: Twayne, 1994. Thoroughly revises French's two other books in this Twayne series. Chapters on Steinbeck's becoming a novelist, his relationship to modernism, his short fiction, his wartime fiction, and his final fiction. Includes chronology, notes, and annotated bibliography.

Hughes, R. S. *John Steinbeck: A Study of the Short Fiction*. Boston: Twayne, 1989. Divided into three sections: Steinbeck's short stories, the author's letters exploring his craft, and four critical commentaries. A good study of some of his lesser known works which includes a chronology, a lengthy bibliography, and an index.

Lisca, Peter. *The Wide World of John Steinbeck*. New York: Gordian Press, 1958. An indispensable guide to Steinbeck's work, published in 1958 and then updated with an "Afterword" examining the writer's last novel *The Winter of Our Discontent* (1961). Admired and imitated, Lisca's work set the standard for future Steinbeck studies.

McCarthy, Paul. *John Steinbeck*. New York: Frederick Ungar, 1980. A short biographical approach to Steinbeck's work that examines each novel against the forces that shaped his life. Includes a useful chronology, notes, a bibliography, and an index.

McElrath, Joseph R., Jr., Jesse S. Crisler, and Susan Shillinglaw, eds. *John Steinbeck: The Contemporary Reviews*. New York: Cambridge University Press, 1996. A fine selection of reviews of Steinbeck's work.

STENDHAL
Marie-Henri Beyle

Born: Grenoble, France; January 23, 1783
Died: Paris, France; March 23, 1842

PRINCIPAL LONG FICTION

Armance, 1827 (English translation, 1928)
Le Rouge et le Noir, 1830 (*The Red and the Black*, 1898)
La Chartreuse de Parme, 1839 (*The Charterhouse of Parma*, 1895)
Lucien Leuwen, 1855, 1894, 1926-1927 (wr. 1834-1835; English translation, 1950)
Lamiel, 1889, 1971 (wr. 1839-1842; English translation, 1929)

OTHER LITERARY FORMS

Stendhal also wrote short fiction, divided by later editors into two groups: his *nouvelles* written between 1829 and 1831, and the short stories *Chroniques italiennes* (1839, 1855; *The Abbess of Castro and Other Tales*, 1926). Stendhal's nonfiction works include musical history and criticism, as in *Vies de Haydn, de Mozart et de Métastase* (1815; *The Lives of Haydn and Mozart, with Observations on Métastase*, 1817), *Vie de Rossini* (1823; *Memoirs of Rossini*, 1824; also as *Life of Rossini*, 1956), and *Notes d'un dilettante* (1824-1827); art history and criticism, as in *Histoire de la peinture en Italie* (1817) and five subsequent volumes of art appreciation; travel diaries, including *Rome, Naples et Florence en 1817* (1817, 1826; *Rome, Naples and Florence, in 1817*, 1818), *Promenades dans Rome* (1829; *A Roman Journal*, 1957), *Mémoires d'un touriste* (1838; *Memoirs of a Tourist*, 1962), and *Voyage dans le midi de la France* (1838; *Travels in the South of France*, 1971); literary theory, including *Racine et Shakespeare* (part 1, 1823; part 2, 1825; *Racine and Shakespeare*, 1962); psychological theory, including *De l'amour* (1822; *Maxims of Love*, 1906); and autobiography and biography, including *Souvenirs d'égotisme*, (1892; written 1832; *Memoirs of an Egotist*, 1949), *Vie de Henry Brulard* (1890; written 1835-1836; *The Life of Henry Brulard*, 1925). In addition, Stendhal's journalism (written between 1822 and 1830), his *Journal* (1888), and his *Correspondance* (1933-1934) occupy some six or seven thousand pages.

ACHIEVEMENTS

Stendhal is frequently referred to, along with Fyodor Dostoevski, as "the forerunner of the modern novel." Insofar as the highest manifestations of the novel form in the twentieth century developed, by way of Thomas Mann, James Joyce, and Marcel Proust, as an exploration of reality that goes beyond the limitations of "realism," the recognition accorded Stendhal is justified. Half a century before Sigmund Freud, Stendhal's power of psychological observation was granting as much scope to subconscious and irrational motivation as to more lucidly conceived manifestations of the compelling forces underlying all major human actions. The conversations between his characters rarely reveal more than the tip of the iceberg; what interests him is the long process of maturation in the mind (the *monologue intérieur*, or "interior monologue") which precedes the spoken word. While his contemporaries Honoré de Balzac and Charles Dickens were realists first and foremost, for Stendhal, realism was at best a means; it was never an end in itself.

The result is an exact and compelling portrait of "reality," which at the same time (particularly in the case of *The Charterhouse of Parma*) is oddly off-key.

(Library of Congress)

All of his full-length novels, without exception, are deeply rooted in the world that he observed about him—in Paris, in small French provincial towns, or else in the cities and plains of northern Italy. Above all, his political and social depiction of the malaise of his time is penetratingly acute—one of the profoundest analyses yet made of a society in a period of political reaction, in which the dominating emotion is that of fear. When the social order is so precarious and at the same time so disillusioned, then virtually every class, and every individual, lives in fear of every other: "We live," he noted—and the phrase has become proverbial—"in an era of suspicion." One of the forces that contributed to this suspicion was that newborn and newly powerful institution, the daily press; Stendhal was the first major novelist to take account of the power of the press in shaping the ideas, the prejudices, the opinions, and the destinies of ordinary people.

However precise this realism was within its own conventional limitations, Stendhal was constantly going beyond it. He was, he admitted, not only repelled but also *bored* by description. Faced with Balzac's Pension Vauquer, he would have given up after the first three lines. Frequently, having embarked on a description, he tails off into "etc., etc.," leaving the rest to his reader's imagination. In the place of description, he preferred what he called *le petit fait vrai*: "the tiny, true fact," the one minute detail of observation so singular that no fiction could have conceived it, yet so revealing that it conjures up a total picture of reality more vivid than could have been vouchsafed by a dozen pages of descriptive journalism. Thus, Fabrice, having strayed almost by accident onto the battlefield of Waterloo, observes his first corpse, already plundered by the still-living: "The corpse had dirty feet"—not the sublime magnificence of the cannonades, but the one "tiny, true fact," evoking a whole panorama of the sordid realities of nineteenth century warfare. In this, Stendhal's realism is at least halfway along the road to the techniques of the Symbolists: The significance of the phenomenon lies in what it reveals beyond itself.

Indeed, the Symbolists, beginning with Charles Baudelaire, recognized Stendhal as an ancestor—although, admittedly, more in the domain of aesthetic theory than in that of the novel. Even within the domain of the realistic novel, however, Stendhal formulated two further principles that are not without significance, even today: first, that the novelist is *not* to be held morally responsible for the immorality of his characters—"A novel is a mirror trundled along beside a highroad"—the mirror is in no way responsible for what it reflects; second, that no individual can be understood, save in terms of the political conditions which alone explain his individuality—"Politics in a novel is like a pistol-shot fired during a concert; something crude, yet which nonetheless *compels* attention." The shot would be awkward material, in fact, but material the novelist could ignore only at his peril.

BIOGRAPHY

Stendhal's experience of life was as rich and as varied as the range of his writings might suggest. Born as Marie-Henri Beyle in Grenoble—a city which he detested all of his life as the very symbol of small-minded provinciality—on January 23, 1783, he lost his mother, Henriette Gagnon, before he was seven, a traumatic experience that left him with a classic Oedipus complex, adoring her memory and everything connected with her and loathing his father, Chérubin Beyle, and everything connected with him. The most abominated of the representatives of his father was a Jesuit priest, the Abbé Raillane, who became his tutor; never, in a single page of his subsequent writings, does Stendhal mention Jesuits without irony and contempt.

No part of Stendhal's writing is wholly separable from his biography. He lived through so many events that, by the time he became a novelist, "history," for him, meant that which he himself had experienced. He was six years old when the French Revolution broke out and eleven when the Terror struck Grenoble; during the latter, he enjoyed himself thoroughly playing cops and robbers and making a dangerous nuisance of himself to his father and to the rest of his family. In spite of everything, however, he received an excellent nonclassical education at the newly established École Centrale at Grenoble, concentrating on modern subjects, on art, and on mathematics, and in November, 1799, he set off for Paris to follow courses at the École Polytechnique, intending to qualify as a military engineer.

This early fascination—on one hand, with the precision of mathematics, and on the other, with the positive aggressivity of military science—was to endure all of his life; it is ironic, therefore, to discover that he never so much as set foot within the walls of the École Polytechnique. Instead, no sooner had he arrived in Paris than he discovered in himself a new ambition: that of becoming a dramatist, "a new Molière"—an extraordinary aberration that was to preoccupy him fruitlessly for the better part of twenty years. On top of this first wrong turn came a second: Alone in his student lodgings, freezing with cold in the depths of a Parisian winter, he developed pleurisy, with complications. Short of a miracle, it would be the end of Marie-Henri Beyle.

The miracle duly occurred. On the day before Stendhal arrived in Paris, November 10, 1799, Napoleon had seized power. Among Napoleon's ablest supporters and administrators—quickly rising to a position of enormous influence as director of the army's Ministry of Supply—was Pierre Daru, a distant cousin of Stendhal's father. The Daru family rescued their seventeen-year-old provincial relative in his distress, and when he had recovered, Pierre Daru found him a job in his own office. Stendhal was so ignorant of letters in that period that the very first time Daru dictated a memorandum to him, he misspelled the word *cela* as *cella*. Thirty years later, Julien Sorel would do the same thing in *The Red and the Black*.

At the beginning of May, 1800, Napoleon opened his second campaign against the Austrians in northern Italy by taking his army over the Saint-Bernard Pass and descending out of the blue onto the plain of Lombardy to beat the enemy at Marengo. Pierre Daru invited his young cousin to participate in the march, and Stendhal accepted with enthusiasm; thus, still in civilian clothes, and decidedly ill-balanced on an awkward "Swiss" horse (falling off horses is a chronic occupational hazard for the Stendhalian hero), Stendhal followed in the baggage train. On May 30, he

came under fire for the first time; two days later, having a free evening in the little township of Ivrea, he paid for a seat to hear a third-rate opera company perform its uninspired version of Domenico Cimarosa's *Il matrimonio segreto* (1792; *The Secret Marriage*). This banal experience was a quasi-mystical revelation that changed Stendhal's life. From that moment on, not France but Italy—above all, Milan—was to be his spiritual home; Marie-Henri Beyle had embarked on the long process of his transformation into the creator of *The Charterhouse of Parma*. In his will, he ordained that his tombstone should bear the inscription, "Arrigo Beyle, Milanese." This stone may still be seen at the Cimetière Montmartre in Paris.

For the next thirty years, his life would be scarcely less adventurous. After eighteen months, he resigned his Italian commission and went back to Paris to write plays, study acting, and fall in love with an actress. The actress, Mélanie Guilbert, accepted an engagement to play in Marseilles; off went Stendhal in her wake, earning his living meanwhile as a grocer's storeman. Then he returned to the Napoleonic service, spending three years (1806-1809) as an administrator in Germany, rising in the ranks and becoming recognized as an enterprising and efficient officer, and traveling widely—to Brunswick, to Berlin, to Dresden (one night, his coach stopped at a little township called Stendhal; the name would seem to have stuck in his mind). He spent seven months in Vienna; returned to Paris, living with an opera singer; and then was in Italy again, in 1811. In 1812, not the most propitious of moments, he volunteered to carry dispatches to Moscow, witnessed the fire that destroyed the city, lost most of his manuscripts, directed a supply column during the Great Retreat, by sheer willpower and hectoring forced his column over the Berezina River the day *before* the disastrous battle, and continued to supply his units as far as Königsberg—but vowed that, thereafter, he would never again experience cold. In 1813, he saw the Battle of Bautzen; in 1814, he was a senior officer in charge of defending the Dauphiné against the advancing Allies. A few weeks later, he was left with the last-minute responsibility of removing all art treasures in Paris from the reach of the oncoming Cossacks. Then came the great collapse.

With Napoleon exiled to Elba, Stendhal's career stood in ruins. He had to choose: either make his peace with the restored Bourbons or remain faithful to his hero and go into exile himself. He chose the latter course, retiring to Milan, penniless and in debt, and there spending the next seven years as a hack writer churning out what he could to help keep himself alive; *The Lives of Haydn and Mozart, with Observations on Métastase, Histoire de la peinture en Italie*, and the travel guide *Rome, Naples, and Florence, in 1817*. The latter sold well: Tourists, after a quarter of a century of political blockade, were pouring back into the peninsula; Stendhal's prospects at last were improving. He had learned Italian, and he was being accepted into young, adventurous literary circles—circles in which, by the year 1818, the word "Romanticism" was coming into fashion, but all too often in conjunction with other words, such as "liberal," *carbonaro*, and "independent Italy." It was to the echo of words such as these that, in 1818, Stendhal met the greatest and most enduring love of his life, Métilde Viscontini Dembowski, friend and protector of the poet Ugo Foscolo. Stendhal loved Métilde passionately and despairingly for three years; she did not ever grant him the least encouragement. In the end, his carbonarist sympathies became too marked for the Austrian authorities to ignore; he was expelled from Milan and, in 1821, returned to Paris. He never again saw Métilde, but her presence is felt in every book he wrote after that point. The essay *Maxims of Love* is an analysis of his feeling for her; Clélia Conti (*The Charterhouse of Parma*) and Madame de Chasteller (*Lucien Leuwen*) both bear her features; his own frustrated feeling of impotence in the presence of the woman he loved is reflected in Octave de Malivert (*Armance*); and it is no accident that the passionate heroine of *The Red and the Black* is named Mathilde.

Now, at last, things became calmer. Stendhal spent nine years in Paris, from 1821 to 1830, as a journalist, an art critic, an acknowledged authority on Italian opera—yet he always found time to be in love. One of his lovers, Clémentine Curial, caused him such despair that he seriously considered suicide; instead, he sat down and wrote his first novel, *Armance*.

Although it was a failure, *Armance* showed Stendhal his true vocation. He was no longer young, but now the creative fury took hold of him. In 1828, he got the first idea for a new novel—"Julien" it was to be called—and although it was not until January, 1830, that he started writing seriously, once he had begun, he worked quickly. "Julien" became *The Red and the Black*, and by July, Stendhal was correcting proofs. On July 28, firing broke out in the street beneath his window: The "Three Glorious Days" were putting a final end to the Bourbon regime. With joy in his heart, Stendhal went on correcting proofs.

Once the new government, that of Louis-Philippe, was established, Stendhal set out to achieve his heart's desire: a post in Italy. He was offered the consulship at Trieste, but Trieste was Austrian territory, and Prince Metternich's files recalled the fact that one Marie-Henri Beyle had already been expelled from Milan for "anti-Austrian activities." Stendhal was refused accreditation. In consolation, he was offered the post of French Consul at Civitavecchia, in the Papal States. There, in this little provincial seaport some eighty miles north of Rome, he was destined to remain for the rest of his career. With no opera, no society, and no intelligent conversation to be found in Civitavecchia, Stendhal had nothing to do but write: *Memoirs of an Egotist, Lucien Leuwen, The Life of Henry Brulard*, the first stories of *The Abbess of Castro and Other Tales*—masterpiece after masterpiece. In the late spring of 1836, he was granted leave, but, back in Paris, the creative mood did not desert him: He wrote *Memoirs of a Tourist, Travels in the South of France*, and another story found in *The Abbess of Castro and Other Tales*, "Vittoria Accoramboni." By what process of ingenuity Consul Beyle contrived to extend his original three months' leave to nearly three years is unknown; in any event, he was still in Paris when, in the last weeks of 1838, he had his greatest moment of inspiration and, in less than two months, set down on paper the entirety of *The Charterhouse of Parma*.

That, however, was virtually the end. "Exhausted," he notes repeatedly in his diaries and jottings during this time. Back in Civitavecchia, he began a new novel, *Lamiel,* but everything seemed to go wrong. In 1842, he was granted a new, short leave, in the course of which he collapsed on the sidewalk of the rue Neuve-des-Petits-Champs in Paris and died the following day, stricken down with apoplexy.

ANALYSIS

It is a primary characteristic of Stendhal as a writer of fiction that he was incapable both of devising a plot and of embroidering characters with the fantasy of his own imagination. He needed to have his fundamental story line laid out for him; only then could he set to work creatively. His genius lay not in fashioning but in refashioning his material.

ARMANCE

This is the pattern found in *Armance.* A certain Madame de Duras specialized in novels in which a pair of lovers are separated by an "insuperable" obstacle. In one of her novels, *Olivier: Ou, Le Secret* (1971, written 1825), this obstacle takes the form of sexual impotence in the hero; the idea for the story was also used by Henri de Latouche for his *Olivier* (1826), which Stendhal reviewed. Stendhal, familiar with both works, had found his basic material; against that, however, was the fact that his whole idealistic sensibility was repulsed by the idea of setting out in black and white the unromantic physiological details of the "obstacle" which, for some four hundred pages, prevents his hero, Octave de Malivert, from marrying the beautiful, half-Russian Armance, and which alone explains the hero's suicide, with the result that the uninformed reader can close the book without even so much as guessing at the mysterious "secret" that alone makes sense of the situation. It is not surprising that, on its first appearance, *Armance* was a failure.

Yet it is precisely to this overcareful concealment of the key to the mystery that the novel owes its most significant qualities. If the secret had been revealed, the tale could have been little more than a medico-psychological casebook of the type popularized by the Goncourt brothers a generation later. As it is, the sense of living with some "inexpressible misfortune" transforms Octave into one of the earliest examples of the true Romantic hero in the French novel: moody, solitary, unpredictable, bored, frustrated by the world, incapable of accepting happiness even when it is offered to him—a Byronic creature whose inner self is at war with his outer semblance, possessed by a demon of inexplicable violence: a true "aristocrat of misfortune." In response, Armance likewise assumes similar characteristics. Already remote, inaccessible, and coldly exotic, thanks to her Russian origins, she alternates between moments of passion and moments of withdrawal, reacting to the "mystery" of her lover by retreating behind the veils of her own mystery.

Among the diaphanous nuances of this game of emotional hide-and-seek, Stendhal weaves a number of other themes characteristically his own. All of Stendhal's writings—even his studies on art and music—are to a greater or lesser degree "committed"; that is, they embody precise critical attitudes toward the political and social issues of his time. The 1820's in France were a period of intense social malaise, as the *ancien régime* aristocracy, supported by the Church, attempted to reassert its control over the country against the temporarily defeated forces of Jacobinism and liberalism. A major victory in this effort to set the clock back came in April, 1825, when the Chamber of Deputies passed an "act of indemnity" granting financial compensation to those aristocratic families who had had their lands and châteaus confiscated during the Revolution. The "reaction" was in the ascendant.

Octave has a title: He is the Vicomte de Malivert. Thus, whether he likes it or not, he is an aristocrat, confined irrevocably within the perimeters of that class. By the very fact of his name, he is stamped indelibly as a reactionary. At the same time, however, he is a highly intelligent, modern, mathematically minded young man, trained at the École Polytechnique and a political idealist into the bargain; today one would call him a progressive intellectual. Thus, in the outcome, the "insuperable" personal and sexual dilemma is transformed into a symbol of something far more significant and universal: the irreconcilable claims of commitment to himself as an individual, on one hand, and to his class, family, and inherited background, on the other. Once again, suicide would appear to be the only solution. Even that, when it comes, bears the same hallmark of "impotence." Octave remains his own divided self even in death. Lord Byron, faced with a parallel dilemma, at least got as far as Missolonghi in his flamboyant gesture of sacrificing himself to a "liberal" cause; not so Octave—a failed Byron if ever there was one. His ship, in Byron's wake, is bound for Greece, and he, to fight the Turks. He dies, however, with careful timing, immediately before the coast is sighted. Octave is indeed a Romantic hero, but he is also the first of Stendhal's antiheroes.

THE RED AND THE BLACK

It was no novel, but the verbatim newspaper report of a murder trial, that provided Stendhal with the plot and the denouement that he needed for *The Red and the Black*. In four consecutive issues dated from December 28 to December 31, 1827, the *Gazette des tribunaux* had carried the story of the trial and subsequent condemnation of Antoine Berthier, twenty-five years of age, a former tutor and a former theological student, who, on July 11, 1827, had entered a church in the little township of Brangues, near Grenoble, where, during the celebration of the Mass, he had drawn and fired a pistol, thereby mortally wounding one Madame Michoud, mother of three children formerly entrusted to his care, and presumed at one time to have been his mistress. As the trial proceeded, more and more singular facts began to emerge, and on these, Stendhal's imagination began to "embroider." The novel, originally called "Julien," was born.

Julien Sorel, youngest son of a peasant sawmill owner and endowed with ambitions well above his station, becomes tutor to the children of Monsieur de Rênal, mayor of the little township of Verrières, in the Jura. There, Julien seduces Madame de Rênal; when suspicions of the relationship are aroused, he leaves the household and enrolls in a theological seminary at Besançon to study for the priesthood. In the seminary, he is befriended by the Director, the Jansenist Abbé Pirard, who recommends Julien as secretary to the Marquis de La Mole, an aristocrat of ancient lineage moving amid the highest circles of Legitimist Paris. Julien seduces the Marquis's daughter, Mathilde—with such success that when she be-

comes pregnant, the Marquis agrees to their marriage. All is set for the supreme realization of Julien's ambitions when the Marquis receives a letter from Madame de Rênal, revealing Julien's former relationship with herself. In a crisis of vengefulness and disillusion, Julien rides off to Verrières and shoots (but does not kill) Madame de Rênal during the celebration of the Mass. He is arrested, tried, condemned to death—and executed.

Julien Sorel is Stendhal's total "egotist," with all that that term implies: intelligence, willpower, and absolute lucidity, yet with so strong a sense of the highest ideal of his own self that no satisfaction of his ambitions or senses is acceptable, unless it should also satisfy that punctilious demand of "honor," without which he is "a mere peasant." Utterly contemptuous of his own peasant-capitalist background, of the provincial bourgeoisie of Verrières, and later even of the right-wing reactionary "high society" of Paris, nothing less than the highest aim of all can seem worthwhile to him. He would be a new Napoleon, a new Danton, yet at the same time he is only nineteen years old, uneducated, unsophisticated, and desperately timid. In the old days, under his hero, his model, Napoleon (he keeps a copy of Emmanuel, Comte de Las Cases's *Mémorial de Sainte-Hélène* hidden under the mattress of his bed—his bible), he might have risen through the ranks to become a marshal of France by the age of thirty (the "red"); but Napoleon is dead, and France, indeed the whole of Europe, lies in the grip of the reaction, controlled by the *ancien régime* aristocracy, by the right-wing bourgeoisie, and above all by the Church. As a soldier now, he would be destined to remain obscurely in the ranks for the rest of his days; but in the Church (the "black"), a man may become a bishop by the age of twenty-five, a cardinal by the age of thirty. In default of opportunity by way of the red, Julien Sorel opts, rationally and mathematically, for the black.

Not only does this situation set out the entire sociopolitical theme of the novel (a devastating condemnation of the whole state of France in the period preceding the July days of 1830, under the right-wing reaction that was perforce to follow a failed revolution), but also it introduces the second theme: hypocrisy. The nineteenth century, in the opinion of those who lived through it, was the most hypocritical century in the history of the world: To succeed, the first requirement was to pay lip service to whatever was in fashion. Thus, Julien Sorel decides to make himself a hypocrite, ruthlessly and lucidly. He is totally atheistic; he believes in no God, in nothing but himself. If the whole of society is corrupt and rotten, then he would be a fool not to profit by this corruption and this rottenness.

Into this pattern of controlled and rationalized egotism there intrude successively two women: Louise de Rênal and Mathilde de La Mole. Each is the absolute antithesis of the other: The first is married, deeply religious, humble, and passionately adoring; the second is a Diana-huntress, a fair-haired virgin inviolate, as implacably Voltairean as Julien himself. Both are infinitely far above Julien in social status; neither can be attacked, save by the stratagems of war. With a degree of male-oriented military objectivity that profoundly shocked Stendhal's contemporaries and that is still more than a little disconcerting even today, Julien prepares his assault on one after another of these "fortresses"—and succeeds. Here, it is the red which is in the ascendant. Cold courage, icy calculation, "devotion to duty"—these are what drive Julien onward, when he would much rather retreat. In each case, when he is "victorious," he is rewarded by no pleasure whatsoever. "Is *that* all it was?" he asks himself after his first subjugation of Madame de Rênal; "she had done her duty" is the only comment that Stendhal allows Julien after his first night with the previously virginal Mathilde de La Mole.

The total cynicism of the assault and the cold, mathematical assessment of the "conquest" are, however, only a beginning. In his essay *Maxims of Love*, Stendhal had written a sentence whose originality, for its time, is easy to overlook: "Sexual intimacy is not so much the climax of happiness, as the last step before reaching it." This apparently simple statement implies the reversal of an entire psychologico-literary tradition in the treatment of the theme of love—the tradition which assumes that, between "true lovers," the physical coming-together is the beginning and the end. For Stendhal, sexual intimacy is only a single step on the road to a complete relationship. Both in the case of Louise de Rênal and in that of Mathilde de La Mole, the lovers only begin to appreciate the significance of their relationship weeks, or even months, after their first moment of physical surrender, and by then it is too late. It is at this point that the irrational begins to take over.

The sheer irrationality of the ending of *The Red and the Black* has puzzled, and continues to puzzle, innumerable commentators—simply because there is no rational explanation. Poor Antoine Berthier could no more explain his actions than could Julien Sorel. Julien, after his assault on Madame de Rênal, could easily have escaped sentence; Madame de Rênal had not died, and powerful friends were working for him. Every chance that is offered to him, however, he refuses. He condemns himself, as it were, against all the evidence. His vaulting ambition appeased at last, he positively exults in the prospect of death. At an earlier point in the novel, meeting the failed revolutionary Count Altamira, condemned to death *in absentia* by the government of his country, Julien had observed significantly: "A death-sentence is the only honour which cannot be bought." Perhaps this is the key. Caught in the toils of an utterly corrupt society, even the sublimest moments of his love for Madame de Rênal and for Mathilde were tainted with corruption: the corruption even of being alive in the nineteenth century in France. Alone in his cell during the final hours, Julien at last finds himself confronted with the only worthy opponent whom his pride acknowledges: himself. This is the ultimate sublimation of "egotism"—an egotism so vast and pure and perfect that it can find satisfaction in nothing less than the Absolute; because there is no Absolute in life, death is the welcomest of lovers.

LUCIEN LEUWEN

Among all of Stendhal's novels, *Lucien Leuwen* is the most immediately and overtly political. In fact, it was probably the realization that to see it in print was likely to cost him his job as French Consul in Civitavecchia that caused Stendhal finally to abandon it two-thirds of the way through. Even so, the two parts that have come down to us are longer than *The Red and the Black*. In spite of their incomplete and unpolished state, they nevertheless represent one of Stendhal's major achievements.

As usual, Stendhal "borrowed" his plot—in this case, from an unpublished "first novel" by one of his oldest friends, Madame Jules Gaulthier. Unfortunately, the original manuscript has vanished; it nevertheless seems to have supplied the material at least for part 1 of *Lucien Leuwen*.

Since July, 1830, when Stendhal had enthusiastically welcomed the Revolution, which brought in the new regime of Louis-Philippe, things had gone very wrong indeed, and, once again, the country stood on the brink of civil war. There were three factions: the aristocracy, supported by the Church (the Legitimists), who had never accepted Louis-Philippe and were conspiring with foreign powers for the return of the Bourbons; the Republicans (mainly intellectuals, but backed by the rising power of the proletariat), determined on a new and definitive revolution; and, sandwiched between the two and loved by no one, the Middle Way (*le juste milieu*), the compromise government actually in power. Early in 1834, a series of incidents had occurred, in which troops had been called in by the bourgeois government to suppress rioting workers. One of these frays, known to history as the Affaire de la rue Transnonain, had caused an explosion of resentment throughout the country. The Affaire de la rue Transnonain not only signaled the beginning of real trouble for Louis-Philippe and gave the term "bourgeois" for the first time its modern, pejorative sense, but also provided the spark in Stendhal's mind that set off *Lucien Leuwen*.

Lucien Leuwen himself is a bourgeois, the sophisticated and intelligent son of a fabulously wealthy banker (modeled on Baron Mayer Rothschild), who, because of his dictatorial powers in the financial world, has every ministry in his pocket. A student at the École Polytechnique, Lucien has been expelled as being suspect of Republicanism; now, to his father's indulgent amusement, he decides for a career in the army, for, like Julien Sorel, he has been brought up on the great Napoleonic legend, besides which, as a handsome young man, he appreciates the elegance of the uniform. His father's influence assures him of a commission as second lieutenant in the Lancers,

and he is stationed in Nancy, a near-frontier garrison town in northeastern France.

With Lucien's arrival in that city, the themes of the novel immediately begin to take shape. Life in the army is anything but that which his romantic imagination had pictured. After nearly twenty years without firing a shot at an enemy, it is boring; in consequence, it is disillusioning, barbaric, inefficient, and philistine. The officers spend their time quarreling, drinking, and seducing; its other ranks are sullen and recalcitrant, because the only time they see action is against their own countrymen "armed with cabbage-stumps." Moreover, there is no longer anything glorious about being an officer: Despised as a "policeman" employed by a corrupt government of financial speculators, the new second lieutenant is lampooned in the press by the Republican Left and systematically snubbed in the aristocratic salons of the Right. Even the latter have little to offer: This is not intellectual, sophisticated Paris, but a remote provincial township bearing a remarkable resemblance to Grenoble—few writers in the entire European tradition have such utter contempt for provincial mediocrity as does Stendhal.

After one farcical "campaign" against the local cabbage-stumps, and a long, drawn-out, inconclusive love affair with an unapproachable Legitimist widow, Lucien is tricked somewhat melodramatically into leaving Nancy, having made himself unpopular in all quarters. Seeing him unemployed, his ever-indulgent father secures for him a post as private secretary to the Comte de Vaise, Minister of the Interior in Louis-Philippe's government. From this point onward, the satire of a corrupt democracy in action becomes progressively more ferocious. It is a society controlled exclusively by two forces: cupidity and fear—on one hand, bribery and peculation; on the the other, spying and a ruthless censorship. Every chance acquaintance, in this first portrait of the modern police state, is a potential government agent; every post-office clerk will open letters and report their contents to the authorities. To be observed reading a suspect article in the press may herald the end of a promising career.

Lucien is wiser now, his early idealism giving way to an utterly ruthless cynicism. (In its own way,

Lucien Leuwen is a *Bildungsroman*: a novel of indoctrination into the manners of a society.) In two memorable episodes, he is first required to "cover up" a failed attempt by a government agent provocateur to portray the workers as dangerous animals intent on destroying the forces of law and order (the "Kortis affair"); then, by a mixture of corruption and intimidation, to manipulate election results in favor of the regime. In the first of these enterprises, Lucien succeeds, almost with the slickness of a modern secret agent; in the second, he fails but emerges with honor. Again, Stendhal asks the question: How can *any* idealism survive amid the unmitigated moral pollution of modern society? Can an honorable man so much as touch politics with his little finger and not be sullied? The answer is an emphatic no.

Into the fabric of this sociopolitical diatribe, which constitutes the essential element of the novel, there are woven two psychological portraits, which are among Stendhal's most fascinating. The first is that of Bathilde de Chasteller—another variation of the Métilde/Mathilde dream figure—a slightly prudish provincial widow who is the great love of Lucien's life and who alone redeems the misery of his sojourn in the garrison town of Nancy. The second, more interesting still, is the portrait of Lucien's own father, the successful banker Monsieur Leuwen, *père*.

François Leuwen is one of Stendhal's finest creations. He is the father Stendhal wished he had had; he is the father, perhaps, that every truly intelligent young man would allot to himself, were the choice his. He is the creative critic to his own son; he is generous, even indulgent; he will accept anything except incompetence or stupidity. He is a banker, but he is totally indifferent to money. For him, banking is a game, just as, later in the novel, when he chooses to indulge in politics, politics is a game. He is brilliant, witty, totally in control of his world, and, after twenty-five years of marriage, still adored by his wife. He is (in a different context) the fifty-year-old Stendhal in relation to his own heroes, for all of them—Octave, Julien, Lucien, Fabrice, Feder de Miossens—are of the age to have been his own sons. All of them, Lucien in particular, are Stendhal as he might have been, had he been born twenty or thirty

years later. Leuwen, *père*, however, is sixty-five years old when the novel opens; by the end of part 2, he is dead. Seemingly, once he had vanished, Stendhal no longer had the courage to go on with his own story.

THE CHARTERHOUSE OF PARMA

Into *The Charterhouse of Parma*, the last and greatest of his completed works, Stendhal poured the entirety of his life's experience: his passionate love of Italy, his cult of energy and unexpectedness, his worship of the young Napoleon, his memories of Métilde, his confrontation of absolutes (the battlefield and the monastery), his contempt for the new, get-rich-quick bourgeoisie of modern Europe, his philosophy of egotism and of the pursuit of happiness ("la chasse au bonheur"), his irony, his cynicism, his frivolity when confronted with anything solemn or pompous, and his unquenchable idealism. The origin of the story lies in an Italian manuscript of the Renaissance, entitled *The Origins of the Greatness of the Farnese Family*: a summary of the manner in which Alessandro Farnese had risen, in 1534, to be elected to the throne of Saint Peter under the name of Pope Paul III. Stendhal had had this narrative in mind for four or five years when, in 1838, some unrevealed incident recalled to him an event which, a decade or so earlier, had moved him deeply: the death of a child, Bathilde, daughter of his sometime mistress Clémentine Curial. This gave him the ending which he needed and, as was so frequently the case, the end was his true starting point. At the same time, he decided to set the story not in Renaissance Rome but in post-Napoleonic Parma. On November 4, 1838, he began to write, or rather, to dictate. By November 8, he had completed the Waterloo episode, and on that same day, he changed his hero's name from Alexandre to Fabrice. By December 26, the novel was complete; it had taken him exactly fifty-two days to write it.

Like *The Red and the Black, The Charterhouse of Parma* falls into two parts, the dominant themes and characters of part 2 being fleetingly, but nevertheless carefully, etched in in part 1. The story opens in 1796, the year in which Napoleon, in the first and most exhilarating of his campaigns, liberated Milan from the Austrians. Into these scenes of delirious rejoicing, Stendhal pours all the excitement of his own first discovery of Milan following the battle of Marengo. A penniless young French officer, Lieutenant Robert, is lodged in the *palazzo* of the noble del Dongo family. There he is welcomed, not by the Marquis (who, being a die-hard, pro-Austrian reactionary, has prudently retreated to his ancestral castle at Grianta on the shores of Lake Como), but by the Marquise, his wife, and by his young sister, the thirteen-year-old Gina del Dongo. This state of euphoria lasts for nearly three years, before the French are driven out once more after the Battle of Cassano, but at some point during the second year, the Marquise has given birth to a son, Fabrice. Stendhal never states, nor even specifically hints, that Fabrice's father is not the avaricious and cantankerous Marquis but rather Lieutenant Robert; nevertheless, the reader is entitled to his or her surmises. At all events, Fabrice's character, as it develops, is a judicious balance between the French and the Italian: He has, on one hand, something of the lucidly calculated egotism and the hypocrisy of a Julien Sorel and, on the other, a degree of spontaneity, of superstition, and of sheer frivolity which, in Stendhal's view, is "typically Italian," although nowhere else does he insist so markedly upon these particular aspects.

Superstition and frivolity: These are the characteristics (in alliance with courage, passion, generosity, and an innate nobility of mind) that distinguish Fabrice from any other Stendhalian hero. Both traits, alternately qualities and defects, Fabrice owes to the total nullity of his education (his is a Jesuit-dominated society that is terrified by ideas, because ideas lead ineluctably to atheism and to revolution)— an education whose supreme achievement is to maintain the child in a state of perfect innocence, that is, ignorance. On the other hand, Stendhal exploits both traits for purposes of his own. The superstition (above all, the faith in omens as guides to decision making or as forewarnings of the future) will gradually evolve into a complex pattern of symbols—trees, towers, walls, prisons, and so on—which themselves form a coherent and autonomous substructure to the novel; the frivolity acquires status as a positive ethic, insofar as it is opposed to all that is humorless and self-important and bourgeois and puritanical in nineteenth century society. In *Lucien Leuwen*, the operations of high finance were redeemed by being "taken as a game"; in *The Charterhouse of Parma*, even the crude machinations of party politics become acceptable, provided that they are conceived as "a game of chess, or whist," or perhaps even as the artfully distracting intrigues of an Italian *opera buffa*.

Fabrice is sixteen years old when Napoleon escapes from Elba and begins the campaign that is to finish at Waterloo. Fabrice, in enthusiasm for his hero, escapes from his gloomy family castle and rushes off to join him as a volunteer—a disastrous impulse of emotional naïveté that culminates in the famous description of the battle itself. These fifty-odd pages offer a truly realistic description of a battle, one which, some twenty-five years later, so impressed Leo Tolstoy that it gave him the first inspiration for *War and Peace* (1865-1869). It is a picture of total chaos, in which no one—least of all Fabrice—has the faintest idea of what is happening: "*Was* that a battle? *Did* I take part in a battle?" This, in the end, as he makes his way out of the rout, is the only question that torments him.

Back in Lombardy, Fabrice finds himself politically suspect as a result of his escapade, and, under the protection of his aunt, the Countess Pietranera, he is smuggled out of the Austrian dominions, first into Piedmont, later to Naples to study theology. This Countess Pietranera is that same Gina who, at the age of thirteen, had first appeared in the *palazzo* of the del Dongo family in the opening scene of the novel. On growing up, she has made a love match with an army officer, General Count Pietranera, subsequently killed in a duel; now an impoverished widow in her early thirties, at the same time that she takes Fabrice under her protection, she attracts the attention of a certain Count Mosca, who is scintillatingly competent, sophisticated, cynical, and middle-aged, currently the power behind the throne of Ranuce-Ernest IV, Prince of Parma. Gina is attracted to him. On his advice, she makes a purely nominal marriage with an aged courtier, the Duke of Sanseverina-Texis, and Count Mosca and the new Duchess Sanseverina take up their residence at the Court of Ranuce-Ernest IV, where they are eventually joined by Fabrice. Fabrice is now a fully fledged *monsignore* (a candidate for higher ecclesiastical office in the Roman Church), with pretensions to succeed, thanks to Mosca's influence, to the Archbishopric of Parma.

The first polarization of the novel is now complete. Against a brilliantly handled background of political intrigue in this comic-opera court, there evolve the emotional relationships of Stendhal's three most complex and convincing characters. Mosca is ever more deeply in love with Gina; Gina progressively falls in love with her own nephew, Fabrice; and Fabrice is in love with no one but quite prepared to have adventures with any pretty woman he meets. In the last analysis, the novel is the most subtle observation of the balance between maturity and immaturity in three completely sincere and generous individuals. Mosca, no less passionate for being past fifty, is able to observe himself lucidly, knowing exactly what he wants from life and how to get it, and is always able to defer immediate and present satisfaction in the interests of some more distant, but more rewarding, end. Gina, a woman at the very height of her maturity and powers, is deeply grateful to Mosca for the richness and excitement of the life he has made for her and is fully aware of the absurdity of falling in love with a man who is fifteen years younger than herself, and who is her own nephew at that, yet is unable to do anything about it. She is given, in consequence, to sudden violent and unpredictable actions that will shake the whole foundation of the state. Fabrice, revering in Mosca the father he might have had, is warmly attached to Gina in a kind of admiring and generous *amitié amoureuse*. At bottom, he is still an adolescent, emotionally dormant, prepared to commit the wildest extravagances for one woman one day, only to make love to another the day following.

One of Fabrice's ephemeral adventures involves him with a little *commedia dell'arte* actress called Marietta, a harmless enough amusement in all conscience, save that Marietta has a "protector," an uncouth lout named Giletti. Giletti, not without reason, becomes jealous of Fabrice, attacks him, and, in the resulting scuffle, gets himself killed. In this (given the prevailing ethos of Parma), there is nothing reprehensible for Fabrice—for a noble del Dongo to dispose of an ignominious, fifth-rate strolling player is, ordinarily, not too unusual. In the hothouse atmosphere of court intrigue that flourishes about Prince Ranuce-Ernest, however, Mosca's enemies recognize the opportunity to topple the all-powerful minister by having his favorite protégé indicted and executed for murder. Thus, Fabrice is arrested and imprisoned in the infamous Farnese Tower.

Fabrice's imprisonment at the very summit of this gigantic fortress (a magnified version of the Castel Sant'Angelo in Rome) marks the beginning of the most hallucinatory episode of the whole novel. From the window of his aerie, Fabrice can glimpse the residence of the Prison Governor, General Fabio Conti, some twenty-five feet below; there he watches the Governor's daughter, Clélia Conti, tending the bird cages on her balcony. Between them springs a love that is so exalted, so ineffable (its very impossibility on the human level carrying it into the domain of the transcendental), that the months of his imprisonment come to represent to Fabrice the sublimest moments of happiness on earth. The devoted and indefatigable Gina arranges his escape, but it takes all of Clélia's powers of persuasion to convince him that he must save his own life. Once restored to the world, he is as a being returned from another dimension, a being allowed a glimpse of Paradise and then wrenched away from it, a being forced to exchange the freedom of imprisonment for the imprisonment of freedom. All appears to him unreal and transparent. His life, his soul, his whole being is "on the other side."

Eventually, the novel draws to its (characteristically abrupt) close. Fabrice and Clélia, amid virtually insuperable difficulties, discover each other again. A child is born to them, a son, Sandrino, but Sandrino dies. A few weeks later, in despair and grief, Clélia dies also. Fabrice renounces the world and retires to a monastery—the Charterhouse of Parma—where his cell recalls to him the sublimest moments of his imprisonment in the Farnese Tower. Then he, too, dies, and his death is followed by that of Gina, yet there is nothing tragic about these deaths.

The Charterhouse of Parma retained its singular density, perhaps, until the Russian novelists achieved its equivalent. Even absolutely minor characters—the Abbé Blanès, the astrologer-priest of Grianta, or Ferrante Palla, the brigand-poet, or "La Vivandière" (the canteen woman following the regiments at Waterloo), or Aniken, the Flemish-speaking innkeeper's daughter at Zonders, where Fabrice recuperates from his wounds—all of these and a score of others have an immediacy that makes them unforgettable. *The Charterhouse of Parma* is Stendhal's last will and testament, embracing all that he knew of good and evil in the world.

Lamiel

The last of Stendhal's novels, *Lamiel*, left unfinished at his death, is of more interest to scholars than to the general reader. Whether Stendhal's creative powers had been exhausted by *The Charterhouse of Parma* or he was experimenting with new narrative forms which he never had time to master is not clear. As the fragments of *Lamiel* have come down to us, there are two quite distinct versions, of which the first (1839) is of greater originality than the second.

The first version of *Lamiel* is an extended novella in the picaresque tradition. It owes much to Voltaire's *contes philosophiques*—particularly to 1748's *Zadig*—and it may well constitute an attempt to write such a tale in a setting of the year 1830. The heroine, Lamiel, an orphan adopted into a family of nouveau riche peasants in Normandy, sets out to discover "what love is all about." With a degree of cynicism redeemed only by absolute naïveté, Lamiel, after each amorous-sexual experience, echoes Julien Sorel's words after his first night with Madame de Rênal: "So *that's* all it was!" After Stendhal's death, a decade or so later, Gustave Flaubert, in *Madame Bovary* (1857), and Edmond and Jules de Goncourt, with *Germinie Lacerteux* (1865), were to tackle similar questions, albeit using a different tonality.

Stendhal's novels concern overall the revolt of the individual against the compulsive forces of conformism; his men and women are utterly and ruthlessly cynical in pursuit of their own self-realization, yet cynicism is only one element in the pattern. Through his novels, Stendhal has bequeathed a philosophy that is frequently known as Beylism and that,

with its inextricable mixture of egoism and idealism, holds an appeal that increases from generation to generation. This philosophy can be summarized as follows: I am Myself, and outside Myself, there is no God, there is nothing. Consequently, my ultimate objective can only be the realization of my own potential, my "happiness." I can realize my ultimate happiness only if this happiness corresponds to the highest ideal that I can conceivably formulate *for* myself; anything less than that is mere vulgarity, sordid, nauseating, and unforgivable. Once that "sublime ideal" is achieved, then there is nothing beyond it: only time, which will destroy its perfection.

It is logical, therefore, that virtually all of Stendhal's novels and stories have the outward form of tragedies, ending in death. Yet they are not tragedies. They are shot through with exaltation: records of men and women striving to realize the highest ideal of themselves in defiance of a faceless, sordid, corrupt, and materialistic society determined to reduce them to its own level of dreary mediocrity.

Richard N. Coe

Other major works

SHORT FICTION: *Chroniques italiennes*, 1839, 1855 (*The Abbess of Castro and Other Tales*, 1926).

NONFICTION: *Vies de Haydn, de Mozart et de Métastase*, 1815 (*The Lives of Haydn and Mozart, with Observations on Métastase*, 1817); *Histoire de la peinture en Italie*, 1817; *Rome, Naples et Florence en 1817*, 1817, 1826 (*Rome, Naples, and Florence, in 1817*, 1818); *De l'amour*, 1822 (*Maxims of Love*, 1906); *Vie de Rossini*, 1823 (*Memoirs of Rossini*, 1824; also as *Life of Rossini*, 1956); *Racine et Shakespeare*, part 1, 1823; part 2, 1825 (*Racine and Shakespeare*, 1962); *Notes d'un dilettante*, 1824-1827; *Promenades dans Rome*, 1829 (*A Roman Journal*, 1957); *Pensées, filosofia nova*, 1981; *Mémoires d'un touriste*, 1838 (*Memoirs of a Tourist*, 1962); *Voyage dans le midi de la France*, 1838 (*Travels in the South of France*, 1971); *Journal*, 1888; *Vie de Henry Brulard*, 1890 (wr. 1835-1836; *The Life of Henry Brulard*, 1925); *Souvenirs d'égotisme*, 1892 (wr. 1832; *Memoirs of an Egotist*, 1949); *Correspondance*, 1933-1934.

MISCELLANEOUS: *The Works*, 1925-1928 (6 volumes).

BIBLIOGRAPHY

Adams, Robert M. *Stendhal: Notes on a Novelist*. New York: Funk & Wagnalls, 1959. Still one of the best critical introductions, written lucidly, with a biographical chapter and discussions of Stendhal's major works. Adams includes an appendix identifying the "major slips, inconsistencies, oversights, and verbal faults" in Stendhal's two major novels.

Alter, Robert. *A Lion for Love: A Critical Biography of Stendhal*. New York: Basic Books, 1979. The biography that best integrates an analysis of Stendhal's fiction into the story of his life.

Bell, David F. *Circumstances: Chance in the Literary Text*. Lincoln: University of Nebraska Press, 1993. Examines the realistic writing of Stendhal and Honoré de Balzac.

Bloom, Harold, ed. *Stendhal*. New York: Chelsea House, 1989. Essays by distinguished critics on women in Stendhal's oeuvre, his use of autobiography, and his love plots. Includes introduction, chronology, and bibliography.

Bolster, Richard. *Stendhal: "Le Rouge et le noir."* London: Grant & Cutler, 1994. A critical guide to *The Red and the Black*.

Brombert, Victor. *Stendhal: A Collection of Critical Essays*. Englewood Cliffs, N.J.: Prentice-Hall, 1962. Essays on Stendhal's Romantic realism, his politics, and his analysis of society. Also an informative introduction by one of the great scholars of French literature, a chronology, and bibliography.

Richardson, Joanna. *Stendhal*. New York: Coward, McCann & Geoghegan, 1974. A sound narrative biography with excellent documentation. Includes a bibliography.

Talbot, Emile J. *Stendhal Revisited*. New York: Twayne, 1993. A revision of a useful introductory work, with a chapter on the man and the writer and separate chapters on Stendhal's major novels. Contains a chronology, notes, and an annotated bibliography.

Wood, Michael. *Stendhal*. Ithaca, N.Y.: Cornell University Press, 1971. A meticulous, scholarly study of Stendhal's style and structure. Includes notes and brief bibliography. One of the standard works of Stendhal criticism in English.

LAURENCE STERNE

Born: Clonmel, Ireland; November 24, 1713
Died: London, England; March 18, 1768

PRINCIPAL LONG FICTION

The Life and Opinions of Tristram Shandy, Gent.,
1759-1767
A Sentimental Journey Through France and Italy,
1768

OTHER LITERARY FORMS

Laurence Sterne began his literary career with political pieces in the *York-Courant* in 1741. Two years later, he published a poem, "The Unknown World," in *The Gentleman's Magazine* (July, 1743). His song, "How Imperfect the Joys of the Soul," written for Kitty Fourmantel, appeared in Joseph Baildon's *Collection of New Songs Sung at Ranelagh* (1765), and a four-line epigram, "On a Lady's Sporting a Somerset," was attributed to Sterne in *Muse's Mirror* (1778). His sermons were published in three installments: two volumes in 1760, another two in 1766, and a final three volumes in 1769. A political satire entitled *A Political Romance* was published in 1759 but quickly suppressed. After Sterne's death, *Letters from Yorick to Eliza* appeared in 1773, and his daughter arranged for the publication of *Letters of the Late Rev. Mr. L. Sterne to His Most Intimate Friends* (1775, three volumes). These volumes include an autobiographical *Memoir* and the *Fragment in the Manner of Rabelais*. In 1935, Oxford University Press published the definitive edition of Sterne's letters, edited by Lewis Perry Curtis. The *Journal to Eliza*, composed in 1767, was not published until 1904.

ACHIEVEMENTS

When Sterne went to London in March, 1760, he was an obscure provincial parson. He rode as a guest in Stephen Croft's cart, and he brought with him little more than his "best breeches." Two months later, he returned to York in his own carriage. Robert Dodsley, who the year before had refused the copyright of *The Life and Opinions of Tristram Shandy, Gent.* (commonly called *Tristram Shandy*) for 50 pounds, now gladly offered Sterne 250 pounds for the first two volumes, 380 pounds for the next two, as yet unwritten, and another 200 pounds for two volumes of sermons. The famous artist William Hogarth agreed to provide a frontispiece to the second edition of volume 1 and another for volume 3; Joshua Reynolds painted Sterne's portrait. Like Lord Byron, Sterne could have said that he awoke to find himself famous. As Sterne did say, in a letter to Catherine Fourmantel, "I assure you my Kitty, that Tristram is the Fashion." Despite the carpings of a few—Horace Walpole thought *Tristram Shandy* "a very insipid and tedious performance," and Samuel Richardson thought it immoral—the novel was the rage of London, inspiring so many continuations and imitations that Sterne had to sign the later volumes to guarantee their authenticity.

After the novel's initial popularity, sales did drop off. In book 8, Tristram complains that he has "ten cart-loads" of volumes 5 and 6 "still unsold." Dodsley abandoned publication of the work after volume 4, and Sterne's new publisher, Thomas Becket, complained in April, 1763, that he had 991 copies of volumes 5 and 6 unsold (from a printing of 4,000). Samuel Johnson's famous comment, though ultimately incorrect, probably reflected the opinion of the day: "Nothing odd will do long. *Tristram Shandy* did not last." Even Sterne may have tired of the work; the volumes grew slimmer, and volume 9 appeared without its mate, volume 10 having, in Sterne's apt words for an obstetrical novel, "miscarried."

Yet *Tristram Shandy* has lasted. It retains its readership, even if it has continued to justify Sterne's complaint of being "more read than understood." Twentieth century readers have made great, perhaps exaggerated, claims for the novel, seeing it as the harbinger of the works of Marcel Proust, James Joyce, and Albert Camus, who, it is said, derived

(Library of Congress)

from Sterne the concept of relative time, the stream of consciousness, and a sense of the absurd. Even if one discounts such assertions, there can be no question of the work's importance in the development of the novel or of *Tristram Shandy*'s place in the first rank of eighteenth century fiction.

Less has been claimed for *A Sentimental Journey Through France and Italy* (commonly called *A Sentimental Journey*), yet this work, apparently so different from and so much simpler than *Tristram Shandy*, greatly influenced Continental, especially German, literature of the Romantic period. Though critics debate the sincerity of the emotions in the work, eighteenth century readers generally did not question Yorick's sentimentality, which contributed to the rise of the cult of sensibility exemplified by such works as Henry Mackenzie's *The Man of Feeling* (1771) and Sarah Morton's *The Power of Sympathy* (1789). Because of its brevity, its benevolence, and its accessibility, *A Sentimental Journey* has enjoyed continued popularity since its first appearance. Though lacking the stature of *Tristram Shandy*, it remains a classic.

BIOGRAPHY

Laurence Sterne was born in Clonmel, Tipperary, Ireland, on November 24, 1713. On his father's side, he could claim some distinction. His great-grandfather, Richard Sterne, had been Archbishop of York, and his grandfather, Simon Sterne, was a rich Yorkshire country squire. Roger Sterne, Laurence's father, was less distinguished. Sterne describes his father as "a little smart man—active to the last degree, in all exercises—most patient of fatigue and disappointments, of which it pleased God to give him full measure." Sterne added that his father was "of a kindly, sweet disposition, void of all design." Many have seen Roger Sterne as the model for Uncle Toby Shandy. At the age of sixteen, Roger joined the Cumberland Regiment of Foot, and on September 25, 1711, he married Agnes Nuttall. Agnes, according to her son, was the daughter of "a noted sutler in Flanders, in Queen Ann's wars," whom Roger married because he was in debt to her father. Actually, she may have been the daughter of a poor but respectable family in Lancashire.

From his birth to the age of ten, Sterne led a nomadic life, wandering from barracks to barracks across Great Britain. During these years, he may have acquired some of the military knowledge that appears throughout *Tristram Shandy*, or at least that fondness for the military which marks the work.

When Sterne was ten, his uncle Richard sent him to school near Halifax, in Yorkshire, and in 1733, Sterne's cousin sent him to Jesus College, Cambridge, where his great-grandfather had been a master and where both his uncle Jaques and his cousin had gone. At Cambridge, Sterne met John Hall, who later renamed himself John Hall-Stevenson. Hall-Stevenson was to be one of Sterne's closest friends throughout his life; his library at "Crazy Castle" would furnish much of the abstruse learning in *Tristram Shandy*, and he would himself appear in both that novel and *A Sentimental Journey* as "Eugenius," the sober adviser. While at Cambridge, Sterne suffered his first tubercular hemorrhage.

After receiving his bachelor's degree in January, 1737, Sterne had to choose a profession. Because his great-grandfather and uncle had both gone into the Church, Sterne followed their path. After Sterne served briefly in St. Ives and Catton, his uncle Jaques, by then Archdeacon of Cleveland and Canon and Precentor of the York Cathedral, secured for him the living of Sutton on the Forest, a few miles north of York. A second post soon followed; Sterne received the prebend of Givendale, making him part of the York Cathedral chapter and so allowing him to preach his turn there.

At York, Sterne met Elizabeth Lumley, a woman with a comfortable fortune. Their courtship had a strong sentimental tinge to it. Indeed, if Sterne actually wrote to Elizabeth the letters that his daughter published after his death, his is the first recorded use of the word *sentimental*, and the emotions expressed in these letters foreshadow both *A Sentimental Journey* and the *Journal to Eliza*. Even if these letters are spurious, Sterne's description of his courtship in the *Memoirs* is sufficiently lachrymose to rival the death of Le Fever in *Tristram Shandy*. Unfortunately for Sterne, he, unlike Tristram, did go on; on March 30, 1741, he married Elizabeth. The unfavorable portrait of Mrs. Shandy owes much to Sterne's less than sentimental feelings toward his wife, whom he called in March, 1760, the "one Obstacle to my Happiness."

The year 1741 was also important for Sterne because it marked his first appearance in print. His uncle Jaques was a strong Whig, and he recruited his nephew to write in support of the Whig candidate for York in that year's election. Sterne wrote, the Whig won, and Sterne received the prebend of North Newbold as a reward. The Whig success was, however, short-lived. When the Walpole government fell in 1742, Sterne wrote a recantation and apology for his part in "the late contested Election," and thereby earned the enmity of his uncle, an enmity that ended only with Jaques's death in 1759.

For the next eighteen years, Sterne lived as a typical provincial clergyman, attending to the needs of his parishioners and publishing two sermons. One of these, "For We Trust We Have a Good Conscience," Sterne reprints in its entirety in the second volume of *Tristram Shandy*. In 1751, he received the commissaryship of Pickering and Pocklington, despite his uncle's efforts to secure this position for Dr. Francis Topham. Sterne and Topham collided again in 1758, when Topham attended to include his son in a patent and thus secure for him a post after his own death. When the dean of York Cathedral blocked the inclusion, a pamphlet war ensued. Sterne fired the final shot; his *A Political Romance* so squashed Topham that he agreed to abandon the fray if Sterne would withdraw his pamphlet. Sterne did withdraw *A Political Romance*, but he was not finished with Topham, who was to appear in *Tristram Shandy* as Phutatorius and Didius.

A Political Romance is little more than a satirical squib, but it shows that Sterne was familiar with the works of Jonathan Swift. In its use of clothes symbolism as well as in its severity it recalls *A Tale of a Tub* (1704), and it shows that Swift's work was running in Sterne's head between 1758 and 1759. He was making other use of Swift, too. On May 23, 1759, Sterne wrote to Robert Dodsley, "With this You will receive the Life & Opinions of *Tristram Shandy*, which I choose to offer to You first." By this time, the first volume of the novel was finished. Al-

though Dodsley refused the copyright for the fifty pounds Sterne requested, Sterne continued to write, completing a second volume and revising the first to remove "all locality" and make "the whole . . . more saleable," as he wrote to Dodsley several months later.

Salable it was. The York edition sold two hundred copies in two days when it appeared in December, 1759, and when Sterne went up to London, he was told that the book was not "to be had in London either for Love or money." Dodsley, who had been unwilling to risk 50 pounds on the copyright, now purchased it for 250 pounds, gave another 380 pounds to publish the still unwritten volumes 3 and 4, and yet another 200 pounds for two volumes of Sterne's sermons. Sterne was honored by the great. Thomas Gray wrote to Thomas Wharton, "Tristram Shandy is still a greater object of admiration, the Man as well as the Book. One is invited to dinner, where he dines, a fortnight beforehand."

In March, 1760, Sterne also succeeded to the curacy of Coxwold, a better position than his earlier one at Sutton. In May, 1760, he therefore settled at Coxwold, renting Shandy Hall from Earl Fauconberg. Here he worked on the next two volumes of *Tristram Shandy*, which he brought to London at the end of the year. In 1761, he repeated this pattern, but he did not return to Yorkshire after delivering the manuscript of volumes 5 and 6. Having suffered a tubercular hemorrhage, he set off for the warmer, milder air of France.

There he repeated his earlier triumph in London, and he incidentally acquired materials for book 7 of *Tristram Shandy* and *A Sentimental Journey*. Sterne remained in France for almost two years; when he returned to England, he hastily wrote the next two volumes of *Tristram Shandy*, which appeared in January, 1765. In October of that year, he brought twelve sermons to London rather than more of his novel. After leaving the manuscript with his publisher, he again set off for the Continent; he would combine the adventures of this trip with those of his earlier one in writing *A Sentimental Journey*.

In June, 1766, Sterne was back in Coxwold, where he wrote what proved to be the last installment of

Tristram Shandy. This he brought with him to London in late December; shortly after his arrival, he met Eliza Draper, the wife of an East India Company clerk twenty years her senior. Though initially unimpressed with her, Sterne was soon madly in love. When Sterne met her, she had already been in England some two years, and she was to return to India less than three months later, yet she was to color Sterne's last year of life. Before she sailed on the *Earl of Chatham* on April 3, 1767, Sterne visited her daily, wrote letters to her, drove with her, and exchanged pictures with her. After their separation, Sterne continued his letters; those he wrote between April 13 and the beginning of August, 1767, constitute the *Journal to Eliza*. When he broke off this journal with the words "I am thine— & thine only, & for ever" to begin *A Sentimental Journey*, her spirit haunted that work, too, as the Eliza upon whom Yorick calls.

By December, Sterne had finished the first half of *A Sentimental Journey* and again set off for London and his publisher. On February 27, 1768, *A Sentimental Journey*, volumes 1 and 2, appeared. Less than a month later, on March 18, Sterne died. He was buried in London on March 22; on June 8, 1769, he was reinterred in the Coxwold churchyard in Yorkshire.

ANALYSIS

Readers may be tempted to see Laurence Sterne's works either as *sui generis* or as eighteenth century sports that had no mate until Marcel Proust and James Joyce. In fact, Sterne was very much a product of his age. His humor owes much to such earlier writers as François Rabelais, Miguel de Cervantes, Michel de Montaigne, Sir Thomas Browne, and Jonathan Swift, all of whom influenced his experimentation with the form of the newly emerged novel. Even this experimentation is typical of the age. Thomas Amory's *The Life and Opinions of John Buncle Esquire* (1756-1766) may have suggested to Sterne his complete title *The Life and Opinions of Tristram Shandy, Gent*. Like *Tristram Shandy*, Amory's book is full of digressions, and its narrator is conceited.

Sterne's experimentation did go beyond the traditional; one need look no farther than the typography, the varying length of the chapters in *Tristram*

Shandy—from four lines to sixty pages—or the unusual location of certain conventional elements—for example, the placing of *Tristram Shandy*'s preface after the twentieth chapter of book 3 or Yorick's writing the preface to *A Sentimental Journey* after chapter 6. At the same time, Sterne relied on the conventions of the novel. He is meticulous in his descriptions of clothing, furniture, and gesture. His characters are fully developed: They walk, sometimes with a limp, they cough, they bleed, they dance. From Swift, Daniel Defoe, and Samuel Richardson, Sterne took the first-person narrator. From Richardson, he adopted the technique of writing to the moment; from Henry Fielding, he got the idea of the novel as a comic epic in prose. From numerous sources—Rabelais, Cervantes, and Swift, to name but three—he learned of the satiric potential of the genre.

A POLITICAL ROMANCE

A Political Romance reveals Sterne's powerful satiric abilities, but this work has little in common with the novels. True, the personal satire of the pamphlet does persist. Sterne lampoons Dr. Burton (Dr. Slop), Dr. Richard Meade (Dr. Kunastrokius), and Francis Topham (Phutatorius, Didius) in *Tristram Shandy*; Tobias Smollett (Smeldungus) and Samuel Sharp (Mundungus) in *A Sentimental Journey*. For the most part, though, Sterne is after bigger game. As he wrote to Robert Dodsley, the satire is general; and, as he wrote to Robert Foley some years later, it is "a laughing good tempered Satyr," another distinction between the novels and the pamphlet.

The objects of this general satire are several: system-makers of all types, pedants, lawyers, doctors, conceited authors, prudes, and self-deceivers. A common thread uniting all these satiric butts is folly, the folly of believing that life should conform to some preconceived notion, of trying to force facts to fit theories rather than the other way around.

Sterne's insistence on common sense and reason is consistent with the Augustan tradition, which itself is rooted in Anglican beliefs that Sterne emphasized in his sermons as well as in his fiction. Although Sterne's satire is good-tempered, it attacks people's tendency to evil, a tendency noted in Article IX of the Thirty-nine Articles of the Anglican

Church. Like his fellow Augustans, Sterne saw this tendency to evil in many spheres. Like them, therefore, he attacked these deviations from the norm as established by religion and reason (which for Sterne are the same), by nature, by tradition, and by authority. The characters in *Tristram Shandy* and Yorick in *A Sentimental Journey* (who is the only sustained character in that work) are laughable because they deviate from the norm and because they refuse to accept their limitations.

Sterne repeatedly reminds the reader of people's finiteness. Thus, death haunts the novels: In *Tristram Shandy*, Toby, Walter, Mrs. Shandy, Yorick, Trim, and Bobby are all dead, and Tristram is dying. In *A Sentimental Journey*, a resurrected Yorick sees death all around him—a dead monk, dead children, a dead ass, dead lovers. Another, less dramatic symbol of the characters' limitation is their inability to complete what they begin. *Tristram Shandy* and *A Sentimental Journey* remain fragments. Trim never finishes his tale of the King of Bohemia and his seven castles. Walter never finishes the *Tristrapaedia*. Obadiah never goes for yeast. Yorick never finishes the story of the notary. Nor can characters communicate effectively with one another: Walter's wife never appreciates his theories, Toby's hobbyhorse causes him to understand all words in a military sense, Dr. Slop falls asleep in the middle of Trim's reading, and Yorick in *A Sentimental Journey* never pauses long enough to develop a lasting friendship.

Death, the prison of the self, the petty and great disappointments of life—these are the stuff of tragedy, yet in Sterne's novels they form the basis of comedy, for the emphasis in these novels is not on the tragic event itself but rather on the cause or the reaction. Bobby's death, for example, is nothing to the reader, not only because one never meets Bobby alive but also because one quickly becomes involved in Walter's oration and Trim's hat. In *A Sentimental Journey*, Sterne focuses on Yorick's reaction to Maria rather than on her poignant tale: Consequently, one laughs at Yorick instead of crying with Maria. The prison of words that traps the characters is not the result of people's inherent isolation but rather of a comic perversity in refusing to accept the plain

meaning of a statement. The tragic is further mitigated by its remoteness. Though Tristram writes to the moment, that moment is long past; Tristram's account is being composed some fifty years after the events he describes, and Yorick, too, is recollecting emotions in tranquillity. The curious order of *Tristram Shandy* and the rapid pace of *A Sentimental Journey* further dilute the tragic. Yorick dies in book 1 but cracks the last joke in book 9. Yorick has barely begun a sentimental attachment with a *fille de chambre* in Paris when he must set off for Versailles to seek a passport. Though the disappointments, interruptions, failures, and deaths recur, individually they quickly vanish from view. What remains are the characters, who are comic because they refuse to learn from their failures.

Sterne's world is therefore not tragic; neither is it absurd. In the world of the absurd, helpless characters confront a meaningless and chaotic world. For Sterne, the world is reasonable; he shares the Augustan worldview expressed so well by Alexander Pope: "All Nature is but Art, unknown to thee,/ All Chance Direction which thou canst not see." The reasonableness of the world is not, however, to be found in the systematizing of Walter Shandy or the sentimentalism of Yorick. People can live in harmony with the world, Sterne says, only if they use common sense. The comedy of these novels derives in large part from people's failure or laziness to be sensible.

TRISTRAM SHANDY

In *Aspects of the Novel* (1927), E. M. Forster writes: "Obviously a god is hidden in *Tristram Shandy* and his name is Muddle." There is no question that the muddle is present in the novel. Chapters 18 and 19 of book 9 appear as part of chapter 25. The preface does not appear until the third volume. There are black, marbled, and white pages. In book 4, a chapter is torn out and ten pages dropped. Uncle Toby begins knocking the ashes out of his pipe in book 1, chapter 21, and finishes this simple action in book 2, chapter 6. The novel begins in 1718 and ends, if it may be said to end, in 1713. Although called *The Life and Opinions of Tristram Shandy, Gent.*, the novel recounts the life of Uncle Toby and the opinions of Walter Shandy.

One must distinguish, though, between the muddle that the narrator, Tristram, creates, and the ordered universe that Sterne offers. Theodore Baird has demonstrated that one can construct an orderly sequence of events from the information in *Tristram Shandy*, beginning with the reign of Henry VIII (III,xxxiii) through the wounding of Trim in 1693 (VIII,xix; II,v), the siege of Namur at which Toby is wounded in 1695 (I,xxv), the conception and birth of Tristram Shandy in 1718 (I-III), the death of Bobby (1719; IV,xxxii and v,ii), the episode of Toby and the fly (1728; II,xii), the death of Yorick (1748; I,xii), and the composition of the novel (1759-1766). Tristram does attempt to impose some order upon these events; the first five and a half books trace his life from his conception to his accident with the window sash and his being put into breeches. He then breaks off to recount the amours of Uncle Toby, which again appear essentially in sequence, with the major exception of book 7, Tristram's flight into France.

Although Tristram attempts to order these events, he fails. He fails not because life is inherently random or absurd, but because he is a bad artist. He pointedly rejects the advice of Horace, whose *The Art of Poetry* (c. 17 B.C.E.) was highly respected among eighteenth century writers. He will not pause to check facts and even refuses to look back in his own book to see whether he has already mentioned something; this is writing to the moment with a vengeance. He refuses to impose any order at all upon his material, allowing his pen to govern him instead of acting the part of the good writer who governs his pen.

In governing his pen, the good writer carefully selects his material. Many a person has told a plain, unvarnished tale in less space than Tristram, but Tristram cannot decide what is important. Must one know what Mrs. Shandy said to Walter on the night of Tristram's begetting, which, incidentally, may not be the night of Tristram's begetting at all, since the night described is only eight months before Tristram's birth rather than nine—does Tristram realize this fact? Does one need so vivid an account of how Walter falls across the bed upon learning of Tristram's crushed nose? Is it true that one cannot

understand Toby's statement, "I think it would not be amiss brother, if we rung the bell," without being dragged halfway across Europe and twenty-three years back in time? Such details serve the purpose of Tristram's creator by highlighting the follies of a bad writer, but they hardly help Tristram proceed with his story.

Tristram's failure to select his material derives in part from laziness. "I have a strong propensity in me to begin this chapter very nonsensically, and I will not balk my fancy," he writes (I,xxiii), for it requires intellectual effort to balk a fancy. In part, too, this failure to select reflects Tristram's belief that everything concerning himself is important. His is a solipsistic rendering of the humanist's credo, *"Homo sum, humani nihil a me alienum puto"*—I am a man, and nothing that relates to man can be foreign to me. He is confident that the more the reader associates with him, the fonder he (the reader) will become. Hence, the reader will want to know about his failure with Jenny, about his aunt Dinah's affair with the coachman, about his attire as he writes, about his casting a fair instead of a foul copy of his manuscript into the fire. Tristram sets out to write a traditional biography, beginning with a genealogy and proceeding to birth, education, youthful deeds that foreshadow later achievements, marriage, children, accomplishments, death, and burial. He becomes so bogged down in details, however, that he cannot get beyond his fifth year. The episode of Toby and the fly must substitute for a volume on education, and the setting up of his top replaces an account of his youthful deeds.

Although Tristram refuses to impose any system on his writing, he is a true son of Walter Shandy in his willingness to impose systems on other aspects of his world. He devises a scale for measuring pleasure and pain, so that if the death of Bobby rates a five and Walter's pleasure at delivering an oration on the occasion rates a ten, Walter proves the gainer by this catastrophe. Tristram has another scale for measuring his own writing; he awards himself a nineteen out of twenty for the design of the novel. Tristram attaches much significance to the way he is conceived, believing that one's conception determines his entire life. His declared method of describing character is similarly reductive, focusing strictly on the individual's hobbyhorse. He has a theory on knots, on window sashes, and on the effect of diet on writing. Tristram thus serves as a satire on systematizers as well as on bad writers.

The more obvious butt of Sterne's satire on system-makers is Walter Shandy. The Augustan Age has also been called the Age of Reason, and Sterne recognizes the importance of reason. At the same time, the Augustans recognized that a person's reason alone is often an insufficient guide because it can be corrupted by a ruling passion, as Yorick's sermon in *Tristram Shandy* reveals. Tristram fails as an author because he trusts exclusively to his own logic instead of following conventional guidelines. Walter Shandy is another example of one who becomes foolish because of his reliance on his own reason. Like Pope's dunces, Walter is well read, and like Pope's dunces, he fails to benefit from his learning because he does not use common sense. He will look in the Institutes of Justinian instead of the more obvious, and more reliable, catechism—part of Sterne's joke here is that the source Walter cites does not contain what he wants. Walter will consult Rubenius rather than a tailor to determine of what cloth Tristram's breeches should be made. From his reading and reasoning he develops a host of theories: that cesarean birth is the best way of bringing a child into the world, that Christian names determine one's life, that auxiliary verbs provide a key to knowledge. Each of these theories rests on a certain logic. Walter is correct that no one would name his child Judas. From this true observation, though, he erects a most absurd theory, proving Tristram's statement that "when a man gives himself up to the government of a ruling passion,—or, in other words, when his Hobby-Horse grows headstrong,—farewell cool reason and fair discretion" (II,v). Neither Walter nor his son will rein in his hobbyhorse, and, as a result, they become ridiculous.

They may also become dangerous. While Walter is busily engaged in composing his *Tristrapaedia* that will codify his theories of child rearing, Tristram grows up without any guidance at all. Walter is willing, indeed eager, to have his wife undergo a cesar-

ean operation because he believes that such an operation will be less harmful to the infant than natural childbirth. That such an operation will cause the death of Mrs. Shandy is a fact that apparently escapes him.

Even the benign and lovable Uncle Toby makes himself ridiculous by yielding to his hobbyhorse. Not only does this hobbyhorse lead him into excessive expense and so deprive him of money he might put to better use, but also it keeps his mind from more worthwhile occupations. Repeatedly, Sterne, through Tristram, likens Toby's garden battlefield to a mistress with whom Toby dallies; the Elizabethan sense of hobbyhorse is precisely this—a woman of easy virtue. As Tristram notes early in the novel, when "one . . . whose principles and conduct are as generous and noble as his blood" is carried off by his hobbyhorse, it is better that "the Hobby-Horse, with all his fraternity, (were) at the Devil" (I,viii). Deluding himself that he is somehow contributing to the defense of England, Toby blinds himself to the real horrors of war. Wrapped up in his military jargon, he isolates himself verbally from those around him; a bridge or a train has only one meaning for him. No less than Tristram, he is betrayed by words, but in his case as in Tristram's the fault lies not with the words but with the individual betrayed.

Nor is Toby's hobbyhorse dangerous to himself alone. It keeps him away from the Widow Wadman and so prevents his fulfilling his legitimate social responsibilities of marrying and begetting children; his hobbyhorse renders him sterile even if his wound has not. This hobbyhorse also comes close to rendering Tristram sterile, for Trim removes the weights from the window sash to make cannon for Toby's campaigns.

Each of the major characters is trapped in a cell of his own making. Tristram can never finish his book because his theory of composition raises insurmountable obstacles. The more he writes, the more he has to write. Walter's and Toby's hobbyhorses blind them to reality and prevent their communicating with each other or anyone else. The Shandy family is well named; "shandy" in Yorkshire means crackbrained. Significantly, the novel begins with an interrupted act of procreation and ends with sterility. As in Pope's *The Dunciad* (1728-1743), the uncreating word triumphs because of human folly.

Sterne's vision is not quite as dark as Pope's, though; the novel ends not with universal darkness but with a joke. Yorick, the voice of reason and moderation, remains to pull the reader back to reality. Yorick is a jester, and the role of the jester is to remind his audience of the just proportion of things as well as to make them laugh. Yorick does not put a fancy saddle on a horse that does not deserve one. He will destroy a sermon because it is too bad (unlike Tristram, who destroys a chapter because it is too good). He makes only modest claims for his sermons and is embarrassed even by these (unlike Tristram, who repeatedly proclaims himself a genius). Yorick thus offers in word and deed an example of living reasonably and happily.

Sterne offers a second consolation as well. Even though characters isolate themselves with their hobbyhorses, even though they cannot or will not understand one another's words, they can and do appreciate one another's feelings. These emotional unions are short-lived, but they are intense and sincere. Walter will continue to make fun of Toby even after promising not to, but at the moment the promise is made, the two are united spiritually and physically. Tristram and Jenny quarrel, but they also have their tender moments. Trim looks for a carriage in a book by shaking the leaves, and he mistakes fiction for reality in a sermon, but he allows his parents three half-pence a day out of his pay when they grow old. The benevolence that Sterne urged in his sermons is capable of bridging self-imposed isolation. Although one laughs at the characters in *Tristram Shandy*, one therefore sympathizes with them as well, seeing their weaknesses but also their underlying virtue. Though they have corrupted that virtue by yielding to a natural tendency to evil, they redeem themselves through their equally natural tendency to kindness.

Tristram Shandy offended many contemporary readers because of its bawdy tales; reviewers much preferred such seemingly sentimental episodes as the death of Le Fever and urged Sterne to refine his humor. *A Sentimental Journey* superficially appears to have been written to satisfy these demands. It is full of touching scenes, of tears, of charity, of little acts of kindness. Moreover, in a letter to Mrs. William James in November, 1767, Sterne describes the novel as dealing with "the gentle passions and affections" and says his intention is "to teach us to love the world and our fellow creatures better than we do." Sterne's letters, and especially his *Journal to Eliza*, reveal him as a man of feeling, and *Tristram Shandy* satirizes all aspects of human life except for benevolence. Sterne's sermons reinforce his image as a believer in the importance of charity. As a Latitudinarian, he believed that the Golden Rule constitutes the essence of religion, that ritual and church doctrine, while important, are less significant than kindness. Because Yorick in *Tristram Shandy* is Sterne's spokesman, it is tempting to see Yorick in *A Sentimental Journey* as having the same normative function. Though the narrator of *Tristram Shandy* is a dunce and a satiric butt, can one not still trust the narrator of *A Sentimental Journey*?

No. In a famous letter to Dr. John Eustace, Sterne thanks Eustace for the gift of a curious walking stick: "Your walking stick is in no sense more shandaic than in that of its having *more handles than one*." Readers could regard *Tristram Shandy* as total nonsense, as a collection of bawdy stories, as a realistic novel, as a satire on the realistic novel, or as a satire on the follies of humankind. Sterne's second novel, too, is "shandaic." The reader can see it as a tribute to the popular spirit of sentimentality or can view it as a satire of that spirit, yet a careful reading of the book will demonstrate why Sterne wrote to the mysterious "Hannah" that this novel "shall make you cry as much as ever it made me laugh." In other words, Sterne is sporting with rather than adopting the sentimental mode.

A SENTIMENTAL JOURNEY

The object of Sterne's laughter is Yorick. The Yorick who recounts his travels is not the same normative parson as appears in *Tristram Shandy*. He is by now twice dead—dead in William Shakespeare's *Hamlet* (1600-1601) and dead again in *Tristram Shandy* some fifteen years prior to the events of *A Sentimental Journey*. This second resurrection may itself be a joke on the reader, who should recall Yorick's death in book 1 of the earlier novel.

This revived Yorick bears a great similarity to Tristram. He is, for one thing, a systematizer. He establishes three degrees of curses; he discovers "three epochas in the empire of a French woman" ("Paris"), he is able to create dialogues out of silence, and he derives national character not from "important matters of state" but rather from "nonsensical minutiae" ("The Wig—Paris"). Like Tristram, too, Yorick is vain. He gives a sou to a beggar who calls him "My Lord *Anglois*" and another sou for *"Mon cher et très charitable Monsieur."* He does not worry about being unkind to a monk but is concerned that as a result a pretty woman will think ill of him.

Even his style, though less difficult to follow than Tristram's, bears some similarities to that of Sterne's earlier narrator. In the midst of the account of his adventures in Versailles, Yorick introduces the irrelevant anecdote of Bevoriskius and the mating sparrows, thus combining Tristram's habit of digressing with Walter's love of abstruse learning. Yorick later interpolates an account of the Marquis d'E****, and while telling about Paris he presents a "Fragment" that does nothing to advance the story. Like Tristram, too, Yorick cannot finish his account, breaking off in mid-sentence. Apparently, he is more governed by his pen than governing.

Yorick also reminds the reader of the narrator in Swift's *A Tale of a Tub*, who believes that happiness is the state of being well deceived. Yorick is disappointed to learn that his small present to Le Fleur has been sufficient only to allow his servant to buy used clothes: "I would rather have imposed upon my fancy with thinking I had bought them new for the fellow, than that they had come out of the *Rue de friperie*" ("Le Dimanche—Paris"). Instead of inquiring about the history of the lady at Calais, he invents a pleasant account of her until he gets "ground enough for the situation which pleased me" ("In the Street—Calais"). He deceives himself into believing that he is accompanying a pretty *fille de chambre* as far as possible to protect her when actually he wants her company. Even his benevolence is self-deception. He conjures up images to weep over—a swain with a dy-

ing lamb, a man in the Bastille, an imaginary recipient of charity. When in this last instance he confronts the reality, his behavior is hardly benevolent, though.

Sterne is not satirizing benevolence as such. In his sermons "The Vindication of Human Nature" and "Philanthropy Recommended" he rejects the notion that people are inherently selfish and stresses his belief in humankind's natural benevolence. Yet he had to look no farther than his own nose to discover that benevolence can become a hobbyhorse that can carry a person away from the path of reason. Yorick's hobbyhorse of benevolence is no less dangerous than Uncle Toby's or Walter Shandy's. Yorick will weep over a carriage, over a dead ass, or over a caged starling. He admits that he does not even need an object for his sympathy: "Was I in a desert, I would find out wherewith in it to call forth my affection" ("In the Street—Calais"). Real human misery, however, he cannot understand. He can weep over his imagined prisoner in the Bastille, but he cannot imagine the real suffering there. He can be callous to the poor, but never to a pretty young woman.

Yorick's benevolence is thus a compound of self-deception and lust. He will give no money to the poor monk until he wants to impress a pretty woman. He gives a sou to a beggar with a dislocated hip, but he gives an unsolicited crown to a pretty *fille de chambre*, and he gives three *louis d'or* to a pretty grisette. He imagines that in offering to share his chaise with another pretty young lady, he is fighting off "every dirty passion" such as avarice, pride, meanness, and hypocrisy. Actually, he is yielding to desire.

True benevolence is guided by reason, and it is not a thing of the moment only, as Sterne points out in his sermon on the Good Samaritan. Yorick's benevolence is impulsive and short-lived. The cry of a caged starling moves him greatly: "I never had my affections more tenderly awakened," he says ("The Passport—The Hotel at Paris"). The hyperbole of the language is itself a warning of Yorick's inability to temper emotion with reason. After such a reaction, his attitude changes abruptly; Yorick buys the starling but never frees it. After tiring of it, he gives it away to another as callous as himself. At Namport, he mourns for a dead ass and praises its owner for his kindness, adding, "Shame on the world! . . . Did we love each other, as this poor soul but loved his ass—'twould be something" ("Namport—The Dead Ass"). By the next page, Yorick is sending his postillion to the devil. Yorick goes out of his way to find the mad Maria, whom Sterne had introduced in book 7 of *Tristram Shandy*. He weeps with Maria at Moulines; she makes such an impression on him that her image follows him almost to Lyon—an entire chapter!

Yorick is humorous because, like Tristram, Walter, and Toby, he is the victim of his hobbyhorse. He gallops away from reason, failing to examine his motivation or to temper his sudden fanciful flights. In "Temporal Advantages of Religion," Sterne provides a picture of the ideal Christian traveler. "We may surely be allowed to amuse ourselves with the natural or artificial beauties of the country we are passing through," Sterne notes, but he warns against being drawn aside, as Yorick is, "by the variety of prospects, edifices, and ruins which solicit us." More important, Yorick forgets the chief end of people's earthly sojourn: "Various as our excursions are—that we have still set our faces towards Jerusalem . . . and that the way to get there is not so much to please our hearts, as to improve them in virtue." Yorick has come to France for knowledge, but he learns nothing. His benevolence is much closer to wantonness than to virtue; it is fitting that he ends his account in the dark, grasping the *fille de chambre*'s end of volume 2.

In *A Sentimental Journey*, as in *Tristram Shandy*, Sterne mocks excess. He shows the folly that results from the abdication of reason. Though he introduces norms such as Yorick in *Tristram Shandy* or the old soldier in *A Sentimental Journey*, the ideal emerges most clearly from a depiction of its opposite—perverted learning, bad writing, and unexamined motives. When Sterne came to London in 1760, Lord Bathurst correctly embraced him as the heir to the Augustan satirists.

Joseph Rosenblum

OTHER MAJOR WORKS

NONFICTION: *A Political Romance*, 1759; *The Sermons of Mr. Yorick*, 1760 (vols. 1-2), 1766 (vols. 3-4); *Sermons by the Late Rev. Mr. Sterne*, 1769 (vols. 5-7); *Letters from Yorick to Eliza*, 1773; *Sterne's Letters to His Friends on Various Occasions, to Which Is Added His History of a Watch Coat*, 1775; *Letters of the Late Rev. Mr. L. Sterne to His Most Intimate Friends*, 1775 (3 volumes); *In Elegant Epistles*, 1790; *Journal to Eliza*, 1904.

BIBLIOGRAPHY

Cash, Arthur Hill. *Laurence Sterne*. 2 vols. London: Methuen, 1975-1986. The definitive biography. The first volume follows Sterne's life to early 1760 and offers many details about his role in the religious and political affairs of York. The second volume treats Sterne the author. Presents a realistic picture freed from Victorian strictures and romantic glosses. The appendices provide a series of portraits and of letters never before published.

_____. *Sterne's Comedy of Moral Sentiments: The Ethical Dimension of the Journey*. Pittsburgh: Duquesne University Press, 1966. Comparing Sterne's sermons with *A Sentimental Journey Through France and Italy*, Cash finds a moral stance in the novel, one that condemns Yorick for excessive sentimentality. Sterne laughs at Yorick, at himself, and at humankind for abandoning reason.

Cash, Arthur Hill, and John M. Stedmond, eds. *The Winged Skull: Papers from the Laurence Sterne Bicentenary Conference*. Kent, Ohio: Kent State University Press, 1971. A collection of essays on a range of subjects, including Sterne's style, his reputation outside England, and his fictional devices. Includes some helpful illustrations.

Hartley, Lodwick. *This Is Lorence: A Narrative of the Reverend Laurence Sterne*. Chapel Hill: University of North Carolina Press, 1943. Still the best general introduction to the man and his work. In a sprightly biography for the general reader, Hartley quotes generously from Sterne and sets him clearly in his age.

Kraft, Elizabeth. *Laurence Sterne Revisited*. New York: Twayne, 1996. Kraft begins her short book with two chapters about Sterne's early writings, then devotes one chapter each to *Tristram*

Shandy and *A Sentimental Journey*. The first chapter is primarily biographical, giving readers an overview of Sterne's life as a cleric before he became a literary celebrity. The second chapter concerns the fruit of Sterne's years as a clergyman, *The Sermons of Mr. Yorick*. Kraft also includes a final chapter on Sterne's changing critical reputation as well as a selected bibliography.

Myer, Valerie Grosvenor, ed. *Laurence Sterne: Riddles and Mysteries*. New York: Barnes & Noble Books, 1984. Contains eleven essays on *The Life and Opinions of Tristram Shandy, Gent.*, covering such matters as the nature of Sterne's comedy, the intellectual background of the novel, and Sterne's influence on the work of Jane Austen. Includes a brief annotated bibliography.

New, Melvin. *"Tristram Shandy": A Book for Free Spirits*. New York: Twayne, 1994. After providing a literary and historical milieu for Stern's most famous work, New explores five different methods of approaching *Tristram Shandy*: "Satire," "Heads" (that is, intellectually), "Hearts" (that is, emotionally), "Joy," and "Tartuffery" (as a humorous attack on hypocrisy). New's approach is somewhat too schematic and too dependent on Friedrich Nietzsche's writings about *Tristram*, but it could act as a helpful guide for students attempting to come to terms with this shifting and slippery text.

Putney, Rufus D. "The Evolution of *A Sentimental Journey*." *Philological Quarterly* 19 (1940): 349-369. Treats the novel as a hoax in which readers could find the sentimentality they were seeking, while Sterne could create the humorous fiction he wanted to write.

Stedmond, John M. *The Comic Art of Laurence Sterne: Convention and Innovation in "Tristram Shandy" and "A Sentimental Journey."* Toronto: University of Toronto Press, 1967. Sterne's novels highlight the comic distance between aspiration and attainment that is endemic in human existence. Provides helpful readings of the novels and an appendix recording Sterne's direct borrowings.

ROBERT LOUIS STEVENSON

Born: Edinburgh, Scotland; November 13, 1850
Died: Vailima, near Apia, Samoa; December 3, 1894

PRINCIPAL LONG FICTION

Treasure Island, 1881-1882 (serial), 1883 (book)
Prince Otto, 1885
The Strange Case of Dr. Jekyll and Mr. Hyde, 1886
Kidnapped, 1886
The Black Arrow, 1888
The Master of Ballantrae, 1889
The Wrong Box, 1889
The Wrecker, 1892 (with Lloyd Osbourne)
Catriona, 1893
The Ebb-Tide, 1894 (with Osbourne)
Weir of Hermiston, 1896 (unfinished)
St. Ives, 1897 (completed by Arthur Quiller-Couch)

OTHER LITERARY FORMS

In addition to his novels, Robert Louis Stevenson published a large number of essays, poems, and short stories, most of which have been collected under various titles. The best edition of Stevenson's works is the South Seas Edition (32 volumes) published by Scribner's in 1925.

ACHIEVEMENTS

A man thoroughly devoted to his art, Stevenson was highly regarded during his lifetime as a writer of Romantic fiction. Indeed, few, if any, have surpassed him in that genre. Combining a strong intellect and a wide-ranging imagination with his ability to tell a story, he produced novels that transport the reader to the realms of adventure and intrigue. After his death, his literary reputation diminished considerably, until he was regarded primarily as a writer of juvenile fiction, unworthy of serious critical attention. With the growth of scholarly interest in popular literature, however, Stevenson is sure to enjoy a reevaluation. Certainly his narrative skill speaks for itself, and it is on that base that his literary reputation should ultimately rest. Anyone who has vicariously sailed with Jim Hawkins in quest of buried treasure or sipped a potion that reduces intellect to instinct with Henry Jekyll can vouch for the success of Stevenson as a writer and agree with what he wrote in "A Gossip of Romance" (1882): "In anything fit to be called reading, the process itself should be absorbing and voluptuous; we should gloat over a book, be rapt clean out of ourselves, and rise from the perusal, our mind filled with the busiest kaleidoscopic dance of images, incapable of sleep or of continuous thought."

BIOGRAPHY

The only child of Thomas and Margaret (Balfour) Stevenson, Robert Louis Stevenson was born on November 13, 1850, in Edinburgh, Scotland. He was in poor health even as a child, and he suffered throughout his life from a tubercular condition. Thomas, a civil engineer and lighthouse keeper, had hopes that Stevenson would eventually follow in his footsteps, and the youngster was sent to Anstruther and then to Edinburgh University. His fragile health, however, precluded a career in engineering, and he shifted his efforts to the study of law, passing the bar in Edinburgh in 1875.

Even during his preparation for law, Stevenson was more interested in literature, and, reading widely in the essays of Michel de Montaigne, Charles Lamb, and William Hazlitt, he began imitating their styles. Their influence can be seen in the style that Stevenson ultimately developed—a personal, conversational style, marked by an easy familiarity.

Between 1875 and 1879, Stevenson wandered through France, Germany, and Scotland in search of a healthier climate. In 1876, at Fontainebleau, France, he met Fanny Osbourne, an American with whom he fell in love. She returned to California in 1878, and in that same year

became seriously ill. Stevenson set out immediately to follow her. Traveling by steerage, he underwent considerable hardships on his journey, hardships that proved detrimental to his already poor health. In 1880, he married Fanny and settled for a few months in a desolate mining camp in California. After a return to Scotland, the couple journeyed to Davos, Switzerland, for the winter.

Again returning to Scotland in the spring, Stevenson worked on his novel *Treasure Island*. Moving back and forth between Scotland and Switzerland was not conducive to improved health, and Stevenson decided to stay permanently in the south of France. Another attack of illness, however, sent him to Bournemouth, England, a health resort, until 1887, during

(Library of Congress)

3081

which time he worked assiduously on his writing. In August of that year he sailed for America, settling at Saranac Lake in New York's Adirondacks. There he wrote *The Master of Ballantrae* in 1889. He finally settled in the islands of Samoa in the South Seas, a setting that he used for *The Wrecker* and *The Ebb-Tide*. He died there on December 3, 1894, ending a short but productive life.

ANALYSIS

By the time that Robert Louis Stevenson published his first novel, *Treasure Island*, the golden age of Victorianism in England was over. The empire was far-flung and great, but the masses of England had more immediate concerns. The glory of the Union Jack gave small comfort to a working class barely able to keep its head above water. If earlier novelists wrote for the middle-class reader, those of the last twenty years of the century revolted against the cultural domination of that class. Turning to realism, they dealt with the repression caused by a crushing environment. Stevenson, however, disdained moral and intellectual topics, preferring the thin, brisk, sunny atmosphere of romance. Consequently, he stands apart from such figures as Thomas Hardy, Arnold Bennett, and George Gissing.

In "A Humble Remonstrance," Stevenson spoke of the function of a writer of romance as being "bound to be occupied, not so much in making stories true as in making them typical; not so much in capturing the lineament of each fact, as in marshalling all of them to a common end." Perhaps, then, Stevenson should be seen not simply as an antirealistic writer of romance, but as a writer whose conception of realism was different from that of his contemporaries.

In his study of Stevenson, Edwin Eigner points out that the novelist's heroes are drawn from real life and are usually failures. Moreover, says Eigner, "very few of the characters, whether good *or* evil, manage even to fail greatly." Stevenson himself wrote in his essay "Reflection and Remarks on Human Life" that "our business in this world is not to succeed, but to continue to fail, in good spirits." His own ill health may have caused him to see life in terms of conflict, and in his case a conflict that he

could not win. This element of failure adds a somber dimension to Stevenson's romances—a note of reality, as it were, to what otherwise might have been simply adventure fiction. It is the element of adventure superimposed on reality that gives Stevenson's writing its peculiar character. A writer's stories, he remarked, "may be nourished with the realities of life, but their true mark is to satisfy the nameless longings of the reader, and to obey the ideal laws of the daydream." In doing this, the writer's greatest challenge, according to Stevenson, is to give "body and blood" to his stories. Setting, circumstance, and character must all fall into place to give a story the power to make an impression on the mind of the reader—"to put the last mark of truth upon a story and fill up at one blow our capacity for sympathetic pleasure." In this way a story becomes more than merely literature; it becomes art.

Stevenson regarded the tales of the *Arabian Nights* as perfect examples of the storyteller's art: tales that could captivate the reader in his childhood and delight him in his old age. Such was the goal that he sought in his own works: to bring the reader to the story as an involved spectator who does not shy away from the unpleasantries or the villainy, but finds in witnessing them the same pleasure he does in witnessing the more optimistic and uplifting aspects of the piece. Perhaps this is Stevenson's greatest achievement: He illustrates with his stories a sometimes forgotten truth—"Fiction is to the grown man what play is to the child."

TREASURE ISLAND

"If this don't fetch the kids, why, they have gone rotten since my day," Stevenson wrote in a letter to Sidney Colvin on August 25, 1881. He was speaking of *Treasure Island*, the novel on which he was then at work. He need not have worried, for since its publication it has been a favorite of children everywhere—and, indeed, of many adults. Stevenson wrote the book, according to his own account, in two bursts of creative activity of about fifteen days each. "My quickest piece of work," he said. The novel was begun as an amusement for his stepson Lloyd Osbourne, then twelve years old. Upon its completion in November of 1881, the novel was serialized in the magazine *Young Folks*; since it did not raise circulation to any degree, it was not considered particularly successful. The book was an altogether different story.

As a tale of adventure, *Treasure Island* stands as one of the best. Buried treasure has always had an aura of mystery and intrigue about it, and this case is no exception. Young Jim Hawkins is the hero of the novel; the adventure starts when Bill Bones, an old seaman, comes to Jim's father's inn, the Admiral Benbow, to wait for a one-legged seaman, who does not arrive. Bones does have two other visitors: a seaman named Black Dog, whom he chases away after a fight, and a deformed blind man named Pew, who gives him the black spot, the pirates' death notice. Bones is so frightened that he dies of a stroke. In the meantime, Jim's father has also died, leaving Jim and his mother alone. Opening Bones's locker, they find an oilskin packet that Jim gives to Squire Trelawney and Dr. Livesey.

Finding in the packet a treasure map, Trelawney and Livesey decide to outfit a ship and seek the treasure. Jim is invited to come along as cabin boy. Just before they sight the island where the treasure is supposed to be, Jim overhears the ship's cook, the one-legged Long John Silver, and some of the crew plotting a mutiny. When Silver and a party are sent ashore, Jim smuggles himself along to spy on them.

When Trelawney and Livesey learn of Silver's duplicity, they decide to take the loyal crew members and occupy a stockade they have discovered on the island, leaving the ship to the pirates. Unable to take the stockade, Silver offers a safe passage home to its defenders in return for the treasure map. The offer is refused, and, after another attack, the party in the stockade is reduced to Trelawney, Livesey, Captain Smollett, and Jim. Jim rows to the ship, shoots the only pirate on board, and then beaches the ship. Returning to the stockade, he finds his friends gone and Silver and the pirates in control. Silver saves Jim's life from the other pirates and reveals the treasure map, which Dr. Livesey had given him secretly when the former had come to treat some of the wounded pirates. What Silver does not know is that Ben Gunn, the lone resident of the island, has already found the

treasure and moved it to his own quarters. When the pirates find no treasure, they turn on Jim and Silver, but Gunn and Jim's friends arrive in time to rescue them. The ship is floated by the tide, and Jim, his friends, and Silver leave the island. Silver jumps ship with only a bag of coins for his efforts, but the rest of the group divide the treasure. "Drink and the devil had done for the rest."

Though Jim may be the hero of the novel, it is Long John Silver who dominates the book. He is an ambiguous character, capable of murder, greed, and double-dealing on one hand and magnanimity on the other. He was Stevenson's favorite character—and the one who ultimately raises the book from a pedestrian adventure story to a timeless, mythically resonant tale which has absorbed generations of readers. The unifying theme of *Treasure Island* is people's desire for wealth. Trelawney and Livesey may be more moral in society's eyes than Silver, but their motivation is certainly no higher. As for Jim, he cannot, like Silver, give a belly laugh in the face of such a world and go off seeking another adventure. One such adventure is enough for Jim, and that one he would rather forget.

THE BLACK ARROW

Serialized in *Young Folks* in 1883, *The Black Arrow* was labeled by Stevenson as "tushery," a term he and William Henley used for romantic adventures written for the market. In a letter to Henley in May, 1883, he said, "Ay, friend, a whole tale of tushery. And every tusher tushes me so free, that may I be tushed if the whole thing is worth a tush." Stevenson had hopes, however, that *The Black Arrow* would strike a more receptive note in *Young Folks* than did *Treasure Island*, and in this respect, his hopes were realized.

Though it lacks the depth of *Treasure Island*, *The Black Arrow* was enormously popular in its time and does not deserve its critical neglect. Set in the fifteenth century against the background of a minor battle of the Wars of the Roses and the appearance of the infamous Richard, Duke of Gloucester, the story recounts the adventures of Dick Shelton as he attempts to outwit his scheming guardian, Sir Daniel Brackley. An unscrupulous man, Sir Daniel has fought first on one side of the war and then on the other, adding to his own lands by securing the wardships of children orphaned by the war.

Planning to marry Dick to Joanna Sedley, an orphaned heiress, Sir Daniel has ridden away to take charge of the girl. In his absence, Moat House, his estate, is attacked by a group of outlaws led by a man with the mysterious name of John Amend-All, who pins a message to the church door of Moat House swearing vengeance on Sir Daniel and others for killing Dick's father, Henry Shelton.

Dick, deciding to remain quiet until he can learn more of the matter, sets out to inform Sir Daniel of the attack. In the meantime, Joanna, dressed as a boy, has eluded Sir Daniel. On his way back to Moat House, Dick meets Joanna in the guise of "John Matcham." Unaware that Sir Daniel has planned the marriage and unaware that John is Joanna, Dick offers to help his companion reach the abbey at Holywood. They eventually arrive at Moat House, where Dick learns that John is really Joanna and that his own life is in danger. He escapes and, after a lengthy series of intrigues and adventures, saves the life of Richard of York, Duke of Gloucester, and rescues Joanna from Sir Daniel, who is killed by Ellis Duckworth (John Amend-All). Dick then marries Joanna and settles at Moat House.

As an adventure story, *The Black Arrow* is thoroughly successful. The movement from episode to episode is swift, and the reader has little opportunity to lose interest. The love story between Dick and Joanna is deftly handled, with Joanna herself a delightfully drawn character. Still, the novel does not venture beyond the realm of pure adventure. Like many adventure stories, it is often contrived and trivial, but this fact does not detract from its readability.

THE STRANGE CASE OF DR. JEKYLL AND MR. HYDE

Stories and theories abound regarding the writing of *The Strange Case of Dr. Jekyll and Mr. Hyde*. In "A Chapter of Dreams" (1888), Stevenson himself gave an account of the composition of the novel, explaining that "for two days I went about racking my brain for a plot of any sort; and on the second night I dreamed the scene at the window; and a scene after-

wards split in two, in which Hyde, pursued for some crime, took the powder and underwent the change in the presence of his pursuers. All the rest was made awake, and consciously." The whole, according to Stevenson, was written and revised within a ten-week period.

The novel is based on the idea of the double personality in every person, an idea with which Stevenson had long been concerned. Referring to Jekyll, he said to Will H. Low, a painter, that "I believe you will find he is quite willing to answer to the name of Low or Stevenson." Not the first to use the idea in literature, Stevenson does give it a different twist. Hyde is not the double of the sinner, a conscience as it were, but, as one reviewer put it, Hyde is a personality of "hideous caprices, and appalling vitality, a terrible power of growth and increase."

As the story opens, Richard Enfield and Mr. Utterson, a lawyer, are discussing the activities of a Mr. Hyde, who has recently trampled down a small child. Both friends of Dr. Henry Jekyll, they are perturbed that the latter has named Hyde as heir in his will. A year later, Hyde is wanted for a murder, but he escapes. Soon after, Dr. Jekyll's servant Poole tells Utterson of strange goings-on in his employer's laboratory. He is concerned that possibly Jekyll has been slain. Poole and Utterson break into the laboratory and find a man dead from poison. The man is Edward Hyde. A note in the laboratory contains Jekyll's confession of his double identity.

Early in life, he had begun leading a double existence: a public life of convention and gentility and a private life of unrestrained vice. Finally, he discovered a potion that transformed him physically into Edward Hyde, his evil self. Though Jekyll wanted desperately to be rid of Hyde, he was not strong enough to overcome his evil side. He finally closed himself in his laboratory, seeking a drug that would eliminate Hyde. Failing in his search, he committed suicide.

As an exploration into the darkest recesses of the human mind, *The Strange Case of Dr. Jekyll and Mr. Hyde* is skillfully constructed. Not only are Jekyll and Hyde presented in a haunting fashion, but Utterson also is a character brought clearly to life. The plot, sensational though it is, does not rely on the standard gothic claptrap to hold the reader. On the contrary, the story is subtly undertold, and the reader is drawn into the horror of it by Stevenson's penetrating imagination and his easy mastery of language and style. The reader, said one reviewer, "feels that the same material might have been spun out to cover double the space and still have struck him as condensed and close knit workmanship. It is one of those rare fictions which make one understand the value of temperance in art."

KIDNAPPED

Stevenson completed *Kidnapped* in the spring of 1886, intending it originally as a potboiler, and it surely has all the ingredients of high adventure: a stolen inheritance, a kidnapping, a battle at sea, and several murders. Having gained an interest in Scottish history from his travels through the Highlands, Stevenson used as his principal source of historical information *Trial of James Stewart* (1753), a factual account of the 1752 Appin murder trial.

Kidnapped is the story of David Balfour, whose only inheritance from his father is a letter to Ebenezer Balfour of Shaws, David's uncle. On the way to see Mr. Rankeillor, the family lawyer, to get the true story of the inheritance, David is tricked and sent off on a ship for slavery in the American colonies. He meets Alan Breck, an enemy of the monarch because of his part in a rebellion against King George, and, though David is loyal to the king, the two become fast and true friends. Escaping from the ship, they have numerous adventures, finally returning to Scotland, where David learns the truth of the inheritance. His father and uncle had both loved the same woman; when David's father married the woman (David's mother), he generously gave up his inheritance to his brother Ebenezer. Ebenezer knew that such an arrangement would not hold up legally, and thus he tried to kill David. David accepts Ebenezer's offer of two-thirds of the income from the inheritance, and, with the money, he helps Alan reach safety from the king's soldiers who are pursuing him.

Kidnapped is rich in its depiction of the Scottish Highlands, and the novel's dialogue is particularly effective. The contrast between David, a Lowlander and a Whig, and Alan, a Highlander and a Jacobite, for example, is well drawn. Ignoring their differences, the two, like Huck and Jim in Mark Twain's *The Adventures of Huckleberry Finn* (1884), prove that their friendship is more important than geographical and political differences.

Whatever Stevenson thought of *Kidnapped*, his friend Edmund Gosse thought it the "best piece of fiction that you have done." Many would argue with Gosse's statement. While it perhaps has more human interest than does *Treasure Island*, it lacks the sharpness and force of Stevenson's masterpiece.

THE MASTER OF BALLANTRAE

Although not as well known as *Treasure Island* and *Kidnapped*, *The Master of Ballantrae* is considered by many to be Stevenson's best novel. Stevenson himself saw it as a "most seizing tale," a "human tragedy." Despite his preoccupation with character delineation in the story, he still regales the reader with a plethora of adventurous incidents. Set in eighteenth century Scotland, *The Master of Ballantrae* recounts the story of two brothers as they compete for title and love. When Stuart the Pretender returns to Scotland in 1745 to claim the English throne, Lord Durrisdeer decides to send one son to fight with Stuart and to keep one at home, hoping that way to make his estate secure regardless of the outcome of the struggle. James, Master of Ballantrae and his father's heir, joins Stuart, and Henry remains behind. When news of Stuart's defeat and James's death comes, Henry becomes Master of Ballantrae. He marries Alison Graeme, who had been betrothed to James.

James, however, is not dead, and, after adventures in America and France, returns to Scotland. Goading Henry and pressing his attentions on Alison, James soon angers his brother to the point of a midnight duel. Henry thinks that he has killed James, but again the latter escapes death—this time going to India. He surprises Henry once more by showing up alive at Durrisdeer. Taking his family, Henry secretly leaves for America, but James, with his Indian servant Secundra Dass, follows. Searching for treasure that he buried on his previous trip to America, James falls sick and dies, but Henry, thinking his brother able to return at will from death, goes to the grave one night and sees Secundra Dass performing strange ministrations over James's exhumed body. Although the servant is unable to revive James, Henry believes that he sees his brother's eyes flutter and dies from heart failure. Thus, both Masters of Ballantrae are united in death.

The Master of Ballantrae, perhaps more than any other of Stevenson's novels, goes beyond the bounds of a mere adventure story. Adventure is a key element in the book, but the characters of James and Henry Durie are drawn with such subtlety and insight that the novel takes on dimensions not usually found in Stevenson's works. Like Long John Silver in *Treasure Island*, James Durie is not an ordinary villain. Henry, who moves from a kind of pathetic passivity in the first part of the novel to a villainy of his own, is unable to assume the true role of Master of Ballantrae. Overmatched and possessed by James, he lacks the dash and charm and strength of personality that makes the latter the real Master of Ballantrae. "In James Durie," wrote one reviewer, "Mr. Stevenson has invented a new villain, and has drawn him with a distinction of touch and tone worthy of Vandyke." With all the attributes of a hateful fiend, James nevertheless has a wit and a courage that are captivating.

Perhaps the novel does, as Stevenson himself feared, leave the reader with an impression of unreality. Still, whatever its shortcomings, *The Master of Ballantrae* has all the trademarks of Stevenson's fiction: an intricately and imaginatively designed plot, power of style, clear evocation of scene, and lifelike characters. G. K. Chesterton felt that Stevenson was the "first writer to treat seriously and poetically the aesthetic instincts of the boy." In his own way, Stevenson contributed a fair number of readable and memorable works to the English literary heritage, and that heritage is the richer for it.

Wilton Eckley

OTHER MAJOR WORKS

SHORT FICTION: *The New Arabian Nights*, 1882; *More New Arabian Nights*, 1885; *The Merry Men and Other Tales and Fables*, 1887; *Island Nights' Entertainments*, 1893.

PLAYS: *Deacon Brodie*, pb. 1880 (with William Ernest Henley); *Macaire*, pb. 1885 (with Henley); *The Hanging Judge*, pb. 1887 (with Fanny Van de Grift Stevenson).

POETRY: *Moral Emblems*, 1882; *A Child's Garden of Verses*, 1885; *Underwoods*, 1887; *Ballads*, 1890; *Songs of Travel and Other Verses*, 1896.

NONFICTION: *An Inland Voyage*, 1878; *Edinburgh: Picturesque Notes*, 1878; *Travels with a Donkey in the Cévennes*, 1879; *Virginibus Puerisque*, 1881; *Familiar Studies of Men and Books*, 1882; *The Silverado Squatters: Sketches from a Californian Mountain*, 1883; *Memories and Portraits*, 1887; *The South Seas: A Record of Three Cruises*, 1890; *Across the Plains*, 1892; *A Footnote to History*, 1892; *Amateur Emigrant*, 1895; *In the South Seas*, 1896; *The Lantern-Bearers and Other Essays*, 1988.

BIBLIOGRAPHY

Bell, Ian. *Dreams of Exile: Robert Louis Stevenson: A Biography*. New York: Henry Holt, 1992. Bell, a journalist rather than an academic, writes evocatively of Stevenson the dreamer and exile. This brief study of Stevenson's brief but dramatic life does a fine job of evoking the man and the places he inhabited. It is less accomplished in its approach to the work.

Calder, Jenni, ed. *The Robert Louis Stevenson Companion*. Edinburgh: Paul Harris, 1980. Forty-one illustrations accompany eight articles by different authors on the life and work of Stevenson. Some of the authors knew Stevenson personally. These topical articles were written between 1901 and 1979.

Daiches, David, *Robert Louis Stevenson and His World*. London: Thames and Hudson, 1973. A standard popular biography written in chronological and narrative style. Complete with 116 illustrations and a chronological page of events pertinent to Stevenson.

Hammond, J. R. *A Robert Louis Stevenson Companion: A Guide to the Novels, Essays, and Short Stories*. London: Macmillan, 1984. The first three sections cover the life and literary achievements of Stevenson and contain a brief dictionary which lists and describes his short stories, essays, and smaller works. The fourth section critiques his novels and romances, and the fifth is a key to the people and places of Stevenson's novels and stories.

Knight, Alanna. *The Robert Louis Stevenson Treasury*. London: Shepherd-Walwyn, 1985. An extremely useful compendium, arranged in eight parts with twenty-eight illustrations. Contains four maps: of Scotland, France, the South Seas, and the United States, as they pertained to Stevenson's life. Includes an alphabetized index of his works, letters, and characters, as well as works published about him in text, film, and radio. Also covers people and places that factored in his life.

McLynn, Frank. *Robert Louis Stevenson: A Biography*. New York: Random House, 1993. Published on the eve of Stevenson's centenary (1994), McLynn's biography seeks to rehabilitate Stevenson's literary reputation. For McLynn, Stevenson is Scotland's greatest writer of English prose. This an accomplished, serious reappraisal of a writer long relegated to the shelves of "boy's books." A final epilogue helps to explain how Stevenson's family squandered his legacy.

Swearingen, Roger G. *The Prose Writings of Robert Louis Stevenson*. Hamden, Conn.: Archon Books, 1980. A complete (350-entry) chronological list of Stevenson's prose writings—from his earliest childhood until his death in 1894—which is concerned with his literary activity as his career progressed. The data include the first appearance of each work, with its particular history of development, and actual locations of the works today.

ROBERT STONE

Born: Brooklyn, New York; August 21, 1937

PRINCIPAL LONG FICTION
A Hall of Mirrors, 1967
Dog Soldiers, 1974
A Flag for Sunrise, 1981
Children of Light, 1986
Outerbridge Reach, 1992
Damascus Gate, 1998

OTHER LITERARY FORMS

Reflecting his particular interest in film, Robert Stone wrote *WUSA* (1970), a screenplay based on his novel *A Hall of Mirrors*; with Judith Roscoe, he also wrote *Who'll Stop the Rain* (1978), a screen adaptation of *Dog Soldiers*. Stone has contributed short stories, articles, and reviews to such periodicals as *The Atlantic Monthly*, *Harper's Magazine*, *The New York Times Book Review*, and the *Manchester Guardian*. Notable among these pieces is "The Reason for Stories: Toward a Moral Fiction," which appeared in *Harper's* magazine in June, 1988. A collection of Stone's short fiction, *Bear and His Daughter*, was published in 1997.

ACHIEVEMENTS

Stone received a Wallace Stegner fellowship to Stanford University in 1962 and a Houghton Mifflin literary fellowship in 1967 for a promising first novel. In 1968 he won the William Faulkner Foundation Award for *A Hall of Mirrors*, a "notable first novel"; reviewers praised his narrative skill, facility for language and dialogue, and strength of characterization. *Dog Soldiers*, in turn, won the National Book Award for 1975 and established Stone's importance as a significant American novelist. In 1979 the Writers Guild of America nominated *Who'll Stop the Rain* for best script adapted from another medium. In 1982 *A Flag for Sunrise* received the John Dos Passos prize for literature and the American Academy and Institute award in literature; was nominated for the American Book Award, the National Book Critics Circle Award, and the PEN/Faulkner Award; and was runner-up for the Pulitzer Prize in Fiction. In 1983 Stone received a National Endowment for the Arts fellowship and a grant from the National Institute of Arts and Letters. Stone is an established artist of high caliber, a political and social critic whose skill has merited comparisons with Graham Greene, Joseph Conrad, John Dos Passos, and Nathanael West.

BIOGRAPHY

Robert Stone was born in south Brooklyn, New York, on August 21, 1937, the son of Gladys Catherine Grant, an elementary school teacher, and C. Homer Stone, who abandoned his family during Stone's infancy. A product of orphanages and Catholic schools, the young Stone, having offended the Marist Brothers by his drinking and his militant atheism, joined the United States Navy's amphibious force before high school graduation. His childhood experiences taught him about the rootless, the psychotic, the irresponsible, and the hypocritical, while his military service prepared him to write credibly of military life, language, and style. While attending New York University from 1958 to 1960, he worked as a copyboy, caption writer, and then editorial assistant for the *New York Daily News*, and on December 11, 1959, he was married to social worker Janice G. Burr. The Stones dropped their conventional life and ended up in New Orleans, where Stone worked at menial jobs for a while, read his own poetry to jazz accompaniment in a French Quarter bar, and moved with the beatnik crowd. His daughter was born at Charity Hospital (a son, Ian, was born later). His experiences in that city provided material for his first novel, *A Hall of Mirrors*.

The Stones became friends with Jack Kerouac and others of the emerging bohemian scene in New York City and with Ken Kesey while Stone was studying and then teaching creative writing at Stanford University in California. His involvement in the drug culture led to his joining the Merry Pranksters' bus in its 1964 cross-country trip.

Stone wrote for the *National Mirror* in New York City from 1965 to 1967 and then freelanced between 1967 and 1971. A Guggenheim fellowship paid his way to London, England. Later, after two months spent gathering material in Saigon, South Vietnam, for his second novel, he moved on to Hollywood, California, to help write the script for *Dog Soldiers*. Next he began a teaching career as a writer-in-residence, mainly at Princeton University but also at Amherst College, Stanford University, the University of Hawaii at Manoa, Harvard University in Cambridge, Massachusetts, the University of California at Irvine, New York University, and the University of California at San Diego. During the 1970's he interrupted this itinerant teaching to travel to Central America three times and to write his third

(Jerry Bauer)

novel. His fourth novel grew out of his experiences with the Hollywood film scene. Stone retained his friendship with Kesey and continued to write short stories and articles for popular journals as well as novels.

After *Outerbridge Reach*, Stone published articles; reviews; a collection of photographs, *Day Hiking in Aspen, Colorado* (1996); a short-story collection, *Bear and His Daughter* (1997); and a novel, *Damascus Gate*. In the 1990's he divided his time between Connecticut and Key West, Florida, where he was featured at the annual Key West Literary Festival. Although Stone did his research for *Damascus Gate* at the Yale Divinity School Library (Stone teaches writing at Yale), much of its imagery resulted from his visits to Jerusalem, where he simply absorbed what he saw.

ANALYSIS

Intrigued by the exotic and by disappointed promises of wealth or adventure, Robert Stone writes as a disillusioned American romantic whose characters unsuccessfully pursue the American Dream in New Orleans, Vietnam, Southern California, Mexico, or Central America. Their failure to choose wisely and to accept responsibility, however, turns their dreams of wealth to ashes, destroys their personal lives, and creates nightmares. Their plight has paralleled that of the national culture as it coped with shattered ideals and governmental corruption in the 1960's and after. In many ways, Stone's works have paralleled the concerns and obsessions of the baby-boom generation.

A HALL OF MIRRORS

A Hall of Mirrors, for example, takes a sharp, satirical look at romantic pessimism in the face of racial prejudice and right-wing extremism in the 1960's. M. T. Bingamon, a "superpatriot" demagogue, exploits the racist fears of poor whites with the aid of Brother Jensen, alias Farley the Sailor, a con man, philosopher, and supposed missionary, head of the Living Grace Mission. A cynical misfit and drifting disc jockey, Rheinhardt, and a naïve and idealistic social worker of wealthy southern parentage, Morgan Rainey, become pawns in Bingamon's power plot.

Rheinhardt espouses Bingamon's cause to preserve his position as the rock disc jockey of WUSA, while Rainey conducts a "welfare" census that brings only pain and loss to those whom he seeks to help. The final third of the novel is an apocalyptic Armageddon, a surreal and nightmarish description of the violent, racist "patriotic" rally the station sponsors and of the ensuing riot. Rheinhardt's parody of reactionary speeches sums up the illusions negated by Stone's novel: "The American way is innocence. In all situations we must and shall display an innocence so vast and awesome that the entire world will be reduced by it. American innocence shall rise in mighty clouds of vapor to the scent of heaven and confound the nations!" Stone's characters have lost their innocence, and all is emptiness, ashes, and betrayal, as the cold-hearted and cold-blooded dominate. Ultimately, Rainey is seriously wounded in the madness of the political rally, but Rheinhardt drifts on. His girlfriend, a basically decent woman brought low by circumstances and misplaced affections, is stunned by Rheinhardt's indifference and, picked up for vagrancy, commits suicide in her jail cell. Rheinhardt, Geraldine, and Rainey's private hall of mirrors reflects the American nightmare wherein civilization proves a farcical hell, dreams are distorted, and action fails.

DOG SOLDIERS

Dog Soldiers and *A Flag for Sunrise*, in turn, capture the naïve cynicism of failed upper-middle-class idealists of the 1970's and their involvement in romanticized drug-dealing or revolutionary plots. *Dog Soldiers* depicts the tragic costs of the Vietnam War in its ongoing effects back home: the difficulty of telling friend from foe and the disintegration of moral certainties, loyalties, and conscience. It argues that the war poisoned American values and produced a loss of faith that infects the survivors. In the novel, former marine Ray Hicks, a drug smuggler from Vietnam, finds in the United States love, betrayal, craziness, and ambiguity. His trusted friend John Converse, a journalist on assignment to Vietnam, enlists his aid to smuggle three kilograms of pure heroin home from Vietnam for a share of the anticipated forty-thousand-dollar profit. Converse classifies Hicks as a usable "psychopath" but does not understand that he himself has been set up from the beginning. Consequently, when Hicks contacts Converse's wife, Marge, a ticket girl for a pornographic cinema and a Dilaudid addict, he finds himself waylaid by hoods and fleeing for his life. Converse too is threatened, tortured, and then forced to deal with a less than honest federal "regulatory" agent, Antheil, who, in on the deal since its Vietnam origins, runs the hoods with "a certain Bohemian flair." As Hicks and Marge flee across Southern California, they meet an array of fringe characters from Hicks's past, characters who make him conclude, "It's gone funny in the states." Hicks envisions himself a serious man, a modern samurai with a worthy illusion, riding the wave until it crashes, but his romantic obsession with Marge and his strong sense of loyalty doom him. After a confused battle scene, heightened by the sounds of Vietnam battles blasted out over loudspeakers, Hicks discovers an escape route but is badly wounded when he returns to rescue Marge and help reunite her with her husband.

The final line of Dieter, Hicks's mentor, sums up the message in all Stone's novels: "We're in the dark ages." The self-centered, amoral Converse, dreaming of personal profit at the expense of friendship and loyalty, confirms this view when he attempts to renege on his agreement to meet Hicks in the desert on the far side of the mountains and then dumps the heroin to save himself. Converse is another of Stone's survivors: an egocentric creature who has sacrificed human feelings and human values to maintain his life. Federal agent Antheil, in turn, epitomizes moral ambiguity as he confiscates for personal profit the smuggled heroin. Ultimately, Stone demonstrates that the end result of the war's by-product, heroin, is nightmare and death—"a chain of victims."

A FLAG FOR SUNRISE

A Flag for Sunrise, set in the fictional Central American country of Tecan, attacks American interference in such countries. As it does so, it continually draws parallels with Vietnam through the memories of the central observer, Frank Holliwell, onetime Central Intelligence Agency operative, now a wandering professor. By exploring the fate of Americans whose lives become entangled in Tecanecan politics, Stone sums up the diverse motives that draw Americans into conflicts that they only vaguely understand. The end result of such involvement is inevitably negative: the importation of the worst from North American culture, support of cruel and murderous regimes, and destruction and death. The novel ends with the statement that "a man has nothing to fear . . . who understands history," yet Stone's characters continually fail to understand history in any of its contexts. A bored and frustrated Roman Catholic nun, the beautiful Sister Justin Feeney, is ordered to close her failed mission and to return to the United States, yet she self-righteously volunteers to aid the revolutionary wounded; the result is that she is senselessly battered to death by a crazed Tecanecan lieutenant. Pablo Tabor, a paranoid psychotic on a rampage of killing, finds his destiny: death underwater. A curious, burned-out drifter, anthropologist Frank Holliwell feels alive only when caught up in the mystery and the horror of conflicts in the threatening and oppressive tropics, but cannot explain why. Holliwell finds survival of the fittest the only value but concludes that outsiders have "no business down there." Everyone is searching for what only the revolutionaries seem to have—a "flag" or purpose—but all are betrayed, tortured, and killed.

CHILDREN OF LIGHT

Children of Light depicts the selling-out in the 1980's of the dreams of the 1960's: Potential artists, novelists, and actors lose their vision and give in to crass commercialism. Stone's characters have buried themselves in drugs, fantasies, sex, and a wealthy lifestyle that leaves them unfulfilled, alienated from their marital partners, their children, and their art. Gordon Walker, once a Shakespearean actor and now a Hollywood writer, writes the screenplay of Kate Chopin's *The Awakening* (1899) and, after his wife's desertion, comes to Bahia Honda, Mexico, to recapture his past bittersweet romance with actress Lee Verger in order to rediscover who he was and what he can still be. Verger, in turn, acts out as her own reality the marital and personal conflicts of her screen character Edna Pontellier. Verger refers to herself and Walker as "Children of Light," the film generation, sitting in darkness and staring at the lighted screen. As "Children of Light," Verger and Gordon cannot distinguish between true relationships and those projected in their art. The "real" Walker and Verger are but empty shadows on the screen.

Verger has given up her medical treatment because it interfered with her acting; she has driven away her psychiatrist husband with her psychic projects and struggled to please director, producer, and press and to deal with sexual advances, blackmail, and threats. At the same time, she has puzzled over the suicide of her screen character, and eventually she accepts suicide as her own destiny. Walker, in contrast, ever the survivor—no matter the cost—returns to family and home and shoddy career. Stone provides no answers to his characters' plight; it is too late.

DAMASCUS GATE

Stone's 1998 novel *Damascus Gate* is set in Jerusalem and captures the complexities of the Middle East. An agnostic American journalist, Christopher Lucas, decides to research and write on the "Jerusalem Syndrome," a condition that causes some visitors to Jerusalem to believe that God has a mission for them, usually a crazy one. Lucas loses his skeptical detachment as he becomes involved with a number of passionate eccentrics. This involvement includes falling in love with Sonia Barnes, an African American Jew whose passions are Sufism and jazz. Lucas finds himself drawn into a plot by Christian fundamentalists and Jewish radicals to bomb all the mosques on Jerusalem's Temple Mount.

The real ambitions of *Damascus Gate* are spiritual, however. Through unexpected plot twists and half-demented characters, Stone shows how close nihilism and belief can be. Although the characters are obsessed with their spiritual torments, they are actually driven by outward events. *Damascus Gate* is a thriller that tantalizes readers with unanswerable spiritual questions but never descends into hopelessness. At its heart is a luminous spirituality and calm that appear to transcend conflict. *Damascus Gate* received praise for its intricate plot, dazzling images, and language. Some critics declared it Stone's best work, while others found fault with its characters ("shallow" wrote one critic, "Indiana Jones and a bimbo" wrote another).

CHARACTERS AND CONCERNS

Throughout his work, most of Stone's characters are blind to their inner motives and to the destructive results of their acts. Converse, in *Dog Soldiers*, says, "I don't know what that guy did or why he did it. I don't know what I'm doing or why I do it or what it's like. . . . Nobody knows. . . . That's the principle we were defending over there [in Vietnam]. That's why we fought the war." Stone's characters ask one another what they are worth and find the answer depressing: "A little cinder in the wind, Pablo—that's what you are." A number of them contemplate or commit suicide.

Overall, Stone's characters are self-destructive men and women of their times, hooked on alcohol, drugs, greed, or egocentricity, paying the price of national and personal ignorance and irresponsibility. They are rootless wanderers of mind and world—sometimes violent, often at the end of their tether, engaging in various forms of sophistry, rationalization, equivocation, or indifference. There is a sense of a cultural breakdown, of misplaced dreams, of despair and loss of hope. Caught up in movements beyond their understanding, they continually betray one another without guilt and without self-knowledge.

In *A Flag for Sunrise* Stone's final image of the world is the cold, hostile one of the sea: at times delicate and beautiful, but always predatory. In fact, Stone relies on this image throughout his canon, with his metaphors and images repeatedly connecting humans to fish and the bleak bottom-of-the-ocean competition. Thereby he captures a sense of cosmic menace, nihilism, and conflict: race wars in *A Hall of Mirrors*, Vietnam and drug wars in *Dog Soldiers*, crazed killers and guerrilla warfare in *A Flag for Sunrise*, and war against inner demons in *Children of Light*. His true villains are casual, feckless individuals who act without thinking or feeling and survive at the cost of others' pain and death.

Stone is one of the most impressive novelists of his generation because of his journalist's sharp eye for detail and for short, intense, dramatic scenes; his poet's ear for dialogue; his English teacher's sense of the subtle nuances of language, images, and interlocking patterns; his imaginative drive; and, most important, his commitment to understanding and facing up to the moral ambiguities of America and Americans.

Andrew Macdonald and Gina Macdonald,
updated by Mary Hanford Bruce

OTHER MAJOR WORKS

SHORT FICTION: *Bear and His Daughter*, 1997.

SCREENPLAYS: *WUSA*, 1970; *Who'll Stop the Rain*, 1978 (with Judith Roscoe).

NONFICTION: *Day Hiking in Aspen, Colorado*, 1996.

BIBLIOGRAPHY

Edwards, Thomas R. "Bear and His Daughter: Stories." *New York Review of Books*, October 9, 1997, 36-38. This favorable review believes that Stone's stories make more clear than his novels Stone's metaphysical bent. Edwards calls the collection "remarkable" for depicting the characters' cries of pain.

Epstein, Jason. "Robert Stone: American Nightmares." In *Plausible Prejudices: Essays on American Writing*. New York: W. W. Norton, 1985. Epstein delineates the violence and destruction in Stone's works and attacks Stone's pessimism.

Gardner, James. "Apocalypse Now." *National Review*, June 1, 1998: 53-54. Gardner reviews *Damascus Gate* favorably, saying that it is informed by a "luminous spiritualism." He comments, however, that the character of Christopher Locus is somewhat bland for a main character in such a substantive book.

Hower, Edward. "A Parable for the Millennium." *World and I* 13, no. 9 (September, 1998): 255-262. This unreservedly positive review of *Damascus Gate* finds Christopher Lucas a credible world-weary hero who finds his redemption in seeking to understand the conflicts in the Middle East.

Hulse, Michael. "All Fortune Cookies to Him." *The Spectator*, October 31, 1998, 50. Hulse is baffled by the plaudits *Damascus Gate* has received, finding it rife with American provinciality and containing ciphers instead of characters. He criticizes the book as having a trite American theme: the right-thinking American and his "bimbo" surviving the odds in an inscrutable foreign country.

Jones, Robert. "The Other Side of Soullessness." *Commonweal* 113 (May 23, 1986): 305-306, 308. Jones shows how Stone chronicles, with cinematic vividness, the country's decay through the voices of its burnt-out cases, always in distant locales, and shows how dangerous and careless people are with one another. In *Children of Light* Stone tries to mirror the American cultural breakdown but provides only meaningless choices.

Moore, L. Hugh. "The Undersea World of Robert Stone." *Critique: Studies in Modern Fiction* 11, no. 3 (1969): 43-56. Moore's thesis is that Stone's recurring images and metaphors of fish-seafloor-evolution are vital to theme and character. They capture a movement toward a new person who can cope with a nightmare environment, cold and immoral. In this hostile world, to survive is immoral, but there is no other choice but despair and death.

O'Brien, Tim, and Robert Stone. "Two Interviews: Talks with Tim O'Brien and Robert Stone." Interview by Eric James Schroeder. *Modern Fiction Studies* 30 (Spring, 1984): 135-164. In this interview Stone talks about the background and research for his books, his sense of American values, his personal interpretation of some of his characters, and the changes in his own perceptions.

Stone, Robert. Interview by Maureen Kaguezian. *TriQuarterly* 53 (1982): 248-258. Stone discusses his characters as representative of different aspects of the American condition, the background out of which his novels grew, his dissatisfaction with the limitations of film and short story, his interest in "the convolutions and ironies of events," and, most particularly, the problem of living in a "meaningful moral way in a world which is apparently godless."

_____. "Robert Stone." Interview by Charles Ruas. In *Conversations with American Writers*. New York: Alfred A. Knopf, 1984. An intriguing interview in which Stone discusses his early influences, the drug culture, the counterculture movement, his writing process, his goals and values, and his characters and plots.

HARRIET BEECHER STOWE

Born: Litchfield, Connecticut; June 14, 1811
Died: Hartford, Connecticut; July 1, 1896

PRINCIPAL LONG FICTION

Uncle Tom's Cabin: Or, Life Among the Lowly, 1852
Dred: A Tale of the Great Dismal Swamp, 1856
The Minister's Wooing, 1859
Agnes of Sorrento, 1862
The Pearl of Orr's Island, 1862
Oldtown Folks, 1869
Pink and White Tyranny, 1871
My Wife and I, 1871
We and Our Neighbors, 1875
Poganuc People, 1878

OTHER LITERARY FORMS

In 1843, Harriet Beecher Stowe gathered a number of her sketches and stories into a volume called *The Mayflower: Or, Sketches of Scenes and Characters of the Descendants of the Pilgrims* (1843). For forty years thereafter, she published short fiction and miscellaneous essays in magazines. In *A Key to Uncle Tom's Cabin* (1853), she assembled a mass of sources and analogues for the characters and incidents of her most famous novel. Her 1869 *The Atlantic Monthly* article "The True Story of Lady Byron's Life" and a subsequent elaboration, *Lady Byron Vindicated* (1870), caused a sensation at the time. She also published a geography for children (1833, her earliest publication, issued under her sister Catharine's name), poems, travel books, collections of biographical sketches, and a number of other children's books.

Stowe's stories and sketches remain readable. Her best collection, *Sam Lawson's Oldtown Fireside Stories* (1872), differs from the novel *Oldtown Folks* mainly in degree of plotlessness. Selections from Stowe's frequently long and chatty letters can be found in the *Life of Harriet Beecher Stowe* (1889), written by her son Charles Edward Stowe, and in more recent biographies, but hundreds of her letters remain unpublished and scattered in various archives.

ACHIEVEMENTS

Known primarily today for her antislavery novel *Uncle Tom's Cabin*, Stowe also interpreted the life of her native New England in a series of novels, stories, and sketches. Along with Ralph Waldo Emerson and Oliver Wendell Holmes, she contributed to the first

(Library of Congress)

issue of the *The Atlantic Monthly* (November, 1857) and for many years thereafter contributed frequently to that Boston-based magazine. As an alert and intelligent member of a famous family of Protestant ministers, she understood the Puritan conscience and outlook as well as anyone in her time, and as a shrewd observer of the commonplace, she deftly registered Yankee habits of mind and speech. All of her novels feature authentic New England characters; after *Uncle Tom's Cabin* and *Dred*, she turned to settings that included all six New England states. Despite a contradictory idealizing tendency, she pioneered in realism.

One of the first American writers to apply a talent for dialect and local color to the purposes of serious narrative, she exerted a strong influence on Sarah Orne Jewett, Mary Wilkins Freeman, and other regionalists of the later nineteenth century. Without a doubt, however, her greatest achievement was the novel that, beginning as an intended short serial in a Washington antislavery weekly, the *National Era*, forced the American reading public to realize for the first time that slaves were not only a national problem but also people with hopes and aspirations as legitimate as their own. Critics as diverse as Henry Wadsworth Longfellow, Heinrich Heine, William Dean Howells, and Leo Tolstoy in the nineteenth century, and Edmund Wilson and Anthony Burgess in the twentieth, have used superlatives to praise *Uncle Tom's Cabin*.

Biography

When Harriet Elizabeth Beecher was born on June 14, 1811, the seventh child of Lyman and Roxana Beecher, her father's fame as a preacher had spread well beyond the Congregational Church of Litchfield, Connecticut. All seven Beecher sons who lived to maturity became ministers, one becoming more famous than his father. Harriet, after attending Litchfield Academy, a well-regarded school, was sent to the Hartford Female Seminary, which was founded by her sister Catharine—in some respects the substitute mother whom Harriet needed after Roxana died in 1816 but did not discover in the second Mrs. Beecher. In later years, Harriet would con-

sistently idealize motherhood. When Catharine's fiancé, a brilliant young man but one who had not experienced any perceptible religious conversion, died in 1822, the eleven-year-old Harriet felt the tragedy. In 1827, the shy, melancholy girl became a teacher in her sister's school.

In 1832, Lyman Beecher accepted the presidency of Lane Seminary in Cincinnati, Ohio, and soon Catharine and Harriet had established another school there. Four years later, Harriet married a widower named Calvin Stowe, a Lane professor. In the years that followed, she bore seven children. She also became familiar with slavery, as practiced just across the Ohio River in Kentucky; with the abolitionist movement, which boasted several notable champions in Cincinnati, including the future chief justice of the United States, Salmon P. Chase; and with the Underground Railroad. As a way of supplementing her husband's small income, she also contributed to local and religious periodicals.

Not until the Stowes moved to Brunswick, Maine, in 1850, however, did she think of writing about slavery. Then, urged by her brother Henry, by then a prominent minister in Brooklyn, New York, and by other family members in the wake of Congress's enactment of the Fugitive Slave Act, and spurred by a vision she experienced at a church service, she began to construct *Uncle Tom's Cabin*. Even as a weekly serial in the *National Era*, it attracted much attention, and its publication in 1852 as a book made Stowe an instant celebrity. After that year, from her new base in Andover, Massachusetts, where her husband taught, she twice visited Europe; met Harriet Martineau, John Ruskin, the Brownings, and Lady Byron, among others; and saw the scope of her fame increase even further.

Stowe wrote another slavery novel, *Dred*, and then turned her literary attention to New England. The drowning of her son Henry, a Dartmouth student, in the summer of 1857, marred for her the successes of these years. In the fall of 1862, infuriated by the lack of British support for the North in the Civil War and skeptical that President Lincoln would fulfill his promise to issue a proclamation of emancipation, Stowe visited Lincoln, who is reported to have greeted her with the words, "So this is the little lady who made this big war." She left Washington satisfied that the president would keep his word.

Following Calvin Stowe's retirement from Andover, the family moved to Hartford, the winters usually being spent in northern Florida. Two of the most sensational scandals of the post-Civil War era involved Stowe, the first arising when she published an imprudent and detailed account of Lord Byron's sins as revealed to her some years earlier by the now deceased widow of the poet, the second being an adultery suit brought against her brother Henry in which Stowe characteristically defended him to the hilt. The Byron affair in particular turned many people against her, although her books continued to be commercial successes throughout the 1870's. The most severe personal abuse ever directed at a respectable nineteenth century woman bothered Stowe far less than another personal tragedy: the alcoholism and eventual disappearance of her son Fred in San Francisco, California, in 1870.

In the last twenty-three years of her life, Stowe became the central attraction of the Hartford neighborhood known as Nook Farm, also the home of Charles Dudley Warner and Mark Twain, the latter moving there in part because of its Beecher connections. Her circle of friends included Annie Fields, wife of *The Atlantic Monthly* publisher; George Eliot, with whom she corresponded; and Holmes, always a staunch supporter. In her final years, her mind wandered at times, but she was still writing lucid letters two years before her death on July 1, 1896, at the age of eighty-five.

ANALYSIS

In 1869, after finishing her sixth novel, *Oldtown Folks*, Harriet Beecher Stowe began a correspondence with George Eliot by sending her a copy. Although an international celebrity, Stowe wanted the approval of this younger and less famous woman who had contributed notably to a movement just beginning to be critically recognized: literary realism. Like Stowe, Eliot came from a deeply religious background and had formed a union with an unromantic and bookish, but supportive, man. Unlike the Ameri-

can novelist, Eliot had rejected religion for rationalism and Romanticism for realism. Had Calvin Stowe's first wife not died, it would have been unthinkable for Harriet Beecher to live with him as Eliot did with George Henry Lewes. In life, the former Miss Beecher cheerfully married the unexciting scholar; in *The Minister's Wooing*, she would not permit her heroine Mary Scudder to marry her scholarly suitor (as Eliot's Dorothea Brooke in *Middlemarch* [1871-1872] was permitted to marry hers, Dr. Casaubon).

Stowe's hope, in a measure fulfilled, that Eliot would like *Oldtown Folks* may be taken as signifying her desire to be recognized as a realist, even though her own realism was strongly tinged with the Romanticism Eliot had come to despise. The young Harriet Beecher had probably learned something from John Bunyan's *The Pilgrim's Progress* (1678, 1684), but most of her other reading—*The Arabian Nights*, Cotton Mather's *Magnalia Christi Americana* (1702), and the works of Sir Walter Scott and Lord Byron—had little to teach an incipient realist. Nor did American literature in the 1830's, when she began to write, furnish any likely models. As a result, the reader finds in her works a mingling of realistic and Romantic elements.

Stowe's settings, particularly the New England ones, ring true. She understood her cultural roots, and she proved able to recollect childhood impressions almost photographically. She possessed a keen ear for dialect and a sharp eye for the idiosyncrasies of people she scarcely seemed to have noticed until they turned up in her writing. She used the novel to probe urgent social issues such as slavery and women's rights. Although she liked nature and worked hard at describing it accurately, she disdained her native region's characteristic transcendental interpretations of it. She displayed the realist's aversion to mystery, mysticism, and the legendizing of history.

On the other hand, the Romantic tendencies of Stowe's fiction stand out against its realistic background. Her heroines are invariably saintly, as are certain of her black males such as Uncle Tom and, in *Dred*, Uncle Tiff. Her recalcitrant heroes often undergo rather unconvincing conversions. Occasionally, she introduces a mythic, larger-than-life character such as Dred. In common with most of the generation of American realists who followed her, she never renounced the heroic but sought to demonstrate its presence among humble and common people. Her heroes differ from those of Twain, William Dean Howells, and Henry James, however, in drawing their strength from a firm Christian commitment: Stowe's piety has been something of an impediment to her modern readers.

The looseness of plotting about which Stowe's critics have complained so much derives in large measure from her inability to develop convincing central characters in most of her novels. Four of her last five novels have plural nouns—words such as *neighbors* and *folks* and *people*—in their titles, but even *Uncle Tom's Cabin* is not about Uncle Tom in the sense that Charles Dickens's *David Copperfield* (1849-1850) or Gustave Flaubert's *Madame Bovary* (1857) is about its title character. In fact, Stowe changed the title of *Dred* for a time to *Nina Gordon*, a more central character but one who dies many chapters from the end. *My Wife and I* and *Oldtown Folks* are narrated by relatively colorless central characters.

One of Stowe's most persistent and indeed remarkable narrative traits also works against her realism on occasions. As she confides at the beginning of chapter 44 of *Dred*, "There's no study in human nature more interesting than the aspects of the same subject in the points of view of different characters." That she periodically allowed this interest to distract her from the task at hand is clear. Although she experimented with different points of view—omniscient, first-person, dramatic, and circulating (the last primarily through the use of the epistolary method)—she worked before the time when novelists such as Joseph Conrad, James Joyce, and William Faulkner developed techniques capable of sustaining this kind of interest. It should be pointed out that Stowe uses the expression "points of view" in the sense of "opinions," and she is more likely to present the conflict of opinions through conversations than through living, breathing embodiments of motivating ideas.

It is as a realist before her time that Stowe is most profitably considered. Even where her realism does not serve a socially critical purpose, as it does in *Uncle Tom's Cabin* and *My Wife and I*, she makes her readers aware of the texture, the complexity, of social life—particularly the conflicts, tensions, and joys of New England community life. Understanding how people grow from their geographic, social, religious, and intellectual roots, she is able to convey the reality of isolated Maine coastal villages and the jaunty postwar Manhattan of aspiring journalists. In her best work, she depicts evil not as the product of Mephistophelean schemers or motiveless brutes but of high-minded people incapacitated by a crucial weakness, such as the irresolute Augustine St. Clare of *Uncle Tom's Cabin*, the temporizing Judge Clayton of *Dred*, and the imperceptive Dr. Hopkins of *The Minister's Wooing*.

UNCLE TOM'S CABIN

Uncle Tom's Cabin: Or, Life Among the Lowly, remains one of the most controversial of novels. Extravagantly admired and bitterly detested in the 1850s, it still arouses extreme reactions more than a century later. An early barrage of challenges to its authenticity led Stowe to work furiously at the assembling of *A Key to Uncle Tom's Cabin* the next year. In 262 closely printed, double-columned pages, she impressively documented horrors that verified "the truth of the work." This book unfortunately encouraged the development of an essentially nonliterary mass of criticism, with the result that the novel early gained the reputation of a brilliant piece of propaganda—even President Lincoln supposedly accepting the Civil War as its legacy—but unworthy of serious consideration on artistic grounds.

It did not help the novel's cause that the inevitable later reaction against this enormously popular story coincided with the effort, spearheaded by Henry James, to establish the novel as a form of art rather than as a mere popular entertainment. A writer who strove too singlemindedly for mere verifiability did not merit consideration as an artist. In the same year that *Uncle Tom's Cabin* began appearing serially, Nathaniel Hawthorne—James's chief example of the American artist—prefaced his *The House of the Seven Gables* (1851) with a firm declaration of its imaginary basis which contrasted sharply with his attempt to provide a "historical" one for *The Scarlet Letter* one year earlier. Hawthorne's star as a writer of fiction gradually rose: Stowe's sank. Like "Old Ironsides," the vigorous youthful poem of Stowe's staunch friend of later years, *Uncle Tom's Cabin* was relegated to the status of a work that made things happen—important historically but damned by that very fact to the region of the second-rate.

In *A Key to Uncle Tom's Cabin*, Stowe herself called *Uncle Tom's Cabin* "a very inadequate representation of slavery," but her excuse is significant: "Slavery, in some of its workings, is too dreadful for the purposes of art." She was acknowledging a problem that would continue to bedevil realists for most of the rest of the century. The most prominent spokesman for realism, Howells, agreed with her, and until the 1890's, realists would generally exclude things considered "too dreadful." As late as 1891, Thomas Hardy induced mass revulsion by allowing his heroine to be raped in *Tess of the D'Urbervilles* (1891) while referring to her in his subtitle as "a pure woman."

Stowe sandwiched the story of Uncle Tom, the meek Christian capable of turning the other cheek even to the sadistic Simon Legree, between the resolute George and Eliza Harris's escape from slavery and the Harris family's fortuitous reunion at the end of the novel. If the plot is untidy and contrived, a number of the individual characters and episodes have remained among the most memorable in fiction. The famous scene in which Eliza crosses the Ohio River ice in early spring is "true" not because the feat had been accomplished (although Stowe knew it had) but because she makes the reader feel Eliza's desperation, the absolute necessity of the attempt, and the likelihood that a person who grew up in her hard school would develop the resources to succeed.

The meeting between Miss Ophelia and Topsy illustrates Stowe's talent for dramatizing the confrontation of stubborn viewpoints. Sold down the river by his first owner, Tom has rescued the angelic daughter of Augustine St. Clare and has been installed to the St. Clare household. Miss Ophelia, a Vermont cousin of St. Clare, has been brought south to take care of Eva, whose mother is languidly incompetent. St.

Clare despises slavery but feels powerless to resist it; Ophelia's intransigent New England conscience will not permit her to acquiese in it. After listening to a considerable amount of her antislavery rhetoric, St. Clare gives his cousin a little black girl rescued from alcoholic parents. Ophelia is revolted by Topsy, so utterly different from the golden, cherubic Eva. Topsy, shrewd and skeptical beyond her years, embodies the insidiousness of slavery itself. Neither was premeditated but simply "grow'd" and now must somehow be dealt with as found. Ophelia must find room in her heart for the little "black spider" or lose face with her cousin. Her struggle with Topsy—and with her own physical aversion—is fierce and richly comical, and its successful outcome believable.

For the modern reader, the death scenes in the novel are more of a problem. Little Eva's protracted illness and beatific death exactly pleased the taste of Stowe's time. Today, her father's senseless and sudden death as a result of his attempt to mediate a tavern brawl seems more like real life—or would if Stowe had not permitted St. Clare to linger long enough to undergo a deathbed religious conversion. Modern reaction to Stowe's climactic scene is complicated by the hostility of writers such as James Baldwin to the character of Uncle Tom, who, in dying at the hands of Legree's henchmen, wins their souls in the process. Whether or not the conversion of Sambo and Quimbo convinces today's reader, Tom's character has been firmly established, and he dies in precisely the spirit the reader expects.

Far less satisfactory is the subsequent escape of two of Legree's slaves from his clutches. Stowe did nothing beforehand to induce belief in a brutal master who could melt into helpless impassivity at the sight of a lock of his dead mother's hair. Finding it expedient to make Legree superstitious, she established this side of his character belatedly and ineptly, and she failed to understand that her conception of the power of motherhood was not universally shared.

In short, the reader's admiration is interrupted by idealistic and sentimental material that does not support Stowe's goal of depicting life as it was. Nor is this inconsistency surprising. No American had ever written such a novel: realistic in impulse and directed at a current social problem of the greatest magnitude. She had no models and could not, like Twain after her, draw upon experiences as Missourian, journalist, western traveler, and—before he wrote his greatest books—neighbor of Stowe and reader of her work.

Like Twain and Howells after her, Stowe did not banish Romanticism from her novels, but her commitment to realism is clear. Thirty years before Twain's accomplishments with dialect in *The Adventures of Huckleberry Finn* (1884), and nearly two decades before Bret Harte popularized the concept of local color, Stowe used dialects—not with perfect consistency but not for the conventional purpose of humor either. For the first time in major American fiction, dialect served the purpose of generating a credible environment for a serious narrative. In the process, she changed the perceptions of hundreds of thousands of readers forever.

Within a year, the book had made Stowe internationally known. When, after several years of minor literary activity, she returned to the subject of slavery, events were unfolding that led inexorably to war. Her brother Henry was outraging North and South alike by holding his own mock slave auction in his Brooklyn church. John Brown was launching his personal civil war in Kansas. In the chamber of the United States Senate, abolitionist Charles Sumner was nearly beaten to death by a southern colleague. Stowe herself had been busy with antislavery petitions and appeals.

DRED

From this context emerged *Dred*, a more somber novel. As it opens, Nina Gordon has returned to her North Carolina plantation from New York upon the death of her father. She has dallied with several suitors but has sense enough to prefer Edward Clayton, an idealistic young lawyer from another part of her native state. After successfully prosecuting a white man who had hired and then physically abused Nina's domestic slave Milly, Clayton's ambition to counteract such abuses legally is checked when an appeals judge—a man of undoubted probity and, ironically, Clayton's own father—reverses the earlier decision on the grounds that no slave has any rights under state law. Meanwhile, Nina's attempt at benign management of her plantation is set back by the appear-

ance of her wastrel brother Tom, who especially enjoys tormenting her able quadroon steward Harry. Although bearing a strong resemblance to George Harris of *Uncle Tom's Cabin*, Harry is different in two important ways. First, Stowe develops the frustration of this educated and sensitive man much more thoroughly. Second, Harry is, unknown to Nina, the Gordon children's half brother.

When Nina dies in a cholera epidemic, Tom asserts control over the plantation, and Clayton returns home with the resolve to press for changes in a legal code that permits a man to own and mistreat his own brother. Harry is driven to rebel and flee into the nearby swamp, where he falls under the influence of Dred, whom the author styles after the son of the famous black rebel Denmark Vesey, but who resembles even more closely that other noted rebel, Nat Turner.

What happens next exemplifies Stowe's familiarity with the clergy and her talent for controversy. Invited by his uncle to a Presbyterian ministers' conference, Clayton seeks there the moral support for legal reform. Even though he finds one minister passionately committed to rights for slaves, the majority of the brethren turn out to be complacent trimmers, and Clayton learns that he can expect no help in that quarter. Stowe strategically places the conference between two scenes of desperation, both of which illustrate the social system's assault on the family. In the former, Uncle Tiff, the black guardian of two white children whose father is a shiftless squatter on the Gordon plantation, vows to preserve them from the corrupting influence of their slatternly stepmother and takes them to Dred's hidden fastness in the swamp. In the latter, another quadroon Gordon offshoot, Cora, confesses in court to the murder of her own two children to "save" them, as she puts it, from being sold away.

In the swamp, Tiff and the children are succored by Dred, who is one of Stowe's most bizarre creations: half Robin Hood, half self-appointed executioner for the Lord. Too mythic a hero for a realistic novel, Dred unfortunately develops quickly into a very tedious one too, ranting interminably in his guise of Old Testament prophet. Even he is no match, however, for the committed Christian Milly, although she can accomplish no more than the postponement of his planned revenge against the hated whites. When Tom Gordon organizes a party to ransack the swamp for Dred and Harry, the former is killed, and Harry and his wife, along with Tiff and his young charges, escape to the North. In an obviously Pyrrhic victory, Clayton, baffled by his neighbors in his attempt to educate the slaves on his own estate, takes them off to Canada, where they continue to work for him in their freedom.

Tiff is another saintly domestic slave, but he has no power to reclaim any Sambo or Quimbo from degradation. There are no spectacular personal conversions in *Dred* and no hope of any social one. Milly, who has had to endure the loss by death or sale of all her numerous children, seems to win a legal victory over a cruel master and a moral one over the vindictive fugitive Dred, but both turn out to be illusory. Not only the fugitive blacks but also Clayton the hero must leave the country. If *Uncle Tom's Cabin* stands as a warning to a divided society, *Dred* is a prophecy of disintegration.

THE MINISTER'S WOOING

Stowe's next two novels have much in common. Both *The Minister's Wooing* and *The Pearl of Orr's Island* are anchored in New England coastal communities, and both put Yankee manners and speech on display. Each novel boasts a saintly heroine who effects the conversion of a dashing young man with a strong affinity for the sea. Although the former novel paints Newport, Rhode Island, less colorfully than the latter does coastal Maine, *The Minister's Wooing* is a more carefully constructed novel which analyzes New England character more profoundly.

More than any other Stowe novel, *The Minister's Wooing* focuses on its principals: Samuel Hopkins, Congregationalist minister of Newport, and Mary Scudder, daughter of Hopkins's widowed landlady. In several respects, the minister is the historical Dr. Hopkins, learned protégé of the great Jonathan Edwards, eminent theologian in his own right and vigorous opponent of slavery in a town consecrated to the slave trade. In the 1780's, when the novel is set, however, the real Hopkins was in his sixties and possessed a wife and eight children; Stowe makes him middle-aged and a bachelor. Another celebrity of the time plays a significant role: Aaron Burr in the years before he became senator, vice president, and killer of Alexander Hamilton in a duel. Burr is depicted as a charming, unscrupulous seducer of women—a distortion of the historical Burr, no doubt, but one based on the man's reputation.

Stowe's motive for involving these men in her story of pious young Mary Scudder is utterly serious. As friend and student of Edwards, Hopkins represents the stern, uncompromising Puritan past. As Edwards's worldly and skeptical grandson, Burr stands for the repudiation of the past. Mary's choice is not—what would be easy for her—between Hopkins and Burr but between Hopkins and her young lover James Marvyn, who resembles Burr only in his impatience with the hard and incomprehensible doctrines of his forebears. James has grown up with Mary but has gravitated to the sea, and he is not quite engaged to her when he is reported lost in a shipwreck. Mrs. Scudder thereafter nudges Mary toward a union with the unexciting minister, himself an admirer of the young lady's ardent—if for his taste too sunny—Christianity.

Stowe neatly balances the claims of Hopkins's exacting Old Testament theology and Mary's simpler faith in the loving kindness of Jesus. In comforting the lost James's mother, long appalled by the minister's remorseless logic and now driven to near-psychosis by her son's supposed death, Mary's cheerful faith receives its first test. She also befriends an aristocratic young Frenchwoman—Burr's intended victim—and learns of the world of adulterous intrigue. As in her previous novels, Stowe introduces a black servant who has looked on life long and maintained a practical Christianity that is proof against all temptation to despair. Having been freed by her master, Mr. Marvyn, under the minister's influence, Candace works freely for the Marvyns and venerates Dr. Hopkins, not failing, however, to draw Mrs. Marvyn gently from "the fathomless mystery of sin and sorrow" to the "deeper mystery of God's love." Meanwhile, Mary's faith deepens, Stowe probably raising more than a few Protestant eyebrows by likening her explicitly to the Virgin Mary, who "kept all things and pondered them in her heart."

In real life, Catharine Beecher's beloved did not survive his shipwreck, and Stowe's elder sister agonized long over the possibility of his having died unregenerate. In life, Henry Stowe did not miraculously escape drowning. James Marvyn, on the other hand, after a considerable interval in which he inexplicably fails to notify either Mary or his family of his survival, returns a week before Mary's scheduled wedding with the minister. After having promised herself to Hopkins, Mary will not of course renege, so it falls to Miss Prissy, her dressmaker and friend, to approach the formidable theologian with the fact—which he is incapable of divining—that James is Mary's true love. Miss Prissy is one of Stowe's well-conceived realistic characters; an incurable gossip and a hypocrite in her professed admiration for the minister's sermons, she is nevertheless willing to assume the unpleasant initiative on behalf of her friend. Apprised of the true situation, the minister releases Mary and promptly marries her to Marvyn.

As she had in her first *The Atlantic Monthly* short story, Stowe depicts in this novel the psychology of bereavement; what she refuses to present is not death itself but the possibility of a good-hearted lad dying unregenerate. She demonstrates how the rigorous faith of a Hopkins can be a barrier, even a poison, to the unstable, but of the efficacy of Christianity to restore lost lambs, she can conceive no doubt. Even the heterodox Burr nearly succumbs to Mary's entreaties to reform. Stowe's less saintly believers, such as Miss Prissy, and her magnanimous skeptics, like Augustine St. Clare of *Uncle Tom's Cabin*, are more credible. As for Hopkins, willing to jeopardize his church financially and socially by his insistence that the most influential of his parishoners renounce his connections with the slave trade, his final renunciation of Mary is quite consistent with his previous rock-ribbed selflessness.

OLDTOWN FOLKS

Oldtown Folks, at which Stowe worked in the postwar years and published whole in 1869—for she refused to serialize it in the usual way—repeats many of the concerns of *The Minister's Wooing* and even reintroduces Jonathan Edwards's grandson, here known as Ellery Davenport. Longer, more varied, and much more rambling, this novel contains a considerable amount of Stowe's best writing. In the preface, her narrator, Horace Holyoke, vows to "interpret to the world the New England life and character of the early republic." Today, no one would choose a loose, leisurely narrative to achieve such an ambition, and perhaps no one but Stowe would have attempted it in the 1860's. It is no coincidence that *Oldtown Folks* attracted the attention of Perry Miller, the distinguished twentieth century interpreter of the New England tradition.

The Minister's Wooing had been a theological novel in which no one had very much fun. As if to redress the deficiency, Stowe widens her focus, invests this work with more of the engaging minor characters of *The Pearl of Orr's Island*, and shows her villagers enjoying themselves. Her twenty-seventh chapter, "How We Kept Thanksgiving at Oldtown," which has become an anthology piece in recent years, argues that Oldtown (based on her husband's hometown of Natick, Massachusetts) has fun precisely because the inhabitants take human life seriously enough "to believe they can do much with it." Sam Lawson—Stowe's most famous character outside *Uncle Tom's Cabin*—far from exemplifying the protestant work ethic, is the town idler, universally valued for his skill at "lubricating" with his humorous andecdotes and relaxed manner the "incessant steampower in Yankee life." By contrast, the character most devoted to work, Miss Asphyxia Smith, is easily the most hateful character in the book.

Sam also serves the tenuous plot interest by coming upon two of its three principals (narrator Horace Holyoke is the other) in an abandoned house to which they had fled from Miss Asphyxia's clutches, for, like Uncle Tiff's young charges in *Dred*, Harry and Tina Percival have been successively deserted by their scalawag father and subjected to the slow death of their mother. Tina, who is adopted by Mehitabel Rossiter, a woman of no physical beauty but much strength of character and intellect, grows into a beautiful and kindhearted but willful woman—exactly the type favored by the unprincipled Davenport. Harry grows up as Horace's companion in the nearby Holyoke household.

Tina, not knowing that Davenport numbers among his previous victims Ellen Rossiter, Mehitabel's younger sister, marries him, and it appears that Stowe will not permit her protagonist the usual eleventh-hour rescue. Tina endures ten years with the erratic Davenport, generously adopting his daughter by Ellen Rossiter, but then, in a switch on the Aaron Burr story, Davenport is killed in a duel. Two years (but only three paragraphs) later, Tina and Horace marry and settle in Boston. At the end of the novel, the Horace Holyokes are discovered back in Oldtown visiting its most durable inhabitant, Sam Lawson.

Any synopsis leaves untouched the merits of *Oldtown Folks*: the interplay of its varied and vital minor characters and the development of its seduction theme. Of the former, Miss Asphyxia, "a great threshing-machine of a woman"; Horace's peppery grandmother, "a valiant old soul, who fearlessly took any bull in life by the horns, and was ready to shake him into decorum"; and Lawson, half nuisance, half good neighbor, are only three of the most memorable. As seducer, Davenport takes advantage of several factors: the intransigence of Calvinism in its death throes, embodied in brilliant but outdated theorizers such as this novel's version of Hopkins, Dr. Stern; the Calvinist legacy of neurosis, skepticism, and rebellion (Miss Rossiter, Tina, and Davenport himself); and the ineffectuality of well-intentioned observers such as Horace and Harry. Thwarted by orthodoxy, which has become a cruel instrument in the hands of its conservative defenders, and averse to the rationalism that played such a large part in the creation of the new republic, the Oldtowners are easily taken in by Davenport, who has turned the passion and intellectual energy inherited from Edwards and the rest of his Puritan forebears to the service of selfish and worldly ends.

MY WIFE AND I and WE AND OUR NEIGHBORS

In *My Wife and I* and its sequel, *We and Our Neighbors*, Stowe turns to contemporary Manhattan life, a frivolous and even more worldly existence dotted nevertheless by young men and women of impulses Stowe characterizes as Christian but which may strike today's reader as more generally humanitarian. The full spectrum of views on women's rights

is on display, including a conviction, expressed by a young woman struggling for the opportunity to study medicine, that "marriage ought never to be entered on as a means of support." The main business of the two novels, however, is to educate Harry Henderson for marriage and thus to provide a base of operations for his wife, who dedicates herself to neighborliness and charitable offices. Stowe retains her observant eye and spicy descriptive powers, but her narrator cannot "interpret" the Gilded Age as Horace Holyoke in *Oldtown Folks* could interpret post-Revolutionary New England.

POGANUC PEOPLE

Pink and White Tyranny, the story of a man who married and must endure a selfish and demanding woman, must rank, along with the earlier *Agnes of Sorrento*, among Stowe's weakest books. Finally, in *Poganuc People*, she returns to the milieu of *The Minister's Wooing*, *The Pearl of Orr's Island*, and her Oldtown books. Poganuc is the Litchfield of her childhood and Dolly Cushing her closet approximation to an autobiographical heroine. The principal conflict is not between the old religion and the new worldliness but between entrenched Congregationalism and upstart Episcopalianism. The novel begins and ends at Christmas, when the liturgical and social differences between the two denominations stand out most sharply. Like Maggie Tulliver in Eliot's *The Mill on the Floss* (1860), Dolly is precocious, sensitive, and consequently often uncomfortable, but instead of developing the crises of her heroine's maturation, as does Eliot, Stowe whisks her off to a fashionable Boston marriage with a successful merchant, after which the author makes a final survey of the Poganuc people going about their business under the immemorial elms of the village.

Stowe seldom brought her psychological insights to bear on the development of her main characters, with the result that the less important ones invariably seem more convincing. Whether because her most productive years antedated the time of the realistic novel and particularly the psychological novel, or because she felt too strongly the nineteenth century prohibition against a woman exploring the conflicts and repressions of her own life, Stowe left unwritten what might have constituted her richest vein of realism. She never wrote a novel expressing what it felt like to be a vocationless Harriet Beecher approaching womanhood or the second Mrs. Calvin Stowe struggling with sickness, poverty, and the multitudinous demands of husband and children. The woman who wrote of domesticity in her time avoided calling attention to its tensions, exactions, and restrictions. Whatever else family life meant to Stowe, it helped prepare her to do what no American novelist had done before: write powerfully and feelingly about slavery.

Robert P. Ellis

OTHER MAJOR WORKS

SHORT FICTION: *The Mayflower: Or, Sketches of Scenes and Characters of the Descendants of the Pilgrims*, 1843; *Sam Lawson's Oldtown Fireside Stories*, 1872.

POETRY: *Religious Poems*, 1867.

NONFICTION: *A Key to Uncle Tom's Cabin*, 1853; *Sunny Memories of Foreign Lands*, 1854; *Lady Byron Vindicated*, 1870; *Palmetto Leaves*, 1873.

CHILDREN'S LITERATURE: *First Geography for Children*, 1833 (as Catharine Stowe).

BIBLIOGRAPHY

Adams, John R. *Harriet Beecher Stowe*. Boston: Twayne, 1989. Part of Twayne's United States Authors series, this is a good introduction to the life and works of Stowe. Includes bibliographical references and an index.

Boydston, Jeanne, Mary Kelley, and Anne Margolis. *The Limits of Sisterhood: The Beecher Sisters on Women's Rights and Woman's Sphere*. Chapel Hill: University of North Carolina Press, 1988. A superb study of Stowe and her sisters, Catharine and Isabella. Brief but insightful essays address each woman as an individual and as a sister. Primary documents are appended to each chapter, providing excellent resources. Illustrations, careful documentation, and a detailed index make this an invaluable text.

Brown, Gillian. *Domestic Individualism: Imagining Self in Nineteenth-Century America*. Berkeley: University of California Press, 1990. Examines themes in works by Stowe, Nathaniel Hawthorne, and Herman Melville.

Donovan, Josephine. *Uncle Tom's Cabin: Evil, Affliction, and Redemptive Love*. Boston: Twayne, 1991. Part of the Twayne Masterworks Series, Donovan's book follows the series format by first placing *Uncle Tom's Cabin* in literary and historical context, then delivering a particular reading of the work. As her subtitle suggests, Donovan views Stowe's masterpiece as a book about evil and its redemption, taking it more or less at face value and reading it with the approach she believes Stowe intended—which has a decidedly feminist bent.

Hedrick, Joan D. *Harriet Beecher Stowe: A Life*. New York: Oxford University Press, 1994. Stowe's family kept a tight rein on her literary remains, and the only previous attempt at a full-scale independent biography, Forrest Wilson's *Crusader in Crinoline* (1941), is now very much out of date. Hedrick's book makes use of new materials, including letters and diaries, and takes fresh approaches to Stowe occasioned by the Civil Rights and women's movements.

Lang, Amy Schrager. *Prophetic Woman: Anne Hutchinson and the Problem of Dissent in the Literature of New England*. Berkeley: University of California Press, 1987. An excellent feminist study, focusing on *Uncle Tom's Cabin* and Stowe's role in the history of Puritan suppression of women who achieve public notice. Stowe's novel constitutes a culmination in this process and presents a model of women as moral superiors who represent the possibility of a future without slavery.

Stowe, Charles Edward. *Life of Harriet Beecher Stowe*. Boston: Houghton Mifflin, 1889. Written by her seventh child, this is the first full-length biography of Stowe, drawn from her letters and her journal. Though not critical, it offers extensive excerpts of her personal writings and of correspondence from other renowned writers. An annotated primary bibliography and a detailed index are included.

Sundquist, Eric J., ed. *New Essays on "Uncle Tom's*

Cabin." Cambridge, England: Cambridge University Press, 1986. An excellent collection of essays on Stowe's most famous novel. The insightful introduction discusses changing literary theories as they relate to *Uncle Tom's Cabin*. The six diverse contributions by notable scholars include analyses of genre and gender issues. A selected bibliography also notes additional criticism.

Tompkins, Jane. *Sensational Designs: The Cultural Work of American Fiction, 1790-1860.* New York: Oxford University Press, 1985. Tompkins addresses *Uncle Tom's Cabin* from the perspective of "the politics of literary history." Nineteenth century popular domestic novels represent attempts to reorganize culture from a woman's perspective, and Stowe's novel is representative of "America's religion of domesticity" as empowerment of women. An excellent and influential study.

AUGUST STRINDBERG

Born: Stockholm, Sweden; January 22, 1849
Died: Stockholm, Sweden; May 14, 1912

PRINCIPAL LONG FICTION

Från Fjärdingen och Svartbäcken, 1877
Röda rummet, 1879 (*The Red Room,* 1913)
Jäsningstiden, 1886 (*The Growth of the Soul,* 1914)
Hemsöborna, 1887 (*The Natives of Hemsö,* 1959)
Tschandala, in Danish 1889, in Swedish 1897
I havsbandet, 1890 (*By the Open Sea,* 1913)
Le Plaidoyer d'un fou, in German 1893, in Swedish 1895 (*A Madman's Defense,* 1912; also known as *The Confession of a Fool*)
Inferno, 1897 (English translation, 1912)
Ensam, 1903 (*Alone,* 1968)
Götiska rummen, 1904
Svarta fanor, 1907
Taklagsöl, 1907
Syndabocken, 1907 (*The Scapegoat,* 1967)
Författaren, 1909

OTHER LITERARY FORMS

August Strindberg was an extremely prolific writer whose collected works total fifty-five volumes. Outside Scandinavia, he is known chiefly as a dramatist, and plays such as *Fadren* (1887; *The Father,* 1899), *Fröken Julie* (1888; *Miss Julie,* 1912), and *Ett drömspel* (1902; *A Dream Play,* 1912) are performed regularly in many parts of the world. Strindberg also wrote several collections of shorter prose pieces; two volumes of short stories entitled *Giftas II* (1886; *Married,* 1913; also known as *Getting Married,* 1973) are particularly well known. He also wrote and published poetry throughout his life.

ACHIEVEMENTS

Strindberg is known throughout the world as one of the fathers of modern drama. In his native Sweden, and increasingly abroad as well, he is also known as a psychological novelist of considerable importance. His second novel, *The Red Room,* is considered the first modern novel in Swedish literature, while another one, *The Natives of Hemsö,* is still one of the best-loved books in Sweden.

Strinberg has also appealed to the smaller audience of the literary establishment. Considered Sweden's greatest writer of belles letters, he has remained the object of critical attention both in his homeland and abroad. All of his important works have been translated into English, and his reputation has long been securely established.

BIOGRAPHY

Johan August Strindberg was born in Stockholm, Sweden, on January 22, 1849. On the side of his father, a steamship agent, he came from a solid middle-class background; his mother, however, was the daughter of a tailor and had been a waitress before coming to the home of her future husband as his servant girl. Strindberg later somewhat romantically referred to himself as "the son of the maidservant," while in fact he was solidly anchored in the Swedish bourgeoisie.

Strindberg grew up around his father's business and early developed an appreciation for matters relating to the sea, especially the Stockholm archipelago.

(CORBIS/Hulton-Deutsch Collection)

Master Olof, 1915), completed in early August of 1872. No theater would accept the play, however, and for the next few years, Strindberg made a living as a journalist and assistant at Stockholm's Royal Library.

In the late spring of 1875, Strindberg was introduced to Siri von Essen, the young wife of Baron Carl Gustaf Wrangel, and a love affair ensued. Siri obtained a divorce in June of 1876, after which she and Strindberg were married in December of 1877. In the same month, Strindberg had a collection of short stories published.

Strindberg's breakthrough as a prose writer came in 1879 with the publication of his novel *The Red Room*. After a period of research into cultural history, he moved with his family to France, where he would spend a considerable portion of his life. In 1884, however, he briefly returned to Sweden to stand trial on the charge of blasphemy; one of the short stories in his just-published collection *Married* was found by the authorities to be disrespectful of the Sacrament of the Lord's Supper. Strindberg was acquitted, but the matter was agonizing for him. A second volume of *Married* stories followed in 1886, however, and the same year saw the publication of the first two volumes of the somewhat fictionalized autobiography *Tjänstekvinnans son: En s äls utvecklingshistoria* (1886; *The Son of a Servant: The Story of the Evolution of a Human Being*, 1966, volume 1 only).

Strindberg returned to Scandinavia in 1887 after a further stay in France, Switzerland, and Germany. This time he settled in Copenhagen, where his naturalistic drama *The Father* was soon to be performed. In the same year, he published his most popular novel, *The Natives of Hemsö*, utilizing memories from an island in the Stockholm archipelago where he had spent several summers. Before returning to Sweden in 1889, he also had established a short-lived experi-

Unlike his several brothers, however, he was not to be prepared for a business career. In 1867, he received his matriculation certificate and soon thereafter took up residence as a student at the University of Uppsala.

Not finding academic life entirely to his liking, Strindberg was only intermittently a full-time student and for a time earned a living as a tutor and as an elementary school teacher. During that time, he wrote several insignificant plays, one of which was performed at Stockholm's Royal Dramatic Theatre in the fall of 1870. After abandoning his studies in 1872, Strindberg began pursuing a career as a writer more aggressively. The first fruit of this activity was the prose version of his drama *Mäster Olof* (1878;

mental theater; had written two more plays, *Miss Julie* and *Fordringsägare* (1888; *Creditors*, 1910); and had finished the manuscript, written in French, of his novel *The Confession of a Fool*, for which his marriage to Siri had provided him with the raw material. Annoyances experienced in Denmark in the summer of 1888 formed the basis for *Tschandala*.

During the summer of 1889, Strindberg stayed on one of the islands near Stockholm and began work on another novel arising from the archipelago, *By the Open Sea*. After a break in his labors, this book was finished in the summer of 1890. Marital difficulties, which had been present for several years, led to the beginning of divorce proceedings, and his marriage to Siri was dissolved in 1891. Strindberg did not remain unmarried for long, however; early in 1893, during a visit to Berlin, he met the Austrian Frida Uhl. They were wed the following year but soon separated, and Strindberg again went to Paris.

The next three years, the so-called *Inferno* crisis, was probably the most difficult period in Strindberg's life. He wanted to conquer Paris not only as a writer but also as a scientist, and he carried on a series of chemical experiments. His experiences during this time became material for his autobiographical novel *Inferno*.

This novel inaugurated another great creative period in Strindberg's life, which produced his well-known play *Till Damaskus* (1898-1904; *To Damascus*, 1913) and, after his final return to Sweden the following year, a series of important historical dramas. In 1901, he married the young Norwegian actress Harriet Bosse; this marriage lasted until 1904. These years saw such great plays as *Dödsdansen* (1901; *The Dance of Death*, 1912) and *A Dream Play*. In 1907, after the establishment of Stockholm's Intima Teatern (intimate theater), Strindberg wrote a series of what he called chamber plays, the best known of which is *Spöksonaten* (*The Ghost Sonata*, 1916). He also wrote a number of prose works, including the infamous satiric novel *Svarta fanor*.

Strindberg had lived a stormy life, and his final years were no exception. A series of newspaper articles begun in April, 1910, set off the most intensive debate in Swedish literary history. Nicknamed the

"Strindberg Feud," this debate resulted from both personal and philosophical differences and became particularly vicious when it was suggested that Strindberg—who, because of his radical views, had not received the Nobel Prize in Literature—ought to receive an equivalent prize from the Swedish people. The author's difficult financial situation made this particularly appropriate. The prize did not materialize, but Strindberg nevertheless succeeded in obtaining financial security through the sale of the rights to the collected edition of his works. Shortly thereafter, he became seriously ill and died from cancer of the stomach on May 14, 1912.

ANALYSIS

August Strindberg's novels constitute a striking illustration of the dialectical relationship between life and art. Strindberg truly lived for his art; he consciously ordered his life in such a manner that he might obtain material for his fiction, much of which was narrated in the first person. This has led several critics to overemphasize the bizarre aspects of his books and to hold that he was mentally ill when in reality he was only experimenting with his sanity. Such is especially the case with two intensely autobiographical novels, *The Confession of a Fool* and *Inferno*. There can be no doubt, however, that Strindberg's art also profoundly affected his life. Popular successes, such as *The Red Room* and *The Natives of Hemsö*, brought him considerable fame and enabled him to improve his standard of living, while *The Confession of a Fool*, which was a fictionalized account of his marriage to Siri von Essen, did much to seal the destruction of that marriage. In *Inferno*, Strindberg deliberately led the reading public to believe that he, the author, was identical with the novel's vacillating and easily frightened protagonist, who with justice was considered mentally ill. Strindberg thus consciously injured his personal reputation for the sake of his art, for he knew that the aesthetic effect of the book would depend on the reader's identification of author and narrator-protagonist during the reading process. Even the lighthearted *The Natives of Hemsö*, which Strindberg thought to be his sanest book, took its toll on the personal affairs of the author. Strindberg had used as models for some of his characters certain people then living on Kymmendö, an island near Stockholm where he had spent many happy summers. His models were offended, and Strindberg was never again welcome on the island.

An important question, therefore, is what it was that drove Strindberg to exploit so ruthlessly both his own life and the lives of those who were close to him. Part of the answer has been suggested by the American Strindberg scholar Eric O. Johannesson, who in his book *The Novels of August Strindberg* (1968) proposes that the fundamental theme of Strindberg's novels is the author's quest for identity. This quest, says Johannesson, takes the form of both an exploration of the author's own self and of the human psyche in general. There is little doubt that Strindberg's desire for truth, along with his need for recognition as a man of letters, was a powerful motivating force behind his artistic activity.

Strindberg's originality as a thinker did not, however, match his quality as an artist, and in his search for truth he relied heavily on ideas that had been generated by others. Constantly in step with the literary and intellectual avant-garde, he tested the validity of the various ideas and standpoints of his age as they became available to him. His development as a novelist thus closely parallels that of European intellectual history. He began as a realist and naturalist who in *The Red Room* criticized social conditions in Sweden. In the stylistically semi-naturalistic *The Natives of Hemsö*, the social satire is absent; its humorous and detailed description of life in the skerries has made it one of Strindberg's best-loved books. *The Confession of a Fool* is likewise heavy with naturalistic detail, but there is also a strong interest in individual psychology which manifests itself in the "battle of the brains" that is taking place between Axel, the book's narrator, and his wife, Maria. The same emphasis on psychology is found in *By the Open Sea*, the protagonist of which is virtually a Nietzschean superman who succumbs only because he possesses the one fatal flaw of allowing himself to be influenced by a woman. The novel *Inferno*, with its interest in mysticism, religion, and other aspects of the

supernatural, places Strindberg squarely within the neo-Romanticism of the 1890's.

Strindberg's desire for truth in all aspects of life, which also manifested itself in his quest for identity, was in part a function of the uneasiness with which he viewed his social position. The mixture of a middle-class background on his father's side and working-class origins on his mother's side created a strong tension in his life. His instincts were those of the bourgeoisie, but he felt considerable loyalty to the lower classes. At the same time, he desired upward mobility, to which he felt especially entitled because of his intellectual prowess. These tensions account for the sociological perspective present in his works.

The desire for an understanding of the self also explains the prevalence of autobiographical elements in Strindberg's novels. *The Confession of a Fool* and *Inferno* have been viewed as straightforward autobiography by many critics, and *The Red Room*, which tells about a group of artists and intellectuals of which Strindberg was a member in the late 1870's, has always been recognized as having numerous autobiographical traits. *The Confession of a Fool* and *Inferno* are first-person novels in which it is difficult to distinguish between author and narrator, and *The Red Room*, which is narrated in the third person, has a young writer as its protagonist. This among other things makes it easy to equate the narrator's point of view with that of Strindberg himself. The point of view in *The Natives of Hemsö* is that of an omniscient, detached narrator who is very similar to Strindberg, the summer guest on Kymmendö, while the fishing inspector Axel Borg, the center of consciousness in *By the Open Sea*, is a man who in most regards corresponds to the Nietzschean ideals that Strindberg advocated at the time.

It is indeed no wonder that the author was so frequently identified with his protagonists. Seemingly oblivious to the cost to his personal happiness and appallingly disrespectful of the right to privacy of those who were close to him, Strindberg consistently turned his life into art.

THE RED ROOM

Strindberg published *The Red Room* in 1879, when he had already had some minor successes as a serious writer, but also after expending much effort on a variety of minor assignments for various newspapers and magazines. He was thoroughly acquainted with life among Stockholm's younger artists and intellectuals, however, and was thus well equipped for the task of writing the book.

Although the short span of narrated time in *The Red Room* (it covers only about a year and a half), together with its episodic structure, makes it difficult to fit the novel completely into the genre of the *Bildungsroman*, the book may well be regarded from that perspective. The main character, Arvid Falk, is a young civil servant turned writer and journalist, and the book tells about his experiences while attempting to come to terms with society. Falk is a naïve idealist whose soul is larger than the destinies that Swedish life in the 1870's have to offer him, and his process of education therefore becomes one of a gradual loss of illusions. As a reporter, he gains insight into the hollowness and deceit of government, the Church, the newspaper industry, book publishing, the insurance industry, banking, charitable organizations, higher education, and the arts. Through this *Bildungsroman*, Strindberg attempts to educate the reader in the true state of contemporary society by portraying his protagonist's education in disillusionment.

The book may also, however, be regarded as a novel experiment akin to the naturalistic novel. Strindberg does not conduct an experiment that, like the typical Scandinavian novel of a few years later, is designed to illustrate the thesis that biological inheritance and social environment determine human development and behavior; rather, *The Red Room* constitutes an experiment with ideas and standpoints. Strindberg tests the validity of the attitudes toward life that inhere in the philosophies of idealism, realism, and nihilism, and it is this process of testing that is of most interest to today's readers.

The standpoint of idealism is represented chiefly by Falk, the protagonist. In the beginning of the novel, he strikes one as a very young, indeed immature, man whose idealism manifests itself as a naïve sympathy with the oppressed and a vague desire for social justice, unaccompanied by serious commitment to specific causes. This naïve idealism is untenable, and

Falk is faced with two choices: He may abandon idealism completely and turn to pessimism and nihilism, or he may subject his idealism to reflection and develop it in the direction of a considered realism, which would entail serious commitment on his part.

The pessimistic, nihilistic stance is represented by two characters, the actor Falander and the sculptor Olle Montanus. Falander is a decadent figure, a seducer of the young whose ideas are transmitted to Falk through Montanus. Montanus commits suicide, which might be a sign of Strindberg's dismissal of his philosophical outlook, but the matter is more complicated than that. Falander is a nihilist in that he attacks societal values, but he is also, as Johannesson has pointed out, a Christ figure: His destiny is to identify himself with others and to suffer with and for them through his compassion. Strindberg's later works show that he was far from finished with this character type.

In *The Red Room*, however, the philosophical possibilities represented by Falander are at least temporarily repressed. Falk's idealism becomes increasingly fanatic, and his demand becomes one of all or nothing. Eventually recognizing this as an impossible situation, he allows himself to be convinced by a more realistic friend to forget all thoughts of improving the world. He reenters polite society as a minor government official and teacher at a school for girls, living only for his coin collection, a few quietistic friends, and later, his fiancée. His end is thus that of the hero of the traditional *Bildungsroman*; namely, apparent integration into society, represented by the acquisition of a respectable position and matrimony. One wonders, however, if this is Strindberg's final word concerning his hero. Falk has passed from a naïve and later desperate idealism to its opposite, an equally desperate quietism. The next stage could be a realistic synthesis of the two, a stance that indeed seems to be implied by Strindberg. The novel is open-ended on this point, for Strindberg's purpose is not as much to suggest answers as to pose questions. The book does so in a most effective manner.

THE NATIVES OF HEMSÖ

The Natives of Hemsö is a novel that fits rather poorly into Strindberg's largely autobiographical authorship, and it may well be regarded, as the author himself regarded it, as an "intermezzo scherzando." Its well-told story, its colorful and uncomplicated characters, and its vivid pictures of life in the Stockholm archipelago have given it the status of a Swedish classic.

The plot is simple. An enterprising farmhand named Carlsson arrives at the island Hemsö in order to help the middle-aged widow Flod put her farm in order. Marriage to the widow would make Carlsson the master of the farm, so he becomes his employer's suitor, and the two are married. Carlsson's main problem is now the widow's son Gusten, who is obviously not interested in being deprived of his inheritance. Gusten becomes a formidable antagonist, especially when Carlsson begins to mismanage the farm and spends most of his time trying to persuade his wife to make a will that would, in effect, disinherit her son. In the end, Carlsson loses in the conflict because of his weakness for one of the servant girls. His wife discovers his infidelity, catches pneumonia, and dies. Carlsson drowns accidentally, and Gusten is left as the farm's unchallenged ruler.

The novel is almost totally free of political and social ideas. It exhibits a kind of limited naturalism, however, for Strindberg depicts his characters as formed by their natural and social environment. At the same time, the book is imbued with a comic spirit, which manifests itself both in the events portrayed and in the depiction of Carlsson's character. Carlsson is uncomplicated and without inner conflicts, and his death is only another instance of the old giving way to youth in life's endless chain. He is simply a man who tried and failed, and his failure has no philosophical implications. As the book's point of view is consistently that of the community, which stands in opposition to the outsider, the ending leaves the reader with a feeling of contentment: The conflict has been resolved in accordance with the order of nature.

THE CONFESSION OF A FOOL

In *The Confession of a Fool*, Strindberg returns to his general artistic project with full force. His search for truth focuses on the human psyche and the effects of interpersonal relationships on it. When read strictly as a work of fiction, the book becomes a powerful and engaging psychological novel. Many critics, however, have found it difficult to regard the book from this perspective. Both the contemporary reading public and later scholars have been painfully aware that the novel tells in detail about Strindberg's relationship with his first wife, Siri von Essen. It can be argued that the book is a piece of autobiography, but if it is to be regarded as such, it quickly becomes clear that many of the events related have been significantly distorted. Strindberg used the experience he had gained in his relationship with Siri, but because he knew that he was writing fiction, not autobiography, he felt no obligation to adhere strictly to what had actually taken place in every instance.

A key to the understanding of both *The Confession of a Fool* and the novel *By the Open Sea* is to be found in an essay written by Strindberg in 1887 on Henrik Ibsen's drama *Rosmersholm* (1886). Entitled "Själamord" ("Psychic Murder"), the essay explores the ways in which modern human beings destroy one another by a variety of means infinitely more sophisticated than old-fashioned physical violence. Today's psychic murderer uses public opinion, hypnotism, and suggestion to destroy his victim; more specifically, he makes the victim ridiculous, robs him of his ability to make a living, and, if possible, drives him insane. *The Confession of a Fool* tells the story of such a crime.

The first-person narrator of the book is a Swedish writer named Axel, who, with his wife, Maria, lives in exile somewhere in central Europe. He suspects that Maria, who he believes has done her best to isolate him from the world in order to destroy his reputation as a writer, is now trying to kill him by causing him to go insane. In order to defend himself both against the rumors that he fears his wife has spread about him and against other and more direct threats to his mind, he begins an investigation into their relationship. The book is the record of this investigation, and it is designed to serve as his final word to the world in case his wife should succeed in her design.

The novel's point of view is consistent throughout; Strindberg never departs from the perspective of his narrator. From this viewpoint, Maria becomes a villain of the highest order who no doubt has been doing everything in her power to rob her husband of his sanity. The discerning reader also understands, however, that there is a considerable difference between the story as told by the narrator and the author's version of it. Because the point of view is consistently that of the first-person narrator, the views of the author can be reconstructed only through a careful reading. Such an analysis will make it clear that Maria is indeed innocent and that her husband, who can be classified only as a madman, is in the process of committing psychic suicide. The value of the novel lies in the tension between these two perspectives and the careful psychological portrayal that is necessary for their creation.

Some critics have argued that Strindberg indeed shared the perspective of his narrator and that he involuntarily revealed the fact that he, like his narrator, was insane during the period when the novel was written. This view is the result of an inability to distinguish between reliable and unreliable narrators. The narrator in *The Confession of a Fool* is insane, but he either does not know it or is unwilling to admit it. The novel's author is, of course, not in the same situation, and he has to find a means of transmitting his view to the reader. This difficult task Strindberg has handled in a sophisticated manner by creating a complex ironic structure. The novel is thus a thoroughly modern one, both in terms of the author's use of psychology and in its narrative technique.

BY THE OPEN SEA

Strindberg continues his search for truth concerning the human psyche in *By the Open Sea*, one of his most underrated novels. Set in the Stockholm archipelago, the book is nevertheless free of the comedy and lightheartedness of its predecessor in the same setting, *The Natives of Hemsö*. The author now has taken up a most solemn subject—namely, the process by which an individual may descend from superhuman strength and intelligence to complete disintegration of the personality. Although the novel's center of consciousness, the fishing inspector Axel Borg, is also the person through whose eyes most of the action is seen, the telling is done by a third-person narrator virtually indistinguishable from Strindberg

himself. This makes the transmission of norms from the author to the reader more easily accomplished than in *The Confession of a Fool*, where Strindberg chose to employ a first-person narrator.

One day in spring, Borg arrives at a tiny, isolated island in the archipelago where he is to teach modern fishing techniques to the inhabitants. Borg is an outsider both geographically and socially; in addition, he views himself as a superman in the spirit of Nietzsche. As a character, he could be attractive only to those who fancy themselves to be of the same kind, and the stage is set for a constant battle between him and the natives. While they are creatures of instincts and feelings, Borg worships logic and reason. The battle thus also becomes one between two different attitudes toward life.

In the first part of the novel, Strindberg describes the intellectual virtues of his protagonist. The fishing inspector is an eminent scientist whose training and native intellect combine to make him an ideal type. Compared to him, the islanders are nothing; they do, however, have the advantage of belonging to a community, a group, while Borg is isolated. Borg's state of isolation constitutes both a strength and a weakness. It is necessary in order to keep him from too much contact with inferior minds, but his lack of access to a community of his equals tends to make him lose the ability to cope with the world of human beings.

A decisive change in Borg's mental state is brought about by his relationship with a young female summer guest. Her name is Maria, and she has a function which is similar to that of the female antagonist by the same name in *The Confession of a Fool*. The cerebral Borg, unable to repress his instincts, seeks Maria's company and, as he believes, allows his intellect to be degraded through their association. Knowing that the relationship is harmful to him, he attempts to liberate himself but discovers that he can accomplish this only by seducing the girl. He does so with the effect that the intended liberation is achieved, but the seduction is also a fatal surrender to his own bodily nature.

Maria leaves, but a new challenger has already arrived. He is a preacher, an old acquaintance of Borg, and his function is to bring the fishing inspector's fears and suppressed feelings of guilt to the surface. Borg's scientifically grounded rejection of religion immediately places him at odds with the man of God, and a battle of the brains follows. The preacher proves to be the stronger; Borg capitulates by asking him to say prayers for him and tell his folktales. At the end of the novel, Borg has receded into insanity. In a moment of clarity, he goes down to the sea, finds a boat, and sails to his death.

By the Open Sea can be read as a novel about the conflict between the conscious and the unconscious and the need to arrive at a state of balance between the two. Borg's personality unravels because the unconscious has been excluded from it. Strindberg, like Carl G. Jung after him, uses the male-female opposition as a metaphor to describe this conflict. When the book's perhaps trivial story is regarded from this perspective, this often underrated work reveals itself to be a powerful psychological novel.

INFERNO

Like *The Confession of a Fool*, the equally autobiographical novel *Inferno* is narrated in the first person. Because the book ostensibly tells about Strindberg's life in Paris during the years from 1894 to 1897, it has been customary not to distinguish between Strindberg and the narrator and Strindberg the author. The lack of distinction between the two is strongly reinforced by the author/narrator, who at the end of the novel offers his diary as proof that the novel is factual. When this claim is taken at face value, however, it becomes clear that Strindberg's perception of reality during the period covered by the novel is such that the author would have to be regarded as mentally ill. The lack of distance between the novel's "experiencing self" and the self that later narrates the events, furthermore, indicates that Strindberg suffered from the same defects at the time of the book's composition.

The reader may accept Strindberg's claims at face value or may subject the book to a less orthodox reading. If, for example, the events of the novel are compared with those that are narrated in Strindberg's diary, it soon becomes clear that the diary strongly discredits the novel's claim to factuality. By

inviting comparison with the diary, Strindberg offers the reader a clue that will lead to the reconstruction of a story that is radically different from that which appears on the book's surface. The novel thus becomes a fundamentally ironic one, and its aesthetic value lies largely in the elegant way in which the irony is constructed. Strindberg's purpose is, in fact, to fool those of his readers who allow themselves to be taken in by the description of his supposed madness, while at the same time he wishes to commune secretly with those who are sufficiently perceptive to realize what he is up to. The structure of the narrative situation thus closely parallels the general structure of irony, with Strindberg being the author and most readers being victims of the irony, and with those few who really understand constituting its audience.

Such a narrative strategy entails a high degree of risk to the author, who by most readers will be considered a madman. Strindberg compensates for this risk by using his persona to express some important verities regarding his perception of his own destiny, much as the medieval fool often was able to express profound truths. Thus, the victims of the irony will simultaneously allow him to experience a sense of intellectual superiority and provide him with an audience that, despite its inferiority, is capable of being instructed. Those who reconstruct the irony and become part of his more sophisticated audience, on the other hand, allow him to feel a sense of community in his exalted intellectual station. At the same time, they have seen through the structure of norms offered to the victims and consequently also possess those truths which Strindberg offers to his least enlightened readers. *Inferno* thus places Strindberg in a position where he cannot lose in his relationship with the reader.

The truths that are expressed by Strindberg's first-person madman concern both how it feels to be losing one's sanity and an antidote against the disintegration of the personality that Strindberg, strictly on an experimental basis, began to administer to himself during the 1890's. This antidote, which was intended both to prevent any loss of mind and to enhance the writer's creative powers, consisted in a religious interpretation of life. Religion was becoming popular among both Scandinavian neo-Romantics and reformed Continental decadents, so Strindberg was in good company. His experimental religiosity was centered on a belief in supernatural powers that were guiding his life and in relationship to which he was a former rebel who was now being chastened and turned into a suffering sacrificial victim not dissimilar to the actor Falander in *The Red Room*. By viewing himself as a proxy for humanity, Strindberg was able to reinterpret his life in Paris as a myth of the human predicament. *Inferno* thus becomes both the story of humanity's passing through Hell and the exceptional individual's rise above his torments by virtue of his intellect.

Strindberg's career stands at the juncture between the nineteenth and the twentieth centuries. Rooted in a Romantic view of the world, he passed through the Scandinavian literary realism of the 1870's and the naturalism of the 1880's, and ended in the neo-Romanticism of the 1890's. His oeuvre is dedicated to the search for truth, particularly with reference to the nature of his own identity. Although his dramas have influenced twentieth century theater to a greater extent than his novels have affected their genre, he is nevertheless an important figure when viewed in the context of the modern psychological novel. Above all, however, Strindberg was a man whose life, in its joy and pain, may well serve as a paradigm for modern people.

Jan Sjåvik

OTHER MAJOR WORKS

SHORT FICTION: *Giftas I*, 1881; *Svenska öden och äventyr*, 1882-1892; *Giftas II*, 1886 (*Married*, 1913; also known as *Getting Married*, 1973; includes *Giftas I* and *Giftas II*); *Utopier i verkligheten*, 1885; *Skärkarlsliv*, 1888; *Legender*, 1898 (*Legends*, 1912); *Fagervik och Skamsund*, 1902 (*Fair Haven and Foul Strand*, 1913); *Sagor*, 1903 (*Tales*, 1930); *Historiska miniatyrer*, 1905; *In Midsummer Days and Other Tales*, 1913; *The German Lieutenant and Other Stories*, 1915.

PLAYS: *Fritänkaren*, pb. 1870; *I Rom*, pr., pb. 1870; *Den fredlöse*, pr. 1871 (*The Outlaw*, 1912);

Hermione, pb. 1871; *Anno fyrtioåtta*, wr. 1876, pb. 1881; *Mäster Olof*, pb. 1878 (*Master Olof*, 1915); *Gillets hemlighet*, pr., pb. 1880; *Herr Bengts hustru*, pr., pb. 1882; *Lycko-Pers resa*, pr., pb. 1883 (*Lucky Peter's Travels*, 1912); *Fadren*, pr., pb. 1887 (*The Father*, 1899); *Marodörer*, pr. 1887; *Fröken Julie*, pb. 1888 (*Miss Julie*, 1912); *Kamraterna*, pb. 1888 (with Axel Lundegård; *Comrades*, 1912); *Fordringsägare*, pb. in Danish 1888, pr. 1889 (*Creditors*, 1910); *Hemsöborna*, pr. 1889; *Paria*, pr. 1889 (*Pariah*, 1913); *Den starkare*, pr. 1889 (*The Stronger*, 1912); *Samum*, pr., pb. 1890 (*Simoom*, 1906); *Himmelrikets nycklar, eller Sankte Per vandrar på jorden*, pb. 1892 (*The Keys of Heaven*, 1965); *Moderskärlek*, pb. 1893 (*Mother Love*, 1910); *Bandet*, pb. in German 1893, pb. 1897 (*The Bond*, 1960); *Debet och kredit*, pb. 1893 (*Debit and Credit*, 1906); *Första varningen*, pr., pb. 1893 (*The First Warning*, 1915); *Inför döden*, pr., pb. 1893 (*In the Face of Death*, 1916); *Leka med elden*, pb. 1893 (*Playing with Fire*, 1930); *Till Damaskus, forsta delen*, pb. 1898 (*To Damascus I*, 1913); *Till Damaskus, andra delen*, pb. 1898 (*To Damascus II*, 1913); *Advent, ett mysterium*, pb. 1899 (*Advent*, 1912); *Brott och Brott*, pb. 1899 (*Crime and Crime*, 1913, also known as *There Are Crimes and Crimes*); *Erik XIV*, pr., pb. 1899 (English translation, 1931); *Folkungasagan*, pb. 1899 (*The Saga of the Folkungs*, 1931); *Gustav Vasa*, pr., pb. 1899 (English translation, 1916); *Gustav Adolf*, pb. 1900 (English translation, 1957); *Carl XII*, pb. 1901 (*Charles XII*, 1955); *Dödsdansen, första delen*, pb. 1901 (*The Dance of Death I*, 1912); *Dödsdansen, andra delen*, pb. 1901 (*The Dance of Death II*, 1912); *Engelbrekt*, pr., pb. 1901 (English translation, 1949); *Kaspers fettisdag*, pr. 1901; *Kristina*, pb. 1901 (*Queen Christina*, 1955); *Midsommar*, pr., pb. 1901 (*Midsummertide*, 1912); *Påsk*, pr., pb. 1901 (*Easter*, 1912); *Ett drömspel*, pb. 1902 (*A Dream Play*, 1912); *Halländarn*, wr. 1902, pb. 1918; *Kronbruden*, pb. 1902 (*The Bridal Crown*, 1916); *Svanevit*, pb. 1902 (*Swanwhite*, 1914); *Genom öknar till arvland, eller Moses*, wr. 1903, pb. 1918 (*Through Deserts to Ancestral Lands*, 1970); *Gustav III*, pb. 1903 (English translation, 1955); *Lammet och vilddjuret: Eller, Kristus*, wr. 1903, pb. 1918 (*The Lamb and the Beast*, 1970);

Näktergalen i Wittenberg, pb. 1904 (*The Nightingale of Whittenberg*, 1970); *Till Damaskus, tredje delen*, pb. 1904 (*To Damascus III*, 1913); *Brända tomten*, pr., pb. 1907 (*After the Fire*, 1913); *Oväder*, pr., pb. 1907 (*Storm*, 1913); *Pelikanen*, pr., pb. 1907 (*The Pelican*, 1962); *Spöksonaten*, pb. 1907 (*The Ghost Sonata*, 1916); *Abu Casems tofflor*, pr., pb. 1908; *Bjälbo-Jarlen*, pr., pb. 1909 (*Earl Birger of Bjälbo*, 1956); *Riksföreståndaren*, pr. 1909 (*The Regent*, 1956); *Siste riddaren*, pr., pb. 1909 (*The Last of the Knights*, 1956); *Stora landsvägen*, pb. 1909 (*The Great Highway*, 1954); *Svarta handsken*, pb. 1909; *Hellas: Eller, Sokrates*, pb. 1918 (*Hellas*, 1970); *Toten-Insel: Eller, Hades*, pb. 1918; *Six Plays*, pb. 1955; *Eight Expressionist Plays*, pb. 1965.

POETRY: *Dikter och verkligheter*, 1881; *Dikter på vers och prosa*, 1883; *Sömngångarnätter på vakna dagar*, 1884.

NONFICTION: *Gamla Stockholm*, 1880; *Det nya riket*, 1882; *Svenska folket i helg och söcken, krig och fred, hemma och ute eller Ett tusen år av svenska bildningens och sedernas historia*, 1882; *Tjänstekvinnans son: En s äls utvecklingshistoria*, 1886 (4 volumes; *The Son of a Servant: The Story of the Evolution of a Human Being*, 1966, volume 1 only); *Vivisektioner*, 1887; *Blomstermalningar och djurstycken*, 1888; *Bland franska bönder*, 1889; *Antibarbarus*, 1896; *Jardin des plantes*, 1896; *Svensk natur*, 1897; *Världshistoriens mystik*, 1903; *Modersmålets anor*, 1910; *Religiös renässans*, 1910; *Folkstaten*, 1910-1911; *Tal till svenska nationen*, 1910-1911; *Världsspråkens rötter*, 1910; *Oppna brev till Intima Teatern*, 1911-1912 (*Open Letters to the Intimate Theater*, 1959); *Zones of the Spirit: A Book of Thoughts*, 1913.

BIBLIOGRAPHY

Bentley, Eric. *The Playwright as Thinker*. New York: Harcourt Brace, 1946. Contains one of the most important assessments of Strindberg as a modern dramatist, but also valuable for insights into the sensibility that created the fiction.

Johnson, Walter. *August Strindberg*. Boston: Twayne, 1976. A solid introductory study, including a chapter on Strindberg's life, his use of autobiography, his fiction, and his early and mature drama.

A concluding chapter assesses his place in literature and the history of drama. A chronology, detailed notes, and annotated bibliography make this a very useful volume.

Krutch, Joseph Wood. *Modern Drama*. Ithaca, N.Y.: Cornell University Press, 1953. Should be read in conjunction with Bentley's discussion of Strindberg's modernism.

Mazor, Yair. *The Triple Cord: Agnon, Hamsun, Strindberg: Where Scandinavian and Hebrew Literature Meet*. Tel Aviv, Israel: Papyrus, 1987. See especially chapters 5 and 6 for a wide-ranging discussion of Strindberg that goes beyond his influence on Hebrew literature.

Mortensen, Brita, and Brian W. Downs. *Strindberg: An Introduction to His Life and Work*. Cambridge, England: Cambridge University Press, 1965. An excellent, accessible guide to both Strindberg's life and his work.

Ollen, Gunnar. *August Strindberg*. New York: Ungar, 1972. A succinct, introductory study, with one-and two-page discussions of his plays and fiction, a chronology, a list and description of Strindberg's stage works, a bibliography, and an index.

Reinert, Otto, ed. *Strindberg: A Collection of Critical Essays*. Englewood Cliffs, N.J.: Prentice Hall, 1971. Divided into three sections: "The Divided Self," "A New Theater," and "Some Major Plays." Reinert's introduction surveys Strindberg's life and career. Includes chronology and annotated bibliography. Section 1 is most helpful for students of Strindberg's fiction.

Robinson, Michael, ed. *Strindberg and Genre*. Norwich, England: Norvik Press, 1991. A good selection of essays on Strindberg's literary form. Includes bibliographical references and an index.

_____. *Studies in Strindberg*. Norwich, England: Norvik Press, 1998. An excellent volume of Strindberg interpretation and criticism. Provides bibliographical references and an index.

Steene, Birgitta, ed. *Strindberg and History*. Stockholm: Almqvist & Wiksell International, 1992. Examines the theme of history in Strindberg's works.